INTRODUCTION TO THE LAW AND LEGAL SYSTEM OF THE UNITED STATES

Fifth Edition

By

William Burnham
Professor of Law
Wayne State University Law School

A Thomson Reuters business

Mat #41046527

© West, a Thomson business, 1999, 2002, 2006

© 2011 Thomson Reuters

      610 Opperman Drive

      St. Paul, MN 55123

      1–800–313–9378

Printed in the United States of America

ISBN: 978–0–314–26610–1

To Marcia —
without whom
all this would have been
done much sooner.

PREFACE

This is intended primarily for people interested in the U.S. legal system who do not have a U.S. legal education. The first group — and the primary inspiration for the book — are law students, lawyers and legal scholars from foreign countries. The second group comprises U.S. undergraduate college students, whether "pre-law" or not, who wish to gain an overview of the law, either for their own edification or for their future study in law school. The third audience are members of the general reading public in the United States and professionals in non-law fields.

A fourth category of readers has emerged in recent years — *law* students in the *U.S.* They find that the book fills them in on subjects they do not have time to study in law school, gives them a "big picture" perspective on the law as a whole, and provides them with a helpful review of "what you would have learned in law school had you been paying attention." In addition, many law students come to law school with an educational, family or personal background devoid of law and lawyers — nurses, engineers, artists, musicians and others. They find that the book gives them background knowledge that their education and work circumstances did not supply them.

The original idea for this book grew out of two frustrations. The first was my effort to find a text for a course, "Introduction to American Law," that I was called upon to teach while on a faculty exchange in Western Europe in the early 1990s. Books for U.S. lawyers and law students were clearly unsuitable because they are too detailed. Books written for undergraduate college students, primarily business law and constitutional law books, are useful only for teaching those two areas of the law and, in any event, are often overly simplistic and "un-lawyerlike" in their presentation. There did not seem to be anything in between. This was confirmed when I spoke with foreign law graduates studying for advanced law degrees at U.S. law schools who felt that the big problem with one year of law study in the U.S. was that they did not get any kind of overview of U.S. law.

The second frustration that led me to attempt this project came from the opposite perspective — my difficulties as a comparativist trying to learn about foreign legal systems. Books on other countries' systems written for foreign audiences tend to deal in generalities that make it hard to picture how the system actually operates and what the principal important legal concepts and doctrines are. At the same time, many such books are quick to give the author's impressions of the differences between systems without giving sufficient detail to allow me, as the reader, to decide for myself how that system fits into my own frame of reference. I found this was true as well of the few books on the U.S. legal system written by U.S. comparative law scholars.

Accordingly, my approach in this book has been to provide a summary of the law and the operation of the legal system in the United States that is sufficiently detailed to allow readers to make their own judgments, without burdening the process with my own comparative observations. When U.S. institutions or laws have been the subject of criticisms, I have sought to set out the arguments from all sides of the question. To aid readers interested in more detail, I have put in many citations to original materials, particularly cases and statutes, and to books and articles that are particularly suited to the non-specialist. The Reader's Guide and Bibliographic Introduction that follows this Preface generally explains the books and cases cited and makes some general comments on the organization of the book. It should help in reading and using the book.

The book is now in its fifth edition and it has evolved over time, though the basic approach remains the same. In the second edition in 1999 I added a chapter on Tax Law and a section on environmental law in the Business Law chapter. In addition, I expanded the Contracts chapter into a chapter on Contracts and Commercial Law by adding expanded treatment of Articles 2 and 9 of the Uniform Commercial Code and new material on federal and state consumer protection laws. I also added a section on intellectual property — copyright, patents and trademarks — to the property chapter. The third edition in 2002 saw the addition of a new chapter, International Aspects of U.S. law. There are no new chapters or major additions in the fourth or fifth editions. However, the text has been thoroughly updated and several revisions of sections or passages throughout have been made. It is current through the 2009-2010 U.S. Supreme Court term with some cases from the 2010-2011 term.

The breadth of this book has required that I write in several areas of law in which I am not a specialist. The noted comparative lawyers Zweigert and Kötz have observed how this is often the fate of comparativists — that they must venture as non-specialists into unfamiliar territory, where certain dangers lurk, including "natives" with sharp arrows in the thickets. But if my fellow "non-native" friends here and abroad receive something worthwhile from this work, it is worth taking the risk.

William Burnham

April 2011
Ann Arbor, Michigan

ACKNOWLEDGMENTS

While writing and revising this book, I have come to realize how understated acknowledgments in the preface of a book are. I simply could not have written this book without the interest, support and assistance of my colleagues and friends. In no particular order, they are Robert Sedler, John Mogk, Thomas Munsterman, Martin Kriegel, Kathryn Heidt, Marcia Major, Leroy Lamborn, Jonathan Weinberg, Janet Findlater, George Feldman, Steven Calkins, Joseph Grano, Frederica Lombard, Kingsley Brown, Stephen Schulman, Diana Pratt, Edward Wise, Peter Henning, Vincent Wellman, Alan Schenk, Michael Sinclair, John Dolan, Margaret Mahoney, Zanita Fenton, Peter Bal, Hans Pijls, Robert H. Abrams, Eric Kades, Peter Henning, Dennis Devaney, Christopher Peters, Katherine White, John Rothchild, David Moran, Michael McIntyre, Erica Beecher-Monas, Ellen Dannin, Jocelyn Benson, Joan Mahoney and Brad Roth.

The special assistance of Martin Kriegel, J.D., LL.M., was absolutely essential in putting together and maintaining the Tax Law chapter.

Prominent among the student assistants who worked on this book were Sheila Kahn, Damon Whitmore, Mary Kosmalski, Kathy Murphy, Tom Bishoff, David Zack, Whitney Veit, Helen Danilenko, and Jonathan Chin. Special thanks to recent University of Michigan law graduates Jason Ryu, Eric Weiler, Chris Machnacki and Rina Wang for work on the fifth edition.

Several lawyers and law students from other countries have provided useful comments and helpful suggestions over the years. Among them have been my students at the University of Utrecht and the University of Maastricht in the Netherlands, the University of Trento (Italy), Moscow Institute of International Relations, Mari State University Law Faculty (Mari Republic, Russia), and Kwansai Gakuin Law Department (Nishinomiya, Japan), my LLM students at the University of Michigan Law School, and the succession of foreign lawyers who have attended the summer programs of the American Institute for Legal Education in Ann Arbor, Michigan.

I also owe a special thanks to Tom Berreman, now retired from West Publishing, who maintained his and my interest in this project through several interruptions and difficulties.

READER'S GUIDE AND BIBLIOGRAPHIC INTRODUCTION

Organization of Chapters   The chapters are arranged in an order that makes sense to me. But readers or teachers may wish to use a different order. In general, there is no great advantage to any particular order. In most situations, where knowledge from a different chapter is needed, there are references to the appropriate pages.

In general, the organization of the book is as follows. Chapters I through VI deal with matters of constitutional, administrative and judicial structure of the legal system and general legal methodology, including caselaw method, the adversary system of adjudication and legal education and the legal profession. Chapters VII and VIII deal with procedural law in civil and criminal cases. Chapter IX, on constitutional law, starts the remainder of the book's focus on substantive law topics. Chapters X through XVII cover most of the major substantive private law areas, plus criminal law.

Within chapters, organization varies. But I have tried to place the more difficult material at the end of each chapter. A teacher who wishes to spare students some of these complexities could have them stop at the appropriate point and go on to the next chapter.

Citations to Cases and Other Authorities   There are many citations to original sources in this book. These citations should facilitate the use of this book as a reference. However, readers who plan to use it in this way should make sure that they consult the original sources cited. A table of case citations is provided in Appendix C.[1]

In most instances where a case is cited in this book, the facts of the case will either be apparent from the text or will be set out in a parenthetical summary following the citation in the footnote. Part of the reason for citing cases is because caselaw is an important source of law in a common law system. But even aside from their precedent-ial value, the fact situations of cases serve as concrete illustrations of how the legal concepts, doctrines or laws discussed in the text are applied in practice. In addition, judicial opinions are often helpful for reference purposes because they tend to be encyclopedic, at least in important cases. Because of this, the reader can often learn about the area of law generally and can find useful citations to more general caselaw, law review articles and treatises.

It is essential that foreign law students or lawyers planning to study in the United States look up and read a few of the principal cases cited here since much of their time studying in U.S. law schools will be taken up by reading and analyzing appellate opinions in preparation for class. Moreover, cases give one a real sense of what kinds of legal disputes arise in the United States and how they arise. I would strongly urge even the casual reader to look up a case that seems interesting from the description in the text and read it.

I would also suggest that teachers using this book edit, copy and hand out one or two cases in each subject matter area for students to read after they have had an overview from the narrative description of the law in the book. Especially useful would be recent cases that have come out since the book was published, especially a case that takes the law in a new direction. Another way to work cases in is to give single students

---

1   Omitted from citations in both the book and the table of cases is any denial of review of the case by a higher court, including denials of certiorari by the U.S. Supreme Court.

or groups of students the task of finding and reading a particular case in the library and then reporting their impressions and analysis of it to the entire class.

Case Citation Form Information on citation form and legal research is set out in the last section of Chapter II.[2] However, some preliminary comments should be made here to facilitate reading.

The basic citation form for a case decision is the following: (1) case name, (2) volume number, (3) abbreviated case reporter series name, (4) page number where the case begins, and (5) the court and year of the decision in parentheses. For example, the case set out in the Appendix on page A1 would be cited as *Hoffman v. Jones*, 280 So.2d 431 (Fla. 1973). This indicates that it is found in volume 280 of West's Southern Reporter, 2d Series, starting on page 431, and that it is a 1973 decision of the Florida Supreme Court. Had the case been from the Florida Court of Appeals, the intermediate appellate court in that state, the abbreviation "Fla.App." would have appeared in the parentheses with the year.

In the federal courts, United States Supreme Court cases are reported in United States Reports (U.S.), its official reporter, so any case with U.S. as the reporter citation is the U.S. Supreme Court. Other parallel cites to commercial reporters, West's Supreme Court Reporter (S.Ct.) and Lawyer's Edition, Second Series (L.Ed.2d), are set out in the Table of Cases at the end of the book. Lower federal court cases are published in the Federal Reporter (F.2d or F.3d) and Federal Supplement (F.Supp. or F.Supp.2d). As with state court citations, right after the citation the court rendering the decision is indicated by an abbreviation in parentheses with the date. For example, (6th Cir. 2006) indicates the Court of Appeals for the Sixth Circuit (Michigan, Ohio, Tennessee and Kentucky) and (WDNY 2006) indicates the U.S. District Court for the Western District of New York.

States often publish official state reporters. However, the official citations are not included because official reporters are often not carried by libraries outside the state that publishes them. The official reporter citation is used for United States Supreme Court Reports since this is the universal practice among lawyers and judges. However, since general public libraries in the U.S. and foreign law libraries often have only the unofficial commercial reporters of United States Supreme Court cases, parallel citations are set out in the table of cases in Appendix C.

Appendix A reproduces a sample common law case decision and the U.S. Constitution. Following them are diagrams of the structure of the federal government, the court system and the floor plan of a jury trial courtroom.

Books Cited The first footnote or so in each chapter or section of this book will contain references to more specialized books on that particular topic. Most of these books are from the "Big Four" in the educational legal publishing business: West Group, Foundation Press (owned by West), Aspen Publishing (owned by Wolters-Kluwer), and the Lexis Law Publishing. Appendix B sets out contacts for these publishers. Consequently, when a book published by any of these four is cited in the text, only the name of the publisher appears. For other books cited, if they are in print or likely to be available in general libraries, I have included the name of the publisher as well.

I have limited my citations to books to those most likely to be useful to the foreign lawyer or U.S. non-law-trained reader. Extended multi-volume treatises exist in most of

---

2 *See infra* pp. 74-78.

the subject-matter areas of law addressed in this book, but they usually tell readers more than they ever wanted to know. "Casebooks" also exist. But they are designed to be used by law students taking a course on the subject. As the title implies, they are primarily full of cases. The cases are then followed by a series of questions which, in the traditional style of such books, are largely unanswerable and designed primarily to stimulate classroom discussion. For the nonspecialist reader, casebooks are an unnecessarily difficult and frustrating way to gain an overview of an area of law.[3]

For these reasons, I usually cite two classes of books that are likely to be helpful: (1) one-volume treatises and (2) law student aids. The one-volume treatises are written by prominent scholars and constitute their attempts at a single-volume narrative treatment of the subject matter area. Treatises of this type are used by law students to review for an examination in a course or for clarification while a course is being taught. They are also used by teachers and practicing lawyers as a departure point for research in an area of law with which they are not familiar. Typically treatises have extensive citations to cases and other authorities for further information and research. The paradigm treatise of this type is West Group's "Hornbook Series," though the other law publishers have some as well.[4] Law student aids take various forms: the "Nutshell Series," "Black Letter Law Series" and "Gilbert's" outlines published by West Group; the "Concepts and Insights" and "Turning Point" series published by Foundation Press; "Examples and Explanations" published by Aspen; and the "Understanding the Law" series published by Lexis. Nutshells are intended to condense an entire law school course into a small pocket-sized paperback of around 300 pages. The Black Letter Series does much the same thing in a larger outline format. The "Examples and Explanations" book contain just that, with some introductory text. The "Understanding the Law" series is somewhere between a Nutshell or Outline and a one-volume treatise.

There is great variation in the quality of writing and clarity of all the books mentioned, and in their suitability for the nonspecialist reader. Single-volume treatises and student aids are at least partly intended for review reading for a course the intended law-student reader has just finished, so they sometimes assume too much knowledge on the part of any other reader Another shortcoming of some student aids, particularly outlines, is that they often do not provide regular citations to cases or statutes. This will frustrate the reader who wants to clarify generalizations about the law by looking at the appropriate caselaw or statute. The "examples and explanations" approach has the benefit of giving the reader both textual material and concrete problems to work through to learn basic concepts and variations on them. However, these books are often selective about what issues they cover within an area of law. They are also designed for supplemental reading in a course or for review and, like nutshells and outlines, may be too detailed and assume too much knowledge. "Understanding the Law" texts are written in narrative form. They are generally not as detailed and comprehensive as hornbooks, though they are more so than nutshells or outlines.

Legal encyclopedias include West's ENCYCLOPEDIA OF AMERICAN LAW, accessed on the Internet at http://www.enotes.com/wests-law-encyclopedia; CORPUS JURIS SECUNDUM (162 vols., updated annually with supplements); and AMERICAN JURISPRUDENCE, 2D SERIES

---

3 Law school classes and the use of casebooks are explained in Chapter IV, pp. 131-132.

4 For the origin of the term "hornbook," *see* Chapter II, p. 76 note 188. West is now publishing a series of shorter "Concise Hornbooks," which will be cited where available.

(140 vols., updated with supplements). The first of the three is designed for the lay reader, while the second two are used by lawyers as a departure point for research.

Access to U.S. Legal Materials on the Internet Since the first edition of this book was published, there has been explosive growth in the amount of U.S. legal materials available free on the Internet. For this reason, Appendix B sets out some of the more prominent web sites where they can be found. However, since there are so many sites and they can be handily located by using general Internet search engines, no attempt at any kind of comprehensive list is attempted. Perhaps the first place to go for free access to legal materials and other legal information would be FindLaw, owned and operated by West Group.[5]

As for doing legal research on the Internet, one should keep in mind that, as of yet, not all the relevant sources of law are available, and finding aids do not yet assure that all the relevant authorities that bear on a given problem will be found. There is also no guarantee that the legal materials found are current. As a result, for any kind of comprehensive research, it is still necessary to gain access to a law library or to use the Westlaw or Lexis computerized legal dabases.[6]

Unfamiliar Terminology There is no glossary of terms in this book as such. However, the index is designed in part to be used as one. In addition to the usual topical listing of subjects and terms discussed, the more important terms have a "defined" entry indicating the page where the term is explained. To assist in finding the term, terms are placed in quotation marks the first time they are used and explained.

An alternative solution is to keep handy one of the many excellent legal dictionaries that have been published over the years. The traditional comprehensive work is BLACK'S LAW DICTIONARY, 9TH ED. (West 2009). More succinct dictionaries are West's student edition of Black's, BLACK'S LAW DICTIONARY, ABRIDGED 9TH ED. (West 2009), BASIC LAW TERMS (West 1998); Mellinkoff's Dictionary of American Legal Usage (West 2009), BRYAN A. GARNER, A DICTIONARY OF MODERN LEGAL USAGE, 2D ED (Oxford U. Press 1995) and ORAN'S DICTIONARY OF THE LAW, 3D ED. (Thomson-Delmar Publishing 1999). There are numerous free legal dictionaries available on the Internet.

I should mention that this book has been published in Russian, Ukrainian and Chinese, so readers fluent in those languages may wish to look for a copy of it in their home countries. The Ukrainian and Chinese translations are of the second edition and the Russian translation is of the third edition. The Ukrainian and Russian editions were financed in part by grants from the U.S. Department of State Bureau of Educational and Cultural Affairs and the U.S. Agency for International Development. The views expressed in this book, however, are my own and are not those of any agency of the U.S. government.

I welcome comments from readers on any aspect of this book. Please address them to me at Wayne State University Law School, 471 West Palmer Street, Detroit, Michigan 48202; w.burnham@wayne.edu.

---

5 The address is http://lp.findlaw.com/.

6 Westlaw and Nexis are explained in Chapter II, *infra* p. 78. While these services are available on the Internet as well, one must subscribe to them in order to use them.

SUMMARY OF CONTENTS

TABLE OF CONTENTS

CHAPTER I

HISTORY AND GOVERNMENTAL STRUCTURE

It is impossible to understand the legal system of the United States without understanding its structure of government. Consequently, it is appropriate to begin this book with that topic.

The Constitution of 1789 established the governmental structure of the United States. The two characteristics of that structure that most directly affect the legal system are "separation of powers" and "federalism." Separation of powers principles assure that none of the three branches of federal government — legislative, executive or judicial — oversteps the bounds of its proper constitutional role and usurps power belonging to the others. We will see later in this chapter that the primary effect on the *legal system* that separation of powers has is on the role of the federal courts.

Federalism means that there are two levels of government in the country, federal and state. In American federalism, the 50 states have a great deal of independence and power. In a real sense, the United States is a country of 51 different governments — 50 states and the federal government. Each of these governments has its own legal system. Indeed, the title of this book is misleading to the extent that it suggests that there is a *single* "legal system of the United States." It would be more accurate to call it an introduction to "the legal *systems* of the United States."

We will first discuss briefly the historical circumstances that led to the adoption of the Constitution and the reasons why the authors of that document — called the "Framers" — chose the governmental structure they did. Then we will trace the development of the constitutional structure by amendment, government practices and court cases since 1789. In reviewing trends and developments since 1789, we will focus first on separation powers and then on the states and federalism. Finally, there will be an overview of the impact of the governmental structure on the legal system.

A. Some Constitutional History

1. Independence From Colonial Rule and Efforts to Achieve Union

The United States began as 13 colonies of Great Britain. From 1760 to 1775, there were protests and then violent clashes between British authorities and dissatisfied American colonists concerning a variety of grievances, chiefly that the British imposed taxes on the colonists yet did not allow colonial representatives to sit in the British Parliament. The dissident colonists identified strongly with their own colonies and thus resistance to British authority began at the local level. However, in 1774 the colonists attempted collective action in Philadelphia at the "First Continental Congress." In response to measures adopted at this Congress, King George III sent troops and the American War of Independence, also called the American Revolution, began in 1775.

On July 4, 1776, the Second Continental Congress adopted unanimously a "Declaration of Independence."[1] Additionally, the Congress adopted a resolution that a "plan of confederation be prepared and transmitted to the respective colonies for their consider-

---

1 The Declaration occupies an important place in political history of the United States and expresses the "enlightenment" political theory of the time: a belief in "natural rights" of human beings, the right of people to throw off an oppressive government, the right of citizens to be free to develop their talents and resources — the right to the "pursuit of happiness" in the document's own words — and other important ideas. *Available at* http://usconstitution.net/declar.html.

ation." In June 1776, a committee was appointed to draft what would later become the Articles of Confederation. After considerable debate, the states ratified the Articles in 1781.

2. The Articles of Confederation

Governmental Structure Under the Articles   The Articles of Confederation failed to provide a viable blueprint for governing the country. Indeed, the Articles provided no truly national government — only a Congress of representatives from the states. When the Congress was not in session, executive power was to be exercised by committees set up by the Congress. Moreover, though the Articles granted several powers to Congress, that body could act in most important matters only on the agreement of 9 of the 13 states. Unanimous approval was needed to amend the Articles themselves. In the Articles, states agreed to abide by congressional decisions, but Congress was given no mechanism to enforce its laws. It could only request that states comply. Finally, the Articles did not give Congress the power to regulate commerce or to tax, reflecting the colonists' experience with the British Parliament's abuse of those powers.

Overall, the Articles established a confederation of separate states — a "firm league of friendship" in which "[e]ach State retains its sovereignty, freedom and independence, and every power, jurisdiction and right, which is not by this confederation expressly delegated to the United States. . . ."[2] As George Washington remarked, the Articles bound the states together with a "rope of sand."[3]

Sources of Disharmony Among the States   Underlying the difficulties with the Articles were differences among the inhabitants of the states over philosophy and social and economic structure, as well as territorial disputes. These differences and disputes predated the Revolution, but had been temporarily forgotten for the duration of the war. They quickly resurfaced once the common enemy of the British crown was defeated. The south was largely rural and agricultural; both economic and social life revolved around large plantations run with slave labor. The northernmost states, called New England, were more oriented toward manufacturing and milling, fishing, shipbuilding, and overseas trade. These kinds of activities led to the creation of urban centers, which were the focus of social and economic life. The middle states engaged in many of the same activities as did New England but had agricultural activity as well. However, farmers usually operated smaller farms without slave labor.

As a direct result of the inadequacies of the Articles, things deteriorated quickly after the end of the War of Independence. Congress negotiated and approved a treaty with Britain in 1784 ending the war, but many states ignored its provisions and Congress could do nothing to force them to honor the treaty. State interference provided Britain with a justification for refusing to carry out many of its obligations under the treaty. More important, it caused friendly foreign countries, which could have provided needed trade and other assistance, to decline to enter into treaties with the largely ineffective national government. Domestically, there was no effective central regulator of disputes about interstate commerce, so trade wars erupted between states. The resulting prohibitively high tariff barriers erected by states caused a sharp drop in trade at a particularly difficult time. States also refused to provide promised funding for the national government. With

---

2   Articles of Confederation, Art. II. *Available at* http://www.usconstitution.net/articles.html.

3   George Washington: A Collection, compiled and edited by W.B. Allen (Indianapolis: Liberty Fund, 1988). *Available at* http://oll.libertyfund.org/Texts/LFBooks/Washington0268/Collection/HTMLs/ 0026_Pt06_Chap06.html.

the army near mutiny because it had not been paid, Congress sought to amend the Articles to allow it to impose a 5% tariff on foreign imports, but the opposition of one state (Rhode Island, the smallest of the 13 states) was sufficient to defeat that proposal.

During the time of the Articles, some states sought to mediate disputes by meeting in conferences, and it was out of one such conference that the idea for a new charter of government emerged.   James Madison, a Virginia delegate to a conference on navigation of interstate rivers suggested that the delegates at that conference call for a convention in Philadelphia in 1787 to discuss the question. All states but Rhode Island sent delegates to what would become the Constitutional Convention.[4]

3. The Constitutional Convention

The delegates to the convention were convinced that a stronger national government was necessary, but they sharply disagreed on just how strong it should be. They had learned the vices of *insufficient* national governmental power from their experience with the Articles of Confederation. But they also had clear memories of the vices of too much national governmental power from their struggles against the British Crown. One group of delegates favored a strong national government capable of rising above regional differences. These "nationalists" ironically and, in a stroke of political genius, chose to be called "Federalists." Other delegates mistrusted strong central control and argued against any greater encroachment on the powers of the states than was minimally necessary to avoid the problems that had arisen under the Articles of Confederation. These "states' rights" delegates, who ultimately opposed the ratification of the constitution as written at the Convention, inherited the label "Anti-Federalists."

For the most part, the Federalists' views prevailed at the 1787 convention. However, they made, significant compromises to accommodate the Anti-Federalists. The debates among the delegates were repeated during the ratification process at ratification conventions in the states. Despite substantial initial opposition, the Constitution was ratified and the new government commenced on March 4, 1789.[5]

4. Ratification of the Bill of Rights

Many Anti-Federalists opposed the Constitution largely because it did not contain a list of individual rights that citizens would have against the new stronger central government. Bills of Rights were a feature of many state constitutions. The Federalists resisted discussing the issue, believing that the most important goal was to establish a basic structure for governing the country as quickly as possible. They urged proponents

---

4   Historians consider James Madison (1751-1836) to be the "father" of the Constitution (a title he rejected) because he played a pivotal role at the 1787 constitutional convention. His notes, taken at the convention, are the primary source of information about the proceedings at the convention. *Available at* http://avalon. law.yale.edu/subject_menus/debcont.asp. In addition, Madison, Alexander Hamilton and John Jay authored a series of anonymous essays, called collectively *The Federalist Papers*, arguing in favor of ratification of the Constitution. *See* THE FEDERALIST (Jacob E. Cooke, ed., Wesleyan U. Press, Middletown, Conn. 1961). *Available at* http://avalon.law.yale.edu/subject_menus/fed.asp. *The Federalist Papers* are a classic in the political literature of the United States and the Supreme Court still uses them today to interpret the Constitution. After ratification of the Constitution, Madison became a member of Congress and in 1808 was elected the fourth President of the United States.

5   For an in-depth discussion of the circumstances surrounding the framing and ratification of the Constitution with excerpts from the original sources and special attention to the Constitution's intellectual origins, *see* DANIEL FARBER AND SUSANNA SHERRY, A HISTORY OF THE AMERICAN CONSTITUTION, 2D ED. (West 2005). *See also* MAX FARRAND, THE FRAMING OF THE CONSTITUTION OF THE UNITED STATES (Yale U. Press 1913). For a collection of documents related to the convention, *see* THE RECORDS OF THE FEDERAL CONVENTION OF 1787 (Max Farrand, ed., Yale U. Press 1913). The debates in the states are collected in JONATHAN ELLIOT, THE DEBATES OF THE SEVERAL STATE CONVENTIONS ON THE ADOPTION OF THE FEDERAL CONSTITUTION (J.B. Lippincott Co. 1836).

of a Bill of Rights to wait until the Constitution was ratified and to add such a Bill by way of amendment — a measure the Federalists agreed to support. The depth of feeling in favor of a Bill of Rights was demonstrated by the fact that 5 of the 13 states submitted demands for a Bill of Rights along with their ratifications. James Madison, one of the Federalists who argued for delaying the question until ratification, drafted a Bill of Rights, which became the first 10 amendments to the Constitution when it was ratified by the people in 1791, shortly after being proposed.

Except for the 10th Amendment, the guarantees of the Bill of Rights relate only indirectly to the structure of government. Consequently, discussion of them is delayed until later chapters on constitutional rights.[6] Including the Bill of Rights, there are 27 amendments, though most are straightforward and warrant little discussion.

B. The Governmental Structure Provided for in the 1789 Constitution

The Constitution has six substantive articles.[7] The most important in terms of governmental structure are Articles I, II and III, which respectively create the legislative, executive and judicial branches of government. Article IV contains miscellaneous provisions that relate mainly to the states and their relationship to each other. Article V sets out the complicated and difficult process needed to amend the Constitution. Article VI sets out miscellaneous provisions, the most important of which declares the supremacy of federal over state law (the "Supremacy Clause").

1. Legislative Power

"Enumerated" Powers of Congress Article I vests "[a]ll legislative Powers herein" in the Congress and later (in §8) lists those powers. This list of powers was a compromise resulting from one of the major differences of opinion at the convention. The Virginia delegation proposed — in direct response to the problems of the Articles of Confederation — that Congress be given the power "to legislate in all cases to which the separate states are incompetent, or in which the harmony of the United States may be interrupted by the exercise of individual legislation."[8] However, other delegates argued that this gave Congress too much power. The final compromise language listed particular subjects in which the delegates *anticipated* that individual state legislation would be disruptive of the "harmony of the United States." Because these powers are listed individually, they are often referred to as Congress's "enumerated powers."

The major powers listed in §8 are those one would expect a national government to have: the powers to issue money, to establish a postal system, to create federal courts, to raise an army and navy, to declare war, to collect taxes and spend money for the general welfare, and the like. As it has developed, the most important of the powers granted is the one empowering Congress to regulate interstate commerce.[9]

Compromise on Representation Another major disagreement among the Framers arose over the composition and the method of selection of the national legislature provided for under Article I. The Federalists wanted representation in the legislature based on population, rather than equal representation for each state. This would

---

6 *See* Chapter VIII, pp. 283-323 (4th, 5th, 6th and 8th Amendments as constitutional requirements in criminal procedure) and Chapter IX, pp. 368-397 (1st Amendment freedoms).

7 A copy of the Constitution is set out in the Appendix, pp. A15-A30.

8 *See* Debates in the Federal Convention of 1787 as reported by James Madison, *supra* note 4, notes for May 29, 1787.

9 In §9 and §10, the Framers listed miscellaneous prohibitions. Most are of little consequence today except prohibitions on retroactive or *ex post facto* criminal laws and laws retroactively "impairing the Obligation of Contracts."

prevent states representing a minority of the population from blocking national legislation, as had happened under the Articles of Confederation. However, strong opposition from the smaller states forced the Framers to compromise and agree to a two-chamber (bicameral) Congress. One chamber, the House of Representatives, would have proportional representation based on population. The other chamber, the Senate, would have equal representation from each state. To assure that the House of Representatives would better reflect the prevailing sentiment of the voters, its members, called "representatives" or simply "members of Congress," were made subject to reelection every 2 years. Senators would serve 6-year terms so as to provide some stability. Both houses would have to agree to legislation before it could become law.[10]

In accordance with this system, today there are 100 Senators (two from each of 50 states) and 435 members of the House of Representatives representing the residents of as many districts throughout the country. Federal territories such as the District of Columbia may elect representatives to Congress but they are not entitled to vote. The 435 House seats are divided among the states based on total population (281,421,906 in 2000) but allowing every state a minimum of one representative. The average size of districts is approximately 640,000 residents. Based on the 2000 census, California, the most populous state (33,930,798 residents) has 53 representatives in the Congress, Michigan (9,955,829 residents) has 15 and Wyoming (493,782 residents) has only one.[11]

Compromise on Slavery In the southern states, an agricultural economy based on slavery had developed and the question of slavery came up several times at the convention. Slavery was not abolished by the Constitution nor was Congress given the power to abolish it. Despite viewing slaves as property rather than human beings, southern delegates insisted that they be counted the same as citizens in determining the number of representatives in Congress. A compromise was reached to count slaves as three-fifths of a free person.[12] Southerners also insisted on a provision requiring the return of escaped slaves from other states.[13] However, many of the Framers hoped that slavery would eventually be abolished and, in another compromise, Congress was authorized to outlaw further *importation* of slaves after the year 1808.[14]

Assuring the Supremacy of Federal Law Another area of disagreement that arose during discussions of the legislative power was how to deal with conflicts between federal legislation and state law. Under the Articles of Confederation, serious problems had arisen when states simply ignored federal laws and treaties which they did not like. Originally, Madison's plan called for a veto procedure whereby Congress could pass resolutions that would annul the effect of particular state laws. Others argued that this means of assuring federal supremacy would be too direct an affront to the states and unwieldy. The Framers settled upon a clause, set out in Article VI, which is referred to as the "supremacy clause":

---

10 Until 1913, Senators were elected by the legislatures of the states. However, this was changed by the 17th Amendment to the current system of election by the entire population of the state. *See* Art. I §3 cl. 1 and footnote thereto in Appendix, p. A14.

11 Redistricting of Congress is required after each decennial census. The 2000 census results reported here represent a loss of one representative by Michigan and a gain of one by California. After the 2010 census, California, Michigan and Ohio each stand to lose a representative, while Texas, Florida and Georgia each stand to gain one or more.

12 Art. I §2 cl. 3.

13 Art. IV §2 cl. 3.

14 Art. I §9. Congress duly passed such a prohibition. The Constitution reflects the embarrassment of some of the Framers about slavery in that it never uses the words "slavery" or "slaves," euphemistically referring to slaves as "other Persons" and "Person held to Service or Labor in one State."

This Constitution and the Laws of the United States which shall be made in Pursuance thereof; and all Treaties made, or which shall be made, under the Authority of the United States, shall be the supreme Law of the Land; and Judges in every State shall be bound thereby, any Thing in the Constitution or Laws of any State to the Contrary notwithstanding.[15]

Congress's "Power of the Purse" One issue upon which the Framers were united was Congress's power to tax and spend. They resolved that the sole power to decide whether and to what extent to tax and fund governmental programs must be lodged in Congress.[16] Furthermore, Article I gives the sole power to originate revenue bills to the House of Representatives — the house most directly representative of the people.[17] This clause assured that there would be "no taxation without representation" — a major complaint about British colonial taxes. In addition, the "power of the purse" would serve as a democratic curb on presidential excesses and adventures, since both would likely need funding. The Framers also gave Congress the ultimate check on executive and judicial power — the power of impeachment and removal from office of any "civil Officers of the United States," including the President and any federal judge.[18]

2. Executive Power

There was little in the Articles of Confederation to use as a departure point for discussion of the executive branch, since the Articles did not provide for an executive at all. The language of Article II of the Constitution is not much more help in determining the structure and powers of the executive. Most of Article II is taken up by qualifications for the office of President and the complicated method of election.[19]

The President as Chief Executive Article II §1 does declare generally that "[t]he executive Power shall be vested in a President of the United States of America," and §3 imposes on the President the duty "to take Care that the Laws be faithfully executed." Article II §3 also gives the President the power, with the "Advice and Consent" of the Senate, to appoint ambassadors, judges, "public Ministers and Consuls" and "all other Officers of the United States" who staff the executive branch of government. Originally the Framers intended to specify in the Constitution various departments of the executive branch, but they changed their minds and decided to leave that to Congress to accomplish by statute. To date, Congress has created 15 departments: Agriculture, Commerce,

---

15 Art. VI cl. 2.

16 Art. I §8 cl. 1.

17 Art. II §7 cl. 2.

18 Art. II §4.

19 Under this method, instead of direct election by popular vote, the state legislature selects "electors" equal in number to the total number of senators and representatives from the state, based on which candidate wins the vote of the people of that state. These electors meet as the "electoral college" and elect the President. Originally, the Framers intended this indirect method of election to operate as a check on extremism or bad judgment of the populace. However, tradition, and in some states the law, requires that the electors vote for the presidential candidate who has won the majority of the popular vote in that state. Because the winner of a majority of votes in a state gets all the electors from that state, it is possible that a President could win sufficient electoral votes to be elected President, but not receive a majority of the vote of all voters in the country (called the popular vote). This happened in the 2000 election, when President George W. Bush won the presidency even though his opponent, Vice President Albert Gore, Jr., won the popular vote. Florida was the final contested state that determined the election and considerable legal controversy arose over who should win the Florida electors. The U.S. Supreme Court finally settled the dispute in *Bush v. Gore*, 531 U.S. 98 (2000). For more on this debacle, *see* E.J. DIONNE, JR. & WILLIAM KRISTOL, *BUSH V. GORE*: THE COURT CASES AND THE COMMENTARY (2001); KARLEN ISSACHAROFF, RICHARD H PILDES & PAMELA KARLEN WHEN ELECTIONS GO BAD, THE LAW OF DEMOCRACY AND THE PRESIDENTIAL ELECTION OF 2000 (West 2000).

Defense, Education, Energy, Health and Human Services, Homeland Security, Housing and Urban Development, Interior, Justice, Labor, State, Transportation, Treasury, and Veterans Affairs. The heads of these departments are called "secretaries" and they are appointed by the President with the advice and consent of the Senate. Collectively, they are referred to as the President's "cabinet."[20]

Veto Power of the President One of the most important and most specific powers of the President, the power to strike down or "veto" legislation, is set out in Article I §7, not Article II. In the discussions over the shape of the powers to be accorded the executive branch, the Framers divided themselves into two camps. Some feared the tyranny of an excessively powerful executive. Others feared that, without a powerful executive to counterbalance Congress, there would be *legislative* tyranny, which had happened already with some state legislatures. It was the latter group whose ideas prevailed. The delegates determined that there should be a single President, elected independently of the Congress for 4-year terms, who would have limited veto power over legislation. Similar to the veto power enjoyed by governors in many states, the President could veto legislation, but Congress could override a veto with a two-thirds majority vote of each house.[21]

The presence of a President with his own direct electoral mandate and veto power makes the U.S. system different from some parliamentary systems. A stalemate between the chief executive officer and the chief legislative body cannot be resolved by a vote of "no confidence" by the legislature, the resignation of the government and a new election. Under the Constitution's system, an adamant President, liberally exercising his veto power against an equally stubborn Congress, unable to muster a two-thirds majority, could often cause a stalemate or "gridlock." Because of this potential, there is a great need for cooperation between Congress and the President.

Presidential Power in Foreign Affairs   The powers granted to the President by Article II are the most specific in the area of foreign affairs. The President has the power to "receive Ambassadors and other public Ministers" (and thus the power to choose whether to recognize foreign governments) and to make treaties with Senate concurrence.[22] The President is also the "Commander in Chief" of the armed forces.[23] The relative specificity of duties in the area of foreign affairs and the fact that the President is head of state show that, at least in foreign affairs, the President has broad authority. A statement made in 1816 by the Senate Committee on Foreign Relations observed that "[t]he President is the Constitutional representative of the United States with regard to foreign nations. He manages our concerns with foreign nations." The statement emphasizes that the executive power is particularly appropriate for international relations because "[t]he nature of transactions with foreign nations . . . requires caution and unity of design, and their success frequently depends on secrecy and dispatch."[24] However, the Framers provided for a shared responsibility with Congress for foreign policy. They gave Congress the power to regulate foreign commerce and to decide whether and to what extent to maintain and regulate the armed forces or to fund foreign

---

20 A chart showing the organization of federal government and its principal agencies and departments appears on pp. A30-A31 of the Appendix.

21 Art. I §7 cl. 2-3.

22 Art. II §2.

23 Art. II §2.

24 *United States v. Curtiss-Wright Export Corp.*, 299 U.S. 304, 319 (1936).

involvements. In addition, Congress has the sole power to declare war and the Senate has the power to ratify treaties.[25]

3. Judicial Power

The Supreme Court and Lower Federal Courts Article III provides: "The judicial Power of the United States, shall be vested in one supreme Court, and in such inferior Courts as Congress may from time to time ordain and establish."[26] The quoted language was the source of a major dispute among the Framers. Some delegates, particularly Madison, felt that the Constitution should establish *lower* federal courts as well as a Supreme Court to assure an effective check on the excesses of the states and the legislative and executive branches of the federal government. Other delegates objected and argued that state courts were sufficient to enforce federal law. They feared that a full complement of federal courts would lead to greater interference in state prerogatives. As a compromise, the Framers agreed that lower federal courts would not be created by the Constitution itself, but that the Constitution would give *Congress* the power to create them if it thought they were needed.

Limited Subject-Matter Jurisdiction of Federal Courts This mistrust of federal courts also led the Framers to limit the types of cases the federal judiciary could decide. Federal courts were limited to cases of two principal types: controversies between citizens of different states or aliens, and cases "arising under" the *federal* Constitution and laws. The first type of jurisdiction, called "diversity" jurisdiction, was relatively uncontroversial, undoubtedly because it was thought appropriate to avoid possible bias by state courts against persons from other states. The Framers conceded that the second category, called "federal question" jurisdiction, was necessary to assure sympathetic and consistent treatment of issues of federal law — but only if Congress determined that state courts could not or would not do so. It is some indication of the mistrust of lower federal courts in federal question cases that Congress gave federal courts diversity jurisdiction almost immediately in 1789, but did not vest them with general federal question jurisdiction until 1875.[27]

The Framers did agree that a Supreme Court had to be established in the Constitution itself. The Supreme Court's *original* jurisdiction was largely limited to suits between states.[28] Its appellate jurisdiction extends to all diversity and federal question cases coming from the lower federal courts and to state court decisions resolving issues of federal law. However, consistent with separation of powers principles, the Court's[29] appellate jurisdiction was established "with such Exceptions, and under such Regulations as the Congress shall make."[30]

---

25 Art. I §8 cl. 3, 11-16. The President and Congress's powers in foreign affairs are discussed in Chapter XVII, pp. 688-693, 692-693, 700-701.

26 For a more complete discussion of the jurisdiction of the United States Supreme Court and the lower federal courts, *see* Chapter V, pp. 174-177.

27 Details of federal question and diversity jurisdiction are discussed in Chapter V, pp. 188-191.

28 *See* Chapter V, p. 177.

29 When referring to the United States Supreme Court in short form, it is common to call it "the Court" with a capital "C," which distinguishes if from references to all other courts.

30 Art. III §2 cl. 2. The meaning of this clause and its possible use as a means of controlling the Supreme Court's power of judicial review are discussed in the chapter on constitutional law, Chapter IX, pp. 335-337. The power of judicial review, which is not explicitly referred to in the Constitution, is also discussed in Chapter IX, pp. 324-329, and later in this chapter where developments since 1789 are considered. *See infra* pp. 9-11.

Judicial Tenure and Selection Concerns for judicial independence at the Convention can be traced to the Declaration of Independence, which stated as one of the colonists' grievances that the King had "made judges dependent upon his Will alone for the tenure of their offices and payment of their salaries." Judicial independence was thought necessary to assure immunity from pressure from the political branches to decide cases a particular way. So, Article III §1 provides that federal judges "shall hold their Offices during good Behaviour," subject only to impeachment by Congress, and that "Compensation . . . shall not be diminished during their Continuance in Office." Many of the Framers' disagreements focused on the method of selection of federal judges. Many delegates wanted Congress to elect federal judges. Others feared that this would make judges too dependent on Congress's will. Ultimately the question was decided by a compromise that spread the responsibility between the President and the Congress: the President would appoint federal judges for life terms with the advice and consent of the Senate, though they could be removed by the entire Congress through the impeachment process.[31]

C. Separation and Balance of Powers Among the Branches of the Federal Government

Separation of powers and "checks and balances" among the three branches of government were a matter of conscious design. The concept derives from the writings of Baron de Montesquieu and John Locke, with whose works the delegates to the convention were familiar.[32] However, the idea as understood in the United States is less one of strictly *separating* powers than it is of *spreading* power among the branches. As Madison observed, the "necessary partition of power among the several departments" in the Constitution will assure that "its several constituent parts may, by their mutual relations, be the means of keeping each other in their proper places."[33] A contemporary commentator has described the Constitution as establishing "separate institutions sharing power."[34] Consequently, it is more appropriate to understand the scheme of the Constitution as a *balancing* of powers or a system of "checks and balances."

Since 1789, governmental structure and relationships between components of government have evolved. Supreme Court decisions have caused some changes. Others have resulted from the natural growth of the size of the country and changes in technology and in the types of challenges facing government. We will discuss four major developments affecting the balance and separation of powers: judicial review, greater presidential power, the growth of administrative agencies, and Congress's modern investigatory oversight role.

1. Establishment and Vigorous Exercise of the Power of Judicial Review

As the discussion of the basic provisions of the 1789 Constitution indicates, the Constitution's "checks and balances" provide means for the executive and legislative

---

31 Art. III §1 and Art. II §4. The modern impact of the lifetime tenure requirement is discussed in Chapter VI, pp. 220-222. Impeachment of federal judges is discussed in Chapter V, pp. 184-185.

32 *See* MONTESQUIEU, THE SPIRIT OF THE LAWS 151-152 (Nugent trans. 1949)(originally published 1748) ("there can be no liberty where the legislative and executive powers are united in the same person or body of magistrates"); John Locke, SECOND TREATISE ON GOVERNMENT: AN ESSAY CONCERNING THE TRUE ORIGIN, EXTENT AND END OF CIVIL GOVERNMENT (1690). *See generally* M.C.J. VILE, CONSTITUTIONALISM AND THE SEPARATION OF POWERS 64-67 (Oxford U. Press 1967) (discussing Locke's role in developing this theory).

33 *Federalist No. 51, supra* note 4, at 347-348.

34 RICHARD NEUSTADT, PRESIDENTIAL POWER: THE POLITICS OF LEADERSHIP 3 (Wiley & Sons 1960).

branches to check the power of the judicial branch, primarily through selection of judges and control of federal court jurisdiction. The constitutional text does not clearly set out what checks the *judicial* branch was to have on *legislative* and *executive* power. Today, we know it is the power of judicial review — the power of the Supreme Court to pass on the constitutionality of laws and actions of the other two branches — but such power is not explicitly set out in the Constitution. Instead, the Supreme Court held in 1803 that judicial review was implicit in the Constitution.

The Basis for Judicial Review   In *Marbury v. Madison*,[35] the Court found judicial review implicit in the nature of a written constitution, in the supremacy clause and in Article III's grant of judicial power. Chief Justice John Marshall reasoned as follows. First, the Constitution is *law* and must be followed; indeed, the supremacy clause makes the Constitution the *supreme* law of the land. Second, the judges of the judicial branch, being vested by Article III with the "judicial Power of the United States," have the power to say *what the law is* in cases that come before them. It follows then that judges, in deciding an issue to which both a statute and the Constitution apply, must follow the hierarchy of law set out in the supremacy clause: they must apply the constitutional provision and disregard the statute. *Marbury* struck down a federal statute, but seven years later in *Fletcher v. Peck*,[36] the Court held that *Marbury's* reasoning also applied to state laws.

Vigorous Exercise of Judicial Review in Modern Times   Judicial review was used sparingly in the first century of the country's history. But beginning at the end of the 19th century, judicial review became a major force in law and government, profoundly affecting the balance of federalism, separation of powers and the relationship between individuals and all levels of government.

In the 75 years from 1789 until 1864, the Court struck down only two Acts of Congress. From 1789 to 1888, a period of 100 years, the total climbs only to 21 invalidations. But during the period 1889-1952, 64 years, there were 55 invalidations, with the Court from 1889-1940, invalidating 52 federal laws in 52 years. In the 52 years between 1953 and 2004, the Court invalidated 97 federal laws, or almost two per year. Though this surge in cases began with the "liberal" Warren Court (1953-1969), the more "conservative" Burger and Rehnquist Courts (1969-1986 and 1986-2005) were no less "activist."[37] While the tenures of the two Chief Justices were approximately the same length (16 years), Chief Justice Burger presided over 34 invalidations of federal law, while Chief Justice Warren presided over only 25. The Rehnquist Court exceeded the Warren Court's rate at 38 cases invalidating federal-laws in 18 years.

The Supreme Court followed a similar pattern in striking down state laws. In the 75 years from 1789 until 1864, the Court held unconstitutional only 39 state laws. From 1789 to 1888, a period of 100 years, the total climbs only to 79 invalidations or less than one a year. But during the period 1889-1952, there were 452 invalidations, with the Court from 1889-1940, invalidating 389 federal laws in 52 years, a rate of over 7 per year. In the 52 years between 1953 and 2004, the Court invalidated 436 state laws, or around 8 per

---

35   5 U.S. 137 (1803).

36   10 U.S. 87 (1810) (Georgia law unconstitutional for violation of prohibition against passing any "Law impairing the Obligation of Contract"). Judicial review is discussed in detail in Chapter IX, pp. 324-326.

37   Historians generally divide the eras of Supreme Court history into periods defined by the tenures of the fourteen Chief Justices. For a brief, readable excerpt dividing the Court's history into four principal periods, *see* DANIEL A. FARBER, WILLIAM N. ESKRIDGE, JR. & PHILIP P. FRICKEY, CONSTITUTIONAL LAW: THEMES FOR THE CONSTITUTION'S THIRD CENTURY, 4TH ED. 3-54 (West 2009). Although it is a casebook, this book has more narrative explanation and analysis than average.

year. Interestingly enough, the biggest surge in state law invalidations began, not with the "liberal" Warren Court (1953-1969), but well before that. In addition, the more "conservative" and "states' rights" oriented Burger and Rehnquist Courts since 1969 have presided over only slightly fewer invalidations per year than the Warren Court.[38]

Numbers do not tell the entire story. But it is as true qualitatively as quantitatively that the constitutional decisions of the Supreme Court and the lower federal courts have become a major source of law in many areas of the law.[39]

Dangers in Activist Judicial Review   While judicial review has generally won praise, it has not usually served progressive interests. Some "low points" in legal history demonstrate the dangers of activist judicial review. The Court's infamous 1857 decision in *Dred Scott v. Sandford*,[40] discussed below, held that under the Constitution blacks were not "citizens" who could take advantage of the diversity jurisdiction of the federal courts. *Dred Scott* also stated that Congress had no power to abolish slavery in its territories. Thus, the Court did not get off to a very good start in its exercise of judicial review: *Dred Scott* was only the Court's second invalidation of a federal law — the first was *Marbury v. Madison* 54 years before.[41]

The Court's most recent difficult period for the Court was the period was 1900 to 1937. During this time, the Court repeatedly used three bases — the due process clause of the 5th and 14th Amendments, a limited view of Congress's power to regulate interstate commerce, and the doctrine against delegation of legislative power — to deny to Congress and the states the power to enact progressive laws regulating business. The Court struck down a New York state law limiting the hours bakers could work per week,[42] federal laws prohibiting child labor,[43] federal laws regulating industry through taxation,[44] federal laws to regulate the economy in the wake of the Great Depression of the 1930s,[45] and a New York law setting minimum wages for women.[46]

Viewing these decisions as a continuing obstacle to meeting the serious social and economic needs of the country, President Franklin Roosevelt and Congress in 1937 considered the possibility of legislation to "pack" the Court — to authorize the President to appoint additional justices to the Court in order to change the balance of power. In

---

38 These statistics are from DAVID M. O'BRIEN, STORM CENTER: THE SUPREME COURT IN AMERICAN POLITICS, 7TH ED. 31 (W.W. Norton 2005). The figures do not include federal laws that Court decisions effectively invalidated because they are identical in all relevant respects to the law involved in a decided case. For example, the figures count *Immigration & Naturalization Service v. Chadha*, 462 U.S. 919 (1983) only once, despite the fact that the decision effectively meant that over 200 other federal statutes with the offending legislative veto provision were also unconstitutional. Nor do the statistics include the decisions of the lower federal courts, which also have the power to hold Acts of Congress and state laws unconstitutional and often do so in cases that never reach the Supreme Court.

39 Constitutional decisions of the Supreme Court are discussed in Chapter IX. To locate the various other places in this book where constitutional decisions are discussed, *see* p. 324 note 1.

40 60 U.S. 393 (1857).

41 *See* discussion *infra* p. 23.

42 *Lochner v. New York*, 198 U.S. 45 (1905).

43 *Hammer v. Dagenhart*, 247 U.S. 251 (1918).

44 *Bailey v. Drexel Furniture Co.*, 259 U.S. 20 (1922) (child labor tax); *Hill v. Wallace*, 259 U.S. 44 (1922) (tax on grain future contracts).

45 *See, e.g., A.L.A. Schechter Poultry Corp. v. United States*, 295 U.S. 495 (1935) (improper delegation of power to develop trade code for industry); *Railroad Retirement Board v. Alton R. Co.*, 295 U.S. 330 (1935) (act setting up retirement program for railroad employees exceeded Congress's commerce clause powers); *Carter v. Carter Coal Co.*, 298 U.S. 238 (1936) (maximum hour labor standards for coal industry beyond commerce clause power).

46 *Morehead v. New York ex rel. Tipaldo*, 298 U.S. 587 (1936).

the alternative, the President considered the possibility of simply disregarding the Supreme Court's decisions. Neither the "Court-packing" plan nor disobedience to the Court was necessary, however. In the Spring of 1937, one Justice switched his vote to favor upholding economic and social welfare programs. Over the next four years, death or retirement of Justices allowed President Roosevelt to appoint seven new justices, all of whom were committed to a more expansive view of Congress's power.[47]

The due process decisions of the Court during this disastrous 1900-1937 period starkly illustrate the nature of the crisis in judicial review then, and what many consider to be a continuing problem with judicial review today. Due process doctrine developed toward the end of the 19th century, when the Court began to define the concept of "liberty" in the 14th Amendment due process clause as including the "freedom of contract." In *Lochner v. New York*[48] the Court held that a New York law that limited the hours that bakers could work to sixty per week violated the due process clause. Such a law, the Court concluded, was an undue burden on "the freedom of the master and employee to contract with each other in relation to their employment."[49] In his dissent in the case, Justice Oliver Wendell Holmes, Jr., protested that the majority's concept of "liberty" imposed its own concept of what was proper economic policy on states. Referring to a popular book by a 19th-century English philosopher of *laissez faire* economic policy, he observed wryly: "[t]he fourteenth amendment does not enact Mr. Herbert Spencer's Social Statics."[50]

The Court regularly suggests that the "Lochner" period provides important lessons for the Court's role today. The Court made this point in its 1992 decision to stick by its 1973 abortion decision despite considerable opposition on the part of the public.[51] The *Lochner* Era teaches that, while the Court is a counter-majoritarian check on political forces, it cannot allow itself and its decisions to stray too far from the mainstream of thought in the country. Unlike the legislative and executive branches of government, the judicial branch's power and influence depend, not on coercion, but on the degree to which society voluntarily respects the Court's decisions. Despite the *Lochner* Era, the Court has recovered its prestige and moral force. Today, society and the other two branches accept the Court's vigorous exercise of judicial review.[52]

2. Growth of Presidential Power

Many Framers were concerned with the *legislative* branch becoming too powerful. Today, however, it is the executive branch that has become a dominating force in

---

47 This history is related in JOHN E. NOWAK & RONALD D. ROTUNDA, CONSTITUTIONAL LAW, 7TH ED. §§11.2-11.3 (West 2004).

48 198 U.S. 45 (1905).

49 *Id.* at 75. There were several other decisions invalidating state laws on due process grounds.

50 198 U.S. at 64. Holmes, known during his tenure on the Court as the "great dissenter," is discussed in another connection in Chapter II, p. 45.

51 *See Planned Parenthood of Southeastern Pennsylvania v. Casey*, 505 U.S. 833 (1992).

52 Some point to *Bush v. Gore*, 531 U.S. 98 (2000) (discussed *supra* note 19), as a serious set-back for the Court's integrity and moral authority. In that case, a majority of the Court composed of Republican appointees prevented a recount of ballots ordered by the Florida Supreme Court pursuant to state election laws, effectively deciding the 2000 election in favor of the Republican candidate. A dissenter in the case observed: "Although we may never know with complete certainty the identity of the winner of this year's Presidential election, the identity of the loser is perfectly clear. It is the Nation's confidence in the judge as an impartial guardian of the rule of law." *Id.* at 129-129, Stevens, J., dissenting). However, the dire predictions of Justice Stevens have not come to pass, at least eyes of the public. The public has largely forgotten the case and criticisms are largely dismissed as partisan rhetoric. It is interesting, however, that Justice Stevens was also a Republican appointee.

government. The President's function in the 19th century — described as "carrying out the will of Congress"[53] — has been supplanted in the 20th century by a model of presidential primacy. Congress bears a good part of the responsibility for what some call the "Imperial Presidency."[54] Although strong Presidents have made "power grabs," more often Congress has willingly delegated its power.[55]

Factors in the Growth of Presidential Power Perhaps the primary factor leading to greater presidential power has been the succession of strong personalities who have occupied the White House in the 20th century, starting with President Theodore Roosevelt in 1901, then Franklin Roosevelt in the 1930s and 1940s, continuing with several strong post-World War II presidents. Although the President shares responsibility for foreign policy with Congress, the differing nature and organization of the two branches make the executive branch more capable of reacting to international crises. United States participation in two world wars, its emergence as a world power, and other international incidents have created a need for quick decisions and responses — something a branch headed by one person and a staff of advisors does better than a 535-member pluralistic legislature. Additionally, the President's control of information about unfolding crises has allowed the President to seize the initiative in foreign policy, often leaving Congress with no choice but to follow the President's lead.

On the domestic front, much of the impetus behind presidential primacy came from the Great Depression of the 1930s. That crisis called for the decisive action of a strong national leader. President Franklin Roosevelt, in response, presented a comprehensive legislative program for Congress to enact. There have also been "spillover" effects from the primacy of the President in wars and foreign affairs. For all these reasons, voters today look to the President for a domestic legislative agenda as much as for foreign policy. A large part of Congress's legislative role, when an active President is in the White House, has been reacting to the President's proposed legislative programs.[56]

Power Over Implementation of Legislative Programs The Constitution directs the President to "take Care that the Laws be faithfully executed,"[57] meaning the President must implement congressional programs.[58] But there is no requirement that the President do so enthusiastically. There are many opportunities for undermining legislative programs, such as interpreting statutory directives more narrowly than Congress might have intended. Such practices are especially likely when Congress

---

53 HARRY A. BAILEY, JR. AND JAY M. SHAFRITZ, EDS., THE AMERICAN PRESIDENCY: HISTORICAL AND CONTEMPORARY PERSPECTIVES vii (Dorsey Press, Chicago 1988).

54 *See* ARTHUR M. SCHLESINGER, JR., THE IMPERIAL PRESIDENCY (Houghton, Mifflin 1973). The impact of this growth in presidential power on separation of powers is discussed in Philip D. Kurland, *The Rise and Fall of the "Doctrine" of Separation of Powers*, 85 MICH. L. REV. 592, 607-613 (1986). In the 20th century, Congress has also *gained* much power as the result of the Supreme Court's willingness to read its powers broadly. But, as discussed below, that gain in power has been at the expense of the states rather than the President.

55 In reaction to some perceived excesses of the Presidents, Congress has made some efforts to reclaim some of its power from the executive branch. This has raised some interesting separation of powers questions. *See* Chapter VI, p. 218 (legislative veto) and Chapter XVII, pp. 700-701 (war powers).

56 Only members of Congress may introduce legislation, but the President has no trouble convincing members of his party in Congress to lend their names to legislation he would like to propose.

57 Art. II §3.

58 *See Train v. City of New York*, 420 U.S. 35 (1975) (President may not "impound" for other uses money Congress has directed to be spent on programs it has enacted).

enacts broad delegations of authority to an executive agency under a secretary in the President's cabinet.[59]

Limits on Presidential Power Despite the growth in presidential power, the President must yield when his actions conflict with the constitutional powers of the other branches. Three cases illustrate this.

In the first case, the *Steel Seizure Case* or *Youngstown Sheet & Tube v. Sawyer,*[60] labor strikes at steel mills threatened steel production needed for the Korean War. Consequently, President Truman issued an executive order instructing the Secretary of Commerce to seize the privately-owned steel mills in the U.S. and operate them under government control. The Supreme Court held the order unconstitutional. Earlier, Congress had passed general labor-management legislation, which rejected the possibility of government seizures of plants in cases of emergencies caused by labor strife. Thus, the executive order was invalid because it conflicted with a policy that Congress had already created.

The second major case concerning presidential prerogatives was *United States v. Nixon,*[61] which involved the Watergate Scandal. During the campaign for the 1972 presidential election, several men identified with the Republican Party were caught breaking into the national headquarters of the Democratic Party in the "Watergate" building. A special prosecutor investigating the break-in subpoenaed tape recordings and documents from President Nixon, who had won reelection after that campaign. Nixon claimed "executive privilege" as the basis for withholding the tapes and documents — the power of the President to conceal information and material regarding the discharge of executive functions that the President believes he and his staff should not disclose. While acknowledging that executive privilege existed, the Supreme Court unanimously affirmed a district court order to produce the tapes, which eventually led to President Nixon's resignation. Thus, the Court confirmed that Presidents, no less than average citizens, must comply with court orders to produce evidence.

The Court decided the third case, *Hamdan v. Rumsfeld,*[62] in 2006. In 2001, Congress granted the President sweeping authority to use "all necessary and appropriate force against those nations, organizations or persons he determines planned, authorized, committed, or aided" the September 11, 2001 attacks on the World Trade Center and the Pentagon.[63] In the ensuing invasion of Afghanistan, the U.S. military captured several hundred combatants and confined them at its base in Guantanamo Bay, Cuba. One of them, Hamdan, was charged with conspiracy to commit terrorist acts in connection with the September 11 attacks. The Bush Administration created a special military tribunal to try Hamdan and others. Hamdan challenged the tribunal's authority and its procedures, which permitted, among other things, the use of secret evidence. Relying on the *Steel Seizure Case*, the Supreme Court held that the President could not create such special military tribunals in the absence of more specific authorization by Congress.[64]

---

59 In fact, there are many influences on both cabinet and independent administrative agencies. *See* Chapter VI, pp. 214-219 (discussing congressional and presidential means of controlling agency action). The two types of administrative agencies are discussed *infra* p. 16.

60 343 U.S. 579 (1952).

61 418 U.S. 683 (1974).

62 548 U.S. 557 (2006).

63 U.S. Public Law No. 107-40, §2(a) (Sept. 18, 2001).

64 Responding to *Hamdan,* Congress specifically authorized the President to create special military tribunals in the Military Commissions Act of 2006, Pub. L. No. 109-366, 120 Stat. 2600. Several other Guantanamo detainees challenged this law in *Boumediene v. Bush*, 553 U.S. 723 (2008). The Court ruled

It also held that the tribunals did not follow the law on procedures for trying U.S. soldiers for crimes.[65]   Furthermore, the tribunal procedures violated Geneva Convention protections concerning prisoners of war, particularly the provision requiring that any trials of prisoners be undertaken "by a regularly constituted court affording all the judicial guarantees which are recognized as indispensable by civilized peoples."[66]

3. The Advent and Growth of Administrative Agencies

Development of Agencies   Nowhere does the Constitution mention administrative agencies.   Yet today, they occupy an important place in governmental structure.[67] Congress established the first powerful federal administrative agency, the Interstate Commerce Commission, in 1887.   But the greatest growth in the power of administrative agencies came in the Great Depression of the 1930s. At the request of President Franklin D. Roosevelt, Congress passed legislation creating a wide variety of administrative agencies to provide relief to victims and to foster future economic recovery. To assure the swift and expert action necessary to accomplish these goals, Congress readily delegated a great deal of its legislative power to those agencies.   Thus began the transformation of the country into "the administrative state."[68] States have taken similar action over the years. Today federal and state administrative agencies manage a wide variety of governmental functions, such as banking, social security, job health and safety, labor organizing and others.[69]

Agencies impact government principally by acting through their delegated legislative power to enact substantive law, in the form of agency regulations or "rules."[70] One can get a rough idea of the impact of agency rules by looking in the law library: federal *regulations* occupy about ten times the space of federal *statutes*.   Federal statutes seldom provide useful guidance to people or companies engaged in federally-controlled activities.   Instead, only consulting masses of administrative rules and interpretive guidelines provides answers. But agencies not only *enact* rules, they also have enforcement divisions that investigate and prosecute violations of those rules. Furthermore,

---

5 to 4 that these military tribunals violated the constitutional right to *habeas corpus*, which requires the executive to bring a prisoner to court and justify the detention. This decision resulted in the release of five Guantanamo detainees. In 2009, President Obama signed the Military Commissions Act of 2009, Pub. L. No. 111-84, 123 Stat. 2190, which amended the original act to conform with the Court's ruling in *Boumediene*.

65 *See also Hamdi v. Rumsfeld*, 542 U.S. 507 (2004) (rejecting the Bush administration's position that it could detain all "enemy combatants" without affording them the opportunity for a hearing to contest this classification was proper) (discussed in Chapter VI, p. 208); *Rasul v. Bush*, 542 U.S. 466 (2004) (rejecting Bush administration's position and holding that judicial remedy of *habeas corpus* is available to test the legality of Guantanamo detainees' detention because while Guantanamo is not within the territory of the U.S., it is under U.S. control).

66 The Court applied the Convention because Congress had directed, in earlier legislation on military courts, that the President follow the "law of war" in creating all military tribunals. Thus, the decision does not change the established rule that treaties do not create judicially enforceable individual rights unless they are self-executing or are implemented by legislation. It also means that if Congress passes a clear statute that is contrary to Geneva Convention rules, that statute will prevail. *See* Chapter XVII, pp. 694-698, 690-691 and note 129.   Congress can, of course, remedy the problem of lack of congressional authorization identified by the Court by passing more specific legislation. However, if it does so, it will have to debate and decide whether the tribunals must comply with international law — a highly charged political issue.

67 *See* Chapter VI, which discusses the law of administrative agencies.

68 A diagram of the structure of the modern federal government showing many of the major agencies appears in the Appendix to this book on pp. A30-A31.

69 The phenomenon is international. *See* MAURO CAPPELLETTI, THE JUDICIAL PROCESS IN COMPARATIVE PERSPECTIVE 16-24 (Oxford U. Press 1989).

70 In general, delegation is proper so long as Congress provides sufficient standards to guide the agency in its rule-making. Courts have approved very general rule-making standards. *See* Chapter VI, p. 219.

agencies have their own administrative hearing officers (often called "administrative law judges" or "ALJ") who adjudicate the disputes resulting from enforcement. Generally judicial review of administrative hearing decisions is limited in scope.[71] Thus, in many areas of law, the only hearing of consequence for litigants is an administrative hearing, not a court hearing.

"Independent" Federal Administrative Agencies   There are two types of federal agencies: "executive" and "independent." Executive agencies are under the general supervision and control of a cabinet officer responsible to the President, though there are limits to presidential control over such agencies. Consequently, the growth of executive agency power coincided with the growth of presidential power. Independent agencies, on the other hand, are not formally subject to supervision by a cabinet member or the President. They are typically headed by collegial bodies. The President, with Senate advice and consent, appoints members of these bodies, but the appointments are for set terms of office that overlap presidential and congressional elections. Such members cannot be removed except for good cause. Among the independent agencies are the Securities and Exchange Commission, which regulates sales of financial securities, the Federal Communications Commission, which regulates licensing of television and radio stations, the Federal Reserve Board, which controls monetary policy, and the Federal Trade Commission, which regulates certain business practices.[72] Congress determines in the relevant enabling legislation whether the agency will be "independent" or "executive."

Congress tends to use independent agencies to regulate in important areas where there is a greater need for continuity of policy and insulation from political control. Independent agencies' structure makes them less vulnerable to the effects of changing presidential administrations, shifting blocks and majorities in Congress, and the influence of congressional committees. However, Congress has exercised inconsistent judgment about what subject matter independent agencies should control. In fact, for many areas of regulation, Congress has split control between an independent agency and a cabinet-controlled executive agency.

The size and practical independence of administrative agencies have led some commentators to refer to them as a "headless fourth branch of government."[73] Considering that unelected administrative agencies exercise a great deal of independent power over citizens, their growth may signal a net loss for democratic values in government.[74] However, congressional and presidential influence on agencies shows some assertion of democratic control.[75]

4. Congress's Investigatory Oversight Role

As modern legislating has become more complex, there has been greater need for legislative committees to give professional assistance. Proposals for legislation, budgets, approval of Presidential appointments, and most other legislative business must

---

71 The Court has largely rejected or ignored separation of powers objections to this mixing of legislative, executive and judicial power in administrative agencies. *See* Chapter VI, pp. 219-223.

72 Others include the National Labor Relations Board, the Federal Maritime Commission, the Consumer Product Safety Council, the Commodity Futures Trading Commission, and the Nuclear Regulatory Commission.

73 *See* Peter Strauss, *The Place of Administrative Agencies in Government: Separation of Powers and the Fourth Branch*, 84 COLUM. L. REV. 573 (1984).

74 *See* CAPPELLETTI, *supra* note 69.

75 *See* Chapter VI, pp. 214-219.

generally survive intensive committee scrutiny before they can be brought to a vote before the entire Congress. The relevant committee's recommendations hold great weight among busy members of Congress who may be only vaguely aware of the details of legislation outside their areas of concern and expertise.[76] There are now 298 standing, special and select committees and subcommittees. Some of the more important standing committees that both houses of Congress have are agriculture, appropriations, armed services, banking, education, energy, foreign affairs, governmental operations, judiciary, labor, small business, and science and technology. Within each committee are standing subcommittees devoted to particular areas.

The original purpose of committees and Congressional agencies was to deal with the increased complexity and specialized nature of legislation in the modern world. But with the changing nature of legislation and the growth of administrative agencies, committees have taken on the more general task of overseeing the operations of government. Before he became President, Woodrow Wilson remarked on the importance of Congress's role in overseeing government and exposing inadequacies, noting that the "informing function of Congress should be preferred even to its legislative function."[77] Committee investigative hearings are nowhere mentioned in the Constitution, but investigations often determine whether there is a need to legislate. Thus, the Court has upheld Congress's right to investigate, including the power to issue subpoenas and to punish disregard of those subpoenas as a "contempt of Congress."[78] However, for some committee hearings, the legislative agenda has not always been obvious. The intense press and television coverage of committee hearings, coupled with the fact that legislators are concerned with reelection, has lead investigations to take on a life of their own. The primary product of many investigations is publicity. Nonetheless, this publicity can be beneficial if the investigations foster greater public awareness of the shortcomings of the government and its officials.

To undertake oversight functions, the legislative branch cannot depend on the executive to provide information. Thus, the growth of the congressional investigative function has led to a growth in congressional staff and other professional assistance.[79] The General Accounting Office (GAO) provides information and assistance essential to Congress's oversight role. The GAO, which has more than 4,000 professional employees, conducts regular audits of agency expenditures while seeking out fraud, waste and mismanagement. It also undertakes special studies at the request of congressional committees. The GAO exerts great influence. Its suggested "corrective measures" instantly get the attention of both Congress and the agency involved. A GAO finding that

---

76 A side effect of the committee system and the requirement that committees approve all proposed legislation has been to give power to those members of Congress who chair important committees to control the legislative calendar and agenda — what bills get discussed and reported out for a vote on the floor. The power of legislative committees is another reason why the question of which party is in the majority in each house of Congress has so much importance, because the majority party names the chairpersons of all the committees and holds a majority of seats on each committee.

77 WOODROW WILSON, CONGRESSIONAL GOVERNMENT 303-04 (Houghton-Mifflin, Boston 1885).

78 *McGrain v. Daugherty*, 273 U.S. 135, 177 (1927). *See* NOWAK & ROTUNDA, *supra* note 47, §§7.4-7.5.

79 In 1989, there were 2,999 congressional staff members assigned to congressional committees. Personal staff for all members of Congress totaled 11,406, averaging 38 for each Senator and 18 for each house member. This represents a 400% growth in personal staff and a 650% growth in committee staff since 1946. In addition to these permanent staff, committees also hire investigative aides each year who, while nominally temporary, often remain with a given committee year after year. CONGRESSIONAL QUARTERLY GUIDE TO CONGRESS 483-484 (1991). *See also* HARRISON W. FOX, JR. & SUSAN W. HAMMOND, CONGRESSIONAL STAFFS: THE INVISIBLE FORCE IN AMERICAN LAWMAKING (Free Press, N.Y. 1977).

a particular expenditure would be improper will make even the most intrepid, independent-minded agency administrator hesitant to spend those funds.[80]

Politically motivated investigations — a common occurrence — tend to be more controversial. Some such investigations have had laudatory results but others have not. Most consider the 1974 Senate committee investigation of the Watergate scandal, which ultimately led to President Nixon's resignation, to have been positive.[81] In that scandal, the Senate committee began investigating to see if officials at the highest levels of the Republican White House were involved in a burglary of the Democratic National Headquarters and the cover up that followed. Ultimately, the committee laid out the incriminating evidence on national television and the President, who had denied involvement, resigned in disgrace. Perhaps the most widely known abuse of the committee investigatory process involved the activities of Senator Joseph McCarthy, who chaired a committee in a 1954 investigation of alleged "Communists" working in the Army and the State Department. The committee produced no substantial evidence, but the accusations of McCarthy, coupled with a brewing anti-Communist hysteria, cost hundreds of people their reputations and careers. For better or for worse, the Congressional investigatory power is well established and has become a potent force in government.

D. The States and Federalism

The Framers carefully planned the system of separation of powers and "checks and balances" between the branches of the federal government. The other great division of power in the United States — between the state and federal governments — emerged from political necessity. Few in the newly independent states would have ratified any constitution that did not provide a vigorous and meaningful role for the states.

Federalism has two dimensions. "Vertical" federalism describes the relationship between the states and the federal government. "Horizontal" or interstate federalism describes the relationship of the states to each other. Both relationships have changed considerably since 1789. The history of vertical federalism has largely been a story of the growth of federal power at the expense of state power. Horizontal federalism has been marked by a steady decrease in the legal significance of state boundaries.

It is an interesting question whether the delegates to the constitutional convention would have approved of these developments. Before reviewing those changes and considering that question, however, we should discuss more generally the nature of state power, the governments of the states and their political subdivisions.

1. State Government Structure and Powers

The Nature of State Governmental Power   The Constitution did not create states, though it often refers to them. There was no need to create them because they already existed in 1787. In fact, states wrote and ratified their own constitutions quickly — all had them by the end of 1776. This fact of states' "aboriginal" existence makes the nature of the power of states significantly different from that of the federal government. The thirteen colonies emerged from the War of Independence as separate sovereign nation-

---

80   For a general discussion of the GAO, *see* ERASMUS KLOMAN, ED., CASES IN ACCOUNTABILITY: THE WORK OF THE GAO (Westview, Boulder Colo. 1979). Another important congressional agency, the Congressional Budget Office, has since 1974 enabled Congress to prepare its own budget proposals and to assist budget committees in analyzing the effect of budget proposals coming from the White House. For a lucid description of the machinery of government with a specific focus on agencies, *see* PETER STRAUSS, AN INTRODUCTION TO ADMINISTRATIVE JUSTICE IN THE UNITED STATES (Carolina Academic Press 1989).

81   *See supra* p. 14.

states. Their status as such was modified only to the extent that they gave up certain rights in the Constitution of 1789 and later amendments to it. Thus, states need not search the federal Constitution for some positive grant of power to act or to make law: they have the power and inherent competence of separate, independent and sovereign nations and may pass legislation on any subject they choose, except as limited by the federal Constitution or their own constitutions.[82] The text of the Tenth Amendment delineates this principle: "The powers not delegated to the United States by the Constitution, nor prohibited by it to the States, are reserved to the States respectively, or to the people."[83]

State Governmental Structure The governmental structure of many states is a state-sized version of federal governmental structure and powers. The Framers "borrowed" many concepts from state constitutions and placed them in the 1789 federal Constitution. In turn, as states framed new constitutions periodically after the ratification of the federal Constitution, they borrowed from it to some extent.

Like federal governmental structure, state constitutions provide for three branches of government, with the chief executive officer having veto power over the legislative branch and the supreme court of the state having the power of judicial review. State legislatures are bicameral (*i.e.*, there are two "houses," usually a "house of representatives" and a "senate"), except for one state, Nebraska, which is unicameral. However, many of the names of state governmental offices and institutions differ from those of their corresponding federal office. The chief executive officer of the state is called the Governor. The person next in line to succeed the Governor is called the Lieutenant Governor. There is usually a Secretary of State[84] and an Attorney General, commonly an Auditor General, and department heads, which often have counterparts in the federal government. The chief legislative body is generally the "state legislature" or "general assembly." The court of last resort is usually the state supreme court.

Some state constitutions reflect their citizens' feeling that the best government is the one that governs least. Many states restrict their governors to short terms of office and forbid them from serving consecutive terms of office.[85] States have also restricted their legislatures as well. For example, one device limits legislative sessions to only one every two years and then for only a given number of days. Another device allows only one house of the legislature to meet one year, the other house meeting the year after. Many states limit the number of bills each member may introduce. However, the tremendous growth of states' responsibilities in the last 40 years has caused most state governments to undergo reorganization along more realistic lines, increasing the ability of legislatures and executives to enact and enforce laws.[86]

---

82 The principle that all states are equal and admitted to the union on the same basis preserves this same status for later-admitted states.

83 In the words of Chief Justice Marshall, "it was neither necessary nor proper to define the powers retained by the States. These powers proceed, not from the people of America, but from the people of the several States; and remain, after the adoption of the constitution, what they were before, except so far as they may be abridged by that instrument. *Sturges v. Crowninshield*, 17 U.S. 122, 193 (1819).

84 The federal Secretary of State's function is very different from that of state secretaries of state. The U.S. Secretary of State's duties are mostly foreign policy and diplomacy. State secretaries of state generally handle administrative matters, such as licensing and records.

85 For example, in Virginia, governors serve a four year term and consecutive terms are not allowed. Term limits in Alabama led Governor George Wallace to run his wife for governor in 1967, with the understanding that he would really be in charge. She was elected, but she died halfway through her term.

86 For more information on state governments and several useful short articles and charts, *see* BOOK OF THE STATES (Council of State Governments, Lexington, Ky. 2005).

Executive power in most states is more diffuse than federal executive power. On the federal level, the President appoints the members of his cabinet, judges, and other high-level executive officials with the advice and consent of the Senate. By contrast, in many states, the people directly elect heads of some major divisions of state government, such as the Attorney General, the Secretary of State or the Auditor General. These officials neither owe their office to the Governor nor can the Governor dismiss them. In fact, these officials are often members of a different political party from the governor. It is even the case in some states that the Lieutenant Governor is from a different political party than the Governor.[87] Such independently-elected officers will often act independently of, and sometimes in opposition to, the Governor. Additionally, state judges tend to be elected rather than appointed. Election systems were present in some states around the time the Constitution was adopted, but elections became more prevalent during the first half of the 19th century. Nonetheless, many states have appointment systems and some have combined systems.[88]

Constitutional Limits on State Governmental Structure   Considering that state governments have a similar structure to the federal government, it is fair to ask whether states are required to have any particular form of government. The answer is "yes and no." Article IV §4 of the Constitution provides that "[t]he United States shall guarantee to every State in this union a Republican Form of Government." However, even assuming one could define precisely the characteristics of a "republican" form of government, the Court has held that this clause is not enforceable by the courts in the same manner as other guarantees in the Constitution, because the clause presents a non-justiciable "political question."[89] Nevertheless, the Supreme Court has forced state governments to conform with republican ideas, albeit through different provisions of the Constitution. For example, the Court held that states must fairly draw boundaries of election districts so as not to dilute the voting strength of people in some regions by creating districts that elect the same number of representatives but with fewer voters. The Court ordered states to create districts that assure "one man, one vote" because to do otherwise would violate the right to equal protection of the laws under the 14th Amendment to the Constitution.[90] The Court distinguished redistricting cases from non-justiciable "political question" cases because redistricting does not affect basic state governmental structure; it simply assures that the *existing* election structure, which the state's citizens had already chosen, does not discriminate.

Local Governmental Structure   The basic political subdivisions of states are counties and cities or villages, though in rural areas, the intermediate township level is also important. All these subdivisions constitute "local" or "municipal" government. Courts generally consider these governmental entities to be creatures of the state and subject to total state control. However, in many states, large cities enjoy considerable independence from state government. This is sometimes the result of political reality (a large percentage of the members of the state legislature may be elected from the largest city in the state) and other times the result of the state constitution granting more independence and "home rule" rights to large cities.

---

87 The 12th Amendment to the U.S. Constitution makes it impossible for the President and Vice President to be members of different political parties.

88 Methods of judicial selection are discussed in Chapter V, pp. 180-184.

89 *See Luther v. Borden*, 48 U.S. 1 (1849). The political question doctrine is discussed in Chapter IX, pp. 333-335.

90 *See Baker v. Carr*, 369 U.S. 186 (1962); *Reynolds v. Sims*, 377 U.S. 533 (1967). The 14th Amendment's guarantee of equal protection of the laws is discussed in Chapter IX, pp. 351-362.

On the city level, the chief executive officer is generally called the mayor and the legislative body is called the "city council." It is common on the local level to have a relatively weak executive in comparison to the legislative body. The laws passed by cities are generally referred to as "ordinances" rather than statutes. They have legal effect only within the city. There is often no "city" judicial branch, because courts that are part of the state judicial system have jurisdiction over offenses within the city limits, including violations of city ordinances.

Counties are geographical areas that usually contain several cities. The state, counties, and cities share overlapping responsibilities, although counties usually manage government functions that are necessarily regional, such as roads, airports, and the county courts. Counties also have their own law enforcement agency, the sheriff, who has power to act in parts of the county that are not in cities.

Powers of Local Governments   Local governments — cities, counties and townships — provide many of the services needed to maintain communities and urban centers. One of the most important and traditional functions of local government is law enforcement. Law enforcement was originally conducted solely by local police forces, which local governments raised and supported through their own revenue. In the 20th century, however, state governments created state police forces to assist in law enforcement. Some other important local government functions are sewage and garbage disposal, water supply, and the control of land use through zoning. A major function of local government is public education on the elementary and secondary school level — schools which the vast majority of children attend. Usually local school boards maintain these school systems, though they must generally meet the requirements of the state department of education. Local governments have the authority to raise revenues by taxation in order to pursue all these programs. In most communities, the largest portion of the local tax burden by far is the school tax. Often local governments fund local community colleges or vocational training centers as well.

2. Changes in Vertical Federalism: The Growth of Federal Power

In the debates on ratification, James Madison described the understanding of federal and state power that many had from reading the "enumerated powers" of Congress and the 10th Amendment to the Constitution:

> The powers delegated . . . to the federal government are few and defined. Those which are to remain in the State governments are numerous and indefinite. The former will be exercised principally on external objects, as war peace, negotiation, and foreign commerce; with which last the power of taxation will, for the most part, be connected. The powers reserved to the several States will extend to all the objects which, in the ordinary course of affairs, concern the lives, liberties, and properties of the people; and the internal order, improvement, and prosperity of the State.[91]

This view has changed considerably since that time.

a. Early Development of an Expansive View of Federal Power

The Implied Powers Doctrine   Chief Justice John Marshall, whose expansive concept of federal power affected constitutional interpretation for many of the early years of the United States, was a principal catalyst in undercutting the above-quoted

---

91 Federalist No. 45 at 313, *supra* note 4. As with all statements made during ratification debates, there is no guarantee that Madison really thought this or was merely saying what was expedient to calm those who were opposed to ratification based on a fear of a strong central government.

view of federal power.[92] He developed the notion of "implied powers" in the 1819 case of *McCulloch v. Maryland*.[93] The issue in *McCulloch* was the constitutionality of Congress's establishment of a Bank of the United States. Chief Justice Marshall admitted that the federal government was a government of limited powers and that Article I did not specifically mention any power to constitute a bank. But he held that the grant of explicit enumerated powers necessarily implied other powers to do what Congress believed appropriate to carry out those enumerated powers. Thus, because Congress had explicit power to lay and collect taxes, to borrow money, to regulate commerce and to raise armies — and a bank would clearly assist legislative programs enacted pursuant to these powers — Congress had the *implied* power to create a bank. In reaching this result, Marshall found support in the "necessary and proper" clause, the last of the enumerated powers, giving Congress the power "[t]o make all Laws which shall be necessary and proper for carrying into Execution the foregoing Powers."[94]

Supreme Court Power to Review State Court Judgments The Court also solidified federal judicial power *vis-a-vis* the states early in U.S. history. As noted above, in the 1810 case of *Fletcher v. Peck*, the Court extended its power of judicial review to acts of state governments. Then, in 1816, the Court made clear that it had appellate jurisdiction over state *court* decisions that interpreted federal law. In *Martin v. Hunter's Lessee*,[95] the Virginia Supreme Court, acknowledging that the supremacy clause of the Constitution bound the court to *follow* federal law, denied that the United States Supreme Court could review the Virginia Supreme Court's *interpretation* of federal law. The United States Supreme Court held that its appellate jurisdiction applied to *all* cases raising issues of federal law, whether those cases came from the lower federal courts or the state courts. Otherwise, the Court noted that great "public mischief" would result as the Constitution or a treaty could mean one thing in Virginia and another in New York. In *Cohens v. Virginia*,[96] the Court also clearly stated its power to review state *criminal* cases in which the defendant alleged his or her conviction violated federal law.

b. State Resistance to Expanding Federal Power, the Civil War and the Civil War Amendments to the Constitution

State Reaction In the period 1800-1860, the growing power of the federal government disturbed many states' rights advocates in the southern states who were concerned that the more populous, urban, anti-slavery northern states controlled the federal government. What frustrated southerners most about federal action displacing state authority was that the federal government's own departments were deciding the limits of federal power, without any meaningful participation by states.

---

92 Chief Justice John Marshall (1755-1835), the fourth and most famous of the fourteen Chief Justices, was a strong Federalist in favor of a strong central government and served on the Court for 34 years. He wrote many of the opinions in landmark cases, including the case that established the power of judicial review, *Marbury v. Madison*, discussed *supra* p. 10 and in Chapter IX, p. 324.

93 17 U.S. 316 (1819).

94 Art. I §8 cl. 18.

95 14 U.S. 304 (1816). At issue in *Martin* was a Virginia law prohibiting aliens from inheriting property in the state, which was challenged on the ground that it violated the 1794 treaty with Great Britain, which guaranteed the rights of British subjects in the United States.

96 19 U.S. 264 (1821). Article III does not give the United States Supreme Court the power to review state supreme court decisions on issues of *state* law, however. Consequently, after *Martin*, state supreme courts have the final say as to the meaning of *their own* law, but the Supreme Court must in all cases be the final arbiter of the meaning of federal law, whether the issue arises in state or federal court. *See* Chapter V, pp. 194-195 and the diagram of federal and state court systems in the Appendix, p. A32. *See also* Chapter II, p. 38.

Starting in the 1830s, resistance to federal authority became increasingly strident. A characteristic incident was South Carolina's attempt to "nullify" a federal tariff law that hurt the interests of southern planters. John C. Calhoun, a former Vice President of the United States, became the head of the South Carolina States' Rights party and called a convention to adopt an "ordinance of nullification" declaring the offending tariffs passed by Congress "null, void, and no law, nor binding on this state, its officers or citizens." The federal government responded to South Carolina's actions with a show of force and the state backed down.

The southern states also deeply resented the Supreme Court's assertion of appellate power, set out in *Martin v. Hunter's Lessee* and *Cohens v. Virginia,* discussed above.[97] An 1830 incident illustrates the depth of the animosity toward the Supreme Court and Congress. Georgia had convicted an Indian named George Tassell of murder and had sentenced him to death. This was a violation of a federal statute prohibiting states from exercising jurisdiction over Indians in certain areas of the state. Tassell appealed his death sentence to the Supreme Court, which was sure to apply the federal statute and reverse the conviction. However, the Supreme Court had to dismiss the appeal as moot when Georgia, in defiance of the Court's exercise of jurisdiction, executed Tassell, an act that Chief Justice Story labeled "indecorous."[98]

The Slavery Question and Civil War The southern states' system of agricultural economy based on slave labor spread into new southern states. The gradual westward expansion of the United States magnified the south's resentment of the federal government. A major expansion added states in the Northwest Territory, now roughly the states of Indiana, Illinois, Wisconsin, Ohio and Michigan. Congress had prohibited slavery in these states and many of their citizens were "abolitionists," meaning that they favored the abolition of slavery. Moreover, these and other northern states became points on an "underground railroad" that assisted slaves to escape to free states or to Canada. Thus, slavery became a national issue in Congress during the first half of the 19th century primarily in relation to the admission of new states into the Union. Each new state's admission raised the question of whether it would be admitted as a "slave" or "free" state. Unable to resolve the question otherwise, Congress compromised and sought to balance the number of new "free" and "slave" states.

One such compromise was the Missouri Compromise of 1820, which admitted the states of Missouri ("slave") and Maine ("free"). The enactment went further and broadly declared that the whole northern part of the Louisiana Territory would be "free" — an immense territory extending as far North and West as the present state of Montana. In an apparent attempt to placate the southern states and head off their threatened withdrawal from the Union, the Supreme Court issued its now-infamous 1857 decision in *Dred Scott v. Sandford*.[99] In that case, a slave, Dred Scott, had sued for his freedom on the ground that he had lived in "free" territory of the United States for years as a result

---

97 Seven states enacted laws denying the Supreme Court's appellate power over their courts. *See* Charles Warren, *Legislative and Judicial Attacks on the Supreme Court of the United States — A History of the Twenty-Fifth Section of the Judiciary Act*, 47 AM.L.REV. 1, 3-4 (1913).

98 *Id.* at 167. In reaction to a case holding the state liable for breach of contract, Georgia enacted a statute in which it declared that anyone enforcing the Court's ruling was "hereby declared to be guilty of a felony, and shall suffer death, without benefit of clergy by being hanged." That decision, *Chisholm v. Georgia*, 2 U.S. 419 (1793), was eventually overruled by the ratification of the Eleventh Amendment to the Constitution. *See infra* p. 37 and Chapter VI, pp. 225-226. "Benefit of clergy" was a defense that essentially enabled literate defendants to avoid the noose.

99 60 U.S. 393 (1857).

of accompanying his "owner" there. The Court rejected Scott's claim on several grounds in several opinions, but in essence the case stood for the proposition that black people were not "citizens" of the United States and that Congress had no power to outlaw slavery in U.S. territories. Nonetheless, this ringing endorsement of slavery in *Dred Scott* was not enough for the south. Eleven states seceded (withdrew) from the Union and formed the Confederate States of America. Civil war broke out in 1861 and ended in 1865 with the surrender of the south.[100]

The Civil War Amendments to the Constitution The south's defeat established that the states were in the Union for better or for worse and that the interests of the union would prevail where they conflicted with those of the states.[101] The three so-called "Civil War Amendments" to the Constitution spelled out the legal impact of the war on states' rights. These amendments effected "a vast transformation from the concepts of federalism that had prevailed in the late 18th century" under the original Constitution.[102] The 13th Amendment (1865) ended slavery, thus overruling the principal holding of *Dred Scott v. Sandford*. The 15th Amendment (1870) assured voting rights to the newly freed slaves. The 14th Amendment (1868) made clear that former slaves were "citizens" of the United States and of the state in which they reside, thus overruling the other part of *Dred Scott v. Sandford*. More broadly, the 14th Amendment provided that a state could not "make or enforce any law which shall abridge the privileges or immunities of citizens of the United States," nor "deprive any person of life, liberty or property, without due process of law," nor "deny to any person within its jurisdiction the equal protection of the laws." All three amendments gave Congress broad power to "enforce" these amendments "by appropriate legislation."[103]

c. Federal Power Since the Mid-20th Century

Impact of the 14th Amendment Perhaps surprisingly, in the years immediately following the Civil War, the Supreme Court rather narrowly read Congress's power under the Civil War amendments and restricted the scope of the individual rights set out in those amendments.[104] It was not until the 20th century that a more expansive view of the amendments prevailed. Congress has used some of its power under the amendments, but the greatest impact of the amendments came through court decisions interpreting their provisions, particularly the due process and equal protection clauses of the 14th Amendment. This has resulted in the "constitutionalization" of many areas of law that

---

100 The rebel "Confederate States of America" comprised Alabama, Arkansas, Florida, Georgia, Louisiana, Mississippi, North Carolina, South Carolina, Tennessee, Texas, and Virginia. As might be expected from this name, the confederate constitution emphasized states' rights much more than did the United States Constitution.

101 After the Civil War, the Supreme Court held that the states had had no constitutional right to secede and that, for the entire time of the war, they remained states of the Union. See *Texas v. White*, 74 U.S. 700 (1869).

102 *Mitchum v. Foster*, 407 U.S. 225, 241 (1972) (1871 civil rights act passed pursuant to 14th Amendment was an exception to 1793 law barring federal court injunction against state court action).

103 Many have unthinkingly heaped praise on the "genius" of the 1789 Constitution without considering the fact that its vagueness about state-federal relations and its failure to deal with the question of slavery set the scene for eventual civil war. *See* Thurgood Marshall, *Reflections of the Bicentennial of the United States Constitution*, 101 HARV. L. REV. 1, 2 (1987). Justice Thurgood Marshall (1908-1993) was the first black justice to sit on the Supreme Court.

104 *See Civil Rights Cases*, 109 U.S. 3 (1883) (beyond Congress's power to pass federal law prohibiting racial segregation in private businesses); *Slaughter-House Cases*, 83 U.S. 36 (1872)(14th Amendment did not protect any right to engage in a profession); *Plessy v. Ferguson*, 163 U.S. 537 (1896)(state-imposed regime of racially segregated facilities not unconstitutional). This paralleled a similar limited view of Congress's commerce clause powers during the same period. *See infra* note 107 and accompanying text.

courts traditionally considered to be solely matters of state concern.[105] Two of the most important areas since 1953 have been criminal due process rights and discrimination based on race and sex.[106]

Impact of the Interstate Commerce Clause The greatest expansion of Congress's power to pass laws displacing state authority has been pursuant to the interstate commerce clause set out in Article I. After a series of decisions reading the interstate commerce power narrowly,[107] the Court took a much broader view in 1938.[108] The commerce clause power of Congress reached its peak in the mid-1990s. The Court upheld federal legislation under the commerce clause whenever Congress had a rational basis for concluding that the regulated activity would affect interstate commerce.[109] Under this test, the Court upheld Congressional regulation of many local activities that only indirectly related to the flow of commerce across state lines. Even if the activity occurred completely within a state, it was properly within Congress's power to regulate if the effect of the activity — when combined with other intrastate activity — could be national. Thus, in *Wickard v. Filburn*,[110] the Court allowed Congress to regulate the amount of wheat a farmer could grow for his own consumption and local sale on a small farm in Ohio on the theory that the "cumulative effect" of *many* small farmers doing the same could have a depressing effect on wheat prices. The Court approved a law banning racial discrimination in public accommodations largely because the effect such discrimination had on interstate commerce. The Court reasoned that discrimination even in small local hotels and restaurants could make it difficult for black citizens to travel on business.[111]

Cutting Back on Federal Power Opponents of federal power have urged that the 10th Amendment to the Constitution, which provides that all powers "not delegated to" the federal government are "reserved to the States," should limit Congress's commerce clause power. However, the Court has dismissed the 10th Amendment, remarking that it "states but a truism, that all is retained that has not been surrendered." This "truism" view of the 10th Amendment still prevails, but recent cases signaled a changed view of what states "retained" and what they "surrendered" upon ratification of the Constitution. In the 58 years between 1937 and 1995, the Court never held a federal statute unconstitutional as beyond Congress's interstate commerce clause power. But in *United States v. Lopez*,[112] the Court struck down a federal criminal law punishing possession of a handgun in or near any school. It rejected arguments that criminals use firearms in violent crime, which has economic impact and discourages individuals from traveling to high crime areas of the country. The Court also rejected the argument that violent crime in schools impedes the educational process, resulting in a "less productive citizenry." Acceptance of these arguments, the Court observed, would allow Congress to legislate against all violent crime and all the activities that might lead to it, as well as

---

105 *See supra* pp. 10-11.

106 *See* Chapter VIII, pp. 283-323 (due process rights); Chapter IX. pp 352-355 (race) and 358-362 (sex).

107 *See, e.g., United States v. E.C. Knight Co.*, 156 U.S. 1 (1895) (manufacturing is not "commerce"); *Veazie Bank v. Fenno*, 75 U.S. 533 (1869) (insurance contracts are not "commerce").

108 It was not purely coincidental that this was also the time when the Court abandoned its "economic due process" limits on federal (and state) legislative power. *See supra* pp. 11-12.

109 *Heart of Atlanta Motel v. United States*, 379 U.S. 241 (1964); *Katzenbach v. McClung*, 379 U.S. 294 (1964) (accepting Congress's conclusion that racial discrimination affects interstate commerce).

110 317 U.S. 111 (1942).

111 *See* cases cited *supra* note 109.

112 514 U.S.549 (1995).

any activity that related to the economic productivity of citizens, including marriage and divorce. This would enable Congress to infringe on the traditional powers of the states.

The *Lopez* Court set out its revised view of Congress's interstate commerce clause power: (1) Congress may regulate "the use of the channels of interstate commerce," as was the case in the racial discrimination cases involving public accommodations for travelers, (2) Congress can "regulate and protect the instrumentalities of interstate commerce, or persons or things in interstate commerce, even though the threat may come only from intrastate activities," such as regulating the rates charged by railroads even for intrastate transportation, and (3) Congress can regulate "activities having a substantial relation to interstate commerce . . . , *i.e.*, those activities that substantially affect interstate commerce," including "intrastate economic activity where . . . the activity substantially affect[s] interstate commerce." Some examples are regulating labor practices of employers with a substantial number of employees or regulating intrastate agricultural activity that had a cumulative effect on interstate commerce.[113]

In a 2000 case, *United States v. Morrison*,[114] the Court struck down the Violence Against Women Act (VAWA), a federal law that authorized victims to bring civil claims if the offender carried out a violent act because of the victim's sex. Since the VAWA did not regulate commercial activity itself, Congress could justify it only under the third *Lopez* category. The Court found the impact on interstate commerce involved in *Morrison* was of the same kind it rejected in *Lopez* — that ordinary crime has an economic impact. Yet, in a 2005 case, the Court retreated somewhat. In *Gonzales v. Raich*,[115] a different majority of the Court upheld the constitutionality of a federal law banning cultivation and use of marijuana, even for medical purposes pursuant to a prescription, as California state law permitted. The Court distinguished *Morrison* and *Lopez* on the ground that the federal drug law overall regulated the "quintessentially economic" activities of production and distribution of drugs. Then, relying on *Wickard v. Filburn*, the Court concluded that "Congress can regulate purely intrastate activity that is not itself 'commercial,' in that it is not produced for sale, if it concludes that failure to regulate that class of activity would undercut the regulation of the interstate market in that commodity."

Congressional Power to Affect States Directly   Congress's commerce and other powers are even more limited when it passes legislation that affects states directly if the effect of such laws is to improperly "commandeer" state governments. In *New York v. United States*,[116] the Court invalidated a federal law that attempted to "encourage" states to develop disposal sites for hazardous radioactive waste produced in the state instead permitting it to be shipped it to other states for disposal. If a state did not permit disposal within its borders, the federal law decreed that state would become the owner of the wastes (which private companies generated) and would become liable for all damages suffered as a result of its failure to take possession of "its" wastes. The Court invalidated this provision as an attempt to "commandeer" the state legislature by coercing it into enacting state laws that Congress wanted. In *Printz v. United States*,[117] the Court applied its anti-commandeering doctrine to administrative agencies of states. In *Printz*, it

---

113 *Id.* at 558-559. *Lopez* and the other post-1995 cases are discussed in Chapter IX, pp. 340-341.

114 529 U.S. 598 (2000).

115 545 U.S. 1 (2005) (Congress had power to prohibit cultivation and possession of marijuana for medical use; drug regulation is "quintessentially economic").

116 505 U.S. 144 (1992).

117 521 U.S. 898 (1997).

invalidated a federal law that required local police officials to investigate the backgrounds of prospective handgun purchasers.[118] Despite these exceptions, however, Congress still has quite broad power to pass legislation affecting the states.[119]

d. Conditional Spending

Any assessment of the federal government's power *vis-a-vis* states must consider "conditional spending." As just discussed, Congress cannot *directly* "commandeer" state legislatures and require states to enact particular laws. However, it often can effectively do so through use of the device of "conditional spending" — offering financial grants to states on the condition that they comply with federal requirements. The power source for this kind of measure is not the commerce clause, but the power to tax and spend to "provide for the general Welfare of the United States."[120] This means that the spending clause can go beyond the subject matter of interstate commerce or any Article I enumerated power. Congress only needs to prove that its enactments are involve "promotion of the general welfare."[121]

The 16th Amendment to the Constitution (1913) greatly enhanced this "spending power" of Congress. This amendment, for the first time, established the right of the federal government to impose a direct tax on income. Federal income tax is generally the most significant tax that inhabitants of the United States pay. Today, it ranges from 15% to 38% of income for individuals.[122] Federal income tax receipts have led to an enormous imbalance in tax revenues received by the federal government on the one hand and the states on the other. It is true, as the Court remarked in a 1947 case, that a state can resist the temptation of federal money by the "'simple expedient' of not yielding."[123] But few states are in a position to do so. Refusing federal money means that the state will, to that extent, experience a disadvantageous "balance of payments" with the federal government: the state will receive less back in federal money than its citizens pay in federal taxes.

To be constitutional, conditions for receipt of particular federal money must be clear to the states and must have some rational relationship to the uses of the federal grant. In addition, the Court has suggested that "in some circumstances the financial inducement offered by Congress might be so coercive as to pass the point at which 'pressure turns into compulsion.'" Nonetheless, the Court has adhered to its view in a long line of cases that "to hold that motive or temptation is equivalent to coercion is to plunge the law into endless difficulties."[124]

---

118 These cases are discussed in more detail in Chapter IX, pp. 337-339. Congress undoubtedly had the power under the commerce clause to regulate these activities itself. Thus, it could have set up a federal agency to accomplish the tasks it sought to foist on the states.

119 *See Garcia v. San Antonio Metropolitan Transit Authority*, 469 U.S. 528 (1985) (federal minimum wage and maximum hour laws apply to state employees; law does not invade reserved powers of states).

120 Art. I §8 cl. 1.

121 *United States v. Butler*, 297 U.S. 1, 67 (1936) (rejecting argument that program of taxing agricultural processors to fund payment of subsidies to farmers who limit production in an effort to raise market prices must find a source in Art. I other than the spending clause).

122 *See* Chapter XVI, where income taxation is discussed in more detail.

123 *Oklahoma v. Civil Service Comm'n*, 330 U.S. 127, 143-144 (1947) (federal funding penalty against state for highway commission member who engaged in partisan political activities was constitutional).

124 *South Dakota v. Dole*, 483 U.S. 203, 212 (1987) (penalty of reduction of 5% of federal highway funding to states that did not pass laws establishing minimum drinking age of 21 is constitutional). Some have suggested that the *Dole* case and other liberal spending clause cases are linked to the pre-*Lopez* liberal commerce clause cases and may therefore be subject to revision in the future.

One example of the effects of federal conditional spending programs is the minimum age of 21 for drinking alcoholic beverages that all states have imposed. This was among the conditions Congress attached to a portion of the federal highway construction money states regularly receive. In addition, the principal reason many states have strong social welfare programs for the poor is that Congress has passed legislation making federal funds available to set up such programs, but only if states follow federal requirements.[125]

3. Changes in Horizontal Federalism: The Blurring of State Boundaries

There has been a psychological blurring of state boundaries resulting from greater urbanization, mobility of the population, and advances in communication and transportation. Travelers barely notice when they cross a state boundary. A *legal* blurring of boundaries has accompanied the psychological blurring. While the legal consequences of state borders are still significant, several constitutional provisions and doctrines make them less important than they have been in the past.

The Right to Travel   The Articles of Confederation expressly protected the right of interstate travel, but inexplicably the Framers included no such provision in the 1789 Constitution. Nonetheless, the Supreme Court has recognized the right based on numerous sources in the Constitution. One of the principal cases involved a Nevada law that imposed a tax on persons leaving the state by means of public transportation. In *Crandall v. Nevada*,[126] the Court held the tax unconstitutional, calling the unrestricted right of interstate travel inherent in the very nature of the federal system.[127] More recently, the Court has spoken of the right to travel to travel as a "fundamental right" and has invalidated even indirect burdens on the exercise of that right. In *Shapiro v. Thompson*,[128] it held unconstitutional a state requirement that all applicants for welfare benefits be able to show that they had resided in the state for at least 6 months. The effect of this law, the Court said, was to prevent the migration of people who might need those benefits to survive in their new state of residence.[129]

The "Dormant" Commerce Clause   A doctrine with even greater impact on state barriers to trade and travel is the "dormant" commerce clause. The "active" commerce clause was discussed above. It is a source of expansive federal power to reach most any private conduct or transaction taking place within the states. But even in its unexercised "dormant state," the commerce clause has an effect. Its mere presence in the Constitution was intended to guarantee the free flow of commerce between the states. As the Court observed, "this Nation is a common market in which state lines cannot be made barriers to the free flow of both raw materials and finished goods in response to the economic laws of supply and demand."[130] From early in the history of the country, the Court has used the dormant commerce clause to invalidate state economic protectionist legislation that discriminates against or unduly burdens the commercial activities of out-

---

125 Federal-state cooperative assistance programs are discussed in Chapter IX, p. 339.

126 73 U.S. 35 (1867).

127 A state or municipality may nonetheless charge *all* travelers a nominal amount for the use of state-provided transportation facilities (such as an airport) to help pay for the cost of those facilities. See *Evansville-Vandenburgh Airport Authority District v. Delta Airlines*, 405 U.S. 707 (1972).

128 394 U.S. 618 (1969).

129 *Shapiro* was decided as a "fundamental rights" equal protection case. *See* Chapter IX, p 356. A more recent case categorized the right to travel as part of substantive due process and the privileges and immunities clause, Art. IV §2, is *Saenz v. Roe*, 526 U.S. 489 (1999).

130 *Hughes v. Alexandria Scrap Corp.*, 426 U.S. 794, 803 (1976)

of-state businesses. The category "out-of-state businesses" includes international firms. In recent years, courts' use of the dormant commerce clause has increased.[131]

Expanded Interstate Reach of State Court Power   Traditionally, the territorial boundaries of a state defined the limits of the power of its courts over defendants. Thus, a court of one state generally had no power to hear a suit against a defendant from another state, unless that defendant was present or owned property in the first state at the time suit commenced.[132] A state court's ability to bind a defendant to its judgments is called "personal jurisdiction" and the ability to bind an out-of-state defendant is called "long-arm" jurisdiction. The Court expanded this power in the second half of the 20th century. Starting in 1945, the "long arm of the law" got longer. The Court expanded the circumstances under which out-of-state residents, particularly out-of-state corporations, are amenable to suit. In *International Shoe v. Washington,*[133] the Court approved subjecting out-of-state defendants to personal jurisdiction so long as the defendant had sufficient "minimum contacts" with the state — in the form of having done business there — such that subjecting the defendant to personal jurisdiction would not be "unfair." Thus today, despite state boundaries that ordinarily would prevent extraterritorial operation of the process of a state court, the courts of California may properly decide a civil case against New York defendants if they have conducted business in California and the suit relates to that business.[134]

The "Full Faith and Credit" Requirement   Article IV requires that states give "full faith and credit" to the judicial proceedings, records, and public acts of other states. This assures that a birth certificate or marriage license in one state will be valid in every other state. The main application of the full faith and credit clause in legal matters concerns the validity and scope of judgments rendered by out-of-state courts. Here, the Court has taken a strict view that a state must give judgments of another state's courts the same effect that that other state would give to them. Only if the courts of the first state did not have the constitutional prerequisite of personal jurisdiction can the courts of a second state refuse to enforce that judgment.[135] It does not matter if the first state's judgment is clearly in error or that it is based on a law that violates the public policy or laws of the second state. The second state must honor the judgment.[136] The combination of long-arm jurisdiction and full faith and credit makes it impossible for people to use state boundaries to evade legal responsibility in a civil case.

Extradition of Fugitives from Justice   The extradition clause of the Constitution assures the validity of a state's criminal convictions in other states.[137] Extradition is the process by which someone charged with or convicted of a crime in one state and arrested in another state may be sent back or "extradited" to the first state upon request. A state must comply with extradition requests. Reversing an old precedent, the Supreme Court in 1987 held that if all necessary paperwork is complete, there can be no other

---

131 The dormant commerce clause is discussed at greater length in Chapter IX, pp. 345-348.

132 *Pennoyer v. Neff*, 95 U.S. 714 (1877).

133 326 U.S. 310 (1945).

134 The fairness limitations on personal jurisdiction come from the due process clause of the 14th Amendment. The circumstances under which a court can constitutionally exercise personal jurisdiction are discussed in Chapter VII, pp. 253-259.

135 *Durfee v. Duke*, 375 U.S. 106 (1963).

136 *See Fauntleroy v. Lum*, 210 U.S. 230 (1908) (Holmes, J.) (Missouri court judgment for gambling debt that arose in Mississippi and was illegal under Mississippi law must be enforced by Mississippi because of full faith and credit). This area of the law is dealt with in more detail in Chapter V, pp. 261-262.

137 Art. IV §2 cl. 2.

proper ground to refuse to extradite and that, if necessary, the requesting state can file a federal action against the other state's governor to compel extradition.[138]

E. The Impact of Governmental Structure on the Legal System: An Overview

Separation of powers and federalism have their advantages in diffusing power among several components of the governmental structure. However, they make for a complex legal system. In later chapters of this book, we will discuss many of those complications in detail, but a brief overview of a few points follows below.

1. The Effects of Vertical Federalism: Concurrent Power to Make Laws and Adjudicate Disputes on the Same Territory

a. Concurrent Federal and State Lawmaking Power

Reasons for Concurrent Lawmaking Power   As discussed, the Supreme Court has not accepted Madison's idea that federal and state power occupy mutually exclusive spheres. Instead, the Court has allowed federal power to expand to the point that the federal government today, under its commerce powers, can broadly regulate most economic activity and a considerable amount of non-economic activity that has economic effects.[139] At the same time, states have retained their traditional sovereign power to make laws for all persons and transactions within their borders. The result is that two different sovereigns — state and federal governments — have overlapping or concurrent power to make law governing transactions and occurrences taking place on the same geographical territory.

Where Congress has chosen to legislate, conflicting state law must give way under the supremacy clause. Some areas of federal law have little occasion to conflict with state law, as where Congress has created a whole new body of law, such as federal tax law or laws dealing with administration of the federal government. But there are many other areas of federal legislative activity that are more general and have the potential of displacing state law. Yet, despite the great increase in federal legislative activity in the last 70 years, Congress has followed a longstanding policy of legislating incompletely — asserting federal power only as far as necessary for the success of some national policy or program — and thus not disturbing the continued application of state law in most areas of the law.

State Law's Traditional Domain   Because of Congress's restraint, there are many areas of law that remain overwhelmingly state law. For example, Congress probably has the power to pass a national commercial code for the entire country and a national law for incorporating companies, but it has shown little interest in doing so. As a result, most of the law that governs ordinary transactions among private citizens or companies remains state law. Contract, tort, property, family and commercial law are virtually all state law. State law regulates professions, from law and medicine to barbers and morticians. State law also establishes and regulates corporations and other business entities. Public utilities supplying gas or electric power to homes and businesses are generally state-regulated private monopolies. Most ordinary crimes, such as murder, robbery, larceny, rape, and assault, are state law.

Incomplete Federal Legislative Intervention   When Congress does choose to intervene in an area in which state law has traditionally governed, the result is most

---

138 *Puerto Rico v. Branstad*, 483 U.S. 219 (1987), *overruling Kentucky v. Dennison*, 65 U.S. 66 (1860).
139 *See supra* p. 26.

often a mix of federal and state law on the same topic. One typical pattern occurs when Congress decides that the resources of the federal government should be brought to bear on a traditionally local problem that has become a national one. An example of this is the problem of collection of child support from responsible parents. Since the 1970s, when the low rate of child support collection became a national disgrace, Congress provided funding and imposed certain minimum standards for child support collection.[140] A second pattern consists of Congress deciding that there is a need for a uniform national rule for some category of transactions that states have already regulated for years. An example of this is consumer credit transactions. The enormous growth in the number of credit cards and other forms of credit, combined with the welter of conflicting state requirements for advertising the terms of credit, led Congress to conclude that it was difficult for consumers to compare credit terms and shop among lenders, so it passed the federal "Truth-in-Lending" Act.[141] Typically then, federal law does not completely take the place of all of state law on a subject. The result is that Congress simply superimposes a layer of federal law on existing state law.

The Doctrine of Preemption The Supreme Court's doctrine of federal "preemption" of state law makes the coexistence of state and federal law on the same subject matter more likely. Congress can and often does explicitly provide for the preemption of state law in the text of federal statutes. In such cases, the scope of the preemption and its effects on particular state laws are issues of statutory interpretation.[142] In other cases, courts must imply the scope of preemption. Thus, federal law will displace state law only if (1) there is a direct conflict between state and federal law or the state law is otherwise an obstacle to accomplishing the federal goals or (2) Congress has expressed an intent to "occupy" an entire "field" of law even though the federal law does not directly conflict or interfere with federal goals. Conflict is relatively clear where the two laws set different standards of conduct and it is impossible to comply with both.[143] However, it is not always clear whether Congress intended the federal standard to be the *only* standard or only a *minimum* standard that state law could supplement.[144] In such a case, the Court looks at whether the state law stands as an obstacle to the accomplishment of Congress's full objectives in light of the federal act's intended purposes and

---

140 *See* 42 U.S.C.A. §§651 *et seq.*, discussed in Chapter XIII, p. 537.

141 15 U.S.C.A. §1601 *et seq.* The same is true of other federal consumer legislation. *See generally* Chapter X, pp. 425-433, where state and federal consumer protection statutes are discussed.

142 However, preemption is not always clear even when the federal statute deals with it explicitly. *Compare Cipolone v. Liggett Group, Inc.*, 505 U.S. 504 (1992) (federal statute providing that "[n]o requirement or prohibition based on smoking and health shall be imposed under State law with respect to the advertising and promotion of cigarettes" did not preempt state-law damages actions for breach of warranty or fraudulent misrepresentation regarding the dangers of smoking other than those contained in advertising) *with Geier v. American Honda Motor Co.*, 529 U.S. 861 (2000) (federal act requiring airbags in cars stated that "[c]ompliance with 'a federal safety standard' does not exempt any person from any liability under common law"; Court held that state damages claims for failure to install airbags preempted).

143 *McDermott v. Wisconsin*, 228 U.S. 115 (1913) (federal law required labeling of maple syrup in a manner that Wisconsin law prohibited).

144 *Wisconsin Public Intervenor v. Mortier*, 501 U.S. 597 (1991) (federal pesticide laws did not preempt stricter local rules). *Compare Rice v. Sant Fe Elevator Corporation*, 331 U.S. 218 (1947) (part of Congress's purpose was to prohibit dual state and federal regulation of grain elevators).

effects.[145] When the issue is not clear, there is a presumption *against* federal preemption.[146]

The Resulting Mix of State and Federal Law Two examples illustrate typical mixes of federal and state law. Taking an example from civil law, in a simple real estate sales transaction in which homeowners are selling their house, state contract and property law (usually common law and a few special statutes) govern the transfer of the property and the rights and obligations of the parties on the contracts for sale of the property and the bank's loan of the money to purchase it. State law or local city or county ordinances regulate the liability of the buyer and seller for property taxes, the zoning of the property for particular uses and whether the building's structure and sanitation are proper. However, federal consumer protection laws regulate the bank's disclosure of the terms of its loan and any report of the problems with the buyer's creditworthiness. If the buyers are eligible for any of the various federal housing assistance programs, the parties will have to follow applicable federal regulations. Federal banking laws control some bank operations while state laws control others.

On the criminal side, bank robbery violates state criminal laws against robbery and larceny. State law governs the robbery and any assaults on police or local inhabitants committed in the process of the robbery, as well as the theft of any "getaway" car. However, the federal government has, since the Great Depression of the 1930s, insured bank deposits against loss and has made robbery of any federally-insured bank a federal crime. If the getaway car the bank robbers stole has moved in interstate commerce, they could be in violation of federal law. Moreover, interstate flight to avoid prosecution, even for a state crime, is a federal offense. Any attack on federal law enforcement agents involved in apprehending the robbers would violate federal criminal laws. City ordinances may even be applicable if the robbers speed away in their getaway car or discharge their firearms within the city limits, though prosecution would not be likely in view of the other offenses committed. If the robbers face prosecution in state court, state law would govern the applicable criminal procedure. However, a large body of specific federal constitutional requirements would also apply. If prosecuted in federal court, both federal statutory and constitutional law would govern the procedure.[147]

The reasons why both state and federal government might choose to regulate the same subject matter vary with the area involved. Sometimes one government deems the measures adopted by the other to be inadequate to protect its interests. But often overlapping regulation is a result of inertia.

---

145 *Crosby v. National Foreign Trade Council*, 530 U.S. 363 (2000) (Massachusetts law barring state agencies from buying goods or services from companies doing business with Myanmar was preempted by federal sanctions against it passed by Congress); *United States v. Locke*, 529 U.S. 89 (2000) (Washington state law governing navigation of oil tankers in Puget Sound preempted by federal law).

146 *See Pacific Gas & Elec. Co. v. State Energy Resources Conservation & Dev. Comm'n*, 461 U.S. 190, 203-204 (1983) (California law prohibiting construction of nuclear power plants until safe method of disposal of nuclear fuel was found was valid even though it had the effect of preventing the building of federally-approved nuclear power plants; federal focus was safety of plant design, while state concern was in part economic feasibility). *See also Medtronics, Inc. v. Lohr*, 518 U.S. 470 (1996) (state tort suit seeking civil damages for defective heart pacemaker device not preempted by federal law regulating such devices); *Silkwood v. Kerr-Magee Corp.*, 464 U.S. 238 (1984) (state tort suit for punitive damages for escape of plutonium not preempted by federal regulation of nuclear materials even though defendant was in compliance with federal law).

147 A person whose single criminal act constitutes both a state and a federal crime may, in most situations, be prosecuted for both violations despite the prohibition against "double jeopardy" for the same offense, guaranteed by the Constitution's 5th Amendment. *See* Chapter VIII, p. 317.

The mix of state and federal law can present a challenge to the lawyer seeking to find all the applicable law. Experienced lawyers will have a good sense of whether a given area is one in which Congress has decided to intervene, but this is not always obvious. Unless already familiar with the area of law, a lawyer will have to do a thorough search of both state and federal law, and then seek to determine how they intersect on the issue in question.

b. Concurrent Federal and State Adjudicatory Power

Concurrent Subject-Matter Jurisdiction   Not only do both state and federal governments exercise concurrent *lawmaking* power; two coordinate *judicial systems* — state and federal — coexist on the same territory. Often federal and state courts in a state are literally across the street from each other. Federal courts naturally have jurisdiction over all federal-law claims and criminal prosecutions, just as state courts have jurisdiction over all state law claims and crimes. At the same time, however, the supremacy clause requires *state* courts to adjudicate most *federal* law claims[148] and *federal* courts routinely handle *state* law claims between citizens of different states under their "diversity of citizenship" jurisdiction. The result is that a plaintiff who has a federal claim or who has a state-law claim against a citizen of a different state has a choice of filing either in state or federal court. The defendant also has a choice: if the plaintiff files a federal question or diversity case in state court, the defendant can in most situations "remove" those cases to federal court if he or she desires.[149]

What Law is Applied by State and Federal Courts   When a *federal* court handles a *state* claim, it must apply *state substantive* law, though it may use its own *federal procedural* law. The federal court must follow state law as declared by the highest court of the relevant state. For example, a federal court handling a diversity medical malpractice case (a state law claim) will follow state law as to the nature of the claim and any defenses, but will apply its own federal rules of procedure.[150] When a *state* court handles a *federal* claim, an approximate reverse mirror image results. The supremacy clause requires that the state court apply *federal substantive* law, but the state court may use its own *state procedural* rules so long as they do not conflict with federal substantive law. Thus, a state court handling a federal civil rights claim will follow federal law as to the substance of that claim, but will apply its own state court rules on matters of procedure.[151]

2. The Effects of Horizontal Federalism: Concurrent Adjudicatory and Lawmaking Powers Among the States

In the typical case involving state-law claims, the law and the courts of only one state are involved. However, if the case involves parties, transactions or occurrences connected with more than one state — as a great and increasing number of cases do — "horizontal" federalism complicates matters. In such interstate disputes, the courts of more than one state may have jurisdiction to decide the dispute and more than one state

---

148 *Testa v. Katt*, 330 U.S. 386 (1947) (invalidating state court's refusal to adjudicate a federal claim because the state's conflicts of law rule provided that the states were not required to entertain penal actions of "foreign sovereign").

149 Details of the subject-matter jurisdiction of state and federal courts appear in Chapter V, pp. 188-191. Of course, because most state law claims involve parties from the same state, diversity jurisdiction will be unavailable and litigants will press the bulk of state law claims in state court.

150 *See* 28 U.S.C.A. §1652.

151 For more detail on state claims in federal court and federal claims in state court, *see* Chapter V, pp. 191-194.

may claim an interest in the dispute sufficient to have its law applied to resolve it. This proceeds from the broadened personal jurisdiction powers of state courts and the variety of state choice of law rules.

Multiple State Forums for Adjudication As discussed briefly earlier in this chapter, a state has the power of "personal jurisdiction" over all its residents and other persons present within its borders, meaning that all such persons are properly subject to suit in its courts. A state's power over non-residents was for years limited to cases where the person had property in the forum state. However, in the last 50 years that understanding has changed. Anyone who has certain "minimum contacts" with a state may be subject to suit in its courts.[152] Because a defendant — especially a corporation — may have the appropriate "minimum contacts" with several states, the defendant may be subject to suit in the courts of more than one state.

Choice of Law Among Multiple State Sources The law can vary from state to state. In interstate litigation, "choice of law" issues can arise — questions of which state's law governs the dispute. Unfortunately, there is no uniform body of federal choice-of-law rules to mediate between the competing state interests involved. Instead, the choice-of-law rules of the state where the case is pending apply to determine the question. One difficulty with this is that state choice-of-law rules are in a great state of flux, so it is difficult to predict what law will be applied to a given dispute.[153]

Even more difficult is the fact that states' choice of law rules have tended recently to favor application of their own law. This trend, when combined with the wider personal jurisdiction powers of state courts, makes it more likely that the choice of *where* one litigates a dispute will often affect *what law* will be applied to resolve the dispute.[154] Interstate cases governed by state law can present the lawyer with a wide variety of courts and bodies of law from which to choose. The decision of where to file suit is often a complicated one. So, for example, in choosing to file suit in Minnesota, one must consider not only the questions of convenient location and other such issues relevant to the deciding where to litigate, but also the possibility that Minnesota law will be applied to the dispute simply because the dispute is filed in its courts.[155]

3. The Effects of Separation of Powers and Federalism on the Federal Courts

Limitations on federal court power under the double banners of separation of powers and federalism are on the rise today as a more conservative Supreme Court reacts to the federal court "activism" of the 1960s and 1970s. Whether one agrees with the Supreme Court's formulation of these limitations on federal court power or not — many of them are controversial — they are consistent with concerns of some of the

---

152 *See International Shoe v. Washington*, discussed *supra* p. 29.

153 The variety of choice of law rules is discussed in Chapter VII, pp. 263-268.

154 Details of personal jurisdiction appear in Chapter VII, pp. 253-259.

155 Laws vary considerably from state to state, but one must not overstate the differences. Often the difference are between majority and minority positions on a legal issue, with relative consistency among states in each camp. In addition, "restatements" of the law by the American Law Institute provide a basis for uniformity when they influence courts or courts adopt restatements outright. *See* Chapter II, p. 76. The Uniform Law Commissioners, a body established in 1892 that is made up of delegates from every state, has also advanced uniformity of statutory law. The Commissioners draft Uniform and Model Acts (*see* http://www.nccusl.o rg/Update/). While they cannot force states to accept the laws they write, their drafts have persuasive force. Their principal success has been the Uniform Commercial Code (UCC) — which every state except Louisiana has adopted — discussed in Chapter X, pp. 414-421. The Commissioners have also had some success in family law (Chapter XIII) and business organizations (Chapter XV).

Framers that a system of lower federal courts parallel to state courts was unnecessary and presented the potential for interference with the states.[156]

The "Cases" and "Controversies" Limitation of Article III   This limitation relates to justiciability of a suit — whether a dispute is of a type that a federal court should decide. Article III states that federal "judicial power" extends to "cases" and "controversies." The Supreme Court has read these terms to limit federal courts to deciding only traditional lawsuits in which there are opposing parties who have a legal claim between them and a concrete "stake" in the controversy. As a result, federal courts may not render advisory opinions or otherwise declare what the law is in some abstract, non-judicial context. In addition, a federal court must carefully evaluate all cases to determine whether the plaintiff has "standing" to raise an issue or whether the case presents a "political" as opposed to a legal question.[157]

Since justiciability limits arise from the special nature of federal courts as defined by Article III, they have no effect on state courts. Some state constitutions have similar limitations on the power of their courts, but others do not. For example, state supreme courts often have the power to issue advisory opinions, even on federal constitutional issues.[158]

Federal Common Law-Making   Federal courts, like state courts, have the power to make "common law." As the next chapter will discuss, the term "common law," when used in this sense, means law that is made completely by judicial decision or caselaw, as opposed to statutory law or even caselaw interpreting statutes.[159] Courts exercising common law powers might be thought of as performing a "legislative" function, because they are creating substantive rules of law that will govern people's conduct in the future. The fact that courts perform such "legislative" functions is not a problem in a common law system as a general matter. However, federal courts differ from state courts in that federal courts' common law-making powers are subject to separation of powers and the grant of "[a]ll legislative Powers" to Congress. As the Court has noted, the common law-making process "involves the balancing of competing values and interests, which in our democratic system is the business of elected representatives."[160]

The Supreme Court long ago limited federal courts' power to punish common law crimes.[161] Federal courts' power to make common law in civil cases exists but is more limited than that of state courts. Federal judicial lawmaking is proper only in a few areas where there are clear and strong uniquely federal interests or Congress directs its application. Thus, federal common law-making is generally limited to cases concerning property and rights and obligations of the United States government (such as government checks and bonds), international relations, and admiralty cases, and those instances where there is clear congressional intent that courts create federal common law or fill gaps in federal legislation.[162]

---

156 *See supra* p. 8. *See* ERWIN CHEMERINSKY, FEDERAL JURISDICTION, 5TH ED. (Aspen 2007), for a discussion of the intricacies of federal court jurisdiction.

157 These justiciability limitations are discussed in more depth in Chapter IX, pp. 329-335.

158 *See* Chapter IX, p. 325. *See also Doremus v. Board of Education*, 342 U.S. 429 (1952) (appeal from state court to U.S. Supreme Court on issue of 1st Amendment freedom of religion dismissed for lack of standing under Art. III; irrelevant that plaintiff had standing in state court under state law).

159 *See* Chapter II, p. 40.

160 *See Texas Industries, Inc. v. Radcliff Materials, Inc.*, 451 U.S. 630, 647 (1981), quoting *Diamond v. Chakrabarty*, 447 U.S. 303, 317 (1980).

161 *United States v. Hudson & Goodwin*, 11 U.S. 32 (1812).

162 *See generally* CHEMERINSKY, *supra* note 156, §§6.1-6.3.

This limitation on federal court common law power also has federalism underpinnings. *Erie, Lackawanna R.R. v. Tompkins*[163] established that federal courts, when handling state law claims, must follow state common law decisions and have no right to make their own independent determinations of what state law is. The *Erie* decision relied in part on the reserved powers of the states over their common law and the fact that common law-making by federal courts interfered with those state powers.[164]

Implied Private Rights of Action   When a statute creates a right, but provides no remedy, a common law court generally creates one in the form of an action for damages. The power to do so is inherent in the ancient maxim *ubi jus ibi remedium*.[165] Congress has created many federal rights by statute but often has failed to provide a private right of action to enforce those rights. If so, federal courts may not create a remedy unless Congress expressly authorizes it to do so or there is some implied congressional direction to do so.[166] According to the Supreme Court, the problem with free judicial creation of remedies is not only that it invades the legislative function, but that it effectively allows federal courts to expand their own jurisdiction, a function the Constitution gives solely to Congress in Article III.[167]

If state courts show a hesitancy to make common law, the disability is one imposed by their own sense of restraint or by their own state constitutions or laws. They are unaffected by federal separation of powers or Article III considerations.

The Anti-Injunction Act and Federal Court Abstention   Under the supremacy clause, federal courts enforcing federal law necessarily enjoy primacy over state institutions, including state courts. However, Congress's concern about federal court interference with state court proceedings caused it to reverse this normal effect of federal supremacy as part of the first legislation enacted under the new Constitution. In 1789, Congress passed the "Anti-Injunction Act," a statutory prohibition on federal courts enjoining state court litigation (ordering that state court litigation cease). Some exceptions to the ban on injunctions have developed over the years, but the general prohibition exists to this day. In addition, the Supreme Court has created several complete or partial "abstention" doctrines. These doctrines, which appear to originate partly from the Constitution, independently require federal courts to abstain from exercising jurisdiction to avoid

---

163 304 U.S. 64 (1938).

164 The Court decided *Erie* at a time when its view of federal power was more restricted than it is today. Consequently, it is unclear today that the Court would hold that federal courts are *constitutionally* incapable of making common law outside of the limited federal areas listed earlier.

165 "For every right, there is a remedy." *See also* RESTATEMENT (SECOND) OF TORTS §874A (1979) (when a statute "protects a class of persons," but provides no civil remedy, a "new cause of action analogous to an existing tort action" may be accorded a person injured by violation of a statute if the court "determines that the remedy is appropriate in furtherance of the purpose of the legislation and needed to assure the effectiveness of the provision").

166 *See Touche Ross & Co v. Redington*, 442 U.S. 560 (1979). *See generally* CHEMERINSKY, *supra* note 156, §6.3.3.

167 *See* Article III §2 and discussion *supra* p. 8. The most complete statement of the rationale for this restrictive rule for federal courts is Justice Powell's dissent in *Cannon v. University of Chicago*, 441 U.S. 677, 730-749 (1979), a position the majority in *Touche Ross, supra* effectively adopted. This apparently constitutionally-based incapacity of federal courts to create rights of actions from federal statutes is a recently "discovered" incapacity. *See Middlesex Sewerage Authority v. National Sea Clammers Assoc.*, 453 U.S. 1, 23-25 (1981) (Stevens, J., dissenting) and *Marbury v. Madison*, 5 U.S. 137, 163 (1803) ("[I]t is a general and indisputable rule, that where there is a right, there is also a legal remedy by suit, or action at law, whenever that right is invaded.")

interference with pending state proceedings or otherwise to avoid a direct affront to the exercise of state judicial, administrative and legislative power.[168]

State Sovereign Immunity from Suit in Federal Court Article III originally provided for federal court jurisdiction over some categories of suits against a *state*. When the Framers debated the Constitution, some questioned whether this provision of Article III would abolish state sovereign immunity from suit, at least when litigants brought suit in federal court. In the 1791 case of *Chisholm v. Georgia*,[169] the Supreme Court decided that Article III did abolish such immunity. It held that the state of Georgia was liable on a supply contract that it had entered into during the Revolutionary War. Congress and the states responded with passage and ratification of the 11th Amendment in 1793, overruling *Chisholm*. State sovereign immunity continues to exist today despite the intervening ratification of the Civil War Amendments, particularly the 14th Amendment's clear limitations on state power. Various fictions have developed to allow suits in federal court to compel states to follow federal law, but suits for money damages remain barred unless the relevant state consents to suit.[170]

---

168 Some of these are discussed in when the judicial system is discussed in Chapter V, pp. 195-197. For more detail, *see* CHEMERINSKY, *supra* note 156, §§12-14.

169 2 U.S. 419 (1793). The decision was not well-received in Georgia. *See supra* note 98.

170 The complicated fictions allowing injunctive relief are necessary because the Supreme Court has declined to hold or even to rule on the perhaps obvious argument that the 14th Amendment (ratified in 1868), of its own force, repealed the 11th Amendment (ratified in 1798). For more on the law of the 11th Amendment, *see* Chapter VI, pp. 225-226. *See also generally* Chapter VI, pp. 223-228, where judicial remedies against state and federal governments and officials are discussed.

CHAPTER II

LEGAL METHODOLOGY

The first task of this chapter is to inventory the various forms that sources of law take in the United States and place them in the appropriate hierarchy of authoritativeness. We will then examine the two most frequently encountered sources of law — common law and statutes — and will explore their interrelationship and methodology. Finally, we will examine briefly the practical questions of how lawyers find and research the law and argue legal points.

A. Sources of Law and Their Hierarchy

1. Enacted Law

Constitutions The structural provisions of the federal Constitution were discussed in Chapter I, as was the increased "constitutionalization" of the law that has taken place since 1953. As will be evident from later chapters, there is scarcely any area of the law that has not been touched by the growth of federal constitutional limitations on government action. Federal constitutional law is discussed in more detail later in this book.[1]

Challenges to state laws and practices based on *state* constitutional grounds have been increasingly successful. Development of state constitutional rights for years was overshadowed and made unnecessary by vigorous development of federal constitutional rights. However, some state courts have chosen to provide their residents with greater protections.[2] Even where federal and state constitutional provisions have exactly the same wording, state courts have sometimes interpreted their state's versions to provide more protection than their federal counterparts.[3] This is important because state action, to be valid, must satisfy both federal and state constitutional requirements. In addition, the United States Supreme Court has no power to decide any issue of state law, so such state supreme court constitutional rulings are immune from reversal by the United States Supreme Court.

Statutes Statutes are laws enacted by federal, state, and local legislative bodies. Generally proposed statutes, called "bills," must survive close scrutiny from specialized legislative committees and gain the approval of the appropriate head executive official. The collection of federal statutes is called the United States Code, while collections of state statutes are called compiled laws or statutes. Statutes and statutory interpretation are discussed in more depth later in this chapter.[4]

Treaties Treaties with foreign nations, concluded by the President and ratified by the Senate, and executive agreements — treaty-like documents that need not be ratified — are another source of law, though not a major one. All treaties are federal law, as states are prohibited by the federal Constitution from entering into treaties with foreign

---

1 *See* Chapter IX.

2 William Brennan, *State Constitutions and the Protection of Individual Rights*, 90 HARV.L.REV. 489 (1977); Jennifer Friesen, *Recovering Damages for State Bills of Rights Claims*, 63 TEX. L. REV. 1269 (1985).

3 *Compare Michigan Dept. of State Police v. Sitz*, 496 U.S. 444 (1990) *with Sitz v. Dept. of State Police*, 506 N.W.2d 209 (Mich. 1993), discussed in Chapter VIII, p. 297, note 165 (unreasonable searches). *See* Utter, *State Constitutional Law, the U.S. Supreme Court and Democratic Accountability*, 64 WASH.L.REV. 19 (1989) (finding 450 such decisions).

4 *See infra* pp. 49-64.

nations.[5] Unlike the situation in some other countries, treaties in the United States are on the same hierarchical level as federal statutes, meaning that Congress can change a treaty by simply passing a contrary statute — arguably not a firm basis on which to build good international relations. In addition, some treaties are not "self-executing" and cannot be enforced unless Congress has passed implementing legislation.[6]

Court Rules   Court rules govern the procedures to be followed in courts. For example, the federal courts are governed by the following bodies of court rules adopted in the following years: Federal Rules of Civil Procedure (1938), the Federal Rules of Criminal Procedure (1946), Federal Rules of Appellate Procedure (1968), and the Federal Rules of Evidence (1975).

Federal court rules are the primary responsibility of the Judicial Conference of the United States, a supervisory and administrative arm of the federal courts. The Conference appoints an Advisory Committee of legal academics, judges and practitioners who draft the rules. The rules are then reviewed and revised by the United States Supreme Court and, if Congress does not intervene, they become law. Federal court rules have the same force as federal statutes. Some of the federal rules related to civil and criminal procedure and evidence are discussed in later chapters.[7]

States also have court rules, which are adopted by various means, usually by the supreme court of the state. Often in states, the court rule (if it truly deals with matters of procedure) has higher status than a statute passed by the legislature and, if there is a conflict, the court rule will prevail.[8]

Administrative Agency Rules and Decisions   Administrative agencies make law primarily through rules they promulgate. In addition, administrative hearing decisions may have some lawmaking effect in the same manner as judicial caselaw, discussed next. Some federal administrative agencies make policy almost exclusively by way of case-by-case adjudication. Agency rule-making and adjudication are discussed in the chapter on administrative law.[9]

2. Caselaw

In a common law system, caselaw court decisions of individual cases are a source of law and are referred to as a whole as "caselaw." Thus, court decisions not only resolve past controversies; a decision of a case is considered to be a "precedent" that has legal effect in the future. This effect comes from the principle of *stare decisis* — the idea that future cases should be decided the same way as past cases.[10] Caselaw is

---

5 Art. I §10. States may, however, with Congressional approval, enter into "compacts" with foreign nations, as they may with sister states. Pursuant to this authorization, some American states have entered into compacts with neighboring Canadian provinces.

6 *See Frolova v. U.S.S.R.*, 761 F.2d 370 (7th Cir. 1985) (U.N Charter and Helsinki Accord concerning the reunification of married couples were not self-executing, so American wife of a Russian citizen could not sue the Soviet Government for its refusal to allow her husband to emigrate) and Chapter 17, p. 690.

7 *See* Chapters VII, pp. 229-242 (Federal Rules of Civil Procedure) and Chapter III, pp. 109-115 (Federal Rules of Evidence).

8 See, e.g. *Winberry v. Salisbury*, 74 A.2d 406 (N.J. 1950) (court rule governing the time period within which an appeal could be taken governed over a contrary statute) and *Ammerman v. Hubbard Broadcasting, Inc.*, 551 P.2d 1354 (N.M. 1976) (since evidence law in New Mexico was considered procedural rather than substantive, statute establishing a privilege in favor of newspaper reporters was ineffective).

9 *See* Chapter VI, pp. 199-204.

10 *Stare decisis* is discussed in greater detail *infra* pp. 65-66.

sometimes referred to as "unwritten" law, because the rule established by the court decision is often only implicit in the decision.

There are two kinds of caselaw: common law caselaw and caselaw interpreting enacted law. The two types of caselaw occupy different places in the hierarchy of sources of law, so they are treated separately here.

a. Common Law Caselaw

"Common Law" as Used Here The term "common law" is sometimes used to refer to *all* judicial decisions in a system where those decisions have precedential effect. In this book, the term is used in a more narrow sense to mean only that body of law developed and articulated *solely* through judicial decisions. As such, unlike caselaw interpreting statutes, common law constitutes a separate and distinct source of law independent of enacted law. The history and nature of common law and its relationship to statutory law are discussed in more detail below.[11]

Common law is on the lowest level of the hierarchy of sources of law in a given legal system. At one point in history, there was a suggestion that the common law prevailed over contrary statutory law.[12] However, the principle of legislative supremacy has won out. Consequently, a legislature has the power to abolish or modify the common law as it sees fit. Common law may also be displaced by a constitutional provision or by an administrative agency rule properly promulgated and within the agency's statutory authority.

State and Federal Common Law As discussed in Chapter I, the legislative powers of the state and federal governments are different in nature. States have the general power to pass legislation in any area and are limited only by limitations imposed on them by the Constitution. The federal government, on the other hand, is one of limited legislative powers. Similar restraints have been said to operate on judicial law-making as a result of both separation of powers and federalism factors.[13] Thus, state common law governs many areas of the law of a given state, such as torts, contracts and property. Federal common law's domain is narrower. Federal judicial lawmaking is proper only under two circumstances: (1) where Congress directs its application pursuant to a proper exercise of its enumerated powers and (2) where there are clear and strong uniquely federal interests that need to be protected.

An example of the first category is Federal Rule of Evidence (FRE) 501, which provides that the privilege of witnesses from testifying, *e.g.*, doctor-patient privilege, "shall be governed by the principles of the common law as they may be interpreted by the courts of the United States in the light of reason and experience." Examples of the second category are as varied as the federal interests involved: maritime and admiralty law, international relations, disputes between the states, and federal government property and financial paper. In addition, in areas where Congress has legislated, even the most comprehensive statutes have gaps. In some cases, those gaps are filled by state common law. However, federal common law built on promotion of the federal interests behind the statute is most often the preferable solution.[14]

---

11 *See infra* pp. 44-48 and 49-54.

12 *See Dr. Bonham's Case*, 77 Eng. Rep. 646 (C.P. 1610) (Coke, J.).

13 *See* Chapter I, pp. 35-36.

14 *See generally* ERWIN CHEMERINSKY, FEDERAL JURISDICTION, 4TH ED. §§6.1-6.3 (Aspen 2003) and sources cited therein.

While state and federal common law deal with different subject matters, they are identical in their methodology. Consequently, no further mention will be made of the distinctions between them in the discussions of common law that follow.

b. Caselaw Interpreting Enacted Law

Caselaw interpreting enacted law, like common law caselaw, follows the rule of *stare decisis*. Consequently, a case decision interpreting a statute is a source of law and will control later cases arising under the statute that involve similar facts.

Caselaw construing enacted law is listed here as a separate source of law apart from the enacted law it interprets. This reflects the understanding that a case decision interpreting and applying enacted law adds something to the law beyond the effect of the enactment standing alone. The amount of law that is added by judicial decision depends on how much interpretation of the enacted law is needed. But that is only a matter of degree. Some lawmaking is taking place.

As a *source of law*, however, caselaw interpreting enacted law is considered to be derivative of the law it interprets. As such, this form of caselaw takes on the hierarchical level of the enacted law that it interprets. Thus, caselaw interpreting the Constitution prevails over a conflicting statute, caselaw interpreting a statute prevails over common law, and so on. Caselaw interpreting a statute can be overruled by later action of the legislature, just as the statute itself can be amended. Caselaw interpreting the Constitution is reversible only by amending the Constitution.

Common law and caselaw interpreting statutes employ much the same reasoning process. For that reason, the two are discussed together when the nature of caselaw reasoning is discussed.[15]

3. The Hierarchy of Sources of Law

Adding the supremacy clause of the Constitution to the points about hierarchy mentioned above, a complete hierarchy of sources of law can be constructed. From highest to lowest, they are (1) the federal Constitution, (2) federal statutes, treaties and court rules, (3) federal administrative agency rules, (4) federal common law, (5) state constitutions, (6) state statutes and court rules, (7) state agency rules, and (8) state common law. It is understood that each level of enacted law includes the caselaw interpreting that enacted law. If two sources of law on the same level of the hierarchy conflict, then the later in time will govern.

This hierarchy of law should be viewed with caution. First, a law's superior position in the hierarchy is not an indication of its importance or the frequency of its use. As discussed in Chapter I, while there is more federal law now than ever before, it is still

---

15 *See infra* pp. 66-74. The precise boundary between common law caselaw and statutory interpretation is sometimes difficult to discern. There are at least three "hybrid" forms. As mentioned earlier in the discussion of federal common law, *supra* p. 40, the legislature may delegate the power to make common law without limitations. Or the legislature may so delegate with the understanding that such common law will be consistent with prevailing legislative principles in the area. *See Textile Workers Union v. Lincoln Mills*, 353 U.S. 448 (1957) (construing §301 of the Taft-Hartley Act as a congressional direction to federal courts to make a federal common law of collective bargaining contracts that is responsive to federal legislative policy on labor-management relations). Or the legislature may use general statutory language and signal its intent that courts interpret that language in accordance with pre-existing common law understandings of its meaning. *See* Sherman Antitrust Act, 15 U.S.C.A. §1, and *National Society of Professional Engineers v. United States*, 435 U.S. 679, 688 (1978) (Congress intended that §1, prohibiting all agreements "in restraint of trade or commerce," would be "shape[d]" by "drawing on common law tradition"). *See also* Chapter XVII, p. 731 (definition of "commercial activity").

true that most everyday transactions and occurrences affecting most people and companies in the United States are governed by state law.[16]

A second caveat regarding this hierarchy is that some conflict combinations in the hierarchy are more likely than others. It is not uncommon for courts to find that a state statute or regulation conflicts with a federal statute and is consequently invalid. It would be rare that a federal administrative rule would override a right guaranteed by a state constitution. The subject matters addressed by the typical federal agency rule and the typical state constitution are so dissimilar that such a conflict is unlikely.

In the next sections, we will focus in more depth on common law and statutes. There are several reasons to do this. First, common law and statutory law together govern the overwhelming majority of legal questions that arise in the legal system. Second, the relationship between common law and statutory law is important, as the role of one affects the nature of the other. Third, the judicial processes involved in common law and statutory interpretation serve as paradigms for dealing with other sources of law: reasoning applied in common law caselaw applies generally to all caselaw, and statutory interpretation principles have applicability to interpretation of other forms of enacted law.

B. Common Law

1. A Very Brief History

After the Norman Invasion of Britain in 1066, the first royal courts developed from the King's Council. The first royal judges, then, were the King's closest advisors who traveled the country checking on local administration and, as part of their duties, deciding disputes. Later their tasks became primarily judicial. They separated from the Council and began to acquire their own jurisdiction as royal courts. These royal judges held court both in Westminster and while traveling throughout the country. Local courts controlled by local nobles continued to resolve most disputes. However, the more important cases were reserved for the King's courts.

The royal judges through their travels acquired in-depth knowledge of local customary law in all parts of the country. However, they believed that cases of "national" interest should be decided — not according to local customary law as applied by the local courts — but in accord with a single national body of law common to the entire country. Meeting in Westminster, they developed such a body of law by selecting from, combining or modifying the local customs that they had learned about. The law thus determined and applied became known as the "common law." This was because it was law that was "common" to the entire country, as opposed to local law, which varied from place to place. Eventually, the royal courts grew and common law displaced a large part of local law.

The instinct of the early common law judges was to keep their decisions as consistent as possible. This principle, called *stare decisis*, dates at least to the 1170s when Richard Fitz-Nigel wrote: "There are cases where the course of events, and the reasons for decisions are obscure; and in those it is enough to cite precedents."[17] A system of precedent is difficult without some written records of earlier decisions, but the small number of common law judges during this period and their central location in

---

16 *See* pp. 30-33.

17 RICHARD FITZ-NIGEL, DIALOGUS DE SCACCARIO (written 1177-1179), quoted in HENRY J. ABRAHAM, THE JUDICIAL PROCESS, 7TH ED. 9 (Oxford U. Press 1998).

Westminster made it possible to maintain some consistency.[18] In addition, lawyers who appeared in the common law courts would assist by reminding the judges of prior cases. This rough system of precedent later gave way to a more sophisticated one once reliable reports of decisions became available.[19]

One might wonder why judge-made law survived in England at a time when it was abandoned in the rest of Europe. The common law survived two major threats to its existence. The first came during the 16th and 17th centuries when the common law faced competition from more accessible Roman-canon law. However, this was also the time of the struggle for supremacy between the King and Parliament — a struggle which Parliament eventually won. The losing Royalists favored Roman-canon law, which was simpler and its procedure and content more easily controlled by the King. The common law, which Parliament favored, represented a guarantee of freedom, in large part because its ponderous, formalistic procedures and strong judges made the courts more difficult for the King to control.[20]

The second threat to the common law's existence was the French Revolution. Its democratic theory maintained that the legislature was the only proper source of positive law in an enlightened democratic age. Strong feeling against judge-made law were also a reaction to the practices of pre-revolutionary French judges, who were members of the aristocracy. When the French Crown enacted moderate statutory reforms in an effort to stave off revolution, these conservative judges sabotaged the effort by giving the statutes with narrow and perverse interpretations.[21] Thus, the powers of judges were strictly limited in order to assure that they do nothing more than strictly apply the law as set out by the legislature. This idea spread from France to other parts of continental Europe as part of the widespread influence of the ideals of the French Revolution.[22]

English common law was well developed when the North American colonies were being settled, primarily by English colonists. Around the time of the Declaration of Independence and thereafter it was formally "received" from England by the newly independent states.[23] Since then, after 200 years of separate existence, common law in the United States has taken on a life of its own. Though common law method is largely the same, there are numerous differences in substantive common law rules in the

---

18 The three courts at Westminster were the Court of Exchequer, the Court of Common Pleas and the Court of King's Bench.

19 *See generally* JOHN P. DAWSON, THE ORACLES OF THE LAW 1-80 (U. of Michigan Law School 1968) and KONRAD ZWEIGERT AND HEIN KÖTZ, AN INTRODUCTION TO COMPARATIVE LAW, 2D ED. 189-191 (Clarendon Press 1992) and authorities cited therein. Assisting in the insularity and cohesiveness of the system was the eventual requirement that common law judges be selected exclusively from the ranks of the lawyers who practiced in their courts. *See* Harry Jones, *Our Uncommon Common Law*, 42 TENN.L.REV. 443, 450-452 (1975); ZWEIGERT & KÖTZ, *id.* at 189-204 and authorities cited therein.

20 ZWEIGERT & KÖTZ, *supra* note 19, *id.*

21 *See* DAWSON, *supra* note 19, at 368-371 and authorities cited therein.

22 *See* JOHN H. MERRYMAN, THE CIVIL LAW TRADITION, 3D ED. 15-16 (Stanford U. Press 2007); DAWSON, *supra* note 19, at 362-379. An important development not discussed here is the appearance of "equity" courts that grew up in England. Equity and law are now combined in one court and equity primarily concerns the form and mode of giving relief in a civil case and whether there is a right to a jury trial in civil cases. Consequently, the development of equity is discussed in the chapter on civil procedure. *See* Chapter VII, pp. 243-243 and 245-247.

23 *See* West's Fla. Stat. Ann. §2.01, quoted in *Hoffman v. Jones*, 280 So.2d 431 (Fla. 1973), set out on p. A12 of the Appendix. *See generally* Harry Jones, *supra*, note 19, at 452-454. Some states received English statutes as well. *See* Ford W. Hall, *The Common Law: An Account of Its Reception in the United States*, 4 VAND.L.REV. 791, 816, 818 (1951).

United States and England and it is rare that courts in the United States rely on English decisions today.[24]

2. The Nature of the Judicial Process in Common Law Adjudication

Common law decisions and rules are based on precedent. However, all cases differ somewhat from prior cases. Consequently, a judge deciding a case must, to a greater or lesser degree, rely on considerations and principles beyond what is set out in prior cases. Moreover, when a court is faced with making the *first* decision in a given area of the law — the "case of first impression" — there is often little precedent on which to rely. This gives rise to the question: what is the ultimate source of common law rules and the nature of the judicial process in common law adjudication? This question has been answered differently at different times.

Current Theory Today, we know that the creative component of the common law comes from judges. Judges "make" common law by applying their conception of what is appropriate public policy. If there is law from prior caselaw to be applied, it should be applied. But whether in applying prior caselaw or striking out in a completely new direction, judges cannot avoid infusing public policy elements into decisions choosing a new rule of law or, for that matter, whenever they decide a case that is not exactly controlled by precedent. Thus, it is customary today to describe judges as "creating" common law or engaging in "lawmaking" activities when they develop common law.

An example of this is *Hoffman v. Jones*,[25] a Florida Supreme Court opinion that is set out in the appendix.[26] *Hoffman* involved a major doctrinal change in the common law of torts — the change from "contributory negligence" to "comparative negligence." Under contributory negligence, an injured plaintiff's negligence, however slight, operated as a complete bar to recovery from even a clearly negligent defendant. Under comparative negligence, the negligence of the plaintiff serves to reduce the amount of damages recovered, but will not stand as a complete bar.[27] In reaching this decision, the majority opinion in *Hoffman* freely considered and weighed considerations of history, economics, and philosophy. It observed that the old rule was developed at a time when tort recovery was thought to pose a serious threat to the development of industry, that today industry is stronger and widespread insurance coverage has made damage awards much less a threat to its existence, and that it is considered unfair and inhumane today to deny recovery for injury because of only slight contributory fault of the injured person.

Consistent with the notion that what is taking place is lawmaking, these kinds of considerations are commonly referred to as "legislative facts" — the kinds of data and public policy considerations a legislature would discuss in deciding whether to pass a statute. This is in contrast to "adjudicatory facts," facts that courts must ascertain to decide whether a particular fact situation fits a settled rule of law.[28]

---

24 Close examination reveals some significant differences in caselaw methodology as well. *See* P.S. ATIYAH & ROBERT SUMMERS, FORM AND SUBSTANCE IN ANGLO-AMERICAN LAW 116-127 (Oxford U. Press 1991). This interesting book makes comparisons between English and American legal methodology in several areas, concluding that English law tends to be "formal" and American law "substantive." *See also* Mortimer N.S. Sellers, *The Doctrine of Precedent in the United States of America*, 54 AM.J. COMP.L. 67 (2006).

25 280 So.2d 431 (Fla. 1973).

26 *See* Appendix, pp. A1-A14.

27 *See* Chapter XI, p. 444.

28 *See generally* WILLIAM REYNOLDS, JUDICIAL PROCESS IN A NUTSHELL, 2D ED §§4.22-4.26 (West 2002). Courts are assisted in fully exploring all the relevant considerations in an important case by permitting *amicus curiae* briefs. Several *amici* appeared in *Hoffman*. *See* Appendix, p. A2. An *amicus curiae*, literally "friend of the court," is a person or organization with an interest in the legal issues being developed in a case, who

Past Theories of Common Law Judicial Process   We acknowledge today that judges make common law, but this was not always the case. In the 18th and 19th centuries, the common law was spoken of as if it existed independently of human action. According to Sir William Blackstone, a judge was simply an "oracle of the law."[29] Thus, judges did not *make* law. They *discovered* and *declared* it. A past case was not law, but only "evidence of the law."[30] In overruling a case, Blackstone noted, "if it be found that the former decision is manifestly absurd or unjust, it is declared not that such was bad law, but that it was not law."[31] Thus, a court overruling a case simply "recognized that the common law has changed" or that the prior case "evinced an incorrect understanding of what the common law rule is."

An allied notion was that the common law method of adjudication was a "scientific" one by which a court would come to a single, correct result in any new case if it located the correct precedents and then used the proper tools of logic in reasoning from that precedent.[32] Christopher Langdell, who introduced the "case method" of law study at Harvard Law School in 1870 and later became Dean, is associated with this view.[33]

Justice Oliver Wendell Holmes, Jr., was an early challenger of this conception of the common law. He mocked the "discovery" approach as perceiving the common law as a "brooding omnipresence in the sky"[34] or as a scientific product of reasoning and logic. His view in 1881 — considered shocking at the time — was that:

> The life of the [common] law has not been logic; it has been experience. The felt necessities of the time, the prevalent moral and political theories, intuitions of public policy, avowed or unconscious, even the prejudices which judges share with their fellow-men, have had a good deal more to do than the syllogism in determining the rules by which men should be governed. . . . The very consideration which judges most rarely mention, and always with an apology, are the secret root from which the law draws all the juices of life. I mean, of course, consideration of what is expedient for the community concerned.[35]

Whatever other purposes the discovery and scientific myths of the common law served, they made judicial lawmaking appear more legitimate. If judges discover the law or use a scientific method to apply it, then judicial decisions are objective and dictated by "the law" rather than policy choices made by judges. The persistence of the myth that judges do not make law can probably be attributed to the fact that judicial lawmaking threatens a basic notion that underlies all legal systems: the fundamental principle that decisions should be made in accord with *preexisting rules* and not by fiat.

---

is permitted to state views and arguments on one side or the other of a case.

29 WILLIAM BLACKSTONE, COMMENTARIES ON THE LAW OF ENGLAND 69 (William S. Hein & Co. 1992) (originally published 1765-1769).

30 *Black & White Taxicab Co. v. Brown & Yellow Taxicab Co.*, 276 U.S. 518, 529-30 (1928). *See also Swift v. Tyson*, 41 U.S. 1 (1842) ("it will hardly be contended that the decisions of Courts constitute laws. They are, at most, only evidence of what the laws are; and are not of themselves laws.")

31 BLACKSTONE, *supra* note 29, at 70.

32 See GRANT GILMORE, THE AGES OF AMERICAN LAW 62 (Yale U. Press 1977).

33 Although the "scientific" method of Langdell's formalism is now largely discredited, his case method of teaching in law school remains. *See* Chapter IV, p. 131.

34 *Southern Pacific Co. v. Jensen*, 244 U.S. 205, 222 (1917) (Holmes, J., dissenting).

35 OLIVER W. HOLMES, JR., THE COMMON LAW 1-2 (1881). Oliver Wendell Holmes, Jr. (1841-1935) was among the most famous of American judges, serving as Chief Justice of the Supreme Judicial Court of Massachusetts and as an Associate Justice of the U.S. Supreme Court. For similar views, *see* BENJAMIN N. CARDOZO, THE JUDICIAL PROCESS 98-141 (Yale U. Press 1921) (discussing the "judge as legislator").

This notion undoubtedly explains the persistence of a parallel myth in civil law countries — that judicial decisions are not a source of law and that judges simply apply code provisions to the case at hand and come up with a decision.[36] Such "folklore," as Professor Merryman has called it, is difficult to eradicate.[37]

The most comprehensive attack on the "folklore" of the common law in the United States was by the Legal Realists in the 1930s, led by Professor Karl Llewellyn and Judge Jerome Frank. The Realists developed both points made by Holmes: first, that the law in judicial opinions is not discovered and declared, it is made; and second, that its content is affected by social, political, economic, historical and other trends in thinking that operate consciously or unconsciously through the judge making it.[38]

Practical Effects of Legal Realism   The demise of the discovery and scientific theories of the common law has made judges self-conscious about their creative functions. An example of this can be found in the *Hoffman v. Jones* case, discussed above and set out in the appendix. Considerable time was spent in the majority opinion and a dissent was sparked on the question of whether it fell to the court or the legislature to change the rule on contributory negligence.[39] And outside the courtroom, whether at public gatherings or confirmation hearings or in judicial election campaigns, judges tend to emphasize their role as law-*interpreters* and to downplay their law-*making* functions.[40] Debates over the nomination of federal judges in recent years have revealed a gross ignorance on the part of the public — and apparently among Senators who should know better — who rail against judges who "legislate from the bench," as if the job of judges in a common law system was one of mechanical application of the law.

The recognition that judges make law based on policy considerations has also led to somewhat greater candor in judicial opinions. Instead of trying to hide policy choices behind intricate discussions of precedents, judges are more likely to forthrightly support the rule they have chosen with arguments based on public policy considerations. The majority opinion in *Hoffman v. Jones*, which, as discussed earlier, openly relies on considerations of history, sociology, economics and philosophy, is an example of this.[41] A demonstration of the older approach of hiding public policy choices behind masterful feats of recasting and distinguishing precedents is Judge Cardozo's opinion in the 1916 case of *MacPherson v. Buick Motor Co.*[42] *McPherson* is often cited as a paradigm of the

---

36 The development of a complex body of tort law in France from only 40 or so words in the French Code Civil demonstrate that civil law judges have just as creative a role as common law judges. *See* MARTIN SHAPIRO, COURTS 136-143 (University of Chicago Press 1981) (discussing French tort law). The fact that a very different body of tort law has developed in the province of Quebec in Canada from essentially the same words shows how codes hardly dictate decisions. *See* H.R. Hanlo, *Here Lies the Common Law: Rest in Peace*, 30 Modern L. Rev. 341, 245-256 (1967).

37 MERRYMAN, *supra* note 22, at 47 ("the important distinction between civil law and common law judicial processes does not lie in what courts in fact do, but in what the dominant folklore tells them they do."); ZWEIGERT & KÖTZ, *supra* note 19, at 272-273. *See also* MAURO CAPPELLETTI, THE JUDICIAL PROCESS IN COMPARATIVE PERSPECTIVE 3-56 (Clarendon Press 1989) (exploring the spread of the domain of judge-made law in civil law countries and the possible reasons for it).

38 *See generally* WILLIAM W. FISHER (ED.), AMERICAN LEGAL REALISM (1993)

39 *See* pp. A8, A11-A14.

40 *But see Republican Party of Minnesota v. White*, 536 U.S. 765 (2002) (state ban on judicial candidates stating views on disputed legal and political issues is unconstitutional as a violation of the 1st Amendment). Judicial election and appointment systems are discussed in Chapter V, pp. 180-184.

41 *See supra* p. 44. This greater candor has been referred to as evidence of the greater overall "substantive" nature of the American as compared to the English approach to law. *See generally* ATIYAH & SUMMERS, *supra* note 24.

42 111 N.E. 1050 (N.Y. 1916).

judicial process in common law. But even though the *McPherson* decision makes radical changes in the nature of liability for defective products, Cardozo's opinion for the court reads as if it were making only the smallest incremental change in the law.

The Limits of the Realist Critique and the "Legal Process" Reaction   Although we are all Legal Realists now, that same realism requires that we recognize grains of truth in both the discovery and scientific theories of common law. Judges are products of the society in which they live and their attitudes and actions reflect more than personal predilections. They reflect society's values in their opinions and decisions. And, to the extent that society's values and a judge's values conflict, conscientious judges will try to discover and choose society's values rather than their own. Practical considerations also support common law rules that reflect widespread customs and conventional morality. Such rules best serve expectation interests of the people governed by them and lessen the concern about notice of the common law's "unwritten" rules. To this extent, much of the law does already exist "out there" in society waiting to be "discovered" by judges.[43]

In addition, accepted "rules" of reasoning from precedent, whether truly "scientific" or not, do count in common law. Judges are expected to write opinions justifying their decisions and those justifications are expected to comply with long-standing judicial conventions. The Legal Process School of jurisprudence which grew up in the 1950s explored the nature of these justificatory constraints on judicial creativity and demonstrated how they are real.[44] According to Legal Process adherents, the common law tradition's demand for "reasoned elaboration" of precedent and other standards of "craftsmanship" in reasoning and opinion writing limit the freedom of judges to decide cases in whatever way they want. Consistent with the Legal Process view, judges in real life sometimes complain that they personally feel inclined to decide a case a particular way, but that "the opinion won't write" that way.

Opinions of courts in real cases often contain both Legal Realism and Legal Process elements. In *Hoffman v. Jones*, the candid Legal Realist side of the opinion has already been mentioned — its considerations of public policy and fairness in deciding to adopt comparative negligence as the rule for negligence cases. But the majority also engages in a close, traditional analysis of precedent in the section of the opinion that determines whether the court should decide the issue of comparative negligence.[45]

---

43 *See generally* RONALD DWORKIN, TAKING RIGHTS SERIOUSLY 22-45 (Harvard U. Press 1977) (discussing how fundamental principles that exist in society and are recognized as binding are themselves law and are used to decide cases that are not directly covered by prior rules).

44 HENRY HART & ALBERT SACKS, THE LEGAL PROCESS: BASIC PROBLEMS IN THE MAKING AND APPLICATION OF LAW (Foundation 1994) (originally released 1958). This casebook, labeled by the authors a "tentative edition" and distributed for years only in duplicated form, has been widely used to teach courses on legal process and is among the most influential books on the subject. *See also* KARL LLEWELLYN, THE COMMON LAW TRADITION: DECIDING APPEALS (Little Brown 1960).

45 *See* p. A4. *See also* A11-A14 (dissent on the issue). Some believe that the constraints imposed by the need for justification are illusory. Among the most critical are those of the Critical Legal Studies movement, principally Duncan Kennedy and Robert Unger. Adherents of the Law and Economics (identified with Richard Posner), assert that courts should strive to develop and effectuate legal rules that are economically efficient. Followers of Feminist Jurisprudence question legal doctrine and all the jurisprudential movements for their failure to reflect the experiences of women. For a review of trends in jurisprudence, *see* Gary Minda, *The Jurisprudential Movements of the 1980s*, 50 OHIO ST. L.J. 599 (1989). For a short collection of readings outlining the principal tenets of these and other contemporary jurisprudential movements, *see* STEPHEN B. PRESSER & JAMIL S. ZAINALDIN, MATERIALS ON LAW AND JURISPRUDENCE IN AMERICAN HISTORY, 4TH ED. (West 2006).

Some Perspective on Judicial Creativity The power of judges to make law should be put into perspective. Virtually all legal issues decided by trial courts, many cases decided by intermediate appellate courts and the majority of cases decided by state supreme courts involve simple application of settled authority or, at the most, choosing between two divergent lines of authority. At a time when the common law still reigned supreme in many areas, Benjamin Cardozo, a judge known to be creative with the common law, remarked that the majority of the cases that came before the highest court of New York "could not, with semblance of reason, be decided in any way but one."[46]

3. The Problem of Retroactivity

Any system that considers judicial decisions to be a source of law should be concerned about problems of retroactive lawmaking.[47] Retroactivity did not trouble Blackstone and other adherents to the "discovery" theory of common law. The announcement of a "new" rule did not change the law; it only declared what the true common law rule was all along. But once one admits that caselaw really does change the law, one must be concerned with the fairness of applying that rule retroactively.

The primary concern about retroactivity is with the rule's application to persons other than the parties to that case. Courts in the United States often resort to the technique of giving decisions prospective effect only or only partial retroactivity.[48] In deciding whether to do so, they evaluate the extent of reliance on the old rule and the degree to which the new rule represents "a clear break with the past."[49] The most common form of prospective application is to apply the new rule to the parties in that case, to other cases pending on the date of the decision, and to all cases arising in the future. This is what the Florida Supreme Court did in *Hoffman v. Jones*, the comparative negligence case in the appendix discussed earlier.[50]

But in a strict sense, the parties in the very case that changes the law are subject to retroactive lawmaking. The appellate decision in a case is made some period of time (often years) after the conduct in question in the lawsuit took place. If the standard of conduct is a new one and especially if the decision overrules some prior clear rule, it would seem unfair to apply it even to the parties in the case, who would have had no notice of such a rule when they engaged in the conduct.[51] Recognizing this, a few cases have given *solely* prospective effect to new caselaw rules, thus not even giving the "winning" party in that case the benefit of the new rule.[52] However, this technique is

---

46 CARDOZO, *supra* note 35, at 164. *See also* Jon O. Newman, *Between Legal Realism and Neutral Principles: The Legitimacy of Institutional Values*, 72 CAL. L. REV. 200, 204 (1984) (in all cases decided in a one year period in 1982-1983, dissenting votes were cast in only 3.7% of them).

47 Retroactivity is a problem with common law, where rules are completely judge-made, but it is also a problem with caselaw interpreting statutes in new directions and particularly with caselaw interpreting the Constitution.

48 English courts generally follow a rule of full retroactivity. But English courts adhere to *stare decisis* more rigidly and are generally not as activist as American courts, thus reducing the unfair effects or retroactivity. *See* ATIYAH & SUMMERS, *supra* note 24, at 147-148.

49 *Desist v. United States*, 394 U.S. 244 (1969).

50 *See* Appendix, p. A10.

51 Jeremy Bentham, a strong supporter of codification of law, explained the problem in a colorful way in answering the question of how judges make common law: "Do you know how they make it? Just as a man makes laws for his dog. When your dog does anything you want to break him of, you wait till he does it, and then beat him for it. This is the way you make laws for your dog and this is the way the judges make law for you and me." Jeremy Bentham, *Truth v. Ashhurst*, 5 WORKS 233, 235 (W. Tait, Edinburgh 1923) (first published 1838).

52 *See Great Northern Ry. Co. v. Sunburst Oil & Refining Co.*, 287 U.S. 358 (1932) (affirming Montana Supreme Court decision reversing case rule for future, but refusing to give appellant benefit of new rule).

rarely used as it gives rise to a host of other objections. Among them is the fact that, without some prospect of gaining some benefit from an appeal, few parties would seek changes in the law, and it would become stagnant. The prevailing view today is that the winning party should get the benefit of the decision, even if it is prospective in all other respects, and that this is an unavoidable cost of a caselaw system.[53]

The retroactivity problem should not be exaggerated, however. As just discussed, changes in doctrine are not that common because of the strength of *stare decisis*. A court must decide that the policies supporting adherence to the established rule — predictability, certainty, fairness and efficiency — are outweighed by the need to overrule an established precedent. Even when there are changes in doctrine, most changes effected by caselaw are incremental and are hardly surprises.

Moreover, although retroactivity is a disadvantage of judge-made law, many argue that the benefits of its flexibility outweigh any such disadvantage. Judge-made law can react to the multitude of situations that could not be foreseen by even the most conscientious legislature. Judges can thus make exceptions to general rules as needed or even rethink and change a rule if it is causing unjust results. And, in any event, any major judicial "mistakes" are subject to change by the legislature.[54]

It should be noted as well that retroactivity is no less a problem in code-based systems with statutory law, since "interpretations" of statutes can change. The sparse 45 or so words of the French Civil Code dealing with civil wrongs have undoubtedly provided little notice to those affected by the judicially created twists and turns of French tort law. Certainly the parties in French tort cases that developed in the law in new directions were no less unfairly surprised than was the defendant in *Hoffman v. Jones*.[55]

C. Statutory Law in a Common Law System

1. Growth of Statutory Law

Calling the United States a "common law" country is misleading to the extent that it suggests that the most prevalent form of law is common law. While this might have been true at one point, it is emphatically not true today. Since the turn of the 20th century and particularly since the 1930s, there has been an "orgy of statute-making"[56] ushering in what has been called the "Age of Statutes." [57] The "center of gravity" of state law has also shifted to statutes. Indeed, it is probably fair to say that the average state in the United States has as many statutes as the average civil law country in Europe. If one multiplies that amount of statutory law by 50 states, one can see just how prevalent statutory law is in the United States.

---

53 *See Stovall v. Denno*, 388 U.S. 293 (1967). Other objections to solely prospective effect are discussed in REYNOLDS, *supra* note 28, §4.29.

54 In England, legislative change is spearheaded by various law reform commissions that keep track of the law in particular areas and report needs for changes to the legislature. This is not generally true in the United States, where the likelihood of legislative intervention in the event of judicial "mistakes" is much lower. *See* ATIYAH & SUMMERS, *supra* note 24, at 29-30, 134-141, 148-149. For a good discussion of the limits and weaknesses of judicial law-making, *see* CAPPELLETTI, *supra* note 35, at 35-46.

55 *See Jand'heur c. Les Galeries Belfortaises*, D.P. 1930.I. 57 (words of the Civil Code imposing liability upon persons for damage caused by "things under their guard" meant that there would be strict liability in automobile accidents), discussed in SHAPIRO, *supra* note 36, at 140-143. *See also* Ruth Redmond-Cooper, *The Relevance of Fault in Determining Liability for Road Accidents: the French Experience*, 38 INT. & COMP. L.Q. 502-509 (1989).

56 GILMORE, *supra* note 32, at 95.

57 *See* GUIDO CALABRESI, A COMMON LAW FOR THE AGE OF STATUTES (Yale U. Press 1985).

Some statutes have replaced common law, but many more have created entirely new areas of law. On the federal level, volumes of federal taxation, social security, environmental, financial securities and banking law fill the United States Code. On the state level, numerous statutes regulating businesses, consumer rights, commercial transactions, and family relations have been enacted. Common law has not disappeared. Many areas of private law in the states — contracts, torts and property law — are governed primarily by common law with some statutory modifications. In most areas of the law, however, statutes are the rule rather than the exception.

2. The Common Law Attitude Toward Statutes

The prevalence of statutory law in the United States does not mean that statutes in the United States and continental Europe are applied the same way or even look the same. A quick glance at federal or state statute books will disclose that U.S. statutes are longer and infinitely more complex than the average civil law code or even most "special legislation" that has grown up in civil law countries outside the codes.[58] Underlying this formal difference is an important conceptual difference in attitudes about statutes.

The Civil Law Approach to Statutes   Because of the influence of the French Revolution throughout continental Europe, the idea of legislative supremacy that developed was really one of legislative *exclusivity* — that legislation was the *sole* legitimate source of law. Judicial lawmaking was formally denied. When legislatures passed codes, they intended those codes to be a comprehensive statement of the entire law on the subject addressed. Thus, when gaps in code coverage inevitably developed, whether through oversight of the drafters or simple obsolescence, judges supplied an answer, but were compelled by the principles of comprehensiveness and legislative exclusivity to justify that answer as an interpretation of the code. This led to a flexible approach to the interpretation of statutes. Flexible interpretation was in turn aided by the fact that the codes, intended as they were to be comprehensive and enduring for years to come, tended to be written in general terms.

The Common Law Approach to Statutes   There is a distinctive "common law attitude" toward statutes that differs from the approach taken in most civil law countries. Common law judges see statutes as containing specific *rules of law* that will be applied fairly according to their terms, but not beyond. Subject matter outside the terms of the statute remains governed by the common law. This means that, as a general rule, U.S. courts will not interpret statutes in two ways that are routine in civil law countries.

First, courts in civil law systems treat the codes as containing germinating principles from which specific rules can be generated. An entire body of French tort law, for example, has been derived from only a few lines of general text in the civil code.[59] Courts in the United States are not likely to find — nor are legislatures likely to write — broad principles in legislation that can be used for the germination of rules.[60] Broad

---

58 An interesting comparison in this respect can be made between the "Model Uniform Product Liability Act" promulgated by the U.S. Department of Commerce as a suggestion for state enactment, U.S. Dept. of Commerce, Uniform Products Liability Act: A Model For the States (U.S. Govt. Printing Off., Washington 1979) and the Federal Republic of Germany's Act of December 15, 1989, on Liability for Defective Products (Product Liability Act — ProdHaftG) (eff. January 1, 1990). Anyone who doubts the potential for complexity of U.S. statutes and has access to federal laws should examine the Clean Air Act, particularly 42 U.S.C.A. §7511a, or most any section of the Internal Revenue Code, 26 U.S.C.A. §1 *et seq.*.

59 The principal section is §1383, which provides: "Everyone is liable for damage he has caused not only by his intentional acts, but also by his negligence or imprudence."

60 The alternative is for the legislature to simply delegate to the courts the power to make common law on the subject. *See infra* p. 63.

principles suitable for germinating rules exist for common law judges, but they are found in the common law.

Second, courts in civil law countries may reason by analogy from a statute and apply it to situations not within its literal terms. An example is the decision the German Federal Constitutional Court that interpreted a statute protecting the rights of a surviving *spouse* of a deceased tenant to continue living in an apartment to grant the same rights to a live-in male companion of a deceased tenant. In doing so, it emphasized the propriety and even the obligation of courts to reason by analogy where appropriate.[61] The average U.S. court will interpret a statute to apply to the extent of its terms, but will generally decline to reason by analogy to a different rule. Indeed, it is likely that a U.S. court considering a statute like the German statute just mentioned would use the maxim *expressio unius est exclusio alterius* and hold that the statute, by specifically including spouses, impliedly excluded persons in other cohabitation relationships.[62]

3. Reasons for the Common Law Approach to Statutes

The common law attitude toward statutes is somewhat ironic, given that common law courts regularly reason analogically from prior cases and germinate specific rules from general *common law* principles, as discussed later in this chapter.[63] There would not seem to be any logical reason why *legislative* principles could not *also* be used to germinate rules.[64] To the extent that judges give a reason for the narrow approach to statutes, it is said to be compelled by legislative supremacy. Any judicial effort to extend a statute beyond a fair reading of its text would add something to the statute that the legislature apparently did not wish to be there. Had the legislature wished to go further than the rule stated in the text of the statute, it would have done so. So any court that adds anything to a statute beyond what is fairly traceable to its text is invading the province of the legislature.

Of course, it is equally logical that the legislature would have wished that courts fill unanticipated gaps in its statutes by reasoning by analogy from the rules set out in the statute and their apparent underlying principles. So, the common law view strikes many as a singularly unhelpful judicial attitude. Where it comes from, however, is understandable. It is the result of the lack of any necessity to view statutes any differently, the basic conception of the relationship between statutes and common law, and a historical judicial hostility toward statutes.[65]

---

61 *See Constitutional Complaint of Building Cooperative "X,"* BVerfGE 82, 6 (First Panel, April 30, 1990). *See also Harty v. Ville de Châlon-sur-Marne*, S. 1878.II. 48 (French Court of Appeals) (interpreting §1386 of the French Code Civil, which makes owners of buildings liable for any damage caused by collapse of their buildings, to apply by analogy to owner of a rotten tree which collapsed causing personal injury) and D. NEIL MACCORMICK AND ROBERT S. SUMMERS EDS, INTERPRETING STATUTES: A COMPARATIVE STUDY 471-472 (Dartmouth Publishing 1991). Reasoning by analogy is inappropriate to expand the reach of criminal or tax statutes, however.

62 The *expressio unius* maxim is discussed *infra* on p. 59.

63 *See infra* pp. 69-72.

64 As long ago as 1908, Dean Roscoe Pound noted the distinctive common law attitude and urged U.S. courts to consider statutes in a more expansive manner. *See* Roscoe Pound, *Common Law and Legislation*, 21 HARV.L.REV. 383 (1908). *See also* Harlan Fiske Stone, *The Common Law in the United States*, 50 HARV. L.REV. 4, 12-15 (1936) and Roger Traynor, *Statutes Revolving in Common law Orbits*, 17 CATH.L.REV. 401, 405-409 (1968). Stone later became Chief Justice of the United States Supreme Court, serving from 1941 to 1946. Traynor was Chief Justice of the California Supreme Court.

65 The common law approach to statutes is especially ironic in the United States, where constitutional interpretation is marked by an extremely flexible view of the text of the Constitution somewhat similar to some continental European courts' approaches to their codes. *See* Chapter IX, pp. 326-327.

Lack of a Need for Expansive Statutory Interpretation   As discussed earlier, a complete system of judge-made common law was developed relatively quickly, over about 100 years.[66] The common law was understood to be the repository of all the "broad and comprehensive principles" that existed in the law.[67] Statutes were enacted on an *ad hoc* basis as needed to address specific problems thought not to be sufficiently addressed by the common law. Thus, common law judges did not search for basic principles in statutes, nor did legislators deem it necessary to set out such principles in the statutes they passed.

Relationship Between Statutes and Common Law   Because common law developed first and statutes dealt with relatively narrow subjects, the common law mind views statutes as being enacted against the comprehensive backdrop of the common law. As a result, there is no need to fill any statutory gaps by extending the reach of the statute. Any gaps have already been filled by the common law. Enacting a statute in a common law system, then, is like placing a rock in a bucket of water. The rock displaces the water as far as it goes, but the water rushes in to fill any holes or cracks in the rock. Judges deciding a case not covered by the statute simply resort to the common law. As a result, common law judges faced with gaps in a statute need not resort to a highly flexible interpretation of the statutory language, such as reasoning by analogy, or to germination of rules from the statutory principles.

Historical Judicial Hostility   The common law reigned supreme for centuries before there were any significant statutory intrusions. As statutory enactments became more frequent, common law judges resented infringements on their domain. In their modest view, statutes were quite unnecessary since the common law had an answer for all important legal questions. Judges viewed Parliament's forays into lawmaking as mistaken and amateurish, and therefore calling for a narrow interpretation. As Pollock observed, "Parliament generally changes the law for the worse, and . . . the business of the judge is to keep the mischief of its interference within the narrowest possible bounds."[68] The maxim that "a statute in derogation of the common law should be strictly construed" is a product of this attitude.[69] In turn, Parliament reacted to narrow and grudging judicial interpretations of its statutes by spelling out its intentions in detail in the statutory language. This then resulted in a complex and specific legislative product unsuitable for expansive interpretation.[70]

Common Law and Statutes in the United States   The above relates to the experience in England. In the United States, discomfort with statutes was perhaps less from the very beginning. States formally "received" English common law by constitutional or statutory enactment, but they freely modified it by statute from the beginning, sometimes in a fit of anti-English pique.[71] However, the notion of strictly construing statutes in

---

66 Dawson, *supra* note 19, p. 6.

67 *Norway Plains Co. v. Boston & Maine R.R.*, 67 Mass. 263 (1854) (Shaw, C.J.).

68 Sir Frederick Pollock, Essays on Jurisprudence and Ethics 85 (1882).

69 *See* Jefferson B. Fordham & J. Russel Leach, *Interpretation of Statutes in Derogation of the Common Law*, 3 Vanderbilt L. Rev. 438, 440-441 (1950).

70 *See* Zweigert & Kötz, *supra* note 19, at 273-278.

71 It is reported that a common toast during the immediate post-Revolutionary United States was: "The Common Law of England: may wholesome statutes soon root out this engine of oppression from America." Evan Haynes, The Selection and Tenure of Judges 96 (Fred B. Rothman & Co., Littleton, Colo. 1981) (originally published in 1944). *See also* Eric Stein, *The Attraction of the Civil Law in Post-Revolutionary America*, 52 Va.L.Rev. 403 (1966). New Jersey and Kentucky statutes prohibited citation of any English common law authorities. Lawrence Friedman, History of American Law, 2d ed., 97-98 (Touchstone Books, N.Y. 1985).

derogation of the common law experienced a surge at the turn of the 20th century in the United States when politically conservative judges narrowly interpreted progressive state social legislation. American legislatures reacted much as Parliament did, by spelling out their intentions specifically.[72]

Courts in both England and the United States have abandoned their general hostility toward statutes, and the legitimacy of statutes as the principal form of law in a modern society is accepted completely. However, the basic concept that "the law" means "the common law with a few statutes added in" continues. Returning to the conceptual analogy of the statutory "rocks" in a bucket of common law "water," the fact that today — in the "Age of Statutes" — the pail is now more full of rocks than water does not alter the basic concept.

4. Attempts at Codification in the United States

Given the common law attitude toward statutes, it is not surprising that efforts at comprehensive legislative codification of the law have failed in the United States. The first codification opportunity presented itself when Jeremy Bentham, a proponent of codification in England, wrote to President James Madison in 1811 offering to codify law in the United States. His offer was politely refused.[73]

The Field Codes Somewhat more fruitful efforts were undertaken in the latter half of the 19th century. This movement was led by David Dudley Field of New York, who in 1847 persuaded the New York legislature to constitute a commission to codify the law. In 1865, the commission presented five codes to the legislature for passage: civil procedure, criminal procedure, penal, civil and political. However, New York enacted only the civil and criminal procedure codes. Much of the reason for the lack of success was the opposition of the organized bar. Another factor was that much of the driving force behind codes — the claim that unwritten caselaw was difficult to understand and apply — had been undercut by the appearance of commentaries on the law, books that summarized caselaw, particularly the commentaries of James Kent and Joseph Story.[74]

Field's codes had greater success in the Western United States, where frontier attitudes about law made the apparent simplicity and accessibility of a code more appealing. Five Western states passed forms of his Civil Codes and still have them today (California, North Dakota, South Dakota, Idaho and Montana). However, legislators and their drafting assistants — themselves products of the common law system — made the codes too specific. In turn, judges similarly steeped in the common law tradition treated these "codes" the same way common law courts have always treated statutes — as

---

72 *Jones v. Milwaukee Elec. Ry. & Light Co.*, 133 N.W. 636 (Wis. 1911) (statute imposing liability on "every railroad company" does not include an "electric interurban railroad company"). It was this conservative judicial attitude that constitutionalized free enterprise that led to the problems generated by the *Lochner* Era discussed in Chapter I, pp. 11-12.

73 ZWEIGERT & KÖTZ, *supra* note 19, at 250. Bentham's view of judge-made law was mentioned *supra* note 51.

74 James Kent (1763-1847) was a judge for many years and then retired to become a professor at Columbia University in 1823, when he published his *Commentaries on American Law*, which went through several editions between 1826 and 1830. Joseph Story (1779-1845) was a Justice of the Supreme Court who taught at Harvard Law School while still a Justice. He published nine commentaries on various subjects of private and constitutional law from 1832 to 1845. Many continued to be updated after his death. These great commentaries inspired many imitators and commentaries became a principal means of gaining access to the law in a system that relied principally on case decisions.

statements of rules to be applied according to their terms, not as sources of germinating principles.[75]

Despite the pervasive common law attitude toward statutes, there has been some move away from it and toward a more expansive view somewhat similar to the European approach. Some of those unusual cases are discussed after the following discussion of more traditional approaches to statutory interpretation.[76]

D. Statutory Interpretation Methods

What follows is a mixture of approaches and "maxims" of statutory interpretation commonly encountered in judicial opinions interpreting statutes.[77] In reading this description, two things should be kept in mind. First, there is no single official approved list of approaches or maxims.[78] Although most of the cases cited here are from the United States Supreme Court, this is done primarily for ease of referencing the opinions cited. State courts are not compelled to follow the Supreme Court's approach except as to *federal* statutes. However, state court approaches are generally similar in any event. Second, many of the maxims discussed contradict each other. In some cases, the court's choice of one maxim over another is left unexplained.[79]

If pressed to give an overall generalization about statutory interpretation in the United States, one could say that courts in the United States generally believe they should interpret the language of the statute in such a way as to give effect to the purpose the legislature sought to accomplish, keeping in mind that ordinarily the best evidence of purpose is the text of the statute. Yet, there are many approaches used that ignore or run counter to this goal.[80]

1. The Plain Meaning Rule

According to this rule, a court should construe a statute so as to give its words their ordinary meaning, unless the result would be absurd. Resort to legislative history or aids to understanding beyond the text is ordinarily not appropriate. The "plain meaning" rule is returning to favor after a period of disfavor.[81]

---

75 FRIEDMAN, *supra* note 71, at 351-354; *See also* ARTHUR T. VON MEHREN, LAW IN THE UNITED STATES 20-21 (Kluwer 1989). *See, e.g., Greenman v. Yuba Power Products, Inc.*, 377 P.2d 897 (Cal. 1963) (notice required by the Civil Code does not apply to warranties arising independently under the common law).

76 *See infra* pp. 61-64.

77 For a taxonomy of methods used in the U.S., *see* MACCORMICK & SUMMERS, *supra* note 61, at 407-459. This excellent book contains chapters on many other countries and a concluding comparative discussion. *See also* HART & SACKS, *supra* note 44, pp. 1111-1380; F. REED DICKERSON, THE INTERPRETATION AND APPLICATION OF STATUTES (Little, Brown 1975) (a classic though theoretical book); KENT GREENAWALT, LEGISLATION: STATUTORY INTERPRETATION: 20 QUESTIONS (FOUNDATION 1999); MICHAEL M.B.W. SINCLAIR, GUIDE TO STATUTORY INTERPRETATION (Lexis 2000).

78 Some state legislatures have attempted to compile lists of rules. *See, e.g.,* Minn. Stat. Ann. §645.16. However, courts tend to ignore them. *See Comment,* "The Effect of the Statutory Construction Act in Pennsylvania," 12 U. PITT. L. REV. 283 (1951 (act used in fewer than 3% of cases involving statutory interpretation). There is also a UNIFORM STATUTE AND RULE CONSTRUCTION ACT, promulgated by the National Conference of Commissioners on Uniform State Laws, and available at http://www.law.upenn.edu/bll/archives/ulc/fnact99/1990s/usrca95.pdf/. *See* Chapter I, p. 34, note 155.

79 The "thrust" and "parry" of a whole host of competing maxims are outlined in Karl Llewellyn, *Remarks on the Theory of Appellate Decision and the Rules of Canons About How Statutes are to be Construed,* 3 VANDERBILT L.REV. 395, 401-406 (1950). One commentator has noted with alarm the Supreme Court's increased use of formal maxims of statutory construction. *See* Daniel A. Farber, *Revival of the Canons,* TRIAL, p. 82 (June 1992). *See also* Daniel A. Farber, *The Inevitability of Practical Reason: Statutes, Formalism and the Rule of Law,* 45 VANDERBILT L. REV. 533, 535 (1992).

80 No attempt will be made here to distinguish between legislative "purpose" and "intent." *See* REYNOLDS, *supra* note 28, §5.5.

81 *See* Phillip P. Frickey, *The New Textualism,* 37 U.C.L.A. L.REV. 621 (1990).

Proponents of the plain meaning approach argue two points in its favor. First, what the legislature passed and the executive signed were the words of the statute, not the committee report or speeches of supporters or opponents. As Justice Jackson put it, "[i]t is the business of Congress to sum up its own debates in its legislation." He viewed going beyond the words of the statute in any case but one where they are "inescapably ambiguous" as allowing the courts to inject themselves and take sides in the "political controversies" that accompanied the enactment, thus subverting the democratic process.[82] Second, ordinary people and most lawyers rely solely on the statutory language and do not have ready access to legislative history materials: "[t]o accept legislative debates to modify statutory provisions is to make the law inaccessible to a large part of the country."[83]

Opponents of a plain meaning rule argue that plain meaning "rests on the erroneous assumption that words have a fixed meaning," pointing out that "[w]ords are symbols used for communication — means, not ends, in the legislative process."[84] As Justice Holmes stated, "[a] word is not a crystal, transparent and unchanged, it is the skin of a living thought and may vary greatly in color and content according to the circumstances and the time in which it is used."[85] Moreover, the plain meaning rule can make for worse judicial meddling than that it seeks to avoid: "Why should a judge be permitted to impose his own reference or that of some hypothetical average person on statutory words instead of inquiring in the first instance as the reference of the enactors?"[86]

The Supreme Court has at one time or another approved the use of the plain meaning rule. A classic application was in *Caminetti v. United States*.[87] There the Court held that the language of a federal criminal statute that prohibited transportation of women across state lines for prostitution or "any other immoral purpose" was clear, and therefore applied to non-commercial debauchery. The decision came over a strong protest that the sole aim of the statute was to stop *commercialized* vice.

Some commentators and judges see a trend in the late 1980s back toward plain meaning in the Supreme Court, largely as a result of Justice Antonin Scalia's influence. In the 1981 Supreme Court term the Court always checked the text against the legislative history.[88] Yet, in the 1989 and 1990 terms, 10 out of 65 and 19 out of 55 statutory interpretation cases were decided without *any* reference to legislative history.[89]

---

82 *Schwegmann Brothers v. Calvert Distillers Corp.*, 341 U.S. 384, 395 (1951).

83 *Id.* at 396.

84 Note, *A Re-evaluation of the Use of Legislative History in the Federal Courts*, 52 COLUM. L. REV. 125, 134 (1952).

85 *Towne v. Eisner*, 245 U.S. 418, 425 (1918).

86 John M. Kernochan, *Statutory Interpretation, An Outline of Method*, 3 DALHOUSIE L. J. 333, 342 (1975).

87 242 U.S. 470 (1917).

88 Patricia Wald, *Some Observations on the Use of Legislative History in the 1981 Supreme Court Term*, 68 IOWA L. REV. 195, 197 (1983). Judge Wald was Chief Judge of the Court of Appeals for the District of Columbia Circuit.

89 Stephen Breyer, *The Uses of Legislative History in Interpreting Statutes*, 65 S. CAL. L.REV. 845, 846 (1992). The author, a proponent of using legislative history, is currently a justice of United States Supreme Court. *See also* MACCORMICK & SUMMERS, *supra* note 61, at 457-458. For a discussion pros and cons of using legislative history, *see* Breyer, *supra*, at 861-869. A recent plain meaning case is *Tyler v. Cain*, 533 U.S. 656 (2005) (plain meaning of "made" retroactive can only mean by the only court empowered to do so; fact that other courts might "hold" a rule retroactive does not mean the same thing).

2. Plain Meaning and Legislative History

The Court has *said* that the plain language of the statute governs when it is unambiguously applicable to the problem[90] and that "[t]he starting point of every case involving construction of a statute is the language itself."[91] It has also cautioned that reliance on legislative history as a means of ascertaining congressional intent is a "step to be taken cautiously"[92] and at one time emphasized Justice Oliver Wendell Holmes's admonition that "[w]e do not inquire what the legislature meant; we ask only what the statute means."[93]

However, the Court has also gone to the opposite extreme. In 1976, it unanimously reversed the Court of Appeals for its invocation of plain meaning and refusal to consult legislative history.[94] Moreover, statutory language apparently has rarely been so clear that the Court does not at least "peek" at that history to verify its reading of the language. Such a "peek" would seem to be required even when the statutory language is clear: one formulation of the plain meaning rule has it that the language of the statute controls "absent a clearly expressed legislative intention to the contrary."[95] Thus, the Civil Rights Act of 1964 was interpreted in *United Steelworkers of America v. Weber*[96] to allow some race-based disadvantageous treatment of white employees (through use of an affirmative action program for minorities) despite the statute's literal prohibition against discriminating "because of . . . race." The legislative history disclosed a purpose to permit reasonable race-conscious attempts to remedy "conspicuous racial imbalance in traditionally segregated categories" of employment.[97]

When legislative history is used, there is a hierarchy of probative value of the various items of that history. Of greatest importance are legislative committee reports.[98] These are descriptions of the legislation written by the legislative committees that have studied it, heard testimony and arguments for and against it, and have voted to send it to the floor for a vote by the relevant house of Congress. Committee reports are thought to be important for statutory interpretation because busy legislators often rely on those reports for their information about the bill in order to decide whether to vote for it or against it. Also important if they exist are conference committee reports. Conference committees are committees with both House and Senate members on them that are set up to work out the differences between versions of bills passed by the House and Senate.[99]

---

90 *American Tobacco Co. v. Patterson*, 456 U.S. 63, 68 (1982).

91 *Ernst & Ernst v. Hochfelder*, 425 U.S. 185, 197 (1976).

92 *Piper v. Chris-Craft Industries, Inc.*, 430 U.S. 1, 26 (1977).

93 Oliver W. Holmes, *The Theory of Legal Interpretation*, 12 HARV.L.REV. 417, 419 (1899), quoted in *S&E Contractors v. United States*, 406 U.S. 1, 14 n.1 (1972).

94 *Train v. Colo. Public Interest Research Group*, 426 U.S. 1 (1976). Indeed, in one case the Court seemed to reverse the usual order of things *See Citizens to Preserve Overton Park, Inc. v. Volpe*, 401 U.S. 402 (1971) ("Because of this ambiguity [in the legislative history], it is clear we must look primarily to the statutes themselves to find the legislative intent.").

95 *Maine v. Thiboutot*, 448 U.S. 1, 6 n.4 (1980), citing cases.

96 443 U.S. 193 (1979). The substance of *Weber* is discussed in Chapter XV, p. 623.

97 *See also Kasten v. Saint-Gobain Performance Plastics Corp.*, ___ U.S. ___, 2011 WL 977061 (2011) (discharge of employee for having "filed a complaint" of a violation of Fair Labor Standards Act includes oral complaints to the employer, given purpose of the Act and other extra-textual considerations).

98 *Lewis v. United States*, 445 U.S. 55, 63 (1980); *Wright v. Vinton Branch Bank*, 300 U.S. 440, 463-64 (1937).

99 *See* Chapter I, p. 16. "Standing" committees of the whole Congress also issue reports, such as the Joint Committee on Taxation, which is active in studying various proposals for tax reform and issues frequent studies and reports describing the current law as well as the reform proposals. At least the Committee's analysis of current reform proposals are used by courts much like other legislative history.

Of a value equal to committee reports are statements of individual legislators responsible for the preparation or drafting of the bill.[100] A statement on the floor of Congress by a representative immediately after introducing an amendment to a bill, which later became part of the final legislation, was held to be "clearly probative of a legislative judgment."[101] Statements in debates on the floor of Congress are considered as somewhat persuasive, though they are not entitled to the same weight as committee reports.[102] Statements "other than by persons responsible for the preparation or the drafting of a bill, are entitled to little weight"[103] and "the fears and doubts of the opposition to a bill are no authoritative guide to the construction of legislation."[104]

Justice Scalia champions the plain meaning rule in large part because he believes that legislative history is a highly unreliable guide to intent. He has noted that statements in debate on the floor of Congress are not probative because they are "ordinarily addressed to a virtually empty floor."[105] It is even concocted to influence courts who may later be called on to interpret the statute. There are many opportunities to "plant" sentences or case citations in committee reports or to engage in rehearsed exchanges on the floor of Congress. This would be bad enough if done out of the legislator's philosophical disagreement with the majority. But the chances are great that such activities would be done at the behest of a lobbyist employed by some special interest group to influence the legislation.[106]

There is considerably less reliance on legislative history in state court decisions construing state statutes. The reason for this is that state legislative histories are usually not published and are otherwise difficult to find and compile. Thus, state courts are more likely to use the plain meaning rule or to resort to the other aids to interpretation discussed here.[107]

Senate and House reports are numbered sequentially for each year without reference to the originating committee. Thus, the 175th committee report in the Senate in the year 1997 would bear a formal citation "S. Rep. 97-175," while the 493rd House report of 1997 would be cited "H.R. Rep. 97-493." Conference reports bear a House number.

100 *Fed. Energy Administration v. Algonquin SNG, Inc.*, 426 U.S. 548, 564 (1976); *United States v. International Union*, 352 U.S. 567, 573-75 (1957).

101 *Simpson v. United States*, 435 U.S. 6, 13 (1978).

102 *Chandler v. Roudebush*, 425 U.S. 840, 858 n.36 (1976).

103 *Ernst & Ernst v. Hochfelder*, 425 U.S. 185, 203 n.24 (1976).

104 *Gulf Offshore Co. v. Mobil Oil Co.*, 453 U.S. 473, 483 (1981).

105 *Crosby v. National Foreign Trade Council*, 530 U.S. 363, 391 (2000) (Scalia, J., concurring).

106 *Blanchard v. Bergeron*, 489 U.S. 87, 98-99 (1989) (Scalia, J., concurring); *Thompson v. Thompson*, 484 U.S. 174 (1988) (Scalia, J., concurring). *See* William S. Moorhead, *A Congressman Looks at the Planned Colloquy and Its Effect on the Interpretation of Statutes*, 45 A.B.A.J. 1314 (1959). *See also Exxon Mobil Corp. v Allapattah Services*, 545 U.S. 546 (2005) (alleged manipulation of House report). Justice Scalia has even railed against the use of legislative history "to confirm what the statute plainly says anyway." In a way, he says, "this utter lack of necessity makes it even worse — calling to mind St. Augustine's enormous remorse at stealing pears when he was not even hungry, and just for the devil of it ('not seeking aught through the shame, but the shame itself!')" (citing *The Confessions of St. Augustine*, Book 2, ¶ 9). *Crosby, supra* note 105 at 391.

107 The official English view before 1993 was not to examine legislative history, although English courts before then could consider committee reports and other preparatory material to determine the evil against which the Act in question was directed. See GLANVILLE WILLIAMS, LEARNING THE LAW 102 (13th ed. 2006) and RUPERT CROSS, STATUTORY CONSTRUCTION 42-52 (1976). This changed in *Pepper v. Hart*, [1993] 1 All E.R. 42, in which the House of Lords adopted the view that it was proper to consider parliamentary legislative history materials in ascertaining the meaning of the statute.

3. The Social Purpose Rule

Under the "social purpose" rule, a statute will be construed to effectuate the social purpose it was designed to accomplish. Traceable to the 1584 English case, *Heydon's Case*,[108] it was used by the United States Supreme Court in the famous case of *Holy Trinity Church v. United States*.[109]

In *Holy Trinity Church*, a federal statute made it unlawful for anyone to assist in the migration of "any alien . . . under contract or agreement . . . to perform labor or service of any kind in the United States . . . ." Holy Trinity Church was prosecuted when it hired an Englishman to come to the United States to be its pastor. Despite the wording of the statute, the Supreme Court held that the church had not violated the statute. It observed that the "evil" at which the statute was directed was importation "an ignorant and servile class of foreign laborers" who agreed to work "at a low rate of wages," thus "break[ing] down the labor market." Since "it was this cheap unskilled labor which was making the trouble" and that it was never suggested that "the market for the services of Christian ministers was depressed by foreign competition," the statute would not apply, despite its clear terms. Clearly the "social purpose" rule can conflict with application of the "plain meaning" rule.

A version of the social purpose rule is the "absurdity" limit on the plain meaning rule. The Court has cautioned that the absurdity exception should be utilized only in "rare and exceptional circumstances."[110] The absurdity limit was used, however, in *United States v. Kirby*,[111] a case in which a state sheriff was prosecuted for violating a federal statute which made it a crime to "knowingly and willfully obstruct or retard the passage of the mail, or of any carrier. . . carrying the same." The defendant sheriff had arrested a federal postal service letter carrier on a warrant issued by a state court. The Supreme Court found that this was an absurd application of the law that could not have been intended by Congress.

In one case, a literal reading of the word "defendant" would have meant that in a civil case evidence of a prior criminal conviction could be introduced to attack the *defendant's*, but not the plaintiff's credibility, a distinction that was simply irrational.[112] The Court declined to read the rule literally, relying in part on the absurdity exception. The case is also notable for the fact that it one of the rare instances when Justice Scalia agreed that use of legislative history was proper.

4. The Context of Statutory Language

The Immediate Context of Terms   Two maxims are used for discerning the meaning of statutory terms from their immediate context. The first is the canon *ejusdem generis*, the concept that "where general words follow an enumeration of specific items, the general words are read as applying to other items akin to those specifically enumerated."[113] For example, in *McBoyle v. United States*,[114] the Supreme Court held that the National Motor Vehicle Theft Act did not apply to airplanes. The definition of "motor

---

108 76 Eng. Rep. 637 (Exchequer 1584).

109 143 U.S. 457 (1892).

110 *Howe v. Smith*, 452 U.S. 473, 483 (1981) (no reason to depart from language of federal statute on prisoner transfer).

111 74 U.S. 482 (1868).

112 *Green v. Bock Laundry*, 490 U.S. 504 (1989) (interpreting Federal Rule of Evidence 609(a)).

113 *Harrison v. P.P.G. Industries, Inc.*, 446 U.S. 578, 588 (1980).

114 283 U.S. 25 (1931).

vehicle" listed "an automobile, automobile truck, automobile wagon, motor cycle, or any other self-propelled vehicle not designed for running on rails." Although an airplane met the literal definition of the statutory language, the Court held that this definition covered vehicles running on land only.[115]

A second, similar rule is *noscitur a sociis* — the notion that "a word may be known by the company it keeps." It was used in *Jarecki v. G.D. Searle & Co.*,[116] in which the Court held that inventions of drugs and photographic devices were not, despite their great novelty, within the definition of "discovery" where the statute used "exploration" and "prospecting" in conjunction with the word "discovery." According to the Court, the context indicated that Congress intended to describe income-producing activity in the oil and gas and mining industries, not in the development of manufactured products, such as drugs and cameras. However, the maxim may not be used to narrow any distinctive meaning intended by the legislature.[117]

Statutes In Pari Materia and Contextual Harmonization   On a broader level of harmonization, courts are supposed to interpret statutes *in pari materia* — "on the same subject" — in a way that is consistent. This device was employed by the Court in *Bowen v. Massachusetts*,[118] in which it held that an action for "damages" included an action for *injunctive* relief that would require payment of money, a form of relief not technically within the definition of "damages."[119] The suit was one against the United States. Another federal statute defining jurisdiction in suits against the United States, had long been construed to include such injunctive actions. The Court consequently found support for its reading from the settled meaning of the other statute. Other harmonization efforts might include intersectional harmony within the same statute or harmonization with a general public policy applicable to that subject matter area.

5. Presumptions About the Use of Language

The Negative Implication Rule   An important maxim close to the heart of the limited common law view of statutes is *expressio unius est exclusio alterius*: the expression of one thing implies the exclusion of others. An example of the *expressio unius* canon is *Tennessee Valley Authority v. Hill*,[120] in which the Court upheld an injunction against completion of a $100 million dam. The injunction was to prevent possible extinction of an endangered species of fish, called "snail darters," in accord with the Endangered Species Act, an act prohibiting destruction of species shown to be on the verge of extinction. The federal agency in charge of the dam argued that there should be a "hardship exemption" from the strict protections afforded to endangered species by the Act, but the Court disagreed. The Act listed several other exemptions, and the Court

---

115 *See also Circuit City Stores, Inc. v. Adams*, 532 U.S. 105 (2001) ("contracts of employment of seamen, railroad employees, or any other class of workers engaged in foreign or interstate commerce" was intended to apply only to transportation workers).

116 367 U.S. 303 (1961).

117 *See Babbitt v. Sweet Home Chapter of Communities for a Great Oregon*, 515 U.S. 687, 702 (1995) (in defining "take" to mean only the direct application of force against an endangered species, the lower court ignored surrounding words, such a "harm," that contemplated indirect effects); *Bilski v. Kappos*, ___ U.S. ___, 130 S.Ct. 3218 (2010) (section of patent law already explicitly defines "process" and nothing about the section's inclusion of "machine" or new states of things suggests that "process" must be tied to them).

118 487 U.S. 879 (1988).

119 Though both forms of relief require payment of money, one is "legal" while the other is "equitable." *See* Chapter VII, pp. 243-243, 245-247.

120 437 U.S. 153, 184 (1978). *Hill* is discussed in another respect in Chapter XV, p. 621.

presumed that the list was exhaustive. *Holy Trinity Church*, discussed earlier, was distinguished.[121]

Specific Language Controls Over the General Another maxim of statutory construction is that specific statutes take precedence over general statutes. For example, in *People v. Ruster*,[122] the defendant was convicted of felony theft under a general theft statute for falsifying his identity in order to receive unemployment benefits. The California Supreme Court reversed the conviction, however, because there existed a more specific statute that made the falsification of unemployment applications a less serious misdemeanor.

6. External Influences on Statutory Interpretation

The Rule of Lenity for Criminal Statutes Another canon of construction that likely underlay the *McBoyle* case, discussed above as an example of *ejusdem generis*, is the "rule of lenity." Under this concept, basic fairness requires that criminal laws give clear notice to possible violators of what conduct is prohibited, so any ambiguity or lack of clarity will be interpreted in favor of the accused. This rule was applied in the early case of *United States v. Wiltberger*,[123] in which the Court interpreted a federal statute extending jurisdiction of American courts over crimes committed on the "high seas" as not extending to crimes committed on rivers in foreign countries.[124]

Deference to Administrative Interpretations The interpretation of a statute by an administrative agency charged with administering that statute is entitled to deference by the courts. If the intent of Congress is clear and the interpretation contradicts that intent, legislative intent controls and a contrary agency interpretation will be struck down. But where the statute or its legislative history is ambiguous or silent on the precise question involved, then a court "does not simply impose its own construction on the statute."[125] Instead, it must defer to the agency's position so long as it is a "permissible construction of the statute."[126] However, statutory "interpretations in opinion letters . . . policy statements, agency manuals, and enforcement guidelines" do not warrant *Chevron*-style deference. They are "entitled to respect," but "only to the extent that they are persuasive" to a court interpreting the statute.[127]

---

121 *See also Leatherman v. Tarrant County Narcotics and Intelligence Coordination Unit*, 507 U.S. 163 (1993) (federal court rule's requirement of higher pleading standard for certain types of claims precludes its application to other types not listed); *Chan v. Korean Airlines, Ltd.*, 490 U.S. 122, 133 (1989) (Warsaw Convention's specifying one sanction for defective notice of limited liability on airline ticket impliedly excluded the sanction of making airline fully liable for damages); *Bruesewitz v. Wyeth LLC*, 562 U.S. ___; 131 S.Ct. 1068 (2011) (Vaccine Act mentioning only defective manufacture and inadequate warnings as basis for suit meant that design-defect liability was excluded).

122 548 P.2d 353 (Cal. 1976).

123 18 U.S. 76, 95 (1820) (Marshall, C.J.).

124 *See also United States v. Thompson/Center Arms Co.*, 504 U.S. 505, 517-518 (1992) (rule applied to scope of definition of prohibited weapons). But *see United States v. Alpers*, 338 U.S. 680 (1950) (statute prohibiting any "book, pamphlet, picture, motion-picture film, paper, letter, writing, print, or other matter of indecent character" was not limited to articles comprehended by sight alone; it included obscene phonograph records).

125 *Chevron, U.S.A., Inc. v. Natural Resources Defense Council, Inc.*, 467 U.S. 837 (1984).

126 *Id. Compare Food and Drug Admin. v. Brown & Williamson Tobacco Corp.*, 529 U.S. 120 (2000) (rejecting FDA conclusion that it could regulate cigarettes; overall statutory scheme, later statutes and common sense dictated otherwise) *with National Cable & Telecommunications Ass'n v. Brand X Internet Services*, 545 U.S. 967 (2005) (upholding Federal Communications Commission's rule determining that broadband cable internet service is not a "telecommunication service," but an "information service").

127 *Christiansen v. Harris County*, 529 U.S. 576, 587 (2000) (rejecting labor department's "opinion letter" interpreting the Fair Labor Standards Act to prohibit employers from requiring employee to take compensatory time to offset overtime); *United States v. Mead Corp.*, 533 U.S. 218 (2001)(same for customs

Interpretation to Avoid Unconstitutionality A court should avoid an interpretation of a statute that might result in its being unconstitutional. In *Kent v. Dulles*,[128] the Court interpreted passport laws as not authorizing the State Department to prohibit persons with "communist backgrounds" from traveling, since such an application would infringe on the fundamental right to travel. In *Webster v. Doe*,[129] the federal Administrative Procedures Act was construed to allow a suit for violation of constitutional rights "in part to avoid the 'serious constitutional question' that would arise if a federal statute were construed to deny any judicial forum for a colorable constitutional claim." Also included in this category are various. Various "clear statement" rules imposed by the Supreme Court require that Congress make absolutely clear its intentions to alter certain aspects of state sovereignty.[130]

Interpretation in Light of Fundamental Values Courts sometimes base a statutory interpretation in whole or in part on the assumption that the legislature did not mean to enact a rule that violates fundamental societal values absent some clear statement. Part of the basis for the Court in *Trinity Church* decision interpreting the statute to permit the church to bring in the English pastor was a supposed policy favoring religion.[131] A more specific fundamental policy may also affect interpretation. In *Santa Clara Pueblo v. Martinez*,[132] the Court declined to imply a private right of action under a federal statute because of the long-standing special policy against judicial interference in Indian affairs.[133]

7. Less Traditional Approaches to Statutory Interpretation

The above aids and approaches to statutory interpretation are generally consistent with the limited "common law attitude" toward statutes identified earlier. However, there has been some movement in recent years toward a more "civil-law" style of reasoning from statutes.[134]

a. Legislatively-Inspired Common Law

Filling "gaps" in statutes with common law is nothing new. This is fully consistent with the conception that statutes are enacted against a common law background. The common law rule that fills the gap may be one that runs counter to the general thrust of the statutory rule.[135] But when a new common law rule must be developed, there is no

---

department tariff classification letters). As the opinions in the *Mead* case indicate, there is sharp disagreement on the Court over just what kinds of agency pronouncements qualify for *Chevron* deference.

128 357 U.S. 116 (1958).

129 486 U.S. 592 (1988).

130 *See also* Chapter I, p. 32, and Chapter IX, p. 338 (statutes preempting state control over core functions) and Chapter VI, p. 226 and note 176 (statutes abrogating 11th Amendment immunity), p. 209 (statutes limiting judicial review of agency action). *Cf.* Chapter IX, p. 348 note 143 (clear statement required for Congress to approve state regulation that burdens interstate commerce). The need to avoid questions of constitutionality trumps *Chevron Oil* deference. *See Solid Waste Agency of Northern Cook County v. United States Army Corps of Engineers*, 531 U.S. 159 (2001).

131 *See supra* p. 58.

132 436 U.S. 49 (1978).

133 Courts are also required to interpret statutes in a manner that will not violate treaties or international law. *See* Chapter XVII, p. 699.

134 A broader approach to statutes has been championed by some scholars and judges. *See supra* note 64.

135 *See, e.g., Norfolk Redevelopment and Housing Authority v. Chesapeake and Potomac Telephone Co.*, 464 U.S. 30 (1983) (telephone company that was required to relocate equipment because of street realignment was not a "displaced person" entitled to relocation benefits within the meaning of federal statute; court applied common law principle that a utility forced to relocate from public right-of-way must do so at its own expense).

reason why it could not be consistent with the statute. Thus, courts have sometimes chosen a *complementary* common law rule analogous to the statutory rule. For example, in *University of Tennessee v. Elliott*,[136] a federal statute required that state *court judgments* be respected by other states and the federal courts. The statute did not by its terms apply to decisions of *administrative agencies*, but the Court was inspired by the principles underlying the statute to create a complementary common law rule analogous to the one stated in the statute that would govern administrative agency decisions.[137]

Other cases involving legislatively-inspired common law move further away from complementary gap-filling cases like *Elliott* and closer to direct reasoning by analogy. In these cases, the "gap" being filled is quite large (if indeed it can be described as a "gap"), and legislative policy is used to *displace* an inconsistent, well-settled common law rule.

A pair of California cases illustrates this. The California legislature had passed Married Women's Property Acts, which abrogated common law disabilities of married women related to property rights.[138] The California Supreme Court relied on the policies underlying those Acts to abolish two common law doctrines that were not within the sweep of the statutes. In one case, the court abolished the doctrine prohibiting tort suits between spouses[139] and in the other, it abolished the rule deeming that husband and wife were incapable of a criminal conspiracy.[140] The court found that the statutes abrogating common law property ownership disabilities had undercut the principle underlying the tort and criminal law doctrines — the fiction that a married woman's person merged with that of the husband upon marriage. The new statutory principle of separate personhood in property matters was applied in a non-property context.

A U.S. Supreme Court case, *Moragne v. States Marine Lines, Inc.*,[141] involved similar reasoning. In that case, an 1886 common law precedent stood in the way of a wrongful death suit by the widow of a longshoreman killed in coastal waters off Florida. Although the common law authorized suits for *injuries*, the 1886 precedent established that *wrongful death* suits by survivors were not permitted unless provided for by statute. Neither Florida nor federal statutes authorized suit in the case. However, the Court overruled the troublesome common law precedent and permitted the suit. It based its decision on the fact that federal and state legislatures in several statutes had consistently granted a statutory right to recover for wrongful death in analogous situations. Justice Harlan's unanimous opinion spoke expansively of the propriety of drawing on legislative policy as a basis for lawmaking.[142]

Legislatively-inspired common law should not seem alien to a common law court. When choosing a common law rule, a court considers *all* possible input into the question of what that rule should be. Public policy choices made by democratically elected legislators are certainly a legitimate part of that data. Indeed, to the extent that

---

136 478 U.S. 788 (1986).

137 It is interesting that the Court in the *Elliott* case did not consider the possible application of the *expressio unius* maxim, which would have dictated the opposite result. *See supra* p. 59.

138 *See* Chapter XIII, p. 520, for a discussion of Married Women's Property Acts.

139 *Self v. Self*, 376 P.2d 65 (Cal. 1962).

140 *People v. Pierce*, 395 P.2d 893 (Cal. 1964).

141 398 U.S. 375 (1970).

142 *See Comment*, "The Legitimacy of Civil Law Reasoning in Common Law: Justice Harlan's Contribution," 82 YALE L.J. 258 (1972).

courts are concerned that judicial lawmaking is undemocratic,[143] legislative sources for common law-making should be all the more attractive to courts.[144]

b. Reasoning by Analogy Without the Common Law Medium

There are a few examples of true application of statutory provisions by analogy without using the medium of common law doctrine. In *Cintrone v. Hertz Trucking Leasing and Rental Service*,[145] and *Newmark v. Gimbel's, Inc.*,[146] the New Jersey Supreme Court found that an implied warranty of fitness for purpose, as set out in the Uniform Commercial Code (UCC) for *sales* of *goods*, applied to the *lease* of a truck and to *services* rendered in a beauty parlor. In the lease case, the court observed that the "development of the warranty doctrine in sales should point the way by suggestive analogy to similar results in cases where a commodity is leased" in view of the fact that the same business ends that can be achieved by selling and buying can be achieved by leasing.[147] The aftermath of the UCC analogy cases, however, shows just how strong a pull the typical common law attitude still has. Other courts have followed the *result* of these cases, but not surprisingly have understood the cases as extending a *common law* rule of strict liability in *tort*. They do not rely on or even mention the Uniform Commercial Code.[148]

One U.S. Supreme Court opinion has reasoned directly by analogy, though over a strong protest from Justice Scalia. In *Agency Holding Corp. v. Malley-Duff & Associates*,[149] the Court had to determine what the time limitation period was for filing actions under the federal Racketeer Influenced and Corrupt Organizations (RICO) statute.[150] The majority opinion applied the limitation period of a different federal statute, an antitrust act, believing that it provided the "closest analogy" to the RICO statute based on its similar structure and purpose. Justice Scalia, voicing the traditional common law attitude, viewed this form of reasoning as illegitimate. If the statute did not provide a limitations period, he argued, then either state law applied or there simply was *no* limitation period. He objected strongly to the Court's "prowling hungrily through the Statutes at Large for an appetizing federal limitations period," absent legislative direction to apply an analogous federal statute. He could "find no legitimate source for the new rule" and argued that picking a limitation period of a certain length was "quintessentially the kind of judgment to be made by the legislature."[151]

---

143 *See supra* p. 46.

144 The development of common law from legislative principles was pointed out several years ago in an essay. *See* James Landis, "Statutes and the Sources of Law," in HARVARD LEGAL ESSAYS 213 (1934).

145 212 A.2d 769 (N.J. 1965).

146 258 A.2d 697 (N.J. 1969).

147 This is consistent with the Uniform Commercial Code's drafters' suggestion that the Code's underlying principles should be applied to decide cases not expressly included in the language of the act. *See* Comment to UCC §1-102, SELECTED COMMERCIAL STATUTES (West 2010).

148 *See Martin v. Ryder Truck Rental, Inc.*, 353 A.2d 581 (Del. 1976). Analogical application of the UCC to leases was rendered largely moot when a new Article 2A covering leases was added in 1990 and adopted in 43 states.

149 483 U.S. 143 (1987).

150 The statute failed to specify any period. Typically, the Court has applied state-law limitation periods of the state where the federal action is brought. This has been justified either on a theory that state law applies of its own force where Congress has not preempted it or because Congress has implicitly directed that courts "borrow" state law.

151 *But see* Traynor, *supra* note 64, at 405-409 (collecting examples from between 1300 and 1800 of English common law courts analogizing from limitation periods in otherwise inapplicable statutes). Traynor was Chief Justice of the California Supreme Court.

The above cases should not lead one to conclude that American courts reason analogically from statutes on a regular basis. Justice Scalia's dissenting position in the *Agency Holding* case is clearly the traditional view. Further, the maxim of *expressio unius est exclusio alterius*, which has seen a resurgence in use by the Supreme Court in recent years, remains an obstacle to much analogical reasoning from statutes. So far, it remains an exotic form of reasoning that is more often rejected than accepted.

E. The Form and General Nature of Caselaw

Having considered statutes in depth, we will now consider caselaw in this and the next section of this chapter. This section will consider the form that caselaw generally takes and the principle of *stare decisis*. In the next section, we will discuss the legal reasoning process used in applying caselaw.

1. Judicial Opinions and Their Structure

Types of Opinions   The most important judicial opinions are appellate court opinions. Appellate courts have multiple judges — usually 3, 5, 7, or 9 judges — and the case is decided by a majority vote of the judges on the court. There is an "opinion of the court" which states the decision and detailed reasons for that decision agreed to by a majority of the judges.[152] This opinion is written and signed by an individual judge who is a member of that majority.[153] Unless the decision is unanimous, one or more "dissenting opinions" may be filed by judges who disagree with the majority's conclusion and reasoning, or a judge may simply indicate the fact of dissent without an opinion. There may also be "concurring opinions" written by judges who agree with the conclusion of the majority, but disagree with its reasoning. Clearly, the majority opinion is the most important opinion, but the attentive lawyer will wish to read concurring and dissenting opinions to clarify the impact of the majority opinion.

The assignment to write the majority opinion is usually made by the chief justice or judge. Drafts of proposed majority, dissenting and concurring opinions are circulated among members of the court. In the process, the majority opinion writer often gets suggestions from other members of the majority and may include responses to criticisms by dissenting and concurring opinions. Sometimes there is a need to "bargain" to accommodate demands from members of the majority. This will force the writer to include ideas that are not his or her own, thus sometimes making for a less-than-completely coherent or consistent opinion. If a majority agrees on the proper result, but less than a majority agrees on a rationale for the decision, no one opinion receives the approval of a majority. The opinion supporting the result in the case that has the most votes is referred to as a "plurality opinion." The precise precedential value of a plurality opinion is not well defined and depends to a large extent on how later majority opinions of the same court treat it. Some have been cited and treated almost like majority opinions while others have been given little weight or have been completely ignored.

Structure and Content of Opinions   There is no set structure for a majority opinion, but it will usually start with a statement summarizing the case and its procedural posture, a statement of the facts and the legal issues presented, a section discussing in detail the reasons supporting the decision, and the action to be taken in the case. The discussion

---

152 The general form of appellate opinions can be seen from *Hoffman v. Jones*, reprinted in the Appendix A.

153 The English style in the 1700s, inherited by American appellate courts, was to have *seriatim* opioions by each judge, giving the reader the task of figuring out who was in the majority and what their reasoning was. Chief Justice John Marshall of the United States Supreme Court, who served from 1801 to 1836, was responsible for breaking with the English practice and requiring a single opinion of the Court.

of the reasoning behind the decision will often be encyclopedic, including extensive citations to and discussions of all prior relevant cases and many secondary authorities, such as law review articles and treatises. Thus, as noted in the Reader's Guide and Bibliographic Introduction to this book,[154] the judicial opinions of some courts — and of the U.S. Supreme Court in particular — are often helpful as references for discovering useful sources in the general area of law to which the case relates.

2. Precedential Effect of Court Decisions

Stare Decisis   The essence of the system by which court decisions are a source of law for later cases is the rule of *stare decisis*. The precise meaning of *stare decisis* is best expressed by the full Latin phrase from which the term comes: "*stare decisis et non quieta movere*," which means "to stand by precedents and not to disturb settled points."

The rationales for having a caselaw or precedential law system have been variously stated.[155] Perhaps the most often-stated justification for following precedent is what Karl Llewellyn called "that curious, almost universal sense of justice which urges that all men are properly to be treated alike in like circumstances."[156] This equality of treatment in turn serves to limit bias and arbitrariness and allows parties to rely with some certainty on how the system has dealt with cases similar to theirs. In addition, following precedent is efficient since similar cases need not be reasoned through "from the ground up." Since statutes can be subject to differing interpretations, the rationales for a system of precedent apply with equal force to judicial decisions interpreting enacted law.

Court decisions can have two types of *stare decisis* effect. The effect can be "binding" or it can be only "persuasive."

Binding Stare Decisis Effect   Binding effect on a court means that the court is obligated to follow the rule established by an earlier case. The decisions of a superior court have binding effect on all lower courts in the same court system. Thus, a decision of the Florida Supreme Court, the highest court in the state, has binding effect on all other state courts in Florida. This form of binding effect is sometimes referred to as "vertical" *stare decisis*. Prior decisions of a court will also bind that *same* court in later cases. This is sometimes referred to as "horizontal" *stare decisis*. However, horizontal binding effect is more flexible than vertical binding effect. It is not unusual that a court would sometimes overrule its own precedent.[157]

Persuasive Stare Decisis Effect   If a court is not obligated to follow precedents established in earlier cases, but may do so if it is persuaded by the reasoning used, the precedential effect is only "persuasive." The decision of a legal question by the courts of one state will have only persuasive effect on the courts of another state. For example, New York courts will follow a Florida Supreme Court decision only if they believe it is correctly reasoned. Similarly, as noted in Chapter I, federal courts must apply state law in suits between citizens of different states.[158] However, their interpretations of state law

---

154 *See* pp. ix-x.

155 *See* LLEWELLYN, *supra* note 44 at 26, where several are discussed..

156 LLEWELLYN, *id.* See also EDGAR BODENHEIMER, JURISPRUDENCE: THE PHILOSOPHY AND METHOD OF THE LAW 425-430 (Harvard U. Press 1974).

157 *Stare decisis* is more closely adhered to in England than in the United States. Indeed, it was only in 1966 that the House of Lords, the highest court in England, formally adopted the principle that it should feel free in appropriate cases to depart from its own prior decisions. 1 W.L.R. 1234 (H.L. 1966) (Lord Gardner L.C.).

158 *See* p. 33.

have only persuasive effect on the state courts of that state, since authoritative interpretations of a state's law may only be rendered by those state courts.

Stare Decisis Effect of Statutory Interpretations Some have argued for a rule of absolute *stare decisis* effect for caselaw interpreting statutes.[159] Among the factors urged in favor is the ease with which the legislature can notice and correct any misunderstanding of legislative intent. In addition, the greater specificity of statutes often means that there are greater reliance interests involved. This has not been the Supreme Court's approach, however.[160]

Stare Decisis Effect of Constitutional Decisions Legislatures have the ability to change both common law caselaw and caselaw interpreting statutes. However, legislative "correction" of *constitutional* caselaw can only take place through the process of amending the Constitution — rarely a successful option. For this reason, the Supreme Court has been somewhat more amenable to overruling cases interpreting the Constitution that have been called into serious question.[161]

F. The Legal Reasoning Process in Caselaw

Two basic types of legal reasoning are used with caselaw: deductive reasoning and analogical reasoning.[162] Deductive reasoning takes caselaw "rules" and applies them in a manner similar to statutes. Analogical reasoning directly compares the facts of the prior precedent to the facts of the case to be decided.[163]

1. Deductive Reasoning from Caselaw Rules

The deductive reasoning process used in caselaw, like the process used with statutes, begins with a rule. However, caselaw involves an added step, because one must first determine just what "rule" has been established by prior caselaw. When dealing with one prior case, that "rule" is the "holding" of a case. In England, the term "ratio decidendi" is used.

a. Determining the Holding or Rule of a Case

The "holding" or "rule" of a case is a one or two sentence statement that summarizes the broader, more abstract principle for which the case stands, and for which the case can be used to decide later cases. A holding must be stated in such a way that it will make sense to a person who has not read the case, so a proper holding will contain shorthand references to the facts which were deemed most important for the decision.

---

159 *See* Lawrence C. Marshall, *"Let Congress Do It": The Case for an Absolute Rule of Statutory Stare Decisis*, 88 MICH. L. REV. 177 (1989) (arguing for an absolute rule and suggesting that *stare decisis* as used today is a "mere rhetorical device").

160 *See, e.g. Monell v. New York Department of Social Services*, 436 U.S. 658 (1978) *overruling Monroe v. Pape*, 365 U.S. 167 (1961) (confessing error in construing the word defining suable defendant "persons" as not including municipalities).

161 *See Burnet v. Colorado Oil & Gas Co.*, 285 U.S. 393, 406-07 (1932) (Brandies, J., dissenting) ("in cases involving the Federal Constitution, where correction through legislative action is practically impossible, this Court has often overruled its earlier decisions"). *But see Planned Parenthood of Southeastern Pennsylvania v. Casey*, 505 U.S. 833 (1992) (declining to overrule its 1973 decision establishing a constitutionally-secured right to an abortion, largely on *stare decisis* grounds).

162 For discussions of the modes of legal reasoning, *see* STEVEN BURTON, AN INTRODUCTION TO LAW AND LEGAL REASONING, 3D ED (Aspen 2007); MELVIN A. EISENBERG, THE NATURE OF THE COMMON LAW (Harvard U. Press 1991); RUGGERO ALDISERT, LOGIC FOR LAWYERS, 3D ED (Clark, Boardman 2001). *See also* Vincent Wellman, *Practical Reasoning and Judicial Justification: Toward an Adequate Theory*, 57 U. COLO.L.REV. 45 (1985). For a comparative study of reasoning from precedents, *see* INTERPRETING PRECEDENTS: A COMPARATIVE STUDY, D. NEIL MACCORMICK & ROBERT S. SUMMERS, EDS. (Dartmouth Publishing 1997).

163 The legal reasoning process is the same for common law caselaw as for caselaw interpreting statutes or other enacted law. Consequently, the two are treated together in this section.

For example, assume A owns a boat. B steals the boat. B then sells the boat to C. C pays B fair market value for it and does not know the boat is stolen. A finds out that C has the boat and sues C for possession.[164] Assume the judge decides for A, the owner. The opinion states in part: "It is argued that C paid fair market value for the boat and had no notice that it had been stolen and therefore acquired title. We do not agree. The seller B acquired the boat by illegal means and thus did not gain any right or title to it. Having no title himself, he was powerless to convey any to C. Moreover, there is benefit in a rule that serves to make it more difficult for thieves to dispose of stolen property. Judgement for A." The holding of the case might be as follows: "Where property is stolen from the owner and sold by the thief to a third person, the owner can recover that property from the third-party purchaser even if the purchaser paid full value and had no knowledge that the property was stolen." This rule can then be applied in the same manner as a statute.[165]

There can be broad and narrow statements of the holding of a case. A broad statement is on a higher level of generalization, while a narrow one will stick more closely to the precise facts of the decided case. The statement of the holding just given above is probably a relatively narrow statement of it, though a statement confining the holding to boats alone, would be even narrower. A broader one would be: "An owner can recover *unlawfully-obtained* property from a subsequent purchaser, even if the subsequent purchaser did not know of the property's illegal origins."

The danger of broad statements of holdings is that they can turn out to be *overly* broad. This is illustrated by assuming that after the above case is decided, which we will call Case 1, a Case 2 arises in the same court. In this case, the boat was bought with a *fraudulent check* and the defrauding purchaser in turn sold it to a third party. The court holds in Case 2 that the original owner may *not* recover from the third party. Without getting into the reasons why a court might so decide (we will discuss that below), it is clear at least one form of "unlawfully-obtained property" may *not* be recovered from the third party purchaser for value. The court has detected a difference between outright theft and fraud and our statement of the holdings in both cases should reflect that fact.

b. Dictum

Judges are expected to give reasons for their decisions. In the process of doing so, they are conscious of the fact that they are not only deciding a case; they are also making law. As a result, they will often seek to elucidate the impact of their decision for future cases. However, not all statements of legal principles by judges deciding a case are part of the holding. Statements that were not necessary to the decision of that case can have no binding authority in a later case, and should be ignored in stating the holding of the case. A statement that is not necessary for decision of the case is called "*dictum*" or "*obiter dictum*."[166] For example, assume that in Case 1 (outright theft of the

---

164 These illustrations are adapted from Lon Fuller, *The Forms and Limits of Adjudication*, 92 HARV.L.REV. 353, 375-76 (1978).

165 Note that this statement of the holding largely ignores the reasoning given in the "opinion" in the earlier case. The extent to which the reasons given by the court in the opinion are to be incorporated into the statement of the holding is a matter of some difference of opinion and the American lawyer is much more likely to include them than the English lawyer. *See* ATIYAH & SUMMERS, *supra* note 24, at 124-125 and sources cited therein.

166 *Dictum* means literally a statement. *Obiter dictum* means a statement uttered in passing. The practical reason why *dictum* should not be relied upon is that both the court and the parties before it have most comprehensively investigated and considered the question actually before the court, and any side issues are not the product of as thorough a process. *See Cohens v. Virginia*, 19 U.S. (6 Wheat.) 264, 399 (1821) (Marshall, C.J.)

boat and later sale; A wins), the court goes on to say that "in a case in which a seller of property obtained that property from the owner fraudulently, the owner could not recover." Or the court might say that "an owner who abandoned his property cannot thereafter sue to recover it from someone who finds it." These comments would not have been necessary to the decision of Case 1 in A's favor and would therefore be *dictum*.

Strictly speaking, *dictum* has no precedential value for future cases. Consequently, it would be improper to say that the above dictum from Case 1 applies to determine later cases of fraudulent sale or abandonment of property. However, no sensible lawyer can ignore *dictum*. It shows that the court has thought about how those other cases should be resolved and would so act if given the chance. The lawyer whose argument in a case is contrary to *dictum* contained in the majority opinion in a recent supreme court case will have a difficult time convincing the court otherwise. On the other hand, it is not unheard of for a court to go against its own earlier *dictum*. The hypothetical nature of *dictum* often means that the court will not have thought about it as deeply and the parties' arguments will not have addressed it as well as points more central to decision of the case.

c. Multiple and Implied Holdings

It sometimes happens that a court rendering a decision does not explicitly state a holding, but one may be implied from the result and the court's statement of the facts. Assume, for example, in boat Case 2 where the seller procured the boat by fraud and then sold it, the court decides that the purchaser wins instead of the owner. However, instead of explaining its reasons, the court merely states the relevant facts of the case, emphasizing the fact that the purchaser of the boat did not know of the fraud. Any statement of the holding in the case must necessarily include the element of lack of knowledge since the context indicates that the court viewed that as important.

A case can have more than one holding. Thus, in Case 1 above involving the stolen boat, the opinion may have also discussed and decided whether the original owner could get specific recovery of the property (as opposed to recovery of the value of the property) as a remedy. A holding that accounted for this part of the case might be: "An owner of stolen property found in the possession of another may obtain an order for specific relief requiring its return so long as the property can be reasonably identified and the person in possession is subject to the jurisdiction of the court."[167]

d. Synthesizing a Rule From Several Cases

There is a second kind of caselaw rule from which lawyers can argue deductively. It is like the holding or rule of a particular case, but represents a "synthesis" of several cases. By putting together or "synthesizing" the holdings of several cases, the lawyer can come up with an overall legal rule for which a line of decisions stands.

To demonstrate this, assume as before that Case 1 involved a *stolen* boat and the owner was *allowed* to recover. Assume as well that Case 2 involved a *fraudulently-obtained* boat and the court held the owner could *not* recover. Now assume a Case 3, in which X has an oil painting. Y obtains the painting from X through fraud. Y then sells the painting to Z. Before this sale, Z had heard rumors that perhaps Y had obtained the painting through some improper means and the price Y was asking was very low. But

---

167 However, if the court had decided that A could *not* recover because A had failed to prove ownership, and then went on to state the circumstances under which an owner *could* obtain an order for specific relief, then such a statement would be *dictum*.

Z bought the painting anyway. The original owner X now sues Z for possession of the painting. Assume that the court in Case 3 holds that X *can* recover this time. In so deciding, the court notes that, unlike Case 2 (where fraud was also involved), in Case 3, Z paid much less than market price for the painting and had heard from others that Y might have obtained the painting unlawfully. These facts, the court observed, should have put Z on notice that there was something wrong with the painting. A synthesis of cases 1, 2 and 3 might be stated as follows: "An owner may recover stolen personal property from a subsequent purchaser for value who did not have notice that it was stolen. However, an owner may not recover fraudulently-obtained property from a subsequent purchaser unless the purchaser knew of the fraud or had reason to question the seller's title to the property." This synthesized rule, like the rule derived from a single case, can then be applied deductively to a later case much the same way that a statute might be applied.

If a synthesis of cases is a broad one and involves the common law, it is sometimes referred to as a "common law rule." Such rules are abstract statements that summarize a "family" of related holdings. The just-stated synthesis of cases 1 through 3 might be treated this way, though most common law rules will cover a broader area. Sometimes a court's opinion will helpfully provide a summarized synthesis of cases.

2. Analogical Reasoning Directly From Prior Caselaw Decisions

There are limits to using holdings and case syntheses deductively like statutes. Deductive reasoning alone is of little use in deciding whether a case *comes within* the rule one has distilled from a prior case, unless the new case involves the same facts as the earlier one. For example, judges who are trying to decide Case 2 (fraudulently obtained boat) can read and reread the *holding* of Case 1, but it will not tell them whether the rule of Case 1 *should* cover Case 2 as well. What the judges need to decide is how Case 2 is similar to or different from Case 1 or any other precedents in the area. To do this requires the application of analogical reasoning directly from the facts of the prior case.

a. The Analogical Reasoning Process

The analogical reasoning process involves a two-step process of (1) identifying the factual similarities and differences between the new case to be decided and the precedent and (2) determining whether the current case is either similar to or different from that precedent in *important* respects relevant to the issue to be decided. If the precedent is deemed similar in those important respects, it will be *followed*. If it is deemed different in important respects, it will be *distinguished*.[168]

Following or distinguishing precedents involves a simple analogical reasoning process used every day. To take an example anyone with children will recognize, assume that you have decided to let your ten-year-old stay up until 10:00 PM (on a non-school night).[169] Your six-year-old feels the sting of injustice when she is forced to go to

---

168 *See* BURTON, *supra* note 162, at 26-27. Professor Edward Levi explains analogical reasoning from precedent as involving three steps: "similarity is seen between cases; next the rule of law inherent in the first case is announced; then the rule of law is made applicable to the second case." *See* EDWARD LEVI, AN INTRODUCTION TO LEGAL REASONING 1-2 (University of Chicago Press 1948). Levi is not specific enough about the nature of the "rule of law" involved to judge, but this seems more like deductive, not analogical reasoning. I believe that Burton's and Golding's view more accurately portrays what lawyers and judges actually do, especially in difficult cases: they make direct comparisons between the facts of each case without the intervention of any clearly formulated intermediate "rule." *See* MARTIN GOLDING, LEGAL REASONING 103 (Alfred Knopf 2001); BURTON, *supra* note 162, at 36.

169 This example is adapted from BURTON, *supra* note 162, at 26-27.

bed at 8:00 PM. She appeals to you to allow her to stay up until 10:00, arguing that you let the ten-year-old child stay up. In developing her argument from precedent, perhaps the six-year-old will point out the factual similarities between their situations, e.g., that they are both children and that neither of them has school the next day. If you find the younger child's appeal to the precedent involving the older child unpersuasive, it will be because you have determined that the difference in their ages is more important than whatever similarities might exist. This difference is important because age directly relates to the issue to be decided — bedtimes for children. The difference in ages is important to bedtimes because younger children need more sleep.

Clearly the most difficult part of the analogical reasoning process is evaluating the importance of the differences and similarities. This question of importance cannot be determined in the abstract. Importance is situational and depends on the issue that is to be decided. In the example with the children, denying the younger child's request to stay up late on the ground that "she's Ann and you're Zelda" is a decision based on an actual difference between them — their names. But different names cannot be a valid basis for deciding the case presented because it is based on a difference that has nothing to do with *bedtimes*. On the other hand, "she's Ann and you're Zelda" *is* a relevant difference in determining where each child should be in a line of children that is arranged alphabetically.

b. Evaluating Factual Variations in Common Law Caselaw

The importance question for common law caselaw is most often determined by examining a "family" of similar cases and principles underlying them. We will return to the example introduced earlier of the dispute between the owners of property and subsequent purchasers to demonstrate the process.

Analogical Reasoning Applied to a Common Law Example Assume that a court has decided Case 1 (boat stolen and sold; owner wins). The Court must now decide Case 2 (boat fraudulently-obtained) where the innocent purchaser has also been sued. On the one hand, underlying Case 1 and similar cases protecting owners of property is the notion that ownership of property is good for society and greater protection will encourage owners to invest in and preserve their property. On the other hand, free commerce in goods is important to society. One could argue that it is unreasonable to burden an innocent purchaser with the risk that the original owner could appear on the scene at any time, even years later, and reclaim the property. The court in Case 1 nonetheless imposed this risk on the purchaser in the case of theft in the name of protecting property ownership and making things more difficult for thieves.[170]

Case 2 is arguably different because owners are more able to protect themselves from fraud than from theft. An owner can prevent fraud by insisting on verification of any tender of payment, while theft can take place at any time and is usually unexpected. At the same time, the subsequent purchaser is *less* able to protect himself from the fraud than from theft. Purchasers in the marketplace in general have limited ability to verify assertions of good title. But purchasers have even more trouble verifying title where their seller has obtained the property by fraud. The transaction has all the outward appearances of a *bona fide* sale, complete with a bill of sale signed by the owner. In fact, but for the fact that the check the owner received for the property later turned out to be worthless, the transaction had all the characteristics of a sale, including the fact that the owner, at the time of transfer of the property, voluntarily parted with possession.

---

170 The "opinion" of the court is set out *supra* p. 67.

On this analysis, assume that the court decides Case 2 in favor of the purchaser. It concludes that, while no title passes by virtue of a theft, many of the elements of a normal sale are present in the fraudulent transaction, including the owner's intent to transfer title, such that it can be said that the defrauding purchaser obtained at least voidable title. Thus, while the owner might be able to sue the *defrauding party* directly to void the title and regain the property, if the property is resold to an innocent purchaser before title is voided, title passes to that purchaser and the owner cannot recover his property from that purchaser.[171]

Now assume that Case 3 arises, the case in which the painting was fraudulently obtained and the buyer paid a low price and had heard rumors about the possibly dubious title of the seller. Case 3 is the same as Case 2 except for the fact that the purchaser seems to have some reason to suspect that there is a problem with the painting. The discussion in Case 2 would seem to make this factual difference an important one, since underlying that decision is a concern that buyers in the market have great difficulty finding out about defective title in fraud cases. In terms of this factor, the purchaser in Case 3 is different from the purchaser in Case 2 and should have been on notice from the low price and rumors that there should be further inquiry. A more subtle basis for deciding Case 3 against the purchaser that might be gleaned from the earlier cases deals with the reprehensibility of the conduct of the actors involved. In Case 1, the Court in part justified its decision on the policy of making things more difficult for thieves. In Case 2, it was undisputed that the owner could recover against the *perpetrator* of the fraud. A person who takes advantage of fraud, as the purchaser in Case 3 did, is only slightly better than the thief or the perpetrator of the fraud and should not be allowed to benefit from that conduct.

"Ghost" Precedents   The analogical arguments made here suggest that there may be more "precedents" involved than just the decided cases. For example, it was argued in Case 2, not only that the fraudulent transfer situation was *distinguishable* from the *theft* situation in Case 1, but that the fraudulent transfer was *similar* to a *true sale*. We were given no *real* case involving a true sale. But we can assume hypothetically that a court would reject the claim of an owner who received the price he asked and completed a sale, but then had second thoughts and sought to reclaim the property from his purchaser. A similar hypothetical "precedent" was used to support the decision in Case 3. The court in Case 3 necessarily assumed that the owner *would* win in a contest between the owner and the *perpetrator* of the fraud. It then used that "ghost" precedent as one of its reasons for denying recovery to the purchaser who took advantage of the fraud.

Recasting Precedent   The arguments made in Case 2 and Case 3 also point out how a court dealing with precedent is not necessarily limited to the rationale given in earlier opinions. The opinion in Case 1 relied in part on a rather formal theory that title had not passed to the thief. The case is recast in the decision of the later cases to fit into a more general theory about safeguarding ownership and purchasers' abilities to protect themselves in the market.[172]

---

[171] Many jurisdictions have distinguished fraud cases from stolen property cases for the reasons stated, as does the UCC. *See generally* RAY A. BROWN, THE LAW ON PERSONAL PROPERTY §§9.4, 9.6 (Callaghan & Co. 1975).

[172] A classic recasting of precedent is Judge Cardozo's opinion in *McPherson v. Buick Motor Co.*, 111 N.E. 1050 (N.Y. 1916) (recasting precedents to broaden protection from harm caused by "imminently" dangerous products, such as mislabeled poisons, to harm caused by products that are dangerous because they are negligently made, such as an automobile).

c. Choice of Deductive or Analogical Reasoning: Easy Cases and Hard Cases

Having outlined both deductive and analogical reasoning in caselaw, it is appropriate to consider when judges or lawyer might choose one mode over the other. Some judicial opinions or arguments go through a complete analogical analysis of the factual differences between the case to be decided and various precedents. Others will synthesize a rule out of the applicable precedents and apply that rule deductively like a statute. Which approach is used depends on a number of factors, including the personal decision-making style of the judge.

Deductive reasoning from general rules established by cases is particularly useful in deciding *easy* cases or easy parts of cases. For example, returning to the property hypothetical, assume that after Case 3 is decided, a Case 4 arises in which the buyer of stolen property actually helped to facilitate the theft of the property. The court could dispose of the case by citing the common law rule set out earlier, followed by a "string cite" of Cases 1 through 3 and other prominent cases in the particular "family" of cases.[173] Because the matter is so clear, there would be no need for any analogical analysis of the facts of the cases.[174]

In fact, deductive reasoning from statements of holdings or rules of prior cases is useful *only* to decide clear or "easy" cases. Arguments in more difficult cases may start out with deductive reasoning, but soon disagreement arises over whether a particular synthesized rule is applicable to the case at bar, or whether such a "rule" exists at all. When that happens, the arguments turn immediately to analogical reasoning directly from the facts of prior cases, seeking to apply them to or distinguish them from the facts of the case to be decided.

3. Reasoning in Caselaw Interpreting Statutes

a. Deductive and Analogical Reasoning in Statutory Caselaw

As already discussed when statutory interpretation was outlined, a court faced with applying a statute must examine the text of the statute and any permitted aids to interpretation allowed to be consulted. The court must also consider prior caselaw interpreting the statute. These holdings and syntheses of holdings serve as "sub-rules" of the statutory rule being interpreted and can be applied deductively to decide easy cases. For example, it is common that a criminal statute will punish assault "with a deadly weapon" more seriously than a simple assault. A case arises in which the defendant, who was stopped by a policeman for a traffic violation, tried to run over the policeman with his car. If there is caselaw holding that a car qualifies (or does not qualify) as a deadly weapon, then that caselaw rule is applied as if it were explicitly provided in the statute.[175]

Courts use caselaw interpreting statutes in much the same way that common law caselaw is used — both deductively and analogically. If the caselaw is clear on the subject of whether a car can be a "deadly weapon" if used to try to kill someone, then

---

173 A "string cite" is where a court or lawyer simply "strings" together in a list the case names and citations of several cases without discussing their facts or reasoning.

174 Use of deductive application of a rule with string cites is so identified with resolving easy questions that intellectually dishonest or lazy judges or lawyers who want the issue involved to seem easier than it is will often misuse the technique. Examination of the facts and holdings of cases in a "string cite" often turn out not to support the proposition claimed.

175 Of course, if there is an explicit definition supplied by the legislature, it must be followed instead.

the case is an "easy" one and the rule established can be applied deductively without any need for direct analogical reasoning.[176] If there is no prior precedent that provides a suitable sub-rule holding that is directly on point, the court must resort to analogical reasoning. Perhaps there are cases involving assaults using other implements that were not originally designed to be used as deadly weapons, but which could be and were used as such. The court will then have to use the analogical reasoning process already outlined for common law decisions and make the factual comparisons and judgments involved.[177]

b. Evaluating Factual Variations in Caselaw Interpreting Statutes

Applying Legislative Policy   The main difference between analogical reasoning in common law and statutory caselaw comes at the point when the court must evaluate the questions of the *importance* of the factual differences and similarities between prior cases and the new case to be decided. In *common law* caselaw, the court refers to principles enunciated in prior cases or in the common law generally. In dealing with caselaw concerning *statutes*, the importance inquiry must generally be confined to criteria set by the *legislature*.

These legislative criteria are usually found by examining the language, purpose and legislative history of the enactment. However, the relevant legislative policy and purpose have often been sifted through several judicial filters. As Professor Shapiro has cogently observed:

> [J]udges [in the United States] often construct their opinions as mosaics of excerpts from, citations of, and comments about earlier judicial decisions. Even when the case is one of statutory interpretation, the wording of the statute may be buried in a footnote. In many instances, of course, the judge will openly proclaim that the source of the basic legal rule being applied is a previous decision rather than a statutory provision.[178]

In the process of this judicial filtering of legislative policy, more general principles sometimes appear.[179]

"Ghost" Precedents in Statutory Interpretation   As we saw earlier when "ghost" common law precedents were discussed, one need not have *actual* prior caselaw to reason by analogy. So strong is the pull of cases and analogical reasoning that judges or lawyers will often create "ghost" cases from which to argue when interpreting a statute. A court will often construct "paradigm cases" that reflect the social ills that the legislature was seeking to eradicate or the kinds of positive behavior it was trying to promote. The court will then compare the instant case with the hypothetical cases and reason from them as if they were real cases. Such "ghost" precedents are especially

---

176 *See supra* pp. 66-69.

177 *See supra* p. 69.

178 MARTIN SHAPIRO, COURTS: A COMPARATIVE AND POLITICAL ANALYSIS 135 (U. Chicago Press 1981).

179 For a discussion of how general principles operate in both common law and statutory caselaw, *see* DWORKIN, *supra* note 43, at 23-24 (discussing both a common law example and one involving a statute). *Cf. Riggs v. Palmer*, 22 N.E. 188 (N.Y. 1899) (grandson could not inherit from the grandparent he had murdered despite lack of such disqualification in the statute; court presumed that legislature had "maxims of the common law" in mind when it passed the statute). *See also supra*, p. 61 (statutory interpretation in light of fundamental values).

easy to generate in statutory caselaw because sponsors and supporters of the bill will often themselves create such examples to illustrate the purpose of the legislation.[180]

G. Legal Research Techniques and the Form of Legal Argument

1. Library Resources for Finding Primary Materials

Caselaw The percentage of appellate court decisions that are published varies widely and has in general been declining in recent years as the number of appeals has increased. Among the federal courts of appeal, fewer than half of their decisions are published. The rest are disposed of summarily or by means of an unpublished opinion. The judges who decided the case make the decision whether to release their decision for publication. Even if not published, opinions are generally available nonetheless from one of the computerized legal research services, discussed below. However, local rules generally prohibit citation to them, maintaining that such opinions have no precedential effect.[181]

Published judicial opinions in cases are published in chronological order and can be found in books known as "reporters" or "case reports."[182] Case reporting in the United States began informally and on a selective basis just as it did in England. However, it soon became more systematic with "official" reports issued by states and the United States Supreme Court. West Publishing Company, a private company, began an effort to be more comprehensive and systematic in the 1880s. Today West publishes "regional reporters" covering all the states. In addition, it publishes the only readily available reporters of lower federal court decisions. Because the West reporters publish all opinions released for publication, many states have abandoned publication of official reports. State trial court decisions are generally not published even on a selective basis except in a few states.

On the federal level, United States Supreme Court opinions are published in three places: the official reporter, United States Reports (U.S.); the Supreme Court Reporter (S.Ct.) published by West Publishing; and U.S. Supreme Court Reports, Lawyer's Edition (L.Ed.), a reporter series published by Lawyer's Cooperative Publishing Company, another private legal publisher.[183] Selected federal district court opinions are reported in reporters entitled Federal Supplement (F.Supp.) and, if they deal with issues of federal court procedure, in the Federal Rules Decisions (F.R.D.). Federal appellate opinions available for publication are published in Federal Reporter, now in its Third Series (F.3d). A federal court of appeals opinion might be cited as *Fligiel v. Samson*, 440 F.3d 747 (6th Cir. 2006). The parenthetical material indicates that the court was the U.S. Court of Appeals for the Sixth Circuit.

---

180 This technique was used by the Court in a statutory context in the *Holy Trinity Church* case, *supra* p. 58. *See also supra* p. 34 ("ghost" precedents in common law caselaw).

181 The issue of unpublished opinions without precedential effect was highlighted when one circuit court of appeals found it to be unconstitutional in *Anastasoff v. United States*, 223 F.3d 898, *vacated as moot on reh'g en banc*, 235 F.3d 1054 (8th Cir. 2000), but another found it constitutional. *Hart v. Massanari*, 266 F.3d 1155 (9th Cir. 2001).

182 Case citation form is discussed in the Bibliographic Introduction and Reader's Guide of this book. For more on legal research *see* ROBERT C. BERRING & ELIZABETH EDINGER, LEGAL RESEARCH SURVIVAL MANUAL (West 2002); MORRIS L. COHEN & KENT C. OLSON, LEGAL RESEARCH IN A NUTSHELL, 8TH ED. (West 2003); RUTH ANN MCKINNEY, LEGAL RESEARCH: A PRACTICAL GUIDE AND SELF-INSTRUCTION WORKBOOK, 5TH ED. (West 2007).

183 Only official U.S. Supreme Court cites are given in the text of this book, but for those whose libraries have one of the other reporting services, parallel cites are set out in the Table of Cases in Appendix C to this book.

Enacted Law State and federal constitutions, statutes, and regulations are published in volumes arranged topically. State and federal statutes are published by governmental publishers and by private publishers in annotated volumes providing reference to cases interpreting the statute, citations to legislative history, pertinent articles in legal periodicals, and references to computer data bases. For example, on the federal level, statutes are contained in the government publication entitled United States Code (U.S.C.) and in two privately published and annotated versions entitled United States Code Annotated (U.S.C.A.) and United States Code Service (U.S.C.S.). Annotations are brief summaries of cases that have been decided that interpret each section of the statute. State statutes are presented in a similar manner, and both federal and state codes are updated regularly by the insertion of a pamphlet known as a "pocket part" into the back of the applicable volume. These pocket parts contain new statutes and summaries of new caselaw explaining existing statutes.

The legislative history accompanying a federal statute is reprinted in two sources. The first is the United States Code Congressional and Administrative News (USCCAN), which contains selected documents pertaining to the statute. The second and more exhaustive source is the Congressional Information Service (CIS). It contains transcripts of committee hearings, committee reports, and congressional debates accompanying the passage of federal laws. This source of legislative history is immense and is contained on microfiche.

Federal regulations promulgated by administrative agencies are contained in the Code of Federal Regulations (C.F.R.) where they are arranged by subject matter. Any changes to existing regulations or the addition of new regulations are published daily in the Federal Register and the C.F.R. is completely revised every year.

2. Secondary Authorities

Secondary authorities are used to supplement the primary sources. These include treatises, hornbooks, restatements of the law, law reviews, and other legal periodicals, which summarize, restate, review, analyze, and interpret the law. Secondary sources are only persuasive authority, that is, they can influence a court to the extent that the court is persuaded by the reasoning in them. They are also consulted as a finding aid by lawyers or judges seeking citations to statutes, cases or other primary sources of law.

Attorney General Opinions In many states state officials have the right to request an opinion of the state's Attorney General on a particular point of law. These opinions are published in a set of books labeled in most states Opinions of the Attorney General (OAG). No such practice exists with the federal Attorney General. These state attorney general opinions are cited and sometimes relied upon by courts and lawyers as secondary authority. However, like other forms of secondary authority, they are influential in courts only to the extent that they demonstrate thorough analysis of the issues involved.

Texts and Treatises Treatises are books written about a particular area of the law with the needs of the practitioner in mind. Many treatises are multi-volume. For example, the treatise on Federal Practice and Procedure by Wright, Miller and Cooper extends to some 23 volumes. Treatises strive to summarize in narrative form all the applicable law touching on a particular area, from statutes and regulations to common law or constitutional law. They also contain analysis and commentary by the authors, including their opinions and criticisms of various rules adopted by courts and legislative bodies.

Restatements of the Law These are compilations or summaries in statute form of the common law in designated areas of the law, such as torts, contracts, property, judgments and conflicts of laws.[184] Restatements are prepared by the American Law Institute, an organization of eminent scholars and practitioners in the given fields. The overall form is a set of statements of the "black letter" law on the subject arranged in sections and stated in the form of a statute.[185] After the "black letter" statement of the law on a particular point, there are scholarly comments on the application of each of the rules just stated, complete with appropriate hypotheticals drawn from actual cases that illustrate the rule stated. These are followed by annotations, updated regularly, that summarize the cases deemed relevant to the subject matter in the section.

Restatements are supposed to do just that — restate or summarize common law rules derived from caselaw. However, that has not prevented some restatement authors from stating what they believe is the more enlightened rule of law, even if it is not the majority view in current caselaw. Thus, some restatements have been less a reflection of *current* law than a statement of what the authors of them think the rule of law *should* be. Restatements have had an influence on the shape of the law. Particularly influential has been the Restatement of Torts, which was largely responsible for establishing strict liability for injuries caused by defective products.[186]

Law Review Articles Law reviews or law journals, usually published by law schools, contain articles by law teachers and scholars analyzing and discussing issues in various areas of the law. If these articles provide a useful analysis of a particular problem that may be facing a court, they can have an impact on the law. Treatises, law review articles and other works by scholars in the United States generally have a greater impact on the law than their counterparts in England do, and less impact on the law than at least some of their counterparts in continental Europe.[187] Generally, in both England and the United States, a judge searching for authority is more likely to turn to another judge's judicial opinion than to a scholar's work.

One-Volume Treatises and Student Texts Single volume treatises and other student texts were introduced in the Bibliographic Introduction and Reader's Guide following the Preface to this book. The "Hornbook" published by West are the most numerous of the one-volume treatises. These works are written primarily by law teachers for law students and therefore are used in judicial opinions only for relatively general propositions of law.[188] However, they are useful as departure points for research and have footnotes that can be used by the reader to locate more specific authority. There are also student aids, such as "nutshells," outlines and review problems, but these are much less likely to be consulted by a lawyer or judge or cited in a judicial opinion. Casebooks

---

184 Currently there are Restatements of Torts, Contracts, Property, Judgments, Agency, Conflicts of Laws, Foreign Relations, Restitution, and Trusts.

185 The expression "black letter" law refers to any clear, simple statement of a rule of law on a particular point without a statement of the reasons for the rule or how to apply the rule to other circumstances. Law students, confused by a conflicting and seemingly endless number of court opinions in a given area of law, often yearn for the professor to give them the applicable "black letter law" on a point, that is, a simple statement of the legal rule established by all those decisions.

186 *See* Chapter XI, pp. 448-450.

187 *See* Chapter IV, p. 135, and pp. A4-A7 of the majority opinion and p. A12 of the dissent in *Hoffman v. Jones*, reprinted in the Appendix.

188 The term "hornbook" was originally defined as "A leaf or written or printed paper pasted on a board, and covered with horn, for children to learn letters by, and to prevent their being torn and daubed." *Pardon's New General English Dictionary* (1758). Later, the hornbook was replaced by primers in book form for children to learn basic information.

— collections of edited cases and statutes with commentary and discussion questions used in law school courses — are rarely relied upon by courts.[189] If a summary of the pertinent law is desired, a treatise will generally be used.

Other Secondary Authorities Legal encyclopedias can be used as secondary sources of law, but they usually serve as a beginning point of research. Legal encyclopedias in the United States contain short general entries written by unnamed authors. The two national encyclopedia series available, Corpus Juris Secundum (CJS) and American Jurisprudence, Second (Am. Jur. 2d), were discussed in the Bibliographic Introduction and Reader's Guide. Most states also have at least one encyclopedia of its own law. These encyclopedias provide a rudimentary description of the law by breaking it into subjects which are arranged and presented alphabetically. Their purpose is to provide background on a particular legal topic and direct the researcher to pertinent case law and enacted law as well as secondary sources such as restatements and legal periodicals.

Somewhat similar to the encyclopedia are the American Law Reports (ALR). The ALR contains "annotations" in the form of short articles with summaries of the law and citations for selected legal topics. ALR started originally as a selective reporter of important cases, but is now used principally for its annotations.[190]

3. How Legal Research is Approached

Lawyers doing legal research are usually in one of two positions. The lawyer may have only a general understanding of the law governing the problem and may wish to find the specific cases and statutes that address the problem at hand. Or the lawyer may already have a specific case or statute that addresses the issue involved — or at least addresses some aspect of the issue — and must find other cases, statutes or authorities and more general support. While the research tools used in both instances are the same, they are used differently.

If the lawyer has a general idea of the law and wants to narrow the issue and the search, the first step is often to refer to a treatise in the general area involved or, if a treatise cannot be found, to one of several legal encyclopedias or the ALR. The researcher can then obtain citations to the principal cases and statutes in the area or to other more specific secondary authorities.

The researcher who already has an applicable case or statute may use one of several finding aids to locate other similar authorities. One way to do this is by looking for cases that cite the cases or statutes with which the researcher is already familiar. This is traditionally done by using Shepard's Citations, which show what other court decisions have cited the particular case, statute, court rule or other source of law. Beneath the citation will be a list of the citations of all the later cases that have cited the case. If these later opinions have discussed the cited case, their treatment of it will be indicated in the margin next to the citation (e.g., criticized, distinguished, followed). Such "Shepardizing" of a case is not just a useful way to find other cases. Before relying on any case, it is essential to "Shepardize" the case to determine whether it has been reversed or overruled.[191]

---

189 One example of a casebook that gets cited relatively frequently by courts is HART & WECHSLER, *supra* note 143.

190 Rules for all forms of citation are set out in two competing books, the "Blue Book" put out by Harvard Law School and the "Maroon Book" put out by the University of Chicago Law School.

191 A competing, completely computerized service since 1997 is West "Keycite" system.

Another method of finding cases is to use state or federal "digests" published by West, the major reporter of opinions. West publishes "headnotes" with every case. Headnotes are brief summaries of the points of law contained in the case that are written by an editor. The headnotes appear at the beginning of the opinion and are serialized with a "key number" assigned to that particular topic throughout all West's publications. The state and federal digests then contain the listings of these headnotes organized by subject matter with the key numbers. The researcher who has a case need only take the pertinent key number from a known case that deals with the issue to be researched and look it up in the appropriate digest, which lists the headnotes from all the other cases that have addressed the same issue. Key numbers and cases may also be found in the digest by looking up key words or terms in the digest's general index similar to the method used for encyclopedias and ALRs.[192]

4. Computerized Legal Research

Clearly, finding authorities and parsing the results of a search are made much easier when done by computer. There are two on-line legal research databases: Lexis-Nexis (by Reed Elsevier) and Westlaw (by West Group and Thomson). Subscribers can access both on the Internet. In addition to speeding up use of traditional methods of legal research just outlined, the computer services permit word searches and have hyperlinks to authorities cited in research results and a wider range of more specific information about how the case has been used or treated in other cases. Computer data bases are also updated more quickly than books and contain materials — particularly unpublished court decisions — that are not available in any books. The disadvantage of computer research services is that they are relatively expensive. There are monthly charges and charges by the minute for time spent doing research.[193]

5. The Form of Legal Argument

There are usually four distinct conceptual components to every legal argument. The lawyer must (1) state the issue involved; (2) state the rule to be applied; (3) apply the rule to the facts of the client's case and (4) state the conclusion reached from the application of the rule to the facts. It is during steps (3) and (4) that the deductive or analogical reasoning processes discussed earlier take place.

The physical form that legal argument generally takes in court is a written "brief," sometimes called a "memorandum of law." There are "trial briefs" submitted to trial courts and "appellate briefs" addressed to appellate courts.[194] Generally, all types of briefs are composed of standard, well defined, sections that correspond with the structure of legal arguments just discussed.

Most argument of legal issues in the United States is in written form. While oral argument of legal points does take place in both trial and appellate courts, it does not serve as a substitute for a written brief in the modern American appellate court. Indeed, it could not so substitute even if the parties wished, since the entire oral argument of the case is customarily limited to 15 or 30 minutes per side. In this respect, American

---

192 Examples of two of the headnotes with key numbers published with *Hoffman v. Jones*, the case in Appendix A, are set out on p. A2. *See also* p. A1, note 4. It is perhaps a continuing legacy of the common law bias against statutes that there is no similar comprehensive system for nationwide indexing and classification of statutes.

193 Access to free legal materials is possible on the Internet. However, search engines are not very sophisticated and there is often no guarantee that those materials are up to date. Appendix B of this book sets out a few of these sites.

194 For a discussion of the nature of trial and appellate courts, *see* Chapter V, pp. 167-171.

appellate legal argument is very different from that of England, where oral arguments in an appellate court develop much of the argumentation that is contained only in written briefs in the United States and can take hours or even days. Oral argument in U.S. appellate courts is limited to the advocate highlighting the most important aspects of the case and answering questions from the appellate judges. It is not uncommon that the questioning of the advocate will occupy almost the entire time allotted for oral argument.

The prevalence of legal argument in written form has caused some to question the need for any oral argumentation and some courts have abolished it. However, most judges still believe that even short oral argument is important for clearing up questions the court has after reading the parties' written briefing, and many judges assert strongly that it should be retained.[195]

Argument of legal points in trial courts during trial is much more likely to be entirely oral, but even during trial, if a legal point is anticipated and is important, most good lawyers will produce at least a short written memorandum or brief discussing the relevant authorities. Pre-trial motions raising legal issues that are made in trial courts outside the immediate context of the trial itself are invariably required to be in writing and are most often accompanied by a written brief. An example would be a pre-trial motion to dismiss for lack of subject matter jurisdiction. In some jurisdictions, a written brief is required by the relevant court rules for all motions made other than those made during trial, and the clerk of the court will not accept any motion for filing that is not accompanied by a brief.

---

195 *See* William H. Rehnquist, *Remarks on the Process of Judging*, 49 WASH. & LEE L. REV. 263, 269 (1992). Rehnquist was Chief Justice of the United States.

CHAPTER III

THE ADVERSARY SYSTEM AND JURY TRIALS

There will be later chapters on civil and criminal procedure in this book, so it may seem somewhat out of place to discuss adversary procedure and jury trials separately here, in the third chapter of the book. The topic is addressed here for two reasons.

First, the adversary trial and juries constitute more than just another step in civil or criminal procedure. These traditions occupy a fundamental place in the United States legal system that is difficult to understate. One reason for this is the high value placed on procedure in general. As Justice Frankfurter has stated, "[t]he history of American freedom is, in no small measure, the history of procedure."[1] It is no coincidence that the overwhelming number of rights the Framers saw fit to include in the Bill of Rights were procedural rights. Moreover, even the more "substantive" freedoms of speech and the press set out in the 1st Amendment have a distinct adversary and procedural component. Thus, a prominent justification for protecting the freedom of expression is the "marketplace of ideas" theory: that "[t]he best test of truth is the power of the thought to get itself accepted in the competition of the market."[2] Even more broadly, an "adversary ethic" prevails in many non-legal contexts. Whether a business management meeting or a political debate, the notion that a particular idea or theory has been exposed to a head-to-head clash with opposing ideas or theories and has been chosen over them gives it real credibility.

Second, discussing the adversary system and jury trials here completes the picture of the tasks that lawyers and judges are called on to perform in the legal system. The last chapter outlined *legal* methodology, that is, how courts in the United States think about and resolve *legal* issues. However, resolving issues of law is only part of the task involved in adjudicating disputes — and it is often the least important part. The facts must also be determined and the law must then be applied to those facts. The process of fact adjudication has particular significance for lawyers who engage in litigation in the United States, since it is the lawyers for the parties who must shoulder the burden of investigating, developing and presenting evidence at trial. The adversary trial process is the core of what might be called the *factual* methodology of the legal system.[3]

We will start with a brief description of adversary theory — the overall characteristics and rationale for an adversary system of adjudication. Then we will examine the institution of the jury in general terms. This will be followed by a relatively detailed description of an adversary jury trial and the lawyer's role in it, including a cursory review of some of the more important limitations on evidence. Thereafter, various criticisms of the adversary system and juries will be considered.

A. The Characteristics and Rationale of the Adversary System

All legal systems strive for decision-making that is impartial and fully-informed. Proponents of an adversary system believe that this is best achieved (1) where the

---

1 *Malinski v. New York*, 324 U.S. 401, 414 (1945).

2 *Abrams v. United States*, 250 U.S. 616, 630 (1919) (Holmes, J.).

3 Although it is essential that practicing lawyers know how to develop the facts in a case, legal education in the United States has tended to emphasize legal analysis and knowledge and traditionally has downplayed the importance of how facts are investigated and adjudicated. As a result, new lawyers may be quite skilled at the legal methodology set out in Chapter II, but may have only a rudimentary understanding of how to investigate and present facts. *See* Chapter IV, pp. 138-140.

decision-maker is neutral and passive, and is charged solely with the responsibility of deciding the case; (2) the parties themselves develop and present the evidence and arguments on which the decision will be based; (3) the proceeding is concentrated, uninterrupted and otherwise designed to emphasize the clash of opposing evidence and arguments presented by the parties; and (4) the parties have equal opportunities to present and argue their cases to the decision-maker.

1. The Need for a Passive Decision-Maker

The most fundamental principle of the adversary system is its insistence upon strictly separating the active function of investigating and gathering evidence from the more passive function of considering the evidence and deciding the case. The theory behind the need for this separation is the belief that performance of the former function necessarily taints the latter: decision-makers who gather the evidence lose their impartiality by reason of their active investigatory role in the case.

The root of the problem, in the words of an often-quoted American Bar Association (ABA) Committee Report on the adversary system, is the "natural human tendency to judge too swiftly in terms of the familiar that which is not yet fully known."[4] We all have a natural urge to impose order on chaos by evaluating and categorizing information as we hear it. But decision-makers are under special pressure to do so, since they must decide the case. The result is a strong inclination in the decision-maker early on — while the information is still being gathered — to start theorizing about what the evidence means. Even passive decision-makers may engage in preliminary theorizing. But decision-makers who actively investigate cannot avoid doing so. An investigator cannot possibly determine what questions to ask or what direction to take the investigation next without first assessing the meaning of the information that is already known.[5]

The main danger of preliminary theorizing is that preliminary theories will become fixed, permanent theories long before they should. As the ABA Committee Report explains, "what starts as a preliminary diagnosis designed to direct the inquiry tends, quickly and imperceptibly, to become a fixed conclusion, as all that confirms the diagnosis makes a strong imprint on the mind, while all that runs counter to it is received with diverted attention." The biasing effects of preliminary theorizing are magnified when the investigator controls *what further* evidence will be investigated — as would be the case if the investigator is also the judge. Ego investment in a preliminary theory provides a strong unconscious motivation to nudge the investigation in the direction of information that confirms that theory, and away from information that conflicts with it.[6]

---

4 *Professional Responsibility: Report of the Joint Conference*, 44 A.B.A.J. 1159 (1958), quoted in Lon Fuller, *The Forms and Limits of Adjudication*, 92 HARV. L. REV. 353, 382-85 (1978) (emphasis added). *See also* Lon Fuller, "The Adversary System" (Chapter III), in HAROLD BERMAN, ED. TALKS ON AMERICAN LAW, 2D ED. 43-44 (Vintage Books 1971). For further discussion of the theory of the adversary system, see STEVEN LANDSMAN, READINGS ON ADVERSARIAL JUSTICE: THE AMERICAN APPROACH TO ADJUDICATION (American Bar Association Section on Litigation) (West 1988); MONROE FREEDMAN, UNDERSTANDING LAWYERS' ETHICS, 4TH ED. 13-42 (Matthew Bender 2010).

5 As Professor Damaska has observed, "You cannot decide which facts matter unless you have already selected, at least tentatively, applicable decisional standards. But most of the time you cannot properly understand these legal standards without relating them to the factual situation of the case." Mirjan Damaska, *Presentation of Evidence and Factfinding Precision*, 123 U.PA. L.REV. 1083, 1087 (1975).

6 Some decision-maker bias is counteracted by a system in which an investigator (usually also a member of the judiciary) investigates the case and delivers the evidence produced to judges who will decide the case. However, if the effect just related is correct, the dossier compiled by the investigator for the judges, while not a final decision, is likely to be similarly skewed.

2. Party Presentation of Evidence and Arguments

Proponents of an adversary system believe that the only way to avoid the skewing effects of the investigative role is to take the responsibility for investigation away from the decision-maker and give it to the parties themselves. Doing so relieves the decision-maker of any need for preliminary theorizing. The decision-maker can relax and simply follow the parties' presentations of the evidence.

But giving the responsibility of investigation to the parties has another beneficial effect: it improves the quality of the decision-making. It does so in two important ways.

First, party investigation increases the amount of information available to the decision-maker. It gives the responsibility of gathering it to those who have the greatest incentive to develop the evidence in their favor. Moreover, the parties have only half the total job a single investigator would have, since they need only concentrate on the evidence in their favor. Second, party presentation assures that the *full potential weight and value* of the evidence will be explored. It is simply impossible for a single investigator to develop in his or her mind, simultaneously and with equal force, completely contradictory theories of a case, and then to maintain those theories in balance until the end of the investigation. While some people are better at this than others, no single person can hold the opposing positions on an issue as well as the opposing parties themselves. Similarly, the weight and value a decision-maker gives to evidence are often affected by *how* the decision-maker first became acquainted with that evidence. Evidence stumbled across in random pieces is not likely to have as strong an impression on the mind as evidence that is presented forthrightly as a logical and coherent whole. Allowing the parties to prepare and present all the evidence in its best light neutralizes the random factor of how the investigator-decision-maker might have encountered that evidence when it first came to light.

The second benefit of placing the burden of investigation and presentation of evidence on the parties is that it promotes the *appearance* of fairness. This is a crucial factor if the stage at which evidence is officially gathered is to be public, as all trials are in the United States. In a public trial, the active involvement of a decision-maker in the investigation and presentation of the evidence can create the appearance that the decision-maker has prejudged the case. An example of this, which often arises in the trial of cases, is where a witness's testimony at trial contradicts an earlier statement given by the witness. There are several different theories about what this could mean. It could be anything from a simple misunderstanding or lapse in thought to a deliberate lie. One has difficulty imagining a series of questions adequately exploring the issue with the witness that would not communicate a preliminary judgment about the contradiction. The investigating official might "bear down" on the witness, pressing the witness for an explanation, but this would convey the impression that the judge doubts the truth of the witness's testimony. Or, more likely, the interrogating judge might *not* "bear down" on the witness in an effort to maintain the appearance of impartiality. But this would convey the impression of a judgment that the contradiction is not important. It is one thing for the parties, the jury or the public to see a *party's lawyer* take one or the other approach and thus convey one or the other impression. But if the *judge* does it, such action communicates the appearance of prejudging the evidence even if no such prejudgment is meant to be communicated.[7]

---

7   This final point shows why active judicial development of evidence is problematic even when the important decision-maker, the jury, remains passive. Juries generally want to do the right thing. Since they cannot depend on the parties before them to give them unbiased advice, they are particularly sensitive to

3.   Structuring the Trial to Induce and Sustain a Clash of Opposing Partisan Views of the Case

The Function of the Adversarial Clash   The simple fact of party presentation of opposing versions and interpretations of the evidence results in a clash before the passive decision-maker. But the clash is more than a by-product of partisan presentations. It is an essential element of adversary procedure. Partisan presentation of opposing viewpoints serves to counteract the tendency toward premature decision-making noted earlier. As the ABA Report notes:

> The [presentations and] arguments of counsel hold the case, as it were, in suspension between two opposing interpretations of it. While the proper classification of the case is thus kept unresolved, there is time to explore all of its peculiarities and nuances.

Structuring the Adversarial Clash   This "suspending" effect is emphasized by the structure of the adversary trial, which requires that the parties' presentations of evidence and arguments alternate. As will be described shortly, each segment of the trial has its plaintiff's part and its defendant's part and the presentations follow shortly after each other.[8] Within a single segment of the trial, "direct examination" of a witness by the proponent of that evidence is followed immediately by "cross examination" by the opponent. The result of this alternating structure is that any proffered analysis of evidence from one side that seems appealing will be followed shortly by a competing view. The clash of competing views of the case is sustained up to the point of jury deliberation, when jury instructions include party-provided summaries of each side's principal contentions, first the plaintiff's and then the defendant's.

"Immediacy" of the Clash of Evidence and Argument   Another important feature of the adversary trial serves to heighten and sustain the clash of evidence. This is the general preference for "immediate" oral evidence and argument rather than "mediate" written evidence and argument. Rules of evidence generally exclude written and other secondary versions of witness observations as "hearsay," thus requiring that the original source of the evidence come to court and testify personally at the trial.[9] Although hearsay is excluded in large part because it is not as reliable as first-hand oral evidence, it is no coincidence that conflicting "immediate" oral first-hand evidence also presents a sharper clash than conflicting written or other secondary evidence.[10] Moreover, the unreliability of hearsay is directly linked to the need for a first-hand adversarial clash. It is mistrusted precisely because the person who uttered it was not subject to a first-hand confrontation in the form of cross examination.[11]

The fact that the parties themselves present and examine the evidence heightens the immediacy of the clash of opposing viewpoints as well. Questions to the witness are

---

any indications from the judge as to what is the right way for them to decide the case. A "solution" to the appearance-of-bias problem might be to exclude the public from the stage of proceedings at which the "raw" facts are gathered and present publicly only a "sanitized" version of the facts. That is not an option in the U.S. system, which generally requires that all judicial proceedings be public. Moreover, it does not eliminate the effect that the appearance of unfairness would have on the parties, lawyers, witnesses or anyone else involved in the closed proceeding.

8   *See infra* pp. 92-109.

9   *See* discussion of evidence law *infra*, pp. 109-115.

10   JOHN MERRYMAN, THE CIVIL LAW TRADITION, 3D ED. 114 (Stanford U. Press 2007). It should be noted that a large part of the original reason for orality of evidence in the common law trial was that juries were often illiterate and would be unable to read written evidence.

11   *See infra* p. 112.

not filtered through a judge or other state official, but are put to the witness directly by the lawyers for the parties. In most cases, the most dramatic first-hand clash of competing views of the evidence comes when direct examination of a party by the party's own lawyer is followed by cross examination of that party by the opposing party's lawyer.

The adversary trial's emphasis on immediacy is not restricted to the *content* of oral testimony, but also takes into account the *manner* in which the witnesses testify. It is acceptable and even expected that a fact-finder (judge or jury) will consider nonverbal clues to credibility that a witness's demeanor on the stand might disclose. This cannot be done with written evidence. This point is emphasized constantly by appellate courts. Even with the aid of verbatim transcripts on appeal, appellate courts will defer to the trial court's evaluation of the evidence in recognition of the trial judge's first-hand opportunity to observe the witnesses and to consider the evidence in the context of a living trial rather than upon a "cold paper record."[12]

Concentrated Hearing The clash of opposing views is also heightened by the use of a continuous and concentrated trial. All the evidence is ready and the persons needed to present it and finally decide the case (judge, parties, jury, lawyers and witnesses) are gathered together in one place. The trial continues uninterrupted until final decision of the case. If the trial were scheduled discontinuously with hearings spread out over several weeks or months, the clash would be greatly reduced. Scheduling the trial as one continuous hearing is also necessary to accommodate the jury, which would likely forget what it had heard if called back for a few hours on scattered days over a span of several weeks. But even trials before the judge alone without a jury are often scheduled continuously. Judges often comment on how the trial's continuous nature and other adversarial features assist them in keeping an open mind throughout the trial. Indeed, consistent with adversary theory, many judges, upon hearing that the case will be tried to them without a jury, make a point of learning as little as possible about the case so as not to prejudge it and to gain the maximum benefits from the clash of adversary presentations of the parties.[13]

4. Structuring the Trial to Assure Equality of Adversarial Opportunities

Equality of "Forensic Arms" It is inherent in the notion of party presentation that the parties' opportunities to present evidence and persuade the decision-maker should be equal. Such "equality of forensic arms," as it is sometimes called, is fundamental to adversary theory. It applies in both civil and criminal cases in the Anglo-American tradition. Thus, the prosecution and defense in a criminal case face identical limitations on presentation of evidence and argument. The prosecution sits at the same kind of table on the same level as the defense and wears the same ordinary clothes as the defense attorney. Whatever prerogatives the prosecutor may enjoy outside the courtroom, they disappear when the prosecutor appears in court in a criminal trial.[14]

---

12 *Gasperini v. Center for the Humanities*, 518 U.S. 415, 421 (1996). The narrow scope of appellate review of facts in the U.S. is discussed in Chapter V, pp. 170-171.

13 In a system of concentrated and continuous trials, the lawyers must prepare their cases thoroughly and completely before the trial starts, since they will be able to make only limited mid-trial corrections.

14 In a civil case, both parties have equal access to the means of investigating and preparing the case for trial. In a criminal case, the prosecution has the investigative resources of the police at its disposal in preparing its case, which the defendant does not have. However, other factors compensate for the imbalance somewhat. First, the defense has the right of compulsory process to subpoena any witness it wants who has relevant testimony (including the victim, a member of the police force or someone else in

Detailed Procedural Rules Administered in an Insular Way   We have already discussed how evidence and trial procedure rules serve to create, heighten and sustain a clash of opposing evidence and arguments. Here we should note how the *nature* of these rules and the *manner in which they are administered* serve to promote equality of adversarial opportunity. First, the procedural and evidence rules applicable to an adversary trial are detailed and relatively rigid.[15] The more detailed and rigid such rules are, the less judicial discretion there is to limit what evidence the parties are allowed to present and how they present it. Second, these procedural and evidence rules are administered in an insular and episodic fashion unrelated to the overall context of the case. This is in part because the rules are detailed and specific and in part because of traditional understandings of the judicial role. It is also a matter of necessity. Given that the parties are responsible for developing the facts at trial, trial judges will usually have only the sketchiest idea of what the facts of the case are. Such a "veil of ignorance" also makes it a virtual necessity that the judge rule in an insular fashion.[16]

This final point on reducing judicial discretion to control what evidence is presented brings us full circle to the first point made with regard to adversary theory. The reason for seeking to limit judicial discretion is to lessen the likelihood of the judge using a premature theory about the merits of the case to control what further evidence is presented, thus skewing the entire direction of the search for evidence. As discussed earlier, this is the most serious danger of judges actively investigating the evidence.[17]

Consistent with this theory, the best trial judges in the U.S. are not those who have the fullest understanding of the facts of the case. The best judges are those who are most knowledgeable about the *rules governing evidence and procedure*, and who administer those rules in an evenhanded fashion *regardless of which side seems to have the better case on the merits*. Trial lawyers in the United States often comment with favor on judges whose ruling on each objection in a trial is made independently of the relative balance of the evidence in the case. Thus, the judge's job in a jury trial might be likened to the job of the referee at a football game, whose job it is to enforce the rules to assure that the sides compete fairly and — to return again to the first point on adversary theory — certainly *not* to kick the ball.[18]

B. Juries

It is possible to have an adversary system without juries and to have juries in a non-adversary system. However, the jury fits well in an adversary system because it is the quintessential passive decision-maker. All the jury does is take in the evidence and decide the case. It has no knowledge of the facts of the case and no right to ask questions, to call witnesses, or otherwise direct the examination of the evidence. Before

---

the prosecution "camp"), but the prosecutor may not compel the defendant to testify or even to answer questions informally because of the privilege against "self-incrimination" guaranteed by the Constitution. Second, the Constitution requires the prosecutor to disclose all exculpatory evidence to the defense that the police might uncover. Finally, the defendant is free to use the services of a private detective and many public defender offices (which represent indigent defendants) have private investigators on their staff. *See generally* Chapter VIII (criminal procedure rights of defendants).

15 The content of evidence rules is discussed *infra* pp. 109-115.

16 Neither the judge nor the jury has any comprehensive summary or dossier of all the facts in the case before the trial starts.

17 *See supra* p. 81. *See also People v. Retamozzo*, 802 N.Y.S.2d 426 (App.Div. 2005) (judge asked too many questions of defendant and prosecution witnesses; conviction reversed).

18 For a work that explores connections between adversarial litigation and more general attitudes about the purposes and functions of a legal system. *See* MIRJAN R. DAMASKA, EVIDENCE LAW ADRIFT (Yale U. Press 1997).

proceeding in the next section to a detailed description of the adversary jury trial, we should examine the institution of the jury more generally.

1. Some History and Comparative Comments

History The historical origins of the jury are obscure and, in any event, a complete history is not needed to understand the modern institution.[19] The jury's origins are considered by many to have been in France, where some form of jury trial was in evidence during the reign of Louis the Pious, circa 829 A.D. It was imported to England by the Normans after the invasion of 1066 and was firmly established as a part of English legal procedure by the twelfth century, probably in reaction to the decline of the medieval forms of procedure, such as trial by battle, ordeal and wager.[20] By the 1400s, the modern characteristic of the jury as a passive and impartial decider of the facts was well established. By 1670, the jury was established as an institution independent of the king and the king's judges, when in *Bushel's Case*[21] it was held that a juror could not be fined or imprisoned for acquitting a defendant. The last characteristic of the modern jury — the need to decide the case based solely on the evidence produced at trial and not on extrajudicial knowledge — was established by the 1700s. The institution of the jury was exported to the United States by English colonists and has been a fundamental part of our jurisprudence ever since despite its decline in recent years England. Right to trial by jury is guaranteed by the 7th Amendment for civil cases and by Article III and the 6th Amendment for criminal cases.[22]

A Comparative Perspective At one point in Europe, inspired by the French Revolution, juries existed in many civil law countries. Today, they have largely disappeared in those countries, except for a recent resurgence in Russia and Spain.[23] But even in civil law countries, the participation of lay persons in deciding cases in court is quite common. In France and Austria, a jury trial of sorts is allowed in some criminal cases and in Germany, there are mixed courts consisting of both law and lay judges. Somewhat parallel to the policies behind juries in the Anglo-American tradition, use of lay judges in these countries is designed to increase the diversity of viewpoints on the proper resolution of cases, to spread the awesome responsibility for decision-making, and to bring a common sense of justice to the legal system.

However, in few systems do lay decision-makers have the degree of independence enjoyed by juries in the Anglo-American tradition. Continental lay judges are fewer in number and are semi-professional, in that they are usually screened for suitability (often being chosen or nominated by a local legislative body) to sit for terms of a year or more. Almost as important, they deliberate together with the legally educated judge and must,

---

19 *See* Stephen Yeazell, *The New Jury and Ancient Jury Conflict*, 1990 U.Chi.Legal Forum 87 *and* Thomas Green, Verdict According to Conscience: Perspectives on the English Criminal Jury Trial, 1200-1800 (U. Chicago Press 1985) (histories of the jury). *See also* John Guinther, The Jury in America 1-35 (Facts on File, N.Y. 1988).

20 *See generally* Theodore F. T. Plucknett, A Concise History of the Common Law (1956) and William S. Holdsworth, I A History of English Law (1956). *See also* Stephen A. Landsman, *The Civil Jury in America: Scenes from an Unappreciated History*, 44 Hastings L.J. 579, 582-587 (1993).

21 124 Eng. Rep. 1006 (1670). The facts behind the decision in *Bushel's Case* are recounted in Guinther, *supra* note 19, at 24-27.

22 The precise scope of the constitutional right to trial by jury is set on in Chapter VII, pp. 243-244, for civil cases and in Chapter VIII, p. 309, for criminal cases.

23 Stephen C. Thaman, The Resurrection of Trial by Jury in Russia, 32 Stanford J. Int'l Law 61 (1995) and Stephen C. Thaman, Spain Returns to Trial by Jury, 21 Hastings Int'l & Comp. L. Rev. 241 (1998).

together with the professional judge, justify their decision in writing.[24] By contrast, the Anglo-American jury numbers up to 12, is chosen from a randomly selected pool drawn from the citizenry at large to decide a single case, deliberates separately from the judge in secret, and usually does not need to justify its decision.[25]

2. The Division of Labor Between Judge and Jury

Fact vs. Law Division Despite their considerable independence, the common law jury does not have the right to decide all the issues in a case. In general, the judge decides issues of law and the jury decides issues of fact. Even on issues of fact, a jury is not free to come to any conclusion it wants. Except for a verdict of acquittal (not guilty) in a criminal case, the trial judge or an appellate court has the power to set aside the verdict if there is no substantial evidence to support it.[26] This power of the trial judge is not an exception to the general rule that judges determine only issues of law. Whether there is any substantial evidence to support a jury's fact-finding is considered to be an issue of law. Stated another way, the question of whether there is enough evidence *for the jury to decide* a fact question is a question of law for the judge.

It is sometimes difficult to tell what is an issue of fact and what is an issue of law. So-called "mixed fact-law" questions arise. In jury trials, the most common mixed questions are issues of "law application" — where a legal standard must be applied to the facts of the case. For example, the question of how fast the defendant was driving at the time of an automobile accident is a pure fact issue clearly appropriate for the jury to decide. It is a mixed fact-law question whether the defendant's driving that speed under the road and weather conditions the jury finds existed constitutes "negligence," thereby entitling the plaintiff to recover. Juries are usually allowed to decide law application questions and would certainly be permitted to decide the negligence question posed. If the law application question is of a type that requires uniform application, such as applying a standard provision of a contract to determine whether there has been a breach of that contract, it is more likely to be deemed an issue of law. On the other hand, if the contract provision is one that laypersons are capable of applying, the jury will be allowed to decide the question.[27]

Jury Nullification Modern juries are told that they must accept the law as given to them by the judge, determine what the relevant facts are, apply the law to those facts and in that manner decide the case. Generally, a verdict at odds with the law will be set

---

24 For example, German lay judges are elected for one-year terms by local legislatures and are supposed to be the "most suitable" in terms of "proven judgment and honorableness." They also deliberate with the professional judges. Not surprisingly, their rate of disagreement with the professional judges is low, around 1.4% *See* Gerhard Casper and Hans Zeisel, *Lay Judges in German Criminal Courts*, 1 J. LEGAL STUDIES 138 (1972).

25 Modern-day juries of comparable independence are the Russian and Spanish juries. *See supra* note 23.

26 See discussion *infra*, p. 108.

27 *See Nunez v. Superior Oil Co.*, 572 F.2d 1119 (5th Cir. 1978) (discussing the fact-law distinction and allowing a jury to decide whether a contract provision excusing failure to pay royalties if that failure was "justified" would include a mistake in paperwork); *City of Monterey v. Del Monte Dunes at Monterey, Ltd.*, 526 U.S. 687 (1999) (question whether the city's decision to reject a particular development plan bore a reasonable relationship to its proffered justifications was properly submitted to jury since question was essentially fact-bound in nature). There may be constitutional restraints on what mixed issues are given to a jury. *See United States v. Gaudin*, 515 U.S. 506 (1995) (reversing a conviction for making false statements on a loan application on the ground that it deprived the defendant of his right to trial by jury when the judge rather than the jury decided whether the statements were "material"). *But see Markman v. Westview Instruments, Inc.*, 517 U.S. 370 (1996) (meaning of the word "inventory" in patent claim held an issue of law for the judge in part because of the need for consistency).

aside by the trial judge. However, a jury acquittal in a criminal case is not reviewable on appeal or otherwise. This means that in this one situation juries have the power of "nullification" — the power to acquit a criminal defendant despite clear evidence of guilt. Sometimes jurors may acquit in such circumstances because they do not believe the evidence. But sometimes a jury acquits in the face of compelling evidence of guilt because it disagrees with the law or with its particular application in that case. When a jury does this, it is judging the law as well as the facts and, by refusing to apply the law, the jury is to that extent "nullifying" it.

There is considerable evidence that the 18th century jury that the Framers of the Constitution had in mind had the right to judge, not only the facts, but the law as well.[28] But the modern view is that they do not have that right.[29] Consequently, neither the judge nor the defendant's attorney may inform the jury of this power. Instead, jurors are instructed by the judge (1) that it would be a violation of their oath as jurors to ignore the court's instructions on the law and (2) that, if the evidence demonstrates beyond a reasonable doubt that the defendant committed the offense charged, they must convict regardless of their personal feelings. However, an acquittal is final and cannot be appealed or otherwise set aside. This is because it would entail ordering a new trial, and the Constitution's double jeopardy clause prevents the defendant from being tried twice for the same offense.[30] So, even if the jury violates the judge's instruction and acquits, the acquittal stands. Because of this, juries have the *de facto power* to nullify. However, they do *not* have the *legal right* to do so.

There are no statistics on how often jury nullification occurs, nor could there be, since the jury is not required to give any reason for its verdict and the question whether the evidence for conviction was compelling is a matter of judgment. When what appears to be nullification takes place, it often attracts great attention from the press, and this makes its frequency seem greater than it probably is. Moreover, the traditional instructions juries are given emphasizing their duty to follow the law as given to them by the judge tend to assure that nullification will take place only in a few extreme cases.[31]

In civil cases, the jury is subject to greater control by the judge and must often give reasons for its verdict through the use of "special verdict" forms or by answering questions about the reasons for its decision.[32] Yet juries can still express their resentment of a legal rule by using their broad power to determine contested issues of *fact*. Indeed, juries can have an effect on the development of the law by consistently and over a long period of time by finding disputed facts a particular way to avoid an unjust legal rule. For example, in *Hoffman v. Jones*, the Florida case changing state law from contributory to comparative negligence, the court supported its decision in part by noting

---

28   *See* Chief Justice John Jay's charge to the jury in *Georgia v. Brailsford*, 3 U.S. (3 Dall.) 1, 4 (1794) and the dissent in *Sparf v. United States*, 156 U.S. 51 (1895). *See generally* Alan Scheflin & Jon Van Dyke, *Jury Nullification: The Contours of a Controversy*, 43 LAW & CONTEMP. PROBS. 51 (1980).

29   *Sparf, supra*.

30   For more detail on double jeopardy, *see* Chapter VII, pp. 315-318.

31   In *United States v. Krzyske*, 836 F.2d 1013, 1021 (6th Cir. 1988), jurors specifically asked the trial judge to explain nullification to them. The trial judge's decision to be less than candid in answer was upheld on appeal. For different views on whether to tell the jury of its nullification power, *see* David C. Brody, *Sparf and Dougherty Revisited: Why the Court Should Instruct the Jury of Its Nullification Right*, 33 AM. CRIM. L. REV. 89 (1995) and Jack. B. Weinstein, *Considering Jury "Nullification": When May or Should a Jury Reject the Law and Do Justice*, 30 AM. CRIM. L. REV. 239 (1993). *See also* Nancy J. King, *Silencing Nullification Advocacy Inside the Jury Room and Outside the Courtroom*, 65 U. CHI. L. REV. 433 (1998) and Darryl K. Brown, *Jury Nullification Within the Rule of Law*, 81 MINN. L. REV. 1149 (1997).

32   *See infra* p. 107.

one scholar's observation that there is "something basically wrong with a rule of law that is so contrary to the settled convictions of the lay community that laymen will almost always refuse to enforce it, even when solemnly told to do so by a judge whose instructions they have sworn to follow."[33]

3. Characteristics of the Modern Jury

Jury Pools and Exemptions from Jury Service The traditional source for jury pools or the "jury venire" — the group of prospective jurors from which jurors are selected — has been voter registration lists.[34] However, not everyone registers to vote — usually fewer than 50% of the population in the United States votes in elections — so most jurisdictions use both voter lists and driver's license lists. In a country that relies so heavily on the automobile, driver's license lists will likely include over 95% of all adults. Whatever list is used for the pool, jurors are selected for the pool at random.

Traditionally, important professionals and others whose services are thought valuable to society, such as physicians, have been exempt from jury duty. Federal law exempts from federal jury service employees of police and fire departments as well as public officials.[35] Lawyers are often exempt from jury service on the theory that their legal knowledge would have a disruptive effect on jury deliberations. However, the trend in recent years has been to abolish all exemptions from jury duty, including any exemption for lawyers or even judges. At the present time, 27 states have no exemptions based on the prospective juror's profession and seven more have only limited exemptions.[36] The idea has emerged that the right of a citizen to a representative jury for decision of court cases overrides any other societal interest and that the burdens and the civic education benefits of jury service should be as widely shared as possible. The concern that lawyers on juries would create problems is thought to be overstated, since the most important work of juries is in resolving factual issues, a task for which legal training is largely irrelevant and, some argue, a detriment.[37]

Avoiding Jury Service Jury duty is mandatory on all those called to serve, but it does not arise very often for the average person. Frequency of service varies with the area of the country, but for a registered voter, serving more than once in ten years is unusual in most areas and many people go their whole life without ever being called. For the average case, jury duty is not that onerous and many people say that they find performance of their "civic duty" to be interesting. Also, a system of "one day, one trial," used in 40% of the states, has made service much easier. Under this system, jurors are in the jury venire for only one day. If they are chosen for a trial, they serve in that trial to conclusion, but if not, they need not return. But some people for one reason or another try to avoid being placed on a jury. Failure to comply with a jury subpoena is contempt of court and is punishable by fine or imprisonment. A prospective juror's statements of an inability to be impartial will be probed by the judge with some disbelief if no concrete reason can be offered. Obvious non-cooperation by a juror may lead one or the other

---

33 *See Hoffman v. Jones*, Appendix, p. A7.

34 "Venire" comes from the original name of the writ used to command the sheriff to summon jurors. Called a *venire facias*, it meant literally "that you cause to come." In federal court, the jury pool is called the "jury wheel."

35 28 U.S.C.A. §1863(b)(5).

36 Source: Center for Jury Studies, National Center for State Courts (1993). Conviction for a felony is still a universal disqualification. *See* ABA STANDARDS RELATING TO JUROR USE AND MANAGEMENT, Part A, Standard 4.

37 In one case with which the author is familiar, a sitting Circuit Court judge of the state of Michigan served as a juror in a criminal case. No problems were reported.

counsel to dismiss the juror from service through a peremptory challenge. Jurors may be excused for "undue hardship or extreme inconvenience."[38]

Diversity of Jury Pools   Inclusive methods for creating jury pools are designed to increase the diversity of juries selected from it. As discussed later, diversity of viewpoints is a key to the success of the group dynamic of jury decision-making.[39] In addition, racial and ethnic, as well as economic and social diversity, are essential in promoting fairness and the appearance of it in trials. Thus, federal law requires "procedures designed to ensure random selection of a fair cross-section of the persons residing in the community" where the court convenes for all federal court juries, and states have similar requirements as well.[40] But sometimes fair procedures do not produce representative pools. In a recent murder case involving the death penalty, a federal court found that higher non-response and undeliverable rates for jury summonses sent to prospective jurors in minority communities had resulted in a yield of black prospective jurors (3%) that was less than half that of the black population of the district (7%). To remedy the problem, the court ordered that, for every jury summons that was undeliverable or otherwise did not produce a response, the clerk was to send a new summons to a different prospective juror in the same postal zip code as that of the undeliverable or not-responded-to summons. However, this plan was disapproved by the appellate court.[41]

Educational Levels of Jurors   Beyond the ability to read and write the English language, there are no educational requirements for being a juror. It is not uncommon for a professor with a Ph.D. to be seated next to a high-school dropout. Each of their votes on the jury counts the same, though the professor may perhaps be more persuasive with other jurors during deliberations.

Because of the lack of any educational requirements, concern has been voiced about juries not understanding complex cases. It is claimed that some cases are impossible for *any* jury to understand, and the federal Courts of Appeal are split on the issue of whether there is a "complexity exception" to the constitutional right to a civil jury trial in federal court.[42] "Blue ribbon" juries, juries made up solely of college graduates, for example, are a possibility, but they are controversial and constitutional doubts have been raised about them.[43] Another suggestion is to increase the amount of juror pay (and charge it to the litigants) so as to attract the better-educated juror.

---

38   28 U.S.C.A. §1863(b)(5) (applicable to federal jury service).

39   *See infra* p. 122.

40   28 U.S.C.A. §1863(b)(3).

41   The non-deliverable rate was 5.8% in wealthier towns, compared to 18.4% in towns with substantial minority populations, and the non-response rate was 23% in minority communities and only 7.6% in more wealthy areas. *United States v. Green*, 389 F.Supp.2d 29 (E.D. Mass. 2005), *rev'd sub nom. In re United States*, 426 F.3d 1 (1st Cir. 2005). *See also United States v. Ovalle*, 136 F.3d 1092 (6th Cir. 1998) (disapproving remedy for under-representation of minorities of removing one in five whites from the pool).

42   *Compare United States Financial Securities Litigation*, 609 F.2d 411 (9th Cir. 1979) (there is no complexity exception to jury trial right in complex securities case) *with In Re Japanese Electronic Products Antitrust Litigation*, 631 F.2d 1069, 1073-74 (3d Cir. 1980)(jury trial request denied in complicated antitrust case where there were millions of documents and jury would be required to analyze Japanese market conditions and business practices over a 30-year period and make price comparisons of many electronic products). These cases and the general problem of jurors' abilities to understand truly complex cases are discussed in SAUL M. KASSIN AND LAWRENCE S. WRIGHTSMAN, THE AMERICAN JURY ON TRIAL: PSYCHOLOGICAL PERSPECTIVES (Hemisphere Publishing, N.Y. 1988).

43   A review of proposals and a general discussion of some of the potential constitutional and other objections is found in Rita Sutton, *A More Rational Approach to Complex Civil Litigation in the Federal Courts: The Special Jury*, 1990 U.CHI.LEGAL FORUM 575.

But many believe the jury's true capacity for accurate fact-finding has not yet been fully tapped. They point out that many traditional jury trial procedures are inconsistent with modern learning theory. One example is the procedure for jury instruction. Jurors traditionally have been given instructions on the law they must apply to the case only at the very end of the trial. The result is that they listen to the evidence throughout the trial without knowing which parts of it are important for deciding the case and which parts are not. And then, when the instructions are finally given, it has been traditional for the judge to read them to the jury rather than to give jurors a written copy. A major effort in recent years has been made to conduct psychological research on the effects of particular jury trial procedures and to seek to change those procedures that interfere with comprehension.[44]

Juror Pay Jurors receive pay from the court for their service, but it is not an amount that would make them rich. At the present time in the federal court system, jurors are paid $40 per day, but in some states, they are paid as little as $5 per day. Whether jurors continue to receive pay from their employers varies. All government employees continue to receive their normal pay. Some states require private employers to continue to pay regular wages or a portion of regular wages to jurors for a certain number of days of jury service.[45] In states without this requirement, the issue of employee pay depends on the agreement between employer and employee. Where employees are unionized, collective bargaining agreements commonly require continuation of employee pay during jury service at least for a limited period. For employees without any of these protections or for people who run their own businesses, jury duty in a trial that goes on for weeks or months can be financially costly. However, statistics indicate that only 25% of all trials in federal court last more than one week and only 0.6% last more than 30 days. Moreover, the prospect of serious financial consequences constitutes "undue hardship" that can excuse the juror from service.

Avoiding Prejudicial Influences When involved in a case, jurors are usually not sequestered (segregated from the public) except while in attendance at trial. They are usually allowed to go home at the end of the day with the admonition that they are not to talk with anyone about the case. But trial judges have the discretion to order any procedures necessary to shelter them from the effect of publicity. In a notorious case, jurors may be sequestered in a hotel during the trial (or at least during deliberations), their access to television or newspapers may be censored and they may be transported to and from court in a van with its windows taped over to prevent them from seeing newspapers on newsstands or signs of protesters. Pre-trial publicity can also make it difficult to find a jury that has not already heard about the facts of the case and formed an opinion. It is not a disqualification that the juror has heard or read about the case. It is only if they have formed an opinion about it that would make it impossible for them to be impartial that they will be rejected.[46]

---

44 For an excellent collection of such changes and proposed changes, the arguments pro and con and citations to the relevant literature, *see* G. THOMAS MUNSTERMAN, PAULA L. HANNAFORD AND G. MARC WHITEHEAD, EDS, JURY TRIAL INNOVATIONS (Nat'l Center for State Courts, Washington, D.C. 1997).

45 *See, e.g.,* Conn. Gen. Stat. §51-247 (requiring employers to pay regular wages for the first 5 days of jury service) and Mass. Gen. Laws Ann. ch. 234A §48 (2010) (first 3 days). *See also Dean v. Gadsden Times*, 412 U.S. 543 (1973) (holding such statutes constitutional). There are also penalties against employers who discharge employees because of jury service. *See* 28 U.S.C.A. §1875 and ROTHSTEIN ET AL., HORNBOOK ON EMPLOYMENT LAW §4.31 (West 2005) (similar laws in every state but Montana).

46 *See generally* THOMAS R. MURPHY, GENERVA KAY LOVELAND AND G. THOMAS MUNSTERMAN, A MANUAL FOR MANAGING NOTORIOUS CASES (Nat'l Center for State Courts. Washington, D.C. 1993).

C. The Adversary Jury Trial and the Lawyer's Role in It

We will now move into a relatively detailed description of the stages of the typical adversary jury trial, with special attention paid to the responsibilities of the lawyers for the parties in presenting and arguing the case.[47]

Civil vs. Criminal Jury Trials Most of the examples used for illustration in the description that follows are from a criminal case. However, there is little difference between criminal trial procedure and civil trial procedure that would strike the casual observer. The only obvious difference would be that in the criminal trial, the plaintiff's side is referred to as "the prosecution" (or "the government") and the lawyer appearing on that side is employed by the government rather than by a private party. Other differences between civil and criminal trials that would not be immediately obvious are: (1) in a criminal case the standard of proof is stricter, (2) criminal defendants cannot be compelled to take the stand or otherwise testify against themselves, and (3) there can be no appeal from a jury verdict of acquittal in a criminal case.[48]

Bench Trial Procedure A non-jury trial, called a "bench trial" or "court trial," follows essentially the procedure outlined here for a jury trial. The main differences are that the steps that concern only the jury would be missing and that the lawyers would modify their arguments to suit a professional decision-maker.

Trial Courtroom Setting A diagram of a typical trial courtroom designed for jury trials is set out in the Appendix.[49] The judge's dais or bench is at the highest level and the witness stand is usually at the next highest level. The judge wears a robe, but no wig. The lawyers do not wear any special dress to distinguish them from others in the courtroom. They usually wear business suits. The parties sit at counsel table next to their lawyers, the better to consult with them during the course of the trial. This is even true of the defendant in a criminal case.[50]

1. Jury Selection

Size of the Jury In criminal felony cases in federal court, a jury of 12 is required by court rule.[51] States usually require 12 jurors in criminal cases as well, though as few as 6 is constitutional.[52] Alternate jurors are chosen in case one of the original jurors cannot serve throughout the trial and deliberations. In civil cases, there is more variation in the required size of juries among states, but most states permit 6-person juries. In federal

---

47 For more information on this and other trial techniques of lawyers, *see* STEVEN LUBET, MODERN TRIAL ADVOCACY: ANALYSIS AND PRACTICE, 3D ED. (Nat'l. Inst. for Trial Advocacy 2004); RONALD CARLSON AND EDWARD IMWINKELREID, DYNAMICS OF TRIAL PRACTICE, 2D ED. (West 1995, 1997); THOMAS MAUET, TRIAL TECHNIQUES, 8TH ED. (Aspen 2010); and ROGER HAYDOCK AND JOHN SONSTENG, TRIAL: THEORIES, TACTICS AND TECHNIQUES (West 1991). For an overview of English trial techniques, *see* KEITH EVANS, ADVOCACY AT THE BAR (Blackstone Press Ltd. 1992). On juries, *see* NANCY MARDER, THE JURY PROCESS (Foundation Press 2005); JEFFREY ABRAMSON, WE, THE JURY (Harvard University Press 2000) and D. GRAHAM BURNETT, A TRIAL BY JURY (Vintage 2001).

48 There are major differences between *pre-trial* procedures in civil and criminal cases. *See* Chapter VII, pp. 229-242 (civil cases) and Chapter VIII, pp. 269-276 (criminal cases).

49 *See* p. A33.

50 For a description of the other aspects of trial court procedure, *see* Chapter V, pp. 167-169.

51 Federal Rule of Criminal Procedure 23(b)(1). The parties can agree to fewer and the judge has the power to permit 11 to decide if there is good cause to excuse one of them (illness, etc.) even without such agreement. Whether 12 in the federal system is required as a constitutional matter has never been decided, since a 12-person jury has always been required by statute or court rule.

52 *See* Chapter VIII, p. 309.

civil cases and in some states, the court must seat between 6 and 12 jurors, but chooses no alternates. The result is that many cases are decided by 8 or 9-person juries.[53]

The Jury Selection Process   The purpose of jury selection, sometimes called "voir dire,"[54] is to determine the qualifications of potential members of the jury and to select an impartial jury to try the case. The format used for jury selection varies from jurisdiction to jurisdiction.[55] In almost all jury selections, by the time of trial the jurors have completed and the lawyers have read questionnaires containing basic information about each juror. The panel of prospective jurors or jury venire is usually given some brief introduction to the case for which they are being selected. This is then followed by questions to members of the panel about their qualifications to serve.

In some jurisdictions, only the judge is allowed to address questions to the jurors directly. In such jurisdictions, the lawyers must submit any questions in writing to the judge, who may or may not choose to ask the question. In other jurisdictions, the lawyers are allowed to address the jury venire directly and, after a few general questions from the judge, to ask questions of prospective jurors, either as a group or individually. Ultimately the extent of lawyer participation is up to the discretion of the individual judge in a given case. But as a general rule, federal courts tend to have judge-conducted jury selection, while state courts allow lawyer-conducted selection. However, several states have limited lawyer questioning.

By whatever method information is obtained, indications that a juror is unable or unwilling to hear and decide the case fairly can be the basis for a "challenge for cause" on which the judge must rule. In addition, the lawyers can make "peremptory challenges," which allow them to exclude a certain number of jurors for no reason at all. The number of peremptory challenges allowed varies from one jurisdiction to another, but federal law is typical. For a 12-person jury in federal court in felonies not involving the death penalty, the prosecution has 6 challenges and the defense has 10. In death penalty cases, the prosecution and defense each has 20 challenges.[56]

Trial Lawyer Techniques in Jury Selection   The primary aim of the lawyers for the parties is to select a jury that is as sympathetic to their side as possible. The ability of the lawyers to influence the composition of the jury is limited at best: by invoking challenges for cause (which are rarely granted) and a set number of peremptory challenges. The pool of jurors that one begins with, however, is randomly determined and beyond the lawyer's ability to influence. Though lawyers often say they are going to court to "select a jury," jury selection is really "juror exclusion" and only a limited number can be excluded in most cases.

Lawyers question jurors to discover their likely predisposition toward the case to be tried. This is most often explored by asking them about experiences they or their close

---

53 Federal Rules of Civil Procedure 47-48. As the Advisory Committee Notes to Rule 47 indicate, alternates were abolished because of complaints that they were "required to listen to the evidence but denied the satisfaction of participating in its evaluation." *See* Chapter VII, p. 243.

54 "Voir dire" comes from the Law French and means "to speak the truth." For an explanation of the Law French, *see* http://en.wikipedia.org/wiki/Law_French.

55 "Jurisdiction" as used here means the judicial systems of the states and the federal government.

56 Federal Rule of Criminal Procedure 24(b). England abolished peremptory challenges for prosecutors in 1305 and for the defense in 1988. Although challenges for cause are permitted, they are made in only 1% of cases. *See* Buston, *Challenging and Discharging Jurors*, [1990] CRIM.L.REV. 225. The exercise of peremptory challenges in the United States was essentially unlimited until the Supreme Court prohibited their use to exclude jurors based on their race, ethnic origin or sex. *See* Chapter VIII, p. 310 (criminal cases) and *Edmondson v Leesville Concrete Co.*, 500 U.S. 614 (1991) (civil cases).

friends and relatives have had that are similar to the facts in the case to be tried. Any questions on sensitive private issues are handled at a bench conference, out of the hearing of the public and other jurors.[57] However, peremptory challenges are often made without regard to the answers given by jurors during *voir dire* and may even be decided before questioning begins. Often the decision is based on assumptions about the person's likely predisposition toward the case based on age, address, education, employment and other basic characteristics disclosed on written juror questionnaires — a socio-economic "portrait" of a juror.

Just what assumptions are drawn from basic information varies from one lawyer to another. In general, however, civil plaintiffs and criminal defendants will represent "anti-establishment" points of view and will lean toward younger, lower class, and ethnically diverse jurors while civil defendants and the prosecution in criminal cases will represent the "establishment" and will usually want the opposite kind of juror.[58]

More sophisticated analysis of potential jurors is available from a growing number of professional jury selection consultants, many of them trained in psychology and other social sciences. They will, for a fee, analyze the lawyer's case and construct a profile of the kinds of jurors to retain or strike, often based on community surveys or the use of focus groups. Use of jury consultants has been touted as very successful in some high-profile cases. One was the 1992 Rodney King case where, despite a videotape showing what appeared to be a rather savage beating, state court jurors acquitted Los Angeles policemen of using excessive force on King. Some research indicates limited effectiveness of such "scientific" jury selection techniques.[59]

Following jury selection, the jury is sworn to decide the case impartially and is given some preliminary instructions on the format of the trial.[60] Jurors are told something about the format of the trial and their duties. Most important, they are admonished to keep an open mind and not to discuss the case with anyone (even among themselves) until the evidence, arguments and final instructions have been completed and they have retired to deliberate. Generally, except in the most complex of cases, the jury is not given any instruction at this point on the law of the claim made or offense charged, because of the belief that such instruction would be confusing or incomplete at this point and might interfere with the jury's listening to all the facts.[61]

---

57 A recent issue of concern is the juror's right to privacy. In one case, a juror objected to a questionnaire that asked such things as her religious preference, her political party affiliation, television shows she watched, whether she classified herself as a political conservative, liberal or moderate, her typical reading material and whether she belonged o the National Rifle Association. *See* David Weinstein, *Protecting A Juror's Right to Privacy: Constitutional Constraints and Policy Options*, 70 TEMPLE L.REV. 1 (1997) (exploring how to protect juror privacy while safeguarding a defendant's right to a fair trial and the public's right of access to court proceedings). In 1998, the American Bar Association added a "Standard on Jury Privacy" to its Standards Relating to Juror Use and Management.

58 As noted earlier, peremptory challenges that appear to be based on race, sex or national origin can be contested and will be allowed only if the judge is convinced that the lawyer has a non-discriminatory reason for excluding the juror. *See supra* note 56 and Chapter VIII, p. 310.

59 *See* GUINTHER, *supra* note 19, at 55-58; KASSIN & WRIGHTSMAN, *supra* note 42, at 57-62.

60 A typical form of the oath taken is as follows: "Each of you do solemnly swear (or affirm) that, in this action now before the court, you will justly decide the questions submitted to you, that, unless you are discharged by the court from further deliberation, you will render a true verdict, and that you will render your verdict only on the evidence introduced and in accordance with the instructions of the court, so help you God."

61 This is changing somewhat, however. *See supra* p. 91.

2. Opening Statements

The Form and Role of Opening Statements After the jury is selected, sworn and seated, the lawyers are permitted to make "opening statements" to the jury. The purpose of the opening statements is to allow the parties to outline the facts in the case and to introduce the jury to their claims or defenses. The evidence in the case will not come before the jury in a clear chronological order, but in a disjointed way dictated by the order in which witnesses testify. Thus, the opening statement is an opportunity to give jurors a clear exposition of the entire "story" of the case. Each side, of course, will have a different "story" to tell. The task facing the lawyers in opening is to set out the story of their case without argument in a way that will appeal to the jury.

Jurors are told that an opening statement is not evidence, only "a guide to the evidence," but studies show just how important a "guide" it is. Research on the decision-making process of jurors shows that they decide cases by constructing a "story" of how the case happened and testing it for accuracy against similar true "stories" from their own lives or experience. Since the opening statement is the opportunity for the lawyers to present their side's "story" in a coherent manner, it is a particularly powerful tool of persuasion.[62]

Lawyer's Approach to Opening Statement The best opening statement will usually present the facts in chronological order. In whatever order presented, the lawyer is supposed to be limited largely to reciting the *facts* the lawyer plans to prove rather than arguing the case. Indeed, one of the few objections allowed during an opening statement is that "counsel is arguing." Nonetheless, each side is permitted to outline its contentions with regard to the evidence so that the jury clearly understands the basic positions of the parties. This may involve some discussion of the applicable law as well. In a criminal case, for example, defense counsel will usually want to spend some time introducing the notion of "reasonable doubt." Clearly, the line between impermissible "argument" and "introducing" one's "contentions" or "position" to the jury is not a clear one.

Because what lawyers say in opening statements is not evidence, but only a guide to the evidence, it has been traditional for lawyers to preface each description of the evidence with the phrase "the evidence will show" or "the prosecution intends to prove that . . . ," instead of just telling the story. Indeed, some judges believe that this is legally required. The modern trend is that it is permissible and much more effective for lawyers to simply tell the story as it will come out. For example an excerpt from an opening in a criminal case might sound like this:

> On Tuesday, May 9th, the defendant John Smith had been drinking beer with his buddies for about four hours at the Dew Drop Inn. At around 10PM, he left his friends at the bar and drove up to the Grand Hotel. He stopped his car in the loading zone and left the motor running. Then, with a loaded pistol in his belt, he walked into the lobby of the hotel and went directly to the hotel night clerk's desk. He passed a note he had written to the night clerk. In the note, he said "I've got a gun. Give me all your 10s and 20s."

3. Presentation of Evidence (Proofs)

Following the opening statements the most important part of the trial starts with the lawyers for the parties presenting their "cases" — the evidence for their side. The

---

[62] Nancy Pennington and Reid Hastie, *The Story Model of Juror Decision Making* in REID HASTIE, ED., INSIDE THE JUROR 192-221 (Cambridge U. Press 1993). Judges probably do the same thing.

plaintiff (or the prosecution in a criminal case) goes first and presents the "plaintiff's case," called the "government's case" or "state's case" in a criminal action. Then the defendant's lawyers present the "defendant's case." Following that, the plaintiff or prosecution has the opportunity to present a "rebuttal case."

It is the responsibility of the lawyers for the parties to assure the attendance of witnesses they need and obtain the appropriate documents for trial. This is generally done by the lawyer simply requesting the court clerk to provide an order requiring the witness to appear, called a "subpoena."[63] The lawyers know what witnesses and other evidence to use at trial because they have investigated the case both through informal means (*e.g.*, talking to witnesses, using private investigators) and through a formal pre-trial process called "discovery." In a civil case, either side in the dispute can compel any member of the public who has knowledge of the case to give "depositions" at the lawyer's office and otherwise to disclose any relevant information or documents. Discovery applies to compel even the opposing party and the opposing party's witnesses to disclose what they know long before trial. In the process of discovery, lawyers will generally hear testimony from all the witnesses who will be called to testify at trial.[64]

In a criminal case, discovery is more limited. Because of their right against self-incrimination, defendants are generally not required to testify or otherwise provide information before trial.[65] The Constitution requires that the prosecution disclose exculpatory evidence to the defense, but the defendant in the United States does not have full access to the prosecution's investigatory file. However, much of the prosecution's file consists of notes and reports of police personnel who will be witnesses in the case. The prosecution is required to produce for the defendant's inspection any writings used by a witness to prepare for testifying.[66]

The lawyers presenting their evidence have three principal tasks: presenting witness testimony, presenting documents or other tangible evidence, and making and defending against objections to evidence. The law and techniques for these activities are outlined next.

a. Witness Testimony

Witness testimony forms the bulk of the proofs offered at most trials. Witnesses may testify based only on personal knowledge and generally witnesses may not testify to "hearsay" — what someone else told the witness.[67] A court stenographer takes down verbatim all the testimony and everything else said in the proceedings.

How Witness Testimony Is Presented   The witness is first "called to the witness stand" by one of the lawyers and takes an oath to tell "the whole truth and nothing but the truth."[68] Despite it being called the witness "stand," the place from which witnesses give evidence is really a chair next to the judge's dais in which the witness sits while testifying. All witnesses testify while seated unless asked to demonstrate something or

---

63 Generally, the court clerk gives the lawyers the requisite subpoenas in blank. However, in some jurisdictions, lawyers in civil cases have the power to issue the subpoenas themselves without any need to go through the court clerk. See FRCP 45(a)(3).

64 *See* Chapter VII, pp. 235-240.

65 However, some defenses require special prosecutorial investigation to rebut, such as alibi or insanity, and are required to be disclosed beforehand. Also, criminal defendants must provide the prosecution with samples for testing, such as handwriting or blood. *See* Chapter VIII, p. 273 and note 37.

66 *See supra* note 14. *See* FRE 612 and FRCrP 26.2.

67 Evidence law is discussed *infra* pp. 109-115.

68 If religious scruples prevent swearing an oath, an alternative "affirmation" may be used.

point something out on a demonstrative aid. This includes the defendant giving testimony in a criminal case.

The side that calls the witness questions the witness first on "direct examination." The opposing side is then given the right to conduct a "cross examination" of the witness. Following the cross examination, the side that called the witness then has the opportunity to conduct a "redirect examination." A "recross examination" and even possibly a second redirect examination may follow, but these are discretionary with the judge. In general, the purpose of direct examination is to get before the jury information that supports the proponent's case; the purpose of cross examination is to bring out contrary facts and to cast doubt on the direct examination.[69]

Witnesses are generally not permitted to testify in a narrative form on either direct or cross examination. They may testify only in response to questions. One reason for this has been discussed: it is thought desirable for lawyers to be able to control and "shape" the witness's testimony by the questions they ask so that the lawyer can present the testimony to the fact-finder in the best (or worst) possible light. Another reason is efficiency. To have a witness simply state everything the witness thinks is relevant to the case will generally result in much that is not really essential. Finally, question-and-answer format is essential to administer limitations on admissibility of evidence. Requiring that witnesses testify only in response to questions gives opposing counsel time to determine from the question asked whether inadmissible evidence is called for, so that an objection can be interposed before the jury hears the answer.[70]

(1) Direct Examination

A direct examination usually has three parts: (1) *background* of the witness (who the witness is, where the witness works, etc.) (2) *setting the scene* by describing the place where the incident occurred, (3) *action*, that is, description of the incident itself. In getting the witness's story out, the witness will usually be answering the five essential "W" questions that any good newspaper story answers — who, what, where, when and why — and most of the lawyer's direct examination questions will begin with one of these five words or with an imperative like "tell me" or "explain."

Form of Questions on Direct Examination In general, the lawyer conducting direct examination will want to ask "open" questions that give the witness the opportunity to talk. An example of an "open" question is "What did you see in the lobby of the Grand Hotel around 10PM on Tuesday, May 9th, of last year?" This is in contrast to "closed" questions that contemplate a limited response from the witness. An example of a closed question would be "How far from the night clerk's desk were you when the robbery was taking place?" or any question that can be answered "yes" or "no." Open questions are in general more efficient in that they ask for more information and allow the witness to

---

69 In general, jurors cannot ask questions, but some judges have permitted them to do so on a limited basis. The questions are submitted to the judge in writing and then are asked by the judge unless it is not a proper question from the standpoint of the law of evidence or if the judge is sure the lawyers will ask it at a later time. Reactions to the practice during a 1984 study in a federal court were positive on the part of judges and jurors, and even some of the lawyers (plaintiffs' lawyers favored the practice more than defendants' lawyers). GUINTHER, *supra* note 19, at 68. *See also* KASSIN & WRIGHTSMAN, *supra* note 42, at 129-131.

70 The Federal Rules of Evidence contain no blanket prohibition against narrative answers. However, the judge has the general power to "exercise reasonable control over the mode . . . of interrogating witnesses and presenting evidence." FRE 611. Consequently, judges will usually sustain an objection to narrative testimony if it is argued that the witness could well blurt out inadmissible evidence before an objection can be interposed.

answer in several sentences at a time. But there is an additional reason why the lawyer will want to use open questions on direct examination — longer answers give the jury more of chance to get to know and to get a "feel" for the witness. This is important, since the jury must decide to what extent to believe the witness and what weight to give the witness's testimony.

Closed questions are appropriate on direct and they are essential to probe matters of detail. For example, in answer to the open question of what happened in the hotel lobby, the witness may start telling about how he was in the lobby waiting for a friend to arrive; how he was leaning against a table reading a newspaper; and that he noticed a person approach the night clerk's desk and hand the clerk a piece of paper. At that point the direct examiner will wish to ask some closed questions, including the example just given about how close the witness was to the clerk's desk. Other closed questions would probably be "How much of man's body could you see: his entire body or just his face?"; "How tall did he appear to be?"; "How was he dressed?"; "What were his facial features like?"; and so on, going into a detailed description that obviously matches the defendant, thus showing in the process that the witness was a careful enough observer to notice details.

"Pacing" a Direct Examination   The mark of a good direct examiner is knowing when to move forward with open questions, thus allowing the witness to get through the story more quickly, and when to slow down the action and focus on details by way of closed questions. This is called the "pace" of the examination. If there are too many narrow questions, important parts of the story will get buried under a mass of unnecessary detail and the slow pace will bore the jury. If there are too many open questions, the story will go by too quickly for the jury to remember or will be described in such a general way that the jury will conclude that the witness did not see much or did not pay much attention to what was there to be seen.

Leading Questions   There is one kind of closed question that is objectionable on direct examination. This is the "leading" question. A leading question is one that suggests to the witness what the answer should be. "Weren't you standing only 10 feet from the night clerk's desk when the defendant walked up?" is a leading question. On direct examination, leading questions are prohibited because it is thought to be unfair to permit the lawyer to "feed" answers to witnesses that support the lawyer's own side. Moreover, the lawyers are permitted and even expected to interview witnesses and review their testimony with them before trial, so leading questions should not be necessary to get the witness's testimony out.[71]

(2) Cross Examination

Purpose of Cross Examination   The purpose of cross examination may in some cases be to seek out information, but more often its main purpose is to undermine the credibility of the witness's direct examination testimony. Such "impeachment" of the witness's testimony may include casting doubt on the witness's ability and opportunity to observe (*e.g.*, it was dark and stormy), exposing any bias or prejudice the witness might have (*e.g.*, the witness dislikes one of the parties), pointing out any interest the

---

[71] Leading questions *are* permitted on direct examination for uncontested material, for foundation material for introducing exhibits into evidence (*see infra* pp. 101-102) and to draw the witness's attention to a particular part of her testimony. They are also permitted in examining a hostile witness, the adverse party or a child or adult witness with impaired communication skills. FRE 611 states a softened version of the rule against leading questions: "Leading questions *should not* be used on direct examination of a witness except as may be necessary to develop the witness' testimony." (emphasis added).

witness has in the outcome of the case (*e.g.*, the witness has "cut a deal" with the prosecution allowing the witness to avoid prosecution if he testifies in this case), and showing bad character for truth-telling (*e.g.*, the witness has been convicted of perjury). Another form of impeachment is to show that the witness made a prior statement that is inconsistent with the witness's testimony at trial.

Form of Questions Not only are leading questions permitted on cross examination; most lawyers believe that proper technique requires that *all* questions on cross examination be leading and answerable by only by "yes" or "no." Assuming the question can fairly be answered "yes" or "no," if the witness tries to go beyond that answer to explain — for example, by answering "yes, but . . . " — the questioner can object that the answer is non-responsive.[72]

The idea behind using leading questions is that they allow the cross examiner to bring out only those items of information that are of value to the cross-examiner's case. Effective cross-examiners will generally ask only questions to which they know the answer and will never ask the witness "why" questions or other questions that give the witness a chance to explain. A cross-examining lawyer, however, is not permitted to argue with the witness or to "badger" the witness. What amounts to argument or badgering is not always clear, but asking the same question over and over or insisting that the answer the witness has given is false will in most circumstances fall into this category.

Effective Cross Examination Techniques A mistake that many beginning lawyers make is to try to accomplish too much on cross examination, expecting that they will be able to get the witness to completely agree with their position.[73] For example, after a direct examination in which the witness identifies the defendant as the robber, the defense lawyer might be tempted to ask "Isn't it true that it was so dark in the lobby that you were really unable to get a good look at the robber?" If the issue in the case is eyewitness identification of the defendant by this witness, this is a valid point to make. However, as a *question*, it is of limited use, since the witness will answer "no" or, worse yet, will feel challenged and thus will repeat once again for the jury just how well he or she could see. The point that it was so dark the witness could not see is a *conclusion* that the lawyer should *argue* in the final arguments in the case (when the witness cannot answer the argument). On *cross examination*, the lawyer is generally only looking for the *facts needed* to make the argument later. Thus, the lawyer, having done the appropriate investigation to determine that affirmative answers will be given, will ask instead: "This took place at 10:00 at night, didn't it?" "So, it was dark outside, correct?" "The only source of light in that lobby was a single light fixture, correct?" "And that single light fixture was hanging from the ceiling *behind* the robber's head, wasn't it?" "And isn't it true that, when you described the assailant to police when they arrived just 10 minutes after the robber left, you told them that it was 'pretty dark' in the hotel lobby?"

---

72 As a control tactic, lawyers sometimes begin their cross examination by instructing the witness that all questions will be answerable only with "yes" or "no" and that the witness should not go beyond that answer. This is generally frowned upon and many judges will sustain objections to it on the ground that it is not counsel's place to instruct the witness, but to simply ask the questions.

73 This unrealistic attitude is undoubtedly influenced by trials in movies and television in which the real murderer is a witness for the prosecution, is exposed by defense counsel during cross examination, and confesses to the crime in open court.

(3) Redirect Examination

Redirect examination is the opportunity for the direct examiner to return to "repair" any "damage" done on cross examination. Redirect examination, like direct examination, must be conducted by way of non-leading questions. This makes it difficult to "repair damage" done on cross unless the direct examiner has anticipated the damage and has prepared the witness for redirect examination. For example, if the redirect examiner wishes to elicit testimony that a prior inconsistent statement the witness signed was signed under time pressure, the most specific question the examiner can properly ask without leading is: "Why did you sign that statement?"

It is in part because of the difficulty of doing an effective redirect with non-leading questions that it is said by some experts in trial advocacy that the "first rule" of redirect examination is "Don't!" Unless there has been damage on cross and that damage can be repaired by way of redirect, redirect will be a waste of time or, worse yet, will serve only to emphasize the damage done on cross.

b. Objections

A jury need not explain the reasons for its verdict. Consequently, the best way to assure that it does not rely on improper evidence in deciding a case is to keep it from hearing that evidence at all.[74] The most common method for doing so in trials is to have the lawyers interpose objections to improper evidence as it is being presented.[75]

Form of Objections Objections are stated orally in open court during the trial. The objecting lawyer is required to state his or her objection and the ground for it, such as "Objection, your honor, hearsay." If in the judge's opinion the objection is clearly well taken or is clearly incorrect, the judge will rule immediately without considering any response from the other side. An objection that is correct will be "sustained" by the judge and one that is not correct will be "overruled."

The judge may choose to hear a brief response to the objection and possibly a brief rejoinder from the objecting lawyer. In the course of argument, an "offer of proof" may need to be made since the judge, in order to rule on the objection, may need to know what answer the witness would give if allowed to answer. Any such offer of proof or extended argument will have to be heard outside the hearing of the jury at a "bench conference" with the judge. When such a conference is needed, the lawyers may ask to "approach the bench." The lawyers then stand close to the judge's bench and may need to speak in whispers if the courtroom is small. If the argument is extensive because the item of evidence is very important and the question of admissibility is a close one, the jury may need to be temporarily removed from the courtroom instead.[76]

Effect of Objections on the Jury Lawyers will seek to avoid unnecessary objections and, when they feel the need to object, will keep in mind that they may be trying the jury's patience. Witness examinations that are constantly interrupted by objections and bench conferences irritate jurors. Not only is the testimony difficult to follow, the jury will think the objecting lawyer is trying to hide something from them.

Motions to Strike Testimony Most objections will be made after a question is asked, but before the witness has a chance to answer. However, sometimes objectionable

---

74 *See* FRCP 52; FRCrP 23(c).

75 The grounds for objecting to evidence are discussed later in this chapter. *See* pp. 109-115.

76 This is also called a "sidebar" conference if the judge has to go to the side of the bench to confer with the lawyers.

evidence comes out before an objection can be interposed. If the jury has already heard the evidence, the lawyer should make a motion to "strike the evidence from the record" and ask that the judge give an "instruction to disregard" the "stricken" evidence.[77] Clearly, it is very difficult for jurors to disregard something they have already heard, so some have characterized such instructions to disregard as attempts "to unring a bell." When the evidence is truly crucial and an instruction to disregard it would be inadequate, it may be necessary to order a new trial.

Motions in Liminé Because objections cannot always be interposed in time and instructions to disregard testimony are imperfect, a better means of assuring that evidence is not disclosed is the "motion in liminé." This motion, literally a motion made "at the threshold," seeks to obtain a ruling on the admissibility of evidence before the trial starts or at any other point before the witness takes the stand.

c. Exhibits: Real, Demonstrative and Documentary Evidence

Importance of Exhibits Exhibits are items of tangible evidence that must be formally authenticated and "admitted into evidence" during the trial. Exhibits are important because juries tend to give them greater weight than testimonial evidence. Tangible evidence cannot forget or exaggerate as witnesses can. Moreover, the jury can read or examine them over and over again in the jury room during their deliberation, while witness testimony lingers only in the memory of the jury.

Types of Exhibits Exhibits are generally of three types: "real" evidence, "demonstrative" evidence and documents. Real evidence comprises actual tangible items involved in the occurrence in dispute, such as the gun or the blood-soaked clothes in a murder case, or the clamp left in the patient during surgery in a medical malpractice case. Demonstrative evidence is anything that is used to represent or demonstrate something that cannot be brought into the courtroom, such as a diagram of the floor plan of a house that was the scene of the crime or a diagram of an intersection where an accident occurred. Documentary evidence comprises any writings relevant to the case. The overall goal for a lawyer seeking to use an exhibit at trial is to get it "admitted into evidence" — formally declared to be part of the official record of the case and thus appropriate for the jury to consider as evidence and take into the jury room at the end of the trial.

Procedures for Exhibits The overall procedural steps that must be followed are that the lawyer must (1) have the court reporter "mark the exhibit for identification" by giving it a number or letter for easy reference, (2) show the exhibit to opposing counsel, (3) "lay a foundation" for its admission and (4) "move the exhibit into evidence." The need to lay a foundation for its admission requires that the lawyer satisfy the judge that the legal prerequisites for its admission into evidence exist. Laying a foundation is usually done by way of witness testimony. After the foundation has been established, to move the exhibit into evidence the attorney simply turns to the judge and says "I move that State's Exhibit No. 34 be admitted into evidence." The judge will then hear any objections to the motion from the other side and will rule.

More than one witness may be necessary to complete the foundation for an exhibit. Thus, for example, if drugs were seized during an arrest, a "chain of custody" must be established to show that the evidence is authentic and was not tampered with from the

---

77 Testimony that is "stricken from the record" still appears in the verbatim transcript of the trial. Striking testimony from the record simply means that the court formally declares that it is not proper evidence and must be disregarded by the jury in reaching a decision.

point that it was seized to the point it is introduced as evidence at the trial. This may involve calling everyone who handled the exhibit as a foundation witness, *e.g.*, the arresting officer, the police courier who delivered the evidence to the police chemist, the chemist, and any custodian of evidence at the police station. As a result, counsel may not be able to complete the last step of moving the exhibit into evidence until after several witnesses are called. Since some of these witnesses will be testifying to matters other than things relating to the particular exhibit, foundation laying can sometimes stretch out over several days of trial.

Effectively Dealing With Exhibits   The key to effectively laying foundations for exhibits is to do it as efficiently and unobtrusively as possible. The point of the foundation-laying — and what the jury is looking forward to — is the *content* of the exhibit. Anything seen by the jury as delaying getting to that content will be resented. One way to make the process more efficient is to mark the exhibits for identification and to show them to opposing counsel before the trial starts, thereby eliminating two of the four steps in the process outlined above. The lawyer can then fit the foundation into the normal direct examination. For example, in seeking to introduce the note the robber passed to the night clerk demanding money, the prosecutor can simply go through the night clerk's description of the robbery, including reference to the note (something that the prosecutor would do in any event). Then all that needs to be done further is to draw the witness's attention to the exhibit and to ask the witness whether the exhibit is the note to which he has been referring to in his description of the robbery. Having thus laid the foundation, the prosecutor can simply move its admission into evidence.

In civil cases, the availability of extensive discovery opportunities means that almost all issues of the admissibility of exhibits will be determined well in advance of trial. This will be done by way of "stipulation" — an agreement between the parties — or by pre-trial rulings of the trial judge.[78] In criminal cases, discovery is more limited, so pretrial resolution of exhibit issues is less likely.

4. Motions for a Directed Verdict

Following the plaintiff's or prosecution's presentation of evidence, the defense may move for a "directed verdict" on the basis of the plaintiff's evidence, even before presenting the defense case.[79] In a criminal case, a similar motion is made after presentation of the prosecution's evidence and it is often called a "motion for judgment of acquittal."[80] The motion seeks dismissal of the case on the ground that the plaintiff or prosecution has failed to produce sufficient evidence for rational jurors to return a verdict in its favor. The defendant has the right to make a second motion for a directed verdict or judgment of acquittal after all the evidence has been presented. This assures that the case that goes to the jury has been screened one final time to assure that there is sufficient evidence for the jury to decide the case.[81]

5. Closing Arguments

The Nature of Closing Argument After both the plaintiff and defendant have "rested their cases" — meaning that they have presented all their evidence — it is time for

---

78 *See* Chapter VII, pp. 229-242 (civil pre-trial procedures).

79 In federal court, this motion is called a Motion for Judgment as a Matter of Law (JML). Federal Rule of Civil Procedure (FRCP) 50(a).

80 *See* Federal Rule of Criminal Procedure (FRCrP) 29(a).

81 A similar motion can be made after a verdict is rendered. *See infra* p. 108.

"closing arguments."[82] Closing arguments are the opportunity given to the lawyers in the case to address the jury directly and seek to persuade the jury to decide the case in their side's favor. Closing is certainly the most "flashy" of all the things that trial lawyers do in trials, but it is not necessarily the most important. If the evidence has not been presented effectively, a brilliant closing argument will not save the case.

Despite how it might sometimes appear to the casual observer, there are in fact limits on what a lawyer can do and say in argument. Generally not allowed are appeals to passion or prejudice, such as arguing or implying that the defendant in a criminal case is guilty because he is black or that a particular verdict will "clean up the drug problem in this city." Counsel may not misstate evidence or "argue off the record." This means that counsel cannot rely on facts that were not introduced into evidence at the trial. Similarly, when evidence is admitted for a limited purpose, the lawyer may not argue a broader use of the evidence. For example, the lawyer may not argue that a prior conviction shows general bad character when it was admitted only to impeach credibility.[83] Finally, a lawyer is not permitted to state the lawyer's personal opinion as to the believability of witnesses or of the correctness of his client's case or of the guilt or innocence of the accused. Generally lawyers will not object even if the other side is transgressing some of these limitations during final argument, but this is not a legal restriction, only a traditional courtesy. Objections should be made if violations of the stated limitations are hurting one's case.

Trial Lawyer Techniques in Closing Argument   The form of closing argument is not specified and there are a wide variety of styles among lawyers. Some are cool and analytical, while others are emotional and intuitive. However, most effective closing arguments will (1) focus the case by setting aside uncontested or less important issues and pointing out the *real* issues in the case; (2) argue the issues that have been brought into focus by carefully organizing the evidence that supports each of them and, where there is a conflict, explaining to the jury why it should accept the arguing party's version over the opposing party's version; and (3) relate the evidence the jury has just heard to the principles of law the jury must apply as set out in the jury instructions.

Closing argument is sometimes referred to as "summation," but that is misleading. A good closing argument will not just summarize the evidence; it will organize it and argue it. In all but the longest and most complicated trials, lawyers who start out their closing argument by announcing that they will now summarize all the evidence the jury has heard will be greeted by anguished facial expressions and then bored looks from jurors who already know the evidence well. What most jurors want and need is some guidance on what the evidence *means*. That is the primary purpose of closing argument.

Trial lawyers will usually try to construct a "theme" for their case. A theme is a shorthand characterization of the case or a "story" of the case that will be easily accepted by the jury as a valid archetype. It may serve to explain the entire case or only important parts of it. A common theme in a medical malpractice case defense would cast the plaintiff as "the ungrateful patient," who makes unreasonable demands and expects miracles. The Bible, Shakespeare, and proverbs provide material for many case themes, but themes can be found in all kinds of everyday experiences as well. A version

---

82   As noted earlier, a motion for a directed verdict may be renewed at this time, and the case will be dismissed by the judge at this point if the plaintiff or prosecutor has not presented evidence sufficient for a rational verdict in its favor.

83   Examples are hearsay statements admitted for a purpose other than their truth. *See infra* p. 113.

of the Biblical saying, "only the wicked flee when no man pursueth," can be used to get the greatest effect out of evidence that the defendant tried to flee. In a similar vein, when a party has overreacted to something the opposing party did, the opposing party may quote Shakespeare: "methinks she doth protest too much." Prosecutors are often faced with trying to prove intent of the defendant circumstantially in the face of believable testimony from the defendant denying that he had such intent. The prosecutor might remind the jury, several times if need be, that "actions speak louder than words."

For a theme to work, it must be anchored in strong evidence, such as an unimpeachable witness or a document.[84] If the evidence on which is it based is weak, the theme will suffer accordingly. For example, the "wicked flee" approach will not work well if there is some doubt that the party *was* in fact fleeing. Moreover, the theme must be one with which the jury can readily identify. For example, a trial lawyer who uses stories about or quotations from famous male sports figures is not likely to get far with a jury of all women. Finally, trial lawyers must always check their case theories to see if their theme can be turned around and used against them.

Analogies, sometimes presented in the form of a "personal anecdote" with which the jury can readily identify, are an extension of this form of theme construction. For example, a prosecutor who wants to encourage the jury to use a relatively small amount of circumstantial evidence to tie the defendant to the crime, can use some variant of the "sugar barrel" story:

> We grew up poor in the south. We didn't have much, but one treat that me and my brother had was that, once a week after supper on Saturday, Mama would give us each a spoonful of sugar from a big barrel where she kept it. That sugar sure tasted good! But we'd sometimes have a yearning for it before Saturday and we'd sneak into the kitchen and take some. Every time we did that, no matter how much we denied it, no matter whether we would sneak down there at midnight when my mama was asleep or when she was gone from the house — she would *always* know we'd done it and we would get a whipping. We began to think she could read our minds!

> But later on, when we were grown up, we found out the reason: each time we would take some sugar, no matter *how careful* we were, we would spill the tiniest bit of it — just a few crystals — on the floor. Since Mama kept the floors real clean, she'd see it and would know we'd been somewhere we shouldn't have been.

> Now, the defendant here thought he had been *really careful* in covering up his crime, but he dropped some sugar crystals, too. Like my Mama, we can learn a lot from looking at those tiny crystals.

At this point the lawyer can go into the small clues left by the defendant and how they connect him with the crime.[85]

---

84 Other guides for constructing themes are suggested in LUBET, *supra* note 47, at 1-14.

85 Some observers have noted that there is often an inverse relationship between the strength of one's case and the amount of theatrics and story-telling that a lawyer engages in. As one trial lawyer confessed, "If the facts of my case are weak, I stand on the law. If the law in my case is weak, I stand on the facts. If both the facts and law of my case are weak, I stand on the *table*." A lawyer facing an entertaining opponent can counter such efforts by arguing that the lawyer is "showing off" to avoid dealing with the serious problems with his case. This can be succinctly illustrated to the jury by using the story of the trial lawyer's confession just related in this footnote.

6. Jury Instructions

Content of Instructions   At the end of all the proofs and usually after closing argument,[86] the judge will provide jury instructions on the law applicable to the case. This is sometimes referred to as the "charge" to the jury. This will include the substantive law related to the claim made or offense charged, such as the requirements for a binding contract or the elements of murder. Many jurisdictions have standard or "pattern" jury instructions that are officially approved by the highest court of that state and which must be given in any case where they are applicable. However, not all points of law that arise in a case are covered by standard instructions and it becomes the task of the lawyers to write and submit proposed instructions to the court.

Instructions will also cover the law governing how the jury is to assess the evidence and decide the case. These instructions are generally not very detailed. The jury is told to elect a "foreperson," who will preside over deliberations and allow everyone a chance to speak. They are also reminded that they are the sole judges of the credibility and weight of the evidence. But no more specific instructions on how to assess particular types of evidence is provided.

Standards of Proof   The jury is told what standard of proof it is to apply in deciding the case. In a criminal case, the standard is "proof beyond a reasonable doubt." Thus, the jury is told that it may find the defendant guilty only if it finds beyond a reasonable doubt that the defendant committed the crime and that it must acquit the defendant if it has a reasonable doubt as to the defendant's guilt. In a civil case, the standard of proof is the "preponderance of the evidence," sometimes referred to as the "greater weight of the evidence." There is also an intermediate standard of "clear and convincing evidence" that is used in some civil cases that have very serious consequences, such as terminations of parental rights and involuntary commitments to mental hospitals. According to some, if the criminal and normal civil standards were expressed as percentages, they would be 95% and 51% respectively, with "clear and convincing" weighing in somewhere around 75-80%.

A typical instruction explaining reasonable doubt tells the jury:

> Reasonable doubt means a doubt based upon reason and common sense that arises from a fair and rational consideration of all the evidence or lack of evidence in the case. It is a doubt that is not a vague, speculative or imaginary doubt, but such a doubt as would cause reasonable persons to hesitate to act in matters of serious importance to themselves.

A typical instruction explaining the civil standard is:

> When I use the expression "by a preponderance of the evidence," I mean that you must be persuaded from a consideration of all the evidence in the case that the issue in question is more probably true than not true. Any findings of fact you make must be based on probabilities, not possibilities. It may not be based on surmise, speculation, or conjecture.

Jury instructions are read to the jury and, until recently, the jury was usually not given a copy of them. Given the inherent weaknesses of reading 15 minutes or more of legal instructions, more and more jurisdictions are allowing or requiring that judges give

---

[86] In some jurisdictions, jury instructions may precede the closing arguments. *See, e.g.,* FRCP 51; FRCrP 30. The reason for this is to allow the lawyers to refer to the instructions during their argument. However, even in jurisdictions where argument comes before the instructions, the lawyer may freely refer to them because the judge will have gone over the instructions with the lawyers prior to closing argument.

the jury a copy. Studies show that, while juries are good fact-finders, they do less well in getting legal standards straight.[87] There is no direct judicial check on jury misunderstanding of the law, unless the jury asks the judge for assistance. However, the judge can set aside any verdict (other than a criminal acquittal) that is not warranted by the facts or the law.[88]

Judicial Comments on the Evidence   Generally, judges in the United States do not summarize the evidence for the jury or comment on it. While federal judges at least theoretically have this power, and commenting on the evidence was at one time an accepted custom, the practice has fallen into disuse today as judges are more concerned lest they improperly influence the jury.[89] The only vestige of the judicial summary and comment that remains is that the judge may read to the jury at the parties' request a brief "theory of the case" instruction written by the parties that outlines each side's principal contentions in summary form.

7. Deliberation and Verdict

Because jury deliberations are undertaken in secret and every jury is unique, little of a general nature can be said about what happens in deliberations. However, there are composite descriptions based on observations of mock juries and some jurors have written about their experiences.[90] At some point, often at the very beginning, a tentative vote is taken to determine the extent of disagreement. This is followed by discussion and more votes until the jury either agrees or is "deadlocked."

Deadlocked and Hung Juries   If the jury reports that it is deadlocked, the judge will usually send the jurors back to deliberate with the admonition to try to see if they can work out their differences. Sometimes, an additional instruction is given to them that is designed to motivate jurors to reconsider their positions. Called an *Allen* charge or a "dynamite charge," it tells the jurors in essence to think seriously about their position and listen carefully to the arguments of the other jurors.[91]

In criminal cases in federal court and all but 5 states, jury verdicts — whether for conviction or acquittal — must be unanimous.[92] In civil cases, unanimity is required in federal court, but the parties can agree to less. And in many states require only a simple

---

87   HARRY KALVEN, JR. AND HANS ZEISEL, THE AMERICAN JURY 149-50 (Little, Brown 1966). *See also* R. P. Charrow and V. R. Charrow, *A Psycholinguistic Study of Jury Instructions*, 79 COLUM. L. REV. 1306 (1979) and KASSIN & WRIGHTSMAN, *supra* note 42, at 144-167. One study shows that jurors' understanding of instructions is increased significantly when they take the opportunity to ask the judge questions. Alan Reifman, Spencer M. Gusick, and Phoebe Ellsworth, *Real Jurors' Understanding of the Law in Real Cases*, 16 Law & Human Behavior 539 (1992).

88   *See infra*, p. 108. *See also* Chapter VII, p. 240, where pre-trial screening devices are discussed. Another standard of proof applied in civil cases with serious consequences (*e.g.*, termination of parental rights, involuntary commitment to a psychiatric hospital) is proof "by clear and convincing evidence."

89   *See Quercia v. United States*, 289 U.S. 466 (1933) (conviction because of trial judge's comment to the jury: "I think that every single word that man [the defendant] said, except when he agreed with the Government's testimony, was a lie"). Not all judges agree that judges should be reticent to summarize and comment on the evidence. Detailed proposals for a broader role for the judge are discussed by a federal judge in Jack Weinstein, *The Power and Duty of Federal Judges to Marshall and Comment on the Evidence in Jury Trials and Some Suggestions on Charging Jurors*, 118 F.R.D. 161 (1988).

90   *See* Phoebe Ellsworth, *Are Twelve Heads Better Than One?*, 52 LAW & CONTEMP. PROB. 205 (1989) (describing a composite picture based on observing mock juries). Two juror accounts are MELVYN ZERMAN, CALL THE FINAL WITNESS 122-42 (Harper & Row 1977), reprinted in part in LANDSMAN, *supra* note 4; VICTOR VILLASENOR, JURY — THE PEOPLE VS. JUAN CORONA (Little, Brown 1977).

91   The *Allen* charge is named for the case in which the Supreme Court approved its use, *Allen v. United States*, 164 U.S. 492 (1896). "Dynamite charge" is a play on words. "Charge" can mean both a jury instruction and an explosive device.

92   Constitutional requirements regarding unanimity are discussed in Chapter VIII, p. 309.

or a two-thirds majority. A jury vote that does not meet the applicable standard for decision results in a "hung jury." If the jury is truly deadlocked, the judge has no choice but to "declare a mistrial."[93] As soon as the jury has reached a verdict, it communicates that to the judge. Everyone assembles in the courtroom, the foreperson of the jury hands the verdict to the judge, who checks it for proper form and then hands it back to the foreperson to read aloud.

Requests for Evidence or Instructions Sometimes the jury will request that certain testimony be read to them or, if written jury instructions are not provided, that certain portions of the instructions be reread. Jurors may request exhibits that have not already been taken into the jury room. Judges are somewhat reluctant to read only the portion of the testimony or instructions that the jury requests for fear that doing so would overemphasize the requested part to the exclusion of other parts. Consequently, to the extent possible, the judge will try to give them the entire testimony of the witness they asked about or the entire instructions, adding the admonition to consider the material they requested in the context of all the evidence and instructions.

Polling the Jury There is little that the lawyers can do during deliberations except appear and argue about any supplemental instructions or other problems that arise in deliberations. However, the losing side has the right to "poll the jury." The judge will then require that each juror answer individually whether in fact the verdict read was the one he or she agreed to. Occasionally a juror who is polled blurts out that it was not his or her verdict. The problem must be ironed out by more deliberation and, if necessary, a mistrial will be declared, resulting in a new trial before a new jury.[94]

Form of the Verdict In all criminal cases and in most civil cases, a "general verdict" stating the bare conclusion of the jury is rendered. In a criminal case, the form for a general verdict will allow the jury to check either guilty or not guilty on each of the charges tried. In a civil case, there will similarly be two choices, either "We find for the plaintiff and award damages of $_____" or "We find for the defendant."

In civil cases, the judge may use a "special verdict" or "general verdict with interrogatories."[95] Special verdict forms direct the jury to answer the component questions that are necessary for a general verdict and, based on those answers, the judge determines what the final resolution of the case is. Thus, in a libel case, the jury may be asked such questions as "Did the Defendant accuse the Plaintiff of taking a bribe in the article published in Smithton Observer on January 10, 1997?" "Did this statement defame the Plaintiff?" "Was the statement privileged?" and so on. Components of damages may similarly be subject to a special verdict. The jury would then state separate amounts for each economic loss suffered, such as lost wages, hospital and medical expenses, impairment of future earning capacity, and for non-economic losses, including fear, shock and pain at the time of the injury, pain and suffering thereafter, loss of companionship or consortium, and whatever other components of non-economic harm are allowed in that jurisdiction.

---

93 Mistrials may also be granted whenever continuation of a trial is impossible or unfair for other reasons, such as misconduct of the lawyers, parties, witnesses or jurors that cannot be "cured" by an instruction to the jury.

94 A mistrial is declared not just when jurors cannot agree, but whenever the trial process aborts. A mistrial can be declared where there is misconduct of the jury or of counsel that cannot be cured. Mistrials also take place when the trial cannot continue because illness or other disaster has reduced the number of jury members to less than the minimum needed or has otherwise made it impossible to continue the trial. Lawyers may move for a mistrial or the judge may declare one on his or her own initiative.

95 *See* FRCP 49.

General verdicts with interrogatories are like ordinary general verdicts in that the jury determines the final conclusion of the verdict itself, but the final conclusion is then followed by questions designed to check whether the jury had the correct reasons for that conclusion. Thus, questions similar to those mentioned above for the special verdict might appear.

It is usually the job of the lawyers to draft a special verdict or a general verdict with interrogatories. To the extent that such verdict forms serve to "rationalize" the jury's decision-making process, they are favored by defendants in civil tort cases to counteract feelings of sympathy for the injured plaintiff. The problem with these devices lies in the difficulty of framing precise, yet understandable, questions for the jury. These verdict forms increase the danger that a verdict that is warranted by the evidence would have to be thrown out just because the jury made mistakes in answering the questions.

8. Post-Trial Motions

Judgment NOV Motions The defense may make a motion *after* a verdict is rendered on the same grounds that a motion for a directed verdict is made earlier in the proceeding.[96] In civil cases, this is called a motion for "judgment notwithstanding the verdict" or "judgment NOV" for the Latin *non obstante verdicto*.[97] However, a directed verdict or judgment NOV may be granted only if there is a "no legally sufficient evidentiary basis for a reasonable jury" to decide for the plaintiff.[98]

New Trial Motions The judge in a civil case may also "set aside" the verdict and grant a new trial if it is "against the great weight of the evidence" or if liability is correct, but the verdict is grossly excessive or inadequate. If it is only the amount of the verdict that is improper, federal and state judges may grant a "remittitur"— ordering a new trial on grounds of excessiveness of the verdict conditioned on the parties consenting to a reduction of the amount awarded by the jury. An "additur," which adds money to a judgment on grounds of inadequacy of the damages, is not recognized in the federal courts. However, the judge may not order a new trial simply because the judge disagrees with it. Thus, it is said that the judge may not sit as a "thirteenth juror."

Post-Trial Motions in Criminal Cases In criminal cases, the defense may also make a motion after a guilty verdict that corresponds to the directed verdict motion or motion for judgment of acquittal made earlier in the trial. It may be called a motion for judgment notwithstanding the verdict or sometimes a renewed motion for judgment of acquittal.[99] The ground for granting such a motion is that the evidence presented at trial was insufficient for the jury to find the defendant guilty beyond a reasonable doubt. The prosecution is not permitted to move to set aside an acquittal.[100]

---

96 *See supra* p. 102.

97 In civil cases in federal court, this motion is called a Renewed Motion for Judgment as a Matter of Law (JML). *See* FRCP 50. This emphasizes the fact that the motion is not a separate motion, but simply delayed consideration of the earlier Motion for JML made before the case was submitted to the jury.

98 FRCP 50(a). As explained by the court in *Boeing Co. v. Shipman*, 411 F.2d 365, 374 (5th Cir. 1969), in considering a motion for judgment NOV, a judge must consider all the evidence "in the light and with all reasonable inferences most favorable to the [plaintiff]," and may reverse the verdict only if the judge "believes that reasonable men could not arrive at a . . . verdict" for the plaintiff. "[I]f there is substantial evidence [for the plaintiff], that is, evidence of such quality and weight that reasonable and fair-minded men in the exercise of impartial judgment might reach" a verdict for the plaintiff, it must be affirmed. The opinion goes on to admonish that "it is the function of the jury as the traditional finder of the facts, and not the Court, to weigh conflicting evidence and inferences, and determine the credibility of witnesses."

99 *See* FRCrP 29(c).

100 Doing so would violate the right against being tried twice for the same offense secured the so-called "double jeopardy" clause of the 5th Amendment. *See infra* Chapter VIII, pp. 315-318.

Impeaching the Verdict A party may also seek to set aside the verdict on the ground that the jury acted improperly during deliberations or trial. This is called "impeaching a verdict." However, motions to impeach the verdict are looked upon with disfavor. Such a rule serves to preserve the secrecy of the jury room and to prevent lawyers from hounding jurors, trying to discover evidence of irregularities.[101] A typical modern rule on the ability of a juror to impeach a verdict is Federal Rule of Evidence 606. It makes an intrinsic-extrinsic distinction: a court may not receive any evidence as to any matter or statement occurring during the course of the jury's deliberations or the effect of anything on deliberations unless it concerns "extraneous prejudicial information" brought to the juror's attention or some "outside influence" on the jury.[102] Thus, testimony would be allowed as to such things as bribery, comments to a juror during deliberation by anyone other than another juror (such as a lawyer, party or court personnel), or exposure of a juror to a newspaper article on the case. The result of this rule is that, so long as there is substantial evidence in the record to support the verdict, it will not be set aside based on misunderstanding of the evidence or the law or on anything else that took place in the jury room.[103]

D. Evidence Law

As already alluded to, the law of evidence is relatively complex. In addition, trial lawyers must be sufficiently familiar with evidence rules to be able to interpose timely objections in the lightening quick pace of the adversary trial. Presented here is a simplified overview of the major evidentiary limitations that apply in jury trials.[104]

1. The Requirement of Personal Knowledge for Testimony

Witnesses may testify only to matters about which they have personal knowledge.[105] In other words, they must have experienced first-hand through one of their senses the events they describe. Personal knowledge may not be assumed. It must be established *by testimony*. Thus, a lawyer who calls a witness to testify to seeing a robber in a hotel lobby will first have to ask questions that show that the *witness* was in the lobby of the hotel and was able to see what was going on there. While all this seems simple in the abstract, it is a problem for many lawyers, because of the natural tendency of people who know the facts of a case well to forget that other people do not share that knowledge. As a result, they often start in the middle of the witness's story without first laying a foundation establishing that the witness has personal knowledge.

---

101 *Vaise v. Delaval*, I.T.R. 11 (1785) (Mansfield, L.J.); *McDonald v. Pless*, 238 U.S. 264 (1915).

102 FRE 606(b). *See In re Beverly Hills Fire Litigation*, 695 F.2d 207 (6th Cir. 1982) (new trial ordered because juror performed his own experiment to test whether the fire could have started as the plaintiff's expert testified and then told other jurors).

103 After the trial is over, jurors may freely talk with whomever they please about what went on in the jury room. Sometimes, lawyers in the case make a point of asking the jurors questions, both to see if there were any extrinsic influences that could lead to impeachment of the verdict and in order to learn from the experience by getting the jurors' impressions of their presentation.

104 For more detailed analysis of the law of evidence, *see* ROGER C. PARK, DAVID P. LEONARD, STEVEN H. GOLDBERG, HORNBOOK ON EVIDENCE LAW, 2D ED. (West 2004); KENNETH S. BROUN, ET AL., MCCORMICK'S HORNBOOK ON EVIDENCE, 6TH ED. (West 2006); MICHAEL H. GRAHAM, FEDERAL RULES OF EVIDENCE IN A NUTSHELL, 7TH ED. (West 2007); ARTHUR BEST, EVIDENCE: EXAMPLES AND EXPLANATIONS, 7TH ED. (Aspen 2009). For a book exploring the stories behind famous evidence cases, *see* RICHARD O. LEMPERT, EVIDENCE STORIES (Foundation 2006).

105 *See* Federal Rule of Evidence (FRE) 602, reprinted in FEDERAL RULES OF EVIDENCE WITH EVIDENCE MAP (West 2010-2011). Trials in federal court are governed by the FRE, first promulgated in 1975. Before 1975, evidence law in federal courts was governed by case law, with a few isolated issues governed by statute. Most state courts have followed the lead of federal courts and have evidence rules very similar to the FRE.

2. Opinion Evidence

Lay Opinions Generally layperson (non-expert) witnesses may testify only to facts and may not testify to conclusions. The reason for this is that it is up to the *jury* to decide what conclusions to draw from the facts. Thus, it is improper for a witness to testify that the defendant "was driving too fast for the existing road conditions" because that is for the jury to decide. But it is hard to tell the difference between facts and conclusions since almost any label language places on an event is a conclusion of sorts.

For example, assume a witness testifies, "the defendant threw a brick." Taking only one word in the sentence as an example, "throwing" is a conclusion based on the fact of the defendant's having the brick in his hand, holding his arm extended behind his head, moving his arm over his head swiftly in a forward direction, and letting go of the brick at some point when his hand came in front of his body. Also, calling the object "a brick" is a conclusion based on the facts that it was square, red and about the size of other things that qualify as bricks, appeared to be made of clay, and appeared to be heavy. Clearly, if people were not allowed to use *any* conclusions, their speech would be very strange indeed. These kinds of "everyday" conclusions must be allowed.

Consequently, the rule against conclusions provides an exception for conclusions that are (1) based on the perception of the witness and (2) "helpful to a clear understanding of the witness's testimony."[106] The first condition is simply a restatement of the personal knowledge requirement. The second requirement of "helpfulness" simply means that using the conclusion would avoid cumbersome and abnormal speech. This second requirement is certainly satisfied in the brick-throwing example above. Other lay conclusions that are permitted are statements such as that a person was "drunk" or that a car was going "thirty-five miles per hour."

Expert Opinions If scientific, technical or other specialized knowledge would be useful to understand a case, an expert witness may testify. Experts have special skills, education, training or experience that permit them to testify to conclusions in their field of expertise that laypersons could not.[107] Physicians testifying in personal injury cases, psychiatrists testifying in criminal cases or child custody cases, and engineers testifying in product liability cases are perhaps the most commonly encountered experts. However, more exotic forms of experts, such as accident reconstruction experts, exist as well.[108]

Court-appointed experts are possible.[109] However, they are not often used. Consistent with adversary principles, each side finds, prepares and presents its own expert testimony. This is a recognition that in specialized and scientific fields, just as

---

106 FRE 701.

107 *See* FRE 702-706.

108 The Supreme Court recently expanded the possibility of a wider variety of experts being permitted to testify by holding that FRE 702 overruled the earlier common law test of expert evidence: whether given evidence meets "general acceptance" in the scientific community. In its place, FRE 702 establishes a more flexible test of whether "(1) the testimony is based upon sufficient facts or data, (2) the testimony is the product of reliable principles and methods, and (3) the witness has applied the principles and methods reliably to the facts of the case." Relevant factors as to the reliability of a particular scientific theory or technique are testing, peer review, error rates, and "acceptability" in the relevant scientific community. *Daubert v. Merrell Dow Pharmaceuticals, Inc.*, 509 U.S. 579 (1993) (admitting testimony of experts that countered published scientific literature that drug Bendectin did not cause birth defects). *See also Kumho Tire, Ltd. v. Carmichael*, 526 U.S. 137 (1999) (*Daubert* applies not just to "scientific" expertise, but also to experts who are not scientists, such as engineers; affirming trial court's rejection of engineers testimony as to the cause of failure of a tire).

109 *See* FRE 706.

when "ordinary" facts are involved, there is often more than one perspective on the issue. To the extent possible, it is appropriate that all sides of the question should be explored.

3. Relevance and Character Evidence

General Relevance Standard   The federal rules and many state evidence rules set a low threshold of probative value, deeming relevant "[e]vidence having *any tendency* to make the existence of any fact that is of consequence to the determination of the action more probable or less probable than it would be without the evidence."[110] But this lax standard of factual relevance must be weighed against other factors, primarily the danger of undue prejudice. The rule states that evidence that is otherwise relevant "may be excluded if its probative value is substantially outweighed by the danger of unfair prejudice, confusion of the issues, or misleading the jury, or by considerations of undue delay, waste of time, or needless presentation of cumulative evidence."[111] For example, gruesome, close-up color photographs of the victim in a murder case probably pass the threshold test of relevancy. However, they are often excluded from evidence in jury cases if their probative value is low, such as where the issue of how the victim died is uncontroverted, and there is great danger that they could inflame the jury and interfere with their ability to be fair to the defendant.

Evidence of Character   The general rule on character evidence is that "[e]vidence of a person's character is not admissible for the purpose of proving action in conformity therewith on a particular occasion."[112] Thus, in a suit for damages for injuries in an automobile collision, evidence of prior accidents the defendant was involved in will not be admissible to prove he was a "bad driver." Similarly, the prosecution in a criminal case generally cannot introduce evidence of the defendant's bad character.[113] The rationale for excluding bad character evidence is that juries may use it to convict criminal defendants or hold civil defendants liable simply for being "bad" people and not because they in fact did what they are accused of doing in a given case.

The prohibition is not complete, however. The prosecution in a criminal case is allowed to present evidence of the defendant's *bad* character to rebut any evidence the *defendant* has chosen to present that shows his *good* character.[114] Also, witnesses who take the stand to testify — including a criminal defendant who chooses to do so — are subject to the possibility that some of their prior felony convictions and perhaps some other prior bad actions will be admitted into evidence to the extent that they bear on the witness's ability to tell the truth (*e.g.*, a prior conviction for perjury or fraud). However, the court is required to weigh carefully evidence of a witness's or party's criminal record to determine whether its probative value is outweighed by its prejudicial effect.[115]

---

110 FRE 401 (emphasis added).

111 FRE 403.

112 See FRE 404(a).

113 *See* FRE 404(a). If character is an element of the offense or claim or defense, then it is fully admissible. Thus, in the example given in the text of proving the character of a "bad driver," such evidence is not admissible in a suit to prove the *driver's* negligence. However, it may be admissible in a suit against the *owner of the car* for negligently entrusting the car to a poor driver if the owner knew of the bad driving history. Character evidence in any event may properly be considered in determining the sentence for a criminal defendant. However, sentencing hearings are proceedings separate from the trial of the case, where only the question of guilt is determined. *See* Chapter VIII, pp. 277-279.

114 FRE 404(a)(1).

115 *See* FRE 608, 609 and 403. Evidence of prior bad acts may be admissible to prove something *other than* the character of the person, such as to show motive, absence of intent, mistake, identity or common scheme or plan. FRE 404(b). Once a witness learns through a pretrial ruling by the judge that the

4. The Rule Against Hearsay and Its Major Exceptions

Hearsay testimony, roughly speaking, is testimony about something someone else said. A more complete definition is that hearsay is evidence of a statement, made earlier out-of-court, that is now being offered to prove the truth of what it asserts.[116] The problem with hearsay is its unreliability based on the lack of opportunity for the party against whom it is offered to confront and to cross-examine the person who made the statement at the time it was made. The rule has ancient beginnings in English law. A common example of hearsay occurs whenever there is an automobile accident, and a witness to the accident describes it to a police officer, but then, in the confusion of the accident, disappears. The police officer generally cannot testify at a later trial as to what the person said. It does not matter that we know the person's name or that what the person told the police officer is consistent with other admissible evidence.[117]

There are two general categories of out-of-court utterances that are admissible despite the hearsay rule. Since hearsay is defined as an out-of-court statement that is offered to prove the *truth of what it asserts*, the first category of admissible statements consists of those that are *not* hearsay because they are offered for some purpose other than their truth. The second category of admissible statements comprises those that meet the definition of hearsay, but fall within some exception to the rule against hearsay.

a. Statements Not Offered for Their Truth

When a statement is offered for a purpose other than that of proving what the speaker intended to assert in it, then it is not subject to the danger that the speaker is lying. This is so because we are ignoring what the speaker asserts and are instead looking at an *unintended* meaning. For example, assume that George Jones seeks to testify that John Smith called him on the telephone on a particular day and in the course of the conversation Smith said "It is raining in Peoria today." This is hearsay *if* it is offered to prove that it was raining in Peoria at that time. However, if the statement is offered in evidence for *any other* purpose, it is not hearsay. It would be admissible, for example, if it were offered to show that the phone line was working, that John Smith spoke the English language, that John Smith was alive that day, that John Smith had not lost his voice, that John Smith knew George Jones's telephone number, or.for some other purpose. The three most common instances of using out-of-court statements indirectly for non-hearsay purposes follow.

Statements Offered to Show an Effect on Hearer Assume Barney is arrested in a building for burglary (breaking into a building with intent to commit a crime therein). He offers evidence that the reason he broke into the building was that a little girl told him that there was a fire in the building and that her mother was trapped inside. Normally what the little girl said would be hearsay.[118] However, Barney is permitted to testify to

---

prosecution will be permitted to bring up his or her prior bad conduct on cross examination, it is a common tactic for the conduct to be brought out first on direct examination in a preemptive effort to "take the sting out" of the jury hearing it for the first time on cross examination. This is risky as it constitutes a waiver of the right to appeal the trial judge's ruling that the evidence is proper. *See Ohler v. United States*, 529 U.S. 753 (2000) (defendant herself brought up her prior convictions; held a waiver of right to appeal the trial judge's pretrial ruling).

116 FRE 801(c) defines hearsay as "a statement, other than one made by the declarant while testifying at the trial or hearing, offered in evidence to prove the truth of the matter asserted." Note that this includes prior out-of-court statements made by the witness as well, *i.e.*, where the "declarant" and the witness at trial are the same person.

117 *But see infra* p. 115, where the "catch-all" exceptions to hearsay are discussed.

118 This would be true even if the little girl was available to testify at the trial. *See supra* note 116.

what she said to him because Barney is *not* offering the statement to prove that there was a fire and that the girl's mother needed to be rescued. He is offering it only to show the *reason* why he broke into the building.

Statements Offered to Attack Credibility Out-of-court statements that are inconsistent with in-court testimony do not violate the rule against hearsay. In the telephone example above, assume John Smith, the person who said on the telephone that it was raining in Peoria, testifies at a later trial that it was *not* raining in Peoria on the day in question. Evidence of his inconsistent statement over the telephone (testified to by anyone who heard it) is not hearsay. The theory is that the out-of-court statement is offered *not* to prove that it was in fact raining, but to impeach Smith's credibility — to show that Smith made a statement contrary to his trial testimony and therefore should not be believed.[119]

Legally Operative Language This includes any out-of-court utterance that has overriding legal significance beyond anything asserted in it. For example, one might wonder why the contents of a contract, which are out-of-court statements, are admissible in evidence. Those contents and any words of offer or acceptance are not hearsay because they are said to have *legal significance without regard to what they assert*. It is the fact that the statements were made that is crucial, not any factual assertions they make. In fact, it is likely that the contract sets out only promises, which do not assert any facts. Other examples of legally operative language are the defamatory statement made by the defendant in a defamation case and the words urging the commission of a crime in a conspiracy or incitement case.

b. Exceptions to the Rule Against Hearsay

There are many exceptions to the rule against hearsay. There are twenty-four in the Federal Rules of Evidence, including a residual exception, discussed below.[120] Because the rule against hearsay contains so many exceptions, some have argued that it should be abolished.[121] However, much to the consternation of law students who have to learn its intricacies, the rule remains. The exceptions discussed here are only some of the major ones.

The exceptions discussed below apply to statements that are clearly hearsay, *i.e.*, statements that are offered to prove what the speaker intended to assert and therefore their reliability depends on the credibility of the speaker. Nonetheless, they are admissible in evidence to prove what they assert, generally because (1) there is something about the nature of the statement or the circumstances in which the speaker utters it that provides some *collateral guarantee of reliability* or (2) there is some *necessity for hearing the statement* in view of the difficulty of proving the matter asserted in any other way.

(1) Party Admissions

Any statement made by a party that *the opposing party* seeks to introduce at trial will be allowed.[122] For example, Dan's dog bites Peter. After the attack, Dan states to Wilma:

---

119 It follows that it would not be proper for the jury to use the inconsistent telephone statement as substantive proof that it *was* raining in Peoria. Jurors are often puzzled by an instruction from the judge explaining that, because the prior inconsistent statement was introduced solely for its relevance to Smith's credibility as a witness, they may use it only for that purpose and not for its substantive content.

120 *See* FRE 803, 804 and 807.

121 This was actually proposed, but quickly dropped when the Federal Rules of Evidence were adopted in 1975.

122 *See* FRE 801(d)(2).

"My dog bit Peter." In a suit by Peter against Dan for damages suffered as a result, Wilma will be allowed to testify to Dan's statement because it is a statement of a party (the defendant) and it is being offered by the plaintiff Peter, an opposing party. Though there are many reasons to allow one party to freely use pre-litigation statements made by the other party, the main one is this. If an *opposing* party is seeking to use the statement, then it must be against the interests of the speaker-party. Therefore, it is likely to be true, since people do not normally say things that are to their detriment unless they are true.[123]

(2) Business Records

Business records potentially include any routinely kept records of any person or organization that keeps such records in the ordinary course of its business activities. Common examples are medical records from doctors' offices or hospitals, records of governmental agencies and accounts and other records of private businesses.[124] The collateral guarantee of reliability for this exception is the *regularity* with which business records are kept. If every time a payment is made, an entry is made in a ledger, then using the ledger to prove payment would seem to be reliable. Necessity is also a consideration, given that it is extremely doubtful a clerk who took the payment would actually remember the amount, when it was made or who made it. However, to protect against falsification or self-serving records, the rule provides that the court can refuse to admit such records if "the source of information or the method or circumstances of preparation indicate lack of trustworthiness."[125]

(3) Excited Utterances

The behavioral assumption behind this exception is that persons who are startled by a sudden event will correctly report that event, since they will not have the time or presence of mind to make up a lie about it. For example, a bomb explodes and Willy, hysterical, screams, "It's a bomb and it was thrown from that car over there!" Willy's statement is an exception to hearsay and a witness who heard it may testify about it to prove that there was a bomb and that it came from a particular car.[126]

(4) Present Sense Impression

The rationale for this exception is similar to the excited utterance, except that there is no requirement of excitement, only a requirement that the description of the event take place while it is going on or shortly thereafter.[127] For example, X and W are standing on the street corner talking to each other with X looking toward the intersection and W facing X. Over W's shoulder, X sees an accident happen and says "That furniture truck just ran the red light." W will be permitted to testify to what X said. Related to present sense impression is the matter of identification of a person after perceiving him, such as a policeman testifying after a lineup that the victim said "that's the man who did it." However, an extra safeguard is provided for identification testimony by the rules, which

---

123 The Federal Rules of Evidence treat party admissions, not as exceptions to hearsay, but as not being hearsay at all. However, admissions are commonly referred to as an exception and that status makes sense, so that is the way they are classified here.

124 *See* FRE 803(6). The definition requires that the entry in the records must be made (1) at or near the time the recorded event took place, (2) by, or from information provided by, a person with knowledge of the event recorded, (3) in records kept in the ordinary course of business (4) by an organization which makes it a regular practice to keep such records. *But see* FRE 803(8) (police reports are not admissible in criminal cases).

125 Police reports of criminal investigations are within the business record exception, but in criminal cases they are excluded from the exception and are thus inadmissible hearsay. *See* FRE 803(8).

126 *See* FRE 803(2).

127 *See* FRE 803(1).

require that the victim who made the statement be available for cross examination about the circumstances of the statement.[128]

(5) State of Mind

Examples of statements regarding one's state of mind are where the witness reports that the person said at some prior time "my leg hurts," "I feel bad," "I'm going to New York tomorrow." Usually people who make such statements do not think about their possible significance in later litigation, although it is always possible that the statement is staged for that purpose. An additional overriding reason they are permitted is the difficulty of proving state of mind by any other method.[129]

(6) Other Exceptions

Merely naming some of the other exceptions to the hearsay rule will suggest what collateral guarantees of reliability exist that make them admissible: statements made for purposes of medical diagnosis, records of vital statistics, marriage and baptismal certificates, market reports, reputation concerning family history and boundaries of land, dying declarations, and statements against pecuniary or penal interest.[130] The Federal Rules of Evidence also provide a residual "catch-all" hearsay exception that allows a court to admit hearsay that is not covered by any existing exception. The residual exception reflects the two bases underlying rationale of the specific exceptions. It provides that a hearsay statement not covered by the specific exceptions that has "equivalent circumstantial guarantees of trustworthiness" and "is more probative . . . than any other evidence which the proponent can procure" is admissible.[131]

E. Criticisms of the Adversary System

There have been and continue to be debates about the assumptions underlying the adversary system. Both the justifications and the criticisms are largely based on untested behavioral assumptions and anecdotal evidence. In addition, proposals for radical change are somewhat pointless given that at least some aspects of the adversary system are enshrined in the Constitution.[132] Nevertheless, we should review some of the major criticisms that have been raised and debated.[133]

1. Abuse of Party-Control

Witness Preparation and Abuse Critics point to all the opportunities for abuse that exist when the parties are in control of investigating and presenting the case. One target is the accepted practice of lawyers preparing "their" witnesses to testify. There are advantages to proper witness preparation: it makes the testimony more to the point. But it is argued that witness preparation allows for the possibility of lawyers prompting the

---

128 *See* FRE 801(d)(1)(C).

129 *See* FRE 803(3).

130 These are set out in other sections of FRE 803 and FRE 804.

131 FRE 807. Another important part of evidence law is the law of "privileges" covered by FRE 501. Information communicated in the course of certain special relationships, such as lawyer-client, doctor-patient, priest-penitent and between spouses is said to be "privileged" and may not be divulged under compulsion at any time. *See also infra* Chapter VII, p. 238 (exemption from discovery) and Chapter IV, p. 163 (attorney-client privilege).

132 *See Herring v. New York*, 422 U.S. 853 (1975) (the constitutional right to counsel "has been understood to mean that there can be no restriction on the function of counsel in defending a prosecution in accord with the traditions of the adversary fact-finding process that has been constitutionalized in the Sixth and Fourteenth Amendments").

133 For a more complete, but somewhat partisan account of criticisms of the adversary system and responses to those criticisms, *see* LANDSMAN, *supra* note 4, at 24-76 and FREEDMAN, *infra* note 156, at 26-42.

witness to testify to things that are not true. And, critics point out, cross examination by the other side is hardly a match for a well-prepared witness. The result, they argue, is likely to be that the other side will feel it necessary to attack the witness in any way possible to undermine their credibility, thus turning the witness stand into a "slaughter-house of reputations" with courts unable to restrain "bullying" of witnesses by lawyers who "forget that they are officers of the court."[134]

Supporters point out that lawyers are prohibited by both professional ethics and the criminal law from suborning perjury or otherwise perpetrating a fraud upon the court. But beyond that, the supposed invincibility of lawyer-prepared witnesses to impeachment ignores the scope and power of cross examination, aided by discovery, to uncover fraud. Moreover, juries are particularly prone to be suspicious of evidence that sounds "too good." Indeed, many lawyers are careful not to "over-prepare" witnesses for this reason. And the amount of preparation the witness has been through can be explored on cross-examination. As for abusive cross-examination tactics, lawyers who conduct themselves in this manner will be admonished by a good trial judge. But the most effective restraint on lawyers is the fact that such tactics are usually counterproductive in front of a jury, which is far more likely to identify with the hapless witness than with the bullying lawyer.

Benefits of Party Control Supporters of the adversary system emphasize that, even if party control may have its risks, it has important benefits. When the parties have extensive and direct input into the process by which their case is decided, they are more likely to feel that their point of view was fully aired and was understood as well as it could be — even if it was ultimately rejected. In this way, party control does two things. First, it promotes the legitimacy of judicial decisions, which depend first and foremost on voluntary acceptance by society as legitimate and only secondarily on state coercion. Second, a system that gives individuals direct participation in and control over litigation affecting their lives affirms human dignity and value. Even if one loses a hearing, active party participation at that hearing "express[es] the elementary idea that to be a *person*, rather than a *thing*, is at least to be consulted about what is done with one."[135] The greater the opportunity to be heard fully in the manner that one wishes to be heard, the greater the respect that is paid to human dignity and worth. Given the threat to individuality posed by expanding governmental power and the pressures of "efficiency" in modern society, supporters of party control argue that there is a greater need today than ever before for individuality-reinforcing institutions.[136]

The Government as Partisan Litigant Special difficulties can arise in an adversary system when the *government* is involved as a party. In many countries, the prosecutor is a quasi-judicial official who is above the partisan fray and "sleeps well even after an acquittal."[137] The prosecutor in the United States is supposed to have a duty "to seek

---

134 Roscoe Pound, *The Causes of Popular Dissatisfaction with the Administration of Justice*, 29 ABA REPORTS 395, 405 (1906).

135 LAWRENCE TRIBE, AMERICAN CONSTITUTIONAL LAW, 3D ED. 666 (Foundation Press 1999).

136 In an interesting study in JOHN THIBAULT AND LAURENS WALKER, PROCEDURAL JUSTICE: A PSYCHOLOGICAL ANALYSIS 77-80, 94-96 (John Wiley & Sons 1975), the authors found that a majority of the subjects of multinational studies thought that adversary procedures were fairer than investigatory procedures for resolving disputes.

137 *See* William J. Pizzi and Luca Marafioti, *The New Italian Code of Criminal Procedure: The Difficulties of Building an Adversarial Trial System on a Civil Law Foundation*, 17 YALE J.INT'L.L. 1, 31 (1992).

justice, not merely to convict."[138] But a realist would have to recognize that once the case reaches the trial stage and even before, prosecutors in the United States see their role as that of a partisan advocate for their client and it is a matter of mere coincidence that that "client" is a powerful government. Thus, prosecutors will in the overwhelming majority of cases do everything in their power to win the case for their client, *i.e.*, to secure the defendant's conviction to the highest possible charge. Sometimes this "win-at-all-costs" attitude has resulted in improper convictions.[139]

The ABA Model Rules of Professional Conduct, which have been adopted in three-fourths of the states, have something to say on the subject, but they equivocate somewhat. Rule 3.8 provides that a prosecutor must refrain from pressing groundless charges, must assure that defendants are advised of their right to counsel, may not take advantage of unrepresented defendants, and must disclose exculpatory information they have to defendants. The official "comment" to this rule explains in general terms that a "prosecutor has a responsibility as a minister of justice and not simply that of an advocate. This responsibility carries with it specific obligations to see that the defendant is accorded procedural justice and that guilt is decided upon the basis of sufficient evidence." However, it concludes unhelpfully, "[p]recisely how far the prosecutor is required to go in this direction is a matter of debate and varies in different jurisdictions."[140]

2. Inadequate Focus on the Truth

This criticism is related to concerns about abuse of party control. It asserts that, contrary to adversary theory, party control of litigation is not likely to result in a fully-informed decision-maker because not all the relevant information will be uncovered. As Judge Frankel, a long-standing critic of the adversary system, has observed, it is a rare case in which either side yearns to have the witness, or anyone, give the *whole truth*.[141] To the extent that incomplete information is supplied, the court will be making a decision based on something other than the real truth about a case. A slightly different version of this critique has it that our "sporting theory of justice" never asks what the truth is; it only asks "have the rules of the game been carried out strictly?"[142] Two responses are usually given to these points.

The Misconceived Quest for "The Truth" The first response admits that the adversary system has a relativistic attitude toward truth, but argues that this is more consistent with reality than any search for "*the* truth." For all the talk in some systems that the "objective truth" must be discovered in legal proceedings, an event cannot be reproduced in court. After it has taken place, unless there is a videotape of it, all that we can rely on are *perceptions* of the event and then only to the extent that those perceptions can be *remembered* by *people* and then *communicated* by them. Given the

---

138 ABA Standards for Criminal Justice, Standard 3-1.1(ABA 1993). These standards are supposed to be "guidelines that have long been adhered to by the best prosecutors and best defense counsel." Federal prosecutors are admonished to "see that justice is done." Department of Justice Manual, Title 9, Chapter 27, §9-27.000 et seq., "Federal Principles of Criminal Prosecution," pp. 9-495-9-559.

139 *See* case examples in Chapter VIII, p. 276, note 35

140 Rule 3.8 of the ABA Model Rules of Professional Conduct and comment (ABA 2010).

141 *See* Marvin Frankel, Partisan Justice 10-20 (Hill & Wang 1980). This book is a succinct, but thorough critique of most all aspects of the adversary system. It is interesting to note that many of the critics of the adversary system and juries are judges with extensive experience with the intricacies of adversary trials. As discussed *infra*, Judge Jerome Frank was also a vigorous critic of the jury system. *See* Jerome Frank, Courts on Trial (Princeton 1949).

142 Pound, *supra* note 64, p.406.

weaknesses of perception, memory and communication, there are often as many "truths" about an event as there are witnesses to it. The idea is not to find "*the* truth" of an event, but to find *which communicated perception* of an event is the *most plausible account* of that event. A system that gives full leeway to competing perceptions of an event throughout the trial and right up until the time for decision is one that accurately reflects reality. By contrast, pursuit of "*the* truth" is not only naive, but ultimately impossible. Defenders of the adversary system would point out that the cause of truth is routinely *better* served in an adversary system since in every case at least two versions of the truth get presented — one more version than would routinely be unearthed in a less adversarial system.[143] In fact, the adversary system *is* concerned with determining the truth, at least as just defined. One has difficulty imagining a case in which the parties collectively would not have the incentive to discover and present all information that is truly relevant to a decision in the matter.

Allocating the Power to Declare Truth Given that there can be competing versions of the truth, it is *equally* important in finding the truth to be concerned about *who has the power to investigate and declare truth*. Given the often elusive nature of truth, the adversary system sees serious dangers if one entity — the state — has a monopoly on the power to discover and declare it. Borrowing from the concept of separation of powers in constitutional theory, proponents of the adversary system believe that the cause of truth is better served if the responsibility for discovering and declaring it is spread between the state, the parties and, where applicable, the jury. While one might doubt how often governments fail their citizens and abuse their power in this respect, mistrust of government is a strong theme in American political history. And one could point to several instances just in the 20th century where governments, unrestrained by countervailing forces, have declared rather monstrous versions of "the truth."

3. The Inefficiency of Adversary Litigation

Complexity, Speed and Values Beyond Efficiency A major criticism of the adversary system, which relates in part to problems with party control, is its slow pace. While some things go quickly, the trial is a slow and complicated process. Presentation of first-hand oral and other "immediate" evidence in a question-and-answer format can take a long time to develop, objections based on complex rules of evidence arise and must be decided, and the judge must remain passive throughout and assure that both sides are heard fully.[144] Even before trial, there must be time for the parties' lawyers to discover and analyze evidence, and then to plan on how to present it in the most persuasive way possible.

It is no secret that all this takes time. However, it does increase the amount of information available to the decision-maker. Moreover, efficiency is not everything. As the Supreme Court has observed:

> The establishment of prompt efficacious procedures to achieve legitimate state ends is a proper state interest worthy of cognizance in constitutional adjudication. But the Constitution recognizes higher values than speed and efficiency. Indeed, one might fairly say of the Bill of Rights in general, and the Due Process

---

143 Some support for the adversary system's more relativistic view of truth can be found in the psychological literature which shows that much of what people perceive is a particular interpretation of the events, rather than a true reflection. *See* DAVID J. SCHNEIDER, ALBERT H. HASDORF & PHOEBE ELLSWORTH, PERSON PERCEPTION (Addison-Wesley Pub. Co., Reading, Mass. 1979).

144 Of course, much of the extra time it takes to try a case is not caused by the adversary system as much as by the right to a jury trial. Criticisms of juries are discussed in the next section of this chapter.

Clause in particular, that they were designed to protect the fragile values of a vulnerable citizenry from the overbearing concern for efficiency and efficacy that may characterize praiseworthy government officials no less, and perhaps more, than mediocre ones.[145]

Some Efficiencies of Adversary Procedure   Adversary systems have efficiencies absent from some other systems. Party control over litigation confers the right to litigate vigorously, but it also permits parties to choose not to litigate. Many civil law systems, at least in criminal cases, require that a trial be held regardless of whether the affected parties want one. In an adversary system, when defendants plead guilty and waive their right to further proceedings, there is no need for a trial. All that is necessary is that they understand that they are waiving their right to a trial and that they admit on the record facts showing that they in fact committed the offense charged.[146] In civil cases, settlements are even easier. Unless a minor or other person in need of special protection is affected, parties have the absolute right to settle whenever and on whatever terms they wish. In the 75 largest counties in the U.S. in 1992, 75% of all civil tort cases were disposed of through an agreed settlement or voluntary dismissal. In criminal cases, 92% of convictions obtained were the result of a guilty plea.[147] There have also been major efforts to urge alternatives to judicial resolution of disputes.[148]

The ability of parties to waive their rights not only disposes of entire cases, it can also dispense with the need for parts of trials. Parties or counsel routinely enter into "stipulations" — agreements about particular facts — or agree to waive objections to particular evidence or procedural requirements. Indeed, a large part of the job of the judge in preparing a civil case at the final pre-trial conference is to explore "the possibility of obtaining admissions of fact and of documents, which will avoid unnecessary proof."[149] It is not uncommon in a civil case that the parties and their lawyers will have stipulated to the admission of almost all documents or tangible evidence in a case, thus removing entirely the need to lay foundations for receipt of those items in evidence at the trial. While stipulations of this type are not as common in criminal cases, their use is increasing.

Recent Anti-Adversarial Reforms   There have been efforts in recent years to limit some "adversarial excesses" and to make litigation more efficient. There have been changes in federal and some state civil procedure rules requiring that the parties automatically disclose basic evidence in support of their claims or defenses to the other side and imposing limits on the extent of discovery. Rules on federal pre-trial proceedings before judges now empower and encourages judges to more actively manage their cases. The use of lower-level "magistrate judges" to keep closer track of litigation in its

---

145 *Stanley v. Illinois*, 405 U.S. 645 (1972). In *Stanley*, the Court held unconstitutional an Illinois law that provided that unwed fathers need not be given a hearing before their parental rights were terminated. For more on the issue of custody of children of unwed parents, *see* Chapter XIII, p. 527, note 48, and Chapter IX, p. 362.

146 *See* Chapter VIII, pp. 280-282, for a description of guilty pleas. The efficiencies gained by guilty pleas were part of what caused Italy to introduce a more adversarial style criminal procedure in 1989. *See* Pizzi & Marafioti, *supra* note 137. Serious limitations on plea bargaining and legal cultural differences have made implementation of the summary guilty plea procedures difficult. Spain and Denmark have enacted similar procedures and informal practices approximating plea bargaining have grown up in France and Germany. *See id.* at 35-37.

147 Source: Bureau of Justice Statistics, U.S. Dept. of Justice. *See* Chapter VII, p. 251 (settlements in civil cases) and Chapter VIII, p. 280 (guilty pleas in criminal cases).

148 *See* Chapter VII, pp. 250-253 (arbitration, mediation and settlement in civil cases).

149 Federal Rule of Civil Procedure 16(c). *See also* Chapter VII, pp. 241 (pretrial conferences).

pretrial stages has increased. Many of these measures are part of a general trend in recent years toward more "managerial judging."[150] Serious sanctions can also be imposed on lawyers who assert groundless positions in litigation.[151]

4. The Costs of Litigation and Inequality of Financial Resources

A Special Problem for Adversary Systems Inequality in litigation because one side has superior resources is undoubtedly a problem in all legal systems. But inequality of resources is a special problem in an adversary system where the parties have so many responsibilities for gathering evidence and presenting the case. Though parties have the right to represent themselves, a party without a lawyer is much more likely to be completely lost in an adversary system than in a system in which the judge is responsible for developing the evidence and legal points. Consequently, it is perhaps much more likely in an adversary system that the party with the more skilled lawyer and more resources for litigation support, such as investigators and experts, will have an advantage. This is exacerbated as well by the "American rule" with regard to litigation costs, under which winning parties may not recover their attorneys fees if they win.[152]

Mitigating Factors The practical need for a lawyer has been met to a certain extent. The 6th Amendment to the Constitution requires that the government provide lawyers and other assistance for the unrepresented in all criminal cases where jail is a possibility.[153] In civil cases, there is no such constitutional right, but efforts have been made since 1964 to provide federal funding for legal services for the poor, and prepaid legal insurance and other plans have grown in recent years.[154] Moreover, the availability of the contingent fee serves as a powerful incentive for good lawyers to handle personal injury civil cases of clients otherwise unable to afford an attorney.[155] In addition, some statutes have changed the "American rule" on litigation costs to one that allows a winning party to recover attorneys fees and court costs from the losing party in some kinds of cases.[156]

In civil cases, many procedural devices are designed to make the outcome in a case less dependent on the skills of the lawyer at trial. The discovery process in civil litigation allows parties to obtain most of the opposing party's evidence well before trial, thereby making it easier for the less well-equipped or less expert lawyer to respond to what greater financial resources or talent may have amassed on the other side of a case. To the extent that a more powerful opponent can use discovery and other procedural

---

150 *See* Chapter VII, pp. 239, 241. For an account of the move toward greater judicial control over fact-finding, *see* John Langbein, *The German Advantage in Civil Procedure*, 52 U. CHI. L.REV. 823, 866 (1988) and Judith Resnick, *Managerial Judges*, 96 HARV.L.REV. 374 (1982). This trend is, to say the least, controversial in the United States. *See* LANDSMAN, *supra* note 4, at 77-121.

151 Some of these measures are discussed in Chapter VII, pp. 229-242.

152 The "American rule" regarding attorney fees is so called to distinguish it from the "English rule," which normally shifts the burden to the losing side. *See* Chapter VII, p. 247.

153 *See* Chapter VIII, p. 312. *See also* Chapter IV, p. 156, for a discussion of public defenders. The criminal defendant also has the right to any necessary experts or investigators at government expense. *See Ake v. Oklahoma*, 470 U.S. 68 (1988) (Defendant has right to a psychiatric evaluation and expert witness assistance where his sanity is at issue in case) and Criminal Justice Act, 18 U.S.C.A. §3006A(c)(1) (providing for payment for defense experts).

154 *See* Chapter IV, pp. 155-156, for a discussion of civil legal services for the poor.

155 In a contingent fee arrangement, the lawyer will not charge the client a fee unless the client wins, in which case the lawyer will take the fee out of the recovery, usually to one-third of the recovery. For a lawyer to be attracted to such a case, of course, there must be a good chance of winning a large enough verdict. Consequently, it is only in personal injury cases where several thousands of dollars or more are at stake that a lawyer will agree to such an arrangement. *See* Chapter IV, p. 145.

156 *See* Chapter VII, p. 248.

devices to "wear down" or increase the litigation costs of a party with fewer resources, changes in recent years imposing limits on discovery and sanctions for misuse of the courts for these purposes, mentioned earlier, are specifically designed to prevent this.[157]

Built-In Safeguards There are also built-in features of the adversary system in the United States that equalize parties with disparate amounts of resources. The presence of a jury makes the trial somewhat more equal since jury members are much more likely to identify with the poor litigant than with the rich corporation or the powerful state. Less well-off parties' lawyers regularly take advantage of the "underdog" status of their client to considerable effect.

But even with all these factors at work, candor requires the admission that inequality based on wealth remains a problem in courts in the United States. It is probably true that, to a certain extent, "what kind of justice a person gets depends on how much money he has."[158] How much more of a problem this is in the United States than anywhere else is hard to say.

5. Criticisms of the Jury System

Most of the criticisms of the jury system are of two types. Critics either point to the relative inefficiency and high cost of jury trials or they question the ability of juries to decide cases properly.[159]

The Expense and Inefficiency of Juries Trials with juries take about 40% longer than bench trials. Enforcing the rules of evidence strictly takes time and the lawyers are more deliberate in presenting their cases. Jurors, not being the "professional listeners" judges are, get tired and need more frequent breaks. And it goes without saying that the decision making process of juries is more protracted. While this may seem like a great loss of efficiency, it should be remembered that around 90% of cases filed do not go to trial at all, and only some of the trials in the 10% of cases that do go to trial are jury trials.

In addition, some of the "anti-adversarial" reforms mentioned earlier have served to make jury trials more efficient. More vigorous pre-trial judicial supervision has the effect of forcing the parties to agree on more facts, thus leaving less for the jury to decide. The use of special verdicts, as discussed earlier in this chapter, can improve efficiency. Such verdicts, instead of just "dumping" the entire case on jurors with no direction other than instructions, can spell out the issues for them by way of specific questions and thus streamline their decision making process.[160] Moreover, the trial judge has always had the power to limit unnecessary proof and to exclude even relevant evidence to prevent "undue delay, waste of time, and needless presentation of cumulative evidence."[161] Many trial judges are exercising this power to a greater degree than before and the result has been improved efficiency.

---

157 *See* Chapter VII, p. 239.

158 *Griffin v. Illinois*, 351 U.S. 12, 18 n.16 (1956).

159 Among the severest critics of juries was Judge Jerome Frank. *See* JEROME FRANK, COURTS ON TRIAL (Princeton 1949). There has been much interest in and criticism of the jury system in recent years. Two books are JEFFREY ABRAMSON, WE, THE JURY: THE JURY SYSTEM AND THE IDEAL OF DEMOCRACY (Harvard University Press 2000) and STEPHEN J. ADLER, THE JURY: DISORDER IN THE COURTS (Main Street Books 1995).

160 *See supra* p. 107. Some of these reforms are addressed in William W. Schwarzer, *Reforming Jury Trials*, 1990 U.CHI.LEGAL FORUM 119, 121-125. *See also* MUNSTERMAN ET AL., *supra* note 44.

161 FRE 403; FRCP 16. The wide-spread use of smaller juries in civil cases makes jury trial somewhat easier. Civil juries of between 6 and 12 may be used in federal court since 1991 and attempts to restore the 12-person jury were defeated in 1996. Close to 40 states provide for juries of fewer than 12 in civil cases.

The Abilities of Juries as Decision-Makers   Critics often argue that only legal specialists, not laypeople, should be involved in decision-making in the legal system. However, it must be remembered that the *legal* issues in a case *are* decided by a judge. The division of labor between judge and jury involves juries in deciding only disputed issues of fact — a task for which a legal education is not necessarily an advantage.[162]

Lawyers who try cases before juries often remark how impressed they are with the abilities of juries at determining fact issues. Though individual jurors may know very little and as *individuals* may not even be particularly good decision-makers, many comment on how the jury, when it sits as a group, is far more than the sum of its parts — how the entire jury seems to acquire abilities that would not be expected from looking at its members individually.

Psychological research on the dynamics of group decision-making tends to support this intuitive observation. One particularly telling study is by Barnlund, who tested the effect of group dynamics on reasoning ability.[163] College students were tested on their syllogistic reasoning ability. Then researchers pitted the *best individual* reasoners against *groups* of the *poorest* reasoners. When it came to dealing with syllogisms whose premises and conclusions were statements that awakened strong emotions and value preferences, such as assertions about Communism, college rule systems, and the like, the *best individual* reasoners did *worse* at solving them than the *groups* of *poor* reasoners. The explanation was that the individual good reasoners were misled by their emotional responses. Members of the groups of *poor* reasoners were also misled initially, but in different directions. As a result, the group was able to set them straight. Those misled in one direction were corrected or balanced out by others who had a different reaction. The operation of this group dynamic is supported by other studies that indicate that accuracy in jury deliberations is improved more by increasing the *social diversity* of jurors than by increasing their average educational level.[164]

Comparing the Alternatives   In evaluating the abilities of the jury, we must remember exactly what fact-finding institutions we are comparing. In all situations other than a criminal acquittal, the judge has the power to set aside lawless or arbitrary jury verdicts. Even if it is reasonable to assume that the average judge would be superior to the average juror, that is not what is being compared. The appropriate comparison is between the judge alone on the one hand and the *entire* jury with the *judge's assistance and control* on the other.

It is interesting to compare the level of judge and jury disagreement in decision-making, especially since the alternative to juries deciding cases is to have judges decide them. In a now-classic study, Kalven and Zeisel found that judges agreed with jury verdicts in 78% of civil and criminal cases.[165] Perhaps more important than the rate of agreement is the fact that many of the 22% of cases where there was disagreement related to a probable different perception of what "justice" required.[166] Among the examples of cases where the jury acquitted, but the judge would have convicted were

162 *See supra* pp. 87, 89.

163 Dean C. Barnlund, *A Comparative Study of Individual, Majority and Group Judgment*, 58 J. AB. & SOC. PSYCH. 55 (1959). Similar studies are cited in Richard O. Lempert, *Uncovering "Non-discernible" Differences: Empirical Research and the Jury-Size Cases*, 73 Mich.L.Rev. 643-708 (1975).

164 *See* Fred L. Strodtbeck, Rita M. James and Charles Hawkins, *Social Status in Jury Deliberations*, 22 Am. Sociological Rev. 713 (1957).

165 KALVEN & ZEISEL, *supra* note 148, at 55-65.

166 *Id.*, p. 116.

the case of a larceny defendant who had stolen $2.50 worth of lumber and who had been in jail for two months awaiting trial and the case of a drunk driving defendant charged with manslaughter in an accident that killed his wife and left him paralyzed for life. And it is possible, given the psychological studies by Barnlund discussed above, that at least in some of the remaining cases where there was disagreement, the jury could have reached the more accurate conclusion.[167]

Juries in Civil Damages Cases There have been special concerns raised about the abilities of juries in civil cases. It has been argued vigorously by defense attorneys and insurance companies that "run-away" juries have been awarding outrageous amounts to undeserving plaintiffs in personal injury cases.[168] However, the reality is quite different. Though the juries in their study tended to side with the defense more than the prosecution in criminal cases, in the 22% of civil cases where judge and jury disagreed, they were almost evenly split. A more recent study examining products liability cases between 1979 and 1988 showed that in nine of the ten years examined, plaintiffs won as many as 58% of all federal products liability cases tried before *judges* and only 29% of federal products liability cases tried before *juries*.[169] Clearly the media have a strong influence on public perceptions of civil juries. A recent study compared federal jury trials described in media accounts with actual figures. In the cases reported by the media, plaintiffs won 98% of jury trials, while in reality only 41% of plaintiffs prevailed. And the median amount jury verdicts reported by the media was $1,100,000, while the actual median amount was $150,000.[170]

Jury awards in civil cases do tend to be higher than judge awards, but the difference is not as striking as one might think. In Kalven & Zeisel's study, judges would have given less than the jury awarded in 52% of cases, about the same in 10%, and more in 38%. And the average dollar amount of disagreement in cases where juries gave more money was only 10%. It should be borne in mind as well that when the amount awarded by a jury is clearly out of line with the damages proven, the fault is not so much with the jury as it is with the judge, who has the power to reduce such awards or to order a new trial.[171] Of course, it is impossible to say whether it is the judge or the jury that is more correct in any objective sense. At least some issues that arise in civil litigation — for

---

167 The American Judicature Society has collected materials on juries: www.ajs.org/jc/index.asp.

168 Similar reasons were given for effectively abolishing the right to a civil jury in England. *See Ward v. James*, [1965] 1 Q.B. 273, 1 All Eng. Rep. 563. Civil cases are triable to a jury only if provided for by statute or if in the judge's discretion there are "in exceptional circumstances" that warrant it. Currently, only twelve or so civil jury trials a year take place in England.

169 Theodore Eisenberg & James A. Henderson, *The Quiet Revolution in Products Liability: An Empirical Study of Legal Change*, 37 U.C.L.A. L.REV 479 (1990). *But see* Kevin Clermont & Theodore Eisenberg, *Do Case Outcomes Really Reveal Anything About the Legal System? Win Rates and Removal Jurisdiction*, 83 CORNELL L. REV. 581 (1998) (advising caution in relying on raw win statistics, since cases that go to trial are a small and skewed sample of all cases). Supposed difficulties with civil juries in tort cases, particularly those with punitive damages, are discussed in Chapter XI, pp. 463-437. The Saks article, *infra* note 172, reviews the major empirical data on the subject. A concern voiced by foreigners doing business in the U.S. has been that they are at a disadvantage before U.S. courts, in part because juries are biased against them. A recent article dispels this myth. Kevin Clermont & Theodore Eisenberg, *Xenophilia in American Courts*, 109 HARV. L. REV. 1120 (1996) (foreigners, whether as plaintiff or defendant, win 63% of the cases, whereas natives win only 37%).

170 Source: American Bar Foundation, as reported in 16 RESEARCHING LAW 3 (2005).

171 *See supra* p. 108.

example, the value of a human life — are arguably issues that judges' legal educations and experience give them no particular superior ability to decide.[172]

Benefits of Juries Beyond Factual Accuracy Some supporters of juries believe that one of the benefits of juries is their very "erroneous" ways in that their decision reflects something more than cold logic and strict law application. As one federal judge explained:

> The law can become rigid. Rules that made sense when adopted may be foolish and unjust in particular cases. The jury can give flexibility to the law, ensuring that it is applied in a way that is consistent with the standards of the community. Because it does not have to explain its reasons, it is able to arrive at appropriate decisions that avoid irrational results but may be difficult for a judge to explain.[173]

Sometimes juries' consistent "tempering" of a legal rule can point the way for law reform. An example of this is *Hoffman v. Jones*, the Florida case changing from contributory negligence to comparative negligence, which was discussed in Chapter II. The Florida Supreme Court relied in part on the fact that it was apparent that juries consistently judged plaintiffs' conduct by a less harsh comparative negligence standard even when told to apply the more strict contributory negligence standard.[174]

Many heros of American political history have been saved by "erroneous" jury verdicts. Peter Zenger, the publisher of criticism against the British Crown who was acquitted by a New York colonial jury in 1734, was probably factually guilty of seditious libel.[175] Later, Northern abolitionists who hid escaped slaves before the Civil War would benefit from jury "inaccuracy." More recently, protesters against the Vietnam War, draft resisters and citizens who hid illegal asylum seekers from El Salvador, whom juries acquitted, were probably factually guilty. Of course, the vast majority of cases are not ones that demand that "the truth" be slighted in favor of justice. But in those cases where truth *and* justice both point toward conviction, the government has ample resources and good lawyers of its own who can make the case for conviction before the jury, if there is one to be made.[176]

Consistent with this, the Supreme Court observed in a 1970 case that the Founders "knew from history and experience that it was necessary to protect against unfounded criminal charges brought to eliminate enemies and against judges too responsive to the voice of higher authority." The right to trial by a jury gives the citizen:

---

172 GUINTHER, *supra* note 19, at 170. In considering increased amounts of jury awards, it is relevant that medical costs constitute the bulk of personal injury damages awards and that medical costs rose by 600% from 1955 to 1985 at a time when per capita income only doubled. Some studies suggest that juries may not be awarding enough damages. In one state, contrary to expectations, where professional decision-makers with medical knowledge were substituted for the jury trial system, the average award *increased* by one-third. *See* Michael Saks, *Do We Really Know Anything About the Behavior of the Tort Litigation System — and Why Not?* 140 U.PA.L.REV. 1147, 1273-1274 (1992).

173 William W. Schwarzer, "Some Observations on the Values of the Jury System" (address at Federal Judicial Center Seminar for Russian Judges and Court Administrators, July 1993).

174 *See* discussion *supra* p. 88.

175 An account of the Zenger case is set out in GUINTHER, *supra* note 19, at 28-30.

176 Juries have also nullified based on racist attitudes, as when southern juries in the past acquitted whites accused of murdering blacks. However, blacks were at that time systematically excluded from jury service. Further, the federal government has often later prosecuted the acquitted defendants for violation of the victim's civil rights. This is allowed under the "dual sovereignty" exception to the ban on multiple prosecutions for the same offense, discussed in Chapter VIII, p. 317.

an inestimable safeguard against the corrupt or overzealous prosecutor and against the compliant, biased, or eccentric judge.... [It] reflect[s] a fundamental decision about the exercise of official power — a reluctance to entrust plenary powers over the life and liberty of the citizen to one judge or to a group of judges. Fear of unchecked power, so typical of our State and Federal Governments in other respects, found expression in the criminal law in this insistence upon community participation in the determination of guilt or innocence.[177]

This role of the jury was eloquently stated by a Maryland farmer in the debates over the constitutional right to a jury trial. He agreed that all the structural controls on the federal government contained in the Constitution, such as separation of power and federalism, were needed to keep it from passing unjust legislation infringing on civil liberties of citizens. But he saw a greater threat to freedom in the *misuse* of otherwise *just* laws on the *local* level, from which the structural protections of the constitution gave no protection. "[T]hose usurpations, which silently undermine the spirit of liberty, under the sanctions of law, are more dangerous than direct and open legislative attack." He argued that the only effective protection from this threat was the jury.[178]

The Value of Civic Participation   Aside from standing as a protection against arbitrary government action, juries also promote democratic values and principles of self-government by enlisting ordinary citizens in the business of government. This popular participation has an indirect benefit similar to one mentioned for party-control over litigation: if citizens have more of a stake in their system, they are more likely to support the decisions of courts, which rely first and foremost on voluntary compliance with their decisions. This consideration played a major role in Russia's 1993 reintroduction of the jury system in that country. It was said to be needed to restore public confidence in a judicial system discredited by 70 years of state and Communist Party control.

The Jury's Effect on Judicial Independence   Some point out that juries help to protect the independence of judges. As explained by the federal judge quoted earlier:

Even under the best of circumstances, a single judge making an unpopular decision comes under public and sometimes official criticism that may have adverse effects on his person, his family and his career. Juries, being anonymous and out of the public eye as soon as the case is over, are well suited to decide controversial cases that could be difficult for judges to decide. And because they hold no office, have no other continuing connection with the government and have no political ambition, they are genuinely independent.[179]

This last point is particularly important for those state courts in the United States whose judges must face reelection, though even federal judges and other appointed judges are not unaffected by these kinds of pressures.[180]

---

177 *Duncan v. Louisiana*, 391 U.S. 145, 156 (1968).

178 HERBERT J. STORING, THE COMPLETE ANTI-FEDERALIST 18-19 (U. Chicago 2007), quoting Federal Farmer (XV, 2, 8, 90).

179 Schwarzer, *supra* note 173. Clearly, there is room for improvement in the jury system. An article by the author of the quotation in the text and director of the Federal Judicial Center, a research arm of the federal courts, surveys various points where improvement have been made and suggested. *See* Schwarzer, *supra* note 160. *See also* MUNSTERMAN ET AL., *supra* note 44.

180 Modes of judicial selection are discussed in Chapter V, pp. 180-184.

As these last few points suggest, juries may have been retained in the United States long after they had been abolished elsewhere precisely because they reflect peculiarly American values. A jury system could well not work in other systems or might work only with major modifications in attitudes and laws.[181]

---

181 There have also been discussions about resurrecting the right to a jury in some criminal cases in Japan. Some have expressed doubts, however, that jury trials would be consistent with Japanese culture and temperament, Richard O. Lempert, *A Jury for Japan?*, 40 AM. J. COMP. L. 37 (1992), and Japan has opted for more of a modified mixed court system.

CHAPTER IV

THE LEGAL PROFESSION

The legal profession in the United States has historically been one of society's most influential professions, if not its most beloved.[1] From the very beginning of the republic, a disproportionate percentage of lawyers have occupied positions of power in political circles. Almost 45% of the Framers of the 1789 Constitution were lawyers. Around 65% of the Senate and well over half the members of the House of Representatives have been lawyers. Alexis de Tocqueville observed in his famous work, *Democracy in America*:

> In America there are no nobles or literary men, and the people are apt to mistrust the wealthy; lawyers consequently form the highest political class and the most cultivated portion of society. . . . If I were asked where I place the American aristocracy, I should reply without hesitation that it is not among the rich, who are united by no common tie, it occupies the judicial bench and the bar.[2]

Judging from the negative public attitudes about lawyers heard today, it is clear that much of the "aristocratic" veneer of the legal profession has worn off.[3] Part of the respect and perhaps a great deal of the dislike of lawyers undoubtedly comes from the nature of law and procedure in the United States. As demonstrated in Chapter II, the legal methodology involved in a caselaw system is complicated and, as discussed in Chapter III, adversarial procedure requires skilled lawyers to fulfill the obligations imposed on parties to investigate and present their own evidence in court proceedings. To this extent, the need to turn to lawyers for help is greater in the United States than in some other systems. Such dependence doubtless results in lawyers being perceived, not only as powerful helper-friends, but also as irritating reminders of powerlessness.

The Profession in Crisis? Even in the most cohesive of times, the legal profession has covered a broad spectrum of lawyers. It includes lawyers in private practice, prosecutors and other government lawyers from every level of government, judges and magistrates, in-house counsel for corporations, public defenders and other lawyers for the poor, and law teachers. Even within the broad category of private practice, lawyers work in a wide variety of settings and often share little in common. Some lack of cohesiveness is also the result of the great increase in the number of lawyers — an increase of 100% between 1970 and 1990. As of 2005, there were 1,104,766 lawyers in the United States. The increase in numbers was accompanied by an increase in the diversity of the profession over the last 30 years in terms of race, ethnicity and sex. This diversity has not only changed the traditional white male "face" of the profession, but has also challenged many aspects of how law is or should be practiced. All these

---

1 For more on the legal profession, *see Legal Education and Professional Development — An Educational Continuum*, REPORT OF THE TASK FORCE ON LAW SCHOOLS AND THE PROFESSION: NARROWING THE GAP (ABA Section of Legal Education and Admissions to the Bar 1992) and RICHARD ABEL, AMERICAN LAWYERS (Oxford University Press 1989) (statistical information on the legal profession).

2 I ALEXIS DE TOCQUEVILLE, DEMOCRACY IN AMERICA 288 (1835-1840) (Vintage Books 1954).

3 According to the Columbia Law Survey, the public thinks lawyers are necessary, but that they are over-paid and dishonest. *See also* Public Perceptions of Lawyers: 2002 Consumer Research Finding (ABA Section on Litigation 2002). For an in-depth analytical approach to the question applicable to civil cases, *see* Marc Galanter, *Predators and Parasites: Lawyer-Bashing and Civil Justice*, 28 GA. L. REV. 633 (1994) (offering a taxonomy of anti-lawyer themes (and some jokes) organized into 4 categories: (1) corrupters of discourse; (2) fomenters of strife; (3) betrayers of trust; and (4) economic predators).

changes have led some to suggest that the legal profession is no longer a single profession but many.[4]

Since almost 75% of the legal profession is engaged in private practice, changes in the nature of private practice have impacted significantly the profession as a whole. The last 40 years have been the era of the law firm, and particularly of the large corporate law firm of more than 250 lawyers. Because of the elite status of such lawyers and the prominence of their firms, the model of the private lawyer has transformed from the single practitioner or small partnership to the large law firm associate. It has resulted in a paradigmatic shift in the private practitioner's work. In the past, private practice centered on the independent professional who worked closely with clients to solve their problems and who exercised comprehensive responsibility over his or her own work. Today, it centers on an employee of a law firm who often has never met his or her client, who is responsible for only part of a client's case, and who gauges his or her worth not by the results obtained for the client, but by the number of hours billed to the client. In addition, the downturns in the business climate in the early 1990s and skyrocketing salaries paid to attract talented lawyers to large firms have brought greater attention to the "business" side of law practice. It is not enough today just to be an excellent lawyer. Lawyers in large firms are under pressure, not only to bill more hours, but also to cultivate and bring in new clients. As a result of some of these changes, many more lawyers are disenchanted with practice at its most elite levels than ever before.

A. Legal Education and Admission to the Bar

1. Legal Educational Requirements and the J.D. Degree

Today in the United States, graduation from law school is the only practical route to becoming a lawyer. This was not always the case. Legal education, as it existed from the time of the Constitution until well into the 20th century consisted of "reading the law," accompanied by an apprenticeship with practicing lawyers. Thomas Jefferson, Chief Justice John Marshall and Abraham Lincoln all became lawyers by this route. In the 20th century, Robert H. Jackson, Attorney General under President Franklin D. Roosevelt, chief U.S. prosecutor at the Nazi war crimes trials at Nuremburg and a justice of the United States Supreme Court, entered the legal profession this way. Though seven states still allow some form of law office study to satisfy educational requirements, few aspiring lawyers use this method of study today.[5] For 2009, in the entire country, just 58 examinees pursued a law license by this method with just 11 of those passing the bar examination of their states.

Educational requirements for lawyers hit an all-time low point in the mid 19th century. This was largely the result of a surge in populist feeling under President Andrew Jackson from 1830 to 1840 that resisted the notion that the bar constituted an elite. In 1860, a specific period of law study was required in only 9 out of 39 states. Bar examinations were uniformly oral and so easy to pass that they were considered by many to be a joke.[6] The American Bar Association (ABA), a voluntary private organization of lawyers founded in 1878, began a long campaign to establish a uniform educational requirement

---

    4   ABEL, *supra* note 1, at 208-211.

    5   Correspondence study is possible only in 3 states. These and other data on bar admission here taken from COMPREHENSIVE GUIDE TO BAR ADMISSION REQUIREMENTS (ABA 2010), prepared by the ABA Committee on Legal Education and Admission to the Bar and the National Conference of Bar Examiners and available at www.abanet.org/legaled/baradmissions/bar.html.

    6   *See* ROBERT B. STEVENS, LAW SCHOOL: LEGAL EDUCATION IN AMERICA FROM THE 1850's TO THE 1980's 25 (U. North Carolina Press 1983).

of attendance at a law school satisfying certain minimum standards as a prerequisite for entry into the legal profession.[7]

There are 193 law schools in the United States that are approved by the American Bar Association (ABA). Other law schools, mostly in California, are not approved by the ABA, but operate under the approval of the government of the state where they are located. Approval by the ABA is very important. Despite the fact that the ABA is a private organization, 18 states permit only graduates from ABA-approved law schools to take their bar examinations.[8] In addition, the 2009 bar passage rate for graduates of ABA-approved schools was 74%, but for graduates of non-ABA-approved schools it was 25%. Of the 193 ABA-approved law schools, 168 are also members of the Association of American Law Schools (AALS), a separate organization interested in quality legal education that maintains a close working relationship with the ABA.[9]

Law school is 3 years. However, the total course of study generally required to graduate law school is effectively 7 years, since almost all law schools require a 4-year undergraduate degree from a college or university for admission. There is no approved "pre-law" course of study for the undergraduate degree, but the typical future lawyer will get his or her degree in the social sciences (31.7%), such as economics or political science, in the humanities (21.1%), such as literature, language, philosophy or the arts, or in business (14.5%). The natural sciences tend not to be heavily represented, but the percentage of engineering graduates has been increasing and is now at 4.3%.[10]

After 3 years of law school, the graduate receives a Juris Doctor or J.D. degree.[11] The overall number of J.D. candidates enrolled at ABA-approved schools in 2008 was 142,922. That same year slightly over 40,000 graduated with a J.D. degree. This number has remained constant over the last 10 years.

Law schools are called "schools" even when they are departments of universities. This is comes from the time in the first half of the 19th century, when law schools were not part of a university, but were instead separate, vocationally oriented institutions.

2. Admission to Law School

Prerequisites Two requirements are the most important in law school admission: the applicant's undergraduate grade-point average (GPA) and scores on the Law School Aptitude Test (LSAT). These two numbers largely determine an applicant's admission into law school and the prestige of his or her law school choices. But efforts to increase the social and ethnic diversity of law students have led to admission systems that consider other factors as well, such as recommendation letters, work experience, ethnic or geographical origin, life experience, a required essay, and reasons for becoming a lawyer. In 2003, the Supreme Court upheld the use of race as one factor, among many

---

7 TASK FORCE REPORT, *supra* note 1, at 105-108. *See also* SUSAN K. BOYD, THE ABA'S FIRST SECTION: ASSURING A QUALIFIED BAR (ABA Section of Legal Education and Admissions to the Bar 1993).

8 Two states permit non-ABA approved law school graduates to take the bar exam only if they have been admitted to practice in another state and have practiced there for several years.

9 Beginning in 1990, a major news magazine began to rank law schools according to their quality and reputation. The methodology used has been criticized by a consortium of ABA, AALS and other committees active in legal education as "meaningless or grossly misleading." In reaction, the ABA has published an OFFICIAL GUIDE TO ABA-APPROVED LAW SCHOOLS each year, which reports data on law schools' faculty, entrance requirements, career placement, bar passage rates and other information.

10 AFTER THE JD: THE FIRST 10 YEARS (NALP Foundation 2004), available from www.nalpfoundation.org/.

11 Before the 1960s, this degree was called an LL.B., or Bachelor of Laws degree. Nothing has changed about the basic degree except its name and many schools have allowed LL.B. degree-holders to exchange that degree for a J.D.

diversity factors, to increase minority representation in law schools against claims that doing so amounted to an unconstitutional racial quota.[12]

Competition for Admission   There was a surge in applications in the late 1960s and early 1970s when the prospect of social change through law was attractive to many. This surge leveled off in the 1980s, but gradually began to climb again despite indications that it was becoming more difficult for law graduates to find jobs. Today, the level is still quite high, with as many as 15 applicants per place in the first-year class at the most prestigious schools and about half that per place at less prestigious schools.

Women and Minorities in Law School   Today women constitute about 47% of law students and racial minority group members comprise 22%, compared to 51% and 29% in the general population. By contrast, in 1966, women constituted only 4% of the law student population and racial minorities constituted less than 1%.[13]

The Cost of Legal Education   The cost of legal education varies widely among law schools. For private law schools (two-thirds of law students attend private schools), the tuition is usually the same for every student unless a scholarship is awarded. However, public law schools, which are funded in part by the government of the state in which they are located, sometimes charge considerably less for students who reside in that state.[14] The average yearly cost of tuition in 2008 was $34,298 at private schools, $16,836 for in-state residents of public schools, and $28,442 for nonresidents. In addition to tuition, a student must pay for living expenses, including room and board and transportation. Average living expenses of students living on campus in 2008 were $12,878.[15] Students with excellent undergraduate college grades and good LSAT scores can expect a certain amount of financial aid from their law school in the form of scholarships, but in 2004 the percentage of students receiving need or merit-based grants was only 21% in public law schools and 17% in private law schools. Fully 87% of students have to take out loans and most graduate with significant debt. About 25% of these had cumulative undergraduate and law school debt of over $100,000 when they graduated. This causes many graduates to seek the highest paying job in private practice they can get, instead of the type of practice they are most interested in or public service.[16]

3. The Basic J.D. Curriculum and Degree

Courses   There is no "official" curriculum mandated by the government for the 3 years of study leading to a J.D. degree. But the content in the first year of law school tends to be dictated by tradition and is surprisingly similar from school to school.

In the first year, all the subjects are usually mandatory. The typical first year student usually takes Civil Procedure, Contracts, Property, Criminal Law, Torts, Constitutional Law and Legal Writing. The subjects in the second and third years are usually all "electives" chosen by the students themselves with the exception of the requirements

---

12   *Grutter v. Bollinger*, 539 U.S. 306 (2003), discussed in Chapter IX, p. 354.

13   Source: ABA Section of Legal Education. The legal *profession* is 27% female and 10% minorities.

14   A state is permitted to favor its own residents in this way and generally justifies such differing treatment on the ground that out-of-state students or their parents have not been paying taxes in that state. The practice has been held constitutional. *See* Chapter IX, p. 342.

15   These and other data are from the ABA at www.abanet.org/legaled/statistics.

16   LIFTING THE BURDEN: LAW STUDENT DEBT AS A BARRIER TO PUBLIC SERVICE (ABA 2002). As a result of this study, the ABA announced that debt forgiveness programs for lawyers in public service jobs would be a lobbying priority. In 2007 Congress passed a bill that forgives the remaining balance of a graduate's federal student loans if he or she has works in the public sector for 10 years and makes timely payments. The bill applies to all graduates with federal loans not just law graduates.

of a research seminar and a course on professional responsibility. Thus, there is no specialization in law school except whatever specialization students themselves may choose by selecting particular courses. The majority of law students choose courses on subjects covered on the bar exam and in the specialty area in which they plan to work. A typical student in the second and third years takes four courses a semester. Popular elective courses include Commercial Transactions, Business Organizations, Tax Law, Labor Law, Wills and Trusts, Evidence, Legal Process, Criminal Procedure, Administrative Law, Legal Ethics, Conflict of Laws, International Law, Environmental Law, Antitrust Law and a research seminar requiring a substantial research paper.[17]

Method of Instruction The method of instruction in law school varies somewhat among law schools, but in most, some form of the "case method" is used. The case method of law study was devised in the 1870s by Christopher Columbus Langdell, a professor and later dean of Harvard Law School. Before that time the primary method of instruction involved lecture and assigned readings from treatises summarizing the law.[18] The main change wrought by Langdell's case method was its focus on original sources of the law and on the methods of case analysis and legal reasoning in caselaw. Some of Langdell's theories of law as "science" have been overtaken by new ideas about the nature of the judicial process.[19] But allowing for modification of the caselaw method to reflect those new ideas, Langdell's method is still the basic model for most modern law school courses.

The main focus of the typical law school course is the "casebook" for the course. The casebook, sometimes called "cases and materials," contains judicial opinions and applicable statutes. Text interspersed among the cases seeks to link the cases together and summarizes less important caselaw or statutory law or scholarly literature. Study questions are inserted following each case to provide hints about what aspects of the case are important, confusing or subject to criticism. Students are assigned cases from the casebook to read and class sessions are devoted primarily to a discussion of those cases. Because of this, students must each have a personal copy of the book.

The rationale for using class discussion rather than lecture as a method of instruction is that students learn more if they learn actively — doing the necessary case analysis and critique themselves rather than listening passively to a teacher's lecture about how to do it. In addition, oral analysis and discussion of legal points are essential skills for a lawyer. Even under this model, teachers sometimes lecture in order to summarize class discussion or to present additional information not covered in the text or class discussion, particularly the teacher's own particular insights or criticisms of the cases assigned.

"Socratic" Method There are many ways to conduct a class discussion, but teachers most often use some variation of a unique teaching method called the "Socratic method" to engage students in discussion of the cases they have read before class. The teacher first calls on a student about the facts of the case and the rule of law represented by the case. Then the questioning explores the ramifications of those rules by posing hypothetical facts ("hypos") that change some of the facts of the principal case. These

---

17 There are 12 states that require that law students take certain courses as a prerequisite to bar admission. Underlying these state educational requirements is a smoldering conflict over who should control the content of legal education — law schools, the courts or the legal profession.

18 The most authoritative of the sources in the 19th century were William Blackstone's 1765-1769 Commentaries on the Laws of England and the treatises on American law by Supreme Court Justice Joseph Story and Chancellor James Kent. *See* Chapter II, p. 53.

19 *See* Chapter II, pp. 44-48.

hypotheticals usually elucidate some aspect of the case and necessitate a deeper analysis of it, often requiring the student to revise his or her view of what rules of law the case stands for. Such revisions may also be called for by questioning the student about the relationship of the case under discussion to other cases being studied. Since "Socratic" interrogation often exposes inadequacies in the student's preparation or thinking, it can be emotionally painful experience for the student, especially if it is conducted aggressively by a domineering teacher. Because of the "Socratic" method of instruction and the heavy workload associated with reading cases and preparing for class, students generally report that the law school experience, at least in the first year, is a difficult and trying one somewhat akin to military training.[20]

The use of the Socratic method in its purest and more aggressive form has declined in the last 25 years. Some teachers have simply modified it to a gentler form of questioning, which some have called "avuncular" Socratic method — questioning conducted as your uncle might do it. The decline of the Socratic method is especially evident in the second and third year courses, where both students and teachers have less patience for it. There has also been a resurgence in use of the lecture method among some teachers, who use the method under the assumption that students have read and understood the readings. Other teachers use a "problem-solving approach" to teaching. Prior to class, students prepare answers to realistic problems presented by the teacher, and the teacher conducts a class discussion of possible solutions to those problems.[21]

Examinations and Evaluation Examinations are invariably written rather than oral and traditionally consist of essay questions that present complex fact situations. In the essay answer, students must analyze the facts and state what legal issues they present. For each legal issue, the student states what the applicable rule of law is, analyzes how the issue should be resolved, in the process considering all the arguments that could be made on both sides of the question, and states what conclusion a court should reach.[22] Such essay exams are typically 3 hours long. In recent years there has been more variety in the format of examinations. The "take-home" exam, which allows students to work at home over a given number of hours or days, is increasingly popular. In addition, some teachers have developed objective examinations with multiple choice and true-false questions.[23] Grading must be done on an anonymous basis to the extent possible and grading duties are performed by the teacher of the course rather than by assistants.

Attrition The percentage of J.D. candidates who dropped out of ABA-approved law schools in 2008 was 4.5%. This includes those who "flunked out," *i.e.* had to leave for academic reasons, as well as those who left for other reasons. More drop out in the first year (3.4%) than in the third year (.15%). However, among some of the weaker and

---

20 The peculiarities and hardship of the law school classroom have had sufficient popular appeal to be the subject of a film, *The Paper Chase* (1973) starring the late John Houseman. It depicts the difficulties of a Harvard law student facing an old-style "Socratic" contracts teacher. Several books are available that give students tips on how to prepare for and survive the law school classroom experience. *See* GEORGE J. ROTH, SLAYING THE LAW SCHOOL DRAGON, 2D ED. (Wiley & Sons 1991); HELENE S. SHAPO & MARSHALL S. SHAPO, LAW SCHOOL WITHOUT FEAR: STRATEGIES FOR SUCCESS, 3D ED. (West 2009); ANN BURKHART & ROBERT STEIN, LAW SCHOOL SUCCESS IN A NUTSHELL, 2D. ED. (West 2008).

21 *See* Myron Moskovitz, *Beyond the Case Method: It's Time to Teach with Problems*, 42 J. LEGAL EDUC. 241 (1992).

22 This method of approaching essay exam questions has been reduced to the acronym "IRAC" by law students who wish to make sure they remember each step: *I*ssue, *R*ule, *A*nalysis, *C*onclusion.

23 The development of objective examinations in law school has in general paralleled the growth of the multistate bar examination, which is a multiple choice examination.

often newer law schools, there is a policy of low admission standards and a high "flunk-out" rate, often resulting in as many as one-third of the entering class failing.[24]

Marks of success in law school are good grades and membership on the editorial board of the law review or law journal. The law school's law review edits and publishes articles written by teachers and scholars, and notes and comments on recent cases written by student members of the law review. In order to be admitted to the law review, the student must either receive outstanding grades in the first year (usually law reviews take only those students with first-year grades in the top 5-10%) or do well in a legal writing competition. The students who are selected to work on the law review do so during their second and third years. The most prestigious law firms strongly prefer former editors and members of law reviews and some large firms interview and consider for employment only graduates who were "on" law review. The majority of the law teachers in the United States were probably members or editors of the law review during their student days.[25]

Summer Clerkships   During the summers after the first and second years, law students try to find some kind of summer work. The preferred work is legal work because it teaches students something about law practice and possibly will assist them in obtaining a job after graduation. Students who work in such positions are called "law clerks" and their summer job is called a "summer clerkship." Law clerks mainly do legal research in the library and write memoranda summarizing the results, but they may be assigned other tasks as well. In recent years, summer clerkships for the best students at many large corporate law firms have not been very demanding, and might better be described as a combination of orientation to the firm and "courtship" of the students to join the firm upon graduation. Indeed, it is not uncommon for a student at an elite law school to be able to "split" a summer between two different firms, an arrangement not exactly conducive to serious work.

Job Prospects of J.D. Graduates   Law review participants, at whichever school, and graduates with high grades from the most prestigious schools tend to fare well in the job hunting process. Generally, for those outside these groups, employment prospects are not so good. While law schools keep and disseminate statistics on their graduates' employment after graduation, those figures are often not what they seem. For example, in the middle of perhaps the worst U.S. economy since the Great Depression, law schools reported an employment rate of 88% for the class of 2009. This is an attractive number that is certain to attract would-be applicants. However, the 88% figure is mostly self-reported and does not include students from whom the law school was unable to obtain employment information. Sometimes law schools even improve their statistics by offering unemployed graduates a job. A stunning 42% of law schools reported that they themselves employed their own graduates.[26]   Of these, 69% were employed in

---

24 Source: ABA Section on Legal Education and Admissions to the Bar.

25 There are a few law reviews that are edited by law teachers and scholars. It seems strange to some that *students* are the keepers of the prominent academic journals of the profession. It is especially strange given that the decision of law faculties to give tenure or to promote a teacher is in large part based on what law reviews accepted and published the teacher's articles.

26 In the big picture, this employment sub-group is small, representing only 3.5% of all law graduate employment. What it may show ultimately, however, is that a conflict of interests exists for law schools to use means (e.g., a tepid effort to track down potentially unemployed graduates or an enthusiastic effort to find any job for unemployed but identified graduates) that magnify the perception of employability.

temporary positions.[27] It seems undeniable that the 88% employment figure does not mean what prospective law students think it means.

4. Advanced Law Degrees

Beyond the J.D., there are higher degrees in law, the Master's Degree in Law (LL.M.) and the Doctor of Science in Law (S.J.D.), but only a few graduates pursue them. This is even true of teachers of law, who need only possess a J.D. degree in order to teach or to receive tenure at their university. Of the 2005 graduating class of law students, only 2.2% enrolled in full-time advanced law degree programs. In 2000, there were about 6,000 students enrolled in masters' programs and just over 3,500 students graduated with masters' degrees. That same year only 50 S.J.D. degrees were conferred.

U.S. law graduates may seek an advanced degree to obtain specialized training, most commonly LL.M. degrees in taxation, corporate finance and intellectual property. A part of the motivation for such study on the part of J.D. degree holders may be to "launder" themselves with an LL.M. from a more prestigious law school after receiving a J.D. degree from a less prestigious one. But a significant portion of the lawyers enrolled in advanced degree programs at U.S. law schools are foreign lawyers seeking a master's degree (M.C.L. or LL.M.) in comparative law. Such degrees are attractive because of their prestige and because the length of study required is only one year. In addition, it can be a "short cut" for the foreign lawyer who wants to be admitted to the bar in the United States, since 10 states permit foreign LL.M. graduates from ABA-approved law schools to take the bar examination.[28]

5. Law Teachers

Titles Unlike European countries, the term "professor" is used in the United States as a general term for almost all full-time teachers of law. There are 3 ranks of professor: assistant professor, associate professor and professor.[29] There is no limit on the number of full professors that a law school may have, and it often happens that over three-quarters of the members of a faculty are full professors.

Academic Administration The law school is headed by a single dean. There is also an associate dean in charge of academic affairs and administrative tasks, an assistant dean for student affairs and an assistant dean in charge of admissions. Law schools are typically not divided into different institutes or subdepartments as in Europe (*e.g.*, civil law, criminal law, state law). This unitary system relieves professors from many of the administrative duties that confront professors in European systems. Even routine administrative matters and the hiring and supervision of support personnel are handled through the dean's office, so that professors can concentrate on teaching and scholarship.

The life of the law teacher is not totally free from administrative burdens, however. Most of the important decisions made at most law schools are not made by the dean, but by the faculty as a whole on the recommendation of various faculty committees. Democracy has its price and that price in law schools is service on these committees.

---

27 Nat'l Association for Law Placement: Employment for the Class of 2009 – selected findings, http://www.nalp.org/uploads/Class_of_2009_Selected_Findings.pdf.

28 *See* Comprehensive Guide to Bar Admission Requirements, *supra* note 5.

29 These roughly correspond to the ranks of lecturer, docent and professor in some European systems. There are also "adjunct" professors, generally practitioners teaching a single course at the law school, and "visiting" professors, full-time teachers from other law schools teaching full-time for a semester or a year at the host institution.

The most important committees are curriculum, faculty appointments, budget, admissions, and tenure and promotions. If a teacher wishes to offer a new course, it must first be proposed to and approved by the curriculum committee and then voted on by the faculty. New teachers are hired only after comprehensive screening and recommendation by the faculty appointments committee and a vote of the entire faculty. Current teachers are promoted or granted tenure only if such action is recommended by the tenure and promotions committee. Then the recommendation must be confirmed by a vote of the entire faculty.

Duties and Career Path   Teaching duties for the average teacher usually involve teaching two courses a semester or four courses a year.[30] In addition, the teacher is expected to engage in scholarly pursuits resulting in books and articles. Because teachers are not confined to a particular institute or subdepartment within the law school, it is not unusual for teachers to teach and write across what lawyers from civil-law countries would consider basic boundaries in the law. Thus, a teacher might teach and write in the areas of corporations, criminal law, civil procedure and constitutional law.

Typically a teacher will start out as an assistant professor, unless considerable practice or other experience calls for beginning at the associate level. After writing 2 or 3 law review articles that prove his or her intellectual mettle and surviving 4 to 6 years in the classroom, the assistant professor will be given "tenure" and promoted to associate professor. This is a serious decision, since tenure assures that the teacher cannot be fired except for the most serious breach or neglect of duties.[31] Then, after 2 or 3 more years of teaching and writing, the teacher is eligible for promotion to full professor. After reaching full professor, the stimulus to continue to do research and writing and to improve one's teaching is largely financial, since it is the most productive scholars and the best teachers who receive the largest share of discretionary pay raises that are bestowed each year.

Each step in the promotion process at the better law schools requires a complete evaluation of the teacher's scholarly work-product by "outside" experts — scholars in the teacher's field from outside the institution. Thus, while law teachers in the U.S. are not required to obtain advanced degrees in law, the tenure and promotion process serves as a substitute for an advanced degree by requiring the teacher to produce substantial scholarship that must be evaluated and approved by experts in the field.

Influence on the Law   Articles and books by legal academics have considerable effect on the development of the law. Law review articles are regularly cited in briefs and judicial opinions and have been responsible for some major changes in the law. In this respect, American academics are more influential on the legal system than their colleagues in England.[32] On the other hand, academic writing does not have the authoritativeness of doctrinal commentaries in continental Europe. Judges in the United States are more likely to be influenced by court opinions written by other judges than by a law review article. In addition, law review articles by professors from many of the elite

---

30 Most courses are "three credit-hour" courses, meaning that they meet three hours a week during a semester of 14 or 15 weeks.

31 Tenure is for the purpose of assuring "academic freedom," the right to teach, write and speak out on any public issue without fear of retaliation.

32 *See generally* P.S. ATIYAH & ROBERT SUMMERS, FORM AND SUBSTANCE IN ANGLO-AMERICAN LAW 398-407 (Clarendon Press 1987). The authors give several reasons for this, not the least of which is the relative lesser ability of English judges to stray far from precedent and inject public policy considerations into their decisions.

law schools have in recent years become oriented toward high theory rather than legal doctrine, thus making them of less interest to courts.[33]

Another way that legal academics affect development of the law is through service in government posts. Professors are frequently tapped to be judges. Some positions in government, such as Solicitor General of the United States — the lawyer who argues the position of the United States government before the United States Supreme Court — and head of the antitrust enforcement division of the Department of Justice, have traditionally gone to law professors. Legal academics from leading law schools also occupy general counsel positions for government agencies or serve as members of or consultants to various government commissions. Moreover, it is relatively common for litigants to retain law professors to argue their cases in the appellate courts and particularly in the Supreme Court.[34]

Pay The salaries of law teachers vary somewhat, with private schools tending to pay more than state institutions, though the range is narrower than the range of salaries of private practitioners.[35] For 2008-2009, most assistant professors' salaries ranged between $85,000 and $105,000 and most full professors' salaries ranged between $130,000 and $150,000, with associate professors somewhere in between. Other possibilities for supplementing income include research grants, representing clients, consulting or writing books. In general, private law schools pay more than public ones.[36]

6. Admission to the Bar

The overwhelming majority of law school graduates in the United States gain admission to the bar and practice law in some form. In this respect, the United States is different from many other countries, where the study of law is completed at the undergraduate level. In these countries, the study of law is considered general preparation for a variety of work in the public and private sectors, and considerably fewer graduates become practicing lawyers.

Types of State Bar Regulation State rather than federal law governs admission to the practice of law and requirements vary from state to state. States have adopted one of two kinds of agencies to oversee the profession. In some states, the agency is an actual governmental one (for example, the supreme court of the state). In others, an "integrated bar" exists and constitutes a form of self-regulation. Under such a system, the state delegates its licensing and regulation authority to an organization, usually called the State Bar Association, which oversees admission to practice and regulates the profession. Membership in the State Bar Association is mandatory in order to practice. In both systems, the supreme court of the state exercises ultimate control over the legal profession.

Bar Examinations All states but one require first-time applicants to the bar to pass a bar examination.[37] The bar examination is given twice a year, in February and July.

---

33 *See* Harry T. Edwards, *The Growing Disjunction Between Legal Education And The Legal Profession*, 91 MICHIGAN L. REV. 34 (1992).

34 *See, e.g., New York Times Co. v. United States*, 403 U.S. 713 (1971), the "Pentagon Papers" case (discussed in Chapter IX, p. 379) wherein Professor Erwin Griswold of Yale Law School as Solicitor General argued against Professor Alexander Bickel of Harvard.

35 *See infra* p. 148.

36 *Source:* Society of American Law Teachers (SALT) Survey of Salaries 2008-2009 (2009).

37 Under a program called the "diploma privilege," Wisconsin exempts students who graduate from the University of Wisconsin or Marquette University from any bar examination requirement in that state. *See* ADMISSION REQUIREMENTS, *supra* note 5.

Usually, it is spread over two or three days. One part of the examination consists of objective multiple-choice questions on general law, which in all but 2 states is the "multistate" bar examination (MBE).[38] The examination is uniform, but each state has the right to set whatever passing score it wishes. The second part of the examination consists of essay questions, either standardized questions from a multistate examination called the MEE (given in 14 states) or questions tailored to the law of the particular state. A third component of the examination, given on a different date, is the Multistate Professional Responsibility Examination (MPRE), required by all but 3 states.[39] Some states, concerned with testing competence for practice more accurately, have departed from the traditional focus on legal knowledge. For example, 21 jurisdictions use an additional Multistate Performance Test (MPT), which requires examinees to do such things as draft a memorandum, write a closing argument for a trial, or outline a deposition.

Before taking the bar exam, almost all graduates take a 6-week "bar review" course offered by private companies. The bar review course is particularly important for the state law part of the bar exam, because most of the better law schools do not focus in any depth on the law of any particular state. The percentage of students who pass the bar exam varies from state to state. For example, in 2009 in California, only 49% passed the bar exam, while in Wisconsin 89% passed. The remaining states fall somewhere in between.[40] Often law graduates complain that states make it difficult to pass the bar exam, not so much to guarantee higher competence among lawyers in the state, but to limit competition with lawyers already practicing in the state.

Interstate Practice Without admission to the bar of a given state, a lawyer has no right to practice there. This prohibition includes all aspects of law practice, including giving legal advice and drafting documents. A lawyer from another state may take part in a trial if the judge gives special permission solely for that case (called appearing *pro hac vice*) and the lawyer works together with a local lawyer. Otherwise, in a majority of states, the lawyer wishing to practice in that state must pass the bar examination of that state. In some states, a lawyer may be admitted to practice without examination if the lawyer has practiced law in another state for a given period of time, usually 5 to 7 years.

Federal Court Practice A license to practice in a state's courts does not authorize the lawyer to practice in the federal courts, even in the federal courts located in that state. Despite the fact that federal law is uniform throughout the country, there is no central place to obtain such certification. Instead, lawyers admitted to practice in a state must go to the local federal district court and obtain a certificate entitling them to practice in that district. Since some states have more than one district, this may involve getting as many as 4 certificates.[41] Fortunately, there is no separate federal bar examination and in most districts obtaining a certificate to practice is simply a matter of money and the formality of being "sworn in" by a federal judge. It is common to arrange "mass"

---

38 *See* COMPREHENSIVE GUIDE TO BAR ADMISSION REQUIREMENTS, *supra* note 5. Links to frequently asked questions about bar admissions, the multistate bar examination, bar examination statistics and other items of interest are available at www.abanet.org/legaled/bar.html.

39 The three states are Maryland, Washington, and Wisconsin.

40 Some others are New York, 65%, Texas, 78%; Illinois, 84%; and Michigan, 81%. Source: THE BAR EXAMINER (2009), available at http://www.ncbex.org/bar-admissions/stats/.

41 There are 91 federal districts in the 50 states and Puerto Rico. *See infra* p. 174. U.S. Courts of Appeal also control admission to their own bars, though like the District Courts, admission is *pro forma*. The U.S. Supreme Court bar is open to anyone who has practiced for at least three years.

swearing in ceremonies in both state and federal courts shortly after the state bar examination results are announced.[42]

A Unified Legal Profession When a lawyer becomes a member of the bar, he or she has the right to fulfill all the duties of the lawyer: consultation, advice, drafting documents, and all other aspects of client representation, both in court and out of court. There is no division of lawyers, as exists in some countries, between barristers, who appear in court, and solicitors, who generally may not. There is also no separate branch of the profession equivalent to the civil-law notary.[43] Lawyers do specialize. A general division of many lawyers is the line between "office lawyers" who do transactional work and "litigators" who handle lawsuits in court. But this and other specializations are informal. All legal professionals, from judges to office lawyers to litigators, are members of the bar, have the same basic legal education and have the same license to practice law.[44]

The generalist nature of the license to practice law means that lawyers have the freedom to change from one type of practice to another. It is not uncommon for lawyers to do so one or more times in the course of their professional lives. Studies show a higher rate of mobility in law than in any other profession.

7. Criticisms of Legal Education in Law School

As stated earlier, the vast majority of law graduates in the United States practice law. Yet, unlike many other countries, U.S. law graduates are not required to undergo any official apprenticeship period of study before practice.[45] Because law school is the only training a new lawyer is required to have before being entrusted with the legal affairs of clients, there has been concern that law schools should better prepare their graduates for practice.

Many of the criticisms are longstanding, dating from the 1930s.[46] More recently, Chief Justice Warren Burger in 1973 focused specifically on inadequacies of lawyers in litigation.[47] In 1992, the American Bar Association turned its attention to legal education and professional development by publishing a critical Task Force Report on the subject.[48] Since the debate has not subsided, it is appropriate to provide a flavor of it.

The Law School Curriculum and Lawyering Skills Essentially the criticism of legal education is that it teaches too narrow a range of skills, primarily concentrating on the

---

42 Some districts have used their power to control admission to impose additional educational or experience requirements on lawyers before allowing them to appear in trials.

43 There is a person called a "notary" or "notary public" in the United States, but a U.S. notary is not a legal advisor and indeed has no formal legal education of any kind. The sole power of a notary in the U.S. is to administer oaths to persons who are to testify or who are to sign sworn documents, and to "notarize" or verify the signatures on such documents. Thus, court reporters, who swear witnesses and take down testimony in court and at depositions, are notaries. Depositions are discussed in Chapter VII, p. 236. The majority of notaries are secretaries in law firms, courts, banks and insurance agencies.

44 There are minor exceptions to this rule, such as patent lawyers. *See* Chapter XII, p. 509, note 194.

45 Two exceptions, Vermont and Delaware, are discussed *infra*.

46 See Jerome Frank, *Why Not a Clinical Lawyer-School?*, 81 U.PENNSYLVANIA L.REV. 907 (1933) Judge Jerome Frank was a judge on the U.S. Court of Appeals for the Second Circuit and is known for his contributions to the school of Legal Realism (see Chapter II, p. 46) and his criticisms of the adversary system and juries (see Chapter III, notes 141 and 159).

47 *See* Warren Burger, *The Special Skills of Advocacy: Are Specialized Training and Certification of Advocates Essential to Our System of Justice?*, 42 FORDHAM L.REV. 227, 230 (1973) (remarking that "we are more casual about qualifying people we allow as advocates in the courtrooms than we are about licensing our electricians").

48 *See* ABA TASK FORCE REPORT, *supra* note 1.

skill of analyzing legal doctrine in cases to the exclusion of other tasks that lawyers are called upon to perform.[49] In an adversary system, lawyers must be able to investigate, analyze and present facts in trials. Yet, courses in trial advocacy, fact investigation and pre-trial motion practice have had no place in the traditional curriculum. Similarly, the non-litigating "office lawyer" must have interviewing, counseling and negotiation skills, and must be able to draft contracts and other documents properly and write opinion letters. Yet, there have historically been few classes that addressed these skills. A major general problem with law schools preparing their students for practice is their presentation of subjects in an atomized fashion. Few courses integrate several different areas of substantive and procedural law in the way that practitioners must deal with them in real life.

Defenders of the traditional curriculum usually respond that law school is not designed to do anything more than teach legal analysis and provide a public policy or interdisciplinary perspective on law. Graduates, they assert, will learn everything they need to know about practice once they start practicing.

The problem with this response is that many graduates do not in fact have the opportunity to learn what they need to know after law school. It is true that the large firms have training programs for new associates that seek to provide the necessary supplemental legal education. However, almost 70% of lawyers in private practice work as solo practitioners or in firms of 5 or fewer lawyers, where there is no training program and often no senior lawyer to protect clients from mistakes. Continuing legal education, discussed in the next section, is a partial solution, but it can be quite expensive.

Skills Courses Progress has been made in adding "skills" courses to the curriculum to address the problem. Most often these courses take the form of "simulation" or "role-play" courses — courses that present the student with realistic simulated problems and require that he or she assume the role of a practicing lawyer and, using practice skills learned in the course, resolve the problem. For example, in a role-play course in trial advocacy, students must present evidence from simulated case files by means of interrogating mock witnesses and presenting documents and other exhibits to a mock judge and jury. While trial advocacy is perhaps the oldest such course offered in law schools, simulation courses exist for interviewing and counseling, negotiation, pre-trial litigation, and arbitration skills.[50]

Under a new ABA standard, effective Fall of 2006, each law school must require that all its students "receive substantial instruction in . . . professional skills generally regarded as necessary for effective and responsible participation in the legal profession." However, the requirement recognizes that law schools will have to "be creative in developing programs of instruction in professional skills . . . using the strengths and resources available to the school."[51] This reflects the realities involved in making such a requirement — few law teachers have practiced for any extended period of time, for most that practice experience was some time ago, and many teachers became academics precisely because they did not like the tumult of law practice. The statement also

---

49 *Id.* at 236-268.

50 The first-year legal writing course usually requires students to write briefs in a simulated case and then argue the case before a panel of "judges" — usually practicing lawyers or teachers. However, this exercise concentrates on case analysis skills in the appellate context — the same orientation toward analysis of appellate cases that is emphasized in traditional substantive law courses.

51 Standard 302(a)(4), 2005-2006 ABA Standards for Approval of Law Schools (ABA 2005).

reflects the fact that skills classes require small classes, which makes them more expensive to offer than the traditional law school course.[52]

Clinical Education　The ultimate "practice skills" courses are the law school "clinics," first introduced in the 1960s. Borrowing the word and idea of a clinic from the medical schools, law schools have established law offices at the law school so students can work as lawyers under the supervision of teachers on real cases.[53] Students do everything that a lawyer would do, from consultation with clients to handling trials.[54] The clients in clinics are poor people who otherwise would not be able to afford a lawyer. Clinics provide a valuable service to poor people and teach students how to practice. They also help law students, who are generally from the middle and upper classes of society, to learn something about the position of poor people in society and to introduce students to their future professional obligation to help those who are unable to pay for a lawyer.[55] Law school clinics have grown in number. Eighty percent of 155 law schools surveyed in 1991 had client-contact clinics and the number of clinics increased by 15% from 1986 to 1991.[56] ABA standards now require (since 2004) that law schools offer courses providing "live-client or other real-life practice experiences" under supervision of law school faculty.[57] However, this can include various kinds of placements in outside agencies with minimal faculty supervision. Moreover, clinics remain elective courses, so students are not required to take them.[58]

8. Legal Education After Law School

Opportunities for "continuing legal education" for practicing lawyers are available both from commercial providers and from non-profit centers that exist in many states. They offer programs of instruction for lawyers who wish to improve their skills or acquire new skills. All but 11 states have made a certain amount of post-law school continuing legal education mandatory for all lawyers, and 22 states have instituted "transition education" or "bridge-the-gap" requirements for new lawyers to help smooth the passage from law school to law practice. The most ambitious is the program in the State of Washington where skills are taught over 9 days in small groups with role-playing exercises. Most other required programs, however, are no more than 3 days long, have a lecture format and do not address lawyering skills. Others may be spread over a three-year period to accommodate the busy schedule of the practicing attorney.

---

52 Computer games provide another avenue for students to develop lawyering skills, either inside or outside the classroom. A consortium of law schools, called CALI (for Computer Assisted Legal Instruction) has been established to promote computer-based learning. *See* www2.cali.org/. CALI is also developing a network for podcasting law school classes, the Legal Education Podcasting Project.

53 The word "clinic" comes from the Greek work "klinigos," meaning "bed." In the medical context clinics have to do with the relationship between a doctor and a sick patient, who is often lying in bed.

54 Law student practice is allowed pursuant to the court rules of the state. *See, e.g.*, Michigan Court Rule 8.120 (providing that students at ABA-approved schools who have completed all first year courses successfully may practice under supervision in a legal aid clinic or prosecutor's or city attorney's office.

55 *See* ABA MODEL RULES OF PROFESSION RESPONSIBILITY, Rule 6.1.

56 TASK FORCE REPORT, *supra* note 1 at 253.

57 Standard 302(b)(1), 2005-2006 ABA Standards for Approval of Law Schools (ABA 2005).

58 It is interesting that large firms, which tend to have the greatest influence on leading law schools, are generally satisfied with a non-skills oriented legal education. They have little faith in the abilities of most teachers, whose practice experience is usually neither substantial nor recent, to teach practice skills. Moreover, the existing system serves their interests by its very failings. If large firms alone have the resources to provide the supplemental post-law school training necessary to ease the transition to practice, that gives their lawyers an advantage over smaller firm lawyers with whom they must contend. In addition, it serves as an additional incentive for law students to seek work at a large firm.

A return to post-law-school apprenticeships has been suggested as a means of assuring better preparation for practice, but it has been largely rejected as infeasible. Among the difficulties are assuring the educational quality of the experience and seeing that it does not become a "form of near-peonage" — problems that have arisen in apprenticeship systems in other countries. Only two states, Vermont and Delaware, require a form of apprenticeship. Delaware's apprenticeship is the only one that must be completed before admission to the bar.[59] Delaware's requirements are quite extensive, requiring the observation of several proceedings in court and completion of a wide variety of lawyering tasks over a 6-month period, from drafting a trial court motion to preparing a will or trust document. However, several other states that have tried apprenticeships have been disappointed in them and have replaced them with required attendance at continuing legal education programs.

B. Issues in the Regulation of Practice

Citizenship and Residency Requirements Constitutional questions have been raised regarding the traditional requirement that lawyers, as "officers of the court," be citizens of the United States. In the case of *Application of Griffiths*,[60] the Court declared that the exclusion of someone from the practice of law based solely upon that person's lack of United States citizenship violated the equal protection clause of the 14th Amendment. And in the case of *Supreme Court of New Hampshire v. Piper*[61] and *Supreme Court of Virginia v. Friedman*,[62] the Court similarly declared unconstitutional states' insistence that lawyers either be domiciled in the state or have a permanent office in the state as a precondition for admission to its bar.

Mandatory Bar Membership and Dues As mentioned earlier, some states have an "integrated bar" system, which requires of all lawyers membership and payment of dues to an official State Bar Association. Under such a system, the state delegates to that Association the power of professional regulation.[63] Consequently, the organization performs self-regulatory functions, such as formulating rules of professional conduct and disciplining members for misconduct, and also engages in activities similar to voluntary organizations like the ABA. State bars have lobbied legislatures and other governmental agencies, filed *amicus curiae* briefs in pending cases, and held conferences on current legal issues. In *Keller v. State Bar of California*,[64] the Supreme Court held that the state bar's use of compulsory dues to finance political and ideological activities with which members disagreed violated their First Amendment right of free speech. While lawyers can be required to join the organization, they can only be charged an amount as dues that reflects expenditures for the purpose of regulating the profession or improving the quality of legal services.

Minimum Fee Schedules Given that the legal profession has a history of self-regulation as a "learned profession," it was assumed for many years that lawyers would be exempt from liability under federal antitrust laws for "ethical" rules designed to limit certain kinds of competition.[65] This assumption proved wrong when the Supreme Court

---

59 Apprenticeships and programs of transition education are discussed in the ABA TASK FORCE REPORT, *supra* note 1, at 287-299.

60 413 U.S. 717 (1973). *See* Chapter IX, p. 355, where discrimination against aliens is discussed.

61 470 U.S. 274 (1985).

62 487 U.S. 59 (1988).

63 *See supra* p. 136.

64 496 U.S. 1 (1990).

65 Antitrust law is discussed in Chapter XV, pp. 609-616.

unanimously decided *Goldfarb v. Virginia State Bar.*[66] In *Goldfarb*, the Court held that a bar association's enforcement of a mandatory minimum fee schedule that set a minimum fee for title searches for residential property sales violated antitrust laws against price fixing. The Court immediately saw through several justifications for minimum fee schedules, including the argument that without them lawyers would engage in unscrupulous competitive efforts and employ shoddy cost-cutting methods to win clients.

Unauthorized Practice of Law Nonlawyers are generally prohibited from practicing law. This was not always the case. For much of colonial history up through the 19th century, many states permitted nonlawyers to practice law and even to represent others in litigation. As the legal profession developed, states made the right to practice law the exclusive province of lawyers to protect the public from legal representation by unqualified persons. However, it is clear that many things that are considered the practice of law can be done by laypersons, such as real estate agents preparing deeds, mortgages and promissory notes, and accountants and others preparing tax returns and giving tax advice. Beginning in the 1930s, bar associations, urged on by the ABA, formed committees to aggressively police unauthorized practice. The result was a whole series of agreements with trade organizations for real estate agents, accountants, law book publishers and others that assured that as much business as possible would be done by lawyers. Much of this came to a halt in 1975 when the *Goldfarb* decision discussed above held antitrust laws applied to lawyers.

Lawyer Advertising Before the 20th century, lawyers were largely unregulated and advertising by lawyers was unrestrained. As professional control developed, more efforts were made to preserve public respect for and the dignity of the legal profession. Since advertising made law sound like just any other commercial endeavor, one of the restrictions imposed was a ban on advertising. In general, all that was permitted was a dignified sign on one's office building and a similarly dignified listing in the telephone book. All this was changed by a 1977 U.S. Supreme Court case, *Bates v. State Bar of Arizona.*[67] In that case, the Supreme Court continued its expansion of the protection of "commercial speech" under the 1st Amendment by holding unconstitutional most state regulations prohibiting lawyers from advertising. The Court held that advertising provides consumer information about legal services and that such information is entitled to 1st Amendment protection almost equal to political and other protected speech. Advertising has created considerable competition at least in legal services for moderate income persons and, as discussed below, has spawned some alternative means of delivering legal services that could not have developed without it.[68]

Specialization Among Lawyers in Private Practice Despite the existence of a general license to practice in all areas of the law, lawyers in the U.S., as elsewhere, tend to specialize in particular areas of the law.[69] Generally, states have prohibited lawyers from holding themselves out to the public as specialists in any particular areas, except trademark, patent or admiralty law. However, the Supreme Court held in *Peel v. Attorney Registration and Disciplinary Comm. of Illinois,*[70] that the 1st Amendment's protection of free speech barred Illinois from prohibiting a lawyer's truthful advertising

---

66 421 U.S. 773 (1975).

67 433 U.S. 350 (1977).

68 The commercial speech doctrine of 1st Amendment law is discussed in Chapter IX, pp. 387-389.

69 *See infra* pp. 144-150.

70 496 U.S. 91 (1990) (plurality opinion).

that he was certified as a specialist by the "National Board of Trial Advocates," a private organization that had promulgated standards for trial lawyers. After *Peel*, specialization programs grew. As of 1991, 15 states had specialization plans in effect for certification of lawyers in up to 25 specialties. However, states have not prohibited non-certified lawyers from practicing in those specialty areas, though some states have required that non-certified lawyers who practice in specialty areas disclose in all advertising that they are not specially certified in that area of practice.[71]

Pay of Lawyers Financially, lawyers do rather well. In 2008, the median annual earnings of lawyers was $110,590, with the middle half earning between $74,980 and $163,320. By comparison, in 2007, the median individual income was $33,452, while the median income for those with a college degree was $46,805 and for those with an advanced degree was $61,287.[72] The median salary for recent law graduates 9 months after graduation was $68,500, but there is considerable variation in pay for different types of practice. In private practice, the median was $108,500, for graduates employed by businesses it was $60,000, and for government lawyers it was $50,000.[73] An interesting characteristic of the salaries of new lawyers is that the data illustrate a striking bimodal distribution rather than a bell curve distribution.[74]

Are There Too Many Lawyers? The number of lawyers in the United States is not regulated in any way except by the market. And it is fair to say that there are so many different law schools in the United States that virtually anyone who has graduated from college and who sincerely wishes to become a lawyer — and who has money — can do so. In 2009, there were 1,180,386 active lawyers in the United States. This works out to one lawyer for every 260 people in the country.[75]

In recent years, some have complained there are too many lawyers. Typical is a report issued in 1991 by the President's Council on Competitiveness. It argues that the ratio of 28 lawyers per 10,000 population in the United States far exceeds the ratio of 11 per 10,000 in Germany, 8 per 10,000 in England, and only 1 per 10,000 in Japan.[76] But comparisons across legal systems are difficult. The cited figure for Japan counts only the 13,000 or so *bengoshi* — the only lawyers who may open an office and represent clients for a fee. It does not include the many more non-*bengoshi* law graduates and others who do legal work as employees of government agencies and business corporations, doing largely the same work that in-house corporate counsel and government lawyers in the U.S. do. The Sony Corporation alone has 150 non-*bengoshi* lawyers on staff. If these are included, as their U.S. counterparts are in the U.S. figure, the result for Japan is around 32 lawyers per 10,000 population — about 4 more lawyers per 10,000 than in the United States. Similarly, in the figures for Germany, only private practitioners were

---

71 *See* ABA Task Force Report, *supra* note 1, at pp. 44-45. In 1993, the ABA established a Standing Committee on Specialization and has a system of accrediting speciality certification programs.

72 U.S. Census Bureau, "Educational Attainment in the United States," http://www.census.gov/prod/2009pubs/p20-560.pdf.

73 Sources: Bureau of Labor Statistics, http://www.bls.gov/oco/ocos053.htm#earnings; NALP, www.nalp.org/press/.

74 See the bimodal graph at http://www.nalp.org/apictureworth1000words.

75 Source: ABA National Lawyer Population by State, http://new.abanet.org/marketresearch/Public Documents/2009_NATL_LAWYER_by_State.pdf.

76 *See* Agenda for Reform in America: A Report from the President's Counsel on Competitiveness (1991), as reported in the New York Times (August 13, 1991).

counted. Adding in government-employed law providers, the revised figure for Germany becomes 34 per 10,000.[77]

C. Types of Practice

The legal profession consists of the following types of practice and percentages of lawyers engaged in each: 74% in private practice; 8% in businesses as "in-house" counsel, 8% in federal, state and local government service, 3% judges, 1% in teaching, 1% lawyers engaged in public interest practice.[78] Judges, who in the United States are also members of the bar, are described in the chapter on the judicial system.[79] The work of law teachers was described earlier in this chapter when legal education was discussed. Below we will discuss the work of lawyers in private practice, as in-house counsel, in government service and in public interest practice.

1. Private Practice

The discussion that follows is organized under two very rough headings. The first is solo practice and smaller firms, including a discussion of their business and non-business-oriented areas of law. Then large corporate firms are discussed. Following that is a brief discussion of non-traditional private legal services that have developed.

a. Solo Practice and Smaller Firms

Solo practitioners and small firms have much in common. Indeed, small firms often operate more as an aggregate of solo practitioners sharing rent than as a true firm. Solo or small-firm practitioners may be new lawyers who aspire to grow and add partners, or they may be experienced practitioners who like the independence and atmosphere of working alone or with a small group of lawyers. Of the divisions of private practitioners, the category of the smallest firms — 1-20 lawyer firms — by far accounts for the greatest number and percentage of lawyers (51%) in the profession.[80]

General Practice Solo practitioners often engage in general practice. As some have said, "I handle anything that walks through that door."[81] As the size of the firm increases, there is greater specialization among the lawyers.[82] In the aggregate, however, smaller firms handle most every kind of legal problem that arises in the life of the average citizen: divorces and related family law matters, residential real estate transactions, wills and trusts, personal injury litigation, consumer disputes, minor criminal matters, and personal financial problems, such as debt problems or bankruptcy. While representation and counsel of small businesses may be involved, smaller firms tend to practice "people" law rather than business law.

---

77 This and the other cross-cultural comparisons are from Ray August, *The Mythical Kingdom of Lawyers*, 78 ABA JOURNAL 72 (September 1992). One must remember as well that lawyers have comparatively greater responsibilities in an adversary system and do much of the work that investigators, magistrates or judges do in more inquisitorial systems. Thus, one would expect more lawyers and fewer judges in a common law country. *See* John Langbein, *Judging Foreign Judges Badly: Nose-Counting Isn't Enough*, 18 JUDGES' JOURNAL (Fall 1979).

78 ABA LAWYER DEMOGRAPHICS (2005) on the ABA website, www.abanet.org/.

79 *See* Chapter V, pp. 177-187.

80 AFTER THE JD study, *supra* note 10.

81 *See* JOEL F. HANDLER, THE LAWYER AND HIS COMMUNITY: THE PRACTICING BAR IN A MIDDLE-SIZED CITY (U. of Wisconsin Press 1967); CARROLL SERON, THE BUSINESS OF PRACTICING LAW - THE WORK LIVES OF SOLO AND SMALL-FIRM ATTORNEYS (Temple University Press 1996).

82 One study found that 55% of solo practitioners spent at least 50% of their time in one area. *See* ABA TASK FORCE REPORT, *supra* note 1, at 41. A 1991 survey of California lawyers indicated that 75% of all lawyers spent at least 50% of their time in one substantive area.

Personal Injury Personal injury litigation firms tend to be either "plaintiffs' firms" or "defense firms" but not both. While most plaintiffs' firms would fall into the category of small and many defense firms are small as well, some defense firms are medium-sized or even large firms. Most personal injury defense is performed pursuant to insurance policy "duty-to-defend" clauses. Insurance companies not only agree to pay the damage the insured is liable for, but also to defend the insured in court. A large firm will sometimes represent a personal injury plaintiff, but it is not a common specialty.

The "American rule" on litigation costs is that the parties must absorb their own legal representation costs.[83] Personal injury defendants' lawyers, and almost all other lawyers, bill their clients by the hour. Win or lose, they receive their pay. Plaintiffs' lawyers use what is called a "contingent fee" arrangement. If the plaintiff receives no money in the case, the plaintiff's lawyer also receives nothing. But if the plaintiff's lawyer succeeds in obtaining monetary damages, either as a result of a trial or through settlement of the case, he or she takes a proportion (usually one-third) of the amount obtained for the client. Of course, it often happens that, in a successful case that is resolved at an early stage of litigation or even without litigation, the lawyer receives a fee that seems large considering the number of hours that the lawyer actually worked on the case. The equity in such system, however, is that in other cases that same lawyer may perform a great deal of work but receive no fee at all.

Many believe that the contingent fee is somehow dishonest and in any event encourages groundless lawsuits. Plaintiffs' lawyers respond that many victims of serious accidents would be unable to gain redress for their injuries without the contingent fee, since they have no money to pay a lawyer by the hour for legal representation. Moreover, there is a disincentive for the lawyer to bring a groundless suit, since the suit has to prevail for the lawyer to get paid. However, there are complaints that lawyers press weak cases to gain a "nuisance" settlement — payment of a small amount of money to avoid the costs of mounting even a successful defense.[84]

Consistent with the entrepreneurial nature of their practice, plaintiffs' lawyers often resort to advertising. Indeed, one cannot watch daytime television in urban areas of the United States today without seeing several such advertisements, some of them in questionable taste.[85]

Criminal Defense One specialty area that is almost always confined to smaller firms is criminal defense work. Privately retained defense counsel in criminal cases typically are sole or small-firm practitioners who limit their practice to such work. Often the lawyers who start such firms do so after they have gained experience as prosecutors or public defenders, discussed later in this chapter.[86] Most "street crime" defendants have little money and qualify for representation by a public defender.[87] However, many

---

83 *See* Chapter VII, p. 255.

84 For a defense of the contingent fee, *see* Elihu Inselbuch, *Contingent Fees and Tort Reform: A Reassessment and Reality Check*, 64 LAW & CONTEMP. PROBS. 175 (2001). In England, contingent fees are permitted in the form of a "conditional fee" agreement. It is similar to a contingent fee in that the lawyer gets no fee if the case loses. In the event of success, however, the lawyer recovers legal fees based on the standard hourly rate the lawyer charges, plus a "success fee" of 100% of that rate up to 25% of the total amount awarded. Since English litigants are entitled to recovery of their legal fees from the opposing party if they win, the client may be able to recover some of the fees paid.

85 The legal basis for personal injury claims is tort law, covered in Chapter XI.

86 *See* discussions *infra* p. 156 (public defenders) and p. 154 (prosecutors).

87 In 1998, 82% of defendants in federal felony cases and 62% of defendants in state cases had appointed counsel. Caroline Wolf Harlow, "Defense Counsel in Criminal Cases" (Bureau of Justice, U.S. Dept. of Justice 2000).

others do not qualify and must seek representation from the private bar. Also, some categories of crime — for example, "white collar" crimes, such as embezzlement, tax fraud, securities fraud, illegal currency transactions and "laundering" drug money — typically involve defendants who have the means to pay for a lawyer.[88] Moreover, in areas where there is no universal public defender system, courts appoint members of the private bar to represent indigent defendants. While court appointments do not pay a great deal, a specialist who does enough of them can generate sufficient income to make pursuit of such cases worthwhile.[89]

Family Law Divorce and related family law matters are often the mainstays of sole and small firm practice. It is said that divorce cases "pay the rent," meaning that the fee in any given case is not that high, but the supply of clients is a steady and dependable one. But some small firms specialize in divorce and particularly in contested divorces. Large firms generally do not bother with divorce cases because there is not much money involved. But in recent years, some of the larger firms in large cities have begun to take divorces where a large amount of money is at stake and wealthy spouses are willing to expend relatively large amounts of money to protect their share of the property or child custody rights.[90]

Labor and Employment Law Firms in this category often deal with issues related to unions and collective bargaining, though the decline of unions in recent years has made such cases less common than they once were. As with the personal injury firms, labor firms can be "management-side" labor law firms or "union-side" labor law firms — both to avoid conflicts of interest and because of personal inclinations of the lawyers. Labor law firms advise management or unions about issues of union recognition and elections, assist in the collective bargaining process, advise on strikes or other labor unrest, and deal with grievances processed under collective bargaining agreements. Lawyers specializing in employment law have increasingly been occupied with a new form of claim by employees — claims for "wrongful discharge." Under this legal theory, employees in many situations are able to argue that they can not be fired without "just cause," generally based on an implied covenant of their employment contract. Firms also specialize in workmen's compensation (administrative remedies for job-related injury) and employment discrimination.[91]

"Boutique" Business Law Firms Lawyers formerly of large firms often leave to create small firms specializing in corporate law. Because these small firms have experienced and capable corporate law specialists, they are able to attract "big name" clients and charge big firm fees. Accordingly, they are often called "boutique" firms.[92] Often these "boutique" firms specialize in a particular kind of practice related to corporations, such as antitrust or securities regulation or representation of businesses before administrative agencies. The growth of such firms has been accelerated by the

---

88 *See* KENNETH MANN, DEFENDING WHITE-COLLAR CRIME: A PORTRAIT OF ATTORNEYS AT WORK (Yale U. Press 1985). "White collar" refers to the fact that perpetrators of crimes of this type are the sort who wear white shirts to work. Such defendants "steal with the pen instead of the gun."

89 Criminal law and procedure are covered in Chapters VIII and XIV.

90 Divorce cases may not be handled on a contingency basis. *See* ABA MODEL RULES OF PROFESSIONAL RESPONSIBILITY Rule 1.5(d)(1). *But see Ballesteros v. Jones*, 985 S.W.2d 485 (Tex. App. 1998) (*en banc*) (contingent fee was not improper in action to establish existence of common law marriage). Family law, including divorces, is covered in Chapter XIII.

91 Labor and employment law are covered in Chapter XV, pp. 616-632.

92 While "boutique" in French simply means a shop, in American English, it has come to mean a small fancy store selling expensive specialty goods.

changing practices of many large corporations seeking legal representation. As noted below, corporations have increasingly spread their work among several legal service providers, often looking for lower fees for the same level of service. For specialized matters particularly, many large corporations find that boutiques, with their smaller overhead costs, are the answer.[93]

b. Large-Firm Practice

The Era of the Large Firm   In 1949, only five firms in the U.S. had more than 50 lawyers; by 1989 there were more than 287. Between 1977 and 1989 the number of firms with more than 100 lawyers increased five times — from 47 to 245.[94] By 2000, there were more than 150 firms that had more than 250 lawyers, and from that number, 57 firms had more than 500 lawyers and 7 had more than 1,000. The largest firm in the United States is DLA Piper, which has 3,785 lawyers in 30 countries and 68 offices.[95] The term "mega-firm" seems more fitting for today's large firms.[96]

Clientele   The largest firms all specialize in representing business corporations. Corporate practice includes matters relating to general business dealings of the corporation, corporate structure, corporate finance, and mergers and acquisitions. Large corporate law firms have various departments that specialize in tax law, antitrust law, real estate law, litigation, banking law, intellectual property, and labor law. Among the clients of these firms one can find the richest and most widely known corporations. In corporate practice, lawyers largely perform the role of advisor, organizer, and negotiator in business matters and draft the necessary documents related to business deals, but if litigation is necessary, the litigation department of the firm will become involved. When it is necessary to represent the company in administrative or criminal matters filed by the government, there are specialists in these areas as well.

Firm Structure   Traditionally, lawyers in firms that are partnerships are either partners or associates. In a professional corporation, they will be shareholders or associates.[97] Partners or shareholders own the firm and receive a percentage of the amount that the firm takes in every year. Associates receive a salary. The ratio of associates to partners-shareholders is approximately one to one in the largest firms, though there may be more associates in some. The path by which an associate may become a partner or shareholder varies from firm to firm, but usually the decision is made between the fifth and the seventh year of an associate's work. The policy has been an "up-or-out" one — either the associate becomes an equity partner or shareholder, or is asked to leave. However, with the explosive growth in the size of law firms, it has become economically difficult to continue to add partners. Many large firms have increasingly used the position of "senior associate" or "tier partner" or "income partner" as an in-between salaried position. In some firms, the position is terminal, while in others it is an additional step toward equity partnership or a title for "lateral hires" while the quality of their work is judged.

---

93 Business enterprise and business regulation law is covered in Chapter XV, pp. 580-616.

94 *See* Stephanie Goldberg, *Then and Now: 75 Years of Change*, 76 A.B.A. JOURNAL 56 (January 1989).

95 These statistics and other information on super large firms are taken from the survey of the 250 largest firms in *The National Law Journal 250*, found at www.law.com/; see also www.dlapiper.com.

96 *See* ROBERT NELSON, PARTNERS WITH POWER (U. of Cal. Press 1988) and MARC GALANTER & THOMAS PALAY, TOURNAMENT OF LAWYERS (U. of Chicago Press 1990).

97 The limited liability of corporations is discussed in Chapter XV, p. 588. Professional corporations have limited liability for ordinary kinds of liability, but the lawyer-shareholders remain personally liable for any malpractice they commit.

Pay and Work Environment   Large-firm lawyers do well financially. In 2009, the median first-year salary for lawyers in firms of 2 to 25 lawyers was $70,000, for lawyers in firms of 501 to 1000 lawyers was $135,000, and for lawyers in firms of more than 1000 lawyers was $160,000. By the eighth year, the figures were $111,625, $180,000, and $258,050, respectively.[98] The figures do not include year-end bonuses, usually given for billing more hours. Bonus payments often depend on overall firm performance, but many firms have a standard bonus schedule. Partners in such firms make even more, of course, and the amount they receive depends on how well the firm performed that year. Profits per partner were in the $2,000,000 to $3,000,000 range at the largest firms.[99]

In return for such pay, firms insist that associates and partners work very hard. Often firms use a system under which associates are required to bill a certain number of hours a year. The "target" hours for large firms average about 2,000 billable hours a year, but 2,200 hour "targets" exist as well. Moreover, there is pressure to bill above these levels. In most firms, the number of hours billed is one of the most important criterion for figuring year-end bonuses for associates and their eligibility for partnership, and for figuring compensation for partners. For example, one firm in Philadelphia pays $5,000 for each 100 hours over 2,000. Another firm requires 2,200 hours just to qualify for any bonus. If one works 2,000 hours, then, taking 2 weeks out of 52 weeks for vacation, 2,000 hours is 40 hours a week. But when one considers that lawyers may spend as much as 15-20% of their time on "non-billable" tasks, a person billing 40 hours a week is working rather hard.[100]

The pay of new lawyers in the large firms seems like high pay, but the law firms, like good investors, "buy low" and "sell high." An associate who makes $80,000 a year and submits 2,000 billable hours is being paid only about $40 an hour plus fringe benefits. If the average billing rate for the lawyer is even as low as $200 an hour, the 2,000 hours billed represent income of $400,000 to the firm.[101]

Prestige and Influence of Large Law Firms   As just seen, large-firm lawyers are better off financially than other lawyers. But more than money is involved. Senior partners of the largest firms often move in powerful governmental and political circles. They regularly serve in governmental positions when their political party is in power and are often tapped for special assignments, such as special counsel to the President or special prosecutors, or nominated to be federal judges. Big firm lawyers are also disproportionately influential in the legal profession. The number of lawyers working in firms of over 100 lawyers comprises only 8% of all lawyers. But senior lawyers from these firms serve with much greater frequency on bar association committees and commissions than sole practitioners or lawyers from smaller firms or in-house counsel. Both because of the high pay and the elite status of large law firms, they attract some of the more able graduates of the most prestigious law schools.

Difficulties for Large Firms   From 1977 to 1990, large firms continued to hire and promote associates because the general business climate was good and companies

---

98 NALP *Associate Salary Survey* (2009), www.nalp.org/press.

99 American Lawyer 100 - "Profits per partner," http://www.law.com.

100 Things were not always this way. In the 1960s and 1970s, associates were generally expected to bill 1,600 and partners 1,300. *See* Goldberg, *supra* note 94.

101 A survey in 2006 among Texas firms indicated average hourly billing rates in firms of over 100 lawyers was $208 for first-year associates, $264 for fourth-year associates, and $488 for partners. Average weekly hours billed were 36 for partners and 38 for associates. Source: THE TEXAS LAWYER (May 3, 2006) as reported in the NATIONAL LAW JOURNAL, www.law.com. Many firms today boast partners charging $1,000 per hour or more, http://www.law.com/jsp/nlj/PubArticleNLJ.jsp?id=1202426491654.

needed representation. However, the economy declined substantially in the period 1990-1993, and many firms cut down on hiring new associates. Some even fired or laid off associates and even partners and shareholders whom they believed were not sufficiently productive. Some large firms disbanded and some even went bankrupt.

An effect of this downturn was greater attention to the business side of law practice. Corporate clients have become more discriminating consumers of legal services, using the lawyers in their own corporate legal departments as sophisticated "shoppers" for legal services, contracting with several different firms on an *ad hoc* basis for discrete tasks or cases and actively negotiating prices.[102] And even when single law firms are retained, corporate clients are much more likely to insist on itemized bills and to require that the firms justify the tasks listed and hours charged.[103] Consequently, large firms usually require their lawyers to bill their work in 6 minute increments, with surprisingly specific descriptions. Many lawyers object to such requirements as inefficient and counter-productive to their legal work. In addition, large firms today place a greater emphasis on their lawyers attracting new business for the firm, sometimes called "rain-making" or "fee origination."

c. Non-Traditional Forms for Delivery of Private Legal Services

"Legal Clinics" and Other Low-Cost Standardized Legal Services   Legal clinics as understood here should not to be confused with the teaching clinics in law schools. The term "clinic" has also been used to describe law offices that specialize in delivery of relatively routine legal services at below-market rates for individuals. Typical types of cases handled are divorce, bankruptcy, real estate transactions, wills and social security cases. Below-market rates are achieved through a high volume of clients, the routine nature of the services rendered, fixed-rate fees, and standardized and streamlined office procedures.[104] Clinics attract the necessary high volume of clients by means of advertising, convenient location in such non-traditional locations as shopping malls, and projecting an informal office atmosphere. They are targeted at middle-income clients who cannot afford traditional rates of lawyers, but are not poor enough to qualify for government-sponsored legal assistance.[105]

The pioneers in this field were two national legal services firms that use the clinic-style approach — Hyatt Legal Services and Jacoby & Meyers. Begun with a great flourish in the wake of the Supreme Court's ruling legalizing advertising in 1977, Hyatt Legal Services pioneered the flat-fee inexpensive legal services office, growing to 200 offices nationally in 1980. Jacoby & Meyers had 150 offices in 6 states with 305 lawyers at that time as well. However, more recent history may indicate limits on such national firms with local offices. Hyatt has now closed, selling off its offices to their attorney-employees. Jacoby & Meyers contracted to just 17 offices by 1999, but has experienced a moderate resurgence recently. No similar national law firms with a clinic approach have emerged to enjoy the level of success these firms experienced in the past.[106]

---

102 In-house counsel are discussed *infra* p. 150.

103 This practice is so widespread that a separate business of auditing legal bills has sprung up. *See* "You Charged How Much?", 85 ABA JOURNAL 20 (1999).

104 *See* GERALD SINGSEN, REPORT ON THE SURVEY OF LEGAL CLINICS AND ADVERTISING LAW FIRMS, ABA Special Committee on Delivery of Legal Services (American Bar Association 1990).

105 Legal services for the poor are discussed *infra* pp. 155-156. The name "clinic" has gradually been disappearing in reaction to the public perception, the result of law school clinics, that the word "clinic" is associated with poor people.

106 Report of the Special Committee on the Law Governing Firm Structure and Operation (2000), www.law.cornell.edu/ethics/mdp1.htm.

Taking their place have been smaller traditional firms and solo practitioners, who began to imitate the pricing and advertising characteristics of the national franchise firms in order to compete with them. Such local, independent small firms — or local chains of them — seem to be the most common form that the clinic approach takes today.

Group Discount and Pre-Paid Legal Services Plans These approaches to providing legal services to middle-income people grew out of the consumer movement of the 1960s. Like advertising, group legal services plans were made possible by decisions of the Supreme Court striking down restrictive state bar regulations on constitutional grounds.[107]

Under a group discount plan, members of a group obtain legal services at below market rates. A typical plan provides free 30 minute consultations on simple matters and a 30% discount on more involved matters. Typically, there is a list of participating lawyers, but some of these plans have offices with staff attorneys employed by the plan.

Pre-paid legal services plans are a form of legal insurance. The basic benefit under pre-paid plans is unlimited legal advice and consultation by telephone by calling a lawyer's office on a toll-free number or on the Internet. In addition, some plans provide for certain simple document preparation or letter-writing and informal negotiation. If further assistance is required, the same sort of discount arrangement used in group plans is available. Prepaid plans are usually offered by employers as part of a benefits package. In addition, some credit card companies have been offering a limited legal-advice-only plan to credit card holders for a small monthly fee. However, with the advent of the Internet, direct purchase of legal insurance by the consumer is also possible. It is estimated by an industry group that in mid-1995, there were 18 million Americans covered by some type of prepaid legal services plan.[108]

2. In-House Counsel

"In-house counsel" are lawyers who are employees of a business who provide legal services solely to that business. Since they are practicing law, they must be admitted to the bar of the state in which they are working. The in-house counsel in charge of the legal department of a corporation usually is called the "general counsel" or "chief legal officer," and is often also a vice president of the corporation.

Work In-house counsel have a legal practice very similar to that of lawyers in corporate firms. They give legal advice, draft documents, negotiate, and, increasingly, handle litigation. Beyond these discrete tasks, their role has been described as one of "managing the legal function of the business enterprise."[109] As already noted above, part of that is the task of negotiating and supervising the relationship of the corporation with "outside counsel," the law firms that represent the corporation in matters that in-house counsel do not handle.

Working Conditions In-house counsel jobs are considered to be among the most pleasant forms of private law practice. Salaries are quite adequate. The median 2007

107 *See Nat'l Ass'n for the Advancement of Colored People v. Button*, 371 U.S. 415 (1963) (1st Amendment freedom of association protects right of organization to obtain legal counsel for its members); *United Transportation Union v. State Bar of Michigan*, 401 U.S. 576 (1971) (state court injunction against union providing legal services to its members violates 1st Amendment right of access to courts).

108 *See* www.abanet.org/legalservices/prepaid/ and the link to the American Pre-Paid Legal Services Institute.

109 J.D. DONNELL, THE CORPORATE COUNSEL: A ROLE STUDY 27-28 (Indiana U. 1970). In addition, some general counsels move out of legal work and into regular management jobs in the business.

base salary of a recent graduate joining the legal staff of a company was $70,000 a year, for managing attorneys was $179,900 and for general counsel was $300,000.[110]

Approximately 75% of the general counsels and 50% of the associates in the legal department of companies worked previously in large corporate firms. The relatively relaxed lifestyle of in-house counsel, rather than the money, often attract these lawyers. But some of the inherent challenges of working in a large organization face them in their new positions as well. While many corporate legal departments comprise only a few lawyers (for example, a small bank or hospital may have only one or two lawyers), others are larger, sometimes numbering in the hundreds of lawyers.

Moreover, in recent years, the responsibilities of in-house counsel have grown. Corporations have begun to use in-house counsel more and outside counsel less in an effort to economize, particularly in the area of litigation. A survey conducted in 2000 showed that the hourly cost per in-house lawyer among survey participants was $170, while the average billing rate for outside counsel at that time was $260.[111] Some areas of practice are more likely to be handled in house than by outside counsel: international law, patents and trademarks, environmental law, labor law, mergers and acquisitions, bankruptcy and antitrust.[112] New responsibilities imposed on lawyers and executive officers of companies by the Sarbanes-Oxley Act, the recent federal statute on corporate governance passed in reaction to high-profile corporate scandals, have served to increase stress levels, but also the importance of in-house counsel.[113]

Potential Conflicts of Loyalty The more active participation of in-house counsel in litigation and generally in contested matters has occasionally led to conflicts between companies and their in-house counsel. Employees of a company must be loyal to their employer, but when those employees work as lawyers, they also must follow the rules of professional responsibility for lawyers. Among those responsibilities is the duty to decline to represent a client or assert a position in a lawsuit whenever the lawyer is convinced that position is groundless.[114] It is much easier for a lawyer in a law firm to decline to represent a client or to refuse to take particular action in a case than it is for an in-house counsel employee. Sometimes the company fires its in-house counsel for refusal to handle a matter. In the last few years, occasions have arisen where courts have awarded damages to in-house counsel for wrongful termination where it was based on just such a conflict with the company.[115]

3. Government Service

a. Federal Government Service

U.S. Attorney General The Department of Justice is the legal department of the federal government and an important part of the executive branch. The head of the Department of Justice is the Attorney General of the United States. The Attorney General

---

110 2007 Altman Weil Law Dept Compensation Benchmarking Survey, www.altmanweil.com. The highest paid general counsel in 2005 in the U.S. worked at General Electric, where he received $4.6 million in salary and cash bonuses, plus various stock options. Slightly more modest was the $1.2 million in salary and cash bonuses received by the general counsel of the AT&T Corporation — ranked 39th in compensation among all general counsel.

111 *Price Waterhouse Coopers Law Department Spending Survey for 2000, Executive Summary*, p. 2.

112 ABA TASK FORCE REPORT, *supra* note 1, at 94.

113 The Sarbanes-Oxley Act is discussed in Chapter XV, pp. 604-606.

114 *See* discussion of lawyer ethics related to adversary representation *infra* pp. 171-174.

115 *See Mourad v. Automobile Club Ins. Assoc.*, 465 N.W.2d 395 (Mich.App.1991). Other courts have refused to allow such suits. *See, e.g., Balla v. Gambro, Inc.*, 584 N.E.2d 104 (Ill. 1991).

is a member of the President's cabinet and is nominated by the President with the advice and consent of the Senate, as required by the Constitution.

U.S. Attorneys The legal powers of the Attorney General and Department of Justice are carried out primarily by local United States Attorneys, sometimes called District Attorneys. The United States Attorneys oversee 91 districts throughout the 50 states and the District of Columbia. Small and sparsely populated states each comprise one district, but most states have two or more districts. These districts are the same districts that define the territories of the federal district courts.[116]

A U.S. Attorney, like the Attorney General, is a political appointee nominated by the President and confirmed by the Senate. When a President of a different party is elected, it is expected that the U.S. Attorney will resign so that the new President can appoint someone from the new President's party. However, the U.S. Attorney is sometimes court-appointed. When President Bush left office, there were 77 U.S. Attorneys who were appointed by him. President Clinton asked for and received their resignations. The rest of the U.S. Attorney's posts were held by court appointees and they were not asked to resign at that time. It happens occasionally that the President declines to change a particular U.S. Attorney despite the fact that the U.S. Attorney was appointed by a previous President of the opposing political party.

Assistant U.S. Attorneys serve under the United States Attorney and carry out the day-to-day work in district offices. Personnel decisions regarding assistant U.S. Attorneys are not generally made on an explicit political basis, but the ability to work under the policies of the U.S. Attorney and division chiefs in the office is important and those policies may have some political overtones. In many U.S. Attorneys offices, except for the top jobs, there are few turnovers in personnel.[117]

Work of U.S. Attorneys United States Attorneys may file criminal charges only for violations of federal criminal law, not state law. Examples of typical federal criminal cases include robbery of a federally insured bank, assault on a federal agent, criminal conduct on a federal reservation, fraud by way of interstate telephone lines, antitrust violations, fraud in sale of securities, violations of federal narcotics laws, possession of certain weapons, and embezzlement of federal funds. As discussed in Chapter I, there is much overlap of state and federal crimes and a violation of federal criminal law in many situations will also be a violation of state criminal law. In the past, the U.S. Attorney in such situations has deferred to state investigation and prosecution in many instances. However, in recent years, there has been much more "federalization" of law enforcement for one category of "ordinary" street crime — illegal sale and distribution of drugs.[118]

Civil actions by or against the United States are also handled by U.S. Attorneys and their assistants or by lawyers from the Department of Justice in Washington, D.C. Lawsuits against the United States and its officials are permitted in many instances.[119]

---

116 *See* Chapter V, p. 174.

117 In *Rutan v. Republican Party of Illinois*, 497 U.S. 62 (1990) and *Branti v. Finkel*, 445 U.S. 507 (1980), the Supreme Court declared that hiring or firing governmental employees according to party affiliation (except for the highest officials whose personal loyalty is essential) violates the First Amendment by penalizing political affiliation and beliefs.

118 Charles Bonner, *Federalization of Crime: Too Much of a Good Thing?*, 32 U. RICH. L. REV. 905 (1998). Prosecution by both state and federal authorities is also a possibility and does not violate the 5th Amendment's right against double jeopardy. *See* Chapter VIII, pp. 315-318.

119 *See* Chapter VI, p. 224. In 1990 alone, there were 787 suits filed against the United States and plaintiffs received approximately $304 million in judgments and settlements.

There are also civil lawsuits regarding the actions of various federal administrative agencies. Judicial review of administrative claims for disability insurance benefits available to permanently disabled workers constitutes a large volume of the cases. There are also matters that arise out of contract disputes with companies working on government projects. Civil suits may also contest the constitutionality of a particular statute, regulation or action of the federal government.[120]

Other Federal Government Lawyers In many other departments of the federal government, there are lawyers who handle the specialized legal business of those agencies. Large employers of lawyers include the Environmental Protection Agency, the Federal Trade Commission, the Internal Revenue Service, the Securities and Exchange Commission, and the National Labor Relations Board. Even the Central Intelligence Agency employs lawyers.

Pay Federal government attorneys receive good salaries, though they are less than those of many private lawyers. Overall, the median pay for U.S. government attorneys was $108,090 in 2004, though Assistant U.S. Attorneys often earn more, the exact amount depending on experience and responsibilities. The range is vast. For example, even among Assistant U.S. Attorneys, the pay scale starts below $45,000 and rises above $130,000.[121] General counsel for the Securities and Exchange Commission (SEC) earned $130,200, while entry level attorneys in that agency earned $51,269 and a general attorney earned $110,028. The salary of the Attorney General of the United States is $191,300.

b. State Attorneys General

The Office In state government, just as in the federal, a lawyer called the Attorney General is the head of the legal department of the executive branch and represents the state both in and out of court. But most attorneys general of states enjoy a greater degree of independence from their governors than their federal colleague enjoys from the President. In a majority of states, the attorneys general are elected by way of a general vote of the citizenry and may not be dismissed by the governor. Often they are members of a different political party than the governor.

Work The attorney general of a state represents the state in all civil matters and gives advice to officials, legislators and agencies of the state. In this capacity, state attorneys general often have an additional way to affect the public policy of the state: they often exercise independent judgment in determining the state's legal position and may decline to assert positions in litigation. In addition, state attorneys general often perform quasi-judicial functions by issuing formal attorney general opinions.[122] Unlike the federal Attorney General, the attorneys general of states do not prosecute or supervise prosecution of ordinary criminal cases. In most states, such prosecutions are handled by local prosecutors, discussed next, who are independent of the state attorney general's office.[123]

Pay The pay of attorneys general varies considerably from state to state. The average for all attorneys general of states was $117,513 in 2008. California and Alabama

---

120 The circumstances under which the United States can be sued are discussed in Chapter VI, pp. 223-224.

121 Department of Justice, http://www.justice.gov/oarm/jobs/10-edva-10.htm.

122 *See* Chapter II, p. 77.

123 However, in the majority of states the office of the attorney general has responsibility for criminal appeals and in half of the states it has the authority to initiate prosecutions at least in some instances. *See* BOOK OF THE STATES: 1998-1999 EDITION (The Council of State Governments).

attorneys general made the most, $184,301 and $163,744, respectively, while Oregon and Arkansas attorneys general made the least, $77,196 and $70,000, respectively.[124]

c. Local Prosecutors

Nature of the Office Although local prosecutors act in the name of the state, they are elected by and responsible to the citizens of a given county, are paid their salary by that county, and are not under the supervision of the attorney general of the state. This reflects a policy that the local community suffering the effects of crimes should be able to express its preferences about enforcement policies through its choice of the lawyers who will prosecute those crimes.[125]

Work Criminal statutes of a state include all of the ordinary forms of criminal activity, and the job of the local prosecutor in large cities is enormous. This does not necessarily mean that the typical assistant prosecutor is always trying cases in court. Just as with civil cases, more than 90% of criminal cases are settled by agreement of the parties. In the majority of criminal cases, this means that the accused pleads guilty to a charge, usually as a result of a plea bargain.[126] Local prosecutors are also responsible for enforcing quasi-criminal laws, such as actions to terminate parental rights for abuse or neglect of children, actions to enforce child support orders, and suits to establish paternity. In some states, prosecutors are even required to make an appearance in all divorce actions where children are involved to insure that the interests of the children are protected. In some areas, prosecutors are active in consumer protection activities, investigating and mediating disputes between consumers and merchants regarding sales of goods or services.

Pay The pay of state prosecutors in 2008 ranged from a $50,000 starting salary to $62,780 after 5 years, to $80,830 for 11 to 15 years experience. While rural prosecutors earned less than those in urban areas, the difference between them was only about 10%. Chief prosecutors earn in the $100,000 to $150,000 range. In sparsely populated counties of many states, the local prosecutor works as a prosecutor only part time and has a private practice in addition.

d. City and County Attorneys

The local prosecutors just discussed handle only criminal and quasi-criminal matters on behalf of the state as a rule. Because of this, counties and cities need another set of lawyers to represent their interests in civil cases and in criminal cases involving violations of municipal ordinances. These lawyers are called city attorneys and county attorneys. In large cities, there are large legal departments under the direction of a city attorney. A majority of counties and small towns do not have enough legal business to justify having a full-time lawyer on staff. Instead, they employ an outside attorney from a private firm when advice or representation in court is necessary.

4. Public Interest Practice

Public interest lawyers are not numerous, but they are important to the legal profession and society because much of their litigation and other activities serve to reform the law. Further, to the extent that public interest lawyers represent clients and

---

124 Source: http://www.legalnewsline.com/news/214122-brown-king-highest-paid-ags.

125 Unlike prosecutors in some other countries, prosecutors in the U.S. are not required to prosecute every violation of the law. *See* Chapter VIII, p. 271.

126 Plea bargaining is discussed in Chapter VIII, pp. 280-282.

points of view that are unpopular or provide representation to poor persons, they remind the profession of one of its highest duties.[127]

a. Legal Services Assistance in Civil Matters

Development of Legal Services Given the complicated character of law and the adversary system of litigation, the assistance of a lawyer is essential in most cases as a practical matter. Persons unable to afford a lawyer then are at a severe disadvantage when dealing with a legal problem. This has led to the establishment and growth of organizations, called "legal services organizations" or "legal aid societies" that are dedicated to providing free civil legal services to the poor.[128]

Legal aid societies have existed since 1876, but the early ones relied on donations by the public and volunteer efforts of private lawyers. In a scathing report issued in 1917, Reginald Heber Smith reviewed the state of legal services for the poor for the Carnegie Foundation and concluded that existing efforts were grossly inadequate even for minimum access to the legal system for the poor. However, the first major effort to try to meet the need did not come until 1964, when President Lyndon B. Johnson's "war on poverty" included funding for such legal aid societies as an essential part of anti-poverty efforts. In that year, Congress passed legislation that appropriated several million dollars to the task of establishing new and strengthening old legal aid societies.

Work Legal services lawyers handle principally two types of cases. Most cases are everyday matters: divorces, custody of children, welfare, consumer disputes, housing disputes (particularly landlord-tenant relations), employment disputes, and so on. The other category of cases consists of so-called "test cases," many of them "class actions" or cases in which a single plaintiff is allowed to represent a group of persons similarly situated.[129] A test case is brought for the purpose of changing the law, generally to broaden constitutional and other important rights. In one case, the constitutional right to notice and a hearing before termination of public benefits was established.[130] In another, the right of a tenant to withhold rent if the landlord has not made necessary repairs to the property was won.[131] In recent years, the frequency of test case litigation has declined as courts and the general atmosphere in the country have become more conservative, and there has been more concentration on efficient delivery of everyday legal services.[132]

Funding By 1981, the amount of the appropriations to the Legal Services Corporation, the agency set up in 1974 to administer legal services programs, had reached $300

---

127 *See infra* p. 165, where the *pro bono* ethical duties of lawyers are discussed. It should be kept in mind that many cases handled by private lawyers could be considered "public interest" cases, such as judgments that serve to gain redress for personal injuries caused by corporations or the government. What distinguishes public interest lawyers from others is that they represent clients principally out of non-material motivations and characteristically limit their practice to such representation.

128 Legal services for the poor in criminal cases are provided by public defender programs and private attorneys appointed by the court. *See infra* p. 156.

129 Class actions are described in Chapter VII, p. 234.

130 *See Goldberg v. Kelly*, 397 U.S. 254 (1970), striking down this policy as violative of the due process clause of the Fourteenth Amendment. *Goldberg* is discussed in Chapter VII, p. 206.

131 *Brown v. Southall Realty Co.*, 237 A.2d 834 (D.C. App. 1968).

132 See Alan W. Houseman, *A Short Review of Past Poverty Law Advocacy*, CLEARINGHOUSE REV. 1514 (April 1990). In addition, restrictions have been added by Congress, including prohibitions on legal services lawyers handling desegregation or abortion cases. *See generally* 42 U.S.C.A. §2996f(b). However, some of those limitations were struck down by the Supreme Court as unconstitutional in *Legal Services Corporation v. Velasquez*, 531 U.S. 533 (2001) (striking down prohibitions on legal services lawyers handling cases involving public welfare benefits as violative of the 1st Amendment).

million for 1,200 organizations, 5,000 lawyers and 2,500 paralegal assistants.[133] But in the 1980s, the administration of President Ronald Reagan tried several times to completely eliminate federal funding for legal services.[134] Congress prevented its abolition, but agreed to cut funding by a third and thereafter raised the appropriation every year by only a very small amount. The amount of appropriations for 1994 was $376 million and local programs handled 1.5 million cases in 1993.[135] By 1999 the level of funding had dropped to $300 million. In 2008, the Legal Services Corporation funded 4,144 full-time staff attorneys and 1,581 paralegal assistants, working at 918 offices.[136] In addition, private lawyers provided volunteer and reduced-fee *pro bono* services under referral programs set up by legal services and under more than 600 other *pro bono* projects.[137] Despite funding setbacks, legal services programs have the solid support of the organized bar and are an established part of the legal landscape.[138]

b. Representation of Indigent Defendants in Criminal Cases

Criminal defendants have a 6th Amendment right to government-provided counsel in all criminal prosecutions in which they face the prospect of being jailed.[139] The government's initial method of discharging this constitutional duty was to assign members of the private bar to represent defendants on an *ad hoc* basis. However, in many parts of the country, federal and state authorities sought to make representation of the poor in criminal cases more effective and its cost more predictable by establishing a system of "public defenders." Under this system, full time lawyers are paid a salary to defend all or most criminal defendants who come before the local courts.

Public defenders working exclusively on criminal cases do not often find themselves involved in class actions.[140] However, important questions of general applicability are decided in criminal appellate cases, in which public defenders often participate. Some states even have a separate defender office that handles criminal appeals exclusively.[141] But the primary contribution of public defenders to the public interest is found in the collective effect of their representation of individual clients. One study of public defenders in Chicago shows that they represent their clients in court vigorously. However, the perception of the quality of their representation by the public and their client population is more negative.[142]

---

133 Paralegals are legal workers who do not have a license to practice law. Most have not attended law school. In practice, however, many perform the same type of functions as junior associates, but paralegals must do so under the supervision of a lawyer. They are widely used in legal services offices and in large law firms.

134 It is said that a good part of President Reagan's dislike for legal services programs was traceable to his experience as Governor of California when he was sued by a legal services organization for taking alleged illegal action in cutting California welfare benefits to the poor.

135 Legal Services Corporation Annual Audit (1994).

136 Legal Services Corp., http://www.lsc.gov/pdfs/LSC_2008_Annual_Report-Highlights.pdf.

137 ABA TASK FORCE REPORT, *supra* note 1, at 53.

138 For a less optimistic view, *see* ABEL, *supra* note 1, at 132-134.

139 *See* Chapter VIII, pp. 302, 312.

140 *But see Gerstein v. Pugh*, 420 U.S. 103 (1975) (class action ordering state sheriff to free all prisoners for whom there has not been a probable cause hearing promptly after their arrest). *See* Chapter VIII, p. 272.

141 Criminal defendants have a right to counsel on appeal as well as at trial. *See* Chapter VIII, p. 322.

142 *See* LISA MCINTYRE, THE PUBLIC DEFENDER: THE PRACTICE OF LAW IN THE SHADOW OF REPUTE (U. Chicago Press 1987). *See also* Caroline Wolf Harlow, "Defense Counsel in Criminal Cases" (Bureau of Justice, U.S. Dept. of Justice 2000) (appointed and retained counsel had same conviction rates).

c. Private Public Interest Organizations

Development of Private Public Interest Groups   The "test case" approach to the problems of disadvantaged persons was first employed by civil rights lawyers working for private public interest organizations, who first brought such suits during the struggles against racial segregation in the 1950s. Foremost among those organizations is the NAACP Legal Defense and Education Fund, which handled perhaps the most important test case in history, *Brown v. Board of Education.*[143]

The ACLU as an Example   The organization best known for using test cases is the American Civil Liberties Union, or ACLU, founded in 1924. In tens of thousands of cases touching on issues of constitutional rights in the Supreme Court and the lower federal and state courts for the last fifty years, lawyers from the ACLU have appeared either as lawyers for a party or in the capacity of *amicus curiae.*[144] The ACLU has comparatively few lawyers on staff, but has great influence because it is more than just a law firm. It has 250,000 mainly non-lawyer "members." More than 10,000 of these members work as volunteers in offices located in all 50 states, publicizing civil rights issues and working on concrete projects that concern civil liberties issues in their regions and cities. In addition, the ACLU has more than 5,000 volunteer lawyers.

The work of the ACLU is controversial even among supporters of civil liberties and indeed among its own members. In the 1970s, it represented the American Nazi party when the town of Skokie, Illinois prohibited the Nazis from organizing a demonstration. Skokie was thought by all concerned to be a special location for the demonstration because it was a city where many survivors of World War II Nazi concentration camps lived. When the Nazis were unable to find a private lawyer who would agree to represent them in their efforts to obtain a parade permit, the ACLU filed suit on their behalf and won.[145] The ACLU represented the Nazis just as vigorously as they defended Communists in the 1950s during a time when many of them were being persecuted for their views. In several situations lately, the position of the ACLU in favor of unlimited freedom of speech was subject to criticism by the public and cost it some of its membership.[146]

Other Groups   Other public interest organizations, such as the Sierra Club and the Natural Resources Defense Council, fight for ecological causes. There are also groups organized around issues of women's rights, consumer protection, the disabled, education, mass media, health care, children's rights and welfare. Historically, most public interest law firms have represented "liberal" or "left" points of view. But in recent years, organizations of different political persuasions have been formed. For example, the Mountain States Legal Foundation is dedicated to protecting "free enterprise." Similarly,

---

143 347 U.S. 483 (1954). *Brown* held that racial segregation in public schools violates the equal protection clause of the Fourteenth Amendment of the Constitution. *See* Chapter IX, p. 353. For a history of *Brown* and the NAACP's litigation strategy regarding civil rights, *see* RICHARD KLUGER, SIMPLE JUSTICE (Knopf 1976).

144 An *amicus curiae* is not a formal party to the case, but an individual or organization that is permitted to file a brief on one or another side of an issue in a case in which it has an interest. *See* Chapter II, p. 44 note 26.

145 *Collin v. Smith*, 578 F.2d 1197 (7th Cir. 1978). *See* Chapter IX, p. 369.

146 For an interesting history of the ACLU that discusses its difficulties with support for some of its positions, *see* SAMUEL WALKER, IN DEFENSE OF AMERICAN LIBERTIES: A HISTORY OF THE ACLU (Oxford U. Press 1990).

the Washington Legal Foundation and the Pacific Legal Foundation have been active in recent cases.[147]

Pay of Public Interest Lawyers   Lawyers who work for either publicly funded or private public interest organizations earn relatively low salaries in comparison with lawyers practicing in private firms. For civil legal services lawyers, median salaries in 2008 were $40,000 for lawyers at entry level, $48,000 for lawyers with 5 years of experience, and $60,000 for lawyers with 11-15 years of experience. For the same three tiers of experience, public defenders made $47,435, $60,000, and $75,000. Directors of programs earn as much as $80,000 to $100,000. Private public interest organizations paid their lawyers between $37,000 and 64,000. On the other hand, legal services and public interest organizations typically provide more paid vacation time than do private firms.[148]

Obviously, lawyers in public interest organizations feel that money is not the most important part of their work. And, despite the fact that high salaries and prestige usually go together, public interest lawyers fighting for civil liberties, rights of minorities or the ecosystem enjoy considerable respect in the eyes of the public.

D. Minorities and Women in the Legal Profession

The Changing Face of the Legal Profession   In 1951, women comprised 3% of the lawyer population, 3.5% in 1960, 8% in 1980, but then 27% in 2000. In 1960, only 1% of lawyers were minorities, but this increased to 7.4% by 1990 and to 10% by 2000. More change is in store because 47% of present-day law students are women and 22% are minorities. As of 2008, 45% of associates and senior/staff attorneys were women, while 19% were racial minorities. However, there still seems to be a "glass ceiling." Only about 19% of partners in major law firms were women and only about 6% were minorities. This represents slow but steady progress since 1993, when the figures were 12.3% and 2.5%, respectively, but is still low compared to women and minority associates.[149]

Racial and Ethnic Minorities   As the profession began to admit women and racial and ethnic minorities in greater numbers in the 1950s, many large firms continued to hire only white males of Anglo-Saxon origin. Black, Hispanic and Jewish lawyers, and generally lawyers from all the immigrant families that came to the United States in the first half of the 20th century, went to work as sole practitioners, for the government, or in small or medium sized firms.[150] The situation for hiring minorities and women has improved considerably in the last 30 years. The main reason for the change was that Congress passed the Civil Rights Act of 1964. That law prohibits discrimination based on race, sex, or ethnic origin in the hiring, promotion or conditions of work of employees of all private institutions and businesses and provides a right to sue and receive monetary compensation from employers who violate the law.[151]

---

147 *Keller v. California*, 496 U.S. 1 (1990) discussed *supra* p. 141, and *Nollan v. California Coastal Commission*, 483 U.S. 825 (1987), discussed in Chapter XII, p. 486, were sponsored and argued in the Supreme Court by lawyers from the conservative Pacific Legal Foundation.

148 Source: NALP, www.nalp.org/, citing 2008 Public Sector and Public Interest Attorney Salary Report.

149 ABA, LAWYER DEMOGRAPHICS (2008), *supra* note 78; and NALP, Law Firm Diversity Demographics Slow to Change (2008).

150 *See generally* ABEL, *supra* note 1, at 85-87, 99-108.

151 *See* Title VII of the Civil Rights Act of 1964, 42 U.S.C.A. §2000e *et seq.* Title VII is discussed in Chapter XV, pp. 620-625. While Title VII has always applied to initial hiring of associates, it was only in 1984 that the Supreme Court made it clear that Title VII applied to *partnership* decisions in law firms. *See Hishon v. King & Spalding*, 467 U.S. 69 (1984).

Women Lawyers   Up until the last quarter of the 19th century, women were prohibited from becoming lawyers in many states. The Supreme Court upheld the constitutionality of that prohibition in 1873 in *Bradwell v. Illinois*, with one justice remarking that "the natural and proper timidity and delicacy which belongs to the female sex unfits it" for law practice.[152] Columbia Law School Dean and later Chief Justice Harlan F. Stone proclaimed in 1927 that women would be admitted to Columbia Law School "over my dead body." Harvard Law School barred women from enrolling until 1950, Washington and Lee Law School barred them until 1972. In the 1970s, though, women began enrolling in substantial numbers, jumping from 8% in 1970 to 34% in 1980.

Yet, as noted above, not many women become partners. And surveys show that they are consistently paid less. Raw data from a recent study showed that, while women who graduated in 1970 started out earning 98% of what their male counterparts earned, after 22 years their pay had shrunk to only 65% of what male 1970 graduates earned. Part of this discrepancy results from the type of legal job (more women than men work in public interest jobs) and more work interruptions, but even accounting for these factors, for women in private firms 29% and 37% of the gender wage gap remains unexplained.[153]

Many believe that the whole system of promotion and admission to partnership in a law firm works against women achieving partnership. Partnership selection takes place usually before the associate's seventh year. And, as already related, in order to become a partner in many firms, one must bill many hours and work many unbilled hours as well. In addition, lawyers are expected to make efforts to bring in new clients for the firm. All this takes up much of the associate's evenings and weekends. For many women, the first 7 years after they finish law school (from the ages of 24 to 31 usually) are also the time when they begin to have children, if they do not already have them. Even in families with relatively progressive views, child care and domestic chores are still done principally by women. Ultimately, it is difficult for working mothers at firms to devote evenings and weekends to their children when their employer requires work to be completed at those times.[154]

A recent suggestion for the problem of balancing career goals and motherhood has been through some version of what has been termed the "mommy track."[155] Under this option, women could arrange alternative work patterns utilizing flexible hours, periods of extended leave and telecommuting. But they would be on a separate track to remain a "permanent" associate rather than become a partner. Some have praised the "mommy track" idea as offering a feasible alternative for women who desire to have a semi-normal relationship with their children, while others have criticized it as institution-alizing "second-class citizen" treatment of women in the firm. It may even spark tensions with male counterparts who desire some form of a "daddy track." However, despite the flaws of a formally recognized "mommy track," many firms recognize the

---

152 83 U.S. 130 (1872) (Bradley, J. concurring). *See* Chapter IX, p. 358.

153 Wynn R. Huang, *Gender Differences in the Earnings of Lawyers*, 30 COLUM. J.L. & SOC. PROBS. 267 (1997).

154 *See* David L. Chambers, *Accommodation and Satisfaction: Women and Men Lawyers and the Balance of Work and Family*, 14 LAW & SOC. INQUIRY 251 (1989) (showing great career and life satisfaction of women who combined career and family life).

155 This notion was spawned by an article in the Harvard Business Review. Felice N. Schwartz, *Management Women and the New Facts of Life*, HARV. BUS. REV. 65 (1989).

benefit of offering some of its features to women in order to recruit and retain good women lawyers.

Aside from the problems just discussed, women lawyers in law firms face a male-oriented atmosphere and social standards. A common complaint is that men in firms spend their social time with other men and make no effort to include women in their network of informal associations. While these "old boys" associations are ostensibly social, the attachments and interactions that result clearly spill over into work.

E. Legal Ethics

1. Regulating the Legal Profession: Sources of Regulation

The last several decades have witnessed an increase in public and professional interest in the ethics and conduct of the legal profession in the United States.[156] Part of this can be attributed to the dramatic increase in the number of lawyers and part of it to the fact that so many lawyers were implicated in the Watergate scandal of the Nixon Administration.[157] In the United States, the conduct of lawyers is subject to regulation from three sources: the judicial branch, self-regulation by the organized bar, and increasing, albeit indirect, regulation through private malpractice actions.

Role of the Judiciary As discussed earlier, the ultimate power of regulation of the profession generally resides in the supreme courts of the states. The judiciary is deemed to have inherent power and the primary role in regulating the legal profession. The connection between legal practice and the judiciary is seen in the common reference to lawyers as "officers of the court." One direct regulatory tool of courts is their power to hold a lawyer in "contempt" or to institute disciplinary proceedings for misconduct. Recently the primacy of judicial control over the profession has been questioned since a high percentage of lawyers today — especially those in large corporate firms — are "office lawyers" who never appear in court. However, much of the power of the judiciary over the profession has been delegated to the profession itself, where "office lawyers" are well-represented.[158]

Self-Regulation Consistent with a long tradition of self-regulation, the ABA has had a strong role in determining the ethical standards of the profession. In 1908, it promulgated its Canons of Professional Ethics which were adopted by many state bar associations. These canons were advisory, but several courts eventually began enforcing them as if they were rules of law. The canons remained in effect until 1970, when the ABA promulgated the Model Code of Professional Responsibility (the "Model Code"). In 1983, the ABA replaced the Code with the Model Rules of Professional Conduct ("Model Rules"). Because the ABA is a private organization and lacks the power to impose its rules on anyone, the code and rules are only "models." However, they have been widely adopted by states as law.[159]

Malpractice Suits Suits against lawyers for malpractice were once a rarity. That is no longer so. The level of competence of lawyers is probably no lower today than in the recent past. The growth in legal malpractice claims is probably due to the same changes

---

156 A good overview of professional responsibility is DEBORAH L. RHODE AND GEOFFREY C HAZARD, JR., PROFESSIONAL RESPONSIBILITY AND REGULATION (2002). A student text by a provocative author is MONROE H. FREEDMAN, UNDERSTANDING LAWYERS' ETHICS, 3D ED. (Matthew Bender 2004). *See also* RESTATEMENT (THIRD) OF THE LAW GOVERNING LAWYERS (American Law Institute 1988). For a book setting out interesting stories behind important ethics cases, *see* DEBORAH L. RHODE & DAVID J. LUBAN, LEGAL ETHICS: LAW STORIES (Foundation 2006).

157 The Watergate affair was discussed in Chapter I, p. 14.

158 *See* ABA Task Force Report, *supra* note 1, at 117-118.

159 These rules with commentary are on the ABA website: www.abanet.org/cpr/mrpc/mrpc_toc.html.

in attitudes toward professionals that has made suing doctors more acceptable — less awe and greater realism about their work and their place in society. Most of the successful malpractice cases have been for especially egregious conduct, such as the deliberate and willful neglect of a client matter to the extreme detriment of the client or gross incompetence. Part of the reason for this is in the legal requirements for a legal malpractice claim. The dissatisfied former client must show both that the attorney was at fault *and* that, but for the attorney's misconduct, the client would have prevailed on the underlying claim — usually shown by a "trial within a trial" on the mishandled claim.[160]

Most lawyers carry malpractice insurance, but the rate for such insurance is far below that of physicians. Bar organizations maintain "client security funds" that are designed to reimburse clients who lose money as a result of improper conduct of lawyers and who are unable to recover their loss otherwise. However, few of these funds provide full compensation.[161]

2. Defining Ethical Behavior: The Duties of the Attorney

The Code and the Model Rules set forth standards and guidelines in the following areas: the attorney-client relationship; the attorney's role as a counselor and an advocate; transactions with persons other than clients; law firms and association of attorneys; pro bono service; and the integrity of the legal profession. Discussion of all these topics is beyond the scope of this chapter, but some are covered here.

a. The Nature of the Attorney-Client Relationship

The attorney-client relationship is the most important aspect of the practice of law. A rhetorical foundation for the nature of the relationship is Lord Brougham's observation that "an advocate, in the discharge of his duty, knows but one person in all the world, and that person is his client."[162] Less dramatically, the Model Rules set forth several of the lawyer's duties to the client, discussed in the next few paragraphs.

Duty of Competent Representation The lawyer has a duty to "provide competent representation" which requires the "legal knowledge, skill, thoroughness, and preparation necessary for the representation."[163] Accordingly, a lawyer whose practice is limited to advising corporations should probably not attempt to try a murder case. Lawyers who do not have sufficient knowledge or experience to handle a matter should either decline representation, associate with an attorney who is knowledgeable on the subject of the representation, or adequately prepare and educate themselves.

---

160 A developing area of liability is bad settlement recommendations. *See Thomas v. Bethea*, 718 A.2d 1787 (Md. 1998) (defendant recommended settlement of $2,500 with landlords for lead paint poisoning of children; "trial within a trial" on underlying tort claim resulted in $125,000 verdict).

161 Such suits also attract the attention of the bar, which may investigate and discipline the offending attorney. For more on malpractice, *see* RONALD E. MALLEN & JEFFREY M. SMITH, PREVENTING LEGAL MALPRACTICE, 2D ED. (West 1996). Another possible approach is to sue the lawyer for violation of consumer protection statutes. *See Latham v. Castillo*, 972 S.W.2d 66 (Tex. 1998) (lawyer misrepresenting that medical malpractice action had been filed perpetrated consumer fraud). *But see Cripe v. Leiter*, 703 N.E.2d 100 (Ill. 1998) (consumer fraud law did not apply to claim that attorney charged excessive fees; excessive fee issues are exclusively remediable by bar disciplinary proceedings).

162 TRIAL OF QUEEN CAROLINE 8 (J. Nightingale ed. 1821).

163 MODEL RULES OF PROFESSIONAL CONDUCT (2008), Rule 1.1. These and other rules are reprinted in JOHN S. DZIENKOWSKI, ED., PROFESSIONAL RESPONSIBILITY: STANDARDS, RULES AND STATUTES (West 2010) and at www.abanet.org/cpr/mrpc/mrpc_toc.html. *See also* ANNOTATED MODEL RULES OF PROFESSIONAL CONDUCT, 6TH ED. (ABA 2008); ABA COMPENDIUM OF PROFESSIONAL RESPONSIBILITY RULES AND STANDARDS (2006 Edition).

Duty to Consult The lawyer has a duty to "abide by a client's decisions concerning the objectives of representation" and "consult with the client as to the means by which they are pursued."[164] The attorney has some authority to make binding decisions for the client, especially concerning technical matters that arise during litigation. But the attorney generally may not make unilateral decisions that will have an impact on the substantial legal rights of the client, such as entering into a settlement without the consent of the client or, in criminal cases, deciding whether the client will testify, plead guilty, or waive the right to a jury trial.[165]

Duty of Diligence An attorney must "act with reasonable diligence and promptness in representing a client."[166] This obligates an attorney to take any action that is legal and ethical to pursue a matter on behalf of a client despite public opposition or personal inconvenience to the lawyer. Procrastination and unreasonable delay must be avoided so that a client's rights are not prejudiced or forfeited due to the expiration of any applicable statute of limitations, the legal time period for filing suit.

Duty to Charge Reasonable Fees The Model Rules require lawyers to charge reasonable fees. Most bar associations provide a fee mediation service to assist in enforcing this provision. The fee should be communicated in writing to the client within a reasonable time after the representation has begun. Contingent fee arrangements are prohibited in domestic relations matters and criminal cases.[167]

Duty of Loyalty and Conflicts of Interest The Model Rules prohibit an attorney from representing a client when the attorney has personal interests that conflict with those of the client, since this would violate the duty of "undivided loyalty."[168] Consequently, an attorney can have no personal interest or stake in the outcome of a suit or matter.[169] Further, if the attorney already has a client whose interests are directly adverse to those of a potential client, the attorney must decline the second representation. Even after an attorney-client relationship ends, an attorney may not later represent a client whose interests are adverse to those of a former client if the attorney obtained confidential information from the former client which relates in a substantial way to the second client's case. As noted next, the attorney owes the first client a continuing duty of confidentiality that survives the termination of the client-attorney relationship.

Duty of Confidentiality An attorney owes a client the important duty of confidentiality. Generally, an attorney may not disclose any information "relating to representation of a client unless the client consents after consultation, except for disclosures that are impliedly authorized in order to carry out the representation."[170]

Faithful adherence to the duty of confidentiality has resulted in what some people feel are repugnant results. For example, during a criminal case in New York, a defendant charged with murder informed his attorneys of the location of the bodies of two other people he had killed. The father of one of the victims begged the attorneys to reveal this information so that he could give his child a decent burial. The attorneys refused because the disclosure of the information would be a breach of their duty of

---

164 MODEL RULES, Rule 1.2.

165 MODEL RULES, Rule 1.2(a).

166 MODEL RULES, Rule 1.3.

167 MODEL RULES. Rule 5.1. Contingent fees were discussed *supra* p. 145.

168 MODEL RULES, Rules 1.7, 1.8, 1.9.

169 This does not prohibit contingent fees, however. *See supra* p. 145.

170 MODEL RULES, Rule 1.6.

confidentiality to their client and would prejudice his chances of plea bargaining with the prosecutor. While the actions of the attorneys in this case may seem heartless, the majority of the legal community agreed that the attorneys acted properly in a morally difficult situation. The foundation of such a strict duty of confidentiality is the need for clients to feel that they can disclose all relevant facts to their attorney, so that they receive the best legal representation possible.[171]

The Model Rules provide three exceptions to the strict rule of confidentiality. First, if the attorney believes that the client is intending to commit a crime that is likely to result in imminent death or substantial bodily harm, the lawyer may inform the authorities.[172] Second, an attorney may reveal client confidences where it is necessary to prove a claim or defense in a controversy between the lawyer and the client.[173] Third, in some states, revealing confidences is permitted to "prevent the client from committing a crime or fraud that is reasonably certain to result in substantial injury to the financial interests or property of another and in furtherance of which the client has used or is using the lawyer's services" and to rectify any such injury.[174] In addition, as discussed next, the duty of candor may override confidentiality in some other situations.

Withdrawal from Representation A lawyer must withdraw from representation of a client if continuation of representation will require a perpetration of a fraud or violation of the rules of professional conduct. In addition, a lawyer may withdraw if the client "insists upon taking action that the lawyer considers repugnant or with which the lawyer has a fundamental disagreement"; the client fails to pay the lawyer and has been given reasonable warning that the lawyer will withdraw unless payment is made; "representation will result in an unreasonable financial burden on the lawyer or has been rendered unreasonably difficult by the client"; or there is other good cause for withdrawal.[175]

b. The Attorney's Duty to the Administration of Justice

Duty of Candor to the Court As was clear from Chapter III, attorneys have major responsibilities in litigation with regard to presentation of evidence and argument before a court on behalf of a client. In performing this public function as an "officer of the court," the lawyer takes on a duty of candor to the court or other tribunal. An attorney may not present evidence the attorney knows to be false. If an attorney discovers that a client intends to commit perjury, the attorney must "take reasonable remedial measures, including, if necessary, disclosure to the tribunal."[176]

---

171 *People v. Belge*, 83 Misc. 2d 186, 372 N.Y.S.2d 798 (Co. Ct. 1975), *aff'd*, 376 N.Y.S.2d 771 (N.Y. App. Div. 1975), *aff'd*, 390 N.Y.S.2d 867 (N.Y. 1976).

172 MODEL RULES, Rule 1.6(b)(1). The exact substance of this rule varies from state to state; some *require* the disclosure while others *permit* it. Further, some states permit the attorney to reveal the client's intention to commit *any* crime. Regardless of what ethical rules might require or permit, lawyers in some jurisdictions may be sued for damages if they do not reveal a client's stated intentions to commit a crime of violence against a particular person. *See Tarasoff v. Regents of the University of California*, 551 P.2d 334 (Cal. 1973) (duty of psychiatrist to warn intended victim of patient's threats of harm).

173 The information is also privileged under evidence law. *See* Chapter III, p. 115, n. 131. The Court recently clarified that the attorney-client privilege survives even the death of the client. *Swidler & Berlin v. United States*, 524 U.S. 399 (1998).

174 MODEL RULES, Rule 1.6(b)(2) (as amended 2003). Not all states have adopted the 2003 amendment permitting disclosure in cases of fraud, most notably California and New York.

175 MODEL RULES, Rule 1.16.

176 MODEL RULES, Rule 3.3. The comment to the Rule states: "If perjured testimony or false evidence has been offered, the advocate's proper course ordinarily is to remonstrate with the client confidentially. If that fails, the advocate should seek to withdraw if that will remedy the situation. If withdrawal will not remedy the situation or is impossible, the advocate should make disclosure to the court. It is for the court then to determine what should be done — making a statement about the matter to the trier of fact, ordering a

Some would argue that this view of the duty of candor violates the client's right to confidentiality and the basic tenets of the accusatorial and adversarial system of justice by requiring, or at the least permitting, defense counsel to assist the prosecution.[177] The Supreme Court has held, however, that it does not violate a defendant's 6th Amendment right to counsel in a criminal case for defense counsel to tell a client who stated his intention to commit perjury that if he so testifies, that defense counsel would have to report it to the court and request to withdraw from the case.[178]

Duty to Refrain from Asserting Frivolous Claims The Model Rules prohibit a lawyer from "defending a proceeding, or asserting or controverting an issue therein" if doing so would be frivolous. The rule makes clear that it is permissible to assert a position that might currently be contrary to legal authorities, but which is based on a good faith argument for an extension, modification or reversal of existing law.[179] This ethical standard has been widely adopted in court rules and legislation as a basis for sanctioning lawyers in litigation when they assert frivolous claims or defenses.[180]

The rule goes on to state, however, that "a lawyer for the defendant in a criminal proceeding . . . may nevertheless so defend the proceeding as to require that every element of the case be established." This exception would include zealous defense of a client the lawyer knows to be guilty and reflects the constitutional principle that the state must prove every element of the crime charged and may not, by procedural rule or otherwise, shift its burden to the defendant. Even when an attorney knows from his client that a witness is providing truthful testimony, the lawyer can vigorously cross-examine the witness about a discrepancy in that witness's testimony and argue that the witness is not telling the truth.[181]

An attorney must also accurately state the law controlling an issue to a court. Even if the opposing counsel fails to disclose and the attorney knows of controlling law directly adverse to this client, the attorney must present that law to the court.[182] This does not prevent the attorney from making creative and good faith arguments to distinguish adverse law in order to persuade the court that existing law is not applicable or sound. This rule is indeed a difficult one for zealous counsel to comply with.

c. Duties to the Profession and Others

Dealing with Represented Parties A lawyer may not communicate on a subject of representation with a person known to be represented by another lawyer without the consent of that person's lawyer.[183] An interesting issue arose regarding this rule when the U.S. Attorney General in 1989 announced that government attorneys could contact people represented by attorneys in certain situations. One provision authorized contact if it is "in the process of conducting an investigation, including, but not limited to, an undercover investigation." Another permitted contact with any employee of a corpora-

---

mistrial or perhaps nothing."

177 *See* FREEDMAN, *supra* note 156, at 109-141 (lawyer should not disclose perjury). Accusatorial and adversarial principles in criminal cases are discussed in Chapter VIII, p. 275.

178 *Nix v. Whiteside*, 475 U.S. 157 (1986). The result was that the client testified, but made no perjurious statements and was convicted. The Court rejected the Court of Appeals approach, which would have required that counsel be silent about any perjury.

179 MODEL RULES, Rule 3.1.

180 An example of this is Federal Rule of Civil Procedure 11, discussed in Chapter VII, p. 232.

181 *United States v. Wade*, 388 U.S. 218, 257-58 (1967). *See also* FREEDMAN, *supra* note 156, at 161-171.

182 Model Rules, Rule 3.3(a)(2).

183 MODEL RULES, Rule 4.2.

tion unless the employee is a "controlling individual" in the corporate organization.[184] The regulations further announced that all contact issues involving government attorneys were solely within the jurisdiction of the Attorney General and that any contrary state rules were preempted. After the ensuing furor and at least two U.S. Court of Appeals cases holding the rule invalid, Congress passed a law placing government lawyers back under the control of state and local rules applicable to all other attorneys.[185] However, opponents have vowed to change that law.

Pro Bono Service The Model Rules recommend that every lawyer "aspire to render at least (50) hours of *pro bono publico* legal services per year."[186] The *pro bono* services contemplated are legal services for "persons of limited means," for public service groups or charities, or "for individuals, groups or organizations seeking to secure or protect civil rights, civil liberties or public rights." In some states, the *pro bono* requirement can be satisfied by a generous donation of money to the local legal aid society. In others, the Model Rule's "aspiration" is a requirement.

Issues in Leaving Firms When a lawyer leaves a firm, disputes over "stolen" clients often arise. It is up to clients to decide who will represent them. However, firms take a proprietary attitude toward long-standing clients and losing several of them can have a major economic impact on the firm. Theoretically, one method of dealing with this problem has been to use non-compete agreements like those used with other employees — an agreement barring departing lawyers from practicing law in competition with the firm they have left for some period of time. However, Model Rule 5.6 prohibits such agreements for lawyers, except when conditioned upon the receipt of retirement benefits. The rule is based on the rationale that choice of counsel is up to the client. Courts have for this reason held that non-compete agreements for lawyers are void as against public policy.[187] However, a partner in a firm owes a fiduciary duty to other partners, so soliciting firm clients — especially before announcing one's departure — could be a breach of that duty, and possibly tortious interference with prospective economic advantage.[188]

Client Solicitation, Advertising and Duty to Report The Model Rules prohibit in-person or live telephone contact to solicit employment for pecuniary gain from a potential client with whom the lawyer has no previous relationship. This limitation is intended to protect vulnerable individuals from undue influence, intimidation and overreaching by an attorney.[189] Further, the Rules impose strict requirements on the content of advertising to insure that it is truthful and that the public will not be misled by it.[190] The Model Rules also impose a duty on lawyers to report any "significant violation"

---

184 *See* 28 CFR §77.1 *et seq.* The quoted language is from §77.7 and §77.10.

185 *See United States ex rel. O'Keefe v. McDonnell Douglas Corp.*, 132 F.3d 1252 (8th Cir. 1998) (prohibiting contact with employees and some former employees of corporation) and P.L.105-277 §801.

186 MODEL RULES, Rule 6.1.

187 *See Cohen v. Lord, Day & Lord*, 550 N.E.2d 410 (N.Y. 1989).

188 *See Dowd & Dowd v. Gleason*, 693 N.E.2d 358 (Ill. 1998) (non-compete agreement is not valid, but breach of fiduciary duty and interference with prospective economic advantage claims possible). Breach of fiduciary duty is discussed in Chapter XV, p. 581, and interference with prospective economic advantage is discussed in Chapter XI, p. 453.

189 MODEL RULES, Rule 7.3.

190 MODEL RULES, Rule 7.1. Some of the ethical restrictions on solicitation and advertising have run afoul of 1st Amendment protections of free speech. *See* Chapter IX, pp. 387-389.

of ethical duties by other lawyers "that raise substantial question as to that lawyer's honesty, trustworthiness, or fitness as a lawyer."[191]

---

191 MODEL RULES, Rule 8.3.

CHAPTER V

THE JUDICIAL SYSTEM

To speak of "the judicial system" of the United States is misleading, because there are in reality 51 different judicial systems in the country: the federal court system and the court system in each state. As to questions of state law, each of the state systems is a separate closed system. In other words, each state system has its own court of last resort that has the last word on what state law is. Only on issues of federal law, arising originally either in federal or state court, can it be said that there is the semblance of a single national judicial system with one court, the United States Supreme Court, serving as the court of last resort.[1]

PART I: An Overview of Court Systems and Judges

A. Trial Courts and Appellate Courts: Their Basic Characteristics and Interrelationship

All the court systems in the United States, state and federal, have two basic types of courts: trial courts and appellate courts. The two have different functions and characteristics.

1. Trial Courts

Functions and Characteristics Judges who staff trial courts "sit" alone without any other judges. They conduct trials either with or without a jury, depending on the type of case and the wishes of the parties. The overall job of trial courts is to reach a decision in the first instance on all disputes filed in a given judicial system. This involves hearing the evidence and arguments presented by the parties, determining the facts in the case and applying the law to those facts. In the process, the trier of fact, whether judge or jury, must resolve conflicts in the testimony and make judgments about the credibility of witnesses and the believability and weight to be given all the evidence. This is an important function because, as discussed below, the facts of a case cannot be relitigated on appeal.[2]

Trials constitute only a part of a trial judge's activities. Pretrial motions must be heard and decided. A great deal of a trial court's time is spent on this activity, which the judge performs alone without the assistance of a jury. In most courts one or two days a week are set aside as "motion days." In addition, trial judges preside over pre-trial conferences in civil cases slated for trial. In those conferences the judge will attempt to persuade the parties to settle the case or, if they cannot settle it, to narrow the factual and legal issues for trial.[3] In criminal cases, a great deal of time is spent on arraignments of criminal defendants (a hearing at which formal charges are presented and bail set) and preliminary hearings (where the prosecution must present enough evidence to warrant binding the defendant over for trial).[4] Judges of trial courts also need time to do legal research and to write the required judicial opinions deciding motions or trials they

---

1 *See* Chapter I, p. 22, and the diagram of the federal and state court systems set out in the Appendix, p. A32. For a short introduction to U.S. courts written especially for a foreign audience, *see* DANIEL J. MEADOR, AMERICAN COURTS, 3D ED. (West 2009) and DANIEL J. MEADOR, APPELLATE COURT IN THE UNITED STATES, 2D ED. (West 2006). *See also* HENRY J. ABRAHAM, THE JUDICIAL PROCESS, 7TH ED. (Oxford U. Press, N.Y. 1998).

2 *See generally* Chapter III, pp. 92-109 for jury trial procedure.

3 *See* Chapter VII, pp. 229-242.

4 *See* Chapter VIII, pp. 273-276.

have already heard. There are also administrative tasks, such as conferences with colleagues on mutual problems, personnel matters, the operation of the clerk of the court's office, and the like.

Trial Judges and Courtrooms   American trial judges wear robes but not wigs as English judges do. The "bench," *i.e.*, the dais where the judge sits when presiding at a hearing, is raised. The judge's secretary or clerk and the court reporter sit in front or to the side of the judge's bench. A jury box, an area with 12 or 14 seats that is enclosed by a one-meter high partial wall, is located to one side. Further out in front of both the judge's bench and the jury box are the counsel tables and chairs, where the lawyers sit when handling a matter before the judge. Nearby is a lectern which the lawyers may use when arguing or conducting witness examinations. Behind counsel tables is a "bar" about a meter high between the area where the lawyers, judge and jury sit, and the rest of the courtroom where the general public sits.[5]

As a show of respect to the judge, all persons present in the courtroom are required to stand when the judge enters and is seated "on the bench." The judge has contempt power to punish summarily any disruption in the courtroom or other display of disrespect to the court. When court is in session, lawyers generally must address the judge from the lectern or counsel table unless they are invited or obtain permission to "approach the bench." This is done usually at trial when matters must be discussed which the jury is prohibited from hearing.

Each judge has a court reporter who takes down verbatim (either in shorthand or by means of a machine) everything that takes place in court at a trial or hearing. In the event of an appeal, this record must be typed up in a transcript that must be filed with the appellate court to apprize it of exactly what happened in the trial court.

Virtually all trial court hearings are open to the public, as a requirement of state and federal constitutional law.[6] However, many trial judges conduct pre-trial conferences "in chambers," meaning the judge's office, usually located behind the courtroom. Also, some matters that are required or permitted to be inquired into confidentially may be heard "*in camera*," *i.e.*, in chambers.

Since trial courts handle all cases filed in a given judicial system, the atmosphere in a trial court in a large city on motion day or the day set for preliminary hearings in criminal cases can be chaotic, with parties, lawyers, police officers and complaining witnesses moving in and out of the courtroom or up to the lectern or bench for conferences with the judge as their cases are called. In the halls, lawyers confer with their clients, worried litigants pace and family members of the litigants gather in groups. In addition, an air of tension is present in view of the fact that disputes are the business of the day and that delay is inevitable as the court tries to handle everything that has been scheduled.

---

5   A diagram of a trial courtroom is set out in the Appendix to this book on p. A33. The bar between the area where the judge and lawyers sit and the area where the public sits gives us the expression that a lawyer, when admitted to practice, is "called to the bar" (English version) or "admitted to the bar" (American version). Lawyers and judges are so identified with their physical place in the courtroom that it is common to refer to judges collectively as "the bench" and to lawyers collectively as "the bar."

6   *See* Chapter IX, p. 386.

At the bottom of the judicial pyramid, trial courts are the most numerous courts in both the state and federal judicial systems. The number of judges staffing trial courts of general jurisdiction varies from a high of 1,498 in California to a low of 16 in Maine.[7]

2. Appellate Courts

Intermediate Appellate Courts and Supreme Courts   Above the trial courts of a judicial system, there are usually two layers of appellate courts: an intermediate court of appeals and a supreme court. The intermediate appellate court is usually called the "Court of Appeals" and the final appellate court is called the "Supreme Court."[8] Judges of supreme courts are usually called "justices," while judges of intermediate courts of appeal and trial courts are called "judges." Appellate courts have no jury or other non-lawyer members. When meeting to hear and decide cases, intermediate appellate courts have three judges while supreme courts usually number five, seven, or nine justices.

This two-tiered structure prevails in the federal system and all but twelve of the states. For most types of cases, there is an appeal as of right from the trial court to the court of appeals, while further appeal to the supreme court is discretionary with that court. However, some categories of cases may qualify for review as of right in a state supreme court, such as cases where the death penalty has been imposed. Where two levels of appellate courts exist, the intermediate court of appeals has the task of assuring that trial court errors are corrected. The supreme court in such a system has the broader task of overseeing the development of the law. Thus, it will generally decide only cases in which the law needs to be clarified or some question of overriding public significance needs to be addressed. A system of granting discretionary review is established to select such cases. To have a case heard in the supreme court of a system, a party must be "granted leave to appeal" or must obtain a writ of "certiorari," the procedure established at common law for a higher court to review the decision of a lower court.[9] Thus, in the ordinary case in most jurisdictions, litigants must be satisfied with only one appeal. However, the courts of final resort of some states with two-level appellate systems, among them New York, retain relatively large categories of obligatory appellate jurisdiction.

Resolving Conflicts Within the Court of Appeals   The "panel" of three judges of intermediate courts of appeal constitutes less than all the judges of that court. This can result in disagreement among different panels of the appellate court. There are many mechanisms for resolving such disagreements. One method, used by the federal courts of appeal and many states, is to convene a court of all of the judges of that court for an *en banc* hearing to resolve the conflict.[10] States handle panel conflicts variously. In some, the first panel to decide an issue binds the entire court until and unless it is

---

7   These figures do not include trial courts of limited jurisdiction. This and other information regarding state courts in this chapter are taken from THE BOOK OF THE STATES (Council of State Governments, Lexington, Kentucky 2005).

8   In some states, among them New York, the court of final resort is called the Court of Appeals and in Massachusetts it is called the Supreme Judicial Court. In Texas and Oklahoma, there are separate supreme courts for criminal and civil appeals.

9   Certiorari practice in the United States Supreme Court is similar and is discussed *infra* p. 182.

10   If the U.S. Court of Appeals of the Ninth Circuit were to meet *en banc*, there would be 28 judges — a rather large court. Legislation enacted in 1978 permits circuits with more than 15 active judges (currently only 3) to conduct limited *en banc* hearings with fewer than all judges. However, only the 9th Circuit has opted to do so. Starting in 1980 it used 11 judges and since January 2006 — after some criticism of the practice — it has used 15 judges. *See* Ct. App. 9th Cir. Rule 35-3 (2006). The practice remains controversial.

reversed by the state supreme court. Another method is to make the first panel's decision binding, but to allow the second panel considering the same issue to indicate that it is following the first panel's decision only because it is required to do so. All the Court of Appeals judges are then polled on whether the potential conflict warrants the convening of a special panel for resolution. Then a special panel of 7 judges, drawn by lot from of all but the judges involved in the two potentially conflicting decisions, rehears and decides the issue.[11]

No such conflict problems attend supreme courts. All judges participate in each case heard unless ill or disqualified. Thus, supreme courts normally sit *en banc*.[12]

3. The Scope of Appellate Review

The scope of appellate review of trial court judgments depends on two factors: whether the issue reviewed is one of fact or one of law, and if one of fact, whether the fact finder was a judge or a jury.[13] An appellate court can review issues of law *de novo* and will reverse a judgment for any non-harmless error, but it is much more limited in its review of the factual basis of a trial court judgment.

Fact Review in General One reason for limited review of facts is one of the tenets of the adversary system discussed in Chapter III: a belief in the superiority of immediate oral evidence over mediate written evidence.[14] Though a verbatim transcript of the entire trial is available to the appellate court, this "cold paper record" of the trial is no substitute for the vantage point of the fact finder at the trial level, who actually sees and hears the witnesses and is therefore in a far superior position to find the facts accurately. Indeed, much of the presumed benefit of the trial-level adversary presentation of the facts would be lost if an appellate court could simply substitute its view of the evidence for that of the trial court.

Standards for Bench Trials and Jury Trials When a trial judge sits as the fact-finder in a bench trial, the judge's findings of fact will be reversed only if they are "clearly erroneous."[15] Review of jury verdicts is even more limited. If the judgment reviewed is based on a jury verdict, a second reason for great deference to trial level findings emerges. The right to trial by jury would not mean very much if either trial or appellate judges could simply reverse jury findings whenever they disagreed with them. The standard for appellate review of jury verdicts is identical to the standard employed by a trial judge in reviewing a jury verdict: the verdict of the jury can be reversed only if there is a complete absence of any substantial credible evidence to support it. Simple disagreement with the verdict is not sufficient. In determining the sufficiency of the

---

11 Michigan Court Rule 7.215(J). Further appeal to the state supreme court is also possible.

12 If one judge cannot hear a particular case for some reason, this can result in an even number on the court and a tie vote. In such a case, the judgment below is affirmed.

13 *See generally* JACK H. FRIEDENTHAL, MARY KAY KANE AND ARTHUR R. MILLER, HORNBOOK ON CIVIL PROCEDURE, 4TH ED. §13.4 (West 2005).

14 *See* pp. 83-84.

15 *See* Federal Rule of Civil Procedure 52(a). "A finding is 'clearly erroneous' when although there is evidence to support it, the reviewing court on the entire evidence is left with the definite and firm conviction that a mistake has been committed." *United States v. United States Gypsum Co.*, 333 U.S. 364, 395 (1948). *See also Anderson v. Bessemer City*, 470 U.S. 564 (1985) (finding of intentional discrimination); *Hunt v. Cromartie*, 532 U.S. 234 (2001) (finding that race, rather than politics, drove the state legislature's legislative redistricting decision). Some states use a standard of "against the manifest weight of the evidence." *Eychaner v. Gross*, 779 N.E.2d 1115 (Ill. 2002).

evidence, the appellate court must be careful not to substitute its view for that of the jury. This would be a violation of the fundamental right to a trial by jury.[16]

It follows from what has been said that an appellate court generally may not receive new evidence on the factual issues in the case.[17] Even if the appellate court determines that more evidence is necessary on a point, it will direct the trial court to take such evidence and make a decision in the first instance.

Review of Decisions Committed to Trial Court Discretion   There are numerous decisions that trial courts make that are committed to their discretion. Most often, there are guidelines for the court to follow, but reasonable judges could differ as to their application to a given set of facts. In such cases, a trial court's decision will be reversed on appeal only if the appellate court finds an "abuse of discretion." This question is essentially one of whether the trial judge's decision was among the rational choices a reasonable judge could make under the circumstances. It is not what the appellate court would have done had it been the trial judge. An example of such decisions is whether to issue a preliminary injunction, an order preserving the *status quo* until the merits of a case can be heard.[18]

Civil vs. Criminal Cases   A narrow scope of appellate review applies to criminal appeals, and it applies to the extent of the standard of proof at issue. Thus, a civil judgment of a jury will be reversed only if the evidence was legally insufficient proof by a *preponderance of the evidence* to support it. In a criminal case, a jury verdict finding the defendant guilty will be reversed on factual grounds only if the record discloses that there was legally insufficient evidence *beyond a reasonable doubt* to support it.[19]

4. Appellate Court Procedure

The issues of law raised on appeal are argued principally by the submission of written briefs by the parties to the appellate court.[20]   Limited oral arguments are permitted. The maximum time for oral argument permitted each side is usually 15 or 30 minutes. Because most of a party's arguments are presented in the written briefs, oral argument generally serves as a time for the attorney to touch on recent developments in the law affecting the case, to highlight the main arguments in his client's favor, and most important, to respond to questions from the bench.[21]

The fact that only issues of law are involved and that they are addressed primarily in written briefs gives the appellate court a much more quiet and erudite atmosphere

---

16 An attempt at explaining the precise difference between the standard of review for judge and jury factual findings is set out in *Hersch v. United States*, 719 F.2d 873 (6th Cir. 1983). The standard for trial judge review of jury verdicts is set out in Chapter III, p. 108 and note 98.

17 For a discussion of the history leading to this almost invariable rule, *see* Robert W. Millar, *New Allegations and Proof on Appeal in Anglo-American Civil Procedure*, 47 NORTHWESTERN U. L. REV. 427 (1952).

18 *See, e.g., William Inglis & Sons Baking Co. v. ITT Continental Baking Co.*, 526 F.2d 86 (9th Cir. 1976) ("the question is not whether or not [the appeals court] would make or would not have made the order. It was to the discretion of the trial court, not to that of the appellate court, that the law entrusted the granting or refusing of these injunctions"). Of course, if the wrong legal test is applied, that is a separate ground for reversal.

19 There can be no appellate review of a verdict of acquittal. *See* Chapter VIII, p. 316.

20 *See* Chapter II, pp. 78-79 (nature of the argumentation style and composition of briefs).

21 Two classic works on the proper purpose and appropriate techniques of oral argument are John W. Davis, *The Argument of an Appeal*, 26 A.B.A.J. 895 (1940), and Robert H. Jackson, *Advocacy Before the Supreme Court: Suggestions for Effective Case Presentations*, 37 A.B.A. Journal 801 (1951). Davis was a well-known and well-connected lawyer who argued many cases in the United States Supreme Court, among them the defense (and losing) side in *Brown v. Board of Education*, 347 U.S. 483 (1954), the school desegregation case. Jackson was a Justice of the Supreme Court.

than prevails in most trial courts. Only the lawyers and their assistants generally attend appellate court sessions. Clients rarely do, in part because the appellate court is often many miles from where they live and in part because they would not understand much of an argument strictly confined to legal issues.

Appellate Court Action   An appellate court decides a case by issuing an order or judgment indicating the winning party and, usually, an opinion of the court setting out the reasons for the decision. As described in Chapter II, there may also be concurring opinions from judges who agree with the result but differ in the reasoning behind it, and dissenting opinions from judges who disagree with the result and the reasoning of the majority.[22] There are various actions that an appellate court can take. It can affirm the judgment of the trial court, meaning that it approves of it. It can reverse that judgment and direct entry of judgment for the opposing side. Or, if the appellate court's opinion depends on further development of facts or the appellate court wishes the trial court to take further action consistent with the opinion, the appellate court will "vacate" the trial court's judgment and "remand" the case to the trial court for "further proceedings consistent with" its opinion.

5.   Trial Court Actions that are Reviewable

The Final Judgment Rule   A final trial court judgment deciding the case on the merits or dismissing it is usually the only kind of judgment or order that can be appealed. The policy behind the final judgment rule is one of efficiency. One "big" appeal takes less time than multiple small appeals. Furthermore, even if many errors are committed, they may be rendered moot if the party suffering from those errors ultimately wins or settles the case.

Interlocutory Appeals   Appeals of non-final orders, called "interlocutory appeals," are often allowed, but they are discretionary. Usually both the trial court and the appellate court must agree that the issue raised by the interlocutory order is a close one and that it would be efficient to address the issue without waiting for a final judgment.[23] For example, if the trial judge denies a motion to dismiss a case for lack of jurisdiction finding that it has jurisdiction, permission to take an interlocutory appeal will often be granted if the issue is a close one since an appellate finding of lack of jurisdiction at that point could avoid an unnecessary trial. There are a few other exceptions to the final judgment requirement, primarily based on an overriding need to have the issue addressed at an early stage of the litigation.[24]

Mandamus   A limited path around the final judgment rule is pursuit of an action for a "writ of mandamus" (an order requiring certain trial court action) or "writ of prohibition" (an order prohibiting certain trial court action).[25] In some state courts these ancient writs are consolidated under the modern label, "writ of superintending control." These forms of action avoid the final judgment rule because they are considered to be an

---

22   *See* p. 64.

23   For example, 28 U.S.C.A. §1292, applicable in federal court, allows an interlocutory appeal from a non-final order if the trial judge certifies that it presents "a controlling question of law as to which there is substantial ground for difference of opinion and that immediate appeal . . . may materially advance the ultimate termination of the litigation," and the appeals court agrees as well.

24   For example, in the federal system an immediate appeal as of right is provided from interlocutory orders granting or denying injunctive relief. 28 U.S.C.A. §1292(a)(1). In addition, some non-final orders that have a "practical finality" about them may be appealed under the "collateral order" doctrine. *See Cohen v. Beneficial Industrial Loan Co.*, 337 U.S. 541 (1949) (order declining to require a bond in stockholder derivative action in which plaintiffs owned few shares of stock).

25   *See* 28 U.S.C.A. §1651 (federal statute authorizing writs).

original action filed against the trial judge (often by name) rather than an appeal. The limited nature of mandamus review must be emphasized, however. It is considered to be an "extraordinary writ" and is available generally only to redress clearly illegal action by the trial judge of a particularly serious sort, most often concerning an improper exercise or abdication of jurisdiction. In the federal system, at least, the occasions for mandamus are narrow and it is said that "mandamus will not lie" for any error that could be remedied adequately by appeal.[26] However, many state systems regularly allow such writs as a supplement to interlocutory appeal.[27]

B. State and Federal Court Structure and Characteristics

1. State Court Structure

Trial Courts of General Jurisdiction   The basic component of all state court systems is the trial court of general jurisdiction. This court has jurisdiction over major civil disputes and all serious criminal offenses, called "felonies."[28] These courts are called by various names. The most common names for this court are the "Superior Court" or the "Circuit Court," though in some states they are called the "District Court." Strangely enough, in New York these trial courts are called the "Supreme Court" (while the highest court in New York is called the "Court of Appeals"). In general the territorial subdivisions over which these state trial courts preside correspond with the county lines of a state.

In most states, there is a layer of trial courts below the circuit or superior court level which exercise limited general jurisdiction. Typically they have jurisdiction over all types of civil cases up to a certain amount of money in controversy and over less serious criminal prosecutions, called "misdemeanors."[29] For example, in California the Superior Court handles all felonies and civil cases of more than $25,000 in controversy, while the Municipal and Justice Courts handle all criminal misdemeanors and civil disputes of $25,000 or less. Sometimes these lower level courts are the descendants of "Justice of the Peace" or other small claims courts. Those less formal courts were gradually "upgraded" and given greater jurisdiction to relieve the increased workload of the superior or circuit court. Appeals from judgments of these lower courts often go to the circuit or superior court rather than to the regular appeals court. In such cases, the circuit or superior court acts as a single-judge appellate court rather than a trial court.

Trial Courts with Specialized Jurisdiction   States have other trial courts with specialized jurisdiction to decide only disputes of a particular type. Among them are probate or surrogate's courts (for overseeing distribution of decedents' estates, for juvenile matters, or for mental commitments and guardianships over adults unable to handle their affairs), juvenile courts (if juvenile matters are not handled by the probate court), and courts of claims (to handle money claims against the state). In some states, some courts with specialized subject-matter jurisdiction are considered the equal of the superior or circuit courts of general jurisdiction. In other states, specialized courts are considered inferior to the circuit or superior court and the latter are sometimes assigned the task of deciding appeals from the former. This is another instance of a trial court exercising appellate court functions through a single judge.

---

26 *See Kerr v. United States District Court*, 426 U.S. 394 (1976) (disapproving mandamus as means of reviewing discovery order, even though irreparable injury was alleged).

27 For a discussion of all these and other devices, *see* FRIEDENTHAL, *supra* note 13, §§13.1-13.3.

28 A felony is generally defined as an offense punishable by more than one year in prison.

29 Misdemeanors are usually crimes punishable by one year or less in jail. *See* Chapter VIII, p. 269.

Small Claims and Other Informal Courts Most states have established small claims divisions either in the courts of general jurisdiction or in the courts just below them. Disputes are limited to those involving less than a specified amount in controversy, such as $300, $500 or $1,000. Sometimes these courts are called "Justice of the Peace" courts, because that is the name of the official who presides over the proceedings. Sometimes these "justices" are not lawyers and have no legal training.[30] Procedure in small claims courts is very informal and there is generally no appeal from a judgment. Sometimes lawyers are prohibited from representing parties in such courts. However, in most jurisdictions, if parties to cases in small claims court wish to utilize a lawyer or to avail themselves of the greater rights afforded by a regular court, they may do so by simply asking that the case be "removed" from small claims court to the regular trial court. In others, there is no right of removal, but the losing party has a right to a "trial *de novo*" in a higher court. A trial *de novo* is a completely new trial that ignores the earlier result in the small claims court.

Appellate Courts The structure of state appellate courts conforms generally to that described above in the general description of appellate courts.[31] However, it bears repeating that the state appellate court of last resort is the final arbiter of the meaning and application of *state* law. While the United States Supreme Court has power to review state court judgments, it may do so only on issues of *federal* law.

2. The Federal Court System

As discussed in Chapter I, federal courts have jurisdiction over federal law claims and state law claims that involve parties from different states. Such claims can arise anywhere, so the federal court system covers the entire country. However, the federal court system is much smaller than the aggregate of all the state systems. In 2008, there were about 340,000 cases filed in federal courts nationwide: 8,000 at the Supreme Court; 58,000 at the Federal Courts of Appeals; and 276,000 at the District Courts.[32] By comparison, over 100 million cases were filed in state courts, just at the trial court level alone.[33] There are about 29,000 state judges but only about 850 federal judges, which is about the same number of state judges just in the California judicial system. Consistent with that disparity, a state judicial system such as California handles about a million cases annually while the nationwide federal judicial system handles about a third of that number annually.

District Courts The basic trial court in the federal system is the United States District Court, located in 94 districts.[34] Districts vary in size. In the more populous states, there are three or even four districts. In the less populous states, the entire state is one district. For example, New York has southern, northern, eastern and western districts, while the entire state of Montana has one district. All district courts have at least two judges (North Dakota and Vermont have only two) and one district (the southern district of New York) has 28. Where necessary to provide better access for litigants and witnesses, judges of

---

30 *See infra* p. 178 and note 49.

31 *See supra* pp. 169-173.

32 This and other statistics come from the Federal Judiciary website set out in Appendix B.

33 Examining the Work of State Courts, 2007, Nat'l Center for State Courts, ncsconline.org.

34 28 U.S.C.A. §§81-131. These districts are in the 50 states, the District of Columbia, the Commonwealth of Puerto Rico, and the territories of Guam, the U.S. Virgin Islands, and the Northern Mariana Islands. For more information on the federal court system, *see* CHARLES A. WRIGHT & MARY KAY KANE, LAW OF FEDERAL COURTS, 6TH ED. §§1-6 (West 2002).

the district court "sit" (*i.e.*, hold court sessions) in various locations. "Magistrate judges," discussed later, also handle some of the caseload at the district level.[35]

Although claims based on federal law are not as numerous as ones based on state law, claims based on federal law are usually of significance when they do arise because they implicate either the federal Constitution or a congressional statute. The substantive importance of the cases, the scarcity in the number of judges, and the lifetime appointment made by the President – all of these characteristics combine to give federal district judges a certain prestige that does not attach to state trial court judges.

Federal Courts with Specialized Jurisdiction   There are several federal courts with specialized jurisdiction.   They are the United States Claims Court, which handles exclusively claims against the federal government; the Tax Court, which handles suits involving federal taxes; the Court of International Trade, which handles civil matters related to tariff and trade agreements; and the system of bankruptcy courts housed with the federal district courts. In addition, there are the District of Columbia Superior Court and the District of Columbia Court of Appeals, both of which act like "state" courts for Washington, D.C. where local law is federal law. There is also a Foreign Intelligence Surveillance Court, which determines applications by the Attorney General for permission to implement domestic wiretaps in the interest of national security and which uses judges from the regular federal courts. Two specialized courts deal with military and veterans matters: the Court of Military Appeals reviews court-martial convictions for military offenses and the Court of Veterans Appeals reviews decisions of the Department of Veterans Affairs on claims for veterans benefits.

The judges of all these specialized courts, except the Court of International Trade and Foreign Intelligence Surveillance Court, are called "Article I judges" and their courts "Article I courts."   Unlike "Article III" judges, they are not appointed for life, but for specific terms.   The differences between the two types of judges and the effect these differences have on their powers are considered in the chapter on administrative law since similar issues arise with administrative agency adjudicators.[36]

The volume of cases these specialized courts handle is insignificant in comparison to district courts. Congress has generally resisted pressures to create more federal courts with specialized jurisdiction, preferring instead that most federal judicial business be handled by "generalist" Article III judges, who handle all kinds of cases.

Federal Courts of Appeals   Above the federal district level are the 13 federal courts of appeals. There is a right to appeal all final judgments of district courts to the circuit courts of appeals of the appropriate circuit. In addition, the circuit courts have jurisdiction to hear appeals from decisions of certain administrative agencies, such as the National Labor Relations Board or the Department of Health and Human Services.[37]

Eleven of these 13 circuits cover several states. For example, the Sixth Circuit covers Ohio, Kentucky, Tennessee and Michigan. The District of Columbia Circuit covers only Washington, D.C. The Federal Circuit is not organized on a geographical basis at all. It has been assigned the task of handling appeals that involve patents and certain damages suits against the United States government from any of the 94 district courts,

---

35   *See infra* p. 186 and note 80, where federal magistrate judges are discussed.

36   Chapter VI, pp. 220-222. *See also infra* p. 186 and note 80, where federal magistrate judges, also Article I judges, are discussed.

37   The federal courts of appeals are sometimes called "circuit" courts of appeals because the judges at one point had to "ride circuit," *i.e.*, to travel through the states under their jurisdiction along a regular route, usually on horseback, and hold court in various places along that route.

as well as appeals from the Claims Court and the Court of International Trade. The smallest number of court of appeals judges is in the First Circuit, which has 6, and the largest is in the Ninth Circuit, which has 28.

The federal circuit courts of appeals have the discretion to disagree with one another and decisions from one circuit have only persuasive precedential effect in another circuit. The result is that there can be and often is a different rule on a point of federal law in New York (a state in the Second Circuit) and in California (a state in the Ninth Circuit). Such a "split in the circuits" forms one basis for the Supreme Court to exercise its power to review decisions of the circuit courts of appeals, as discussed below.

3. The United States Supreme Court

Nature and Dual Function The Supreme Court of the United States is part of the federal court system, but has a hybrid function. As one might expect, it exercises appellate jurisdiction over cases appealed from the United States Courts of Appeals, but it also exercises appellate jurisdiction over state courts as to *federal issues*.[38]

The Supreme Court is the only court that is specifically created by the Constitution. However, its composition and jurisdiction are determined by Congress. Since 1868, the Court has consisted of 9 judges: 8 associate justices and one "Chief Justice of the United States." In its entire history, it has had as few as 5 and as many as 10 justices. The Court is located in Washington, D.C. and hears every case *en banc*, meaning that all 9 justices sit together and make final decisions in all cases.

Certiorari and Appeals There are two routes to review in the U.S. Supreme Court: an appeal as a matter of right and the discretionary grant of a writ of certiorari. Very few cases fall into the category of appeals as of right, so as a practical matter certiorari is the only way to gain Supreme Court review.[39] Certiorari means to "bring up the record," an essential first step for review of a case by an appellate court. By exercising its appellate certiorari jurisdiction over cases involving issues of federal law coming from the lower federal courts and the highest state courts, the Court maintains the supremacy and consistency of federal law.

Certiorari Procedure In a private conference held each week during the active term, certiorari grants are decided according to the "Rule of Four," meaning that it takes a vote of four Justices to grant certiorari. Like the state supreme courts exercising discretionary jurisdiction, the Supreme Court does not view its role as one of correcting error, but as one of serving the broader interests of the law and the legal system. Thus, its rules provide that certiorari will be granted only when a federal appeals court or a state supreme court has decided a federal law question in conflict with another federal appeals court or state supreme court, or where "a state court or a United States court of appeals has decided an important question of federal law that has not been, but should

---

38 *See* 28 U.S.C.A. §§1254, 1257 and *supra* note 1. For a readable and more detailed description of the Supreme Court and how it operates, *see* ABRAHAM, *supra* note 1, 170-244. For even greater detail on how the Court selects and decides case, *see* SUSAN L. BLOCH & THOMAS G. KRATTENMAKER, SUPREME COURT POLITICS (West 1994). *See also* DAVID M. O'BRIEN, STORM CENTER: THE SUPREME COURT IN AMERICAN POLITICS, 8TH ED. (W.W. Norton 2008).

39 28 U.S.C.A. §§1251-1259. Appeals as of right directly to the Supreme Court are allowed only from special three-judge district court decisions. *See* 28 U.S.C.A. §1253 and §2284. The court is made up of two district judges and one circuit court of appeals judge and is authorized only when reapportionment of legislative districts is ordered and occasionally when Congress desires speedy resolution of a constitutional issue. *See, e.g., United States v. Eichman*, 496 U.S. 310 (1990) (regarding the constitutionality of a federal statute that made the burning of the U.S. flag illegal), discussed in Chapter IX, p. 378.

be, settled by this Court, or has decided an important federal question in a way that conflicts with relevant decisions of this Court."[40] Of the 7,738 petitions for certiorari the Court received in 2008, only 87 cases were argued and 83 of them were decided in 74 signed opinions — about 1%.[41]

Original Jurisdiction The Constitution provides that the Supreme Court has original jurisdiction "[i]n all Cases affecting Ambassadors, and other [foreign] public ministers and consuls, and in cases in which a State shall be a party."[42] These cases form a negligible part of its business, usually less than one-tenth of certiorari grants. By far the greatest number of original jurisdiction cases are disputes between states, although there is an occasional suit by a state against the federal government.[43] Most suits by states against another state are territorial disputes, usually arising as a result of a river changing its course.[44] A notable non-territorial dispute was the seemingly interminable litigation between Texas, California and Utah over which state had the right to tax the estate of multi-billionaire Howard Hughes.[45]

As the court of first instance in these cases, the Supreme Court acts as a trial court. Since a trial before the Supreme Court would be unwieldy, the Court appoints a "special master," usually a retired federal judge, to hear proofs and make a recommended decision in such disputes.[46]

C. Judges and Methods of Judicial Selection

1. Characteristics of Judges

Experience as Members of the Bar Federal and state judges are members of the bar. Thus, they have gone through the same legal education and procedures for acceptance into the bar described in Chapter IV.[47] At one point in United States history, judges were neither members of the bar nor even trained in law. From colonial times until well into the nineteenth century, "lay judges" were not uncommon in the United

---

40 Supreme Court Rule 10.

41 2009 Year-End Report on the Federal Judiciary, http://www.uscourts.gov/ttb/2010-01/index.cfm. This represents a sharp downward trend, both in percentage and absolute terms. As recently as the 1996 term, the Court decided 158 cases out of 6,695. And 30 years ago, when the Court had only 5,000 petitions, it decided between 150 and 180 cases a year. For description and analysis of the Court's certiorari practices, *see* BLOCH & KRATTENMAKER, *supra* note 38, at 325-380.

42 Art. III §2.

43 *South Carolina v. Baker*, 485 U.S. 505 (1988) (suit against the Secretary of the Treasury challenging the constitutionality of a federal law that prohibited states from issuing unregistered bearer bonds).

44 *See, e.g., Arkansas v. Tennessee*, 310 U.S. 563 (1940) (holding that Arkansas through acquiescence had given up its legal claim to land that had cut away from Arkansas and attached to Tennessee due to avulsion caused by the Mississippi River in the early 1800s).

45 *See California v. Texas*, 437 U.S. 601 (1978) and *California v. Texas*, 457 U.S. 164 (1982). The litigation finally ended in 1991. A recent case of note was litigation between New Jersey and New York over their claims to filled portions of Ellis Island, the famous entry point for many waves of immigrants to the United States. *New Jersey v. New York*, 523 U.S. 767 (1998).

46 *See Kansas v. Colorado*, 533 U.S. 1 (2001), where objections to the special master's report are considered in a case involving upstream overuse of water from an interstate river.

47 *See* pp. 128-140. A few state judges of courts of limited jurisdiction may be non-lawyers.

States.[48] Things are different today, although there are still a few non-lawyer judges in some rural areas.[49]

Judges in the United States almost always come to the bench following several years of law practice, whether as private lawyers, prosecutors, or public defenders. Because of this, new judges in the United States tend to be older than their counterparts in civil law countries, most of whom start out on the judicial ladder shortly after finishing their legal education.[50] Part of the Anglo-American tradition of preferring older judges has to do with the need for the judge to have gained adequate knowledge of the law and the complexities of court procedure, including handling a relatively complicated adversary trial process, which is mastered only after a some years in practice. But it is more than that. Experience, not just as a lawyer but in life, is deemed essential for the exercise of mature judgment, which many view as the hallmark of a good judge in the United States. This is particularly so in a common law system where judges have lawmaking powers.

Career Paths of Judges   Career paths of judges in the United States differ from the career paths of judges in civil law countries and of judges in England.[51] Judges in the United States usually do not start at the bottom of the judicial ladder and work their way up to positions on higher courts with more responsibility. A judge in the United States who starts out at the trial level is likely to remain there unless he or she makes some effort to gain the attention of the electorate or political appointing authorities. There is no official "performance review" system. Similarly, a judge can start a judicial career at any level in the judiciary, depending on his or her ability to influence the voters or the inclinations of the appointing authorities. Thus, a lawyer who has no prior judicial experience can become a justice on a court of last resort in a state or even the United States Supreme Court. Felix Frankfurter came to the Court after a law-teaching career, as did Elena Kagan. The late Chief Justice William Rehnquist was an Assistant Attorney General at the Office of Legal Counsel at the Department of Justice before ascending to the Court. In fact, fewer than half of the justices who have served on the United States Supreme Court had prior judicial experience of any kind. Interestingly, there is no legal requirement that federal judges even be lawyers.[52]

Judges as Political Beings   As will be discussed shortly, under most judicial selection systems in the United States, judges either run for election by the general

---

48 Of the eleven judges of the Massachusetts Superior Court from 1760 to 1774, nine had never practiced law and six had never studied it. New York included the governor and legislators on its highest court until well into the nineteenth century. *See* LAWRENCE FRIEDMAN, A HISTORY OF AMERICAN LAW, 2D ED. 125 (Touchstone Books, New York 1985). Use of lay judges was consistent with English practice of having trial courts run by layperson squires and having a legislative body, the House of Lords, as the court of last resort in the system.

49 The Supreme Court has held that it does not violate the due process clause of the Constitution for a defendant to be tried before a non-lawyer judge in a petty criminal case, at least where there is a right to *de novo* re-trial in a higher court with a lawyer-judge. *North v. Russell*, 427 U.S. 328 (1976). In reaction to erratic and legally questionable behavior of some lay judges, several states have enacted laws requiring that all judges in the state be lawyers. *See generally* ABRAHAM, *supra* note 1, at 21, 138-140.

50 For a further description of courts and judges in the United States with comparisons to other countries, *see* ABRAHAM, *supra* note 1.

51 For a more detailed comparison of the career paths of English and American judges, *see* P. S. ATIYAH AND ROBERT S. SUMMERS, FORM AND SUBSTANCE IN ANGLO-AMERICAN LAW 347-353 (Clarendon Press 1987).

52 A useful summary of the backgrounds of recent United States Supreme Court justices is set out in DANIEL A. FARBER, WILLIAM ESKRIDGE, JR. & PHILIP FRICKEY, CONSTITUTIONAL LAW, 3D ED. 55-58 (West 2003). Justice Frankfurter once remarked that "the correlation between prior judicial experience and fitness for the functions of the Supreme Court is zero." Felix Frankfurter, *The Supreme Court in the Mirror of Justice*, 105 U. PA. L. REV. 781, 795 (1957).

population or are appointed by elected officials. Consequently, whether the post is that of federal or state judge, becoming a judge depends in large part on the candidate's ability to attract political support. It is thus not surprising that many judges in the United States are "political people" — people who have been involved in politics on a regular basis in some capacity, whether as office holders, political organizers, fund-raisers, campaign managers or party chairs. It is sometimes the case, especially for judicial candidates for appellate courts, that the political career of such candidates is much longer and more substantial than their legal career. Whatever their past political background, however, once on the bench, judges are not supposed to engage in partisan political activity.

But while a judge may have to cease partisan political activity after going on the bench, the political orientation of judges continues to make its mark after appointment through a judge's "judicial philosophy." A central component of that philosophy is a concept of the proper role of courts in society. Judicial philosophy may be a "liberal-activist" one that emphasizes the role of courts in fighting social injustice and expanding individual rights. Or it may be a "conservative" philosophy of "judicial restraint," which maintains that courts should rarely intervene to upset a legislative judgment or interfere with administrative action. Or it may be a "conservative activist" philosophy — one that has characterized the Supreme Court at several points in its history and in recent years.

A judge's judicial philosophy is not necessarily what could be understood as overtly political, and certainly judges are not supposed to make decisions on political grounds. However, judicial philosophy necessarily includes attitudes about such "non-political" issues as the proper limits of tort recovery for personal injury, the rights of consumers against manufacturers, the rights of criminal defendants or even the rights of shareholders in a corporation against management. More generally, all people — including judges — have a natural tendency to be sympathetic toward one side or the other when they learn of a dispute between the government and an individual, the government and a business, rich and poor, businesses and individuals, or even state and federal governments. When the case is a close one and a decision can be justified either way by the law and the facts, these general inclinations can have a crucial influence.[53]

It should be emphasized that many of these elements of judicial philosophy are often unconscious or, when conscious, are not thought of as being political. They are in any event no different from the kinds of attitudes that often influence judicial decision-making in other legal systems. But the fact that judges in the United States have a well-developed political "past" makes the connection between political viewpoint and judicial decision more transparent. It is not uncommon for lawyers in an important case to read the judicial opinions and research the political background of the judge assigned to their case for some insight into the judge's political attitudes, so that they may better frame their arguments and assess their chances of success.

Judicial philosophy can grow and change, especially when nurtured by the lifetime tenure guarantees of the federal system and some state systems. For example, U. S. Supreme Court justices have produced surprises for Presidents who nominated them. The most notable of these was Earl Warren, a former Republican governor of California who was appointed as Chief Justice by Republican President Dwight D. Eisenhower. Following the appointment, the Warren Court proceeded to issue liberal opinions on civil

---

53 Of course, when there is a jury present, issues of fact or the application of law to fact are resolved by the jury and the judge has limited power to reverse jury findings. *See* Chapter III, pp. 87, 108.

rights, rights of the accused in criminal cases and in other areas, much to the dismay of conservatives. This led the plain-spoken war hero President Eisenhower to remark that his appointment of Earl Warren was the "worst damn-fool mistake I ever made as President."[54] Similarly, both William Brennan, appointed by Eisenhower, and Harry A. Blackmun, appointed by Republican President Richard M. Nixon, were Republicans who turned liberal on the Court. On the other side, Justice Byron White, appointed by Democrat John F. Kennedy, was a disappointment to liberals as he often sided with the conservative faction of the Supreme Court in criminal procedure and other cases involving constitutional rights of the individual.

Judicial Pay In 2008, United States district judges earned $169,300, court of appeals judges $179,500, Supreme Court associate justices $208,100 and the Chief Justice of the United States $217,400. According to a 2009 survey of the salaries of state judges conducted by the National Center for State Courts, judges of trial courts of general jurisdiction averaged $134,826, but their pay varied widely from $104,170 to $178,789. The average judge of an intermediate state appeals courts earned $145,665 and justices of state supreme courts had salaries averaging $150,633. Although the salaries of judges are certainly not modest, they are less than those of many experienced and established private lawyers, from whose ranks judicial candidates are most often chosen. Clearly, for many lawyers, the attraction of being a judge is found in other aspects of the position, primarily power, prestige and a less-pressured work life.[55]

2. Judicial Selection Methods in the Federal System

As discussed earlier, to assure independence of the federal judiciary, the notion of their election (even by Congress) was rejected in favor of lifetime appointment by the President with "advice and consent" of the Senate.[56] Where the path to the bench is by way of executive appointment, the power of appointment, at least on the federal level, is generally exercised along political lines. More than 90% of judgeships bestowed by recent Presidents have been to members of their own political party, except for Gerald Ford, who appointed only 82% from his own party. The precise way that the appointment process works in the federal system varies depending on whether it is for the lower federal courts or the Supreme Court.

Lower Federal Court Appointments   Generally, the President consults with the Attorney General and other advisors, to come up with a list of nominees. In addition, because of the need for Senate approval, certain customs and practices have arisen with regard to appointments to the lower federal courts. Senators with the same party affiliation as the President have a great deal of power to "suggest" nominees to the President for district court posts in their state and have virtually an absolute right to "veto" nominees the President may be considering if they are "personally obnoxious" to the Senator. Arrangements vary from state to state and there are even compromise agreements in some states that allow a Senator of the opposite political party of the

54 JOHN D. WEAVER, WARREN: THE MAN, THE COURT, THE ERA 342-343 (Little, Brown & Co. 1967). On the democratic side, President Harry Truman considered his appointment to the court of Justice Tom Clark a poor choice. "Tom Clark was my biggest mistake. It isn't so much that he's a bad man. It's just that he's such a dumb son of a bitch." His attitude is attributed to Clark's vote to invalidate Truman's seizure of the nation's steel mills to avert a strike. When he was attorney general, Clark had advised Truman that he had legal authority to do so. En.wikipedia.org/wiki/Tom_C._Clark. The *Steel Seizure Case* is discussed in Chapter I, p. 14.

55 The salaries of the highest paid private lawyers are discussed in Chapter IV, p. 148.

56 *See* Article II §2 cl. 2 and Chapter I, p. 9. For more information on judicial selection, *see* ABRAHAM, *supra* note 1, at 22-39.

President to "suggest" judicial candidates. The President has more latitude in naming judges for the courts of appeal, since circuits cover more than one state, but even there seats are in practice thought of as "belonging" to one or another state, thereby assuring a major role for the Senators from that state.[57]

United States Supreme Court Appointments   The President's problem with Supreme Court nominees is less one of placating individual Senators than one of surviving the scrutiny of the Senate Judiciary Committee (which conducts hearings on judicial nominees) and the full Senate in its exercise of its right of "advice and consent." For better or for worse, the nomination and confirmation process has been a political one from the beginning. George Washington's nomination of John Rutledge to the Supreme Court in 1795 was rejected by the Senate because of the nominee's opposition to a treaty with Great Britain. Since that time, the Senate has rejected one out of every five nominations, though most of the rejections were before 1900. Earlier in this century, there was opposition to Justice Louis D. Brandeis, the first Jewish member of the Court, from railroad and business interests concerned with his past public interest advocacy activities. This delayed approval of his nomination for some five months.

In recent years, as the Supreme Court has become polarized into liberal and conservative camps and a long line of Republican Presidents has sought to name more and more conservative justices to the Court, Senate "advice and consent" has once again come to the forefront of the public consciousness. The defeat before the Senate in 1987 of President Reagan's nomination of Robert Bork caused some of the greatest controversy in recent years.[58]

The degree to which there have been complaints about "politicization" of the selection process depends on whose nominee is being held up at any given time. Senator Strom Thurmond, who complained the loudest when President Reagan's nomination of Robert Bork was rejected in 1987, had led an ideological campaign in 1967 against appointing Justice Thurgood Marshall, the first black justice on the Court, largely on the basis of Marshall's career as a fighter for "liberal" civil rights causes.

Some Presidents seem to purposely choose nominees who will not cause a political stir. One way to do that is to pick a nominee about whose attitudes very little is known. President George H. W. Bush did this with Justice David Souter. Souter was dubbed the "stealth" candidate by the press, the reference being to the United States warplane that is constructed in such a way as to be undetectable on radar. And the political nastiness of recent times has obviously inclined some Presidents to nominate moderate candidates. President Bill Clinton nominated Ruth Bader Ginsburg, a former law professor who had demonstrated moderate views while serving on the Court of Appeals, and picked Stephen Breyer, who was confirmed by an almost unanimous Senate vote, over more controversial choices he had been considering.[59]

---

57 A deputy attorney general under President Kennedy once remarked that, in light of the realities of judicial selection, the Constitution "reads backwards" — that it should say "the Senators shall nominate and with the consent of the President appoint judges . . . ." *See* ABRAHAM, *supra* note 1, at 22, n.5.

58 The Bork debacle is all the more notable for the fact that the nominee took his defeat to the public by way of a book and regular newspaper articles seeking to "expose" the process that defeated his nomination as an illegitimate political move by the Senate that has no place in the process. *See* ROBERT BORK, THE TEMPTING OF AMERICA (Touchstone Books 1990) and Chapter IX, p. 327, note 20. It also has the distinction of having added a new verb to American English — "to Bork," meaning to attack in an unrestrained manner. There was also acrimonious debate over Clarence Thomas in 1991. While the Thomas hearings had some political overtones, they were largely focused on the judges' non-political activities — alleged sexual harassment of a female employee in his office.

59 *See* O'BRIEN, *supra* note 38, pp. 33-102, for these and other appointment stories.

The fact that political considerations enter into judicial selection should not be taken as an indication that those appointed are not qualified. At the very least, an incompetent judge is a political liability for the appointing politician. Especially as to the federal bench, there exists a convention of appointing highly qualified candidates. The American Bar Association (ABA) has been active in rating federal judicial candidates, but has not often found nominees unqualified. Since taking office, President Barack Obama has made 54 nominations of Article III judges. Of those, 41 have been declared "well-qualified" by the 15-member ABA judicial rating committee; the remaining 13 have been declared "qualified." Of the 54 nominees, only 4 received any vote of "non-qualified" from the 15-member committee.[60]

3. State Judicial Selection Systems

States have different types of systems for selection of judges. Some are the same for all courts in the state, while others have different selection systems depending on the level of court involved.[61]

Executive Appointment Systems An executive appointment system, whereby the governor of the state appoints judges, exists in some states. The appointment is sometimes from a pre-screened slate of candidates, sometimes with input from the legislature, and sometimes without any limitation. Judicial terms of office can be for life or for a term of years from as short as 4 or 6 years or as long as 12 to 15 years.

Electoral Systems for Judicial Selection Many state systems provide for the election of judges by a vote of the general populace. Election of judges is based on the notion that judges, no less than any other public official exercising power in a democracy, should ultimately be answerable to the people. Today electoral systems are in decline, but still enjoy widespread use in the states.[62]

There are several different versions of electoral systems for judges. Sometimes judges are elected by a vote of the general populace and sometimes by a vote of the state legislature. In some states where the general electorate chooses judges, judicial candidates run by party affiliation just as executive and legislative candidates do. In others, they run as non-partisan candidates.

Modified "Missouri" Plans An interesting system for judicial selection was developed in the state of Missouri in 1940 and has been adopted in one form or another in almost half the states. The "Missouri Plan" is said to combine the best features of an election system and the best features of an appointment system, with additional measures taken to assure non-partisan selection of candidates based on merit. Under this plan, judicial candidates are screened by a nominating committee composed of lawyers, judges and laypersons. The committee selects three candidates for every judicial vacancy on the basis of their credentials and merits, and submits these nominees to the state's governor who must select one of the three. The appointment is for at least a year and until the next general election, at which time the question is placed on the ballot as to whether the judge should be "retained" in office. If the judge is retained, then the judge serves for a 12-year term on the appellate courts or for a shorter

---

60 For more detail on the federal judicial selection process, *see* HENRY J. ABRAHAM, JUSTICES AND PRESIDENTS: A POLITICAL HISTORY OF APPOINTMENTS TO THE SUPREME COURT (Oxford U. Press 1992)

61 For a chart summarizing state systems, *see* BOOK OF THE STATES, *supra* note 7, pp. 318-321.

62 Some states have always provided for an electoral system. However, many states began with executive appointment systems and then changed to an electoral system in the mid-19th century, a time of great populism in the country, reflected and magnified by the presidency of Andrew Jackson, a popular general who championed "the common man." *See* FRIEDMAN, *supra* note 48, at 371.

term in the trial courts. Statistics show that the electorate votes to retain virtually all judges. Some form of an appointment and retention system has been adopted in almost half the states.

Evaluating Judicial Selection Systems   Election of judges has been criticized on several grounds. An obvious one is its failure to assure adequate judicial independence as judges will worry more about popular reaction to their decisions than the proper application of the law. Another concern is that the general population does not know enough about law or judicial qualifications to choose their judges wisely. Often the sophisticated voter and even the average lawyer will not be familiar with all the judicial candidates on the ballot. The question of how to finance judicial election campaigns complicates matters. Lawyers are a natural source of campaign contributions, but there is the danger of judges treating contributing and non-contributing lawyers differently after they are elected. This is possible not only with respect to the decision of cases, but also as to other discretionary functions that judges perform, such as appointments of lawyers to represent indigent defendants. In addition, many think it is unseemly for judges or judicial candidates, who are often identified with political parties even in non-partisan elections, to participate in election campaigns.

With all their difficulties, however, electoral systems have managed to select qualified judges to many appellate courts. For example, judgeships on the highest court of New York, the New York Court of Appeals, were filled by election until 1978, and that court was known as perhaps the best state court in the nation.[63] Appointment systems also have their own problems. While the tradition with federal judges has been generally to avoid the appointment of unqualified candidates, governors of states have sometimes used their appointment powers to reward political supporters without sufficient concern for their judicial qualifications.

Recent developments have raised new questions about electoral systems. First, there has been a substantial increase in television advertising funded by industry and other special interest groups. Many of these ads are of the "attack" sort, more typical of a partisan executive or legislative election than a dignified judicial selection process.[64] Second, while states with election systems prohibit judges and judicial candidates from engaging in "inappropriate political activity" and from "mak[ing] pledges, promises or commitments that are inconsistent with the impartial performance of the adjudicative duties of the office,"[65] the Supreme Court in 2002 in *Republican Party of Minnesota v. White*[66] cast doubt on the constitutionality of such limits, striking down as a violation of 1st Amendment free speech a ban on judicial candidates announcing their views on disputed legal and political issues.

It should also be noted that many states that supposedly have electoral systems operate under a *de facto* modified appointment and retention system. The executive has the power to make interim appointments if judges die or resign in the middle of their term. The interim appointed judges who complete the unexpired term are listed as "judge" on the ballot in the upcoming election and they can argue that they have proven that they can do the job. These factors likely give them an almost insurmountable

---

63 Chief Judge Stanley H. Fuld, considered an exceptional judge, was so popular that he was nominated by all four political parties for reelection in 1966.

64 *See* THE NEW POLITICS OF JUDICIAL ELECTIONS 2004 (Nat'l Center for State Courts 2005).

65 ABA Model Code of Judicial Conduct, Canon 5(A)(3)(d).

66 536 U.S. 765 (2002). *See* J.J. Gass, *After White: Defending and Amending Canons of Judicial Ethics*, *Brennan Center for Justice at NYU School of Law* 5 (2004), www.brennancenter.org/resources/ji/ji4.pdf.

advantage over other candidates. In some states there is a tradition of elected judges resigning before the end of their terms just so that the governor can appoint a replacement who will then have an advantage in the next election.[67]

4. Removal and Discipline of Judges

Impeachment of Federal Judges   The only constitutional method of removing federal judges is impeachment by the House and conviction in the Senate for "Treason, Bribery, or other high Crimes and Misdemeanors."[68] The first judge to be impeached and removed was John Pickering in 1803, who was charged with misconduct in a trial and being drunk while on the bench. Justice Samuel Chase was impeached in 1804 for what could be described as political reasons, but he was acquitted in the Senate. Since then, Congress has used impeachment as a means of removing or attempting to remove federal judges from office only 7 times.[69] Hostility to judicial decisions has not been the motivating force in most impeachments. Indeed, most removals of federal judges from office in recent years have followed the judge's conviction of a serious crime.

Congress has removed three federal judges recently and each case presented its memorable aspects. Harry Claiborne of Nevada, the first federal judge in some 50 years to be impeached, had been convicted of the crime of federal income tax evasion. He was serving a prison sentence in a Louisiana federal prison, but steadfastly refused to resign from office. He continued to draw his salary until Congress voted by a wide margin to remove him. Judge Alcee Hastings of Florida was acquitted of bribery before a jury in 1983, but Congress felt there was sufficient evidence of guilt to proceed with impeachment. Congress impeached him and removed him from office in 1987. Hastings was subsequently elected to Congress and some people joked that he might get to vote on his own impeachment. Most recently, the 1989 impeachment of Judge Walter Nixon is notable because it resulted in a constitutional challenge to the impeachment process. The Senate did not convict Nixon by way of a trial before the *entire* Senate. Instead, it appointed a committee of twelve Senators to hear the evidence and to report that evidence to the full Senate, which then voted on the impeachment charge. In *Nixon v. United States*,[70] the Court rejected Nixon's challenges to this procedure, holding that the lawsuit presented a non-justiciable political question solely within the power of Congress to determine.[71]

Authorization for lesser sanctions than impeachment was instituted in 1980, setting up a system for fielding complaints against federal judges within the Judicial Council of each circuit, a body that sets administrative policy within the circuit and includes district and circuit judges.[72] Investigations of all non-frivolous complaints can be ordered and certain sanctions short of dismissal imposed, such as a private or public reprimand or censure, certification of disability, a request for voluntary resignation, or prohibition against further case assignments. The system has been upheld against arguments that

---

67 Just how much advantage is enjoyed by incumbent judges is testified to by the fact that many of them, particularly trial judges, consistently face no opposition at election time. For a comparative look at American and English judicial appointment practice, *see* ATIYAH & SUMMERS, *supra* note 51. For a web site with useful links on judicial selection, *see* www.ncsconline.org/WC/FAQs/Print/Prt_JudSelFAQ.htm.

68 Article II §4. For impeachment, a majority vote in the House is needed. For conviction and removal from office, a two-thirds majority is needed in the Senate. Article I §3 cl. 6.

69 However, several more judges have resigned rather than face impeachment.

70 506 U.S. 224 (1993).

71 Three Justices took the position that judicial review of the challenge was not barred by the political question doctrine, but that the practice was constitutionally permissible.

72 Judicial Conduct and Disability Act of 1980, 28 U.S.C.A. §§351-364.

the system is unconstitutional because impeachment is the only constitutional sanction against a federal judge, and because it violates 1st Amendment free speech rights.[73]

Removal of State Judges For states with electoral systems or systems providing for electoral retention of judges, removal is possible at each general election. However, incumbent judges — even more than incumbent legislators — tend to be reelected over and over again with little trouble. A recent exception to matter-of-course retention took place in California. There the Chief Justice Rose Bird and two other justices were ousted by the voters, who did not like their record of voting to overturn death penalty sentences.[74]

Whatever the judicial selection system, states also provide for midterm removal for criminal behavior, incompetence, "lack of judicial temperament," and other good cause. Review of a judge's behavior is generally undertaken by a state commission on the complaint of a lawyer, litigant or member of the public. The commission has power to take or recommend to the supreme court of the state appropriate disciplinary action, including removal from the bench. Most often these commissions are referred to as the Judicial Tenure Commission or Board of Judicial Standards. Some of these organizations make recommendations for discipline or removal, but others, such as the California Commission on Judicial Performance and the New York State Commission on Judicial Conduct, are themselves empowered to impose sanctions, including removal. Impeachment by the legislature is usually an additional possible alternative.[75]

Civil and Criminal Liability of Judges Judges in the United States have no immunity from criminal investigation, prosecution or conviction, either for actions related to their judicial functions (such as taking a bribe) or otherwise. They can be investigated and prosecuted like any other citizen. Fortunately, relatively few instances of systemic corruption have arisen, the most notable being the FBI's "Operation Greylord" in the 1980s, when several judges in Chicago were convicted for bribery. However, prosecutions for individual corruption and other criminal acts do occur with somewhat more frequency.[76]

Judges are, however, very broadly protected by judicial immunity from civil liability for anything done as part of their judicial functions. This is deemed essential to protect judicial independence, though the facts of some of the cases cause some to doubt whether that aim is served in all cases.[77] Immunity from civil liability does not extend to orders for injunctive relief, mandamus or other such relief.[78]

---

73 *See McBryde v. Comm. to Review Circuit Council Conduct and Disability Orders*, 264 F.3d 52 (D.C. Cir. 2001) (upholding constitutionality of public reprimand based on finding that judge for years had engaged in a "pattern of abusive behavior"; challenge to sanctions of not assigning any new cases for a year and not assigning cases involving 23 lawyers who had cooperated in Council proceedings determined moot).

74 *See* ABRAHAM *supra* note 1, at 36.

75 *See* BOOK OF THE STATES, *supra* note 7, pp. 235-241 for a chart listing removal procedures for all states. For more detail, *see* FISHER, *supra* note 59, at 143-149.

76 *See* cases cited in Geoffrey P. Miller, *Bad Judges*, 83 TEX. L. REV. 431, 435-436 (2004). This article discusses all kinds of judicial misconduct and organizes examples into categories.

77 *See, e.g., Stump v. Sparkman*, 435 U.S. 349 (1978) (judge not liable for violation of civil rights when, at behest of teenager's mother, he ordered that teenager be surgically sterilized; law did not give power to enter such order, no case file was opened, no case number assigned, and no holding held); *Mireles v. Waco*, 502 U.S. 9 (1991) (judge not liable for injuries to lawyer when he ordered court officer to forcibly bring lawyer before the court and to use excessive force in doing so).

78 *See* John O. Haley, *Civil, Criminal and Disciplinary Liability of Judges*, 54 AM. J. COMP. L. 281 (2006).

D. Other Judicial Officials and Assistants

1. Magistrates

The term "magistrate" can have a general meaning, referring to any kind of judge. However, it also has a more specific meaning, referring to a lower level judicial officer who is under the supervision of a judge. Thus, in the federal system, the federal Magistrates Act creates the office of "magistrate judge."[79] In contrast to the political selection process for Article III judges, federal magistrate judges are selected on a merit basis after screening by a committee of lawyers and non-lawyers. The district judges in a district make a choice from a list provided by the committee. Magistrate judges serve 8-year terms. If they do well, they are usually offered the opportunity to serve additional 8-year terms.

Magistrate judges can hold hearings on all non-dispositive motions (decisions that do not decide a case on the merits or dismiss it). Without consent of the parties they have the power to hold hearings on dispositive motions and make recommended decisions, which must then be reviewed by the district judge. With consent, they can try civil cases (including jury trials) to final judgment just as a district judge would. The degree to which federal magistrate judges are given responsibility varies from district to district and depends in large part on the attitude of the judges of that district toward delegating judicial duties. Magistrate judges are used much more widely in the federal system today than in the past as the caseload of the federal courts has increased and the need for supervision of pre-trial proceedings has grown.

The limited nature of the duties of federal magistrate judges results from their limited tenure. Article III of the Constitution requires that the "judicial power of the United States" be exercised by federal judges who have lifetime tenure. The theory that permits magistrates to exercise judicial functions at all is the idea that they are "adjuncts" to the "Article III" district judge — helpers who assist the district judge by hearing evidence and making recommendations. Under this arrangement, they may hold hearings and write recommended decisions, but responsibility for the ultimate decision must reside in an Article III judge.[80] Magistrates then are "Article I" judges. The largest category of Article I judges are administrative agency adjudicators. Consequently, the limits on the powers of Article I judges are discussed in more depth in the chapter on administrative law.[81]

Many state trial courts have magistrates and give them similar duties. Sometimes lower level judicial officers in states are called "commissioners" or "referees." Often on the state level, such officers are attorneys in private practice who work part time in their judicial role.

2. Bankruptcy Judges

Bankruptcy law is entirely federal, though state issues arise to the extent that state contract, property and tort law are relevant to the debtor's rights and obligations.[82] Bankruptcy cases are handled by a special corps of federal bankruptcy judges attached

---

79 28 U.S.C.A. §631 *et seq.* Federal magistrate judges have existed in some form since the first statute setting up the federal court system in 1789, but were called "commissioners" until 1968.

80 *United States v. Raddatz*, 447 U.S. 667 (1980) (Article III not violated by magistrate conducting hearing and making recommended decision on suppression motion in criminal case so long as district judge has *de novo* review power). *But see Gomez v. United States*, 490 U.S. 858 (1989) (absent consent, magistrate may not preside over jury selection in criminal trial).

81 *See* Chapter VI, pp. 220-222.

82 Bankruptcy law is discussed in Chapter XV, pp. 606-608.

to federal district court and appointed for 14-year terms by means of a merit selection process similar to that employed for magistrate judges. Because of their term limitations, bankruptcy judges are Article I judges like federal magistrate judges and are subject to some of the same limitations. Thus, absent consent of the parties, bankruptcy judges are limited to rendering recommended decisions on many issues. However, on matters directly concerning bankruptcy discharge and administration of the bankruptcy case, they may render final decisions like any other trial court. Such decisions are subject to a right of appeal to the district court, which then sits as an appellate court and provides the same scope of review and deference to fact-finding due in an appeal to an appellate court.[83]

3. Administrative Adjudicators

Administrative agencies exercise considerable judicial power when they adjudicate disputes arising in the programs they administer. Consequently, no understanding of the "judicial system" of the United States would be complete without consideration of their important functions. As already indicated, their functions and the limits on powers of other Article I judges are discussed in the next chapter on administrative law.

4. Court Clerks, Law Clerks and Other Court Officials

Administrators Each court, trial or appellate, has a chief "clerk of the court" who is in charge of administrative matters and in whose office all litigation documents are filed and kept. In addition, other clerks or secretaries assist the judge with typing and filing documents, drafting routine orders and correspondence, and other chamber functions. Also important are court reporters, who keep a record of all proceedings before the judge.

Law Clerks The person of greatest direct assistance to a judge on any level is a "judicial clerk" or "law clerk," also called "law secretaries" in some jurisdictions. All federal trial and appellate judges and all state appellate judges and justices have full-time law clerks to do legal research and draft opinions and memoranda of decisions. Most often judicial law clerks are recent law school graduates who work for the judge (or for the entire court if that is the system) for a short period of time, usually one or two years. Judicial clerks, especially those working for federal judges and state supreme court justices, usually have excellent law school records and often have writing and research experience as members of their school's law review. Pay for such clerks averages between $40,000 and $60,000, though permanent judicial clerks in the federal system can receive up to $82,000.[84] While many law clerks could conceivably get higher paying jobs in private practice, they choose to be law clerks because of the experience and education they will gain and because of the prestige attached to such service. The most prestigious of judicial clerkship posts are those held by law clerks for justices of the United States Supreme Court, many of whom go on to impressive careers as private lawyers or law teachers. In order to entice such clerks to work for them, many firms are willing to pay high signing bonuses, some as high as $250,000. Some Supreme Court law clerks return later in life to the Supreme Court as Supreme Court justices. For example, the late Chief Justice William Rehnquist was clerk to Justice Robert Jackson.

---

83 28 U.S.C.A. §§157-158. The areas of law where decision by Article I judges are permissible are explained in Chapter VI, pp. 221-221, in conjunction with *Northern Pipeline Co. v. Marathon Pipeline Co.*, 458 U.S. 50 (1982) (entire bankruptcy Article I judge system is unconstitutional).

84 What Lawyers Earn, www.law.com/special/professionals/nlj/earn/earns_1.html#3.

The vast majority of state trial judges do not have full-time law school graduates as law clerks. However, many state trial court judges in urban areas regularly employ at least law-student law clerks on part time basis. The reason for not providing clerks (aside from the high cost) is the assumption that state trial judges need them less, since most of their work deals with factual issues and the exercise of discretion within known legal parameters rather than with fine legal points. Many state trial judges disagree and point to the fact that they handle many of the same kinds of cases that their colleagues on the federal trial bench do.

E. Subject-Matter Jurisdiction of State and Federal Courts

1. State Court Subject Matter Jurisdiction

In Chapter I, when the nature of state power was discussed, we saw how states before the Constitution had all the inherent powers of sovereign international states and, upon ratification, lost only those powers that they gave up in the Constitution. Consistent with this concept, state courts potentially have general and unlimited subject-matter jurisdiction over disputes of every conceivable type that are not prohibited to them by federal law. The symbol of such broad jurisdiction is the state trial court of general jurisdiction — the superior or circuit court — which has power to handle the widest range of cases. State court subject matter jurisdiction definitions may require that certain kinds of disputes be handled by one of its specialized courts, but for every type of case there is some state court that has the power to hear it.[85]

2. Federal District Court Subject Matter Jurisdiction

In contrast to state courts, federal courts are courts of *limited* jurisdiction. As with any other organ of federal power, federal courts must trace their jurisdiction to some affirmative source of power in the Constitution. Federal judicial power is confined to cases "arising under [the] Constitution, the Laws of the United States, and Treaties," and controversies "between Citizens of different states."[86] The first category is generally referred to as "federal question" jurisdiction and the second as "diversity" jurisdiction.

Federal Question Jurisdiction   Today, federal question cases comprise by far the most numerous category of cases in federal court. This was not always true. A lingering effect of the mistrust that some Framers had of the lower federal courts was that they were not given general federal question jurisdiction until 1875 — after the Civil War.[87] Before then, state courts were relied upon to enforce what federal law there was. The history of state court enforcement of federal law before the Civil War was marked by evasion, hostility and interference with federal policy at every turn.[88] The rationale for federal question jurisdiction is that federal courts will give a more consistent and more sympathetic interpretation of federal law than state courts. However, state courts retain concurrent jurisdiction over all federal question cases so that, if the parties wish to go to state court, they may. There are a few categories of federal question cases, however,

---

85 States may limit the jurisdiction of their own courts, for example, as a matter of *forum non conveniens*. *See* Chapter VII, pp. 259-261.

86 Art. III §2. For more detail on subject matter jurisdiction, *see* WRIGHT, *supra* note 34, §§17-22A, and ERWIN CHEMERINSKY, FEDERAL JURISDICTION, 5TH ED. (Aspen 2007).

87 28 U.S.C.A. §1331. *See* Chapter I, p. 8.

88 *See generally*, John Gibbons, *Enforcement of Federal Law in State Courts 1789-1860*, 36 RUTGERS L. REV. 399 (1984). *See also* Chapter I, p. 23.

where Congress has made federal court jurisdiction exclusive.[89] Federal question jurisdiction is most commonly invoked in such areas as civil rights, antitrust, federal criminal law, bankruptcy, patent and copyright infringement, securities violations and labor law.

Article III is not self-executing, so it does not itself grant jurisdiction. Congress must pass a statute conferring jurisdiction.[90] In the case of federal question jurisdiction, Congress has passed a statute that tracks the "arising under" federal law language of Article III, quoted above. This language might seem to include every case in which a federal issue comes up. However, the federal question jurisdiction *statute* — despite using the same language — has been interpreted narrowly to mean that jurisdiction exists only for cases where the federal question presented is necessary to make out the *plaintiff's claim*. This rule, called the "well-pleaded complaint" rule, excludes any case where the federal issue is presented as part of a *defense*.[91] It does not matter that a defensively asserted federal issue is the most important or even the only real issue in the case. For example, a state-law defamation claim (a claim for damage to reputation caused by untrue statements) is sometimes met with a defense based on the free speech guarantees of the 1st Amendment to the Constitution.[92] Such a case can be handled only in state court. The wisdom and legitimacy of the well-pleaded complaint rule of federal question jurisdiction have been questioned.[93] Clearly the rule abandons many important federal law issues to state courts. However, its advantages are that it is simple to administer and it allows jurisdiction to be determined at the very beginning of the lawsuit by looking only at the plaintiff's complaint.[94]

The well-pleaded complaint rule means in most cases that there is federal question jurisdiction only when federal law authorizes the plaintiff's claim. However, the Supreme Court recently reaffirmed that even when state law authorizes the claim, federal question jurisdiction exists if an essential element of the state-law claim requires resolution of a "substantial" federal issue. Exactly when the issue of federal law is sufficiently "substantial" is not exactly clear.[95]

Diversity Jurisdiction Federal court jurisdiction also applies to disputes between citizens of different states or between a citizen and an alien.[96] Congress has always limited diversity cases to major disputes, providing a requisite minimum amount that

---

89 Exclusive federal jurisdiction is given in admiralty cases (28 U.S.C.A. §1333), bankruptcy cases (28 U.S.C.A. §1334), patent and copyright cases (28 U.S.C.A. §1338), claims arising under the securities exchange laws (28 U.S.C.A. §78aa), federal criminal law (18 U.S.C.A. §3231), and antitrust actions (28 U.S.C.A. §1337), though the exclusion from antitrust cases is only implied.

90 With regard to the Supreme Court, it has always been assumed that Art. III is self-executing and thus grants jurisdiction, without the need for a statute, in the narrow categories of cases over which the Court has original jurisdiction. *Kentucky v. Dennison*, 65 U.S. 66 (1860).

91 28 U.S.C.A. §1331, as interpreted in *Louisville & Nashville Railroad v. Mottley*, 211 U.S. 149 (1908).

92 *See* Chapter IX, p. 380, and Chapter XI, pp. 457-459.

93 *See* Donald Doernberg, *"There's No Reason For It; It's Just Our Policy": Why the Well-Pleaded Complaint Rule Sabotages the Purposes of Federal Question Jurisdiction*, 38 HASTINGS L.J. 597 (1987).

94 Although Article III uses the very same words, it has been interpreted as potentially including jurisdiction over cases where the federal issue arises in the defense or even in some other context. *See Verlinden B.V. v. Central Bank of Nigeria*, 461 U.S. 480 (1983) (approving statutory grant of jurisdiction where federal issue arose as an anticipation of a defense). *See* WRIGHT, *supra* note 34, §20.

95 *See Grable & Sons Metal Products v. Darue Engineering & Mfg.*, 545 U.S. 308 (2005) (suit to obtain title to real property based on state law, but essential element required plaintiff to prove federal tax lien invalid under federal law). *Compare Merrell Dow Pharmaceuticals v. Thompson*, 478 U.S. 804 (1986) (no jurisdiction where state law tort claim included issue of whether drugs violated federal regulations).

96 28 U.S.C.A. §1332.

must be in controversy. In 1789, the amount was $500; today it is $75,000. Diversity cases make up about 20% of the federal district court case load.

The Framers of the Constitution created diversity jurisdiction out of a concern that state courts would favor their own citizens over citizens of a different state or country. It was thought that federal judges would be more neutral in such disputes, in part because they would not identify so strongly with any particular state and in part because lifetime appointment would mean that they would not have to face the wrath of the voters for unpopular decisions. There have been attempts in Congress in recent years to eliminate diversity jurisdiction based on the argument that state prejudice against outsiders is no longer a problem in the modern, mobile age. Proponents of diversity jurisdiction dispute this and, to date, diversity jurisdiction remains.

Natural persons' citizenship is their place of domicile, or their permanent home, at the time suit is filed.[97] A corporation has dual citizenship: it is considered a citizen both of the state where it is incorporated and the state in which it has its principal place of business.[98] Since diversity cases are based on state law, it goes without saying that there is concurrent jurisdiction of all diversity cases in state court.

Like federal question jurisdiction, the identical phrase in both Article III and the diversity jurisdictional statute — suits "between Citizens of different States" — has been interpreted more narrowly in the statute. As used in Article III, it is interpreted to permit Congress to create jurisdiction where there is only "minimal diversity," *i.e.*, where only one party is from a different state.[99] As used in the statute, however, the Court has held that the phrase requires "complete diversity." In other words, *all* the plaintiffs must be from different states than *all* the defendants. Thus, there would be no diversity jurisdiction over a suit in which New York, Ohio and Michigan plaintiffs sued Florida, California and Ohio defendants, despite the fact that several out-of-state parties would be involved. This is true regardless of the federal district chosen for filing suit.[100]

Removal Where subject matter jurisdiction would exist in either state or federal court, the initial court choice is made by the plaintiff. However, defendants can choose the federal forum as well through a procedure called "removal." A defendant sued in state court on a claim that would have qualified for federal court jurisdiction may remove the case from state court to the local federal court.[101] However, if removal is based solely on diversity of citizenship, the defendant may remove the case only if no defendant is a citizen of the state in whose courts the action was brought. The rationale

---

97 In an effort to limit diversity jurisdiction in cases involving aliens, Congress amended §1332 in 1988 to provide that "an alien admitted to the United States for permanent residence shall be deemed a citizen of the state in which such alien is domiciled." Thus, an alien admitted for permanent residence living in New York could not sue a U.S. citizen of New York in the federal court as had been permitted before, but would have to sue instead in state court.

98 If a corporation has places of business in more than one state, the principal place of business is its "nerve center" — where the corporation's high level officers direct, control, and coordinate the corporation's activities. *Hertz Corp. v. Friend*, ___ U.S. ___, 130 S.Ct. 1181 (2010).

99 Congress has so provided in some cases. *See State Farm Fire and Casualty Co. v. Tashire*, 386 U.S. 523 (1967) (upholding constitutionality of 28 U.S.C.A. §1335, the interpleader statute). *See also* the Multiparty, Multiforum Trial Jurisdiction Act of 2002, 28 U.S.C.A. §1369 (mass accidents where at least 75 people have died) and the Class Action Fairness Act of 2005, 28 U.S.C.A. §1332(d) (class actions based on diversity).

100 *Strawbridge v. Curtis*, 7 U.S. 267 (1806) (Marshall, C.J.). Excepted from federal court jurisdiction are domestic relations and probate cases. *See Ankenbrandt v. Richards*, 504 U.S. 689 (1992).

101 28 U.S.C.A. §1441. The case is removed to the federal court of the district where the state court is located.

for this rule is that diversity is designed to ensure that out-of-state parties are treated fairly, so it makes little sense to allow defendants sued in their home state's courts to have access to federal courts. Thus, if a New York plaintiff sues a California defendant in the state court in *California*, the defendant may *not* remove the case, but if the same case is filed in any other state court (*e.g.*, New York), it *is* removable.

Supplemental Jurisdiction Federal courts are authorized to assume jurisdiction over some claims that involve neither diverse parties nor federal questions if those claims arise out of a "common nucleus of operative fact" as claims asserted over which they have jurisdiction. "Supplemental jurisdiction" is based on the idea that it is uneconomical and unfair to the parties to require that they litigate such related claims in two court systems.[102] Under some circumstances, "pendent parties" on related claims can be added — parties as to whom no claims sufficient for federal jurisdiction exist.[103]

PART II: Federalism Complications in the Judicial System

Concurrent overlapping competence of state and federal courts to handle both state and federal claims can give rise to complexities and inefficiencies.[104] We will consider two issues that arise when federal courts adjudicate state-law claims and state courts adjudicate federal-law claims: (1) which body of law, state or federal, applies to what issues in such "mixed" cases and (2) the structure for appellate review of issues in mixed cases. Another feature of overlapping jurisdiction is the potential for simultaneous litigation of the same dispute in both state and federal court. That issue will also be examined briefly.

A. Law Applied in Federal and State Courts

1. Law Applied When State-Law Claims Are Adjudicated in Federal Court

The Rules of Decision Act As already alluded to in Chapter I, Congress has provided since 1789 in the Rules of Decision Act that federal courts handling state-law claims must follow state law.[105] The Act has been interpreted to mean that federal courts must follow state law on all *substantive* issues, but that they may follow their own federal *procedural* law. This is consistent with the traditional conflict-of-laws notion that a forum court is permitted to apply its own procedural rules even if the substantive issues are governed by foreign law. The precise scope of the command of the Rules of Decision Act was made clear in the 1938 case of *Erie, Lackawanna R.R. v. Tompkins*, and issues under the Act are referred to as "*Erie* questions."[106]

---

102 *See United Mine Workers v. Gibbs*, 383 U.S. 715 (1966) and 28 U.S.C.A. §1367.

103 *Exxon Mobil Corp. v Allapattah Services*, 545 U.S. 546 (2005).

104 Overlapping jurisdiction in the courts of *different states* also causes complication. This topic is discussed in the chapter on civil procedure. *See* Chapter VII, pp. 253-268.

105 *See* 28 U.S.C.A. §1652.

106 304 U.S. 64 (1938). *Erie* made clear that federal courts must follow *all* of state law, both statutory and common law. This "corrected" an old case interpreting the Rules of Decision Act that held that the phrase "laws of the several states" in the Act required federal courts to follow state law meant only state *statutory* law, not common law decisions. *Swift v. Tyson*, 41 U.S. (16 Pet.) 1 (1842). The holding in *Swift* was understandable given the "discovery" view of the common law prevalent at that time: since there could only be one correct common law view, all courts, state and federal, should come to the same result. In Chapter II, we saw how Justice Holmes's realism about common law exploded the discovery myth. His view was ultimately adopted by the Court in *Erie*: that the common law, like any other law, is the command of a particular sovereign and uniformity of decisions is possible only if federal courts are required to follow the state courts' *own version* of the common law. *See* Chapter II, pp. 45-46.

Erie's dichotomy of substantive state law but procedural federal law is consistent with general conflict-of-laws principle that the forum court is permitted to apply its own procedural rules. But the special policies behind the *Erie* decision may cause the substantive-procedural line to be drawn in a different place than might be expected in the conflicts situation.

Anti-Forum-Shopping Policy   The first relevant policy is the policy against "forum-shopping." The Framers of the Constitution made federal courts available as an alternative to state courts to provide a more neutral *forum* for disputes between citizens from different states. They did not intend that federal courts provide a different *body of law* to decide those disputes. Thus, parties should not be able to "forum-shop" between state and federal courts in order to obtain a better result in their cases, based on the state court applying state law and the federal court applying federal law.[107] Consistent with this policy, the substance-procedure question for *Erie* purposes is decided according to the "outcome determinative" test: an issue is considered to be a "substantive" one calling for application of state law if (1) applying federal law would cause the court to come to a different result and (2) that difference is the kind of difference that would influence the parties to choose federal court over state court.[108]

This test is easy to apply in most situations. For example, the law relating to the standard of conduct by which a court judges the defendant's actions in a tort case is clearly substantive under this standard. Other issues are less clear. For example, the law may provide that the "burden of proof" is on one party or the other in a particular kind of case. Burden of proof sounds "procedural" in an intuitive sense, but it clearly can affect the outcome of the case. Consequently, burden of proof is classified as "substantive," and the federal court must apply state law rather than federal on the issue of burden of proof.[109] The Court has held that all the following issues are substantive law issues calling for the application of state rather than federal law: time limitation periods within which suit must be filed,[110] a requirement that a bond be posted by shareholders before they may sue their corporation,[111] and laws prohibiting suit by any corporation not licensed to do business in the state.[112] Significantly, the Court has held that *choice-of-law* rules are substantive, thus calling for the federal court to apply the choice-of-law laws of the state where it sits.[113]

---

107 Such "forum-shopping" was rampant before *Erie* required federal courts to follow state common law as well as statutory law. *See Black & White Taxi Co. v. Brown & Yellow Taxi Co.*, 276 U.S. 518 (1928) (plaintiff Kentucky corporation reincorporated in Tennessee to create the diversity of citizenship that would allow it to sue in the Kentucky federal court and thus avoid Kentucky state common law that would have defeated its claim in state court).

108 *Guaranty Trust Co. v. York*, 326 U.S. 99 (1945). Since defendants have the power to remove many diversity cases to federal court, defendants as well as plaintiffs can engage in "forum-shopping." *See* discussion of removal, *supra* p. 190.

109 *Palmer v. Hoffman*, 318 U.S. 109 (1945).

110 *Ragan v. Merchants Transfer & Warehouse Co.*, 337 U.S. 530 (1949); *Walker v. Armco Steel Corp.*, 446 U.S. 740 (1980). These periods are referred to as "statutes of limitations."

111 *Cohen v. Beneficial Indus. Loan Corp.*, 337 U.S. 541 (1949). Shareholder suits are discussed in Chapter XV, p. 594.

112 *Woods v. Interstate Realty Co.*, 337 U.S. 535 (1949).

113 *Klaxon Co. v. Stentor Electric Mfg. Co.*, 313 U.S. 487 (1941). *See, e.g., Day & Zimmermann, Inc. v. Challoner*, 423 U.S. 3 (1975) (in a diversity suit brought by the parents of a soldier killed in Cambodia against manufacturer of artillery shell, the federal court located in Texas had to apply Cambodian tort law since that is the body of law that Texas choice-of-law rules indicated would be applied had the suit been brought in the Texas state court). *See generally* Chapter VII, pp. 263-268, where choice-of-law rules are discussed. However, some federal appeals courts have applied *federal* common law conflicts rules to state law claims arising under a federal law giving federal courts jurisdiction over claims arising out of international banking

It is important to emphasize that the Rules of Decision Act is concerned only with one kind of forum-shopping: parties seeking to take advantage of the difference between *federal and state* law. It has nothing to say about parties taking advantage of a difference between the *law of two different states.* Shopping *between states* for more favorable law, made possible by state choice-of-law rules, does not offend the need for federal and state courts in the same state to apply the same substantive law.

Supremacy of Federal Law   Despite the importance of preventing forum-shopping, that policy may conflict with the supremacy of federal law. Some state laws or practices, regardless of how "substantive" they appear, may disrupt important and well-established federal court procedures. If so, the supremacy of federal law requires they be displaced. In some cases, this is so even if applying federal law might change the outcome of the case and lead to forum-shopping. For example, in one case, state law required that a particular mixed fact-law issue be determined by the judge, while federal law would normally give such an issue to the jury to determine. The Court held that the "strong federal policy against allowing state rules to disrupt the judge-jury relationship in the federal courts" required that the federal court apply the federal rule.[114] It was also clear that who determined the issue would not in most cases affect how the issue was resolved and the state's choice of the judge was a matter of historical accident. In *Gasperini v. Center for Humanities,*[115] a New York law affected the judge-jury relationship directly by requiring its judges to reduce jury awards that "deviate materially from what would be reasonable compensation." The federal standard allows reduction only if the verdict was so excessive as to "shock the conscience" of the court. The Court upheld application of the New York rule by federal courts in diversity cases because it was clearly outcome-determinative and the state had substantive policy reasons for enacting it.

The strongest expression of federal procedural interests occurs when the federal law on the subject is set out in one of the Federal Rules of Civil Procedure or its equivalent. In such cases, the Supreme Court has followed a policy of presumptive application of the federal rule regardless of how "outcome-determinative" its effects might be.[116] This policy has resulted in differing outcomes between state and federal courts and to that extent encourages forum-shopping.[117]

2. Law Applied When Federal Law Claims are Adjudicated in State Court

The procedural-substantive dichotomy also arises when a *federal claim* is filed in *state court,* and the Court has imposed a rough "reverse-*Erie*" rule: the forum state court applies its own procedural law even while applying substantive federal law. However,

---

transactions. *See Edelman v. Chase Manhattan Bank,* 861 F.2d 1291 (1st Cir. 1988). *See also* Donald T. Trautman, *Toward Federalizing Choice of Law,* 70 TEXAS L. REV. 1715 (1992).

114 *Byrd v. Blue Ridge Rural Electrical Cooperative,* 356 U.S. 525 (1958) (issue was whether the plaintiff was an "employee" of the defendant; if so, he was entitled only to Workmen's Compensation administrative remedy; if he was not an "employee," he could sue in court for damages).

115 518 U.S. 415 (1996).

116 *Hanna v. Plumer,* 380 U.S. 460 (1965). *See generally* FRIEDENTHAL, KANE & MILLER, *supra* note 13, §§4.1-4.3.

117 *See, e.g., Stewart Organization, Inc. v. Ricoh Corp.,* 487 U.S. 22 (1988) (federal statute allowing transfers of cases permits transfer pursuant to forum-selection clause of contract even though applicable state law would render such clause unenforceable as a matter of state contract law); *Business Guides, Inc. v. Chromatic Communications Enterprises, Inc.,* 498 U.S. 533 (1991) (FRCP 11 imposing liability on represented parties for prosecution of a groundless suit will apply to a suit in federal court regardless of whether such liability exists in state law for a suit filed in state court).

the supremacy of federal law can pre-empt a procedural state rule that "unduly" interferes with assertion of a federal claim. For example, in *Brown v. Western Railway of Alabama*, the plaintiff brought suit on a federal claim in the Georgia state court. The plaintiff's complaint was dismissed based on a Georgia state pleading rule that provided that pleadings would be "construed strictly against the pleader."[118] Despite the fact that rules about pleadings would seem intuitively to be "procedural," the Supreme Court held the Georgia rule invalid as applied to the federal claim on the ground that it "unduly interfered" with assertion of the federal claim. This was so despite the fact that the state court applied the rule evenhandedly to all claims that came before it, whether state or federal.

3. Appeals of Federal Law Issues in State Court and State Law Issues in Federal Court

As can be seen, state courts routinely decide issues of federal law and federal courts routinely decide issues of state law. If a state court is wrong on an issue of federal law, the Supreme Court has the power to review that state court's judgment on issues of *federal* law.[119] However, if a federal court in a diversity of citizenship case is wrong on an issue of *state* law, there is no comparable appeal to a state court with final authority to decide the issue of state law. An appeal to the United States Supreme Court is to no avail, since it has always disclaimed the power to review issues of *state* law arising in either state or federal courts. No appeal from the federal court to the state supreme court of the relevant state is possible. There is no mechanism for it and the supremacy of federal law and institutions over the states would seem to deny any such power.[120] Thus, while federal courts are supposed to follow state law as declared by the state's highest court, state law is not always clear, and there is no provision for definitive appellate review. Federal courts then are sometimes relegated to a "best guess" as to the content of state law.

The danger of lower federal court mistakes on issues of state law is lessened considerably by the fact that federal district judges are admitted to the bar of the state where the federal court is located, are usually experienced lawyers, and are often former state court judges from that state. In addition, many states have a procedure for federal courts to "certify" unclear issues of state law to the state supreme court.[121] But there is no federal certification law and not all states have a certification procedure. Moreover, certification sometimes runs into several practical problems. First, certification is optional for the federal judge, who may resist admitting inability to determine an issue of state law. Second, from the state side, state supreme courts often resist deciding legal issues in the abstract, and may even be prohibited by their constitutions or laws from doing so. Third, a state supreme court may issue an abstract answer that is unclear.[122] The result is that mistakes are sometimes made in forecasting how an issue would be decided by a state court, especially on an issue of first impression.[123] Because of the

---

118 338 U.S. 294 (1949). *See also Felder v. Casey*, 487 U.S. 131 (1988) (state pre-suit notice of claim requirement when suing the government unduly interferes with assertion of federal civil rights claim).

119 *See Martin v. Hunter's Lessee*, discussed in Chapter I, p. 22.

120 *See infra*, p. 195 and note 127, and Chapter VI, p. 225.

121 *See, e.g.*, Mich. Ct. Rule 7.305(B).

122 *See Sun Insurance Office v. Clay*, 319 F.2d 505, 509-510 (5th Cir. 1963), where the federal court of appeals was somewhat puzzled by the Florida supreme courts answer to a question it had certified, so it went on to interpret state law on its own.

123 *See Pierce v. Cook & Co.*, 518 F.2d 720 (10th Cir. 1975) (setting aside federal court judgment based on state supreme court's overruling of caselaw on which federal court relied).

quality of some federal court decisions on state law issues of first impression, those federal decisions are sometimes followed by state courts, even though the federal decisions technically qualify only as persuasive precedential authority.[124]

B. Simultaneous Litigation in State and Federal Court

Concurrent jurisdiction gives rise to the potential for conflict between state and federal court where both are asked simultaneously to assume jurisdiction over essentially the same dispute. Parties tend not to litigate in two forums at once, so the question does not arise often, but when it does, it raises difficult issues of federalism. Duplicative litigation is wasteful and it may be somewhat surprising that there is no prohibition *per se* against a party litigating in both state and federal court simultaneously. However, duplicative litigation is seen as one of the costs of federalism. Indeed, the Supreme Court has emphasized that federal courts should not abstain from exercising their jurisdiction in order to avoid duplicative litigation except in the most exceptional circumstances.[125] Conflicts in the exercise of jurisdiction are determined as follows.

1. Resolution by First Entry of Judgment

Under the requirement of "full faith and credit" federal and state courts must respect each others final judgments. So in the case of simultaneous litigation, the first judgment controls the result in the subsequent case and the issue of which court's judgment will prevail is determined by which court wins the "race" to judgment.[126] But the question arises as to what a state or federal court may do — while litigation is pending — to *prevent* a judgment from being entered first in the other court. This raises the question of what power state and federal courts have to enjoin parties from litigating in the other forum.

2. Injunctions Against Litigation in Another Court

Because of the nature of the federal system, particularly the supremacy clause, state courts may not enjoin federal litigation, unless it is necessary to protect state court jurisdiction over real property located in the state.[127] Similarly, since 1789, the federal Anti-Injunction Act has generally prohibited *federal* courts from enjoining state proceedings.[128] This would seem to leave things at an impasse. However, there are three important exceptions in the federal Anti-Injunction Act. Federal courts may enjoin state court proceedings if "expressly authorized by Act of Congress or where necessary in aid of its jurisdiction or to protect or effectuate its judgments."[129] Thus, in the event of a clash of jurisdiction, federal courts have substantial power to enjoin state litigation. However, several doctrines of "abstention" have developed to limit federal courts in their exercise of this power.[130]

---

124 For a positive review of certification, *see*. Lillich and Mundy, *Federal Court Certification of Doubtful State Law Questions*, 18 UCLA L. REV. 888 (1971). For an example of the U.S. Supreme Court certifying a question to a state supreme court, *see United States v. Juvenile Male*, ___ U.S. ___, 130 S.Ct. 2518 (2010).

125 *Moses H. Cone Memorial Hospital v. Mercury Construction Co.*, 460 U.S. 1 (1983).

126 *See* Chapter VII, pp. 261-262. One exception to this rule, however, is a federal suit for writ of *habeas corpus*. A state prisoner convicted in state court whose federal constitutional claims have already been rejected by the state trial and appellate courts can get a fresh hearing of those claims in federal district court under certain circumstances. *Habeas corpus* is discussed in Chapter VIII, pp. 279-280.

127 *Donovan v. Dallas*, 377 U.S. 408 (1964).

128 28 U.S.C.A. §2283.

129 *Id.*

130 For a discussion of these abstentions and others, *see* CHEMERINSKY, *supra* note 86 §§11.1-14.4.

3. Abstention

Given the supremacy of federal law and federal institutions and the fact, as just discussed, that the federal court may even enjoin state court litigation in some circumstances, it may seem surprising that the most common result when the same controversy is pending in both federal and state court is that the federal court must defer to the state court. In such cases, it is said that the federal court must "abstain" from addressing the dispute. There are several different types of abstention and each has a different effect. In some a state case must be pending at the same time as the federal case and in others it is simply sufficient that the action *could* be filed in state court. The three major abstention doctrines are outlined here.

"Younger" Abstention One situation where simultaneous litigation is possible is where a party who has been sued or prosecuted in state court believes that the state proceeding is barred by federal law, but has no confidence that the state court will give proper consideration to the federal-law defense. Most often this involves situations where a state criminal defendant has a federal constitutional law defense to the state criminal prosecution — for example, when a state prosecutes a person for conduct asserted to be protected by 1st Amendment free speech rights. Federal civil rights laws give the person a claim in federal court to enjoin the prosecution on the ground that it violates federal rights.[131] But if the person seeks an injunction against the state proceeding, the federalism-based abstention doctrine of *Younger v. Harris*[132] requires that the federal court "abstain" in favor of the state court deciding the federal law issue. As a result, the person must rely on the state court to vindicate any federal rights by way of a defense to the state court prosecution. The only way that a federal court will become involved is if the person is able to convince the U.S. Supreme Court to grant *certiorari* after all state appeals are exhausted or if the criminal defendant seeks *habeas corpus* review in the lower federal courts.[133] A narrow exception to the *Younger* doctrine is where it can be shown that the state prosecution is in bad faith.[134]

"Pullman" Abstention Another form of abstention applies when a federal suit challenges a state law as unconstitutional, but there are unclear issues of state law involved. Unclear state-law issues are generally of two types: (1) the challenged state law *could* be interpreted by a state court in a way that would make it constitutional, or (2) there is a plausible argument that the law is invalid as a matter of state-law. In either event, clarification of state law could result in a plaintiff victory on state-law grounds, thus rendering federal court decision of the constitutional challenge unnecessary. This form of abstention applies even if no state court action is pending in which clarification of the state law issue could be obtained. Plaintiffs must file another suit in state court to obtain that clarification. Then, if they lose on that issue, they can return to federal court to press their federal constitutional claims.[135]

This form of partial abstention is named for *Pullman v. Texas Railroad Comm'n*,[136]

---

131 The claim would be based on 42 U.S.C.A. §1983, discussed in Chapter VI, pp. 226, 227. Section 1983 has been held to fall within the exception to the Anti-Injunction Act for injunctions "expressly authorized by Act of Congress."

132 401 U.S. 37 (1971).

133 *Habeas corpus* is discussed in Chapter VIII, pp. 279-280.

134 The *Younger* doctrine has been extended to some civil cases. Generally, *Younger* applies only to civil judicial and administrative proceedings that seek some coercive remedy *against* the federal plaintiff. *See* Chapter VI, p. 226.

135 *England v. Louisiana Board of Medical Examiners*, 375 U.S. 411 (1964).

136 312 U.S. 496 (1941).

the facts of which illustrate the typical case. In *Pullman*, a regulation of the Texas Railroad Commission segregated railroad employees by race according to their job description and reserved the higher status jobs for whites. Black railroad porters challenged the regulation, claiming that it constituted unconstitutional race discrimination. Texas law appeared to allow a basis for challenging the regulation on the ground that it was beyond the powers of the commission set out in state statutes, but the law was unclear on the point. Because of this, the plaintiffs were required to go to the Texas state courts to resolve that state law issue. If that challenge was rejected, they would be allowed to return to federal court to renew their federal constitutional challenge. Since *Pullman* abstention gives the state the first chance to take care of the plaintiff's problem on the basis of state law, it is said to promote harmony between state and federal courts.

"Colorado River" Abstention Where there is parallel litigation on the same subject pending in both state and federal courts and neither *Younger* nor *Pullman* abstention applies, *Colorado River* abstention is possible.[137] Unfortunately, this form of abstention is not well-defined. On the one hand, the Court has emphasized that federal courts should abstain only in the most exceptional circumstances. On the other hand, the lower federal courts do not seem to follow this principle, commonly dismissing pending cases before them. The Court has on several occasions had to reverse trial court decisions to abstain from exercising jurisdiction. It seems likely that this is because lower federal court judges feel overwhelmed by the ever-increasing number of cases, and feel that duplicative litigation, whatever the reason for it, is not a high priority in the allocation of scarce judicial resources.[138]

---

137 *See Colorado River Water Conservation District v. United States*, 424 U.S. 800 (1976) (simultaneous litigation over water rights in state and federal court; federal court abstention warranted).

138 *See, e.g., Moses H. Cone Memorial Hospital v. Mercury Construction, supra* note 125.

CHAPTER VI

ADMINISTRATIVE LAW

Administrative law is the study of the law governing administrative agencies and officials.[1] Included are the proper procedures for promulgating legislative rules and adjudicating disputes, legal issues raised by less formal actions of agencies, the problem of improper conduct of administrative officials, and the judicial remedies available in all these areas.[2]

This chapter will focus primarily on the law of federal administrative agencies and the requirements of the federal Administrative Procedures Act (APA) and caselaw thereunder. Federal agencies play a pivotal, and ever-growing, role in facilitating governance, and many of the laws pertaining to state agencies reflect those pertaining to federal agencies.[3]

PART I: Law and Procedures of Administrative Agencies

A. Types and Purposes of Administrative Agencies

Types of Agencies Broadly defined, virtually every non-military government organ other than the courts and the legislature is considered an "agency."[4] There are two general types of agencies: regulatory and social welfare. Regulatory agencies set and enforce standards of conduct in private relations in various areas, such as transportation or food and prescription drugs. An example is the federal Interstate Commerce Commission, the first administrative agency. Social welfare agencies dispense government assistance for veterans, the aged, the disabled and others. An example is the federal Social Security Administration within the Department of Health and Human Services. Regulatory and social welfare agencies exist on both the state and federal levels. Both have the power to make rules, to enforce them and to adjudicate disputes arising under their jurisdiction.

Federal agencies are also distinguished by whether they are "executive branch" agencies or "independent" agencies. The former are responsible to a cabinet "Secretary," while the latter are headed by administrators, boards or commissions not formally subject to executive branch supervision. When it creates the agency, Congress determines whether the agency is executive or independent.

Advantages and Disadvantages of Agencies Agencies serve three essential purposes. First, agencies bring expertise to bear on problems in a way that generalist

---

1   The advent and expansion of administrative agencies is one of the major changes in the structure of government since 1789. *See* Chapter I, pp. 15-16.

2   For more on administrative law, *see* ALFRED C. AMAN, JR. & WILLIAM T. MAYTON, HORNBOOK ON ADMINISTRATIVE LAW, 2D ED. (West 2001); BERNARD SCHWARTZ, ROBERTO L. CORRADA & J. ROBERT BROWN, JR., ADMINISTRATIVE LAW, 7TH ED. (Aspen 2010); ROBERT J. PIERCE, SIDNEY A. SHAPIRO & PAUL R. VERKUIL, ADMINISTRATIVE LAW AND PROCESS, 5TH ED. (Foundation 2009). *See also* A BLACKLETTER STATEMENT OF FEDERAL ADMINISTRATIVE LAW (ABA 2004). *See also* PETER STRAUSS, AN INTRODUCTION TO ADMINISTRATIVE JUSTICE IN THE UNITED STATES, 2D ED. (Carolina Academic Press 2002) and Dominique Custos, *The Rulemaking Power of Independent Regulatory Agencies*, 54 AM. J. COMP. L. 615 (2006), works written especially for the foreign lawyer. *See* Appendix, pp. A30-A31, for an outline of governmental structure with major federal agencies shown. Major federal and state laws on administrative agencies are collected in SELECTED FEDERAL AND STATE ADMINISTRATIVE AND REGULATORY LAWS (West 2007).

3   Also having strong influence on state practice is the Uniform Law Commissioners' Model State Administrative Procedure Act (1981), www.nccusl.org/Update/. *See* Chapter I, p. 34, note 155.

4   *See* 5 U.S.C.A. §551(1).

executive officials, legislators and judges cannot. The highly technical fields of economic and market regulation, for example, require expert knowledge and flexibility to react quickly to changing conditions. In the social welfare area, programs are complex and the number of recipients is so great that it is only through specialized and expert administration that benefits can be properly distributed. The second reason for agencies is efficiency. Considerable efficiency results naturally from expertise in administration. But further efficiency gains come from the nature of agency structure, which combines legislative, executive and judicial functions "under one roof" unlike the traditional "separation of powers" government structure.[5] A third attraction of agencies is that their self-contained structure makes them more independent, insulating them from the "political winds that sweep Washington."[6] Thus, it is hoped, government policy and actions in a given area will be more consistent and more rational than those that would be produced by the political branches.

The disadvantages of agencies grow directly out of the three advantages just stated. Expertise can breed a narrow vision and arrogance. Undue concern for efficiency can trample individual rights. Insulation from political control can lead to a lack of accountability for actions and lawlessness. Much of administrative law struggles to enhance the positive side of agency expertise, efficiency and independence while controlling their more negative consequences.

The first half of the 20th century saw unrestrained growth in the size, number and variety of practices of federal agencies. A scathing report issued in 1937 complained that they had become "a headless 'fourth branch' of government, a haphazard collection of irresponsible agencies and uncoordinated powers."[7] Following a presidential commission investigation, steps were taken in 1946 to deal with such problems though passage of the Administrative Procedures Act (APA), a comprehensive statute regulating federal agency procedures for rule-making, adjudication and other activities.[8]

Agencies have two basic functions beyond their obvious executive mission: rule-making and adjudication. Statutory and constitutional aspects of these two functions will be outlined first.

B. Rule-Making Functions of Agencies

1. Legislative Rules and the Rule-Making Process

Legislative "rules" set the substantive and procedural laws that must be followed by both the agency and those subject to its jurisdiction. Under the APA, rule-making can be formal or informal, but it is almost always informal.

Informal Rule-Making   For informal rule-making, the APA requires a "notice-and-comment" procedure.[9] A federal agency must first publish a notice of proposed rule-making in the Federal Register, a daily government publication, and invite public comments on its proposal. "[A]n agency's notice must 'provide sufficient detail and rationale for the rule to permit interested parties to comment meaningfully.'"[10] Rule

---

5   The separation of powers problems inherent in such an arrangement are discussed *infra* pp. 219-223.

6   *Commodity Futures Trading Commission v. Schor*, 478 U.S. 833, 835 (1986).

7   President's Commission on Administrative Management, Report with Special Studies (1937), quoted in AMAN & MAYTON, *supra* note 2, at 3.

8   *See* 5 U.S.C.A. §§551-559, 701-706, 1305, 3105, 3344, 5372, 7521.

9   5 U.S.C.A. §553. *See* JEFFREY S. LUBBERS, A GUIDE TO FEDERAL RULE-MAKING, 4TH ED. (ABA 2006).

10   *Fertilizer Institute v. Environmental Protection Agency*, 935 F.2d 1303, 1311 (D.C. Cir. 1991).

introductions require the agency to deal meaningfully with the public comments by providing its reasons for the final rule, and it cannot ignore any point of view.[11] It must respond specifically to significant negative comments either by modifying the proposed rule or explaining its refusal to do so.[12] Overall, the agency must show that it has "genuinely engaged in reasoned decision-making."[13] At the end of the notice and comment period, the agency promulgates and publishes the final version of the rule.

If the notice-and-comment procedures have been followed and the rule is an interpretation of statutory language or fills in gaps in the statute within the scope of the agency's delegated power, a reviewing court must defer to the agency's interpretation of the statute under the *Chevron* rule, discussed in Chapter II. The reviewing court "may not substitute its own construction for a reasonable interpretation" by the agency.[14]

Formal Rule-Making Congress does not require that formal rule-making procedures be followed very often. For formal rule-making, testimony and other evidence must be taken "on the record" before final rules can be promulgated.[15] Formal rule-making is generally reserved for such matters as rate-making, in which an agency must make a general decision on what prices or rates to allow in an industry that it regulates. The Court has made it clear that rule-making procedures more formal than the notice-and-comment procedure may be imposed only by *Congress* and that courts do not have any power to impose more stringent procedures where Congress has not.[16]

The public has the right to petition for rule-making. There is no requirement that the agency respond with rule-making.[17] In one case, however, the Court held that a state had standing to appeal an agency's denial of a petition for rule-making.[18]

Final federal agency rules are compiled yearly in Code of Federal Regulations (C.F.R.), where they are organized by subject matter. However, C.F.R. compilations are notoriously late in being published, so it is often necessary to find the final rule in the Federal Register.

Both state and federal administrative procedure acts contain "good cause" exceptions to the normal notice and comment procedure. Under the federal APA, "good

---

11 *See Kennecott Copper Corp. v. Environmental Protection Agency*, 462 F.2d 846 (D.C. Cir. 1972) (rule sent back to agency for reconsideration of why it reached a particular standard for air quality when tests showed a different standard was sufficient). In addition, Congress has required that all major agency actions consider specific items. One is the requirement of an environmental impact statement. *See* 42 U.S.C.A. §4321, discussed in Chapter XV, p. 639.

12 *United States v. Nova Scotia Food Products Corp.*, 568 F.2d 240 (2d Cir. 1977) (agency did not respond sufficiently to comments that current health standards were adequate and that new rule would make commercial marketing of whitefish unfeasible).

13 *Greater Boston Television Corp. v. Fed. Communications Comm'n*, 444 F.2d 841, 851 (D.C. Cir 1970) (decision on license renewal upheld). If a court vacates a rule, the agency can re-publish the same rule and follow the proper procedures the second time, but it cannot make the rule retroactive. *Bowen v. Georgetown Univ. Hospital*, 488 U.S. 204 (1988) (retroactive recoupment of Medicare payments already made to hospitals).

14 *See* Chapter II, p. 60, and *Chevron, U.S.A., Inc. v. Natural Resources Defense Council, Inc.*, 467 U.S. 837 (1984) (EPA rule defining the statutory term "stationary source" of air pollution upheld).

15 *See* 5 U.S.C.A. §557.

16 *Vermont Yankee Nuclear Power v. Natural Resources Defense Council, Inc.*, 435 U.S. 519 (1978) (reversing lower court order requiring agency to implement additional procedures, including suggestion of possible cross-examination of agency personnel who produced report on which agency relied).

17 5 U.S.C.A. §553(e). *See WWHT, Inc. v. Fed. Communications Comm'n*, 656 F.2d 807 (D.C. Cir. 1981) (by providing petition procedure, Congress did not mean to compel rule-making).

18 *Massachusetts v. Environmental Protection Agency*, 549 U.S. 497, 127 S.Ct. 1438, 167 L.Ed.2d 248 (2007).

cause" is said to exist when the notice and comment procedures would be "unnecessary, impracticable or contrary to the public interest." These are generally interpreted as requiring some sort of emergency need for the rule. The rules adopted pursuant to this exception are called "interim final" rules. The agency then goes through the comment procedure before finalizing the rule, although the interim rule may take effect upon its first publication.

2. Interpretive Rules and Statements of Policy

Agencies also issue "interpretive rules." As the name suggests, these rules interpret some existing legal standard. They often deal with the application of legislative rules to particular facts and are expected to apply to a general category of cases of that type. Interpretive rules are exempt from the procedural requirements for rule-making applicable to legislative rules.[19] Interpretive rules may be promulgated in the same style as legislative rules, but they may also be promulgated in a less formal style, such as a question-and-answer format.[20] It is sometimes difficult to draw the line between an interpretive rule and a new legislative rule, but the basic principle is clear: an interpretive rule is improper if it sets out what is effectively a new requirement.[21]

"Statements of policy" are also issued. They need not follow any particular form. They relate principally to the future intentions of the agency, often with regard to what enforcement action it will take in particular situations. Interpretive rules or policy statements can be disputed as incorrect interpretations of existing law. If the dispute is successful, the agency must refrain from applying them to the complaining party or to other similarly situated parties.[22]

Agencies also give advice to the public on how to comply with their regulations. When that advice is correct, it is a great service to the public. When it is incorrect, agencies will seek to protect reliance interests to the extent possible. However, it is clear that in general there is no obligation to do so.[23]

C. Adjudicatory Functions of Agencies

Adjudication determines the rights and obligations of a particular party based on the application of some legal standard to particular facts. Understood in a broad sense, adjudication happens every time an agency takes action that is not in the form of a rule. However, in this section we will focus on *formal* adjudication, by which affected parties are afforded a trial-type hearing before the agency. Examples of formal adjudication by federal agencies are claims before the Social Security Administration for disability insurance benefits, unfair labor practice claims against an employer or union before the National Labor Relations Board or enforcement proceedings before the Securities and

---

19   *See* 5 U.S.C.A. §553(d).

20   The Equal Employment Opportunity Commission issues both. *See Newport News Shipbuilding and Dry Dock v. Equal Employment Opportunity Comm'n*, 462 U.S. 669 (1983), where examples of both forms of interpretive rules (on sex discrimination in medical disability insurance) are quoted.

21   *Compare Cabias v. Egger*, 690 F.2d 234 (D.C. Cir. 1982) (agency letter simply construed the language and intent of statute) *with Chamber of Commerce v. Occupational Safety & Health Admin.*, 636 F.2d 464 (D.C. Cir. 1980) (requirement announced in agency head's speech and later published as an interpretive rule enunciated a new requirement that must be promulgated as a rule). *See American Mining Congress v. Mine Safety & Health Admin.*, 995 F.3d 1106 (D.C. Cir. 1993) (setting out a widely cited definition).

22   Agencies may also waive their rules in individual cases where it appears the rule is not appropriate, a part of what has been called "administrative equity." *See* Jim Rossi, *Making Policy Through the Waiver of Regulations at the Federal Energy Regulatory Commission*, 47 ADMIN. L. REV. 255 (1995).

23   *Office of Personnel Management v. Richmond*, 496 U.S. 414 (1990) (incorrect advice caused plaintiff to lose 6 months of his pension; yet, equitable estoppel did not operate against the government).

Exchange Commission to revoke the license of a securities broker. The formal adjudicatory functions of administrative agencies are an important part of their work. Indeed, Congress has established several agencies whose sole responsibility is adjudication, with no responsibility to issue rules.[24]

Statutes determine whether formal adjudication is necessary. Requirements can vary. For example, while all the proceedings mentioned in the last paragraph require formal adjudication, no such process applies to a decision of the Secretary of Transportation to order an automobile manufacturer to recall a particular car for safety defects. Although the primary focus here will be on formal adjudication, more informal agency action will be discussed later when judicial review is considered.[25]

1. Administrative Adjudication Procedure under the APA

Hearing Before the Administrative Law Judge   The centerpiece of formal APA administrative adjudication is the hearing before an administrative law judge (ALJ) of the agency in question.[26] The ALJ is well versed in the intricacies of the agency's subject matter and decides cases only from that agency. To assure a fair hearing, the APA mandates strict separation of ALJs from employees of the agency's investigatory and adjudicatory branches, including prohibitions on *ex parte* contacts and undue influence. In addition, it prohibits any "interested person outside the agency" from engaging in such activity.[27]

Nature of Agency Hearings   The ALJ's decision must be made based solely on the "record" compiled by that ALJ.[28] The written decision will include findings of fact and conclusions of law much like the decision of a judge following a bench trial in court. In some agencies, the administrative hearing process resembles traditional courtroom proceedings, while in others it is more inquisitorial. An observer dropping in on a contested hearing before an ALJ from the National Labor Relations Board would probably see little to distinguish it from a bench trial in a courtroom. On the other hand, an observer of most administrative hearings involving Social Security benefits would witness ALJ interrogation of the claimant and other indices of judicial control that would be inappropriate in a courtroom. Indeed, it is said that the Social Security ALJ, as the only government representative present at the hearing, is supposed to "wear three hats": to represent the claimant's interests, to represent the agency and to decide the case.[29] Whatever procedure is afforded by the agency, the standard by which a decision must

---

24 Among them are the Occupational Safety and Health Review Commission, the Federal Mine Safety and Health Review Commission and the National Transportation Safety Board.

25 *See infra* p. 213.

26 *See* 5 U.S.C.A. §§554, 556, 557. *See* MICHAEL ASIMOV, A GUIDE TO FEDERAL AGENCY ADJUDICATION (ABA 2002). The question of what kinds of agency decisions require these formal adjudication standards is one that is often disputed and is not entirely clear from the statute. ALJs are called referees or hearing examiners in some state systems.

27 5 U.S.C.A. §554(d), §557(d) and *infra* p. 223. *Ex parte* contact is contact between adjudicators and others without all the parties to the dispute being present. The prohibition applies to the President and White House staff, *Portland Audubon Society v. Endangered Species Comm'n*, 984 F.2d 1534 (9th Cir. 1993), and to members of Congress, *Pillsbury Co. v. Fed. Trade Comm'n*, 354 F.2d 952 (5th Cir. 1966).

28 5 U.S.C.A. §556(e).

29 This is contrary to the basic adversary principles discussed in Chapter III and has been criticized on that ground. However, it has been upheld by the Supreme Court. *See Richardson v. Perales*, 402 U.S. 389, 410 (1971). *See* SCHWARTZ, *supra* note 2, §5.29. Nonetheless, the non-adversarial nature of Social Security hearings was one basis for the Court holding that failure of the claimant to raise an issue during administrative proceedings did not result in their forfeiting the right to raise it on judicial review. *See Sims v. Apfel*, 530 U.S. 103 (2000) (claimant failed to raise before the Appeals Council two errors of the ALJ).

be made is the same standard as in civil cases in court: whether the factual contentions have been proven by a preponderance of the evidence.[30]

One difference between administrative hearings and court proceedings is that there is no absolute right to an oral hearing or cross examination of witnesses at the administrative hearing. The APA provides that the party "is entitled to present his case or defense by oral or documentary evidence" and "to conduct such cross-examination as may be required for a full and true disclosure of the facts."[31] The opportunity for cross examination is more likely to be provided if the issues at the hearing are factual and depend on witness credibility.[32] However, in many other situations, such where resolution of the case requires the application of technical or scientific data, cross examination would not be useful. Some courts have required that the necessity for cross examination "be established under specific circumstances by the party seeking it."[33] Pretrial procedures differ, however. In the administrative case, there usually has been a full investigation conducted by the enforcement division of the agency, so there are full statements of witnesses in the file for all parties to examine before the hearing.[34]

Rules of Evidence The Federal Rules of Evidence do not generally apply to agency hearings.[35] The APA provides that all oral or documentary evidence is admissible except irrelevant, immaterial or unduly repetitious evidence.[36] So hearsay evidence is fully admissible and a decision may be based solely on hearsay evidence if it is trustworthy.[37] Even when hearsay evidence is suspect, it is admitted, evaluated and given such weight as appears appropriate.[38] But if hearsay is contradicted by other direct trustworthy testimony, it will be deemed insufficient to support a decision.[39] When material evidence relevant to the issues in the case is excluded, reversal is appropriate.[40] Courts have also reversed agency decisions when the agency has not articulated on the record any reason why it did not find certain testimony credible.[41]

The Final Agency Decision The status of ALJ action varies from agency to agency. ALJs are considered the designees of the director of the agency who are appointed for the purpose of gathering evidence, but beyond that, practice varies. In some agencies

---

30 *See* Chapter III, p. 105 (standards of proof in civil and criminal cases). The burden of proof in administrative hearings is also on the claimant. *Schaffer v. Weast*, 546 U.S. 49 (2005) (burden of proof on student's parents in hearing on adequacy of school's placement of disabled student under Individuals with Disabilities in Education Act).

31 5 U.S.C.A. §556(d).

32 *See* SCHWARTZ, *supra* note 2, §7.7.

33 *Cellular Mobile Systems of Pa. v. Fed. Communications Comm'n*, 782 F.2d 182, 198 (D.C. Cir. 1985). *Compare Giant Food Inc. v. Fed. Trade Comm'n*, 322 F.2d 977 (D.C. Cir. 1963) (agencies cannot refuse or limit cross examination).

34 This makes less necessary the formal "discovery" process that is used in civil cases in court. *See* Chapter VII, pp. 235-240.

35 *But see* 29 U.S.C.A. §160(b) (proceedings before the National Labor Relations Board "shall, so far as practicable, be conducted in accordance with the rules of evidence applicable in the district courts of the United States under the rules of civil procedure.") *See* Chapter III, pp. 109-115 (evidence rules for courts).

36 5 U.S.C.A. §556(d).

37 *Richardson v. Perales*, 402 U.S. 389 (1971) (medical reports were properly relied on in disability hearing at least where claimant did not subpoena doctor for cross examination).

38 *See Calhoun v. Bailer*, 626 F.2d 145 (9th Cir. 1980) (8 factors to consider in evaluating hearsay).

39 *Hoska v. Dep't of the Army*, 677 F.2d 131 (D.C. Cir. 1982).

40 *Catholic Medical Center v. Nat'l Labor Relations Board*, 589 F.2d 1166 (2d Cir. 1978) (evidence that employer did not refuse to bargain was improperly excluded).

41 *Tieniber v. Heckler*, 720 F.2d 1251 (11th Cir. 1983) (claimant's testimony as to his disability).

the ALJ makes only a recommended decision that is then submitted to the agency head for acceptance, rejection or modification. In others, the ALJ decision is a final initial decision that may be subject to modification by higher authority in the agency. In yet others, the ALJ decision is the final agency action.[42]

By whatever means the decision of an ALJ becomes final, the final adjudicatory decision is deemed the decision of the head of the agency.[43] This does not mean that the head of the agency must personally participate in reviewing the ALJ decision. Instead, the agency is likely to have an "appeals council" or other body comprising persons at the policy-making level in the agency.

Agency Decisions as Precedents The practice of citing and relying on prior administrative adjudications varies among agencies. Use of administrative decisions as precedent is hampered by the fact that agencies that set out agency policy primarily by rule-making often do not publish their decisions in a form that is easily accessible to the public or even to lawyers. However, if prior decisions can be found, the law of judicial review effectively requires that they be given precedential effect by the agency. This follows from a long-established common law and statutory basis for courts to reverse administrative action on the ground that it is "arbitrary and capricious."[44] If it can be shown that an agency has decided seemingly identical cases in different ways without distinguishing the cases, the agency's actions are considered arbitrary and capricious by definition. In practice, however, the facts of agency decisions are often unique, thereby making it easy for the agency to distinguish apparently similar cases. Some types of decisions, such as individual disability adjudications, for example, are so unique that it may not be worth the effort to try to research them.

Case Adjudication As Lawmaking Despite the obstacles to using agency decisions as precedents, some administrative agencies give full *stare decisis* effect to their adjudicatory decisions and use those decisions to establish agency policy much in the way that courts make law. For example, the National Labor Relations Board (NLRB), makes policy almost exclusively through its administrative hearing decisions — despite pleas from several quarters that it do so by rule.[45] Administrative adjudication as a means of making agency policy raises all the problems that attend judicial lawmaking on a case-by-case basis, including the problem of retroactive lawmaking.[46] However, it has been upheld by the Supreme Court. This is so even when an agency decision clearly announces new principles.[47] As with judicial lawmaking, however, it is easy to overstate the problem. The routine administrative adjudication involved in the average case affords even less opportunity for lawmaking than routine judicial adjudication, since the legal standards set out in administrative rules are relatively more specific.

---

42 Consistent with the movement toward alternative dispute resolution (ADR) in the courts, *see* Chapter VII, pp.250-253, 1990 amendments to the APA require agencies to use ADR in all their functions.

43 *See* 42 U.S.C.A. §405(g) (referring to the final decision subject to judicial review as "the final decision of the Commissioner of Social Security").

44 5 U.S.C.A. §706(2)(A).

45 *See, e.g.,* Merton C. Bernstein, *The NLRB's Adjudication-Rule Making Dilemma Under the Administrative Procedure Act,* 79 YALE L.J. 571, 589-98 (1970). *See also Nat'l Labor Relations Bd. v. Wyman-Gordon Co.,* 394 U.S. 759 (1969) (plurality, concurring and dissenting opinions addressing the legitimacy of NLRB practices). *But see American Hospital Ass'n. v. Nat'l Labor Relations Bd.,* 499 U.S. 606 (1991) (unsuccessful challenge to the first substantive rule issued by the NLRB since 1935).

46 *See* Chapter II, pp. 48-49.

47 *Nat'l Labor Relations Bd. v. Bell Aerospace Co.,* 416 U.S. 267 (1974); *Securities & Exchange Comm'n v. Chenery Corp.,* 332 U.S. 194 (1947). *See generally* AMAN & MAYTON, *supra* note 2, §4.5.

2. Minimum Due Process Requirements for Agency Action

The APA requirements for hearings apply only to actions of federal agencies. State statutes on administrative procedure impose similar standards on some state agencies. Generally, these requirements provide for hearing rights that are well above the constitutional minimum. However, state statutes may not apply to some state and local administrative actions. And certain federal or state statutory hearing rights may not in some circumstances comport with due process. In these instances, the person affected will have to resort to the minimum procedural due process protections afforded by the due process clauses of the 5th and 14th Amendments to the Constitution as developed in court decisions.

The due process clause states that no person may be "deprived of . . . liberty, or property, without due process of law."[48] There are two steps in the procedural due process analysis. The first is to determine whether there is a "deprivation" of "liberty or property." If there is no such deprivation, the due process clause is inapplicable and no procedural safeguards are required. If there is a deprivation, then due process applies and a second question arises: what "process" is "due," *i.e.*, what procedural safeguards are required to protect the individual against an erroneous or unjust deprivation?

Defining "Liberty" or "Property" Interests When the government confines a person or takes away his or her property, it clearly "deprives" that person of liberty or property. But liberty and property for due process purposes include something less than a vested right to "pure" liberty (*i.e.*, freedom from confinement) or an ownership-type property interest. For example, due process applies to a welfare recipient's "right" to continue to receive welfare benefits. This is so even though the state is not required to have welfare programs for relief of poor people and could abolish them tomorrow if it chose. If the government *has* chosen to have welfare programs and a person is eligible to receive those benefits as long as certain factual conditions are met, then that recipient has a *legitimate claim of entitlement to continue* receiving those benefits. That is sufficient to constitute "property" that cannot be "deprived" without affording due process.[49]

Similarly, prisoners who are granted parole from prison on the condition that they follow certain rules have a liberty interest subject to due process protections. Properly convicted prisoners have already had their liberty seriously and validly restricted in compliance with the highest due process standards when they were convicted and sentenced to prison. While on parole, their liberty interests are clearly less than those of a free person on the street. However, their liberty interests qualify for protection if they have a *legitimate claim of entitlement* to stay out of prison *unless* they violate the rules of their parole. If they do, as is generally the case with parolees, then they have a liberty interest that is subject to due process protections.[50] Even in prison, inmates

---

48 The due process clause also protects "life." However, deprivations of life (and the most common form of "pure" liberty deprivation — conviction of a crime) may be accomplished only by way of the criminal process consistent with all the criminal due process safeguards specified in the Bill of Rights. *See* Chapter VIII, pp. 283-323, where constitutional criminal procedural rights are discussed.

49 *Goldberg v. Kelly*, 397 U.S. 254 (1970).

50 *Morrissey v. Brewer*, 408 U.S. 471 (1972). *Compare Connecticut v. Doe*, 538 U.S. 1 (2003) (sex offenders had no conditional liberty interest since all were required to register, even if not dangerous) and *Town of Castle Rock v. Gonzales*, 545 U.S. 748 (2005) (no property interest in enforcement of restraining order because state law did not make enforcement mandatory).

have a liberty interest in avoiding a further restraint that "imposes atypical and significant hardship on the inmate in relation to the ordinary incidents of prison life."[51]

Also treated as protected "deprivations" are revocation of a driver's license[52] and suspension of a student from school for misbehavior.[53] On the other hand, a state university teacher who had a one-year contract was held not to have a legitimate claim of entitlement beyond that year.[54] Similarly, temporary public employees would generally have no legitimate expectation that they would be continued in their positions indefinitely. In the welfare assistance context, there are emergency assistance programs that provide funding for temporary housing and that contemplate a one week limit on such assistance. Termination at the end of that week would not deprive the recipient of any protected property interest (assuming the recipient has been advised of the one-week limit), but termination *before* the end of that week would be subject to some form of due process.[55]

Defining the Content of Procedural Safeguards Required Once it is determined that liberty or property interests have been deprived by administrative action, the next question in the procedural due process analysis is: what "process" is "due" for there to be "due process"? Obviously, there are many procedural protections that might be required. The proper process could range from an informal opportunity to state one's objections in writing to the full range of rights comparable to those enjoyed by a person facing a criminal charge in court — a full adversary hearing with rights to counsel, confrontation, proof beyond reasonable doubt, and so on.[56]

The standard "bundle" of due process rights that have been afforded when a very important property interest is at stake in the administrative context is set out in the 1970 decision in *Goldberg v. Kelly*,[57] a case involving termination of welfare benefits based on financial need. According to *Goldberg*, a person facing such a loss is entitled to (1) notice of the action a reasonable time *before* it is scheduled to take effect, together with the reasons therefor and (2) the opportunity for a trial-type hearing *before* the deprivation becomes effective.[58] The hearing must be (3) conducted by a neutral administrative official not involved in making the original decision. At the hearing, the affected person has (4) the right to have a lawyer or other person present to assist him or her at the

---

51 *Sandin v. Conner*, 515 U.S. 472, 484 (1995) (finding 30-day punitive segregation involved no "dramatic departure from the basic conditions of [the inmate's] sentence"). *See also Meachum v. Fano*, 427 U.S. 215 (1976) (no liberty interest at stake in transfer from medium to maximum security prison). *Compare Wilkinson v. Austin*, 545 U.S. 209 (2005) (prisoners facing assignment of indefinite length to "supermax" prison with solitary confinement had protected liberty interest). *See also Vitek v. Jones*, 445 U.S. 480 (1980) (transfer from prison to mental hospital affects liberty interest because of stigma and greater restrictions on activities).

52 *Bell v. Burson*, 402 U.S. 535 (1971). *See also Barry v. Barchi*, 443 U.S. 55 (1979) (jockey's license); *Memphis Light, Gas and Water Div. v. Craft*, 436 U.S. 1 (1978) (municipal utility service).

53 *Goss v. Lopez*, 419 U.S. 565 (1975).

54 *Roth v. Bd. of Regents*, 408 U.S. 564 (1972).

55 The issue has arisen as to whether a person who *applies* for a benefit or license is *denied* is entitled to a hearing. Hearings are routinely given, so the issue does not often arise whether there is any liberty or property interest that must be protected by due process. *But see American Manufacturers Mutual Insurance Co. v. Sullivan*, 526 U.S. 40 (1999) (no protected interest arose until workers compensation insurance benefits began to be received).

56 *See generally* Chapter VIII, pp. 307-315.

57 397 U.S. 254 (1970).

58 Notice must be by a method that is likely to actually inform the person. *See Jones v. Flowers*, 547 U.S. 220 (2006) (sale of property for taxes after notice published in newspaper and two unclaimed letters, and without posting notice at address to which notice was sent, violated due process).

hearing; (5) the right to confront and cross-examine the witnesses against him or her when credibility is at issue; (6) the right to a written decision based solely on the evidence produced at that hearing; and (7) the right to have a complete record of the hearing, including a record of the testimony and other evidence offered. By contrast, a secondary school student facing a short suspension from school for misconduct is entitled only to "oral or written notice of the charges against him and, if he denies them, an explanation of the evidence the authorities have and an opportunity to present his side of the story."[59]

While *Goldberg* establishes the baseline due process standard, due process overall is a flexible standard. The test for determining the content of procedural safeguards required is set out in *Mathews v. Eldridge*.[60] The *Eldridge* standard imposes a "cost effectiveness" test that balances three factors: (1) the seriousness of the deprivation; (2) the risk of erroneous deprivations and the likely effectiveness of the proposed additional protections in reducing that risk; and (3) the government's interest in avoiding additional procedural protections, including the cost and administrative burdens involved in providing them and considering the governmental function involved.

Balancing these three factors may involve adding to or subtracting from any of the baseline elements identified in *Goldberg v. Kelly*. For example, in *Mathews v. Eldridge*, Mr. Eldridge was receiving benefits from the Social Security Administration's disability program before they were terminated. Regulations entitled him to a hearing, but only a *post-deprivation* hearing. Although *Goldberg* had held that a *pre-deprivation* hearing was required for *need-based* welfare benefit terminations, the Supreme Court found an important distinction in the fact that Social Security disability benefits are government *insurance* benefits payable regardless of whether the disabled person is financially needy. Thus, the seriousness of the deprivation (factor (1) above) in Eldridge's case was less than in *Goldberg v. Kelly*. The *Eldridge* opinion also relied on factor (2), pointing to the fact that the decision on disability was a medical one. Consequently, according to the Court, a face-to-face hearing before an ALJ would not improve greatly on the accuracy of the initial agency decision, which was made in consultation with medical experts. This was contrasted with situations like *Goldberg*, where factual questions involving credibility are central.[61]

The *Eldridge* factors also explain why the government may act in an emergency without first affording a hearing. The fact of an emergency gives overwhelming weight to factor (3), the government's interest in summary action. Summary action has been allowed to stop strip mining, to seize property for the war effort, to protect against a bank

---

59 *Goss v. Lopez, supra* note 53. Expulsion from school or even suspension for a long period would require more process than *Goss* affords. But academic dismissals require less process than disciplinary ones. *Bd. of Curators v. Horowitz*, 435 U.S. 78 (1978) (dismissal from medical school, "like the decision of an individual professor as to the proper grade for a student in his course . . . requires expert evaluation of cumulative information and is not readily adapted to the procedural tools of judicial or administrative decision-making"). *See also Wilkinson v. Austin, supra* note 51 (process for determining that inmate should be in "supermax" prison satisfied due process, even though it provided only notice of summary of facts with opportunity for inmate to respond, but no right to call witnesses, given prison's interest in controlling gang activities in prison).

60 424 U.S. 319 (1976).

61 For other applications of the *Eldridge* test, *see Cleveland Bd. of Education v. Loudermill*, 470 U.S. 532 (1985) (public employee); *Wilkinson v. Austin, supra* note 51 (inmate assignment to "supermax" prison); *Martinez-De Bojorquez v. Ashcroft*, 365 F.3d 800 (9th Cir. 2005) (deportation proceedings).

failure and to protect the public from misbranded drugs or contaminated food.[62] However, the fact the government is conducting a war does not justify dispensing with due process protections.

In *Hamdi v. Rumsfeld*,[63] a U.S. citizen captured in the U.S. invasion of Afghanistan sued for release from detention. The Court acknowledged the President's power to capture and detain enemy combatants in wartime — even if they are U.S. citizens — but held that *Eldridge* nonetheless required that detainees be provided with hearings to determine whether they were in fact enemy combatants. The Court rated *Eldridge* factors (1) and (3) very high — (1) unqualified freedom from confinement balanced against (3) "weighty and sensitive governmental interests in ensuring that those who have in fact fought with the enemy during a war do not return to battle against the United States." Then, applying factor (2), it held that a detainee must receive notice of the factual basis for being considered an enemy combatant and a prompt and fair opportunity to rebut that basis before a neutral decisionmaker. The Court adverted to the "possibility" that the decisionmaker could be "an appropriately authorized and properly constituted military tribunal," and it would permit hearsay evidence and a presumption in favor of the military's initial designation as an enemy combatant. But the detainee would have to have a fair opportunity to present evidence to rebut the presumption. It left it to the lower courts to work out the details.[64]

Procedural Due Process and Judicial Proceedings The due process clause provides minimum standards for *all* adjudicatory actions of government — judicial as well as administrative. Consequently, the *Eldridge* test has relevance to civil and criminal cases in courts. For example, procedural due process has been held to require a prior judicial hearing before personal property can be seized by a creditor under an installment sales contract.[65] When "pure" liberty interests are at stake, the protections are even greater. Persons facing imprisonment for civil contempt of court may be entitled, not just to the opportunity to bring a lawyer at their own expense, but to the right to have a lawyer, appointed and paid for by the state, to represent them at their hearing.[66] Conceptually, the due process continuum reaches all the way up to criminal cases. Criminal cases are generally governed, not by the procedural due process test of *Eldridge*, but by the specific guarantees of the Bill of Rights.[67] But one could well imagine that the *Eldridge* factors, if applied to criminal cases, could cause a court to apply many of the same strict safeguards found in the Bill of Rights as a matter of procedural due process.[68]

---

62 *See Hodel v. Virginia Surface Mining Ass'n*, 452 U.S. 264, 300 (1981) (strip mining); *Phillips v. Comm'r of Internal Revenue*, 283 U.S. 589 (1931) (tax collection); *Coffin Bros. & Co. v. Bennett*, 277 U.S. 29 (1928) (bank failure); *North American Cold Storage Co. v. Chicago*, 211 U.S. 306 (1908) (contaminated food).

63 542 U.S. 507, 528-539 (2004) (plurality opinion).

64 For other cases on the Guantanamo detainees, *see* Chapter I, p. 14.

65 *Fuentes v. Shevin*, 407 U.S. 67 (1972) (secured creditor's seizure of debtor's kitchen stove pursuant to state law that did not provide for a pre-seizure hearing violated procedural due process).

66 *See Mead v. Batchlor*, 460 N.W.2d 493 (Mich. 1990). The contempt power is discussed in Chapter VII, p. 247. *But see Lassiter v. North Carolina Dep't of Social Services*, 452 U.S. 18 (1981) (appointed counsel not *per se* required for parents facing termination of parental rights to their children).

67 *See* Chapter VIII, p. 283, where the sources of criminal due process rights are discussed. As noted there, the 5th and 14th Amendment due process clauses are also sources of procedural rights in criminal cases, but the Court has not applied the *Eldridge* test in criminal cases.

68 In actuality, the due process clause *does* result in the application of most Bill of Rights guarantees to state court criminal cases, but it is generally said instead that those right are "incorporated" against the states by the due process clause rather than being the product of a weighing of due process factors. *See* Chapter VIII, p. 283.

Criticism of the Eldridge Test The *Eldridge* test has been criticized for its attempt to "balance" completely dissimilar factors. How much weight one gives, for example, to the *individual interests* versus *governmental interests* implicates the most fundamental of political attitudes and cannot be weighed according to any objective legal standard. One could well ask if the test is any better than a judge simply deciding whether a given procedure "sounds fair under the circumstances." Another criticism of the *Eldridge* test is that it is too cold and objective: as a "cost-effectiveness" test of procedural safeguards, it fails to include the intangible concepts of justice and respect for individual autonomy that due process represents.[69] Thus, it fails to consider that forcing the government to justify deprivations it seeks to impose may serve valid constitutional and social purposes regardless of the *result* of the process.[70]

D. Judicial Review of Agency Action

One major value of administrative agencies is their expertise. However, they must apply that expertise within the confines of the law. Judicial review is deemed necessary to assure a rational and legally appropriate decision, both when agencies adjudicate and when they make rules. In the United States, this judicial review is undertaken by the ordinary courts — not by special administrative courts, as is the case in some other systems. Review by generalist judges is thought to be a benefit since it counteracts tendencies toward a narrow agency perspective.

1. Right to Judicial Review of Agency Action

Right to Review in General The right to judicial review of agency action is provided by statute, either by the specific statute that governs that agency or by the APA.[71] Where there is no specific statute and the APA is the only possibility, a court will "begin with the strong presumption that Congress intends judicial review."[72] The question of whether there is a *constitutional* right to judicial review of all administrative action is one that has been debated, but not definitively resolved.

Interpretation of Statutes to Permit Review The issue of a constitutional right to judicial review has not been resolved, in part because courts have tended to interpret statutes in such a way as to permit judicial review even when those statutes appear on their face to preclude it. For example, despite the fact that the Immigration and Nationality Act provides that all agency decisions in deportation cases "shall be final," judicial review was held to be available.[73] Congress later provided expressly for review by statute. However, in 1996 Congress removed the right to judicial review for aliens

---

69 *See* Jerry L. Mashaw, *The Supreme Court's Due Process Calculus for Administrative Adjudication in Mathews v. Eldridge: Three Factors in Search of Value*, 44 U. CHI. L. REV. 28, 46-57 (1976) (offering an alternative "value-sensitive approach"). *Cf. Saleeby v. State Bar*, 702 P.2d 525 (Cal. 1985) (including in California due process "the dignitary interest in informing individuals of the nature, grounds, and consequences of the action" and "freedom from arbitrary adjudicative procedures").

70 *See* Chapter III, text at note 135, where the individuality-reinforcing values of procedural fairness are discussed. Due process hearing rights apply only to adjudicative determinations and not to legislative changes. Thus, if an agency were promulgating a rule the effect of which would be to deprive a person of liberty or property, the trial-type procedures of *Goldberg v. Kelly* are not required before such a rule can be adopted. SCHWARTZ, *supra* note 2, §§5.6-5.8. For more on procedural due process rights, *see* JOHN E. NOWAK & RONALD D. ROTUNDA, HORNBOOK ON CONSTITUTIONAL LAW, 8TH ED. §§13.1-13.10 (West 2010).

71 5 U.S.C.A. §§701-706. *See* JOHN F. DUFFY & MICHAEL HERZ, A GUIDE TO JUDICIAL AND POLITICAL REVIEW OF FEDERAL AGENCIES (ABA 2005).

72 *Bowen v. Michigan Academy of Family Physicians*, 476 U.S. 667, 670 (1986).

73 *Shaughnessy v. Pedreiro*, 349 U.S. 48 (1955). *See also Kucana v. Holder*, ___ U.S. ___, 130 S.Ct. 827 (2010) (immigration law limiting court's authority to review any action within the attorney general's discretion, does not apply to preclude judicial review of refusal to reopen deportation case).

subject to deportation for having been convicted of committing certain aggravated felonies. The Court held that the right to direct appeal of the agency's decision had been removed. But it also held that review by means of *habeas corpus* was still available. This was so despite the fact that Congress had entitled its repealing sections "Elimination of Custody Review by Habeas Corpus." The Court held that the result was necessary in view of the lack of clarity in the statute's *text* and the desire to avoid the serious constitutional question that would arise should it interpret the amendments involved as removing all judicial review of the deportation orders involved.[74]

The statutory interpretations involved have on occasion appeared strained.[75] However, if Congress has clearly prohibited review, the Court has acquiesced, even when the challenged decisions are claimed to be arbitrary and capricious or in clear violation of the law.[76] A more difficult question is whether judicial review of *constitutional* issues could ever be denied. This issue is discussed in more depth in the chapter on constitutional law.[77] The Court has never decided the issue, but it has interpreted ambiguous statutes in such a way as to permit review "in part to avoid the 'serious constitutional question' that would arise if a federal statute were construed to deny any judicial forum for a colorable constitutional claim."[78]

2. Procedural Aspects of Judicial Review

Exhaustion of Administrative Remedies Generally, claimants aggrieved by agency action must obtain a final decision of the agency before resorting to judicial review.[79] This means that the claimant faced with a negative action by an agency must exhaust the appeal procedures the agency provides. This is said to assure economical use of judicial and administrative resources, to promote administrative autonomy and responsibility by providing the agency with the opportunity to correct its own mistakes, and to further the legislative purpose of granting authority to the agency by requiring that its procedures be respected. However, exhaustion is not required if it would be futile, such

74 *Immigration and Naturalization Service v. St. Cyr*, 533 U.S. 289 (2001); *Calcano-Martinez v. Immigration and Naturalization Service*, 533 U.S. 348 (2001). *Cf. Zadvydas v. Davis*, 533 U.S. 678 (2001) (interpreting statute as not providing for indefinite detention of aliens subject to deportation orders because a contrary interpretation would raise potential constitutional problems).

75 *Lindahl v. Office of Personnel Management*, 470 U.S. 768 (1985) (statute providing that Navy disability determinations were "final and conclusive and are not subject to review" held not to preclude some judicial review of "misconstruction of the governing legislation" going "to the heart of the administrative determination").

76 *See, e.g., United States v. Wunderlich*, 342 U.S. 98 (1951) (decision of agency in government contract dispute), *But see* SCHWARTZ, *supra* note 2, §8.6 at 485-486 (criticizing lack of review as making agencies "virtual laws unto themselves").

77 *See* Chapter IX, pp. 335-337.

78 *Webster v. Doe*, 486 U.S. 592, 603 (1988). *See also Johnson v. Robison*, 415 U.S. 361, 366 (1974) (prohibition of review of veterans benefit cases did not prohibit review of constitutional issue). *But see* Scalia, J., dissenting in *Webster v. Doe, supra. Cf. Reno v. American-Arab Anti-Discrimination Comm.*, 525 U.S. 471 (1999) (Congress can properly bar review of attorney general's decision to commence deportation proceedings against illegal aliens even if that decision is alleged to constitute unconstitutional selective enforcement, since illegal aliens have no right to argue selective enforcement as a defense).

79 5 U.S.C.A. §704. *McKart v. United States*, 395 U.S. 185 (1969) (military draft classification not appealed administratively, so judicial review is barred). However, exhaustion is not required where the administrative remedies are inadequate to award the relief the plaintiff seeks. *McCarthy v. Madigan*, 503 U.S. 140 (1992) (federal prisoner who sued prison officials for money damages was not required to exhaust prison administrative remedies).

as where the agency is bound by applicable law to decide against the claimant and the claimant wishes to challenge that law.[80]

Means of Obtaining Review   Judicial review may be obtained by any available means. Usually, a petition for review is required to be filed within a certain number of days after the final decision.[81] In other cases, the agency may have to bring an enforcement action in court to gain compliance, at which time judicial review occurs. This is the case with some decisions of the NLRB, which must bring an action for enforcement in the Court of Appeals.[82] In some cases, review will be by way of defense against administrative enforcement and appeal from any negative decision in that proceeding. In addition, an action for an injunction or for declaratory relief may be used.[83] *Habeas corpus* was used in deportation cases until review under the APA was recognized.[84]

Standing   A person seeking judicial review of agency action in federal court must have "standing" to contest that action. Standing generally requires that the person be one who is actually injured by the agency action.[85] However, when review is sought under the APA, an additional requirement beyond simple injury must be met. The APA provides for review only if the claimant's injury qualifies as an injury "within the meaning of a relevant statute."[86] This has been understood as requiring that the injury complained of be one that is within the "zone of interests" defined by the statute governing the agency action.

This requirement is most relevant when the injured plaintiff is not the party who was the direct subject of the administrative action. Such plaintiffs must show that the relevant statutes were intended to protect them from the type of injury they complain of. For example, when the Comptroller of Currency approved the applications of two banks to sell securities, the banks did not complain, but stock brokers and dealers who would face competition from the banks filed suit. The Court found that an arguable basis for the National Bank Act limiting securities brokerage activities of banks was to prevent competition with established securities dealers — the precise injury complained of by the plaintiffs.[87] Had the Court found that the sole purpose of the Act was to assure that banks did not fail by overextending their operations, then injury to competitors would not have been within that zone of interests. An example of a negative zone of interests case is one involving the decision of the federal Postal Service to permit certain private courier companies to engage in some international mail delivery. The postal workers' union sued to contest the decision, claiming that it was unlawful. The Court held that the zone of interest test was not satisfied: Congress's purpose in prohibiting private

---

80 *Bethesda Hospital Ass'n v. Bowen*, 485 U.S. 399 (1988) (agency had no power to award reimbursement hospitals sought). *See generally* SCHWARTZ, *supra* note 2, §§8.33-8.40.

81 *See, e.g.,* 42 U.S.C.A. §405(g) (60 days for Social Security appeals).

82 29 U.S.C.A. §160(e), (f).

83 An injunction is a court order stopping the defendant from doing something or requiring the defendant to do something. Declaratory relief is a declaration that the defendant's actions are unlawful. Both are discussed in greater detail in the chapter on Civil Procedure. *See* Chapter VII, pp. 245-247.

84 *Shaughnessy v. Pedreiro, supra* note 73. *Habeas corpus* is discussed in Chapter VIII, pp. 279-280.

85 Constitutional aspects of standing are discussed in Chapter IX, pp. 329-332.

86 5 U.S.C.A. §702.

87 *Clarke v. Securities Industry Ass'n*, 479 U.S. 388 (1987). Clearly, application of the zone of interest test can lead to varying results depending on the analysis of the relevant purposes of the statute — an analysis that often comes close to deciding the merits of the case.

competition with the Postal Service was to assure that the Service received sufficient revenues, not to protect government postal workers' jobs.[88]

3. Scope of Review of Agency Action

Review of Fact Determinations   The general rule is that a reviewing court must affirm the agency determinations of issues of fact made after a trial-type hearing if they are supported by "substantial evidence."[89] Substantial evidence has been defined as "such relevant evidence as a reasonable mind might accept as adequate to support a conclusion."[90] Many courts have held that this is largely the same standard used when trial judges review jury verdicts or appellate courts review a trial judge's factual findings to see if they are "clearly erroneous."[91] However, courts give great deference to the findings of agencies because of the agencies' expertise in the subject matter. Accordingly, the Supreme Court has observed that the "court/court standard of review has been considered somewhat stricter (*i.e.*, allowing somewhat closer judicial review) than the APA's court/agency standards."[92] However, it has also been observed that applying the "substantial evidence" test — like reviewing jury verdicts and trial court findings of fact — is "more of an art than a science."[93]

Some agency decisions may be reviewed *de novo* by a court. This means that the court can examine the record as if it were the finder of fact in the first instance.[94] In some cases, *de novo* judicial review of fact issues is required by the Constitution.[95]

Review of Legal Issues   Courts have the primary responsibility to say what the law is and thus have the power, in general, to determine *legal* issues *de novo* based on their own analysis of the law. But an agency interpretation of a statute that is embodied in an agency's legislative rule that was adopted through the notice-and-comment rule-making process is entitled to *Chevron* deference, and a court may not substitute its own view for that agency interpretation.[96] Similarly entitled to deference is an agency's interpretation of its own ambiguous rule,[97] so long as that interpretation is within the scope of the agency's delegated authority.[98] If an agency's legal interpretation is embodied in a ruling in a particular case and it does not fall within the categories just noted, then *Chevron*

---

88   *Air Couriers Conference of America v. American Postal Workers Union*, 498 U.S. 517 (1991). *See also Block v. Community Nutrition Institute*, 467 U.S. 340 (1984) (denying standing to consumers of milk products to challenge minimum prices set for milk handlers and producers).

89   5 U.S.C.A. §706(2)(E) and *Universal Camera v. Nat'l Labor Relations Bd.*, 340 U.S. 474 (1951).

90   *Consolidated Edison Co. v. Nat'l Labor Relations Bd.*, 305 U.S. 197, 229 (1938).

91   *See* Federal Rule of Civil Procedure 52 and Chapter V, p. 170 and Robert L. Stern, *Review of Findings of Administrators, Judges and Juries: A Comparative Analysis*, 58 HARV. L. REV. 70 (1944).

92   *Dickinson v. Zurko*, 527 U.S. 150, 153 (1999) (requiring that Federal Circuit Court of Appeals review patent and trademark office decisions under the APA standard and not the "clearly erroneous" standard).

93   AMAN & MAYTON, *supra* note 2, at 446. The *Dickinson* case cited in the last footnote contains a detailed discussion of the evolution of the APA standard of review.

94   This is true of many civil rights claims. *See Chandler v. Roudebush*, 425 U.S. 840 (1976) (employment discrimination).

95   *Agosto v. Immigration and Naturalization Service*, 436 U.S. 748 (1978) (*de novo* trial of citizenship issue in deportation proceeding required both by statute and the Constitution).

96   *See supra* p. 200 and Chapter II, p. 60.

97   *Auer v. Robbins*, 519 U.S. 452, 461-463 (1997) (whether sergeants were executive employees exempt from overtime pay requirements of Fair Labor Standards Act). But *Auer* deference would not apply to a "*post hoc* rationalizatio[n]" advanced by an agency in response to litigation challenging past agency action.

98   *Gonzales v. Oregon*, 546 U.S. 243 (2006) (attorney-general's interpretive rule prohibiting doctors from prescribing drugs to assist suicide under Oregon law was beyond his power under federal drug control laws, which are aimed at illicit drug trafficking).

deference does not apply and the agency's interpretation "'is entitled to respect' only to the extent that it has the 'power to persuade.'"[99]

Review of Mixed Fact-Law Issues Some issues of law are not "pure" law or fact issues. They seem legal, but have factual aspects to them, as where a legal standard is applied to the facts of the case to reach a conclusion that those facts are sufficient under the statutory language — commonly referred to as "mixed" fact and law issues. In such instances, the reviewing court must affirm the finding if the application is reasonable.[100] The questions of whether the statute is clear or how "pure" an issue is one of law are issues about which there is considerable room for disagreement.[101]

4. Review of Discretionary Agency Actions or Inaction

Many agency decisions are matters of discretion not dictated by the law or facts. Examples are the numerous decisions on funding, refusals to grant exceptions, "no-action" letters and other refusals to take action. The questions of whether such actions are subject to review and the scope of that review are important.

The APA appears on the surface to provide contradictory answers to the question of reviewability. On the one hand, it provides that a court may set aside agency action that is "arbitrary, capricious, *an abuse of discretion*, or otherwise not in accordance with law."[102] On the other hand, it prohibits judicial review of any matter "committed to agency discretion by law."[103] If action is truly committed to agency discretion, then it is difficult to see how a court is to determine whether the administrator's discretion was "abused." In other words, if there are *no* statutory standards limiting an administrator's actions, then it is difficult to see how judicial review would be anything more than a court arbitrarily substituting its decision for that of the administrator. The Court has determined that, unless "statutes are drawn in such broad terms that in a given case there is no law to apply" — no standards by which a reviewing court could judge the propriety of the decision — then the matter is "committed to agency discretion" and is not reviewable. But if there is some law to apply, then the decision is reviewable and those standards are applied to determine whether there was an abuse of discretion.[104]

The principal case in the area illustrates how both the question of reviewability is decided and the standard of "abuse of discretion" is applied. In *Citizens to Preserve Overton Park v. Volpe*,[105] the Secretary of Transportation released federal money to local authorities to fund construction of a highway through a park. A provision of the governing statute allowed such construction unless a "feasible and prudent" alternative route existed. If no alternative existed, the statute mandated that all possible steps be

---

99 *See United States v. Mead Corp.*, 533 U.S. 218, 226-227 (2001) (customs service reclassification of goods in tariff ruling), quoting *Skidmore v. Swift & Co.*, 323 U.S. 134 (1944) (administrator's bulletin).

100 *Nat'l Labor Relations Bd. v. Hearst Publications, Inc.*, 322 U.S. 111 (1944) (determination of whether "newsboys" who distributed papers on the street were "employees" within the meaning of the National Labor Relations Act).

101 *See generally* AMAN & MAYTON, *supra* note 2, §13.7. A similar fact-law distinction arises with respect to the division of labor between judge and jury. *See* Chapter III, p. 87.

102 5 U.S.C.A. §706(2)(a) (emphasis supplied).

103 5 U.S.C.A. §701(a).

104 *Citizens to Preserve Overton Park v. Volpe*, 401 U.S. 402 (1971). Professor Schwartz disagrees with the premise that there must be statutory standards to apply, citing English practice as support. *See* SCHWARTZ, *supra* note 2, §8.11, at 495. Examples of discretionary actions not subject to review are the President's decision to accept or reject a list of miliary base closings, *Dalton v. Spencer*, 511 U.S. 462 (1994), and an agency's decision to discontinue funding a health program out of its lump sum appropriation. *Lincoln v. Virgil*, 508 U.S. 182 (1993).

105 401 U.S. 402 (1971).

taken to "minimize harm" to the park. The Secretary took the position that the question of whether any alternative route was "feasible and prudent" was clearly non-reviewable discretionary action. The Supreme Court held that there was in fact "law to apply." The statute clearly indicated Congress's intent that park land be protected. Consequently, the standard to be applied was whether the Secretary had fully considered alternative routes and had properly determined that there were special problems with them. Thus, while a court in a case involving discretionary action cannot dictate what decision an administrator must reach, it can assure that the decision made is a rational one that takes into account the factors that the law requires the agency to consider.[106]

APA also permits suit to "compel agency action unlawfully withheld or unreasonably delayed."[107] However, the agency must be clearly required by law to take "discrete action." Thus, in *Norton v. Southern Utah Wilderness Alliance*,[108] the Supreme Court held that the requirement that the Bureau of Land Management manage wilderness areas "in a manner so as not to impair the suitability of such areas for preservation as wilderness" did not require prohibition of off-road vehicles or any other "discrete action." The Court emphasized that the holding served to avoid undue judicial interference with agencies' lawful discretion and judicial entanglement in abstract policy disagreements about which courts lack both expertise and information.

5. Attorney Fees and Costs

The Equal Access to Justice Act was passed by Congress in recognition of the high cost of contesting actions of agencies and the beneficial effects of redressing lawless agency action or inaction. Consequently, in any case against the United States or one of its agencies, a federal court "shall award" attorney fees to any prevailing private party "unless the court finds that the position of the United States was substantially justified or that special circumstances make an award unjust."[109]

E. Presidential and Congressional Controls on Federal Agency Action

Federal agencies are subject to statutory commands and owe their continued existence to Congress and the President. Consequently, complete control of agencies is always available through legislation abolishing them or limiting their power. However, these means of control are not often exercised. Instead, Congress and the President use less drastic and less direct means. These efforts, however, are not completely successful. This is in part because many agencies have been set up as independent precisely to avoid the effects of political influence. In addition, presidential and congressional influences often pull agencies in opposite directions, so they effectively cancel each other out.

1. Power Over Tenure of Agency Officials

Presidential Power of Appointment A major way to influence agency policy and rules is through the power to appoint the agency head or cabinet secretary whose department supervises the agency. The "appointments clause" of the Constitution provides that Congress shall establish the offices of government, that higher-level or

---

106 It is important to emphasize that the "substantial evidence" rule and great deference to administrative agency fact-finding would not apply to discretionary decisions such as the one in *Overton Park*, because there was no trial-type administrative hearing. Indeed, the problem with the administrator's decision in *Overton Park* was that there was *no* record of reasons for it.

107 5 U.S.C.A. §706(1).

108 542 U.S. 55 (2004).

109 28 U.S.C.A. §2412(d)(1)(A). However, the maximum rate for attorney fees is $125 per hour.

"principal officers" will be appointed by the President subject to Senate confirmation, and that "inferior officers" may be appointed by the President, by the courts of law, or by department heads without need for Senate involvement, if Congress so provides.[110] The President's choice and the process of Senate approval of a Cabinet Secretary or agency head present opportunities to pick administrators who have particular views about the way the agency should be run and to extract promises regarding the future direction of the agency.

Presidential Removal Power There is not explicit power in the President to remove federal administrative officers, but Article II's provision that "[t]he executive Power shall be vested in" the President has been understood to empower the President to keep executive officers accountable — by removing them from office, if necessary.[111] But as noted in Chapter I, there are many "independent" administrative agencies. This independence is assured by providing for appointment terms that extend beyond the term of office of the President who appointed those officers and by limiting the presidential ability to remove them.[112]

The original caselaw on removal drew a distinction between administrative officials who perform "executive" functions and those who performed "quasi-judicial" and "quasi-legislative" functions. While the President retained the right to dismiss "those who are part of the Executive establishment" and who perform purely executive functions, he could not dismiss those "whose tasks require absolute freedom from Executive interference."[113] This test has been replaced by a more flexible, functional one under which the President can freely dismiss only those officials who are essential to the President's performance of core presidential functions.[114] Thus, the distinction is drawn between executive branch officials performing "administrative" functions, whose dismissal Congress can regulate, and executive branch officials exercising "political" functions, whom the President can not dismiss at will.[115]

Civil Service Employees Below "inferior officers" are employees whose appointment and tenure are not subject to any constitutional restraints.[116] This provides a constitutional justification for the existence of a competitive, merit-based civil service

---

110 Art. II §2 cl. 2.

111 Art. II, §1, cl. 1. *See Myers v. United States*, 272 U.S. 52, 164 (1926); *Free Enterprise Fund v. Public Co. Accounting Oversight Bd.*, ___ U.S. ___, 130 S.Ct. 3138 (2010). The removal power has been a sore point between the President and Congress. The famous impeachment of President Andrew Johnson and his narrow acquittal in the Senate in 1867 were based on his refusal to accede to a Tenure in Office Act passed by Congress that would have changed the tenure of all his cabinet officials (most of them inherited from President Lincoln) from service at the pleasure of the President to dismissal only with the concurrence of the Senate. Under *Myers, supra*, the Act violates separation of powers.

112 *See* Chapter I, p. 16.

113 *Humphrey's Executor v. United States*, 295 U.S. 602 (1935) (prohibiting presidential dismissal where Congress had provided by statute that a member of the Federal Trade Commission could be removed mid-term only for poor job performance).

114 *Morrison v. Olson*, 487 U.S. 654 (1988) (appointment and removal procedure for special prosecutor not invalid just because limits were placed on presidential power to dismiss her, since such limits did not "impede the President's ability to perform his constitutional duty").

115 *See* STRAUSS, *supra* note 1, at 68.

116 *Buckley v. Valeo*, 424 U.S. 1, 126, n. 162 (1976).

system.[117] It is these individuals, who are protected from dismissal except for cause, who perform the daily functions of government administration.

Congressional Control Over Tenure of Agency Officials Though the Senate must approve presidential agency appointments, it is clear that Congress does not have the power itself to appoint executive officials. In *Buckley v. Valeo*,[118] the Supreme Court considered the constitutionality of provisions of the Federal Election Campaign Act. The Act authorized a Federal Election Commission to make rules regulating campaign practices and to investigate and prosecute violations of them. In an effort to achieve a political balance on the Commission in this sensitive political area, the Act provided for appointment of some commissioners by the President (without participation of the Senate) and some by the President *pro tempore* of the Senate and the Speaker of the House of Representatives.[119] The Supreme Court held the Commission so constituted violated the appointments clause. Since the Commissioners would be enforcing the law and would therefore be *executive* officers, they could only be appointed by the President with approval of the Senate and could not be appointed by legislative officials. The decision was supported by reference to the policy that underlies all separation of powers problems: the notion that "the same persons should not both legislate and administer the laws."[120]

Just as Congress cannot appoint executive agency personnel, it violates separation of powers for Congress to vest executive power in an official over whose tenure it already has control. In *Bowsher v. Synar*,[121] Congress passed a law intended to reduce the federal deficit. The law assigned certain duties to the Comptroller General, the official in charge of the Government Accounting Office, a legislative bureau that investigates and evaluates internal operations of government. The law instructed the Comptroller, upon being notified of certain fiscal information, to determine what spending cuts to make based on standards set out in legislation. These spending cuts were then to be transmitted to the President who was required to put them into effect. The Comptroller General's exercise of this kind of judgment, the Court held, was clearly executive action. The problem was that the Comptroller General, as head of a legislative agency, was subject to removal by Congress before expiration of his 15-year term. It violated separation of powers for Congress to vest executive decision-making power in an official under its control.[122]

---

117 Another reason why the civil service is constitutional is that civil service employees are "inferior officers" whose appointment and dismissal are vested in department heads whose discretion to hire and fire is controlled by the merit requirements of the statute establishing the civil service. *See* STRAUSS, *supra* note 2, at 64 and *United States v. Perkins*, 116 U.S. 483 (1886) (when Congress vests appointment power in department heads, it may restrict the manner of removal).

118 424 U.S. 1 (1976).

119 These officials are the presiding officers of the two houses of Congress elected by their members.

120 424 U.S. at 272. The act had also provided that all appointees would need to be approved not just by the Senate, but by both houses of Congress — a provision that the Court struck down as well.

121 478 U.S. 714 (1986).

122 *See also MWAA v. Citizens for the Abatement of Aircraft Noise*, 501 U.S. 252 (1991) (unconstitutional for members of Congress to serve on a board overseeing administration of federal airports because the board's power would be executive, not legislative power). It also violates separation of powers to vest the power to dismiss in federal officials not subject to dismissal by the President. *Free Enterprise Fund v. Public Co. Accounting Oversight Bd.*, *supra* note 111.

2. Ongoing Presidential and Congressional Influence on Agency Action

Presidential Means of Control   Beyond the power to appoint agency officials, the President has many opportunities to exercise ongoing control over agency policy and action. The degree of a President's control varies with the agency and depends in part on whether the agency is an executive agency, which is responsible to a presidential cabinet Secretary or other presidential appointee, or an independent agency. Actions of executive agencies can be supervised closely. "Major rules" generally must be cleared with the White House's Office of Management and Budget (OMB) and may result in considerable debate, negotiation and compromise.[123] The content and timing of the administrative rules may be affected. Enforcement priorities of agencies can be made to reflect the President's views. A policy of agency *inaction* is the easiest to implement. There is a long history of executive branch officials and agencies reading statutory commands narrowly or "dragging their feet" in promulgating needed regulations or pursuing enforcement actions with which they disagree. To give a recent example, the Reagan and the first Bush administrations were repeatedly criticized for failing to enforce vigorously civil rights and environmental protection laws.

Presidential influence should not be overstated, however. Most federal administrative agencies are housed in the executive branch. However, of the approximately 5 million civilian and military personnel in the 14 departments of the government, the President gets to appoint only the top 3,000 or so. The remaining administrators who actually do the work carrying out policy are not so easy to control. They are part of the merit-based civil service system.[124] Generally the President cannot fire them and they have specialized knowledge and strong feelings about "their" agency's policies and practices. Further, the President and his staff or appointees are only one form of influence on agency personnel. As pointed out below, congressional committees have great influence over agencies.

President Harry S. Truman, who served from 1945 until 1953, was considered by many to have been a very strong President. But in dealing with the bureaucracy, he described his task as being "to bring people in and try to persuade them to do what they ought to do without persuasion. That's what I spend most of my time doing. That's what the power of the President amounts to."[125] Truman also commented on the eve of his successor, former Army General Dwight D. Eisenhower, becoming President: "He'll sit here and he'll say 'Do this! Do that!' and nothing will happen. Poor Ike — it won't be a bit like the Army."[126]

There are some legal limits to presidential intervention in agency matters even in those agencies whose heads the President has appointed. For example, the President may not seek to "impound" funds Congress intended that the agency spend.[127] In *Train v. City of New York*,[128] Congress had passed the Clean Water Act of 1972 over President

---

123 *See* OMB Executive Order No. 12291, 46 Fed. Reg. 13193 (Feb. 17, 1981) (requiring that all executive agency action be cleared through OMB).

124 *See supra* p. 215.

125 Quoted in STRAUSS, *supra* note 2, at 61 n.32.

126 ALEX AYRES, ED., THE WIT AND WISDOM OF HARRY S. TRUMAN 43 (Meridian Books 1998).

127 Impoundment dates from 1803, when President Thomas Jefferson refused to spend $50,000 on defense of the Mississippi River. President Nixon was perhaps the biggest impounder of funds, at one point impounding as much as $25 billion.

128 420 U.S. 35 (1975).

Nixon's veto, but Nixon continued his opposition to the program and impounded funds by ordering the administrator of the Environmental Protection Agency to withhold several billion dollars that Congress had directed should go to fund construction of sewage treatment plants for New York City. The City of New York sued for release of the money. The Court held that the President had no power to order the agency to withhold the funds and that the agency must spend those funds as Congress directed.[129]

Congressional Power and Influence Over Agencies   Congressional oversight of agencies has its source in the "power of the purse" given by the Constitution — the power to decide whether and to what extent to fund government operations.[130] The means by which congressional influence is most commonly exercised is through congressional committees. As noted in Chapter I, the original purpose of committees was to deal with the increased complexity and specialized nature of legislation in the modern world. But with the growth of administrative agencies, committees have developed a strong supervisory influence on their operations. Because committees are organized according to subject matter, their members develop expertise and a strong interest in an area of agency action, making it difficult for agencies to use their superior knowledge to escape scrutiny. Most important, since Congress has control over agency budgets, Congressional committee members can be very persuasive in convincing agency heads to alter the way they are carrying out a particular Congressional program.[131]

To assist it in carrying out this oversight role, Congress has established powerful agencies of its own to do research and investigative work and to make recommendations in particular areas. Among them are the Government Accounting Office (GAO), the Congressional Budget Office and the Library of Congress. The GAO regularly issues reports on the performance of federal agencies.[132]

Congress at one point reserved to itself the power of "legislative veto" of agency action or rules through use of a resolution or vote of one house or, in some cases, even a committee vote. However, in *Immigration & Naturalization Service v. Chadha*,[133] the Court held that a legislative veto by a single house of Congress violated the separation of powers and the "presentment" and "bicameralism" clauses of the Constitution, which require that legislation be passed by both houses of Congress and presented to the President for approval or veto.[134] Legislation since 1996 provides in general that any "major" agency rule (as defined, there are around 80-100 major rules a year) must be presented to both houses of Congress and may not take effect for at least 60 days

---

129 A "settlement" of the impoundment dispute between Congress and the President enacted after *Train* is set out in 2 U.S.C.A. §681 *et seq.* (allowing the President to delay spending and propose recission of budgetary amounts, but prohibiting outright impoundment).

130 *See* Chapter I, p. 6.

131 Even the influence of individual members of Congress on agency decisions have been tolerated at least before the adjudication stage. *DCP Farms v. Yeutter*, 957 F.2d 1183 (5th Cir. 1992).

132 Another tool that facilitates accountability of agencies is the federal Freedom of Information Act (FOIA), which gives individual citizens the right to obtain records held by a federal agency, 5 U. S. C. §§552, unless the documents fall within enumerated exemptions, see §§552(b). "[C]onsistent with the Act's goal of broad disclosure, these exemptions have been consistently given a narrow compass." *Dept. of Justice v. Tax Analysts*, 492 U. S. 136, 151 (1989). *See also Dept. of the Interior v. Klamath Water Users Protective Ass'n*, 532 U.S. 1 (2001) (exemption for certain "inter-agency or intra-agency memorandums or letters").

133 462 U.S. 919 (1983).

134 *See* Art. I §7 cl. 2 & 3. One method of avoiding presidential veto is to attach a "rider" affecting particular administrative action to a bill the President wants. The President has no "line-item veto" power and must either approve or veto the entire bill presented to him. *See infra* note 138.

thereafter to give Congress the chance to pass a joint resolution — approved by both houses and signed by the President — rejecting it. If this happens, the agency may not thereafter re-issue the same rule unless Congress enacts legislation allowing it to do so.[135] Congress is not often able to mobilize itself sufficiently within 60 days to stop even a significant percentage of these rules and the President may well refuse to sign the joint resolution. The device was first used successfully in 2001 to stop rules on ergonomics injuries in the workplace promulgated by the Occupational Safety and Health Administration (OSHA), after a major lobbying effort by business interests.[136]

PART II: Separation of Powers and Federalism Issues Involving Agencies

A. Administrative Agencies and Separation of Powers

From all that has been discussed, it is clear that administrative agencies exercise *executive* power when they enforce the law, exercise *legislative* power when they engage in rule-making and exercise *judicial* power when they adjudicate disputes under governing law. One might suppose that a system of government that purports to be based on separation of powers would have some difficulty with this mix of functions in administrative agencies.[137] In fact, all these separation of powers questions have been settled by the Supreme Court in a way that has permitted longstanding agency practice to continue.

There are three dimensions to the separation of powers critique of federal administrative agencies: (1) that executive agencies are exercising legislative power, (2) that executive agencies are exercising judicial power, and (3) that one governmental organ, regardless of what branch it belongs to, combines executive, legislative and judicial functions "under one roof."

1. Agencies Exercising Legislative Power

The Court has viewed the problem of agencies exercising legislative power by promulgating rules as one of "delegation" of legislative power. The Court's position is that a statute does not improperly delegate legislative power so long as Congress provides "intelligible standards" to limit the discretion of the agency and to provide a basis for meaningful judicial review.[138] Only then can it be assured that the essentials of the legislative function of determining policy are being exercised by Congress and not by the agency. Thus, in *A.L.A. Schechter Poultry v. United States*,[139] the Court unanimously invalidated a statutory grant of administrative authority to establish "codes of fair competition" in various segments of business and industry with no indication of what the content of those codes should be.

The Court has never overruled the *Schechter* case, but the Court has sustained as sufficient direction from Congress that the Federal Communications Commission

---

135 *See* 5 U.S.C.A. §§801-808.

136 Pub. L. 107-5 (2001). While OSHA had spent 10 years developing the rules, Congress took only a week to examine and vote to disapprove them.

137 *See* Chapter I, pp. 9-18, 34-37, where other separation of powers issues are discussed.

138 *Yakus v. United States*, 321 U.S. 414 (1944). *See also Touby v. United States*, 500 U.S. 160 (1991). The Court has consistently rejected the idea that Congress may properly give away whatever power it wants. *See Clinton v. City of New York*, 524 U.S. 417 (1998) (the "line item veto" case, holding that Congress's attempt to give the President the power to cancel certain appropriations that have been enacted into law violated the "presentment" clause, Art. I §7, which permits only two actions of the President "before it become[s] a Law": the President, who "shall sign it" if he approves it or "return it," *i.e.*, "veto" it, if he does not).

139 295 U.S. 495 (1935).

regulate broadcast licensing in accord with the "public interest";[140] that a government department define and recover "excess profits";[141] and that the federal Price Administrator fix "fair and equitable" commodities prices.[142] In the recent case of *Whitman v. American Trucking Associations, Inc.*,[143] the Clean Air Act directed the Environmental Protection Agency to set maximum air pollution levels that would be "requisite to protect the public health" with "an adequate margin of safety." The Court interpreted the phrase as supplying "intelligible principles" to guide the agency in promulgating air standards that were "sufficient, but not more than necessary" to protect public health. It pointedly rejected the Court of Appeals requirement that Congress provide "determinate criterion" for saying "how much [harm] is too much."[144]

Anti-delegation rules have somewhat more force on the state level, where one can find an occasional case decision striking down a state administrative rule for improper delegation of legislative power. But most states follow an approach similar to that used for the federal government.[145]

2. Agencies Exercising Judicial Power

In a common sense meaning of "judicial power," the hearing divisions of agencies clearly exercise judicial power when they hold hearings and decide disputes. If this is so, a potential problem arises with Article III of the Constitution, which specifies that "[t]he judicial Power of the United States, shall be vested in" federal courts staffed by "Article III" judges — judges whose independence in decision-making is protected by lifetime tenure subject only to removal by impeachment. Administrative adjudicators, sometimes referred to as "Article I" judges, do not have lifetime tenure.

The Court has had some difficulty with this issue. On the one hand, administrative agencies are a practical necessity in the modern age. On the other, there must be *some* limits on Congress's ability to assign the task of adjudicating disputes to adjudicators without lifetime tenure. Otherwise, Congress could give *all* federal judicial business to agencies or other non-life-tenured judges over whom it has greater influence. This would render the lifetime tenure requirements of Article III a nullity and defeat the Framers' purpose to establish a federal judiciary that is independent of Congress's will.[146]

---

140 *National Broadcasting Co. v. United States*, 319 U.S. 190, 225-226 (1943).

141 *Lichter v. United States*, 334 U.S. 742, 778-786 (1948).

142 *Yakus v. United States*, 321 U.S. 414, 426-427 (1944). *See generally* Peter H. Aranson, Ernest Gellhorn, Glen O. Robinson, *A Theory of Legislative Delegation*, 68 Cornell L. Rev. 1 (1982). Some have suggested that the *Schechter* case might still be good law on its facts since it involved a grant of open-ended power directly to the President (rather than to an agency) to make rules in a vast area (reorganization of the economy) without any of the procedural requirements for promulgating rules that agencies must follow today. Others have suggested even more broadly that the anti-delegation doctrine might be on its way back. *See* AMAN & MAYTON, *supra* note 2, at 23-27, and *National Cable Television Ass'n, Inc. v. United States*, 415 U.S. 336 (1974).

143 531 U.S. 457 (2001).

144 Concurring Justices chided the majority for "pretend[ing]... that the authority delegated to the EPA is somehow not 'legislative power,'" rather than "frankly acknowledging that the power delegated to the EPA is 'legislative' but nevertheless conclud[ing] that the delegation is constitutional because adequately limited by the terms of the authorizing statute. Acknowledging this is no different, they maintained, than what occurs routinely within the executive branch, where "the authority granted to . . . federal law enforcement agents is properly characterized as 'Executive' even though not exercised by the President." 531 U.S. at 488 (Stevens, J., concurring).

145 *See* AMAN & MAYTON, *supra* note 2, at 7.

146 Federal magistrate judges, bankruptcy judges and many of the judges on federal courts with specialized jurisdiction are also Article I judges. *See* Chapter V, pp. 175, 186-187. As such, the same constitutional difficulties and solutions that justify agency adjudicators apply to them.

There are three theories under which administrative adjudication by agencies is permitted, none of them entirely satisfying.

Public vs. Private Rights   The traditional approach to the problem has been to divide potential judicial business into two categories: "public rights" and "private rights."[147] According to the Court, Article III judges are required only for adjudication of disputes over *private* rights. "Private rights" cases are tort, contract, property or other suits between private parties, including claims for damages between private parties provided for in federal statutes. The category also includes all criminal cases. These private rights are thought to be at the "core" of "judicial business" that cannot be handled by agencies, but must instead be adjudicated — even at the initial trial level — by an Article III judge or by a state court. "Public rights" are said to arise in matters between the government and individuals where the rights have been created by Congress and are thus subject to its control.[148] Public rights are said to include public benefits and privileges, such as Social Security payments, veterans' benefits, food stamps, and licenses. Congress can constitutionally create public rights, and therefore it can assign determinations regarding public rights to purely administrative Article I adjudicators.

The categories of public rights just listed are certainly the most numerous types of cases that administrative agencies handle and the private rights cases are the kinds of cases judges traditionally handled before the advent of the modern administrative state. However, the public-private rights distinction does not make much sense in terms of the purpose of Article III's lifetime tenure requirement as a safeguard against congressional influences on federal judges.[149] Under this view, cases particularly vulnerable to congressional interest and intervention should be protected from congressional interference by assigning them to independent, Article III judges. Yet, many *public* rights cases, such as suits to protect and expand government healthcare and welfare assistance or to stop pollution or deforestation on federal lands, are exactly the kinds of cases that invite political interference. At the same time, many *private* rights cases, such as contract disputes between corporations and suits by creditors on debts, are not likely to attract much political attention and are therefore the least in need of a judge who has lifetime tenure. In many ways, the public-private distinction would make more sense if it were *reversed*.

Agencies as "Adjuncts" to Courts   An alternative rationale explains Article I agency adjudicators as "adjuncts" to an Article III court. Under this theory, agencies are allowed to adjudicate cases, even cases centered on private rights, on the principle that they are "assisting" the Article III court in deciding the case, with the Article III court making the *ultimate* decision. Thus, in the typical agency arrangement, the agency adjudicates the case in the first instance, but there will be *judicial review* of that decision by an Article III court. Thus, "the essential attributes of judicial power" are reserved to Article III courts, and the rule against non-Article III adjudication of private rights is not offended.[150]

---

147 *See Northern Pipeline Co. v. Marathon Pipeline Co.*, 458 U.S. 50 (1982) (legislation authorizing bankruptcy judges with 14-year terms to adjudicate private rights cases violates Article III).

148 *Atlas Roofing v. Occupational Safety and Health Review Comm'n*, 430 U.S. 442, 450 (1977). Thus, under this theory Congress need not afford *any* judicial or administrative hearing remedies in public rights cases other than those required by procedural due process. *See supra*, pp. 205-209.

149 *See* Chapter I, p. 9.

150 *See Commodity Futures Trading Comm'n v. Schor*, 478 U.S. 833 (1986), quoting *Crowell v. Benson*, 285 U.S. 22, 51 (1932).

The problem with this theory is that it does not comport with reality. Most administrative agency adjudications are really final and binding when rendered without any need for the agency to seek approval of an Article III court.[151] Even when there is judicial review, virtually conclusive effect is given to the Article I adjudicator's administrative fact-finding and courts give great deference even on issues of law.[152] Indeed, with respect to agency decisions, one could argue that it is the Article III court, not the administrative agency, that operates as the adjunct.

The Functional Approach   Because of difficulties with the public-private right test and the adjunct theories, the Supreme Court has seemed to back off both theories. It has taken a "functional" approach similar to that employed to resolve other separation of powers problems: it has interpreted Article III's judicial qualifications requirement in a manner that may not do complete justice to its wording, but generally serves the constitutional *function* it was designed to serve.[153] Applying the functional approach to Article I adjudicators, the Court has sought to balance two opposing factors: (1) Congress's interest in efficiency and expertise in having a particular category of cases decided by an Article I adjudicator and (2) the danger of congressional influence over that category of cases. Using this standard, the Court allowed Congress to assign some private rights disputes to administrative adjudication.[154]

The "functional" approach is subject to the usual criticisms of balancing tests — that it is impossible to balance dissimilar values against each other on any principled basis. Also, it ignores the relatively clear text of the Constitution that vests "[t]he judicial Power" in Article III judges. Indeed, the Court's "functional" approach could be seen as nothing more than a device that allows the Court to switch to a higher level of generalization to avoid clear language. As such, it effectively reduces Article III's command to a standardless test of whether a particular arrangement offends the *general idea* of separation of powers as that idea is understood by a given majority of the Court at a given time.[155]

3. Intra-Agency Separation of Powers Problems

Even if the *inter-branch* separation of powers problems just discussed can be resolved, many argue that surely there must be an *intra-branch* separation of powers problem when rule-making, enforcement and adjudication functions are located "under one roof." As James Madison stated in Federalist No. 47, "[t]he accumulation of all powers, legislative, executive, and judiciary, in the same hands, whether of one, a few, or many, and whether hereditary, self-appointed, or elective, may justly be pronounced

---

151 An exception is the NLRB, which must seek enforcement of its decisions. *See supra* p. 211.

152 *See supra* pp. 212-213. The "adjunct" theory works somewhat better in describing federal magistrates, also classified as non-tenured Article I adjudicators, who work under the close supervision of an Article III district judge and for the most part only recommend decisions. *See* Chapter V, p. 186.

153 This approach can be directly traced to Justice White's dissent in *Northern Pipeline*, the last case to take the pure public-versus-private rights approach. *See supra* note 147.

154 *See, e.g., Thomas v. Union Carbide Agricultural Products Co.*, 473 U.S. 568, (1985) (approving administrative system of reimbursement for development costs of chemical); *Commodity Futures Trading Comm'n v. Schor*, 478 U.S. 833 (1986) (approving administrative adjudication of disputes between federally-licensed securities brokers and their clients). Another constitutional objection to administrative adjudication has been that it violates the 7th Amendment right to a jury trial in civil cases. The Court has rejected this argument. *See Atlas Roofing Co. v. Occupational Safety and Health Review Comm'n*, 430 U.S. 442, 461 (1977); *Granfinanciera, S.A. v. Nordberg*, 492 U.S. 33, 61 (1989). See also AMAN & MAYTON, *supra* note 2, at 143-145 (criticizing the Court's view).

155 *See Morrison v. Olson*, 487 U.S. 654, 697 (Scalia, J., dissenting).

the very definition of tyranny."[156] In addition there are the fundamental notions that "no man shall be a judge of his own cause" and that "the same persons should not both legislate and administer the laws."[157]

Professor Strauss has observed that "[i]t is hard to say as a theoretical matter why these arrangements satisfy the structural requirements of 'separation of powers,' although it is clear beyond doubt in the eyes of courts that they do."[158] The true reason why agencies have been sustained against constitutional challenge probably lies in the fact that they serve important functions in modern government, and that hobbling them by insisting on purity in separation of powers would not be wise policy.

However, there is no need to resort to reasons of expediency, since, as just noted, separation of powers cases tend to require only that federal government power structures not offend the *functions* served by separation of powers. Under this functional approach, agencies do not violate separation of powers because they simply do not present the threat of tyranny that concerned Madison and the other Framers. First, modern agencies are relatively independent of all three branches and are not "captives" of any one branch. A greater threat would be presented if legislative, executive and judicial functions were combined in the President, the Congress or the courts. Second, while agencies enjoy a certain independence from any *one* branch, they are subject to the external and often competing influences exerted by *all three* branches noted earlier: the President appoints many agency heads and top officials, supervises their activities and may fire some of them; Congress monitors their operations through committee oversight and legislative mandates; and the courts review the legality of agency actions. This makes agencies less likely to threaten the tyranny that Madison feared.[159]

A third argument that mitigates separation of powers concerns is that the consolidation of enforcement, rule-making and adjudicative functions exists *only at the top levels*. The head of the agency and top advisors exercise these consolidated powers. Below the top level, however, functions are separated into different divisions of the agency. The most dangerous threat to fairness is probably influence by the enforcement division on the adjudicative division. Under the APA, however, ALJs may not be "responsible to or subject to" the "supervision or direction" of agency enforcement personnel, and there may be no *ex parte* contact between them regarding a pending case.[160]

B. Federalism and Sovereign Immunity Limits on Suits to Redress Illegal Federal and State Agency Action

1. Suits Against Agencies

When judicial review was discussed, we considered several situations in which agencies were sued by individuals. Suits against agencies, however, can sometimes conflict with sovereign immunity — the doctrine under which a sovereign cannot be

---

156 THE FEDERALIST PAPERS at 324 (Jacob E. Cooke ed.) (Wesleyan U. Press 1961) (originally published 1788).

157 *Buckley v. Valeo*, 424 U.S. 1, 272 (1967).

158 STRAUSS, *supra* note 2, at 16.

159 *See* STRAUSS, *supra* note 2, at 14-17. The Supreme Court has also rejected due process challenges to combining investigative and adjudicative functions in one agency. *See Withrow v. Larkin*, 421 U.S. 35 (1975) (rejecting physician's argument that due process was violated because the agency that handled charges of professional misconduct against doctors had the power to investigate those charges, present them, and then rule on their validity, unless a risk of actual bias or prejudgment could be shown).

160 5 U.S.C.A. §554(d) and *supra* p. 202. ALJs are also exempt from agency performance review and have their tenure and compensation determined by the chief civil service commission. *See generally* AMAN & MAYTON, *supra* note 2, §8.5.2.

sued without its consent. When a statute provides for judicial review, as is often the case, the sovereign arguably gives "consent." However, consent does not cover all forms of action against governmental agencies.

It is somewhat ironic that a country that threw off the yoke of monarchism and ratified a written constitution to assure a government that follows the rule of law, retains the doctrine of sovereign immunity.[161] Since sovereign immunity could make the government effectively unaccountable to the Constitution and laws, the tension between rule of law and sovereign immunity has produced caselaw and legislation that modifies immunity concepts sufficiently to allow actions for most forms of *injunctive relief*. This at least allows a court to halt an illegal practice and to order that the government conform its conduct to the law in the future.[162]

The kind of injunctive relief that is allowed varies depending on the court (whether it is state or federal) and the level of government being sued. Consequently, it is necessary to consider all possible permutations of courts and defendants.

a. Suits Against *Federal* Agencies in *Federal* Court

For actions in federal court "seeking relief *other than money damages*," the APA operates as a waiver of sovereign immunity and allows the United States to be named as a defendant.[163] Actions against the United States or its agencies for money damages are generally barred by sovereign immunity, but may be brought pursuant to certain statutes. Primary among them are the Federal Tort Claims Act (FTCA) and the Tucker Act. The FTCA, enacted in 1946, provides for tort liability of the federal government "in the same manner and to the same extent as a private individual under like circumstances."[164] The Tucker Act, first enacted in 1855, provides for recovery of damages in "cases not sounding in tort," meaning primarily government contracts cases.[165] However, in keeping with the notion that there could be no suit in the absence of a congressional waiver of sovereign immunity, Congress has made exceptions to its waiver of immunity and exempted the United States from trial by jury and punitive damages.[166] In general, "[w]hen the United States enters into contract relations, its rights and duties therein are governed generally by the law applicable to contracts between private individuals."[167]

b. Suits Against *Federal* Agencies in *State* Court

The APA's waiver of federal sovereign immunity explicitly waives it only for suit in *federal* court. Moreover, because of the nature of the federal structure contemplated by the Constitution and particularly the supremacy of federal law, state courts have no

---

161 *See* ERWIN CHEMERINSKY, FEDERAL JURISDICTION, 5TH ED. §9.2.1 (Aspen 2007).

162 *See supra* note 83.

163 5 U.S.C.A. §702 (emphasis supplied). Before the APA was amended to waive immunity, suits against the U.S. for injunctive relief were permitted against the responsible officers, similar to the state officer suits described *infra* p. 225. *See Larson v. Domestic & Foreign Commerce Corp.*, 337 U.S. 682 (1949). *See generally* GREGORY C. SISK, LITIGATION WITH THE FEDERAL GOVERNMENT, 4TH ED. (ALI-ABA 2006).

164 28 U.S.C.A. §§2671-2680. The FTCA in §2680 excludes certain kinds of claims, including claims arising in a foreign country, claims that involve the exercise of a "discretionary function," claim arising out of military activity during time of war, claims concerning fiscal operations, or any claim for intentional torts committed by non-law enforcement personnel.

165 28 U.S.C.A. §1491(a)(1).

166 For a discussion of the FTCA and the Tucker Act, *see* CHEMERINSKY, *supra* note 161, §§9.2.3-9.2.4.

167 *Mobil Oil Exploration & Producing Southeast v. United States*, 530 U.S. 604 (2000) (government must refund $158 million paid for oil exploration rights by oil companies after it breached contract by following law imposing new requirements for approval of leases).

power to review or order relief with respect to the actions of federal officials or agencies. This rule was established in *Tarble's Case*.[168] In that case, the Supreme Court held that a state court in Wisconsin could not issue a writ of *habeas corpus* against a federal army recruiting officer ordering the release of an allegedly underage soldier. In addition, Congress has provided that federal officials may remove any state court suits against them to federal court.[169]

c. Suits Against *State* Agencies in *Federal* Court

Plaintiffs seeking redress for state violations of federal law have traditionally sought relief in federal rather than state court. Three factors account for the popularity of federal courts in such cases: the fact that federal judges are not part of the state governmental machinery; the expertise of federal judges on issues of federal law; and, the insulation of federal judges from political pressure due to life tenure. As discussed in Chapter I, when the Constitution was being debated, the question of whether states gave up their sovereign immunity from suit in *federal* court arose. In the 1791 case of *Chisholm v. Georgia*,[170] the Supreme Court decided that Article III's grant of federal judicial power over suits in which a state is a party abolished state immunity from suit in the *federal* courts, regardless of whatever immunity the state might enjoy in its own courts. Congress and the states responded with passage and ratification of the 11th Amendment in 1798, reinstating that immunity. The immunity continues to exist today despite the diminution in states' rights wrought by the Civil War and the 14th Amendment's limits on state action.[171]

The literal wording of the 11th Amendment does not bar suits for enforcement of *federal rights* brought by citizens against their *own* states. Nonetheless, the Supreme Court in the 1890 case of *Hans v. Louisiana*, held that, notwithstanding the wording of the 11th Amendment, such suits were nonetheless barred.[172] However, caselaw interpreting the 11th Amendment has worked a division between permissible injunctive relief and prohibited damages relief roughly similar to the division created by the APA for federal court suits against the federal government. The Supreme Court in *Ex parte Young*[173] held that, while sovereign immunity prevents suits against *states*, it does not bar federal law claims against state *officials in their official capacities* at least where the suit is for prospective injunctive relief. *Young* created the fiction that an official acting contrary to superior federal law was for that reason no longer a state official and could be subjected to suit for such "individual conduct." However, this theory is a "legal fiction" since the relief awarded in an official-capacity officer suit binds the state and

---

168 80 U.S. (13 Wall.) 397 (1871).

169 28 U.S.C.A. §1442(a)(1). *But see Mesa v. California*, 489 U.S. 121 (1989) (removal is proper only if the defendant official has some defense to the suit or prosecution based on federal law). *Tarble's Case* followed and resolved issues raised by the vigorous use of state courts to protect escaped slaves from being recaptured and sent back to the south on order of federal "slave commissioners." This history is related in the Gibbons law review article cited in note 88 of Chapter V.

170 2 U.S. (2 Dall.) 419 (1793). *Chisholm v. Georgia* was discussed in Chapter I, p. 37.

171 These limits are primarily the due process and equal protection clauses. The argument has been made that the 14th Amendment of its own force repealed the 11th Amendment, but the Court avoided deciding the question. *See Milliken v. Bradley*, 433 U.S. 267, 290 n.2 (1977).

172 134 U.S. 1 (1890). The 11th Amendment also applies to claims against states brought in federal *administrative agencies* as well. *Federal Maritime Comm'n v. South Carolina State Ports Authority*, 535 U.S. 743 (2002). Sovereign immunity under the 11th Amendment does not bar suits against municipal subdivisions of states — cities, counties, townships and the like — unless those municipalities are acting as the "alter ego" of the state, *i.e.* serving simply as the agent of the state in carrying out what is really a state program. *Pennhurst State School and Hospital v. Halderman*, 465 U.S. 89 (1984).

173 209 U.S. 123 (1908).

thus has the same effect as relief ordered against the state itself.[174] Moreover, the "officer-suit" fiction does not go so far as to allow an official-capacity officer suit for *damages* collectable from the state treasury.[175]

Congress has the power, if it chooses, to override state sovereign immunity from damages relief by passing a statute, if it makes clear on the face of that statute its intent to abrogate state immunity. However, Congress may do so only if it acts pursuant to powers granted to it by amendments ratified after 1798 — when the 11th Amendment was ratified. Since most of Congress's powers come from Article I (ratified 1789) and it does not qualify, the most important power for abrogation purposes is in section 5 of the 14th Amendment (ratified 1868).[176] As noted in Chapter IX, this power has been interpreted narrowly.[177]

Official capacity suits against state officials in federal court are generally asserted pursuant to 42 U.S.C.A. §1983, the Civil Rights Act of 1871, which makes "[e]very person" acting "under color of" state law liable for injunctive or damages relief in federal court for violations of federal law. Suits for relief against administrative agency heads are facilitated by the fact that there is no requirement that the §1983 plaintiffs exhaust state administrative or judicial remedies.[178] However, there are three limits on the use of §1983 as a method of federal judicial review of state agency action. The first is that the plaintiff can raise only federal constitutional or statutory issues since the statute is addressed only to deprivations of federal rights. Second, relief may not include any accrued retroactive money judgment against a state agency, as discussed above. Third, if the state administrative proceeding is an enforcement action brought *against* the would-be federal plaintiff by the state agency, the federal court will be required to abstain from jurisdiction to permit the state proceeding to take its course. If those proceedings are decided against the party, that party will be relegated to state court judicial review.[179]

d. Suits Against *State* Agencies in *State* Court

As stated in Chapter I, states retain whatever rights and powers they had as sovereign international states, except to the extent that they gave up those rights and powers in the Constitution. Among the rights retained is a state's sovereign immunity from suit in its own courts absent consent. However, many states have allowed suit on

---

174 The concept of suing the government by suing its officials was borrowed from English practice where a similar fiction was employed to allow some suits against the Crown. *See* Louis Jaffe, *Suits Against Governments and Officers: Sovereign Immunity*, 77 HARV. L. REV. 1 (1963).

175 *Edelman v. Jordan*, 415 U.S. 651 (1974).

176 *Seminole Tribe v. Florida*, 517 U.S. 44 (1996), *overruling Pennsylvania v. Union Gas Co.*, 491 U.S. 1 (1989). One example of the exercise of this power is 42 U.S.C.A. §2000d-7 (allowing suits against states for discrimination under several civil rights laws). *See generally* CHEMERINSKY, *supra* note 161, §§7.1-7.7.

177 *See* pp. 343-344 and *Board of Trustees of the University of Alabama v. Garrett*, 531 U.S. 356 (2001) (reading Congress's §5 powers narrowly as not authorizing it to abrogate state sovereign immunity in the absence of specific findings that such abrogation is a proportionate response to the problem).

178 *Patsy v. Florida International University*, 457 U.S. 496 (1982). The plaintiff may be bound by certain findings of fact made at any trial-type state administrative hearing, if the federal plaintiff did in fact pursue state administrative remedies. *See University of Tennessee v. Elliott*, 478 U.S. 788 (1986).

179 *See Ohio Civil Rights Comm'n v. Dayton Christian Schools*, 477 U.S. 619 (1986) (federal court must abstain in favor of pending state civil rights administrative proceeding against federal plaintiff). This is part of "*Younger* abstention," discussed in Chapter V, p. 196.

terms similar to those allowed by the federal government, discussed above. Other states have abolished or waived their sovereign immunity completely.[180]

Nonetheless, the Supreme Court has extended 11th Amendment immunity — just discussed above — to bar suits filed in *state* court, despite the terms of that Amendment limiting its application to suits in federal court.[181] The rationale was that states were protected by an unspoken constitutionally-based sovereign immunity from suit, of which the 11th Amendment was only one manifestation. Thus, for *state-law* claims in state court, state law sovereign immunity governs the permissibility of those claims. For *federal-law* claims in state court, the same 11th Amendment that applies in federal courts determines the circumstances under which suits are permitted — usually limited to prospective injunctive relief.[182]

2. Suits Against Administrative Officials for Personal Liability

Despite the sovereign immunity of governmental bodies, it is sometimes possible to recover a *personal* money judgment against an administrative *official* for bad faith illegal actions. These suits are not barred by sovereign immunity because the suit is solely against the official and does not result in any government liability.[183]

Suits Against State Officials for Violating Federal Rights It should be noted as well that personal damages suits are generally possible *only* against administrative officials. The 1871 Civil Rights Act, discussed above, provides broadly for suit in state or federal court for damages liability against "every person" acting under color of state law who violates federal rights. However, there are several common law immunities that the Court has presumed that Congress meant to continue to apply despite the broad statutory language. Legislators,[184] judges[185] and prosecutors are immune for action taken in those capacities.[186] However, they are liable to suits for personal damages when they take action in their *administrative* capacities.[187]

---

180 *See* PROSSER & KEETON'S HORNBOOK ON TORTS, 5TH ED. §§131-132 (West 1988). More detail about the immunity of states from tort liability is set out in Chapter XI, p. 413.

181 *Alden v. Maine*, 527 U.S. 706 (1999) (suit by state employees under federal Fair Labor Standards Act is barred by state sovereign immunity).

182 If 11th Amendment jurisprudence proves too much for literal-minded readers, its incongruities have amused others as well. *See* William Burnham, *"Beam Me Up, There's No Intelligent Life Here": A Dialog on the 11th Amendment with Lawyers from Mars*, 75 NEBRASKA L. REV. 551 (1996).

183 *See Scheuer v. Rhodes*, 416 U.S. 232 (1974) (suit for personal injuries by college students against Ohio governor and National Guard soldiers called out to quell student unrest not barred by 11th Amendment). *See generally* CHEMERINSKY, *supra* note 161, §7.1-7.7.

184 *Tenney v. Brandhove*, 341 U.S. 367 (1951) (state legislators); *Eastland v. United States Serviceman's Fund*, 421 U.S. 491 (1975) (federal legislators); *Bogan v. Scott-Harris*, 523 U.S. 44 (1998) (local legislators). High-level administrators or judges who act as "legislators" by promulgating rules may also be entitled to legislative immunity. *See Supreme Court of Virginia v. Consumers Union*, 446 U.S. 719 (1980). Legislative immunity applies to bar not only damages, but injunctive relief as well.

185 *Stump v. Sparkman*, 435 U.S. 349 (1978) (state judge who illegally ordered sterilization of minor was immune from damages; though order was not authorized by law, it was a judicial act); *Butz v. Economu*, 438 U.S. 478 (1978) (federal administrative law judge entitled to same judicial immunity as regular judges).

186 *Imbler v. Pachtman*, 424 U.S. 409 (1976); *Buckley v. Fitzsimmons*, 509 U.S. 259 (1993). *See also Briscoe v. LaHue*, 460 U.S. 325 (1983) (police officer witnesses).

187 *See Davis v. Passman*, 544 F.2d 865 (5th Cir. 1977), *rev'd on other grounds* 442 U.S. 228 (1979) (congressman may be liable for sex discrimination in hiring his staff since that action was administrative rather than legislative); *Burns v. Reed*, 500 U.S. 478 (1991) (prosecutor not entitled to immunity for giving erroneous advice to police, since that was an administrative act not connected with representation of government in court). A clear and concise summary of the complicated law in this area can be found in CHEMERINSKY, *supra* note 161, §§8.1-8.11.

Administrative actors are liable only if they acted in "bad faith" — defined as action which the official reasonably should have known would violate the plaintiff's rights.[188] The determination of bad faith is an objective one and has nothing really to do with the actual state of mind of the defendant. It is a purely legal question of whether the official's actions violated clearly established federal rights. The Court has recently stated that "[t]he qualified immunity standard gives ample room for mistaken judgments by protecting all but the plainly incompetent and those who knowingly violated the law."[189] Compensatory damages may be awarded and punitive damages are available if evil motive or intent or recklessness is shown.[190]

Suits Against Federal Officials There is no statute like §1983 providing for a private right of action for damages for violation of the Constitution or federal law against *federal* officials. However, the Court in *Bivens v Six Unknown Named Agents of the Federal Bureau of Narcotics*[191] implied a private right to sue for damages for bad faith constitutional violations. All the common law immunities set out above for state officials apply to their federal counterparts.[192] For all other claims, if federal officials are acting within the scope of their official capacity, the suit is treated as if it were against the United States and is handled in accordance with the FTCA. If the federal employees involved are determined not to have been acting within the scope of their employment, then suit may proceed in state court under applicable state law.[193]

---

188 *See Harlow v. Fitzgerald*, 457 U.S. 800 (1982) (suit against Department of Defense officials for retaliatory discharge of plaintiff who exposed cost overruns).

189 *Hunter v. Bryant*, 502 U.S. 224 (1991) (*per curiam*).

190 *Smith v. Wade*, 461 U.S. 30 (1983).

191 403 U.S. 388 (1971).

192 One that is unique to the federal context is that the President is absolutely immune from any damages liability for actions taken pursuant to his office. *Nixon v. Fitzgerald*, 457 U.S. 731 (1982). However, there is no immunity for a President, even temporary immunity while President, from suit for actions taken before becoming President. *See Clinton v. Jones*, 520 U.S. 681 (1997).

193 28 U.S.C.A. §2679.

CHAPTER VII

CIVIL PROCEDURE

Part I of this chapter traces the course of a typical civil lawsuit. Trial procedure was discussed extensively in Chapter III, so the emphasis here is on pretrial procedures, relief available after trial and the effect of judgments. Part II of this chapter considers some of the complexities that a federal system creates for litigation of civil claims as a result of multiple overlapping laws and court systems. Under this heading, we consider the questions of the proper court for filing a lawsuit and what body of law must be applied.

PART I: The Course of a Civil Lawsuit

As noted in Chapter III, procedure during trial is quite similar in civil and criminal cases. There are substantial differences in pretrial procedure, however.[1]

The rules of civil procedure vary among the states, but most state rules are similar to the Federal Rules of Civil Procedure (FRCP). Passed in 1938, the FRCP have been adopted virtually unchanged by half of the states and the other half have borrowed significantly from them. Consequently, in the material below, procedure is explained by reference to the FRCP.[2]

A. The Pleading Stage of the Case

1. Plaintiff's Complaint

A civil action begins when the plaintiff files a "complaint" with the clerk of the court's office. The FRCP requires that the complaint contain (1) a statement of the grounds upon which subject matter jurisdiction of the court is based, (2) "a short and plain statement of the claim showing that the pleader is entitled to relief" and (3) a demand for the relief that the pleader seeks.[3]

At common law, one wrong step in pleading meant that the litigant's case was dismissed or a defense was lost. This has given way to a more liberal view that facilitates getting to the merits of the dispute — what has been called "notice pleading." Notice pleading, as the term implies, requires only enough facts, in the words of a leading case, "to give the defendant fair notice of what the plaintiff's claim is and the grounds on which it rests."[4]

The appendix of forms of the FRCP sets out the following example of such "notice pleading" with a complaint for negligence arising out of an automobile accident:

1. Allegation of jurisdiction.

2. On June 1, 1936, in a public highway called Boylston Street in Boston, Massachusetts, defendant negligently drove a motor vehicle against plaintiff who was then crossing said highway.

---

1 For more detail on civil procedure *see* JACK H. FRIEDENTHAL, MARY KAY KANE & ARTHUR R. MILLER, HORNBOOK ON CIVIL PROCEDURE, 4TH ED. (West 2005). A student text is JOSEPH W. GLANNON, CIVIL PROCEDURE: EXAMPLES AND EXPLANATIONS, 6TH ED. (Aspen 2008). *See* also CHARLES ALAN WRIGHT, HORNBOOK ON THE LAW OF FEDERAL COURTS, 6TH ED. (West 2002) and ERWIN CHEMERINSKY, FEDERAL JURISDICTION, 5TH ED. (Aspen 2007). An incisive volume providing a perspective on civil litigation in the United States is STEPHEN N. SUBRIN & MARGARET Y.K. WOO, LITIGATING IN AMERICA; CIVIL PROCEDURE IN CONTEXT (Aspen 2006).

2 The Federal Rules of Civil Procedure, other rules and selected federal statutes related to federal courts are collected in FEDERAL RULES OF CIVIL PROCEDURE - 2009-2010, EDUCATIONAL EDITION (West 2009).

3 FRCP 8(a).

4 *Conley v. Gibson*, 355 U.S. 41, 47 (1957).

3. As a result plaintiff was thrown down and had his leg broken and was otherwise injured, was prevented from transacting his business, suffered great pain of body and mind, and incurred expenses for medical attention and hospitalization in the sum of one thousand dollars.

Wherefore plaintiff demands judgement against defendant in the sum of _____ dollars and costs.

Since complaints are written by lawyers, few are quite this succinct and to the point, but there is no requirement that the complaint go much beyond these conclusory allegations. Pleadings of this sort are of limited use in determining the facts underlying the claim. Instead, the facts are explored directly through the device of "discovery." An exchange of "notice" pleadings also does little to distill out the issues to be tried or to screen out insufficient claims. Instead, these functions are performed by pretrial conferences and summary judgment procedures, discussed below.

Some states, among them California, require "fact" pleading. While fact pleading is somewhat more demanding of the pleader than "notice" pleading, these systems also provide all the modern advantages of liberal discovery and pretrial procedures. In addition, even the FRCP require that some matters be pleaded "with particularity," such as fraud, mistake and special damages.[5]

Service of Process When the plaintiff files the complaint with the court clerk, the clerk issues a "summons." This is an order of the court directing the defendant to respond to the complaint or suffer a "default judgment."[6] The plaintiff must arrange to have the summons and complaint "served" on the defendant by physically handing them to the defendant or leaving them at his or her home or office with an adult residing or working there with instructions to give them to the defendant. Many jurisdictions allow mailing of the summons and complaint to the defendant with a request that the defendant waive the necessity of in-hand service. When the defendant resides out of state, service by mail is permitted.[7] In addition, a court may expressly order that other means be used.[8] By whatever means accomplished, service of the summons and complaint is necessary to establish "personal jurisdiction" of the court over the defendant, which is necessary for the court to issue a binding judgment against the defendant.[9]

---

5 *See* FRCP 9(b) and (g). Despite the Supreme Court's overall insistence that general allegations are sufficient except as otherwise provided in FRCP 9 or by statute, *see, e.g., Leatherman v. Tarrant County Narcotics Unit,* 507 U.S. 163 (1993) (no specific pleading rule for civil rights cases), the Court in recent years has insisted on specific pleading in anti-trust cases. *See Bell Atlantic Corp. v. Twombly,* 550 U.S. 544 (2007) (in an antitrust conspiracy case requiring that the complaint set out "enough factual matter" to demonstrate "plausible grounds to infer an agreement" among the defendants). *See* Chapter XV, p. 609 n. 164. In a later case, it indicated *Twombly* could well apply to other types of cases. *Ashcroft v. Iqbal,* ___ U.S. ___, 129 S.Ct. 1937 (2009) (applying *Twombly* to reject vague allegations that high federal officials were responsible for plaintiff's harsh incarceration). At present, it is unclear when the *Twombly* standard will be invoked and when it will not. The Court has not yet settled on a clear rule for ascertaining what kinds of allegations must be pleaded specifically and what kinds may be pleaded generally.

6 FRCP 55. A default judgment is a judgment entered against a defendant for failure to contest a case. The amount of the judgment is determined by the clerk of the court when it is for a liquidated sum (such as for a loan plus interest) and is determined by the judge or jury in a summary trial if it is for an unliquidated amount (such as for personal injuries in a tort case).

7 *See* FRCP 4.

8 One federal court permitted service of process by e-mail for an international defendant. *See Rio Properties, Inc. v. Rio International Interlink,* 284 F.3d 1007 (9th Cir. 2002).

9 Personal jurisdiction was introduced in Chapter I, p. 28, and is discussed in its interstate context *infra* pp. 253-259.

2. The Defendant's Response to the Complaint

The defendant responding to the complaint has two options. The first is to raise one or more procedural defenses that are allowed to be raised by a "motion to dismiss." The second option is to contest the complaint on its merits by filing an "answer."[10] Whichever of the two alternatives is chosen, the defendant's response must be filed with the court within 20 days after service of the complaint unless an extension of time is obtained from the plaintiff or the court.[11]

Motion to Dismiss   The defendant has the option of asserting certain procedural defenses in a motion to dismiss. Those grounds are challenges to the court's jurisdiction (personal or subject-matter), improper venue (location of the court where the case is filed), improper service of process, failure of the plaintiff to join an indispensable party, or failure of the plaintiff to state a legal claim.[12] Asserting these grounds by motion is not required and the defendant could just as well include them in the answer. However, proceeding by motion allows the defendant to adopt a more aggressive posture by forcing the plaintiff to respond to the motions immediately. In addition, the court must dispose of these procedural objections before the defendant is required to file an answer responding to the plaintiff's complaint on its merits. If the motion to dismiss is granted, of course, the defendant may never have to file an answer.

The ground of "failure to state a claim upon which relief can be granted"[13] deserves some further discussion. It is the only ground relating to the merits of the case that is allowed to be raised by motion this early in the suit. A motion made on this ground is an important early screening device for claims. It tests whether, assuming hypothetically that all the facts alleged in the complaint are true, the plaintiff would be able to recover.

Complaints dismissed for failure to state a claim generally fall into two categories. The plaintiff may have alleged facts sufficient to make out a claim if such a claim existed in the law, but the law does not provide for claims of this type. For example, a complaint alleging all the elements of intentional infliction of emotional distress would be dismissed on this basis in a state that does not recognize that particular tort.[14] Or the plaintiff may have failed to allege sufficient facts to make out all the essential elements of a claim that *is* authorized by the law. For example, the plaintiff's complaint may assert facts that otherwise sound like a case calling for the application of the well-established tort of negligence, but the acts or omissions of the defendant that are alleged do not amount to negligence.

Answer   The defendant's answer contests the plaintiff's claim on the merits. The main parts of the answer are the responses to the allegations in the plaintiff's complaint and "affirmative defenses." In the responses to the allegations, the defendant is required to admit, deny or state lack of knowledge as to each allegation in the complaint (lack of knowledge is treated as a denial). Affirmative defenses stated in the answer may include such grounds as contributory negligence, satisfaction of the claim, estoppel or

---

10 *See* FRCP 8 and 9.

11 FRCP 12(a). Sixty days is allowed for response if the defendant agrees to waive service of process. FRCP 4(d)(3) and 12(a)(1)(B).

12 *See* FRCP 12(b).

13 FRCP 12(b)(6).

14 Thus, many appellate cases that make new law are appeals from grants or denials of a motion to dismiss for failure to state a claim. Similarly, a plaintiff can challenge a legally insufficient defense by filing a "motion to strike." FRCP 12(f).

fraud,[15] or they may be one or more of the procedural defenses mentioned above. Affirmative defenses are so called because alleging them usually requires that the defendant go beyond simply denying the plaintiff's allegations and set out additional affirmative facts that avoid the claim.

In a third part of the answer, the defendant may include any "counterclaims" against the plaintiff.[16] The federal courts, as well as most state courts, make counterclaims compulsory if they arise out of the same transaction or occurrence as the plaintiff's claim. Thus, failure to assert related counterclaims will bar their later assertion in a separate suit. All other counterclaims are merely "permissive counterclaims," meaning that the defendant may choose to bring them in response to the plaintiff's claim or bring them later in a separate action. Also possible are "cross-claims," claims that are filed by one co-party against another co-party, usually co-defendants. For example, assume in a three-car collision among A, B, and C, that A sues B and C. If B has injuries and thinks the accident was C's fault, B may file a cross-claim against co-defendant C. If B thinks the accident was A's fault, B may counterclaim against the plaintiff A.[17]

A final method of defense applies if a defendant in a suit believes that someone not joined as a party to the lawsuit has a duty to indemnify the defendant for all or part of what the defendant may have to pay the plaintiff. In such a situation, a "third-party claim" may be asserted by way of "impleading" the responsible party into the lawsuit. For example, if P sues D because D's truck hit P and the accident happened because the brakes on the truck failed, D may implead the company that repaired the brakes on that truck as a third party defendant.[18]

Amendment of Pleadings   If a motion to dismiss for failure to state a claim is granted for failure to allege sufficient facts, the plaintiff usually is allowed to "amend" the complaint if there is reason to believe the facts exist, but were simply left out of the complaint. The defendant has a similar opportunity to amend if the defendant has omitted or has inadequately set out a defense in the answer. The rules also provide generally that permission to amend pleadings "shall be granted freely when justice so requires."[19]

"Rule 11" Duties and Sanctions   Under FRCP 11, lawyers and parties who file pleadings, motions or other papers, or otherwise assert a position in court thereby certify that they have investigated the grounds for the relief requested and that the request is well-grounded in law and fact or is supported by non-frivolous arguments for a change in law. If documents filed or positions asserted in court do not live up to this standard, the judge may award "sanctions" against the attorney or party, including the full amount

---

15   FRCP 8(c).

16   *See* FRCP 13(a) and (b). For simplicity's sake, the discussion in the text refers to a defendant's counterclaiming against the plaintiff in response to the plaintiff's claim. However counterclaims may be filed against *any* opposing parties.

17   *See* FRCP 13(g).

18   *See* FRCP 14(a). Impleader enforces only an indemnity relationship between the existing defendant and the third party defendant. Thus, an existing defendant cannot implead a third-party defendant on the ground that the third party is liable to the plaintiff directly, not to the existing defendant.

19   FRCP 15(a). A plaintiff can also amend a complaint without court permission before an answer is filed and a defendant can similarly amended an answer as of right within 20 days after it is filed. New claims added through amendment "relate back" to the date the original complaint was filed when they arise out of the same transaction or occurrence as the original claim, thus avoiding any problems with statutes of limitations. FRCP 15(c).

of the opposing party's attorney fees that were made necessary by the groundless lawsuit or defense.[20]

These provisions of FRCP 11, first approved in 1983, have been the source of some controversy. Critics have charged that the rule as applied discriminates against plaintiffs, particularly those who assert novel constitutional and other claims or those who face uncooperative defendants from whom they need information to substantiate their claim. Other criticism has been over the vast amount of "satellite litigation" it has spawned over whether and to what extent sanctions should have been imposed. As a result, amendments have softened the rule's impact somewhat. Sanctions have been made optional with the judge and any monetary sanctions usually are paid to the court rather than the other party, thus reducing the incentive to pursue them. There is also set a 21-day "grace period" within which a party can withdraw the offending paper and avoid sanctions. Further, unsupported factual allegations are allowed to be made if they "are likely to have evidentiary support after a reasonable opportunity for further investigation or discovery."[21]

3. Joinder of Claims and Parties

Joinder of Claims   Joinder of multiple claims is very liberal. At the plaintiff's option, a complaint may combine all the claims the plaintiff has against the defendant even if they are unrelated. Thus, claims for negligence, breach of contract and slander, all arising from different events occurring at different times, may all be joined in one suit against a single defendant or they may be sued upon separately.[22] However, if multiple theories of recovery or forms of relief arise from the *same* transaction or occurrence, the plaintiff must combine them in the same complaint or be barred from raising them later in a separate suit. For example, claims for strict liability, negligence and breach of a warranty, as redress for a single injury from a defective product, must be asserted in the same lawsuit.[23]

Joinder of Parties   Joinder of parties is somewhat more limited, but still liberal. Plaintiffs may join together or may join multiple defendants on their claims if all the claims arise out of the same transaction or occurrence and have an issue of law or fact in common. If the case becomes too complex to try in one proceeding, the court has the discretion to order separate trials.[24] Similarly, if there are separate actions pending with overlapping facts that could beneficially be tried together, those cases can be consolidated or, in some circumstances, can be consolidated for pretrial proceedings.[25]

Interpleader   "Interpleader" allows a party holding a disputed sum of money to deposit that money in court and join all the claimants to it as defendants. The court will

---

20 This is an exception to the usual rule in the U.S. that each side has to bear its own legal costs regardless of outcome. *See infra* p. 247.

21 FRCP 11(b)(4). Discovery is discussed *infra* pp. 235-240.

22 FRCP 18(a).

23 This mandatory joinder result is not required by the FRCP, but by the doctrine of claim preclusion or *res judicata*, discussed below in the section on the effect of judgments, which prohibits "claim splitting." *See infra* p. 248.

24 FRCP 20(a) and (b), and FRCP 42(b).

25 *See* FRCP 42(a) and 28 U.S.C.A. §1407. In complex cases, consolidations for pretrial proceedings under the cited statute are administered by the Judicial Panel on Multi-District Litigation. Mass disaster cases typically are processed by the Panel. *See, e.g., In re Air Disaster at Lockerbie, Scotland*, 709 F.Supp. 231 (Jud. Pan. Mult. Lit. 1989). *See also* Multiparty, Multiforum Trial Jurisdiction Act of 2002, 28 U.S.C.A. §1369, which provides for federal jurisdiction over "accidents" in which over 74 people are killed at a single "discrete location."

determine who is entitled to the money and has the power to enjoin all other litigation involving that particular money. The advantage of interpleader is that it forces the claimants to litigate their claims in a single suit, thus saving the stakeholder from having to defend multiple litigation in multiple forums. An example is an insurance company that is uncertain which of several beneficiaries to pay.[26]

Class Actions A "class action" is a suit in which one or more representatives of a group of people with similar claims file suit on behalf of the entire group.[27] These individuals representing the class, called the "named plaintiffs," then request "class certification," which allows the action to proceed on behalf of the entire class. To order certification, the judge must find that the class is so large that joinder is not practicable, that the claims of class members have common legal or factual issues and are similar in nature, and that the named plaintiffs will adequately represent the interests of the unnamed class members.[28] Adequate representation is essential for the judgment to be binding on the unnamed class members as a matter of due process.[29] When money damages are sought, notice to absent class members must be provided to allow class members to "opt out" of the class and file their own suit if they choose. In the event of a settlement, the judge must determine that the settlement is fair to the class.[30]

Most class actions fall into two categories. The first comprises actions for injunctive relief against a defendant who has acted or will act in a manner that affects an entire class of people in pretty much the same way. This form of class action is often used in suits against government officials challenging the constitutionality of laws, though it is also used against private defendants, such as an employer with an alleged discriminatory employment policy or practice. Two of the most important constitutional cases decided by the Supreme Court, the *Roe v. Wade*, the abortion case, and *Brown v. Bd. of Education*, the school desegregation case, were class actions of this type.[31] The second type of class action is a suit seeking redress for a large number of monetary losses that are so small that individual pursuit of the claims would be impractical. An example is a consumer class action against a drug company for small overcharges on its medicines that it has made over the years.[32]

---

26 Congress has passed the Federal Interpleader Act liberalizing subject-matter and personal jurisdiction for many interpleader cases. *See* 28 U.S.C.A. §1335 (minimal diversity among claimants and $500 in controversy); §2361 (nationwide service of process).

27 *See* FRCP 23 and FRIEDENTHAL, KANE & MILLER, *supra* note 1, §§16.1-16-8.

28 *See Amchem Products v. Windsor*, 521 U.S. 591 (1997) (in class action against former asbestos makers filed solely for settlement purposes, class was too broad where it included currently injured class members seeking immediate payment and exposure-only members seeking ample, inflation-protected fund for the future).

29 *Hansberry v. Lee*, 311 U.S. 32 (1940) (black residents of neighborhood not bound by prior judgment upholding racially discriminatory deed restrictions on residential property because representation of their interests was inadequate and violated their due process rights).

30 When notice of pendency and opt-out rights is required to be sent, the named plaintiff must pay for it. *See Eisen v. Carlisle & Jacqueline, infra* note 32.

31 *Roe v. Wade*, 410 U.S. 113 (1973) and *Brown v. Board of Education*, 349 U.S. 294 (1955). If a class action is filed, the case will continue even if the named plaintiffs' individual claim becomes moot — a useful feature for the pregnant plaintiff in *Roe* and the public school student plaintiffs in *Brown*. *See Sosna v. Iowa*, 419 U.S. 393, 397-403 (1974) (class action case challenging the constitutionality of a waiting period for divorce was not moot despite the fact that the original plaintiff had obtained a divorce elsewhere) and Chapter IX, p. 326. This type of injunctive class action is provided for in FRCP 23(b)(2).

32 *See Eisen v. Carlisle & Jacqueline*, 417 U.S. 156 (1974) (suit by class of 2.25 million odd-lot traders against brokerage firm for overcharging). This type of class action is provided for in FRCP 23(b)(3). While usually it is small losses that are involved, this type of class action has increasingly been used in mass tort cases involving significant personal injuries, mainly to protect the defendant from future liability. *See*

Consumer class actions to redress large numbers of small losses hold the promise of bringing unscrupulous businesses to justice when they would otherwise avoid liability. However, such class actions have come in for criticism in recent years. When small claims are aggregated, the potentially ruinous exposure risk for defendants means there is great pressure on them to settle even doubtful claims. And even when the claim is meritorious — and also when it is not — the defendant and the plaintiffs' lawyers often collude in a settlement that leaves class members with token relief, usually in the form of coupons for future discounts on the defendant's products, while the plaintiff class's lawyers receive massive amounts of cash in attorney fees.[33] In part in reaction to such "coupon" class actions, Congress recently passed legislation addressing this and other perceived problems with class actions.[34]

B. The Discovery Stage

After all matters of preliminary defenses and pleading are resolved, the facts of the case are investigated and developed through a pretrial process called "discovery."[35] In discovery, the parties have the power to require anyone who has knowledge relevant to the case, including the opposing party, to come forward and divulge that knowledge under oath. Discovery is largely conducted by the lawyers themselves independently of the court or a judge.[36] Any necessary discovery meetings, including the taking of testimony, are generally held in the office of one of the discovering party's attorneys. It is routine for a lawyer *via* the discovery process and long before trial to interrogate virtually every witness the other side expects to call at trial and to obtain copies of every document and to examine all other tangible evidence the other side expects to offer as proof at trial.

The need for pretrial discovery grows out of the fact that the adversary system in the United States uses a single, concentrated, continuous trial. It is undoubtedly useful in any system for the lawyers to know as much about a case as possible early in the proceedings. But the typical civil law system's discontinuous hearing process, which spreads the "trial" over several hearings over a period of time, makes it easier to react to surprise facts introduced by an opposing party. There is time to find rebuttal evidence and present it at a later hearing. In the United States, the single concentrated trial is the only opportunity the parties have to prove their cases and rebut the opposing party's evidence. Discovery allows the party to be completely prepared on all aspects of the case by the time the trial starts.

Though discovery aids trial preparation, it has other purposes. First, it promotes settlement. Pretrial knowledge of all the facts compels the parties to undertake a more realistic evaluation of the strengths and weaknesses of their cases. Second, discovery can disclose where there is agreement on the facts, if not on their legal meaning in terms of liability. This can form the basis for resolving the case without trial by way of

---

Amchem v. Windsor, supra note 28. *See also* the "mass action" statute *supra* note 25.

33 In a suit against Blockbuster Video challenging the amount it charged in late fees for returned movies, the settlement provided class members with coupons for discounts and free rentals, but no change in the late fee policy. However, the plaintiff class's counsel were to receive $9.25 million in fees.

34 Class Action Fairness Act of 2005, 28 U.S.C.A. §1332(d) and other parts of Title 28. The basic technique used by the Act is to make many such actions removable to federal court, where there will be greater scrutiny of claims and class action certification and greater oversight of settlements. *See also* Chapter XV, p. 602, where shareholder class actions for securities fraud are discussed.

35 FRCP 26-37 regulate discovery. Discovery in state systems may differ slightly from state to state, but the differences are minor.

36 *See* Chapter III, pp. 84-85.

summary judgment, discussed below. Third, if trial is ultimately necessary, the trial will be simpler and fairer. It will be simpler because undisputed issues will not have to be tried. And trial of disputed issues will be fairer because the lawyers will be better prepared to address them. Thus, resolution of the case will depend less on the relative strength of the trial skills of the parties' lawyers.[37]

1. Discovery Methods

There are five discovery devices that the parties may use. All these devices may be used against parties to the case (plaintiff or defendant), while a few may be used against a non-party witness.

Depositions The first and most widely used discovery device is the oral "deposition."[38] Any person who has information relevant to the case, can be compelled to undergo a deposition, or be "deposed." Parties to the case can be deposed without a court subpoena so long as "reasonable notice" is given. People who are not parties must be served with a "subpoena" (a court order to appear), but lawyers may obtain subpoenas from the court clerk easily or, in some jurisdictions, may issue subpoenas themselves.[39] Depositions usually take place in the office of one of the attorneys in the case. A notary is present to swear the deponent (the person being deposed) and most commonly a court reporter makes a verbatim record of the examination as in court. The deponents are interrogated by the lawyers just as they would be in court. Any objections to testimony will be on the record for later ruling by the judge should a party seek to use the deposition at trial.

Answers given in depositions are inadmissible hearsay if they are later sought to be offered in evidence at trial. However, at trial a deposition of a *party* may be used for any purpose by the adverse party since all the statements therein are party admissions. The deposition of a non-party witness may be used at trial if it is inconsistent with the witness's trial testimony.[40] In addition, the deposition of any witness may be used as a substitute for live testimony if the witness is unavailable, defined as when the witness is dead or too ill to testify, cannot remember what happened, cannot be subpoenaed or persists in refusing to testify even though ordered to do so by the court.[41]

Depositions are useful tools for preparing for trial. They allow the lawyers to directly question the opposing witnesses and parties well before trial, thereby providing a trial preview. The oral format facilitates finding out information, since the witness's answers are uncoached and the questioner can immediately follow up on the answers given with further questions. However, depositions tend to be expensive.[42]

---

37 Discovery may also be used to preserve testimony for later use at trial if the witness will not be available to testify. *See* FRCP 27.

38 *See* FRCP 30. Written depositions are possible as well, but are rarely used.

39 *See* FRCP 45(a)(3) ("attorney as officer of the court may . . . issue and sign a subpoena").

40 FRCP 32, referencing the Federal Rules of Evidence (FRE). Hearsay and other limitations on evidence as set out in the FRE were discussed in Chapter III, pp. 109-115. Unlike unsworn prior statements of witnesses that were not given at a prior hearing or deposition, inconsistent deposition testimony can be used as substantive evidence, not just to impeach the witness. *See* FRE 801(d)(1)(A).

41 FRE 804(a)(1). Most often, the witness's refusal to testify or exemption from testifying at trial is motivated by a claim of privilege, such as the privilege against self-incrimination.

42 This largely results from the need for the presence of all the lawyers and the inefficiencies of oral interrogation. FRCP amendments in 1993 made depositions less expense by permitting non-stenographic means (audio or video taping), thus eliminating the need for a court reporter. FRCP 30(b)(7); FRCP 32(c).

Interrogatories Written "interrogatories" sent to the opposing party are the second most common discovery device.[43] Interrogatories must be answered under oath in writing. They may be addressed only to a party, and parties usually respond only after consultation with their attorney. At the later trial, an interrogatory can be used for any purpose, whether as substantive evidence or as a means of impeaching a party's testimony. The advantage of interrogatories is that they are cheap and easy to use. All one needs is a word processor and an imagination. On the other hand, written interrogatories are a much more cumbersome way to obtain information than depositions, where the questioner can immediately follow up on any unclear answers. Moreover, interrogatory answers are filtered through the opposing party's attorney, who can assure that the answers impart as little useful information as possible.

Requests to Produce Documents and Things Like interrogatories, "requests for production of documents" can be sent only to an opposing party.[44] This device is often used in conjunction with interrogatories, thus allowing a party to ask about documents and then require that appropriate copies be attached. To get documents from a *non-party*, a subpoena must be issued, either in conjunction with a deposition or separately. This device is also the method by which a party can inspect land or real evidence in the possession of the opposing party. A subpoena for documents is called a subpoena *duces tecum*.[45]

Order for Physical or Mental Examination An order of this type is used to verify a party's physical condition by requiring that the party be examined by a doctor chosen by the opposing party. Because such examinations are very invasive, they are permitted only with special court permission and only if the court finds that the mental or physical condition of the party is truly "in controversy" and there is "good cause" for the examination.[46] These requirements effectively require that the issue of the party's health be essential to proper resolution of the lawsuit. They are easily satisfied in the most common situation where such orders are granted — examinations of plaintiffs by defendants' doctors in personal injury cases to verify the extent of the plaintiffs' claimed injuries. It bears emphasizing that an order for physical or mental examination applies only to parties and cannot be used to determine the physical or mental condition of a non-party witness, no matter how useful such information might be.

Requests for Admissions The final form of discovery discussed here is final in another sense, because it is generally used after all the other discovery devices have uncovered the facts of the case. "Requests for admissions" are written requests asking the opposing party to admit the truth of certain facts which discovery shows are essentially undisputed.[47] While a party may refuse to admit a fact, an unreasonable refusal is grounds for reimbursing the requesting party for the costs of proving that fact at trial. Failure to respond to a request for admissions is taken as an admission of the facts on which the admissions were sought. An admission is viewed as conclusively establishing the matter admitted, though only for the purposes of that particular case.

---

43 FRCP 33.

44 FRCP 34.

45 FRCP 45(a)(1).

46 FRCP 35(a). *See Schlagenhauf v. Holder*, 379 U.S. 104 (1964) (insufficient grounds for battery of mental and physical exams of bus driver defendant whose bus collided with a truck).

47 FRCP 36.

2. Scope of Discovery

Relevance and Privilege   The scope of discovery is very broad: the parties "may obtain discovery regarding any matter not privileged, which is "relevant to the claim or defense of any party" in the pending action. Even if the information or material being sought ultimately would not be admissible evidence at trial, discovery may still be had if the information is "reasonably calculated to lead to admissible evidence."[48] The reference to "privileged" matter is to information protected by a "privilege" — information given in confidence in the course of a special relationship, such as doctor-patient, lawyer-client, priest-penitent or spousal relationships, or others established by law.[49]

Protection of Confidential Commercial Information   A "trade secret or other confidential research, development or commercial information," though not privileged, may be protected from discovery by means of a "protective order." Such information is not completely exempt from discovery if it is directly relevant to the lawsuit, but even if it is required to be disclosed to the opposing party, a protective order can be used to prevent disclosure outside the lawsuit.[50]

Attorney Work Product   Potentially exempt from discovery is "attorney work product" material.[51] This includes much of the material that lawyers generate when they prepare a case for trial, such as witness interviews, analyses of the facts and law applicable to the case, witness and trial preparation notes, and observations and impressions of the strengths and weaknesses of the case. Allowing discovery of such materials is thought to be unfair and disruptive of the trial preparation process. The attorney's mental impressions, conclusions, and legal theories can never be discovered. However, the lawyer may be required to share some factual work product material with the other side if the other side cannot, without "undue hardship," acquire the materials from another source. For example, if the defendant's lawyer finds and interviews an eyewitness right after an accident, that witness's statement is generally not discoverable by the plaintiff since it is work product and the plaintiff can simply obtain the same information from the witness by way of a deposition. However, if the plaintiff's lawyer got involved in the case late and the witness, on being deposed by the plaintiff, cannot recall the details of the incident because of the passage of time, the defense would probably have to give the witness's written statement to the plaintiff.

The work product exception does not exempt a party from disclosing all relevant *information* that party may have found if it is requested by the opposing party. If requested, parties and their lawyers are always required to reveal the names and locations of anyone they know of who has information relevant to the lawsuit so that the opposing party can depose the person. This is so even if finding the witness involved major expense and investigative efforts. They must also disclose what *information* they have as a result of interviewing that witness since that is information about the subject

---

48 FRCP 26(b)(1). With court permission, discovery of "any matter relevant to the subject matter involved in the action" may be obtained.

49 Issues of federalism complicate privilege in federal courts. Privilege is determined according to state law for state-law claims and according to federal common law for federal claims. *See* FRE 501.

50 FRCP 26(c)(7). *See Coca-Cola Bottling Co. of Shreveport, Inc. v. Coca-Cola Co.*, 110 F.R.D. 363, 366 (D. Del. 1986) (secret formula for Coca-Cola ordered to be revealed because it was essential to determining lawsuit; when Coca-Cola Co. refused to comply, all inferences from the formula would be assumed to be in plaintiff's favor at trial).

51 FRCP 26(b)(3) and (4). *See also Hickman v. Taylor*, 329 U.S. 495 (1947) (discussing the basis for the work product exception).

of the lawsuit that is within the knowledge of the party. What is protected is the very document that the lawyer produced in working with the witness.

Expert Witnesses Expert witnesses present a special problem for the lawyer who must cross-examine them since their testimony deals with specialized knowledge and complex concepts. This is particularly true of medical experts. To aid in cross-examination by the other side, a party is required to disclose the name of any expert witness it plans to use at trial and provide a report describing the expert's probable testimony at trial. After receiving the report, the opposing party is permitted to depose the expert. However, disclosures and depositions are allowed only for experts whom the party has decided to call to testify at trial. Discovery is generally not allowed with respect to experts whom the party has decided not to call to testify at trial.[52]

3. Enforcement of Discovery

Discovery is generally conducted without court supervision and relies heavily on voluntary compliance with the discovery rules. When problems arise, they may be taken up with the court. This system avoids wasting the court's time. Consequently, judges are often impatient with recalcitrant parties who are not cooperating in divulging information or who are overreaching by seeking to gain information to which they are not entitled under the rules.

Discovery Disputes Discovery disputes come before the court in two ways. First, a "motion to compel discovery" may be filed by the party *seeking discovery* when that party receives objections or inadequate responses to its discovery requests.[53] The second way is when the party *against whom* discovery is sought raises the issue by seeking a "protective order" prohibiting or limiting the discovery sought.[54] In both situations, any court order resolving the dispute is enforceable by contempt of court.[55] In addition to ordering that particular questions be answered or particular documents be produced, a court in extreme cases of resistance can order that the facts sought to be established by discovery are deemed admitted, that recalcitrant plaintiffs' claims be dismissed or that recalcitrant defendants defenses be stricken.[56] Another encouragement to informal discovery compliance is that, unlike the general "American rule" under which each side absorbs its own litigation costs, the party that loses a discovery dispute before the court must pay the attorney fees incurred by the winner unless the loser's position was "substantially justified."[57]

Abuse of Discovery Because discovery is conducted mostly without court supervision, it can be misused to harass the opposing party or to drive up the opposing party's costs of litigating. Perceived problems with abuse of discovery has been foremost in the minds of the Supreme Court and the Advisory Committee on the Federal Rules. Amendments in 1993 addressed discovery abuse specifically. Parties are now required

---

52 FRCP 26(b)(4). A party may be especially interested in finding out about experts that the other side has consulted, but has decided not to call as witnesses. This is because the party probably decided not to call them because they gave an opinion that undercut that party's case. Prohibiting discovery from non-testifying experts is based on the ideas that (1) one side should not "freeload" the other side's work and (2) parties should consult a wide variety of experts without fear that the other side will have access to their opinions. The non-discovery rule is relaxed in "exceptional circumstances," such as where one party has hired all the experts in a given field.

53 FRCP 37(a).

54 FRCP 26(c).

55 Contempt is discussed *infra* p. 247.

56 FRCP 37(b) and (d).

57 FRCP 37(a)(4). Attorneys fees as part of the costs are discussed *infra* p. 247.

to meet early in the case and disclose to each other, without the need for any request, all the principal evidence they have to support their claims or defenses.[58] The rules also now limit the total number of interrogatories in a given case to 25 and the depositions to 10. These changes have been severely criticized by many as contrary to adversary principles and as imposing impossible burdens.[59] However, some limits may be overridden by agreement of the parties or court order.[60] Perhaps as important as rule changes in avoiding discovery abuse has been the growth in the number and powers of magistrate judges. Virtually all discovery matters are now handled by magistrate judges in the first instance, since they have more time to devote to supervision of the discovery process than do district judges.[61]

C. Motion for Summary Judgment and the Final Pretrial Conference

1. Summary Judgment

Earlier we discussed the motion to dismiss for "failure to state a claim on which relief can be granted" as a rough screening device on the merits of the plaintiff's claim. This dismissal motion tests only the sufficiency of the complaint, however. All the facts alleged there are assumed to be true for purposes of the motion. A second screening device, the "motion for summary judgment," tests whether the plaintiff, after a sufficient opportunity for discovery, has sufficient evidence to support the claims stated. Summary judgment will thus be granted against a party if "there is no genuine issue as to any material fact and . . . the moving party is entitled to judgment as a matter of law."[62]

The relevant facts for purposes of the motion are those revealed in the discovery process, plus any affidavits — written statements of witnesses made under oath — that the parties might submit. The defendant seeking summary judgment must point out how the facts negate or fail to support the plaintiff's claims. Then the plaintiff must respond by showing, through counter-affidavits or discovery, what facts support the claims made.[63] Summary judgment must be denied if there is sufficient evidence for a rational jury to decide the case in favor of the plaintiff.[64] This is the same standard that is used for a directed verdict at trial. The difference between the two is that the summary judgment decision is made on the basis of *written versions* of the evidence set out in the affidavits and discovery materials, while the directed verdict motion is decided based on the judge's evaluation of *actual trial testimony and evidence*. If after considering the affidavits and discovery, the judge is convinced that, if such evidence were presented at trial, no rational jury could decide for the plaintiff, then the judge should enter summary judgment for the defendant. On the other hand, if there is substantial

---

58 *See* FRCP 26(a)(1).

59 Three justices dissented from promulgation of the federal automatic disclosure requirements on the ground that such rules do not "fit comfortably within the American judicial system, which relies on adversarial litigation to develop the facts." *See* dissenting statement of Scalia, J., with whom Justices Thomas and Souter concurred. *See* 146 F.R.D. 401, 507 (1993).

60 For a different view, *see* Linda S. Mullinex, *The Persuasive Myth of Pervasive Discovery Abuse and the Consequences for Unfounded Rulemaking*, 46 STANFORD L. REV. 1393 (1994).

61 Federal magistrate judges are described in Chapter V, p. 186.

62 FRCP 56(c). The rule allows summary judgment to be entered if liability is clear even if the amount of damages is still in dispute. This simply means that there will be a later trial, but it will be limited to the issue of damages.

63 *See Celotex Corp. v. Catrett*, 477 U.S. 317 (1986) (discussing the parties's responsibilities on summary judgment).

64 The standard for a directed verdict is discussed in more detail in Chapter III, pp. 102, 108.

evidence that would support a rational verdict in the plaintiff's favor, the judge must deny summary judgment and order a trial.

For example, assume that P sues D in an automobile accident case, claiming that D ran a red light. D denies this in an answer. D moves for summary judgment, attaching affidavits or depositions of three witnesses who state, contrary to what P has alleged, that they saw the accident and that D had a *green* light at the time. If P files a counter-affidavit or a deposition from another witness who saw the accident or his own affidavit stating that the light was *red* for D, then the judge should deny summary judgment. There is conflicting evidence that must be resolved at trial. But if P is not able to produce any proof to support his allegation that D ran the red light, then the judge should grant summary judgment to D. In looking at the proof on both sides, the judge must give the benefit of the doubt to the party defending against the motion, in this example, to P. This is essential to preserve the constitutional right to a trial by jury.

The most common summary judgment situation is where the defendant seeks to test the plaintiff's claim. The examples above reflect this. However, a *plaintiff* may also win summary judgment on a claim if facts are overwhelmingly in the plaintiff's favor.[65] But summary judgment is less likely to be granted to a plaintiff where the state of mind of the defendant is an element of the plaintiff's claim and is denied, such as in discrimination cases.[66]

2. Pretrial Conferences

Though not required, almost all judges hold pretrial conferences and the lawyers are required to attend. The purpose of pretrial conferences is to manage the case so as to assure that all settlement opportunities are explored, that wasteful pretrial activities are avoided, and that the quality of the trial is improved through more open discovery and better case preparation.[67]

Issues Raised There is no limit on the number of pretrial conferences that a judge may require. Pretrial conferences held early in a case tend to focus on settlement and discovery, including setting "discovery cut-off" dates. Later pretrial conferences and particularly the final pretrial conference are devoted to expediting and simplifying the trial of the case, including the possibility of obtaining stipulations (agreements) regarding uncontested facts to avoid wasting time on unnecessary presentations of evidence. The parties are typically required to exchange lists of all the witnesses they will call at trial and copies of all the documents they will present at trial. They will also be required to agree on as many issues of admissibility of evidence as possible. The judge will then decide as many remaining evidence issues as possible before the trial begins so that the trial is not unnecessarily interrupted by objections.

Role of the Judge How active a judge is in pretrial conferences varies from judge to judge. Some judges "push" the parties to settle or to agree on limiting the issues to be tried, while others are content to accept at face value the parties' assertions that further settlement negotiations or attempts to gain stipulations to particular facts would be fruitless. In general, federal judges are quite active and state judges are moving in

---

65 *American Airlines v. Ulen*, 186 F.2d 529 (D.C. Cir. 1949) (summary judgment properly granted to plaintiff passengers when facts showed airline's flight plan effectively called for plane to fly through a mountain).

66 *See Hunt v. Cromartie*, 526 U.S. 541, 119 S.Ct. 1545, 143 L. Ed.2d 731(1999) (summary judgment improperly granted based on determination that race was a motivation in legislative redistricting). *See also Reeves v. Sanderson Plumbing Products, Inc.*, 530 U.S. 133 (2000) (JNOV in age discrimination case).

67 *See* FRCP 16(a).

that direction.[68] This has been fueled by complaints about the slow pace and inefficiency of civil litigation caused by insufficient attention to case management on the part of the lawyers. This trend toward a more active judge departs from the classic adversarial view of judges as passive referees.[69]

Final Pretrial Order After the final pretrial conference, the judge enters a "final pretrial order." Again, styles vary from judge to judge, but this order is usually comprehensive. It will recite all the facts and law applicable to the case that are not in dispute (including matters settled by stipulation or by pretrial rulings of the court), set out the remaining issues to be tried, and list the witnesses to be called and exhibits to be presented at trial. No witnesses may be called except those listed in the pretrial order. No exhibits may be offered except those ruled admissible or designated as eligible to be offered at trial in the pretrial order. No legal or factual issues and theories may be gone into at trial beyond those set out in the order. The order may be changed only as necessary to "prevent manifest injustice."[70]

D. Trial Procedure

Chapter III provided a full description of the procedures involved in an adversary jury trial as well as a discussion of various trial techniques used by lawyers in such trials.[71] Most of the examples given there were from a criminal trial, but civil trials are virtually identical in their overall form and structure. However, two matters should be discussed here in addition to what was said in Chapter III: the impact of civil pretrial procedures on civil trials and the scope of the right to a jury trial in civil cases.

1. Impact of Civil Pretrial Procedures on Trials

Despite the similarities between civil and criminal trials, discovery and the other extensive pretrial procedures available in civil cases alter some aspects of the trial. First, these procedures, and particularly the final pretrial conference before an active judge, can focus the civil trial more specifically on the disputed issues. Often it is possible to submit much of the case to the jury on stipulated facts, reserving testimony and other evidence only for disputed issues. At the very least, it is possible to shorten or eliminate laying foundations for many exhibits, since most judges will have required that the parties agree on the admissibility or at least the authenticity of all exhibits at the pretrial conference. Second, witness examinations, even as to disputed issues, should go much more smoothly since the lawyers have already questioned the witness in deposition. Copies of depositions are available to impeach the witness, should the witness contradict or "improve upon" what was said in the deposition. Third, as discussed earlier, if a witness is not available, a deposition may be used in place of live testimony, and a deposition of a party may be used for any purpose by an opposing party.[72] Answers to interrogatories or responses to requests for admissions operate as party admissions and may completely remove the need for proof on some issues. In keeping with the oral

---

68 For an example of an active "settling" judge, *see Lockhart v. Patel,*115 F.R.D. 44 (E.D. Ky. 1987). The legal issue in the case — whether the court can order the parties to attend a settlement conference — was resolved in favor of that power in 1993 amendments. *See* FRCP 16(c) (last sentence) and (f).

69 *See* Chapter III, p. 81. This more active function of judges has been dubbed "managerial." *See* Judith Resnik, *Managerial Judges*, 96 HARV. L. REV. 374 (1982).

70 FRCP 16(e). Modern pretrial practice renders unlikely a favorite dramatic technique in some movies about trials in the United States — the "surprise witness" who appears at the last moment in a trial and saves what seems to be a hopeless trial. While this might happen in a criminal case, the modern pretrial order makes it virtually impossible in federal and most state civil cases in the United States.

71 *See* Chapter III, p. 92-109.

72 *See supra* p. 236.

tradition of the adversary trial, if these written substitutes for testimony form a part of the proofs in the trial, they are usually read to the jury rather than being given to them to read.

2. Scope of the Right to a Jury Trial in Civil Cases

Law vs. Equity Distinction The 7th Amendment to the Constitution "preserves" the right to a trial by jury for civil cases only"[i]n Suits *at common law*." This makes all-important a distinction that would otherwise be largely of historical interest only: the distinction between "law" and "equity." Law and equity at one time defined two separate court systems in England and in some of the United States. There were the common law courts staffed by common law judges and equity or chancery courts staffed by "chancellors." The procedures followed in law and equity were quite different. Among the various differences, common law courts used juries to decide contested fact issues, while equity chancellors decided the case alone without a jury.[73]

Consequently, to determine whether the right to a jury trial exists in a given civil case, a court must refer to the division between law and equity as it existed in 1791 — the year the 7th Amendment was ratified. This was not difficult when law and equity were administered by two different courts. But the dual court systems of law and equity were merged into one in the modern system, typically into one unified "civil action."[74] Moreover, legislatures and courts have been active in creating new claims beyond those authorized by the common law and equity in 1791. For these new claims, courts today employ a historical approach that analyzes whether the cause of action is most directly *analogous* to common law or equitable actions that existed in 1791.[75]

A general rule of thumb is that an action is "legal" if money damages are sought and "equitable" if some other form of relief is sought.[76] The rule works in most cases because money damages were the traditional form of relief offered in the courts of law. However, there are exceptions going both ways. Money can be awarded in an action for breach of fiduciary duty, but the action is historically equitable, so no jury trial is possible.[77] And actions for replevin (return of personal property wrongfully taken) and suits to evict a tenant from property are "legal" even though they entail court orders for specific non-monetary relief, so a jury is available as of right.

Civil Jury Size Juries of less than 12 and non-unanimous verdicts are permitted under the Seventh Amendment and are common in civil cases in both federal and state

---

73 The 7th Amendment applies only to civil cases in *federal* court, as it has not been "incorporated" against the states *via* the due process clause of the 14th Amendment. Incorporation is discussed in Chapter VIII, p. 283. However, state constitutional provisions, the source of the right to a jury trial in state courts, almost uniformly make the same distinction between law and equity. In the federal system, 6th Amendment's guarantee of a jury trial in *criminal* cases has been incorporated against the states, though not in all its particulars. A distinction between the criminal and civil jury trial rights in both state and federal systems is that in criminal cases, trial by jury is assumed unless the defendant affirmatively waives the right to a jury, while in civil cases, the party must make a timely demand for jury trial. FRCP 38.

74 *See* FRCP 1 and 2. In some states, a vestige of separate systems of law and equity is preserved by having the same judges sit as "chancellors" or "judges" depending on the claim they are hearing.

75 The analysis demanded sometimes borders on the absurd as the sides trade abstruse historical references. *See Chauffeurs, Teamsters & Helpers, Local No. 391 v. Terry*, 494 U.S. 558 (1990) (suit against union for breach of duty of fair representation required jury trial even though unions did not exist in 1791).

76 *City of Monterey v. Del Monte Dunes at Monterey, Ltd.*, 526 U.S. 687 (1999) ("in suits sounding in tort for money damages, questions of liability were decided by the jury, rather than the judge"; holding right to jury trial in suit against city for violation of constitutional rights).

77 *See also Curtis v. Loether*, 415 U.S. 189, 196 (1974) (claim for back pay in employment discrimination case was "equitable restitution," though damages for housing discrimination was "legal").

court.[78] A variety of winning verdict votes exist in the states, from unanimous 12-person jury verdicts (9 states) to 5 members of a 6-person jury (6 states) and even 6 members of an 8-person jury (5 states).[79]

E. Judgments in Civil Cases: Money Damages, Equitable Relief and Costs

After the trial, a "judgment" is entered on the jury verdict, subject to any post trial motions.[80] In a bench trial, the judge must deliver an opinion or findings of fact and conclusions of law on the basis of which a judgment is entered.[81] There are several kinds of relief that may be granted in a judgment.[82]

1. Money Judgments

Types of Damages Money judgments may reflect damages of three types: compensatory, punitive and nominal. Compensatory damages are designed to compensate — to place the party in the position the party would have been in but for the actions of the defendant. Compensatory damages are available in all kinds of cases. The question of what elements are included in compensatory damages varies with the type of claim and is discussed in the appropriate substantive law chapters.[83]

Punitive damages may sometimes be awarded to punish the defendant beyond the requirement of paying compensation. Punitive damages focus less on the extent of the harm done to the plaintiff and more on the culpable behavior of the defendant. And in order to punish that behavior, such damages necessarily look to the economic resources of the defendant in deciding the measure of its sanctions. Some jurisdictions (including federal law) allow punitive damages to be awarded even when there are no compensatory damages. Other jurisdictions require some compensatory damages before any award for punitive damages can be made. They may be awarded only in tort cases involving either intentional or reckless harm. Mere negligence is not sufficient. Of course, if the same act that constitutes a breach of contract constitutes an intentional tort, punitive damages may be awarded. In addition, a breach of the implied covenant of good faith and fair dealing established in a contract relationship is considered an intentional tort and is thus remediable by punitive damages.[84]

A judge or jury may award a plaintiff nominal damages in the amount of one dollar. Nominal damages are not often awarded, but are possible in cases where the jury determines that the plaintiff has made out a claim and proved the defendant violated the plaintiff's rights, but there was no real harm suffered.

Enforcement of Money Judgments If a defendant fails to pay a judgment, the plaintiff may have to take action to enforce it. One common way to enforce a judgment against an employed person is to use a writ of a garnishment — an order to the defendant's employer to pay a percentage of the defendant's wages to the plaintiff until the judgment is satisfied.[85] If liquid assets are not available, but the defendant has property, a "writ of execution" must be obtained from the court authorizing a sheriff to seize the

---

78 *Colgrove v. Battin*, 413 U.S. 149 (1973) (federal court). *See supra* note 65.

79 Source: Center for Jury Studies, National Center for State Courts. *See also* Chapter III, p. 92.

80 *See* Chapter III, pp. 108-109.

81 FRCP 52.

82 *See generally* DAN B. DOBBS, HORNBOOK ON THE LAW OF REMEDIES, 2D ED. (West 1993).

83 *See* Chapter X, pp. 411-412 (contract breaches) and Chapter XI, pp. 460-466 (torts).

84 *See* Chapter X, p. 406; Chapter XI, p. 463 (torts) and pp. 464-464 (constitutional limits).

85 Federal law limits the weekly amount to 25% of wages. 15 U.S.C.A. §1673(a).

defendant's nonexempt property and sell that property in order to satisfy the judgment. Any proceeds in excess of the judgment are then returned to the defendant.[86]

The plaintiff can use discovery or other supplemental procedures to require that the defendant disclose where assets are located or to turn over certain property for execution. Failure to comply with such an order can could result in imprisonment for contempt of court.[87]

2. Equitable Relief

Forms of Equitable Relief Generally, damages are "substitutionary relief" as they provide a money substitute compensative for the harm suffered. But sometimes a court can provide "specific relief" — relief that actually prevents harm from taking place or undoes harm that was suffered by restoring the rights violated or by requiring the defendant to turn over the very thing the plaintiff is entitled to. Such specific relief is most often equitable in nature.[88]

The most common form of equitable relief is the injunction. An injunction can be simple, such as one ordering a defendant to stay off the plaintiff's property or a city official to stop enforcing an ordinance. Other forms of equitable relief include "reformation" or "rescission" of a contract, and "specific performance" — an order requiring the breaching party in a contract case to perform obligations required under the contract.[89] Historically, since equity courts were developed to avoid the rigid strictures on relief imposed on common law courts, equity's hallmark is its flexibility and the forms of equitable relief possible are as varied as the wrongs it remedies.[90] If necessary, equitable relief can be very complex, such as an order completely restructuring a company or reorganizing a school system to stop racial discrimination and to eradicate its continued effects.[91]

Grounds for Equitable Relief Traditionally, to obtain equitable relief, a plaintiff must demonstrate: "(1) that it has suffered an irreparable injury; (2) that remedies available at law, such as monetary damages, are inadequate to compensate for that injury; (3) that, considering the balance of hardships between the plaintiff and defendant, a remedy in equity is warranted; and (4) that the public interest would not be disserved by a permanent injunction."[92]

The first two requirements shade into each other in that an "irreparable" injury is one that no "remedy at law" in the form of money damages would redress adequately. This prerequisite for equitable relief is inherited from a compromise worked out between the common law courts and the chancery courts in 17th century England to avoid conflicts — chancery would not step into a dispute unless the common law courts

---

[86] Each state has laws which identify property that is exempt from execution. Most provide that clothing and other personal items and tools of the defendant's trade are exempt, as well as a portion of the value of the defendant's home, if the defendant owns a home. Exemptions vary widely from state to state.

[87] Contempt of court to enforce court orders is discussed *infra* p. 247. In this instance, the resulting imprisonment is not for debt, but for violating the court order to disclose or turn over assets.

[88] *See supra* p. 243 (distinction between law and equity).

[89] *See* Chapter X, p. 412. Perhaps the most numerous invocations of equitable powers are in divorce cases, from the decree itself to orders for child support, restraining orders and other ancillary relief.

[90] For a history of the development of equity, *see* ALFRED H. MARSH, HISTORY OF THE COURT OF CHANCERY AND OF THE RISE AND DEVELOPMENT OF THE DOCTRINES OF EQUITY (Carswell 1890, reprinted 1985).

[91] For an example of such a detailed "structural" injunction in a school desegregation case, *see Carr v. Montgomery County Bd. of Education*, 289 F.Supp. 647 (M.D. Ala. 1968), *aff'd* 395 U.S. 225 (1969). *See generally* OWEN FISS, INJUNCTIONS (Foundation 1972).

[92] *eBay Inc. v. MercExchange, L.L.C.*, 547 U.S. 388 (2006).

could not afford adequate relief.[93] Today, the same court and judge determines the appropriate relief, so conflicting jurisdiction is no problem. Instead, the requirement today serves to impose a hierarchy of relief in which damages is "ordinary" relief, while equitable relief is "extraordinary" relief.[94] Especially given that specific relief can be intrusive and disruptive in some cases, courts often emphasize that an injunction should be ordered only if it is truly a necessary and appropriate resolution of the dispute. The third "balance of hardships" requires balancing the burdens on the plaintiff if the relief is denied against the hardship on the defendant if relief is granted.[95] The fourth "public interest" requirement is rather open-ended and can include all manner of considerations.

Consistent with the flexibility of equity, equitable decrees are generally modifiable at a later time if circumstances change. Thus, an order granting equitable relief in cases involving prospective and ongoing judicial supervision of the defendant's conduct may be modified as necessary to assure that it is still fair and accomplishing what it was intended to achieve. In one case, the Supreme Court allowed a sheriff to seek a modification of the order pertaining to jail several years after it was entered on the ground that interim changes in the factual circumstances and law made it inequitable to continue the decree.[96] If the purposes of the decree have been carried out, the defendant may even have it rescinded.[97]

There are inherited verbal nuances used in suits for equitable relief that should be mentioned. The initial pleading in a suit in equity is often called a "petition" instead of a complaint. The judgment rendered is often called a "decree" rather than a judgment. Judges discussing what relief to order will sometimes refer to their powers "as chancellor." Finally, ancient equity "maxims" may sometimes appear in opinions. For example, a judge may deny relief under the "clean hands" doctrine, under which a petitioner "who seeks equity, must do equity," meaning that the petitioner will not get any relief from the court if his own conduct in the controversy has been improper. Today judges will most likely simply "balance the equities" of the case without any felt need to invoke equity maxims.

Provisional Relief The flexible nature of equity allows for certain kinds of provisional relief, mainly relief aimed at preserving the *status quo* until a final trial of the dispute can be held. Thus, a "preliminary injunction" preventing a defendant from taking certain action may be entered. Generally the plaintiff must show a reasonable likelihood of success on the merits of the claim and a clear need for protection pending a decision on the merits.[98] A "temporary restraining order" is also possible to avoid immediate serious irreparable harm to the plaintiff until a hearing can be held on a

---

93 This was the solution of the "Coke-Ellesmere" dispute, named for the common-law judge and equity chancellor involved in it. *See* J. H. BAKER, AN INTRODUCTION TO ENGLISH LEGAL HISTORY 92-93 (2d ed. 1979).

94 This notion of a remedial hierarchy has been challenged in view of the ease with which courts give injunctions in certain kinds of cases without much inquiry into the actual effectiveness of substitutionary relief. *See* and *compare* Douglas Laycock, *The Death of the Irreparable Injury Rule*, 103 HARV. L. REV. 688 (1990) *and* Doug Rendleman, *The Inadequate Remedy at Law Prerequisite for an Injunction*, 33 FLA. L. REV. 346 (1981).

95 *See, e.g., Sigma Chemical Co. v. Harris*, 605 F.Supp. 1253 (E.D. Mo. 1985) (entering injunction enforcing agreement not to compete), *injunction modified on appeal* 794 F.2d 371 (8th Cir. 1986).

96 *Rufo v. Inmates of the Suffolk County Jail*, 502 U.S. 367 (1992).

97 *Board of Education v. Dowell*, 498 U.S. 237 (1991) (court-ordered remedy to end *de jure* racial segregation of schools should be terminated when the effects of *de jure* discrimination have ended).

98 *See William Inglis & Sons Baking Co. v. ITT Continental Baking Co., Inc.*, 526 F.2d 86 (9th Cir. 1975) (discussing alternative formulations of the preliminary injunction test).

motion for a preliminary injunction.[99] For example, a temporary restraining order would be appropriate in a divorce case to keep a husband who has threatened physical violence away from the wife.[100]

Enforcement of Equitable Decrees If the losing party in a suit for equitable relief refuses to comply with an order, that party is said to be "in contempt of court" and can be fined or imprisoned. It is important to note that imprisonment for civil contempt is not a means of punishment; it is a coercive measure. Thus, the imprisoned party "carries the keys to the prison in his own pocket," meaning that his compliance will "purge" his contempt and result in immediate release.[101]

3. Declaratory Relief

Another form of relief similar to an injunction and often awarded along with it is "declaratory relief." A declaratory judgment establishes the rights of the parties based on the facts and law, but does not require either party to do anything.[102] Perhaps the most common declaratory judgment actions are actions filed by insurance companies seeking a determination that an insured who suffered a loss arguably covered in an insurance policy has no claim under the policy. This issue would normally be determined in a suit by the insured against the company for money, but if the insured does not sue and the company wants the matter settled, a declaratory judgment is the appropriate way to get a definitive ruling. Declaratory judgments are also used when laws or practices are sought to be declared unconstitutional and there is no need for injunctive relief. Thus, if there is an ordinance of a city that the plaintiff contends violates the Constitution and there is no indication of any immediate harm to the plaintiff that requires injunctive relief, the court may simply enter a judgment declaring that the ordinance is unconstitutional and declaring what conduct the plaintiff has a right to engage in.

The Supreme Court has been less than clear as to the precise effect of a declaratory judgment:

> [E]ven though a declaratory judgment has the "force and effect of a final judgment," it is a much milder form of relief than an injunction. Though it may be persuasive, it is not ultimately coercive; noncompliance with it may be inappropriate, but is not contempt [of court].[103]

Whatever the effectiveness of declaratory relief by itself, it can form the basis for an injunction should the trial court deem that necessary.[104]

4. Awards of Costs

Costs Recoverable Most judgments award "court costs" to the prevailing party. In the U.S. legal system, these costs include fees of the clerks and marshals, witness fees

---

99 *See* FRCP 65.

100 Much to the chagrin of creditors, federal courts do not have the power to preliminarily enjoin a debtor from disposing of assets until a judgment can be obtained and executed. *See Grupo Mexicano De Desarrollo, S.A. v. Alliance Bond Fund, Inc.*, 527 U.S. 308 (1999).

101 *See* RONALD L. GOLDFARB, THE CONTEMPT POWER (Anchor Books 1971).

102 The federal Declaratory Judgment Act is found at 28 U.S.C.A. §§2201-2202.

103 *Steffel v. Thompson*, 415 U.S. 452, 471 (1974), quoting from *Perez v. Ledesma*, 401 U.S. 82, 126 (1971) (separate opinion of Brennan, J.). In *Steffel*, the Court approved entry of a declaratory judgment that held that a state statute against hand-billing could not be constitutionally enforced against an anti-Vietnam War protester.

104 28 U.S.C.A. §2202.

and docket fees.[105] Unlike the "English rule" on fees and costs and the prevailing rule in many civil law countries, the "American rule" on costs recoverable by a prevailing party is that attorney fees are not normally included in the absence of some specific statutory authorization. Thus, both parties must normally pay their own attorney fees, which will usually represent the largest portion of litigation expenses.[106] However, the FRCP and analogous state court rules have "offer of judgment" rules. If a party offers to settle a suit by entry of judgment in a particular amount, the offeree fails to accept the offer and the result at trial is at least as favorable as the offer, the offeree is liable for the actual costs incurred by the offeror after the date of the offer. Thus, if a prompt, realistic offer is made early in a suit and is not accepted, successful parties may be able to recover most of their attorney fees.[107]

Attorney Fees Award Statutes There are several special statutory authorizations for attorney fee awards in both state and federal law. These statutes generally relate to claims that the government wants to encourage people to bring because successful individual suits benefit society in general. Common among these are civil rights claims, suits to protect consumer rights, actions to gain redress for stock market manipulation, antitrust suits, and suits to protect the environment.[108]

F. Effect of Judgments

Judgments not only award relief but also settle disputed claims, defenses and issues between the parties. The system needs to avoid litigating these claims and issues a second time, because doing so is both unfair to the defending parties and a waste of valuable judicial resources. The law that defines the effect that final judgments will have on any subsequent litigation is the common law doctrine of *"res judicata." Res judicata* is divided into two separate doctrines, claim preclusion and issue preclusion.[109] The traditional name for claim preclusion is *"res judicata"* and the traditional name for issue preclusion is "collateral estoppel."

1. Claim Preclusion (*Res Judicata*)

Claim preclusion means that the plaintiff gets only one chance to sue the defendant regarding a single transaction or occurrence.[110] This means that in a case where there could be several legal theories upon which to base a claim, all such theories must be included in one lawsuit. For example, assume the plaintiff is injured when hit by the defendant's truck and sues based on *negligence.* Once that suit is over, that plaintiff cannot sue the defendant again based on the same accident even if a new theory of recovery is alleged, such as *strict liability* (liability without fault) based on the fact that the defendant's truck was overloaded. The plaintiff is barred by the first judgment whether he or she won or lost the first suit. This application of *res judicata* is called the rule against "claim splitting." Similarly, a plaintiff may not "split" damages. This means that the plaintiff must assert a claim for the entire loss in one suit and may not generally

---

105 28 U.S.C.A. §1920 (allowable costs in federal court).

106 *See Alyeska Pipeline Service v. Wilderness Society,* 421 U.S. 240 (1975) (reaffirming "American Rule" against attorney fee awards in the absence of statute).

107 *See* FRCP 68. However, the rule does not apply if the defendant offeror prevails. *Delta Air Lines, Inc. v. August,* 450 U.S. 346 (1981) (defendant offered $450 and plaintiff lost; plaintiff is not liable for costs).

108 *See, e.g.,* 42 U.S.C.A. §1988 (civil rights suits) and the numerous consumer protection statutes discussed in Chapter X, pp. 425-433.

109 *See generally* RESTATEMENT OF JUDGMENTS, 2D (American Law Institute 1982-1988) [hereafter "RESTATEMENT"].

110 *See* RESTATEMENT §§18-20.

claim property damage in one suit and personal injuries in another. *Res judicata* also operates against defendants. Compulsory counterclaims — counterclaims that arise out of the same transaction or occurrence — are barred if not asserted by the defendant in response to a claim.[111]

2. Issue Preclusion (Collateral Estoppel)

Defensive and Offensive Uses of Issue Preclusion Issue preclusion does not bar relitigation of entire claims. It bars relitigation of certain *issues* that have already been litigated in an earlier lawsuit. If an issue of fact or law has been (1) actually litigated and determined (2) by a final and valid judgment and (3) the determination was essential to the judgment, then that determination binds the parties in any later proceeding (4) as to the same issue, whether it arises on the same or a different claim.[112] For example, assume that P holds a patent and sues D Co. for infringement. The court finds that P's patent is invalid and enters judgment for D Co. P then files suit for infringement of the same patent against X Co. X Co. can use the doctrine of issue preclusion to have the second suit dismissed. The issue of the validity of P's patent has already been determined against P, so P is precluded from re-litigating that issue. This is *defensive* use of issue preclusion, *i.e.*, its use by the defendant in the second suit to defeat a claim.[113]

In some jurisdictions, issue preclusion can be used *offensively*, *i.e.*, by the plaintiff to establish a claim. Assume that there is a plane crash and 100 passengers are injured. If a passenger, P1, sues Airline Co. and wins, the judge or jury necessarily determined that the Airline Co. was negligent and that the negligence led to the plane crash. P2, P3, P4 and all the rest of the passengers through P100 can now sue Airline Co. and use issue preclusion offensively against it on the issues of negligence and causation. Effectively this means that the only thing remaining for P2 through P100 to prove at trial is the amount of their damages.[114]

Mutuality of Estoppel A common limitation on the application of issue preclusion is the requirement of "mutuality of estoppel." Mutuality requires that the parties in the first and any later suits be identical before the losing party in the first suit will be bound in the later lawsuit. Thus, if a jurisdiction follows mutuality, in neither of the examples given above (the patent infringement or the plane crash cases) would issue preclusion be allowed to be used. The second patent case involved a different defendant company and the later plane crash cases involved different plaintiffs. It would violate due process if a person not a party to a case could be bound by the judgment in that case.[115]

Mutuality is based on the principle that it is unfair for a person to *take advantage* of a ruling *in favor* of his or her position in a case if that person would not have been *bound* had the ruling gone *against* his or her position. For example, supporters of mutuality would argue that, since X Co., sued by P in the second patent case, would not have been *bound* by a judgment in the first case *in favor of P* that the *patent was valid*, it should not

---

111 *See* RESTATEMENT §22.

112 RESTATEMENT §27.

113 *See Blonder-Tongue Laboratories, Inc. v. University of Illinois Foundation*, 402 U.S. 313 (1971).

114 *See In re Air Crash at Detroit Metropolitan Airport*, 776 F.Supp. 316 (E.D. Mich. 1991).

115 *Richards v. Jefferson County*, 517 U.S. 793, 801-802 (1996); *South Central Bell Tel. Co. v. Alabama*, 526 U.S. 160 (1999) (so holding even though the same lawyer represented one of the parties in both cases). It does not violate due process to bind non-parties in a class action or if they are "in privity" with a party, if their interests were adequately represented in the litigation. Class actions were discussed *supra* pp. 234-235. A non-party is in privity with a party if the two are closely related legally, such as where one is the successor in interest, assignee, insurer, surety or agent of the other, unless their interests are conflicting.

be allowed to *take advantage of* the determination *in favor of D Co.* that the *patent was invalid.* Similarly, since passengers P2 through P100 would not have been *bound* by a determination against P1 that Airline Co. was *not negligent* — since P2 through P100 were not parties to the suit — they should not be able to *take advantage* of a determination in P1's favor that Airline Co. *was negligent.* Opponents of mutuality argue that it is a waste of judicial resources to require the very same issue to be tried over again when it has already been determined once against someone who *was* a party. Stated otherwise, the parties who lost in the first case have had their "day in court" and it is unfair to allow them a second opportunity to prove differently just because the current plaintiff is new. Persuaded by this logic, the mutuality rule has been abolished for federal court judgments and for many state judgments, and it is the position of the second Restatement of Judgments.[116] However, several states still require mutuality in some form.[117]

Exceptions to Issue Preclusion Whatever the scope of basic issue preclusion, there are exceptions to it. For issue preclusion to apply to a litigated issue, it must have been "fully and fairly litigated."[118] This means that if the procedural protections available in the first court were not very good or for some other reason the party was limited in its ability to fully litigate the issue, then re-litigation may be allowed. For example, the determination of a small claims court where no lawyers are permitted and no appeal is allowed would not be given issue preclusion effect. Also, application of issue preclusion will not be allowed if the issue comes up again in an unusual and unanticipated context, if its application would have an adverse impact on the public interest, if the standard of proof in the first action was lower (as where the first case is civil and the second criminal), or if prior determinations of the issue are conflicting.[119]

G. Resolving Cases Without Litigation

Litigation according to the procedures outlined above can take a great deal of public and private time and money, and each year approximately 18 million civil cases are filed. The judicial system could not long survive if even a substantial minority of these cases went to trial. A major study of the state courts across a national sample of urban, suburban, and rural jurisdictions in 2005 showed that only 2.8% of civil cases filed went to trial.[120] With increasing costs of litigating, the need for alternative dispute resolution (ADR) has been emphasized. And courts and legislatures have gone beyond

---

116 *See Blonder-Tongue Laboratories v. University of Illinois Foundation,* 402 U.S. 313 (1971) (defensive use) and *Parklane Hosiery v. Shore,* 439 U.S. 322 (1979) (offensive use) and RESTATEMENT, *supra* note 109, §27.

117 *See Howell v. Vito's and Trucking and Excavating Co.,* 191 N.W.2d 313 (Mich. 1971) (criticizing and rejecting offensive non-mutual issue preclusion). Typically, states that have relaxed the mutuality requirement have done so first for defensive use.

118 RESTATEMENT §28.

119 *See* RESTATEMENT §§28 and 29 (setting out these and other exceptions). Section 29 exceptions apply only if the person seeking to use issue preclusion was not a party to the first action, as was the case in both the examples above of the patent infringement and the plane crash.

120 Source: Bureau of Judicial Statistics, U.S. Dept. of Justice, http://bjs.ojp.usdoj.gov/content/pub/pdf/cbjtsc05.pdf. Disposition without trial does not necessarily mean that the case settled. "[C]ases dismissed for want of prosecution, grant of default or summary judgment, withdrawal by party, or transfer to another court" also amount to disposition without trial. Although a more detailed breakdown is not provided in this 2005 study, in a 1992 study, the DOJ data show that about 75% of cases filed were disposed by settlements or dismissals. http://bjs.ojp.usdoj.gov/content/pub/pdf/cjcavilc.pdf. Thus, there is strong evidence that the majority of the cases outside the 2.8% figure are settled or dismissed cases.

merely encouraging ADR methods. In some cases, they have required that those methods be pursued.[121]

1. Voluntary Settlements

Private Negotiation and Settlement Parties can reach negotiated settlements at any time in the litigation process, including during trial or appellate review. Unless a minor child or other dependent person is a party or the case is a class action, there is no need for the judge to scrutinize the settlement.

Lawyers representing clients in negotiation must evaluate their clients' legal position and advise them of the probable trial outcome. Though it is sometimes difficult to shake clients from an overly optimistic view of their chances of success, ultimately the decision is the client's to make after considering the advice of the lawyer. Lawyers are ethically bound to communicate all offers to their clients for their consideration.[122] It is some measure of the importance that negotiation and settlement have attained that there are now courses at some law schools and many continuing legal education programs for lawyers that focus on negotiating skills.[123]

Mini-Trials A twist on voluntary settlement procedure is the "mini-trial." This process follows a trial-like procedure and is often used in disputes involving highly technical or complex matters that are otherwise hard to evaluate. During a mini-trial, counsel for both parties present a shortened version of their client's case before their clients and a "jury" hired for the occasion, which then "deliberates" to a "verdict." What happens next can vary. In some instances, the lawyers simply continue to negotiate, having been informed of what at least one jury would determine were the case to come to trial. In other instances, and especially where the clients are resistant to settlement, the lawyers may leave and allow their clients and a neutral advisor to discuss the possibility of a settlement. The mini-trial is beneficial because it gives the parties and the lawyers a realistic view of the strength of their case and makes them more aware of the risks involved in going to trial. As with informal negotiations, the mini-trial is usually a private affair and does not involve the court system.

Mediation Mediation is similar to private negotiation except that the settlement is facilitated by an impartial third party, or mediator. The mediator does not decide the dispute for the parties; the mediator simply acts as a supervisor of the negotiation between the parties by convening the negotiations and helping to find common ground. The fact that parties maintain control over the process means that mediation, like negotiation, has no rules except those that the parties decide to set up for themselves in the process. Mediation is a popular method of resolving disputes between parties who have an ongoing relationship and want to maintain that relationship, whether it is husband and wife, management and labor, or manufacturer and supplier. Once the parties reach a settlement, it is incorporated into a written agreement that has the same effect as a contract between two parties.[124]

---

121 For more, *see* STEVEN J. WARE, HORNBOOK ON ALTERNATIVE DISPUTE RESOLUTION, 2D ED. (West 2007); JACQUELINE NOLAN-HALEY, ALTERNATIVE DISPUTE RESOLUTION IN A NUTSHELL, 3D ED. (West 2008).

122 ABA Model Rules of Professional Conduct, MR 1.4(a) and (b) and comments.

123 Two texts are DONALD G. GIFFORD, LEGAL NEGOTIATION: THEORY AND PRACTICE 2D ED. (West 2007) and MARK SCHOENFIELD & MICK SCHOENFIELD, THE MCGRAW-HILL 36-HOUR NEGOTIATION COURSE (McGraw-Hill 1991). For an interesting book on negotiation not limited to the legal context, *see* ROGER FISHER, GETTING TO YES (Penguin Books 1991).

124 The ABA has approved a Model Standards of Conduct for Mediators (ABA 2005). The standards and the Reporter's Notes on them can be found at www.abanet.org/dispute.

Arbitration   Unlike a mediator, an arbitrator decides the dispute between the parties. The arbitration hearing is generally conducted like a trial. Attorneys for both sides present their evidence and arguments to the arbitrator and the arbitrator renders a decision, usually in written form. Many arbitration agreements incorporate the rules of the American Arbitration Association, a private organization that serves as a clearing-house for arbitration. Though arbitration is similar to judicial resolution of the case, it can have the advantage of being less formal, less expensive, and less time-consuming. A major advantage of arbitration is that the parties can design their own procedure and choose decision-makers who have specialized knowledge useful in deciding their dispute.[125] If the parties have agreed that the arbitration decision is to be binding, both federal and state courts will honor that agreement and will refuse to review a dispute that has been settled by arbitration.[126]

Arbitration was first used only to resolve commercial contract disputes and labor-management disputes, since it was usually only in those contexts that the parties agreed beforehand to arbitrate. Arbitration has since expanded to include all manner of legal claims, including rights under employment discrimination and other statutes that implicate important public interests. Objections to this use have been rejected by the Supreme Court so long as the claimant "effectively may vindicate [his or her] statutory cause of action in the arbitral forum."[127]

Nonetheless, the validity of arbitration agreements entered into by consumers or employees can be challenged as amounting to an "unconscionable" or "adhesion" contract.[128] A major issue is the substantial cost of arbitration. Low-income consumers can obtain the right to litigate in court *in forma pauperis* — without prepayment of court filing fees — but there is no similar solution in arbitration. Arbitration fees are based on the size of a claim, unlike court filing fees, which are modest set amounts that do not vary with the size of the claim. State and federal judges are paid by the government and do not charge for their services, while experienced arbitrators can charge hundreds and even thousands of dollars a day. Prohibitively high costs of arbitration may relieve consumers of their contractual duty to arbitrate.[129]

2. Court Sponsored Settlement Procedures

Because of the overburdened, and consequently slow, judicial process, many states have developed ADR programs sponsored by the courts and to some extent require their

---

125 *See, e.g., Ferguson v. Writers Guild of America, West, Inc.*, 277 Cal. Rptr. 450 (Cal. App. 1991) (in dispute over screen-writing credits for film, *Beverly Hills Cop II*, parties filed written submissions to expert arbitrators whose identities were unknown both to the litigants and to each other).

126 This is required by the Federal Arbitration Act, 9 U.S.C.A. §§2 *et seq. See Shearson-American Express, Inc. v. McMahon*, 482 U.S. 220 (1987) (federal courts); *Southland Corp. v. Keating*, 465 U.S. 1 (1984) (state courts).

127 *Gilmer v. Interstate/Johnson Lane Corp.*, 500 U.S. 20, 28 (1991) (age discrimination). *See Floss v. Ryan's Steakhouses, Inc.*, 211 F.3d 306 (6th Cir. 2000)(recounting the expansion).

128 *Compare Floss v. Ryan's Steakhouses, Inc., id.* (arbitration agreement invalid as unfair) *with Lyster v. Ryan's Steakhouses, Inc.*, 239 F.3d 943 (8th Cir. 2001) (arbitration agreement not invalid). *See* Chapter X, p. 410 (adhesion contracts and unconscionability). The validity of an arbitration clause may be litigated in court, but challenges to the entire contract must be decided by the arbitrator. *Buckeye Check Cashing, Inc. v. Cardegna*, 546 U.S. 440 (2006) (claim that usury voided entire contract).

129 *Green Tree Financial Corp. v. Randolph*, 531 U.S. 79 (2000) (so stating, but finding insufficient proof of prohibitive costs in that case). *Compare Mendez v. Palm Harbor Homes, Inc.*, 45 P.3d 594 (Wash. App. 2002) (finding arbitration prohibitively expensive). A partial solution for some disputes may be found in the American Arbitration Association's Consumer Arbitration Rules, under which consumers in small-claims arbitration incur no filing fee and pay only $125 of the fees charged by the arbitrator.

use.[130] All federal courts must provide litigants with at least one ADR process including, but not limited to, mediation, early neutral evaluation, mini-trials, and arbitration. In addition, all federal courts may require pursuit of mediation or neutral case evaluation and 20 districts can require arbitration.[131]

Typically court required arbitration or case evaluation programs require a summary submission of cases — sometimes with key witnesses and sometimes not — to a panel of lawyer-evaluators. The panel renders a decision. If both parties accept the decision, the case is settled. If either side rejects, the case goes to trial. If one side accepts and the other rejects the panel's decision, and the rejecting side does not win at least as much as the amount the panel recommended, the rejecting side must pay the attorney fees and costs incurred at trial by the accepting side. This attorney fee-shifting is significant in a system in which attorney fees at trial represent the largest part of the costs in the case and the normal rule is that each side absorbs its own attorney fees.[132]

PART II: The Complicating Effects of Federalism on Civil Procedure

The concepts discussed so far have considered court systems in isolation. However, as noted in Chapter I, federalism complicates the legal system. Two coordinate *judicial systems* with substantial overlapping jurisdiction — state and federal — coexist on the same territory in each state. Furthermore, *50 state lawmaking and judicial* systems exist side by side in the country. In cases involving parties, transactions or occurrences that concern more than one state, the reach of these laws and court power often overlaps. This can make litigation in some cases very complex.[133]

There are four areas of the law that deal with these problems of conflicts of laws and court power. The first is the law of personal jurisdiction. It defines which courts have the power to adjudicate the liability of a given defendant. Personal jurisdiction is usually based on the defendant's connection to the territory of the state where the action is filed. The second area is the law of *forum non conveniens*. Under this doctrine, a court may decline to exercise jurisdiction it otherwise has, because a court in another judicial system (another state or country) is much more convenient and has a greater interest in handling the case. The third is the law of interstate recognition of judgments. This is sometimes called "full faith and credit" after the choice of words used in the constitutional provision that sets the general rule of recognition. The fourth area is "choice of law." Choice-of-law rules determine what law a court will apply to resolve a particular case on the merits when the law of more than one jurisdiction has been identified as potentially applicable.

A. Personal Jurisdiction in State and Federal Courts

1. Personal Jurisdiction in State Courts

One example given in Chapter I of the legal blurring of state boundaries that has occurred in the 20th century has been the growth of state courts' powers of "personal jurisdiction" over out-of-state defendants. Personal jurisdiction is a court's authority "to determine the personal rights and obligations of the defendant."[134]

---

130 For further information, *see* www.ncsconline.org, the National Center for State Courts website.

131 *See* 28 U.S.C.A. §§ 651-658 and 28 U.S.C.A. §§ 471-482.

132 For an example of such a fee-shifting case evaluation program, *see* Michigan Court Rule 2.403-.404.

133 Some of these problems were introduced briefly in Chapter I, pp. 32-36.

134 *Pennoyer v. Neff*, 95 U.S. 714, 727 (1877). The term "jurisdiction," then, can be used in different ways. Subject matter jurisdiction (discussed in Chapter V, pp. 188-191) differs from personal jurisdiction in that subject matter jurisdiction grants power to hear a particular *type of case*. For more detail on

Personal Jurisdiction and Territoriality At its most basic level, personal jurisdiction is founded on the concept of territoriality. It starts with the proposition that a state or country has power to adjudicate only matters that concern persons and property within its borders. The concept of territorial limits on a court's jurisdiction is most often associated with *international* states, but the same concept applies to the states within the United States.[135] Under a strict view of territoriality, personal jurisdiction can exist only if (1) the defendant is physically located in the state where suit it filed and is appropriately served with process in the state (*in personam* jurisdiction) or (2) any property in dispute is physically located in the state where suit is filed and the property is properly seized by means of attachment (*in rem* jurisdiction).

The "Contacts" Test The Supreme Court, in its seminal 1945 decision in *International Shoe Co. v. Washington*,[136] departed from this strict territorial view of personal jurisdiction. It formulated a test that focused instead upon the *fairness* of the particular state court's exercise of jurisdiction over the defendant in light of the defendant's connection with the state. For personal jurisdiction to exist over an out-of-state defendant, the *International Shoe* test required only that there be "certain minimum contacts" with the forum state such that exercising jurisdiction over the defendant would "not offend traditional notions of fair play and substantial justice" embodied in the 14th Amendment due process clause. Under this rubric, the Court has approved exercises of personal jurisdiction pursuant to state statutes establishing "long-arm" jurisdiction over out-of-state defendants based on certain kinds of past actions taken by them or effects caused by them in the forum state.

How many contacts are sufficient to constitute the requisite "minimum contacts" clearly depends on the circumstances. One contact will do if it is direct and the claim is related to that contact, such as driving into a state and hitting a state resident with one's car.[137] Or, if a person owns land in a state and the dispute relates to that land, the presence of that land in a state is a sufficient single contact with the state that permits its courts to adjudicate that claim.[138]

"General" and "Specific" Jurisdiction Later refinements of the doctrine have divided personal jurisdiction into "general" and "specific" jurisdiction. If there is general jurisdiction over the defendant, then the defendant may be sued on any claim — even claims unrelated to the defendant's contacts with the state. For an individual, general jurisdiction exists if the person is served with process while physically in the state or if the person is domiciled in the state.[139] For corporations, general jurisdiction exists if the defendant has its principal place of business in the state, is incorporated there or carries on "a continuous and systematic . . . part of its general business" in the state.[140] Thus,

personal jurisdiction, *see* FRIEDENTHAL, KANE & MILLER, *supra* note 1, §§3.1-3.28. For the special personal jurisdiction aspects when non-U.S. defendants are sued, *see* Chapter XVII, pp. 714-716.

135 *See* Chapter XVII, pp. 705-714 (international extraterritorial reach of U.S. law).

136 326 U.S. 310, 316 (1945).

137 *Hess v. Pawloski*, 274 U.S. 352 (1927) (using a consent theory of jurisdiction based on road use).

138 *Shaffer v. Heitner*, 433 U.S. 186 (1977).

139 *Burnham v. Superior Court*, 495 U.S. 604 (1990) (upholding constitutionality of "transient jurisdiction," service on defendant who is only temporarily in the state); *Milliken v. Myer*, 311 U.S. 457 (1940) (domiciliary of state is subject to personal jurisdiction even if living out of state); *Blackmer v. United States*, 284 U.S. 421 (1932) (U.S. citizen domiciled abroad is subject to subpoena power of U.S. federal court).

140 *Helicopteros Nacionales de Columbia, S.A. v. Hall*, 466 U.S. 408 (1984), quoting *Perkins v. Benguet Mining Co.*, 342 U.S. 437, 438 (1952). *Hall* held that the mere purchase of helicopters in Texas for use in Peru and Colombia and a trip to Texas by a manager was not sufficient for general jurisdiction over a Colombia company sued for crash in one of those helicopters. *Perkins* involved a Philippine company that

if a person slips and falls in the hotel of a national hotel chain that has hotels in every state, general jurisdiction over the hotel exists in the courts of every state.[141]

"Specific" jurisdiction exists when the defendant's contacts with the forum state are more limited, but the claim involved *arises out of or relates to* those contacts. An example of this is the one given above of a person hitting a state resident while driving.

The Requirement of "Directed" Contacts Specific jurisdiction cases are by far the most numerous ones in which personal jurisdiction is contested. The most important requirement for the relevant contacts is that they must be directed toward the forum state by the defendant. In the words of an often-cited case, a state cannot force a nonresident to litigate in its courts unless there is "some act by which the defendant purposefully avails itself of the privilege of conducting activities within the forum State, thus invoking the benefits and protections of its laws."[142]

Product Liability Cases Cases involving manufactured goods that travel across state lines and injure consumers are among the most difficult. The Court has emphasized that a defendant's contacts must be truly "voluntary" and "purposefully directed" toward the forum state. Thus, a state may "assert personal jurisdiction over a corporation that delivers its products into the stream of commerce with the expectation that they will be purchased by consumers in the forum State."[143]

The problem is that Supreme Court is not of one mind as to what this "stream of commerce" idea means. In *Asahi Metal Industry Co., Ltd. v. Superior Court*,[144] there was a 4-4 split of the justices on this point. In *Asahi Metal*, suit was brought by a California motorcyclist for injuries sustained when he lost control of his motorcycle after a sudden loss of air and an explosion of its rear tire. He alleged that the motorcycle tire and tube were defective. He sued Cheng Shin, the Taiwanese manufacturer of the motorcycle tire's inner tube, which promptly joined a claim against Asahi Metal Co., the Japanese manufacturer of the valve stem used in the tube. The plaintiff's claims against Cheng Shin were eventually settled and dismissed, leaving only Cheng Shin's indemnity action against Asahi. The Japanese defendant contested jurisdiction. Asahi certainly knew that its valve stems, while sold to a Taiwanese company and incorporated into tire tubes in Taiwan, were being installed on motorcycles sold in the United States. For four justices, this was enough — that if a corporation "is *aware* that the final product is being marketed in the forum State, the possibility of a lawsuit there cannot come as a surprise." A different four justices believed that "placement of a product into the stream of commerce, without more, is not an act of the defendant purposefully directed toward the forum State," even if the defendant is aware that the "stream of commerce may or will sweep the product into the forum." There must, in addition, be "an *intent or purpose to serve the market* in the forum State," such as designing products for its market, advertising there or marketing products through an agent.[145] The case was decided on

---

maintained its main, if temporary, office in Ohio during the Japanese occupation of the Philippine Islands during World War II. This was deemed sufficient for general jurisdiction in Ohio.

141 Venue or *forum non conveniens* requirements may limit suit to a particular state, however. *See infra* pp. 259-261.

142 *Hansen v. Denckla*, 357 U.S. 235, 253 (1958) (Delaware trustee's passive receipt of orders from settlor in Florida is insufficient basis for Florida to exercise jurisdiction over trust). *See also McGee v. International Life*, 355 U.S. 220 (1957) (facts that Texas insurance company sent policy to California resident and received premiums from him is sufficient basis for jurisdiction over suit to recover under the policy).

143 *Wordwide Volkswagen, infra* note 146, 444 U.S. at 297.

144 480 U.S. 102 (1987).

145 *Asahi Metal*, 480 U.S. at 111 (emphasis added).

another basis, as discussed below, but the split of opinion on the Court has not been resolved.

Those who would require voluntary and purposeful direction of contacts toward the forum state argue that potential defendants should be able to structure their conduct in such a way as to know where they will be subject to suit and where they will not. Those who would require simple awareness argue that it is unfair for a corporation to profit from a distant market, but to avoid the risks of suit when their products injure people there simply by refraining from sending personnel or licensing distributors there or avoiding advertising there.

Another variant of this problem occurs when the product is in the forum state only because the *consumer-plaintiff brought* it there. The Court has held that such a contact with the forum state cannot be considered a "voluntary" one that is "purposefully directed" by the defendant toward the forum state. In *Worldwide Volkswagen Corp. v. Woodson*,[146] a couple bought a car from a seller in New York and a design defect in the car caused serious injury in an accident in Oklahoma. The Supreme Court held that there was no personal jurisdiction over the New York seller except in New York and neighboring states. The contacts with Oklahoma were the product of the buyer's voluntary action and the seller could not have reasonably foreseen that it would be subjected to suit in Oklahoma. Clearly, if a seller or manufacturer has service facilities or other agents in the forum state, the foreseeability requirement is satisfied — even under the more restricted view stated in *Asahi Metal*. For that reason, the Oklahoma court clearly had jurisdiction over Audi, the *manufacturer* of the car, even though it did not have jurisdiction over the seller.[147]

Intentional Torts When a defendant commits an intentional tort and the defendant has reason to know that its effects will be on the plaintiff in the plaintiff's home state, then the plaintiff's state usually has jurisdiction. Thus, in *Calder v. Jones*,[148] the Supreme Court approved jurisdiction in California — where the plaintiff lived and worked — based on the effects that a defamatory article written in Florida had on the plaintiff there. The "effects test," as it has been called, permits jurisdiction even when the defendant has had no physical contact with the forum state.

Contracts Cases In contract cases, the contacts and overall reasonableness and fairness test is applied in a similar manner. If the contract has connections with more than one state, the course of negotiation and performance of the contract are considered, along with any other indications of reasonable expectations of the parties about where suit might be filed. Thus, in *Burger King Corp. v. Rudzewicz*,[149] Michigan franchisees were subject to personal jurisdiction in Florida because they voluntarily entered into long-term contractual relationship with a Florida corporation and received benefits from it. But in contract cases, the parties often agree on personal jurisdiction by means of a "forum selection clause" in the contract, and there is a "strong presumption" in favor of

146 444 U.S. 286 (1980).

147 *Compare Gray v. American Radiator & Sanitary Corp.*, 176 N.E.2d 761 (Ill. 1961) (Illinois courts had jurisdiction over manufacturer of defective valve, installed by water heater manufacturer, that caused injury to consumer in Illinois).

148 *Calder v. Jones*, 465 U.S. 783 (1984) (article written in Florida about entertainer Shirley Jones and distributed in National Enquirer magazine, which had its largest circulation in California).

149 471 U.S. 462 (1985).

such provisions.[150] Forum selection clauses in consumer contracts may be invalid if found to be unconscionable.[151]

The Overall Reasonableness Factor Even if a court finds the requisite contacts for personal jurisdiction, that court must also test the exercise of such jurisdiction on the facts of that case against an overall reasonableness standard to see if it comports with "traditional notions of fair play and substantial justice." The additional factors generally considered are (1) the actual burden on the defendant of defending in the forum, (2) the interests of the forum state in the case, (3) the plaintiff's interest in getting relief, and (4) systemic interests in "efficient resolution of controversies" and "fundamental substantive social policies."[152] It was the application of these overall reasonableness factors that was the only point on which a majority of the Supreme Court could agree in *Asahi Metal Industry Co. v. Superior Court.* While split 4-4 on whether the sufficient "minimum contacts" existed, eight justices agreed that assertion of jurisdiction by the California courts would be "unreasonable and unfair" in an overall sense because the only claim left in the case was a claim by a Taiwanese company against a Japanese company. The Court emphasized that the Taiwanese tube manufacturer had settled by paying the plaintiff, who was then dismissed from the suit, and that the only claim left in the California court was the Taiwanese company's claim against the Japanese defendant for indemnification of what it had paid the plaintiff.[153]

State "Long-Arm" Statutes Due process is a limit on state court assertions of personal jurisdiction, an issue of federal constitutional law. However, for jurisdiction to be sustained, states must also authorize their courts as a matter of state law to assert jurisdiction over out-of-state defendants. This is done by way of state "long-arm" statutes that specify the extent of their power. Some state long-arm statutes define state-law authority as coextensive with the due process limits.[154] If so, there is no separate issue of whether the assertion of jurisdiction is authorized as a matter of state law. However, a state might choose to limit the powers of its courts to less than the full scope of power that due process would permit.[155]

Internet Contacts The problem with applying the above law to operators of websites on the Internet is that it is difficult to satisfy the requirement that the defendant have purposely directed its contacts toward any particular state, given that a website can

150 *Mitsubishi Motors Corp. v. Soler Chrysler-Plymouth, Inc.*, 473 U.S. 614, 631 (1985) (arbitration clause). *See also The Breman v. Zapata Off-Shore Co.*, 407 U.S. 1 (1972) (dismissing action in Florida federal court in favor of U.K. jurisdiction as specific in maritime contract); *National Equipment Rental, Ltd. v. Szukhent*, 375 U.S. 311 (1964) (appointment of agent in New York for service of New York court process on Michigan defendants with no New York contacts upheld against constitutional attack).

151 *See* Chapter X, p. 410. *But see Carnival Cruise Lines, Inc. v. Shute*, 499 U.S. 585 (1991) (in admiralty suit against cruise ship company for injury sustained on ship, consumer-passenger was held bound by forum selection clause printed on back of her ticket) *superceded by* 46 U.S.C. App. §183c (permitting passengers in maritime cases to sue in any court of competent jurisdiction).

152 *Asahi Metal*, 480 U.S. at 113.

153 *Asahi Metal*, 480 U.S. at 115.

154 *See, e.g.*, Cal. Code of Civ. Pro. §410.0 ("A Court of this state may exercise jurisdiction on any basis not inconsistent with the Constitution of this state or of the United States.")

155 For example, New York gives personal jurisdiction to its courts over cases where there is misconduct outside the state causing "injury to person or property within the state," but only if the defendant (1) "regularly does or solicits business, or engages in any other persistent course of conduct or derives substantial revenue from goods used or consumed or services rendered *in the state*" or (2) "expects or should reasonably expect the act to have consequences in the state and derives substantial revenue from interstate or international commerce." N.Y. Civ.Prac.Law & Rules §302(a)(3) (2008). *See Ingraham v. Carroll*, 687 N.E.2d 1293 (N.Y. 1997).

be accessed by anyone in any state. But some Internet cases are easier to resolve than others. First, if the Internet is used as a means for the defendant to enter into contracts with the residents of the forum state, then contract negotiation, formation and performance that take place over the Internet are treated the same as if mail or telephone communications were used, and *Rudzewicz v. Burger King*, discussed above, is applied.[156] Second, purely "passive" websites that do nothing more than advertise are controlled by the earlier print advertising cases that hold that mere advertising is not sufficient purposeful direction of contacts to any particular state.[157] Third, intentional torts committed on the Internet can usually be resolved by applying the "effects test" of *Calder v. Jones*, discussed above.[158] Cases involving interactive web sites have proven more difficult. In these, courts have tried to determine whether there is "something more" beyond simply maintaining a web site that shows that the defendant purposefully directed his or her activities toward the forum state. In doing so, courts look at the "nature and quality of commercial activity that an entity conducts over the Internet" to see if forum state contacts figure prominently.[159]

A difficult case is one where people respond to a website's invitation to subscribe and receive an electronic publication. Analogy to non-Internet cases is difficult because, in *Keeton v. Hustler Magazine*,[160] a print-medium defamation case, the Supreme Court, noting that the effects of defamation are felt in every state where it is circulated, not just the state where the plaintiff lives, permitted jurisdiction over a magazine that sold 10,000 to 15,000 copies in the forum state, which had no other relationship to the plaintiff or the subject matter of the defamation. Courts have focused in such cases on the "level of interactivity and commercial nature of the exchange of information that occurs on the Web site." Thus, if the only interactivity is providing an e-mail address and the number of subscribers from the forum state is minimal, there is less likely to be jurisdiction. But if there is greater depth of interactive activity with those who respond to invitations to subscribe and substantial numbers of contracts to supply information, services or goods to forum state residents, a finding of jurisdiction is more likely.[161]

2. Personal Jurisdiction Powers of Federal Courts

In contrast to the state courts, the "territory" of federal courts is the entire country. Consequently, one might think that federal courts would have nationwide personal jurisdiction powers and that barriers posed by state borders would be inapplicable to suits in federal court. However, Congress and the Supreme Court in the Federal Rules

---

[156] *See CompuServe, Inc., v. Patterson*, 89 F.3d 1257 (6th Cir. 1996) (jurisdiction existed over Texas resident who contracted with Ohio company to distribute its software and electronically uploaded files to company's computer in Ohio).

[157] *Bensusan Restaurant Corp. v. King*, 937 F.Supp. 295 (S.D.N.Y. 1996), *aff'd* 126 F.3d 25 (2d Cir. 1997) (web advertising); *Witbeck v. Bill Cody's Ranch Inn*, 411 N.W.2d 439 (Mich. 1987) (tour book advertising).

[158] *Panavision Int'l, L.P. v. Toeppen*, 141 F.3d 1316 (9th Cir. 1998) (Toeppen registered Panavision's trademarks as his domain names on the Internet to force Panavision, located in California, to pay him money for them). *Compare* Revell v. Lidov, 317 F.3d 467 (5th Cir. 2002) (Texas plaintiff could not sue New York university's interactive website or Massachusetts contributor to that site in Texas courts, since alleged defamatory contribution did not focus on Texas or any of plaintiff's activities in Texas).

[159] *Cybersell, Inc. v. Cybersell, Inc.*, 130 F.3d 414 (9th Cir. 1997) (use of same registered service mark of Arizona company not sufficient to show purposeful direction and collecting cases).

[160] *Keeton v. Hustler Magazine*, 465 U.S. 770 (1984).

[161] *Zippo Mfg. Co. v. Zippo Dot Com, Inc.*, 952 F.Supp. 1119 (W.D. Pa. 1997) (finding purposeful direction toward Pennsylvania on interactive site that resulted in contracts with 3000 individuals and 7 Internet access providers). The *Zippo* case has been influential in Internet jurisdiction law.

of Civil Procedure have chosen a more limited view that draws a distinction between diversity cases and federal question cases.[162]

State-Law Diversity Claims In diversity cases, state-law claims are being asserted and a federal court may, in general, exercise no more power of personal jurisdiction than may a *state court* of general jurisdiction of the state where the federal court is located.[163] Thus, a plaintiff would gain no advantage in terms of personal jurisdiction by filing a diversity suit in the New York federal court rather than in the New York state court. Keeping federal courts on par with state courts when they handle state-law claims discourages forum-shopping — plaintiffs turning to federal courts solely to extend the reach of personal jurisdiction on a state claim.

Federal Claims When a claim is based on federal law, federal courts are not so confined. If there are sufficient contacts with any one state for personal jurisdiction, the federal court in that state has jurisdiction. If there are insufficient contacts for the general jurisdiction courts of any one state to have jurisdiction, then the federal court may exercise jurisdiction in any manner "consistent with the Constitution and laws of the United States."[164] A federal court handling a federal law claim, then, will have personal jurisdiction over all defendants residing in the United States and all foreign defendants who have the appropriate minimum contacts with the United States as a whole.[165] When both state and federal claims are asserted, personal jurisdiction acquired based on contacts with the entire United States for federal claims permits the court to proceed with the state claims as well.[166]

B. *Forum Non Conveniens*

The common law doctrine of *forum non conveniens* allows a court to decline to exercise jurisdiction if that court "is a seriously inconvenient forum for the trial of the action" and "a more appropriate forum is available to the plaintiff."[167] The question of convenience is committed to the discretion of the trial court, which applies a wide variety of "public" and "private" factors. These are summarized and discussed in the seminal case of *Gulf Oil Corp. v. Gilbert*.[168]

---

162 *See* Chapter V, pp. 188-191 (discussion of diversity and federal question jurisdiction).

163 FRCP 4(k)(1).

164 FRCP 4(k)(2). The provision has been referred to as a federal long-arm statute, since it serves as an affirmative authorization for asserting personal jurisdiction.

165 The relevant Court of Appeals cases are discussed in Chapter XVII, p. 716. Congress has provided for nationwide service of process in certain special kinds of cases. *See, e.g.,* 28 U.S.C.A. §1391 (suits against officials and agents of the U.S. government); 28 U.S.C.A. §2361 (interpleader cases, where there are several claimants to a single fund of money). The Court has upheld interpleader jurisdiction provision as constitutional. *State Farm Fire & Cas. Co. v. Tashire*, 386 U.S. 523 (1967). The applicable due process limitation would be the due process clause of the *5th* Amendment rather than the due process clause of the 14th Amendment, since the 14th Amendment applies only to state courts. *See* Chapter VIII, p. 285.

166 *ESAB Group, Inc. v. Centricut Inc.*, 126 F.3d 617, 628-629 (4th Cir. 1997). For an Internet case aggregating contacts with the entire United States, *see Quokka Sports, Inc. v. Cup Int'l Ltd.*, 99 F.Supp.2d 1105 (N.D. Cal. 1999) (site using .com domain name from U.S. registrar rather than .nz domain, banners with advertising from U.S. companies, quoting advertising rates in U.S. dollars, offering travel packages in U.S. dollars, and offering books in affiliation with Amazon.com showed intent to target U.S. markets).

167 RESTATEMENT (SECOND) OF CONFLICTS OF LAWS §84 (1969). The origin of the doctrine is obscure, but it appears to have originated in Scotland. *See* Barrett, *The Doctrine of Forum Non Conveniens*, 35 CALIFORNIA LAW REV. 380 (1947) and *Zurick v. Inman*, 426 S.W.2d 767, 769 (Tenn. 1968).

168 330 U.S. 501 (1947). They include both "public" administrative difficulties for the court and general appropriateness of handling the case and "private" factors related to practical problems including difficulties of access to evidence.

Forum Non Conveniens in Context Personal jurisdiction is somewhat like *forum non conveniens* in that it deals with where a suit can handled and with convenience. In addition, both state and federal judicial systems have "venue" requirements that assure that trial in the case is held at a place *within that system* that is convenient for parties and witnesses. The state and federal court systems allow for free venue transfer within them for convenience.[169] Thus, personal jurisdiction and venue together have a "funneling" effect: personal jurisdiction determines the state suit can be filed in and venue then narrows it down further, typically to a particular county in a state system or to a particular district in the federal system. Where *forum non conveniens* comes in is when the *most convenient* place within a given judicial system has been found, but that place is *still* inconvenient as compared to a place *outside that judicial system* (another state or another country). In such an event, *forum non conveniens* permits the court to dismiss the lawsuit so that it can be brought in that more convenient judicial system.[170]

In the United States, *forum non conveniens* issues can arise in both interstate and international contexts and in both federal and state courts. However, because federal courts have the power to transfer a case between districts throughout the country,[171] *forum non conveniens* dismissal issues arise in federal court only when the competing, more convenient jurisdiction is a foreign country.

An interstate example of *forum non conveniens* would be as follows. P, from the state of Ohio, is driving his car in Michigan when his brakes fail and he is seriously injured. P sues the manufacturer, one of the "Big Three" auto companies in Michigan, in his own Ohio state court. P does so because Ohio holds defendants strictly liable in product liability cases, while Michigan requires proof of fault.[172] Since all the witnesses, the hospital personnel who treated P, the wrecked vehicles and the accident scene are all in Michigan, it is likely that the Ohio courts will consider dismissing the case so that it can be filed in Michigan. An international example is the case involving the Union Carbide chemical disaster in Bhophal, India, that killed and injured thousands. Instead of suing in the courts of India, the plaintiffs sued in the U.S. federal court in New York City. The main reason was the more advantageous procedural and substantive law that would be applied in the New York federal court, particularly liberal discovery rights and the right to a jury trial. The federal appeals court ordered the action dismissed so that it could be refiled in India. Among other things, it considered the fact that virtually all the witnesses were in India, all the plant records were in Hindi and Indian law would undoubtedly govern liability in the case.[173]

Forum-Shopping and Forum Non Conveniens As these examples indicate, in most *forum non conveniens* cases the plaintiffs involved have chosen to file their case in an inconvenient place in order to avoid unfavorable substantive or procedural law. The incentives to "shop" for better law have increased as the revolution in choice-of-law

---

169 *See* 28 U.S.C.A. §1391 (venue rules) and 28 U.S.C.A. §1404 (transfers among permissive venues).

170 Dismissal rather than transfer is the appropriate remedy for *forum non conveniens*, since one sovereign cannot transfer its cases to another in the absence of some special agreement to that effect.

171 *See supra* note 169.

172 Personal jurisdiction exists in Ohio because the defendant is a national manufacturer and there is general personal jurisdiction. Plaintiff residence venue is allowed in many state courts.

173 *In re Union Carbide Corp. Gas Plant Disaster*, 809 F.2d 195 (2d Cir. 1987). One might add that juries in large cities, such as New York, tend to be more sympathetic to plaintiffs in personal injury cases than are juries from suburban or rural areas. Perhaps part of the reason for the result in the case was that the Indian government, which had argued in the trial court that the case should stay in the U.S. courts because Indian courts could not handle such a large, complex case, changed its position and argued for dismissal in the court of appeals after negative political reaction at home to its implied criticism of Indian courts.

rules has increased the number of instances when a forum court will apply its own law to a dispute.[174] However, the Supreme Court has ruled that the possible loss of advantageous procedural or substantive law if a *forum non conveniens* dismissal is granted "should ordinarily not be given conclusive or even substantial weight."[175] A negative change in law matters only if the more convenient forum does not provide any realistic possibility of recovery.[176] While courts at one point maintained that, if at least one party to the lawsuit is from the forum state, that was sufficient to defeat a *forum non conveniens* dismissal, this view is generally not followed anymore.[177]

Conditional *forum non conveniens* dismissals are possible to deal with potential barriers to suit in the more convenient forum, particularly personal jurisdiction or statute of limitations problems. Thus, the federal court in the Union Carbide Bhophal disaster case made its dismissal conditional upon Union Carbide consenting to the jurisdiction of the Indian courts and waiving any applicable statute of limitations.[178]

C. Recognition of Judgments: The "Full Faith and Credit" Requirement

1. Enforcement and Effect of Out-of-State Judgments

The "full faith and credit" clause of the Constitution states that "Full Faith and Credit shall be given in each State to the public Acts, Records, and judicial Proceedings of every other State."[179] This requires states to enforce judgments rendered in other states.[180] *Federal* courts must also recognize *state* court judgments, though this results not from constitutional requirements, but from a statute.[181] Federal courts in one part of the country give preclusive effect to judgments of federal courts in other parts of the country because they are all part of the same court system.[182]

Traditionally and still in some states, a plaintiff who wins a judgment and finds that the defendant has property in another state can enforce that judgment by filing a "suit on the judgment" in that other state. This suit converts the judgment of the first state into a judgment of the second and the plaintiff can proceed to enforce it against the defendant's property. However, 39 states have adopted the Uniform Enforcement of Foreign Judgments Act, which provides that, upon completing certain filing and notice require-

---

174 *See infra*, pp. 265-268 (trends in choice-of-law doctrine).

175 *Piper Aircraft Co. v. Reyno*, 454 U.S. 235, 247 (1981) (in suit arising out of a plane crash in Scotland, the absence of strict liability under Scottish law and lower damage awards in its courts afford no basis to keep case in Pennsylvania federal court). This decision affects only federal courts, as state courts can have their own standards. *See* FRIEDENTHAL, KANE & MILLER, *supra* note 1, §§2.15-2.17 (venue and *forum non conveniens*).

176 Some courts disagree even with this exception and have prohibited permitting the plaintiff to proceed even if suit would be impossible in the more convenient forum. *See Shiley, Inc. v. Superior Court*, 6 Cal. Rptr. 2d 38 (Cal. Ct. App. 1992) (claim would have been barred by statute of limitations).

177 *See, e.g., Silver v. Great American Ins. Co.*, 278 N.E.2d 619 (N.Y. 1972) (residence of defendant only one factor to consider); *Russell v. Chrysler Corp.*, 505 N.W.2d 263 (Mich. 1993) (same). *See also Gulf Oil Corp. v. Gilbert, supra* (New York is inconvenient forum even though defendant was licensed to do business there).

178 Statutes of limitations provide time periods within which a person with a claim must bring that claim or be barred.

179 Article IV §1. *See also* 28 U.S.C.A. §1738 (judgements "shall have the same full faith and credit in every court within the United States . . . as they have by law and usage in the courts of such State.")

180 The procedure for enforcing judgments within a state was discussed *supra* p. 244.

181 28 U.S.C.A. §1738.

182 For recognition of judgments from foreign countries, *see* Chapter XVII, pp. 726-728.

ments in the second state, the judgment will have "the same effect" as a judgment of that second state. This eliminates the need for filing a suit on the judgment.[183]

A second function of "full faith and credit" is that it serves as an interstate preclusion device. Thus, an out-of-state judgment has the same claim and issue preclusion effects discussed earlier that it does in the state that rendered it.[184]

2. Exceptions to Full Faith and Credit

Direct and Collateral Attacks The grounds for avoiding the effects of the rendering state's judgment in the courts of the enforcing state are few and narrow. No defenses to liability under the law of the rendering state that could have been raised in the proceedings in the rendering state can be raised. And it is no ground for challenge that the rendering state's laws that permitted recovery violate the public policy or laws of the enforcing state. For example, in *Fauntleroy v. Lum*,[185] the Supreme Court required Mississippi courts to enforce a Missouri judgment based on a gambling debt incurred in Mississippi — a debt that was illegal and unenforceable under Mississippi law. The Court noted that, "as the jurisdiction of the Missouri court is not open to dispute, the judgment cannot be impeached in Mississippi even if it went upon a misapprehension of Mississippi law."

The reason for the Court's last statement is that the law makes a distinction between "direct" attacks on judgments and "collateral" attacks. A direct attack is a challenge to a judgment that is mounted in that very lawsuit. An example is a timely appeal, which is a continuation of the same lawsuit in the appeals court. A collateral attack is any challenge to the validity of a judgment that is mounted in a different case after the judgment in the first case is final. Usually collateral challenges are barred by *res judicata* and allied finality doctrines. A defendant's opposition to proceedings to enforce a judgment based on its invalidity is considered a collateral attack. If a collateral attack would not be permitted in the *rendering* state's courts, then full faith and credit would prohibit the *enforcing* state from permitting one.

The Jurisdiction Exception A major exception to the rule against collateral attacks is a challenge to the judgment based on absence of personal jurisdiction. The enforcing state is required by the Constitution to entertain arguments that the rendering court did not have personal jurisdiction. However, this is permitted only if the defendant did not appear in the original action, since this would have afforded the defendant an opportunity to mount a direct attack on jurisdiction.[186] A challenge based on the allegation that the judgment was procured by fraud is possible as well.[187]

---

183 *See* www.nccusl.org/Update/. *See also* Chapter I, p. 34, note 155 (Uniform Law Commissioners). *See generally* EUGENE F. SCOLES, PETER HAY, PATRICK J. BORCHERS & SYMEON SYMEONIDES, HORNBOOK ON CONFLICT OF LAWS, 4TH ED. §§24.8-24.32 (West 2004).

184 *See supra*, pp. 248-250, and RESTATEMENT OF JUDGMENTS, 2D, *supra* note 109, §86 (effect of state court judgment in another state) and §87 (effect of federal court judgment in state court) and RESTATEMENT OF CONFLICTS, 2D §103 (American Law Institute 1969) (effect of judgment of one state in another state). However, when a federal court decides a state law claim, usually in a diversity case, it is federal common law of judgments that applies, but federal common law adopts the law of the *state where the federal court is located*. *Semtek International, Inc. v. Lockheed Martin Corp.*, 531 U.S. 497 (2001).

185 210 U.S. 230 (1908).

186 *See Pennoyer v. Neff*, 95 U.S. 714 (1877). Collateral challenges to *subject-matter* jurisdiction are also possible, but only if the rendering jurisdiction permits them to be raised collaterally after judgment. *Aldrich v. Aldrich*, 378 U.S. 540 (1964). However, this sort of challenge is rarely provided for under state law. Federal subject-matter jurisdiction is generally not subject to collateral challenge. *See Chicot County Drainage Dist. v. Baxter State Bank*, 308 U.S. 371 (1940) and WRIGHT, *supra* note 1, at 84-85.

187 *See* SCOLES ET AL, *supra* note 183, §24.17.

D. Choice-of-Law Rules

In Chapter I, we observed how the existence of 50 coordinate state lawmaking jurisdictions side-by-side can complicate litigation that involves people, transactions or occurrences connected with more than one state. A major complication is the question of which state's law will be applied in such a case — the question of choice of law. It would be useful if this issue were governed by *federal* law instead of the law of each individual state. Federal law would better mediate between the competing interests of the states involved and would provide a single consistent body of choice-of-law doctrine to apply that would be ultimately resolvable by the U.S. Supreme Court. However, Congress has enacted no federal statute on conflict of laws. Each state court in which a case is filed applies its own choice-of-law rules. And, as discussed in Chapter V, even *federal* courts adjudicating state-law claims apply the choice-of-law rules of the state where it sits.[188]

There are a few modest federal constitutional limitations on choice of law, which are discussed next. After that, we will consider the variety of state conflicts rules that can be applied.[189]

1. Constitutional Limitations on State Choice-of-Law Rules

Choice-of-law decisions implicate state sovereignty since one state is, in effect, "reaching out" to apply its law to a dispute having a substantial connection with another state. Choice of law also concerns fairness since substantial connections with one state may well create reliance interests that can be violated when the law from a different state is suddenly applied. Given these considerations, one might expect that constitutional limitations related to interstate federalism or due process would limit state choice-of-law rules in a major way. In fact, their limitations are modest.

The due process clause of the 14th Amendment prevents application of the law of a state when a dispute has *no connection at all* to that state (other than the fact suit was filed there).[190] In *Allstate Ins. Co. v. Hague*,[191] the Supreme Court held that "that State must have a significant contact or significant aggregation of contacts, creating state interests, such that choice of its law is neither arbitrary nor fundamentally unfair."[192] However, the facts of *Hague* demonstrate how minimal those contacts can be and how it does not matter that there is another state with comparatively greater contacts. *Hague* permitted Minnesota to apply its own law to a claim against an insurance company

---

188 *See* Chapter V, p. 192 and *Klaxon Co. v. Stentor Electric Mfg. Co.*, 313 U.S. 487 (1941).

189 A standard treatise on choice of law discussing in depth many of the issues covered in this section is SCOLES ET AL., *supra* note 183. A previous edition of an introductory chapter of this book, written for a European audience, appeared as PETER HAY & RONALD ROTUNDA, THE AMERICAN FEDERAL SYSTEM (Giuffrè, Milan, Italy and Oceana Press, Dobbs Ferry, N.Y. 1982). For a more succinct summary *see* WILLIAM M. RICHMAN & WILLIAM L. REYNOLDS, UNDERSTANDING CONFLICT OF LAWS 3D ED. (Matthew Bender 2002).

190 *Home Insurance Co. v. Dick*, 281 U.S. 397 (1930) (Texas could not apply its own law to a dispute over an insurance policy where nothing in any way relating to the policy sued on was done or required to be done in Texas). *See also Phillips Petroleum Co. v. Shutts*, 472 U.S. 797 (1985) (Kansas could not constitutionally apply its own law to claims of class members in class action who had no connection with Kansas). The Court at one time held that the full faith and credit clause of Article IV provided an independent and stricter limitation on a state's refusal to apply the law of another state, but it has since abandoned the idea, essentially merging it into the due process test. *See* SCOLES ET AL., *supra* note 183, §3.24.

191 449 U.S. 302 (1981). *See also Franchise Tax Bd. v. Hyatt*, 538 U.S. 488 (2003) (*Hague* contacts test applied to approve application of Nevada law in suit against California tax agency in Nevada courts).

192 449 U.S. at 313. While this "contacts" test sounds similar to the test for personal jurisdiction over out-of-state defendants, the contacts needed are much less, as the facts of the *Hague* case make clear. *Compare* discussion, *supra* pp. 254-257.

arising out of a motorcycle accident that caused the death of the insured. The contract of insurance was taken out in Wisconsin, the accident was in Wisconsin and both people involved in the accident were residents of Wisconsin. However, the Supreme Court found three sufficient "contacts" between the suit and Minnesota: the insured victim had worked in Minnesota for years before his death, the plaintiff widow had moved to Minnesota *after* his death, and the defendant insurance company did business (unrelated to the suit) in Minnesota.

2. The Variety of State Choice-of-Law Rules

Freed from significant constitutional or federal statutory restraints, states have taken three basic approaches to choice of law: the traditional "vested rights" doctrine, the various "interest" and "policy" analysis approaches, and the "most significant relationship" theory of the Second Restatement.

Vested Rights Approach to Conflicts The traditional "vested rights" doctrine dominated the view of courts in the United States during the period 1900-1950 and was the approach taken by the 1934 First Restatement of the Conflict of Laws. It was based on the notion of "legislative jurisdiction" of a particular sovereign — the idea that a state has the power to prescribe rules of conduct for transactions or occurrences taking place on its own territory. Once the "last event" of the transaction or occurrence takes place on the territory of that state, the parties to it acquire vested rights under the law of that jurisdiction that cannot be taken away. For instance, in the case of an airplane crash, if the crash occurred in California and the plaintiff sued claiming that the pilot was negligent, the law of California would govern because that was where all the acts or omissions constituting the tort took place (*lex loci delicti*). In contract cases, the place the offer was accepted and, therefore, where the contract was formed, would govern. Similarly, the law of the jurisdiction where a marriage was performed determined its validity, and the law of the place where land was located determined title.[193]

One problem with the vested rights approach is its malleability. What law applies depends on how the claim is characterized and different characterizations are often possible. For example, a suit by the passenger-survivor of an airplane crash could be characterized as a *tort* claim, pointing to the law of the place of crash. But it might also be characterized as a suit for *breach of contract* for transportation, pointing to the law of the place the ticket was purchased — often and not coincidentally the forum state and the state where the plaintiff resides.[194] By approaching choice-of-law issue by issue, called "*dépeçage*," even more manipulation was possible. Thus, in one case, the court avoided a defense of interspousal immunity to a tort claim by characterizing the issue as one of *family* law calling for application of law of place of marriage, while applying a different body of *tort* law to remaining aspects of the claim.[195] Vested rights can thus be manipulated to provide "escape devices" to allow application of the forum state's law or some other law favorable to one or the other party.

193 *See generally* SCOLES ET AL., *supra* note 183, pp. 557-1256 (applying of the "vested rights" and other choice-of-law theories over a wide spectrum of subject-matter areas). *See also* RESTATEMENT OF CONFLICTS (American Law Institute 1934) §377 (torts), §311 (contracts), §§215, 255 (property).

194 This characterization was attempted, but rejected by the court in *Kilberg v. Northeast Airlines, Inc.*, 172 N.E.2d 526 (N.Y. 1961), which reached the same result by characterizing the foreign jurisdiction's limitation on suit as "procedural." *See also Levy v. Daniels' U-Drive Auto Renting Co.*, 143 A. 163 (Conn. 1928) (tort claim re-characterized as contract claim).

195 *See Haumschild v. Continental Cas. Co.*, 95 N.W.2d 814 (Wis.1959).

A more fundamental criticism of the "vested rights" theory is that it focuses on a territorial connection to some state that is artificial and often coincidental. Too often it points the forum court away from its own law, despite the existence of strong forum state interests in having its law applied. In tort cases, victims and survivors of torts suffered in other states often seek to sue in the courts of their own state. Since the forum state will be responsible for supporting those victims should they be unable to obtain adequate compensation, it has a strong interest in having its law applied. In light of this interest, many would argue that, in the case of an interstate airplane flight that crashed in California, it is a mere fortuity that the crash took place in California, or in any other state the plane might have flown over on its way to California.

Interest Analysis and Policy Approaches to Choice of Law Dissatisfaction with the vested rights approach led to the formulation by academic commentators of several different theories, which have been adopted, in whole or in part, by some state courts. There are many varied descriptions of these approaches, but most of them require the judge to resolve choice-of-law questions by (1) determining the policies behind the laws involved and (2) deciding the extent to which the states involved have an interest in applying law reflecting those policies to the issue presented in the suit.[196]

Primary among the interests asserted in many of these theories are the interests of the forum state. Thus, the net result of most such analyses is to increase the number of occasions when a *forum* court will apply its *own* law. Setting the tone for many of these interest-oriented reactions to vested rights is Professor Currie's "nihilist" statement: "We would be better off without choice-of-law rules. Normally, even in cases involving foreign elements, the court should be expected as a matter of course to apply the rules of the forum."[197]

One contribution to interest analysis, provided by Professor Currie, is the concept of "false conflict," which has become "an integral part of all modern policy-based analyses."[198] A "false conflict" describes the situation when an analysis of the *policies* underlying apparently conflicting laws discloses that those *policies* do not conflict. For example, assume that in the California airplane crash hypothetical posited earlier a wrongful death suit is brought in New York against a Minnesota-based airline company. Assume further that New York law allows recovery by the surviving children of the present value of the decedent's future earnings, while California, the place of the crash, does not allow recovery of that category of damages.[199] A court could well decide that the two different rules present a false conflict. If the purpose of California's damages limitation is to protect *California courts* from speculative computations of future damages and to protect *California defendants* from excessive verdicts, then that purpose is inapplicable where suit is brought outside of California and against a non-California corporation. Since there is no "true" conflict, the forum state (New York) should apply its own law.[200]

The false conflict idea does not invariably point to the forum state's law, however. This is illustrated by a New York case in which a Boy Scout was sexually assaulted by a supervisor on an outing. The suit against the Boy Scout organization alleged that it was

196 For an overview of these various theories, *see* SCOLES ET AL., *supra* note 183, at 25-68.

197 Brainerd Currie, *Notes on Methods and Objective in the Conflict of Laws*, 1959 DUKE L.J. 171, 177.

198 SCOLES ET AL., *supra* note 183, at 29.

199 These assumptions should not be taken as representing the true state of the law in any of the states mentioned.

200 *See Griffith v. United Airlines*, 203 A.2d 796 (Pa. 1964).

negligent in selecting the offending supervisor. The issue was whether New Jersey's charitable immunity would bar suit. The defendant organization and the plaintiffs were from New Jersey and the negligent selection of the supervisor took place in New Jersey. However, the incident and the outing were in New York, and the plaintiffs brought suit in New York, probably in an attempt to avoid New Jersey law. The New York court determined that the policy underlying immunity — regulating or encouraging charities — was solely an interest of New Jersey. Since the apparent conflict with New York's abolition of charitable immunity was a false one, New Jersey law applied and the suit was dismissed.[201]

In the case of a "true conflict," an interest analysis approach attempts to weigh the interests of the various states involved.[202] These interests may reflect such policies as protecting local victims, protecting local defendants, or other more specific interests arising from the particular wrong involved. One method of weighing competing states' interests is California's "comparative impairment" test. Under this test, a court compares the extent of damage that application of one or the other legal rule to the case would inflict on the competing states' interests. The court should choose the rule that causes the *lesser* degree of impairment. A leading case involved liability of a bar for injuries caused by drunk customers (referred to as "dram shop" liability). California plaintiffs were injured in California by a drunk California patron who was driving home from a Nevada bar. Plaintiffs sued the bar in the California courts. The bar claimed that Nevada law, which did not provide for liability in such a case, applied. The California Supreme Court first identified the respective interests: California's interest was in protecting its residents from the acts of intoxicated individuals while Nevada's policy was to protect its bar owners from ruinous liability. The court concluded that California's interests would suffer greater impairment from *not* imposing liability than Nevada's interests would suffer from *imposing* liability. California's interest was greater, the court said, because its interest extended to harm caused by persons who became intoxicated *both in California and out of state*. It seemed to the court that Nevada's attempt to protect *local* businesses was much less seriously impaired since the defendant Nevada bar in that case had advertised in California to attract California residents. The court noted that there might be more serious impairment of Nevada's local interests if the case involved a truly "local" bar that did no advertising and did not otherwise seek to attract California residents.[203]

When freely evaluating competing states' interests, there is clearly the tendency of a forum court to prefer its own state's interests. An even stronger "homing tendency" is provided by theories that state a preference for the "better rule of law," associated with Professor Leflar.[204] In the absence of objective criteria for determining when one legal rule is "better" than another, the chances are great that the forum state, which has chosen to adopt the legal rule it has over all other choices, will modestly find its own law to be "better" than others. It is true that there are often other "choice-influencing considerations" that might counterbalance any "homing tendency," but these factors

---

201 *Schultz v. Boy Scouts of America*, 480 N.E.2d 679 (N.Y. 1985). The other situation where a "false conflict" exists is where the non-forum state explicitly disclaims an interest in applying its own law outside its borders by providing for a *renvoi* to the forum state's law or an *envoi* to the law of a third jurisdiction. There is substantial overlap in the functions performed by these two doctrines and the "false conflict" idea.

202 Professor Currie's approach would refuse to resolve "true" conflicts since it assumes that it is a legislative rather than judicial function to weigh truly conflicting interests.

203 *Bernhard v. Harrah's Club*, 546 P.2d 719 (Cal.1976).

204 *See* SCOLES ET AL., *supra* note 183, §2.13.

tend to be vague and contradictory. Professor Leflar's factors would take into account predictability of results, maintenance of interstate and international order, simplification of the judicial task, advancement of the forum's governmental interests, as well as the application of the better rule of law.

Second Restatement Approach to Conflicts The most recent approach to choice of law is the Second Restatement of Conflicts, promulgated in 1971, which seeks to determine which state has the "most significant relationship" to the case. It provides specific presumptive rules for types of cases that are applied in the absence of strong countervailing indications pointing in a different direction. Clearly, the Second Restatement edges away from the overwhelming tendency of the forum court to favor application of its own law and seeks to provide more stability to choice of law than existed with pure interest analysis.

For example, §146 on torts states that "the local law of the state where the injury occurred determines the rights and liabilities of the parties, unless, with respect to the particular issue, some other state has a more significant relationship under the principles of §6 to the occurrence and the parties." Section 6 significantly leaves out any "better rule of law" factor and includes a "protection of justified expectations" factor.[205] What contacts are counted to determine a "more significant relationship" are set out in a non-exhaustive list in §145(2): place of the injury, place of the conduct causing the injury, residence or place of business or incorporation of the parties, and the place where any relationship between the parties is centered. Regarding contracts, §188 lists as appropriate contacts generating interests the place of negotiation, formation or performance of the contract, the place where the object of the contract is located, and the parties' domicile, nationality, residence place of business or incorporation — all to be considered in light of the §6 factors. Similar to torts, it provides a presumptive rule that, whenever the place of negotiation and performance are in the same state, that state "will *usually* be the state that has the greatest interest in the determination of issues arising under the contract."[206]

If the forum state's choice-of-law rules point to the law of another state, that other state's choice-of-law rules may sometimes point back to the forum state's law, "returning" the case or issue back to the forum state. For example, State A's choice-of-law rules may indicate that State B's standard of liability (strict liability) should apply, but State B's choice-of-law rules, if applicable, would apply State A's standard of liability (negligence). This "return" of the case to State A, called *"renvoi,"* is generally not applicable in the United States.[207] However, some of the purposes of *renvoi* are accomplished through the device of the "false conflict": if State B's law points back to State A's law, that could be seen as a disclaimer by State A of any interest in applying its own law. In addition, §8 of the Second Restatement of Conflicts, allows for *renvoi* when "the objective of the particular choice-of-law rule is that the forum reach the same result on the very facts

---

205 The Second Restatement requires consideration of the needs of the interstate and international system, the relevant policies of the forum, the relevant policies of the other interested states and their interests in the determination of a particular issue, the protection of justified expectations, the basic policies underlying the particular field of law, and the certainty, predictability and uniformity of result.

206 §188(3) (emphasis added). Other sections provide presumptive rules for different kinds of contracts. The 1980 Convention on the Law Applicable to Contractual Obligations of the European Communities adopts a test similar to the Second Restatement, providing that the law of the "most closely connected" country should apply and setting out rules with rebuttable presumptions. *See* SCOLES ET AL., *supra* note 183, §18.40.

207 This has been criticized. *See* SCOLES ET AL., *supra* note 183, §3.13. Similarly, there can be an *envoi*, a direction by a non-forum state to follow the law of a third state.

involved as would the courts of another state" or "when the state of the forum has no substantial relationship to the particular issue or the parties."

3. Trends in Conflicts Law in the Courts

Lack of Clarity in the Courts Some states still apply some version of "vested rights," some use a pure interest analysis approach, while yet others have adopted the Second Restatement. The choice-of-law approach in many states is unclear. Confusion is increased by the fact that academic commentators advocating conflicting theories lay claim to the same judicial decisions as representing their favorite approach. New York has employed an approach that combines elements of straight policy choices, interest balancing and the notion of a lawsuit's "center of gravity."[208] But later New York cases demonstrate more certainty through use of specific rules distilled from policy analysis.[209]

While the vested rights theory had its faults, many are coming to realize that even more damage is done by the trend toward applying the forum state's law. When the result in litigation depends on the place suit is filed, plaintiffs will do their best to forum-shop for favorable law. Since the Supreme Court has effectively abdicated any constitutional control over choice of law and has abandoned choice of law to state prerogatives, the answer to this problem will come slowly, if at all.[210]

Some Stability for Contracts and Property The problem of unpredictability of choice of law is less in contracts situations since the parties can and often do agree on what law will apply in the event of a breach. For example, §1-105 of the Uniform Commercial Code provides that "when a transaction bears a reasonable relationship to this state and also to another state or nation the parties may agree that the law of either this state or of such other state or nation shall govern their rights and duties." Similar party autonomy is recognized in §187 of the Second Restatement. Choice of law is also more predictable in property cases since the rule that the law of the place where the property is located will govern, is well established.[211]

Other Mitigating Factors It should also be pointed out that the problem of over-application of the forum's law is somewhat ameliorated by the "minimum contact" requirement of personal jurisdiction, which limits the number of states in which a plaintiff may sue.[212] The doctrine of *forum non conveniens* provides some protection as well.[213] However, for companies whose products or services bring them into contact with residents of every state in the United States, it is possible that the law of any of the fifty states could be applied to judge their conduct.

---

208 *See Babcock v. Jackson*, 191 N.E.2d 279 (N.Y. 1963).

209 See *Neumeier v. Kuehner*, 286 N.E.2d 454 (N.Y. 1973) (rules for liability of car drivers to passengers) and *Cooney v. Osgood Machinery, Inc.*, 612 N.E.2d 277 (N.Y. 1993) (law governing contribution between joint tortfeasors is the law of the state where the insurance to cover the loss was taken out). *See* Symposium on *Cooney v. Osgood Machinery, Inc.*, 59 BROOKLYN L. REV. 1323 (1994).

210 *See* discussion *supra* p. 263 (*Hague*).

211 *See* SCOLES ET AL., *supra* note 183, §19.2.

212 *See supra* pp. 253-259.

213 *See supra* pp. 259-261.

CHAPTER VIII

CRIMINAL PROCEDURE

This chapter is divided into two parts. Part I outlines the procedural steps in the criminal justice process. Part II deals with constitutional criminal procedure law — limitations on the criminal justice process imposed by the Constitution.

PART I: An Outline of the Criminal Justice Process

The system of criminal procedure in the United States is both adversarial and accusatorial.[1] The adversarial aspects have been discussed: the parties themselves develop and present the evidence for their side before the jury, and the judge acts only as necessary to assure overall fairness of the contest between the sides.[2] Accusatorial principles are not the same as adversarial principles, but they complement each other. Accusatorial principles require the "government in its contest with the individual to shoulder the entire load,"[3] while adversarial principles require that the prosecutor, as the government's representative, present the case against the defendant. Thus, the prosecutor generally must bear the entire burden of proving the defendant's guilt on every element of the crime without the compelled assistance of the accused or the helping hand of the judge. The U.S. system allows for exceptions to the accusatorial principle, just as it contemplates exceptions to the adversarial principle, but it remains primarily accusatorial and adversarial.[4]

A. Arrest, Formal Charges and the First Appearance

Crimes are divided into "felonies" and "misdemeanors." The classification is determined by the potential sentence: felonies are crimes punishable by death or by imprisonment for a year or more, and misdemeanors are punishable by less than a year in jail. However, some states have what are called "high misdemeanors," crimes punishable by up to two years in jail. The felony-misdemeanor distinction has an impact upon the nature of pre-trial procedure, as noted below.[5]

Police Investigation and Arrest As in most countries, the police are usually the first to arrive at the scene of a crime or to receive a report of one.[6] If the report is based upon

---

1 *See generally* JOHN H. MERRYMAN, THE CIVIL LAW TRADITION, 2D ED. 126-128 (Stanford University 1985) and WAYNE R. LAFAVE, JEROLD H. ISRAEL & NANCY KING, HORNBOOK ON CRIMINAL PROCEDURE, 4TH ED. 31-34 (West 2004, 2005), the standard treatise on criminal procedure. *See also* JOSHUA DRESSLER, UNDERSTANDING CRIMINAL PROCEDURE, 2D ED. (Matthew Bender 1997). *See also* ROBERT M. BLOOM AND MARK S. BRODIN, CONSTITUTIONAL CRIMINAL PROCEDURE: EXAMPLES AND EXPLANATIONS, 4TH ED. (Aspen 2004). For an excellent comparative guide, *see* FLOYD FEENEY & JOACHIM HERMANN, ONE CASE — TWO SYSTEMS (Transnational 2005) (comparison of handling of same case in California and Augsberg with specific factual detail and forms).

2 *See* Chapter III, pp. 80-85.

3 *Murphy v. Waterfront Commission*, 378 U.S. 52, 55 (1964). *See* LAFAVE, ISRAEL & KING, *supra* note 1, §1.4(d).

4 Examples of exceptions from the pure form of accusatorial justice include requiring the defendant to give pretrial notice of certain defenses (such as alibi and insanity), to bear the burden of proof on some defenses, and to supply blood, handwriting samples, and fingerprints. *See infra* note 37.

5 Violations of traffic regulations and city ordinances constitute a third category: offenses that do not normally result in arrest and are often considered "civil infractions," rather than crimes. These violations are usually disposed of by the payment of a fine, often by mail.

6 The description here presents a composite picture of procedure that would be typical in most states, with occasional references to federal procedure. *See generally* LAFAVE, ISRAEL & KING, *supra* note 1, §§1.2-1.5. For a detailed description of the federal criminal process, complete with transcripts of hearings and forms, *see* HARRY L. SUBIN, BARRY BERKE & ERIC TIRSCHWELL, THE PRACTICE OF FEDERAL CRIMINAL LAW PROCESS:

police observation and the police believe that they have "probable cause" to believe the suspect committed a crime, the suspect is immediately arrested. "Probable cause" to arrest exists when "the facts and circumstances within [the officers'] knowledge and of which they had reasonably trustworthy information [are] sufficient in themselves to warrant a man [sic] of reasonable caution in the belief that an offense has been or is being committed."[7] If the report of a crime is based on information provided by a victim, the police will conduct a pre-arrest investigation to determine if there is sufficient evidence to support charges against a suspect. The police may also seek an arrest warrant from a judge if they submit written affidavits (sworn statements under oath) showing that there is probable cause to believe the accused committed the crime. However, the vast majority of arrests are made based on probable cause, without a judicial warrant. Police still regularly seek warrants are because a court is more likely to uphold the legality of warranted arrests, especially where the issue of probable cause is a close one. After an arrest, the police will also carry out any necessary investigation to gather further evidence against the person arrested.

After an arrest is made, a higher ranking police official, followed by a prosecutor will informally review the sufficiency of the evidence to determine whether to charge the accused with the crime. These reviews are not impartial or even quasi-judicial. The arrestee does not appear and the only information comes from the police working on the case, usually in the form of an arrest report and any additional evidence discovered. In some jurisdictions, police decide not to file charges in 10 to 15% of their arrests, most of them misdemeanors. After the police file the charges, the prosecutor reviews them. The prosecutor generally decides not to continue the case in 30 to 50% of felony charges.

Police Independence In general, the police carry out both pre-arrest and post-arrest investigations without any direct supervision by or assistance from the prosecutor. Although the police eventually have to justify their arrests and criminal charges before the prosecutor will institute a criminal case in court, the prosecutor does not normally get directly involved in the police investigation, except in very important cases.[8] Judicial involvement is also episodic and only at the request of the police. It mainly takes the form of the issuance of search warrants or arrest warrants as needed, for which the police apply directly to a judge, again without the involvement of the prosecutor. No judge or any other judicial officer has responsibility for overall supervision of the investigation.

Witness Assistance in Investigations. Police do not have the power to issue subpoenas or otherwise to compel unwilling witnesses or victims to give statements or even to talk to them. Instead, the police must resort to persuasion, pressure or charm, as the situation demands, to obtain information.[9] Court subpoenas are only permitted

---

PROSECUTION AND DEFENSE (West 2005).

   7   *Brinegar v. United States*, 338 U.S. 160, 175-76 (1949). The Court observed that it "mean[s] more than bare suspicion," but "less than evidence which would justify . . . conviction." *See also Maryland v. Pringle*, 540 U.S. 366 (2003) (officers had probable cause to arrest all 3 men in a car for possession of cocaine found hidden in the car as to which all denied any knowledge).

   8   The police may occasionally seek the prosecutor's legal advice on how to proceed, but even this degree of involvement is rare.

   9   *See Davis v. Mississippi*, 394 U.S. 721, 727 n. 6 (1969) ("while the police have the right to request citizens to answer voluntarily questions concerning unsolved crimes they have no right to compel them to answer."); *Kolender v. Lawson*, 461 U.S. 352 (1983) (police may stop a person who is a suspect or a material witness "for the purpose of asking investigation questions" and "may ask them in such a way calculated to obtain an answer. But they may not *compel* an answer and must allow the person to leave after a reasonable period of time unless the information they have acquired during the encounter has given them

to compel witness attendance at trials or other hearings. Prosecutors also have no subpoena power. However, federal law and the law of most states provide for arrest and detention of a "material witness" — a prosecution or defense witness who may not appear at a trial or hearing in response to a subpoena.[10] In the federal system, the material witness must be released after a deposition has been taken and the testimony is preserved. However, the material witness detention power has often been used as a general administrative and investigative tool in a manner that exceeds its real purpose of preserving testimony and assuring witness attendance at trial. For instance, the material witness detention power has been used to detain illegal immigrants extensively.[11] Beyond the material witness power, the only way prosecutors can compel a witness to come forward is if a *grand jury* conducts the investigation and issues a subpoena, as discussed in the following paragraph.

The Investigative Grand Jury   Generally, grand juries take a more passive role — screening cases after the prosecution decides it has enough evidence to charge a suspect.[12] But some jurisdictions provide for *investigative* grand juries, which can issue subpoenas to witnesses, including potential defendants. Grand juries do not routinely investigate ordinary criminal cases because their investigations, compared to police investigations, are "expensive, time consuming, and logistically cumbersome."[13] Nonetheless, investigative grand juries often used in three kinds of cases: (1) organized crime cases, in which a complicated criminal structure must be unraveled and victims and potential witnesses are particularly wary of cooperating; (2) cases involving political figures (*e.g.*, corruption), in which use of the grand jury would allay any public suspicions about the objectivity and thoroughness of the investigation;[14] and (3) cases involving abuse of private corporate power, both because they are complicated and because there is substantial public interest in them.

Persons called before the grand jury, however, can decline to testify on grounds of self-incrimination under the 5th Amendment of the Constitution. If the prosecution believes the witness's evidence is crucial to the investigation, the prosecutor can obtain a court order compelling testimony. However, the prosecution must first grant the witness immunity from prosecution for any crimes derived from the compelled testimony.[15]

Prosecutorial Discretion   Once prosecutors become involved in a criminal case, they enjoy a great degree of discretion in their decision to drop charges or dismiss cases

---

probable cause sufficient to justify an arrest."). Only in 2004 did the U.S. Supreme Court decide that a person stopped on reasonable suspicion can be criminally punished for refusing to give his or her name when so requested by a police officer. *Hiibel v. Sixth Judicial District Court*, 542 U.S. 177 (2004). For more on "reasonable suspicion," *see infra* p. 295, where *Terry* stops are discussed.

10 *See* 18 U.S.C.A. §3144 (federal statute) (permitting arrest of any person whose "testimony . . . is material in a criminal proceeding . . . if it is shown that it may become impracticable to secure the presence of the person by subpoena").

11 Stacey M. Studnicki, Material Witness Detention: Justice Served or Denied?, 40 WAYNE L. REV. 1533 (1994). *See United States v. Valenzuela-Bernal*, 458 U.S. 858 (1982) (detention of illegal aliens as materials witnesses in prosecution of smuggler who transported them).

12 *See infra* pp. 273-275.

13 LAFAVE, ISRAEL & KING, *supra* note 1, p. 405.

14 For example, the investigation of President Clinton by the Special Prosecutor for financial irregularities in matter involving the Whitewater Development Corporation.

15 *See, e.g.*, 18 U.S.C.A. §6002. For this reason, the immunity given is called "use and derivative use" immunity. For a case applying this immunity to dismiss an indictment — also involving the Whitewater investigation — *see United States v. Hubbell*, 530 U.S. 27 (2000). The law of investigative grand juries is explained in LAFAVE, ISRAEL & KING, *supra* note 1, Chapter 8.

(called *nolle prosequi*), and in their overall control of the case throughout judicial proceedings. Under the fundamental concept of "prosecutorial discretion," the prosecutor is not required by law to prosecute a case, even if there is sufficient evidence to support a conviction. Prosecutors in the U.S. never lose control of their cases and can drop charges at any time prior to final judgment and sentencing. Cases can be dropped even during an appeal. Judicial review of the exercise of prosecutorial discretion is rare. But if a defendant can show clear and convincing evidence of selective prosecution based on race, religion or other impermissible factors, a court may find an abuse of discretion based on an equal protection violation.[16] However, not all constitutional rights create a strong ground for challenging abuses of prosecutorial discretion. The Supreme Court has held in the context of a civil suit for damages for alleged retaliatory prosecution for the defendant's exercise of his 1st Amendment rights, the existence of probable cause for pressing the criminal charges is a complete defense.[17] "Desuetude," an objection to prosecution because of the law's long and continued nonuse, is generally not a basis for contesting the decision to prosecute.

Filing the Complaint Against the Defendant If the prosecutor authorizes charges, a "complaint" is filed in court. A judge or magistrate then conducts an *ex parte* review of the complaint and supporting information to insure that there is probable cause to proceed against the defendant. This review must take place within 48 hours after an arrest.[18] *Ex parte* in this context means that the prosecutor may participate, but neither the defendant nor the defendant's lawyer is present. The judge reviews the evidence from police reports and the complaint. The judge may also require that the victim or arresting officer testify to fill in details. If the supporting information is not sufficient, the judge will direct the prosecutor to produce more information or release the arrestee.

The complaint operates as the initial charging instrument. In a misdemeanor case, the complaint serves as the charging instrument throughout the proceedings. In a felony case, an indictment or information replaces the complaint, as discussed below.

The First Appearance The next stage is the defendant's "first appearance" before a judge or magistrate.[19] This first appearance has several purposes. One is to assure that the person arrested is actually the person named in the complaint. Another is to advise the defendant of the charges and of his or her rights in future proceedings. These include the right to a lawyer. For most defendants, this is the point at which a lawyer is appointed.

The judge also decides whether the defendant may be released pending trial, which has traditionally been referred to as "release on bail." Release can be financial, requiring payment of money, or non-financial. Financial release involves setting a bond amount that the defendant must pay to secure release. If the defendant fails to appear after release, he or she forfeits the bond. The defendant may be required to pay the full bond amount to the court, called a "cash bond." Or the court may also allow the defendant to pay only a portion of the bond amount (usually 10%) to secure release, either through

---

16 *United States v. Armstrong*, 517 U.S. 456 (1996) (there must be evidence of both discriminatory effect and purpose; for a race-based claim, defendant must show that similarly situated individuals of a difference race were not prosecuted).

17 *Hartman v. Moore*, 547 U.S. 250 (2006) (suit against postal inspectors who urged prosecution of Moore because he had engaged in lobbying to influence postal services decisions on adopting software dismissed because there was probable cause to prosecute).

18 *Gerstein v. Pugh*, 420 U.S. 103 (1975); *County of Riverside v. McLaughlin*, 500 U.S. 44 (1991).

19 This step is also called an "arraignment on the warrant" or "initial presentment" in some states.

a "deposit bond" to the court or by a "surety bond" underwritten by a bail bond agent. Factors affecting the amount of bond a judge will set include the nature and circumstances of the offense, the evidence against the accused, the character of the accused, and the ability of the accused to "make bond," *i.e.* to pay the amount necessary to secure release. While financial inability to post bail is not a reason for release without bail, the judge must still consider the financial ability of the defendant as a factor in setting the bond amount.[20]

Non-financial release takes three forms. "Release on recognizance" means that the defendant simply signs a promise to return for any later hearings. "Conditional release" requires the defendant to comply with certain conditions during release, such as drug monitoring or reporting. In an "unsecured bond," the defendant pays no money, but is obligated to pay the full amount of bail in the event of non-appearance. The technology revolution has given courts the option of using an "electronic tether" — a device worn by the defendant that informs police where the defendant is at any given moment and alerts the police if the defendant tampers with the device. In 2002, 34% of state felony defendants were granted financial release and 28% were released on non-financial; 32% could not meet their bail conditions and 6% were denied bail. Of those released, 78% appeared at all later court dates and 22% did not. Of the 22%, 16% eventually returned to court while 6% remained at large a year later.[21]

If the case is a felony, the judge sets a date for a "preliminary examination," discussed in the next section. If the case is a misdemeanor, preliminary examination is not necessary, and the case may be tried immediately. However, often there is no time for a trial the day of the first appearance because of other cases or the need for trial preparation, so a pre-trial conference date or trial date is set for some future time.

B. Preliminary Hearings, Indictments or Informations, and Pre-Trial Motions

In felony cases, the next step following the first appearance is to determine whether the evidence against the defendant supports a formal charge. Depending on the jurisdiction, this is done either: (1) by a judge or magistrate after a preliminary hearing or (2) by a grand jury. If the preliminary hearing route is used and the case survives scrutiny, a "prosecutor's information" is filed. If the case passes muster with the grand jury, a "grand jury indictment" is filed. The two documents are similar in setting out the formal charges against the defendant. The only difference is who signs the documents. The 5th Amendment to the Constitution requires that federal prosecutors proceed by grand jury indictment in all felony cases. However, the U.S. Constitution does not require states to provide either grand jury or even a preliminary hearing to screen charges. In fact, some states have moved toward elimination of the preliminary hearing.[22] Currently,

---

20 *Stack v. Boyle*, 342 U.S. 1 (1951). *See generally* LAFAVE, ISRAEL & KING, *supra* note 1, Chapter 12. In minor cases, the defendant may be able to obtain release by means of "stationhouse bail," *i.e.* by posting cash as security with the police at the police station and promising to appear before the judge at the next hearing date in the case. *Id.* p. 20.

21 Felony Defendants in 75 Large Urban Counties, 2002, Tables 14 and 20 (Bureau of Justice Statistics 2006), www.ojp.usdoj.gov/bjs/.

22 *Lem Woon v. Oregon*, 229 U.S. 586 (1913) (absence of preliminary hearing does not violate due process). A typical proposal is one that was suggested in Michigan. Instead of a preliminary hearing, a "conference" would be held at which all investigative reports, witness statements and confessions would be required to be disclosed to the defense. No showing of probable cause would be required, nor would a judge be required to preside over the conference. Exceptions would be provided for certain very serious felony cases. One reason for eliminating the requirement was the finding that of the 75,000 or so felony cases filed each year, defendants waived preliminary examination in 75% of them and in 86% of serious

18 states require grand jury indictments in at least in some categories of offenses, while 28 are "information states" with a preliminary hearing system. The remaining 4 states permit proceeding by information for all felony cases, except those punishable by life imprisonment or the death penalty.[23]

Preliminary Hearings and Prosecutor's Information The preliminary examination or hearing takes place before a judge or magistrate a few weeks after the first appearance. Both sides are present and represented by counsel. The issue at the preliminary hearing is whether there is enough evidence to "bind over" the defendant for trial.[24] For a "bind-over," the court must find that (1) a crime has been committed and (2) there is "probable cause" to believe that the defendant committed it. "Probable cause" means that there must be reasonable and trustworthy information sufficient to show a good probability that the defendant committed the crime.[25]

Charges are rarely dismissed at the preliminary hearing stage. The defendant has the right to present evidence, but also has a constitutional right not to produce any evidence, and will rarely do so at this stage.[26] The prosecutor does not need to present all available testimony or evidence, but is required to present enough evidence to establish probable cause. The effect of this requirement is that the defendant and defense counsel get a "preview" of the evidence that will face them at trial and the opportunity to test its strength through cross-examination. Because of this, the preliminary hearing is an important indirect form of "discovery" for the defense.[27]

Because the preliminary examination protects the defendant by screening charges, the defendant can waive it.[28] Despite the discovery value of a preliminary hearing, defendants commonly waive it and the case proceeds directly to arraignment, described below. This most often occurs when the prosecutor has offered a concession to the defendant for his waiver in a "plea bargain."[29] The defense may also waive the examination when it is aware of a curable defect in the prosecution's case and does not want to alert the prosecutor to it, or if the defense feels that a preliminary hearing will strengthen the resolve and memory of the prosecution's witnesses by putting their testimony on record. However, the most common situation in which a preliminary hearing does not

---

felony cases. Moreover, defendants did not waive the examination until the very day it was scheduled to begin, resulting in wasted time and effort, as police officers and other witnesses were required to appear to testify and the case was subject to possible dismissal if important witnesses did not appear.

23 *See* LAFAVE, ISRAEL & KING, *supra* note 1, pp. 734-737. The arguments for and against grand jury indictments are outlined *id.* §15.3. England has abolished its grand jury.

24 The preliminary hearing in state cases is usually conducted by a lower level trial court. Thus, in a state that vests trial jurisdiction over felonies in the circuit or superior courts, the district or municipal court will usually hold preliminary examinations. *See* Chapter V, pp. 173-174.

25 *See, e.g., People v. Harlan,* 669 N.W.2d 872, 876 (Mich. App. 2003) ("probable cause standard is not a very demanding threshold"; "a magistrate may bind a defendant over for trial even while personally entertaining some reservations regarding his guilt"; it is "sufficient that the prosecutor presents some evidence with respect to each element of the offense charged, or evidence from which the elements may be inferred."). *See also supra* note 7.

26 The defendant has the absolute right not to testify in this or any other proceeding based on the right against self-incrimination under the 5th Amendment of the Constitution. *See infra,* p. 310.

27 Compare discovery procedures in civil cases. *See* Chapter VII, pp. 235-240. Generally, the prosecutor may only use evidence at the preliminary examination that would be admissible at trial, so the preliminary exam may afford the opportunity for the defense to challenge the admissibility of evidence.

28 In some states, both the defendant and the prosecution have the right to a preliminary examination, so the prosecution may choose to hold it even if the defense would prefer to waive it.

29 Plea bargaining is discussed *infra,* pp. 280-282.

take place is where a grand jury indictment has preceded it, as explained below. Of course, this occurs only in jurisdictions with grand jury systems.

Grand Jury Indictments The grand jury is a group of 23 private citizens selected to review criminal cases for a period of several months to one year. To return an indictment, the grand jury must determine, by a majority vote, that there is probable cause to believe that the defendant committed a crime. Thus, the grand jury has a function roughly equivalent to that of the judge at the preliminary hearing. However, the grand jury hears only the prosecution's evidence, and the defendant and defense counsel have no right to attend the proceeding, to present evidence or to cross-examine the prosecution's witnesses.[30] Although on rare occasions grand juries exercise independence and refuse to issue an indictment, they usually follow the wishes of the prosecutor. Grand juries refuse to indict even less frequently than judges refuse to bind the defendant over in preliminary hearings.

Where the grand jury procedure is required or available as an option, a preliminary hearing date will be set, but the prosecutor will seek and obtain a grand jury indictment *before* any preliminary hearing is held. Since grand jury review is considered to be an adequate screening of the charges, this makes the preliminary hearing unnecessary. If given a choice, prosecutors prefer the grand jury route to formal charges for perhaps obvious reasons. Often a grand jury indictment is obtained even before the defendant is arrested, which allows the prosecutor to proceed directly to the arraignment.

Arraignment on the Indictment or Information Within a short time after the indictment or information has been filed with the trial court, the defendant is "arraigned" before that court. This means that the defendant is brought before the court to be formally charged with the crime as specified in the indictment or information. At the arraignment, the defendant is informed of the charges and asked to plead guilty or not guilty. In some circumstances, the defendant may plead *nolo contendere* (no contest), which is essentially a guilty plea except that it cannot be used as evidence of the defendant's liability in future civil suits by crime victims. Even though there has been prosecutorial screening at earlier stages, new information results in between 5% and 15% of cases being dismissed pursuant to a *nolle prosequi* motion.[31] Of the remaining cases, the vast majority will be disposed of by a guilty plea, as discussed below in the section of this chapter dealing with plea bargaining. If the defendant does not plead guilty at the arraignment, the judge sets a date for a trial.

Pre-Trial Motions Prior to the trial, a defendant has the right to raise several motions.[32] A common motion is a motion for discovery of the prosecution's evidence. The comprehensive discovery procedures available in civil cases are inapplicable to a criminal case.[33] Prosecutors are in general not required to turn over their entire file to the defendant, so how much information or documents the defense obtains varies with the jurisdiction and even with local practice. However, the due process clause of the 5th Amendment of the Constitution, as interpreted in *Brady v. Maryland*,[34] requires that the

---

30 Some states allow counsel to attend and to ask questions. Even states that do not so provide, give the defense the right to a copy of the testimony of any witness who testified before the grand jury.

31 LaFave, Israel & King, *supra* note 1, p. 21.

32 A motion is simply an application to the court for an order.

33 For example, depositions, which are routine in civil cases (discussed in Chapter VII, p. 236), may be ordered only in exceptional circumstances to preserve testimony for trial. FRCrP 15(a).

34 373 U.S. 83 (1963) *See also United States v. Bagley*, 473 U.S. 667 (1985) (standard for reversal for failure to disclose). *See* Chapter III, p. 87, note 14.

prosecution at least turn over to the defense all the *exculpatory* evidence in its possession, so the defense will file a pre-trial *Brady* motion if the prosecution has not previously turned over such evidence.[35]

Motions to suppress evidence obtained through unconstitutional police methods are also common. The grounds for these motions are discussed in Part II of this chapter on constitutional criminal procedure. The defense may demand a hearing on any such issues and has the right to compel the attendance of any necessary witness, including the police. These hearings are usually held several weeks before trial.

C. Trial

Jury trial procedures were discussed in Chapter III.[36] As stated there, civil and criminal trials are conducted very similarly. However, the standard of proof in a criminal case requires that the case be proven "beyond a reasonable doubt," in contrast to the civil standard of "preponderance of the evidence." In addition, a criminal defendant, consistent with accusatorial principles, has an absolute right not to testify.

There are major differences, however, in the extensiveness of civil and criminal *pretrial* procedures, and this has an impact on the trial. As noted earlier, the comprehensive formal civil discovery procedures are inapplicable to a criminal case. Although under *Brady v. Maryland*, as just discussed, the defendant has a constitutional right to obtain discovery of any *exculpatory* evidence, there is generally no absolute right to discover *incriminating* evidence in the hands of the prosecution. At the same time, the prosecutor usually has only limited rights of discovery from the defendant.[37] Before the trial starts, then, the prosecution will have only such information as the police investigation might have uncovered, including any statements the defendant might have given to police investigators voluntarily after appropriate warnings on the right to remain silent. The defense will have only the information from the prosecutor's abbreviated version of its case presented at the preliminary examination, plus any exculpatory *Brady* material

---

35 *See, e.g., Kyles v. Whitley*, 514 U.S. 419 (1995) (reversing death sentence because of prosecution's failure to disclose various items, including initial statements of eyewitnesses who initially described the killer as 5 feet 3 inches tall and of "medium build," while the defendant was 6 feet tall and thin); *Banks v. Dretke*, 540 U.S. 668 (2004) (reversing robbery conviction where prosecutor failed to disclose that informant-witness against the defendant had initiated the idea of getting a gun to commit the robberies they were charged with and that he would have been arrested on drug charges if he had not helped put together a case against the defendant). For reversal, however, there must be a "reasonable probability . . . that the result of the trial would have been different" or that "the favorable evidence could reasonably be taken to put the whole case in such a different light as to undermine confidence in the verdict." *Strickler v. Greene*, 527 U.S. 263 (1999) (concluding that the defendant "would have been convicted of capital murder and sentenced to death, even if [the eyewitness] had been severely impeached or her testimony excluded entirely"). There is no ongoing *Brady* duty after trial and conviction. *District Attorney's Office v. Osborne*, ___ U.S. ___; 129 S.Ct. 2308 (2009) (after his conviction, *Brady* was not applicable to require access to DNA evidence used at his trial to test it).

36 *See* pp. 92-109.

37 The defendant may be required to notify the prosecution of the intent to rely on certain defenses that require substantial pre-trial investigation to rebut. Thus, notices of a claim of alibi (that the defendant was elsewhere during the crime) or a claim of insanity are typically required. *See* Federal Rule of Criminal Procedure (FRCrP) 12.1, 12.2. In addition, the defendant may be compelled to provide handwriting samples, fingerprints, and blood samples for comparison purposes. Also, if the defense seeks discovery, it may have to submit to reciprocal discovery of any exhibits or scientific analyses that it plans to introduce at trial. *See* FRCrP 16(b). However, in Minnesota, New Jersey and Massachusetts, judges can also compel defense lawyers to give the prosecution evidence that they plan to use to cross-examine prosecution witnesses. *See, e.g., Commonwealth v. Durham*, 843 N.E.2d 1035 (Mass. 2006).

turned over. Given that this is far less information than is available in a civil case, the trial of the average criminal case can hold more surprises for the lawyers involved.[38]

The prosecution at trial has the duty to prove each and every element of the offense against the defendant beyond a reasonable doubt, and that burden may not be shifted to the defendant.[39] As a result, another difference between civil and criminal trials is that it is less common in a criminal trial to have "stipulations." Stipulations are agreements between the parties, which obviate the need to present proof on some elements of the case or which concede the admissibility of evidence, particularly exhibits. Stipulations are routine in civil trials and are often entered into under pressure from the trial judge who does not want to waste time on unnecessary proofs. This is generally inappropriate in a criminal trial. The absence of stipulations will often mean that the lawyers in a criminal trial will have to spend more time laying the necessary foundation for admission of evidence.

D. Sentencing Procedures in Criminal Cases

Sentencing Hearings Upon the defendant pleading guilty or being found guilty after a trial, the next step is to determine what punishment is appropriate — to impose a "sentence." In some systems the judge sentences the defendant immediately after the trial is over. In the U.S. the judge will set a separate date for sentencing and order the preparation of a "pre-sentence report." This report is prepared by an agency attached to the court, generally the "probation department." The report addresses the defendant's background as it relates to factors relevant to sentencing.

On the date set for sentencing, the defendant appears once more before the judge and has the right to address the judge personally or through defense counsel on the question of sentence. A prime determinant of the severity of the sentence is the defendant's prior history of crime. However, the judge may consult all kinds of evidence, including hearsay and lay opinions, and even evidence of uncharged crimes or crimes of which the defendant was acquitted.[40] The judge may hear witness testimony or statements.

Victim Impact Statements Traditionally, the victim's role at the sentencing hearing has not been very important, since the focus is not on what to do for the victim, but what to do with the defendant. However, this is changing. A recent movement in favor of greater victims' rights has arisen and has convinced some states to enact statutes allowing or requiring the use of "victim impact statements." The Supreme Court initially held such evidence unconstitutional, but reversed itself almost immediately, and held that such statements are permitted.[41] Courts have the power to order that the defendant pay restitution to the victim as part of the punishment ordered after conviction, and some

---

38 Criminal defense attorneys sometimes employ private investigators to assist them in investigating the facts of a case. *See* Chapter III, p. 85, note 14.

39 *See In re Winship*, 397 U.S. 358 (1970), discussed *infra* p. 313. However, the burden of proof on defenses may be shifted to the defendant. *See infra* p. 314.

40 *See* 18 U.S.C.A. §3661; *United States v. Watts*, 519 U.S. 148 (1997) (use of acquitted conduct does not violate the ban on multiple prosecution for the same offense and may be proven by the prosecution by a preponderance of the evidence, not beyond a reasonable doubt). *But see United States v. Booker*, 543 U.S. 220 (2005), discussed below (holding that where facts mandating a sentence beyond the maximum authorized by a jury's verdict must be determined by the jury).

41 *See Payne v. Tennessee*, 501 U.S. 808 (1991), (overruling *Booth v. Maryland*, 482 U.S. 496 (1987) and *South Carolina v. Gathers*, 490 U.S. 805 (1989)).

jurisdictions require the court to consider restitution.[42] However, no jurisdiction permits the victim to file a civil claim as part of the criminal case, as is permitted in the legal systems of some other countries. Instead, victims seeking an award of damages for a crime committed against them must file a separate civil suit. It is not difficult to recover a judgment against a criminal defendant in a civil suit, because the guilty judgment in the criminal court automatically proves liability in the civil case based on issue preclusion.[43] However, civil suits are not often filed by victims, mainly because criminal defendants rarely have money or property from which a judgment can be collected.[44]

The Jury's Role in Sentencing Traditionally, the jury has had a limited role in sentencing. Its work is usually complete when it determines guilt. However, in recent years, the Court has expanded that role, requiring that juries determine any "sentencing factors" that enhance punishment other than the defendant's past criminal record. In *Apprendi v. New Jersey*,[45] the Court held that it violates both due process and the right to a jury trial to have the trial judge, rather than the jury, determine whether the defendant acted with a racially biased purpose when he fired shots at black family's house. The Court thought it irrelevant that the law labeled racial bias as a "sentencing factor" rather than an "element" of a distinct hate crime offense.[46] Then, in *Blakely v. Washington*,[47] the Court held that the jury must decide whether the defendant acted with "deliberate cruelty" — a sentencing factor that the judge had determined under state law. Finally, in *United States v. Booker*,[48] the Court held the federal "sentencing guidelines" unconstitutional for their failure to require that mandatory sentencing enhancement factors be determined by the jury. As a result, those formerly mandatory "guidelines" are now only advisory. The choices for Congress or the many states that have such determinate sentence mechanisms are to require prosecutors to charge and prove any sentencing enhancements before a jury at the trial, to be content with such their guidelines being purely advisory, or providing for one or the other depending on the nature of the offense.[49]

Death Penalty Cases Even before the Supreme Court enhanced the jury's role in sentencing, it had been common for the jury to participate in deciding whether to impose the death penalty. At the guilt stage of the trial, evidence related to punishment is inadmissible. However, if the jury decides that the defendant is guilty, then the same jury is reconvened for a punishment stage. The prosecution presents all additional evidence bearing on punishment, including evidence on the defendant's background, character and other crimes. The defense may also introduce mitigating evidence to demonstrate that the defendant is not worthy of a death sentence. The jury considers

42 Restitution is required for most federal crimes, 18 U.S.C.A. § 3663A, but in most states it is optional. In addition, since the 2004 Federal Crime Victims Rights Act federal crime victims have had the right "to be reasonably heard at any public proceeding in the district court involving release, plea, sentencing or any parole proceeding." 18 U.S.C.A. §3771(a)(4). This has been interpreted to include the right to make an oral statement. *Kenna v. U.S. District Court*, 435 F.3d 1011 (9th Cir. 2006). However, other courts have disagreed. Other rights of victims are set out in other subsections of the cited statute.

43 *See* Chapter VII, pp. 249-250, where preclusion is discussed.

44 *See* Chapter VII, pp. 244, where enforcement of civil judgments is discussed.

45 530 U.S. 466 (2000).

46 *See also Castillo v. United States*, 530 U.S. 120 (2000) (presence of a "machinegun" could not be a sentencing factor that a judge could determine; it had to be an element of a more serious crime).

47 542 U.S. 296 (2004).

48 543 U.S. 220 (2005). *See* Chapter XIV, p. 575 (how guidelines determine the final sentence).

49 Juries would not only have to make any mandatory sentencing enhancement decision. They would also have to make that determination beyond a reasonable doubt. *See infra* p. 313.

all of the evidence presented in the case in deciding whether the death penalty should be imposed. In some states the jury has only advisory input, in others it decides the question, and in yet others death is imposed only if both judge and jury agree.[50]

E. Appellate Review of Convictions

Direct Appeal Defendants convicted in a state trial court generally have a statutory right to one appeal, usually to the intermediate appellate court of the state. If the state's intermediate appellate court affirms the conviction, they have the right to petition for leave (permission) to appeal to the state supreme court. Defendants may also file a petition for *certiorari* in the United States Supreme Court to gain review any *federal* issues in their appeal, such as a violation of constitutional rights. Defendants convicted in a federal district court have a statutory right to appeal to the United States Court of Appeals for the circuit in which they were convicted. If unsuccessful in the court of appeals, they may petition for *certiorari* in the Supreme Court.[51]

Review on Federal Habeas Corpus Under certain circumstances, after exhausting all direct appeals — including appeals to the state and United States supreme courts — a prisoner may be able to gain additional review of federal constitutional issues by filing a *habeas corpus* petition in the federal District Court.[52] *Habeas corpus* is not an appeal. It is an entirely new civil lawsuit filed against the warden of the prison where the prisoner is confined. It is thus a "collateral attack" on the prisoner's conviction. What is sought is a "writ of *habeas corpus*" — an ancient common law remedy that requires the authorities to justify why a particular prisoner is being held. The reasons given for confinement are usually that the prisoner was properly convicted of a crime and sentenced to prison. Consequently, to gain release, the prisoner must show that his or her conviction was obtained in violation of the Constitution. If the court determines there was such a violation, it orders the prisoner to be released. If the court rules in favor of the warden, the prisoner may, in some circumstances, appeal to the United States Court of Appeals and petition for *certiorari* in the United States Supreme Court.

The overall purpose of federal *habeas corpus* review has been to assure enforcement of federal constitutional rights by allowing anyone held in confinement to test the constitutionality of that confinement at any time. State courts have the power to adjudicate prisoners' claims of constitutional error and will have done so on the prisoner's direct appeal. But releasing convicted felons is not a popular thing for a judge to do and presents special difficulties in states where judges are elected. Federal judges' lifetime tenure insures a more dispassionate review of constitutional issues. In addition, some feel that federal judges are more sensitive to and often more knowledgeable about issues of federal law. Not surprisingly, many of the important constitutional criminal procedure decisions the Supreme Court has made — some of which are discussed below — have been in *habeas corpus* cases.

Despite the illustrious history of the "Great Writ," as it has been called, there has been a recent trend in both the Court and Congress to limit its scope and availability.

---

50 *See* Model Penal Code §210.6, providing states a choice of differing versions of this procedure that vary depending on how much control the judge or jury have. Methods of execution and statistics are discussed in Chapter XIV, pp. 577-579. *See also* pp. 574-576 (length of sentences of imprisonment).

51 The scope of appellate review was discussed in Chapter V, pp. 170-171.

52 28 U.S.C.A. §§2254-2255. *See also* Art. I §9 cl. 2 of the Constitution ("The Privilege of the Writ of Habeas Corpus shall not be suspended, unless when in Cases of Rebellion or Invasion the public Safety may require it.") *See* LaFave, Israel & King, *supra* note 1, Chapter 28. It is estimated that the success rate for prisoners who file for *habeas corpus* is about 4%.

Some years ago, the Supreme Court removed all issues of unconstitutional searches and seizures from *habeas* review, by limiting review to cases in which the state court denied the opportunity for full and fair litigation of the issue.[53] The Court recently effectively limited prisoners to only one *habeas* petition.[54] It has also held that if the prisoner's lawyer failed to raise a constitutional issue on direct appeal in state court, the prisoner is barred from any later challenge based on that issue on federal *habeas corpus*.[55] Congress has since adopted these and other limitations on the writ by statute, including limiting the time period during which a writ of *habeas corpus* can be sought to one year after all state appeals (if any) are exhausted.[56] Finally, *habeas* petitions must meet a very high standard of review. The federal district court reviewing a *habeas* case may not disturb a state court's determination of constitutional issues unless it is "contrary to" or "involved an unreasonable application of, clearly established Federal [constitutional] law" as determined by past decisions of the Supreme Court.[57]

F. Resolving Criminal Cases Without Trial

One of the consequences of an adversary system giving the parties control over litigation is that parties can choose to give up their right to litigate. In criminal cases, this most often happens when defendants choose to waive their right to contest the charges at a trial and instead admit their guilt. Guilty pleas are not only consistent with adversary principles; they are a matter of necessity for the criminal justice system. If even a third of criminal defendants actually insisted on having a trial, especially a trial by jury, the system would collapse. Of the 47,556 criminal defendants convicted in federal court during 1995, 91.7% pleaded guilty. Similar results obtain in state court.[58]

Procedure for Guilty Pleas The process for accepting a guilty plea is summary. The defendant stands at the lectern with defense counsel and the judge questions the defendant personally about his or her plea. The judge's purpose in inquiring is twofold: (1) to assure that the decision to plead guilty is voluntary and fully informed and (2) to set out sufficient facts to show that the defendant is in fact guilty of the offense. Without establishing both these matters on the record, the plea cannot be accepted by the court and the case will be set for trial.[59] However, the defendant need not admit his or her

---

53 *Stone v. Powell*, 428 U.S. 465 (1976). *Stone* is based on the theory that the exclusionary rule has little deterrent effect when applied several years after a conviction on *habeas corpus* review. Somewhat inconsistently, the Court has declined to extend the doctrine of *Stone* to federal court review of *Miranda* violations despite the fact that the exclusionary rule is involved in both confession and search and seizure cases. *Withrow v. Williams*, 507 U.S. 680 (1992) (distinguishing *Stone* largely on the ground that the evidence excluded in 4th Amendment cases is reliable, while there may be some doubt as to reliability of confessions obtained in violation of *Miranda*).

54 *McCleskey v. Zant*, 499 U.S. 467 (1991) (second petition that was filed after death row prisoner found out that police had placed an informant in his cell should be dismissed even though government had withheld information about informant at time of first petition).

55 *Coleman v. Thompson*, 501 U.S. 722 (1991) (fact that death penalty defendant missed state court appeals time limit by 3 days prohibits federal habeas review of possible constitutional errors).

56 *See* Antiterrorism and Effective Death Penalty Act of 1996, codified in 28 U.S.C.A §§2244, 2253, 2254, 2255, 2261-66.

57 *See* 28 U.S.C.A. §2254(d)(1); *Williams v. Taylor*, 529 U.S. 420 (2000).

58 Source: Bureau of Justice Statistics, U.S. Dept. of Justice.

59 *Bradshaw v. Stumpf*, 545 U.S. 175 (2005). One of the rights defendants who plead guilty give up is the right to contest the legality of evidence that might have been introduced at trial. However, the federal system and most states allow a "conditional plea," whereby defendants can plead guilty subject to the outcome of a suppression motion and any subsequent appeals if agreed to by the court and prosecutor. *See, e.g.*, FRCrP 11(a)(2).

guilt, and may in fact claim innocence while still pleading guilty, so long as the judge determines there is enough evidence of guilt in the factual record.[60]

No Contest Pleas It is also possible for a defendant to plead *nolo contendere* or "no contest" to charges. This means simply that the defendant is choosing not to contest the charges. This plea has the same result as a guilty plea — a finding of guilt by the court. The main advantage is that the admission inherent in the no contest plea, unlike a guilty plea, is not admissible to prove any element of the offense in a civil trial.[61] This consideration is of no consequence to most defendants who, because they have no money, will probably not be sued civilly. But civil liability can be a serious consequence of a guilty plea to some business crimes, such as antitrust violations, or in some criminal offenses involving automobile accidents if the defendant has insurance or other assets sufficient to pay a civil judgment. No contest pleas are possible only with the approval of the prosecution and the judge.

1. Plea Bargaining

Although defendants sometimes plead guilty without receiving anything in return, especially in misdemeanor cases, guilty pleas in most felony cases are the result of a "plea bargain" struck by the prosecution and the defendant. A plea bargain is an agreement by which the defendant agrees to plead guilty in return for either a reduction in the charge or some special dispensation regarding the sentence. The advantage from the defendant's position is clear: the disposition of the case is made more certain and usually more lenient than if the defendant went to trial. The advantage of plea bargaining for the prosecutor and the court is that the plea agreement saves time and resources because once a defendant pleads guilty, there is no need for a trial.

The Bargaining Process Bargaining often occurs at some time prior to the arraignment on the indictment or information, though in the federal system, it is usually after indictment. The prosecution may approach the defense, or the defense may suggest a plea to the prosecution. There can be charge bargaining and sentence bargaining (or a combination of both). An example of charge bargaining is where the defendant is charged with armed robbery, but is permitted to plead guilty to unarmed robbery, a lesser offense, because the case is weak or there are special considerations. In a sentence bargain, on the other hand, charges are not reduced. Instead, the prosecutor and the defendant agree on a sentence range or a particular recommendation the prosecutor is willing to make in return for a guilty plea. To start in as strong a bargaining position as possible, many prosecutors initially charge a defendant with the greatest number of the most serious charges warranted by the facts, with the idea that some of the weakest of them can be traded away in bargaining.[62]

Role of the Judge in Plea Bargaining In both charge bargaining and sentence bargaining, the judge is informed of the bargain before taking the guilty plea and must agree. However, the judge does not usually become involved in the plea bargaining discussions and most often allows the prosecutor and defendant to reach whatever

---

60 *North Carolina v. Alford*, 400 U.S. 25 (1970). So called "Alford pleas" remain controversial because they allow an innocent defendant to plead guilty in order to avoid the risk of harsh punishment. In *Alford*, the defendant, claiming innocence, pleaded guilty to second degree murder in order to avoid a possible conviction of first degree murder after trial and the death penalty.

61 This effect, called issue preclusion or collateral estoppel, is discussed in Chapter VII, pp. 249-250.

62 If the highest charge possible has not been filed, it is even permissible for the prosecutor to threaten to file more serious charges in order to "persuade" the defendant to plead guilty. *Bordenkircher v. Hayes*, 434 U.S. 357 (1978).

agreement will dispose of the case.[63] As with all other guilty pleas, when defendants plead guilty, they must state on the record facts that show that they are guilty of the bargained offense or it must otherwise be shown that the evidence is consistent with guilt. Unless this occurs, the judge will reject the plea and the case will be set for trial. If the judge accepts the plea bargain, but the defendant does not receive what was promised, the defendant can compel specific performance of the plea agreement in accord with basic contract principles.[64]

Criticisms of Plea Bargaining Plea bargaining has come under considerable attack. Some critics feel that plea bargaining is too lenient on the criminal. Others fear that it induces defendants who may be innocent or have a defense to the charge to plead guilty anyway for fear that they might nonetheless be convicted at trial.[65] But a series of U.S. Supreme Court rulings has upheld plea bargaining as constitutional. Plea bargaining, it has declared, "is an essential component of the administration of justice" and, "[p]roperly administered, it is to be encouraged."[66]

2. Programs for Diversion from the Criminal Justice System

Several programs are available to divert the offender from being processed through the criminal justice system. These programs were developed to alleviate the harshness of incarceration of first-time offenders and juvenile offenders for non-violent crimes. They seek to rehabilitate offenders, instead of punishing them. They have the added benefit of helping to reduce case backlogs and relieving overcrowding in prisons.

Programs for diversion from the criminal justice system can be an alternative to prosecution or they can be a substitute for incarceration. Programs that are an alternative to prosecution are usually directed toward juvenile offenders and adult first-time offenders, who often have drug or alcohol addiction problems. Programs vary from city to city, but most require offenders to undergo counseling, psychotherapy, drug or alcohol treatment as a condition for dropping the criminal charges. Offenders can be diverted into these programs prior to prosecution if their characteristics and background meet the criteria of the program and they have been referred by the local prosecutor. Similar programs are also available for offenders who may be rehabilitated through a vocational and job placement program.[67]

Most of the programs mentioned above are also available as an alternative to incarceration for convicted offenders. Thus, a first-time offender found guilty of a

---

63 Some controversy exists over whether the court should participate in any discussion of plea bargaining. The Federal Rules of Criminal Procedure prohibit court involvement in any plea discussion, as do many state court rules, but New York permits it.

64 *Puckett v. United States*, ___ U.S. ___; 129 S. Ct. 1423 (2009); *Santobello v. New York*, 404 U.S. 257, 260 (1971). The defendant must also be properly advised by counsel, even on issues on collateral consequences of the plea, including the possibility of deportation if the defendant is not a citizen. *Padilla v. Kentucky*, ___ U.S. ___, 130 S.Ct. 1473 (2010).

65 *See North Carolina v. Alford*, 400 U.S. 25 (1970) (defendant's plea of guilty to second degree murder to avoid death penalty is proper if it is intelligently and voluntarily made and if there is sufficient evidence to support guilt, even though defendant later protested his innocence).

66 *Santobello v. New York*, *supra* note 64. *See also Brady v. United States*, 397 U.S. 742 (1970) (voluntary plea bargaining is constitutional). The defendant also has a right to effective assistance of counsel in the plea bargaining process. *See infra* note 287.

67 For a description of one such program in Colorado, *see* Herbert C. Covey and Scott Menard, *Community Corrections Diversion in Colorado*, 12 J. Crim. Just. 1 (Winter 1984). A study of a community correctional program in Allegheny County, Pennsylvania, showed that in 1984, 38% of all criminal cases filed in that county were disposed of through a program called Accelerated Rehabilitation Disposition. This program offered both drug and alcohol treatment, as well as educational and vocational training. *Comment*, 24 DUQUESNE L.REV. 253 (1985).

nonviolent crime is often given the choice of serving time in prison or completing substance abuse treatment or vocational training.

PART II: Constitutional Criminal Procedure

A. Introduction and Preliminary Comments

Among the most important rights that suspects and defendants enjoy in the criminal process are federal constitutional rights.[68] The law in this area is complicated. It is governed exclusively by court decisions that interpret the Constitution. The number of published appellate decisions is staggering. While many Supreme Court cases are cited or discussed below, there are many more Supreme Court decisions that are not. Furthermore, no mention is made here of any of the many decisions of United States Courts of Appeals, both in direct appeals and *habeas corpus* cases, or the intermediate appellate or supreme courts of the states.

Before delving into the substance of the law, a few preliminary points should be made.

Constitutional Source of Criminal Procedural Rights   The content of the federal constitutional criminal procedure rights applied in federal and state legal systems is virtually the same. However, the immediate constitutional source of those rights is different. For federal prosecutions, the major sources are (1) the specific Bill of Rights guarantees in the 4th, 5th, 6th, and 8th Amendments and (2) separate rights protected by the general wording of the due process clause of the 5th Amendment, such as the requirement of proof beyond a reasonable doubt for a criminal conviction.

For state prosecutions, the Bill of Rights does not directly apply because its drafters intended it to apply only to the *federal* government.[69] However, in a series of decisions beginning in the 1960s, the Supreme Court has held that the 14th Amendment due process clause "incorporates" most of the protections of the Bill of Rights against the states.[70] In addition, parallel to the rights secured by the due process clause of the 5th Amendment, the due process clause of the 14th Amendment directly protects more general rights for criminal defendants.[71]

State Action   The United States Constitution defines and limits the power and authority of the government (be it federal or state) and in all but one instance its provisions are applicable only to government actors.[72] This limitation has an important

---

[68] State constitutions, to the extent that they provide more or different protection to defendants, can be important on some issues. *See* Chapter II, p. 38, and *infra* note 165 and accompanying text. However, state constitutional provisions largely track federal constitutional provisions and court decisions, so constitutional criminal procedure remains overwhelmingly federal.

[69] *Barron v. City of Baltimore*, 32 U.S. (7 Pet.) 243 (1833). *See* Chapter I, p. 4.

[70] The relevant portion of the 14th Amendment states "nor shall any *State* deprive any person of life, liberty, or property, without due process of law." Through this clause, the Court has held that nearly all of the specific Bill of Rights guarantees mentioned above apply against the states, because to deny criminal defendants these rights would deprive citizens of due process of law.

[71] See *infra* pp. 313-315. Some provisions of the Bill of Rights have not been incorporated at all: the 3rd Amendment's protection against quartering troops in private homes, the 5th Amendment's requirement of grand jury indictment, and the 7th Amendment's right to a jury trial in civil cases. Incorporation is important beyond the question of criminal procedural rights, as it applies to the entire Bill of Rights. Indeed, the first Bill of Rights provision to be incorporated was the 1st Amendment right of freedom of speech. *See Gitlow v. New York*, 268 U.S. 652 (1925). The latest amendment to be incorporated was the 2d Amendment right to keep and bear arms. *See McDonald v. City of Chicago*, ___ U.S. ___, 130 S.Ct. 3020 (2010).

[72] Only the 13th Amendment has been interpreted to apply to private actors. *Runyon v. McCrary*, 427 U.S. 160 (1976). The 13th Amendment, enacted after the Civil War, bans slavery and involuntary servitude.

significance for constitutional criminal procedure. Private citizens acting on their own initiative could break into someone's home, retrieve evidence, and give it to the police, and the 4th Amendment provides no protection.[73] However, if government officials knew and approved of the private conduct and the private actor intended to assist the police, private action is considered to be state action.[74]

General Trends in the Law The Supreme Court is the ultimate interpreter of the Constitution, so the history of criminal due process rights has largely been a history of the views of particular majorities of the Supreme Court, subject to the effects of *stare decisis*.[75] Under the Court's influence, the United States, like many other countries, has moved back and forth between the two "models" of a criminal procedure system: the "crime control model" and the "due process model."[76] The Court under Chief Justice Earl Warren in the 1960s leaned more toward the due process model, emphasizing the rights of individuals against the government. A drift in the opposite direction began under Chief Justice Warren Burger in the 1970s, and the Court under Chief Justice William Rehnquist in the 1980s and 1990s sharply turned toward the "crime control" end of the spectrum.[77]

Whatever level of protections of defendants' rights is appropriate, scientific advancements in deoxyribonucleic acid (DNA) testing of evidence have forced a reexamination of the ability of the criminal justice system to avoid conviction of the innocent. An editorial in the American Judicature Society's journal raises serious questions, noting that in the past 15 years, over 170 persons nationwide (including a significant number who had been on death row) have been exonerated by post-conviction DNA testing.[78] While there is DNA evidence to test only in homicides, rapes, and some assaults, the exonerations in those cases suggest that mistakes take place in non-DNA cases as well. In a random review of cases in Virginia where DNA was available post-conviction, but had not been used in the trial, fully 6% of the cases had resulted in erroneous convictions. Of cases where the convicted defendants are later exonerated, in 80% there were mistaken eyewitness identifications, in 20% false or coerced confessions, in 50% the police or prosecuting attorney failed to disclose exculpatory evidence, in 40% defense counsel were ineffective, and in 20% jailhouse informants provided false information.

B. Limitations on Investigative Techniques and Apprehension of Suspects

1. Search and Seizure

The 4th Amendment provides that "[t]he right of the people to be secure in their persons, houses, papers, and effects, against unreasonable searches and seizures, shall not be violated, and no Warrants shall issue, but upon probable cause, supported by Oath or affirmation, and particularly describing the place to be searched, and the persons or things to be seized." There are two issues that must be resolved in a

---

73 *Burdeau v. McDowell*, 256 U.S. 465 (1921).

74 *United States v. Leffall*, 82 F.3d 343 (10th Cir. 1996) (insufficient government involvement when airline employee thought is was airline policy to open all suspicious packages, became suspicious of an air express package and called airport police, who witnessed him open it).

75 Literally "to stand by things decided." *Stare decisis* is the principle that the Supreme Court should not overturn its earlier decisions. See Black's Law Dictionary (8th ed. 2004), stare decisis.

76 *See* HERBERT PACKER, THE LIMITS OF THE CRIMINAL SANCTION 149-246 (Stanford University Press 1968).

77 Only trends since the 1960s are mentioned because it was only in the 1960s that the Supreme Court began to develop and protect individual rights in earnest.

78 *See* Editorial, 89 JUDICATURE 244 (2006), www.ajs.org/ajs/ajs_editorial-template.asp?content_id=493.

challenge to police investigative action alleged to constitute an unconstitutional search or seizure. The first is whether the action constituted a "search" or a "seizure." If there was a search or seizure, then the second issue is whether that search or seizure was "unreasonable," considering among other things whether prior judicial approval in the form of a warrant was obtained.

a. What is a "Search"?

The Katz Test One might think that determining whether a search has taken place would be a simple matter. It is not. At one point, "search" was defined in terms of a physical intrusion into a "constitutionally protected area."[79] The Supreme Court in 1928 held that a telephone wiretap, whereby incriminating conversations were recorded and used against the defendant, was not a search because a conversation was not a physical object and there was no physical penetration of any constitutionally protected area.[80] In *Katz v. United States*,[81] a 1967 case, the Court abandoned its property-oriented approach. It held that an electronic listening device attached to the outside of a public telephone booth to record a defendant's telephone conversations *did* constitute a search subject to 4th Amendment protections. The Court held that the 4th Amendment is designed to protect *people*, not *places*. What people seek to keep private should be protected without reference to whether a "public" place or a physical trespass was involved. Conversely, what people "knowingly expose to the public, even in [their] own home[s] or office[s]" is outside the protection of the 4th Amendment.[82] Because Mr. Katz had a reasonable expectation that his telephone conversations would be private, the interception of them was a search, and the police should have obtained a search warrant. Therefore, under the *Katz* rule, when law enforcement officials have invaded a person's "reasonable expectation of privacy," there is a "search" subject to 4th Amendment protections.

"False Friends" When one has a confidential conversation with a trusted friend, one undoubtedly expects privacy, and that "expectation" on some level might be thought to be "reasonable." However, the Supreme Court has held that people cannot reasonably expect that their conversation partner will not relay the conversation to the police.[83] Nor may they reasonably expect that their conversation partner is not an agent of the police.[84] Similarly, the Court has held that police do not violate the 4th Amendment when they equip an informer with a recording device or a transmitter by which the police can hear the conversation.[85] Additionally, the Court has held that use of a "pen register" device, which records numbers dialed from a particular telephone, but does not record conversations, does not constitute a search. It explained that this is because there was no reasonable expectation that the telephone company did not keep records of the numbers dialed and would not turn such information over to the police.[86]

---

[79] *Boyd v. United States*, 116 U.S. 616 (1886).

[80] *Olmstead v. United States*, 277 U.S. 438 (1928).

[81] 389 U.S. 347 (1967).

[82] *Katz, supra* note 83, at 351.

[83] *United States v. White*, 401 U.S. 745 (1971).

[84] *Hoffa v. United States*, 385 U.S. 293 (1967) (defendant's acquaintance in a hotel room was paid government informant; defendant assumed the risk that his "false friend" would inform on him).

[85] *United States v. White*, 401 U.S. 745 (1971).

[86] *Smith v. Maryland*, 442 U.S. 735 (1979).

"Open Fields" Doctrine Despite the Supreme Court's rejection in *Katz* of a property-based concept of "search," in *Oliver v. United States*,[87] it reaffirmed the so-called "open fields" doctrine established before *Katz*. An open field is any land outside the "curtilage" of a house. The "curtilage" of a house is, in the city, the lot upon which the house is located and all other things on the lot — sidewalks, garages, porches, driveways and lawns. The curtilage of a farm house includes some land around the house, but does not include the entire acreage of a farm. The notion is that "open fields do not provide the setting for those intimate activities that the Amendment is intended to shelter from government interference or surveillance." Thus, on the facts of *Oliver* it was held not to be a search when police ignored "no trespassing" signs, got around a locked gate and stone wall and observed marijuana plants that were not visible without trespassing on the land.[88] A large part of the justification for assuming that activity in "open fields" is beyond 4th Amendment protection is that the general public regularly trespasses on such areas, even though such intrusions are technically illegal. Moreover, the decision in *Oliver* noted, police and non-police alike could have flown over the property in an airplane and looked at it lawfully, so the fact they viewed it by illegally trespassing on foot did not matter.

Aerial Surveillance The last comment suggests that aerial surveillance is not a search. Aerial photography of an industrial plant did not constitute a search of an industrial plant due to the nature of the premises, but the Supreme Court has indicated that such surveillance of the curtilage of a home, "where privacy expectations are most heightened," might constitute a search.[89] Yet, where police officers flew in an airplane at 1,000 feet over a defendant's residence within public navigable airspace and observed marijuana plants growing within the curtilage of the defendant's home, no search occurred. This was so even though six-foot high fences surrounding the curtilage prevented the officers from observing the marijuana from the ground.[90] The defendant had no reasonable expectation of privacy, because "any member of the public flying in this airspace who glanced down could have seen everything that these officers observed." In a case involving a police helicopter flying lower, the Court held there was no search, but indicated that the result might have been different if the helicopter had interfered with the normal use of the curtilage by causing excess noise, wind, or dust, or had allowed the police to observe "intimate details connected with the use of the home or curtilage."[91]

Other Enhanced Senses A theory similar to that involved in the aerial surveillance cases allowed police to use a "beeper" tracking device, an instrument attached to an object in the suspect's possession that emits signals enabling police to track the location and movement of the suspect and the object.[92] The theory is that the defendant was traveling on public roads and was there for anyone to see as he drove along, if they

---

87　466 U.S. 170 (1984). *See also Hester v. United States*, 265 U.S. 57 (1924) (original open fields case).

88　*See also United States v. Dunn*, 480 U.S. 294 (1987) (holding no search took place when federal agents went to defendant's farm, climbed over an outer fence that enclosed the entire farm, then climbed over an inner fence around a barn, smelled the odor of drug manufacturing coming from the barn, went to the barn and peered inside without entering the barn and saw incriminating evidence).

89　*Dow Chemical Co. v. United States*, 476 U.S. 227 (1986).

90　*California v. Ciraolo*, 476 U.S. 207 (1986).

91　*Florida v. Riley*, 488 U.S. 445 (1986) (helicopter flying at lawful altitude of 400 feet, from which marijuana plants were observed in greenhouse within curtilage of house).

92　*See also United States v. Knotts*, 460 U.S. 276 (1983). *But see United States v. Karo*, 468 U.S. 705 (1984) (illegal search when beeper tracked item in suspect's possession into homes).

wished to pay any attention. Allowing a dog trained for drug-detection to sniff luggage in a public airport when government agents had reasonable suspicion that the luggage owner possessed illegal drugs was held not to be a search.[93] The dog sniff disclosed the presence of contraband only, and not the nature of any noncontraband items in the luggage. Similarly, a government agent's in-the-field chemical test of a substance he suspected was cocaine was held not to be a search. Where possession of the substance in question is outlawed, no "legitimate interest in privacy" is "compromise[d]" when the field test merely reveals its contraband nature.[94]

A technological innovation that has recently raised 4th Amendment issues is the "thermal imaging" device, which measures the heat generated by a house. Its significance for law enforcement is that excessive heat generated by a particular house is often an indication of the use of high-intensity lamps to grow marijuana. In *Kyllo v. United States*,[95] a police thermal scan of Kyllo's residence showed that his garage roof and a side wall were relatively hot compared to the rest of his home and substantially warmer than the neighboring units in the same building. A federal magistrate issued a warrant based on the information and the search resulted in seizure of marijuana and prosecution of Kyllo. However, the Supreme Court held that the initial thermal imaging of Kyllo's dwelling amounted to a search without a warrant or probable cause. It rejected the idea that, like the luggage sniffed by the dog and the car passing through city streets with a beeper attached, the exterior of Kyllo's house was there for all to see. It did so because the imager permitted police to get information on the interior of the home that could not otherwise have been obtained without physical intrusion into a constitutionally protected area. Consequently, such sense-enhancing technology constitutes a search at least where the device is not in general public use. The Court noted that it was making its decision in the case keeping in mind that law enforcement is developing even more sophisticated technology for "seeing" through walls.[96]

Trash The 4th Amendment does not protect one's trash because "plastic garbage bags left on or at the side of a public street are readily accessible to animals, children, scavengers, snoops, and other members of the public," and the owners have no "subjective expectation of privacy" in garbage "that society accepts as objectively reasonable." Where police suspected a homeowner of drug violations, their inspection of trash bags left outside the curtilage for collection was held not to be a search.[97]

Premises of Others A person who is present briefly in another person's apartment for commercial (drug-dealing) purposes with no other connection to the householder has no legitimate expectation of privacy. Consequently, no 4th Amendment interests were infringed when police officers looked in the window through a gap in the closed blind and observed the defendants and the apartment's lessee bagging cocaine.[98]

---

93 *United States v. Place*, 462 U.S. 696 (1983). *See also Illinois v. Caballes*, 543 U.S. 404 (2005) (narcotics dog sniffing trunk of care stopped for traffic violation). *But see id.*, (Souter, J., dissenting) ("[t]he infallible dog . . . is a creature of legal fiction," citing studies that showed that dogs "return false positives anywhere from 12.5% to 60% of the time").

94 *United States v. Jacobsen*, 466 U.S. 109 (1984).

95 533 U.S. 27 (2001).

96 Another device in development would permit police to electronically "frisk" anyone for weapons from a distance of 3 to 7 meters. *See* David Harris, *Superman's X-Ray Vision and the Fourth Amendment: The New Gun Detection Technology*, 69 TEMPLE L.REV. (1996).

97 *California v. Greenwood*, 486 U.S. 35 (1988).

98 *Minnesota v. Carter*, 525 U.S. 83 (1998).

b. Whether a Search is "Reasonable"

If it is determined that a search took place, it must next be determined whether the search was "reasonable" within the meaning of the 4th Amendment. Generally, for a search to be reasonable, there must be "probable cause" to search and the searchers must have obtained a search warrant. "Probable cause" to search in the context of the 4th Amendment exists when there is reasonable and trustworthy information indicating that particular evidence will be found in a particular place.[99] Search warrants are judicial orders permitting a search. However, there are exceptions to both these requirements. Thus, "reasonable" searches may be categorized as (1) searches requiring both probable cause and a warrant, (2) searches requiring probable cause, but no warrant and (3) searches requiring neither probable cause nor a warrant.

(1) Searches With Probable Cause and a Warrant

The Warrant Requirement According to the Supreme Court, "searches outside the judicial process, without prior approval by a judge or magistrate, are *per se* unreasonable under the 4th Amendment — subject only to a few specifically established and well-delineated exceptions."[100] The government bears the burden of showing that the search comes within one of the exceptions. This general rule is based on the fact that the "reasonableness clause" and the "warrant clause" of the 4th Amendment are linked. The Amendment provides that the right "against unreasonable search and seizure shall not be violated, *and no Warrants shall issue* but upon probable cause, supported by Oath or affirmation, and particularly describing the place to be searched, and the persons or things to be seized." However, the 4th Amendment could not reasonably be read to require that a warrant be obtained in *every* instance, because police often have no time to get a warrant. Nonetheless, the Court has read the 4th Amendment as expressing a clear preference for searches with warrants.[101]

Warrant Procedure To get a warrant, the police must submit an application for a warrant to a judicial officer. No assistance, permission, or request from the prosecutor is required. In most states, that judicial officer is a lower-level trial court judge. Whatever the judicial officer's title, that officer must qualify as a "neutral and detached magistrate" who is independent of the police.[102] The warrant application must describe the place, person, and the things to be searched and seized and must be supported by an affidavit (a statement made under penalty of perjury). In that affidavit the police or a witness must explain the circumstances constituting "probable cause." If the "totality

---

99 *Carroll v. United States*, 267 U.S. 132, 162 (1925). The issue of probable cause is subject to *de novo* review on appeal. *Ornelas v. United States*, 517 U.S. 690 (1996).

100 *Katz v. United States*, 389 U.S. 347, 357 (1967). *See also Chimel v. California*, 395 U.S. 752 (1969); *Mincey v. Arizona*, 437 U.S. 385, 390 (1978).

101 Some members of the Court read the warrant clause differently. They maintain that it was directed at assuring that *warrants that are issued* are not like the abusive "general warrants" issued by colonial judges that allowed searches of general areas for any evidence of criminal activity. Thus, only warrants that "particularly describ[ed] the place to be searched, and the persons or things to be seized" are permitted. For proponents of this view, failure to get a warrant is only one factor to consider in deciding whether a search is reasonable and any *per se* requirement of a warrant is "judicially created" and not constitutionally compelled. For proponents of this position, the "constitutional test is not whether it is reasonable to procure a search warrant, but whether the search was reasonable." *Robbins v. California*, 453 U.S. 420 (1981) (Rehnquist, J., dissenting), *overruled by United States v. Ross*, 456 U.S. 798 (1982).

102 *Johnson v. United States*, 333 U.S. 10, 14 (1948). *See Coolidge v. New Hampshire*, 403 U.S. 443 (1971) (state attorney general could not issue search warrant acting as Justice of the Peace); *Connally v. Georgia*, 429 U.S. 245 (1977) (magistrate without regular salary, who was paid a fee for each warrant issued, but was paid nothing for each warrant denied, was not neutral and detached).

of the circumstances" discloses probable cause, the magistrate or judge should issue the warrant.[103]

In large metropolitan areas, police officers often seek out "easy" judges who do not make pointed inquiries as to the precise nature of the evidence supporting probable cause. Often, judges consider warrant applications while on the bench presiding over a trial or other hearing. The question arises whether the warrant procedure provides much protection. Some judges do deny warrants, but the simple fact that a warrant *application* must be made provides some protection. Since the application stands as a *record* of the facts allegedly constituting probable cause as they existed *before* the search is carried out, there can be no dispute over what the facts constituting probable cause were. When there is no warrant application, it is open to the police to exaggerate the amount of evidence they had *before* the search, sometimes from facts learned as a result of the search.[104]

(2) Searches With Probable Cause But Without a Warrant

Exigent Circumstances Most of the exceptions to the warrant requirement come under the general category of "exigent circumstances," meaning that there was an emergency situation that made it impracticable for the police to get a warrant. Any emergency will suffice, but in every such situation, the trial judge on motion of the defendant must review whether there was an emergency and whether the police had probable cause.[105] Thus, police may enter a home without a warrant when they have an objectively reasonable basis for believing that an occupant is seriously injured or imminently threatened with such injury.[106]

The "Automobile Exception" The Court has recognized that when police stop a car and suspect criminal activity in the car, the car and the evidence in it can rapidly be moved out of the jurisdiction.[107] As a result, the automobile exception to the warrant requirement might seem to be included in the above general "exigent circumstances" category. However, the presence of exigent circumstances need not be shown in every case involving an automobile. The only thing that need be shown is probable cause to believe that the car contains contraband or other evidence of a crime.[108] If an additional justification for an automobile exception is needed, it is that people have a reduced

---

103 *See also Los Angeles County v. Rettele*, 550 U.S. 609, 615 (2007) (probable cause is "a standard well short of absolute certainty"; officers do not always violate the 4th Amendment when they make errors in the warrant application). For an example of the kind of information that constitutes probable cause, *see Illinois v. Gates*, 462 U.S. 213 (1983) (approving issuance of search warrant based on anonymous tip with some corroboration from police sources). *See also supra* p. 270. For an example of a warrant that was defective for failure to comply with the "particularity" requirement, *see Groh v. Ramiriz*, 540 U.S. 551 (2004). "Anticipatory" warrants are possible where the object sought has not yet arrived at the defendant's home, but officers know it will arrive soon. *See United States v. Grubbs*, 547 U.S. 90 (2006) (videotape).

104 It is true that there is a "good faith" exception to exclusion of evidence under which officers who could not be expected to know that the evidence they had was insufficient for a warrant. *See infra* p. 304. This exception somewhat undercuts the "record-keeping" aspects of the warrant process argued above.

105 The Court has held that the police, if they have probable cause to search, have the right to prevent the suspect from entering the premises and destroying the object of their search while other officers go get a warrant. *See Illinois v. McArthur*, 531 U.S. 326 (2001) (police prevented McArthur from entering his home unaccompanied by an officer for about two hours). In *McArthur*, the Court used the same approach as it has done with administrative searches. *See infra* pp. 297-298.

106 *Brigham City v. Stuart*, 547 U.S. 398 (2006) (police saw violence inside home). *See also Michigan v. Fisher*, ___ U.S. ___; 130 S. C. 546 (2009) (police saw evidence of violence inside home, thus entitling them to enter the home even though the tenant told them to leave and get a warrant).

107 *Carroll v. United States*, 267 U.S. 132 (1925). Any vehicle comes within this exception: mobile homes, boats, trucks, and airplanes are included. *California v. Carney*, 471 U.S. 386, 393 n.2 (1985).

108 *Pennsylvania v. Labron*, 518 U.S. 938 (1996).

expectation of privacy in automobiles. This arises from the facts that there is extensive regulation of motor vehicles[109] and that such vehicles are used only for transportation and not for residential or personal storage purposes.[110]

The most common automobile search occurs when a person is stopped for traffic violations and, during the stop, evidence of non-traffic offenses is observed, thus leading to a search of the car. Often narcotics or other officers will look for traffic violations to use as a basis for stopping a motorist suspected of a non-traffic offense. This tactic was approved by the Court in *Whren v. United States*,[111] where the Court unanimously held that if there is probable cause to stop for a traffic violation, it does not matter that the officer has a non-traffic motive for the stop or that a reasonable traffic officer would not have stopped a motorist under the circumstances. An automobile search may include any part of the automobile that contains criminal evidence, including any container found therein that is large enough to hold the object of the search.[112] Officers making a traffic stop can order the driver and any passengers out of the car.[113]

An automobile may be searched where it is stopped or parked, if not parked in a residential setting (*e.g.*, in a parking lot or on a street).[114] Or the vehicle may be seized and removed to another location for search. Removal for search is permitted whenever a law enforcement officer would have been permitted to search the automobile where it was stopped or first discovered.[115] However, the police may not search an automobile merely because a suspect is *arrested* as a result of a traffic stop. The police must have probable cause to believe there is evidence in the car of the offense for which the driver is being arrested.[116]

Plain View Doctrine This warrantless search situation comes into play whenever a police officer is conducting a lawful search or is otherwise present at a place the officer has a right to be and observes incriminating evidence in "plain view." If so, the officer may seize it without getting a warrant. The three requirements of the doctrine are: (1) the officer's presence in the area where the item is seen must be lawful; (2) the officer must have lawful access to the item; and (3) it must be immediately apparent to the

---

109 *Cady v. Dombrowski*, 413 U.S. 433 (1973).

110 *Cardwell v. Lewis*, 417 U.S. 583 (1974).

111 517 U.S. 806 (1996). *Compare United States v. Botero-Ospina*, 71 F.3d 783 (10th Cir. 1995) (Seymour, C.J., dissenting) (such a rule "frees a police officer to target members of minority communities for the selective enforcement of otherwise unenforced statutes"). *See also* Henry Louis Gates, Jr., "Thirteen Ways of Looking at a Black Man," THE NEW YORKER 56, 59 (Oct. 23, 1995) ("there's a moving [traffic] violation that many African-Americans know as D.W.B. — Driving While Black," a play on the words and abbreviation for the real traffic offense of DWI — Driving While Intoxicated).

112 *California v. Acevedo*, 500 U.S. 565 (1991). This includes containers that clearly belong to passengers. *Wyoming v. Houghton*, 526 U.S. 295 (1999).

113 *Pennsylvania v. Mimms*, 434 U.S. 106 (1977)(driver; bulge in pocket was observed; pat-down was proper); *Maryland v. Wilson*, 519 U.S. 408 (1997) (passenger; bag of cocaine fell when passenger got out).

114 *California v. Carney*, 471 U.S. 386 (1985). If the automobile is parked within the curtilage of a residence, a warrant generally must be obtained. *Coolidge v. New Hampshire*, 403 U.S. 443 (1971).

115 *Chambers v. Maroney*, 399 U.S. 42 (1970). Police should search the vehicle within a few days of seizure. *Chambers, supra*; *Cardwell v. Lewis*, 417 U.S. 583 (1974); *United States v. Johns*, 469 U.S. 478 (1985).

116 For example, if an officer makes a traffic stop and arrests the driver for driving with a suspended driver's license, and then handcuffs and places the driver in a police car, the officer is not entitled to search the vehicle because there would be no evidence that offense in the vehicle. *Arizona v. Gant*, ___ U.S. ___; 129 S. Ct. 1710 (2009). The police may search a vehicle for weapons when arresting the driver for *any* offense, but the *Gant* Court restricted the scope of "protective sweeps" to situations in which the driver or passengers still had access to the vehicle. See the discussion of searches incident to lawful arrest, *infra*, p. 291.

officer that the item is contraband in nature or evidence of a crime. A typical case would involve officers who enter a home pursuant to a warrant to search for a murder weapon. While searching the living room of the home, they see several clear plastic bags full of what looks like rock cocaine on top of a coffee table. The officers may seize the bags. The officers' presence in the home was lawful because they had a search warrant authorizing them to enter and search the home; they had lawful access to the bags because the bags were in plain view for all who entered the living room to see, and it was not necessary to disturb anything in order to see the bags; and finally, it was immediately apparent to the officers that the bags were filled with contraband, so they had probable cause to seize them.

If it is not immediately apparent that the item is contraband, then the seizure is improper. In one case, the occupant of an apartment reported that a bullet came through the ceiling and injured him. Officers entered the apartment above looking for the shooter, other victims, or guns. While there, one officer saw two expensive stereo sets and suspected that they were stolen. The officer lifted up a stereo turntable to check its serial number, called the police station and matched the number with that of a stolen item, and then seized the turntable. The Supreme Court held that reading serial numbers that were in plain view would be justified, but that the act of picking up the turntable to see and record the number constituted a separate search, for which the officers needed separate probable cause.[117]

Like the automobile exception to the warrant requirement, "plain view" seems like just another example of "exigent circumstances," because evidence in "plain view" situations could easily be removed or tampered with by someone before the police could return with a search warrant. However, as with the automobile exception, the police need not show in each case that it was essential that they seize the evidence immediately to prevent its loss.

(3) Searches Without Probable Cause or a Warrant

Inventory Searches   The police often have authority to impound vehicles for non-investigatory reasons. These might include instances when vehicles are improperly parked and blocking traffic, the owner has a mass of unpaid parking tickets, or the vehicle has been abandoned for some period of time on a public street. When police impound a car, they have a right to inventory its contents. If in the process of such inventory criminal evidence is found in "plain view," such evidence may be seized.[118] Inventory searches should not be a pretext for investigative searches and are reasonable only if conducted pursuant to established, uniformly-applied law enforcement department procedures.[119] Similarly, the police have the right to inventory the possessions of an arrested person in preparation for jailing.[120]

Search Incident to Lawful Arrest   A search incident to (*i.e.*, in connection with) a lawful arrest may be made without a warrant. Under this exception to the warrant requirement, the arrested person and the area within the arrestee's immediate control may be searched. This exception has been justified by law enforcement agents' need to protect themselves and others by preventing an arrestee from acquiring a weapon,

---

117 *Arizona v. Hicks*, 480 U.S. 321 (1987). The state conceded that the officer's initial suspicions before checking the serial number did not amount to probable cause.

118 *South Dakota v. Opperman*, 428 U.S. 364 (1976).

119 *Colorado v. Bertine*, 479 U.S. 367 (1987); *Florida v. Wells*, 495 U.S. 1 (1990).

120 *Illinois v. Lafayette*, 462 U.S. 640 (1983).

and to prevent the destruction of evidence.[121] While searching an arrestee, law enforcement agents may seize anything (not just a weapon) that they have probable cause to believe is evidence of a crime, even a crime unrelated to the arrest.[122] When arresting someone in a private home, law enforcement agents may automatically conduct a "sweep" of "spaces immediately adjoining the place of arrest" to ensure that the arresting officers will not be attacked by others present in the home.[123]

The "search incident" exception has expanded beyond its original rationale of protecting officers or preserving evidence of the crime for which the defendant was arrested. In one case it was used to justify a full search of a person under arrest for a traffic violation, after the officer felt heroin capsules inside a cigarette pack and then emptied them out during a pat-down search of the defendant.[124] The Court rejected arguments that whatever the officer felt in the cigarette package was obviously neither a weapon nor evidence of the traffic violation, observing broadly that it was not necessary to tie authority for a search to one of the reasons behind the exception. The "search incident" exception also permits the police to search the passenger compartment of an automobile when arresting a driver or passenger, but only if the arrestee still has access to the vehicle.[125] Furthermore, officers may not conduct a warrantless search of a car or a person incident to the issuance of a traffic citation or "ticket," because such a search is justified by neither officer safety or preservation of evidence.[126] Nonetheless, officers who suspect a motorist is armed may order that person out of the car and conduct a pat-down search of the motorist's person.[127] Additionally, police may bring a drug-sniffing dog to sniff an automobile regardless of the reason for the stop, so long as they do not detain the motorist longer than necessary to complete the traffic stop and make reasonable inquiries.[128]

Consent Searches Searches conducted with the suspect's consent similarly require neither probable cause nor a warrant. However, consent to a search must be voluntary. Consent may not be obtained through coercion (threats, intimidation, shows of force). Consent obtained as a result of the police falsely informing a person that they have the right to search is not valid. For example, in *Bumper v. North Carolina*,[129] the police falsely claimed to a homeowner that they had a warrant to search her home. She opened the door and said "go ahead." When no warrant was ever produced, the prosecutor claimed that the homeowner had consented to the search. The Supreme Court found that her consent was invalid, as it was obtained through coercion, by "acquiescence to a claim of lawful authority." Additionally, consent is not established

121 *Chimel v. California*, 395 U.S. 752 (1969).

122 *United States v. Robinson*, 414 U.S. 218 (1973).

123 *Maryland v. Buie*, 494 U.S. 325 (1990). This right flows from the fact of arrest. There need not be separate probable cause for this search. *See* DRESSLER, *supra* note 1, §68[C].

124 *United States v. Robinson*, 414 U.S. 218 (1973). A pat-down search is explained *infra* p. 295.

125 *Arizona v. Gant*, ___ U.S. ___; 129 S. Ct. 1710 (2009) (if arrestee is handcuffed and in the police car, there is no safety justification to search the arrestee's vehicle). *But see Thornton v. United States*, 541 U.S. 615 (2004) (the fact that arrestees are outside the car does not prevent officers from performing a protective sweep of the car as a search incident to arrest, especially when the arrestees outnumber police). *See also New York v. Belton*, 453 U.S. 454 (1981) ("passenger compartment" does not include the trunk or engine compartment).

126 *Knowles v. Iowa*, 525 U.S. 113 (1998).

127 Pat-down searches based on reasonable suspicion are authorized by the "stop and frisk" rule of *Terry v. Ohio*, discussed *infra* p. 295.

128 *Illinois v. Caballes*, 543 U.S. 405 (2005).

129 391 U.S. 543 (1968).

to search a home where one co-occupant consents, but the other objects.[130] However, police officers need not inform people of their right to refuse consent.[131] Similarly, a search conducted during a traffic stop pursuant to consent was still valid despite the fact that the police officer did not tell the defendant that he was "free to go."[132] Consent is determined based on all the surrounding facts and circumstances.[133]

Border Searches In *United States v. Flores-Montano*,[134] the Court unanimously held that searches at the border, where "[t]he Government's interest in preventing the entry of unwanted persons and effects is at its zenith," need not be based on reasonable suspicion or probable cause. It approved the suspicionless disassembly of the gas tank of the defendant's car at the border, in which marijuana was found.

(4) Means of Executing Searches: The "Knock and Announce" Rule

The police have the right to break down the door of a dwelling to carry out a search or an arrest.[135] However, they must first knock and announce their presence. In *Wilson v. Arkansas*,[136] the Court unanimously held that the common law rule that officers must "knock and announce" is part of 4th Amendment law. There may be "countervailing law enforcement interests" that could create exceptions to the rule, but the Court in *Wilson* did not indicate what these might be. What is clear, however, is that a blanket exception for police officers executing a warrant in a felony drug investigation is not constitutional.[137] However, in a recent case, the Court approved a warrantless entry when police witnessed a brawl going on inside a house and they entered through an unlocked back screen door, and it was not likely that knocking on the front door would have produced a response.[138] How long officers must wait after knocking was the subject of the Court's decision in *United States v. Banks*,[139] where the Court, while admitting the "call is a close one," held that 15 to 20 seconds was sufficient time to wait before using a battering ram to break into the defendant's apartment to serve an arrest warrant. Banks was in the shower at the time and did not hear the police knocking.[140]

c. Unreasonable "Seizures" of Persons: Illegal Arrests

The Significance of the Illegality of an Arrest The fact that an arrest is illegal will not result in a suspect being released from custody if the illegality can be cured. Once it is cured, the suspect can simply be "rearrested" while in custody. The legality of the original arrest is important mainly because it affects the application of two warrantless

---

130 *Georgia v. Randolph*, 547 U.S. 103 (2006) (wife consented; husband objected).

131 *Schneckloth v. Bustamonte*, 412 U.S. 218, 248 (1973). As discussed *infra*, pp. 396-398, police *are* required to inform suspects of their 5th Amendment right against self-incrimination.

132 *Ohio v. Robinette*, 519 U.S. 33 (1996).

133 Usually, if consent is given, it is given just before the search. However, blanket consent may required as a condition of release on parole. *See Samson v. California*, 547 U.S. 843 (2006).

134 541 U.S. 149 (2004).

135 Officers also have the right to prevent interference with a search by detaining any occupant of the dwelling searched. *Michigan v. Summers*, 452 U.S. 692 (2005). However, excessive force may not be used. *But see Muehler v. Mena*, 544 U.S. 93 (2005) (not excessive to hold petite 5-foot-2-inch woman found on premises in handcuffs for 3 hours).

136 514 U.S. 927 (1995).

137 *Richards v. Wisconsin*, 520 U.S. 385 (1997).

138 *See Brigham City v. Stuart*, *supra* note 106.

139 540 U.S. 31 (2003).

140 After taking such care in the cases to define the scope of the knock-and-announce rule, the Court in 2006 held that exclusion of any evidence seized in violation of it is not required. *See Hudson v. Michigan*, discussed *infra* p. 306.

search categories just discussed: the "search incident to arrest" exception and the "plain view" exception. Searches incident to arrest cannot be valid if the arrest to which they are "incident" was illegal. Similarly, evidence is often in "plain view" of a police officer only because that officer is in a particular place making an arrest. If the arrest is illegal, there may be no other justification for the officer's presence at that place.

For the arrest to be "reasonable," there must be probable cause and, in some instances, an arrest warrant. Whether a warrant is required depends in large part on where the arrest takes place.[141]

Arrests in the Home Because "physical entry of a home is the chief evil against which the wording of the 4th Amendment is directed," police officers may not enter a person's home to arrest that person unless they have an arrest warrant and good reason to believe that the suspect is there, unless there is consent or "exigent circumstances."[142] Exigent circumstances exist if (1) the police are in "hot pursuit" of a fleeing felon;[143] (2) there is probable cause to believe that evidence will be destroyed if the police do not enter the home immediately; (3) the suspect will escape if police do not enter the home immediately; or (4) harm will occur to the police or others if the police do not enter the home immediately.[144]

Because the sanctity of the home is so important, the police, in seeking to arrest a suspect, may not enter the home of an acquaintance of the suspect in order to arrest that suspect, even if they have an arrest warrant. To enter any house other than the suspect's, they must have a *search* warrant allowing them to enter that house to search for the suspect. Without this rule, police officers could engage in devious tactics: they could wait to arrest the suspect until he or she visited a house the police wanted to search, but did not have probable cause to search, or they could use the arrest warrant as a basis for entering *any* house on the pretext that they thought the suspect might be there.[145]

Arrests Outside the Suspect's Home Outside the home, although a warrant is preferred, felony suspects may generally be arrested without a warrant, but on probable cause. The Supreme Court approved a federal statute authorizing the warrantless arrest of suspected felons based on probable cause. In that case, federal agents had probable cause to arrest the suspect, who was in a restaurant. The arrest was valid, even though federal agents had plenty of time to obtain an arrest warrant, but did not do so.[146] However, under common-law principles, misdemeanants may not be arrested without a warrant, unless the misdemeanor occurs in the arresting officer's presence, though some have doubted whether this is a constitutional requirement.[147]

Reasonableness of Means of Arrest The means used to effectuate an arrest must be reasonable. This can include the application of deadly force, such as a gun. However, "use of deadly force to prevent the escape of all felony suspects, whatever the circumstances, is constitutionally unreasonable." Application of deadly force is justified only if "the officer has probable cause to believe that the suspect poses a threat of

---

141 *See supra*, p. 270 (warrant procedures).

142 *Payton v. New York*, 445 U.S. 573 (1980).

143 *Warden v. Hayden*, 387 U.S. 294 (1967); *United States v. Santana*, 427 U.S. 38 (1976).

144 *Minnesota v. Olson*, 495 U.S. 91 (1990).

145 *Steagald v. United States*, 451 U.S. 204 (1981).

146 *United States v. Watson*, 423 U.S. 411 (1976). This is consistent with the common law rule which did not require a warrant to arrest suspected felons.

147 *See Atwater v. City of Lago Vista*, *infra* note 150, at 340, fn 11.

serious physical harm, either to the officer or to others."[148] This rule applies even if the officer risks injury or death. In *Scott v. Harris*,[149] a police officer forced the suspect's vehicle to crash, rendering the suspect a quadriplegic. The Court found that the officer had acted reasonably in using deadly force because the fleeing suspect posed an imminent threat to pedestrians and other motorists.

Beyond limiting use of deadly force, the Court has been reluctant to limit the means of arrest, even when police use harsh arrest techniques for relatively minor offenses. In *Atwater v. City of Lago Vista*,[150] a woman was subjected to a full custodial arrest for not wearing her seatbelt, a misdemeanor punishable only by a fine. She was actually taken into physical custody, fingerprinted, photographed, and placed in a cell for an hour before being taken before a magistrate, who released her on bond. Nonetheless, the Court ruled in favor of the state, finding that common-law practice at the time the 4th Amendment was ratified to be unclear, but thought it unworkable to draw a line between "arrestable" and "non-arrestable" offenses.

d. The "Terry" Stop and Frisk

"Seizure" includes other forms of detention that fall short of arrests. A "seizure" occurs whenever police restrict the subject's freedom of movement, either by physical force or show of authority. The test is whether a reasonable person would have believed he or she was free to leave or end the encounter.[151]

"Stop and Frisk" An important form of temporary detention that is permissible under the 4th Amendment is the *"Terry* stop," named for *Terry v. Ohio*.[152] In *Terry*, a police officer observed two men walking back and forth in front of a furniture store multiple times, peering into the window and conferring together. His experience as a police officer told them that such conduct is often an indication of robbers "casing a job" — planning how they will rob a store. The officer approached the men, asked their names and, after receiving a mumbled response, felt the exterior of the overcoat of one the men and felt a pistol in the pocket. The Court approved the officer's actions as consistent with the 4th Amendment. While the conduct of the men did not amount to "probable cause" for a full "arrest" or "search," it did amount to "reasonable suspicion" sufficient for a "stop and frisk," a less invasive form of a "search."

Reasonable suspicion is defined as "specific and articulable" facts that "disclose unusual conduct which leads [the officer] reasonably to conclude in light of his experience that criminal activity may be afoot"[153] While the defendants' conduct in *Terry* was not a violation of the law in itself and may have been ambiguous in its meaning, *"Terry* recognized that the officers could detain the individuals to resolve the ambiguity."[154] If the same level of reasonable suspicion leads the officer to believe "that the persons with whom he is dealing may be armed and presently dangerous,"[155] the officer may "frisk" the person. A frisk, also called a "pat-down," is when an officer pats the outside of a person's clothing all over the person's body feeling for objects that might be weapons. *Terry* frisks were originally limited to officers searching for and seizing

---

148 *Tennessee v. Garner*, 471 U.S. 1 (1985).
149 550 U.S. 372 (2007).
150 532 U.S. 318 (2001).
151 *Brendlin v. California*, 551 U.S. 249 (2007).
152 392 U.S. 1 (1968).
153 *Terry v. Ohio*, 392 U.S. at 21, 30. Compare the definition of probable cause, *supra* p. 270.
154 *Illinois v. Wardlow*, 528 U.S. 119 (2000).
155 *Terry v. Ohio*, 392 U.S. at 21.

weapons in order to protect themselves. However, the Supreme Court held in 1993 that a police officer could, while conducting a proper *Terry* frisk for weapons, seize an item that the officer — using his sense of touch — could immediately discern was contraband. Thus, the Court engrafted a "plain feel" rule onto *Terry* analogous to the "plain view" rule. However, officers must limit the extent of their frisk once they feel an object beneath the suspect's clothing. If the object is obviously not a weapon and it is only after squeezing, sliding or otherwise manipulating the object that it became apparent that it was contraband, then the seizure is invalid.[156]

Because "reasonable suspicion" is not susceptible to precise definition, numerous cases have arisen testing its threshold. One issue that has arisen has been the status of anonymous tips. In a recent case, the Court made clear that the requirement of "specific and articulable facts" observed by the police officer excludes reliance on anonymous tips alone, since in such cases any suspicions arise, not from observations by the police officers involved, but from the anonymous source.[157] Other issues have involved the significance of the location of the observed conduct — whether in a "good" neighborhood or a crime-ridden one — and the subject's reaction when the police appear, *i.e.,* whether fleeing from police creates reasonable suspicion. Both issues appeared in a recent case, *Illinois v. Wardlow*, a decision as ambiguous as the conduct it involved.[158] Police in a caravan of police vehicles drove into an area known for a high level of narcotics activity. Officers observed Wardlow standing next to a building with an opaque plastic bag in his hand. When Wardlow saw the caravan, he immediately fled with two police officers in pursuit. When the officers caught up with Wardlow, they frisked him because it was often their experience that drug dealers were armed, and found a pistol. Since feeling the pistol obviously gave them probable cause for a full search and seizure of the pistol and Wardlow, the only issue was the propriety of the original *Terry* stop and frisk. The Court rejected a *per se* rule that flight from police officers always constitutes reasonable suspicion. It even reaffirmed the propositions that "when an officer, without reasonable suspicion or probable cause, approaches an individual, the individual has a right to ignore the police and go about his business"[159] and that "refusal to cooperate [with the police], without more, does not furnish the minimal level of objective justification needed for a detention or seizure."[160] However, "headlong flight" is not going about ones business: "it is not necessarily indicative of wrongdoing, but it is certainly suggestive of such." The Court also reaffirmed that an "individual's presence in an area of expected criminal activity, standing alone, is not enough to support a reasonable, particularized suspicion that the person is committing a crime." However, it held that officers are "not required to ignore the relevant characteristics of a location." It then concluded that the combination of the high-crime

---

156 *Minnesota v. Dickerson*, 508 U.S. 366 (1993). One problem with *Terry* stops is that they can be used disproportionately against minorities. *See* David A. Harris, *Factors for Reasonable Suspicion: When Black and Poor Means Stopped and Frisked*, 69 IND. L.J. 659 (1994). *See also supra* note 111 (traffic stops).

157 *Florida v. J.L.*, 529 U.S. 266 (2000) (frisk based on anonymous report that a young black male in a plaid shirt was carrying a gun held invalid even though defendant was wearing a plaid shirt and was standing at the very bus stop the informant indicated he would be). The Court in *J.L.* also rejected creation of a blanket "firearm exception" that would make anonymous tips sufficient in light of the dangers presented by firearms.

158 528 U.S. 119 (2000).

159 Citing *Florida v. Royer*, 460 U. S. 491, 498 (1983), discussed in the next paragraph.

160 Citing *Florida v. Bostick*, 501 U. S. 429, 437 (1991) (police seeking to find illegal drugs routinely boarded buses when they stopped and asked passengers whether they could look in their luggage; held that coercive context could make resulting consent inoperable).

neighborhood and Wardlow's "headlong flight" justified the stop and frisk. Four members of the Court dissented.

Another issue for *Terry* stops is the use of "drug courier profiles." In one case, a nervous young man paid cash for an airline ticket from Miami to New York under an assumed name and carried heavy bags. He was stopped and his bags were searched. The Court suppressed the evidence. It held that the defendant could be stopped by police and they had grounds to temporarily detain him and his luggage while they attempted to verify or dispel their suspicions that he was a drug courier. However, the police exceeded the limits of an investigative stop where they asked the defendant to accompany them to a small police room, retained his ticket and driver's license, and did not indicate in any way that he was free to depart.[161] In a later case, the Court refused to suppress drugs found in a search following a similar stop. The defendant paid $2,100 for two round-trip tickets between Honolulu and Miami — source city for illicit drugs — with a roll of $20 bills. He traveled under a name that did not match the name under which his telephone number was listed; he stayed in Miami for only 48 hours, even though a round-trip flight from Honolulu to Miami takes 20 hours; he appeared nervous during his trip; and he checked none of his luggage. Upon stopping the defendant, having a dog sniff the defendant's luggage and obtaining a warrant, they found evidence of involvement in drug trafficking in one bag, which led them to search the other bags.[162]

e. Administrative Searches and Seizures

The government is allowed to detain and search in circumstances that would otherwise violate the 4th Amendment if it is pursuing "special needs" beyond an interest in detecting and prosecuting crimes.[163] Such administrative detention and searches are valid if "reasonable," determined "by balancing the need to search against the invasion which the search entails."[164] Thus, in *Michigan Department of State Police v. Sitz*, the Court approved of police detaining drivers briefly at random checkpoints on the highway to determine whether those drivers were intoxicated. While drunk driving is a criminal offense, the roadside checkpoints also served the administrative purpose of removing drunk drivers from the road.[165] The Court has also suggested that a similar roadblock to verify drivers' licenses and registrations would be permissible to serve a highway safety interest.[166] Fixed Border Patrol highway checkpoints were approved 66 miles inland from the border with Mexico for the purpose of checking for illegal aliens.[167] Also falling into this category are airport security checks, justified by the interest in the safety of civil aviation.

The difficulty with administrative searches lies in the fact that, if evidence of a crime happens to be found, it may be and often is used in a criminal prosecution. This reduces

---

161 *Florida v. Royer*, 460 U.S. 491 (1983).

162 *United States v. Sokolow*, 490 U.S. 1 (1989).

163 *See generally* LAFAVE, ISRAEL & KING, *supra* note 1, §3.9. Sometimes these searches are called "regulatory or "inspections."

164 *Camara v. Municipal Court*, 387 U.S. 523 (1967) (routine inspections of housing for fire, health and safety code violation are proper if made pursuant to a warrant based, not on probable cause, but on passage of time, the nature of the building and the condition of area where the building is located), *followed in Marshall v. Barlow's, Inc.*, 436 U.S. 307 (1978) (worker safety inspections).

165 496 U.S. 444 (1990). The Michigan Supreme Court subsequently held the same alcohol check points unconstitutional under the *Michigan* Constitution. *Sitz v. Dept. of State Police*, 506 N.W.2d 209 (Mich. 1993). *See* Chapter II, p. 35 and note 3.

166 *Delaware v. Prouse*, 440 U. S. 648, 663 (1979).

167 *United States v. Martinez-Fuerte*, 428 U.S. 543 (1976).

the issue to the elusive question of what the primary purpose of a given checkpoint program is. In a recent case the Court held that a "narcotics checkpoint" program of the city of Indianapolis conducted by police officers was not justifiable as an administrative search because it "unquestionably" had the primary purpose of "detecting evidence of ordinary criminal wrongdoing," rather than protecting an interest such as highway safety.[168]

The Court has also approved drug testing as proper administrative searches in some contexts, such as drug tests of high school athletes in public schools[169] and of certain government employees.[170] However, the Court invalidated a state statute that required that all candidates for public office submit to drug testing. It noted the absence of special needs, given that there was "no evidence of a drug problem among the State's elected officials," that such officials did not perform tasks that were "safety sensitive" and that elected officials are subject to intense day-to-day scrutiny, unlike others who have been subject to such tests.[171] Most recently, the Court invalidated a state university hospital's policy, developed in cooperation with local police, of surreptitiously testing pregnant patients to determine whether they were using illegal drugs that could have an effect on their unborn baby. The "special needs" of protecting maternal and infant health were not sufficient, the Court held. Consequently, the 4th Amendment's "general prohibition against nonconsensual, warrantless, and suspicionless searches necessarily applies to such a policy."[172]

2. The Law of Confessions

Voluntariness Requirement The self-incrimination clause of the 5th Amendment provides that no person "shall be compelled in any criminal case to be a witness against himself." At the very least, this clause and the due process clauses of the Constitution prohibit involuntary confessions.[173] In general, a confession is voluntary if it is the

---

168 *Indianapolis v. Edmond*, 531 U.S. 32, 40 (2000). *But see Illinois v. Lidster*, 540 U.S. 419 (2004) ("information-seeking" roadblocks permitted where the focus of the criminal investigation is not on the drivers stopped and questioned, but someone else).

169 *Vernonia School District 47J v. Acton*, 515 U.S. 646 (1995). Also in the public school context, the Court approved a public school official's search of the purse of a 14-year-old student whom the school official suspected of selling marijuana. Such searches of public school students were permissible, it held, if made on "reasonable grounds" for suspecting a violation of school rules or the law and if "the measures adopted are reasonably related to the objective of the search and not excessively intrusive in light of the age and sex of the student and the nature of the infraction." *New Jersey v. T.L.O.*, 469 U.S. 325 (1985). The Court pointedly did not address the issue of what standards might apply to searches of students' lockers, desks or other storage facilities. *But see Safford Unified School District No. 1 v. Redding*, ___ U.S. ___; 129 S. Ct. 2633 (2009) (school administrator's strip search of 13-year-old student on suspicion she possessed drugs was unreasonable, but school staff was not civilly liable to the student due to qualified immunity).

170 *Treasury Employees v. Von Raab*, 489 U.S. 656 (1989)(drug testing of federal customs officers who carry guns approved); *Skinner v. Railway Labor Executives' Assoc.*, 489 U.S. 602 (1989)(drug testing of railway train drivers approved). *See also Griffin v. Wisconsin*, 483 U.S. 868 (1987)(search of convict on probation without warrant and on less than probable cause approved due to "special interests" of the state); *United States v. Biswell*, 406 U.S. 311 (1972) (warrantless unannounced inspection of firearms dealer's business during working hours proper).

171 *Chandler v. Miller*, 520 U.S. 305 (1997).

172 *Ferguson v. City of Charleston*, 532 U.S. 67 (2001).

173 *Bram v. United States*, 168 U.S. 532 (1897) (self-incrimination); *Brown v. Mississippi*, 297 U.S. 278 (1936) (due process). Originally, the notion of excluding confessions came from English practice. *See King v. Rudd*, 168 Eng. Rep. 160, 161, 164 (K. B. 1783) (Lord Mansfield, C. J.) (stating that the English courts excluded confessions obtained by threats and promises); *King v. Warickshall*, 168 Eng. Rep. 234, 235 (K. B. 1783) ("A free and voluntary confession is deserving of the highest credit, because it is presumed to flow from the strongest sense of guilt . . . but a confession forced from the mind by the flattery of hope, or by the torture of fear, comes in so questionable a shape . . . that no credit ought to be given to it; and therefore it is rejected").

product of an essentially free and unconstrained choice of its maker. To determine this, a court must examine the "the totality of all the surrounding circumstances — both the characteristics of the accused and the details of the interrogation."[174] These circumstances include any coercive conduct by police, and the characteristics and status of the confessor. Physical brutality, such as beating, deprivation of food, water, or sleep, or threats of violence, can constitute coercive police conduct without regard to the defendant's individual characteristics.[175] Extended periods of incommunicado interrogation can also be coercive.[176] Promises of leniency can invalidate a confession, as can some forms of police deception, usually misrepresentations of law. For example, telling suspects that their fingerprints were found at the scene, or that accomplices have already confessed and implicated them, are deceptions that are tolerated by courts. However, telling suspects that their confession cannot be used against them is not proper.

Due process requires "that a jury [not] hear a confession unless and until the trial judge has determined that it was freely and voluntarily given."[177] However, even if the *judge* determines in pretrial proceedings that the confession was voluntary, the *jury* at trial must be permitted to assess on its own whether and to what extent it will believe the confession.[178] Thus, a distinction is made between *admissibility* and *weight* of confessions as evidence. Admissibility, determined by the judge, considers whether a confession is sufficiently voluntary that it is eligible to be considered as evidence in the case at all. Evidentiary weight involves the question of what evidentiary value to assign the confession in light of all the evidence in the case. Weight is decided by the jury when it makes its determination of whether the defendant guilty.

Miranda Warnings In *Miranda v. Arizona,*[179] the Supreme Court decided that the voluntariness test alone was an insufficient protection against police overreaching in interrogating suspects and extracting involuntary confessions. The Court held that statements obtained during custodial interrogation may not be used against the suspect in a criminal trial unless the police first provide procedural safeguards to ensure that the privilege against self-incrimination is not violated. Under *Miranda*, the police are required, upon arresting and interrogating a suspect, to advise the arrestee of certain rights, or as police shows on television have popularized it, to "read him his rights." The suspect must be advised: "You have the right to remain silent. Anything you say can and will be used against you in a court of law. You have the right to consult an attorney and have an attorney with you during questioning. If you cannot afford an attorney, one will be appointed for you." Police do not have to use this exact formula, so long as the warnings reasonably convey the substance of the rights to the suspect.[180]

As the *Miranda* warnings suggest, a suspect may waive the right to remain silent, as well as the right to have an attorney present during interrogation, but such a waiver must

---

174 *Schneckloth v. Bustamonte,* 412 U.S. 218, 226 (1973).

175 *Brown v. Mississippi, supra* note 173 (first case to bar use of a confession in a state court; police brutally beat suspects).

176 Ashcraft v. Tennessee, 322 U.S. 143 (1944) (36 hour interrogation was inherently coercive).

177 *Sims v. Georgia,* 385 U.S. 538, 543-544 (1967). *See generally Jackson v. Denno,* 378 U.S. 368 (1964).

178 *Crane v. Kentucky,* 476 U.S. 683 (1993).

179 384 U.S. 436 (1966).

180 *Florida v. Powell,* ___ U.S. ___; 130 S. Ct. 1195 (2010) (advice of "the right to talk to a lawyer before answering any of [police] questions," and that he can invoke this right "at any time . . . during [police] interview," satisfies Miranda)

be knowing and voluntary.[181] Studies show that most suspects do choose to talk. However, a *voluntary* waiver of the right to remain silent is one made without threats, trickery, or cajoling by police. A "lengthy interrogation or incommunicado incarceration before a statement is made is strong evidence" of an involuntary waiver of the suspect's rights. A suspect can make a knowing and intelligent waiver only if he or she is given the *Miranda* warnings. Circumstantial evidence that the suspect was aware of his rights will not suffice.[182] Nonetheless, a suspect's waiver of *Miranda* rights need not be expressly made. When a police officer reads a suspect the *Miranda* warnings, the suspect apparently understands the warnings, and the suspect then makes incriminating statements, waiver can be inferred.[183] However, once a suspect "indicates in any manner, at any time prior to or during questioning, that he wishes to remain silent, the interrogation must cease."[184]

If the suspect indicates a desire to speak to a lawyer, the interrogation must cease until a lawyer is present or the suspect initiates further communications.[185] Unlike an assertion of the right to remain silent, an assertion of the right to counsel prevents police from questioning the suspect about *any* crime, even one that is completely unrelated to the initial subject of the interrogation.[186] If the suspect consults with a lawyer, the police may not reinitiate questioning without the lawyer present.[187] However, if there is a sufficient "break in custody," the subject's previous assertion of the right to counsel does not apply and interrogation may resume.[188]

The *Miranda* warnings are required only if there is "custodial interrogation." This is defined as "questioning initiated by law enforcement officers after a person has been taken into custody or otherwise deprived of his freedom of action in any significant way."[189] The prerequisite that the suspect be in custody means that statements elicited in casual contact between the police and citizens or statements volunteered by a person on the street are unaffected by *Miranda*. Also, no *Miranda* warnings are needed before police interrogate a suspect in the suspect's home if the suspect is not under arrest, but is free to leave or ask the police to leave.[190] "Interrogation" includes express questioning or its "functional equivalent," *i.e.*, "any words or actions on the part of police (other than

---

181 *Miranda, supra; see Johnson v. Zerbst*, 304 U.S. 458 (1938).

182 After *Miranda* warnings are given and waived, police trickery and deceit are more tolerated. It is not at all unusual that the police will lie to the suspect to try to induce a confession. *See Frazier v. Cupp*, 394 U.S. 731 (1969) (suspect falsely told co-defendant said something); *State v. Barner*, 486 N.W.2d 1 (Minn.App. 1992) (suspect falsely told his fingerprints were found on a knife).

183 *North Carolina v. Butler*, 441 U.S. 369 (1979).

184 *Miranda, supra* note 179. But see *Michigan v. Mosley*, 423 U.S. 96 (1975) (no violation when suspect cut off questioning and 2 hours later a different officer asked about a different crime after giving *Miranda* warnings again).

185 *Edwards v. Arizona*, 451 U.S. 477 (1981). *But see Davis v. United States*, 512 U.S. 452 (1994) (no violation where defendant initially waived his rights, then after some interrogation said "Maybe I should talk to a lawyer," but then, when asked to clarify his intentions, said "No, I don't want a lawyer.").

186 *Arizona v. Roberson*, 486 U.S. 675 (1988). *See also McNeil v. Wisconsin*, 501 U.S. 171 (1991). Compare *Michigan v. Mosley*, 423 U.S. 96 (1975) (interrogation about a different crime following a second set of *Miranda* warnings were given was constitutional).

187 *Minnick v. Mississippi*, 498 U.S. 146 (1990).

188 *Maryland v. Shatzer*, ___ U.S. ___; 130 S.Ct. 1213 (2010) (14 day gap in interrogations was enough of a "break in custody" to negate the suspect's earlier assertion of his right to counsel during interrogation).

189 *Miranda, supra* note 179. The fact that the person interrogated is the "focus" of the investigation is irrelevant, if this fact is not communicated to the person and custody is not involved. *Stansbury v. California*, 511 U.S. 318 (1994) (per curiam).

190 *Beckwith v. United States*, 425 U.S. 341 (1976).

those normally attendant to arrest and custody) that the police should know are reasonably likely to elicit an incriminating response from the suspect."[191]

A police technique used to avoid the *Miranda* requirements has been the "two-step interrogation." The suspect is first questioned without warnings and incriminating statements are elicited, then *Miranda* warnings are administered and a second interrogation takes place covering the same ground. Where this technique is used to evade *Miranda* requirements, all incriminating statements must be suppressed.[192]

Miranda Exceptions In recent years, the Supreme Court has created exceptions to the requirement that *Miranda* warnings be given before a defendant's statements may be used against him in a criminal trial. The Supreme Court recognized a "public safety exception" to the *Miranda* requirement in *New York v. Quarles.*[193] In that case, police had been informed that a rapist had fled into an all-night grocery store armed with a weapon. When police found him in the store, they frisked him and found his holster empty. Without reading *Miranda* warnings to him, an officer asked where the gun was, and the defendant indicated its location. Because this "custodial interrogation" occurred under circumstances posing a threat to public safety, the Supreme Court reversed the lower courts' suppression of the statement about the gun. The Court reasoned that the defendant's right to his *Miranda* warnings was outweighed by the interest in public safety.

Another exception is the "covert custodial interrogation" exception established in *Illinois v. Perkins*:[194] "*Miranda* warnings are not required when a suspect is unaware that he is speaking to a law enforcement officer and gives a voluntary statement." In *Perkins*, an undercover police officer was placed in a jail cell with the defendant and engaged the defendant in a conversation in which the defendant made incriminating statements. The rationale of this exception is that the purpose of *Miranda* is to protect against the coercion that can inhere in the "interplay between police custody and police interrogation." When the suspect does not know that he is speaking to a police officer, there is no such interplay and therefore no coercion.

A plurality of the justices of the Court recently carved out a "routine booking" exception. "Booking" is the process by which a suspect who has been arrested is processed administratively through the collection of personal information and taking of fingerprints and photographs. Under this exception, *Miranda* warnings need not be given prior to asking questions designed to elicit "biographical data necessary to complete booking or pre-trial services." Thus, incriminating statements given in response to such questions are admissible in evidence against the defendant, so long as the booking questions were not designed to elicit incriminating information.[195]

---

191 *Rhode Island v. Innis*, 446 U.S. 291 (1980) (conversation between police officers within hearing of suspect that it would be bad if handicapped children from nearby school were to find weapon defendant had abandoned did not constitute interrogation). *Compare Brewer v. Williams*, 430 U.S. 387 (1977), discussed *infra* p. 302.

192 *Missouri v. Seibert*, 542 U.S. 600 (2004). Apparently, this technique was so widespread that it was taught in police training programs. *Compare Oregon v. Elstad*, 470 U.S. 298 (1984) (good faith initial omission of *Miranda* warnings based on doubts whether suspect was in custody).

193 467 U.S. 649 (1984).

194 496 U.S. 292 (1990).

195 *Pennsylvania v. Muniz*, 496 U.S. 582 (1990) (plurality opinion) (statements by drunk driver whose processing was videotaped at police station with his knowledge, but without *Miranda* warning, is admissible).

A battle has raged since the *Miranda* decision over the issue of whether it has had an adverse effect on law enforcement and should be overruled.[196] Despite the furor, the Supreme Court recently reaffirmed *Miranda* as a constitutional rule.[197]

3. Pre-Trial Right to Counsel

The 6th Amendment provides that "[i]n all criminal prosecutions, the accused shall enjoy the right . . . to have the Assistance of Counsel for his defence." Although an important part of this right to counsel is the right to a lawyer to defend the accused in court at trial, as discussed below, the right to counsel must be afforded at all "critical stages" of a criminal prosecution. This includes the important period between being formally charged and trial. During this period, the right to counsel includes the right to have a lawyer present whenever there is any contact with government agents or officials outside the context of court hearings.

In a seminal case in this area, *Massiah v. United States*,[198] the defendant, indicted on federal narcotics charges, retained counsel, pleaded not guilty, and was released. A co-defendant was cooperating with the federal authorities, but Massiah did not know about it. The co-defendant allowed government agents to install a listening device in his car, and he engaged the defendant in an incriminating conversation, tapes of which were used against the defendant at his trial. The Supreme Court held that the 6th Amendment was violated by the government's "deliberate elicitation" of incriminating statements after indictment and in the absence of counsel. The Court reasoned that the period after indictment and before trial was "the most critical period of the proceedings," and denial of counsel at this stage would be denial of "effective representation by counsel at the only stage when legal aid and advice would help him." The *Massiah* rule attaches "at or after the time that judicial proceedings have been initiated against [the accused] — whether by way of formal charge, preliminary hearing, indictment, information, or arraignment."[199] Thus, *Miranda* protects against interrogation without counsel *before* formal charges have been brought, while the 6th Amendment protects against "deliberate elicitation" without counsel *after* formal charges have been brought.[200]

In a controversial 1977 case on "deliberate elicitation," *Brewer v. Williams*,[201] a defendant suspected of murdering a little girl was being transported between jails. His appointed counsel had instructed the police officers not to question his client. However,

---

196 *See* Richard A. Leo, *Inside the Interrogation Room*, 86 J.CRIM.L & CRIMINOLOGY 263 (1996) (study of three California cities "does not support the assertion that *Miranda* has exercised an adverse impact on law enforcement"), Paul G. Cassell, *Miranda's Social Costs: An Empirical Reassessment*, 90 Nw.L.REV. 387 (1996) ("*Miranda* has led to lost cases against almost 4% of all criminal suspects who are questioned") and Stephen J. Schulhofer, *Miranda's Practical Effect: Substantial Benefits and Vanishingly Small Social Costs*, 90 Nw.L.REV. 500 (1996) (lost case rate is "*at most* only 0.78%").

197 *See Dickerson v. United States*, 530 U.S. 428 (2000). The Court laid to rest the theory that *Miranda* was not constitutionally based, holding that it was unaffected by a federal statute, 18 U.S.C.A. §3501(c), that provided that a confession "shall be admissible in evidence if it is voluntarily given." However, the Court continues to refer to *Miranda* as only a "prophylactic rule" designed to *prevent* violations of the 5th Amendment. *See United States v. Patane*, 542 U.S. 630 (2004) (plurality opinion), discussed *infra* p. 306, and *Chavez v. Martinez*, 538 U.S. 760 (2003) (plurality) (violation of *Miranda* is no basis for recovery of damages for any constitutional violation).

198 377 U.S. 201 (1964).

199 *Brewer v. Williams*, 430 U.S. 387 (1977).

200 *See supra* p. 300, where *Miranda* interrogation is discussed. Since statements given by a defendant before and after formal charges are brought are equally harmful, some have suggested that there is no need for a separate 6th Amendment right to counsel — that *Miranda* should just apply to both situations. The two developed separately largely because *Massiah* was decided two years before *Miranda*.

201 *Supra* note 199.

one of the officers started talking to the defendant about the victim. The officer did not ask any questions, but lamented that the murdered child's parents would not be able to give the girl a proper "Christian burial," as it was winter and her body would soon be covered by snow. The defendant, an escaped mental patient who was deeply religious, was overcome with emotion and told the police where the little girl's body was. The Court held that this statement had to be suppressed at trial.[202]

Until recently, it was clear that police could not initiate an interrogation of defendants who for whom counsel had been appointed pursuant to the 6th Amendment right to counsel, *i.e.*, after critical stages in the proceeding had begun.[203] Effectively, this meant that the 6th Amendment right to presence of a lawyer could not be waived. However, the Supreme Court held recently that this was true only if the defendant had at one point personally invoked the right to counsel.[204] The Court reasoned that the rule prohibiting police-initiated interrogations after counsel had been appointed is meant to prevent police from badgering defendants into changing their minds about the right to counsel once they have invoked it. But for the rule to apply, it must be clear that the suspects have at some point invoked their to counsel.

4. The Exclusionary Rule

Basis for Exclusionary Rule   If police obtain evidence in violation of constitutional rights, the normal remedy is to exclude the evidence from trial. This "exclusionary rule" was first announced by the Supreme Court in 1914, in *Weeks v. United States*.[205] *Weeks* applied only to federal trials, but the Court extended the rule to the states in 1961 in *Mapp v. Ohio*.[206] The *Mapp* Court set out two justifications for the exclusionary rule: (1) to deter law enforcement officers from violating Constitutional rights by removing their incentive to do so; and (2) to preserve "judicial integrity," *i.e.*, to ensure that courts do not become accomplices in the violation of constitutional rights by accepting and relying on evidence derived from such violations.

Criticism of the Exclusionary Rule   The exclusionary rule has been under attack in recent years as pressures for a more "crime control" regime in criminal procedure have grown. Part of that attack has come from members of an increasingly conservative Supreme Court. The criticisms of the rule emphasize the enormous social costs when criminals are released. Moreover, critics say, the rule seriously retards the truth-finding process of courts and erodes public respect for the judiciary when criminals are set free on "legal technicalities." Supporters of the exclusionary rule argue that exclusion of

---

202 The right to counsel is "offense specific." Thus, if a defendant is charged with and has been appointed counsel on one offense and is then arrested for but not charged with a different offense, the presence of counsel for the first offense is not required unless the uncharged offense is duplicative of the charged one. *Texas v. Cobb*, 532 U.S. 162 (2001).

203 *Michigan v. Jackson*, 475 U.S. 625 (1986).

204 *Montejo v. Louisiana*, ___ U.S. ___; 129 S.Ct. 2079 (2009). In *Montejo*, the trial court had appointed counsel for the defendant shortly after his arrest, but it did so on its own, not at his request. The Court remanded the case to the lower courts to determine whether the defendant had at some other point invoked his right to a lawyer.

205 232 U.S. 383 (1914). Before *Weeks*, the Court had wavered on the issue. In *Boyd v. United States*, 116 U.S. 616 (1886), it held that certain papers of the defendant in that case seized in violation of the 4th Amendment had to be suppressed. However, in *Adams v. New York*, 192 U.S. 585 (1904), it declared that the "weight of authority as well as reason" supported application of the common law view that all evidence, whatever its source and however obtained, should be admissible. Nonetheless, U.S. courts have always followed the English rule that *coerced confessions* were not admissible. *See The King v. Warickshall*, 168 Eng. Rep. 234 (K.B. 1783).

206 367 U.S. 643 (1961). *Mapp* thus "incorporated" 4th Amendment rights into the due process clause of the 14th Amendment so that they could be applied against the states. *See supra* p. 283.

unconstitutionally seized evidence is the only effective redress for the person whose rights were violated and the only means of insuring that 4th Amendment and other constitutional rights are respected. They also point out that there are social costs imposed when illegal police conduct is routinely tolerated by the courts. Moreover, abolishing the rule would create even greater cynicism about judicial institutions, since it is hard to justify the notion that one has a particular *right*, but has no effective *remedy* for its violation.[207] Even apart from what the true measure of the relative social costs would be, supporters of the rule assert, the balance struck by the Constitution is clearly in favor of protection of individual rights.[208]

Instead of abolishing the exclusionary rule, the current Supreme Court has chosen to preserve it, but to narrow its application. Most of these limitations have been tied to the first reason given in the *Mapp* case — deterrence of police misconduct. The result has been that, unless the application of the rule to a particular kind of case directly and substantially furthers the policy of deterrence, the rule will not be applied to bar the evidence involved. As the Court observed in a recent case, "[t]he exclusionary rule operates as a judicially created remedy designed to safeguard against future violations of Fourth Amendment rights through the rule's general deterrent effect. As with any remedial device, the rule's general application has been restricted to those instances where its remedial objectives are thought to be efficaciously served."[209] The second basis of *Mapp* — that "judicial integrity" is compromised when courts use unconstitutionally obtained evidence — has been largely forgotten.

"Good Faith" Exception Primary among the exceptions linked directly to deterrence is the "good faith" exception. Under this concept, if the police officers did not know or could not reasonably have been expected to know that their actions were unconstitutional, the evidence is admissible. Courts have applied this exception to defective search warrants and searches incident to *unlawful* arrests. In *United States v. Leon*,[210] the Court upheld admission of evidence a police officer obtained in reliance on a invalid search warrant that appeared valid on its face, but which was later determined to be invalid. The Court expanded the exception to searches incident to invalid *arrests*. In *Arizona v. Evans*, a police computer listed an arrest warrant as valid when in fact it had been quashed. The police arrested the defendant and searched him, finding contraband. Despite the illegal arrest, the Court held that the exclusionary rule did not apply, in part because court personnel, rather than police, made the computer mistake.[211] In a subsequent case involving a defective arrest warrant, the Court went further and held that the good faith exception applies even to the negligence of police themselves. The Court reasoned that punishing negligence would not further the exclusionary rule's goal

---

207 According to a study of California cases, the frequency with which the exclusionary rule actually results in freeing the defendant is between 0.6% and 2.35% of felony arrests, though in drug cases, the number rose to 7% or 8%. NATIONAL INSTITUTE OF JUSTICE, THE EFFECTS OF THE EXCLUSIONARY RULE: A STUDY IN CALIFORNIA (1982), cited in *United States v. Leon*, 468 U.S. 897, 907 & n.6 (1984).

208 For a cogent summary of the exclusionary rule debate, *see* DRESSLER, *supra* note 1, §120. Two cases in which various justices debate the merits of the exclusionary rule are *Stone v. Powell*, 428 U.S. 465 (1976) and *United States v. Leon*, 468 U.S. 897 (1984). *See also Bivens v. Six Unknown Named Agents*, 403 U.S. 388 (1971) (Burger, C.J., dissenting) (arguing for monetary compensation to innocent victims in place of an exclusionary rule).

209 *Arizona v. Evans*, 514 U.S. 1 (1995).

210 *United States v. Leon*, 468 U.S. 897 (1984). The decision in *Leon* sparked a spirited dissent that defended the exclusionary rule against much of the criticism to which it has been subjected.

211 *Arizona v. Evans*, *supra* note 209.

of deterring police misconduct. Only the police's "systematic error or reckless disregard of constitutional requirements" would cause the exclusion of evidence.[212]

The Impeachment Evidence Exception Even when the exclusionary rule applies to bar use of unconstitutional evidence as proof of guilt, it may be used on cross-examination to impeach the defendant's credibility in front of the jury if the defendant chooses to testify at trial and makes any statement that is inconsistent with that illegal evidence.[213] In the case of a confession obtained in violation of *Miranda*, this means that a defendant who takes the witness stand in his own defense and testifies that he was not involved in the crime must anticipate that the jury will also hear his illegally-obtained confession. The rationale the Court has given for the impeachment exception is that violations of constitutional rights do not give defendants the right to commit perjury. The value of truthful testimony outweighs "the speculative possibility" that using suppressed evidence to impeach a defendant would encourage police to violate the constitution.[214] Illegally obtained evidence may not be used to impeach other defense witnesses, however.[215] In addition, despite the impeachment exception, an *involuntary* confession or a confession obtained by torture is inadmissible in evidence for any purpose.[216]

Exceptions for Derivative Evidence Important to the effective operation of the exclusionary rule is the notion that any additional evidence that is derived from the evidence unconstitutionally obtained should also be excluded at trial. This is the doctrine of the "fruit of the poisonous tree."[217] Under this doctrine, if the tree is "poisoned" (*i.e.*, evidence is unconstitutionally obtained), then the "fruits" of that tree (any items or information derived from the use of the unconstitutional evidence) are also "poisoned." For example, if an unconstitutional search reveals an address book that contains a map describing where other evidence is located, the court must exclude not only the address book, but also the other evidence described in it. As the Court observed long ago, "[t]he essence of a provision forbidding the acquisition of evidence in a certain way is that not merely evidence so acquired shall not be used before the Court but that it shall not be used at all."[218]

However, if the connection between the illegal police conduct and the discovery and seizure of the evidence is "so attenuated as to dissipate the taint," the challenged evidence will be permitted to be used.[219] If the prosecution can demonstrate that the derivative evidence has a source independent of the tainted source, it will be permitted to use it.[220] Another important limitation is "inevitable discovery" exception created by the Court in *Nix v. Williams*.[221] If the prosecutor can prove by the civil *preponderance of the evidence* standard that the challenged evidence "ultimately or inevitably would have been discovered by lawful means," then the evidence is admissible. The prosecutor in

---

212 *Herring v. United States*, ___ U.S. ___; 129 S.Ct. 695, 704 (2009) (what sheriff's department thought was a valid arrest warrant from a neighboring county turned out to have been recalled five months earlier).

213 *See Walder v. United States*, 347 U.S. 62 (1954) (4th Amendment violations); *Harris v. New York*, 401 U.S. 222 (1971) (*Miranda* violations); *Kansas v. Ventris*, ___ U.S. ___; 129 S. Ct. 1841 (2009) (violation of 6th Amendment right to counsel).

214 *Harris v. New York, supra.*

215 *James v. Illinois*, 493 U.S. 307 (1990).

216 *Mincey v. Arizona*, 437 U.S. 385 (1978); *New Jersey v. Portash*, 440 U.S. 450 (1979).

217 *Nardone v. United States*, 308 U.S. 338 (1939).

218 *Id.*, quoting *Silverthorne Lumber Co. v. United States*, 251 U.S. 385, 392 (1920).

219 *Nardone*, 308 U.S. at 341.

220 *Murray v. United States*, 487 U.S. 533 (1988).

221 467 U.S. 431 (1984).

Nix admitted that the police secured information from the defendant about the location of the murder victim's body in violation of the defendant's 6th Amendment right to counsel. The Supreme Court held that the evidence was admissible because, under the circumstances in that case, the police had organized an extensive search, were only a few miles from the body, and would have eventually found the body without relying on the unconstitutionally-obtained information.

The "fruits" doctrine has a more limited application to *Miranda* violations. *Testimonial* evidence from the suspect or others obtained as a result of a *Miranda* violation must be suppressed, but *physical* evidence is treated differently. Thus, in *United States v. Patane*,[222] a gun obtained as a result of interrogating the defendant after defective *Miranda* warnings was held to be admissible, but the rationale for doing so divided the Court. A plurality of 4 justices reasoned that the 5th Amendment, which *Miranda* is designed to enforce, proscribes compelling a defendant to be a "*witness* against himself" — thus making it inapplicable to physical evidence derived from a *Miranda* violation. Clearly, this provides an incentive for the police to ignore *Miranda*.

Exception for Proceedings Other Than Criminal Trials The exclusionary rule applies to some forfeiture proceedings in which criminal activity is alleged,[223] but it does not apply to civil tax proceedings[224] deportation hearings,[225] grand juries,[226] preliminary hearings,[227] parole revocation proceedings,[228] or bail determination proceedings.[229]

"Knock and Announce" and the Future of the Exclusionary Rule In *Hudson v. Michigan*,[230] the state admitted that the police had violated the "knock-and-announce" rule. The Court had unanimously confirmed that the 4th Amendment imposed this rule in 1995 and several cases thereafter.[231] Nonetheless, the Court did not exclude the evidence in *Hudson*. It maintained that there was an insufficient causal link between the violation and the evidence seized, because the same amount or only slightly less evidence would have been seized even if officers had knocked, and that the defendants had no legitimate interest in taking advantage of the time afforded them to dispose of evidence. Thus, the interests behind the knock-and-announce rule were sufficiently protected without excluding the evidence. However, the Court also observed that "the exclusionary rule has never been applied except 'where its deterrence benefits outweigh its substantial social costs,'" thus suggesting that its application in every case should be determined by a free balancing of social costs against deterrence benefits.[232]

C. Rights at the Charging Stage and Pre-Trial Release

Charging Procedures The 5th Amendment requires "presentment or indictment of

---

222 542 U.S. 630 (2004).

223 *One 1958 Plymouth Sedan v. Pennsylvania*, 380 U.S. 693 (1965).

224 *United States v. Janis*, 428 U.S. 433 (1976).

225 *Immigration & Naturalization Service v. Lopez-Mendoza*, 468 U.S. 1032 (1984).

226 *United States v. Calandra*, 414 U.S. 338 (1974).

227 *Giordenello v. United States*, 357 U.S. 480 (1958).

228 *Pennsylvania Board of Probation v. Scott*, 524 U.S. 357 (1998).

229 18 U.S.C.A. §3142(f) (applicable to federal cases).

230 547 U.S. 586 (2006).

231 *See supra* p. 293.

232 *Cf. Sanchez-Llamas v. Oregon*, 548 U.S. 331 (2006) (assuming that Vienna Convention's requirement that arrestee's home country's consulate be notified of the arrest is judicially enforceable, exclusionary rule does not apply because the Convention does not provide for exclusion).

a Grand Jury" in all felony cases. However, this provision is one of the few provisions of the Bill of Rights that has not been incorporated into the due process clause and applied against the states.[233] Thus, states may bring charges by using grand juries, or by filing a prosecutor's information.[234] Some states either require, or allow as an option, indictment by a grand jury as a matter of state law.

Pre-Trial Release Procedures for pre-trial release on bail were discussed earlier.[235] The 8th Amendment guarantees that "[e]xcessive bail shall not be required."[236] Traditionally, persons charged in all non-capital crimes had a right to be considered for release on bail pending trial. The Supreme Court has stated that bail set in an amount higher than that which would secure a defendant's appearance at trial may be excessive.[237] However, in the 1980s "preventive detention" of defendants who were not a flight risk, but who might commit other crimes while on bail began to be used. For example, the 1984 amendments to the Federal Bail Reform Act of 1966[238] gave federal magistrates the power to hold without bail any defendant as to whom "no condition or combinations of conditions [of release] will reasonably assure the appearance of the person as required *and the safety of any other person and the community.*"[239] The act lists offenses that imply high flight and community safety risks. The preventive detention provisions of the Act were held constitutional in *United States v. Salerno.*[240]

D. Rights at Trial

1. Right to Speedy Trial

The 6th Amendment provides that "[in] all criminal prosecutions, the accused shall enjoy the right to a speedy . . . trial." In *Smith v. Hooey*, the Supreme Court noted three purposes of the speedy trial right: "(1) to prevent undue and oppressive incarceration prior to trial, (2) to minimize anxiety and concern accompanying public accusation and (3) to limit the possibilities that long delay will impair the ability of an accused to defend himself."[241] A claim that a state has violated this constitutional guarantee is a fact-intensive inquiry requiring the balancing of (1) "whether [the] delay before trial was uncommonly long," (2) "whether the government or the criminal defendant is more to blame for that delay," (3) "whether, in due course, the defendant asserted his right to a speedy trial," and (4) "whether he suffered prejudice as the delay's result."[242] The right to a speedy trial attaches at the time of arrest or formal charge, whichever comes first. The remedy for violation of the right is dismissal of the charges.[243]

Speedy trial issues comes up most often in the context of "detainers." Detainers notify prison officials in one state that authorities in another state want the prisoner

---

233 *Hurtado v. California*, 110 U.S. 516 (1884). *See* discussion *supra* p. 283.

234 *See supra* pp. 273-275, where indictments and informations are discussed.

235 See *supra* p. 272.

236 The Supreme Court has never squarely held, though it has observed in passing that the excessive bail clause of the 8th Amendment is applicable to the states through the due process clause of the 14th Amendment. *Schlib v. Kuebel*, 404 U.S. 357 (1971).

237 *Stack v. Boyle*, 342 U.S. 1 (1951).

238 18 U.S.C.A. §§3146-3152, repealed in part, 18 U.S.C.A. §§3141-3150.

239 18 U.S.C.A. §3142(b).

240 481 U.S. 739 (1987). *See also United States v. Goba*, 240 F.Supp.2d 242 (W.D.N.Y. 2003) (ordering detention of U.S. citizens arrested for conspiracy to provide material support to al-Qaeda).

241 393 U.S. 374, 377 (1969), quoting *United States v. Ewell*, 383 U.S. 116, 120 (1966).

242 *Doggett v. United States*, 505 U.S. 647, 651 (1992). *See also Barker v. Wingo*, 407 U.S. 514 (1972).

243 *Strunk v. United States*, 412 U.S. 434 (1972).

turned over to them for trial on other criminal charges at the end of the prisoner's current sentence. A prisoner against whom detainers have been "lodged" is likely to be treated differently in prison. Detainers also affect eligibility for parole.[244] Consequently, upon a prisoner's demand, the state must make a diligent effort to bring the prisoner to trial within 180 days of the date of the detainer.[245]

Outside the detainer area, speedy trial issues come up less often as a constitutional matter because Congress passed the Speedy Trial Act of 1974 for the federal system,[246] and the states have implemented rules of court or statutes that require prompt trials.[247] Issues still do arise, however. In *Klopfer v. North Carolina*,[248] the defendant's first trial ended in a hung jury and the prosecutor failed to bring the defendant to a prompt retrial, instead deciding to take a *"nolle prosequi* with leave" — a device by which the defendant remained under indictment, but was released, subject to the prosecutor retrying the defendant at any time in his discretion. The Court held that this violated the right to a speedy trial.[249] In *Vermont v. Brillon*,[250] the Court found no violation of the speedy trial right when a three-year delay in bringing the defendant to trial was in part caused by the defendant forcing several attorneys assigned to represent him to withdraw, the first withdrawing on the eve of trial and the third withdrawing because the defendant threatened to kill him. Other delays were caused by defense counsel not moving the case along expeditiously. Even though defense counsel are assigned and paid for by the state, their delays are chargeable, not to the state, but to the defendant.

2. Right to Public Trial

The 6th Amendment guarantees the right to a "public trial." The defendant's right extends to all criminal prosecutions and all phases of them, from jury selection to the final verdict.[251] It has even been held to extend to pre-trial evidence suppression hearings.[252] The Supreme Court has stated that the right to a public trial safeguards against attempts to use "courts as instruments of persecution" and as checks on "possible abuse of judicial power." In addition, a public trial may encourage potential witnesses to come forward and may make testifying witnesses more truthful, for fear of contradiction by others with knowledge of the case who are sitting in the audience and

---

244 Parole is conditional release before the end of the prisoner's sentence. *See* Chapter XIV, p. 574.

245 *Smith v. Hooey*, 393 U.S. 374 (1969). Procedures are governed by the Interstate Agreement on Detainers (IAD)a compact entered into by 48 States, the United States, and the District of Columbia. 18 U. S. C. App. §§2. Compacts between states are authorized by Art. I §10 cl. 3 of the Constitution.

246 18 U.S.C.A. §§3161-3174. This act provides that information or indictment is to be issued 30 days after a defendant is arrested or served with a summons, and trial is to commence within 70 days of the filing of the information or indictment. There are numerous exceptions to the time requirements. The remedy for a violation of the Act is dismissal of the charges, sometimes with and sometimes without the right to reinstate charges.

247 LaFAVE, ISRAEL & KING, *supra* note 1, at 865-866. States typically require trials to commence anywhere from 75 to 180 days arrest, indictment, or the filing of an information, whichever comes first. In most states, where a defendant has shown by timely motion that the time required by the statute or court rule has elapsed, the remedy for violating the statute or court rule is dismissal with prejudice.

248 *Klopfer v. North Carolina*, 386 U.S. 213 (1967)

249 Like most constitutional rights, the right to speedy trial can be waived. A recent detainer case holds that defense counsel's agreement to a trial date beyond the 180 day limit in the Interstate Compact on Detainers constituted a waiver of the defendant's right to be tried within that period. *New York v. Hill*, 528 U.S. 110 (2000). *See also Wilson v. Mitchell*, 250 F.3d 388 (6th Cir. 2001) (22-year delay between charge and arrest was not violation of speedy trial act because defendant had been eluding capture).

250 ___ U.S. ___; 129 S.Ct. 1283 (2009).

251 *Presley v. Georgia*, ___ U.S. ___; 130 S.Ct. 721 (2010).

252 *Waller v. Georgia*, 467 U.S. 39 (1984).

might come forward.[253] The public trial requirement is met so long as the public in general has free access to a defendant's criminal trial. The right is not violated just because all persons who wish to attend a trial cannot be accommodated.

To show that the right has been violated, a defendant need not show prejudice to his case; he need only show that the public was improperly excluded, and he will be granted a new trial.[254] The 6th Amendment right to a public trial is the defendant's alone, and exclusion of the public is not a violation if the defendant has waived his right. However, the press and members of the public may have a separate *1st Amendment* right of access to court proceedings.[255]

3. Right to a Jury Trial

The 6th Amendment guarantees the right to trial by jury in criminal prosecutions for all "non-petty" offenses, defined as crimes for which the potential punishment is more than 6 months.[256] Historically, the number of jurors on a jury was 12. However, the Supreme Court has held that it is constitutional for states to convene juries of as few as 6 in criminal cases, concluding that having 12 jurors was nothing more than "historical accident."[257] Today, 33 states have authorized juries of less than 12 in at least some kinds of criminal cases.[258] The number of jurors for federal criminal cases remains at 12 as a matter of non-constitutional law, so there has never been the occasion to determine definitively if the federal government is required to use a jury of 12. Although the right to a jury trial is generally thought to be for the protection of the defendant, the prosecution has a right to a jury trial even if the defendant does not want one in the federal system and in 25 states.[259]

As for the vote margin needed to decide a case, the Supreme Court has held that unanimity is not a constitutional requirement for states. The Court has approved a 10-2 vote as sufficient for conviction, and certain members of the Court have hinted that a 9-3 vote might be constitutional.[260] However, if the state uses six-person juries, unanimity is required.[261] Notwithstanding the constitutional latitude states enjoy with criminal juries, all but 5 states require unanimous verdicts as a matter of their own law, as does the federal government.[262]

---

253 *In re Oliver*, 333 U.S. 257 (1948).

254 *Waller v. Georgia*, 467 U.S. 39 (1984).

255 *See, e.g., Gannett Co., Inc. v. DePasquale*, 443 U.S. 368 (1979); *Richmond Newspapers, Inc. v. Virginia*, 448 U.S. 555 (1980); *Globe Newspaper Co. v. Superior Court*, 457 U.S. 596 (1982). *See also* Chapter IX, p. 386.

256 *Bloom v. Illinois*, 391 U.S. 194 (1968). Multiple petty offenses may not be added together to reach the six-month period. *Lewis v. United States*, 518 U.S. 322 (1996).

257 *Williams v. Florida*, 399 U.S. 78 (1970). In *Ballew v. Georgia*, 435 U.S. 223 (1978), the Court disapproved use of a five-person jury.

258 Empirical studies have shown that 6-person juries are substantially worse than 12-person juries in their ability to decide cases properly. *See* Lempert, *supra*, Chapter III, p. 126, note 144. *See also* p. 122 (greater diversity improves jury accuracy more than greater average education).

259 *Singer v. United States*, 380 U.S. 24, 34 (1965). Stated another way, there is no right to a judge trial.

260 *Apodaca v. Oregon*, 406 U.S. 404 (1972); *Johnson v. Louisiana*, 406 U.S. 356 (1972).

261 *See Burch v. Louisiana*, 441 U.S. 130 (1979) (5-1 vote for conviction held unconstitutional).

262 As with the issue of the required size of the jury, the fact that unanimous verdicts have always been required by statute and common law has made it unnecessary to determine if a federal jury is required to be unanimous as a constitutional matter.

4. Right to an Impartial Jury

In *Duncan v. Louisiana*,[263] the Supreme Court held that the 6th Amendment right to an "impartial jury" was applicable to the states through the 14th Amendment's due process clause. In *Taylor v. Louisiana*,[264] the Court held that all defendants are entitled to be tried by juries drawn from a pool representing a fair cross-section of the community. A "jury pool made up only of segments of the populace [or excluding] large, distinctive groups" does not serve the purpose of a jury, which is "to guard against the exercise of arbitrary power." Though the jury *pool* must represent a cross-section, the actual jury that is eventually selected need not represent a fair-cross section.[265] However, if peremptory challenges are being used to exclude prospective jurors on grounds of their race, ethnic or national heritage, or gender, such action by either the prosecution or the defense is unconstitutional. To succeed in peremptorily challenging any juror, the prosecutor or the defense may be called upon to justify the challenge as based on a non-discriminatory reason.[266]

The 6th Amendment also states that defendants have the right to be tried by a jury "in the State and district wherein the crime shall have been committed." State constitutions often provide that trial by jury should take place in the county where the crime charged was alleged to have been committed.

5. Right Not to Testify

The 5th Amendment's self-incrimination clause has been discussed as it applies to interrogations by the police. The clause is also applicable at the trial stage, where it prevents defendants from being called to testify at their criminal trial. The setting in which the privilege may be claimed may be anywhere — at a police station, a civil trial, a legislative or administrative hearing, or a grand jury proceeding.[267] However, the word "witness" in the self-incrimination clause means that compelled incriminating statements must be "testimonial." Thus, the privilege against self incrimination does not prevent the compelled disclosure of documents containing incriminating assertions of fact or belief, because the creation of those documents was not "compelled" within the meaning of the privilege.[268]

---

263 391 U.S. 145 (1968).

264 419 U.S. 522 (1975).

265 *Fay v. New York*, 332 U.S. 261 (1947); *Lockhart v. McCree*, 476 U.S. 162 (1986); *Holland v. Illinois*, 493 U.S. 474 (1990).

266 *See Snyder v. Louisiana*, 552 U.S. 472 (2008)(race); *Batson v. Kentucky*, 476 U.S. 79 (1986)(race); *Hernandez v. New York*, 500 U.S. 352 (1991) (Latin American heritage); *J.E.B. v. Alabama ex rel. T.B.*, 511 U.S. 127 (1994) (sex). The Court extended the prohibition to defense challenges in criminal cases in *Georgia v. McCollum*, 505 U.S.42 (1992). *See also Purkett v. Elem*, 514 U.S. 765 (1995) (clarifying procedures for implementing *Batson*); *Johnson v. California*, 545 U.S. 162 (2005) (prosecutor used 3 of his 12 peremptory challenges to remove prospective black jurors; describing what leads to an inference of discrimination) and *Miller-El v. Dretke*, 545 U.S. 231 (2005) (lower courts' conclusion challenges were not racially determined was "an unreasonable determination of the facts"); *Rivera v. Illinois*, ___ U.S. ___; 129 S.Ct. 1446 (2009)(trial judge's good faith error in denying a defendant's peremptory challenge does *not* deprive the defendant of the right to an impartial jury). *See also Dretke, supra* (Breyer, J., concurring) (suggesting that peremptory challenges be eliminated entirely). Peremptory challenges were discussed in Chapter III, p. 93.

267 Fear of prosecution under the laws of a foreign country are not sufficient to invoke the privilege. *United States v. Balsys*, 524 U.S. 666 (1998) (suspected Nazi collaborator could not refuse to testify in a investigation that could lead to his deportation and prosecution in Lithuania or Israel).

268 *Fisher v. United States*, 425 U.S. 391 (1976) (tax records). *But see United States v. Hubbell*, 530 U.S. 27 (2000) (acts of identifying, producing and verifying records were testimonial).

The right not to testify necessarily includes within it the right not to have that silence used against the defendant. The trial court must instruct the jury on this point and the prosecutor is not allowed to comment on the defendant's silence. For example, in *Griffin v. California*,[269] the trial judge had instructed the jury that when a defendant does not testify in his own defense, but it is reasonable to expect him to deny or explain evidence presented against him because of facts within his knowledge, the jury may consider his failure to testify as proof against him. The prosecutor argued at the close of the case that the defendant "certainly" knew what had happened to the victim, but had refused to tell the jury what he knew. The Supreme Court held that such a comment on a defendant's refusal to testify, whether made by a court or a prosecutor, violates the self-incrimination clause.[270]

Despite these advantages of the right against self-incrimination, defendants who choose to take the stand must take the same oath to tell the truth as any other witness. Theoretically then, a criminal defendant could be prosecuted for perjury for taking the stand and falsely denying involvement in the crime. This rarely happens in practice, however, as prosecutors are usually satisfied with the verdict of guilty in the principal case and know the difficulties of proving perjury beyond a reasonable doubt.[271]

The right against self-incrimination applies to everyone, not just to defendants in criminal cases. However, witnesses may be forced to testify against a defendant if the prosecutor has granted those witnesses "immunity" from prosecution based on the evidence they give.[272] Since immunity removes any self-incriminating effect of their testimony, witnesses may not decline to testify. If a witness still refuses to testify even after being granted immunity, that witness can be held in contempt of court and punished accordingly. One method of enforcing orders to testify is to jail the witness until the witness agrees to testify.[273]

6. Right to Confront Accusers

The 6th Amendment also guarantees that the accused "shall enjoy the right . . . to be confronted with the witnesses against him . . . ." This means, meaning the defendant must have the opportunity to see his or her accusers face to face and to cross-examine them. In *Davis v. Alaska*,[274] the trial court refused to allow the defendant to cross-examine the prosecution witness, a juvenile delinquent on probation for burglary. The Supreme Court held this to be a violation of the right of confrontation. However, preliminary hearing testimony that is subject to cross examination may be admitted against the defendant if the witness becomes unavailable.

Over the years, the Court's confrontation jurisprudence got away from a strict requirement of the opportunity to cross-examine and began to permit statements of a missing witness to be admitted at trial if the statements bore "adequate indicia of

---

269 380 U.S. 609 (1965).

270 *See also Carter v. Kentucky*, 450 U.S. 288 (1981) (jury instruction on defendant's silence).

271 Not only may perjury be prosecuted, an untrue denial of guilt under questioning by a Federal investigator can be prosecuted as a crime under the Federal false-statements law. *Brogan v. United States*, 522 U.S. 398 (1998).

272 *See supra* p. 271 (grand jury testimony). Such a grant of immunity is only from *use* of the compelled statements to prosecute the person; it does not bar a prosecution that is based on evidence *independent* of the compelled statements. *Zicarelli v. New Jersey*, 406 U.S. 472 (1972).

273 Imprisonment until the person complies would be civil contempt. *See* Chapter VII, p. 247.

274 415 U.S. 308 (1974).

reliability." But in a 2004 case, the Court exhaustively reexamined the history of the clause and went back to its roots, reaffirming that the prosecution may not use any statement against the defendant unless the defendant had the opportunity to cross-examine that witness at the time the statement was made.[275] However, it is only statements that are "testimonial" that are subject to the confrontation requirement. Thus, a domestic battery victim's statements recorded in a telephone call to the police while the crime was going on were not testimonial and, therefore, admissible, since they were intended to enable the police to resolve the existing emergency, not the product of post-incident police investigation efforts.[276] On the other hand, a domestic battery victim's written statements in an formal complaint and affidavit given to police officers investigating the crime were testimonial, and therefore, inadmissible.[277]

The right to a face-to-face confrontation with accusers can be waived by obstreperous behavior. In one case, the Court held that a judge properly excluded the defendant from his own trial after he used vile language and engaged in other disruptive behavior, had been repeatedly warned and was told he could return to the trial anytime if he agreed to behave himself.[278] If a defendant absconds *during* his or her trial, this also constitutes a waiver of confrontation rights. Thus, in general, no defendant can be tried *in absentia* unless he or she is present at the beginning of the trial and later voluntarily absconds.[279] Additionally, if the defendant causes a witness to be unavailable to testify, the defendant forfeits the right to confrontation and the prosecution can use the witness's previous statements. However, the defendant must have acted with the intent of preventing the witness from testifying.[280]

7. Right to Counsel at Trial

Relying on the 6th Amendment right to counsel, the Supreme Court has held that state and federal governments must appoint an attorney for anyone accused of a felony who cannot afford an attorney. The Court held that "lawyers in criminal courts are necessities, not luxuries," and that "in our adversary system of criminal justice, any person haled into court, who is too poor to hire a lawyer, cannot be assured a fair trial unless counsel is provided for him."[281] Counsel must also be appointed for one accused of a misdemeanor where a conviction could result in even one day in jail.[282]

---

275 *Crawford v. Washington*, 541 U.S. 36 (2004) (excluding recorded statement of defendant's wife's obtained by the police in his absence).

276 *Michigan v. Bryant*, ___ U.S. ___, 131 S.Ct. 1143 (2011) (statement of mortally victim to police that defendant shot him was not testimonial because "primary purpose" was to enable police assistance to meet an ongoing emergency, not "to establish or prove past events potentially relevant to later criminal prosecution").

277 *Davis v. Washington*, 547 U.S. 813 (2006).

278 *Illinois v. Allen*, 397 U.S. 337 (1970).

279 *United States v. Crosby*, 506 US 255 (1993) (trial may not be held if defendant absconds before trial starts); *Taylor v. United States*, 414 US 17 (1973) (per curium) (trial may continue if defendant absconds after trial has started). *See also* Federal Rule of Criminal Procedure 43.

280 Thus, the Court held that where a defendant murdered his ex-girlfriend in a domestic dispute, the prosecution could *not* introduce her testimonial statements to police three weeks before the murder, because although the defendant had "caused" her to become unavailable, he had not murdered her with the intent of preventing her testimony at trial. *Giles v. California*, 554 U.S. 353 (2008).

281 *Gideon v. Wainwright*, 372 U.S. 335 (1963) (state); *Johnson v. Zerbst*, 304 U.S. 458 (1938) (federal).

282 *Argersinger v. Hamlin*, 407 U.S. 25 (1972). However, if the case involves a misdemeanor for which only a fine is to be imposed, there is no right to appointed counsel. *Scott v. Illinois*, 440 U.S. 367 (1979). Moreover, the uncounseled conviction may be used to enhance the sentence of a later crime. *Nichols v. United States*, 511 U.S.738 (1994) (drunk driving conviction punished only by a fine used to enhance prison sentence on conviction of later federal drug charges).

A person has the right to waive his right to the assistance of counsel and represent himself at his criminal trial, no matter how ill-advised that choice might be. In *Faretta v. California*,[283] the defendant had been granted permission to represent himself. Later, the trial judge appointed a public defender, because he felt that the defendant was not knowledgeable enough to defend himself. The defendant was convicted, but the Supreme Court reversed the conviction, holding that "the right to defend is given directly to the accused."[284] However, if a defendant is competent enough to stand trial, but suffers from severe mental illness to the point that he or she is not competent to conduct trial proceedings by themselves, the judge may insist on appointed counsel.[285]

The right to counsel means the right to the *effective* assistance of counsel. As the Supreme Court observed in *Strickland v. Washington*,[286] the mere fact "[t]hat a person who happens to be a lawyer is present at trial alongside the accused" will not alone meet the requirements of the 6th Amendment. However, the 6th Amendment standard for counsel's performance is rather low. A conviction will be reversed only where "counsel's conduct so undermined the proper functioning of the adversarial process that the trial cannot be relied on as having produced a just result."[287]

8. Burden of Proof

Closely related to the right not to testify is the due process requirement articulated in *In re Winship*[288] — that the prosecution has the burden of proof as to "every fact necessary to constitute" the charged crime and that those facts must be proved "beyond a reasonable doubt."[289] It is perhaps strange that so fundamental a right is not set out explicitly in the Bill of Rights, but instead had to be inferred from the due process clauses of the Constitution. The *Winship* requirement imposes two different requirements. First, it imposes a quantum of proof requirement on judge and jury, prohibiting them from using any lower standard of proof of facts necessary for conviction than proof "beyond a reasonable doubt."[290] Second, it assures that the burden of proof on the elements of an offense may not be shifted to the defense in a way that forces defendants to prove their innocence.[291]

---

283 422 U.S. 806 (1975).

284 There is no corresponding right to represent oneself on appeal, nor does the 6th Amendment require the assistance of counsel on appeal. *Martinez v. Court of Appeal of California*, 528 U.S. 152 (2000). However, appointed counsel on appeal is constitutionally required by equal protection and due process for the defendant's first appeal as of right on the ground that failure to do so would result in an improper disparity between rich and poor defendants. *See infra* p. 322.

285 *Indiana v. Edwards*, 554 U.S. 164, 128 S.Ct. 2379 (2008).

286 466 U.S. 668, 685 (1984).

287 A defendant's right to effective assistance of counsel applies to plea bargaining as well. *Hill v. Lockhart*, 474 U.S. 52 (1985); *United States v. Gordon*, 156 F.3d 376, 380 (2d Cir.1998) (attorney breached his duty as a criminal defense lawyer "to advise his client fully on whether a particular plea to a charge appears desirable" when the attorney "grossly underestimat[ed his client's] sentencing exposure"). However, the defendant may waive counsel just as in the case of a trial. *See Iowa v. Tovar*, 541 U.S. 77 (2004) (waiver must be "intelligently" made, but no particular warnings need be given by the court). The right also applies during sentencing, though the Court has set a low standard. *See Schriro v. Landrigan*, 550 U.S. 465 (2007) (failure to present mitigating evidence during sentencing is not ineffective assistance).

288 397 U.S. 358 (1970).

289 This includes any element that can result in an increase in the defendant's sentence beyond the maximum specified in the law. *See* discussion of the jury's role in sentencing, *supra* p. 278.

290 *See* Chapter III, p. 108, where jury instructions explaining the criminal standard of "beyond a reasonable doubt" and the civil standard of "preponderance of the evidence" are set out.

291 *Mullaney v. Wilbur*, 421 U.S. 684 (1975) (in murder prosecution, defendant could not be required to negate malice by proving sudden provocation). *Compare Patterson v. New York*, *infra* note 295.

This shifting may not be done indirectly through presumptions either.[292] Thus, in *Sandstrom v. Montana*,[293] the Court held invalid a jury instruction given in a deliberate homicide case that stated that "the law presumes that a person intends the ordinary consequences of his voluntary acts." This violated the *Winship* rule because it could be understood by the jury as shifting the burden to the defendant to disprove intent once the prosecution had proved his voluntary act of causing the death of the victim. Even more problematic are mandatory presumptions. Thus, in *Carella v. California*,[294] the Court unanimously struck down a California law providing that anyone who fails to return a rental vehicle within 5 days of its due date is presumed to have stolen it.

Despite *Winship*'s close regulation of burden shifting as to the *elements* of an offense, it does not prevent the state from placing the burden of proof on the defendant as to *defenses*.[295] What standard of proof the defense may constitutionally be required to meet in proving defenses is not completely clear. The issue does not often come up, since most jurisdictions impose a "preponderance of the evidence" standard — the most lax standard and the one used in civil cases.[296] The Court in a 1952 case approved Oregon's requirement that the defense prove insanity "beyond a reasonable doubt," but that case predates the due process revolution of the 1960s.[297] Moreover, the Court in 1996 held that the defense's burden of proving mental incompetence *to stand trial* may not be higher than the civil "preponderance of the evidence" standard.[298]

The Court has also made clear that the *Winship* requirement does not prevent a state from prohibiting the defense from introducing certain kinds of evidence in defense of a criminal charge. In *Montana v. Egelhoff*,[299] the defendant in an intentional homicide case sought to prove that he was so intoxicated that he was unable to form the intent to kill, but he was barred from doing so by a statute prohibiting any evidence of a defendant's state of alcohol intoxication. The Court upheld the statute.[300]

---

292 *Winship* also does not affect either the burden or the standard of proof in suppression hearings. *See Colorado v. Conelly*, 479 U.S. 157 (1986) (prosecution need only prove waiver of *Miranda* rights by a preponderance of evidence).

293 442 U.S. 510 (1979).

294 491 U.S. 263 (1989).

295 *Patterson v. New York*, 432 U.S. 197 (1977) (defendant in a murder prosecution can be required to prove the affirmative defense of extreme emotional disturbance that reduces the crime to manslaughter); *Dixon v. United States*, 548 U.S.1 (2006) (defendant may be required to prove defense of duress in case in which she bought a firearm because her boyfriend forced her to).

296 This was the case in *Patterson, supra* note 295.

297 *Leland v. Oregon*, 343 U.S. 790 (1952).

298 *Cooper v. Oklahoma*, 517 U.S. 348 (1996). *But see United States v. Amos*, 803 F.2d 419 (8th Cir. 1986) (upholding on authority of *Leland* federal statute's imposing on the defense the burden of proving insanity by "clear and convincing"). The different treatment of insanity as a defense to a crime and incompetence to stand trial may lie in the fact that the insanity defense is not constitutionally required, while it violates due process to try a person who is so incompetent to stand trial.

299 518 U.S. 37 (1996). The case is also discussed in Chapter XIV, p. 562.

300 A plurality of four justices held exclusion of relevant evidence was constitutional because it did not offend any "principle of justice so rooted in the traditions and conscience of our people as to be ranked as fundamental." Justice Ginsberg, the fifth vote necessary for a majority, reasoned more simply that the state had a broad constitutional right to define the elements of criminal offenses and could change its concept of the moral culpability of defendants to equate sober and intoxicated defendants. Justice Ginsberg's opinion suggests a difficulty with the *Winship* doctrine: that it seems to turn on whether the state defines a given issue as an *element* of the offense or as a *defense*. If this is correct, then the state could presumably avoid the *Winship* problem by simply redefining the offense in most cases.

9. Other Constitutional Protections

Other rights not explicitly mentioned in the Bill of Rights — like the right in *Winship* — have been found in the 14th Amendment and the 5th Amendment due process clauses. Some of the practices prohibited that are not discussed elsewhere in this chapter include: defense discovery rights,[301] improper closing argument by the prosecutor,[302] violation of the right to counsel at parole revocation proceedings,[303] prohibiting a defendant's access to evidence,[304] entrapment,[305] improper conduct of the prosecutor in grand jury proceedings,[306] judicial bias,[307] prejudicial publicity,[308] and charges motivated by prosecutorial vindictiveness.[309] Since due process is a flexible concept, this list is not exhaustive.[310]

E. The Effect of Prior Proceedings: The Double Jeopardy Guarantee

The 5th Amendment provides that no one may "be subject for the same offence to be twice put in jeopardy of life or limb."[311] Double jeopardy problems typically occur in two instances: (1) when the prosecution is disappointed in an acquittal and seeks to try the defendant once again for the same crime, or (2) when the prosecution obtains a conviction, but is dissatisfied with the severity of that conviction or sentence and wishes to try a second time to convict the defendant of a more serious crime, or to obtain a higher or additional sentence. The essence of double jeopardy's protection against retrial is not just the possibility of a worse result for the defendant in the second trial, however. It is also the "continuing state of anxiety and insecurity" and the "embarrassment, expense, and ordeal" of a second trial.[312]

1. When Jeopardy Attaches

It is important to know when jeopardy "attaches" to the first prosecution, since it is only if the first prosecution is terminated after that point that it "counts," and thus will bar a second trial. If the case is tried to a jury, jeopardy attaches when the jury is empaneled and sworn.[313] When the case is tried before the judge alone, jeopardy attaches when

---

301 *Pennsylvania v. Ritchie*, 480 U.S. 39 (1987).

302 *Donnelly v. DeChristoforo*, 416 U.S. 637 (1974).

303 *Morrissey v. Brewer*, 408 U.S. 471 (1972) (appointed counsel required only under certain circumstances).

304 *Arizona v. Youngblood*, 488 U.S. 51 (1988).

305 *United States v. Russell*, 411 U.S. 423 (1973) (dictum). Entrapment is a defense based on the claim that the police caused the defendant to commit a crime he would not otherwise have committed. *See* Chapter XIV, pp. 568- 569.

306 *Bank of Nova Scotia v. United States*, 487 U.S. 250 (1988).

307 *Tumey v. Ohio*, 273 U.S. 510 (1927) (fees paid to judge for each conviction); *Mayberry v. Pennsylvania*, 400 U.S. 455 (1971) (defendant insulted judge and same judge held defendant in contempt).

308 *Sheppard v. Maxwell*, 384 U.S. 333 (1966).

309 *Blackledge v. Perry*, 417 U.S. 21 (1974).

310 *See* Chapter VI, pp. 206-209, which discusses what procedural protections due process requires.

311 *See generally* LAFAVE, ISRAEL & KING, *supra* note 1, Chapter 25. Despite the somewhat archaic reference to "jeopardy of life or limb," double jeopardy applies to all crimes, from misdemeanors to capital felonies. *Ex parte Lange*, 85 U.S. 163 (1873).

312 *Green v. United States*, 355 U.S. 184 (1957). *See also United States v. DiFrancesco*, 449 U.S. 117 (1980) (discussing at length the purposes and history of the double jeopardy clause). Double jeopardy applies only to criminal prosecutions, so it has no effect on an ordinary civil suit following conviction. In addition, if the first acquittal was the result of bribing the judge in the first trial, a second trial is not barred on the theory that the defendant had never truly "in jeopardy" of conviction the first time.

313 *Crist v. Bretz*, 437 U.S. 28 (1978).

the prosecution begins its opening statement.[314] Therefore, multiple criminal complaints based on the same crime that are dismissed *before the trial stage* do not violate the prohibition against double jeopardy.

2. Retrial After a Completed Trial or Other Ruling on the Merits

Once a trial has started and jeopardy has attached, a jury *acquittal* presents the clearest bar to a second prosecution.[315] A dismissal by the judge for lack of sufficient evidence or any other form of judicial acquittal also bars re-prosecution. This is so regardless of how erroneous the judge's determination of lack of evidence might be.[316] A *conviction* after trial also bars retrial for the same offense. However, if after a conviction, a new trial takes place because the trial judge set aside the original verdict at the defendant's request, double jeopardy will not bar the second trial because the defendant sought the new trial.[317] Similar waiver results when a defendant wins a reversal of a conviction on appeal.[318] Nonetheless, double jeopardy *bars* retrial if the defendant wins reversal of the first verdict from the trial or appellate court because there was insufficient evidence to support that verdict.[319]

Double jeopardy necessarily means that the prosecution cannot appeal an acquittal regardless of what errors were committed at trial, since a reversal of the acquittal would result in a second trial.[320] However, double jeopardy does not prevent the prosecution from appealing a *trial judge's order setting aside* a jury conviction — even one that is on grounds of insufficiency of the evidence. The reason for this is that reversal of the judge's order would not subject the defendant to a second trial: it would simply reinstate the original jury conviction.[321] In addition, the double jeopardy clause is not violated when the prosecution appeals the imposition of a particular *sentence* (as opposed to a judgment of guilt) that the prosecution thinks is illegal or too lenient, when that is permitted by statute. The rationale is that no retrial of the case is needed. Also, re-

---

314 *See* Chapter III, pp. 92-95, for a description of trial procedure as it relates to empaneling the jury and opening statements.

315 *See also Green v. United States*, 355 U.S. 184 (1957) (where defendant was charged alternatively with first and second degree murder, conviction for second degree murder operated as an acquittal of first degree murder); *Bullington v. Missouri*, 451 U.S. 430 (1981) (where jury had convicted defendant, but declined to impose the death penalty in first trial, death could not be imposed on retrial after defendant successfully appealed because first verdict was tantamount to a partial acquittal).

316 *Smalis v. Pennsylvania*, 476 U.S. 140 (1986) (judicial direction of acquittal was based on an erroneous understanding of the applicable law). *See also Smith v. Massachusetts*, 543 U.S. 462 (2005) (directed verdict as to one charge was final despite fact judge changed her mind after defense had presented its case). For a discussion of the circumstances under which a judge may direct the verdict or judgment in the defendant's favor, see Chapter III, pp. 102, 108.

317 *United States v. Scott*, 437 U.S. 82 (1978).

318 *Ball v. United States*, 163 U.S. 662 (1896). *See also North Carolina v. Pearce*, 395 U.S. 711 (1969) (any more severe sentence imposed after retrial must be based on conduct occurring since the first sentence).

319 *McDaniel v. Brown*, ___ U.S. ___; 130 S.Ct. 665 (2010); *Burks v. United States*, 437 U.S. 1 (1978). *Cf. United States v. Watts*, 519 U.S. 148 (1997).

320 *Ball v. United States*, 163 U.S. 662 (1896); *Fong Foo v. United States*, 369 U.S. 141 (1978).

321 *See United States v. Wilson*, 420 U.S. 332 (1975). Thus, a distinction is drawn between a judicial acquittal *following* a jury verdict (usually referred to as a judgment notwithstanding the verdict) and one ordered mid-trial *before* a jury verdict (directed verdict of acquittal). Only if the trial is aborted *before* the verdict is retrial necessary, so that is the only situation in which double jeopardy bars a prosecution appeal from a judicial acquittal. *See* Chapter III, pp. 102, 108, for the distinction in general between judgment notwithstanding the verdict and a directed verdict.

sentencing does not involve the same sort of government oppression as successive trials on the issue of guilt.[322]

3. Retrial After a Mistrial

Not all trials end in convictions or acquittals. Trials can abort for many other reasons, resulting in the judge declaring a mistrial.[323] If the defendant moves for or consents to the mistrial, this is often deemed a waiver of double jeopardy protections,[324] but there is no waiver when the prosecution's actions at trial provoked the defense motion for a mistrial.[325] But even mistrials granted over the defendant's objection will not bar re-prosecution of the defendant if there was "manifest necessity" for the judge to stop the trial. Such necessity exists whenever "an impartial verdict cannot be reached, or if a verdict of conviction could be reached, but would have to be set aside on appeal due to an obvious procedural error in the trial."[326] But consistent with the concern for prosecutorial oppression underlying double jeopardy, retrial is not allowed after a mistrial granted on a ground that "lend[s] itself to prosecutorial manipulation" and could "allow the prosecution the opportunity to strengthen its case."[327]

4. What is the "Same Offence"

For double jeopardy to apply, the second prosecution must be for the "same offence." A single criminal action can violate several criminal statutes, thus raising the possibility that prosecutions brought and tried separately for each "offense" would violate double jeopardy. The overall test of whether the second prosecution is the same offense was set out in *Blockburger v. United States*.[328] That test states that crimes under different statutes are different offenses if any element is different: if each offense "requires proof of an additional fact which the other does not." This would mean at the very least that a crime and any of its "lesser-included offenses" would be considered to be the same offense. A lesser-included offense of a crime is any offense that is less serious than that crime and whose elements are all included within the definition of the more serious crime. Thus, the Supreme Court has held that it violated double jeopardy to try a defendant first for operating a car without permission and then to charge him with stealing the same car, because operation of a car without permission is included within the definition of auto theft.[329]

---

322 *United States v. DiFrancesco*, 449 U.S. 117 (1980).

323 *See* Chapter III, p. 107, for a discussion of mistrials.

324 *United States v. Dinitz*, 424 U.S. 600 (1976).

325 *Dinitz, supra*; *Oregon v. Kennedy*, 456 U.S. 667 (1982) (second trial not barred after defense motion for mistrial was granted based on prosecutor asking witness whether witness did not do business with the defendant "because [he] is a crook?").

326 *Illinois v. Somerville*, 410 U.S. 458 (1973) (indictment did not allege essential element and could not be amended under state law; retrial allowed). For examples of cases involving "manifest necessity," *see United States v. Perez*, 22 U.S. (9 Wheat.) 579 (1824) (jury deadlocked); *Simmons v. United States*, 142 U.S. 148 (1891) (juror was found to have known the defendant personally); *Brock v. North Carolina*, 344 U.S. 424 (1953) (prosecution witnesses unexpectedly invoked their right against self-incrimination), overruled in part on other grounds in *Benton v. Maryland*. 501 U.S. 957 (1991).

327 *Downum v. United States*, 372 U.S. 734 (1963) (retrial barred after mistrial granted to prosecution on ground that prosecution had not subpoenaed one of its witnesses).

328 284 U.S. 299 (1932). *See also United States v. Dixon*, 509 U.S. 688 (1993).

329 *Brown v. Ohio*, 432 U.S. 161 (1977). However, *Brown* made clear that if the lesser included offense were prosecuted first before facts constituting the more serious offense developed, then a second prosecution on the more serious charge is not barred. For example, if a defendant is convicted of attempted murder for shooting the victim and the victim dies from those injuries, a second prosecution for murder is not barred.

5. Collateral Estoppel

The classic *Blockburger* definition of "same offense" would make kidnaping, robbery, and murder arising out of a *single* criminal episode all "different offenses." Thus, it would seem that the prosecution could proceed to trial on the kidnaping charge first and, if the defendant is acquitted, it could follow up with a second prosecution for robbery or even a third trial for murder, should the defendant be acquitted of robbery. What may prevent this is the doctrine of issue preclusion or collateral estoppel.[330] The leading case is *Ashe v. Swenson*,[331] where the defendant was prosecuted for robbing one of 6 players at a card game.[332] At his first trial, his defense was that he was elsewhere at the time of the crime, and he was acquitted by a jury. The prosecution then tried to prosecute him for robbery of the second card player. The Supreme Court held that, since it was clear that the jury acquitted the defendant because it was convinced that the government had not shown that the defendant participated in the robbery, the government was bound by that determination in any later proceedings involving that defendant.[333] However, the Court has also held that evidence of a defendant's participation in a burglary for which he was acquitted may be introduced in a later trial for bank robbery to bolster identification of the defendant as the bank robber and to show his connection with another person implicated in the bank robbery.[334] Additionally, where the defendant in a multiple-count trial is acquitted on some counts but the jury fails to reach a verdict on other counts, double jeopardy may bar retrial on the deadlocked counts if the jury determined the same issues involved in the counts for which it acquitted the defendant.[335]

6. Double Jeopardy and Dual Sovereignty

Successive prosecutions by *state* and *federal* governments for criminal offenses arising out of the same criminal episode are not barred by double jeopardy. These are permitted under the "dual sovereignty" doctrine. That doctrine is based on the notion that "an act denounced as a crime by both national and state sovereignties is an offense against the peace and dignity of both and may be punished by each."[336] The federal government may prosecute a defendant for the same conduct for which the defendant had already been convicted by a state,[337] and a state may prosecute a defendant for the same conduct for which the defendant had already been convicted by the federal government.[338] However, when the first prosecution was in state court, federal policy requires that a later federal prosecution should be undertaken only if there is a compelling federal interest in pursuing it.[339] A recent example of the operation of the "dual

---

330 For a general discussion of collateral estoppel or issue preclusion, *see* Chapter VII, pp. 249-250.

331 397 U.S. 436 (1970).

332 The robbery of each card player was a different offense because each was committed against a different victim.

333 The prosecution cannot *take advantage* of a prior finding against the defendant. *Simpson v. Florida*, 403 U.S. 384 (1971). *Compare* Chapter VII, pp. 249-250 (offensive use allowed in civil cases).

334 *Dowling v. United States*, 493 U.S. 342 (1990). FRE 404(b) permits proof of other wrongful acts if offered to prove, not bad character, but identity. *See* Chapter III, p. 111.

335 *Yeager v. United States*, ___ U.S. ___; 129 S.Ct. 2360 (2009).

336 *United States v. Lanza*, 260 U.S. 377 (1922).

337 *Abbate v. United States*, 359 U.S. 187 (1959)

338 *Bartkus v. Illinois*, 359 U.S. 121 (1959)

339 LaFave, Israel & King, *supra* note 1, p. 1192, n. 8, citing U.S. Attorneys' Manual §9-2.142. *See also Petite v. United States*, 361 U.S. 529, 530 (1960) (*per curium*).

sovereignty" doctrine was the prosecution of Los Angeles police officers in federal court for civil rights violations for the beating of motorist Rodney King following their acquittal on state assault charges in state court. Issues of dual sovereignty are likely to increase as the number of federal crimes increases.

The same notion of dual sovereignty permits two states to prosecute the defendant for the same conduct. In *Heath v. Alabama*,[340] the victim had been kidnaped in Alabama, taken to Georgia and murdered. The Court held that it did not violate double jeopardy for the defendant to be convicted of felony murder in Alabama and ordinary murder in Georgia. However, dual sovereignty does not work where there is a violation of both state law and a city or county ordinance, since cities are subdivisions of the state and are considered to be the same sovereign. In one case, the defendant stole a mural from the city hall and damaged it. He was prosecuted and convicted under city ordinances for destruction of city property and for disorderly breach of the peace. Then he was prosecuted and convicted of felony grand larceny under state law. The Court held that conviction on the city ordinance charges barred the state larceny prosecution.[341] Native American tribal governments are also considered separate sovereigns from state and the federal government for purposes of double jeopardy.[342]

F. Limitations on Punishment

1. The Death Penalty

The Eighth Amendment states that "cruel and unusual punishments [shall not be] inflicted." Based upon this and the due process clause, the Supreme Court in 1972 struck down death penalty statutes in Georgia and Texas on the ground that those statutes left juries with untrammeled discretion to impose or withhold the death penalty.[343] By 1976, however, states had revised their laws to limit the discretion of judges and juries and to require them to consider relevant aggravating and mitigating circumstances specified by statute. In *Gregg v. Georgia*, the Court upheld these new laws.[344] While the Court admitted that the death penalty was "cruel" punishment, it denied that it was "unusual" — either in modern times or in 1791, when the 8th Amendment was ratified. Some years later, the Court rejected the argument that the death penalty was racially discriminatory just because blacks are sentenced to death at a higher rate than whites.[345] The Court also rejected a challenge to the means of execution. In *Baze v. Rees*[346] the Court ruled that the three-drug "lethal injection" protocol was not cruel and unusual because although sometimes incorrect dosages could cause the prisoner pain before death, the state had sufficient safeguards in place to ensure proper administration of the drugs.

While the constitutional problem with many death penalty laws has been the wide discretion permitted, death as an *automatic* punishment upon conviction for certain crimes has also been struck down. The Supreme Court has struck down statutes

---

340 474 U.S. 82 (1985)

341 *Waller v. Florida*, 397 U.S. 387 (1970).

342 *United States v. Lara*, 541 U.S. 193 (2004).

343 *Furman v. Georgia*, 408 U.S. 238 (1972). There were 9 separate opinions, but 5 of them found defects in the statutes involved. *Furman* voided some 40 death penalty statutes and 629 death sentences.

344 428 U.S. 153 (1976).

345 *See McCleskey v. Kemp*, 481 U.S. 279 (1987).

346 553 U.S. 35 (2008). *See also Provenzano v. Moore,* 744 So.2d 413 (Fla. 1999) (use of electric chair does not violate 8th Amendment).

providing for mandatory death for all first-degree murder[347] and for killing a police officer or firefighter.[348] Nor is the death penalty constitutionally applied to defendants for any offense committed before they were 18 years old.[349] Consistent with the common-law tradition, an insane person may not be put to death has been held to be enshrined in the 8th Amendment.[350] A plurality of the Court has held that a death sentence for rape of an adult woman or a child, unless coupled with an intentional killing, is unconstitutional because it does not involve the killing of another human being.[351]

Most of the Supreme Court's death penalty cases have focused on the procedure for juries to determine whether death is the appropriate punishment. One problem has been assuring that states afford the defendant the opportunity to show all relevant mitigating circumstances to the jury and that they are presented in a fair manner. For example, in *Eddings v. Oklahoma*,[352] the Court reversed the death sentence because the trial judge had refused to consider evidence of the defendant's turbulent family history, of beatings by a harsh father, and of his serious emotional disturbance. However, in Kansas v. Marsh, the Court upheld an instruction that required the jury to impose the death penalty if aggravating and mitigating circumstances were equally balanced.[353] A second problem has been assuring that jurors have complete information on the alternatives to a death sentence. Thus, the Court has insisted that juries be told whether a sentence of life in prison in a given state means that there is no chance the defendant' could be released on parole, since this could have a strong influence on jurors who are concerned about the defendant's future dangerousness.[354]

Another issue that has come up is that of the so-called "death-qualified" jury. Jurors have the power, though not the legal right, to "nullify" the law — to ignore the law as given to them by the judge and acquit the defendant.[355] Consequently, states have sought to exclude jurors who are opposed to capital punishment. In *Witherspoon v.*

---

347 *Woodson v. North Carolina*, 428 U.S. 280 (1976).

348 *Roberts v. Louisiana*, 431 U.S. 633 (1977).

349 *Roper v. Simmons*, 543 U.S. 551 (2005).

350 *Ford v. Wainwright*, 477 U.S. 399 (1986). This results in what has been called a "cure-to-kill" situation, whereby a prisoner is treated in order to be sufficiently sane to be executed. *See also Atkins v. Virginia*, 536 U.S. 304 (2002) (retarded person may not be executed); *Panetti v. Quarterman*, 551 U.S. 930 (2007) (insane person may not be executed even if sane at the time of the crime and trial).

351 *Coker v. Georgia*, 433 U.S. 584 (1977) (rape); *Kennedy v. Louisiana*, 554 U.S. 407 (2008) (child rape). Commentators believe that this nonetheless leaves open the possibility that a death sentence is constitutional for some non-murder offenses, such as treason, airplane hijacking or kidnaping, as pointed out by the dissenters in *Coker*. *See* LAFAVE, *supra* note 1, at 191.

352 455 U.S. 104 (1982). *See also Lockett v. Ohio*, 438 U.S. 586 (1978) (Ohio's limiting mitigating factors to a statutory list deprived defendant of the individualized approach she is entitled to); *Smith v. Spisak*, ___ U.S. ___; 130 S.Ct. 676 (2010) (judge or jury may not impose death penalty if they are prevented from considering any aspect of defendant's character or circumstances of the offense that the defendant proffers as a basis for mitigation).

353 *Kansas v. Marsh*, 548 U.S. 163 (2006). *But see People v. LaValle*, 817 N.E.2d 341 (N.Y. 2004) (jury instruction on consequences of inability to agree gave jury incentive to impose life without parole or death in violation of state constitution's due process clause).

354 *Simmons v. South Carolina*, 512 U. S. 154 (1994); *Shafer v. South Carolina*, 532 U.S. 36 (2001) (instruction required even if prosecution does not argue future dangerousness). *See also Penry v. Johnson*, 532 U.S. 782 (2001) (effect of jury instruction could have precluded jury from considering some of defendant's mitigating evidence). *See also Brown v. Sanders*, 546 U.S.212 (2006) (appeals court's invalidation of jury finding of two aggravating factors not sufficient to doubt sentence, where two others were properly found).

355 *See* Chapter III, p. 87.

Illinois,[356] the Court reversed a death sentence because Illinois had excluded all prospective jurors who had "conscientious scruples" against the death penalty. The Court approved in general the idea of inquiring into prospective jurors' views on the death penalty, but required such a juror state unambiguously that he or she would vote against imposing the death punishment no matter what facts were shown at trial.[357]

2. Other Forms of Cruel and Unusual Punishment

Arguments that the 8th Amendment prohibits terms of imprisonment that are disproportionately long in light of the offense have generally been difficult to win. In *Harmelin v. Michigan*,[358] the Supreme Court held 5-4 that it did not violate the 8th Amendment for a state to impose a sentence of mandatory life imprisonment without parole for simple possession of 650 grams (1.56 pounds) of cocaine.[359] The majority did not agree on a rationale. The four dissenters vehemently disagreed with the judgment, finding the sentence to be disproportionate to the offense.[360]

Another issue is treatment of prisoners while they are serving their sentence. The Supreme Court has held that when a prisoner alleges use of excessive force by prison personnel, the test is not the severity of the prisoner's injury, but rather whether prison personnel used force in a good faith effort to maintain discipline. Guards violate a prisoner's 8th Amendment rights only when they act maliciously with intent to harm.[361]

3. Civil Forfeitures

Prior to 1970, civil forfeiture of property was available as an additional but seldom used remedy in criminal cases. Its increased popularity among prosecutors recently has raised several constitutional questions. For constitutional purposes, a distinction must be drawn between *in personam* civil penalties and *in rem* forfeiture actions.

In personam civil forfeitures are for the purpose of punishing the owner for transgressions against the criminal law and typically involve seizure of property unrelated to the offense. In pursuing them the government must afford the property owner the same panoply of due process rights applicable to a criminal case.[362] In addition, any such punitive forfeiture that is "grossly disproportional" to the offense violates that 8th Amendment's ban on "excessive fines." The Court recently so held in a case where federal prosecutors sought the forfeiture of $357,144 in cash from a man and his family, who tried to bring it with them on a flight to Cyprus in order to repay a family debt. He had failed to report it in accordance with a Federal law requiring that all currency being taken out of the country in excess of $10,000 be declared. Given that there was no

---

356 391 U.S. 510 (1968).

357 *See also Uttecht v. Brown*, 551 U.S. 1 (2007) (defendant's rights not violated when prosecution excluded juror who would be substantially impaired in his ability to impose a death sentence).

358 501 U.S. 957 (1991).

359 For a rare instance of a successful challenge based on length of sentence, *see Graham v. Florida*, ___ U.S. ___, 130 S.Ct. 2011 (2010) (8th Amendment does not permit a juvenile offender to be sentenced to life in prison without parole for a nonhomicide crime).

360 *But see Solem v. Helm*, 463 U.S. 277 (1983) (requiring sentences to be proportional to the offense). It is interesting to note that the Michigan Supreme Court, reviewing the same law in question under the *Michigan* Constitution, held such a sentence unconstitutional. The Michigan Constitution forbids "cruel *or* unusual" punishments, unlike the "cruel *and* unusual" punishments prohibited by the federal Constitution. *People v. Bullock*, 485 N.W.2d 866 (Mich. 1992).

361 *Wilkins v. Gaddy*, ___ U.S. ___; 130 S.Ct. 1175 (2010).

362 *One 1958 Plymouth Sedan v. Pennsylvania*, 380 U.S. 693 (1969).

evidence that the money was the product of any illegal conduct, the Court affirmed the lower court's determination that $15,000 was sufficient.[363]

By contrast, *in rem* civil forfeitures are actions directly against "guilty" property — property used in the commission of crime. Such actions are "remedial" rather than punitive since their purpose is simply to remove the offending property from circulation without regard to any sanction against a criminal defendant. As remedial procedures, they are not subject to the excessive fines clause because the forfeiture, not being punishment, is not a fine.[364] In addition, it does not matter that innocent owners or co-owners of the property may lose their interest as a result of the forfeiture. This was demonstrated in a recent case where Michigan seized an automobile a man had used to have sex with a prostitute. The car was titled in both the man's and his wife's names and the wife sought to claim at least her half of the car. The Supreme Court determined that the state's deprivation of her interest did not violate due process. The Court did note that if the property used was stolen from the owner or if the owner did everything possible to avoid having the property put to the unlawful use, a constitutional question about forfeiture might arise, but there was no general "innocent owner" defense.[365]

G. Rights on Appeal

Right to Appeal Criminal defendants have no constitutional right to appeal their convictions.[366] However, state and federal defendants by statute have the right to at least one appeal. Statutory appeal rights are relatively recent in the federal system.[367]

Right to Counsel on Appeal Even if the right to appeal is only statutory, the Supreme Court held in *Douglas v. California*[368] that a combination of the equal protection and due process guarantees requires that states provide counsel to convicted indigent criminal defendants on their first appeal of right. *Douglas* involved a California rule that gave appellate courts the discretion to appoint or deny counsel to indigent appellants, depending on the appellate court's determination of whether or not the appointment of appellate counsel would be advantageous to the appellant or "helpful" to the court. No such preliminary review of the necessity of appellate counsel was made when an appellant could afford to hire appellate counsel. The Supreme Court held that states were required to afford adequate and effective appellate review to indigent defendants by affording them with counsel in every case.

---

363 *United States v. Bajakajian*, 524 U.S. 321 (1998).

364 *See United States v. Ursery*, 518 U.S. 267 (1996) (*in rem* civil forfeiture of property used in a crime does not constitute double punishment for purposes of the double jeopardy clause). A purportedly remedial forfeiture may become a punitive one if it goes beyond instrumentalities of the crime to those that merely "facilitate" the crime, in which case it is subject to the excessive fines limitation. *Austin v. United States*, 509 U.S. 602 (1993). *See also United States v. Bajakajian*, *supra* note 363.

365 *Bennis v. Michigan*, 516 U.S. 442 (1996). *See also Calero-Toledo v. Pearson Yacht Leasing Co.*, 416 U.S. 663 (1974) (innocent lessor-owner of yacht used in drug smuggling has no defense to forfeiture). The Court has held that procedural due process requires prior notice and opportunity for hearing before seizure if there is no emergency. *United States v. James Daniel Good Real Property*, 510 U.S. 43 (1993).

366 *McKane v. Durston*, 153 U.S. 684 (1894); *Abney v. United States*, 431 U.S. 651, 656 (1977).

367 Appeals as of right in criminal cases were first permitted in 1889 when Congress enacted a statute allowing such appeals "in all cases of conviction of crime the punishment of which provided by law is death." Act of Feb. 6, 1889, 25 Stat. 656. A general right of appeal in criminal cases was not created until 1911. Act of March 3, 1911, 36 Stat. 1133. Before 1889 all federal criminal cases ended in the trial court. In England appeal rights in criminal cases were not established until 1907.

368 372 U.S. 353 (1963). *See also Griffin v. Illinois*, 351 U.S. 12 (1956).

Douglas assures that a lawyer appointed to represent the defendant will review the case looking for errors to appeal rather than the appellate court itself. Difficulties arise, however, when appointed appellate counsel determines that there are no meritorious issues to raise. In such cases, counsel is caught between the ethical duty of zealous representation and the duty not to file a frivolous case.[369] The Court disapproved a California procedure in which counsel simply filed a brief stating that an appeal would be frivolous and asking to withdraw as counsel.[370] In a recent case, the Court approved a California procedure for frivolous appeals whereby counsel's brief to the appellate court summarizes the procedural and factual history of the case, with citations of the record, and attests that counsel has reviewed the record, explained his evaluation of the case to his client, provided the client with a copy of the brief, and informed the client of his right to file a *pro se* supplemental brief. Counsel further requests that the court independently examine the record for arguable issues.[371]

There is no right to appointed counsel beyond the first appeal as of right, however.[372] There is similarly no right to appointed counsel for collateral attacks on convictions by way of federal *habeas corpus* or state discretionary post-conviction remedies,[373] even when a death sentence is involved.[374]

Appeals by the Government   As discussed earlier, because of the double jeopardy clause, the government does not have the right to appeal an acquittal. It may, however, appeal sentences, reversals of convictions and orders for new trials.[375]

Harmless Error   Just because a defendant is able to show on appeal that constitutional violations took place at the trial level, this will not result automatically in the reversal of the defendant's conviction. Such violations might have constituted "harmless error."[376] Because of accusatorial principles and the importance of constitutional rights, the burden is generally on the prosecutor to show that the error was harmless and was harmless beyond a reasonable doubt.[377] Certain kinds of "structural" constitutional errors will automatically call for reversal despite the *Chapman* rule, however. This is particularly true of errors that could have affected the fact-finding process.[378]

---

369 *See* Chapter IV, p. 164.

370 *Anders v. California*, 386 U.S. 738 (1967).

371 *Smith v. Robbins*, 528 U.S. 259 (2000).

372 *Ross v. Moffitt*, 417 U.S. 600 (1974). Appointed counsel must be afforded to defendants wishing to apply for review of a conviction based on a guilty plea if that is the only appeal route possible. *Halbert v. Michigan*, 545 U.S. 605 (2005).

373 *Pennsylvania v. Finley*, 481 U.S. 551 (1987). *Habeas corpus* was discussed *supra* p. 279-280.

374 *Murray v. Giarratano*, 492 U.S. 1 (1989) (plurality opinion). States, however, must make legal materials reasonably available so that inmates can prepare their own petitions. *Bounds v. Smith*, 430 U.S. 817 (1977).

375 *See supra*, p. 309.

376 *See, e.g.*, the harmless error rule in FRCrP 52(a): "Any error, defect, irregularity, or variance that does not affect substantial rights must be disregarded."

377 *Chapman v. California*, 386 U.S. 18 (1970).

378 *See Sullivan v. Louisiana*, 508 U.S. 275 (1993) (constitutionally deficient jury instruction on reasonable doubt required reversal despite harmless error argument by the state); *United States v. Gonzales-Lopez*, 548 U.S.140 (2006) (denial of right to counsel of defendant's choice).

CHAPTER IX

CONSTITUTIONAL LAW

Constitutional law pervades virtually every area of law in the United States, as should be clear from the number of constitutional issues already discussed.[1] This chapter will deal with some of the more important areas of constitutional law that have not been discussed. It is necessarily a cursory treatment of the subject. As with constitutional criminal procedure, the cases discussed in this chapter are only a small portion of the relevant caselaw.[2]

PART I: Judicial Review, Structure and Powers

A. Judicial Review

Judicial review was officially recognized in 1803 in *Marbury v. Madison*.[3] The rationale of *Marbury* and some pitfalls of judicial review were mentioned in Chapter I and will not be repeated here. Here we will discuss the nature of judicial review in more detail and methods of constitutional interpretation.

1. The General Nature of Judicial Review

Constitutional Review as a By-Product of Private Litigation The basic idea behind *Marbury* is that constitutional judicial review of laws is nothing extraordinary. As the Court observed, the first "province and duty" of all courts is to determine "what the law is" in any case before them. "The law" includes the Constitution and, in particular, its supremacy clause, which establishes the hierarchy of laws. Consequently, when a court discovers that a statute violates the Constitution, it simply engages in a "choice-of-law" determination, applying the Constitution and ignoring the statute.

This rationale for judicial review has three effects on how such review is carried out. First, unlike some countries, the United States has no special constitutional tribunal separate from the ordinary courts. Any court at any level may and indeed *must* engage

---

[1] Constitutional law issues discussed elsewhere in this book include the following: separation of powers (pp. 4-9); judicial review (pp. 9-11); federalism and Congressional power (pp. 21-27); state sovereign immunity (pp. 37, 225-227); jury trial right in civil cases (pp. 309-310); jury trial right in criminal cases (pp. 243-244); constitutional doctrines affecting the legal profession (pp. 141-142); appointment and impeachment of federal judges (pp. 220-222); procedural due process (pp. 205-209); separation of powers as related to administrative agencies (pp. 219-223); due process limits on state court power (pp. 253-259, 263-268); the "full faith and credit" clause (pp. 261-262); defendants' rights in the investigation and prosecution of criminal cases (pp. 283-323); constitutional limits on tort recovery for libel by public officials (pp. 457-460); constitutional limits on punitive damages (pp. 463-465); constitutional limits on condemnation of property (pp. 482-487); and the powers of Congress and the President in international affairs (pp. 688-693, 692-693, 700-701).

[2] Standard one-volume treatises on constitutional law are JOHN E. NOWAK & RONALD D. ROTUNDA, HORNBOOK ON CONSTITUTIONAL LAW, 8TH ED. (West 2009) and ERWIN CHEMERINSKY, CONSTITUTIONAL LAW: PRINCIPLES AND POLICIES, 5TH ED. (Aspen 2007). An unusually helpful casebook is DANIEL FARBER, WILLIAM ESKRIDGE & PHILIP FRICKEY, CONSTITUTIONAL LAW, 4TH ED. (West 2009). *See also* Robert A. Sedler, "Constitutional Law of the United States," in INTERNATIONAL ENCYCLOPEDIA OF LAWS (Kluwer Int'l and Taxation 1994). An excellent Internet source is http://www.findlaw.com/casecode/constitution/. *See also* and MICHAEL C. DORF, CONSTITUTIONAL LAW STORIES 2D ED. (Foundation 2009) (the stories behind famous cases).

[3] 5 U.S. (1 Cranch.) 137 (1803).

in constitutional judicial review — from the lowest municipal court to the U.S. Supreme Court. Thus, judicial review in the United States is decentralized.[4]

Second, courts decide constitutional issues when they arise in ordinary lawsuits. Any person may challenge the constitutionality of any law or other governmental action that adversely affects that person. The right is not limited to certain public officials or entities as it is in some countries.[5] Moreover, federal courts may decide constitutional issues *only if* they arise in an actual concrete "case or controversy."[6] Federal courts and most states courts may not render advisory opinions.[7]

Finally, judicial review is supposed to be judicial in the sense that when a court decides a constitutional question, it makes a *legal* rather than a *political* determination. A court does so by doing what courts normally do — interpreting enacted law. Indeed, the "political question" doctrine is designed to prevent courts from doing anything else.[8]

Judicial Review as a Special Public and Political Process   Nonetheless, some evidence undercuts the three points in the preceding paragraphs. Because judicial review is decentralized and available in any court, the U.S. Supreme Court is simply another "ordinary" court. However, there is a reverence with which lawyers and lower court judges treat even *obiter dictum* in Supreme Court constitutional decisions that gives those decisions the aura of being, not just the "final word," but the "only word" on the meaning of the Constitution. The feeling is that an issue of constitutional law is not *really* settled until the Supreme Court resolves it. Thus, the decisions of the lower federal and state courts (not to mention the opinions of legislators or executive officials) are somehow only "best guesses" about what the Constitution means.

The Supreme Court has not exactly discouraged this impression. For example, in a 1992 decision, the Court affirmed a 1973 abortion case, saying it involved "the sort of intensely divisive controversy" that "has a dimension that the resolution of the normal case does not carry." Such "rare precedential force" occurs when "the Court's interpretation of the Constitution calls the contending sides of a national controversy to end their national division by accepting a common mandate rooted in the Constitution." Whatever this statement means, it goes beyond the normal preclusive and precedential effects a judicial decision would have in an ordinary non-constitutional case.[9]

Second, any attempt to pass off judicial review as a by-product of ordinary litigation does not consider "test case" litigation that appears routinely in the Supreme Court and the lower federal courts. Many suits are truly "public law litigation" that go beyond the

---

4   Separate constitutional tribunals are the norm in Europe. *See* Louis Favoreau, "Constitutional Review in Europe," in Louis Henkin and Albert J. Rosenthal, eds., Constitutionalism and Rights: The Influence of the United States Constitution Abroad 40-42, 56 (Columbia U. Press 1990); Mauro Cappelletti, The Judicial Process in Comparative Perspective 132-143 (Oxford U. 1989).

5   *See* Favoreau, *supra* note 4, at 51-53. The government makes its views known by filing *amicus curiae* briefs. *See* Chapter II, p. 44, note 28.

6   *Liverpool, N.Y. & P. Steamship Co. v. Comm'rs of Emigration*, 113 U.S. 33, 39 (1885) (federal courts may not "pronounce any statute . . . void, because irreconcilable with the constitution, except as it is called upon to adjudge the legal rights of litigants in actual controversies."). *See infra* pp. 329-332.

7   *See* Nowak & Rotunda, *supra* note 2, §2.12 (describing the Court's 1793 refusal to answer a list of legal questions involving the United States' attempts to remain neutral in the war between France and England) and *infra* pp. 329-332. *But see* Mass. G. L. A. Const., pt. 2, c. 3. art. 2, Amend., Art. 85 and Mich. Const. Art. 3 §8 (empowering courts of Massachusetts and Michigan to render advisory opinions).

8   The political question doctrine is discussed *infra* pp. 333-335.

9   *Planned Parenthood of Southeastern Pennsylvania v. Casey*, 505 U.S. 833, 866 (1992). The Court evinced a similar attitude with regard to its racial desegregation decision in *Brown v. Board of Education*, 347 U.S. 483 (1954). *See Cooper v. Aaron*, 358 U.S. 1 (1958).

private interests of any party.[10] Instead, the focus is almost exclusively on the issues raised and their impact on the public at large. An example is the class action suit, in which the original plaintiff and his or her problem may be all but forgotten, but the lawsuit continues on behalf of an undetermined class of persons similarly situated.[11]

Finally, as cases demonstrate and the next section discusses, interpretation of constitutional provisions is quite different from more "ordinary" interpretations of enacted law. Indeed, some have suggested that constitutional review in the United States is not "judicial" at all; instead it is a political function that has been "carefully disguised" behind the "fiction" of courts determining the law.[12] We have already seen how "judicial philosophy" is perceived to play an important role in judicial decision-making. It is clear that many of the elements of "judicial philosophy" touch on basic political values. For evidence, one need look no further than the judicial selection process, particularly for the Supreme Court, which is almost as politicized and rancorous as any partisan election campaign.[13] Readers must determine for themselves which of the competing models of constitutional judicial review is more accurate, after considering the remainder of this chapter.

2. Constitutional Interpretation

Modes of Interpretation   Constitutional interpretation takes various forms.[14] Sometimes it is textual and mirrors the approach courts take when interpreting statutes. In other cases, the Court uses a "functional" approach, moving to a higher level of generalization than the text employs and seeking only to give effect to the overall functions a particular provision or structural limitation serves. We saw an example of this when separation-of-powers objections to administrative agencies were discussed in Chapter VI.[15] Other cases have been the subject of a "structural" approach, in which the Court reasons from the overall structure and purpose of the entire Constitution. The Court used this technique to some extent in *Marbury v. Madison.* In part, the type of analysis courts employ depends on the clarity of the Constitution's text — the clearer the text, the greater the attention to its wording. But different members of the Court have different views as to what constitutes a "clear" textual command.

Flexibility of Interpretive Methods   Whatever labels we might apply to the Court's approaches to constitutional interpretation, one of their characteristics is that they are

---

10 *See* Abram Chayes, *Public Law Litigation and the Burger Court*, 96 HARV. L. REV. 4 (1982).

11 *See Sosna v. Iowa*, 419 U.S. 393, 397-403 (1974) (determining constitutionality of waiting period for divorce after original plaintiff had obtained a divorce elsewhere because case was certified as a class action). Class actions were discussed in Chapter VII, p. 234. *See also infra* p. 332; *U.S. Parole Commission v. Geraghty*, 445 U.S. 388 (1980) (action brought on behalf of a class does not become moot upon expiration of named plaintiff's substantive claim, even though class certification has been denied; prisoner had been released from prison, but was allowed to appeal class action issue).

12 CAPPELLETTI, *supra* note 4, at 149. Richard Posner, a federal appellate judge and a prominent legal scholar, also takes this position and discusses several examples of Supreme Court cases illustrating the point. *See* Richard A. Posner, The Supreme Court, 2004 Term: Foreword, 119 HARV.L.REV. 31, 40 (2005) ("it is rarely possible to say with a straight face that a Supreme Court constitutional decision . . . was decided correctly or incorrectly," because such cases "can be decided only on the basis of a political judgment, and a political judgment cannot be called right or wrong by reference to legal norms.").

13 *See* Chapter V, pp. 179-180.

14 For books discussing and excerpting principal works on constitutional theory, *see* JOHN H. GARVEY, T. ALEXANDER ALIENIKOFF & DANIEL FARBER, MODERN CONSTITUTIONAL THEORY: A READER, 5TH ED. (West 2004). *See also* PHILIP BOBBITT, THE MODALITIES OF CONSTITUTIONAL ARGUMENT 12-22 (Blackwell, Oxford 1991) and WALTER E. MURPHY, JAMES E. FLEMING & SOTIRIOS A. BARBER, AMERICAN CONSTITUTIONAL INTERPRETATION, 4TH ED. (Foundation Press 2008).

15 *See* pp. 219-223.

very flexible.[16]   Thus, much constitutional law cannot be traced to the text of the Constitution by traditional means used to interpret other forms of enacted law.[17] In many cases, it is more accurate to say, not that a particular statute violates *the Constitution*, but that it violates a principle that *courts say* the Constitution *represents*. In the process of ascertaining what principles underlie the Constitution, there is ample room for judges — consciously or unconsciously — to inject all manner of political, economic or social theory into their constitutional decision-making. This often leads commentators to criticize courts in general, and the Supreme Court in particular, for engaging in "political activism" rather than applying the law.

There are at least two characteristics of the Constitution that invite judicial activism. First, much of the Constitution's text is very general. And many of those general terms, such as "liberty," "due process" and "equal protection of the laws," require anyone seeking to define them to draw on one political vision or another. Second, the Constitution is 200 years old. Issues the Framers deemed important have become non-issues today and new important problems have arisen that the Framers could not have foreseen. Amendment is not a realistic option for changing basic constitutional values, given the Constitution's extremely difficult amendment process, so the task of "updating" the Constitution has fallen to the courts. The tendency toward such "updating" is accelerated by the nature of the job of the judge, who in the process of hearing cases, is presented daily with concrete examples of laws and government practices that seem to operate in an unjust way. And common law judges are especially comfortable with judicial law-making.[18]

The tendency toward a flexible and expansive approach to constitutional interpretation is most often associated with the constitutional "rights explosion" of the 1960s. But in many ways, it has existed virtually from the beginning. In 1819, in *McCulloch v. Maryland*, Chief Justice Marshall found "implied powers" behind those specifically enumerated to sustain the constitutionality of a federal statute. Further, he reasoned from the overall structure of the Constitution to find an immunity of the federal government from oppressive state taxation. He felt it sufficient to justify such action by his famous statement: "we must never forget that it is *a constitution* we are expounding."[19] He emphasized that the Constitution does not have the "prolixity" of a statute. Many parts of it are written in generalities, the better to endure for the "ages to come."

Debate Over Interpretive Methods In recent years, many have questioned whether it is legitimate for judges interpreting the Constitution to rely on values not directly traceable to its text or its history. "Originalists" argue that it is illegitimate to go beyond the "original intent" of the Framers of the Constitution. Similar to originalists are "strict interpretivists."[20] Both argue that referring to the text and intent of the Framers is logical

---

16 This is in sharp contrast to the approach common law courts take in their interpretation of *statutes*. *See* Chapter II, pp. 50-53.

17 The lack of close connection to text is evident in the typical law school constitutional law course which requires students to digest hundreds of pages of caselaw, but not to read the Constitution itself.

18 *See* Chapter II, pp. 42-48. It is interesting to observe that the aging Codes of some continental European countries have similar problems of obsolescence and similarly general provisions, thus leading to greater judicial activism. CAPPELLETTI, *supra* note 4, at 45.

19 17 U.S. (4 Wheat.) 316 (1819) (emphasis in original). *See* Chapter I, p. 21 (*McCulloch's* holding).

20 A unique public debate on the question of using extra-textual constitutional values took place during the hearings before the Senate Judiciary Committee on the (non) confirmation of Robert Bork to be a Supreme Court justice. *See* Chapter V, p. 327 and note 58. For development of Bork's views, *see* Robert Bork, *Neutral Principles and Some First Amendment Problems*, 47 IND.L.J. 1 (1971). A large part of the Senate's decision not to confirm Bork was his disapproval of any approach to constitutional adjudication

because that is the approach courts use in interpreting statutes. Moreover, they assert, once judges abandon text and original intent, there are no limits to what values they could ascribe to constitutional provisions. And the pre-1937 "Lochner Era" illustrates starkly the danger of judges choosing the "wrong" values.[21]

These views are controversial, however. Originalism is difficult to justify because the original intent of the Framers is undiscoverable. There is no official history of what the Framers discussed during the constitutional convention in 1787, and unofficial sources — mainly James Madison's notes — account for perhaps 10% of what went on during the convention. And there is no guarantee that Madison's account is accurate or balanced. Madison had strong views on many issues and his views often did not prevail. His opinions and his participation in the debates could have biased his report.[22] Moreover, Madison's notes show that the Framers often exchanged a wide range of opposing views and then approved compromise wording, leaving us to wonder *which* of the Framers' original intentions to follow. A pragmatic argument is that originalism and close textual interpretivism are not practical, because they will mean that the Constitution will not reach many important questions that are important today, but which the Framers could not have foreseen. And if the Constitution cannot be invoked to challenge a legislative rule or executive action unless it is clearly contrary to the text and original intent of the Framers, then the Constitution will seldom be invoked to deal with the problems of modern society.

On the opposite end of the spectrum from originalists and strict interpretivists are "non-interpretivists" or "fundamental rightists." Non-interpretivists maintain that it is proper for judges to "find" in the general provisions of the Constitution "fundamental rights" that the government must respect, and to use contemporary notions of fairness and rights in determining what those fundamental values are. Non-interpretivists point to the fact that the Framers placed several "open-ended" provisions into the Constitution — the "due process" clause, for example — that they could only have intended for judges to apply with a contemporary frame of reference. This, the non-interpretivists claim, is supported by the 9th Amendment, which proclaims that "[t]he enumeration in the Constitution, of certain rights, shall not be construed to deny or disparage others retained by the people." In this respect, non-interpretivists claim essentially to be both "originalists" and "strict interpretivists." They assert that both the text of the Constitution and the "original understanding" of the Framers show that unwritten fundamental principles should have constitutional status.[23]

The debate between the originalists and strict interpretivists on the one hand, and fundamental rightists and non-interpretivists on the other, is often overshadowed by the political views of their adherents. It is no coincidence that most originalists and strict interpretivists are political conservatives who believe that courts should defer to the majority will as represented by the legislature. Thus, opponents argue, originalism is just

---

other than that of an originalist or strict interpretivist.

21 *See* Chapter I, pp. 11-12.

22 Interestingly enough, Madison intended that his notes be destroyed upon his death because he was concerned that they might be misused by succeeding generations. RALPH L. KETCHAM, JAMES MADISON: A BIOGRAPHY 660-671 (U. Va. Press 1990).

23 *See* Thomas C. Grey, *Do We Have an Unwritten Constitution?*, 27 STAN.L.REV. 703 (1975). For a challenge to originalism and a response, *see* Paul Brest, *The Misconceived Quest for the Original Understanding*, 60 BOSTON U.L.REV. 204 (1980) and Richard A. Kay, *Adherence to the Original Intentions in Constitutional Adjudication: Three Objections and Responses*, 82 NW.U.L.REV. 226 (1988). These and other articles on constitutional theory are excerpted in GARVEY & ALEINIKOFF, *supra* note 14.

a mask for a conservative political agenda. On the other hand, originalists and strict interpretivists charge that open non-interpretivism, at least as practiced in the 1960s and 1970s, is no less "result-oriented" and is designed to advance a "leftist" political vision. In the *Lochner* era, the political positions were reversed; political conservatives supported the Court intervening to strike down "leftist" business regulation by Congress and state legislatures to protect workers, while the "progressive" forces of the time condemned the conservative "activism" of the "nine old men" on the Supreme Court.

As specific cases discussed in this chapter will show, the Supreme Court has decided cases using all these modes of interpretation and several in between. In addition, both the Court and commentators have used several other modes of constitutional decision-making that could be classified as hybrids of the types just discussed.

Recently, a debate has arisen about the legitimacy of the use of foreign and international law in constitutional decision-making. In *Atkins v. Virginia*,[24] the Court held that the Eighth Amendment's prohibition of "cruel and unusual punishments" forbids the execution of mentally retarded individuals. In examining "the evolving standards of decency that mark the progress of a maturing society," the Court considered the practices in American states, but also cited a brief of the European Union which catalogued the overwhelming repudiation of such executions by other countries. Then, in *Lawrence v. Texas*,[25] the Court invalidated a state law criminalizing "homosexual sodomy." While it relied on U.S. sources, the Court also cited a 1967 Act of the English Parliament and a 1981 ruling of the European Court of Human Rights invalidating criminal prohibitions on sodomy to refute Texas's claim that criminal punishment of homosexual sodomy was universally accepted within Western civilization. Three justices objected, citing one of the justice's earlier opinions protesting the Court's "impos[ing] foreign moods, fads, or fashions on Americans."[26]

B. Limits on Judicial Review by Federal Courts

Both state and federal courts at all levels exercise the power of constitutional judicial review. However, litigants have traditionally resorted to the federal courts for protection of federal constitutional rights. Moreover, the United States Supreme Court, the final arbiter of federal constitutional issues coming from state or federal court, is a federal court subject to separation of powers limits. Consequently, it is appropriate to start our discussion of separation of powers issues with a review some of the limitations on federal judicial power that can affect judicial review.

1. Standing

Standing requires that plaintiffs in any case in federal court be able to demonstrate that they have some "personal stake" in the outcome of the controversy: (1) a "distinct and palpable injury" (2) caused by the defendant.[27] Standing is generally a problem only in cases seeking injunctive or declaratory relief, because a claim for damages will always allege a sufficient tangible injury caused by the defendant's conduct.

Injury in Fact The Court has not set out a clear theory of how to determine what constitutes appropriate injury. It is clear that ideological or philosophical satisfaction or disappointment do not qualify, no matter how sincerely upset or jubilant the plaintiff

---

24 536 U.S. 304 (2002).

25 539 U.S. 558 (2003).

26 *Id.* at 598 (Scalia, J., dissenting) (quoting *Foster v. Florida*, 537 U.S. 990 (2002) (Thomas, J., concurring) (denying certiorari in a challenge to a 27-year delay in execution of a death sentence).

27 *Simon v. East Kentucky Welfare Rights Org.*, 426 U.S. 26, 41 n.2 (1976).

would be over the court's decision. Injury to a citizen's interest in the government acting legally is also insufficient for standing.[28] Furthermore, Congress is without power to bestow such "citizen standing." Congress passed a federal environmental statute that granted "any person" the right to enjoin violations of the statute. But the Court viewed the violation of this "abstract, self-contained, non-instrumental 'right' to have the Executive observe the procedures required by law" as an insufficient injury.[29] Members of Congress did not have standing to challenge the constitutionality of the Line Item Veto Act, which allowed the President to "cancel" certain spending and tax benefit measures with which he disagreed after he had signed them into law, rather than having to veto the whole bill. The members' alleged injury was insufficient because it was not personal, but common to all members of Congress and because it amounted to an abstract dilution of institutional legislative power rather than palpable personal injury.[30] However, where the harm is concrete, even if widely shared, there is injury in fact. Thus, pollution over a wide area that affects the health of a great number of people is no less actionable merely because many share the injury.[31]

At the same time, the injury required for standing is not limited to concrete, economic interests. It includes some intangible injuries, such as injury to the "aesthetic, conservational and recreational interests" of users of a national park. Such users had standing to challenge the proposed construction of an entertainment facility in a park when that facility would have interfered with their use of the park.[32]

Causation and Redressability The plaintiff must prove not only that the injury bears a "fairly traceable causal connection" to the challenged law or governmental action, but also that a favorable court decision invalidating the law or action is likely to redress the injury. For example, in *Warth v. Seldin*,[33] the Court denied standing to low-income residents living in an urban area adjoining a suburban area, who had sued the suburb for refusing to grant permits for the construction of low-income housing, claiming discrimination. The Court denied the plaintiffs standing because they could not point to any tangible injury that the suburb's action had caused to them. They could not identify a particular housing project that the suburb had blocked and could not show that, if such

---

28 *United States v. Richardson*, 418 U.S. 166 (1974) (no "citizen" standing to challenge law that prohibited public disclosure of CIA expenditures).

29 *See Lujan v. Defenders of Wildlife*, 504 U.S. 555 (1992) (Endangered Species Act bestowing on "any person" the right to commence a civil suit for violations of the law). *But see Bennett v. Spear*, 520 U.S. 154 (1997) (ranchers could use citizen suit provisions where injury from reduced water for irrigation could result from drawing water from reservoir) *and Massachusetts v. Environmental Protection Agency*, 549 U.S. 497 (2007).

30 *Raines v. Byrd*, 521 U.S. 811 (1997). *See* Chapter VI, p. 219 note 138 (line item veto is unconstitutional). *See also Elk Grove United School District v. Newdow*, 542 U.S. 1 (2004) (non-custodial parent did not suffer injury in fact by his child's recitation of the Pledge of Allegiance "under God," where custodial parent favored it; no standing to challenge recitation as violative of Establishment Clause).

31 *See also Fed. Election Comm'n v. Akins*, 524 U.S. 11 (1998) (where citizens challenged government's classification of organization as not a "political committee," which meant it did not have to disclose its membership, contributions and expenditures, citizens suffered injury of denial of information).

32 *See Sierra Club v. Morton*, 405 U.S. 727 (1972). *Compare Lujan v. Defenders of Wildlife, supra* note 29 (DOW members' "some day intentions" to visit endangered species in faraway countries insufficient injury in challenge to agency rule limiting overseas application of the Endangered Species Act) *and Summers v. Earth Island Institute*, ___ U.S. ___; 129 S.Ct. 1142 (2009) (no member of organization had concrete plans to visit a site where the challenged regulations were being applied) *with Friends of the Earth v. Laidlaw Environmental Services, Inc.*, 528 U.S. 167 (2000) (affidavits and testimony of FOE members describing effects of pollutant discharges on their recreational, aesthetic, and economic interests demonstrated sufficient injury).

33 422 U.S. 490 (1975).

a project had been approved and constructed, they would have been able to move into it. Such a showing *was* made in *Arlington Heights v. Metropolitan Housing Development Corp.*,[34] where the intended residents of a particular project that had been denied approval by a suburb had standing to challenge the denial of approval for that project as being racially discriminatory.[35]

On the other hand, the Court held in *Northeastern Florida Chapter of the Association of General Contractors of America v. City of Jacksonville*[36] that injury in fact may be the deprivation of the *opportunity to compete* for a governmental benefit. Thus, a contractor that regularly bid on government contracts had standing to challenge the constitutionality of a law that prevented the contractor from bidding on a certain percentage of the contracts that were "set aside" for contracting firms owned by racial minorities and women — even if the contractor could not show that it would be awarded one of those contracts if the law were struck down.[37]

Taxpayer Standing As a general proposition, a federal taxpayer lacks standing as a taxpayer to challenge the constitutionality of the expenditure of federal funds. The same is true of a state taxpayer seeking to the challenge the constitutionality of the expenditure of state funds. The individual taxpayer's interest in the expenditure of such funds is said to be "comparatively minute and indeterminate."[38] However, older cases, which the Supreme Court has not overruled, have held that a taxpayer of a *local* governmental unit, such as a city, does have a "direct and immediate" interest in the expenditure of local funds.[39] The Supreme Court has also allowed taxpayer standing to challenge the expenditure of governmental funds in aid of religion as constituting an impermissible "establishment of religion," in violation of the 1st Amendment.[40] While this exception is difficult to reconcile with the "distinct and palpable injury" requirement, the causation-redressability requirement and the Court's rejection of "citizen standing," it nonetheless remains viable at the present time.[41]

Rationale for Standing Standing is said to be justified by Article III's limiting the federal courts to "Cases" and "Controversies" and *Marbury v. Madison* — that courts engaging in constitutional judicial review are doing nothing unusual, but are simply determining what the law is and applying it to the issues in an ordinary lawsuit. The Court and commentators have often mentioned two other factors. The first is that in a democracy, unelected judges present a purported "anti-majoritarian difficulty" because they are not accountable to the voters. This should lead judges to practice "judicial restraint" and make decisions, particularly constitutional ones, only when necessary to

---

34 429 U.S. 252 (1977).

35 *See also Simon, supra* note 27 (fact that tax authorities had lowered the amount of free medical care that hospital had to give to the poor to retain its tax exemption was not shown to be causally related to any denial of care to poor plaintiffs).

36 508 U.S. 656 (1993).

37 *See also Duke Power Co. v. Carolina Environmental Study Group*, 438 U.S. 59 (1978) (plaintiffs had standing to challenge limitation on liability of nuclear plants in event of catastrophe despite fact no catastrophe had taken place and no one had been denied recovery based on the challenged limitation).

38 *Frothingham v. Mellon*, 262 U.S. 447 (1923) (federal); *Asarco, Inc. v. Kadish*, 490 U.S. 605 (1989) (state).

39 *See Crampton v. Zabriskie*, 101 U.S. 601 (1879).

40 *Flast v. Cohen*, 392 U.S. 83 (1968).

41 Taxpayer standing was undercut further in a recent case. *Arizona Christian School Tuition Organization v. Winn*, ___ U.S. ___ (April 4, 2011) (taxpayers did not have standing to challenge tax credit as opposed to governmental expenditure).

resolve actual concrete disputes.[42] In turn, when judges determine what the law is only in concrete cases, judicial law making is incremental because it is limited by the facts of the case. A second rationale for standing is the adversary system's assumption that the best way to assure fully informed decisions is to rely on the parties themselves to gather and present the evidence and arguments on both sides. Requiring that parties have a personal stake in the outcome of their case, it is argued, assures the requisite motivation to explore and present all relevant facts and law, which aids the court in making a fully informed decision.[43] However, the behavioral assumption behind this is questionable because parties motivated by purely ideological concerns, such as environmental activists (who would *not* have standing), are much more likely to vigorously pursue a lawsuit than someone who stands to lose only $25.00 (who *would* have standing). Many commentators have criticized the Court's standing doctrine as unprincipled and as a disguised method of deciding the merits of the case.[44]

2. Ripeness and Mootness

Ripeness and mootness are related to standing and might be understood roughly as standing in a time frame. Ripeness issues arise in cases where the plaintiff may in time face redressable harm, but that harm has not yet developed. Thus, plaintiffs who challenge the validity of an ordinance against distributing political leaflets may not sue until they have engaged in the activity and have been threatened with arrest.[45]

Mootness issues arise when the redressable harm has occurred and the case therefore no longer presents a live controversy. In a leading "mootness" case, an applicant to a state university law school challenged the law school's refusal to admit him as unconstitutional. He prevailed in the lower court, which ordered the school to admit him. By the time the case reached the United States Supreme Court, he was in his final term at the law school, and the school stipulated that he would be permitted to graduate regardless of the outcome of the case in the Supreme Court. The Supreme Court held the case was moot.[46]

The most common exception to mootness occurs when an issue is "capable of repetition, yet evading review." In the 1973 abortion case, *Roe v. Wade*,[47] the state defendants argued that the case was moot because the plaintiffs were no longer pregnant. The Court rejected this argument because pregnancy lasts only nine months, and it would be impossible for anyone challenging an anti-abortion law to stay pregnant until the Court finally decided the case. In this and other situations, the Court has not

---

42 This concept underlies one of the more influential modern theories of judicial review that counsels judicial restraint in all but a few "democracy-reinforcing" areas. *See* JOHN HART ELY, DEMOCRACY AND DISTRUST (Harvard Univ. Press 1980). For the classic debate on the subject, *compare* ALEXANDER BICKEL, THE LEAST DANGEROUS BRANCH 16-26 (Bobbs-Merrill, Indianapolis 1962) *with* Gerald Gunther, *The Subtle Vices of the "Passive Virtues" — A Comment on Principle and Expediency in Judicial Review*, 64 COLUM. L. REV. (1964). For a broader discussion of the problem, *see* CAPPELLETTI, *supra* note 4, at 40-46.

43 *See* Chapter III, pp. 80-85. For an argument that this is not an essential ingredient for constitutional cases, *see* Abram Chayes, *Foreword: Public Law Litigation and the Burger Court*, 96 HARV. L. REV. 4 (1982).

44 *See, e.g.*, Gene Nichol, *Causation as a Standing Requirement: The Unprincipled Use of Judicial Restraint*, 69 KY. L. J. 185 (1981). Another standing limit, discussed in the chapter on administrative law, is used exclusively in administrative law cases is the "zone of interests" test. *See* Chapter VI, p. 211.

45 *Steffel v. Thompson*, 415 U.S. 452 (1974). *See also Socialist Labor Party v. Gilligan*, 406 U.S. 583 (1972) (political party's challenge to loyalty oath requirement not ripe since they had not yet been denied place on ballot). *Compare Duke Power Co.*, *supra* note 37 (challenge to law limiting liability for nuclear power companies for disaster was ripe despite fact there had not been a disaster that exceeded limits).

46 *DeFunis v. Odegaard*, 416 U.S. 312 (1974).

47 410 U.S. 113 (1973).

held a case moot if the issue presented is "capable of repetition, yet evading review."[48] In the normal course of things in the *Roe* case, the plaintiffs could again become pregnant and could again seek an abortion, which would continue to be prohibited by the challenged law. Consequently, the Court ruled that the case presented a live controversy.[49] Even if the defendant voluntarily ceases the challenged activity, this "does not moot a case or controversy unless 'subsequent events ma[ke] it absolutely clear that the allegedly wrongful behavior could not reasonably be expected to recur.'"[50]

Despite its connection to constitutionally based standing doctrine, mootness is a non-constitutional "prudential" limitation on federal court power. This means that a federal court has discretion whether to invoke a mootness exception.[51]

3. The "Political Question" Doctrine

Under this doctrine, the Court has stated that it will refuse to decide some disputes on the ground that they present a *political* question incapable of judicial resolution — as opposed to a *legal* question that a court can resolve. While this seems appropriate on its face, it is unclear what the precise distinction is between a non-justiciable political question and a justiciable legal one.[52] It is hard to see how some of the issues the Court has dismissed as "political" are any less political than other issues it routinely decides. As Justice Jackson once commented, "all constitutional interpretations have political consequences."[53] Nonetheless, the Court has identified two primary situations where it considers a question "political" rather than "judicial."[54]

Lack of Judicially Manageable Standards The first "political question" is where a court lacks manageable standards to apply to resolve the issue. An example is *Coleman v. Miller*,[55] in which the Court faced the question of whether the states properly ratified an amendment to the Constitution prohibiting child labor where opponents claimed that Kansas had ratified it too late. Congress had imposed no time limit on ratification, as it had done for some other proposed amendments. The issue on the merits of the cases was whether this meant that there was a limit of a "reasonable time" and, if so, whether

---

48 *Federal Elections Comm'n v. Wisconsin Right to Life*, 551 U.S. 449 (2007) ("Capable of repetition, yet evading review" mootness exception applies where: (1) challenged action is in its duration too short to be fully litigated prior to cessation or expiration, and (2) there is reasonable expectation that same complaining party will be subject to same action again; election cycle was over, but case not moot).

49 Voluntary cessation of challenged activity is not sufficient to moot a case. If it were, dismissal would "leave '[t]he defendant . . . free to return to his old ways'". *Friends of the Earth, supra* note 32 (quoting *United States v. W. T. Grant Co.*, 345 U.S. 629, 632 (1953)).

50 *Parents Involved in Community Schools v. Seattle School Dist. No. 1*, 551 U.S. 701, 719 (2007) (quoting *Friends of the Earth, supra* note 32 at 189) (defendant school district abandoned race-based student assignment plan during litigation, but Court allowed case to continue because district could have reinstated plan at any time).

51 *Compare Erie v. Pap's A. M.*, 529 U.S. 277 (2000) *with City News & Novelty Inc. v. Waukesha*, 531 U.S. 278 (2001) (cases involving adult bookstores challenging city ordinances who later ceased doing business; one case declared moot and the other not).

52 One noted commentator suggested that there is really no such thing as a political question doctrine because all decisions in the area can be explained according to well-accepted axioms already applicable to courts. *See* Louis Henkin, *Is there a "Political Question" Doctrine?*, 85 YALE L.J. 597, 622-623 (1976).

53 ROBERT JACKSON, THE SUPREME COURT IN THE AMERICAN SYSTEM 56 (1955).

54 *See generally Baker v. Carr*, 369 U.S. 186, 217 (1962). *Baker* was a voting rights cases decided under the equal protection clause of the 14th Amendment in which the Court rejected arguments that the case seeking reapportionment of state legislative districts presented a political question. *Baker* was discussed briefly in Chapter I, p. 20.

55 307 U.S. 433 (1939)

Kansas's ratification some 13 years after passage by Congress was too late. Instead of deciding the case, the Court dismissed it on political question grounds, partially because of the lack of judicially ascertainable standards to determine what a reasonable time was. In deciding that question, the Court would essentially be making a political judgment reserved for the other two branches.[56] The Court also cited a lack of standards in *Luther v. Borden*,[57] which held that the determination of whether a particular government of a state constituted a "Republican Form of Government," as Article IV §4 of the Constitution requires, presented a non-justiciable "political" question.

Commitment to a Political Branch A question can also be political when the Constitution entrusts its resolution to one of the two "political" branches of government. The Court has held that Article I's grant to the Senate of the "sole Power to try all Impeachments" created an unreviewable power to determine what procedure to follow.[58] It dismissed a federal judge's challenge to the Senate's decision to conduct his impeachment trial by appointing a committee of 12 Senators to hear evidence and report it to the full Senate, which then voted on the impeachment charge.[59] On the other hand, Article I §5 provides that each House of Congress is to be the "judge of the elections, returns and qualifications of its own members." Yet, in *Powell v. McCormack*,[60] the Court held that *this* provision was *not* a grant of an unreviewable power to the House to decide whether to seat a Member whom voters had elected and who met age, citizenship and residency qualifications imposed by the Constitution.[61]

Foreign policy disputes between Congress and the President often fall into the political question category. When Congress and the President disagree on foreign policy, they often use the powers the Constitution has given them to advance those views. Congress uses its "power of the purse" and the President uses his various foreign policy powers, including his power as commander-in-chief of the armed forces.[62] In *Goldwater v. Carter*,[63] some Senators sued the President, contending that he lacked the power to terminate a treaty with Taiwan without Congressional approval. The Supreme Court dismissed the suit, but disagreed on the reason. A plurality of four Justices found that the case presented a non-justiciable political question, because the parties asked the Court to settle a dispute between "coequal branches of our government, each of which has resources available to protect and assert its interests." The plurality also emphasized the lack of judicially manageable standards, given the absence of any constitutional provision on treaty termination. Justice Powell reasoned similarly, but under a "ripeness" rubric. He argued that the courts should not intervene *until* each

---

56 The latest amendment to the Constitution perhaps proves how "political" a question the issue was in *Coleman v. Miller*. Congress imposed no time limit for the 27th Amendment, which languished over 200 years before 38 states ratified it. The amendment, proposed in 1789 but not ratified until 1992, prevents Congress from voting itself an immediate pay raise by delaying raises until the next election. Congress, concerned about voter reaction if it showed itself unwilling to accept a limit on its ability to give itself a raise, immediately voted to "accept" the ratification.

57 48 U.S. (7 How.) 1 (1849). *Luther v. Borden* was discussed briefly in Chapter I, p. 20.

58 Art. I §3 cl. 6.

59 *See Nixon v. United States*, 506 U.S. 224 (1993).

60 395 U.S. 486 (1969).

61 *See* Art. I §2 cl. 2.

62 Foreign policy powers of the President and Congress are discussed in Chapter XVII, pp. 692-693, 700-701.

63 444 U.S. 996 (1979).

branch has "taken action asserting its constitutional authority." Because neither house of Congress had expressly acted to reject the President's claim of authority to terminate the treaty, Powell would have held that the constitutional issue was not "ripe."

4. Congressional Limits on Judicial Review

Article III specifies that the judicial power of the Supreme Court in its appellate form is subject to "such Exceptions, and under such Regulations as the Congress shall make." It also gives Congress the right to decide whether to "ordain and establish" the lower federal courts and to specify what their jurisdiction will be.[64] Some have read the "regulations and exceptions" clause and Congress's plenary power over the existence and jurisdiction of lower federal courts as effectively giving it absolute control over the content of court decisions, in essence, giving Congress has the "last word" on constitutional judicial review. Under this theory, if Congress does not like what the Supreme Court or lower federal courts are doing in particular kinds of cases, it can simply deprive those courts of jurisdiction over that category of disputes. Members perennially propose such "jurisdiction-stripping" legislation. In the 1950s, bills were aimed at decisions striking down anti-subversion laws, loyalty oaths and other practices. In the 1960s, they targeted expansions of criminal due process rights. In the 1970s and 1980s, they concerned the Court's decisions on abortion rights and religious activities in public schools. None of these bills passed, but scholars maintain that this control over jurisdiction is a constitutional "check and balance" on the unrestrained exercise of judicial review. Others disagree, suggesting several grounds upon which jurisdiction-stripping is unconstitutional.[65]

Essential Function Theory Some opponents of jurisdiction-stripping argue that the terms the Constitution uses, "regulations" and "exceptions," denote only "procedural" rules that address administrative problems or increase the efficiency of the courts.[66] They argue that "the exceptions must not be such as will destroy the essential role of the Supreme Court in the constitutional plan."[67] The followers of this "essential function" theory further argue that it is not likely that the purpose of the regulation and exceptions clause was to provide control over the substantive content of Supreme Court decisions, because the form of control it provides is clumsy and counterproductive. First, depriving the Court of jurisdiction in *future* cases does not erase the effect of decisions the Court has already made, which would continue to govern the lower courts. Indeed, depriving the Court of jurisdiction would have the *opposite* effect desired. It would assure that the Court would *not* have jurisdiction to accept review of a *future* case to *overrule* the decision Congress did not like. Second, these commentators read the Constitution as

---

[64] The federal court system Congress has created is discussed in Chapter V, pp. 174-177.

[65] The points of view are set out, discussed and criticized in Gerald Gunther, *Congressional Power to Curtail Federal Jurisdiction: An Opinionated Guide to the On-Going Debate*, 36 STAN. L.REV. 201 (1984).

[66] Congress has the power to control other procedural aspects of the Supreme Court's operations, such as its size, which has fluctuated between 5 and 10 justices. The "procedural" nature of this aspect of the Court has not prevented Congress from manipulating it for political purposes. Congress reduced the Court's number from 10 to 6 in 1866 in part to prevent President Andrew Johnson from filling a vacancy. Angry about Johnson's opposition to Congress's post-Civil War policies toward the south, Congress had earlier impeached Johnson, but he avoided conviction by one vote.

[67] Henry Hart, *The Power of Congress to Limit the Jurisdiction of Federal Courts: An Exercise in Dialectic*, 66 HARV. L.REV. 1362, 1365 (1953). *See also* Leonard G. Ratner, *Congressional Power Over the Appellate Jurisdiction of the Supreme Court*, 109 U.PA.L.REV. 157 (1960). For the application of a similar theory to the lower federal courts, *see* Lawrence Sager, *Forward: Constitutional Limitations on Congress's Authority to Regulate the Jurisdiction of the Federal Courts*, 95 HARV. L. REV. 17 (1981).

requiring at the very least that Congress leave *state* courts free to decide the issues it has removed from Supreme Court jurisdiction. This would result in different states' courts taking conflicting positions on what the Constitution means with no means of resolving those conflicts.

Limits Imposed by Substantive Rights Another view, identified with Professor Tribe, does not reason from Article III, but points out that jurisdictional statutes, no less than any other statute, may violate the rights-securing provisions of the Constitution if they unduly burden the exercise of a constitutional right.[68] For example, it would certainly violate equal protection for Congress to pass a statute denying federal courts jurisdiction over all suits brought by black people. Similarly, a statute depriving the Court of the power to hear cases involving abortion would impermissibly burden the right of women to obtain an abortion, just as any other law that provided some other obstacle to the right to an abortion, such as requiring a husband's consent.[69]

The Supreme Court has held that jurisdiction-stripping statutes are unconstitutional where they deprive federal courts of jurisdiction over a substantive constitutional right, at least where federal courts are the only remedy available to the plaintiff. In 2006, Congress passed the Military Commissions Act of 2006 (MCA),[70] which authorized the Bush Administration to create special military tribunals to try Guantanamo Bay detainees. The Constitution, however, gives prisoners the right to *habeas corpus* — a common law writ that compels the government to bring a detainee before a *court* and justify the detention.[71] In *Boumediene v. Bush*,[72] Guantanamo detainees, who had been held for years without trial, sued for *habeas corpus* in federal court. The Bush Administration responded that the court had no power to hear the claim because the MCA stripped its jurisdiction in favor of the military tribunals. The Supreme Court struck down the statute, holding that the statute unconstitutionally suspended the writ of *habeas corpus* and reinstated federal courts' jurisdictions over the detainees' petitions.

Boumediene concerned a specific grant of jurisdiction to federal courts in the Constitution itself. It is unclear whether Congress can pass jurisdiction-stripping statutes limiting jurisdiction over claims of statutory rights or that only *indirectly* burden constitutional rights. The Court has never squarely faced this question. Two Civil War-era cases are inconclusive. One upheld the jurisdiction-stripping statute, but it was clear that the statute left other jurisdictional routes to appeal open.[73] The other struck down the statute, but the Court's reasons for doing so would have been sufficient even without considering its jurisdiction-stripping aspects.[74] *Dictum* statements in the opinions in

---

68 *See* Lawrence Tribe, *Jurisdictional Gerrymandering: Zoning Disfavored Rights Out of the Federal Courts*, 16 HARV. C.R.-C.L.L.REV. 129 (1981). The term "Gerrymandering" actually refers to drawing legislative districts in a manner that allows one to promote the election of one party's candidates — a tactic identified with Governor and later Vice President Elbridge Gerry of Massachusetts (1744-1814). This is ironic, given that Gerry had nothing to do with the politically-shaped Massachusetts election districts. Racial gerrymandering is discussed *infra*, p. 343.

69 *Planned Parenthood*, *supra* note 9 (striking down husband consent law).

70 Pub. L. No. 109-366, § 3930, 120 Stat. 2600 (amended by National Defense Authorization Act for Fiscal Year 2010, Pub. L. No. 111-84, 123 Stat. 2190, enacted October 28, 2009).

71 "The privilege of the writ of habeas corpus shall not be suspended, unless when in cases of rebellion or invasion, the public safety may require it." U.S. CONST. Art. I, § 9.

72 553 U.S. 723 (2008).

73 *Ex parte McCardle*, 74 U.S. (7 Wall.) 506 (1868).

74 *United States v. Klein*, 80 U.S. (13 Wall.) 128 (1872).

these two cases speak broadly of Congress's plenary power under the regulations and exceptions clause. More recently, however, the Court construed a federal statute to allow a government employee to sue for violation of his constitutional rights "in part to avoid the 'serious constitutional question' that would arise if a federal statute were construed to deny any judicial forum for a colorable constitutional claim."[75]

The lack of clarity on the issue may be healthy. Congress can communicate its displeasure with the Court's decisions by threatening to pass such a statute, because strong arguments in favor of this power make the threat credible. On the other hand, there is enough basis for the Supreme Court to strike the statute down that Congress will probably never go past the "communication" stage and actually pass one.[76]

C. Legislative Powers of the Federal Government and the Relationship Between the States and the Federal Government: Vertical Federalism

Federalism most often limits *state* power. Chapter I outlined this aspect of federalism, discussing the scope of federal legislative power,[77] the preemption doctrine,[78] and conditional spending programs.[79] In addition, the structural limitations of federalism prohibit states from taxing federal instrumentalities. *McCulloch v. Maryland*,[80] also discussed in Chapter I, prohibited the State of Maryland from taxing a federal bank.[81] But federalism sometimes limits the *federal* government's ability to act.

Collisions of federal and state power happen in two instances: when federal laws seek to regulate the activities of the *states themselves* and when those laws seek to regulate *private conduct within* states. As one might expect, federalism limits have most often posed a problem for laws that regulate the states themselves. Recently, however, courts have increasingly scrutinized laws regulating private conduct within states.

1. Regulating the States Themselves

The "Clear Statement" Rule   Since 1985, the Court has taken the position that federalism limits are essentially self-enforcing. In *Garcia v. San Antonio Metropolitan Transit Authority*[82] the Court held that the federal Fair Labor Standards Act, which governs minimum wages and overtime pay, applied to state employees despite arguments that it invaded powers reserved to the states. Any federalism-based objections to the use of the federal commerce power, *Garcia* held, had already been factored in "through state participation in federal government action." In this way "[t]he political

---

75 *See Webster v. Doe*, 486 U.S. 592, 603 (1988), discussed in Chapter II, p. 60.

76 Separation of powers issues that arise between Congress and the President are addressed in Chapter I, pp. 12-15, and Chapter VI, pp. 219-223.

77 *See* Chapter I, pp. 21-27.

78 *See* Chapter I, p. 32 and note 146.

79 *See* Chapter I, p. 27.

80 17 U.S. (4 Wheat.) 316 (1819). *See* Chapter I, p. 22.

81 State taxation of federal employees' income is permitted so long as it is even-handed. *See Davis v. Michigan Department of Treasury*, 489 U.S. 803 (1989) (state exemption of state, but not federal, retirement pay is impermissibly discriminatory). States may also tax federal instrumentalities that are not "so closely connected to the Government that the two cannot realistically be viewed as separate entities." *Director of Revenue of Missouri v. CoBank ACB*, 531 U.S. 316 (2001) (federally established banks for farm cooperatives may be taxed).

82 469 U.S. 528 (1985).

process ensures that laws that unduly burden the States will not be promulgated."[83] Consequently, the Court reasoned, there is no need for the Court to further protect states with a *judicial* doctrine of federalism limitations.[84]

Nonetheless, the Court in *Gregory v. Ashcroft*[85] recognized the value of requiring a "clear statement" by Congress of its intention to affect state governmental functions. *Gregory* presented the question of whether the federal Age Discrimination in Employment Act barred state laws mandating retirement of state judges at age 70. Given the central role of the state judiciary in state government, the Court presumed that Congress did not mean to include state judges, because it did not mention them specifically in the Act. The Court noted that there was an exception in the Act for state employees who are "appointee[s] on the policy-making level" and determined that state judges fell within that exception. *Gregory* is only a rule of statutory interpretation. It assumes that Congress could pass an amendment to the Act specifically making state judges subject to the it and federalism would not stand in the way.[86]

"Commandeering" State Governmental Bodies and Officials   The concept of "commandeering" state governments applies where Congress attempts to force state officials to pass laws or perform other tasks. In *New York v. United States*,[87] Congress confronted the growing problem of states impeding development of hazardous radioactive waste disposal on their territory. Instead, companies in those states were encouraged to ship the waste to other states for disposal. One part of the federal law provided economic incentives for states that permitted private development of safe disposal sites within the state. But behind such persuasion were more coercive consequences. States that did not enact laws permitting disposal within their borders became owners of all wastes generated in the state — even that produced by private companies. Thus, states would become liable for all damages if they failed to properly dispose of "their" wastes. The Court held this latter provision unconstitutional. Though the federal government did not directly order states to pass in-state disposal laws, the alternative of taking possession of all wastes produced within its borders was so undesirable that Congress had effectively coerced state legislatures into enacting in-state disposal laws.

While many thought the *New York* rule applied only to "commandeering" the state *legislature*, the Court soon applied the doctrine the *executive* branch of state government. In *Printz v. United States*,[88] a federal gun control law required local police to investigate the background of all prospective handgun purchasers to determine whether

---

83 *Id.* at 556. *See* Herbert Wechsler, *The Political Safeguards of Federalism: The Role of the States in the Composition and Selection of the National Government*, 54 COLUM. L.REV. 543 (1954). Some evidence that political safeguards are working is found in the fact that Congress has refrained from exercising its considerable power to regulate private conduct in states, thus leaving state law to govern vast areas of conduct. *See* Chapter I, pp. 30-33.

84 Before 1937 and for 10 years between 1976 to 1985, the Court used the federalism policies embodied in the 10th Amendment to invalidate federal legislation affecting states in areas of "traditional state functions." *See National League of Cities v. Usery*, 426 U.S. 833 (1976) (holding that Fair Labor Standards could not be applied to state and local government workers). *Usery* was overruled by *Garcia*. Nonetheless, the 10th Amendment remains a bar to some federal legislation affecting states. *See Coyle v. Smith*, 221 U.S. 559 (1911) (Congress may not dictate location of the Oklahoma's capital city).

85 501 U.S. 452 (1991).

86 The Court had earlier held that the act applied to bar mandatory retirement of more ordinary state employees in *Equal Employment Opportunity Comm'n v. Wyoming*, 460 U.S. 226 (1983).

87 505 U.S. 144 (1992).

88 521 U.S. 898 (1997).

they satisfied federal requirements regarding age, residency, and absence of a criminal felony record. The Court held that Congress could not require local police to perform such "background checks." It distinguished *Garcia* and similar cases, which involved the "incidental application to the States of a federal law of general applicability," while "here, it is the whole object of the law to direct the functioning of the state executive."

The Impact of the New York and Printz Cases   It bears emphasizing what the Court's decision in *New York* and *Printz* do *not* do. First, they do not affect Congress's right to regulate directly the conduct of *individual waste producers or waste management companies* that are located *in* the states. So, if Congress *itself* had passed the waste regulation program as *federal* legislation with *federal* enforcement of its provisions — rather than trying to force the states to enact it — Congress could have attained the same goal.[89] Second, the decision did nothing to affect Congress's power to accomplish the same aim through a conditional spending program — offering federal funding to states contingent on their acceptance of federal conditions. The Court does not consider the financial impact of not receiving federal grants to be "coercion" of states. This is true even if the state feels compelled to participate in the federal program in order to "get back" federal tax money its own citizens paid and even if a condition of receipt of federal money is that the state pass certain laws.[90]

The Court revealed another limit on *New York* and *Printz* in *Reno v. Condon*.[91] In that case, the Court upheld a federal law that prohibited states from selling driver's license information to commercial businesses. The law did not violate the principles of *New York* or *Printz*, because the law "regulate[d] state activities," rather than "seek[ing] to control or influence the manner in which States regulate private parties."[92] Unlike *New York*, the law did not require South Carolina to enact any laws or regulations and, unlike *Printz*, it did not require state officials to assist in the enforcement of federal statutes regulating private individuals. The Court also found that Congress had the power under the interstate commerce clause to pass the law.[93]

2. Federal Regulation of Private Conduct Within States

The Post-1937 Standard   From the end of the Civil War until 1937, the Court viewed the scope of the interstate commerce power as being very narrow.[94] However, a more liberal perspective replaced this view as justices and their philosophy changed in the wake of the Court's dispute with the Roosevelt administration, briefly recounted in Chapter I.[95] From 1937 until only recently, the commerce clause cases established the rule that federal legislation is valid under the interstate commerce power so long as Congress could have had a "rational basis" to believe that the activity it chose to regulate affected interstate commerce in some way. Congress need not have conducted a study to reach such a conclusion and it did not seem to matter what the immediate object of

---

89 In the event it did so, Congress would also have to set up a mechanism to administer it. Avoiding the need for creating a new federal bureaucracy could well have been the reason Congress chose to pass the statute in the form that it did.

90 *See* Chapter I, p. 27.

91 528 U.S. 141 (2000).

92 *Id.* at 150 (quoting *South Carolina v. Baker*, 485 U.S. 505, 514-515 (1988)).

93 *See infra* note 113.

94 *See* p. 25.

95 *See* pp. 11-12.

congressional regulation was or in what area of the law Congress sought to pre-empt state law.

Thus, in *Wickard v. Filburn*,[96] the Court allowed Congress to regulate the amount of wheat a small-scale farmer in the middle of Ohio could grow for his own consumption and local sale, on the theory that the "cumulative effect" of *many* small farmers doing the same could have a depressing effect on wheat prices. And in *Katzenbach v. McClung*,[97] the Court upheld the application of the Civil Rights Act of 1964, which banned private racial discrimination in all public accommodations, to a small local restaurant. The Court concluded that Congress could have rationally decided that the cumulative effect of local incidents of racial discrimination would affect interstate commerce and that some of the food served there had moved in interstate commerce. Similarly, in *Perez v. United States*,[98] the Court employed a similar "cumulative effect" theory to uphold a federal law prohibiting extortion by local racketeers threatening violence to recover loan payments from local citizens.[99]

The Lopez Case In 1995, *United States v. Lopez*[100] threw these cornerstones of modern federal power into doubt. The Court resurrected an admonition from an earlier case that had been largely forgotten:

> [T]he scope of the interstate commerce clause power must be considered in the light of our dual system of government and may not be extended so as to embrace effects upon interstate commerce so indirect and remote that to embrace them, in view of our complex society, would effectually obliterate the distinction between what is national and what is local and create a completely centralized government.[101]

The federal law challenged in *Lopez* prohibited the possession of any firearm within 1,000 feet (307 meters) of any public or private school. The Supreme Court struck down the law as not within the commerce power because it "is a criminal statute that by its terms has nothing to do with 'commerce' or any sort of economic enterprise, however broadly one might define those terms."

The *Lopez* Court rejected arguments that the use of firearms in violent crime produced economic impact both by discouraging individuals from traveling to high crime areas and by impeding the educational process, which created a "less productive citizenry." Acceptance of these arguments, the Court observed, would allow Congress to legislate against all violent crime and all the activities that might lead to it, as well as any activity that related to the economic productivity of citizens, including marriage and divorce. This would enable Congress to infringe improperly and unconstitutionally on the traditional powers of the states.

The Court set out its revised view of Congress's interstate commerce clause power: (1) Congress may regulate "the use of the channels of interstate commerce," as in the

---

96 317 U.S. 111 (1942).

97 379 U.S. 294 (1964).

98 402 U.S. 146 (1971).

99 *See* Chapter I, p. 25.

100 514 U.S. 549 (1995).

101 *Lopez, supra* note 100 at 556-557 (quoting *Nat'l Labor Relations Bd. v. Jones & Laughlin Steel Corp.*, 301 U.S. 1, 37 (1937)).

racial discrimination cases involving public accommodations for travelers;[102] (2) Congress can "regulate and protect the instrumentalities of interstate commerce, or persons or things in interstate commerce, even though the threat may come only from intrastate activities," such as regulating safety standards for railroads, even for intrastate transportation;[103] and (3) Congress can regulate "activities having a substantial relation to interstate commerce . . ., i.e., those activities that substantially affect interstate commerce," including "intrastate economic activity where . . . that activity substantially affect[s] interstate commerce."[104] Thus, for example, under (3) Congress could regulate labor practices of employers with a substantial number of employees or intrastate agricultural activity that has a *cumulative* effect on interstate commerce.[105]

The Court admitted that earlier commerce clause cases upheld legislation that regulated "activities that arise out of or are connected with a commercial transaction." But the gun law "is not an essential part of a larger regulation of economic activity, in which the regulatory scheme could be undercut unless the intrastate activity were regulated." The defendant in *Lopez* "was a local high school student at a local school; there is no indication that he had recently moved in interstate commerce, and there is no requirement [in the statute] that his possession of the firearm have any concrete tie to interstate commerce."[106]

The Role of Congressional Findings The *Lopez* Court also noted that there were no congressional findings in either the law or the legislative history demonstrating the connection Congress had found between gun possession near schools and interstate commerce. The Court admitted that it had not generally required such history, but such findings would have assisted it "in evaluat[ing] the legislative judgment that the activity in question substantially affected interstate commerce." While *Lopez* was pending, Congress passed an amendment to the law adding congressional findings that outlined the necessary ties to interstate commerce. The Court was aware of this amendment but deemed it irrelevant because the government did not rely on this after-the-fact justification in its argument.[107] Furthermore, a later case, *United States v. Morrison*,[108] cast doubt on Congress's ability to satisfy commerce clause requirements merely by coupling a law with congressional findings.

The VAWA Case In *Morrison*, a rape victim sued her attackers in federal court under the federal Violence Against Women Act (VAWA), which authorized victims to bring civil claims against attackers if the attacker targeted the victim because of her sex. Clearly the VAWA did not regulate commercial activity itself. And the Court rejected the argument that violent crimes against women have an economic impact, finding that justification identical to the one it rejected in *Lopez*. The cases dealing with *effects* on interstate commerce — cumulative or otherwise — did not save the VAWA, because those cases all involved *economic* activities, not non-economic activity. It is noteworthy

---

102 *Heart of Atlanta Motel, Inc. v. United States*, 379 U.S. 241, 256 (1964).
103 *Southern Railroad Co. v. United States*, 222 U.S. 20 (1911).
104 *Lopez, supra* note 100 at 558-559.
105 *Nat'l Labor Relations Bd. v. Jones & Laughlin Steel Corp., supra* note 101 (labor practices of business affecting interstate commerce); *Wickard v. Filburn, supra* note 96 (cumulative effect of small-scale intrastate farming on national prices Congress sought to regulate).
106 *Lopez*, 514 U.S. at 561, 566.
107 *Id.* at 563 n. 4.
108 529 U.S. 598 (2000).

that, unlike the original law in *Lopez*, Congress had analyzed the question carefully and had made extensive findings about violence against women and its effects on interstate commerce. The Court rejected those findings because they merely documented the aggregate impact of *non-commercial* criminal activity.[109]

It is truly hard, however, to distinguish the VAWA case from the civil rights cases, in which the Court upheld the Civil Rights Acts under the commerce clause because racial discrimination prevented black people from traveling freely and transacting business. There is evidence that women's fear of sexual violence similarly limits them from traveling and transacting business. Thus, 4 dissenting justices in *Morrison* found that the justifications for the VAWA and Civil Rights Acts were identical.

The Future of the Commerce Power There are many federal criminal laws that, like those in *Lopez* and *Morrison*, focus on localized activity of a non-commercial sort. In one case, the Court interpreted the language of a federal statute punishing arson of any structure "used in interstate or foreign commerce."[110] The defendant had been convicted of burning down his cousin's house. The Court rejected the government's argument that the house, which was used solely as a residence and not to carry on any trade or business, was "used in" interstate commerce because it was the subject of a mortgage and insurance from out-of-state providers and used natural gas from out of state. In view of the "serious constitutional question" that would arise if the statute were interpreted so broadly, the Court held that "used in interstate commerce" must mean active employment for commercial purposes. Otherwise, "hardly a building in the land would fall outside the federal statute's domain."[111]

In *Gonzales v. Raich*,[112] the Court determined the constitutionality of applying the federal Controlled Substances Act (CSA) to prohibit home cultivation of marijuana for medicinal use within the state of California. The CSA conflicted with California state law, which expressly permitted cultivation and use of marijuana pursuant to a doctor's prescription. However, the Court upheld the federal law as a valid regulation of interstate commerce, even as applied to medicinal use wholly within the state of California. The Court distinguished *Morrison* and *Lopez* on the ground that the overall federal drug law, which applied to all manner of production and distribution of "controlled substances" throughout the country, regulated "quintessentially economic" activities. Then, relying on *Wickard v. Filburn*, the Court concluded that "Congress can regulate purely intrastate activity that is not itself 'commercial,' in that it is not produced

---

109 Among the findings Congress made and supported with research were: "Violence is the leading cause of injuries to women ages 15 to 44; Since 1974; the assault rate against women has outstripped the rate for men by at least twice for some age groups and far more for others; An estimated 4 million American women are battered each year by their husbands or partners; [The incidence of] rape rose four times as fast as the total national crime rate over the past 10 years; [T]hree-quarters of women never go to the movies alone after dark because of the fear of rape and nearly 50 percent do not use public transit alone after dark for the same reason; [A]n individual who commits rape has only about 4 chances in 100 of being arrested, prosecuted, and found guilty of any offense; [A]lmost 50 percent of rape victims lose their jobs or are forced to quit because of the crime's severity."

110 18 U.S.C.A. §844(i).

111 *United States v. Jones*, 529 U.S. 848 (2001). *Compare Perez v. United States, supra* p. 340.

112 545 U.S. 1 (2005).

for sale, if it concludes that failure to regulate that class of activity would undercut the regulation of the interstate market in that commodity."[113]

3. Congressional Power Under §5 of the 14th Amendment

The 14th Amendment to the Constitution prohibits states from depriving anyone of life, liberty or property without due process of law or denying equal protection of the laws. Section 5 of that Amendment states that "Congress shall have power to enforce, by appropriate legislation, the provisions of this article." While this power does not help Congress battle economic problems, one might wonder why Congress relied on the commerce clause instead of §5 in passing laws against racial discrimination. The big question regarding §5 is whether Congress's power is limited to passing "procedural" laws that provide the *means* for redressing violations of *existing* due process and equal protection rights, or whether §5 empowers Congress to create additional *substantive rights* beyond those the Court has declared to be part of due process or equal protection.

Katzenbach v. Morgan[114] upheld a federal prohibition on state laws requiring literacy tests to vote, despite the fact that the Court had never held that such tests, administered properly, constituted racial discrimination. The Court held that "it is enough that we perceive a basis upon which Congress might predicate a judgment that the application of New York's literacy requirement to deny the right to vote to [Puerto Ricans fluent in Spanish] constituted an invidious discrimination in violation of the Equal Protection Clause." Some though this decision authorized Congress to go beyond the rights the Court had declared to exist under the 14th Amendment so long as Congress had a rational basis to believe that those additional rights were appropriate to supplement existing constitutional rights.

In *City of Boerne v. Flores*,[115] however, the Court took a narrower view of congressional power under §5. In *Flores*, the Court considered the validity of the Religious Freedom Restoration Act (RFRA). Congress passed RFRA after its disagreement with a Supreme Court decision that narrowed the scope of the 1st Amendment guarantee of the "free exercise" of religion. The Court had changed the free exercise test to remove 1st Amendment protections for any religiously motivated conduct that a state law of general applicability criminalized.[116] Congress wished to reestablish as a federal *statutory* matter the earlier constitutional test of state laws, providing in RFRA that a state law of general applicability that burdens religious practices is valid only if it "(1) is in furtherance of a compelling governmental interest, and (2) is the least restrictive means of furthering that compelling interest." In *Flores*, the archbishop of a Catholic church in Texas sued under RFRA when the city, acting under a local historic preservation ordinance, denied the church a permit to enlarge the building.

The Court held that RFRA was beyond Congress's power. In its view, there were two types of statutes that were valid exercises of §5 powers: (1) "procedural" laws that provide a civil or criminal remedy for violations of 14th Amendment rights that the Court

---

113 The Court did sustain the constitutionality of a federal statute that prohibited states from selling driver's license information to businesses, which would then use it to solicit sales of products and services, on the ground that it was a "thin[g] in interstate commerce." *Reno v. Condon, supra* note 91.

114 384 U.S. 641 (1966).

115 521 U.S. 507 (1997).

116 The "free exercise" clause is discussed in more detail in this chapter *infra* pp. 394-397. The Supreme Court case in question is the *Smith* case, discussed *infra* p. 394, in which Smith was fired for using drugs as part of religious observances in the Native American Church.

had already established and (2) laws that establish new substantive statutory rights that are "prophylactic," in that they were designed to prevent constitutional violations, such as the law in *Katzenbach v. Morgan*. Clearly, RFRA could not be justified as the first type, because it sought to restore 1st Amendment law that the Court had rejected.

The law also failed as a prophylactic rule because — unlike the law in *Katzenbach v. Morgan* — there was "a lack of proportionality or congruence between the means adopted and the legitimate end to be achieved." The Court noted that before enacting the RFRA, Congress conducted no study of the need to prevent state legislatures from passing laws out of religious bigotry. In *Katzenbach*, there was "evidence in the record reflecting the subsisting and pervasive discriminatory — and therefore unconstitutional — use of literacy tests." The federal Voting Rights Act in *Katzenbach* targeted states with a long history of intentional discrimination in voting. The act required pre-implementation administrative approval of electoral practices, with this strict review ending after 7 years. In contrast, the RFRA was not so focused in time, geographical area or design. It allowed anyone who could show some substantial burden on his or her religious practices to force the state to demonstrate both a "compelling interest" in its law and that its law was "the least restrictive means of furthering [that] interest."[117]

The Court took a similarly limited view of Congress's §5 powers in response to arguments that §5 justified the Violence Against Women Act (VAWA) in *United States v. Morrison*, discussed above.[118] The Court did not reach the issue of "proportionality" of Congress's response to the problem, however, because the 14th Amendment only reaches state action, while the VAWA targeted private individuals.[119] Although Congress found that state law enforcement and courts often treated women victims of criminal violence poorly because of their sex, the VAWA did not authorize claims against states or their officials — only against the private perpetrators of violence.[120]

D. The Relationship Between the States: Horizontal Federalism

American states retain all the powers of nation-states except those they surrendered in the Constitution. In exercising their independent powers in the federal system, American states act in many ways like separate countries. However, in other instances the Constitution requires states to act more like simple subdivisions of a single country. In Chapter I, we discussed how the right to interstate travel, the "dormant" commerce clause, state court jurisdiction over out-of-state defendants, the "full faith and credit" clause and the extradition clause have blurred state boundaries.[121] In Chapter VII we considered the issues of personal jurisdiction and the "full faith and credit" due federal

---

117 RFRA is nonetheless valid as applied to the actions of the federal government. *See, e.g., Gonzales v. O Centro Espirita Beneficente Uniao Do Vegetal*, 546 U.S. 418 (2006) (RFRA prohibits government from prosecuting sect's use of a tea containing a hallucinogen in its religious ceremonies).

118 *See supra* p. 341.

119 *See supra* p. 349 and Chapter VIII, p. 283 (state action in constitutional criminal procedure).

120 Even if a law properly regulates state conduct under §5, there may be no remedy in damages for those injured by state action, because the state may have immunity from suit for damages under the 11th Amendment. Nonetheless, Congress can, in some situations, abrogate state immunity provided its intention to do so is evident in the statute. *United States v. Georgia*, 546 U.S. 151 (2006) (federal Americans with Disabilities Act abrogated state immunity; paraplegic prisoner permitted to sue the state for failing to provide access for the disabled). *See* Chapter VI, pp. 225-226, for more on the 11th Amendment and sovereign immunity.

121 *See* pp. 28-30.

and state court judgments.[122] This section discusses two of these topics in greater detail: the "dormant" commerce clause and the related requirement that states respect the privileges and immunities of citizens of other states.[123]

1. The "Dormant" Commerce Clause

Source and Purpose The interstate commerce clause provides Congress with broad powers to pass legislation. Such legislation preempts state law whenever the two conflict. But even when Congress has not acted, the commerce clause has a limiting effect on state regulation. The clause's mere existence, in its "dormant" state, creates a negative implication that states may not interfere with interstate commerce in certain ways. Its purpose is to prevent a state from engaging in economic protectionism — from "establishing an economic barrier against competition with the products of another state or the labor of its residents."[124]

Tests Applied to State Laws The Court's current dormant commerce clause doctrine has two tests: it invalidates state laws that "discriminate against interstate commerce" without substantial justification or that impose an "undue burden" on interstate commerce. The clearest cases of discrimination occur where the state regulation discriminates on its face. But the Court will invalidate neutral laws that have a discriminatory effect if it detects either a discriminatory motivation or if "reasonable non-discriminatory alternatives adequate to conserve legitimate local interests are available."[125] The "undue burden" test will invalidate state action that impedes commerce when "the burden imposed on such commerce is clearly excessive in relation to the putative local benefits," considering "whether [local interests] could be promoted as well with a lesser impact on interstate activities."[126]

In recent years, the Court has shown a preference for the "discrimination" test over the "undue burden" test.[127] But from the statements of the tests above, one can see that the two tests amount essentially to the same thing. A state law that imposes an "undue burden" on interstate commerce because it brings few legitimate (*i.e.*, non-protectionist) local benefits could be discriminatory, because the small measure of non-protectionist local benefit suggests strongly that it is simply a pretext for discrimination. Similarly, a law that discriminates on its face or has a discriminatory impact on interstate commerce without any substantial local non-protectionist benefits imposes an "undue burden," because the non-protectionist local interests will seldom outweigh the burden imposed.

---

122 *See* pp. 253-259 and 261-262.

123 Extraterritorial application of state law in other states is discussed in Chapter VII, pp. 263-268. International extraterritorial application of state and federal law is discussed in Chapter XVII, pp. 705-714.

124 *Philadelphia v. New Jersey*, 437 U.S. 617, 624 (1978). Other provisions of the Constitution that similarly operate in their dormant state to preempt state regulation are those vesting foreign relations power in the federal government. *See* Chapter XVII, p. 695. In considering the cases that follow, the reader should know that three justices have opined that "[t]he negative Commerce Clause has no basis in the text of the Constitution, makes little sense, and has proved virtually unworkable in application." *Camps New-found/Owatonna, Inc. v. Town of Harrison*, 520 U.S. 564, 610 (1997) (Thomas, J., dissenting).

125 *Dean Milk Co. v. City of Madison*, 340 U.S. 349, 354 (1951). *Dean Milk* also shows that the dormant commerce clause applies to local governments, which cannot justify burdening out-of-state interests merely because their laws also discriminate against in-state residents from other parts of the state.

126 *Pike v. Bruce Church, Inc.*, 397 U.S. 137, 141 (1970).

127 *See generally* Don Regan, *The Supreme Court and State Protectionism: Making Sense of the Dormant Commerce Clause*, 84 Mich. L. Rev. 1091 (1986).

Three General Categories of State Practices Most dormant commerce clause cases fall into three general categories. The first category is cases in which a state tries to "fence out" items of commerce that compete with local products. A state may bar "harmful" products from another state, such as cattle with disease that could infect in-state herds.[128] However, barring non-health threatening out-of-state products based on their origin is prohibited. For example, the Court invalidated New York's prohibition of the sale of milk purchased from farmers in other states at lower prices than the New York minimum price.[129]

A second category of cases involves states "fencing in" valuable local resources. The Court has struck down laws prohibiting a privately owned hydroelectric power in the state from exporting power to other states,[130] prohibiting exportation of certain fish caught in the state,[131] prohibiting exportation of ground water to adjoining states that grant no reciprocal water rights[132] and prohibiting giving licenses to milk processing facilities that would divert local milk supplies to other states.[133] Also included in this category are laws fencing out unattractive out-of-state items, such as garbage and other wastes, in order to preserve the state's landfill space for in-state trash. Thus, in *Philadelphia v. New Jersey*,[134] the Court struck down New Jersey's prohibition on private landfills accepting out-of-state waste. Except for the waste's out-of-state origin, it was no different from New Jersey waste, so the Court found no threat to public health to justify the law. Less-than-complete or "indirect" restrictions on interstate commerce also run afoul of the dormant commerce clause.[135] For example, the Court relied on this line of cases to strike down a state law granting a general exemption from real estate taxes solely to state residents. In the Court's view, this amounted to giving state residents "a preferred right of access" to land in the state.[136]

The third category is where states use means short of prohibition either to burden out-of-state or to prefer in-state businesses or products. In *Hunt v. Washington State Apple Advertising Commission*,[137] the Court invalidated a North Carolina law on advertising for apples. The law in effect prohibited the display of Washington state apple grades on packages of apples shipped to North Carolina. Washington state had developed a grading system that the apple industry considered superior to the federal Department of Agriculture grading system. Because the Washington grade marked superior apples,

---

128 *Mintz v. Baldwin*, 289 U.S. 346 (1933).

129 *Baldwin v. G.A.F. Seelig, Inc.*, 294 U.S. 511 (1935). *See also Lewis v. B.T. Investment Managers, Inc.*, 447 U.S. 27 (1980) (state prohibition on out-of-state banking institutions controlling in-state investment advisory firms invalid); *Granholm v. Heald*, 544 U.S.460 (2005) (invalidating state law providing that in-state wineries could ship directly to consumers, but out-of-state wineries could not).

130 *New England Power Co. v. New Hampshire*, 455 U.S. 331 (1982).

131 *Hughes v. Oklahoma*, 441 U.S. 322 (1979).

132 *Sporhase v. Nebraska*, 458 U.S. 941 (1982).

133 *H.P. Hood & Sons v. DuMond*, 335 U.S. 808 (1948).

134 *Supra* note 124.

135 *See Chemical Waste Management, Inc. v. Hunt*, 504 U.S. 334 (1992) (higher fee for disposal of out-of-state hazardous waste). It is also no excuse that a state is retaliating for discriminatory treatment by another state. *Great A.& P. Tea Co. v. Cottrell*, 424 U.S. 366 (1976).

136 *Camps Newfound/Owatonna, Inc. v. Town of Harrison*, 520 U.S. 564 (1997).

137 432 U.S. 333 (1977).

prohibiting its display on apple containers had the effect of depriving Washington apples of the competitive advantage they would otherwise enjoy.[138]

Dealing With Discriminatory Effect To base a finding of state discrimination on improper discriminatory *effect*, rather than purpose, a litigant must identify benefitted and burdened groups that are similarly situated except for the fact that one group is identified with interstate commerce or located out-of-state. The fact that the regulation benefits one kind of *economic interest* at the expense of another does not make it "discriminatory" for negative commerce clause purposes, even though the benefitted economic interest is primarily local while the burdened economic interest is primarily interstate. Thus, in *EXXON Corp. v. Maryland*,[139] Maryland law prohibited oil refining companies from owning retail service stations. The Court held that the law did not violate the dormant commerce clause, even though its effect was to favor retail service station owners, most of whom were local, over oil companies, all of which were out-of-state.[140] Maryland also had a relatively strong non-discriminatory reason for its law;. In the oil crisis of 1973, the oil refining companies favored their own service stations over independents, selling gasoline to their own stations while not filling orders from the independents.

Why a Preference for a Discrimination Test If a state law burdens both out-of-state and in-state interests, a discrimination charge is harder to prove even if there is some disproportionate impact. But if *in-state* interests are *also* affected, "a State's own political processes will serve as a check against unduly burdensome regulations."[141] This is one reason why the Court prefers the discrimination rather than the "undue burden" test. With the "undue burden" test, the *Court itself* must evaluate the burden, a task for which a court is not well equipped. With the discrimination test, it need only insure that — whatever burden there is on out-of-state interests — the state imposes that burden equally on in-state interests. This leaves it to the political process of the state to evaluate the burdens and benefits of the law in response to complaints from in-state residents affected by it.[142]

"Tentative" Judicial Review Judicial review of legislation on dormant commerce clause grounds differs somewhat from review on other constitutional grounds. Because Congress's power to regulate interstate commerce is plenary, it has the power to authorize any form of state regulation of commerce that it chooses, including discriminatory or burdensome state laws that would otherwise violate the dormant commerce clause. As a result, a Supreme Court case striking down state regulation is really a form of "tentative" judicial review: even though the Court has struck down the state regulation as violative of the dormant commerce clause, Congress has the power to "overrule" the

---

138 *See also Pike v. Bruce Church*, 397 U.S. 137 (1970) (requirement that cantaloupes picked in Arizona be packed there violates dormant commerce clause). *Pike* was decided on the ground that the packing requirement was an "undue burden," rather than on discrimination grounds. But it is easily understood as a discrimination case when one realizes that requiring packing in the state attracts additional business to the state at the expense of other states.

139 437 U.S. 117 (1978)

140 *See also Minnesota v. Clover Leaf Creamery Co.*, 449 U.S. 456 (1981) (Minnesota regulation barring use of plastic non-refillable milk containers not discriminatory even though permitted use of paperboard non-refillable milk containers favored instate pulpwood industry).

141 *Kassel v. Consolidated Freightways Corp. of Delaware*, 450 U.S. 662, 675 (1981).

142 *See CTS Corp. v. Dynamics Corp. of America*, 481 U.S. 69, 94-97 (1987) (Scalia, J., concurring in part and concurring in the judgment).

Court and determine that the state's regulation *is* an appropriate regulation of interstate commerce.[143]

Market Participant Exception One category of discriminatory state action that does not violate the dormant commerce clause consists of cases in which the state acts as a "market participant." Thus, when the state purchases goods from suppliers or sells goods produced at state-owned facilities or distributes its own property, it can prefer its own residents. For example, in *Reeves v. Stake*[144] South Dakota owned its own cement factory and properly limited sales to state residents. The notion is that a state is using its tax revenues to benefit its own people and need not share those resources with non-citizens. Another market participant case was *White v. Massachusetts Council of Construction Employers, Inc.*,[145] where the Court upheld a city's rule requiring that contractors on city-funded projects employ at least 50% city residents.

Government Function Exception The Court is likely to uphold state laws that favor in-state *public* entities at the expense of out-of-state *private* business. In *Haulers Ass'n, Inc. v. Oneida-Herkimer Solid Waste Management Authority*,[146] county "flow control" ordinances required private waste haulers to deliver waste to state-operated landfills, although out-of-state landfills were cheaper. The private haulers sued, but the Court sided with the state, despite the burden on interstate commerce, because "treating public and private entities the same under the dormant Commerce Clause would lead to unprecedented and unbounded interference by the courts with state and local government."

2. The Privileges and Immunities Clause of Article IV

Like the dormant commerce clause, the "privileges and immunities" clause of Art. IV §2 cl. 1 prevents states from discriminating against out-of-state citizens. But it protects "basic rights," not just commerce rights. It provides that "[t]he citizens of each State shall be entitled to all Privileges and Immunities of Citizens of the several States." However, two obstacles face litigants building a privileges and immunities claim. First, it is difficult to identify some "basic right" that the targeted state policy affects.[147] Second, even as to rights that are clearly "basic," such as the right to vote, a state can justify disparate treatment of non-residents so long as it has a "substantial reason" for the discrimination. For example, the right to vote in state and local elections is "basic," but a state can properly restrict non-residents from voting.

---

143 *See, e.g., Prudential Ins. Co. v. Benjamin,* 328 U.S. 408 (1951) (state regulation of insurance); *Northeast Bankcorp, Inc. v. Bd. of Governors of Fed. Reserve System,* 472 U.S. 159 (1985) (state regulation of interstate banking). However, Congress must clearly state its intention to approve the state regulation. *See South-Central Timber Development., Inc. v. Wunnicke,* 467 U.S. 82, 91 (1984). Also, a separate challenge to the state statute could be made under the equal protection clause of the 14th Amendment. *See Metropolitan Life Ins. Co. v. Ward,* 470 U.S. 869 (1985), discussed *infra,* text at note 211.

144 447 U.S. 429 (1980).

145 460 U.S. 204 (1982).

146 550 U.S. 330, 332 (2007). *See also Department of Revenue of Kentucky v. Davis,* 553 U.S. 328 (2008) (state law exempting interest income from Kentucky state and municipal bonds but assessing taxes on interest income from out-of-state bonds did not violate dormant commerce clause because raising revenue by issuing bonds is a traditional government function).

147 *Baldwin v. Fish & Game Commission of Montana,* 436 U.S. 371, 383 (1978) (elk hunting for sport was not a "basic right," so state may charge higher hunting license fee for non-residents).

Nonetheless, the Court has applied the privileges and immunities clause to prevent states from restricting admission to the practice of law solely to residents of the state[148] and from subjecting out-of-state residents to higher taxes.[149]

Moreover, a state has the right to reserve its tax *revenue* and other resources for its own residents. The justification is self-evident: tax revenues of a state would not last long if everyone in the country had an equal right to them. Consequently, a state may charge non-resident students higher tuition to attend its public universities.[150] However, the policy must directly involve preservation of the resources *of the state*. Discriminatory state regulation of *private* conduct violates the privileges and immunities clause. For example, a state may not require *private* employers to give employment preference to state residents in all oil and gas operations connected with state-owned oil and gas reserves.[151] Yet, state-required hiring preferences for state residents on *state-funded* construction projects are constitutional so long as the preference is based on a welfare motive, such as the need to provide employment for unemployed workers.[152]

PART II: Individual Rights Protected by the Constitution

The subject of individual rights and liberties protected by the Constitution is vast. The discussion here will be limited to the most important constitutional provisions and doctrines outside the areas of procedural due process rights and criminal due process rights, which have already been discussed in other chapters.[153]

A. State Action

The Constitution only secures rights against action by governments, state or federal. Consequently, a threshold question in every case involving individual constitutional rights is whether the challenged conduct is attributable to the government. This concept is called "state action" because most issues have concerned state, rather than federal government. However, the test is the same when applied to either.

Private Action Entangled with the State When the challenged action is taken by a state official, there is little question in most instances whether it is the action of the state government. However, private entities or persons often take action that is sanctioned, facilitated or entangled with the state in some manner. The question in such cases is whether there is such a "close nexus between the State and the challenged action" that seemingly private behavior "may be fairly treated as that of the State itself."[154] In general, courts consider a nominally private entity to be a "state actor" when it is entwined with

---

148 *Supreme Court of New Hampshire v. Piper*, 470 U.S. 274 (1985), discussed in Chapter IV, p. 141.

149 *Lunding v. New York Tax Appeals Tribunal*, 522 U.S. 287 (1998) (invalidating a New York law permitting only New York residents a tax deduction of alimony payments).

150 *See Vlandis v. Kline*, 412 U.S. 441 (1973). *See also McCready v. Virginia*, 94 U.S. 391 (1877) (upholding a state's exclusion of non-residents from planting oysters in state-owned tidelands).

151 *Hicklin v. Orbeck*, 437 U.S. 518 (1978).

152 *United Building and Construction Trades Council v. City of Camden*, 465 U.S. 208 (1984). Art. IV privileges and immunities overlap somewhat with the dormant commerce clause. However, there are some differences: under Art. IV, discrimination must be overt (not just in effect); only "basic rights" are protected; corporations are not "citizens" protected; there is no "market participant" exception; and Congress cannot validate discriminatory state action. *See* FARBER, *supra* note 2, at 899-900.

153 *See* Chapter VI, pp. 205-209 (procedural due process) and Chapter VIII, pp. 283-323 (criminal due process rights).

154 *Jackson v. Metropolitan Edison Co.*, 419 U.S. 345, 351 (1974) (privately owned electric utility heavily regulated by the state that enjoyed a state-created monopoly was not a state actor).

governmental policies or when government is entwined in its management or control.[155] *Brentwood Academy v. Tennessee Secondary School Athletic Association*[156] illustrates this. In that case, a private, non-profit athletic association with a voluntary membership of 84% of the state's public schools was deemed to be a state actor when it disciplined a member for violations of its rules, because it was closely "entwined" with the state. State education officials sat on the Association's committees as nonvoting members and the state permitted Association employees to join its retirement system. Moreover, it was clear that the state education officials in fact relied on the association to police athletics in the public schools.[157]

Ad Hoc Private Action in Concert With State Officials   Private persons can also be state actors when they act in concert with state officials. Thus, in *Lugar v. Edmondson Oil Co.*,[158] a private creditor's joint participation with state officials in obtaining a state court order for seizure of a debtor's property made the creditor a "state actor" on the debtor's claim that the state seizure statute was unconstitutional. Similarly, when state law *requires* private persons to take certain actions, those actions are deemed to be state action.[159] However, the mere fact that state law *authorizes* private creditors to take particular action on their own does not make their action state action.[160]

The Court has even held in one case that the action of a private person enforcing a private contract in court constitutes state action. In a 1948 case, *Shelley v. Kraemer*,[161] white property owners sued to enforce a racially restrictive covenant — provisions of deeds to private residential property — that prohibited sale of those parcels to "people of the Negro or Mongolian Race."[162] The defendants asserted, however, that such racially discriminatory restrictions violated the equal protection clause of the 14th Amendment.[163] The Court held that the contractual provision itself was not a violation of equal protection, because it was a private agreement between private persons. However, the Court held that *enforcement by the courts* of the provision, even if private property owners sought it, *did* involve state action, so the resulting court judgment would violate equal protection. As such, *Shelley v. Kraemer* stands for a rather broad proposition. If judicial enforcement of provisions of private contracts constitutes state action, then all private contracts must comply with the Constitution. The Court has never held that *Shelley*'s state action holding is limited to racially restrictive covenants, but most lawyers treat it that way.

---

155 *See Burton v. Wilmington Parking Authority*, 365 U.S. 715 (1961) (private restaurant located in a publicly owned and operated automobile parking building operating pursuant to license from city was a state actor when it discriminated on grounds of race).

156 531 U.S. 288 (2001).

157 *But see National Collegiate Athletic Ass'n v. Tarkanian*, 488 U.S. 179 (1988) (college athletic association was not a state actor when it investigated coach for violations of its rules; state university had adopted association's rules as its own and fired coach when rules violations were found, at least where rules were the product of membership that included colleges from other states).

158 457 U.S. 922 (1982). This would also characterize most of the state action questions in criminal cases where private persons gather evidence in cooperation with the police. *See* Chapter VIII, p. 283.

159 *Adickes v. S.H. Kress Co.*, 398 U.S. 144, 170 (1970) (state law required private businesses to maintain separate facilities based on race).

160 *Flagg Bros., Inc. v. Brooks*, 436 U.S. 149 (1978) (sale by storage company of belongings for non-payment of storage bill pursuant to state statute was not state action).

161 334 U.S. 1 (1948).

162 Restrictive covenants in real property are discussed in Chapter XII, p. 26.

163 The substance of equal protection doctrine is discussed *infra* pp. 351-362.

Public Functions Performed by Private Entities A private entity performs a "public function" when it "exercises powers traditionally exclusively reserved to the State."[164] The rationale is that the state should not be able to avoid complying with the Constitution by simply delegating its power to private persons. For example, when the Texas Democratic Party, a private political organization, only permitted white people to participate in its primary elections to determine its candidates for political office, the Supreme Court held that the party's actions constituted state action, because running an election for government office was a public function.[165] In a case involving a "company town"—a municipality entirely owned by a shipbuilding company—the Court held that running the city was a public function,[166] as is managing a city park.[167] The modern shopping center, which is in some ways the new "town square," has presented some challenges to the application of the public function doctrine. At first, the Court in 1968 held, on authority of *Marsh*, that shopping centers did approximate the company town. Thus, their action in excluding striking workers from picketing a store in the mall violated the 1st Amendment's freedom of speech.[168] The Court reversed this view in 1976, however, and permitted such exclusions in *Hudgins v. National Labor Relations Bd.*, holding that shopping centers were entirely private.[169]

B. Rights to Equal Protection of the Laws

The equal protection clause of the 14th Amendment provides that no *state* shall "deny to any person within its jurisdiction the equal protection of the laws." Though there is technically no equal protection clause applicable to the *federal* government, the Supreme Court has held that the *due process* clause of the 5th Amendment contains an equal protection component that imposes the same limitations on the federal government that the 14th Amendment imposes on the states.[170] Consequently, everything that follows applies equally to actions of federal and state governments.

Modern equal protection doctrine is really three different doctrines, because courts apply three levels of scrutiny to determine if particular legislation or other government action denies equal protection of the laws. In short, they are: (1) for a classification that burdens fundamental rights or affects "suspect classes" of people (primarily racial groups), the Court applies "strict scrutiny" and requires a compelling governmental interest to justify the classification; (2) for a classification that relates to business, economic or welfare matters that does not burden particular races or fundamental rights, the Court applies lax scrutiny and requires only that the legislature have had some conceivable "rational basis" for the classification; and (3) for classifications that

---

164 *Jackson v. Metropolitan Edison Co.*, 419 U.S. 345, 352 (1974) (private electric company not a state actor when it terminated service because providing electric services is not traditionally a state function).

165 *Nixon v. Condon*, 286 U.S. 73 (1932); *Smith v. Allwright*, 321 U.S. 649 (1944); *Terry v. Adams*, 345 U.S. 461 (1953).

166 *Marsh v. Alabama*, 326 U.S. 501 (1946) (shipbuilding company could not prohibit Jehovah's Witness from distributing literature in town run by it where its employees lived).

167 *Evans v. Newton*, 382 U.S. 296 (1966) (park bequeathed to city by private person on condition that it be used only by white people was transferred by city to a private entity; held that the private entity was performing a public function and could not exclude anyone based on race).

168 *Amalgamated Food Employees Union v. Logan Valley Plaza, Inc.*, 391 U.S. 308 (1968).

169 424 U.S. 507 (1976). However, it does not violate a shopping center's 1st Amendment rights for a state to create a state constitutional right for speakers with points of view it does not like to have access to shopping centers. *PruneYard Shopping Center v. Robins*, 447 U.S. 74 (1980).

170 *Bolling v. Sharpe*, 347 U.S. 497 (1954). This holding, of course, is nonsensical as an interpretation of constitutional text. However, the Court has shown no inclination to retreat from it.

distinguish on grounds of sex, the Court applies "middle-level scrutiny" and requires that the classification bear a substantial relationship to an important governmental interest to be sustained. The following sections examine these tests.

1. Strict Scrutiny for Suspect Classifications and Burdens on Fundamental Rights

Under the strict scrutiny test, a law that distinguishes along "suspect" lines or that discriminates with regard to a "fundamental right" is unconstitutional unless it is necessary to promote a compelling governmental interest. This test thus has both an "ends" and a "means" aspect: the end sought to be achieved must be extremely important and the means chosen to achieve it (the classification in the challenged statute) must involve the least possible burden on the suspect class or the fundamental right. Thus, even if the state identifies a compelling governmental interest, if there is an alternative means of achieving that interest that would be less burdensome to the fundamental right or the suspect class, the classification will be struck down.[171]

a. Suspect Classifications

Because the equal protection clause of the 14th Amendment was one of the three post-Civil War amendments designed to assure the benefits of full citizenship to the newly freed slaves (it was ratified in 1868), race has always been considered to be at the core of the "equal protection of the laws" that it guaranteed. Consequently, almost all government discrimination based on race or ethnicity violates equal protection.[172]

Discriminatory Purpose and Discriminatory Effect For discrimination to violate equal protection, it must have been intentional.[173] When the discrimination results from an explicit classification set out on the face of the law itself, there can be no doubt that the different treatment is intentional. The Court will in most circumstances invalidate explicit suspect classifications, because there can be few compelling justifications for them.[174] However, when the statute or regulation is neutral on its face, but has a disproportionate impact on a suspect class, intent to discriminate may be difficult to prove. Of course, substantially disproportionate effect and a lack of a racially-neutral explanation for that effect is good circumstantial evidence of intent to discriminate.[175]

Where a neutral statute gives an administrator broad discretion, courts are more likely to find discrimination. In *Yick Wo v. Hopkins*,[176] a law prohibited laundries from being located in wood buildings without a special permit. The city consistently refused permits to Chinese laundries while granting them to others. Because the authorities could offer no racially neutral explanation for their conduct, the Court held that the law's

---

[171] The requirement of a close ends-means "fit" is a common characteristic of other constitutional tests in other areas, such as 1st Amendment rights. *See infra*, p. 375 (freedom of expression) and pp. 394-393 and note 471 (free exercise of religion).

[172] *Strauder v. West Virginia*, 100 U.S. 303 (1879) (law prohibiting blacks from serving on grand or petit juries unconstitutional); *Yick Wo v. Hopkins*, 118 U.S. 356 (1886) (discriminatory denial of laundry license to Chinese); *Hernandez v. Texas*, 347 U.S. 475 (1954) (exclusion of Mexican-Americans from jury service);

[173] *Arlington Heights v. Metropolitan Housing Development Corp.*, 429 U.S. 252, 267 (1977) (racially disproportionate impact of zoning ordinance not sufficient to show intent).

[174] *But see infra*, pp. 354-355 (affirmative action programs).

[175] *Compare* dormant commerce clause discrimination, *supra*, p. 345. Both equal protection and dormant commerce clause challenges are discussed in a case involving a law that has disproportionate impact on interstate commerce in *Minnesota v. Clover Leaf Creamery*, *supra* note 140.

[176] 118 U.S. 356 (1886).

purpose was to discriminate against Chinese.[177] On the other hand, where disproportionate racial impact resulted from administration of a written objective test for employment, that was not sufficient to show a discriminatory purpose.[178]

Proving intent is especially difficult when the challenged state action is a statute because determining the motives of the legislature is a "sensitive inquiry." In such cases, courts consider the general historical background of the law, the prevalence of other prior discriminatory laws, the sequence of events leading to the particular law, and statements of lawmakers. *Hunter v. Underwood*,[179] the question was whether a section of the Alabama constitution, adopted in 1901, constituted intentional discrimination against blacks when it provided that persons convicted of crimes of "moral turpitude" lost their right to vote. The Court held that the history of the constitutional convention and other historical studies demonstrated an intent to disqualify blacks from voting.[180]

Racial Segregation Despite the fact that the equal protection clause was ratified in 1868, the Court did not hold that racial segregation violated that clause until 85 years later. In 1896, the Court settled on a definition of equality in the case of *Plessy v. Ferguson*,[181] holding that "separate but equal" treatment of minorities was all that equal protection required. In *Plessy*, the Court upheld a Louisiana law separating train passengers according to race. Only in *Brown v. Board of Education*[182] in 1954 did the Court finally accept the idea that separate treatment based on race constitutes racial discrimination regardless of how equal the separate facilities are, because such segregation — imposed by the majority to insulate itself from the minority — stigmatizes the minority group. *Brown* involved racial segregation of public schools.

It is impossible to overemphasize the dehumanizing effects of the racial segregation system imposed on black people in the United States for almost 100 years after the Civil War had ended. Especially in the southern states, laws and a multitude of customary practices that accompanied them operated to perpetuate an entire separate system of inferior schools, housing, churches, businesses, transportation, and hotels. A black person seeking to find a place to eat would have to find a "black" eating place. Public restrooms were divided into "Men," "Women," and "Colored." There were even "White" and "Colored" public drinking fountains. Northern states enshrined fewer segregation practices in law, but whites, as individuals and business owners uniformly chose to segregate non-whites. Famous black musicians, such as Lena Horne and Louis Armstrong, even when performing in the North, could not stay overnight in the very hotel where they performed.

It is similarly impossible to over-emphasize the importance of the Court's 1954 decision in *Brown v. Board of Education*. Most lawyers in the United States identify

---

177 *See also Louisiana v. United States*, 380 U.S. 145 (1965) (literacy tests for prospective voters in the south were discriminatory; they were administered loosely and the results were invariably that blacks failed in large numbers while whites did not).

178 *Washington v. Davis*, 426 U.S. 229 (1976). Disproportionate effect *is* sufficient to prove discrimination under federal statutes prohibiting discrimination in some instances. *See* Chapter XV, pp. 621-623 (employment discrimination in violation of Civil Rights Act of 1964).

179 471 U.S. 222 (1985).

180 Though the Court found that the lawmakers had an *additional* motive of discriminating against poor *whites*, this was not sufficient to save the provision because it was clear that it would have been adopted in any event to disenfranchise blacks, the overwhelming majority of whom were poor.

181 163 U.S. 537 (1896).

182 347 U.S. 483 (1954).

Brown as the single most important decision of the Supreme Court. *Brown* invalidated all states' dual systems of public schools, which were either mandated by law or established and maintained through consistent practices of school administrators. But *Brown* applied by analogy to all other governmental racial segregation.[183]

Affirmative Action Given this history, it is perhaps ironic that the most important issue in racial discrimination cases today concerns discrimination against whites. "Affirmative action" programs — designed to remedy past discrimination by giving advantages to minorities in jobs, school admissions, and government contracts — have been attacked as unconstitutional discrimination against whites. The Court has held that affirmative action programs are subject to strict scrutiny analysis because they classify based on race. However, they may be justified by a compelling state interest.

A general desire to remedy past "societal discrimination" will not justify outright racial quotas for contracts or school admissions.[184] However, using "race as one among many factors" in an admissions or other program can be constitutional. In *Grutter v. Bollinger*,[185] the Court approved, as a compelling interest, a state's "commitment to racial and ethnic diversity" as part of its "interest in attaining a diverse student body" in its universities. At issue was the law school admissions policy at the University of Michigan, which considered race among several other factors the school deemed important in creating a diverse student body. The Court emphasized that the system provided for "highly individualistic, holistic review of each applicant's file, giving serious consideration to all the ways an applicant might contribute to a diverse educational environment." It was not fatal that the law school monitored the number of minority students it admitted to assure admission of a "critical mass" of minority students — "meaningful numbers" sufficient to encourage them to participate in the intellectual life of the law school and to assure that they would not feel isolated. This was not an impermissible quota, the Court noted, because it did not involve reserving a fixed number or percentage of slots for minority students.[186] However, the Court recently held that the same "critical mass" reasoning does not apply to race-conscious admissions and placement policies in secondary or elementary schools. In 2007, in *Parents Involved In Community Schools v. Seattle School District No. 1*,[187] parents challenged a school district assignment

183 The equal protection clause has no effect on racially discriminatory action by *private* individuals because the Constitution generally applies only to governmental action. Private discrimination is outlawed by several federal statutes, starting with the Civil Rights Act of 1964. Title VII of this law, which prohibits discrimination in employment, is discussed in Chapter XV, pp. 620-625. Other titles prohibit discrimination in private housing, public accommodations and credit extensions, and in any federally-funded activity.

184 *Richmond v. J.A. Croson Co.*, 488 U.S. 469 (1989) (city requiring all contractors with city contracts employ minority-owned firms for 30% of work because of history of few minority contractors being so employed was unconstitutional). However, the Court held that true remedial affirmative action awarding contracts to minority contractors who could prove that they had been denied contracts in the past on racial grounds would have been permissible.

185 539 U.S. 306 (2003).

186 By contrast, the Court held in a companion case that Michigan's undergraduate admissions rules, which gave 20 points (of a total of 100 points necessary for admission) to all minority applicants, did amount to a virtual quota, because it assured the admission of all minimally qualified minority applicants. *Gratz v. Bollinger*, 539 U.S. 244 (2003). *Grutter* essentially approved the approach of Justice Powell 25 years earlier in his separate opinion in a contentious case with no majority opinion, *Regents of the University of California v. Bakke*, 438 U.S. 265 (1978), in which the Court upheld a medical school admissions system that considered race as a factor in admissions. *See also Wygant v. Jackson Board of Education*, 476 U.S. 267 (1986) (race used as a factor in assignment of secondary school teachers).

187 *Supra* note 50.

plan that set aside slots in high schools for children of minority races. The Court struck down the plan, holding that a diverse student body was not a compelling government interest in high schools, though it was in higher education.

Racially-Conscious Decisions Affecting Voting Rights   A similar controversy exists where states use race to draw the boundaries of congressional and state legislative districts. The federal Voting Rights Act prohibits "diluting" the political power of racial minorities. Consequently, states have frequently drawn legislative district borders in such a way that racial minorities constitute a majority of the voters in a percentage of districts equal to the percentage of minority voters in the general population of the state. In the past, the Supreme Court has approved this deliberate creation of "minority-majority" districts where the purpose is to provide minority voters with a fair share of political power.[188] However, in *Shaw v. Reno*,[189] a 5-4 majority invalidated an improbably shaped "majority-minority" congressional district that was 160 miles long and, for much of that length, no wider than a highway. The Court held that a majority-minority district could be so irrational on its face that it could only be understood as an effort to segregate voters into separate districts on the basis of race. It remanded to the lower court to determine whether race was the "predominant factor" in drawing the district, as that would violate equal protection.[190] In a case the following year, however, the Court emphasized that there is a strong presumption that the line-drawing was proper, and that an attack on racial grounds would succeed only if the plaintiff was able to show "that the legislature subordinated traditional race-neutral districting principles, including but not limited to compactness, contiguity, respect for political subdivisions or communities defined by actual shared interests, to racial considerations."[191] States redraw district lines every 10 years, following the constitutionally-mandated decennial census. However, states may redraw their boundaries at any time in the interim, though they must comply with *Reno* and other cases.[192]

Discrimination Based on Alienage   Distinctions based on alienage are treated differently depending on whether it is the federal government or state or local government that is discriminating. If a state or local government treats aliens differently, the Court applies strict scrutiny. When the *federal* government deals with aliens, the classifications are subject only to rational basis scrutiny.[193] This double standard is based on the federal government's plenary power over immigration and naturalization.[194] However, the rational basis standard also applies to state or local exclusion of aliens from certain government jobs that are "intimately related to the process of democratic self-government."[195] Thus, the Court has applied strict scrutiny and struck down state

---

[188] *United Jewish Organizations of Williamsburgh v. Carey*, 430 U.S. 144 (1977).

[189] 509 U.S. 630 (1993).

[190] In a second appeal following a remand, the Supreme Court held the district invalid, noting that it was not narrowly tailored to serve any compelling state interest. *Shaw v. Hunt*, 517 U.S. 899 (1996).

[191] *Miller v. Johnson*, 515 U.S. 900 (1995).

[192] *League of Latin American Citizens v. Perry*, 543 U.S. 941 (2006) (Texas state legislature's mid-census redistricting violated the Voting Rights Act by diluting the Latino vote, but such mid-census redistricting is permissible provided it does not dilute minority voting power).

[193] *See, e.g., Mathews v. Diaz*, 426 U.S. 67 (1976), as explained in *Nyquist v. Mauclet*, 432 U.S. 1, 7 n.8 (1977) (upholding federal durational residency requirements for welfare benefits imposed on aliens, but not citizens).

[194] Art. I §8 cl. 4.

[195] *Bernal v. Fainter*, 467 U.S. 216, 220 (1984).

laws disqualifying aliens from obtaining welfare benefits and from becoming lawyers or civil servants.[196] However, states *may* prohibit aliens from becoming state police officers, probation officers, and public school teachers.[197]

b. Classifications Affecting Fundamental Rights

The Court applies strict scrutiny to classifications that affect the exercise of "fundamental rights." These include any of the explicit rights in the text of the Constitution (such as in the 1st Amendment),[198] plus any that the Court has held to be fundamental under the general provisions of the Constitution (such as the right to vote or the right to privacy).[199] Like suspect classifications, the Court will strike down classifications based on the exercise of a fundamental right unless the government can show that they are necessary to pursue a compelling governmental interest. In many cases, the major issue is whether the classification burdens fundamental rights. Thus, even though abortion is a fundamental right, the Court did not apply strict scrutiny to a federal welfare statute prohibiting federal funding for medical costs of abortions, while funding the cost of live births. The Court held that that classification did not affect a fundamental right because it did not place any obstacles in the path of a woman seeking an abortion. Consequently, the Court upheld the statute under rational-basis review.[200]

Perhaps the seminal case in fundamental rights equal protection is *Skinner v. Oklahoma*.[201] Skinner was convicted of larceny for the third time. The state sought to apply a law allowing it to sterilize habitual criminals convicted of certain crimes. The Supreme Court struck down the law as violative of equal protection because it only applied only to *some* crimes, such as larceny and manslaughter, but not to others, such as fraud or embezzlement. The Court hinted that the state may have had a rational basis for distinguishing among offenses, but this was irrelevant because sterilization affected the *fundamental right* to procreate. Thus, the Court applied strict scrutiny.[202]

2. Lax "Rational Basis" Scrutiny for Economic and Business Regulation or Social Welfare Programs

The Court applies a "rational basis" test in all classifications involving economic, social welfare or business regulation that do not otherwise relate to the exercise of fundamental rights or suspect classifications. The Court has stated it will uphold a law under the rational basis test "if any state of facts reasonably may be conceived to justify it."[203] It is not necessary for the legislature to have actually had such facts in mind. Counsel or the court can suggest the rational basis during the lawsuit. In essence, unless the classification is completely irrational, a court will sustain it. The Court uses a lax test

---

196 *Graham v. Richardson*, 403 U.S. 365 (1971) (welfare benefits); *Application of Griffiths*, 413 U.S. 717 (1973) (admission to law practice); *Sugarman v. Dougall*, 413 U.S. 634 (1973) (civil service jobs).

197 *Foley v. Connelie*, 435 U.S. 291 (1978) (police officer); *Cabell v. Chavez-Salido*, 454 U.S. 432 (1982) (probation officer); *Ambach v. Norwick*, 441 U.S. 68 (1979) (public school teacher).

198 *See, e.g., Carey v. Brown*, 447 U.S. 455 (1980) (statute prohibiting all picketing near residences unless related to a labor dispute violates both 1st Amendment and strict scrutiny equal protection).

199 *See Shapiro v. Thompson*, 394 U.S. 618 (1969) (state welfare residency requirement violates strict scrutiny equal protection because it affects fundamental right to travel). *See also Attorney General of New York v. Soto Lopez*, 476 U.S. 898 (1986) (both right to travel and equal protection violated by employment preference solely for veterans living in the state when they entered military service).

200 *See Harris v. McRae*, 448 U.S. 297 (1980).

201 316 U.S. 535 (1942).

202 Other fundamental rights are discussed *infra* pp. 352-355.

203 *Sullivan v. Stroop*, 496 U.S. 478 (1990).

because "[t]he Constitution presumes that . . . even improvident decisions will eventually be rectified by the political process and that judicial intervention is generally unwarranted no matter how unwisely we may think a political branch has acted."[204] As an "ends-means" test, then, the end need only be a legitimate one and the means chosen need only be one that a rational person might conceive of as furthering that end.

Under these conditions, it is relatively easy to think up a rational basis for a classification, so this test has the effect of presuming the validity of the legislation. In this respect, it is the opposite of the suspect classification test, which presumes that the legislation is invalid. Thus, in these two areas, the battle over the validity of a challenged classification is largely over once the court determines into which category the legislation falls.

The Court applied the rational basis test in *Dallas v. Stanglin*,[205] in which it unanimously upheld a city ordinance that limited the use of certain dance halls to persons between the ages of 14 and 18. The Court first found that the law did not limit any rights to association protected by the 1st Amendment or the due process clause and thus did not warrant strict scrutiny. It then applied the rational basis test. The city argued the purpose of the ordinance was to protect children from the corrupting influences of persons over 18. The plaintiffs responded that the ordinance did not apply to other gathering places in which teenagers might encounter "corrupting influences," such as roller skating rinks. Nonetheless, the Court sided with the city, observing that the difference "may not be striking, but the differentiation need not be striking in order to survive rational basis scrutiny."[206]

The rational basis test is indeed a lax one and — given a legitimate legislative purpose — it is hard to argue that the classification could not conceivably be thought to further the aim of the statute. However, the legislative purpose must be *legitimate*. In *City of Cleburne v. Cleburne Living Center*,[207] the city denied a permit to use a house as a home for a group of mentally-retarded persons. However, the city would have permitted an identical number of *non-retarded* unrelated persons to live together. While rejecting the argument that mentally retarded persons were a "suspect" class, the Court nonetheless found that the ordinance violated equal protection. The only conceivable basis for the ordinance was the city's desire to keep retarded persons out — a purpose that was not legitimate. The Court used similar reasoning in *Romer v. Evans*,[208] where it struck down a popular referendum in Colorado that prohibited the state or local governments from enacting any law giving protected status or other preference to persons based on their sexual orientation. Because homosexuals do not constitute a suspect class and there was no fundamental right to engage in homosexual activities,[209] only rational basis scrutiny applied. However, the referendum did not pass the rational basis test because "imposing a broad and undifferentiated disability on a single named

---

204 *Vance v. Bradley*, 440 U.S. 93 (1978).

205 490 U.S. 19 (1989).

206 *Id.* at 28.

207 473 U.S. 432 (1985).

208 517 U.S. 620 (1996).

209 *See Bowers v. Hardwick*, 478 U.S. 186 (1986) (plurality), *overruled by Lawrence v. Texas*, 539 U.S. 558 (2003) discussed *infra* p. 367.

group" is an "invalid form of legislation." "[A]nimus toward [that] class" lacks any rational relationship to *legitimate* state interests.[210]

The Court used similar reasoning in the business context in *Metropolitan Life Insurance Co. v. Ward*.[211] That case involved a state law that imposed a higher tax on *out-of-state* insurance companies doing business in the state than on *in-state* insurance companies. The Court held that the law would be invalid if the sole reason for the distinction was a desire to protect local businesses from out-of-state competition, which is not a permissible governmental purpose. Dissenting justices in the case asserted that a possible reason for favoring local companies could be consumer protection: *i.e.*, local companies would be more likely to have local offices through which companies could help local consumers. While the city did not argue this consumer protection rationale, the Supreme Court nonetheless considered it and remanded the case to the lower court to consider consumer protection as a possible rational basis for sustaining the law.[212]

3. The Middle-Level Test for "Semi-Suspect" Classifications

Why a Middle-Level Test   Before the 1970s, the Court seemed satisfied with only two levels of scrutiny for legislative classifications. However, as the Court began to deal with more and more challenges to sex-based classifications, it became clear that neither the strict nor the lax test would work very well. For example, a Michigan law prohibited women from working as bartenders unless they were the daughter or wife of the bar owner. The Court found a rational basis in that most bar patrons are men, potentially creating a detrimental atmosphere to women. Additionally, the law inhibited prostitution. One could have readily criticized this basis for the law because bars are no worse in these respects than any other places that the legislature allowed women to work. However, this justification probably would have satisfied rational basis.[213] On the other hand, this law would clearly be invalid under strict scrutiny. But then so might many other laws, such at those that exempt women from compulsory military service or protect them from sexual exploitation, because the government would have to show a compelling interest in the classification and prove that it could not achieve that interest in any other way.

The common law has discriminated against women for centuries. A married woman had few rights.[214] The common law treatment of women carried over into constitutional law. In an 1873 case, *Bradwell v. Illinois*,[215] the Court held that it was constitutional for Illinois to deny women the right to practice law in the state. A concurring justice was moved to write:

---

210 517 U.S. at 632 (emphasis added). Irrational discrimination against a "class of one" also violates equal protection. *See Village of Willowbrook v. Olech*, 528 U.S. 562 (2000) (woman who was denied water service by municipal offices was "intentionally treated differently from others similarly situated" without any "rational basis for the difference in treatment" and thus constituted a "class of one" denied equal protection). *But see Engquist v. Oregon Dept. Of Agriculture*, 553 U.S. 591 (2008) ("class of one" claim not cognizable in the area of public employment).

211 470 U.S. 869 (1985).

212 Incidentally, there was no dormant commerce clause problem with the law because Congress has given states the power to regulate the insurance industry, even if such regulation burdens interstate commerce. *See* discussion, *supra* p. 347.

213 *See Goesaert v. Cleary*, 335 U.S. 464 (1948), *overruling recognized by Payne v. Tennessee*, 501 U.S. 808 (1991).

214 *See* Chapter XIII, p. 520 (legal disabilities of married women at common law).

215 83 U.S. 130 (1873).

> The natural and proper timidity and delicacy which belongs to the female sex evidently unfits it for many of the occupations of civil life. . . . The paramount destiny and mission of woman are to fulfill the noble and benign offices of wife and mother. This is the law of the Creator.[216]

Much has happened in constitutional law since 1873. Indeed, exactly 100 years after *Bradwell*, four members of the Court were in favor of holding that sex-based classifications were suspect and called for the application of strict scrutiny.[217]

The Standard Today   In the end, the Court settled upon a middle-level scrutiny test halfway between strict scrutiny and rational basis. A law distinguishing among the sexes must "serve important governmental objectives and must be substantially related to achievement of those objectives."[218] Unlike rational basis, the governmental objective cannot be an after-the-fact justification, but must have actually been relied upon by the legislature when it drew the distinction.[219] As a test of "ends" and "means," the end must be substantial — halfway between a "compelling" interest and a merely "legitimate" interest. The "fit" between that end and the means to accomplish it must be that the classification "substantially" furthers the end. The Court has emphasized that the state must show an "exceedingly persuasive justification" for differing treatment based on sex.[220] This is halfway between the "fit" required for a suspect classification and rational basis. By contrast, a suspect classification must be the only reasonable way to achieve the governmental end while the rational basis test requires only that it be rationally possible that the means chosen will advance the governmental interest.

Using this intermediate standard, the Court invalidated an Oklahoma law that set the legal age for drinking at 18 for females and 21 for males.[221] It also struck down an Idaho law preferring men over women among the relatives of a deceased person in the choice of an administrator of the estate,[222] rejecting generalizations about women's lesser ability to understand law, business or commerce as a basis for the irrebuttable preference. In *Mississippi University for Women v. Hogan*,[223] the Court struck down a state "women-only" nursing school admissions policy as based on "archaic and stereotypic notions" concerning the abilities of males and females. In *United States v. Virginia*,[224] the Court required that a state military academy with a reputation for tough training admit women, despite arguments that the presence of women would disrupt its "adversarial" approach to training. The Court equated these arguments to those made in the 19th century against women becoming lawyers. It observed that "generalizations about 'the way women are,' estimates of what is appropriate for *most women*, no longer justify denying opportunities to women whose talent and capacity place them

---

216 *Id.* at 141 (Bradley, J., concurring). Ms. Bradwell was not deterred from a legal career. For 30 years she was the editor and publisher of a very influential legal journal, The Chicago Law Journal. Ms. Bradwell was admitted to the Illinois bar after her death, as Illinois and several other states finally began to abolish their bans on women becoming lawyers. *See* Jane M. Friedman, America's First Woman Lawyer: The Biography of Myra Bradwell (Prometheus Books, N.Y. 1993).

217 *Frontiero v. Richardson*, 411 U.S. 677 (1973).

218 *Craig v. Boren*, 429 U.S. 190 (1976).

219 *United States v. Virginia*, 518 U.S. 515 (1996).

220 *Id.* at 523.

221 *Craig v. Boren, supra* note 218.

222 *Reed v. Reed*, 404 U.S. 71 (1971).

223 458 U.S. 718 (1982).

224 518 US 515 (1996).

outside the average description."[225] In *Orr v. Orr*,[226] the Court struck down a statute that provided for alimony to be awarded to wives, but not to husbands. It found that the presumption that husbands were never as needy as wives stemmed from impermissible sexual stereotypes. Similarly, the Court invalidated statutes based on assumptions that when both spouses are employed, the husband is the superior wage-earner and that men have a need for more education than women.[227]

Laws Disadvantaging Men As the *Orr* and *Hogan* cases indicate, men can also use the equal protection clause to challenge sex-based distinctions. Thus, the Court invalidated a law providing child support benefits to the surviving wife of a deceased male worker, but not to the surviving husband of a deceased female worker.[228] Similarly, the Court struck down a law providing survivors' benefits to all wives of deceased male workers, without a showing of actual dependency on the deceased spouse, but providing such benefits to the husband of a deceased female worker only upon a showing that he was actually dependent on his wife's earnings.[229] However, statutes that give *advantages* to women are valid, if designed to compensate women for *past unequal treatment by society*. Thus in *Kahn v. Shevin*,[230] the Court upheld a Florida law that gave property tax exemptions to widows, but not to widowers. Similarly, in *Califano v. Webster*,[231] federal Social Security laws permitted women to disregard more years of lower earnings than men in determining the rate of payment of their retirement benefits. The Court noted that it was common knowledge that working women have historically been paid much less than men. Congress's attempt to correct this imbalance was a sufficiently substantial governmental objective. These cases seem to make the constitutionality of affirmative action programs for women less problematic than affirmative action for racial minorities.

Permissible Sex-Based Distinctions Laws based on true biological differences, sometime referred to as "sex-specific traits," will also be upheld so long as they satisfy the less restrictive "rational basis" standard of review. For example, the biology of human reproduction is such that the mother of a child is easily identified by the birth process, while the father is not so easily identified. Consequently, the Court upheld in *Tuan Anh Nguyen v. Immigration and Naturalization Service* a statutory provision under which children born of a U.S.-citizen *mother* automatically become U.S. citizens, while those born of a U.S.-citizen *father* do not.[232] Similarly, a state may permit the unmarried *mother* of a child to bring an action for the child's wrongful death, but deny that right to

---

225 518 U.S. at 549.

226 440 U.S. 268 (1979).

227 *Frontiero v. Richardson*, 411 U.S. 677 (1973) (invalidating federal law that automatically gave military men a "dependency allowance," but required military women to prove actual dependency of their spouse to qualify); *Stanton v. Stanton*, 421 U.S. 7 (1975) (invalidating state law that required parents to support male children until age 21, but female children only until age 18).

228 *Weinberger v. Weisenfeld*, 420 U.S. 636 (1975).

229 *Califano v. Goldfarb*, 430 U.S. 199 (1977). These laws could also be viewed as discriminating against the female workers involved by not providing them with the protection that male workers get.

230 416 U.S. 351 (1974).

231 430 U.S. 313 (1977).

232 533 U.S. 53 (2001). The father could have made the child a citizen by filing an acknowledgment of paternity at any time before the child reached 18.

the *father* unless the father has "legitimated" the child by acknowledging paternity.[233] However, the fact that DNA tests can conclusively prove paternity forced the Court in *Tuan Anh Nguyen* to rely on an interest that "the child and the citizen parent have some demonstrated opportunity or potential to develop . . . a relationship that . . . consists of the real, everyday ties that provide a connection between child and citizen parent."[234] Tying all this to biological differences seems to reintroduce factors that sound strangely like the very stereotypes about the sexes that have been rejected in other cases.

Biological differences have prompted the Court to hold as well that a state may constitutionally exclude pregnancy from its medical insurance plan for state workers even though it is only women who get pregnant.[235] The Court also has upheld the constitutionality of Congress's limiting the draft (compulsory military service) to males.[236] From that decision, it appears likely that the Court would hold that military regulations banning women from frontline combat duty are constitutional. In the draft case, the Court approved Congress's reliance on the lesser physical strength of women, the difficulties of maintaining separate facilities under combat conditions, as well as the effect on public morale that sending women into combat might entail.[237]

Differing Views of Women's Rights and Equality Criticisms of the Court's approach to women's rights are as varied as viewpoints about women's position in society. Even feminists are divided. Some feminists believe that the Court should have determined that sex was a suspect classification and should strike down all sex-based classifications, even those that are designed to assist women. The theory is that such protections, while they provide some temporary assistance to some women, are harmful in the long run because they perpetuate the stereotype of women as being dependent and inferior. They argue that these meager advantages become excuses for perpetuating even greater disadvantages or encouraging women to follow the traditional path of homemaker, rather than building a career.

Other feminists support statutes that provide women with special protections on the ground that they are necessary as a practical matter. Such statutes are needed to counteract disabilities that society has imposed in the past and maintains in the present. They argue that treating women the same as men simply allows those societal inequalities to continue to oppress women until such time as society changes its expectations of women, something that could be a long time in coming.

This conflict in views was evident in a case challenging a California law that required employers to provide all female employees with an unpaid pregnancy leave of up to four months and the right to be reinstated into a "substantially similar job" upon return from that leave. *Amicus curiae* briefs filed by two feminist organizations, the National Organization for Women (NOW) and the Equal Rights Advocates, took opposing positions on the law. NOW argued that the law should be struck down because it was

---

233 *Parham v. Hughes*, 441 U.S. 347 (1979). *But see Caban v. Mohammed*, 441 U.S. 380 (1979) (mother-only consent to adoption unconstitutional where biological father had lived with mother and child and established a relationship with the child).

234 *Tuan Anh Nguyen, supra* note 232 at 54.

235 *Geduldig v. Aiello*, 417 U.S. 484 (1974). However, Congress has since provided statutory protection against such discrimination with the Pregnancy Discrimination Act, 42 U.S.C.A. §2000e(k).

236 *Rostker v. Goldberg*, 453 U.S. 57 (1981).

237 Women receive more effective protection from sex discrimination from Title VII of the Civil Rights Act of 1964, 42 U.S.C.A. §2000e *et seq. See* Chapter XV, pp. 620-625.

yet another piece of "protective" legislation based on assumptions about the weakness of women. Equal Rights Advocates argued that the law should be upheld, claiming that the special treatment afforded by the statute was not discrimination; it was necessary to *assure equality* of employment opportunity given the disadvantages that women face in the workplace. The Court upheld the law.[238]

Presumably, the Equal Rights Amendment (ERA) to the Constitution would have required true sex-neutrality, had it been ratified. The ERA provided that "[e]quality of rights under the law shall not be denied or abridged by the United States or by any State on account of sex." Congress passed it in 1972 after a 55-year struggle and sent it to the states for ratification with a 7-year limit. Though 30 of the necessary states quickly ratified the ERA, a more conservative mood later swept the country and the ratification process stalled. Five more states ratified, but three that had previously ratified withdrew their approval. Though Congress extended the time for ratification until 1982, no additional states ratified and the amendment died for lack of support.

Discrimination Against "Illegitimate" Children   The Supreme Court has held that a middle-level test like that used to strike down some sex-based classifications applies to discrimination against "illegitimate" children or children born of parents who are not married to each other. The Court has invalidated many of the traditional legal disabilities imposed on such children. It has held unconstitutional denials of the right to inherit from the father;[239] the right to receive workers' compensation benefits;[240] the right to wrongful death recovery for the death of a parent;[241] the right to welfare benefits;[242] and the right to child support from the natural father.[243] The Court has held, however, that if governmental benefits are based on past "actual dependency" on a deceased parent, the government may require that illegitimate children establish actual dependency, even though it presumes that *legitimate* children were dependent on the father.[244] It also rejected a challenge to a federal statute bestowing U.S. citizenship automatically upon birth to a child born out of wedlock to an American citizen *mother*, though not to the same child born of a citizen *father* unless a paternity decree was entered before the child turned 18.[245]

C. Substantive Due Process Rights

The Varieties of Due Process   As pointed out in the chapter on criminal procedure,[246] there are two due process clauses in the Constitution: one in the 5th Amendment, which applies only to the federal government, and the other in the 14th Amendment, which applies only to the states. Collectively, they provide that a person may not be "deprived of life, liberty or property without due process of law" by any governmental body in the

---

238 *See* FARBER, *supra* note 2, at 353-356 (briefs) and *California Federal Savings and Loan Association v. Guerra*, 479 U.S. 272 (1987).

239 *Trimble v. Gordon*, 430 U.S. 762 (1977).

240 *Weber v. Aetna Casualty & Surety Co.*, 406 U.S. 164, 175 (1972).

241 *Levy v. Louisiana*, 391 U.S. 68 (1968).

242 *New Jersey Welfare Rights Organization v. Cahill*, 411 U.S. 619 (1973).

243 *Gomez v. Perez*, 409 U.S. 535 (1973). *See also Clark v. Jeter*, 486 U.S. 456 (1988) (6-year limitation on the time for filing paternity action was constitutionally impermissible). *But see Lalli v. Lalli*, 439 U.S. 259 (1978) (state may require that paternity be established in a judicial proceeding during the father's lifetime as precondition for inheriting from father).

244 *Mathews v. Lucas*, 427 U.S. 495 (1976).

245 *Miller v. Albright*, 523 U.S. 420 (1998). *See also* Chapter XIII, p. 527 note 48.

246 *See* Chapter VIII, p. 283.

United States. The generality of this wording has led the Court to use due process for many purposes. Due process establishes three distinct sets of rights. The first, "incorporated" due process rights, have already been discussed in the criminal procedure chapter.[247] The second are "procedural" due process rights, which were discussed in the chapter on administrative law.[248] The third set of rights, discussed here, are "substantive" due process rights.

Definitions "Substantive due process" seems to be a contradiction in terms. In fact, the doctrine has little to do with "process" and a great deal to do with "substance." While the due process clause states that the government shall not "deprive any person of life, liberty or property *without due process of law*," substantive due process holds that there are certain rights encompassed within the term "liberty" that the state may not infringe no matter what "process" it provides. Indeed, we might more accurately describe the rights protected in this area not as *due* process rights, but as "*no process*" rights. If the "without due process" portion of the clause means anything in the substantive due process context, it can only be that a court presumes that there was a failure in the *legislative* process if it produced a law that violates fundamental rights. However, the Court has simply ignored the "process" reference and has never explained what role it plays in the substantive due process context.

Overlap With Equal Protection There is considerable and perhaps complete overlap between substantive due process and the top and bottom levels of three-tier equal protection doctrine discussed earlier. "Fundamental rights" substantive due process corresponds to strict scrutiny equal protection in that it requires a compelling governmental interest to sustain any infringement on fundamental rights.[249] There is also a lax form of substantive due process identical to rational basis equal protection: it applies to business, welfare or economic legislation and invalidates a law only if it is completely irrational. As such, lawyers rarely use economic substantive due process and even more rarely use it successfully.[250] Today, courts judge the validity of business, welfare and economic laws almost always under the equal protection rubric rather than due process. Consequently, this section will discuss only the fundamental rights side of substantive due process.[251]

Substantive Due Process and Judicial Review Substantive due process has become the major source of unwritten "fundamental rights" outside the more specific rights-bestowing provisions of the Constitution. As such, substantive due process raises — more than any other constitutional doctrine — the question of the Court's legitimate role

---

247 *See* Chapter VIII, pp. 283-323

248 *See* Chapter VI, pp. 205-209. While procedural due process standards are most often applied to administrative action, they also apply to judicial action. *See* Chapter VI, p. 208. As discussed in Chapter VII, due process is also used to test the limits of personal jurisdiction (*see* pp. 253-259) and choice of law (p. 263).

249 *See supra* p. 356.

250 *See, e.g., North Dakota State Board of Pharmacy v. Snyder's Drug Stores, Inc.* 414 U.S. 156 (1973) (law requiring pharmacies to be controlled by pharmacists is not completely irrational and thus does not violate due process). *Compare supra* pp. 356-358 ("rational basis" equal protection).

251 At one point it seemed that strict scrutiny equal protection rather than substantive due process would be the major vehicle for protecting fundamental rights. Some texts reflect this in their organization. *See* NOWAK & ROTUNDA, *supra* note 2, §14.29 (discussing the abortion cases under equal protection).

in applying its power of judicial review to invalidate governmental action through"non-interpretivist" methods.[252]

The history of substantive due process dates from the embarrassing 1900-1937 period, discussed in Chapter I.[253] Cases in this era, the most famous (or infamous) being *Lochner v. New York*,[254] "found" in the "liberty" guaranteed by the due process clause, the tenets of 19th-century *laissez faire* capitalist philosophy. *Lochner* invalidated state laws setting maximum working hours on the ground that the law interfered with the "liberty" of employers and employees to freely contract with each other. *Lochner* lead to a series of "economic" substantive due process cases that favored business interests, which ended in 1937 when the Court upheld a state minimum wage law because "regulation which is reasonable in relation to its subject and is adopted in the interests of the community" did not deprive individuals of "liberty."[255] Eventually, substantive due process would reemerge, but not to protect economic or business interests. Rather, the Court has and continues to confine its elaborations on what is included in "liberty" to individuals' right of privacy. Whether this revised return to substantive due process is any better than *Lochner* is hotly debated.[256]

1. The Right to Privacy

Birth Control and Abortion In developing the right to privacy, the Court initially avoided reliance on substantive due process analysis, explicitly rejecting arguments "suggest[ing] that *Lochner* be our guide" and disavowing any power to "sit as a super-legislature to determine the wisdom, need, and propriety of laws." Thus, the Court tried to avoid relying on substantive due process in *Griswold v. Connecticut*,[257] where it struck down a state statute that prohibited all use of birth control devices as infringing on the "right to privacy." The majority opinion relied on the cumulative effect of "penumbras, formed by emanations from" the Bill of Rights defining "zones of privacy" that protected the right of a married couple to use birth control devices. A concurring opinion emphasized the 9th Amendment's reservation of unspecified "other [rights] retained by the people." Two concurring opinions relied on substantive due process. But despite its disclaimers, the majority opinion relied on two cases from the *Lochner* period: *Meyer v. Nebraska*[258] and *Pierce v. Society of Sisters*.[259] In *Meyer*, the Court struck down a Nebraska law that prohibited teaching young children any language other than English in any public or private school. The Court held that "liberty" in the due process clause included "certain fundamental rights which must be respected." In *Pierce*, the Court followed *Meyer* in striking down an Oregon law that required all children to attend public schools based on the right of the parents to choose a private school for their children if they wanted.

---

252 *See supra* p. 328.

253 *See* pp. 11-12.

254 198 U.S. 45 (1905).

255 *West Coast Hotel Co. v. Parrish*, 300 U.S. 379, 391 (1937).

256 The opinions of Justices O'Connor, Chief Justice Rehnquist and Justice Scalia in dissent in an abortion case constitute a classic debate about the role of the Court in "fundamental rights" substantive due process doctrine and what dangers to its authority exist in light of its experiences in the pre-1937 years. *See Planned Parenthood of Southeastern Pennsylvania v. Casey*, 505 U.S. 833 (1992).

257 381 U.S. 479 (1965).

258 262 U.S. 390 (1923).

259 268 U.S. 510 (1925).

In *Roe v. Wade*,[260] the abortion rights decision, the majority relied directly on a substantive due process rationale. As if to make sure that it was choosing the "correct" set of values to infuse into the term "liberty," Justice Blackmun's opinion undertook an exhaustive examination of the history of abortion law, beginning with the ancient Greeks, and considered all manner of medical, philosophical and religious input on the questions involved. The opinion held that the right to privacy included the right to an abortion, but recognized two countervailing interests of the state: an interest in the mother's health and an interest in "potential human life." Based on this and medical information on fetal development, the Court divided pregnancy into three trimesters.[261] Because in the first trimester childbirth is more of a threat to the woman's health than an abortion and the fetus is not viable outside the mother's body, neither of the two state interests is very strong. At the other end of the gestation period, last trimester abortions involve both interests: a substantial threat to the mother's health and a fetus capable of surviving outside the mother's body. Thus, the state's interest in regulating abortions in this final three months of pregnancy becomes "compelling" and it can prohibit abortions altogether except to save the life or health of the mother. During the middle trimester, the state's interest in the health of the mother is stronger than in the first trimester, so it can regulate as necessary to protect that interest, such as requiring that the procedure be performed in an adequate medical facility like a hospital or clinic.

Since *Roe*, there has been almost endless litigation over the issues it raised. Several state regulations attempting to make abortions more expensive and requiring them to be performed in hospitals were struck down.[262] The Court invalidated on vagueness grounds a statute requiring a doctor to determine viability of the fetus before performing an abortion,[263] but then later approved a more specific viability test requirement aimed at abortions past the 20th week of pregnancy.[264] In other cases it struck down consent requirements that required the father's consent or the mother's parents' consent if she was a minor,[265] but later approved a statute requiring that a minor either notify both parents or obtain judicial approval before getting an abortion.[266] The Court also rejected challenges to federal and state welfare laws that prohibited funding for abortions for poor women, while allowing such funding for live childbirth. The Court held that the government may not place obstacles in the path of a woman seeking an abortion, but it is not required to *fund* her exercise of her right.[267] Finally, after almost 20 years of *Roe* and increasing anti-abortion protests across the country, the Court agreed to consider the question of overruling *Roe* in 1992 in the case of *Planned Parenthood of Southeastern Pennsylvania v. Casey*.[268]

In *Planned Parenthood*, the joint opinion of the Court affirmed two limits on the right to an abortion contained in the Pennsylvania law. One, which had been approved

---

260 410 U.S. 113 (1973).

261 A trimester is one of the three three-month periods that make up the 9 months of gestation in the normal pregnancy.

262 *See Planned Parenthood v. Danforth*, 428 U.S. 52 (1976); *Akron v. Akron Center for Reproductive Health*, 462 U.S. 416 (1983).

263 *Colautti v. Franklin*, 439 U.S. 379 (1979).

264 *Webster v. Reproductive Health Services*, 492 U.S. 490 (1989).

265 *Danforth, supra* note 262.

266 *Hodgson v. Minnesota*, 497 U.S. 417 (1990).

267 *Maher v. Roe*, 432 U.S. 464 (1977); *Harris v. McRae*, 448 U.S. 297 (1981).

268 505 U.S. 833 (1992).

in earlier cases, was a requirement of parental consent or judicial approval for minors. The other was a 24-hour waiting period after the doctor had provided specified information about abortions and fetal development — a limitation that the Court had previously invalidated as an undue burden on exercise of the right.[269] However, a bare majority of the Court refused to overrule *Roe*. In doing so, the Court relied heavily on *stare decisis*. Justice O'Connor's majority opinion observed that "[a]n entire generation has come of age free to assume *Roe*'s concept of liberty in defining the capacity of women to act in society" and that *Roe*'s doctrinal basis is "not at odds with other precedent for the analysis of personal liberty." Consequently, "the stronger argument is for affirming *Roe*'s central holding, with whatever degree of personal reluctance any of us may have . . . ." The Court also referred to the public protests against *Roe*, considering that factor not just irrelevant, but a reason *not* to overrule it, because "surrender[ing] to political pressure" would damage the Court's moral authority and prestige.[270]

In the process of rejecting challenges to *Roe*, the Court summarized the right to an abortion, avoiding the strict three trimester analysis of *Roe*. The Court held that before fetal viability, a woman has a right to terminate her pregnancy, and a state law is unconstitutional if it imposes an "undue burden" on the woman's decision, *i.e.*, if it has the purpose or effect of placing a substantial obstacle in the woman's path. After viability of the fetus, the state, in promoting its interest in the potentiality of human life, may regulate, and even proscribe abortion, except where "necessary, in appropriate medical judgment, for the preservation of the [mother's] life or health."[271]

Since *Casey*, the Court has enforced various aspects of the *Roe* decision without making any major changes in doctrine. In a 2000 case, *Stenberg v. Carhart*, it struck down Nebraska's criminal prohibition on so-called "partial birth" abortions.[272] It did so on two grounds. First, the statute had an exception only for when such a procedure was necessary to save the mother's life, but not when it was necessary to protect her health. Second, the definition of the prohibited procedure was so broad as to cover many post-viability abortion procedures that are widely used and clearly protected by *Roe*.[273] In 2006, it similarly approved a lower federal court's injunction against a parental notification statute in New Hampshire that had no such exception for threats to the mother's health.[274] In 2007, however, the Court upheld the federal Partial-Birth Abortion Act of 2003. The Court distinguished *Stenberg* because the federal statute's language was more specific and the procedure it proscribed was never medically necessary.[275]

2. Other Privacy Rights

Beyond abortion and contraception, the right to privacy has expanded to cover some other aspects of family life and marriage. The Court struck down a zoning law that

---

269 *See Akron, supra* note 262.

270 *Planned Parenthood*, 505 U.S. at 860-861 (joint opinion). Justice Scalia's dissent argued that the Court's prestige and authority was undermined more by continuing to operate in an "area, where we have no right to be, and where we do neither ourselves nor the country any good by remaining." *Id.* at 1002.

271 *Planned Parenthood, id.* at 870-879.

272 These are procedures in which the fetus is removed later in the pregnancy, when the fetus is more developed and possibly viable outside the mother's womb. They are controversial because they often require the doctor to crush or dismember the fetus before removing it from the uterus.

273 530 U.S. 914 (2000).

274 *Ayotte v. Planned Parenthood of Northern New England*, 546 U.S. 320 (2006).

275 *Gonzalez v. Carhart*, 550 U.S. 241 (2007).

reserved a neighborhood for "nuclear" families of parents and children only, thus prohibiting a grandmother from living with her grandsons for its interference with family privacy.[276] Declaring the right to marry to be fundamental, the Court also struck down a law that required, as a precondition of marriage, that a parent show that he or she did not owe unpaid child support.[277] By a 4-4 vote in 1986, the Court had declined to extend the right to privacy to protect private consensual sexual conduct of homosexuals. But the Court overruled that decision in 2003, holding that a state "cannot demean [homosexuals'] existence or control their destiny by making their private sexual conduct a crime" without violating their "right to liberty under the Due Process Clause."[278]

Litigants have argued the right to privacy is broad enough to include a "right to die." In *Cruzan v. Director, Missouri Dept. of Health*,[279] Nancy Cruzan was in an irreversible coma. Her parents wanted doctors to remove her feeding tube to let her die naturally. The Missouri Supreme Court held that they could not remove the tube because they had failed to meet Missouri's "clear and convincing evidence" standard for showing that Nancy would have decided to remove the tube were she conscious. The U.S. Supreme Court held that (1) artificial feeding is a form of medical treatment that may be terminated to fulfill the patient's desire to die with dignity, but (2) Missouri had a strong state interest in preserving human life and assuring against hasty decision-making. Thus, the high standard of proof was constitutional.[280] In 1997, the Court faced the right-to-die issue again when mentally competent, terminally ill patients sought to receive lethal medicine from their doctors. The case involved a Washington state law that prohibited causing or aiding a suicide. The lower federal court found the law unconstitutional on privacy grounds. The Supreme Court reversed, recasting the issue, not as a "right to die," but as a "right to *assistance*" in dying. Relying on a long history of state prohibition on assisted suicides and what it saw as abuses of the practice in the Netherlands, the Court concluded that Washington had the right to ensure against the risks of abuse by totally banning, rather than regulating, assisted suicides.[281]

Oregon went in the opposite direction, passing the Death with Dignity Act, which permitted physicians to dispense or prescribe lethal doses of drugs at the request of a terminally ill patient. In reaction, the U.S. Attorney General issued an interpretive rule declaring that using controlled substances to assist suicide is not a legitimate medical practice and that dispensing or prescribing them for this purpose is unlawful under the federal Controlled Substances Act. The Court invalidated the interpretive rule as beyond the scope of the federal statute, which, it determined, was aimed at recreational use of drugs and drug addiction, not regulation of physicians licensed to practice medicine

---

276 *Moore v. City of East Cleveland, Ohio*, 431 U.S. 494 (1977). The Court had upheld a more inclusive city ordinance in *Belle Terre v. Boraas*, 416 U.S. 1 (1974) that limited a "family" to not more than two unrelated persons.

277 *Zablocki v. Redhail*, 434 U.S. 374 (1978). *See also supra* p. 356 (right to procreate).

278 *Bowers v. Hardwick*, 478 U.S. 186 (1986), *overruled by Lawrence v. Texas*, 539 U.S. 558 (2003). Cf. *Romer v. Evans*, 517 U.S. 620 (1996), discussed *supra* p. 357.

279 497 U.S. 261 (1990).

280 Most states only require proof by a preponderance of the evidence that the incapacitated individual would have wanted to terminate life support. *But see Washington v. Harper*, 494 U.S. 210 (1990) (liberty interest in refusing unwanted medical treatment did not allow prisoner to refuse administration of antipsychotic drugs).

281 *Washington v. Glucksberg*, 521 U.S. 702 (1997); *Vacco v. Quill*, 521 U.S. 793 (1997). *See Symposium: Physician-Assisted Suicide*, 82 MINN. L.REV. 885 (1998).

under state law.[282] However, Congress probably has the constitutional power to pass a statute with the same content as the rule.[283]

D. First Amendment Freedoms of Expression

The 1st Amendment protects the rights of free speech, press and assembly — the freedoms of expression. Included in freedom of expression are not only oral, written and other direct modes of expression, but also "symbolic speech" — conduct intended to express a point of view, such as wearing armbands or burning flags.[284]

Why Protect Free Expression There are several reasons typically given for protecting free expression. Principal among them is the notion that in a democracy people must be informed to govern themselves, and that freedom of expression is essential to this informing function.[285] Coupled with this idea is the conviction that the free flow of discussion and criticism of the performance of those in power serves as a check on abuses of governmental power.[286] Another theory is the "marketplace of ideas" — that "[t]he best test of truth is the power of the thought to get itself accepted in the competition of the market."[287] Repression of expression causes "market distortion" and does so in two different ways. If it is successful, it removes some points of view from the "market." If it is not successful, it may give "forbidden" points of view more appeal than they would otherwise have.[288] A related idea concentrates on perhaps the most immediate benefit of free expression: it is healthy for people — it allows them to express their individuality and to "blow off steam." People will make speeches in the park instead of making revolution in the streets. As Justice Brandeis observed in *Whitney v. California*, "it is hazardous to discourage thought, hope, and imagination; . . . repression breeds hate; . . . hate menaces stable government; . . . the path of safety lies in the opportunity to discuss freely supposed grievances and proposed remedies."[289]

These various theories have their detractors. If limited to their rationales, the informed self-government and the "marketplace of ideas" theories would presumably protect only "idea" or "political idea" speech.[290] And some have noted that the "marketplace of ideas" theory posits a peculiarly archaic *laissez-faire* form of the marketplace that society abandoned long ago as unworkable for goods and services. After all, dangerous *consumer products* are banned in the *real* market, so why not ban dangerous *ideas* — such as racial hatred and genocide — from the marketplace of *ideas*. As for the idea of people "blowing off steam," critics charge that we have ignored the real harm that words can cause. The use of "free expression" to degrade women or members of racial minorities, thus keeping them "in their place," is a serious social, economic and

---

282 *Gonzales v. Oregon*, 546 U.S. 243 (2006).

283 *See Gonzales v. Raich, supra* note 111, the medical marijuana case, discussed *supra* p. 342.

284 For a lucid and thought-provoking explanation of 1st Amendment law *see* DANIEL A. FARBER, THE FIRST AMENDMENT, 2D ED. (Foundation 2003).

285 *See* ALEXANDER MEIKLEJOHN, FREE SPEECH AND ITS RELATION TO SELF-GOVERNMENT (Harper, New York, N.Y. 1948).

286 *See* Vincent Blasi, *The Checking Power of the First Amendment Theory*, 1977 AM. BAR FOUND. RES. J. 521.

287 *Abrams v. United States*, 250 U.S. 616, 630 (1919) (Holmes, J.). *See* JOHN STUART MILL, ON LIBERTY (Hacket Pub. Co., Indianapolis, Ind. 1978) (originally published in 1859).

288 *See* NOWAK & ROTUNDA, *supra* note 2, §16.6 (discussion of justifications for freedom of speech).

289 274 U.S. 357 (1927) (Brandeis, J., concurring).

290 *See* Robert Bork, *Neutral Principles and Some First Amendment Problems*, 47 IND. L. J. 1 (1971).

political problem.[291] Nonetheless, at present these objections have not prevailed in 1st Amendment law.

Content and Viewpoint Neutrality   A first principle of government regulation of expression is that it must be content neutral. "If there is any fixed star in our constitutional constellation, it is that no official, high or petty, can prescribe what shall be orthodox in politics, nationalism, religion, or other matters of opinion or force citizens to confess by word or act their faith therein."[292] Content regulation requires the greatest burden of justification — a compelling governmental interest. Thus, the Court held in *Boos v. Barry*[293] that a law that prohibited the display of any sign in front of a foreign embassy that "tends to bring the foreign government into public odium or public dispute," while allowing signs praising the foreign government, violated the First Amendment, because it directly regulated content. Similarly, in *United States v. Playboy Entertainment Group, Inc.*,[294] the Court invalidated a federal law that required cable television operators either to block all "sexually oriented" programs or to show them only between 10PM and 6AM. This principle of content neutrality underlies cases holding "anti-flag-burning" laws unconstitutional. Those laws punished burning the U.S. flag as a sign of contempt or desecration, but allowed burning as a respectful means of disposal of a worn or soiled flag.[295]

A second "bedrock principle underlying the 1st Amendment," which is related to content neutrality, is that "the government may not prohibit the expression of an idea simply because society itself finds the idea itself offensive or disagreeable."[296] Just as the government cannot *itself* condemn speech for its content, it cannot use offensiveness to the *public* as a basis for prohibiting it. Consistent with this principle, the Court in *Cohen v. California*[297] held that a Vietnam War protester could not be arrested for wearing a jacket in a courthouse that displayed the "unseemly expletive" of "Fuck the Draft." Even self-styled Nazis, who sought to march in uniform with swastikas in a section of town where survivors of Nazi concentration camps lived, could not be prohibited from marching merely because it would have offended residents.[298] And in *United States v. Playboy Entertainment Group, Inc.*, discussed above, the Court "assum[ed] that many adults themselves would find the [sexual] material [banned by

---

291 *See* Richard Delgado, *Words that Wound: A Tort Action for Racial Insults, Epithets and Name-Calling*, 17 HARV. CIV. RTS.-CIV. LIB. L. REV. 133 (1982) and Catherine MacKinnon, *Pornography, Civil Rights, and Speech*, 20 HARV. CIV. RTS.-CIV. LIB. L. REV. 1 (1985). *See also infra* p. 366 (discussion of obscenity and feminist view of pornography).

292 *West Virginia State Bd. of Education v. Barnette*, 319 U.S. 624, 642 (1943) (state could not require school children of Jehovah's Witnesses faith to salute the American flag). The difficulty and controversial nature of the case is shown by the fact that *Barnette* overruled a 3-year-old precedent, *Minersville School District v. Gobitis*, 310 U.S. 586 (1940), and was decided during the war, when feelings of patriotism were high.

293 485 U.S. 312 (1988).

294 529 U.S. 803 (2000).

295 *See Texas v. Johnson*, 491 U.S. 397 (1989); *United States v. Eichman*, 496 U.S. 310 (1990).

296 *Texas v. Johnson*, 491 U.S. 397, 414 (1989) (burning of the U.S. flag).

297 403 U.S. 15 (1971).

298 *See Collin v. Smith*, 578 F.2d 1197 (7th Cir. 1978), discussed in Chapter IV, p. 157. *See also Snyder v. Phelps*, ___ U.S. ___, 131 S.Ct. 1207 (2011) (civil suit by father of soldier killed in Iraq war for infliction of emotional distress against persons who picketed his son's military funeral using signs stating "Thank God for Dead Soldiers" to communicate their belief that God hates the United States for its tolerance of homosexuality, particularly in the military, is barred by the 1st Amendment).

the federal law] highly offensive" and many more certainly would not want their children to view it.

1. Content Regulation

In view of the almost *per se* rule of invalidity of government regulation of expression based on content, prohibiting expression based on content can generally take place only in areas of expression that do not fall within the 1st Amendment's protections at all. Despite the 1st Amendment's absolute command that there shall be *"no Law . . . abridging the freedom of speech,"* there are several categories of speech that are not protected at all by the 1st Amendment. The Supreme Court has taken the view that the Framers of the Constitution intended to exempt several categories of speech from 1st Amendment protection.[299]

Seditious Speech Because the central purpose of freedom of expression is to foster spirited political debate, the problem of seditious speech must be handled carefully. Unfortunately, regulation of sedition got off to a bad start in the United States — actually two bad starts. The first was the Sedition Act of 1798, which mandated fines and imprisonment, *inter alia*, for making any "false, scandalous and malicious writing against the government or members of the government with intent to defame . . . or to bring them . . . into contempt or disrepute." The Act was passed on the eve of war with France by a Congress controlled by the Federalist Party to use as a tool for suppressing its Democratic-Republican opponents. Several opponents of Federalist government policy were fined and imprisoned. Although James Madison and Thomas Jefferson condemned the Sedition Act, it was never subject to challenge in the Supreme Court and it expired in 1801. However, as the Court noted in a 1964 case, "the attack upon its validity has carried the day in the court of history."[300] Fines levied in its prosecution were repaid by Act of Congress on the ground that it was clearly unconstitutional.

The second "bad start" with regard to sedition laws was over a hundred years later. Congress enacted the Espionage Act of 1917 during a period of "Red hysteria" following the Russian Revolution and in the midst of World War I. In *Schenck v. United States*,[301] the Court upheld the conviction of Schenck, a socialist, who published and distributed leaflets opposing U.S. involvement in World War I, attacking the draft as slavery and encouraging young men to resist. Similarly, in *Abrams v. United States*,[302] the Court upheld the conviction and 20-year sentence of Abrams, who was passing out leaflets opposing U.S. involvement in the Russian Revolution. Both cases used a "clear and present danger" test. Under this test, the government has the right to punish those who advocate the overthrow of government if their advocacy represents a clear and present danger that such overthrow will happen. It is difficult today to see how Schenck's leafleting could have satisfied this test.[303]

---

299 According to some, this is reflected in the language chosen. The 1st Amendment says that *freedom* of speech may not be abridged, not that *speech* may not be abridged. The *freedom* of speech excludes several categories of speech. *See* MEIKLEJOHN, *supra* note 285, at 19.

300 *New York Times v. Sullivan*, 376 U.S. 254 (1964).

301 249 U.S. 47 (1919).

302 250 U.S. 616 (1919).

303 *See also Gitlow v. New York*, 268 U.S. 652, 658 (1925). The anti-communist hysteria of the 1950s provided another occasion for suppression of political expression. In *Dennis v. United States*, 341 U.S. 494 (1951) and *Scales v. United States*, 367 U.S. 203 (1961), the Court approved convictions of members of the Communist Party of the USA, because the Court thought they represented a real threat. The fact that all these cases were decided in the 20th century should not be taken as suggesting that suppression of speech

The current standard for judging seditious advocacy was set forth in the 1969 case of *Brandenberg v. Ohio*,[304] which created a revised "clear and present danger" test. The Court held that a state may not "forbid or proscribe advocacy of the use of force or of law violation except where such advocacy is directed to inciting or producing imminent lawless action and is likely to incite or produce such action." Relying on the "marketplace of ideas" theory, the Court justified governmental interference with a speaker's calls to *immediate* action on the ground that the immediate incitement left no time for more speech to counteract it. At the Ku Klux Klan meeting in *Brandenberg*, crosses were burned and some people had weapons. They talked about marching to Washington, but there was no indication that they were immediately going from their meeting to attack a government installation.[305] Consequently, their expression was protected under the 1st Amendment.

Speech as Illegal Conduct   Criminals often carry out crimes through speech. Prosecution of these speakers based on the content of their speech is constitutional. For example, criminals use speech to commit perjury, bribery, fraud, solicitation to commit murder, extortion, and threats to kill public officials.[306] In a less extreme situation, it does not violate freedom of speech to prohibit a newspaper from publishing sex-designated employment opportunity advertisements, because publication amounts to sex discrimination prohibited by federal law.[307]

Even speech with more expressive content is punishable under some circumstances. "Fighting words" — words that are "likely to provoke the average person to retaliation and thereby cause a breach of the peace" — are exempt from 1st Amendment protection. In *Chaplinsky v. New Hampshire*,[308] the Court held that this speech is "of such slight social value as a step to truth that any benefit that may be derived from them is clearly outweighed by the social interest in order and morality." However, unless "fighting words" are limited solely to face-to-face personal insults of an especially confrontational type, the government could use the exception to punish speech just because it represents an unpopular point of view. Thus, in *Cohen v. California*, discussed above,[309] the Court rejected application of the exception to Mr. Cohen's expression of his sentiments about compulsory military service on his jacket. While the message might have offended some veterans, it was not the kind of direct face-to-face statement that would qualify as "fighting words."

Even when a law punishes speech that is clearly "fighting words," the law must not do so on the basis of content or viewpoint. In *R.A.V. v. St. Paul*,[310] a juvenile burned a

---

and political activity did not take place until recent times. In fact, considerable evidence exists that such suppression occurred on a regular basis between the 1798 and 1917 acts. *See generally* David Rabban, *The First Amendment in Its Forgotten Years*, 90 YALE L. J. 514 (1981).

304 395 U.S. 444 (1969).

305 *See also Hess v. Indiana*, 414 U.S. 105 (1973) (threats made by university students during an anti-war demonstration to "take the fucking street later" did not reach the point of "likely to incite or produce imminent lawless action").

306 *Watts v. United States*, 394 U.S. 705 (1969) (threats on the life of the President are punishable, but statement by Watts that he would shoot the President if he were ever given a rifle was not a true threat, only "political hyperbole").

307 *Pittsburgh Press v. Pittsburgh Comm'n on Human Rights*, 413 U.S. 376 (1971).

308 315 U.S. 568, 574 (1942).

309 403 U.S. 15 (1971).

310 505 U.S. 377 (1992).

cross on the lawn of a black family. He was convicted under a "Bias-Motivated Crime" ordinance, which proscribed cross-burning and similar action if it "arous[ed] anger, alarm or resentment in others on the basis of race, color, creed, religion or gender." The Court held the ordinance unconstitutional because it punished abusive expression only on the stated basis, leaving people free "to express hostility, for example, on the basis of political affiliation, union membership, or homosexuality." However, in *Virginia v. Black*,[311] the Court approved a state statute punishing cross burning "with the intent of intimidating any person or group of persons." Unlike the statute at issue in *R.A.V.*, the Virginia statute did not "single out for opprobrium only that speech directed toward 'one of the specified disfavored topics.'" Instead, it flatly proscribed all cross-burning when used to intimidate as a "particularly virulent form of intimidation." The fact that no other virulent forms of intimidation were punished was not a problem, given "cross burning's long and pernicious history as a signal of impending violence."[312]

Obscenity Obscenity is excluded from 1st Amendment protection, not so much on a theory that it presents a danger to society, but because of historical understandings that the Framers of the 1st Amendment did not intend to protect it.[313] While there is no question that obscenity is unprotected speech, the Court has struggled to define exactly what is "obscene" while ensuring the definition does not encompass valuable speech. Whenever the Court has refined the definition, a local prosecutor somewhere in the country has used it to suppress books and films that are recognized as good literature or even classics.[314] Generally, the Court has undertaken *ad hoc* analyses of the allegedly obscene material on a case-by-case basis. In the 1960s, a Boston court found an 18th century book, John Cleland's *Fanny Hill: Memoirs of a Woman of Pleasure*, obscene. The Court reversed the lower court, as it did in a number of similar decisions in the 1960s.[315] In each case, the justices had to watch the movie or read the book to see if it met the test of obscenity. Some justices essentially gave up after several attempts to define what was obscene. Justice Potter Stewart famously stated that he was unable to define obscenity, but "I know it when I see it."[316]

The current obscenity test comes from *Miller v. California*.[317] Under *Miller*, a book, magazine or film is obscene if: (1) the "average person, applying contemporary community standards," would find that the work as a whole, "appeals to the prurient interest" in sex; (2) the work depicts "in a patently offensive way" sexual conduct specifically defined by the applicable state law; and (3) the work, taken as a whole, "lacks serious

---

311 538 U.S. 343 (2003).

312 Cross burning was used by the Ku Klux Klan following the Civil War as a means of terrorizing blacks and their supporters, primarily as a threat of future violence. *See id.* at 352-357.

313 *Roth v. United States*, 354 U.S. 476, 484-485 (1957). Another important point resolved in *Roth* was that novels and other artistic works are protected by the 1st Amendment even though they do not directly relate to the self-governance policies behind protecting free expression. A summary of the history of obscenity regulation is recounted in NOWAK & ROTUNDA, *supra* note 2, §16.56.

314 Interestingly enough, though the government may punish *distribution* of obscene materials, a person has a substantive due process right of privacy that protects private possession of such materials in one's home. *Stanley v. Georgia*, 394 U.S. 557 (1969). How one gets those materials to one's home is a problem, however. *See United States v. 12,200 Ft. Reels*, 413 U.S. 123 (1973) (not unconstitutional to punish mailing, transporting or importing obscene materials even if they are for private use).

315 *A Book Named 'John Cleland's Memoires Of A Woman of Pleasure' v. Attorney General*, 383 U.S. 413 (1966).

316 *Jacobellis v. Ohio*, 378 U.S. 184 (1964).

317 413 U.S. 15 (1973).

literary, artistic, political, or scientific value." Aside from its vagueness, this test has at least three problems. First, it requires judges and local juries to determine what the local "community standards" are regarding sex and to engage in literary criticism — matters about which they are not necessarily experts. Second, the Court has never explained what it means by the phrase "appeals to the prurient interest" in sex. It has held that the phrase does not include appeals to "normal" interest in sex, only to "shameful or morbid interest in sex." However, there is no clue as to how one distinguishes between the two.[318] Third, the reference to "contemporary community standards" means *local* standards. Thus, the Constitution effectively has a different meaning in rural Georgia than it does in New York City.

The problems of the *Miller* test are evident in subsequent cases. Almost immediately after the Court decided *Miller*, a Georgia jury found a highly-acclaimed film, *Carnal Knowledge*, starring Jack Nicholson and Candice Bergen, to be obscene. The Supreme Court reversed, pointing out that the nudity and "ultimate" sex acts depicted were not what it had in mind in *Miller* and that "there was no exhibition of the actors' genitals."[319] More recently, in *Ashcroft v. Free Speech Coalition*,[320] the Court struck down a federal law banning computer-generated images that *appeared* to depict a minor engaging in sexually explicit activity. While acknowledging that "sexual abuse of a child is a most serious crime and an act repugnant to the moral instincts of a decent people," the Court found that the statute failed all three parts of the *Miller* test: (1) by banning any depiction of sexually explicit activity of children — even a picture in a psychology manual — the law was not limited to portrayals appealing to a "prurient interest" in sex; (2) by failing to require that the image be patently offensive, it applied to any pictures of what appeared to be 17-year-olds engaging in sexually explicit activity, a depiction that would not in every case contravene community standards; and (3) given that teenage sexual activity and child sexual abuse have been common artistic and literary subjects throughout history, from Shakespeare plays to the 2000 Academy Award-winning film, "American Beauty," the law failed to consider the work's redeeming artistic value, but instead banned any work that contained a single scene portraying sexual activity of minors. Thus, "virtual child pornography" — the use of youthful actors or computer generated figures portraying sexual activity of minors — cannot be prohibited even if it meets the *Miller* test. However, a ban on photographs of *actual* children in sexual situations — even if they are not obscene under *Miller* — is permitted based on the need to protect the children involved in the making of the films or pictures.[321]

Nonetheless, Congress may have found a partial way to suppress virtual child pornography despite the *Free Speech Coalition* case. In response to that case, Congress passed an amended statute which criminalized "advertising," "promotion," or "solicitation" of *virtual* child pornography in a "manner that reflects the belief, or that is intended to cause another to believe, that the material or purported material is, or contains" *actual* child pornography."[322] Thus, the new statute criminalized not the underlying material itself, but the offer of such material either believing it to be actual child pornography or intending pass it off as actual child pornography. The Court upheld the new law by

---

318 *Brockett v. Spokane Arcades, Inc.*, 472 U.S. 491 (1985).
319 *Jenkins v. Georgia*, 418 U.S. 153 (1974)
320 535 U.S. 234 (2002).
321 *New York v. Ferber*, 458 U.S. 747 (1982).
322 18 U.S.C.A. §2252A(a)(3)(B).

analogy to criminal statutes punishing the sale, not just of illegal drugs, but of fake illegal drugs that are actually legal substances.[323] It seems, therefore, that one way around the problem of defining obscenity is to remove the material from the equation, and instead focus on the intent of the defendant to distribute obscenity.

A new approach to defining obscenity, based on feminism rather than traditional morality, emerged in the 1980s. This theory asserts that obscenity should be curbed because it "is central in creating and maintaining the civil inequality of the sexes," from employment opportunities to crimes directed at women, such as rape, battery and prostitution.[324] Feminists Andrea Dworkin and Catharine MacKinnon, a law professor, drafted a model city ordinance in 1983 that suppressed "pornography," defined as "the sexually explicit subordination of women, graphically depicted, whether in pictures or words." The ordinance listed several examples of pornography, such as where "women are presented dehumanized as sexual objects, things or commodities" or as enjoying being raped, beaten or otherwise degraded or humiliated. These types of laws would have given *any* woman the right to sue various persons trafficking or otherwise responsible for pornography for damages arising from their activities. However, in one case involving a version of the model ordinance enacted in Indianapolis, the U.S. Court of Appeals held that it violated the 1st Amendment on the ground that it regulated material, based on its content, that was not obscene under the *Miller* test. The Supreme Court summarily affirmed this decision.[325]

Under yet another recent approach, states and cities have dealt with sexually explicit expression, not by trying to close "adult" establishments under anti-obscenity laws, but by using zoning laws to confine them to certain areas cities and towns. Often this holds more promise of success because municipalities enjoy wide zoning powers and such measures are not complete prohibitions on expression.[326]

2. Time, Place and Manner Restrictions on Protected Expression

Different Rules for Different Places of Expression The government may completely prohibit speech that is seditious, a mechanism of illegal conduct, or obscene, provided it meets the Court's definitions of these categories. While the 1st Amendment protects all other forms of speech, the government may regulate it depending on the setting in which it occurs. For example, the government may not regulate expression on one's private property. If expression takes place on the private property of another, the private owner – but not the government – may prohibit the expression.[327] Most commonly, however, speakers use public property for expression. In such cases, some regulation

---

323 *United States v. Williams*, 553 U.S. 285, 297 (2008).

324 Proposed ordinance of the City of Minneapolis, Minnesota. To view the ordinance, which the city council passed but the mayor vetoed in 1984, see Nadine Strossen, *Is Minnesota Progressive? A Focus On Sexually Oriented Expression*, 33 WM. MITCHELL L. REV. 51 (2006).

325 *American Booksellers Ass'n v. Hudnut*, 771 F.2d 323 (7th Cir. 1985), *aff'd mem.* 475 U.S. 1001 (1986). A summary affirmance is considered to have precedential value. For opposing viewpoints of commentators, *see* MacKinnon, *supra* note 291, and Nadine Strossen, *The Convergence of Feminist and Civil Liberties Principles in the Pornography Debate* (Book Review), 62 N.Y.U. L.Rev. 201 (1987). A more feminist definition of pornography discussed has met with better favor in Canada. *See Butler v. Regina*, 134 Nat'l Rep. 81 (Sup. Ct. of Canada 1992).

326 *See infra* p. 380, where the use of zoning and other incomplete prohibitions are discussed.

327 *See Lloyd Corp. v. Tanner*, 407 U.S. 551 (1972) and *Hudgens v. Nat'l Labor Relations Bd.*, 424 U.S. 507 (1976) (expressive activity properly prohibited by owners of private shopping malls despite their having some of the characteristics of a public forum).

may be constitutional. To what degree the government may regulate expression depends on whether it takes place in a "traditional public forum," a "designated public forum," or a "non-public forum." The Court established these three categories of public property in *Perry Education Association v. Perry Local Educators' Association.*[328]

Traditional Public Forums A traditional public forum includes public streets and parks, which "have immemorially been held in trust for the use of the public and time out of mind, have been used for purposes of assembly, communicating thoughts between citizens, and discussing public questions."[329] The right to expression is at its broadest in public forums. The government generally may not prohibit any form of expression protected by the 1st Amendment. It may impose reasonable time, place and manner regulations unrelated to content, but then only if those restrictions leave open sufficient alternative means for expression.

The most common content-neutral governmental interest that expressive conduct affects is disruption of traffic. However, laws allowing officials to deny permits must be narrowly drawn to prevent abuse under the pretext of time, place and manner regulation.[330] In *Heffron v. International Society for Krishna Consciousness,*[331] religious proselytizers sought to distribute their literature by walking among the crowd at a state fairground. A state fair regulation required that distribution of all merchandise, including written materials, take place only from approved booths on the fairground. The Court held that crowded conditions at the relatively congested fairground area were a sufficient reason for such regulation. The Court noted that the rule regulated only one means of communication — distribution of merchandise and materials — thus leaving open other means of communication.[332]

Complete prohibition of some expressive activity is possible if a substantial government interest supports the restriction and it is not content-based. The Court held in *Boos v. Barry*[333] that a law prohibiting critical picketing of foreign embassies (but permitting more positive picketing) was content-based and therefore invalid. However, the Court also approved, in that same case, a complete ban on congregations of persons within 500 feet of a foreign embassy if such gatherings posed a security threat. However, the absence of any such substantial interest led the Court to invalidate a law prohibiting all signs and leaflets on the sidewalk in front of a federal building.[334]

Picketing in residential areas has been a controversial issue partly because anti-abortion activists use it to "expose" doctors who perform abortions. Streets and sidewalks of a residential area, no less that the streets in a business district, are traditional public forums. However, the Court held in *Frisby v. Schultz*[335] that a city can ban

---

328 460 U.S. 37 (1983).

329 *Hague v. Congress of Industrial Organizations*, 307 U.S. 496 (1939).

330 *See and compare Cox v. New Hampshire*, 312 U.S. 569 (1941) (upholding denial of permit for religious organizers to parade to advertise a religious meeting) *with Shuttlesworth v. Birmingham*, 394 U.S. 147 (1969) (holding unconstitutional city's denial of a permit for a civil rights march organized by Martin Luther King).

331 452 U.S. 640 (1981).

332 *See also Grayned v. City of Rockford*, 408 U.S. 104 (1972) (a ban on loud picketing on sidewalk near schools is permissible); *Ward v. Rock Against Racism*, 491 U.S. 781 (1989) (city noise regulation of sound system at outdoor concert is permissible).

333 485 U.S. 312 (1988).

334 *United States v. Grace,* 461 U.S. 171 (1983).

335 487 U.S. 474 (1988).

"all focused picketing taking place solely in front of a *particular* residence." The rationale was that "focused" picketers "do not seek to disseminate a message to the general public, but to intrude upon the targeted resident, and to do so in an especially offensive way." Another abortion-related case, *Hill v. Colorado*,[336] involved a state law that made it unlawful, within 100 feet (30 meters) of any health care facility, to "knowingly approach" within eight feet (2.5 meters) of another person, without that person's consent, "for the purpose of passing a leaflet or handbill to, displaying a sign to, or engaging in oral protest, education, or counseling with such other person." The law primarily applied to abortion protesters who would harass patients and workers entering abortion clinics. Noting that the law was content neutral and left open many other avenues for expression, however, the Court upheld it.

Designated Public Forums A designated public forum is any public property other than a traditional public forum that the government has designated as a public forum by opening it for use by the public as a place for expressive activity. Generally, the same rules govern designated public forums and traditional public forums. However, the government has more control over designated public forums in two ways. First, it may "undesignate" the forum, *i.e.*, cancel its designated status as a public forum, thus subjecting it to the less permissive rules applicable to non-public forums. Second, the government may limit the groups of people who have access. For example, a state university can limit its public forum facilities solely to its own students, provided these limitations are not based on the viewpoint of the excluded speech.[337] Thus, it violated the 1st Amendment when a public school district's regulation permitted after-hours use of school facilities for "social, civic and recreational purposes" by private organizations, but denied access to a religious organization that wanted to show a film on family values and child rearing that represented a religious viewpoint. The Court held that the school's policy discriminated on the basis of viewpoint because it permitted the presentation of all views about family issues and child rearing except those dealing with the subject from a religious standpoint.[338] Similarly, in *Rosenberger v. Rector and Visitors of the University of Virginia*, the Court invalidated a state university's policy of excluding religious groups from a program funding student organization publications.[339]

Non-Public Forums A non-public forum is any other government property accessible to the public that is not generally suited for expressive activities, but is capable of being used that way. The government may "reserve [such non-public forum property] for its intended purposes . . . as long as the regulation on speech is reasonable and not an effort to suppress expression merely because public officials oppose the speaker's views."[340] Thus, the Court has allowed bans on all partisan political activity on a military

---

336 530 U.S. 703 (2000).

337 *Widmar v. Vincent*, 454 U.S. 263 (1981).

338 *Lamb's Chapel v. Center Moriches Union Free School District*, 508 U.S. 384 (1993). *See also Good News Club v. Milford Central High School*, 533 U.S. 98 (2001) (same).

339 515 U.S. 819 (1995). *See also Bd. of Regents of the University of Wisconsin v. Southworth*, 529 U.S. 217 (2000) (upholding system of funding student organizations, but only if funding is distributed on a viewpoint-neutral basis); *Christian Legal Soc. Chapter v. Martinez*, ___ U.S. ___, 130 S.Ct. 2971 (2010) (law school's requirement that Christian Legal Society accept anyone as a member regardless of religion or sexual orientation if it wants to be an official student organization is a reasonable, viewpoint-neutral condition).

340 *Perry Education Association, supra* note 328 at 46.

base[341] and on non-profit political advocacy groups from charitable solicitation drives in federal government offices.[342] The government justified the bans on its interest in avoiding the appearance of political favoritism. Thus, the government may constitutionally impose content-based, but viewpoint-neutral, restrictions on access to a non-public forum, so long as the restriction is reasonably related to the purpose for which the property is being used. The non-public forum in the *Perry Education Association* case was the school district's interschool mail system. The Court found nothing wrong with the school district allowing the union that represented its teachers to send materials through the system, while denying access to other groups, including a rival union.

Problems with the Perry Test The *Perry* three-category test seems tidy, but there are problems, both in categorizing the forum and applying the test. Two cases illustrate this point. In a 1990 case, the Court tried to apply the *Perry* test to a sidewalk connecting a post office to a parking lot. A badly split Court held that the post office could ban solicitations on the sidewalk, but the justices could not agree on whether the particular sidewalk was a public or non-public forum.[343] In a1992 case, it held that authorities could prohibit Hare Krishna proselytizers from soliciting funds and handing out leaflets in New York airports.[344] A majority of the Court reasoned that the"traditional public forum" test was purely *historical* and that airports — a relatively new phenomenon — were not *traditional* public forums. The restriction on soliciting funds was reasonable because passengers would have to stop, engage the solicitor in conversation and perhaps reach into a pocket or purse, thus disrupting passenger pedestrian traffic. However, a different majority of the Court struck down the airport's ban on *distributing leaflets* as unreasonable because leafleting is not as problematic as soliciting funds. Four dissenting justices argued that an airport was a public forum because "expressive activity has been a commonplace feature of our Nation's airports for many years." However, despite its public forum status, the dissent agreed that solicitation of funds *could* be banned, thus appearing to endorse a test for public forums that is more restrictive than that underlying *Perry* and other cases.

Two other crucial issues relating to designated public forums are: what power the government has *in its designation* to deny access to certain categories of persons or organizations, and precisely what are "content-neutral," as opposed to "viewpoint-neutral," regulations.[345] These issues arose in *Arkansas Education Television Commission v. Forbes*.[346] In that case, the Court upheld a state-owned public television station's decision to exclude a candidate from a televised debate because he had little popular support. The debate was a non-public forum, from which the station could exclude him "in the reasonable, viewpoint-neutral exercise of its journalistic discretion." The Court used —— but did not wholeheartedly endorse —— the *Perry* test.[347] Dissenters objected that the station had created a designated public forum for political discourse and could

---

341 *Greer v. Spock*, 424 U.S. 828 (1976).

342 *Cornelius v. NAACP Legal Defense & Education Fund*, 473 U.S. 788 (1985).

343 *United States v. Kokinda*, 497 U.S. 720 (1990).

344 *International Society for Krishna Consciousness Inc v. Lee*, 505 U.S. 672 (1992).

345 *See* the duel between the majority and the dissent in *Rosenberger, supra* note 339.

346 523 U.S. 666 (1998).

347 In discussing the applicable law, the Court in *Forbes* noted dryly: "[f]or our purposes here, it will suffice to employ the [*Perry*] categories of speech fora already established and discussed in our cases." *Forbes, supra* note 345 at 677.

not "undesignate" certain ballot-qualified candidates except pursuant to clear, objective, predetermined standards, not by an *ad hoc* decision. Otherwise, officials could exclude a speaker based on viewpoint and then to make up a viewpoint-neutral category to cover the real reason for the exclusion.

3. Regulating Symbolic Expression

Words are clearly a form of expression, but one can express a political or other viewpoint by engaging in conduct. Such action is commonly referred to as "symbolic speech." But the 1st Amendment does not protect all expressive conduct. A politically motivated assassination is clearly expressive conduct, but no one would suggest it is protected. In a prominent symbolic expression case, *United States v. O'Brien*,[348] the Court held that the government could constitutionally punish burning a draft registration card — a popular form of protest against the Vietnam War. According to the Court, draft card burning involved more than just expressive activity; it also involved disruption of an administrative system. In *O'Brien*, the Court developed a test for judging activity that involves both protected symbolic "speech" and unprotected "non-speech elements." Regulation of non-communicative elements of conduct will be valid if (1) "it furthers an important or substantial governmental interest," (2) that interest is "unrelated to the suppression of free expression" and (3) the "incidental restriction" on the activity "is no greater than is essential to the furtherance of that interest."

The requirement that the government interest be "unrelated to suppression of free expression" has been the basis for striking down several laws punishing particular conduct. For example, in *Texas v. Johnson*,[349] the defendant was prosecuted for burning a U.S. flag. Texas asserted its interest was preserving the flag as a symbol of nationhood and national unity. However, the Court rejected this as directly "related to the suppression of free expression." It reasoned that, if destruction of a flag had a negative impact on these interests, it was *precisely because* the conduct communicated a message of casting contempt on the flag.[350] There was a spirited dissent in the case and a public furor over the decision that included calls to amend the Constitution to overrule the Court. Congress passed a federal "anti-flag-burning" statute that punished the simple act of destroying or defacing without reference to casting contempt or "desecrating" — in essence an attempt to come within the *O'Brien* guidelines. The Court nonetheless held that statute unconstitutional.[351]

4. Means of Regulating Expression

Prior Restraints There are various ways that the government can try to regulate expression. Most often the government does not anticipate the expression. But when it does, the government sometimes seeks an injunction. Generally, any such form of "prior restraint" is unconstitutional. Civil or criminal liability *after* expression takes place is normally the only means of obtaining redress for harm done. In *Near v. Minnesota*,[352] a newspaper planned to publish an article accusing city officials and the mayor of

---

348 391 U.S. 367 (1968).

349 491 U.S. 397 (1989).

350 *See also Tinker v. Des Moines School District*, 393 U.S. 503 (1969) (secondary school's ban on students wearing black armbands to protest Vietnam War, but not on wearing other political symbols was improper regulation of expression not otherwise justified).

351 *United States v. Eichman*, 496 U.S. 310 (1990).

352 283 U.S. 697 (1931).

corruption. A state court issued an injunction against publication, finding that the charges in the article were unsubstantiated. The Supreme Court reversed the injunction. It held that, if the statements in the article were not true, city officials could sue later for libel. But even untrue publication could not be enjoined beforehand.

Another landmark case on prior restraint was *New York Times Co. v. United States*,[353] the "Pentagon Papers" case. There the Court invalidated an injunction prohibiting publication, during the Vietnam War, of a secret government study on the war that a disgruntled defense department employee had leaked to the press. The Court rejected the government's argument that publication would endanger national security or embarrass U.S. allies. Absent the government proving that the study contained specific information on movements of troops or other material the enemy could have used, an injunction was unconstitutional.

The Court has permitted injunctions in other areas of expression. For example, an injunction may properly restrict dissemination of obscenity because it is not protected expression at all,[354] so long as there is an opportunity for a prior hearing on the issue of whether the material is obscene under the 1st Amendment.[355] The Court has also approved injunctions against anti-abortion protesters seeking to disrupt the operations of abortion clinics and to discourage patients from going there. In one case, protesters had set up numerous blockades and disruptions of clinic operations. The Court upheld part of the injunction, which banned certain disruptive conduct near the clinic and *all* demonstrations within a "buffer zone" of 15 feet around the clinic. However, the Court struck down the "floating buffer zone" around all patients entering or leaving the clinic as burdening more speech than necessary. The normal rule against prior restraints was inapplicable because the injunction was unrelated to content, left other channels of communication open and was based on prior unlawful conduct of the demonstrators.[356]

Taxation and Forfeiture of Profits The government is limited in its ability to impose financial burdens on speech based on its content. In *Arkansas Writers' Project v. Ragland*,[357] the Court invalidated a tax scheme that taxed "general interest" publications, but not religious, professional, trade or sports publications. The law was unconstitutional because it was content-based even though the state did not intend to hinder expression by the burdened category of publications. Also held unconstitutional was a New York law that allowed the State Crime Victims Compensation Board to seize all profits from publication of a book about a crime written by the perpetrator. In *Simon &*

---

353 403 U.S. 713 (1971).

354 *Paris Adult Theatre v. Slaton*, 413 U.S. 49 (1973).

355 *Kingsley Books, Inc. v. Brown*, 354 U.S. 436 (1957); *Freedman v. Maryland*, 380 U.S. 51 (1965).

356 *Schenck v. Pro-Choice Network of Western New York*, 519 U.S. 357 (1997). *See also Madsen v. Women's Health Center*, 512 U.S. 753 (1994) (36-foot buffer zone in front of clinic and noise restrictions upheld; restriction on approaching patients within 300 fee of the clinic invalid). *But see Hill v. Colorado*, 530 U.S. 703 (2000) (approving 8-foot zone around persons within 100 feet of any health care facility), discussed *infra* p. 376. The Court distinguished *Madsen* on the grounds that only unwilling listeners were covered, that the zone was smaller and that protesters could remain stationary in the path of a listener and not violate the statute.

357 481 U.S. 221 (1987).

Schuster, Inc. v. Members of the N.Y. State Crime Victims Comm.,[358] the Court struck down the law because it singled out certain publications based on content.

Private Tort Actions The 1st Amendment prohibits courts, from enforcing certain private damages claims. In *New York Times Co. v. Sullivan*,[359] the Court held that when public officials and "public figures" bring defamation and similar tort actions 1st Amendment concerns arise because these claims could "chill" or discourage discussion of public issues. To sustain such claims, public officials or public figures must prove with "convincing clarity" that the defendant writer or publisher's statement was knowingly false or made with "reckless disregard" for its truth or falsity.[360]

Zoning At least in the area of sexually explicit expression, the Court has given governments broad powers to regulate the location of shops selling sexually explicit materials, even though those materials are not obscene. The Court has approved a city ordinance prohibiting adult theaters within 1,000 feet of any residence, church, park or school based on the government interest in regulating the "secondary effects" of such theaters, such as crime, lowered property values and spoiling the quality of neighborhoods.[361] Nude dancing, though not necessarily obscene, may be completely banned, at least in state-regulated bars. In *Barnes v. Glen Theater, Inc.*,[362] the Court admitted that there was undoubtedly some 1st Amendment protection for nude dancing, but the Indiana law was content-neutral in its prohibition of all public nudity and applied only to bars, thus permitting such activities in other establishments. States enjoy broad power when it comes to liquor regulation because of the 21st Amendment of the Constitution.[363] However, not all protected expression is equal in this regard. Protected sexually explicit expression probably ranks lower than other protected forms of expression. One would have difficulty imagining the Constitution allowing a state to ban political debates in bars or within 1,000 feet of any school or residence.

Unconstitutional Conditions and Conditional Funding The classic unconstitutional condition case is *Speiser v. Randall*.[364] In that case, California required veterans to sign a statement disavowing any belief in overthrowing the government by force as a condition for receiving their veteran's property tax exemption. The Court struck it down, maintaining that denial of an exemption to those who would not sign served to "penalize" them for their views and "coerce" them to refrain from the proscribed speech. Since *Speiser*, however, the Court has been less than consistent in its application of the

---

358 502 U.S. 105 (1991). *But see Snepp v. United States*, 444 U.S. 507 (1980) (per curiam) (approving government seizure of profits from book published by a former CIA employee in violation of pre-employment agreement to obtain prepublication clearance).

359 376 U.S. 254 (1974). *See also Philadelphia Newspapers, Inc. v. Hepps*, 475 U.S. 767 (1986); *Gertz v. Robert Welch, Inc.*, 418 U.S. 323 (1974) (cases involving public figures rather than public officials). The *New York Times* rule applies as well to actions for invasion of privacy and for infliction of emotional distress, as discussed in Chapter XI, pp. 457-460.

360 *Time, Inc. v. Hill*, 385 U.S. 374 (1967); *Hustler Magazine, Inc. v. Falwell*, 485 U.S. 46 (1988). For more detail on the *New York Times* standard, *see* Chapter XI, pp. 457-460.

361 *City of Renton v. Playtime Theaters*, 475 U.S. 41 (1986), disagreement recognized by *Boos v. Barry*, 485 U.S. 312 (1988).

362 501 U.S. 560 (1991).

363 *California v. LaRue*, 409 U.S. 109 (1972). The 21st Amendment repealed the 18th Amendment, which had established "prohibition," a complete ban of alcoholic drink in the entire United States, which existed from 1920 to 1933. Despite efforts to enforce it, liquor was widely sold and consumed in the country. The 21st Amendment ended prohibition by giving liquor control to the states.

364 357 U.S. 513 (1958).

doctrine. The problem is that it is impossible for the government to subsidize all expression, so funding less than all expression can be recast simply as not being "coercion" against anyone or any viewpoint, but as an inevitable and unavoidable choice. For example, in *Rust v. Sullivan*,[365] the Court upheld a funding program for family planning services projects that prohibited employees of funded projects (primarily doctors and other health-care professionals) from "provid[ing] counseling concerning the use of abortion as a method of family planning" or from referring a pregnant woman to an abortion provider, even upon her specific request. The Court reasoned that Congress had not discriminated against viewpoints on abortion, but had "merely chosen to fund one activity to the exclusion of the other." The program sought to fund only family planning services prior to pregnancy and excluded abortion as a method of family planning, thus rendering advice about abortion beyond the scope of the program. The restrictions were considered necessary "to ensure that the limits of the federal program [were] observed."

In *Legal Services Corp. v. Velazquez*,[366] the Court took a different stance and revised the *Rust* rationale. *Velazquez* struck down conditions on federal funding of legal services for the poor that prohibited lawyers employed by programs funded under the law from representing clients in any effort to amend or otherwise challenge existing welfare law. The Court distinguished between *Rust*, which involved the funding of a governmental message, and *Velazquez*, where the government sought to fund private expression — communication of advice to and representation of clients. Thus, in *Rust*, the government decided on a particular policy and spent money to espouse it, but did not choose to espouse the opposite view. Supposedly this is more permissible than funding private expression of a given viewpoint, because in the case of government speech, those who dislike the message can vote the officials who created the policy out of office. However, the Court's distinction is not very satisfying because voters have an equally effective — or ineffective — remedy when the government funds private speech with which voters disagree. Indeed, one could argue that direct government sponsorship of a message is more pernicious for the government's obvious sponsorship of it.[367]

In a case involving subsidy of artistic projects, *National Endowment for the Arts v. Finley*,[368] the Court upheld a federal statute Congress had passed in reaction to the National Endowment for the Arts (NEA) funding art projects that many members of Congress considered offensive.[369] The statute, passed after bitter debate, required that the NEA, in making its funding decision, "tak[e] into consideration general standards of decency and respect for the diverse beliefs and values of the American public," as well as the "artistic worth" of proposed projects. The Court observed that the NEA's decision was a group one that was necessarily subjective and took into account a wide variety of factors, including various ideas of what "decency and respect" meant. The Court also

---

365 500 U.S. 173 (1991).

366 531 U.S. 533 (2001).

367 *Compare Fed. Communications Comm'n v. League of Women Voters of California*, 468 U.S. 364 (1984) (holding unconstitutional federal statute prohibiting grantees of federal public broadcasting corporation from broadcasting editorials) *with Regan v. Taxation with Representation of Washington*, 461 U.S. 540 (1983) (holding constitutional denial of tax exemptions for non-profit organizations that seek to influence legislation).

368 524 U.S. 569 (1998).

369 Among the works were *The Perfect Moment*, which included homoerotic photographs, and *Piss Christ*, a photograph of a crucifix immersed in urine.

felt that the nature of the criteria did not expressly "threaten censorship of ideas," so there was no realistic danger that the criteria would compromise 1st Amendment values.[370]

Compelled Speech　As some of the cases above suggest, the 1st Amendment prevents the government from "compelling speech" with which a person disagrees. The classic case is *Wooley v. Maynard*,[371] in which a Jehovah's Witness was prosecuted for putting tape over the motto of New Hampshire, ironically enough "Live Free or Die," which appeared on all New Hampshire car license plates. The Court held the prosecution unconstitutional. And in *West Virginia State Bd. of Education v. Barnette*,[372] the Court invalidated a state law requiring that school children either salute the U.S. flag or recite a pledge honoring it. More commonly, cases in this genre have involved government requirements that individuals pay subsidies for speech to which they object. Thus, in *Abood v. Detroit Board of Education*,[373] the Court held that a state public employees' union could not use the dues of employees, over their objection, to pay for ideological causes not germane to its duties as a collective-bargaining representative. In *Keller v. State Bar of California*,[374] California lawyers, who were required by state law to become a member of the State Bar of California in order to practice law, won the right to avoid paying that portion of their dues that financed activities of the organized bar beyond those connected with regulating the profession and improving the quality of legal services. The Court has even applied the concept to commercial speech. In *United States v. United Foods, Inc.*,[375] federal law required mushroom producers to pay into a fund used to advertise the benefits of eating mushrooms. The Court struck down this part of the law at the behest of a mushroom grower who believed its mushrooms were superior. The fact that the speech in this case was arguably commercial made little difference to the Court. In *Rumsfeld v. Forum for Academic and Institutional Rights, Inc.*,[376] however, the Court held that the federal government did not compel speech by requiring, on penalty of losing federal funding for education, that law schools permit military recruiters to interview on their premises, even though the schools objected to the military denying homosexuals the right to serve in the military.

Indirect "Chilling" of 1st Amendment Rights　Whenever the government passes criminal laws, those laws must be specific and clear. If a law is either vague or is so broad as to include some activity that *may* be protected by the 1st Amendment, courts can strike down the law on the doctrines of "vagueness" or "overbreadth." These doctrines stem from the due process clause, rather than the 1st Amendment, but often appear in free speech cases. Thus, a city ordinance that prohibited anyone from standing on a sidewalk in the city and "there conduct[ing] themselves in a manner annoying to persons passing by" was invalidated on its face as overbroad.[377] Though some such activity might be punishable consistent with the Constitution, much of this

---

370 *See* Kathleen Sullivan, *Unconstitutional Conditions*, 102 HARVARD LAW REV. 1413 (1989).

371 430 U.S. 705 (1977).

372 319 U.S. 624 (1943).

373 431 U.S. 209 (1977).

374 496 U.S. 1 (1990).

375 533 U.S. 405 (2001). *But see Glickman v. Wileman Brothers & Elliott, Inc.*, 521 U.S. 457 (1997) (federally mandated assessments for similar advertising in tree-fruit industry constitutional where ancillary to a more comprehensive program restricting marketing autonomy in a volatile market).

376 547 U.S. 47 (2006).

377 *See Coates v. Cincinnati*, 402 U.S. 611 (1971).

kind of activity could well be protected by the 1st Amendment. Similarly, in *City of Chicago v. Morales*,[378] the Court struck down an "anti-gang" ordinance that, among other things, required police officers to order people who were "loitering" — defined as "remain[ing] in any one place with no apparent purpose" — to disperse. Such an order was appropriate if the officer "reasonably believe[d]" one of the loiterers "to be a criminal street gang member." The statute was so broad that it covered a "substantial amount of innocent conduct" and "necessarily entrust[ed] lawmaking to the moment-to-moment judgment of the policeman on his beat."

The Court has resorted to overbreadth and vagueness when it is not yet ready to specify the boundaries of protected 1st Amendment behavior. For example, flag-burning has been with us for some time as a means of protest. Yet, it was only in 1986 in *Texas v. Johnson* that the Court provided a definitive answer to the 1st Amendment question. The Court had sidestepped the 1st Amendment issue several years earlier using vagueness. It reversed the conviction of a man who had sewn a flag on the seat of his pants, doing so on the ground that the statutory phrase "treats [the flag] contemptuously" was unconstitutionally vague under the due process clause.[379] Similarly, in 1987 the Court held that a resolution banning all "First Amendment activities" in an airport terminal was unconstitutionally overbroad, thus making it unnecessary to decide whether the 1st Amendment would have protected the activities. Then in 1992, the Court in the *Hare Krishna* case discussed above decided the question of what expressive activities in airport terminals are protected by the 1st Amendment.[380]

5. Some Special Issues in Freedom of Expression

Regulation of Electronic Media   Because the airwaves needed for broadcasting television and radio signals are limited and belong to the public, the 1st Amendment does not prohibit the Federal Communications Commission (FCC) from regulating broadcasting "in the public interest," as Congress has authorized it to do. Thus, many forms of governmental regulation that would be unconstitutional as applied to newspapers or books can be properly applied to the broadcast media. For example, the FCC can require broadcast media to provide "equal time" to political spokespersons with differing views, even though newspapers may not.[381] The FCC's power is considerable. In *Federal Communications Comm'n v. Pacifica Foundation*,[382] the Court upheld the FCC's power to ban "patently offensive" (but not obscene) words, noting the special nature of radio transmission, which "confronts the citizen, not only in public, but also in the privacy of the home." One the other hand, the Court in 1996 struck down a federal statute that required cable television operators to "block and segregate" all sexually explicit programs, meaning that they were required to provide a separate channel for such broadcasts and block transmission of them unless they received a written request from a cable subscriber. While protection of children was a "compelling interest," the

---

378 527 U.S. 41 (1999). *See also United States v. Stevens*, ___ U.S. ___; 130 S.Ct. 1577 (2010) (striking down as overbroad a federal law criminalizing the sale or possession of "depictions of animal cruelty").

379 *See Smith v. Goguen*, 415 U.S. 566 (1974).

380 *See and compare Board of Airport Commissioners of Los Angeles v. Jews for Jesus*, 482 U.S. 569 (1987) and *International Society for Krishna Consciousness v. Lee*, 505 U.S. 672 (1992).

381 *Compare Red Lion Broadcasting Co. v. Fed. Communications Comm'n.*, 395 U.S. 367 (1967) ("fairness doctrine" for broadcast media) *with Miami Herald Publishing Co. v. Tornillo*, 418 U.S. 241 (1969) (rejecting "fairness" limits on print media). *See also Turner Broadcasting System v. Federal Communications Comm'n*, 520 U.S. 180 (1997).

382 438 U.S. 726 (1978).

Court concluded that the government could protect that interest using less restrictive means.[383]

The Court has treated the Internet differently. In *Reno v. American Civil Liberties Union*,[384] the Court struck down the Communications Decency Act of 1996, which prohibited Internet transmission of indecent communications to persons under age 18. The Court held that the Internet is fully subject to the 1st Amendment, observing that it is not as invasive as radio or television, nor could a person come across sexually explicit materials on the Internet by accident. Then, in *Ashcroft v. American Civil Liberties Union*,[385] the Court held in the context of a motion for a preliminary injunction that the Child Online Protection Act, which Congress passed in reaction to *Reno*, was likely unconstitutional because there were less drastic means of preventing dissemination of material "harmful to minors."[386] However, in *United States v. American Library Association*,[387] the Court upheld a federal law requiring libraries receiving federal funds to use software to block obscenity, child pornography and sex-related material "harmful for minors," so long as the statute permitted adults to request unblocking.

Political Campaign Funding Scandals in political campaigning have led Congress and the states to impose limitations on various campaign practices. However, speech in the electoral process is at the heart of the 1st Amendment, so some of these restrictions have had a difficult time in the Supreme Court. In general, the Court has distinguished between limits on campaign *expenditures*, which it has generally struck down, and limits on campaign *contributions*, which it has generally permitted.[388] The reason for the distinction is that contributions are more clearly linked to political corruption than political spending. However, it was easy to make "disguised contributions" by having a would-be contributor simply spend the money on advertising or other efforts to support the candidate, rather than contributing directly to his or her campaign. Anticipating this problem, federal election laws have sought to limit "coordinated expenditures" — "expenditures made by any person in cooperation, consultation, or concert, with, or at the request or suggestion of, a candidate, his authorized political committees, or their agents." In *Fed. Election Comm'n v. Colorado Republican Federal Campaign Comm.*,[389] political organizations argued that this limit should not apply to political parties. The Court disagreed and upheld limits on political party coordinated expenditures on behalf of candidates.

Until recently, the Court allowed much more regulation of campaign contributions from corporations, because corporations generate immense wealth unrelated to the degree of political support for the ideas espoused by the corporation. The Bipartisan

---

383 *Denver Area Education Telecommunications Consortium, Inc. v. Fed. Communications Comm'n*, 518 U.S. 727 (1996).

384 521 U.S. 844 (1997). *Cf. Sable Communications v. Fed. Communications Comm'n*, 492 U.S. 115 (1989) (holding unconstitutional a federal law that prohibited "sexually oriented prerecorded telephone messages," because the messages did not come into the home involuntarily).

385 542 U.S. 656 (2004).

386 For a preliminary injunction, only a showing of *likelihood* of success on the merits is required. *See* Chapter VII, p. 246.

387 539 U.S. 194 (2003).

388 *Buckley v. Valeo*, 424 U.S. 1 (1976) (federal law limits); *Nixon v. Shrink Missouri Government PAC*, 528 U.S. 377 (2000) (state law limits). *Cf. Fed. Elections Comm'n v. Nat'l Conservative Political Action Comm.*, 470 U.S. 480 (1985) (federal limit of $1,000 on spending by political action committees invalid).

389 533 U.S. 431 (2001).

Campaign Reform Act of 2002 (BCRA) prohibited corporations and labor unions from using their general treasury funds to make "electioneering communications," those which expressly advocate the election or defeat of a candidate.[390] However, in a landmark 2010 case,[391] the Court held that the 1st Amendment prohibited the government from suppressing political speech on the basis of the speaker's corporate identity. Although the Court upheld provisions requiring corporations to disclose their expenditures and identify the source of political advertisements, the fact that corporations may now draw on their vast treasuries to influence political campaigns will certainly affect politics in the United States.

Expressive Association Implicit in the right to engage in activities protected by the 1st Amendment is "a corresponding right to associate with others in pursuit of a wide variety of political, social, economic, educational, religious, and cultural ends."[392] Government action that directly suppresses such organizations is unconstitutional, as is indirect action that has that effect. Thus, in *NAACP v. Alabama ex rel. Patterson,*[393] the Court struck down a court order requiring that the NAACP disclose the names and addresses of its members, because the order could have induced members to withdraw from the NAACP and dissuade others from joining it because they feared the consequences of this exposure.[394] On the other hand, the Court has held that the right to free association does not prohibit compulsory union "service fees" paid by nonmembers in "closed shops" and used to benefit the labor union,[395] laws banning payroll deductions from public employees for political causes,[396] and laws regulating how political parties select candidates who will appear on the ballot.[397]

State laws requiring that organizations admit persons whose views clash with the organization can run afoul of the 1st Amendment if the law "impose[s] serious burdens" on the group's "collective effort on behalf of [its] shared goals."[398] For example, in *Boy Scouts of America v. Dale,*[399] a New Jersey law prohibited discrimination against

---

390 2 U.S.C.A. §441b.

391 *Citizens United v. Federal Election Comm.,*___ U.S. ___; 130 S.Ct. 876 (2010).

392 *Roberts v. United States Jaycees,* 468 U.S. 609, 622 (1984).

393 357 U.S. 449 (1958).

394 "NAACP" stands for the National Association for the Advancement of Colored People. It is a racial minority rights advocacy group. The NAACP case was decided in 1958 — in the midst of the of struggle of blacks in the south to end segregation — when the possibility of violence against members of any civil rights groups was real. *See supra* p. 353, where segregation in the south is in the 1950s is discussed. *Compare Doe v. Reed,* ___ U.S. ___, 130 S.Ct. 2811 (2010) (in face of 1st Amendment challenge, state interest in integrity of electoral process justifies disclosure of referendum petitions seeking repeal of same-sex domestic partner law, with names and addresses of persons who signed them; if specific harm to signers could be shown, 1st Amendment might dictate different result).

395 *Locke v. Karass,* ___ U.S. ___; 129 S.Ct. 798 (2009) (use of compulsory union dues from nonmembers by national union organization to fund its non-political national litigation does not offend 1st Amendment). *Cf. Davenport v. Washington Educ. Ass'n,* 551 U.S. 177 (2007) (upholding state law requiring labor union to obtain approval of nonmember before spending fees for political purposes).

396 *Ysursa v. Pocatello Educ. Ass'n,* ___ U.S. ___; 129 S.Ct. 1093 (2009) (state law prohibiting public employee payroll deductions for political causes has rational basis and does not offend 1st Amendment).

397 *Washington State Grange v. Washington State Republican Party,* 552 U.S. 442 (2008) (state law establishing "blanket primary" system for choosing which candidates appear on the ballot does not affect associational rights, even if there is a risk of voter confusion); *New York State Bd. of Elections v. Lopez Torres,* 552 U.S. 196 (2008) (New York statute regulating selection process for state judicial candidates does not offend their associational rights).

398 *Roberts v. United States Jaycees,* 468 U.S. at 622, 626-627.

399 530 U.S. 640 (2000).

homosexuals. A Boy Scout leader filed a claim under the law when the Boy Scouts fired him for being a homosexual. The Court held that the organization stood for values so antithetical to homosexuality that the presence of a gay activist as scoutmaster would seriously undercut the organization's ability to advocate its views. However, in *Roberts v. United States Jaycees*[400] and *Board of Directors of Rotary Int'l v. Rotary Club of Duarte*,[401] the Court rejected similar arguments made by the Jaycees and the Rotary Club in support of their men-only membership rules. The Court permitted states to apply their sex discrimination laws against these organizations, forcing them to admit women.[402]

Press Access to Criminal Trials The press and the public have a right under the 1st Amendment to attend criminal trials, even over a defendant's objection. At the same time, the accused in a criminal case has the right to an impartial jury and a fair trial.[403] However, courts may not control the press in a way that infringes on 1st Amendment rights unless it is absolutely essential to prevent a serious threat to the fairness of the proceedings.[404] A "prior restraint" on publication of information adduced at trial is presumptively invalid.[405] Privacy interests of participants are an insufficient justification for closing a proceeding or prohibiting publicity. Thus, in *Globe Newspaper Co. v. Superior Court*,[406] the Court invalidated the routine exclusion of the press and public during testimony of child victims of sexual abuse. A state may even permit television broadcast of a criminal trial over a criminal defendant's objection.[407] Today, in Florida, California and many other states, one can watch court proceedings on television. A cable television network, Court TV, broadcasts trials across the nation

Reporter Privileges The press and the courts have also clashed where prosecutors demand that journalists relinquish criminal evidence that only they possess. In *Branzburg v. Hayes*,[408] a reporter was jailed for refusing to comply with a subpoena for his notes on a news story on illegal drug manufacturing. The reporter argued that he had promised his sources confidentiality and that no one would talk to him if the police could get his notes. The Court held that the interest of the police in investigating criminal activity justified the interference with his interest in reporting the news. However, a concurring opinion of Justice Powell, purporting to endorse the majority opinion, adopted a case-by-case balancing test suggesting that, where the needs of law enforcement were small and infringements on freedom of the press great, a court should decline to enforce such a subpoena. Similarly, in *Zurcher v. Stanford Daily*,[409] police obtained a warrant to search a student newspaper for photos of a student riot in an effort

---

400 *Roberts v. United States Jaycees, supra* note 392.

401 481 U.S. 537 (1987).

402 In an analogous situation involving political parties, the Court invalidated a California voter initiative that permitted non-party members to vote in elections for the purpose of selecting the party's candidate in the general election. *California Democratic Party v. Jones*, 530 U.S. 567 (2000).

403 *See Sheppard v. Maxwell*, 384 U.S. 333 (1966) (conviction of prominent doctor for murder of his wife reversed where press was so unrestrained that "carnival atmosphere" was created). The "right to a speedy and public trial" under the 6th Amendment also gives the press and public the right to attend a trial and certain pretrial proceedings. *Presley v. Georgia*, ___ U.S. ___; 130 S.Ct. 721 (2010).

404 *Waller v. Georgia*, 467 U.S. 39 (1984).

405 *Nebraska Press Assoc. v. Stuart*, 427 U.S. 539 (1976). *See also supra* p. 378 (prior restraints).

406 *Globe Newspaper Co. v. Superior Court*, 457 U.S. 596 (1982).

407 *Chandler v. Florida*, 449 U.S. 560 (1981).

408 408 U.S. 665 (1972).

409 436 U.S. 547 (1978).

to identify the participants. A similar alignment of justices upheld the legality of the search, rejecting 1st Amendment arguments. Again, Justice Powell's "swing" vote suggested qualifications on the right to conduct such searches. In response to the *Zurcher* case, Congress passed a federal statute prohibiting searches of newsrooms and seizures of "work product" of reporters except as "necessary to prevent the death of, or serious bodily injury to, a human being" and in other exceptional circumstances.[410]

Issues of the Source of Published Materials   The landmark case discussed above in the section on prior restraints, *New York Times Co. v. United States*, dealt with publication of the Pentagon Papers but did not consider the fact that a Department of Defense employee had stolen the materials. Clearly, if one uses legal means to obtain truthful information, the state cannot prohibit publication even if it has an appropriate interest in suppressing the information. Thus, where a journalist heard information about a juvenile crime over police radios, the state could not prohibit publication of the juvenile's name in the media.[411] A similar result was reached with regard to a state law that prohibited publication of the names of victims of sexual assaults because the police freely supplied this information in its pressroom.[412] The remedy in these situations is to cut off the information at the source by ensuring that the police do not release it.

Although the Court did not decide the issue, *New York Times Co.* presented the question whether the government can punish publication of unlawfully obtained information, when the publisher obtained the information lawfully. *Bartnicki v. Vopper*[413] involved a 1934 federal law that prohibited interception of telephone calls by private persons. The law punished anyone who disclosed the private interceptions if he or she had a reason to know that the interceptions were obtained in violation of the act. During labor negotiations between teachers and a public school, someone intercepted and recorded a cell phone conversation between a union negotiator and the union president. A local radio host obtained the tape and played it on the air as part of his news program. The Court held that prosecutors could not apply the federal law's sanctions to the radio commentator, even if the unknown interceptor had violated the statute. The Court dismissed the government's interest in deterring wrongful interceptions, because the punishment in question would not apply to the interceptor. The Court had more difficulty with the government's asserted interest in protecting the privacy of telephone conversations. However, the Court noted that the subject was a matter of public importance and it had to balance this fact against the interest in individual privacy. Analogizing the libel cases, in which public figures can recover damages only if they prove "actual malice,"[414] the Court observed that "[o]ne of the costs associated with participation in public affairs is an attendant loss of privacy."

Commercial Speech   Before 1976, speech involving the exchange of goods or services for profit, called "commercial speech," was among the categories of speech excluded from 1st Amendment protection, like obscenity and seditious speech. However, the Supreme Court opened an new area of 1st Amendment law when it decided in *Virginia State Board of Pharmacy v. Virginia Citizens Consumer Council* that

---

410 Privacy Protection Act of 1980, 42 U.S.C.A. §2000aa.
411 *Smith v. Daily Mail Publishing Co.*, 443 U.S. 97 (1979).
412 *Florida Star v. B.J.F.*, 491 U.S. 524 (1989).
413 531 U.S. 990 (2001).
414 *See supra* p. 380 and Chapter XI, pp. 457-460.

a ban on pharmacists advertising prices of prescription drugs violated free speech.[415] Shortly thereafter the Court decided *Bates v. Arizona State Bar*,[416] which struck down an absolute ban on lawyer advertising. In the pharmacy case, the Court reasoned that society has a strong interest in the free flow of commercial information. While the interest in protecting commercial speech is not as strong as protecting expression of ideas, it is nonetheless substantial and deserves protection. The Court considered it ironic that the 1st Amendment would protect the same information about drug prices if the pharmacist "cast himself as a commentator on store-to-store disparities in drug prices, giving his own and those of a competitor as proof." Commercial advertising, however tasteless it may be at times, contains information. As such, it is important in a system of free enterprise. Commercial speech relates to both to the private economic decisions of the purchasing public and to formation of intelligent opinions of voters as to how the government should change or regulate the economic system.

The current commercial speech test is the 4-part rule of *Central Hudson Gas & Electric Co. v. Public Service Comm'n*. A court must determine: (1) whether the speech concerns lawful activity and is not be misleading; if the speech passes this test, then the asserted governmental interest in limiting it must be examined to determine; (2) whether that interest is substantial; (3) whether the challenged regulation directly advances that interest; and (4) whether the regulation is not more extensive than necessary to serve that interest.[417] For example, a state could not prohibit all commercial billboards because of the interests of preserving aesthetics and enhancing traffic safety.[418] A court should question the asserted governmental interest when the challenged law permits some forms of speech but bars others that are no less problematic in terms of the asserted interest. Thus, in *City of Cincinnati v. Discovery Network, Inc.*,[419] a Cincinnati ordinance permitted publishers to place news racks containing newspapers on public sidewalks, but prohibited news racks containing advertising and promotional materials. The Court found that there was no valid basis to distinguish between news racks based on the content of the material in them.[420] Similarly, in *Greater New Orleans Broadcasting Association, Inc. v. United States*,[421] the Court struck down a federal regulation that banned all casino advertising. The Court found the justifications for the regulation wanting, because both the federal government and some states had legalized casino gambling. Further, even if limiting demand for casino gambling might be an appropriate "substantial interest," the fit of the means to that end was not sufficient to justify the ban, especially because the ban applied only to private casinos and exempted state-run or Indian tribal casinos.[422]

---

415 425 U.S. 748 (1976). *See also 44 Liquormart v. Rhode Island*, 517 U.S. 484 (1996) (striking down state statute banning price advertising for alcoholic beverages except at the store selling them).

416 433 U.S. 350 (1977). *See also* Chapter IV, p. 142.

417 447 U.S. 557 (1980) (invalidating prohibition on advertising by state-regulated monopoly utility).

418 *Metromedia, Inc. v. City of San Diego*, 453 U.S. 490 (1981) (plurality opinion).

419 507 U.S. 410 (1993).

420 For a detailed discussion of the *Central Hudson* test, *see Lorillard Tobacco Co. v. Reilly*, 533 U.S. 525 (2001).

421 527 U.S. 173 (1999).

422 *See also Lorillard Tobacco Co. v. Reilly*, 533 U.S. 525 (2001) (interest in preventing children from using tobacco is substantial, but prohibitions on all outdoor advertising within 1000 feet of any school and in-store advertising below 5 feet from the floor were too broad); *Thompson v. Western States Medical Center*, 535 U.S. 357 (2002) (prohibition on pharmacists advertising availability of compounded drugs).

Advertising is relatively impersonal. Direct in-person solicitation of business also raises 1st Amendment issues. In *Edenfield v. Fane*,[423] the Court invalidated a ban on certified public accountants' direct in-person solicitation of prospective business clients. However, the Court has held that the state *may* prohibit *lawyers* from engaging in direct in-person solicitation of prospective clients because of the peculiar dangers inherent in direct solicitation by lawyers.[424] In one Florida case, the Court even upheld a ban on "targeted mailings" from lawyers. The letters offered specific legal services that were addressed to specific people injured in an accident or to the survivors in case of death. Florida did not completely ban these letters, but only prohibited mailing them within 30 days after the accident. The Court stated this rule was properly designed "to forestall the outrage and irritation with the state-licensed legal profession that the practice of direct solicitation only days after accidents has engendered."[425]

E. First Amendment Religious Freedoms

There are two "religion clauses" of the 1st Amendment. One guarantees a right to the "free exercise" of religion, while the other prohibits any "law respecting the establishment of religion." Interpreting these clauses is problematic in light of their history because the Framers had divergent views on their meaning.[426] Furthermore, the clauses created a paradox because "free exercise" and "establishment" are ultimately contradictory. For example, if a state provides scholarships to students studying to be pastors, it could violate the establishment clause. But if the state, in an effort to avoid "establishment of religion," denies general scholarships to students studying to be pastors, they could accuse it of interfering with the free exercise of religion.[427] Emerging from this essential dilemma is the notion that the government must be *neutral* in its attitude toward religion.[428] However, courts have struggled to define "neutrality."

1. The Establishment Clause

To determine whether a law or practice is sufficiently neutral toward religion, courts must apply the three-part test developed in *Lemon v. Kurtzman*:[429] (1) the law or action must have a secular purpose; (2) the primary effect of it must be that it neither advances nor inhibits religion; and (3) it must not foster "excessive government entanglement" with religion. Lawyers and courts often say that the establishment clause creates a "wall of separation between Church and State."[430] However, the *Lemon* test and cases applying it show that complete non-involvement with religion is impossible.

---

[423] 507 U.S. 761 (1993).

[424] Public interest lawyers are permitted to solicit on behalf of their organizations because the profit motive is absent. *Ohralik v. Ohio State Bar Association*, 436 U.S. 447 (1978); *In re Primus*, 436 U.S. 412 (1978). Public interest lawyers were discussed in Chapter IV, pp. 154-158.

[425] *Florida Bar v. Went For It, Inc.*, 515 U.S. 618 (1995).

[426] *See* ARLIN ADAMS & CHARLES EMMERICH, A NATION DEDICATED TO RELIGIOUS LIBERTY: THE CONSTITUTIONAL HERITAGE OF THE RELIGION CLAUSES 6-26 (U. of Philadelphia Press, Philadelphia, Pa. 1990). For a succinct review of the religion clauses, *see* THOMAS C. BERG, THE STATE AND RELIGION IN A NUTSHELL, 2D ED. (West 2004) and FARBER, *supra* note 284, at 243-285.

[427] *Cf. Witters v. Washington Dept. of Services for the Blind*, 474 U.S. 481 (1986), discussed *infra* p. 392 (no violation of establishment clause to provide scholarship for religious education as part of a program funding all other areas of study) and *Locke v. Davey*, 540 U.S. 712 (2004) (free exercise clause not violated by state refusing to fund educational training to become a pastor while funding all other disciplines).

[428] *See Wallace v. Jaffree*, 472 U.S. 38 (1985).

[429] 403 U.S. 602 (1971). *See* NOWAK & ROTUNDA, *supra* note 2, §§17.1-17.16 (religion clauses).

[430] *Everson v. Board of Education*, 330 U.S. 1, 16 (1947) (quoting Thomas Jefferson).

By far, the greatest number of establishment clause cases involve the nexus between religion and schools. These cases have two aspects. First, because the government runs the public school system in the United States, it may not use the schools to "establish" any particular religion or even to encourage religion in general. Second, there is a healthy system of private schools that educate a substantial minority of children in the country. Religious institutions operate many of these schools, but they often rely on general government subsidies for education. The government must not assist these private schools to the extent that it violates the establishment clause.

Religion in Public Schools While public schools may require students to study religion or the Bible as part of a secular program on the subject, a public school may not require religious exercises in class. It does not matter whether the exercises are denominational (associated with one or another religious group) or non-denominational.[431] The same rule applies to prayers at graduation ceremonies and other school events — even if they are student-initiated and student-led.[432] Even a period of silence for "meditation or voluntary prayer" is prohibited, at least when it is implemented to "return voluntary prayer to the public schools."[433] Excusing children who object from such activities is not a solution. In fact, the Court has held that excluding students exacerbates the problem because it has a negative effect on the students' relationship with their classmates or teacher based on religious differences.[434] Though a school has broad discretion in selecting its curriculum, it may not use that discretion to advance religion. Thus, a state statute prohibiting the teaching of Charles Darwin's theory of evolution of humans from lower animals violated the establishment clause.[435] In reaction, some states passed statutes allowing the teaching of evolution but requiring equal class time devoted to "creation science" or "intelligent design," the notion that a supernatural being created humankind. But the Court held that these laws violate the secular purpose part of the *Lemon* test because their purpose was to counterbalance the teaching of evolution, thus advancing the religious viewpoint.[436]

Religious instruction in school is prohibited even if the teacher comes from outside the school system.[437] However, other "accommodations of religion" by public schools are not prohibited, such as releasing children from their schoolwork during the school day to attend religious classes off school premises.[438] And as discussed above in the section on freedom of expression, when public schools open their facilities to community groups for use as a public forum, they may not exclude religious groups.[439] It follows

---

431 *See Engel v. Vitale*, 370 U.S. 421 (1962) (New York statute required prayer: "Almighty God, we acknowledge our dependence upon Thee, and we beg Thy blessings upon us, our parents, our teachers and our Country"). *See also Stone v. Graham*, 449 U.S. 39 (1980) (posting of 10 commandments from Old Testament of Bible violated establishment clause).

432 *Lee v. Weisman*, 505 U.S. 577 (1992) (rabbi invited to recite non-sectarian prayer at graduation on invitation of school officials); *Santa Fe Independent School Dist. v. Doe*, 530 U.S. 290 (2000) (students voted whether to have an "invocation" before all football games and who would deliver it).

433 See *Wallace v. Jaffree*, 472 U.S. 38 (1985). Presumably, such a moment of silence, which is not religious by itself, would have to be sustained if it was not enacted for a religious purpose.

434 *School District of Abington Twp. v. Schempp*, 374 U.S. 203 (1963).

435 *Epperson v. Arkansas*, 393 U.S. 97 (1968).

436 *Edwards v. Aguillard*, 482 U.S. 578 (1987).

437 *Illinois ex rel. McCollum v. Board of Education*, 333 U.S. 203 (1948).

438 *Zorach v. Clausen*, 343 U.S. 306 (1952).

439 *See supra*, p. 376.

that permitting such access does not violate the establishment clause.[440] On the other hand, the Court found a violation of the establishment clause when New York "accommodated" a community of Hassidic Jews by authorizing them to form their own school district so their children would not have to attend regular public schools.[441]

Financial Assistance to Religious Schools Cases dealing with governmental assistance to religious schools (also called "parochial" schools) have followed a tortuous path, as members of the Court sharply divide on the proper approach. The Court found state programs met the *Lemon* test's neutrality requirement when they provided reimbursement to parents for the expense of public bus transportation to private schools;[442] loans of state-approved secular textbooks to children in religious schools;[443] and funding to parochial schools for state-required standardized tests.[444] However, the Court disapproved state salary supplements for private (including religious) school teachers of secular subjects. Though the purpose was secular and it did not promote religion as such, there was "excessive entanglement." Religious school teachers were subject to religious supervision by their schools and distributing aid required a continuing close involvement of the government with religious schools.[445]

Recently, courts have sharply disagreed on the issue of offering public school programs on the premises of religious schools. In *School Dist. of Grand Rapids v. Ball,*[446] remedial and enrichment programs were being taught to *religious* school students at public expense in *public* classrooms, and a community education program was being taught by *public* school teachers in *religious school* classrooms. The Court worried that teachers would become inadvertently involved in teaching particular religious beliefs, that the program might provide a "crucial symbolic link between government and religion" in the "eyes of impressionable youngsters," and that the programs would, in general, indirectly promote the "primary religious mission" of the religious institutions involved. However, in *Zobrest v. Catalina Foothills School Dist.*[447] a school district supplied sign-language interpreters for deaf students in public schools. A deaf student wished to continue to have such an interpreter after transferring to a parochial school. A sharply divided Court held 5-4 that it did not violate the establishment clause for the school district to continue to provide the interpreter. Then in *Agostini v. Felton,*[448] an extraordinary 5-4 decision, the Court vacated an injunction that prevented New York City from sending public school teachers into parochial schools to provide remedial education. It overruled its previous decision upholding the injunction — and overruled such parts of the *Ball* decision as prevented the state from offering secular public school

---

440 *Widmar v. Vincent,* 454 U.S. 263 (1981). *Widmar* involved a state college, but Congress passed an Equal Access Act in 1984 extending *Widmar* to public secondary schools. In *Board of Education of Westside Community Schools v. Mergens,* 496 U.S. 226 (1990), the Court held that the Act did not violate the establishment clause.

441 *Board of Education of Kiryaz Joel Village School District v. Grumet,* 512 U.S. 687 (1994).

442 *Everson v. Bd. of Education,* 330 U.S. 1 (1947).

443 *Bd. of Education of Central School Dist. No. 1 v. Allen,* 392 U.S. 236 (1968).

444 *Committee for Public Education and Religious Liberty v. Regan,* 444 U.S. 646 (1980).

445 *Lemon v. Kurtzman,* 403 U.S. 602 (1971).

446 473 U.S. 373 (1985).

447 509 U.S. 1 (1993).

448 521 U.S. 203 (1997).

programs in religious schools. The most recent Supreme Court case in this area had an even more pronounced split of opinion on the relevant test of government aid.[449]

Because college student minds are not as "impressionable," the Court has been more forgiving of governmental aid to religious colleges, so long the school uses the funds for secular purposes only.[450] If assuring such secular use requires on-going monitoring by the government, however, that may be "excessive entanglement" with religion. Nonetheless, the Court approved funding for sex counseling services for adolescents in religious schools and other institutions, dismissing as inconsequential problems with religious school counselors promoting religious views on sex.[451]

Financial benefits that do not go to religious schools but directly to students or their parents, who exercise their own "free choice" to use them for a sectarian school are more likely to be constitutional. The Court has theorized that if the parents or students choose to use neutrally available state aid to pay for a religious education, this private choice does not confer any message of state endorsement of religion. Thus, tax deductions for school expenses to parents of both public and private schoolchildren do not violate the establishment clause, even if the greatest beneficiaries of such subsidies are parents sending their children to religious schools.[452] The same "free choice" idea sustained the constitutionality of a blind student using his state educational grant to attend a Christian college, at least where the grant was only a small part of a grants program for the blind that applied to all forms of study at both public and private schools.[453] Nonetheless, a tax deduction for tuition paid to parochial or other private schools is unconstitutional when designed "to provide desired financial support for nonpublic, sectarian institutions."[454]

Establishment Clause Issues Outside the Educational Context Government recognition of religious holidays satisfies the *Lemon* test's second requirement that government action be supported by a secular purpose. "Blue laws," common in some parts of the United States, require that businesses close on Sundays. These laws stem from Sunday being the day of worship for Christians and a "day of rest." Despite this original religious purpose, however, the Court's view is that Sunday closing laws are constitutional because their *present* purpose is secular — having a uniform day of rest. Any benefits to religion are incidental.[455] Secular purpose also justifies government recognition of Christmas, the most important holiday of the year in the United States for

---

449 *Mitchell v. Helms*, 530 U.S. 793 (2000) (splitting 3-2-3 on the applicable test, but agreeing on the result that a federal program for distributing library and media materials and computer software and hardware, to public and private elementary and secondary schools to implement "secular, neutral, and nonideological" programs was constitutional).

450 *See Tilton v. Richardson*, 403 U.S. 672 (1971) (20-year limit on the assurance of secular use of property deemed insufficient to avoid an establishment clause challenge). *See also Roemer v. Board of Public Works of Maryland*, 426 U.S. 736 (1976) (grants to private colleges, including sectarian schools, with assurances of secular use of funds upheld).

451 *Bowen v. Kendrick*, 487 U.S. 589 (1988).

452 *Mueller v. Allen*, 463 U.S. 388 (1983). *See also Zelman v. Simmons-Harris*, 536 U.S. 639 (2002) (upholding program of tuition assistance to low-income families of children attending public or private schools and tutorial aid for needy students in public schools).

453 *Witters v. Washington Dept. of Services for the Blind*, 474 U.S. 481 (1986).

454 *Committee for Public Education v. Nyquist*, 413 U.S. 756 (1973).

455 *McGowan v. Maryland*, 366 U.S. 420 (1961). However, a state law giving employees the right not to work on the sabbath of their choice does violate the establishment clause because it has the primary effect of advancing religion. *Estate of Thornton v. Caldor, Inc.*, 472 U.S. 703 (1985).

most people. As the Court has noted, despite its religious origins, Christmas is really observed as a holiday of gift-giving and other secular activities. However, the government may not "endorse" the original Christian religious significance of Christmas by way of public display of a nativity scene of Jesus's birth on public property.[456] On the other hand, displaying a nativity scene as part of an overall "holiday display" of a Santa Claus, toy animals, gifts and other secular symbols of Christmas, does not endorse Christianity. The Court has noted more broadly that there is no establishment problem with "the government's acknowledgment of our religious heritage and government sponsorship of graphic manifestations of that heritage."[457]

A recent pair of cases dealt with government displays of the Ten Commandments from the Bible. In *Van Orden v. Perry*,[458] the Court allowed Texas to display a monument setting out the Ten Commandments on the grounds of the state capitol building. The display was one of several monuments on the capitol grounds "representing the several strands in the State's political and legal history," which had "a dual significance, partaking of both religion and government," and had been there for some 40 years. However, in *McCreary County v. American Civil Liberties Union*,[459] the Court held such a display in a Kentucky county courthouse unconstitutional because it was created for religious purposes and was not together with other secular historical materials. Although, in the course of the litigation, the county added to the display to make it more educational, this did not negate the original religious purpose of the display.

As *Van Orden* suggests, a long history of routine use of religious rituals may demonstrate a secular purpose. The Court upheld on historical grounds the practice of having a state-paid chaplain open the legislative session with a prayer. It observed that the first United States Congress, at the time the states adopted the 1st Amendment, did the same and it did not see legislative prayer as a violation of the establishment clause.[460] Similar reasoning would presumably support the use of "In God We Trust" on United States currency and "God Save This Honorable Court" in the official announcement of the opening of the sessions of all federal courts, including the Supreme Court. Probably these references are "interwoven so deeply into the fabric of our civil polity that [their] present use may well not present the type of involvement which the First Amendment prohibits."[461]

Recently, the Court created a new justification for allowing the government to seemingly favor some religions over others. *Pleasant Grove City, Utah v. Summum*[462] concerned a Ten Commandments monument in a public park. A private organization had paid for the monument and placed it in the park with the city's permission. When"Summum," a small religious group, sought the city's permission to place a

456 *Allegheny County v. American Civil Liberties Union*, 492 U.S. 573 (1989).

457 *Lynch v. Donnelly*, 465 U.S. 668 (1984).

458 545 U.S. 677 (2005).

459 545 U.S. 844 (2005).

460 *Marsh v. Chambers*, 463 U.S. 783 (1983).

461 *Abington Township School District v. Schempp*, 374 U.S. 203, 304 (1963) (Brennan, J., concurring). In another establishment clause case, Congress required by statute that all burdens on prison inmates practicing their religion serve a "compelling governmental interest" and be the "least restrictive means" possible. Citing the history of "frivolous and arbitrary" burdens imposed on "non-mainstream" religious observances by prisons officials, the Court upheld the law as neutral. *Cutter v. Wilkinson*, 544 U.S. 709 (2005).

462 555 U.S. ___; 129 S.Ct.1125, 1130 (2009).

monument of its "Seven Aphorisms of Summum" in the same park, the city denied permission, even though the group would have paid all the costs of erecting it. The Court held that the city was entitled to favor the Ten Commandments monument because "the placement of a permanent monument in a public park is best viewed as a form of government speech and is therefore not subject to scrutiny under the Free Speech Clause." Thus, it is sometimes constitutional when the government itself "speaks" and favors one religion over another. In reality, the Court may have feared that ruling in favor of Summum would have resulted in public parks across the nation being congested with monuments from thousands of religious organizations. The case teaches that the establishment clause must, at times, yield to practicality and favor majority religions.

2. The Free Exercise Clause

The paradigm violation of the free exercise clause occurs when the government disadvantages people because of their religion.[463] Laws that do this explicitly are rare. Most free exercise claims involve laws that pursue a permissible public purpose but burden religious beliefs *indirectly*. What the challenger seeks is an *exemption* from a *general* law. While the Court has been quite solicitous of accommodating religion in the past, some recent cases trend toward the view that any law of general applicability is constitutional even though it interferes with the religious practices of some people.

Traditional vs. New Free Exercise Standards   For years, the Court applied a strict scrutiny test under which it would first determine whether the burden on religious beliefs was significant and, if it was, would sustain the law only if it was narrowly drawn to achieve a *compelling* state interest. In determining the question, the Court considered the availability of less restrictive alternatives.[464] Thus, in *Sherbert v. Verner*,[465] a woman had been fired because she refused to work on Saturday, the Sabbath day of her religion. The state denied her unemployment benefits because of a general prohibition on awarding benefits to those who refuse offers of "suitable work." The Court held that the law as applied violated her right of free exercise of religion because it forced her to choose between getting unemployment compensation and following her religious beliefs — something the state had no compelling interest in doing.[466] However, in *Employment Division, Department of Human Resources v. Smith*,[467] the Court announced that it would no longer follow this process of balancing the burden on religion against a compelling state interest. Instead, so long as the *purpose* of the law is not to burden the exercise of religion, a "generally applicable and otherwise valid law" is constitutional regardless of its "incidental" effects on religious practices. In *Smith*, the Court upheld

---

463 *See, e.g., McDaniel v. Pay*, 435 U.S. 618 (1978) (striking down law prohibiting clergy from serving as legislators) and *Torasco v. Watkins*, 367 U.S. 488 (1961) (law requiring declaration of belief in God as a condition of public office unconstitutional).

464 This test is similar to the test involved in strict scrutiny equal protection (*supra*, pp. 352-356), substantive due process (*supra*, pp. 362-368), and 1st Amendment freedom of expression (*supra* pp. 368-389).

465 *Sherbert v. Verner*, 374 U.S. 398 (1963).

466 To the same effect are *Thomas v. Indiana Employment Security Comm'n*, 450 U.S. 707 (1981) and *Hobbie v. Unemployment Appeals Comm'n*, 480 U.S. 136 (1987). *Thomas* rejected asserted state interests in preventing unemployment and avoiding probing inquiries into religious beliefs of applicants for unemployment as not compelling enough. It also rejected the state's claim that *paying* unemployment compensation would violate the *establishment* clause.

467 494 U.S. 872 (1990).

Oregon's denial of unemployment benefits to a drug counselor who was fired for using peyote (a naturally occurring hallucinogenic drug) as part of his religious practices as a member of the Native American Church. Peyote use violated state drug laws and those laws made no exception for religious use. The Court did not overrule the *Sherbert v. Verner* line of cases. It noted, however, that the Oregon case involved violation of a *criminal* law, unlike its earlier cases.[468]

The Court similarly declined to use the strict scrutiny test in *Lyng v. Northwest Indian Cemetery Protective Assoc.*[469] Native Americans challenged the federal government's decision to permit timber harvesting and road construction in a national forest. The Native Americans used, for religious purposes, an area of forest that the government owned, but that was open to public use. The proposed development would have virtually destroyed the religious use of the forest. The Court declined to apply strict scrutiny, however, pointing out that such an incidental effect on religion was far from a government "prohibition" of the free exercise of religion. Since *Smith* and *Lyng*, the Court has offered little guidance on which test to apply. In *Church of Lukumi Babalu Aye, Inc. v. Hialeah*,[470] a church that performed animal sacrifice rituals claimed that city ordinances prohibiting such practices were unconstitutional. All the justices agreed that strict scrutiny applied in that case because the ordinances, while neutral on their face, were passed for the purpose of stopping the religious practice in question. The Court rejected, as not sufficiently "compelling," the city's interest in public health and preventing cruelty to animals. Concurring opinions in the case debated the propriety of the *Smith* standard and demonstrated how *Smith* could have been based on the state's compelling interest in prohibiting use of hallucinogenic drugs.[471]

Past Uses of the Traditional Test Whatever the status of the strict scrutiny test after *Smith* and *Lyng*, a long line of pre-*Smith* cases used the compelling state interest test to invalidate application of neutral statutes or policies that affect religion. In *Wisconsin v. Yoder*,[472] the Court held that compulsory education laws, which required children attend school until age 16, could not be applied to children of the Amish faith, which considered any formal education beyond 8 years to be an interference with religious training. The state's interests in assuring children would be productive members of society and protecting their well-being were insufficient because the Amish system of home-based vocational training prepared children for life. The Court has also exempted religious organizations from federal civil rights laws prohibiting employment discrimination based on religion, on the ground that forcing religious employers to hire non-adherents to their

---

468 In an analogous case decided in 1878, before the Court established much of today's free exercise doctrine, the Court decided that the government did not offend the 1st Amendment when it prosecuted a Mormon for bigamy despite the fact that his faith required that he have more than one wife. *Reynolds v. United States*, 98 U.S. (8 Otto) 145 (1878).

469 485 U.S. 439 (1988).

470 508 U.S. 520 (1993).

471 Congress responded to *Smith* by passing the Religions Freedom Restoration Act of 1993, 42 U.S.C.A. §2000bb, imposing the pre-*Smith* standard as a statutory matter. However, the Court struck down the act as applied to the states in *City of Boerne v. Flores, supra* note 115, discussed *supra* p. 343. But there has been more success asserting rights under the statute against the federal government. *See Gonzales v. O Centro Espirita Beneficente Uniao Do Vegetal*, 546 U.S. 418 (2006) (under RFRA, federal narcotics law can not be applied to stop religious sect from important hallucinogenic tea central to its observances).

472 406 U.S. 205 (1972).

faith violated the free exercise clause.[473] The Court has also held that church-affiliated schools are not subject to federal unemployment compensation laws[474] and has construed federal labor laws narrowly, making them inapplicable to protect unionization activities of lay faculty at religious schools on the ground that government intervention would present "serious constitutional questions."[475]

On the other hand, the Court has used the traditional free exercise test to *reject* claims for exemptions from generally applicable governmental requirements. These cases are most certainly still good law after *Smith*. Thus, the Court has upheld forcing an Orthodox Jewish merchant who closed his store on Saturday to comply with a Sunday closing law as well on the grounds of a governmental need for a uniform day of rest for all employees.[476] The Court also has upheld a military regulation prohibiting a Jewish officer from wearing a yarmulke while in uniform;[477] child labor laws applied to a child distributing religious literature with her guardian;[478] a law requiring immunization of children despite a parent's religious objections;[479] and a law requiring that children be assigned Social Security numbers against the religious wishes of their parents.[480]

Taxation and Free Exercise Many free exercise cases have dealt with tax policy. The Court has upheld the application of a general sales tax to religious goods and literature offered for sale,[481] denied exemption from Social Security taxes to the Amish who do not believe in compulsory insurance programs,[482] and upheld denial of tax exemptions to non-profit religious organizations that practice racial discrimination, even if it is done for religious reasons.[483] On the other hand, in a pair of older cases, the Court, on free exercise grounds, prohibited cities from applying a flat-fee licensing tax (charged all "solicitors") to persons distributing religious literature and from applying a flat "bookseller" fee to a minister who earned his living selling religious literature.[484]

In some taxation cases, free exercise claims meet the countervailing force of the establishment clause. For example, the Court held that a state tax *exemption* to all religious publications violateds the *establishment* clause.[485] Yet, it has held that exempting church property from taxes based on market value — along with the property of other educational and charitable institutions — does not violate the establishment clause. Such an exemption represents a neutral position toward religion that would be

---

473 *Corporation of the Presiding Bishop of the Church of Jesus Christ of Latter-Day Saints v. Amos*, 483 U.S. 327 (1987). But the Court has sustained the application of federal wage and hour laws to commercial businesses operated by religious organizations. *Tony and Susan Alamo Foundation v. Secretary of Labor*, 471 U.S. 290 (1985). General employment discrimination laws are discussed in Chapter XV, pp. 620-625.

    474 *St. Martin Evangelical Lutheran Church v. South Dakota*, 451 U.S. 772 (1981).

    475 *Nat'l Labor Relations Bd. v. Catholic Bishop of Chicago*, 440 U.S. 490 (1979). For a discussion of law relating to labor organizing, *see* Chapter XV, pp. 625-632.

    476 *Braufeld v. Brown*, 366 U.S. 599 (1961).

    477 *Goldman v. Weinberger*, 475 U.S. 503 (1986), *superceded by statute*, 10 U.S.C.A. §774.

    478 *Prince v. Massachusetts*, 321 U.S. 158 (1944).

    479 *Jacobson v. Massachusetts*, 197 U.S. 11 (1925).

    480 *Bowen v. Roy*, 476 U.S. 693 (1986).

    481 *Jimmy Swaggart Ministries v. Board of Equalization*, 493 U.S. 378 (1990).

    482 *United States v. Lee*, 455 U.S. 252 (1982).

    483 *Bob Jones University v. United States*, 461 U.S. 574 (1983).

    484 *See Murdock v. Pennsylvania*, 319 U.S. 105 (1943); *Follett v. McCormick*, 321 U.S. 573 (1944).

    485 *Texas Monthly, Inc. v. Bullock*, 489 U.S. 1 (1989).

destroyed by the "entanglement" that would result from government determining the value of church property and enforcing the tax.[486]

Government Resolution of Religious Questions The need for government neutrality most starkly appears in lawsuits that turn on the resolution of a religious question. In one case, two competing religious groups sought possession of church property. The church charter gave the property to the group that followed the "true faith." The Court held that it would violate the 1st Amendment if it decided this issue and that it had to defer to the highest tribunal of the church.[487] If no such tribunal existed and if a court could apply neutral principles of contract and property law to the dispute, it could do so.[488] If not, neither the state court nor any federal court could become involved.

Another fundamental potential "entanglement" with religion occurs when a court must decide what constitutes a "religion," either for 1st Amendment or other purposes. The Court has not limited religion to theistic beliefs and has held that a person claiming an exemption on religious grounds need not be a member of an organized religion or sect.[489] In cases involving exemption from military service on religious grounds, the Court has held that a belief is "religious" if it is "sincere and meaningful . . . [and] . . . occupies in the life of its possessor a place parallel to that filled by the God of those admittedly qualifying for the exemption."[490]

---

486 *Walz v. Tax Commission*, 397 U.S. 664 (1970).

487 *Presbyterian Church v. Hull Church*, 393 U.S. 440 (1969). The Court noted, however, that the decisions of church tribunals *are* reviewable by civil courts if they are based on "fraud, collusion, or arbitrariness," quoting from *Gonzalez v. Roman Catholic Archbishop of Manila*, 208 U.S. 1, 16 (1929).

488 *Jones v. Wolf*, 443 U.S. 595 (1979).

489 *Frazee v. Illinois Dept. of Employment Security*, 489 U.S. 829 (1989) (unemployment claimant with "sincerely held" religious views on Saturday work entitled to *Sherbert v. Verner* protections).

490 *Welsh v. United States*, 398 U.S. 333, 339 (1970), quoting from *United States v. Seeger*, 380 U.S. 163, 176 (1965).

CHAPTER X

CONTRACTS AND COMMERCIAL LAW

Contract law originated in the English common law courts and remains today largely governed by common law. However, as in other areas of the law, state and federal statutes play an increasing role. For example, every state has adopted most or all of the Uniform Commercial Code (UCC) which sets out a standardized set of rules for many types of commercial agreements, such as the sale of goods. In addition, federal and state governments have created consumer protection laws which regulate many consumer transactions.[1] The result is a mix of common law and federal and state statutes. Transactions often have to be examined carefully to determine what laws apply.[2]

PART I: The Common Law of Contracts

A. Formation of Contracts

A contract is a promise between two or more parties that the law recognizes as binding by providing a remedy in the event of breach. The common law states that for promises to be enforceable there must be "mutual assent" between the parties. Mutual assent exists if there was an offer and an acceptance of the offer, supported by mutual consideration, defined below. When focusing on offer and acceptance, it is common to refer to the parties as the "offeror" and the "offeree." An offeror is a person who makes an offer and the offeree is a person to whom the offer is made.

Although mutual assent is frequently referred to as a "meeting of the minds" and courts speak freely of the "intent" of the parties, actual subjective intent is irrelevant. Instead, an objective test is used and the intent that a reasonable person would infer from a party's words and acts is assigned to the parties. For example, an offeree may receive an offer and, without reading it, send an acceptance. Since the acceptance would lead a reasonable offeror to conclude that the offeree had read and accepted the offer's terms, there is a contract with all of the offeror's terms, despite the fact that the offeree could not possibly have intended subjectively to accept those terms. One result of an objective standard is that an offer which is made in jest can be enforced if a reasonable person would have concluded that a real offer was intended, unless the offeree actually knew that the "offer" was a joke.[3]

1. Offer and Acceptance

Offers An offer is "a manifestation of willingness to enter into a bargain so made as to justify another person in understanding his assent to that bargain is invited and will conclude it."[4] An offer must be sufficiently definite such that, if accepted, there would be a sufficient "basis for determining the existence of a breach and for giving an

---

1   *See infra* pp. 426-429, where Truth in Lending and other federal consumer laws are discussed.

2   The UCC is discussed *infra* pp. 414-421. Single-volume treatises on contract law are E. ALLAN FARNSWORTH, CONTRACTS, 4TH ED. (Aspen 2004), JOHN D. CALAMARI & JOSEPH M. PERILLO, HORNBOOK ON CONTRACTS, 6TH ED. (West 2009); BRIAN A. BLUM, CONTRACTS: EXAMPLES AND EXPLANATIONS, 4TH ED. (Aspen 2007).

3   *See Lucy v. Zehmer*, 84 S.E.2d 516 (Va. 1954) (seller claimed he "was high as a Georgia pine" and that the transaction "was just a bunch of doggoned drunks bluffing to see who could talk the biggest and say the most"; written contract to sell his farm was valid nonetheless as a "serious business transaction").

4   RESTATEMENT (SECOND) CONTRACTS §24 (American Law Institute 1981) [hereafter RESTATEMENT]. Restatements were discussed in Chapter II, p. 76.

appropriate remedy."[5] This will often require that the offer specify essential elements such as quantity and price. The offeror must manifest an intent to give the offeree the power to "close" the deal by accepting the offer. Thus, the statement "I will sell you my car for $300" is an offer. The offeree can accept by promising to pay the $300 or by paying it.

Agreements are often arrived at only after a series of negotiations. In such cases, a party might make a statement which is not an offer, but a manifestation of an intent to negotiate. For example, a person might say: "It would not be possible for me to sell my old car to you for less than $300." Viewed objectively, this statement is not an offer to sell for $300, but an intent to open negotiations.

Often statements resemble offers but do not meet the necessary requirements. For example, advertisements are generally not offers, in part because they do not contain sufficient language of promise or commitment to sell. Instead, they are usually considered invitations to bid or make an offer. But some advertisements may be offers. For example, in one case, a retail store's advertisement read: "Saturday, 9 A.M., . . . 1 black lapin stole, . . . $1, First come first served." It was held to be an offer because the words "First come first served" are promissory, there is a price and quantity element, and it is directed toward a particular person — the first person to tender $1 on Saturday after 9 A.M.[6]

Acceptance   The offeree accepts the offer by agreeing to the proposed bargain. Early common law required that the acceptance be a "mirror image" of the offer, *i.e.*, the acceptance cannot add terms or change any terms of the offer. If it did, then it is not an acceptance at all, but a rejection of the original offer and a counteroffer. In one well-known case, the seller sent an offer on its form, which listed the terms of sale. The buyer responded with its order form. That form corresponded to the seller's form with one minor exception. The buyer decided not to go through with the contract for other reasons and the court excused the buyer because of the discrepancy.[7] This strict rule has been modified in most jurisdictions.

Means of Acceptance   The common law makes a distinction between "bilateral" contracts (where the offeror seeks acceptance through a *promise* of performance) and "unilateral" contracts (where the offeror seeks acceptance through actual *performance*). The offeror, as the master of the offer, may prescribe the method by which the offer will be accepted. For example, if an offeror promises to sell a car to the offeree for $300, the offeror can specify whether the acceptance will be by a promise to pay the $300 or by actual payment of the $300. If the offeror does not specify the mode of acceptance, the offeree can accept "in any manner and by any medium reasonable in the circumstances."[8] In a unilateral contract, where the offer specifically invites acceptance by performance, the offer can be accepted only by full performance. For example, assume an offeror promises to pay $100 if the offeree paints the offeror's house. The offeree cannot accept this offer by *promising* to paint the house, nor can the offeree accept by paint. The offeree can accept the offer only by *completely painting* the house. Until the offeree has completely painted it, there is no acceptance and therefore no contract. This rule may cause unfair results by allowing the offeror to receive partial performance and

---

5   RESTATEMENT §33(2).

6   *Leftkowitz v. Great Minneapolis Surplus Store, Inc.*, 86 N.W.2d 689 (Minn. 1957).

7   *See Poel v. Brunswick-Balke-Collender Co.*, 110 N.E. 619 (N.Y. 1915).

8   RESTATEMENT §30(2).

then revoke the offer before the acceptance is complete. Consequently, the law generally protects those who partially perform in one of two ways. First, the offeree may recover the value of any work performed under an equity doctrine of *in quantum meruit*. Second, some courts hold that once the offeree has started to perform, the offer becomes an "option contract," which cannot be revoked until the offeree has had the chance to perform.

Time for Acceptance   The power to accept an offer does not belong to the offeree forever. The period of acceptance can be terminated by lapse, rejection, revocation, or the death of a party. Often the offer specifies the amount of time in which the offer may be accepted by the offeree. If the offeree does not accept within that time, the offer has lapsed, and the offeree can no longer exercise the power to accept and close the deal. If no period is specified in the offer, it lapses after a reasonable time or until the offeror revokes the offer. What is a reasonable time depends on the circumstances. For example, unless specified otherwise, an offer made in a face-to-face conversation is usually deemed to continue only to the close of the conversation, and cannot be accepted thereafter.[9]

The power to accept an offer also ends when the offeree rejects the offer. After rejecting the offer, the offeree cannot reconsider and accept. An offeree's counteroffer terminates the power of acceptance just as if the offeree had rejected the offer, unless the original offer is irrevocable (discussed below). An offeree can avoid this result by using language which does not reject the offer. For example, the offeree can keep the original offer open by replying "we are considering your offer. In the meantime, would you consider . . . ."

Before the offeree accepts or rejects the offer, the offeror can terminate the offeree's power of acceptance by revoking the offer. When an offer or acceptance is mailed, the "mail-box" rule applies, under which transmittal is effective upon sending the offer or acceptance. However, a revocation sent by the offeror is effective only upon *receipt* by the offeree. Thus the issue of when the acceptance becomes effective may be an important question in determining if the offeror still has the power to revoke the offer or if it has already been accepted and a contract has been formed. Since an acceptance is effective when mailed, a contract is concluded at that time. Thus the offeror will only learn of the acceptance and existence of the contract when the offeror actually receives it. If an offeree mails an acceptance, but later reconsiders and communicates a rejection, the rejection is not valid even if it arrives before the acceptance. This rule prevents an offeree from accepting an offer using, for example, slow mail service, while knowing that if market prices suddenly change or a better offer is submitted by someone else, the offeree can quickly dispatch an overtaking rejection. But if a rejection is sent first and the offeree after reflection sends an overtaking acceptance, the acceptance will be effective if it arrives before the rejection.

Option Contracts   For the protection of the offeree, there are some situations in which an offer is irrevocable for a period of time. An offer is irrevocable if the offeree gives the offeror "consideration" for a promise not to revoke the offer for a period of time. Giving consideration means that the offeree pays or otherwise gives value to the offeror to keep the offer "open" for some period of time. An offeree in this position is

---

9   *See Akers v. J.B. Sedberry, Inc.*, 286 S.W.2d 617 (Tenn.App. 1955) (employer's acceptance of employees' offers to resign after the end of the face-to-face conversation was too late).

said to have an "option contract," and may consider the offer for the period of time agreed upon without fear of revocation.[10]

Another occasion when an option contract is formed is when the offeror wants acceptance by performance and the offeree begins the invited performance.[11] The length of this option contract is a "reasonable time." Since an offer for a unilateral contract has not been accepted until the offeree has fully performed, this rule protects the offeree from revocation after beginning performance in reliance on the offer. Returning to the house-painting hypothetical mentioned earlier, the offeree would be protected from revocation if painting the house had begun.

Under some circumstances, an offer can be irrevocable when the offeree *relies* on the offer, but has not yet begun performance. Thus, "an offer which the offeror should reasonably expect to induce action or forbearance of a substantial character on the part of the offeree before acceptance and which does induce such action or forbearance is binding as an option contract to the extent necessary to avoid injustice."[12] For example, assume a general contractor receives an offer from a subcontractor — often called a "bid" — to do the electrical work of a building that the general contractor is seeking to build. The general contractor uses the subcontractor's bid to calculate its own bid to construct the building. If the subcontractor were then able to revoke the offer, and the general contractor wins the contract, the general contractor would be responsible for completing the building at the contract price but would likely have to hire a more expensive electrician. The quoted rule protects the general contractor in this situation by making the subcontractor's bid irrevocable.[13]

2. Consideration

General Requirement Consideration plays a broad role in contracts. Generally, no promise is enforceable unless it is supported by consideration. Consideration is a bargained-for exchange between the promisor and the promisee. "Promisee" refers to the person benefitting from a given promise, while the "promisor" is the person who made the promise and is being called on to carry it out. Generally, anything that is given in exchange for a promise will constitute consideration, as long as it was bargained for.[14] Thus, a promise or performance given by the promisee to the promisor must be "sought by the promisor in exchange for his promise and . . . given by the promisee in exchange for that promise."[15] Therefore, the mere fact that the promisee gave something to the promisor does not in itself satisfy the requirements of consideration.

All legal systems look for a serious intent to be bound when determining which promises will be enforced as contracts. But the requirement of consideration is unique to the common law countries and it may sometimes restrict what the law considers to be an enforceable contract. The consideration requirement reflects a discomfort that common-law judges feel in determining parties' subjective intent. Consideration provides an objective manifestation of agreement.

---

10   Consideration is discussed more generally in 2. below.

11   RESTATEMENT §45.

12   RESTATEMENT §87(2).

13   *See, e.g, Drennan v. Star Paving Co.*, 333 P.2d 757 (Cal. 1958) (paving subcontractor's bid is binding even if based on a mistake, in the absence of the bid stating a specific right to revoke it).

14   The modern view is that the consideration need not convey a benefit to the promisor or a detriment to the promisee. RESTATEMENT §79.

15   RESTATEMENT §71(2).

Promises to Make a Gift One situation affected by the consideration requirement is a promise to make a gift. Such a promise is usually unenforceable. This is because the nature of a gift is that the promisor wants nothing in return for the promise. Sometimes it may sound as if the promisor of a gift wants something in return. For example, a man may tell a neighbor: "If you come over to my house, I'll give you some suits that I have outgrown." By going to the house, the neighbor has performed an action to get the suits. However, performing this act is not really sufficient consideration to make the promise binding because the promisor was probably not seeking a visit to his or her house in exchange for the promise to hand over the suits. Instead, the promisor probably meant, "you can have the suits but you have to come and get them." In other words, the promisor probably did not make the promise in exchange for the neighbor's act of going to the house. If this is the case, there is no consideration for the promise and it is unenforceable.[16]

Illusory Promises A promise which appears to promise something, but in fact does not commit the promisor to anything at all, is known as an "illusory" promise and is insufficient consideration. For example, it has been held that the promise of a creditor not to collect the debt "until such time as I want my money" is illusory.[17] A promise is similarly illusory when one of the parties reserves an unrestricted right to terminate the agreement at any time. With such a reservation, the party has not committed to anything and the promise is void for lack of consideration. On the other hand, a termination clause that requires the party to give notice some period of time before the termination becomes effective does not make the promise illusory, because the duty to give notice is a detriment. There are some cases, however, that have enforced seemingly illusory promises by implying a duty to use "good faith" in performing the promise. In one case, an employee in a contract promised to work only as much "as he in his sole judgement shall deem necessary." This promise was not illusory, since there was an implied promise to "render some substantial services" and "to act in good faith."[18]

Pre-Existing Duty Rule Consideration may be absent when the promise is in exchange for performing a "pre-existing duty." A promise to do something that is already legally required is not valid consideration for a new promise. The pre-existing duty rule seeks to prevent extorted modifications of contracts. For example, assume a builder agrees to construct a building for an owner for one price. The builder then threatens to halt construction unless the owner agrees to pay more money. The additional amount is generally not enforceable. The promise to build the structure is not consideration for the owner's promise to pay the additional amount since the builder was already obligated to build the structure in accordance with their first agreement. Thus a promise to pay an additional amount requires "fresh" consideration. If, for example, the builder agrees in return for the higher amount to complete the structure one month earlier than originally agreed or to expand it, the additional amount is enforceable.[19]

The pre-existing duty rule has been criticized because it interferes with the parties' freedom to modify their agreements as they see fit. As a result, some jurisdictions have

---

16 If there is consideration, then there is an enforceable contract. *See Barron v. Cain, infra* note 41.

17 *Strong v. Sheffield*, 39 N.E. 330 (N.Y. 1895).

18 *See Seymour Grean & Co. v. Grean*, 82 N.Y.S.2d 787 (App. Div. 1948) (dictum; court held other consideration sufficient).

19 *See* RESTATEMENT §73. *W.E.Koeler Construction Co. v. Medical Center of Blue Springs*, 670 S.W.2d 558 (Mo.App. 1984) (subsequent agreement allowing contractor to substitute cheaper materials and promising to award later work to that contractor were not enforceable in return for contractor keeping bid price firm, because contractor already had a duty to complete the building for the bid amount).

found exceptions to the rule, and a few have abolished the rule all together. The modern trend is to enforce modifications to contracts not fully performed that are fair and equitable in view of unanticipated circumstances.[20]

Promissory Estoppel At first glance it may appear that the requirement of consideration could lead to rather harsh results. For example, it may seem unfair to allow a promisee, thinking a binding contract existed, to incur an expense, only to discover later that the law would not enforce the contract for lack of consideration. Such problems are dealt with through a doctrine known as "promissory estoppel." Promissory estoppel is an alternative to consideration. It provides that reliance on a promise can make the promise binding or enforceable to some extent, even without consideration, but only if it was foreseeable to the promisor that the promisee would rely on the promise.[21]

3. Formal Requirements

Once there is mutual assent supported by consideration, an enforceable contract exists. There is no requirement for any formal ceremony to make the agreement "official," no requirement for a seal (an embossed marker), and, in some cases, no requirement that the contract even be in writing. If the contract is in writing it does not have to be in any particular form. However, some types of contracts are required to be in writing under the "Statute of Frauds."

a. The Statute of Frauds

All of the states (except Louisiana) have adopted a close form of the English Statute of Frauds (1677), which requires that certain types of contracts be in writing in order to be enforceable. The primary purpose of the Statute of Frauds is to ensure that certain contracts are not enforced unless there is sufficient proof that the contract exists. There are four types of contracts that typically fall within the Statute of Frauds and must therefore be in writing. These are (1) a suretyship contract (a contract to answer for the debt or obligation of another), (2) a contract to transfer or buy any interest in land, (3) a contract that cannot be performed within one year of its making, and (4) a contract for the sale of goods worth $500 or more.[22]

Under both the common law and the UCC, the Statute of Frauds requires that the writing must be "signed by the party against whom enforcement is sought."[23] This generally means that the signature must be written on a paper copy of the contract. However, in 1997 the Information Security Committee of the American Bar Association's Science and Technology Section proposed a relaxation of the requirement that signatures be written on paper. The Committee suggested that digital signatures could replace physical signatures and would facilitate global commerce by avoiding having mail hard copies of the written contract back and forth.[24] The recent revisions of the

---

20 RESTATEMENT §89. *See Angel v. Murray*, 322 A.2d 630 (R.I. 1974) (upward modification of compensation under garbage collection contract due to unexpected increase in number of residential units served was effective).

21 RESTATEMENT §90. *See State Dept. of Highways v. Woolley*, 696 P.2d 828 (Colo.App. 1984) (landowners were estopped from revoking their promise to grant state highway department right to enter their land where department spent money and labor in reliance on promise). *But see Local 1330, United Steel Workers v. United States Steel Corp.*, 631 F.2d 1264 (6th Cir. 1980) (not foreseeable that the union would rely on a promise to keep plants operating if fixed costs of the plants were met).

22 This amount is raised to $5000 under the proposed revisions of Article 2 of the Uniform Commercial Code (UCC). *See infra* p. 414 for more on the UCC.

23 UCC §2-201.

24 Information Security Committee, American Bar Ass'n, *States' Role in Developing Digital Signatures Policies and Standards* (July 31, 1997). *See* www.abanet.org/scitech/ec/isc/stateds.html.

Uniform Commercial Code (UCC) adopt this view. The new UCC substitutes the word "authenticate" for "sign." "Authenticate" means to sign or "to execute or otherwise adopt a symbol, or encrypt or similarly process a record . . . with present intent of the authenticating person to . . . adopt or accept a record."[25]

When it would be extremely unfair to one of the parties to hold a contract invalid due to its failure to satisfy the Statute of Frauds, courts have made exceptions. For example, courts have enforced oral agreements for the sale of land if the purchaser has paid a considerable portion of the price or made significant improvements to the land.[26]

b. Resolving Problems with Incomplete or Indefinite Written Agreements

The Parol Evidence Rule A frequent problem occurs when a contract has been reduced to writing, but one of the parties claims that their actual agreement included a term which is not in the writing. The "parol evidence rule" generally prohibits the introduction of extrinsic evidence that contradicts terms of a written contract. The purpose of the parol evidence rule is to promote certainty by preventing written agreements from being contradicted by less reliable accounts of the agreement and by encouraging parties to make their written agreements complete.[27]

The parol evidence rule applies only if a written contract is intended to be the final expression of the entire agreement and to include all of the terms and details of the agreement. If the writing is not intended to constitute the full agreement, then parol evidence can be used to supplement or even contradict the terms of the writing. In the past the decision of the question of whether a written contract embodies the complete agreement of the parties was made by looking solely at the document and determining if the terms sought to be added by parol evidence would naturally and normally have been left out of the writing. But under the more modern approach a judge balances the actual intentions of the parties against the document itself.[28]

Exceptions to the Rule The parol evidence rule applies only to extrinsic agreements that were made prior to or contemporaneous with the written agreement. Evidence of terms that *contradict* the written contract will *not* be allowed. However, the party may show evidence that there were *additional* terms that do not contradict the writing or that the contract was orally modified after the writing. The rule also does not prevent parties from proving fraud, duress, lack of consideration, or anything else that would make the contract void or voidable.

B. Interpretation of Contracts

Plain Meaning Rule One approach to interpretation, called the "plain meaning rule," provides that the meaning of any writing or term which appears to be plain and unambiguous on its face will be determined without using any extrinsic evidence whatsoever. The plain meaning rule does not allow the parties to show what they

---

25 UCC §1-201(1). The UCC is explained in greater detail *infra* pp. 414-425.

26 *See, e.g., Holt v. Katsanevas,* 854 P.2d 575 (Utah App. 1993) (oral modification of contract for the sale of land enforceable notwithstanding the statute of frauds if the party has performed in part in reliance on the modification).

27 Although "parol" literally means "oral," the parol evidence rule acts to exclude not only oral evidence, but all forms of evidence extrinsic to the written agreement.

28 *See Sierra Diesel Injection Service, Inc. v. Burroughs Corp.,* 890 F.2d 108 (9th Cir. 1989) (computer seller's printed form contract was not a final complete statement of the agreement despite the fact that it so stated; most important factor was the parties' intent). *See generally* CALAMARI & PERILLO, *supra* note 2, §3-2.

thought the term meant, and does not even allow evidence of trade usage to interpret the words. Although this rule is widely criticized, "it is undoubtedly still employed frequently or on occasion by the great majority of the jurisdictions in this country."[29]

Interpretation Focusing on the Parties' Intent The common law maintains a strong position that terms of a contract should be interpreted by their external expression and not by the subjective intentions of one party. Even so, recognizing the importance of the parties' intentions and the imprecisions of language, a more modern approach allows the parties to introduce evidence of what they subjectively thought the terms in the writing meant.[30] Parties may have directly conflicting ideas about what the terms meant. When this happens, the court may find that there was no mutual assent and therefore no contract. But if one party knows of or should have known of the meaning attached by the other party to a term, a court will find that there was mutual assent.[31]

When parties have conflicting interpretations of a term in the contract, courts may also make use of some general principles of law, or maxims, in deciding which interpretation should be followed. The Restatement suggests some of these general principles. For example, an ambiguous term will be construed against the drafter of the agreement.[32] All terms will be interpreted, where possible, to have a reasonable, lawful, and effective meaning.[33] A term that has been negotiated between the parties will control over one that is part of the standardized, non-negotiated part of the contract, or "boilerplate."[34] Another maxim, the primary purpose rule, provides that if the court can determine what the parties' "primary purpose" for making the contract was, that purpose should be given great weight in the interpretation of the terms.[35]

Court-Supplied Terms Often parties enter into contracts without expressly or implicitly providing all the terms of their agreement. When this occurs, courts are often willing to supply the missing term. "When the parties to a bargain sufficiently defined to be a contract have not agreed with respect to a term which is essential to a determination of their rights and duties, a term which is reasonable in the circumstances is supplied by the courts."[36] Such court-supplied terms usually deal with an issue that the parties never even thought about. A reasonable supplied term is one that the parties would have agreed to or which conforms to commercial standards of fairness. For example, if a person hires a painter to paint a house but the parties did not discuss price, the court may supply the term "reasonable price," and define it as the painter's usual

---

29 CALAMARI & PERILLO, *supra* note 2, at 167. The "plain meaning" rule in contract law is similar to the "plain meaning" maxim of statutory interpretation. It has many of the same benefits and difficulties as does the statutory interpretation maxim, noted in Chapter II, pp. 54-57.

30 The parol evidence rule does not bar the use of parol evidence to interpret or explain terms contained in a complete written agreement, but the use of extrinsic evidence to interpret or explain terms may be limited by rules of contract interpretation.

31 RESTATEMENT §§18, 20, 201. *See Wells v. Weston*, 326 S.E.2d 672 (Va. 1985) (property settlement agreement providing for spousal support payments to wife for as long as she lived valid as written; husband's uncommunicated intent that payments stop upon her marriage was not part of the contract).

32 RESTATEMENT §206.

33 *Id.*, §203(a).

34 *Id.*, §203(d).

35 *Id.*, §202(1).

36 RESTATEMENT §204. *See Barco Urban Renewal Corp. v. Housing Authority*, 674 F.2d 1001, 1007 (3d Cir. 1982) (right of first refusal deemed to continue for a commercially reasonable time where no time was stated by contract).

charges. Thus a court will look to trade usage, course of performance, and course of dealings when deciding what is a fair term.[37]

Courts are often unwilling to supply certain kinds of missing terms. For example, quantity terms will generally not be filled in, because an objective standard is difficult to find for this usually subjective expectation.

C. Issues in Performance of Contracts

1. Order of Performance

Ideally, parties to a contract will tender their promised performances simultaneously. This preferred order provides the security that both parties' expectations will be met because both parties can defer their performance until there is adequate certainty that the other party will perform. It is especially common for parties to follow this order of performance when selling and buying real estate. On the agreed date for performance, the seller tenders a deed and the buyer tenders the purchase price. This is referred to as "closing" the transaction.

Often circumstances make it impractical for parties to tender their performance at the same time. This is the case where the performance of one party will take longer than the other party's. This is especially true of construction contracts where the builder's promised performance is providing a completed building and the owner's performance is payment for that completed building. But under such circumstances the builder can regain the security of simultaneous performance by requiring in the contract that payments be made at stated intervals for work completed. It is also very common for one party to tender performance first in reliance on the other party's promise to tender its performance at a later date. This is common when parties have dealt with each other before and one party is willing to perform first.

2. Conditions and Duties

Although a party to a contract has a duty to perform the tasks promised, that duty to perform may be conditional. A "condition" is "an event, not certain to occur, which must occur, unless its nonoccurrence is excused, before performance under a contract becomes due."[38] A party whose performance is conditional does not have to perform the promised act until and unless the condition has been satisfied or excused.

Express and Implied Conditions When the parties have agreed to the condition (expressly or impliedly), the condition is an express condition. For example, suppose a party has contracted to buy a house "subject to and conditional upon" obtaining a mortgage to finance the $100,000 sale price. If no bank will approve such a mortgage, the buyer's duty to perform does not arise. Explicit conditions are applied strictly. Thus, even if a bank is willing to lend $90,000 and the seller is willing to make separate arrangements for the remaining $10,000, the buyer does not have a duty to perform.[39] Implied conditions may also arise where they logically flow from the nature of the contract or it performance.[40]

---

37 *See, e.g., Columbia Nitrogen Corp. v. Royster Co.*, 451 F.2d 3 (4th Cir. 1971) (evidence of trade usage allowing phosphate buyers to ignore contractually stipulated minimum quantities should have been allowed by court).

38 RESTATEMENT §224. These conditions are sometimes called "contingencies."

39 *See Luttinger v. Rosen*, 316 A.2d 757 (Conn. 1972) (purchases unable to find mortgage at a certain rate, so contract condition was not satisfied).

40 *See Kingston v. Preston*, 99 Eng. Rep. 437 (K.B. 1773) (seller of shop not obligated to deliver possession if the buyer has not paid).

Excuse of Conditions A party may be excused from performing a condition if there is a good reason for non-performance, such as where the party is prevented from doing so by the other party's wrongful conduct. In one case, a nephew agreed to live with his uncle and take care of him for the rest of his life in exchange for payment after the uncle died. The nephew performed his part of the agreement for several years, during which the uncle was constantly drunk and abusive to the nephew, eventually forcing the nephew to leave. The nephew was still permitted to recover under the contract.[41]

Difference Between Condition and Duty A condition differs from a duty. A duty results from a promise, and the breach of a promise will give the other party a cause of action for damages. For example, an insurance policy agreement provides that the homeowner *must notify* the insurance company of any fire within seven days. The homeowner has made a promise and therefore has a duty to inform the insurance company. If the homeowner fails to notify the insurance company within seven days after a fire, the homeowner has breached the contract. The insurance company may sue for damages for that breach (if there are any). But it still has to perform, *i.e.*, it must still pay the agreed-upon insurance coverage amount. If, however, the agreement had provided that the insurance company will pay the coverage amount *if and only if* it is notified of the fire within seven days, then there is a condition. The condition qualifies the insurance company's duty to perform. If the homeowner does not inform the insurance company within seven days, the insurance company does not have to pay the coverage amount.[42]

D. Grounds for Nonperformance of Contracts

1. Mistake

A party may be released from a contract if the contract was based upon a mutual mistake, and the party seeking release did not bear the risk of that mistake. The mistake must concern a basic assumption on which the contract was made, such as the nature, identity, or existence of the subject matter. For example, if a buyer unfamiliar with livestock sees a steer and thinks it is a cow, and agrees to buy it, the buyer will still have to perform. The mistake here was not mutual; it was unilateral. Also, the buyer bore the risk of this mistake, since the buyer admittedly knew little about livestock, but chose to proceed anyway. On the other hand, if two parties agree to the sale of a live cow, but unknown to them, the cow had died before their agreement, the mistake is mutual and the seller will not have to perform.[43]

2. Changed Circumstances: Impossibility, Impracticability, Frustration of Purpose, and Reformation

Impossibility A party might also be released from a contract where, through no fault of the parties, the performance has become impossible or the principal purpose of one of the parties in entering into the contract has become frustrated. For example, assume a painter is hired to paint a building. Through no fault of either party, the

---

41 *Barron v. Cain*, 4 S.E.2d 618 (N.C. 1939).

42 Such efforts may run afoul of the "presumption against forfeiture." *See Ferguson v. Phoenix Assurance Co.*, 370 P.2d 379 (Kansas 1962) (condition in insurance policy required that there be forceful entry into safe evidenced by "visible marks made by tools, explosives, electricity or chemicals upon the exterior of . . . the doors of the vault or the safe . . ."; when burglar opened safe by manipulating combination lock without such visible marks, court refused to interpret the clause literally, holding that it really only imposed condition that the loss not be an "inside job").

43 *See Sherwood v. Walker*, 33 N.W. 919 (Mich. 1887) (seller of cow could avoid contract for sale of cow when both buyer and seller erroneously believed the cow to be infertile).

building burns down before the painter starts painting. The painter is excused from performing because of impossibility.

Impracticability In some cases, the performance has not become literally impossible, but unforeseeable circumstances have made performance extremely costly or burdensome. This is known as "impracticability," and the modern trend is to release a party from a contract if performance becomes extremely impracticable. But impracticality requires that the economic loss be both substantial and unforeseen at the time the contract was made. Many of the modern cases dealing with impracticability have involved drastic increases in energy costs resulting from the oil embargo of the 1970s. These cases show that courts are generally unwilling to release parties from their obligations simply because of lost profits.[44]

Frustration of Purpose Frustration of purpose occurs when a change in circumstances makes one party's performance virtually worthless to the other. For example, the parties enter into a lease of a building. The lease specifies that the building is to be used for the sole purpose of operating a casino. During the period of the lease, gambling is declared illegal. The lessee cannot claim any right to discontinue paying rent due to impossibility, because it is still legal for the lessee to rent the building. But the main purpose of the lease has been frustrated, so the lessee might be excused from continuing to perform.[45]

Reformation of Contracts Instead of declaring the contract invalid because of changed circumstances, a court may try to "reform" it. However, U.S. courts generally feel that they have no power to impose unbargained-for terms upon parties when the parties agreed on different terms. Such action is seen as a direct interference with a free market and the right of parties to contract freely to guarantee their own expectations. One can nonetheless find occasional cases where contracts have been reformed.[46]

3. Lack of Capacity: Minors and Mental Incapacity

Persons lacking legal capacity include those who are too young (below the age of majority) or mentally incompetent. A person who lacks the legal capacity to enter into an agreement can be released from the duty to perform.

Minors A minor may enter into a contract, but may disaffirm the contract at any time during minority or within a reasonable time after majority, even if the other party has fully performed. To disaffirm a contract, the minor has only to indicate an intent not to be bound by the contract. For example, a minor may buy a car, drive it for a few months, and then decide to disaffirm the contract. The minor can return the car for a refund even if the car has been damaged.

There are limitations on the minor's power to disaffirm. One limitation concerns contracts for necessaries. In most jurisdictions, if the minor disaffirms after having already received the necessary, the seller can recover the reasonable value of the

---

44 *Laclede Gas Co. v. Amoco Oil Co.*, 522 F.2d 33 (8th Cir. 1977). *See also Missouri Public Service Co. Peabody Coal Co.*, 583 S.W.2d 721 (Mo.App. 1979) (upholding specific performance of contract to supply coal to utility after price had increased dramatically, because change was foreseeable).

45 *But see Scottsdale Road General Partners v. Kuhn Farm Machinery*, 909 P.2d 408 (Ariz. App. 1996) (doctrine did not excuse non-payment for resort facilities after organizer canceled convention because participants were canceling due to fear of flying during the Gulf War).

46 *See ALCOA v. Essex Group, Inc.*, 499 F.Supp. 53 (W.D. Pa. 1980) (long term contract for aluminum ingots held to have failed of its essential purpose due to energy price increases; it was reformed by changing the price to reflect the original intentions of parties and court's sense of fairness).

necessary, which will likely be lower than the contract price.[47] Contracts to pay child support, military enlistments, and educational loans are other areas where a minor's power to disaffirm is usually limited. Additionally, even when the contract can be avoided, some courts hold the minor liable for the benefit received from the subject matter of the contract or for the deterioration of its value.[48]

After reaching the age of majority, the former minor can ratify the contract that was previously voidable, and make it enforceable. Failure to disaffirm is considered ratification of the contract. The former minor can also ratify the previously voidable contract by words, even oral, after reaching the age of majority. Finally, the former minor can ratify the contract by conduct, such as by insisting that the other party perform, or by beginning to perform after reaching the age of majority.

Mental Deficiency   Like a minor, a person who is mentally infirm lacks legal capacity. A person lacks capacity who, because of mental disease or defect, does not have the ability to understand the contract. Some jurisdictions also deem persons to lack capacity if they are unable to make a reasonable judgement, even if they understand the contract.[49] A contract is voidable by a party who contracted while mentally infirm. In close cases, the court looks at the "substance of the bargain" to see whether the bargain was fair.

4. Duress and Undue Influence

Duress   A contract entered into under duress is voidable at the option of the victim of the duress. If the victim has already performed, damages or other suitable relief may be obtained in court. Duress is an action that compels another to do something that person would not otherwise do, so there can be no mutual assent when duress is present. Duress can be committed by violence, imprisonment, wrongful taking and keeping of a person's property, or the threat of any of those acts. Under some circumstances, a threat to breach a contract unless it is modified may be duress. The modern rule is that such a threat is duress if the threat would result in irreparable injury and if it is made in "breach of the duty of good faith and fair dealing." The same applies to threats to exercise legal rights in an oppressive way. For example, an employer employs duress by threatening to fire an at-will employee (which the employer has a legal right to do) unless the employee signs an agreement to sell back all shares of stock the employee has in the company. Under the circumstances, the contract to sell the stock is unenforceable.[50]

Undue Influence   This defense is like duress in that it involves pressure on a party. But it is generally invoked only when someone takes advantage of the party's particular

---

47   This would not be a recovery under a contract, since the contract cannot be enforced against the minor. Instead, the recovery would be in "quasi-contract" (discussed *infra* p. 414), which is not a contract at all, but a term that refers to recoveries that are imposed in the absence of enforceable contracts when justice so requires.

48   *See Dodson v. Shrader*, 824 S.W.2d 545 (Tenn. 1992) (minor who bought and wrecked pickup truck allowed to avoid the contract and could only recover the price paid, but truck's deterioration in value and the benefit received would be deducted from recovery); *Vichnes v. Transcontinental & Western Air, Inc.*, 18 N.Y.S.2d 603 (1940) (minor could not disaffirm contract to purchase airline ticket where she received benefit of ticket purchased). *But see Adamowski v. Curtiss-Wright Flying Service, Inc.*, 15 N.E.2d 467 (Mass. 1938) (money paid for flying lessons must be refunded because they are not necessaries).

49   *See, e.g., Lloyd v. Jordan*, 544 So.2d 957 (Ala. 1989) (annuity owner suffering from dementia held incapable of understanding change of beneficiary form, so change was void).

50   RESTATEMENT §176(D) *See Reiver v. Murdoch & Walsh, P.A.*, 625 F.Supp. 998, 1011-1014 (D.Del. 1985) (law firm's threats to fire at-will employee to force release of part of employee's bonus could support claim of economic duress).

vulnerability to pressure. In one case, a teacher had been arrested and had not slept for 40 hours when the principal of his school and the district superintendent arrived at his house and persuaded him to resign his position. The court held that the physical and mental condition of the teacher, the intrusion into the home and the lack of time given to think about it or consult a lawyer showed undue influence.[51]

5. Misrepresentation

A party to a contract that was procured by misrepresentation or concealment may avoid the contract. Only misrepresentations of fact, not of opinion, qualify, and the victim of the misrepresentation must have justifiably relied on the misrepresentation. Generally the misrepresentation must have been intentional. But if it concerns a material fact, unintentional misrepresentation may be sufficient.

Concealment of a fact, rather than the misrepresentation of it, is tolerated, because there is generally no duty to disclose anything to the contracting party. But there are several exceptions that result in the party's having a duty to disclose. If only part of the truth is told such that an overall misleading impression is created, this non-disclosure of the entire truth may constitute misrepresentation. Positive action taken in concealment, such as sweeping up evidence of termites and painting the affected area just before the sale of a house, can also constitute misrepresentation. Disclosure of a fact is also required where it is needed to prevent some previous assertion from being misleading. For example, if the seller of a house truthfully states that the house has no termites, but later discovers termites before the sale takes place, the seller must disclose this later discovery. A party who knows that the other is making a mistake as to a basic assumption also has a duty to disclose. The party's failure to correct that misunderstanding constitutes a misrepresentation if the non-disclosure amounts to a failure to act in good faith.

6. Unconscionable and Adhesion Contracts

A party may be excused from performance under a contract if the contract or a particular term therein is found to be unconscionable or an "adhesion contract." A contract may be unconscionable if there was "an absence of meaningful choice on the part of one of the parties together with contract terms which are unreasonably favorable to the other party."[52] Signs of unconscionability or adhesion can include harsh, one-sided contract terms set out in a standardized contract, gross inequality of bargaining power and contract provisions hidden in fine print. If a court finds all or part of the contract unconscionable, it may refuse to enforce the unconscionable part or it may decline to enforce the whole contract. In the words of the Restatement, where one party has reason to believe that the other party agreeing to the contract "would not do so if he knew that the writing contained a particular term, the term is not part of the agreement."[53]

7. Illegal Contracts and Contracts Against Public Policy

A contract that involves illegal subject matter or illegal means of performance is

---

51 *Odorizzi v. Bloomfield School District*, 54 Cal.Rptr. 533 (Cal.App. 1966).

52 *Williams v. Walker-Thomas Furniture Co.*, 350 F.2d 445 (D.C.Cir. 1965).

53 RESTATEMENT §211(3). *Mills v. Agrichemical Aviation, Inc.*, 250 N.W.2d 663 (N.D. 1977) (voiding exclusion of liability for crop spraying in insurance policy because insured would reasonably expect coverage for crop spraying in such a policy). The UCC provides for the obligation of good faith in all contracts, UCC §1-203, and for the removal of unconscionable terms, UCC §2-302. However, it applies only to contracts for the sales of goods.

void for illegality. Examples are contracts for gambling debts or prostitution or a contract to gain a competitive advantage by destroying the property of a competitor. The illegality may also spring from civil law. Thus, contracts to defame another person or to infringe on someone's trademark are also void. In addition, courts have found contracts void simply because they are against the "public policy" of the state. For example, in some states, agreements by employees who leave their employment not to compete with their former employer are void because of the public policy in favor of free competition and full productivity of its citizens.[54]

E. Breaches and Repudiations of Contracts

Breaches A party who fails to perform when performance is due under a contract has breached that contract. The non-breaching party may sue for damages or another remedy. Any of the grounds for non-performance discussed earlier will excuse a breach and relieve the breaching party of the duty to pay damages.

Repudiation Today, the other party does not always have to wait until performance is due to see whether the first party will breach. When one party clearly communicates unwillingness or inability to perform the contract and the threatened breach is material, the other party may treat this potential breach as a "repudiation" of the contract. For example, assume a landowner enters into a contract under which that owner is to convey the land to the buyer on May 1st. On April 15, the landowner tells the buyer that he or she will not convey the land. The owner has not yet breached the contract because the duty to convey the land has not yet arisen, but there has been a repudiation. When one party repudiates, the other party may suspend performance and may sue for damages immediately as if a breach had already occurred. Allowing the innocent party to act based on a repudiation prevents the unnecessary accrual of damages that could take place while the innocent party waited until the performance was due.

Repudiation must be unequivocal, so there is no repudiation if one party merely states vague doubts about willingness or ability to perform or if circumstances make it appear that performance may not be forthcoming. However, since such circumstances may give the other party reasonable ground for insecurity, the other party may demand an assurance of due performance. For example, if a seller finds out that the buyer is having financial difficulties and has failed to perform its contracts with other sellers, the seller may demand that the buyer provide some kind of assurance of performance. If the buyer fails to provide the demanded assurance, this failure will be considered a repudiation entitling the seller to suspend performance and sue for damages.[55]

F. Remedies for Breaches of Contracts

1. Damages and Their Limitations

Expectation Damages The most common kind of relief that is awarded in a suit for breach of contract are "expectation damages," so called because they remedy the unfulfilled expectations of a party. Expectation damages should put the aggrieved party in the same position the party would have been if the contract had been fully performed. This generally means, in a sales context, that the measure of damages will be the market price minus the contract price. For example, assume a buyer agrees to buy 100 pairs of jeans for $8 a pair for a total of $800. The seller agrees to deliver the jeans on May 1, but

---

54 *See Diaz v. Indian Head, Inc.*, 402 F.Supp. 111 (N.D. Ill. 1975) (applying New York law).

55 *See Kaiser Francis Oil Co. v. Producer's Gas Co.*, 870 F.2d 563 (10th Cir. 1989) (where contract required buyer to make certain payments and buyer did not do so when demanded by seller, seller was entitled to suspend performance). UCC §2-609 and §2-610.

fails to deliver. The price of jeans has risen to $10 a pair or $1000 for 100 pairs. The buyer is entitled to $200 in damages. But the award will not compensate for all losses that the aggrieved party may sustain from the breach. Two limits on this general rule are "mitigation" and "foreseeability"

Mitigation of Damages Injured parties are under an obligation to take reasonable steps to mitigate or minimize their damages to the extent that this can be done without "undue risk, burden or humiliation."[56] For example, when a seller fails to deliver components needed to manufacture a product, the manufacturer-buyer must try to get the components elsewhere if this can reasonably be done. This is called "cover" and if a price higher than the contract price must be paid, the difference is recoverable as damages. The buyer may not simply do nothing and let its manufacturing plant remain idle and then sue for the shutdown of production. The theory of mitigation is that the additional damages a non-mitigating injured party allows to accumulate are the fault of that party and not of the breaching party.

Foreseeability Damages are not recoverable for loss that the party in breach did not have reason to foresee as a probable result of the breach when the contract was made. For example, assume once again a seller who fails to deliver components of a product to the manufacturer-buyer. The buyer is able to purchase the components from another seller and production is resumed after a one-week delay. However, unknown to the seller, the buyer was counting on taking that very week's production to a major trade fair at which it usually concludes several contracts with prospective purchasers. Because the plant had to be shut down, the buyer had no products to take to the trade fair and could not go. The breaching seller could foresee that the buyer would "cover," by buying the components elsewhere, and must pay the buyer the difference between the contract price and the price of the cover. And, if the buyer covered as promptly as possible, the seller is liable for the normal loss of profits during one-week halt in production. But the seller is not liable for the loss of the contracts that the buyer could have signed at the trade fair because such a consequence was not foreseeable by the seller.

A breaching party may be liable for unforeseeable and unusual losses if that party had actual notice of the possibility of special losses. Thus, had the buyer in the above example told the seller of the upcoming trade fair and the necessity of having the components on time and the seller had then agreed to the contract, the seller would be liable for the lost profits.[57]

Generally, the plaintiff in an action for breach of contract cannot recover any damages beyond the foreseeable benefits of the contract bargain — the expectation damages discussed above. In this respect, contract damages are more limited than damages recoverable for violations of non-contractual tort duties, which may include compensation for emotional distress and in some cases punitive damages.[58]

2. Equitable Relief

Specific Performance Another possible remedy for a breach of contract is specific performance. Specific performance is an equitable remedy in which the court orders

---

[56] RESTATEMENT §350.

[57] RESTATEMENT §351. *Hadley v. Baxendale*, 156 Eng. Rep. 145 (1854) (shipper not liable for its delay in delivering a miller's shaft for repair because it was not foreseeable that the miller would not have another shaft).

[58] *See* Chapter XI, pp. 460-463.

the breaching party to perform duties under the contract. This remedy is usually used only where remedies at law will not adequately compensate the innocent party for the breach of the contract.[59] For example, if a contract to sell goods is breached by the seller, a legal remedy is adequate because damages awarded to the buyer will cover the cost of replacing the goods. But the buyer will not be adequately compensated by money if the contracted-for item is unique and irreplaceable.[60] In this case, the court may order the seller to deliver that item in accordance with the terms of the contract. Land is usually considered "unique" and specific performance is appropriate in real estate contracts. In contracts involving services, specific performance will generally not be ordered, because ordering a person to perform a service is considered to be imposing "involuntary servitude" prohibited by the 13th Amendment. However, a defendant may be enjoined from performing services *elsewhere*. For example, a professional athlete who refuses to play for the team he or she has contracted to play for cannot be ordered to play, but can be enjoined from playing for any other team.[61]

Restitution Remedies   A court order of "restitution," also an equitable remedy, places the parties back in the positions they were in before the contract was made.[62] Restitution is based on the principle that "one person is accountable to another on the ground that otherwise he would unjustly benefit or the other would unjustly suffer loss."[63]

There are two distinct uses of restitution. The first is to "undo" a contract that is void or voidable for fraud, duress, mistake, non-compliance with the Statute of Frauds, or any of the other such reasons. The second use of restitution is as an alternative to suing for damages for breach of contract. However, restitution is an option only if there is a complete breach of the contract, *i.e.*, one that goes to the essence of the contract. If there is, instead of suing for damages for breach of contract, the innocent party can elect to "cancel" the contract and sue for restitution. The advantage of restitution over expectation damages is that the amount awarded in restitution may exceed the contract price if the value that the breaching party has received is more than the contract price. The basic difference between restitution and expectation damages, is that restitution is measured by the gain the breaching party obtains, while expectation damages are measured by the benefit the innocent party should expect according to the contract. The difference is said to be justified because wrongdoers should suffer the consequences of their own wrongdoing and should not be permitted to be protected by the very contract that they breached.[64]

For example, suppose a builder enters a contract to build a building for $100,000. When the builder is halfway through and has been paid $25,000, the owner refuses to pay any more on the contract and orders the builder off the premises — a total breach of the contract. The owner then sells the uncompleted building for $200,000. If the builder sued for expectation damages, they would amount to only $75,000, the balance of the contract price not yet paid. However, restitution would total $175,000, the value

59 Equitable relief was discussed in Chapter VII, pp. 245-247.
60 UCC §2-716.
61 *See Dallas Cowboys Football Club v. Harris*, 348 S.W.2d 37 (Tex.Civ.App. 1961).
62 *See generally* DAN B. DOBBS, HORNBOOK ON THE LAW OF REMEDIES, 2D ED. §12.7 (West 1993).
63 *See* RESTATEMENT OF RESTITUTION 1 (American Law Institute 1937).
64 *See* CALAMARI & PERILLO, *supra* note 2, §15-1-15-15-4.

of the building that the builder built minus what the builder had already been paid.[65] However, if the owner's breach was a delay in making an installment payment on time, the builder would not be justified in canceling the contract and suing for restitution, since this is not a total breach of the contract.[66]

Quasi-Contract Theories of Recovery In cases where there is no contract, but the defendant has nonetheless been enriched by the plaintiff's action, the plaintiff may recover under "quasi-contract." For example, if a physician happens upon an injured child and renders medical assistance, the physician can recover against the child's parents for the value of that assistance in quasi-contract. Despite the terminology, quasi-contractual recovery has nothing to do with contracts. Such recovery comes from duties imposed by the law as a means of ensuring justice by preventing one party from being unjustly enriched at the expense of another.[67]

PART II: Commercial Law

A. The Uniform Commercial Code

There have been attempts in the past to codify commercial law, but none has succeeded like the Uniform Commercial Code (UCC). Although it was proposed in 1952, the UCC was not adopted widely until the 1960s.[68] It is now in effect in every state except Louisiana, where major portions have been enacted. The UCC's principal purposes are "to simplify, clarify, and modernize the law governing commercial transactions" and "to make the law uniform among the various jurisdictions."[69] Where there are gaps in the UCC, the common law rules of contracts apply.[70]

Space limitations require that we limit our discussion to two articles of the UCC — Article 2 on transactions in goods and Article 9 on security interests in personal property.[71] The discussion of Article 2 focuses mainly on the ways in which the UCC's Article 2 alters the common law rules of contracts, outlined above, when transactions

---

65 *See Boomer v. Muir*, 24 P.2d 570 (Cal.App. 1933) (affirming judgment for contractor of $258,000 when contract rate would have yielded only $20,000).

66 *Integrated, Inc. v. Alec Fergusson Electrical Contractors*, 58 Cal.Rptr. 503, 509 (Cal.App. 1967) ("slight deviation either in time or amount of progress payments should not justify rescission or abandonment"; only "an extended and unreasonable delay, imposition of new and onerous conditions to payment, outright refusal, or a total repudiation of the contract" is sufficient to justify cancellation).

67 *See* CALAMARI & PERILLO, *supra* note 2, §1-12. Quasi-contract is to be distinguished from actual implied contracts. Thus, if the parents of an injured child asked a physician to treat their child, they would be liable to pay, but it would not be on a quasi-contract theory. There was an actual contract, because the request for treatment implied that they would pay for that treatment.

68 Earlier efforts were the Uniform Sales Act (1906) and the Negotiable Instruments Law (1896). The UCC is a joint product of the National Conference of Commissioners on Uniform State Laws and the American Law Institute and was finished in 1952. Chapter I, p. 34, note 155. Louisiana has not adopted Article 2 on sales.

69 UCC §1-103(a).

70 UCC §1-103(b).

71 The other articles and their subject matters are: Articles 1 (general provisions), 2A (leases of goods), 3 (negotiable instruments), 4 (bank deposits and collections), 4A (funds transfers), 5 (letters of credit), 7 (documents of title) and 8 (investment securities). Article 6 on bulk sales was eliminated in 1989. Excellent succinct treatments of the UCC are JOHN F. DOLAN, COMMERCIAL LAW: ESSENTIAL TERMS AND TRANSACTIONS, 2D ED. (Aspen 1997); and CLAYTON P. GILLETTE & STEVEN D. WALT, SALES LAW: DOMESTIC AND INTERNATIONAL 2D ED. (Foundation 2008) (also discussing the U.N. International Sales of Goods Convention). The standard treatise is JAMES J. WHITE & ROBERT S. SUMMERS, UNIFORM COMMERCIAL CODE, 6TH ED. (West 2010). The UCC and many other statutes are in SELECTED COMMERCIAL STATUTES (West 2009). An extensive survey of the UCC is found in UCC Survey, 51 BUSINESS LAWYER 1339 (1996). For a guide to the recent changes in Article 9, *see* CORRINE COOPER, ED., THE NEW ARTICLE 9 OF THE UNIFORM COMMERCIAL CODE, 2D ED. (American Bar Assoc. 2001) and RUSSELL HAKES, THE ABCS OF THE UCC ARTICLE 9 (American Bar Assoc. 2001).

in goods are involved. Article 9 treats the parallel issue of a creditor's security interest in personal property of a debtor.

1. Contracts for Sales of Goods Under the UCC

Article 2 of the UCC applies to sales of goods, not to sales of real property, services or securities.[72] Issues of coverage arise when there are "mixed" contracts. For example, a mixed contract of services and goods may involve a builder who provides the service of installing goods such as cabinets and appliances. In such cases, most courts seek to determine whether the "predominant purpose" of the contract was the provision of services or sale of goods.[73] If the court determines that the predominant purpose of the contract is the sale of goods, then Article 2 applies to the entire contract.[74] Other courts apply a more particularized test by determining whether the contractual breach involved services or goods.[75] Under this minority approach, courts would apply Article 2 only if the breach itself involved goods. Courts apply similar treatment to mixed contracts of real property and goods, with the majority of courts again applying the predominant purpose test.[76]

a. Special Rules for "Merchants"

To assure that the UCC works for both the business community and ordinary consumers, it defines a special class of "merchants" to which it applies a different standard of conduct. "Merchants" are those who "deal in the goods" involved or who "hold themselves out as having knowledge or skill peculiar to the practice or goods involved."[77] The UCC's comments disclose an intent to distinguish between a "professional in business" and the "casual or inexperienced seller or buyer." Typical merchants would include the jewelry or hardware store as well as their owners. The definition tends to be more inclusive than not, but the entity or person is considered a merchant only in his mercantile capacity. For example, the jewelry store owner is a merchant to the extent that he trades in jewelry; he is not a merchant in transactions outside the jewelry profession. The sales volume at which a casual seller or buyer turns into a merchant-dealer of such goods is unclear.[78]

---

72 In addition, as of 1988, the United States is subject to the United Nations International Sale of Goods Convention, so the UCC does not apply to international sales of goods when the other country is also a party to the Convention. *See generally* GILLETTE & WALT, *supra* note 71, at 25-41 and *passim.*

73 *See Bonebrake v. Cox*, 499 F.2d 951, 960 (8th Cir. 1974) (applying the test to determine that installation of bowling lanes and equipment was a sale of goods). *But see Ward v. Purego Co.*, 913 P.2d 582 (Idaho 1996) (contract for application of fertilizer on crops was one for services, not goods).

74 *See Midwest Mfg. Holding v. Donnelly Corp.*, 975 F.Supp. 1061 (N.D. Ill. 1997) (stating that if contract predominantly involves the sale of goods, then the entire contract is subject to the UCC).

75 *See Foster v. Colorado Radio Corp.*, 381 F.2d 222 (10th Cir. 1967) (in sale of radio station, UCC applied to goods, but not to non-goods, such as good will, real estate, studios and transmission tower). *But see Hudson v. Town & Country True Value Hardware*, 666 S.W.2d 51 (Tenn. 1984) (applying two different measures of damages would pose "insurmountable problems of proof").

76 By contrast to the case law on mixed contracts of goods and services, there is statutory and case law support for the position that mixed contracts of goods and realty can be governed by different applicable laws depending on the aspect of the contract at issue. Farnsworth, *supra* note 2 §6.6.

77 UCC §2-104(1).

78 *See Nelson v. Union Equity Cooperative Exchange*, 548 S.W.2d 352 (Tex. 1977) (farmer selling his wheat to silo held to be a "merchant"; dissent argued farmer made only one "casual sale" a year). Most cases agree with the majority. *See also infra* note 80. *Compare Dixon v. Roberts*, 853 P.2d 235 (Okla. App. 1993) (amateur ostrich raisers with little experience in that business are not merchants).

b. Contract Formation

Formation and the Requirement of a Writing Article 2's "statute of frauds" requires that all contracts for sales of goods $500 or more be in writing. But not much writing is required. An enforceable contract exists if there is some writing "signed by the party against whom enforcement is sought" that "indicates" that a contract was made and that sets out the quantity of goods involved.[79] Between merchants, even oral agreements are enforceable if "within a reasonable time a writing in confirmation of the contract . . . is received" and no "written notice of an objection to its contents is given within 10 days."[80] In addition, under §2-204(1), "conduct . . . which recognizes the existence of a contract" is sufficient — most often performance by the parties. Under §2-204, the fact that the contract is missing terms, except for quantity,[81] does not invalidate a contract if the parties had intended to enter a binding agreement.

Acceptance of Offers Under §2-206(1), acceptance of an offer may be made in "any reasonable manner" unless the offeror has made it "unambiguously" clear that the offer may be accepted only in a certain manner. Section 2-207(1) provides that an acceptance is effective even if it contains terms additional or different from the offer. Thus, the UCC rejects the common law "mirror image" rule.[82] However, there must be some "definite and seasonal expression of acceptance," so if an acceptance differs so much from the offer as to indicate absence of agreement on basic terms, no contract is formed. For example, in an attempted sale of surplus factory equipment, there was an exchange of telegrams that agreed on price, but the seller proposed a sale "as is — where is," while the buyer proposed "F.O.B. our truck your plant loaded." In effect, the buyer's F.O.B. (free on board) statement proposed that the seller load the equipment onto the buyer's truck as part of the sale price. The Court held that there was no contract.[83]

Consideration The UCC eliminates the requirement of consideration for some option contracts for merchants. Called a "firm offer," a merchant's signed written offer to buy or sell goods that assures that it will be held open is irrevocable for the period of time stated or for a reasonable time, even absent consideration.[84] The UCC also abolishes any need for fresh consideration for modifications in contracts, thus rejecting the common law "pre-existing duty" rule.[85] The UCC rule makes it easier for parties to adjust their contracts to meet commercial exigencies. The problem of extortionate modifications, as where a builder threatens to slow down construction unless the

---

79 UCC §2-201(1). There need not be a single writing; an exchange of letters will do.

80 UCC §2-201(2). It was this provision that underlay the dispute over whether the farmer in the *Nelson* case was a merchant. *See supra* note 78. Nelson had an oral agreement to sell his wheat to a silo at a stated price. The silo followed this up with a §2-201(2) confirmatory letter. The price of wheat suddenly increased, Nelson refused to perform and the silo sued him and won. Another exception to the writing requirement is where goods specially ordered have begun to be manufactured or there is part performance. *See* §2-201(3).

81 UCC §2-201(1).

82 *See* discussion *supra* p. 399.

83 *Koehring Co. v. Glowacki*, 253 N.W.2d 64 (Wis. 1977). *Compare Idaho Power Co. v. Westinghouse Electric Corp.*, 596 F.2d 924 (9th Cir. 1979) (acceptance containing additional warranty disclaimer was "seasonable expression of acceptance").

84 UCC §2-205. A three-month limit on irrevocability is imposed.

85 UCC §2-209. Pre-existing duty was discussed *supra* p. 402.

contract price is raised, is handled by the UCC's unconscionability (§2-302) and good faith (§1-203) requirements.[86]

c. Determining Contract Content Under the UCC

Some sales contracts are fully negotiated in a deliberate manner, reduced to an integrated writing and signed by the parties. The content of such contracts is easy to determine. Other contracts pose greater challenges in determining their content. A contract may be complete, but the terms may be incomplete or unclear. Other contracts may not even be complete but become enforceable contracts by virtue of the subsequent conduct of the parties.[87] So, the UCC is often called upon to determine contractual content in two common situations: (1) when the parties' communications reflect an agreement, but the terms are incomplete or unclear; and (2) when the parties' correspondence does not reflect any true agreement, but the parties nonetheless perform.

Missing Terms   Missing terms in the contract are supplied by a set of gap-filler default terms set out in the UCC. Part 3 of Article 2 provides gap fillers based on prevailing commercial practices for such basic terms as price, place for delivery, time for performance and duration, and time and place of payment.[88] It also imposes quality standards through an implied warranty of merchantability, as well as rules for creating express warranties and implied warranties of fitness for purpose, and for excluding warranties.[89] In addition, Part 3 provides definitions for standard terms, such as F.O.B., C.I.F., Ex-Ship, "letter of credit" and "sale on approval." Part 5 sets out standards for performance, including issues of risk of loss in transit. Parts 6 and 7 set out default rules for breaches and remedies.[90]

Additional and Different Terms   A more complicated problem than missing terms are "additional" and "different" terms. This problem results from widespread use of standard business form contracts. Sellers' forms favor sellers and buyers' forms favor buyers. When the offer is on one such form and the acceptance is on a different one, there is usually agreement on the basic terms actually negotiated and a contract is formed based on those terms. But other terms on the opposing forms often conflict. When problems arise in the performance of the contract, the parties will pull out their forms and actually read them — perhaps for the first time — to see what they "agreed" to. Such a "battle of the forms" is regulated by §2-207.[91]

An "additional term" is a term set out in a form offer or acceptance for which there is no corresponding term on the other form. For example, the offer may provide that the parties will submit all disputes to arbitration, while the acceptance is silent on the subject. Under §2-207(2), *additional* terms are treated as "proposals for addition to the

---

86 *See Roth Steel Products v. Sharon Steel Corp.*, 705 F.2d 134 (6th Cir. 1983) (modifications must be consistent with commercial standards of fair dealing in the trade and the modifier must have a valid commercial reason for seeking the modification; raising steel prices because of market changes was not a proper modification on facts of the case).

87   UCC §2-204(1).

88   UCC §2-305 (reasonable price); UCC §2-308 (delivery at the seller's place of business); UCC §2-309 (reasonable time for performance); UCC §2-310 (payment due at time and place buyer is to receive the goods or documents of title; other provisions govern inspection and goods shipped on credit).

89   Warranties are discussed in greater detail *infra* pp. 419-421.

90   *See infra* p. 421.

91   Only a few of the types of "battles of the forms" can be discussed here. White and Summers discuss 8 common types and warn that many other combinations are possible. WHITE & SUMMERS, *supra* note 71, §1-3. Also, as will be seen, §2-207's meaning and application are not self-apparent. The Kansas Supreme Court has dubbed it a "murky bit of prose." *Southwest Engineering Co., Inc. v. Martin Tractor Co.*, 473 P.2d 18, 25 (Kan. 1970). *See also Roto-Lith, infra* note 97 (§2-207 "not too happily drafted").

contract." They become part of the contract unless the offeree objects to them within a reasonable time.[92]

A "different term" is a term in the offer or acceptance that conflicts with a counterpart term in the other. For example, the offer may provide for arbitration, but the acceptance provides that there will be no arbitration. Most courts agree that *conflicting* terms cancel each other out and are "knocked out" of the contract.[93]

Express Terms at Odds With Gap Fillers When different terms are knocked out of the contract, a UCC default gap filler will be inserted if there is one on the subject. In instances where an express term in the offer conflicts with a gap filler, the conflict is not viewed as one between different terms that would necessitate the knock-out rule. Instead, the express term in the offer is considered simply an "additional" term that becomes part of the contract for lack of objection to it within a reasonable time.[94]

A different result may obtain if it is the *acceptance* that introduces an express term at odds with a gap filler. For example, assume that the *offer* is silent as to damages, while the *acceptance* seeks to limit damages that are ordinarily available under the UCC. Since a term that conflicts with a gap filler is an "additional" term rather than a "different" term, the disclaimer would ordinarily become part of the contract unless the offeror objects.[95] However, §2-207(2) sets out a second exception in addition to objections by the offeror: additional terms in an *acceptance* do not become part of the contract if they "materially alter" the terms of the offer.[96] Comments to the Code indicate that a limitation on damages is usually not such a material alteration. However, a remedy limitation can be deemed a "material alter[ation]" of the offer terms if it is a severe limitation.[97] Other examples of material alterations include the addition of a warranty disclaimer, the addition of a clause securing cancellation rights, or the addition of a clause unreasonably restricting the time period for making complaints. If deemed a material alteration, the additional term in the acceptance stands only as a *proposal* for addition to the contract. It cannot become part of the contract without the other side

---

92 UCC §2-207(2). *See Polyclad Laminates, Inc., v. VITS Maschinenbau GmbH*, 749 F.Supp. 342 (D.N.H. 1990) (arbitration clause in seller's offer accepted by buyer's form that did not address the issue). In a merchant-consumer situation, any additional or different terms do not become part of the contract unless the consumer expressly consents to them.

93 *See Daitom, Inc. v. Pennwalt Corp.*, 741 F.2d 1569, 1580 (10th Cir. 1984) (disclaimer of warranty knocked out; knock-out rule essential to avoid giving unfair advantage to the person who sent the first form and it at least results in a Code gap filler being applied). Oddly enough, the two major experts on the UCC, White and Summers, disagree on how even this basic issue of conflicting terms should be resolved. *See* WHITE & SUMMERS, *supra* note 71, at 8-12.

94 *Idaho Power Co., supra* note 83 The court also held that the statement in the acceptance that it would be "deemed to constitute an agreement to the conditions named hereon and supersedes all previous agreements" did not make the buyer's acceptance of the offer conditional on the seller's assent to its terms.

95 This assumes that the acceptance evinces sufficient agreement with the offer to form a contract or that the parties' conduct in performing the contract indicates an contract exists. *See supra* text at note 83, where the *Koehring* case is discussed.

96 *See* §2-207(2), discussed in text *supra* at note 92. Note that §2-207(2)(a)-(c) pertain only to merchants. Additional terms set out in an acceptance by a consumer are always considered mere proposals for addition to the contract.

97 *See Altronics of Bethlehem, Inc. v. Repco, Inc.*, 957 F.2d 1102 (3d Cir. 1992) (in sale of security systems, seller's acceptance which limited remedies solely to repair or replacement was a material alteration; therefore not part of the contract). *But see Roto-Lith, Ltd. v. F.P. Bartlett & Co.*, 297 F.2d 497 (1st Cir. 1962) (acceptance with warranty disclaimer held to be expressly conditional and assented to by buyer's acceptance of goods).

expressly accepting it. The contract made then is the agreed-to terms plus any applicable gap fillers.

Expressly Conditional Acceptances In some instances, an acceptance may be made expressly conditional to the offeror assenting to additional or different terms. Such acceptances operate as counteroffers, and in order to form a contract, an acceptance of the additional or different terms by the original offeror is required. There are a few things to note here. First, the offeree must unambiguously express the conditional nature of his or her acceptance such that it "clearly reveals that the offeree is unwilling to proceed with the transaction unless he is assured of the offeror's assent to the additional or different terms therein."[98] Second, mere lack of objection by the offeror is not sufficient to form a contract on the terms of the conditional acceptance. Third, despite obstacles to contract formation in a situation involving an expressly conditional acceptance, subsequent conduct by the parties that indicates the existence of an agreement between the parties is sufficient to form a contract. The UCC's view is that if the parties act like there is a contract then there should be a legally enforceable contract. Thus, even if there has been no offer and acceptance consummation, a new contract is formed under terms agreed-to by both parties during their communications; conflicting or missing terms are supplied by the UCC.

d. Warranties

The UCC goes well beyond the common law in its provisions on "warranties." Warranties are promises of the seller pertaining to the sold goods that become part of the contract for sale under Article 2. Warranties may be express or implied.

Express Warranties Under §2-313, "[a]ny affirmation of fact or promise made by the seller to the buyer which relates to the goods and becomes part of the basis of the bargain creates an express warranty that the goods shall conform to the affirmation or promise." The assertion of fact can be written or oral. It may include a description of the goods or even a nonverbal affirmation, such as the showing of a sample to the buyer. The seller need not use "formal words such as 'warrant' or 'guarantee'" and "a specific intention to make a warranty" is not necessary. However, "an affirmation merely of the value of the goods or a statement purporting to be merely the seller's opinion or commendation of the goods" — generally called "puffing" — is not a warranty.[99]

The requirement that the seller's warranties be "part of the basis of the bargain" has given courts some trouble. The presumption, according to the official comments to §2-313, is that the affirmations made by the seller are part of the bargain; thus actual reliance by the buyer need not be shown. Case law varies on this issue.[100] Some courts,

---

98 *See Dorton v. Collins & Aikman Corp.*, 453 F.2d 1161 (6th Cir. 1972). *See also Idaho Power Co.*, *supra* note 83 (noting that the expressly conditional acceptances provision "has been construed narrowly"). *Compare Roto-Lith* case, *supra* note 97 (buyer's acceptance of goods was assent). Once more, not only the courts, but White and Summers disagree on how this situation should be resolved. *See* WHITE & SUMMERS, *supra* note 71, at 13-20.

99 UCC 2-313(2). *See Fitzner Pontiac-Buick-Cadillac v. Smith*, 523 So.2d 324 (Miss. 1988) (description of used car as in "first class shape" was not a warranty); *But see Hauter v. Zogarts*, 534 P.2d 377 (Cal. 1975) ("Golfing Gizmo" statement "completely safe ball will not hit player" held an express warranty that was breached when golf ball hit the plaintiff) and *Acme Equipment Corp. v. Montgomery Cooperative Creamery Ass'n.*, 138 N.W.2d 729 (Wis. 1966) ("in good shape and good working order" a warranty as applied to dairy equipment).

100 *Compare Speed Fastners, Inc. v. Newsom*, 382 F.2d 395 (10th Cir.1967) (sale of stud fasteners; plaintiff not entitled to recover in breach of express warranty where there was no evidence that plaintiff's employer relied on statements in seller's pamphlet before purchase) *with Hawkins Construction Co. v. Matthews Co.*, 209 N.W.2d 643 (Neb. 1973) (sale of scaffolding; express warranty created even if buyer did

in contrast to the UCC, state that the "basis of the bargain" requirement is met in the case of an advertisement or a brochure so long as there is evidence the plaintiff read the item before the deal was concluded.[101] Issues arise when there is evidence that the buyer had independent knowledge that the seller's representations were not true. In the case of the sale of a painting, the seller argued that the buyer had known about authenticity challenges to the painting at the time of the sale, so he should not have relied on the seller's representations that there had been no challenges. The court rejected this argument, holding that representations form a "basis of the bargain," not just when "the buyer believe[s] in the truth of the warranted information," but also when the buyer believes he is "purchasing the [seller's] promise as to its truth."[102] It has even been argued that statements of the seller made *after* the goods are sold are enforceable warranties, at least where the buyer could return the goods and the post-contract assurances forestalled or prevented such return.[103]

Implied Warranty of Merchantability Section 2-314's "implied warranty of merchantability" is perhaps the most important warranty under the UCC. The section states that every sale of goods by a "merchant" seller shall contain an implied warranty that the goods are merchantable.[104] "Merchantable" is defined as goods that are "fit for . . . ordinary purposes," are of "fair average quality" and "pass without objection in the trade." Perfection is not the standard. If a defect can be reasonably expected with regard to a particular good, it is considered merchantable even if the defect causes injury to someone. For example, fresh New England fish chowder is not "unfit" for eating just because it has fish bones in it, even if those bones cause personal injury.[105] Trade usage may have to be consulted to determine the appropriate standard of merchantability. For instance, hormone additives in cattle feed make it unmerchantable only in light of trade usage establishing that such additives are not usually included unless requested and that their addition is always disclosed on the label.[106] Even if there is evidence of a defect not reasonably expected by the user, it must be proven that the seller caused the defect. For example, a drug manufacturer was not liable for injuries caused when poison was injected into its medicine by a third person, even though the medicine clearly was unfit for its intended purpose.[107]

Implied Warranty of Fitness for Purpose Under §2-315, if a seller "has reason to know any particular purpose for which the goods are required and that the buyer is relying on the seller's skill or judgment to select or furnish suitable goods," an implied warranty arises that the goods the seller selects will be fit for that purpose. Unlike the

---

not rely on statements in seller's brochure).

101 *Interco v. Randustrial Corp.*, 533 S.W.2d 257 (Mo.App. 1976) (advertising statement in brochure that flooring "will absorb considerable flex" read by buyer was a warranty).

102 *Rogath v. Siebenmann*, 129 F.3d 261 (2d Cir. 1997) (applying New York law). Reliance has been an issue in tobacco litigation based on manufacturers' warranties that cigarettes did not harm one's health. Compare *Cipollone v. Liggett Group*, 893 F2d 541 (3d Cir. 1990) (only knowledge of advertising claims required) *with American Tobacco Co. v. Grinnell*, 951 S.W.2d 420 (Tex. 1997) (reliance on advertising claims required and negated by showing plaintiff had other reasons for starting to smoke).

103 WHITE & SUMMERS, *supra* note 71, at 342-343.

104 *See* discussion of who a "merchant" is, *supra* p. 415. When the seller is not a merchant, the buyer must rely solely on express warranties or perhaps implied warranties of fitness for purpose.

105 *See Webster v. Blue Ship Tea Room*, 198 N.E.2d 309 (Mass. 1964) (plaintiff choked on fish bones in fish chowder).

106 *Kassab v. Central Soya*, 246 A.2d 848 (Pa. 1968).

107 *Elsroth v. Johnson & Johnson*, 700 F.Supp. 151 (S.D.N.Y. 1988).

implied warranty of merchantability, there is no requirement here that the seller be a merchant.[108]

Remedies Buyers who suffer a breach of warranty have several possible remedies, but the most common is a suit for damages.[109] Damages are available both for personal injury and for commercial loss or property damage. As discussed in the next chapter, warranty theories of recovery for consumers injured by defective products form a significant part of "products liability."[110] Indeed, in some ways warranty liability is broader.[111]

Warranty Disclaimers and Remedy Limitations A seller may disclaim any of the above warranties or may limit the remedies available.[112] Disclaimers will often state that the buyer takes the item "as is" or that "the seller disclaims any warranties express or implied." However, any disclaimer of merchantability must "mention merchantability" and must be "conspicuous," meaning that it must be in a type face that is larger than that used in the rest of the contract or is in a contrasting color. As for remedy limitations, an important and common remedy limitation is the exclusion of any recovery for "consequential damages."

"Unconscionability" is a specific limit on remedy limitations and the UCC presumes that limiting "consequential damages for injury to the person in the case of consumer goods" is unconscionable.[113] However, unconscionability is more difficult to show when it comes to warranty disclaimers. There is a general provision on unconscionability in UCC §2-302, but most courts have held that it is "preempted" by the more specific provisions of §2-316, which describes how a seller can properly disclaim warranties.[114] But some courts have held warranty disclaimers unconscionable even when the provisions of §2-316 have been satisfied.[115]

A typical disclaimer and remedy limitation provision in a contract will disclaim all implied warranties and substitute a limited express warranty of freedom from manufacturing defects for one year after purchase, and will limit remedies to replacement or repair. Courts routinely uphold such disclaimers and limitations on remedies.

Third Party Beneficiaries of Warranties An important common law principle is the notion of "privity of contract." This means that in general, only persons who are parties

---

108 *Leal v. Holtvogt*, 702 N.E.2d 1246 (Ohio App. 1998) (selling chronically lame stallion when seller knew that buyers were interested in a horse good for breeding beached implied warranty of fitness).

109 UCC §§2-714, 2-715. Rejection and revocation of acceptance are also possible. *See* §§2-601, 2-605 and §2-608. The buyer can then recover any price paid, the costs of purchasing substitute goods, called "cover," and consequential damages. §§2-711(1), 2-712. However, the seller has the right to "cure" the defect under §2-508 in the event of rejection and revocation of acceptance is possible only when the goods' "non-conformity substantially impairs [their] value." §2-608(1).

110 *See* Chapter XI, pp. 448-450. In addition to the warranties discussed, the UCC provides for a warranty of title, under which sellers automatically warrant that they own the goods and have a legal right to sell them and that the goods do not infringe upon any patent or trademark. UCC §2-312.

111 *See* Chapter XI, p. 450, note 95. Other warranty remedies for consumers may be available under the federal Magnuson-Moss Warranty Act, discussed *infra* p. 431.

112 UCC §2-316 (disclaimers of warranties); UCC §2-719 (limitations of remedies).

113 UCC §2-719(3). *See Collins v. Uniroyal*, 315 A.2d 16 (N.J. 1964) (warranty against tire "blow-outs" that was limited to tire replacement or repair held presumptively unconscionable as applied to death caused by blow-out). The presumption does not apply to limits on commercial losses. *But see Majors v. Kalo Laboratories, Inc.*, 407 F.Supp 20 (M.D.Ala. 1975) (limiting warranty claims to those raised within 10 days of sale was unconscionable where hidden defect in soybean seeds caused loss of farmer's crop).

114 *Marshall v. Murray Oldsmobile Co.*, 154 S.E.2d 140 (Va. 1967) (disclaimer upheld in new car sale).

115 *Martin v. Joseph Harris Co.*, 767 F.2d 296, 299 (6th Cir. 1985) (waiver of cabbage seed warranties that complied with §2-316 was unconscionable when seeds contained "black leg" disease).

to a contract, and thus "in privity with" each other, may claim the benefits of that contract. This principle presents a problem when the person injured by defective goods is a third party — someone other than the original buyer. The UCC generally abolishes privity as a requirement for recovery. However, in deference to the controversy over third-party recovery, it provides three alternative rules that offer varying degrees of coverage to third parties. The alternatives differ on which third parties may sue (just natural persons or anyone), what injuries are compensable (only personal injury or property damage as well) and who may recover (only household members or anyone who is injured).[116]

In addition, none of the options for third-party recovery permits recovery for "pure economic loss," such as lost profits. This makes abolition of privity of limited use to businesses which did not actually purchase the defective goods that damaged them. Thus, a third-party consumer can often recover for personal injuries caused by a defective product, but a third-party business cannot recover for lost profits caused by the same breach. For example, assume the builder of a new airport terminal uses defective steel beams in its construction, which results in a delay in the airport being opened because the beams have to be replaced. A restaurant in the terminal that loses profits because of a delay cannot recover against the steel beam manufacturer. By contrast, if the defective beams cause personal injury to restaurant customers, those customers can recover for their injuries from the manufacturer.[117]

2. Security Interests in Personal Property Under the UCC

a. The Nature of Security Interests

Article 9 of the UCC governs "security interests" in personal property.[118] A security interest is an interest in property, granted by a debtor to a creditor, which secures a debt.[119] It provides security to the creditor because it permits the creditor to take the secured property in the event that the debtor does not repay the debt.[120] The encumbered property is referred to as the "collateral." Collateral may be tangible, such as consumer goods or equipment, or it may be intangible, such as patents or promissory notes.

Security interests are used in a variety of contexts. A manufacturer may give a security interest in its machinery to borrow money to purchase raw materials needed in manufacturing. The supplier of goods to a retail store may insist on retaining a security interest in those goods as inventory of the store until they are sold. Or, a consumer may borrow money from a bank or credit union to purchase an automobile and grant a security interest in the car to secure the loan. If the security interest secures the loan

---

116 UCC §2-318, Alternatives A, B, and C.

117 *See Minnesota Mining and Manufacturing Co. v. Nishika Ltd.*, 565 N.W.2d 16 (Minn. 1997) (plaintiff camera manufacturer, who never bought chemicals from manufacturer, could not recover for lost profits unaccompanied by personal injury or property damage when chemicals failed to develop film properly). *Nebraska Innkeepers, Inc. v. Pittsburgh-Des Moines Corp.*, 345 N.W.2d 124 (Iowa 1984) (hotel owners could not recover for loss of business from steel manufacturer when defective beams caused a bridge to be closed to traffic). When combined with the similar ban on recovering in tort for pure economic loss, *see* Chapter XI, p. 461, this rule serves to limit all claims by businesses for pure economic loss caused by defective goods to claims based on a warranty theory where the warranty is made to the immediate buyer. This makes it subject to waiver or modification in the contract between the seller and the buyer.

118 As noted earlier, *supra* p. 415, a revised Article 9 went into effect in most states on July 1, 2001. Security interests in real property are discussed in Chapter XII, p. 488.

119 UCC §9-109.

120 UCC §9-103.

used to purchase the collateral, as in the automobile example, it is called a "purchase money security interest" (PMSI).[121]

b. Requirements for Valid Security Interests

To have a valid enforceable security interest, three requirements must be met: (1) the parties must authenticate a security agreement that describes the collateral or the debtor must give possession of the collateral to the creditor; (2) the creditor must give value for the security interest (normally a loan of money); and (3) the debtor must have an interest in the property.[122] Once these requirements are met, the security interest has "attached," *i.e.*, it is enforceable by the creditor against the debtor. In order for the creditor to have "priority" over other creditors, buyers, and other third parties, the creditor must "perfect" the security interest. Perfection means attachment, plus another step, usually an act that gives the world notice of the security interest.[123] Such steps include filing a "financing statement,"[124] taking possession of the collateral[125] or, in the case of an automobile, noting a lien on the certificate of title.[126] The most common means of perfecting a security interest is by filing a financing statement.[127] A "financing statement" is a short form that is filed with the office of the Secretary of State of the state where the debtor lives or is located.[128] A sufficient financing statement provides the debtor's name, the secured party's name, and a description of the collateral.[129] It is a document containing minimal information, and it serves mostly as a guide for further inquiries.

c. Enforcing Security Interests

If the debtor fails to repay the creditor and does not voluntarily give up the property to the creditor, the creditor has the right to take the collateral upon default by either judicial or non-judicial means. Judicial means usually involve an action for "replevin" or "claim and delivery" — a claim used in any situation where one seeks to gain possession of personal property that is in the possession of another.[130] The secured party may also seize the property without going to court if the seizure can be accomplished without a "breach of the peace."[131] Clearly non-judicial means are simpler and less expensive, so many creditors regularly use them. Since security interests are regularly taken in sales of automobiles, some creditors resort to such "self-help repossession" on a regular basis and employ persons who are specialists in the art of locating cars of defaulting debtors and then driving or towing them away.

d. Disputes Over Secured Property

Disputes Between Secured Creditors and Other Creditors   Article 9 boasts many

---

121 UCC §1-201(37).

122 UCC §9-203(b).

123 UCC §9-308(a).

124 UCC §9-310(a).

125 UCC §9-313(a).

126 UCC §9-311(a)(2), (b). Title notation is usually provided for in motor vehicle registration laws.

127 The security agreement made between the creditor and debtor may also be used. Because that document provides greater detail than required to put others on notice regarding the security interest, most parties choose not to file the security agreement.

128 UCC §9-301(1); §9-501(a)(2).

129 UCC §9-502(a).

130 *See* Chapter XI, p. 439. Procedural due process requires that the debtor be given notice before judicial seizure and an opportunity for a hearing. *See* Chapter VI, pp. 205-209.

131 UCC §9-609.

intricate details in adjudicating priority disputes. Here is a general overview. In resolving priority disputes, Article 9 categorizes creditors into hierarchical classes. Two general concepts govern this hierarchy: a secured creditor beats all others to rights in the collateral unless a specific UCC provision states otherwise,[132] and within a class, first in time equals first in right.[133] At the top of the hierarchy are buyers in the ordinary course, discussed in more detail below. Such buyers are not secured creditors, and thus ordinarily would be subordinate to a secured creditor's rights in the collateral. §9-320, however, provides a specific provision giving such buyers priority even over perfected secured creditors. Next in line are perfected secured creditors, followed by lien creditors. A lien creditor is an unsecured creditor who has made the effort to obtain a judicial lien on the collateral through the court system.[134] After lien creditors, next in line are buyers not in the ordinary course, discussed below. After them, there are attached but unperfected creditors. Generally, these are creditors who attached their interests to the collateral by executing a security agreement but failed to perfect their interests by filing successfully. At the bottom of the hierarchy are general unsecured creditors.

Disputes Between Secured Creditors   When a debtor gives a security interest in the same property to multiple creditors, priority is given to the creditor who has perfected the security interest and, if both have perfected, to the one who perfected first. Since most security interests are perfected by filing a financing statement, the first secured creditor to file a financing statement is usually the one who prevails.[135] Before lending money, a creditor can research the public record to look for prior financing statement filings. If no financing statement is found, the creditor can be sure that it will have first priority in the collateral when it files its financing statement.

Disputes Between Secured Creditors and Buyers   The UCC generally provides that a security interest continues in the property even if it is sold, unless the secured party authorizes the disposition.[136] Thus, the creditor with a security interest will win a dispute with someone who buys the collateral from the debtor. As discussed above, however, a buyer in the ordinary course takes goods free of encumbrance. To enjoy this provision, the buyer must give new value to a seller who ordinarily sells goods of that kind.[137] Thus, a clothing store may give a security interest in its inventory of clothes to a bank in order to obtain a loan. If the store sells a sweater, the purchaser will take that sweater free of the bank's interest. However, if the clothing store has granted a security interest in its office equipment and it sells some of that equipment, the purchaser will not be protected because the clothing store does not ordinarily sell office equipment.[138] Such a purchaser is considered a buyer not in the ordinary course. It should be noted that the secured party in each of these sales is not without recourse since the security interest in the collateral automatically attaches to the proceeds of the sale.[139] In some

---

132 UCC §9-201.

133 UCC §9-322.

134 UCC §9-102(52). *See* Chapter VII, p. 244, where procedures for execution of judgments are discussed.

135 UCC 9-322(a)(1). In fact, creditors may and often do file a financing statement before the loan is made or the debtor has signed a security agreement in order to ensure that they will have priority.

136 UCC §9-315(a).

137 UCC §9-320(a). In addition, in inventory financing, the creditor usually also gives permission to the debtor to sell its inventory.

138 Most sales of secured property between consumers are valid against the secured creditor, unless the creditor has filed a financing statement. UCC §9-320(b).

139 UCC §9-315(a).

cases, perfection will continue in the proceeds, and in other cases the secured party has to perfect its new interest.[140]

Disputes Between Secured Creditors and Bankruptcy Trustees   Bankruptcy is a judicial proceeding in which a debtor can apply remaining assets to pay debts and be discharged from any further obligation on those debts.[141] The bankruptcy trustee gathers all the assets of the debtor on behalf of the *unsecured* creditors. In the process, the trustee seeks to enlarge the pool of assets available to pay unsecured creditors (the debtor's "estate"). One way to enlarge the estate is to contest and invalidate the security interests of secured creditors.

In a contest between the trustee and the secured creditor, a secured creditor with a fully valid and perfected security interest will generally have priority over the bankruptcy trustee. However, if the creditor has not perfected its interest (usually by failing to file a financing statement), it will lose to the trustee.[142] Thus, creditors must be sure that they do not delay in filing their financing statements.

The creditor will also lose if the creditor's transaction amounted to a "fraudulent transfer" of an interest in property or constituted a voidable "preference." These rules prevent creditors from using their leverage with the debtor to gain an advantageous position shortly before bankruptcy. Fraudulent transfers are transfers of property interests, including security interests, (1) made within the *year* before filing bankruptcy; (2) if done with the intent to defraud or if less than reasonable value was given to the debtor; and (3) if done while the debtor was insolvent or which caused the debtor to become insolvent. "Preferences" are transfers, including security interests, (1) made to creditors within the 90 days before the bankruptcy was filed (2) that enabled the transferee to receive more than it otherwise would receive in the bankruptcy proceeding.[143] This means that an already attached security interest perfected within the 90-day period will be voided as a preference.[144]

B. Consumer Protection Laws

By distinguishing between merchants and consumers and making commercial transactions subject to the unconscionability doctrine, the UCC makes some effort to protect consumers in their purchases of goods. Other laws go even further.

1. Consumer Credit Transactions

The consumer economy of the United States runs on credit. Not only does the United States have one of the lowest savings rates in the industrialized world, the use of credit to live beyond one's immediate means is taken for granted. The eagerness of consumers to obtain credit usually means that they do not shop for it and they often will not bargain over credit terms. This makes the area of consumer credit transactions particularly subject to abuse by lenders and therefore the object of several consumer protection laws.

---

140 UCC §9-315(d).

141 Bankruptcy is discussed in Chapter XV, pp. 606-608.

142 *See* 11 U.S.C.A. §544 (trustee has the status of a lien creditor); UCC §9-317(a)(1) (lien creditor has priority over an unperfected secured party). One might wonder why a secured creditor would ever fail to file a financing statement. But a creditor whose debtor is having difficulty may intentionally refrain from filing because it could prevent the debtor from borrowing new money to pay off old debts. In addition, sometimes filing is simply overlooked.

143 11 U.S.C.A. §547(b).

144 11 U.S.C.A. §547(e).

a. Federal Laws

The Truth in Lending Act Since 1968, consumer credit transactions have been subject to the Truth in Lending Act (TILA), part of the Consumer Credit Protection Act (CCPA).[145] The TILA does not regulate the actual terms of credit, such as how much interest a lender can charge.[146] States regulate such terms. TILA requires that, whatever the terms of an extension of credit may be, they must be disclosed clearly and in a uniform way so that prospective consumer borrowers can shop for the lowest cost credit. The principal disclosures are the "finance charge" — defined broadly to include not just interest, but many of the "hidden" costs of borrowing, such as loan application fees, mortgage broker fees, and required insurance — and the resulting "annual percentage rate," expressed as a percentage of the "amount financed."[147] In addition, in one-time closed end credit transactions, the lender must disclose the sum of the amount financed and the finance charge as the "total of payments"; the lender must also disclose late payment fees and details regarding any rebate of the finance charge in the event of an early debt payoff. In the case of credit cards and other open-end credit accounts, the TILA requires disclosure of the rate of the finance charge and the conditions under which it will be imposed.[148]

Another provision of the TILA is the right of any consumer to cancel within 3 days transactions that involve a security interest in the consumer's home; some transactions, such as the purchase money mortgage, are excluded.[149] If the creditor does not properly disclose the 3-day rescission right at the time of the transaction, as required by TILA, the 3-day period is extended up to, but not exceeding, 3 years.[150] This TILA provision has as its focus home improvement contractors and bill consolidators peddling "home equity loans," with high rates and high fees.[151] The rationale behind the right of rescission is that borrowers need to understand and think particularly seriously about a transaction that could ultimately lead to the loss of their home if they default.[152]

The TILA is enforceable by a consumer suit in federal court without regard to diversity of citizenship or amount in controversy. Depending on the TILA violation at issue, recovery rules vary, but a successful suit will always include actual damages and sometimes include reasonable attorney fees, with a minimum damages amount specified for some categories of violations where actual damages are not likely to be

---

145 15 U.S.C.A. §1601 *et seq.* Also of importance is Regulation Z, promulgated under the TILA by the Federal Reserve Board. 12 CFR §226.1 *et seq.* The TILA, Regulation Z and virtually the entire CCPA are set out in SELECTED COMMERCIAL STATUTES, *supra* note 71.

146 *But see* 15 U.S.C.A. §1615 (outlawing the "Rule of 78s," a method of computing the unearned portion of the finance charge to be rebated to the debtor in the event the debt is paid off early that allows creditors to receive a high amount of unearned interest) and §1639 (certain terms of home equity loans).

147 *First Acadiana Bank v. Fed. Deposit Ins. Corp.*, 833 F.2d 548 (5th Cir. 1987) (when bank required all car loan applicants to use bank-approved attorneys to draw up loan documents, attorney fees paid were part of the finance charge); *Lawson v. Reeves*, 537 So.2d 15 (Ala. 1988) (difference in price between cars sold for cash and cars sold on installment contracts was a hidden finance charge).

148 *See* 15 U.S.C.A. §1638 (closed end) and §§1637 and 1637a (open end).

149 15 U.S.C.A. 1635(e).

150 15 U.S.C.A. §1635(a) and (f). *See Jenkins v. Landmark Mortgage Corp.*, 696 F.Supp. 1089 (E.D. Va. 1988).

151 Development of home equity loans was also spurred by changes in tax laws that prohibited deduction of interest on consumer debts, but continued to permit deduction of mortgage interest.

152 *See also* 15 U.S.C.A. §1637a (home equity loan disclosures). For an example of a successful class action attacking many of the excess "garbage fees" in home equity loan transactions, *see Rodash v. AIB Mortgage Co.*, 16 F.3d 1142 (11th Cir. 1994). Class actions of this type were so successful that Congress established stricter standards for home equity loans in 1995. *See* 15 U.S.C.A. §§1640(a), 1649.

very much.[153] Various federal agencies responsible for supervising different classes of creditors may also take action. They could sue to enforce compliance or could order institutions under their supervision to adjust accounts of consumers so that they do not pay a finance charge higher than what was disclosed.[154]

Credit Card Issuance, Liability and Billing It used to be common practice for merchants or credit card companies to simply send out credit cards to potential customers. The CCPA puts a stop to this by prohibiting the issuance of any credit card except at the request of the consumer.[155] The CCPA also limits the liability of consumers whose credit cards are used fraudulently to the first $50 of such charges.[156] As for credit card billing, the CCPA provides a procedure for card holders to protest errors on their credit card bill within 60 days of the error appearing. The credit card issuer must make the required corrections, including crediting any finance charges imposed, or send the card holder an explanation denying the error. If the billing error is the result of goods not being delivered, the card issuer may not deem the amount correct unless it verifies that the goods were sent. No action may be taken to collect the disputed amount nor may the card issuer restrict or cancel the account while the dispute is being investigated.[157]

An interesting feature of the Act with regard to credit cards is that it allows card holders to assert against the credit card issuer any claims they have against the seller of goods as to the quality of goods purchased. However, the right is limited to transactions exceeding $50 in which the seller is located in the same state or within 100 miles of the card holder.[158]

CARD Act "The Credit Card Accountability, Responsibility, and Disclosure Act" of 2009 (CARD Act) implemented myriad changes designed to strengthen consumer protections in open end credit plans. Sharing the same core principles of TILA, such as fairness and transparency in consumer credit transactions, the CARD Act takes the cause even further and in the process amends and expands aspects of TILA. Of note, the CARD Act requires advance notice, not less than 45 days before the effective date, of any rate increases;[159] forbids over-limit fees unless consumer expressly permits his account to process transactions over the credit limit;[160] and prohibits credit card issuance to those under 21 years of age unless the underage applicant supplies sufficient evidence of ability to pay or a co-signer, who is at least 21 years old.[161] Significant to those carrying heavy credit card burdens, a CARD Act provision directs card issuers to apply payments in excess of the minimum first to the balance carrying the highest interest rate, then in descending order of interest rates to other balances.[162]

Electronic Funds Transfers Electronic funds transfer (EFT) cards and other EFT deductions from bank accounts are becoming increasingly popular as a means of

---

153 15 U.S.C.A. §1640(a). This changes the normal "American rule" on fees. *See* Chapter VII, p. 247.

154 *See, e.g., Acadiana Bank, supra* note 147. TILA advertising requirements may be enforced only by a federal agency, the Federal Trade Commission. Consumer leasing is also covered by the TILA, which imposes requirements similar to those discussed here. *See* 15 U.S.C.A. §1667 *et seq.*

155 15 U.S.C.A. §1642.

156 15 U.S.C.A. §1643. The Act also makes fraudulent use a federal crime punishable by 10 years in prison or a $10,000 fine. 15 U.S.C.A. §1644.

157 *See* 15 U.S.C.A. §1666 *et seq.*

158 15 U.S.C.A. §1666i.

159 15 U.S.C.A. §1637(i).

160 15 U.S.C.A. §1637(k).

161 15 U.S.C.A. §1637(c)(8).

162 15 U.S.C.A. §1666c.

making payments. The CCPA has provisions on EFT billing errors that are similar to those on credit card billing errors. A $50 consumer liability limit is imposed as well.[163]

Consumer Credit Reporting   Gathering and reporting information on consumer creditworthiness is a big business. In response to widespread abuses in the industry, the CCPA (1) limits the type of information that may be included in a consumer's file, particularly old information, such as bankruptcies more than 10 years old and judgments against the debtor, accounts placed for collection or arrests or convictions of crime that are more than 7 years old; (2) restricts the uses to which reports can be put, usually only for credit transactions, insurance applications and employment; (3) requires notification whenever a report is or may be requested; (4) provides consumers the right to view their file, to challenge the accuracy of information in it, to force deletion of unverifiable information and to add statements disputing the accuracy or completeness of any information that is then required to be included in any future reports; (5) requires disclosure of the sources of information and the identity of credit report inquirers in the previous year; and (6) imposes verification requirements for particularly sensitive information, such as public records of convictions, and for potentially suspect sources of information, such as personal interviews with the consumer's neighbors, friends or associates.[164] In the event credit is denied, lenders are required to give applicants a written statement of reasons for the denial as well as the name and address of any credit reporting agency used by the lender. Civil suits by consumers may be filed in federal court on the same basis generally as under the TILA.[165]

Equal Credit Opportunity   The CCPA also provides for "Equal Credit Opportunity."[166] It prohibits any discrimination against applicants for credit (1) on grounds of race, color, religion, nationality, origin, sex or marital status, or age; (2) because all or part of the applicant's income is from public assistance; or (3) because the applicant has exercised rights under the CCPA.

Debt Collection   The CCPA also includes a Fair Debt Collection Practices Act.[167] It regulates practices of debt collectors, sometimes called "collection agencies." The Act prohibits collectors from contacting debtors at unusual or inconvenient times (usually periods outside 8:00 AM to 9:00 PM) or inconvenient places, including place of work, or at any time after being told in writing that the debtor will not pay the debt or wishes that no further contact be made. Contact with anyone else but the debtor regarding the debt is prohibited, except when the debt has been reduced to a court judgment and such contact is necessary. Harassment and abuse of the debtor are prohibited, such as threats of violence or injury to the debtor's reputation, use of obscene or profane language, publishing a "shame list" of debtors who allegedly refuse to pay their debts or repeated use of the telephone to annoy or harass any person. Further, debt collectors may not do anything that would give the false impression that they are law enforcement officers or lawyers, that nonpayment of the debt could result in arrest or imprisonment or that documents they use in collection efforts are related to judicial proceedings. In the event of a dispute, collection agencies must inform debtors of their right to seek

---

163 Civil liability provisions similar to the TILA also apply.

164 *See* 15 U.S.C.A. §1681 *et seq.*

165 For an example of a successful suit, *see Stevenson v. TRW, Inc.*, 987 F.2d 288 (5th Cir. 1993) (credit reporting company's placing burden on consumer to deal with fraudulent accounts it was reporting was inadequate reinvestigation; damages of $30,000 and attorney fees of $20,700 approved).

166 15 U.S.C.A. §701.

167 15 U.S.C.A. §1692 *et seq.*

"validation" of the debt from the creditor. There is a defense to an action by a consumer if the debt collector's violation was not intentional and "resulted from a bona fide error," but that defense does not include errors of law based on a misunderstanding of the CCPA's provisions.[168] States have regulated collection agencies for a long time, requiring, among other things, a state license to do business.[169] Thus, another possible remedy for a consumer is to challenge the license of the offending collection agency. The CCPA does not preempt state debt collection laws.[170]

Federal Trade Commission "Holder in Due Course" Regulations   Whenever a consumer finances the purchase of goods, the financing contract or note is considered negotiable, meaning that it can be sold to another party, usually a bank or other financial institution, which then has the right to collect on it from the consumer. This is a useful device for sellers, who are in the business of selling goods not financing credit. Sellers prefer to purchase more inventory and expand their markets than to tie up money in financing sales. This useful device, however, also presents a challenge when a consumer no longer desires to make payments because of a problem with his or her purchase. If the seller of the goods is still the holder of the contract, the consumer can put pressure on the seller, who presumably can solve the problem, by withholding payment. However, if the seller has sold the contract, that transaction now separates the contract holder and the party perceived to be responsible for the problem.

The new contract holder, who has purchased it without notice of any problems in the original sale, is considered a "holder in due course" (HDC) under the UCC. The HDC can enforce payment even if the goods are defective or the original seller made misrepresentations when he or she sold the goods to the consumer.[171] The consumer-buyer, hoping to recover the money paid to the HDC, may bring an action against the seller. It may be a harsh rule for the consumer-buyer, but it is a rule intended to promote a policy of free trade in negotiable instruments.

Some states, either by legislation or case law, permit the consumer to assert any defense against a later holder that could be asserted against the seller. However, much of this state law has been rendered moot by regulations of the Federal Trade Commission (FTC). The FTC has not changed state law. Instead, it has proclaimed that the use of the HDC rule to shield a holder from the consumer-buyer's defenses is an "unfair trade practice." FTC rules prohibit any holder from taking or receiving any consumer credit contract that does not include a notice that "any holder [of the contract] is subject to all claims and defenses which the debtor could assert against the seller of the goods or services obtained." This contractual language is embedded in a transfer to an HDC, and therefore is enforceable as a matter of state contract law.[172]

---

168 *See Jerman v. Carlisle, McNellie, Rini, Kramer & Ulrich LPA*, ___ U.S. ___, 130 S.Ct. 1605 (2010) (law firm filed complaint in court that erroneously stated that mortgage debt would be assumed valid unless consumer disputed it in writing; not a bona fide error).

169 *See Miller v. Payco-General American Credit*, 943 F.2d 482 (4th Cir. 1991) (printing notice of validation right in gray ink on reverse of letter demanding immediate payment was not proper disclosure).

170 In a decision that caused some consternation in the legal profession, the Supreme Court held that lawyers who normally collect debts for clients through litigation are subject to the Act. *See Heintz v. Jenkins*, 514 U.S. 291 (1995). Congress then amended the Act to provide that litigation papers need not set forth the disclosures required for all communications with a debtor.

171 *See* UCC §9-302(a), §9-305(b).

172 16 CFR §433.2. *See Ford Motor Credit Co. v. Morgan*, 536 N.E.2d 587 (Mass. 1989) (buyer of car permitted to use defense of misrepresentations of seller against holder, but a buyer's affirmative claim for rescission of the contract is possible only if the goods are not delivered or are totally worthless).

b. State Laws

The Uniform Consumer Credit Code The Uniform Consumer Credit Code (UCCC or "U-triple-C") was first promulgated in 1968, with major revisions in 1974. It is in effect in some form in only 9 states. Its unpopularity with states is largely because many of the consumer protections it affords have either already been enacted as separate state laws or implemented nationally by FTC rules, already discussed, such as federal limitations on the "holder in due course" rule, regulations of debt collection practices, and various disclosure requirements in consumer credit and lease transactions, as well as limitations on garnishment and "cooling-off periods" for home solicitation sales, discussed below. While the UCCC adopts a maximum ceiling rate for consumer credit of 24%, many states have long ago imposed even lower ceilings.

Some of the UCCC's provisions do not overlap of state other laws. For instance, the UCCC prohibits contract provisions that require consumers to pay creditors' attorney fees, take excessive collateral as security for payment, or impose "balloon payments," default charges or excessive charges for credit life, property and liability insurance. Under the UCCC, unconscionability is a basis for rescinding consumer credit transactions.[173] The UCCC also provides statutory penalties and attorney fees for successful private suits and administrative enforcement actions, similar to federal TILA provisions.

Other State Laws on Consumer Credit Before Congress got involved in consumer credit in 1969 with the TILA, states regulated consumer credit, imposing both licensing and disclosure requirements. State licensing and regulation continue unaffected by federal law. Often, state laws require disclosures that supplement TILA.

2. Deceptive and Unfair Trade Practices

a. Federal Laws

The Federal Trade Commission Act and Regulations As noted above when HDC was discussed, the FTC has stepped in to regulate various aspects of consumer credit transactions. But its authority extends even more broadly to policing all "unfair and deceptive trade practices."[174] In addition, where it appeared necessary, Congress passed statutes dealing with consumer protection problems unrelated to credit.

Home Solicitation Sales Sales by a salesperson who has come to the consumer's home present a difficult psychological dimension for many people. The typical consumer is not expecting a sales pitch and may feel "cornered" even in his or her own home. FTC regulations and many state laws provide a mandatory "cooling-off" period to permit such consumers to reconsider their decision and cancel the sale without any penalty. The cooling-off period mandated by federal law is three days, but federal law provides that state laws with more protection apply instead.[175]

Mail or Telephone Transactions The FTC regulates all mail order sales and any sales using telephone lines that are initiated by the buyer — including computer shopping. Sellers are required to ship orders within a reasonable time, to notify the

---

173 Unlike the UCC, the UCCC sets out 5 "considerations" to guide courts in determining unconscionability. They are applied in *Besta v. Beneficial Loan Co.*, 855 F.2d 532 (8th Cir. 1988).

174 15 U.S.C.A. §45.

175 16 CFR §429 *et seq.* As mentioned earlier, if the door-to-door sale involves granting a security interest in the consumer's home, other recission laws may apply as well. *See supra* p. 426.

buyer promptly if the order cannot be shipped on time and to provide prompt refunds when the consumer cancels.[176]

Magnuson-Moss Warranty Act   Warranties on consumer products continue to be regulated primarily by state law, principally the UCC. However, Congress deemed it necessary to step in with the Magnuson-Moss Warranty Act to improve on state law as it relates to *express written* warranties on consumer products.[177] The Act creates no new warranties. Like the TILA, it primarily regulates how warranty terms are used and disclosed to facilitate comparison shopping. The Act provides that, if a written warranty is given, its terms and conditions must be "fully and conspicuously disclose[d] in simple and readily understood terms" and must be available for inspection before sale. The Act defines what terms a warranty must have to be a "full warranty" and requires that anything less be "conspicuously designated" a "limited warranty." A full warranty (1) must provide for prompt remedy of any defect or other failure to conform to the warranty without charge; (2) may not limit the duration of implied warranties and must conspicuously disclose any limitations on remedies; (3) must provide a refund-or-replacement guarantee if a reasonable number of attempts at repair do not succeed; (4) must extend to all consumers who use the product, not just the immediate buyer; and (5) must require no action other than consumer notification to effectuate its terms.[178]

The Act creates remedies for violations of the Act and any breach of consumer warranties, including express and implied warranties created under the UCC. But unlike the UCC, the Act provides for the award of attorney fees in successful suits.[179] Once the consumer proves that the product does not conform to the warranty, the burden of proof shifts to the warrantor to prove that the failure of the product was caused by consumer misuse or other damage not attributable to the warrantor.[180]

Warrantors are encouraged to enter into agreements with third parties, such as consumer groups, to set up informal dispute resolution mechanisms as specified in the Act. As an incentive for doing so, the Act provides that the seller can require that the consumer go through that mechanism before suing in court if such a requirement is stated in the seller's warranty.[181]

---

176 16 CFR §§435.1-435.2. Other FTC actions include the Used Motor Vehicle Regulation Rule, 16 CFR §§455.1-455.5 and Regulation of Funeral Industry Practices, 16 CFR §§453.1-453.9. In addition to making rules, the FTC can pursue unfair and deceptive practices whether or not contained in a rule, adjudicate whether they are unfair or deceptive and, if so, order appropriate relief. *See Arthur Murray Studio of Washington v. Fed. Trade Comm'n*, 458 F.2d 622 (5th Cir. 1972) (enjoining high-pressure tactics and long-term contracts in selling of dance lessons).

177 15 U.S.C.A. §2301 *et seq.*; 16 CFR §700 *et seq.* The Act and regulations are set out in SELECTED COMMERCIAL STATUTES, *supra* note 71. UCC warranties were discussed *supra* pp. 419-421.

178 15 U.S.C.A. §2304(a)-(b). In addition, if the seller also sells the buyer a service contract for servicing and repair, then the seller may not disclaim any implied warranties. For a used car case involving a service contract that generally shows the interrelationship between the federal Act and the UCC, *see Ismael v. Goodman Toyota*, 417 S.E.2d 290 (N.C.App. 1992).

179 *See generally* 15 U.S.C.A. §2310(d). Suit is possible in federal court only if individual claims total at least $25 and all claims in the case total at least $50,000. Otherwise suit must be in state court. Despite the right to sue for damages under this section, courts have construed another section of the Act to bar suits for personal injuries that are otherwise available under state law. *See, e.g., Gorman v. Saf-T-Mate, Inc.*, 513 F.Supp. 1028 (N.D. Ind.1981) (noting the "poor drafting" of the Act made decision difficult).

180 15 U.S.C.A. §2304(c); *Universal Motors, Inc. v. Waldock*, 719 P.2d 254 (Alaska 1986) (consumer's proof that BMW engine failed because of damaged timing tensioner was sufficient to shift the burden to the defense to prove that the damage was caused instead by consumer's overreving the engine; jury verdict for consumer affirmed).

181 15 U.S.C.A. §2310(a).

Labeling Laws Federal labeling laws range from those on fur, wool and flammable fabrics to smokeless tobacco and butter.[182] Smokers will be familiar with the federally mandated Surgeon General's warnings on cigarette packages.[183] Everyone is familiar with the standardized labeling of nutritional content on food products.[184] Medicinal labeling laws may be perhaps the most important, since incorrect labels can have deadly consequences.[185]

A drawback of many federal labeling laws is that they do not provide consumers with a right to sue for damages. Instead, the injured person must invoke a state-law-based right to sue for negligence and argue that the fact that the mislabeling violated federal standards — like any other violation of a regulatory statute — constitutes grounds for *per se* negligence.[186]

Limitations on Garnishment One method of executing on a civil judgment is garnishment, the process whereby the judgment creditor can obtain an *ex parte* order from the court requiring the debtor's employer to pay a portion of the debtor's wages directly to the creditor.[187] Because such disruption of the debtor's household budget can be devastating to the debtor and his or her family, the CCPA limits garnishment to 25% of "disposable" wages (after taxes and other mandatory deductions).[188] Garnishment is not popular with employers, who must now report the debtor-employee's wages to the court, calculate the withheld amount and reprocess checks to make payment to both creditor and debtor in the correct proportions. Recognizing this unpopularity, the CCPA makes it illegal for an employer to discharge an employee by reason of garnishment for any one indebtedness.[189]

Unsolicited Merchandise A tactic used by some unscrupulous sellers was to send consumers unordered goods by mail and then to bill them when the goods were not returned. A federal statute has provided, since 1970, that consumers may keep any such goods or throw them away without incurring any obligation to pay for them.[190]

Telemarketing Telephone solicitation of sales, referred to as "telemarketing," was subjected to regulation in 1991. Prohibited practices include the use of automatic telephone dialing systems and the playing of prerecorded messages. In contrast to some other federal laws, a private right of action is provided for, and actual damages with a minimum of $500 for each violation may be sought in state or federal court, with the

---

182 *See* 15 U.S.C.A. §69 (fur products); 15 U.S.C.A. §68 (wool); 15 U.S.C.A. §4401 *et seq.* (smokeless tobacco); 21 U.S.C.A. § 321a (butter).

183 15 U.S.C.A. § 1331 *et seq.*

184 15 U.S.C.A. §1451 *et seq.*

185 21 U.S.C.A. §331.

186 Despite the need to determine whether the drug was mislabeled under federal law, such a suit is not a "federal question" suit that can be brought in federal court. *See Merrell Dow Pharmaceuticals. v. Thompson*, 478 U.S. 804 (1986), discussed in Chapter V, p. 189, note 95. Another difficulty with federal labeling laws is that manufacturers can argue that they preempt state law remedies. *See Cipollone v. Liggett Group, Inc.*, 505 U.S. 504 (1992) (state law failure-to-warn claims are preempted by federal cigarette warning requirements; misrepresentation and other claims are not).

187 *See* Chapter VII.

188 15 U.S.C.A. §1673. *See* SELECTED COMMERCIAL STATUTES, *supra* note 71, at 1396.

189 15 U.S.C.A. §1674. This section makes such discharge a criminal offense (misdemeanor). No explicit private right of action is created.

190 39 U.S.C.A. §3009.

additional possibility of the court granting treble damages in the event of wilful or knowing violations.[191]

b. State Laws

Consumer Protection Acts Many states have comprehensive consumer protection acts that seek to protect consumers from a wide variety of deceptive and unfair practices. Representative of some of these laws is the Uniform Consumer Sales Practices Act (UCSPA).[192] The Act has been adopted in only three states. The reasons for its limited adoption parallel those that apply to the UCCC — many states have their own consumer protection acts that borrow to some degree the text, ideas and purposes of the UCSPA. The FTC also covers some of the more urgent consumer protection issues.

Aside from their substantive provisions, the most effective consumer protection laws provide minimum damage recovery, attorney fees, and the possibility of class action as a litigation device. All three remedies address the important fact that most consumer protection violations involve small amounts of money.[193]

The Importance of State Law in Enforcing Federal Rights Some of the rights set out above are secured by FTC rules. But the rules can be difficult to enforce because the only enforcement remedy provided in the FTC Act is an enforcement proceeding brought by the FTC itself.[194] The FTC can prosecute only a tiny fraction of the complaints that are brought to its attention,[195] so state laws become crucial for effective relief. Some state statutes use language similar to the "deceptive and unfair trade practices" language of the FTC Act and state that "[i]t is the intent of the legislature that . . . the courts will be guided by the interpretations given by" the FTC of the Act. Other state laws provide that any practice that is subject to an FTC cease and desist order affirmed by a federal court is also a violation of state law.[196]

---

191 47 U.S.C.A. §227. The Act's constitutionality under the 1st Amendment has been sustained by at least one Circuit Court of Appeals. *Moser v. Fed. Communications Comm'n.*, 46 F.3d 970 (9th Cir. 1995).

192 Available at www.nccusl.org/Update/ The Uniform Act has been adopted only by Kansas, Ohio and Utah, but other states have "borrowed" portions of it. *See, e.g.,* §§V.T.C.A.Bus. & C. 17.41 to 17.63 (Texas).

193 *See, e.g.,* UCSPA §§11-13. Mich.Comp.L.Ann. 445.911(2) ("actual damages or $250.00, whichever is greater, together with reasonable attorneys' fees")

194 There is general agreement that this means that there is no private right of action by a consumer to enforce FTC rules or the FTC Act itself. *Holloway v. Bristol-Myers Corp.*, 485 F.2d 986 (D.C. Cir. 1973). *But see Guernsey v. Rich Plan of the Midwest*, 408 F.Supp. 582 (N.D. Ind. 1976) (FTC had found that this very seller's practices violated federal law, so a consumer affected by those practices had a right to sue).

195 An example of an FTC prosecution is *Kraft v. Fed. Trade Comm'n*, 970 F.2d 311 (7th Cir. 1992) (cheese maker deceptively advertised amount of calcium in its cheese). See also *supra* note 176.

196 Mass.Gen.L.Ann. 93A §2 (quoted language); Mich.Comp.L.Ann. 445.911(2)(c) (FTC cease and desist order). An FTC rule that is quite effective without a right to sue to enforce it is the HDC rule, since it is most commonly used by the consumer as a defense when the creditor sues. *See supra* p. 429.

CHAPTER XI

TORT LAW

The word "tort" simply means "wrong." The law of torts concerns civil wrongs: wrongful acts which injure the body, property, or reputation of a person that can result in civil liability.[1]

A. Torts in Perspective

Torts Distinguished from Contracts   Tort law in the Anglo-American tradition is distinguished from contract law, which enforces duties set out in parties' agreements. This is in contrast to the civil law's unified approach that considers both contractual and non-contractual civil wrongs under the heading of the "law of obligations." Tort law requires no express agreement between the parties for a duty to arise, but instead simply assumes that all members of society have a common, unspoken duty to refrain from behavior that creates an unreasonable risk of harm to other people.

Though tort law and contract law are distinct, there is some overlap. Parties to a contract owe certain duties to each other as specified in the contract, but parallel obligations may flow from tort law which would apply to them even in the absence of a contract. Consequently, in many cases both tort and contract theories of recovery can be alleged. A tort theory of recovery will in most instances provide broader relief and will be the primary claim pressed. Generally, in a contract case, the plaintiff may not receive damages for emotional distress or punitive damages, while in some tort cases, such categories of damages are permitted.[2] A common example of overlap is in the area of liability for personal injuries caused by defective products — "products liability" — where the plaintiff may often sue either in tort for strict liability or negligence, or in contract for breach of warranty.[3]

Torts Distinguished from Criminal Law   Torts and criminal law are similar in that both focus on wrongful acts and those wrongful acts can often be both criminal and tortious. Torts also has some elements of concern with society's and the government's interests, particularly with respect to the question of deterring future wrongful behavior. The nexus is felt particularly strongly in tort cases where punitive damages are allowed. However, close examination shows significant differences. The most common type of tort is negligence, while most crimes require intent or at least recklessness. Punitive damages are generally not allowed in negligence cases. Moreover, tort law's primary focus is the relationship between private parties and assuring that compensation is paid to the injured individual, while criminal law is concerned with vindicating society's interests. Symbolic of the separation between criminal law and torts is the fact that, unlike some countries, a civil claim for damages cannot be appended to a criminal

---

1   A standard hornbook on torts is DAN DOBBS, ROBERT E. KEETON & DAVID G. OWEN, PROSSER & KEETON ON TORTS, 5TH ED. (West 1984, 1988). A more concise summary is Marshall S. Shapo, Principles of Tort Law, 3d (West 2010). *See also* EDWARD J. KIONKA, TORTS IN A NUTSHELL, 5TH ED. (West 2010). An excellent comparative work is JOHN G. FLEMING, THE AMERICAN TORT PROCESS (Oxford U. Press 1991). For an interdisciplinary perspective, *see* SAUL LEVMORE, FOUNDATION OF TORT LAW (Oxford U. Press 1994).

2   Punitive damages and their limits are discussed *infra* pp. 463-465.

3   *See* Chapter X, pp. 419-422, and *infra* p. 448. For more on the overlap, *see* PROSSER & KEETON, *supra* note 1, §92 and KIONKA *supra* note 1, §10-1. *See also* Chapter XV, p. 618, where the possibility of *tort* liability based on breach of an implied "covenant of good faith dealing" inherent in all *contracts* is discussed.

prosecution. Instead a crime victim who wishes to get monetary compensation must file a separate civil lawsuit.[4]

Sources of Tort Law   Tort law in the U.S. is largely common law. This means that courts have the power to shape and change the elements of claims and defenses of existing torts and the power to create new torts.[5] Statutes have been passed, particularly in recent years, in attempts to "reform" the tort system, but most of those have related to procedural matters and amounts and categories of damages.[6] With a few exceptions, legislatures appear content to leave basic tort elements and defenses to the courts.[7]

State and federal legislatures regularly create new civil wrongs by passing regulatory statutes and providing a private claim for damages for their breach. Examples are federal statutes on employment discrimination or various consumer protection acts.[8] However, these statutory wrongs are generally not referred to as "torts." Similarly, persons injured by violations of constitutional rights can sue the government officials involved for civil liability.[9] This area is sometimes referred to as "constitutional torts," but it is generally considered part of civil rights or constitutional law rather than torts.[10]

As common law, tort law is primarily state law and there is some variation from state to state. However, most of the bases for civil liability came from a common core of common law and are roughly similar in all states. Yet, despite relative uniformity among states, torts remains an area that does not contain an overall unifying principle. This is in large measure the result of the common law development of tort law: *seriatim* recognition by courts of rights to recover damages under specific headings — trespass, slander, conversion, and others — each containing its own unique requirements for recovery.

Organization of this Chapter   It is traditional to divide torts into three categories based on the degree of fault attributable to the tortfeasor: intentional torts, negligent torts, and liability without fault.[11] After this, we will consider torts vindicating particular kinds of interests, which involve more than one state of mind. Following that will be a consideration of relief available in tort cases and an overall view of the tort system of compensation, including the role played by liability insurance, recent efforts at "tort reform" and substitutes for tort recovery that have been developed.

---

4   The criminal victim as civil plaintiff in a later suit for damages will have little trouble establishing liability because of the doctrine of issue preclusion or collateral estoppel. *See* Chapter VII, pp. 249-250. Because many criminals have no money, some states have instituted crime victim compensation boards before which a crime victim can file an administrative claim for compensation from a state fund. *See, e.g.,* N.Y. Exec. Law §622 *et seq.*; Cal. Gov. Code §13959 *et seq.*

5   Examples of relatively new torts include intentional and negligent infliction of mental suffering, infliction of prenatal injuries and the alienation of the affections of a parent. *See* PROSSER & KEETON, *supra* note 1, §1.

6   *See infra* p. 467.

7   In recent years in the United States, however, some courts have expressed hesitancy in making judicial changes in tort law. *See* discussion in Chapter II, p. 46.

8   *See* Chapter XV, pp. 620-625 (employment discrimination) and Chapter X, pp. 425-433 (consumer protection).

9   The basis for suit in these situations was discussed in Chapter VI, pp. 227-228.

10   In fact, the line between constitutional and regular common law torts is sometimes difficult to discern. *See* William Burnham, *Separating Constitutional and Common law Torts: A Critique and a Proposed Constitutional Theory of Duty*, 73 MINN. L. REV. 515 (1989).

11   "Tortfeasor" simply means the person who committed the tort.

B. Types of Torts by Degrees of Fault

1. Intentional Torts

Intent is defined in terms of the tortfeasor's probable attitude toward the *conse-quences* of an act. Thus, a person acts *intentionally* with respect to injury when that person desires to cause a certain injury or where that person is substantially certain that the injury would occur.[12] This definition of intent is subjective to the extent that the defendant must have at least been aware that the injury was substantially certain to occur. Since many defendants will not admit to such intent, however, it may be proved by circumstantial evidence. The test of intent is ultimately objective since the law presumes that a defendant intends the natural and probable harmful consequences of his or her acts. Thus, a person who fires a gun directly at someone may testify to their fervent hope that the bullet would not injure the victim, but it is not likely that such testimony would be believed, and liability for the intentional shooting would be properly imposed.[13]

In general, intentional conduct is more morally reprehensible than negligent conduct, so the law tends to impose greater responsibility on intentional tortfeasors. Thus, the amount of compensation, degree of causation and the issue of who bears the burden of proof required will often be more liberal for the plaintiff in intentional tort cases than in negligence cases.

a. Most Common Types of Intentional Torts

Battery   A battery is an intentional harmful or offensive contact the defendant makes with the plaintiff.[14] The nature of intent has already been discussed. It is further relevant to emphasize, however, that battery does not require that the defendant intended a *particular injury*, only that the person intended the contact. For example, assume a victim's leg is peculiarly susceptible to injury because of prior injury. Not knowing this, the defendant kicks the victim's leg in a way that would not seriously injury a healthy leg, but causes serious injury in this case. The defendant is liable even though there was no intent to cause an injury that serious.[15]

The contact required for battery must be "harmful or offensive." Harmful contact is obvious when the defendant physically attacks the plaintiff causing injury. Offensive contact is contact that would be considered offensive by the average person and that the defendant knows will be offensive to the plaintiff. Examples of offensive contact include being spit upon, being kissed by a stranger, or being pushed. The circumstances of the situation help define whether the contact is "offensive."[16] It is irrelevant that the defendant intended the contact to benefit the plaintiff if it was not consented to. For

---

12 RESTATEMENT (SECOND) OF TORTS §8A (American Law Institute 1965) [hereafter RESTATEMENT].

13 *See* PROSSER & KEETON, *supra* note 1, at 35-36.

14 *See* RESTATEMENT §13.

15 *Vosburg v. Putney*, 50 N.W. 403 (Wis. 1891).

16 *See Estate of Berthiaume v. Pratt*, 365 A.2d 792 (Me. 1976) (doctor who moved dying patient's head to get a better photograph of it over patient's objections held liable for battery and invasion of privacy); *Fidler v. Murphy*, 203 Misc. 51, 113 N.Y.S.2d 388 (1952) (cause of action for assault and battery properly stated when police officer had plaintiffs photographed and fingerprinted when this was not allowed by law); *Gallela v. Onassis*, 487 F.2d 986 (2d. Cir. 1973) (bumping and touching Jackie Kennedy Onassis while attempting to take photographs was offensive contact and therefore battery). *See also* RESTATEMENT §§15, 18, 19.

example, a doctor who operates on a plaintiff without informed consent commits a battery.[17]

The contact required for battery is generally actual contact with another person's body. American courts have, however, allowed battery claims where the contact was only with an extension of the body. For example, knocking off a hat or striking a car in which someone is riding may be sufficient to constitute contact.[18] The contact does not need to be violent. All that is required is harmful contact of something against the body of the plaintiff. For example, poisoning someone's food is considered a battery, as is transmission of a sexual disease and withdrawal medical treatment.[19]

Assault Assault is closely related to battery but does not require contact. An assault occurs when the defendant intentionally acts in a way that is sufficient to cause reasonable apprehension of an immediate battery. The required apprehension of battery must be such that a normal person would feel threatened. This generally means that the defendant must have the apparent ability to carry out the threat. However, actual fear on the plaintiff's part is not required. Thus, plaintiffs who are too brave to be frightened can still recover if they perceived a threat. However, plaintiffs must be aware of the threatening act at the time.[20] Generally, mere words alone, unaccompanied by a physical act, will not be enough to establish reasonable apprehension. For the threatened contact to be immediate, there must be a manifestation of the threatened act. Thus, a threat to injure someone tomorrow is not immediate. Similarly, a threat to shoot someone, when it is clear that no gun is present, is not an "immediate" threat sufficient for an assault claim.[21]

It is common for people to refer to "assault and battery," as if they were the same thing or always go together. This is not the case. They often do go together, but there can be an assault without a battery and a battery without an assault.

False Imprisonment False imprisonment is the unlawful intentional confinement of a person against that person's will.[22] The essence of the tort is the natural mental harm that results when one's freedom is restricted without justification. The confinement may be a result of physical force or of a threat to person or property. Confinement may be the result of withholding or failing to provide a means of escape.[23] The threat or physical barrier that restrains the plaintiff must be one that would restrain a reasonable person. For example, false imprisonment would not occur if a person was told to stay

---

17 *See, e.g., Blanchard v. Kellum*, 975 S.W.2d 522 (Tenn. 1998) (battery suit proper where patient was not informed by dentist that all 32 of her teeth would be pulled in one sitting). Usually the duty to obtain informed consent is imposed by statute. The duty requires that all the risks and alternative, non-experimental procedures be explained. *See Moore v. Baker*, 989 F.2d 1129 (11th Cir. 1993) (doctor's failure to explain alternative therapy that was not generally accepted did not vitiate consent).

18 *See Crossman v. Thurlow*, 143 N.E.2d 814 (Mass. 1957) (battery when defendant rammed police officer's car with his car while officer was in it).

19 *See Kathleen K. v. Robert B.*, 198 Cal.Rptr. 273 (Cal.App. 1984) (battery when genital herpes contracted through sexual relations with the defendant who knew he had the disease); *Causey v. St Francis Medical Center*, 719 So.2d 1072 (La.App. 1998) (battery when physician and hospital withdrew life-sustaining care to comatose patient over strongly expressed objections of patient's family).

20 RESTATEMENT §22.

21 *See, e.g., Brooker v. Silverthorne*, 99 S.E. 350 (S.C. 1919) (statement made over telephone that defendant would break plaintiff's neck not an assault because defendant was not in close proximity to plaintiff). *See also* RESTATEMENT §24.

22 *See* RESTATEMENT §35.

23 *See Whittaker v. Sandford*, 85 A. 399 (Me. 1912) (defendant leader of a religious cult agreed to take a defecting follower back to America aboard his private yacht; upon arrival he told plaintiff she was free to leave but refused to provide a boat to take her ashore).

in a room but there was no threat of harm or physical barrier to prevent the person from leaving. A common suit for false imprisonment involves merchants detaining people suspected of shoplifting. Recovery is often made more difficult, however, by state statutes granting immunity if the merchant had probable cause to detain and detained in a reasonable manner.[24]

Trespass to Land   Trespass to land involves entry onto the land of another.[25] The intent requirement for trespass is only that the trespasser intended to enter the property. It is irrelevant whether the trespasser knew that the property belonged to the plaintiff, or even if the trespasser believed it was his or her own property. There is also no requirement of actual damages. Damages are presumed. The strict rules of trespass reflect the high value that was placed on land ownership in feudal times. They also reflect the fact that at common law an action for trespass was the only way to determine title to land. Today that can be done by way of a suit to quiet title, though trespass actions are used even today to prevent a habitual trespasser from acquiring title through adverse possession or an easement by prescription — methods of gaining property rights through continued usage.[26]

A trespass can also occur when the defendant causes an inanimate object to enter the plaintiff's land. Courts have allowed claims of trespass in cases where smoke or pollution has entered the plaintiff's land and has caused damage.[27] Thus, the ancient torts of trespass and nuisance have been adapted to provide a common law basis for modern environmental protection. Even objects crossing over or under the plaintiff's land may, in some cases, constitute a trespass. This rationale developed from the common law rule that the property owner owned the piece of land from the center of the earth all the way up to "the heavens." This view of property has changed in modern times, especially with the advent of aircraft which requires the ability to fly freely over privately owned land.[28]

Conversion   Conversion is one of the many common law torts that relate to interferences with possessory interests in personal property, called "chattels." It is closely associated with a "trespass to chattels" and is a more serious version of it. Thus, trespass to chattels is available for any intentional interference with personal property of any substantial kind, while conversion is an interference so serious that the value of the personal property is essentially lost to the original owner. Whenever personal property is wrongfully taken or retained, the owner is entitled to appropriate damages. The measure of damage is determined by the length of time the defendant had control

---

24 *See Hainz v. Shopko Stores, Inc.*, 359 N.W.2d 397 (Wis.App. 1984) (reversing jury verdict for plaintiff on basis of such a statute).

25 The original common law understanding of trespass imposed liability without fault. Even today, reckless or negligent trespass are actionable as well. However, most trespass actions involve an intentional entry onto land and the only real question is whether that entry was lawful. RESTATEMENT §166.

26 *See* Chapter XII, p. 478, for a discussion of title by adverse possession.

27 *See Borland v. Sanders Lead Co., Inc.*, 369 So.2d 523 (Ala. 1979) (lead smelting company held liable in a trespass case for damages caused to a farmer's crops when airborne lead particles escaped from their plant).

28 RESTATEMENT §159(2) states that "[f]light by aircraft in the air space above the land of another is a trespass if, but only if, (a) it enters into the immediate reaches of the air space next to the land, and (b) it interferes substantially with the other's use and enjoyment of his land." In one case, the court held that poison sprayed from an airplane that otherwise was at the appropriate altitude was part of the flight and its invasion of the lower reaches of the plaintiff's airspace constituted a trespass because it interfered with his use of his land. See *Schronk v. Gilliam*, 380 S.W.2d 743 (Tex.Civ.App. 1964).

over the property, whether the defendant acted in good faith, how much actual damage was done, and the amount of inconvenience inflicted upon the true owner.[29]

Replevin As an alternative remedy, the owner whose personal property has been taken may seek a court order requiring return of the property by way of an action for "replevin," sometimes called "claim and delivery." A plaintiff will seek replevin when it is especially difficult to assign a price to a chattel or the chattel is unique and irreplaceable. However, replevin is most often used by creditors who sell personal property on credit and retain a security interest in the property. When the debtor fails to pay, the creditor can regain possession or "repossess" the item through replevin.[30]

b. Defenses to Intentional Torts

Consent Consent can be used as a defense against any intentional tort when the plaintiff has expressly or impliedly agreed to the harm inflicted. Consent can also be implied when plaintiffs place themselves in situations where it is obvious that harm will result. For example, boxers consent to being struck just by entering the ring and could not successfully claim assault and battery. However, they do not consent to their opponents using bricks inside their gloves. This exceeds the scope of the consent given.[31]

Most states follow the rule that a person who consents to a criminal act is barred from bringing a tort action arising from the criminal act. But if a statute exists to prevent harm to a certain class of individuals, such as children, from their inability to appreciate the consequences of the act, consent will not bar a tort action.[32]

Self-Defense Self-defense, defense of others, and defense of property are used as defenses to assault, battery and false imprisonment and can be used if the party claiming the defense responded in a reasonable manner and in a manner proportionate to the threat presented. Therefore, a person who is the victim of a beating cannot shoot the batterer and claim self defense unless the victim reasonably fears for his or her life. The victim may use only such force as is necessary to stop the battery. In other words, deadly force can be used only to meet deadly force.[33] Use of deadly force is generally not allowed to protect property unless there is some threat of harm to the owner. Defense of property is available only to protect it or to recover it immediately after it has been stolen so long as the response is reasonable.

Necessity The defense of necessity is sometimes used as a defense to trespass and conversion. Necessity is the privilege to use, and damage if necessary, a person's property in order to prevent greater harm to a person or the public as a whole. There are two categories of necessity — public necessity and private necessity.

---

29 *See* RESTATEMENT §222A.

30 Security in and repossession of personal property are discussed in Chapter XII, p. 422-419.

31 *See Hackbart v. Cincinnati Bengals Inc.*, 601 F.2d 516 (10th Cir. 1979) (after the referee in a football game had stopped play, one football player struck another player in the back of the head, causing his neck to be broken; injured player never consented to being struck after the play was over).

32 An example of statutes enacted to protect a certain class of persons is statutory rape. Under statutory rape laws a female under a certain age may sue for battery even if she consented to sexual intercourse. *See* Chapter XIV, p. 561.

33 RESTATEMENT §65 states that deadly force is never allowed unless there is a threat of death and no means of retreat. But there is a great deal of variation among the states as to when deadly force is authorized. *See Silas v. Bowen*, 277 F.Supp. 314 (D.S.C. 1967) (self-defense held proper where the defendant shot the plaintiff in the foot after the plaintiff verbally threatened him; situation was such that the defendant could well have perceived himself in danger of death even though the defendant never threatened to kill the plaintiff).

Public necessity occurs when it appears reasonably necessary that an individual's property will have to be damaged to prevent greater damage to the community. A famous case from the American Civil War illustrates what "reasonably necessary" can include. Upon learning that Union Troops were approaching, the citizens of a town in Tennessee destroyed all the whiskey of a local distillery for fear that the Union troops would get drunk on the whiskey and pillage the town. The distillery sued in conversion to recover the value of the whiskey, but the town successfully raised the defense of public necessity.[34]

Private necessity is similar to public necessity except that an individual's property is harmed in order to prevent a greater harm to another individual or to property. Private necessity prevents property owners from resisting the use of their property by claiming trespass.[35] However, a person who exercises private necessity will be required to pay for any actual damages caused.[36]

2. Negligence

To qualify as intentional injury, the injury must be substantially certain to occur. By contrast, negligence involves actions (or omissions) that create an *unreasonable risk* that the injury will occur. Negligence, like intent, might be thought of as reflecting a tortfeasor's mental attitude toward the consequences of his or her actions, thus ensnaring only careless or inattentive people. But we *presume* that everyone, by virtue of their living in society, knows what acts or omissions create unreasonable risks of harm. As a result, negligence is best understood as conduct that falls below the *standard of care deemed by the law* as necessary to protect others from unreasonable risks of harm — regardless of the actor's actual subjective state of mind.[37] Negligence, then, is generally expressed as a "breach of a duty."[38]

a. Negligence as the Breach of a Duty of Care

Reasonable Person Standard The standard of care to which people are expected to conform their conduct is defined in terms of how a "reasonable person" would have acted. Any special traits of the tortfeasor are taken into account, but the standard otherwise remains unchanged. Thus, a child or a person with a disability will be held

---

34 *Harrison v. Wisdom*, 54 Tenn. 99 (1872). If the *city itself* had taken the property today based on public necessity, it would have to pay reasonable compensation under the "just compensation" clause of the 5th Amendment to the Constitution. *See* Chapter XII, pp. 482-487.

35 *See Ploof v. Putnam*, 71 A. 188 (Vt. 1908) (boat moored to a dock to avoid a storm was set adrift by the owner of the dock; dock owner was liable for damages because the boat owner was exercising private necessity).

36 *See Vincent v. Lake Erie Transp. Co.*, 124 N.W. 221 (Minn. 1910) (defendant owner of cargo ship that had moored to plaintiff's pier to ride out a violent storm was liable for damage caused by ship during the storm when ship smashed against the pier). These forms of necessity bear some resemblance to the defense of necessity in the criminal law. *See* Chapter XIV, p. 566.

37 RESTATEMENT §282.

38 Somewhere between intent and negligence is "reckless" or "grossly negligent" conduct. RESTATEMENT §8A, comment b. In certain categories of negligent torts, for social policy reasons, tortfeasors qualify for some greater protection than the negligence standard affords. For example, in automobile torts, although negligence is usually sufficient to hold a driver liable for injuries resulting from an accident, some states have enacted "guest" statutes protecting a driver from liability except for reckless or grossly negligent driving when sued by a "guest" passenger in the car, a protection designed to encourage giving rides to people. *See, e.g., Roe v. Lewis*, 416 So.2d 750 (Ala.. 1982) (explaining basis for guest statute). However, many such statutes have been held unconstitutional as denying equal protection to injured riders in cars. *Manistee Bank & Trust v. McGowan*, 232 N.W.2d 636 (Mich. 1975).

to the standard of a "reasonable person" of that age or with that disability.[39] The standard of what a reasonable person would do is most commonly established by examining prior judicial decisions, by referring to standards of conduct set out in regulatory statutes (*e.g.*, safety codes for construction or traffic laws). But there need not be any prior decision on similar facts or a statutory standard, as the jury (or trial judge) may determine even in a unique case whether the risk of injury was one that a reasonable person would have foreseen.[40]

Violation of a Regulatory Statute In most jurisdictions, if the defendant has violated a statutory duty of care, the mere violation of the statute is *per se* negligence. The classic example is the driver who runs a red light, in violation of traffic laws. However, the statute must have as its purpose protecting against the type of harm that resulted from its violation.[41] In most tort cases, this means that the statute must have been enacted for a public safety purpose. For example, it has been held that "[t]he evident purpose of requiring motor vehicles to be locked is not to prevent theft for the sake of owners or the police, but to promote the safety of the public in the streets." Consequently, failure to do so is negligence *per se* in a personal injury action against the car owner by a person injured by the stolen vehicle following its theft.[42]

Negligence of Professionals When the negligence standard is applied to a professional, such as in a medical malpractice case, a "professional version" of the reasonable person standard is applied. The standard becomes that of a reasonable professional in that field possessing the training and skills of a member in good standing of that profession.[43] Just as in a negligence case involving a non-professional defendant, the standard of care in a medical malpractice case can be established by prior court decisions and any applicable regulatory rules. But if the doctor follows what was ordinary and customary in the profession, it is rare that a court will view that conduct as negligent.[44] The standard of care is further limited in some jurisdictions by requiring that the standard be that of reasonably qualified physicians *in the locality where the defendant practices*, though the trend is away from this limitation. The appropriate standard of care is most often determined with the assistance of expert witnesses, such as other doctors in the field who can give their opinion as to whether the care met appropriate standards.[45]

---

39 *See, e.g., Roberts v. Ring*, 173 N.W. 437 (Minn. 1919) (child plaintiff not contributorily negligent for walking in front of moving car because a reasonable child of the same age and maturity would have behaved the same way).

40 RESTATEMENT §285. *See Weirum v. RKO General, Inc.*, 539 P.2d 36 (Cal. 1975) (radio station liable for actions of radio listeners who drove their cars recklessly to arrive first at radio station to claim prize).

41 *Gorris v. Scott*, L.R. 9 Ex. 125 (1874) is the principal case applying this limitation. The owner of sheep that were washed overboard and lost at sea during shipment sued the shipper. The owner claimed the shipper was negligent because he failed to place the sheep in pens as required by law. However, the court held that the owner could not rely on violation of the law as proof of negligence. While penning would have prevented the sheep from being washed overboard, the penning law was enacted to prevent the transmission of disease, not to protect the animals from being washed overboard.

42 *Ross v. Hartman*, 139 F.2d 14, 15 (D.C.Cir. 1943). *See also Elliott v. Michael James, Inc.*, 559 F.2d 759, 764 (D.C.Cir. 1977) (stabbing of restaurant employee; escape prevented because doors were unlawfully locked on inside contrary to industrial safety board regulations).

43 *See* PROSSER & KEETON, *supra* note 1, at 185-192.

44 *But see Helling v. Carey*, 519 P.2d 981 (Wash. 1974) (holding ophthalmologist negligent as a matter of law for failing to give test for glaucoma despite expert testimony that standard practice was not to give it to patients under age 40).

45 *See* Chapter III, p. 110, for a discussion of expert witnesses.

Res Ipsa Loquitur   Proof of negligence can be accomplished directly or through circumstantial evidence. The concept of *res ipsa loquitur* ("the thing speaks for itself") is sometimes used to shift the burden of proof to the defendant in situations where the facts constituting negligence are more accessible to the defendant.[46] Thus, where the defendant had control of the situation or instrumentality that injured the plaintiff and harm of this type would not ordinarily occur without the defendant being negligent, the jury may be instructed that it may infer that the defendant was negligent as long as the plaintiff was not contributorily negligent.[47]

The Nature and Extent of Tort Duties   Generally, the law imposes duties to refrain from acting, but it tends not to impose affirmative duties to take action. One area where such questions have arisen is in "failure to aid" cases. In the United States, a person generally owes no duty to aid or rescue another person in peril. However, such a duty may arise if there is a special relationship, such as an innkeeper's duty to aid guests in case of fire or a school's duty to aid its pupils.[48] Special relationships can also be created if the rescuer placed the person in the predicament.[49] Also, a person who begins rendering aid may not discontinue that aid if it would place the victim in a worse position than if no aid had been rendered.[50]

The duties of land owners to people who enter their property are discussed when property law is outlined. However, special mention should be made here of suits for "attractive nuisances" because of their prevalence. A land owner is liable for injury even to trespassing children that results from a dangerous condition on the land, which is particularly attractive to children, such as a flooded gravel pit "swimming hole." In essence, however, the "attractive nuisance" doctrine is nothing more than a negligence standard imposing a duty on property owners to take into account the special circumstances of their property's allure to children and children's lack of judgment.[51]

b. Causation in Negligence Cases

To prove the element of causation, the plaintiff must prove that the defendant's act or breach of duty was both the "cause-in-fact" and the "proximate cause" of the plaintiff's injuries.

Cause-in-Fact   Cause-in-fact is usually determined by applying a "but for" test: if the plaintiff would not have been injured "but for" the act of the defendant, the defendant's act is determined to be a cause-in-fact of the injury. Another standard for determining actual cause is the "substantial factor" test, which attempts to determine if the defendant's action was a substantial factor in causing the injury. Cause-in-act is very broad in its scope. If this were the only type of causation required, liability would

---

46 *See* RESTATEMENT §328D.

47 *See Ybarra v. Spangard*, 154 P.2d 687 (Cal. 1944) (*res ipsa loquitur* applied to claim of plaintiff who sustained traumatic injury to his shoulder while unconscious during appendectomy surgery performed by defendants; burden of proof shifted to defendants).

48 *See* PROSSER & KEETON, *supra* note 1, at 376. *But see Parra v. Tarasco, Inc.*, 595 N.E.2d 1186 (Ill. App. 1992) (restaurant not liable for failing to aid diner who choked to death on food because it was not responsible for putting him in danger).

49 *But see Yania v. Bigan*, 155 A.2d 343 (Pa. 1959) (no liability where defendant incited victim to jump into water and then stood by while he drowned). *See* PROSSER & KEETON, *supra* note 1, at 375-376 for other "unappetizing" decisions.

50 *See Zelenko v. Gimbel Bros.*, 287 N.Y.S. 134 (Sup.Ct.1935) (store liable where customer became ill, employees took her to store's infirmary and left her there unattended for six hours resulting in injury).

51 *See* RESTATEMENT §339. *See, e.g., Gregory v. Johnson*, 289 S.E.2d 232 (Ga. 1982) (unfenced swimming pool 3 blocks from elementary school). *See also* Chapter XII, pp. 479-481 (other duties of landowners to those who come on their property).

be extended to some absurd situations. Thus, people could say that whoever introduced their parents to each other is a "but for" cause of everything that happens to them in life. The broad scope of cause-in-fact is narrowed by applying the concept of proximate cause.

Proximate Cause Some argue that proximate cause has little to do with proximity or nearness of the defendant's conduct to the result. Rather it is better thought of as *legal* cause — the sort of causal relationship the law will accept as sufficient. As such, proximate cause may have less to do with "cause" than with the scope of the defendant's duty. The case of *Palsgraf v. Long Island R.R.* discusses this very issue.[52] A railroad's employees assisted a passenger to get on board a moving train. That action knocked loose a package the passenger was carrying, which contained fireworks. The fireworks exploded causing shock waves that knocked over a heavy scale at the end of the railroad platform which fell on Mrs. Palsgraf injuring her. Judge Cardozo of the New York Court of Appeals wrote the majority opinion reversing a judgment for the plaintiff on the ground that the actions of the employee were not negligent since the employee did not owe a duty to Mrs. Palsgraf for such unforeseeable consequences. Judge Andrews in dissent viewed the issue more traditionally as one of proximate cause and found liability.

Whether viewed as a matter of duty or of proximate cause, courts in situations like the *Palsgraf* case usually consider the question to be one of the foreseeability of the injury. If the injury was a foreseeable consequence of the defendant's actions, the law will deem it to be proximately caused by those actions. The question is not whether the defendant *in fact* foresaw the harmful results. It is sufficient if a *reasonable person would have* foreseen the harmful results. Another test of proximate cause that has been suggested is a test of the "directness." The question under this test is whether there is an unbroken sequence of events between the act and the harm.[53] The directness test and the foreseeability test have been criticized as not being tests at all, but simply restatements of the court's intuitive conclusion that liability would be fair or unfair under the circumstances.

Intervening Cause A complicating factor in causation is "intervening cause." An intervening cause is an event which occurs after the defendant's negligent act has occurred and which contributes to the injury. If the intervening cause was the *proximate* cause of the plaintiff's injury, the defendant's act will not be considered the proximate cause. But if the intervening cause was a foreseeable consequence of the defendant's conduct, the defendant will often be held liable for this additional harm. For example, a person who allows gasoline to spill on the sidewalk may be liable for the resulting harm if a third person drops a lighted cigarette into the gas. This is because a reasonable person could foresee such a thing happening. A defendant may even be held liable for injury resulting from an Act of God as long as it is foreseeable.[54]

---

52 162 N.E. 99 (N.Y. 1928). The exchange between Judges Cardozo and Andrews is perhaps the most famous judicial exchange of views in all of tort law.

53 *See In re Polemis and Furness, Withy & Co.*, [1921] 3 K.B. 560, All E.R. Rep. 40 (defendant's act of dropping plank on a ship which caused a spark which ignited fuel which destroyed a ship was proximate cause of ship's destruction regardless of whether fire was foreseeable consequence of dropping plank).

54 *See Chase v. Washington Water Power Co.*, 111 P.2d 872 (Idaho 1941) (power company spaced wires close enough that it was foreseeable that something could connect them, so it was liable when wingtips of two hawks connected wires causing a fire that destroyed the plaintiff's barn).

c. Defenses to Negligence

The defendant facing a negligence action will seek to negate causation and breach of duty, but may also assert affirmative defenses. Affirmative defenses to a negligence action include "contributory negligence" and "comparative negligence," "assumption of the risk" and various immunities.

Contributory and Comparative Negligence At least beginning in 1809, the common law defense of contributory negligence provided that plaintiffs who contribute to their injury through their own negligence, however slight, are completely barred from any recovery.[55] This all-or-nothing rule shifts the loss even to plaintiffs who are less at fault than the defendant. The feeling has grown in the last 35 years that this produces unfair and harsh results. Beginning in the 1970s, state courts began modifying their common law and state legislatures passed statutes adopting comparative negligence. Today, 46 states follow some form of comparative negligence. In 34 states, the change was made legislatively and in 11 it was made judicially.[56]

There are two forms of comparative negligence, pure and modified. Pure comparative negligence apportions liability between the plaintiff and the defendant exactly in accord with their relative percentages of fault. For example, if a jury finds that the plaintiff's negligent act accounted for 30% of his or her injury, the plaintiff will still be allowed to recover the remaining 70% from the defendant. If the plaintiff was 70% negligent and the defendant 30%, plaintiff can still recover 30%. Pure comparative negligence is the form most commonly adopted by judicial opinion and endorsed by commentators.[57]

Modified comparative negligence is the most common legislative approach. There are different versions of it, but the most common is to provide that the plaintiff may recover for that percentage that the defendant was at fault, but only if the plaintiff's degree of fault is 50% or less. Other versions employ an "equal fault bar" rule, under which a 50%-50% tie will bar any recovery.[58]

Assumption of Risk The defense of assumption of risk applies as a defense when the plaintiff voluntarily consented to take the risk that a certain harm would occur. To invoke this defense, the defendant must prove that the plaintiff knew and appreciated the potential danger but consented to take the risk. This consent can be either express or implied. For example, the plaintiff in one case used a motel's side door where the ice has obviously not been cleared away to bring things in from her car. She made one trip

---

55 For a review of the history of contributory negligence, *see Hoffman v. Jones*, 280 So.2d 431 (Fla. 1973), the Florida Supreme Court case that changed Florida law from contributory to comparative negligence, which was discussed in Chapter II. *See* Appendix, p. A4.

56 The states that retain contributory negligence as a complete bar are four southeastern states: Maryland, Virginia, North Carolina and Alabama. *See McIntyre v. Balentine*, 833 S.W.2d 52 (Tenn. 1992), which collects citations to all the relevant cases and statutes as of 1992.

57 *Hoffman v. Jones, supra* note 55, and the majority of judicial adoptions of comparative negligence have been in pure form. *See* Appendix, p. A9. *But see McIntyre v. Balentine, supra* note 56 (adopting comparative negligence, but barring recovery if the plaintiff is more at fault than the defendant). For a recent case deciding to retain contributory negligence as a complete bar, *see William v. Delta International Machinery*, 619 So.2d 1330 (Ala. 1993). An interesting empirical study on jury reaction to modified comparative fault is set out in Jordan H. Leibman, Robert B. Bennett Jr. and Richard Fetter, *The Effect of Lifting the Blindfold from Civil Juries Charged with Apportioning Damages in Modified Comparative Fault Cases: an Empirical Study of the Alternatives*, 35 AM. BUS. L.J. 349 (1998) (concluding jurors find greater fault on the defendant's part when they know the result of their finding).

58 For a guide to the debate over pure versus modified comparative negligence, *see* David C. Sobelsohn, *"Pure" vs. "Modified" Comparative Fault: Notes on the Debate*, 34 EMORY L. REV. 65 (1985).

without mishap, but fell and broke her ankle during the second. She was held to have assumed the risk.[59] A spectator at a baseball game, by sitting in the stands, assumes the risk of being hit by a ball hit into the stands.[60] But a person does not assume risks not reasonably contemplated. So if a spectator at a baseball game is trampled by an unruly crowd chasing a baseball hit into the stands, the spectator cannot be said to have consented to that type of risk, because most people would not anticipate that type of risk at a baseball game.[61]

A person can assume a risk by signing a written agreement. Such agreements are commonly upheld where there is open and free bargaining between the parties. However, if one party is at an obvious disadvantage in terms of bargaining power, courts may refuse to recognize the agreement.[62] Courts also consider the degree to which the consenting person actually understood the consent form.[63]

Immunities An immunity is a defense to tort liability that is granted to a particular class of people for reasons of social policy. The most common immunities in tort law are husband and wife immunity, parent and child immunity and governmental immunity. While these immunities were created by common law, many have been eliminated or modified by statute or overruled by judicial decisions.

At common law husbands and wives could not sue each other because they were considered to be the same person in the eyes of the law.[64] The same reason was given for child and parent immunity. But today this distinction has eroded to the point that most states allow suits between husbands and wives or children and their parents.[65]

Governmental immunity came from English common law and was based on the notion that "the king can do no wrong." Both the United States and state governments enjoy common law sovereign immunity. In 1946, however, Congress enacted the Federal Tort Claims Act (FTCA) waiving federal sovereign immunity except for intentional torts. The state's immunity extends to local municipalities at least to the extent that they are exercising governmental (as opposed to proprietary) functions. Governmental acts include functions that are uniquely governmental and could not be provided by a private organization. For example, police and fire departments are uniquely governmental and enjoy a wide range of immunity. County hospitals or airports, on the other hand, are not so uniquely governmental and are, therefore, not usually extended immunity.

With the widespread introduction of liability insurance, many states abolished state and municipality immunity in the 1960s and 1970s. Some saw this as a positive step

59 *Schroyer v. McNeal*, 592 A.2d 1119 (Md.App. 1991). Clearly, cases like this could also be decided on the basis of contributory negligence.

60 *Arbegast v. Board of Education, South New Berlin Cent. School*, 480 N.E.2d 365 (N.Y. 1985) (plaintiff admitted she was told that "participants are at their own risk" before she participated in basketball game played while riding donkeys).

61 *Lee v. National League Baseball Club of Milwaukee, Inc.*, 89 N.W. 2d. 811 (Wis. 1958).

62 *Union Pacific Railroad Co. v. Burke*, 255 U.S. 317 (1921) (where shipper was offered only one price, waiver of liability would not be honored, since no off-setting benefit was offered in return for it).

63 *Conservatorship of Estate of Link, Inc.*, 205 Cal.Rptr. 513 (Cal.App. 1984) (convoluted 193-word disclaimer sentence in fine print held insufficient). The validity of consent forms parallels the unconscionability defense in contract actions. *See* Chapter X, p. 410.

64 *See* Chapter XIII, p. 520.

65 *See Self v. Self*, 376 P.2d 65 (Cal. 1962) (abolishing interspousal tort immunity) discussed in Chapter II, p. 62. *See generally* JOHN DEWITT GREGORY, PETER N. SWISHER & SHERYL L. WOLF, UNDERSTANDING FAMILY LAW §§6.01, 6.02 (Lexis 2005)

toward government being accountable for its wrongs and as a proper application of the same loss-spreading and compensation policies applicable to private tortfeasors.[66] However, there has been a backlash against this trend and immunity has reappeared in recent years.[67] But states that have governmental immunity generally make exceptions for some of the most common kinds of torts, such as personal injuries caused by traffic accidents involving state vehicles or improperly maintained public buildings. In addition, many states do not extend their immunity to their *employees* who can be held personally liable. And in many situations where there is employee liability, the government routinely steps in to pay any judgment.[68]

d. Some Special Issues in Negligence Liability

(1) Joint Torts

Nature of Joint Tortfeasor Liability Conduct of more than one person may lead to injury. When this is the case, it is possible that there will be "joint tortfeasors." The issue of whether multiple wrongdoers are joint tortfeasors is important because joint tortfeasors are "jointly and severally" liable for injury that was caused by *all* of them. This means that any *one* of several joint tortfeasors can be held liable for the full amount of the plaintiff's injury. Thus, the plaintiff needs to sue only one of several joint tortfeasors to obtain a judgment for the entire amount of the damage caused by all of them. The hapless joint tortfeasor who is sued alone has a "right of contribution" from the other joint tortfeasors, meaning that he or she can obtain a judgment against the other joint tortfeasors for their proportional share.[69] However, the other tortfeasors may well be "judgment-proof" — without assets sufficient to pay any judgment.[70]

Concurrent Action There are two circumstances in which persons acting concurrently will be deemed joint tortfeasors. First, if their concurrent acts are independent of each other, they are joint tortfeasors only if the injury is not "divisible," meaning that it cannot be shown which part of the injury was caused by one actor and which by the other. Thus, where a fire of unknown origin merged with a fire set by the defendant and the combined fires destroyed the plaintiff's home, it is impossible to divide the damage between the two fires and a single defendant is liable for the entire amount of the damage.[71] A more common example of an indivisible single injury is where the passenger in a car is injured in a crash caused by the concurrent negligence of the driver of the passenger's car and the driver of another vehicle. If the injury *is* divisible, the concurrent actors will not be joint tortfeasors. For example, assume that A and B, members of two different hunting groups, fire their guns simultaneously and negligently

---

66 *See infra* pp. 466-467, where the role of liability insurance is discussed.

67 Usually the courts will abolish common law governmental immunity and the legislature will reestablish it by statute. *See, e.g., Pittman v. City of Taylor*, 247 N.W.2d 512 (Mich. 1976) (abolishing common law governmental immunity) and Mich.Comp.L.Ann. §691.1401 (reasserting immunity).

68 *See* PROSSER & KEETON, *supra* note 1, §§131-132. *See generally* Chapter VI, pp. 223-228, where sovereign immunity and its exceptions are discussed.

69 Thus, the defendant joint tortfeasor in a lawsuit has the right to implead the other tortfeasors in the same suit. *See* the discussion of impleader in Chapter VII, p. 232.

70 *See* Chapter VII, p. 244. Another reason for not suing all joint tortfeasors is that some of them may be relatives or friends. For example, the negligence of the driver of one car may combine with the negligence of the driver of another car to injure the passenger in the first car. If the driver of the first car is the passenger's teenage son, the passenger may not wish to include him as a defendant.

71 *See Kingston v. Chicago & N.W. R. Co.*, 211 N.W. 913 (Wis. 1927).

in P's direction while shooting at game. A's shot hits P in the leg and B's shot hit P in the arm. P's injury is divisible, so A is liable for the leg injury and B for the arm injury.[72]

Action in Concert The second joint tortfeasor situation is where two tortfeasors act "in concert," meaning that they cooperate or coordinate their actions. They are considered joint tortfeasors regardless of whether the injury is divisible. Thus, modifying the example above, if A and B are in the same hunting party and agree that they will fire their guns in P's direction to scare him, but their shots accidentally hit P in the arm and leg, A and B are joint tortfeasors. This is so even though it is possible to determine which injury A caused and which injury B caused.

Multiple Serial Actions Where the actions of tortfeasors are not concurrent, but take place one after the other, joint and several liability may also be imposed. For example, A injures P and P is taken to the hospital where Dr. B aggravates P's injury with negligent treatment. Since negligent medical treatment is a risk that is a foreseeable consequence of injury, A is liable to P for the entire injury and Dr. B is jointly and severally liable with A for the aggravated portion of the injury.

(2) Vicarious Liability: Liability for the Negligence of Others

Respondeat Superior A person has "vicarious liability" when that person is responsible for injury caused by the tortious actions of another. Most often this is based on some relationship between them. The most common kind of vicarious liability is *respondeat superior* — the liability of an employer for the torts of its employees committed while acting within the scope of their duties.

Liability of Owners of Cars Owners of automobiles are also responsible for the negligence of persons driving their car with their permission. Most often, this form of liability is imposed by statute.[73] As with *respondeat superior*, the principal tortfeasor remains liable, but it is generally more fruitful to sue the employer or owner, since they are more likely to have insurance.

(3) Dram Shop Liability

Many states have passed "Dram Shop" acts, which establish liability for taverns for injuries inflicted by a person who became intoxicated at a given tavern or who was already intoxicated when served by that tavern.[74] And even in states without such special statutes, a negligence action can be brought, assisted by regulatory prohibitions on serving drunk patrons.[75] This form of liability has been extended by judicial decision to social hosts of parties, though the trend is against it.[76]

3. Liability Without Fault

Liability without fault, or strict liability, occurs when the law imposes liability without requiring proof of intent, negligence, recklessness or any other fault. The defendant in a strict liability action may even have taken all precautions possible to prevent an injury to the plaintiff.

---

72 If there is only one injury, such as where only one shot hits P, and P cannot prove whose shot it was, the courts have shifted the burden of proof to the defendants on the issue of causation, imposing liability on both unless they can prove their innocence. *See Summers v. Tice*, 199 P.2d 1 (Cal. 1948).

73 *See* KIONKA, *supra* note 1, §8-16.

74 "Dram shop" is an 18th century term for a tavern used today only to refer to this kind of liability.

75 *Rong Yao Zhou v. Jennifer Mall Restaurant, Inc*, 534 A.2d 1268 (D.C. 1987). Violations of regulatory statutes as *per se* negligence were discussed *supra* p. 441.

76 *See, e.g., Kelly v. Gwinnell*, 476 A.2d 1219 (N.J. 1984) *superceded by* N.J.S.A. 2A:15-5.6a.

a. Abnormally Dangerous Activities

Strict liability was first applied in cases involving owners of dangerous animals. The theory was later expanded to cover abnormally dangerous activities. The origin of this branch of the doctrine was the famous English case of *Rylands v. Fletcher*.[77] That case imposed strict liability on the owner of a water reservoir when the water broke through a mine shaft and flooded adjacent land. In determining whether an activity is abnormally dangerous, courts have considered the degree of risk of some harm, the likelihood that the harm that results from it will be great, the inability to eliminate the risk by exercise of reasonable care, the extent to which the activity is not a matter of common usage, the inappropriateness of the activity to the place where it is carried on, and the degree to which the dangerous nature of the activity outweighs any value of the activity to the community.[78] To the extent that each of these factors is rated high, a given activity is more likely to be declared eligible for strict liability treatment. Modern examples of ultra-hazardous activity are fumigation of residences, fireworks displays and gasoline storage.[79]

b. Products Liability

Nature of Liability Strict liability is applied commonly to dangerously defective or unsafe products.[80] It was pioneered by a California Supreme Court decision in 1963 and the Second Restatement of Torts §402A in 1965.[81] Under this concept, a supplier of a product (manufacturer, distributor or seller) is liable for personal injury or property damage suffered by the ultimate consumer or user of that product as a result of the product being "in a defective condition unreasonably dangerous to the user."[82] A manufacturer can be held liable even if it maintained reasonable quality control and there was no negligence in the design process. A retail seller can be held liable even though it was in no way involved in the manufacturing or design process. However, the seller can pass on the liability to the manufacturer.[83]

The policy reasons behind strict liability for products are numerous. As products and production methods have become more complex, consumers are less able to inspect products and determine their safety. Strict liability will also motivate manufacturers to make their products safer. Moreover, the cost of injuries from defective products can be spread over all of society by imposing that cost on suppliers, because they then

---

77 L.R. 3 H.L. 330 (1868).

78 RESTATEMENT §520.

79 *Old Island Fumigation v. Barbee*, 604 So.2d 1246 (Fla.App. 1992) (fumigator held liable for residents becoming ill even though the reason fumes reached them was a defect in the buildings that the fumigator could not have noticed); *Klein v. Pyrodyne Corp.*, 810 P.2d 917 (Wash. 1991) (spectators injured by fireworks display put on by pyrotechnic company); *Yommer v. McKenzie*, 257 A.2d 138 (Md. 1969) (maintaining underground gasoline tank that contaminated water in nearby well was ultra-hazardous activity). *But see Arlington Forest Assoc. v. Exxon Corp.*, 774 F.Supp. 387 (E.D. Va. 1991) (applying Virginia law to conclude use of underground gasoline tanks is not ultra-hazardous).

80 *See* JERRY J. PHILLIPS, PRODUCTS LIABILITY IN A NUTSHELL, 5TH ED. (West 1998).

81 *Greenman v. Yuba Power Products, Inc.*, 377 P.2d 897 (Cal. 1963).

82 RESTATEMENT §402A. Limitations on this sweeping liability are that (1) it applies only to merchant suppliers, meaning suppliers who regularly deal in the product, and (2) the product must not have been altered after it left the supplier's control and must be used in a normal and proper manner. All but 6 jurisdictions (Delaware, Massachusetts, Michigan, North Carolina, Virginia and the District of Columbia) have adopted some version of the Restatement formulation. So have many European civil law countries. *See* Jon R. Maddox, *Products Liability in Europe; Towards a Regime of Strict Liability*, 19 J. WORLD TRADE LAW 508-521 (1985).

83 To conserve legal resources, some states provide by statute that if the manufacturer is solvent and can be sued, other suppliers in the distribution chain may not be joined.

pass that cost on to all consumers by purchasing insurance and increasing prices of the product to reflect the cost of the premiums.[84]

Defining "Defective" A product is considered defective if it contains some irregularity that renders it not reasonably safe. The defect can exist through (1) defective manufacturing, (2) defective design or (3) a failure to warn of a potential hazard associated with the product. Defective manufacturing occurs when one item of a line of products is improperly built, making it different from the rest. Examples are a jar of baby food with glass in it or missing bolts on an airplane wing.[85] With defective design, an entire line of products contains the same harmful quality making it unnecessarily dangerous. Examples are a lack of proper support bars on a scaffold or exposed electrical wires.[86] Failure to warn of a potential hazard in using a product is a defect when the risk of harm is foreseeable and a warning to the consumer or user would substantially reduce the risk of that harm occurring.[87]

These three categories of defects were developed over the years by courts refining the definition of "defective" in §402A of the Second Restatement. In 1997, a Third Restatement was promulgated. Its §2 explicitly divides defects into the three categories and seeks to provide a clearer definition of design and warning defects.[88] Product design is defective "when the foreseeable risks of harm posed by the product could have been reduced or avoided by the adoption of a reasonable alternative design . . . and the omission of the alternative design renders the product not reasonably safe."[89] Some have criticized this definition as departing from the strict liability regime of §402A in its apparent requirement that it be shown that a "reasonable design alternative" was available. However, §2 is not the only route to a finding of defectiveness. Under §3, there need not be proof of any specific defect if it can "be inferred that the harm sustained by the plaintiff was caused by a product defect . . . when the incident that harmed the plaintiff . . . was of a kind that ordinarily occurs as a result of product defect." Thus, if the back of the driver's seat of a car suddenly collapses causing the driver to lose control of the car, the plaintiff need not prove as a prerequisite to recovery that specific alternative designs were available to the manufacturer that would have made the seat less likely to collapse. Also a plaintiff can recover for "manifestly unreasonable design" — a design that is so unreasonably dangerous that the product simply should not be marketed at all. For example, if someone is injured by an exploding cigar, the novelty company that manufactured the exploding cigar could be held liable without the plaintiff having to prove that an alternative design would not have been as dangerous, but would have been equally effective as a prank.

The Third Restatement approach to the issue of warnings is that a product "is defective because of inadequate instructions or warnings when the foreseeable risks of

84 *See* PROSSER & KEETON, *supra* note 1, §98. For an early influential judicial articulation of this view, *see Escola v. Coca-Cola Bottling Co.*, 150 P.2d 436, 440-444 (Cal.1944) (Traynor, J. concurring).

85 *See also Embs v. Pepsi-Cola Bottling Co.*, 528 S.W.2d 703 (Ky.App. 1975) (several bottles of 7-Up carbonated soft drink exploded injuring bystander; recovery allowed).

86 *See, e.g., Leichtamer v. American Motors Corp.*, 424 N.E.2d 568 (Ohio 1981) ("roll bar" on jeep not strong enough to protect passengers when jeep pitched over in an accident); Dura Corp. v. Harned., 703 P.2d 396 (Ala. 1985) (pressure tank could not hold more pressure than 180 pounds per square inch).

87 *See Jackson v. Coast Paint and Lacquer Co.*, 499 F.2d 809 (9th Cir.1974) (failure to warn of inflammability of epoxy paint fumes in enclosed areas could render paint unreasonably dangerous).

88 Section 2, RESTATEMENT (THIRD) OF TORTS: PRODUCT LIABILITY (American Law Institute 1997). Because of the breadth of tort law, the ALI has decided to update the torts restatement in segments.

89 *See, e.g., Uniroyal Goodrich Tire Co. v. Martinez*, 977 S.W.2d 328 (Tex. 1998) (possible alternative tire design in case where tire exploded, causing brain damage to mechanic trying to mount it).

harm posed by the product could have been reduced or avoided by the provision of reasonable instructions or warnings . . . and the omission of the instructions or warnings renders the product not reasonably safe." Comments make clear, however, that warnings alone are not sufficient to make a product reasonably safe if other measures, such as alternative design, could have been used to reduce its danger. This is a variance from the Second Restatement, which provided in its comment j that a product bearing a warning "which is safe if the warning is followed, is not in a defective condition."[90]

The question of whether a product is "reasonably safe" enters into all categories of allegedly defective products. This determination clearly involves a balancing of the risk involved against the social utility of the product. A car that will only go 25 miles per hour is infinitely safer than one capable of going 70-plus miles per hour, but the social utility of the faster car saves it from being held defective. On the other end of the social utility spectrum is the hypothetical of the exploding cigar. The low social utility of playing pranks using explosives is a key consideration in determining that all exploding cigars are probably "unreasonably dangerous."

"Misuse" can be a complete defense to a products liability claim. For example, a person might use a kitchen knife to try to pry the top off a jar. The blade breaks and a piece of it shoots into the person's eye. The knife maker might claim this was misuse. However, if the particular misuse was a foreseeable one, the defendant will usually be liable.[91] On the other hand, if the plaintiff knowingly assumed the risk of the foreseeable misuse, the misuse is not a defense. The plaintiff's contributory negligence may also be used to assess comparative fault or to permit the defendant to prove that it was the plaintiff's conduct that was the proximate cause of the plaintiff's injuries, not any defect in the product.[92] By whatever name the plaintiff's misconduct goes, the overall issue is whether it is fair in light of all the facts to place the responsibility on the plaintiff user or the manufacturer.

Other Product Liability Theories　Strict liability in tort is not the only theory that a plaintiff can pursue if injured by a defective product. Two others are a contract theory of recovery based on implied or express warranties[93] and a tort theory claiming negligent design or manufacture.[94] Usually, strict liability is the easiest of the three available theories of recovery. Indeed, it was developed because of dissatisfaction with the difficulties of recovery under a warranty or negligence theory. But these other methods of recovery are a matter of necessity for plaintiffs from jurisdictions that do not have strict liability.[95]

90　An example of the Third Restatement approach being used to hold a tire manufacturer liable even when the user ignored a warning, *see Uniroyal Goodrich Tire Co. v. Martinez, supra* note 89.

91　*Price v. BIC Corp.*, 702 A.2d 330 (N.H. 1997) (parent could maintain action for child's injury because butane lighter lacked child restraint device; misuse by another child was foreseeable).

92　*Madonna v. Harley Davidson, Inc.*, 708 A.2d 507 (Pa. 1998) (intoxication of driver of motorcycle). One defective product for which strict liability and warranty liability have been excluded in most states is bad blood, usually blood contaminated with the AIDS virus. *See Kozup v. Georgetown University*, 663 F.Supp. 1048 (D.D.C. 1987). However, some states allow recovery on a negligence theory. *United Blood Services v. Quintana*, 827 P.2d 509 (Colo. 1992).

93　*See Goldberg v. Kollsman Instrument Corp.*, 191 N.E.2d 81 (N.Y. 1963) and Chapter X, p. 401.

94　*See supra* pp. 440-443.

95　*See supra* note 82. Other reasons to use a warranty theory are (1) warranty claims have a 4-year statute of limitations, UCC §2-725(1), which is longer than the typical tort limitations period; (2) pure economic losses may be recoverable if not disclaimed (see *infra* p. 461 and note 156) and (3) §402A provides for recovery only by the ultimate *consumers and users* of products, while Alternatives B and C of UCC 2-318 (enacted in 14 states) permit recovery by anyone "who may *reasonably be expected to . . . be affected . . .* by the goods . . . ." *But see Giberson v. Ford Motor Co.*, 504 S.W.2d 8 (Mo. 1974) (§402A liability

A federal statutory remedy may exist for products with designs regulated by federal product safety standards. In 1972, Congress passed the federal Consumer Product Safety Act (CPSA)[96] establishing the Consumer Product Safety Council (CPSC), a 5-person regulatory body that sets safety standards for various products, including required warnings labels where appropriate. The CPSC regulations cover many products, to name but a few — swimming pool slides, cribs and pacifiers for babies, power lawn mowers, bicycles, cigarette lighters, paint, products propelled by chlorofluorocarbons, toys, pajamas and fireworks. Like the Food and Drug Administration and other federal agencies, the CPSC has the power to conduct research and investigations into possibly dangerous products, to order recalls and to sue to enjoin distribution. Unlike federal food and drug standards, however, a violation of CPSA and CPSC product standards forms the basis for damages liability for any resulting injury if the violation was a "knowing" one.[97]

Market-Share Liability In some product liability cases it is not possible to tell what company manufactured the defective product. In such cases, under limited circumstances "market-share" liability may be imposed in some states. If the products of all manufacturers are identical and the plaintiff cannot reasonably be expected to identify the particular manufacturer, the plaintiff can hold liable *all* the manufacturers who produced a substantial amount of the product in question when the plaintiff was exposed to it, with each manufacturer being liable for the proportion of the judgment that corresponds to its share of the market. The facts of the first case to impose this form of liability, *Sindell v. Abbott Laboratories*,[98] illustrates its application. *Sindell* involved DES, a drug marketed from 1941 to 1971 and given to pregnant women to prevent miscarriages. While the drug did not harm the mother and had no immediate effect on the fetus or child, it did cause female children to develop certain kinds of cancers when they reached adulthood. Because all the DES marketed was made from the same formula and the passage of time made it impossible to tell which manufacturer made any given dose of DES, the California Supreme Court held that liability would be shared by all manufacturers on a market-share basis, unless a particular manufacturer could prove that it could not have made the product that injured the plaintiff. Market-share liability remains controversial and many states do not impose it. And even courts that agree with it in principle have been reluctant to extend it to products other than drugs with latent effects.[99]

C. Torts Vindicating Particular Interests

The torts discussed so far have dealt with general interests in freedom from physical harm or property damage. There are other torts, however, that are designed to protect special kinds of interests.

---

applied to bystanders injured when car motor exploded in traffic causing collisions).

96 15 U.S.C.A. §§2051 *et seq.* Regulations of are found at 16 CFR §1000 *et seq.*

97 15 U.S.C.A. §2072. Food and drug standards are not enforceable by a private civil suit, except indirectly where they afford a basis for tort liability under state tort law, *See* Chapter X, p. 432, note 186. The CPSA is not a complete boon for plaintiffs, however. If the CPSC has promulgated a standard for a particular product, any state-law-based suit seeking to impose a higher standard is preempted. *See* 15 U.S.C.A. §2075(a) and *Moe v. MTD Products*, 73 F.3d 179, 182 (8th Cir. 1995) (in lawn mower injury case, federal standards preempted state-law failure-to-warn claim, but not defective design claim).

98 607 P.2d 924 (Cal. 1980).

99 *See Smith v. Eli Lilly & Co.*, 560 N.E.2d 324 (Ill. 1990) (encyclopedic opinion rejecting market-share liability for drugs and citing cases rejecting its application to drugs in other states and to other products).

1. Injuries to Economic Interests

a. Fraud and Misrepresentation

Fraud The common law action for fraud or deceit is the intentional version of the tort of misrepresentation. Its elements are (1) a misrepresentation by the defendant, (2) knowledge by the defendant that the statement was false, (3) intent by the defendant to induce the plaintiff to rely on the false statement, (4) reasonable reliance by the plaintiff, and (5) actual damages resulting from the plaintiff's reliance.

Misrepresentation can be either false statements or the intentional concealment or failure to disclose information. For example, if a seller knows that a home is termite-infested, but tells the buyer it is not infested, the seller has made a false statement. If the seller, on the other hand, covers up any evidence of termite infestation and does not tell the buyer of the termites, this action could be considered intentional concealment or failure to disclose information.[100]

Negligent Misrepresentation Negligent misrepresentation is a relatively new tort. Courts were at first reluctant to allow recovery, permitting such actions to proceed only when tangible injury to person or property had occurred. As the concept gained more recognition and support, however, courts allowed the action where the damages were intangible economic interests such as lost profits or a disadvantageous contract. Today, negligent misrepresentation cases are often brought in situations involving business relations when one party relies on wrong information supplied by another party. An action for negligent misrepresentation requires the same elements as any other negligence action.[101]

Innocent Misrepresentation In a few jurisdictions, innocent misrepresentations are actionable. This is based on the judgment that, as between the injured party and the innocent representor, it is fair to require that the latter absorb the loss.[102] This strict liability theory is now accepted in the majority of jurisdictions when the misrepresentation involves the sale of an item or service. Thus, a manufacturer of an item may be held strictly liable for physical harm if a product does not meet performance standards advertised, even if the manufacturer thought in good faith that the claims were true.[103]

b. Interference with Economic Advantage

Intentional Interference with Contract Rights This tort has its origin in the English case of *Lumley v. Gye*, in which the defendant induced an opera singer to breach her contract to perform at the Queen's Theater.[104] The interference must be shown to be intentional and for an improper purpose, including economic benefit to the defendant. A noted recent case was *Texaco, Inc. v. Pennzoil*,[105] in which Texaco was sued for

---

100 *Obde v. Schlemeyer*, 353 P.2d 672 (Wash. 1960). Because fraud is a serious allegation, even liberal "notice" pleading regimes often require that the circumstances constituting the fraud be stated "with particularity" in the complaint. *See* FRCP 9(b) and Chapter VII, p. 230.

101 *See Seagraves v. ABCO Manufacturing Co.*, 164 S.E.2d 242 (Ga.App.1968) (defendant held to reasonable person standard where he stated that tank was clean before plaintiff made repairs, when in fact it had been used to store flammable materials).

102 *See* SECOND RESTATEMENT §552C and Alfred Hill, *Damages for Innocent Misrepresentation*, 73 COLUM. L. REV. 679 (1973). Clearly many misrepresentation cases will overlap with contract law imposing express or implied warranties. *See* Chapter X, p. 419.

103 *See, e.g., Hawkinson v. A.H. Robbins*, 595 F.Supp. 1290, 1310 (D.Colo. 1984) (manufacturer of inter-uterine contraceptive device that seriously injured users held strictly liable for misrepresentation that its product was a "carefree contraceptive device").

104 118 Eng.Rep. 749 (Q.B. 1853).

105 729 S.W.2d 768 (Tex.App. 1987).

interfering with a deal whereby Getty Oil would purchase Pennzoil. The case was primarily noted for its award of major damages against Texaco: $7.53 billion in actual damages and $1 billion in punitive damages.[106]

Interference with Prospective Economic Advantage It is also tortious to otherwise interfere with another's prospects for commercial success even when those are not secured by contract if such action is wrongful or undertaken solely to cause harm. For example, standing in the door of another's store, seeking to persuade customers to go to one's own store instead would be actionable. However, it should be noted that "fair" economic competition that is designed to disadvantage a competitor is proper. Also close to the boundaries of this tort are other actions for economic wrongs under antitrust laws, unfair competition laws, and trademark, copyright and patent infringement.[107]

2. Misuse of Legal Procedures

Misuse of legal procedure occurs when a person is unjustifiably subjected to legal action. Under this heading are the three torts of malicious prosecution, wrongful institution of civil proceedings, and abuse of process.[108]

Malicious Prosecution Malicious prosecution takes place when a person is subjected to criminal proceedings, those proceedings terminate in that person's favor, and the defendant instituted those proceedings without probable cause and for an improper purpose, defined as a purpose other then bringing a criminal to justice. A common example is where a store has the plaintiff prosecuted for shoplifting even though there was no reasonable basis for it.[109] The final requirement of improper purpose is sometimes referred to as a requirement of "malice." Although it is analytically distinct from the question of absence of probable cause, malice or improper purpose can be inferred from the absence of probable cause.[110]

Wrongful Institution of Civil Proceedings Wrongful institution of civil proceedings is similar to malicious prosecution but applies when the defendant brings an unfounded *civil* lawsuit. As with malicious prosecution, this tort is established by showing that the action terminated in favor of the plaintiff and was brought for an improper purpose.[111] Thus a suit brought to harass a person or to solicit a settlement with no real chance of success, is brought for an improper purpose.[112]

Abuse of Process Abuse of process occurs when a civil or criminal suit is warranted, but a party uses the litigation for an improper purpose. An example of this would be threatening to subpoena a person to testify in an ongoing suit unless the person pays a debt or performs some service.[113]

---

106 Punitive damages are discussed *infra* pp. 463-465.

107 Another use of the tort is to sue departing lawyers who "steal" firm clients. *See* Chapter IV, p. 165. An encyclopedic opinion on the tort is *Della Penna v. Toyota Motor Sales*, 902 P.2d 740 (Cal. 1995).

108 *See* PROSSER & KEETON, *supra* note 1, §§119-121.

109 *Tweedy v. J.C. Penny Co.*, 221 S.E.2d 152 (Va. 1976).

110 *Martin v. City of Albany*, 364 N.E.2d 1304 (N.Y. 1977).

111 SECOND RESTATEMENT §676 states that the only proper purpose for bringing a civil law suit is to adjudicate the issue upon which the claim is based.

112 Summary sanctions may be ordered against litigants and lawyers who file suits or assert positions in lawsuits that are groundless or are asserted for improper purpose. *See* Chapter VII, p. 232.

113 *See, e.g., Czap v. Credit Bureau of Santa Clara Valley*, 86 Cal.Rptr. 417 (Cal.App. 1970) (plaintiff stated a cause of action for abuse of process where credit agency sought to execute on debtor's property in order to pressure her to use funds that were exempt by law from seizure by creditors to pay her debt).

3. Invasions of Dignitary Interests

a. Defamation

Elements Defamation is concerned with injury to the reputation of another person. The elements are (1) the defendant made a defamatory statement concerning the plaintiff; (2) the statement was "published"; and (3) the statement damaged the plaintiff's reputation. The damaging statement need not be shown to be intentional or negligent; if caused to be published, it is actionable. "Publication" is a special term that does not have its usual meaning, but simply means that the statement was communicated to some other person. Defamation can either be written (libel) or oral (slander). One who "re-publishes" (repeats) a defamation is subject to liability equally with the original person who uttered it. Consequently, the author, editor and owner of a newspaper, journal, book or radio or television company are all subject to liability, as are radio and television broadcasters.[114] The original source of the defamation will usually be held responsible for the damage caused by such re-publication.[115]

A "defamatory" statement is a statement that damages a person's reputation by lowering the person in the estimation of the community or deterring other people from associating with that person.[116] What counts is not so much the plaintiff's own feeling about the statement, but whether others would consider it a mark of disgrace. Some statements are defamatory on their face, such as accusing a person of committing a crime. Others depend on the context in which they are uttered. Unlike English law, U.S. law considers a statement defamatory that injures the plaintiff's reputation within any subgroup, not just the community in general.[117] Pure expression of opinion and simple name-calling — as opposed to an assertion of fact — can never be defamatory.[118] The question of whether a statement is defamatory is one of law for the judge to determine, not the jury.[119] However, if language used is fairly susceptible of two different meanings only one of which is defamatory, then that is a question of fact for the jury.[120]

Defenses One defense to defamation is "privilege." "Absolute privilege" protects the speaker who is carrying out certain important duties, regardless of that person's motive or the truth or falsity of the statement. Absolute privilege usually arises from involvement in judicial or legislative proceedings, or by virtue of being a high-level governmental official.[121] Also, husband and wife are absolutely privileged to defame

---

114 SECOND RESTATEMENT §578. *See also* §581(2) (radio or television broadcaster).

115 SECOND RESTATEMENT §§576, 622A.

116 SECOND RESTATEMENT §559.

117 *Ben-Oliel v. Press Publishing Co.*, 167 N.E. 432 (N.Y. 1929) (complaint was sufficient when it alleged that plaintiff was defamed when false statements about the customs of Palestine were attributed to her even though her reputation would be tarnished only among those familiar with those customs).

118 SECOND RESTATEMENT §566. *See Curtis Publishing Co. v. Birdsong*, 360 F.2d 344 (5th Cir. 1966) ("bastards"). However, if the ridicule or insult is serious enough, an action for infliction of emotional distress may be proper. *See infra* p. 459.

119 *See Great Coastal Express v. Ellington*, 334 S.E.2d 846 (Va. 1985) (whether accusation of commercial bribery was an accusation of a crime involving moral turpitude is an issue for court, not jury); *Nichols v. Item Publishers*, 132 N.E.2d 860 (N.Y. 1956) (reversing a jury determination that a statement that a pastor had been removed from his office in church was defamatory). *See* Chapter III, p. 87 (division of labor between judge and jury).

120 *See Rovira v. Boget*, 148 N.E. 534 (N.Y. 1925) (jury question whether "cocette," which can mean either a prostitute or a poached egg, is defamatory).

121 *See* SECOND RESTATEMENT §§585-591. *See, e.g., General Electric Co. v. Sargent and Lundy*, 916 F.2d 1119, appeal after remand, 954 F.2d 724 (6th Cir. 1992) (absolute privilege extends to comments made by defendant in anticipation of litigation regarding allegedly defective anti-pollutant devices).

each other.[122] An important special privilege that affects the media is the privilege of fair reporting of an official action or proceeding, or of meetings open to the public that deal with matters of public concern.[123]

"Qualified privilege" may also be a defense to defamation. Qualified privilege is qualified in that it will not defeat a defamation claim if the defendant claiming it made the defamatory statement with actual malice, recklessness, or knowledge of falsity. Qualified privilege applies to communication related to a matter of public interest or where it is necessary to protect one's own interest. For example, defendants who reasonably believe that the plaintiff has stolen their property may communicate that belief to the police without incurring liability. Qualified immunity is also granted to protect the interest of a third person, such as reporting suspicions that the plaintiff stole someone else's property. Reports by former employers are also covered by qualified immunity in many states. Thus a former employer who tells a potential employer that the plaintiff was a bad worker is protected, so long as the communication was made without malice, recklessness or knowledge that the statement is false.[124]

A defamatory statement must be false to be actionable.[125] But the common law has considered truth to be a *defense* to defamation rather than an element of the plaintiff's case. Thus, the defendant has the burden of proving the statement was true rather than the plaintiff having to prove that it was false. However, this rule is modified by 1st Amendment considerations in cases involving "public concern," as discussed below.

Damages Generally, if defamation is shown, damages are presumed and if the defamation was intentional, then punitive damages may be assessed. However, like placing the burden of proving truth on the defendant, this rule is modified by 1st Amendment considerations in cases involving "public concern," as discussed below.

b. Infliction of Emotional Distress

Infliction of emotional distress is a relatively new tort and the limits of liability are still being defined. In the past, for a plaintiff to recover for emotional distress, there had to have been some kind of physical contact involved (a battery). The modern tort of infliction of emotional distress does not require actual physical contact. Although this tort is sometimes discussed with intentional torts, the mental state required can be intent or recklessness and, most recently, even negligence.[126]

Intentional Infliction Intentional infliction of emotional distress occurs whenever a defendant's behavior toward the plaintiff is so outrageous and extreme that it causes serious emotional distress. Proof of actual damages is often a barrier to a plaintiff attempting to bring an emotional distress case. It is not sufficient to prove that the defendant's actions were extreme and outrageous; the plaintiff must prove that the acts caused severe distress. While there is generally no requirement that the emotional distress manifest itself as a physical symptom, courts will sometimes look to see whether the plaintiff has sought medical attention.

---

122 Second Restatement §592.

123 Second Restatement §611.

124 *See, e.g., Russell v. American Guild of Variety Artists*, 497 P.2d 40 (Haw. 1972) (union official's letter to plaintiff's booking agent stating that plaintiff had been committed to mental facility covered by qualified privilege because not made in bad faith or with malice).

125 Second Restatement §581A.

126 Second Restatement §46.

There is some disagreement among jurisdictions as to when a third person, such as a person who witnesses an outrageous act, can recover for emotional distress. For example, a person may witness a murder and become ill as a result. The Second Restatement requires generally that the third party suffer some kind of physical symptoms in order to recover damages. A close family member, however generally need not prove physical symptoms.[127]

Negligent Infliction Negligent infliction of emotional distress is a new concept and has met with a varied reception. Most of the states that allow this cause of action require that the act which causes the distress be in some way directed toward the plaintiff and that the resulting distress be reasonably foreseeable. For example, courts have allowed recovery in a case where a mother witnessed a car running over her child. This is because people who are driving negligently should reasonably foresee that, if they run over a child, the child's mother may be nearby and witness the accident, and that witnessing the injury would upset the mother.[128] However, under the same circumstances most courts will not allow a stranger to recover after seeing the same accident nor do they allow a parent to recover if the parent does not actually witness the injury.[129]

In contrast to intentional infliction of emotional distress, *negligent* infliction usually requires that the plaintiff suffer a physical symptom as a result of the emotional distress.[130] But some states, most notably California, have allowed recovery even when there is no physical symptom.[131] It remains to be seen whether this is a growing trend.

c. Invasion of Privacy

Four Component Torts of Invasion of Privacy Invasion of privacy is divided into four separate torts: "appropriation," "intrusion," "publicity of private life," and "displaying in a false light."[132] "Appropriation" is the use of a person's name or picture for financial gain without his or her consent, such as where a famous person's name or picture is placed in an advertisement for a product without consent.[133] "Intrusion" is the invasion of a person's solitude which would be highly offensive to the reasonable person, such as taking a photograph of a person through a window of the person's house. However, it is not an actionable intrusion to take another's picture in a public place, such as a public beach, or with permission in a private place.[134] "Publicity of private life" involves making public details of a person's private life. "Displaying in a false light" occurs when the plaintiff is placed before the public in a way that would be offensive to a reasonable person. "False light" cases are similar to defamation cases. However, recovery for

---

127 *See* SECOND RESTATEMENT §46(2).

128 *See Dillon v. Legg*, 441 P.2d 912 (Cal. 1968) (mother who witnessed her daughter being struck by a car allowed to recover).

129 *Thing v. LaChusa*, 771 P.2d 814 (Cal. 1989) (mother who learned of her child's accident and rushed to the scene may not recover because she was not actually present when the accident occurred).

130 SECOND RESTATEMENT §436(A). *See Johnson v. West Virginia University Hospitals*, 413 S.E.2d 889 (W.Va. 1991) (policeman who was bitten by AIDS-infected patient whom he tried to subdue was allowed to recover from hospital for emotional distress over his exposure to AIDS when hospital negligently failed to inform him of the patient's infected status when they called on him to assist).

131 *See Molien v. Kaiser Foundation Hospitals*, 616 P.2d 813 (Cal. 1980) (husband allowed to recover for emotional distress when defendant misdiagnosed him as having syphilis and wife's suspicions of marital infidelity caused their marriage to break up).

132 *See* SECOND RESTATEMENT §§652A-652E.

133 *See Midler v. Ford Motor Co.*, 849 F.2d 460 (9th Cir. 1988)(advertising firm which had singer sing in a way that resembled Bette Midler's voice liable for appropriation).

134 *But see Dieteman v. Time, Inc.*, 449 F.2d 245 (9th Cir. 1971) (actionable claim where reporter took photograph from concealed camera while in plaintiff's house under false pretenses).

being displayed in a false light does not require that it be proven that the portrayal would injure a person's reputation, as is the case with defamation.

d. Constitutional Limits on Dignitary Torts

(1) The 1st Amendment and Defamation

The policy behind the 1st Amendment is to encourage robust public debate of issues affecting society. If the normal common law of defamation applied, with its strict liability, its requirement that the defendant prove truth and its rule of presumed damages, defamation actions or the threat of them could "chill" the exercise of 1st Amendment rights. Though not entirely free from doubt, the amount of protection due an alleged defamatory statement has generally depended on the extent to which the victim of that defamation is a "public figure" and the extent to which the subject of the libel involved a matter of "public concern." "Public figures" are all public officials in supervisory positions and any private persons who voluntarily "thrust themselves to the forefront of particular public controversies in order to influence the resolution of the issues involved."[135] What is an issue of "public concern" is less clear, though it clearly includes government officials' performance of their duties or criticism of the views of other public figures on the subject matter that made them a public figure.

Public Figure, Public Concern   When a *public figure* sues regarding defamation related to a matter of *public concern* the 1st Amendment severely restricts that figure's ability to recover. The principal case of this type is *New York Times Co. v Sullivan*.[136] In that case, a city police commissioner sued several black ministers and the New York Times when the ministers published an advertisement in the paper seeking support for their civil rights struggles. The advertisement made critical comments about law enforcement's handling of civil rights demonstrators. It also contained some factual errors.[137] *New York Times* held that the 1st Amendment has three effects on the common law elements of defamation when public figures sue: (1) it shifts the normal common law burden of proof on truth to require that the *plaintiff* prove *falsity*, (2) it imposes a higher degree of culpability by requiring the plaintiff to prove that the defendant acted with "actual malice" and (3) it requires a higher proof standard, requiring that the plaintiff prove such actual malice "with convincing clarity."[138] To prove actual malice, the plaintiff must prove that the defendant either knew that the statement was false or evinced a reckless disregard for whether it was true or false. The standard

---

135 *See Rosenblatt v. Baer*, 383 U.S. 75 (1966) (supervisor of county-owned ski resort). On non-government public figures, *compare Gertz v. Robert Welch, Inc.*, 418 U.S. 323, 345 (1974) (attorney representing plaintiffs in civil rights suit against a city police officer was not a public figure) *with Curtis Publishing v. Butts*, 388 U.S. 130 (1967) (athletic director of a privately incorporated athletic association attached to a state university, who was accused of "fixing" football games, was a public figure).

136 376 U.S. 254 (1964). *See also* Chapter IX, p. 380.

137 Perhaps influencing the decision was the fact that the mistakes were minor. For example, the advertisement said that civil rights leader Martin Luther King had been arrested 7 times, when he had in fact been arrested only 4 times.

138 The "convincing clarity" standard is somewhere in between the normal civil standard of "preponderance of the evidence" and the criminal standard of "beyond a reasonable doubt." *See* Chapter III, p. 105, where standards of proof are compared. At the very least, *New York Times* holds that this requires that the plaintiff prove he was referred to directly by name or title —something not done in that case. *See also Bose Corp. v. Consumers Union of the United States*, 466 U.S. 485 (1984) (appellate court must scrutinize facts on actual malice carefully to assure that it is has been established with convincing clarity).

is subjective, meaning that it must be proven that the editor or writer "in fact entertained serious doubts as to the truth of his publication."[139]

Private Figure, Public Concern   Where a *private figure* sues regarding alleged defamation that relates to what is clearly a *public concern*, the 1st Amendment has a limiting effect, but not to the extent that it does in the case of public figures. The principal case in this category is *Gertz v. Robert Welch, Inc.*[140] In that case, a police officer had been convicted of murdering a young man. Elmer Gertz, a private lawyer, represented the family in a highly publicized civil rights suit against the policeman. A John Birch Society publication accused Gertz of orchestrating a "communist frame-up" of the policeman for murder. It also claimed falsely that Gertz had a criminal record and asserted that Gertz, as a "Leninist" and "communist fronter," was participating in a communist conspiracy to discredit local police departments, apparently an essential step in a communist conspiracy to enslave the country. The Court held that Gertz was a private figure and that the *New York Times* standard would not apply. Nonetheless it held that the 1st Amendment (1) shifts the common law burden of proof as to truth to the plaintiff, as discussed above, (2) permits recovery of compensatory damages only if the plaintiff actually proves such damages based on at least a standard of negligence, and (3) prohibits any award of presumed or punitive damages unless the plaintiff proves "actual malice" in compliance with the *Sullivan* standard.

Similarly, in *Philadelphia Papers, Inc. v. Hepps*,[141] a private businessman sued a newspaper that had accused him of having links to organized crime and using them to influence legislation. The state court imposed the common law burden of proof that required the defendant to prove truth. The Court disagreed and applied the *Gertz* standard to the case, labeling the subject matter of the defamation "speech of public concern" and noting that it was "against a media defendant."

One might criticize *Gertz* and *Hepps* for distinguishing between public and private figures, at least when the defamation deals with matters of public concern, since vigorous discussion of public concerns is at the core of 1st Amendment protections regardless of whether a public figure is involved. The *Gertz* court found different treatment of public and private figures to be warranted for two reasons. First, people who become public figures do so voluntarily and assume the risk of sharp public criticism. Second, public figures' celebrity status and high positions give them a ready access to the media that private figures do not have. This allows public figures to respond publicly to defamatory attacks, thereby reducing their need to resort to defamation suits for protection.[142]

Private Figure, Private Concern   In the absence of evidence that the plaintiff is a public figure or that the defamation related to a public concern, the 1st Amendment has

---

139 *St. Amant v. Thompson*, 390 U.S. 727, 731 (1968). *See also Harte-Hanks Communications v. Connaughton*, 491 U.S. 657 (1989) (newspaper accused judgeship candidate of using "dirty tricks" to influence a witness by offering her and her sister a trip to Florida; evidence was sufficient to support jury finding of actual malice where the paper failed to attempt to contact the witness's sister, the editor refused to listen to taped interviews of the witness, and jury rejected testimony that the paper thought that the witness was credible). *But see Masson v. New Yorker*, 501 U.S. 496 (1991) (fact that quotations ascribed to plaintiff public figure were fabricated was not sufficient to show actual malice unless fabricated quotes substantially change the meaning of what was actually said).

140 418 U.S. 323 (1974).

141 475 U.S. 767 (1986).

142 *Gertz*, 418 U.S. at 344-345.

no effect. Thus, in *Dun & Bradstreet v. Greenmoss Builders*,[143] the private figure plaintiff sued over a false credit report disseminated to only 5 business clients that incorrectly asserted that the plaintiff company had filed for bankruptcy. A plurality of the Court maintained that the case involved only a matter of private concern, so no 1st Amendment protections were due, and a majority of the Court affirmed a judgment for presumed compensatory and punitive damages without compliance with the *Gertz* standard.

Public Figure, Private Concern   Few cases have involved this category, perhaps because it is hard to imagine any aspect of a public figure's life that would not be automatically be a public concern. Certainly, the Clinton sex scandal suggests that today most any private matter can be related to an official's fitness for office.

A Caveat   Although the various combinations of public and private figures and issues are set out neatly above, it must be stated that things are not quite this clear. The principal problem is that the Court has not been clear on what a "public concern" is and if it is relevant. In the *Gertz* case, the Court specifically denied that there was any public-private concern distinction, thus suggesting that the *Gertz* protections apply to all private issue defamation. Another source of uncertainty is the phrase quoted above from *Hepps* — the suggestion that it made a difference that the suit was "against a media defendant." *Gertz* also stated that it was imposing a minimum negligence standard for compensatory damages in defamation suits against "a broadcaster or publisher." Yet, the Court has not attempted to define who belongs to the "media," nor has it taken the position that the media are somehow different because "the press" is mentioned in the 1st Amendment.

Protection of Opinion   One thing the Court has made clear is that there is no general privilege for all expressions of *opinion* on matters of public concern. Some have argued that, since name-calling, epithets and rhetorical hyperbole are a normal part of the discussion of matters of public concern, such a privilege based on the 1st Amendment should be afforded. The Supreme Court has rejected any such blanket rule, noting that rephrasing "Jones is a liar" as "in my opinion, Jones is a liar" does little to change its effect on Jones's reputation. Thus, even a statement of opinion is actionable if it contains some provable false factual implication.[144]

(2) The 1st Amendment and Other Dignitary Torts

Intentional Infliction of Emotional Distress   Most defamation is intended to hurt its target, so public figures could easily avoid *New York Times* limitations in many defamation cases by simply switching to the tort of intentional infliction of emotional distress instead. Consequently, it is essential that the *New York Times* standard apply to this tort as well. Thus, in *Hustler Magazine, Inc. v. Falwell*,[145] Falwell, a nationally known minister and founder of the "Moral Majority," could not recover for emotional distress caused by mock interview with him in which he stated that his first sexual encounter was a drunken incestuous rendezvous with his mother in an outhouse. Falwell's defamation claim failed because the jury found that no reasonable person would have believed the "facts" in the mock interview to be true. However, the jury awarded substantial damages for intentional infliction of emotional distress. The Court reversed, holding that intentionally inflicting emotional distress on public figures is a time-honored

---

143 472 U.S. 749 (1985) (plurality opinion).

144 *Milkovich v. Lorain Journal Co.*, 497 U.S. 1 (1990) (newspaper columnist's statement that high school coach, a private figure, committed perjury presents factual issue of whether it was true; there is no separate constitutional privilege for "opinion").

145 485 U.S. 46 (1988).

tradition in the United States and that the 1st Amendment prohibits any liability in suits by public figures regarding issues of public interest unless a false statement of fact is made and the *New York Times v. Sullivan* "actual malice" standard is met with regard to it.

Invasions of Privacy   The four components of invasion of privacy have been handled somewhat differently in terms of 1st Amendment protections. The *New York Time* rule has been applied to cases where the public figure plaintiff claims to have been portrayed in a false light, requiring proof that the defendant acted with "actual malice."[146] But appropriation cases have not been held subject to 1st Amendment limitations. It has likened them to copyright suits, in which the appropriation decreases the commercial value of someone else's speech and invades "the right of the individual to reap the reward of his endeavors."[147] As for publicity of private life, if the private details are already part of the public record, any prohibition of further dissemination violates the 1st Amendment rights of free speech and press. In one case, the Court reversed a judgment for damages in favor of a rape victim whose name had been published by a newspaper in its "Police Reports" section, based on a state statute prohibiting publication of the name of any victim of a sexual assault. If a newspaper "lawfully obtains truthful information about a matter of public significance," it violates the 1st Amendment to prohibit or penalize its publication.[148] No 1st Amendment issues have yet arisen in intrusion cases.

D. Relief Available in Tort Cases

What damages are recoverable for torts varies by jurisdiction. In general, aside from nominal damages, two types of damages are available in tort cases: compensatory damages and punitive damages.[149] A plaintiff may recover both compensatory and punitive damages in the same case.

1. Compensatory Damages

Awards of damages are generally made in a lump sum, not by way of periodic payments, as is the case with most administrative compensation systems. The elements of compensatory damages available vary from state to state, but the overall purpose of compensatory damages everywhere is to compensate the plaintiff monetarily for the actual damage suffered. This is generally subject to a duty of the plaintiff to "mitigate damages," meaning that the plaintiff must take steps to prevent damages from continuing or getting worse if that can be done by reasonable action. Compensatory damages include both economic and non-economic losses resulting from personal injury or property damage.[150]

---

146 *Time, Inc. v. Hill*, 385 U.S. 374 (1967) (holding *Sullivan* standard applicable to false light cases). The actual holding in *Hill*, that non-public figure plaintiffs had to meet the *Sullivan* standard, has since been undercut by the *Gertz* case, as discussed above under defamation. Consequently, lower courts are divided over what approach to use for private figures.

147 *Zacchini v. Scripps-Howard Broadcasting Co.*, 433 U.S. 562, 573 (1977) (television station broadcast a 15 second tape of plaintiff's "human cannonball" act, which was the entire performance). The Court rejected 1st Amendment limits on copyright suits in *Harper & Row v. Nation Enterprises*, 471 U.S. 539 (1985) (copying 300 words from a 200,000 word manuscript of President Ford's memoirs).

148 *Florida Star v. B.J.F.*, 491 U.S. 524 (1989). *See also Cox Broadcasting Corp. v. Cohn*, 420 U.S. 469 (1975) (rape victim's name made public by open records of the trial proceedings) and *Smith v. Daily Mail Publishing Co.*, 443 U.S. 97 (1979) (name of juvenile delinquent lawfully obtained).

149 *See* Chapter VII, p. 244.

150 *See generally* DAN B. DOBBS, LAW OF REMEDIES §8.1 (West 1993).

Economic Loss Economic losses are the actual expenses that the plaintiff incurred. Damaged property, medical bills, and lost wages are typical examples. Medical expenses can be substantial in the United States, which has no free national health program.[151] Property damage and past medical expenses and lost wages are relatively easy to measure. Future medical expenses and future employment income losses are more difficult to determine. To project these losses, expert testimony from doctors and economists is required. An injured homemaker, most often the female spouse who is not employed outside the home and takes care of the home, may claim for the cost of replacement services.

Until recently, it was a universal rule that benefits received by a plaintiff from a "collateral source" may not be used to reduce the defendant's liability for damages. Consequently, a plaintiff who is out of work for a period of time may recover lost wages for that period even if the employer paid the plaintiff wages under a disability or sick leave benefit for all or part of that time. A plaintiff can also recover for medical expenses even if they have been paid by a medical insurance policy or were provided free of charge. While this may seem like overcompensation, one theory behind the rule is that the wrongdoing defendant should not be the beneficiary of the plaintiff's or plaintiff's employer's foresight in purchasing insurance. Today, about half the states have enacted statutes modifying or abolishing the collateral source rule in at least some categories of cases. Thus, the amount of a judgement is reduced by any amount the plaintiff has received from insurance policies or governmental compensation programs such as worker's compensation.[152]

The Pure Economic Loss Rule In negligence and product liability cases, a plaintiff usually cannot recover for "pure economic loss" — lost profits or other financial opportunities. These may be recoverable for *intentional* torts designed to remedy such losses, such as interference with contractual relations.[153] And even in negligence and product liability cases, as just discussed, economic losses can be recovered if they are the result of personal injury or property damage.[154] But lost profits and other such economic losses do not qualify for recovery under a tort theory.

Several reasons have been given for the pure economic loss rule, both theoretical and practical. On the more theoretical side, recovery for pure economic loss seems more appropriate to contract law's concept of expectation damages — giving the parties the "benefit of their bargain"[155] — than tort law's policy of seeking to return injured parties to the position they occupied before the injury. Moreover, making pure economic losses solely an issue of contract law makes it subject to negotiation between the parties. Permitting commercial parties to allocate their liability beforehand in the event of breach results in greater efficiency and predictability. As the Supreme Court stated in applying the pure economic loss rule in an admiralty case:

---

151 *See* Chapter XV, p. 620 (cost of private medical insurance).

152 Some of these statutes have been held unconstitutional. *Smith v. Department of Insurance*, 507 So.2d 1080 (Fla. 1987). The impact on the plaintiff of deducting private medical or disability insurance proceeds from the judgment is often negligible. Most of the deducted amounts would have gone to the plaintiff's medical or disability insurance carriers anyway because of subrogation agreements — agreements under which insureds agree to reimburse their insurance carrier from any recovery they received in order to reimburse the carrier for payments it has made to the insured.

153 *See supra* pp. 452-453.

154 The product damaging itself is not considered compensable property damage, however. *See East River Steamship Corp. v. Transamerica Delaval, Inc.*, 476 U.S. 858 (1986) (defective turbines rendered ships inoperable causing economic damage; no recovery in admiralty case).

155 Chapter X, p. 411.

Contract law, and the law of warranty in particular, is well suited to commercial controversies . . . because the parties may set the terms of their own agreements. The manufacturer can restrict its liability, within limits, by disclaiming warranties or limiting remedies. . . . In exchange, the purchaser pays less for the product.[156]

As for practical reasons for the rule, any serious disruption of business operations caused by negligence or a defective product will often have many, varied and expensive consequences that would satisfy the tort law's broad standard of foreseeability, thus resulting in massive liability judgments. Moreover, if tort recovery were permitted for pure economic loss, tort law would completely displace the parties' commercial contractual relations, thus permitting commercial parties to ignore their contractual obligations.

Whatever its rationale, the result of the pure economic damages rule is that commercial parties often have no meaningful tort remedy, since sellers of goods and services often require their business customers to agree to waivers and limitations on remedies. For example, the typical contract for sale of goods disclaims liability for consequential damages and limits remedies for defects to repair or replacement of the item.[157]

Non-Economic Loss The largest component of non-economic loss is "pain and suffering." As the phrase indicates, this category of damages is designed to compensate the plaintiff for the conscious physical pain and mental suffering that come with physical injury. This included not only physical pain, but mental anguish over disfigurement or shorter life expectancy and other consequences. Also often included within pain and suffering are compensation for loss of enjoyment-in-life, such as the inability without pain or complete inability to have sex, play the violin, jog or any other customary activity that gave the victim pleasure in life before the injury. It is often difficult to place a dollar value on these losses and it is thought that this amount is best evaluated by a jury.

Cross-country and cross-cultural comparisons are difficult to make, but it is probably true that the United States is more generous than Western European countries when it comes to compensation for non-economic harm. In one study, actual awards for cervical spine injuries in Germany and New York state were studied. While the average recovery was €3,777 in Germany, it was the equivalent of €214,855 euros in New York state. The medians were €1,175 and €80,750, respectively.[158] In another study, using figures provided by experts in the U.S. and 19 West European countries, the median award for loss of a leg was €41,000 in Europe, while it was €750,000 in the U.S. For a plaintiff rendered a quadiplegic, the respective expected median awards were €92,000 and €2,550,000. One thing that accounts for the higher amounts in the U.S is the difference in how lawyers fees are paid. In Europe, the loser pays the winner's fees, so the European plaintiff gets the full amount awarded for non-economic damages. In the

---

156 *East River Steamship*, *supra* note 154, 476 U.S. at 872-873, where other sources are also cited. *See also* THIRD RESTATEMENT OF TORTS §21 and commentary thereto. Contract remedies for economic harm are discussed in Chapter X, pp. 412, 421 (contract remedies). *Compare Seely v. White Motor Co.*, 403 P.2d 145, 151 (Cal. 1965) (defective truck; recovery of economic loss from loss of use permitted on warranty, but not on negligence or product liability theory) *with Oppen v. Aetna Ins. Co.*, 485 F.2d 252 (9th Cir. 1973) (major oil company negligently caused oil pollution on the California coast killing many fish; commercial fishermen allowed to recover economic losses.)

157 *See* Chapter X, p. 421.

158 Anthony J. Sebok, *Translating the Immeasurable: Thinking about Pain and Suffering Comparatively*, 55 DEPAUL L.REV. 379, 396 (2006).

U.S., the parties are responsible for their own legal fees, win or lose, and in the case of a win by a plaintiff this means that typically one-third of the total award is paid to the lawyer in the form of a contingency fee. Since non-economic damages average one-half of the total award, one can reduce that portion of the award by one third. In cases where non-economic damages are less than one-third of the total award, U.S. plaintiffs worse off than their European counterparts and in a few cases end up with no compensation at all for their non-economic losses and perhaps a deduction from the economic damages portion of their award.[159]

2. Punitive Damages

a. Nature of Award and Grounds

Punitive damages are awarded only for particularly egregious behavior and are designed to punish the tortfeasor and deter a repetition of that conduct.[160] They are usually awarded in addition to compensatory damages, though some jurisdictions permit an award of punitive damages even in the absence of compensatory damages. For a punitive damage award, the plaintiff generally must prove either an intentional tort or reckless, willful or wanton behavior. The size of punitive damage awards is usually determined by a jury, though it is subject to review by the judge. Punitive damages are typically awarded in intentional tort cases, but have also been awarded in some products liability actions where the manufacturer knew of a defect in its product and the potential for serious injury and death, and yet made a conscious decision not to correct the defect. For example, in *Grimshaw v. Ford Motor Co.*,[161] a woman was badly burned when the car she was riding in burst into flames when it was struck in the rear end. Evidence introduced at the trial showed that the defendant was aware of the defect before the car was introduced on the market, but chose not to remedy the defect. The jury awarded the plaintiff $2,500,000 in compensatory damages and $125,000,000 in punitive damages. This amount was later reduced to $3,500,000 by the court because of the gross disparity between the compensatory and punitive damages.

Despite popular belief to the contrary based on the publicity given to punitive awards, they are somewhat of a rarity. For example, in Cook County (which includes the City of Chicago), the number of punitive damage awards averaged 1.8 per year during the 1960s and 1970s, 2.8 per year during 1980-1984, and 2 per year during 1990-1994. During the entire 25-year period of 1960-1984, only 50 punitive damage awards were made. San Francisco averaged even fewer: 0.2 awards per year from 1960 to 1980, 1.2 per year from 1980 to 1984, 4 per year from 1990 to 1994, and an overall total of 10 over the 25 years. Also contrary to popular belief, the amounts of punitive awards have not "skyrocketed" as some have asserted. Awards have increased, but have obviously not reached the height most assume. In the 1990-1994 period, the mean punitive damage award in Cook County was $6.8 million and the mean San Francisco award was $1.6 million. But the median award was $250,000 in Cook County and $97,000.[162] This

---

159 On attorney fees, *see* Chapter IV, p. 145, and Chapter VI, p. 248. Stephen D. Sugarman, *A Comparative Look at Pain and Suffering Awards*, 55 DEPAUL L.REV. 399, 418 (2006).

160 *See generally* DOBBS, *supra* note 150, §3.11.

161 174 Cal. Rptr. 348 (Cal.App. 1981).

162 DEBORAH HENSLER AND ERIK MOLLER, TRENDS IN PUNITIVE DAMAGES: PRELIMINARY DATA FROM COOK COUNTY, ILLINOIS AND SAN FRANCISCO, CALIFORNIA (Rand Corp. 1995). In products liability and medical malpractice cases, in Cook County there was one product liability punitive damage award for the 1960-1979 period, one such award during the 1980-1984 period, and three such awards during the 1990-1994 period. For medical malpractice, there were no such awards in 1960-1979 and three in 1980-84.

suggests that the typical punitive damages case does not involve awards of millions of dollars.

b. Constitutional Requirements

The Supreme Court has rejected the notion that punitive damage awards violate the 8th Amendment's prohibition on excessive fines, holding that that Amendment does not apply to suits between private parties.[163] However, it has held that awards are subject to scrutiny under the due process clause. The due process objection can apply either to the procedure used in arriving at the amount of the award or to the amount itself.

Procedure In *Pacific Mutual Life Insurance Co. v. Haslip*,[164] the Court held that due process requires that the jury be given specific standards as to the grounds for and amount of punitive damages. *Haslip* was a suit against an insurance company for bad faith denial of medical insurance coverage. The Court upheld the award, pointing out that evidence of the defendant company's wealth was excluded from evidence, that jury instructions gave guidance as to the nature and function of punitive damages. The Court also noted that both the trial and appellate courts had supervisory power to revise such awards. In *Honda Motor Co., Ltd. v. Oberg*,[165] the Court stuck down an Oregon constitutional provision that prohibited any judicial review of a jury's punitive damages award unless there was a complete absence of evidence to support it. Then, in *Cooper Industries, Inc. v. Leatherman Tool Co., Inc.*,[166] the Court held that due process required that appellate courts review punitive damages awards *de novo*, despite the fact that appellate review of a trial court's review of a jury's award of *compensatory* damage awards is only "abuse of discretion." The Court reasoned that compensatory damages compensate for an identifiable loss, so their determination is essentially a factual one. Punitive damages, on the other hand, are to punish. The issue on appellate review is a constitutional one — whether the award is grossly excessive or arbitrary punishment — and therefore is for the appellate court to assess *de novo* as a matter of law.

Amount In the *Haslip* case above, the Court approved an award of $800,000 punitive damages and $200,000 compensatory damages. This was a 4-to-1 ratio of punitive to compensatory damages and a 200-to-1 ratio of punitive damages to out-of-pocket expenses. As such, it was much in excess of the criminal fine that the state could have imposed for insurance fraud. The Court indicated that such a ratio "may be close to the line . . . of constitutional impropriety." However, in a 1993 case, a plurality of the Court affirmed a judgment of $10 million in punitive and $19,000 in compensatory damages for a ratio of 526 to 1 in a slander of title case.[167]

The Court finally reversed an award as excessive in *BMW v. Gore*.[168] *Gore* holds that such awards may not be "grossly excessive" in relation to the state's "legitimate inter-

---

163 *Browning-Ferris Industries of Vt., Inc. v. Kelco Disposal, Inc.*, 492 U.S. 257 (1989). The excessive fines clause does apply to civil forfeiture actions brought by the government. *See* Chapter VIII, p. 321.

164 499 U.S. 1 (1991).

165 512 U.S. 415 (1994).

166 532 U.S. 424 (2001).

167 *TXO Productions v. Alliance Resources Corp.*, 509 U.S. 443 (1993). Slander of title is an intentional tort in which the plaintiff owner of property suffers damages (usually in the form of loss of business) because the defendant has in bad faith cast doubt on the plaintiff's title to property. A colorful opinion by an eccentric West Virginia Supreme Court Justice approved the award and divided punitive damages cases into those involving "really mean defendants," "really stupid defendants," and "really stupid defendants who could have caused a great deal of harm by their actions but who actually caused minimal harm." *See TXO Productions v. Alliance Resource Corp.*, 419 S.E.2d 870 (W.Va. 1992).

168 517 U.S. 559 (1996).

ests" in punishing unlawful conduct and deterring its repetition. *Gore* involved BMW's practice of repainting cars damaged in transit and then selling them as new cars without telling the purchaser that the car had been damaged and repainted. The award must be judged by the application of three "considerations": (1) the degree of reprehensibility of the defendant's conduct, (2) the disparity between the compensatory award and the punitive damages award amount and (3) the disparity between the punitive damage award and other civil and criminal penalties authorized by state law. In striking down the award in *Gore*, the Court determined on the facts of *Gore* that the damage inflicted was purely economic and in the amount of only $4,000, that the $2 million award represented a 500-to1 ratio to actual damages, and was greatly in excess of the $2,000 fine and penalties imposed by the state for similar conduct. The Court also noted that in some states, BMW's practices were legal. This was relevant to the amount because a state's "legitimate interests" in punitive damages awards cannot, consistent with territoriality principle, extend to punish conduct in other states.

Finally, in *State Farm Mutual Insurance, Inc. v. Campbell*,[169] the Court settled on a maximum ratio of 9 to 1 as the presumptive due process limit, but emphasized that "there can be no rigid benchmarks that a punitive damages award may not surpass." In cases where "a particularly egregious act has resulted in only a small amount of economic damages," a higher ratio would be appropriate, but when substantial compensatory damages are awarded, "then a lesser ratio, perhaps only equal to compensatory damages, can reach the outermost limit" of due process. The Court then reversed a punitive award with a 145-to-1 ratio to compensatory damages of $1,500,000, where plaintiffs were subjected to callous treatment by their insurance company that caused them emotional distress for a year and half, but caused no physical injury.

3. Wrongful Death and Survival Actions

At common law, a plaintiff's claim expired on the death of the plaintiff. Thus, it was, as some said, "cheaper to kill than to maim." To counter this rather harsh common law rule, most states have enacted statutory modifications providing for "wrongful death" claims and "survival" actions to be prosecuted beyond death by certain designated relatives.[170]

Wrongful Death Claims Wrongful death statutes generally provide that the entity or person who would have been liable had the victim not died continues to be liable despite that death. Only certain "heirs at law" of the victim can sue — those who according to statute would inherit from the deceased should the deceased die intestate, *i.e.*, without a will. Usually, those heirs at law are the spouse, children and parents of the deceased.[171] The damages that may be recovered are the damages suffered by the heirs at law, not those suffered by the deceased before death. This would include economic losses, such as medical bills and loss of support in the form of income the deceased would have received. It also includes non-economic damages, such as emotional loss in the form of loss of companionship. Because the measure of damages is the effect on the surviving plaintiff, it can vary considerably depending on how significant the deceased was, actually or potentially, in the life of the plaintiff. Thus, a 12-year-old girl

---

169 538 U.S. 408 (2003).

170 In at least one instance, a wrongful death claim was created by judicial decision, though that decision was inspired by enactment of wrongful death statutes. See *Moragne v. States Marine Lines, Inc.*, 398 U.S. 375 (1970), discussed in Chapter II, p. .

171 This is so even if there was a will. Intestate succession is discussed in Chapter XIII, p. 494.

who loses her mother will be awarded considerably more than the adult brother of the deceased who has been out communication with the deceased for years.

A wrongful death claim exists only if the deceased would have had a claim had death not ensued, so claims are subject to all the various defenses applicable to live victims. Most commonly, the issue is the contributory negligence of the deceased.

Survival Actions All states have enacted survival statutes. Unlike wrongful death statutes which permit recovery of losses suffered by surviving relatives, these statutes provide for the *estate* of the deceased person to recover damages for losses the *deceased* suffered before dying. This includes all the economic and non-economic damages outlined above that a live plaintiff can recover, including pain and suffering the deceased experienced before death. The rationale of survival statutes is that it is only fair for the estate of the deceased to recover the amount the deceased would have had, had death not intervened. Some states have gone further than this and allow recovery for what the estate of the deceased would have been had the deceased died a natural death after a normal life span.

4. Specific Relief

In situations where monetary damages are inadequate to remedy a civil wrong, a court may instead grant specific relief rather than money damages. Injunctions are commonly granted in trespass cases or to "abate" a nuisance.[172] Otherwise injunctions will be awarded only when monetary damages are difficult to fix. However, an action for replevin for recovery of property is commonly used as a remedy to repossess personal property pledged as security.[173]

E. Administration of the Tort System of Compensation

1. The Role of Liability Insurance

Most potential defendants purchase liability insurance under which an insurance company agrees to pay for losses for which the insured may be held liable, up to a given policy limit. Without tort liability, insurance would not be needed. But just as clearly, without insurance coverage, tort liability would largely be unavailing, as few would have assets sufficient to pay judgments.[174]

Spreading Costs Insurance coverage provides a way to spread the costs of accidents and other injuries over the entire society. The tort system shifts costs to defendants, and insurance further shifts and spreads the loss over all in society when prospective defendants pass on the cost of the insurance premiums by raising the price of the products and services they sell. Viewed broadly then, the expenses of accidents are just one of the costs of living in an industrialized society. Since we all reap the benefits of having that kind of society, it is fair that we all share its costs.

Duty to Defend Clauses As important as the insurance company's obligation to pay liability is its "duty to defend" — its obligation to provide the insured with legal representation in defending any lawsuit for liability insured under the contract. Disputes arise over the duty to defend, mainly over the question of whether the claims made are for liability that is covered under the policy. The general rule is that if *any* of the claims made are for a liability compensable under the policy, then the insurance company must

---

172 Trespass and nuisance are discussed in Chapter XII, pp. 479-481.
173 *See supra* p. 439 and Chapter XII, p. 423 (repossession through replevin).
174 For more on liability insurance, *see* PROSSER & KEETON, *supra* note 1, §§82-85.

defend the entire suit.[175] Because the insurance company is in charge of the defense of the lawsuit, the presence of insurance increases the number of out-of-court settlements. While individual defendants' pride may cause them to balk at settling a case by paying the plaintiff something on the claim, insurance companies look at it as a simple business question of whether the risk of losing plus the costs of defending are greater than the cost of settling. In a dispute between the insured and the insurance company over whether to settle, the company will generally win out because most insurance policies contain a clause that allows the insurance company to settle without the consent of the insured. However, there are numerous conflict-of-interest situations that can arise between the company and the insured in the settlement process.[176]

Prevalence of Liability Insurance The development and widespread use of the automobile have been the catalyst for the widespread use of liability insurance. Whenever a business engages in an activity that might cause serious personal injury, it purchases the requisite insurance. It is common as well for individuals to purchase a comprehensive "homeowner's insurance" policy, a broad policy that insures home owners against loss of their home, but also insures against liability for torts connected with ownership of the property and "off-premises" torts committed by the insured. Most on and off-premises torts covered by liability insurance policies cover only negligent acts and not intentional acts of the insured. Other common types of liability insurance include insurance for landlords and other property owners, medical and legal malpractice and other professional insurance, and commercial liability insurance.

2. The "Crisis" in the Tort Compensation System and Recent Attempts at Reform

The Litigation "Explosion" In recent years, many have argued that society's burden in absorbing the cost of injuries through insurance has become too great. Led by the insurance industry, objections have been heard most often in the area of medical malpractice cases where the cost of insurance is very high and adds to the already high cost of health care in the United States. In the area of products liability, critics argue, increased awards and numbers of suits have posed a severe impediment to the growth of business and scientific research within the United States. The constant fear of liability makes insuring high risk ventures almost impossible and thwarts the development of new research that developers fear could expose them to liability. They argue that this is the result of easy liability rules, contingent fees for lawyers, the presence of insurance, "runaway juries" and a culture in which everyone with even the hint of injury sues for compensation without thinking twice about it.

Types of Tort Reform Measures Based on these perceptions and arguments, numerous "tort reform" measures have been pushed through state legislatures. While most of the basic grounds for liability have remained untouched, there have been numerous limits in the amount that can be recovered and other procedural aspects, such as modification of joint and several liability, modification or elimination of the collateral source rule, limits on recoveries of both non-economic compensatory

---

175 *See Maryland Casualty Co. v. Peppers*, 355 N.E.2d 24 (Ill. 1976) (both intentional and unintentional bases of liability were alleged; policy covered only unintentional wrongs, but company had a duty to defend both).

176 *See Merritt v. Reserve Insurance Co.*, 110 Cal.Rptr. 511 (Cal.App. 1973) (discussing conflicts).

damages and punitive damages, and regulation of attorney contingent fees.[177] In 1997, Congress debated a "Products Liability Reform Act" that would establish uniform laws and procedures for resolving and compensating parties injured by defective products that would be generally much more restrictive that the law existing in the states now.[178] A Model Punitive Damages Act was adopted in 1996 by the Uniform Law Commissioners that would, if adopted, further restrict punitive damage awards. While the Act largely codifies current law on the subject as set out in the *BMW v. Gore* case, it would change the law in most states by requiring a heightened standard of "clear and convincing" evidence that the defendant "maliciously injured" the plaintiff.[179]

Validity of Assumptions About Tort Litigation   Despite these enactments and proposals, decisions on reforms are being made without any solid information about how the tort system of compensation works and what needs fixing. An article surveying studies about the tort litigation system demonstrates that what everyone assumes is the case is not necessarily the true state of things. The article concludes that there is much about the tort system that is simply unknown, but the data that exist undercut the popular conceptions about it.[180] As for the complaint of a "litigation explosion" and the propensity of Americans to "sue at the drop of a hat," the evidence shows that tort filings have actually decreased in the last 7 years and that, barring automobile accident cases, only a tiny fraction of accidental deaths and injuries become claims for compensation. Studies further show that most cases filed are settled and on average these settlements undercompensate plaintiffs.[181] In medical malpractice, studies consistently show that only a small percentage who receive seriously unsatisfactory medical care sue and plaintiffs win such suits only 30% of the time.[182] As for "runaway" juries, as discussed in Chapter III, in the great majority of cases that are tried, the extent of disagreement between judge and jury on amount of recovery is not that great. The "problems" with punitive damages have already been discussed: such awards are infrequent and modest in amount.[183]

Most studies conclude that there is a problem with the cost of the tort litigation system and with the fact that it undercompensates most successful litigants and does not compensate at all the vast majority of people with deserving claims. But the tort reform packages that have been enacted attack the perception of "too many suits and

---

177 A common step that several states have taken is to limit non-economic damages to a set amount, often $250,000. However, Wisconsin's limit for medical malpractice cases was held unconstitutional under its state constitution. *Ferdon v. Wisconsin Patients Compensation Fund*, 701 N.W.2d 440 (Wis. 2005).

178 Products Liability Reform Act, Senate Report No. 105-32, 105th Cong. 1st Sess. (1997). The majority and minority portions of the report also set out the arguments on both sides of the issue on the need for and advisability of such reforms.

179 *See* Model Punitive Damages Act, available at www.lectlaw.com/files/leg19.htm.

180 *See generally* Michael Saks, *Do We Really Know Anything About the Behavior of the Tort Litigation System — and Why Not?*, 140 U.Pa.L.Rev. 1147 (1992).

181 An in-depth study completed by the Rand Corporation in 1991 indicates that only about 10% of accident victims in the study sought some form of compensation. While 7% of these did so by contacting an attorney, only 4% actually hired the attorney and only 2% filed suit. DEBORAH R. HENSLER ET AL., COMPENSATION FOR ACCIDENTAL INJURIES IN THE UNITED STATES 121-22 (Rand Corp. 1991).

182 In a 1990 study, researchers examined the cases of a group of patients whom medical experts determined were subjected to seriously deficient medical care. Of them, 26% did nothing, 46% changed doctors, 25% complained directly to the doctor and 9% contacted a lawyer, but none actually filed suit. Marylynn L. May & Daniel B. Stengel, *Who Sues Their Doctors? How Patients Handle Medical Grievances*, 24 Law & Soc'y Rev. 105, 107-108 (1990).

183 *See supra*, p. 463.

runaway juries" rather than seeking to address what should be the focus of such reform — how to compensate deserving injured people more fairly and more efficiently.[184]

3. Substitutes for Tort Recovery

Workers' Compensation A relationship with enormous potential for tort litigation is the employer-employee relationship. For years, however, strict enforcement of contributory negligence, assumption of the risk and the "fellow servant" rule[185] kept the chances of recovery low. Even cases of clear liability were difficult to litigate against the superior legal resources of the employer and in any event the litigation process consumed years before the injured worker would actually receive any money. As a result, states began to pass "workers' compensation" acts at the turn of the 20th century.[186] These laws set up an employer-financed administrative system for compensating work-related injuries without the need for the worker to prove fault. The amounts paid are limited to wage loss and medical expenses, with no provision for pain and suffering, punitive damages or other elements of damages recoverable in tort. The remedy is exclusive of any tort remedy against the employer that might otherwise arise out of the employment relationship. The advantage of worker compensation awards to the employee is that money is paid quickly shortly after the injury — when it is most needed — and recovery is assured without any need to show fault. The advantage of worker compensation to employers is that the costs of industrial accidents are made certain and predictable.[187]

No-Fault Automobile Insurance Systems The no-fault concept has been applied as well to automobile accidents, the most numerous tort cases in the courts. About half the states have laws that provide that, instead of proving fault and collecting damages from the *other* party's insurance company, all parties involved in an accident are compensated by *their own* insurance company. This eliminates the need for litigation to gain compensation for most traffic accidents — litigation that often did little more than shuttle money back and forth between insurance companies, pursuant to subrogation agreements.[188]

Most no-fault plans allow an injured motorist to receive payment of medical costs and lost wages caused by injury in an automobile accident and for any property damage. These amounts reflect only economic compensatory damages. Non-economic damages, such as pain and suffering, are not allowed for most ordinary injuries. However, there is an exception for injuries that result in death or serious disfigurement or permanent impairment of bodily functions. For those, the traditional tort remedies are

---

184 A strong critic of the existing tort system of compensation even makes this point and agrees that the Reagan-Bush administration initiatives to "reform" the tort system have been "one-sided." Stephen D. Surgarman, *Doctor No*, 58 U. CHI. L. REV. 1499, 1513 (1991), reviewing PAUL C. WEILER, MEDICAL MALPRACTICE ON TRIAL (1991).

185 Under this rule, if the immediate cause of an injury at work was the action or omission of a fellow employee, the employer could not be sued. *See Priestley v. Fowler*, 150 Eng. Rep. 1030 (Ex. 1837).

186 For a more detailed discussion of Worker's Compensation, *see* MARK A. ROTHSTEIN ET AL., EMPLOYMENT LAW §§7.1 *et seq.* §§10.6 *et seq*. (West 2005) and JACK B. HOOD, BENJAMIN A HARDY, JR., & HAROLD S. LEWIS, JR., WORKER'S COMPENSATION AND EMPLOYEE PROTECTION LAWS IN A NUTSHELL 1-140 (West 2004).

187 The constitutionality of worker's compensation systems was upheld in *New York Central R.R. v. White*, 243 U.S. 188 (1917). Within in 3 years of the *White* decision, all but 8 states had adopted workers' compensation laws. For an account of the interesting history of workers' compensation, *see* Richard A. Epstein, *The Historical Origins and Economic Structure of Workers' Compensation Law*, 16 GA. L. REV. 775 (1982).

188 An essential ingredient for the success of a no-fault system, however, is that automobile insurance coverage be mandatory. Subrogation agreements were discussed *supra* note 152.

available against the defendant directly as they existed before. No-fault statutory schemes have been challenged as unconstitutional in several states, but have generally been upheld.[189]

No-Fault Tort Systems? Because, as noted above, the actual problems of the tort compensation system are its high cost and failure to reach many injured people, some states have considered a no-fault approach to torts. These programs purport to deliver compensation to a higher number of deserving injured people and to do so with greater efficiency and lower cost than the current tort system. Florida and Virginia have tried to apply the no-fault concept to babies who suffer neurological damage during delivery. Congress has done the same with regard to injuries resulting from vaccinations.[190] However, none of these schemes has been used very much. More generally, there is doubt that no-fault is the answer, given the high cost and workability in areas as complicated as injuries from medical treatment and the fact that the elimination of fault and greater efficiency of the system would attract a greater number of claims.[191]

---

189 The basis for attack has generally been equal protection or due process. However, when the subject of regulation is economics, welfare and business and does not involve invidious discrimination or infringement on a fundamental right, all that is needed is a rational basis to uphold it. *See* Chapter IX, pp. 356-358. The first major decision upholding the constitutionality of a no-fault law was *Pinnick v. Cleary*, 271 N.E.2d 592 (Mass. 1971). In addition to discussing the various constitutional objections, the case outlines in detail the operation of Massachusetts's no-fault law.

190 *See, respectively,* Fla.St.Ann. 766.301-.316 (2001); Va. Code Ann. §38.2-5000 *et seq.*; 42 U.S.C.A. §300aa-10 *et seq.*

191 *See and compare* MAXWELL J. MEHLMAN, SAYING "NO" TO NO-FAULT: WHAT THE HARVARD MEDICAL MALPRACTICE STUDY MEANS FOR MEDICAL MALPRACTICE REFORM (1991) (costs would be greater than the current tort system) *with* William G. Johnson et al., *The Economic Consequences of Medical Injuries*, 267 J. Am. Med. Assoc. 2487 (1992) (costs would not be significantly costlier than tort system).

CHAPTER XII

PROPERTY LAW

In this chapter we will discuss the legal forms that property rights take in the United States. We will consider both real and personal property, including intellectual property. We will look at issues of property taxation, zoning and other land use restrictions, government takings of property for public purposes, as well as mortgages and other security interests in property. To provide a concrete context for the subject, we will set out a real estate purchase transaction. Landlord-tenant relations, as well as more recent forms of home ownership, such as condominiums and cooperatives will be discussed. Gifts, testamentary transfers and trusts are also discussed.

PART I: Real and Personal Property

A. The Nature and Forms of Property

Types of Property The U.S. legal system, like most others, distinguishes between "real property" and "personal property." Real property, also called "realty," is land and the structures built upon it. All other property is personal property or "personalty." These correspond roughly to the civil law notions of immovable and movable property. The manner in which the law views these two types of property varies, especially in regard to transfer or sale. Because of this difference, each will be discussed separately, starting with real property. However, the nature of interests or rights in property discussed in this first section applies generally to both. The examples given relate primarily to real property, but most definitions of interest and rights have their counterpart in personal property. Special features that relate to personal property will be indicated.[1]

The Nature of Property Rights Property law concerns the rights and obligations of people with respect to things. The aggregate of such rights and obligations is sometimes analogized to a bundle of sticks. Each "stick" can be seen as a specific right: (1) the right to possess, (2) the right to use, (3) the right to exclude others and (4) the right to alienate (sell). The right of possession allows a person to possess property, but does not give that person the right to sell it. For example, a landowner may give another person the right to possess his or her land for a limited time pursuant to a "lease." In effect, the landowner transfers to the other person the "right-to-possession stick," but keeps all the other rights. Once the term of the lease expires, the right to possess expires and the "stick" is returned to the bundle.

A fundamental principle of property law is that an owner generally may not convey a greater interest than that owner has. Thus, in the example of the owner above who leased property, if that owner sells the property, the buyer of the property would still be subject to that lease.

B. Defining Interests in Real Property

A person who owns or possesses a piece of real property is said to have an "estate" or an "interest" in the property. From the following outline, it can be seen that U.S. property law is very flexible in its ability to define property interests — to allocate the "sticks" in the "bundle." Property interests can be defined in terms of (1) the degree of

---

1 For more on property law *see* WILLIAM B. STOEBUCK & DALE A. WHITMAN, HORNBOOK ON THE LAW OF PROPERTY, 3D ED. (West 2000). *See also* ANN BURKHART & ROGER BERNHARDT, REAL PROPERTY IN A NUTSHELL, 5TH ED. (West 2005); BARLOW BURKE, JR., PERSONAL PROPERTY IN A NUTSHELL, 3D ED. (WEST 2003).

control the owner of that interest has, (2) the duration of the interest (time), (3) physical space allocated to the owner, and (4) the way the ownership interest is held (single or shared title).

1. Property Interests Defined by Degree of Ownership or Control

Ownership Interests: Fee Simple Absolute The greatest interest in terms of degree of control over the property is called "fee simple absolute" or "fee simple."[2] The owner of the fee simple estate holds all the possible rights and interests associated with property in a single bundle. The fee simple estate is freely transferable during the life of the owner/holder and can be passed from generation to generation by inheritance. A fee simple estate may thus be transferred by a "deed" or a "will." A deed is a written document that conveys title and ownership, either through sale or gift. A will is a written instrument that passes property upon the death of a person according to the wishes of the deceased.

Fee simple ownership is the most common interest in land. Consequently, the rights, limitations and obligations associated with it will be discussed in more detail in a later section.[3] In addition, sales of fee simple ownership are the most common method by which interests in real estate are transferred, so modern real estate sales transactions will also be discussed.[4]

Possessory Interests in Property: Leases The owner of a property can convey to another person the right to possess the property for a limited period of time. The owner of the property is called the "lessor" or "landlord." The person using the property is called the "lessee" or "tenant." The interest of the tenant is called the "leasehold" and it is generally created by way of a document called a "lease." At the end of the lease term, the right to possess the property returns to the landlord and the tenant's rights are extinguished. During the term of the lease the tenant can transfer or assign the tenant's possessory interests to another or may sublease or sublet the premises. In an assignment, the transferee tenant takes the place of the original tenant. In a sublease situation, the lessee conveys the right of possession to the sub-lessee, but remains liable to the landlord under the lease. Because of this, the original lessee retains the right to intervene and even evict the sub-lessee should the sub-lessee act contrary to the original lessee's interests. The landlord also has a similar right to intervene. Leases between landlords and tenants often restrict the tenant's ability to transfer all or part of the tenant's interest.[5]

The landlord may convey ownership interests in leased land. However, when the property is leased, all the landlord retains is a "reversionary" interest in the property. This means that the possessory rights that the owner-landlord conveyed to the tenant will return to the owner only at the end of the leasehold. Thus, a landlord who sells leased property conveys only this reversionary interest, so the buyer takes the land subject to the lease.

---

2 The holder in fee simple also holds the property for the longest period of time — an indefinite period.

3 *See infra* pp. 476-481. As discussed there, an owner can hold property in fee simple absolute, but have other interests from the bundle outstanding, such as easements, security interests, covenants, servitudes, or other transferable rights.

4 *See infra* pp. 488-490.

5 Because many people rent their place of residence in the U.S., modern landlord-tenant law will be addressed later in a separate section. *See infra* pp. 492-493.

Leasing personal property — from cars to heavy equipment — has become an increasingly common substitute for outright ownership, which generally entails a greater outlay of money and other burdens. Personal property leases follow the same basic concepts as real property leases. Because of the greater frequency of leasing, the authors of the Uniform Commercial Code have added a new Article 2A, which parallels Article 2's regulation of sales of goods.

Use and Access Rights: Easements An easement is the right to use land owned by another. Easement rights to land are discussed under the heading of limitations on ownership rights.[6]

Splitting Legal and Equitable Title: Trusts A fee simple owner of property can transfer property into a "trust." The transferor is referred to as the "settlor," "trustor" or "grantor." When this is done, one person, the "trustee," controls and manages the property, while another person, the "beneficiary," is entitled to receive the benefits from the property. The trustee receives "legal title" to the property, but must manage and allocate its benefits according to the terms of the trust agreement. The beneficiary, on the other hand, has the beneficial interest in the property and is generally considered to have "equitable title" to the property.

Trusts are widely used to give someone — often the settlor's children or other relatives — some of the benefits of ownership of property (such as the income from property) without the burdens or rights of such ownership. Because of their widespread use, trusts are discussed in greater detail later in this chapter.[7]

2. Property Interests Defined by Physical Limits

Boundaries of Land Physical boundaries represent the most common way that interests in real property are defined. Historically, the landowner was said to possess the space below the surface of the land "to the center of the earth" and the space above the land "up to the heavens." In modern society, however, ownership rights are exercised within more confined parameters. The invention of the airplane has made ownership of air space infeasible;[8] interference with underground water supplies may be a cause of action;[9] local zoning ordinances significantly restrict land use possibilities, especially in residential zones; and, nuisance laws proscribe a wide array of activities both below and above the land surface.

Physical Structures on Land Physical structures located on land, such as buildings, are part of the real property. Included as well are items of personal property that have been affixed to those structures, called "fixtures." Despite the fact that such items of property might otherwise be considered personal property before they became affixed, they become part of the realty when they become fixtures. For example, before being installed, a roll of carpeting is personal property. After that roll of carpeting is cut and tacked down as wall-to-wall carpeting, it becomes a fixture.[10]

---

6 *See infra* p. 477.

7 *See infra* pp. 495-497.

8 *See* Chapter XI, p. 438 and note 28, concerning the question of what interference with the airspace above land is considered wrongful.

9 *See Flowers v. Northhampton Bucks County Mun. Auth.*, 57 Pa. D. & C.2d 274 (Pa. D. & C. 1972) (stating that even if landowner is drilling solely on his own property, he may not appropriate another's percolating water for unlawful purposes including for commercial sale).

10 *See, e.g., Dean Vincent, Inc. v. Redisco, Inc.*, 373 P.2d 995 (Or. 1962) (carpeting a fixture where there is "annexation, adaption, and [the] functional intention" for it to be a permanent part of the structure).

Space Inside Buildings: Condominiums Real property interests are not just limited to the ownership of land and buildings, but may also include ownership of space inside a building. A building can be divided into "condominiums" — separate units in a building, each of which may be separately owned. The condominium owners own both the space between the interior walls of the unit and a part interest in the building by way of their membership in an association, which owns the entire building. Because of the increasing popularity of condominiums, they will be discussed in more detail, along with the somewhat similar "cooperative," in a later section of this chapter.[11]

3. Property Interests Defined by Time

Present Indefinite Continuous Ownership Fee simple ownership is ownership that continues for an indefinite period of time.

Property Interests of Limited Definite Duration Leasehold interests terminate at the end of the leasehold period. At that point the possessory right which the tenant had "reverts" back to the owner. Commercial leases for business property are almost always leases of a definite duration (sometimes with an option to renew), as are most residential leases.

Interests of Periodic Renewable Duration Despite the fact that most leases have a definite end date, it is common to have a "periodic" tenancy. Such a tenancy is for a certain period of time, but that period of time automatically renews unless notice is given by either landlord or tenant of an intention to terminate the tenancy. Thus, in a "month-to-month" tenancy, the time period of the tenancy is one month, but each month a new tenancy arises unless notice is given. Many people remain in apartments for years under a month-to-month tenancy arrangement.

Life Estates Terminating Upon Death A life estate is a possessory property interest that terminates on the death of the estate holder or another designated person. Upon such death the interest returns to the grantor or goes to another person in accord with the wishes of the grantor as expressed in the instrument that created the life estate. Life estates are usually freely transferable. But the basic principle of property transfer — that a transferor can transfer no greater estate than the transferor's interest — means that the life estate will terminate upon the death of the person who transferred the interest. Thus, life estates, in light of these transferability issues, have little commercial value. They are often used, however, by elderly parents who sell or give their home to their children while reserving a life estate in themselves so that they may continue to live there until their death.[12]

Future Interests A future interest is a present interest to enjoy possession of the property some time in the future. Future interests are true present property rights in that they are inheritable, are generally freely transferable, and must be compensated for if taken by the government. A simple example of a future interest is the landlord's reversionary interest during a lease, as described above. The landlord's "reversion" presently exists, but does not give the landlord the right to possession of the property until the term of the lease expires. Another example is the remainder interest of the property owner subject to a "life estate," as just discussed.[13]

---

11 *See infra* pp. 491-492.

12 Today, this arrangement is more likely to be accomplished through a trust, since it provides for more flexibility. *See infra* pp. 495-497.

13 For more information on future interests, see CHARLES I. NELSON & PETER T. WENDEL, A POSSESSORY ESTATES AND FUTURE INTERESTS PRIMER. 3D ED (West 2007); THOMAS F. BERGIN & PAUL G. HASKELL, PREFACE TO ESTATES IN LAND AND FUTURE INTERESTS, 2D ED. (West 1991).

Discontinuous Periodic Ownership Interests: Time-Share Properties A "time-share" interest is an ownership in property that grants the owner the right to possession of that property for a specific period of time every year. For instance, an owner may buy a time-share interest in a condominium located at a ski resort for the third week in January every year. Time-share units are usually furnished and managed by the condominium developer. Owners of units often have the right to trade their time-share (period of possession) with another owner.[14]

4. Property Interests Defined by How the Interest Is Held

Single Ownership A property interest may be held by one person or entity. Included are natural persons, partnerships, corporations or trusts.[15] Fee simple single ownership gives the person or entity full rights to the entire property for an indefinite period. As such, it is the highest form of property ownership.

Joint Tenancy In a joint tenancy, owners ("joint tenants") own an undivided, equal portion of the property. A joint tenancy creates "concurrent estates" in more than one person. This means that all the owners have the right to possess and enjoy the entire piece of property. Joint tenants also enjoy the "right of survivorship." In other words, if a joint tenant dies, that tenant's interest in the property does not descend to the tenant's heirs, but is extinguished.[16] As a result, the interests of the surviving joint tenants expand in equal proportions. For example, if three people own a property as joint tenants, and one of the owners dies, the surviving owners will each own an undivided one-half interest in the property. If joint tenants cannot agree about how to manage or use the land, a joint tenancy may be extinguished by court action called a "partition" action. This action may be brought by one of the joint tenants. A partition of the property can result in an actual physical division of the property giving each joint tenant an undivided fee simple interest in a physical portion of the property, or in a court-ordered sale of the entire property, with a division of the proceeds of the sale. If a joint tenant sells his or her interest, the joint tenancy is severed as to that tenant's interest and is converted into a tenancy in common, described below, with respect to the buyer of that interest.[17]

Tenancy by the Entirety Tenancy by the entirety refers to the method by which a husband and wife may jointly own property. It is similar to a joint tenancy because when one spouse dies the surviving spouse automatically takes the entire estate in fee simple. However, unlike a joint tenancy, there is no unilateral right to division of the property. Divisions can be made only in a divorce action or by mutual agreement.[18] A major advantage of tenancy by the entirety is that the creditors of an individual spouse cannot reach the entireties property.

Tenancy in Common A tenancy in common establishes a concurrent estate in land, but tenants in common do not enjoy the right of survivorship. Thus, if a tenant in common dies, that tenant's interest descends to his or her heirs and the tenancy in

---

14 The common law provided for only a limited set of leaseholds. Today, contract law governs creations of interests in land, so the parties can create whatever interests they want.

15 For a discussion of partnerships and corporations, *see* Chapter XV, pp. 580-600.

16 "Heirs" are the persons who have rights to the property upon the death of the owner. *See infra* pp. 493-495.

17 For example, suppose that there are three joint tenants. If one joint tenant sells his or her interest, the buyer is now a tenant in common with the other two joint tenants. The two non-transferring joint tenants, who are in a tenancy in common with the new buyer, still remain in a joint tenancy with respect to each other. If one of the two remaining joint tenants sells his or her interest, then no joint tenancy exists. All parties are now tenants in common.

18 *See* Chapter XIII, pp. 466-468, for a discussion of property division in divorce actions.

common continues. When the ownership interest is ambiguous, the law prefers a tenancy in common over a joint tenancy. In general, absent the expressed intent of a grantor to create a joint tenancy, a court will presume that the grantor intended to create a tenancy in common.[19]

C. Personal Property

Personal property is all property that is not real property or a "fixture," as defined earlier. Examples of personal property are books, utensils, cars, furniture, stocks, bonds, patents and copyrights. Personal property may be either "tangible" or "intangible." "Tangible" personal property consists of material objects that have intrinsic value — objects that are valuable in and of themselves, such as jewelry. "Intangible" property is made up of those "things" that lack material form. Examples of intangible property are stocks in corporations, copyrights, patents, and bank accounts.[20] The documents that these are printed on are only evidence of the ownership interest and are not in themselves the "thing" possessed. However, an item of personal property may embody both tangible and intangible property rights. For example, educational materials such as books and films have the tangible property qualities of a physical existence as well as the intangible property qualities of ownership of the ideas that go into them.[21]

Like real property, personal property can be held by multiple owners by means of the concurrent ownership interests mentioned above. For example, a joint tenancy bank account is useful because it gives the right of survivorship to the other tenant.

D. Rights and Obligations of Owners of Real Property

1. Rights Included in Ownership of Real Property

Right of "Quiet Enjoyment" An owner has the right to possession and control of the property. This right is called a right of "quiet enjoyment" of the premises. This includes the right to exclude trespassers (anyone who comes on land without permission). Multiple owners of real property, such as joint tenants, tenants in common and tenants by the entireties, are entitled to equal and undivided possession of the property. Thus, each owner has the right to possess the whole property unless that possession interferes with the possessory rights of the other owners.[22]

Oil, Gas and Mineral Rights Fee simple ownership of a property includes the ownership of resources both below and above the surface of the land. Not only can the resources themselves be conveyed by the owner, but also the right to enter the land and remove these resources may be conveyed separately by the owner. An owner may convey the outright ownership of subsurface resources to another by deed. More commonly, an owner will grant, by means of a lease, the right to remove resources for a limited period of time. Obviously, the process of actually extracting oil, gas or minerals from land can involve a major disruption of the possessory rights to the surface of the

---

19 Some commentators reason that this presumption is justified because the right of survivorship that would attach to a joint tenancy would have the effect of cutting off the rights of the joint tenant's heirs. However, the law's preference for tenancies in common is probably more historical than rational.

20 Coins and other currency are considered tangible, however. Intellectual property, which includes patents, copyrights and trademarks, is intangible personal property.

21 *Simplicity Pattern Co., Inc. v. State Board of Equalization*, 161 Cal. Rptr. 558 (Cal. Ct. App. 1980) (sale of collection of original film negatives was not a sale of "tangible personal property" because the value of the negatives was in their content), *opinion vacated by*, 615 P.2d 555 (Cal. 1980) (court held that sale of film negatives was a sale of tangible personal property because the negatives were physically useful in making the finished product).

22 The right of an owner to sue another for trespass is discussed in the chapter on torts. *See* Chapter XI, p. 438.

land. Thus, an owner who has granted mineral rights to another has substantially decreased the value of the land.

Water Rights As a general rule, landowners have the right to use the water that is located on their property. The terms "riparian rights" (rivers) and "littoral rights" (seas, oceans and lakes) refer to the rights of a landowner with respect to bodies of water bordering on the landowner's property. The nature of water rights in the United States varies depending on whether the property is East or West of the Mississippi River.

The climate east of the Mississippi River is relatively wet and humid, and there are numerous rivers and a high water table. The climate West of the Mississippi River is drier with fewer rivers and a lower water table. East of the Mississippi River there was sufficient water to meet the needs of human consumption, agriculture and manufacturing. Consequently, a rule of riparian rights developed that requires that water be shared equally. No priority is given to the first user of the water. West of the Mississippi River there was often not enough water to satisfy the needs of all property owners in a particular area. As a result, a "prior appropriation" rule developed. Under this rule, the first user of the water was allowed to use all the water he or she needed. Subsequent settlers could not demand that the water be shared. The prior appropriation rule was developed as an incentive to settle the land. It assured the first settlers to arrive that they would not have to worry about later settlers demanding that they share scarce water.

Right to Lateral and Subjacent Support Landowners have a right to the support afforded their land through adjacent or subterranean land. If a person removes either the lateral or subjacent support from another person's property, either through excavation or mining, that person is liable for any damage should the other property slide or fall. The liability arising from the removal of lateral or subjacent support is "strict liability" so long as the damaged property was in its natural state. If there is a building or other structure on the property and the weight of that building contributes to the movement of the land, the person who removed the support will only be liable if negligent in the removal of the support.

2. Consensual Limitations on Ownership

Easements An easement is the right to *use* part of another person's land for a specific purpose without actually owning it.[23] For example, a landowner may grant the gas or electric utility company the right to use part of the landowner's property so that the utility company can lay gas pipes or install electric cables. The landowner maintains ownership of the property while the utility company has a right to use the land for the specified purpose. An easement that grants the right to do something, as shown in this example, is considered an affirmative easement. There are also negative easements, which require a landowner to refrain from specified actions. For example, a negative easement may forbid a landowner from increasing the height of his or her building, which could impede the light received by the holder of the negative easement. An easement can be perpetual or for a limited time. If it is perpetual, the right to use it remains with the easement holder even if the property is sold. However, for this to occur the easement must be recorded. An easement may be terminated by a written agreement between the property owner and the easement holder.

Licenses A license is the permission of a landowner to use his or her property in some specific way. A license can be distinguished from an easement in that it is

---

23 *See* STEPHEN A. SIEGEL, A STUDENT'S GUIDE TO EASEMENTS, REAL COVENANTS AND EQUITABLE SERVITUDES, 2D ED. (Matthew Bender 1999).

generally revocable by the grantor at any time. By contrast, an easement cannot be revoked by the grantor without the agreement of the grantee. Licenses and easements both differ from leases in that they only grant the right to engage in some sort of activity on the land, not the right to possession. Although a license is considered an interest in land,[24] it need not comply with the Statute of Frauds and may therefore be granted orally.[25] This characteristic of licenses distinguishes them from easements, which must comply with the Statute of Frauds. As a result, there are situations where a party intending to create an easement instead creates a license because the conveyance fails to meet Statute of Frauds requirements.[26]

Covenants Covenants are promises made by landowners with respect to use of their land. In contrast to easements, which involve the grant of a property interest, covenants signify a contractual promise or restriction related to the land. These promises usually appear in deeds to the property or in subdivision plans. Like easements discussed above, covenants also may be classified as affirmative or negative. A promise to pay dues to a homeowners' association is an affirmative covenant. A promise not to establish a business on one's land is a negative covenant, also known as a restrictive covenant. The most common use of covenants is to establish "building and use restrictions" which bind all the homeowners in a neighborhood to a set of rules for building and living in that neighborhood. The building restrictions are established for the purpose of ensuring that all homes in the area are of similar size, quality and esthetic value. A covenant generally "runs with the land." This means that a covenant binds all subsequent landowners.

At one point in the United States, "racially restrictive covenants" were used to keep homeowners from selling their houses to members of a minority race. The Supreme Court held these invalid as a violation of the equal protection clause of the Constitution in the 1948 case of *Shelley v. Kraemer*.[27]

Equitable Servitudes Equitable servitudes function similarly to covenants except that they provide an equitable remedy instead of a contractual one. A legal action under a covenant seeks money damages, whereas an action under an equitable servitude seeks injunctive relief.[28] Another distinction is that privity is not required to bind successors to an equitable servitude, whereas covenants require privity to bind successors. The doctrine of privity in the common law of contract provides that a contract cannot confer rights or impose obligations arising under it on any person or agent except the parties to it. Thus, an equitable servitude applies beyond the immediate parties who agree to it.

3. Limitations Arising By Operation of Law

Adverse Possession Adverse possession is a means of gaining ownership of property, without the consent of the owner, by physically possessing that property adverse to the owner's interest for a statutorily specified time. Possession must be actual, hostile to the owner's interests, open and notorious, exclusive and continuous for a statutory period, typically 15 or 20 years. The theory of adverse possession is that

---

24 RESTATEMENT OF PROPERTY §512 (1944, 1998) Comment C.

25 *See* Chapter X, p. 403, for a discussion of the Statute of Frauds.

26 *See Kitchen v. Kitchen*, 641 N.W.2d 245 (Mich. 2002) (holding that oral conveyances cannot transfer an irrevocable interest in land because such conveyances fail to satisfy the Statute of Frauds).

27 334 U.S. 1 (1948). *Shelley* raises interesting issues of whether there was really "state action" in violation of the Constitution. *See* Chapter IX, pp. 349-351, particularly p. 350, where *Shelley* is discussed.

28 *See* Chapter VII, pp. 244-247.

the prescribed period of time is essentially a "statute of limitations" on the owner's right to sue to recover the property. Once the land has been possessed for the required period of time and all the elements of adverse possession have been fulfilled, the adverse possessor can bring an action to "quiet title" to gain title to the land.[29] The policy behind adverse possession is to prevent land from remaining unused and to assure that owners are vigilant in protecting their rights.

Adverse possession issues do not often arise as to entire parcels of land, given that the owner is likely to notice continuous open and notorious possession of the property and do something to evict the trespasser. However, adverse possession issues arise quite often with respect to portions of a parcel, where there is encroachment by a neighboring owner that is not noticed or, if noticed, is ignored. Common examples are improper placement of a fence or driveway. Owners must be alert to such encroachments and take action before the statutory period runs on pain of losing that part of their land.

Easements by Prescription and Necessity In limited situations, an easement may be established by prescription, which shares generally the same requisite elements of adverse possession. An easement also may be acquired by necessity. Such an easement arises where a landowner sells a part of the land and thereby cuts off the new parcel from access to a public road or utility line. The new owner of the parcel is granted an easement by necessity through operation of law. The owner whose land is subject to this easement may choose the access location insofar as it is a reasonable location.

Mechanics Liens When builders and contractors are not paid for work performed, the law creates a lien on the property. In most states, for the lien to be valid, it must be recorded within a certain period of time following completion of the work.[30]

4. Duties of Owners of Real Property

Nuisance Every person has a duty to refrain from creating or allowing a "nuisance" to exist on property that person controls. A nuisance is any activity that adversely affects adjacent owners or the general public, such as a factory that releases toxic fumes into the atmosphere.

The most common remedy is "judicial abatement" of the nuisance. This means that the court grants an injunction ordering the property owner who is creating the nuisance to cease the activity that is interfering with the rights of others. In rare cases, however, the courts have awarded money damages and allowed the nuisance to continue, for instance when an injunction would stop a factory from operating thereby causing great detriment to the community through the loss of jobs and revenue.[31] In deciding whether to abate a nuisance, courts balance the importance of the interfering activity against the harm caused by it.

A contextual analysis is applied both in the characterization of an activity as a nuisance and the degree of its interference. For example, noise and air pollution are expected in a large city and are not necessarily unreasonable. On the other hand, a person who lives in the country may reasonably expect quiet and clean air. A factory

---

29 Indeed, this judicial action is a requirement of any adverse possessor who seeks marketable title for purposes of selling his adversely gained property interest.

30 For an explanation of recording, *see infra* p. 489.

31 *See Boomer v. Atlantic Cement Co.*, 257 N.E.2d 870 (N.Y. 1970).

emitting smoke and noise that is erected near a residence in a rural area is more likely to be considered a nuisance that should be abated.[32]

Owners' Duties to Persons Who Enter the Property An owner has duties with regard to persons who enter his or her property. There are two kinds of duties, one pertains to activities conducted on the land and the other to dangerous conditions of the land. With respect to activities, most jurisdictions apply a standard of reasonable care under the circumstances.[33] With respect to conditions, traditionally jurisdictions apply varying standards based on the relationship between the person entering the property and the owner of it. "Invitees" are persons whom the owner has invited explicitly or implicitly to come onto the premises. Typically, invitees are customers or employees. Since invitees are there for the owner's benefit, the owner owes the highest duty to them — a duty to protect them from all unreasonable risks. In practice, this duty entails not only the provision of adequate warnings for already known risks, but also a duty to make reasonable inspections of the premises.[34] "Slip-and-fall" cases are a common example of invitee lawsuits. For example, the owner of a store has a duty to clean up promptly or provide adequate warning of any spilled liquids or other hazards in the store aisles.[35] The landowner does not need to eradicate the dangerous condition; instead, the landowner needs only to provide adequate warning. This distinction explains why businesses often mop the floors of a premise then put up a yellow "Caution" sign. "Licensees" are people who enter the property with the owner's permission, but are not there for the owner's benefit. Licensees include party guests and neighbors retrieving their errant pets. Here, the owner has no duty to make reasonable inspections, but the owner still owes a duty to warn of dangerous conditions.[36] "Trespassers" generally have no right to be on the owner's property, but even as to them the owner must keep the property free from unreasonable dangers that the trespasser might not expect. However, the owner has no duty to warn of any hidden dangers. And in any event, the owner of land may not set a trap employing deadly force to repel a trespasser.[37]

Courts have increasingly expressed dissatisfaction with this "trichotomy" approach based on the status of the person entering the property. The main reason has been the difficulty of classifying the injured persons. Nearly one half of all jurisdictions have either abandoned or substantially modified the trichotomy approach in favor of a unified analysis based on reasonableness of the owner's action or inaction in light of all the surrounding circumstances.[38]

---

32 *See Spur Industries, Inc. v. Del E. Webb Development Co.*, 494 P.2d 700 (Ariz. 1972) (feed lot located next to a residential neighborhood, with odor and flies from the feed lot made living in the neighborhood unhealthy; injunction forcing lot to move). For general law on injunctions and other equitable relief, *see* Chapter VII, pp. 245-247.

33 *See Cleveland-Cliffs Iron Co. v. Metzner*, 150 F.2d 206 (6th Cir. 1945) (holding that mining company must exercise reasonable care in its activities even as to trespasser-plaintiff).

34 *See Maehlman v. Reuben Realty Co.*, 166 N.E. 920 (Ohio Ct. App. 1928) (finding that duty of reasonable inspection requires beach proprietors to examine below water areas for broken glass if broken glass is discovered above water along the shoreline).

35 Invitees may include persons other than paying customers. *See Bray v. Kate, Inc.*, 454 N.W.2d 698 (Neb. 1990) (plaintiff can recover for slipping on ice in front of restaurant even though he fell just as he was about to open the door to enter).

36 *Thacker v. J.C. Penny Co.*, 254 F.2d 672 (5th Cir. 1958) (store owner could be liable for actions of child climbing on balcony and falling).

37 *See Katko v. Briney*, 183 N.W.2d 657 (Iowa 1971) (trespasser on unoccupied house injured by trap with gun set by owner may recover for injuries).

38 North Carolina most recently did so in an opinion that reviews the entire area, the competing authorities and difficulties with the old approach. *Nelson v. Freeland*, 507 S.E.2d 882 (1998).

A special duty applies to owners of hotels or motels. Innkeepers have had a special duty to protect guests under the common law from the time of the Middle Ages. This duty extends to protection against intentional actions of third parties under some circumstances. Thus, an innkeeper can be held liable for injuries to guests caused by robbers who broke into the guests' room, shot the husband, caused the wife emotional distress and robbed them, where there was evidence that a prudent innkeeper would have installed better doors and locks.[39]

Liability of Owners and Creditors for Environmental Cleanups Several state and federal laws mandate the clean up of hazardous waste, and some impose the costs of the cleanup on those landowners or those involved with the contamination of the property. An example is the federal Comprehensive Environmental Response Compensation and Liability Act (CERCLA).[40] Under CERCLA, any present or past owner of contaminated property is liable for the costs incurred in the cleanup of hazardous waste on the property. There is, however, a defense for subsequent purchasers of contaminated property who were ignorant of the contamination when they purchased the property. This defense is available only to those purchasers who have made adequate inquiries about the ownership and uses of the land.[41]

5. Property Taxes on Ownership of Real Property

Most states and municipalities impose taxes on real property. These taxes are used to support community services such as education, parks, police and fire departments, as well as other local services. Generally, the largest portion of local property taxes fund the local public school system.

Property taxes are due at least once every year. They are based on the value of the property as determined by a municipal tax assessor, so they are often called "*ad valorem*" taxes. To determine the amount of the tax, the "assessed value" of the property is multiplied by the tax rate, called the "millage rate" because it is expressed in "mills."[42] The millage rate is usually determined by community vote in general elections. The rate of property tax differs significantly from state to state depending on the proportion of local governmental functions derived from property taxes. Such taxes can cost homeowners anywhere from a few hundred to tens of thousands of dollars a year, depending on the region of the country and the value of the homes in the neighborhood.

Since the tax is based on the value of the real property, richer communities, despite often enjoying a lower millage rate, have more money to spend on their public schools than poorer communities. The result can be inferior educational opportunities for children in poor communities. The Supreme Court has rejected constitutional challenges to these unequal educational opportunities.[43] However, some state courts have held such systems for financing public schools unconstitutional as discriminatory under their own state constitutions.[44]

---

39 *Kveragas v. Scottish Inns*, 733 F.2d 409 (6th Cir. 1984) (applying Tennessee law).

40 42 U.S.C.A. §§9601-9675.

41 *See generally* KATHRYN R. HEIDT, ENVIRONMENTAL OBLIGATIONS IN BANKRUPTCY (West 1993, 2002).

42 A "mill" is one tenth of a cent.

43 *San Antonio Independent School District v. Rodriguez*, 411 U.S. 1 (1973) (rejecting equal protection challenge under 14th Amendment).

44 *See, e.g., Serrano v. Priest*, 557 P.2d 929 (Cal. 1976) (school financing by property taxes invalid under the equal protection clause of California's constitution).

E. Government Control Over Real Property

1. Regulating Land Use

Some land use regulation occurs at the federal level. For example, there are federal regulations designed to preserve the quality of the environment. But the majority of land use regulation is by local governments.[45] Although the right to regulate land is considered to be among those "reserved" by the states, states generally delegate most of their regulatory power to local municipal governments. However, some states have adopted comprehensive land use management acts to ensure that local regulation is consistent with statewide planning goals.[46]

Zoning Zoning is the principal means of land use regulation in America today. A typical municipal zoning ordinance divides the municipality into "zones." The ordinance specifies which uses are permitted in each zone and which uses are prohibited there. For example, one zone may be designated as a "single family housing" zone, while another zone may be designated as an "industrial use" zone. This means that a factory may not be built in the single family housing zone and that a residence may not be built in an industrial zone. Zoning ordinances have been held to be a constitutionally valid use of the state's authority to regulate land use as long as the ordinances promote the public health, safety, morals and general welfare.[47]

Building Requirements In most areas of the country, a building permit is needed before beginning any construction or demolition of structures on land. Plans must be submitted, and methods of construction must comply with complex regulations, as required by counties and cities. However, most regulations are based on a model code promulgated by the Building Officials and Code Administrators International, Inc. (BOCA). There is variation depending on the special needs of particular areas. For example, earthquake-resistant construction methods and design are required in California, and hurricane-resistant methods are required in Florida.

Subdivision Regulation Subdivision regulation is directed at developers who subdivide large tracts of land into smaller lots. The developer is usually required to submit a plan showing how a subdivision will connect with existing utilities and streets. In addition, the developer may be required by the municipality to "dedicate" (donate) a part of the land for a community purpose, such as for a school or a park. However, as indicated below where regulatory takings are discussed, there are some limits to what state and local governments can require.

2. Governmental Takings of Land: Eminent Domain

The government's power to take private property for public use is known as the power of "eminent domain."[48] The government most often exercises its power of eminent domain to "condemn" property needed for public improvements, such as for the construction of a highway or a park. However, the 5th Amendment's "takings"

---

45 *See generally* DANIEL R. MANDELKER, LAND USE LAW, 5TH ED. (Lexis 2003, 2007).

46 *See, e.g.,* Oregon's statute, Or. Rev. Stat. §§197.005-197.860, passed in 1991.

47 *Village of Euclid v. Amber Realty Co.,* 272 U.S. 365 (1926).

48 For more on takings and eminent domain, *see* THOMAS E. ROBERTS, ED., TAKING SIDES ON TAKINGS ISSUES (Am. Bar Ass'n 2002) and THE IMPACT OF *TAHOE SIERRA* (Am. Bar Ass'n 2003); Steven Greenhut, Abuse of Power: How the Government Misuses Eminent Domain (Steven Locks Press 2004).

clause provides that "private property [may not] be taken for public use, without just compensation."[49]

The "Public Use" Requirement When property is transferred to the government for the purpose of constructing a highway or government building, the "public use" of the taking is clear. But the government may also use its takings authority to transfer property from one private owner to another. Some transfers are relatively uncontroversial: a railroad company builds a station or railway tracks; a public utility runs gas or electric lines or builds a plant; or, a developer builds a stadium that benefits the entire city. In these instances, the property itself or the services promoted by the transfer are literally available for "public use." But some transfers to private ownership are permitted even where public use is not contemplated, so long as the transfer is for a "public purpose." Thus, in *Hawaii Housing Authority v. Midkiff*,[50] the Supreme Court upheld Hawaii's transfer of the property of certain landlords to their tenants. The Court noted that the government may not take private property from one private owner and transfer it to another simply to confer a private benefit on the new owner. However, Hawaii's redistribution of property had a public purpose because there was a great concentration of land ownership in the hands of relatively few owners — a product of Hawaii's unique history — and this had skewed the real estate market and inflated prices.[51] The Court also emphasized that it was deferring to the legislative judgment that such an "oligopoly" of private land ownership had created a public problem in the state.

A public purpose has also been found to support transfers of property from one private owner to another in efforts at "urban renewal" or "economic development." In a 2005 case, *Kelo v. City of New London*,[52] the Court approved New London's takings of Ms. Kelo's and her neighbor's houses pursuant to the city's plan for "economic revitalization," promulgated in reaction to decades of economic decline that had resulted in high unemployment and departures of residents. The plan called for a park, a museum, a marina, retail and office space, and a waterfront hotel, as well as residential use. Ms. Kelo and her neighbors objected that their homes were being taken to enrich other private owners. But the Court found that the takings were pursuant to a "carefully formulated . . . economic development plan that [the city] believes will provide appreciable benefits to the community, including — but by no means limited to — new jobs and increased tax revenue." The fact that the plan effectively transferred property from one private homeowner to another did not defeat this public purpose.[53]

Midkiff and *Kelo* were decided under the federal constitution. "Public use" may be developing in the opposite direction under state law.[54] For example, the Michigan

---

49 Although the 5th Amendment technically applies only to the federal government, this protection for "takings" applies equally to state and local governments because it has been "incorporated" against the states through the due process clause of the 14th Amendment. *See* Chapter VIII, p. 283.

50 467 U.S. 229 (1984).

51 In Hawaii, 47% of all of the state's private land was in the hands of only 72 private landowners, and on the state's most urbanized island, Oahu, 22 landowners owned 72.5% of the fee simple titles.

52 545 U.S. 469 (2005).

53 *See also Berman v. Parker*, 348 U.S. 26 (1954) ("non-blighted" department store could be taken to redevelop an overall blighted area in order to create "better balanced, more attractive community"). A basis for distinguishing *Kelo* from *Midkiff* and *Berman* is suggested by the principal dissenting opinion in *Kelo*, which suggests that in *Midkiff* and *Berman* the purpose was to cure an existing evil, while in *Kelo*, elimination of the existing bad use of the land was not the purpose of the taking. *Kelo*, 545 U.S. at 500. *Kelo* was a 5-4 decision.

54 State takings law is important because state and local government actions must comply with both federal and state constitutional and statutory requirements. *See* Chapter II, p. 38.

Supreme Court in 1981 found in *Poletown Neighborhood Council v. City of Detroit*[55] that the City of Detroit's condemnation of an entire neighborhood and transfer of the land to a private automobile manufacturer to build a factory was for a public purpose, since the factory would create new jobs and reduce unemployment in a depressed area. However, in 2004, the court overruled its earlier decision and disapproved a county's efforts to condemn private homes in order to clear the way for development of a business and technology park The Michigan court observed:

> To justify the exercise of eminent domain solely on the basis of the fact that the use of that property by a private entity seeking its own profit might contribute to the economy's health is to render impotent our constitutional limitations on the government's power of eminent domain. [It would make] one's owner-ship of private property . . . forever subject to the government's determination that another private party would put one's land to better use.[56]

The "Just Compensation" Requirement The "just compensation" requirement has as one of its primary purposes barring the government "from forcing some people alone to bear public expenses which, in all fairness and justice, should be borne by the public as a whole."[57] By requiring that the government pay for what it takes, the burden of public improvements is spread to all taxpayers.[58] Fairness also requires that compensation be based on fair market value — what a willing buyer would pay a willing seller for the property.

3. Regulatory "Takings"

Government regulation often has an economic impact, and regulation of land use is particularly likely to have such an impact. A rule that required compensation for every such economic effect would make the process of governing expensive indeed. At the same time, a government should not be able to avoid paying compensation for disrup-tions of property interests almost as severe as outright seizure merely by the expediency of labeling its actions "regulation." Consequently, in a seminal case decided in 1922, the Supreme Court began to recognize "regulatory takings." It observed that, "while property may be regulated to a certain extent, if regulation goes too far it will be recognized as a taking."[59] When property owners sue for compensation for a regulatory taking, the suit is referred to as an action for "inverse condemnation." The rationale for the phrase is that the property owner is in essence seeking a judicial declaration of condemnation, which would then trigger the government's duty to compensate the owner.

Categorical Regulatory Takings: "Total Takings" and Physical Intrusion Two types of government regulation will automatically be considered regulatory takings. The first is a "total taking" — where the owner is left with title, but the regulation denies the owner all "economically viable use" of the property. In *Lucas v. South Carolina Coastal Commission*,[60] a state law limiting coastal development to prevent further erosion of the

---

55 304 N.W.2d 455 (Mich. 1981).

56 *County of Wayne v. Hathcock*, 684 N.W.2d 765, 786 (Mich. 2004) (no public purpose served by condemning land to create a business and technology park). *See* Timothy Sandefur, A Gleeful Obituary for *Poletown Neighborhood Council v. Detroit*, 28 HARV. J.LAW & PUB. POLICY 651 (2005).

57 *Armstrong v. United States*, 364 U.S. 40, 49 (1960).

58 Takings law applies to any form of property, not just to real estate. *See Ruckelshaus v. Monsanto Co.*, 467 U.S. 986 (1984) (taking pesticide research data, including trade secrets, and allowing competitor access to it considered valid so long as just compensation is provided).

59 *Pennsylvania Coal Co. v. Mahon*, 260 U.S. 393 (1922) (Holmes, J.). For more on regulatory takings, *see* STEVEN J. EAGLE, REGULATORY TAKINGS (Matthew Bender 2005).

60 505 U.S. 1003 (1992).

coast line prevented the owner of ocean-front lots from building houses on them. The Court found that this foreclosed all viable economic use of the land. Consequently, however laudable the aesthetic and environmental goals of the state law might be, the state could not pursue them by banning all construction without compensating owners such as Lucas. By contrast, in *Palazzolo v. Rhode Island*,[61] a case with somewhat similar facts, total taking was not found. Rhode Island's Coastal Resources Management Agency designated 18 acres of salt marshes on Palazzolo's land as protected "coastal wetlands." Because of this, his application for a permit to fill in the marshes and build a beach club was denied. Palazzolo lost in his effort to get compensation, however, because an "economically viable use" for the land remained. The Court found he could still build a residence on the parcel.[62]

The other category of *per se* regulatory takings are physical intrusions. In *Loretto v. Teleprompter Manhattan CATV Corp.*,[63] the Court held that New York effected a taking of landlords' property when it required that they permit cable television companies to place cable facilities in their apartment buildings. This was so even though the facilities occupied at most only 1 ½ cubic feet (.5 cubic meters) of the landlords' property. As a result, compensation for use of that space had to be paid.[64]

Non-Categorical Takings: Diminution in Economic Value   Where government regulation does not eliminate all economically beneficial use of the property, but only diminishes its value, a taking still may have occurred depending on the circumstances. Under the test of *Penn Central Transportation Co. v. New York*,[65] a court should consider (1) the "economic impact of the regulation on the claimant . . . , particularly, the extent to which the regulation has interfered with distinct investment-backed expectations" and (2) "the character of the governmental action," particularly "whether it is [a] public program adjusting the benefits and burdens of economic life to promote the common good," while keeping in mind (3) the overall purpose of the takings clause — preventing the government from "forcing some people alone to bear public burdens which, in all fairness and justice, should be borne by the public as a whole." This "test" is certainly not a model of clarity. In fact, the Court admitted in *Penn Central* after stating the test that it involves "essentially *ad hoc* factual inquiries."[66]

The facts of *Penn Central* illustrate one application of the test. New York City's Landmarks Preservation Committee declared Penn Central's railroad station in Manhat-

---

61 533 U.S. 606 (2001).

62 It remanded to the Rhode Island courts to determine whether there might nonetheless be a non-categorical taking under *Penn Central*, discussed next. The only defense to a total taking is that it is nothing more than affirmation of an already existing use limitation on the property. In *Lucas*, South Carolina claimed that its ban on beachfront construction did nothing more than enforce an already existing limitation growing out of "background principles of the State's [common] law of property and nuisance already place upon land ownership." While expressing some skepticism about the existence of such a "background principle," the Court remanded to the state courts to explore that possibility. *Id.* at 1029. In *Palazzolo*, 533 U.S. at 627-630, the Court made clear that this part of *Lucas* did not mean that "any new regulation, once enacted, becomes a background principle of property law which cannot be challenged by those who acquire title after the enactment." The effect of this ruling in *Palazzolo* was to eliminate a "notice" argument that had been made — that property owners who bought their property after a regime of regulation had been enacted could not challenge the regulation because they had "notice" of the regulatory limits when they purchased the property.

63 458 U.S. 419 (1982).

64 *See also United States v. Causby*, 328 U.S. 256, 265 (1946) (physical invasions of airspace by military planes that killed plaintiffs' chickens and caused them to go out of business).

65 438 U.S. 104 (1978).

66 438 U.S. at 123-124, in (3) quoting *Armstrong v. United States*, 364 U.S. 40, 49 (1960).

tan a historic landmark. This designation forced the railroad to get permission to alter its exterior. Because the station was unprofitable, the railroad sought to build a 50-story office building above it. The Commission denied permission, so Penn Central sued for compensation. The Court held that there was no taking. It found that (1) New York's historical designation system was legitimate given that "preservation of landmarks benefits all New York citizens and all structures, both economically and by improving the quality of life in the city as a whole," (2) the City permitted continued use of the station as a station, so it was not interfering with Penn Central's "primary expectation concerning the use of the parcel," (3) a smaller development for the station that clashed less with its architecture was not ruled out by the Commission, and (4) Penn Central could develop other properties it owned in the same historical district, thus assuring a "reasonable return" overall for the company. On the last point, the Court emphasized that it focused on "the nature and extent of the interference with rights in the parcel as a whole — here, the city tax block designated as the 'landmark site.'"[67]

Another application of *Penn Central* is *Keystone Bituminous Coal Ass'n v. DeBenedictis.*[68] In that case, a coal company sold land, but retained the mineral rights to the coal beneath it. A state law limited how much coal could be extracted from beneath the surface so that mining did not undermine support under the buildings that had been built on the surface of the land. The Court found that investment-backed expectations were not seriously eroded, since the mining company still had a great deal of coal it could mine without violating the state law. At the same time, the public purpose of "providing for the conservation of surface land areas" and the "public interest in health, the environment, and the fiscal integrity of the area" that underlay that purpose, justified whatever diminution in the value of the property rights involved. Thus, there was no taking.[69]

Nexus and Proportionality   Sometimes when a state law requires a permit to develop property, the governmental entity that issues the development permits — usually a municipality — will grant the permit, but will impose conditions designed to compensate for the negative effects of that development. These conditions can also effect a taking if (1) there is no connection between the conditions imposed and the effects they are designed to ameliorate or (2) even if there is such a nexus, the burdens the conditions impose on the developer are out of proportion to the negative effects they are designed to compensate for.

The "nexus" requirement was established in *Nollan v. California Coastal Commission.*[70] Nollan sought a building permit from the Commission to demolish his beachfront house and construct a larger one in its place. The Commission conditioned the permit

---

67 438 U.S. at 130-131. The Court approvingly cited older cases where the diminution in value caused by the regulation was substantial, including *Village of Euclid v. Amber Realty, supra* note 47 (ban on all industrial use resulting in 75% loss in value); *Hadacheck v. Sebastian*, 239 U.S. 394 (1915) (ban on plaintiff continuing to operate his brickyard in the city, resulting in 87.5% diminution in value of property).

68 480 U.S. 470 (1987).

69 *Compare Pennsylvania Coal Co. v. Mahon*, 260 U.S. 393 (1922) (limits on coal mining resulted in taking where state interest was simply to help some private surface owners). *Tahoe-Sierra Preservation Panel v. Tahoe Regional Planning Agency*, 535 U.S. 302 (2002), involved a complete, but temporary, ban on any development of property — a 32-month moratorium imposed by a regional authority while it developed a comprehensive land-use plan. The Court found that this was not a categorical taking, so it had to be evaluated according the *Penn Central* regulatory taking factors. Taking into account the "planners' good faith, the landowners' reasonable expectations, [and] the moratorium's actual impact on property values," the Court determined that there was no compensable taking.

70 483 U.S. 825 (1987).

on Nollan providing a public easement across his property that would allow the public to walk between two public beach areas on each side of his property. The nexus between the easement and the grant of the building permit was that the larger house Nollan planned to build would block the public view of the ocean. Although the Court agreed that this was a legitimate state interest, it thought that there was no reasonable connection between simply *viewing* the ocean and granting an easement allowing the public to walk across Nollan's property. The Court observed that "unless the permit condition serves the same governmental purpose as the development ban, the building restriction is not a valid regulation of land use but 'an out-and-out plan of extortion.'"[71]

"Proportionality" grew out of *Dolan v. City of Tigard*.[72] Dolan, the owner of a commercial property sought a permit to expand her building and add a paved parking lot. The city granted the permit on the condition that she (1) deed a portion of her property to the city for use as a "public greenway" along an adjoining creek and (2) grant a public pedestrian and bicycle pathway easement across a portion of her property. The Court struck down these conditions, holding that there must be some "rough proportionality" between the conditions imposed and the nature and extent of the burden caused by the owner's proposed development. In addition, to aid in judicial review, the city must make "some sort of individualized determination" of the connection between the conditions imposed and the burden. On the facts of *Dolan*, the owner *could* be required to maintain a "greenway" along the creek, since that would assist in preventing the increased danger of flooding from water running off the owner's new parking lot. But the Court could find no reason why the city had to *own* that greenway. As for the bicycle and pedestrian easement, the Court admitted that the property owner's expanded store would create more traffic, but found that the city's generalized conclusion that the easement "could offset some of the traffic demand" did not comply with the required "individualized determination."[73]

Nollan and *Dolan* involved, respectively, a single home and a single business. Conditions are also imposed on larger scale developments. Developers of large residential subdivisions are routinely required to "dedicate" to the municipality roads, sewers, alleys, playgrounds and even property for public schools. Also, exactions may be imposed to compensate for the burdens that new residents will place on the governmental services and infrastructure outside the boundaries of the subdivision. Even "controlled growth" plans designed to forestall "urban sprawl" have been approved.[74]

---

71 483 U.S. at 837. A property owner is not entitled to a jury trial in a condemnation action. However, the owner is entitled to a jury trial in an action for inverse condemnation, since that is a suit to establish liability for wrongful action by the government. *City of Monterey v. Del Monte Dunes at Monterey, Ltd.*, 526 U.S. 687 (1999). Both the question of whether the regulation left any economically viable use and, if so, whether the city's action substantially furthered a legitimate interest were, respectively, fact and mixed fact-law questions appropriate for the jury. *See* Chapter III, p. 87.

72 512 U.S. 374 (1994).

73 The relationship between the proportionality requirement and the non-categorical takings cases of the *Penn Central* type is not clear. *Nollan* and *Dolan* involved conditional approvals. But outright denial cases can be seen as involving proportionality. Thus, in *Penn Central* the Historical Preservation Commission's outright denial of the original plan and its was willingness to approve a "less ambitious development proposal for the station that clashed less with its architecture" could be seen as proportional responses to the respective burdens those plans would have on the historic architecture of the station.

74 *Golden v. Planning Bd. of Ramapo*, 285 N.E.2d 291 (N.Y. 1972).

PART II: Transfers of Property Interests

A. Real Estate Purchase Transactions

The steps in a typical residential real estate purchase transaction are outlined here. Commercial real estate transactions follow much the same process except that financing may be more complicated.[75]

1. The Purchase Contract

An interested buyer makes a written offer in the form of a proposed agreement. The Statute of Frauds requires that all agreements related to real estate be in writing.[76] The modern purchase agreement is governed by the same rules as other contracts: there must be an offer, acceptance and consideration bargained for. Once the seller and the purchaser have agreed on the terms and signed the agreement, the agreement becomes a binding legal contract. After the purchaser has had an opportunity to investigate the condition of the property, research the status of the title of the property, and obtain financing, the parties arrange for the "closing" or "settlement" of the sale. The closing is the final step in the sale, when the title of the property (deed) is given by the seller to the purchaser in exchange for the balance of the money due the seller.

2. Financing

Because of the large amount of money involved in the purchase of real estate, most buyers have to seek financing from a third party such as a bank, or less frequently, arrange for installment payments with the seller.[77] If the buyer obtains a mortgage loan, the buyer pays the seller a down payment, usually 10-20% of the purchase price, and pays the balance with the mortgage loan. The seller thereby receives the entire purchase price and conveys the deed to the buyer. The buyer uses the purchased property as security for the loan and makes regular payments to the bank until the loan is repaid. The three principal documents signed at the closing are (1) the deed, which the seller signs conveying the title of the property to the purchaser, (2) the note, which is the purchaser's promise to pay the loan back to the bank, and (3) the mortgage, which pledges the property as collateral for repayment of the note.

The buyer is given the deed, which grants legal title to the property. However, as long as there is an outstanding balance on the loan, any ownership interest granted is subject to the bank's right to "foreclose" on the mortgage if the purchaser defaults. In a foreclosure action, the bank may have the property sold at a "sheriff's sale" and have the proceeds used to pay off the loan. In about one-half of the states, this sale is subject to a statutory right of the purchaser to "redeem" the property up to a certain time after the sheriff's sale. The statutory right of redemption is exercised by matching the foreclosure sale price and meeting other statutory requirements such as the payment of interest accrued during the process.[78]

---

75 For more, *see* GRANT S. NELSON & DALE A. WHITMAN, LAND TRANSACTIONS AND FINANCE, 4TH ED. (West 2004); D. BARLOW BURKE, JR., REAL ESTATE TRANSACTIONS: EXAMPLES AND EXPLANATIONS, 4TH ED. (Aspen 2006); GRANT S. NELSON & DALE A. WHITMAN, REAL ESTATE TRANSFER, FINANCE & DEVELOPMENT, 8TH ED. (West 2009). The last book, while a casebook, has excellent text material and examples of documents.

76 *See* Chapter X, p. 403, for a discussion of the Statute of Frauds.

77 The installment payment contract is generally referred to as a "land contract."

78 The buyer's pre-foreclosure right of redemption, called the "equity of redemption," has traditionally been protected by the common law. Recognized in all states, the equity of redemption is exercised by making good on all past payments, as well as specified costs and accrued interest. The equity of redemption is a non-waivable right, but it ends at the foreclosure sale. By contrast, starting at the foreclosure sale is the statutory right of redemption, a right added by state legislation.

3. Title Assurance

If the seller does not deliver "merchantable" or "marketable" title upon closing the sale, the buyer has the right to rescind the purchase contract. As a result, the verification of good title is pivotal to the process.

Unlike many countries, the vast majority of localities in the United States do not have a central title registration system, but only a "recording" system for real property transactions.[79] Under this system, local governments, usually counties, maintain a records office, commonly called a "register of deeds," that *records* transactions presented to it. But the fact that the office has accepted a deed for recording does not guarantee good title. The office is a mere custodian of legal documents produced by others. Whether the latest deed reflects the true owner of the property can be determined only through a "title search" of the records — tracing the chain of owners back to the original conveyance of the land from a sovereign, usually the federal or state government.[80]

Recording is not required for title to pass. If the rules of contract and property law for a conveyance of real property have been met, title passes regardless of whether it is recorded.[81] If there are title contests, however, recording statutes determine the winner. Assume that O (owner) conveys to A, and A does not record. Assume O then conveys to B. In about half the states, recording statutes provide that B will win if B is a good faith purchaser, without notice of the O-to-A conveyance, who paid value for the property. This recording system is called a "notice" statute, and it imposes the rule that the last good faith purchaser without notice wins. This purchaser wins even if he or she does not record. However, this victorious purchaser still desires to record quickly so as to protect himself or herself from future good faith purchasers. In approximately the other half of states, "race-notice" statutes are applied instead. Under these statutes, the first good faith purchaser, without notice, who records wins. Applying the preceding illustration, the race is on between A and B, both good faith purchasers, without notice, who paid value.[82]

Thus, recording statutes do two things. First, they provide an obvious incentive for people to record their transactions promptly. As a result, virtually every informed party to a real property transaction records the transaction as soon as it is concluded. Second, they assure that the documents that are recorded take priority over documents that are not. So, a title searcher of the public records can be confident that the "record owner" revealed by a search is the real owner *vis-a-vis* claimants with unrecorded interests. However, some unrecorded interests may still prevail over record title, such as adverse

---

79 The records in which the deeds are recorded also show the presence of liens, mortgages and covenants to which the property is subject. For greater detail on title assurance, *see* NELSON & WHITMAN, *supra* note 75, pp. 213-261.

80 For states with colonial histories, title may be traced back to English (or other) royal grants.

81 *See Woodward v. Bowers*, 630 F.Supp. 1205, 1208 (M.D. Pa. 1986) (explaining recorder's functions). A few localities in the United States have true title registration systems or "Torrens" systems.

82 A typical "race-notice" statute provides: "Every . . . conveyance not . . . recorded is void as against any subsequent purchaser or mortgagee in good faith and for valuable consideration from the same vendor . . . of the same real property . . . whose conveyance is first duly recorded." West's Revised Code of Washington 65.08.070. A "notice" statute would omit the last phrase. Three states, Delaware, Louisiana and North Carolina, have a "race" system, whereby the first to record wins regardless of whether C paid anything for the property. For a case demonstrating the different effects of notice and race notice and touting the superiority of a notice system, *see Frees-Krey, Inc. v. Page*, 591 P.2d 1339 (Colo.App. 1978), *rev'd on other grds*, 617 P.2d 1188 (Colo. 1980).

possession, prescriptive easements and interests created by any instrument not eligible (or required) to be recorded, such as a lease for less than a year.

The system for assuring marketable title to real property has changed over the years. Originally the purchaser had to hire a lawyer to do a title search. In most states today the purchaser simply buys a "title insurance" policy at the closing of the sale. Under this arrangement, the title insurance company does the title search and insures the purchaser against defects in title. However, it is common for the title company to make exceptions for the unrecorded interests just mentioned.[83]

4. Transfer Taxes on the Sale of Property

The sale or transfer of real property is taxed on both the state and federal level. Typically, states will levy a "transfer tax," similar to a sales tax, at the time of property sale. The transfer tax varies among states. It can be a set sum of a few hundred dollars or a percentage of the property sale price, running into the thousands of dollars. The revenues from these transfer taxes usually are included in the state's "general revenues." Thus, these tax revenues are not dedicated for a particular purpose, but may be spent by the state for any legitimate state function. Transfer taxes are usually lower than the annual *ad valorem* property taxes discussed earlier.

5. RESPA Disclosures to the Purchaser-Borrower

All the above procedures result in a broad array of charges made to the purchaser at the closing — attorney fees, taxes, property insurance, title insurance and brokers' fees. In an effort to insure that purchasers are fully informed as to these charges, Congress passed the Real Estate Settlement Procedures Act (RESPA), which requires that lenders give prospective borrowers, within three days of mortgage application, a booklet prepared by the U.S. Housing and Urban Development Agency (HUD) and a good faith estimate of closing charges. The HUD booklet explains closing procedures, charges and the applicant's rights. The finance charge for the loan, expressed as an "Annual Percentage Rate" (APR), as defined by federal law, must also be disclosed. In reaction to lenders steering the borrower to certain lawyers or title insurers, who charged inflated rates and gave "kick-backs" to the lender, RESPA prohibits any "kick-back" payments and requires clear disclosure of any persons or companies the consumer is required to use for legal and other real estate services.[84]

6. Income Tax on Gains Realized From Sale of Real Property

Federal and state governments provide substantial income tax incentives to support home ownership, which is viewed by many as an essential part of the "American dream." Of the approximately 105 million residences in the United States, approximately 64% are owned by the occupants. Residential property taxes paid by the homeowner are deductible from his or her income for tax purposes. Further, interest paid on a loan for a personal residence is also deductible, contrary to the general rule against deducting interest.

Generally, profit from the sale of property is taxable income under the federal tax code. However, a major exclusion to that rule permits most homeowners to keep their gains tax-free. Recent changes in the tax code provide an exclusion of gains up to

---

83 As this discussion indicates, what sales contracts require to be delivered in almost all transactions is not true marketable title, but "marketable title subject to easements and restrictions of record."

84 12 U.S.C.A. §2601 *et seq.* APR disclosures are required in other extensions of credit by the Truth in Lending Act, which was discussed in Chapter X, p. 426.

$250,000 for a single person and $500,000 for a couple.[85] And even when there is a sale of investment property or property used for business purposes, the proceeds of such a sale can be reinvested in "like-kind" property, and taxation of any gain will be deferred until the new property is sold.[86] Like the federal government, most states impose income taxes, and home sellers may owe state tax on any profits from the property sale. However, the rates of state income taxes are generally much lower than the federal rates.[87]

B. Development and Sale of Condominiums and Cooperatives

1. Condominiums

The basic concept of a condominium was introduced earlier in this chapter. A condominium is typically a building that has been divided into individual "units," with the space between the interior walls of each unit being owned separately. The building itself, including the land, exterior walls, mechanical systems, hallways, and any other common facilities, called the "common elements," are owned by an association of the unit owners as tenants in common. Unit owners become members of the association by virtue of owning their unit.[88] This entitles them to vote on association matters. The association is responsible for the maintenance, repair and management of the common elements of the building, such as halls, walks, elevators and roofs. Owners are charged a monthly assessment for these services. In addition to the monthly association assessment, owners are responsible for property tax assessed on their unit.

Condominium development is governed by state statute. Typically the statute requires condominium documents (including the "master deed," the bylaws of the condominium association, and the condominium subdivision plan) to be prepared and recorded with the register of deeds. The documents must describe the units and common elements, the rules by which the association is run, and the restrictions for the use of the units. Owners are bound by these restrictions and rules, which can be quite specific. Restrictions on pets (size, type, or number), parking, renting, and usage of common areas are typical. In recent years, courts have started to circumscribe these restrictions. Similarly, while condominium documents often provide that owners cannot transfer their interest to anyone not approved by the owners' association, courts have stepped in to control these limitations as well .[89]

Condominium projects include older buildings that were formerly apartments, new buildings designed as condominiums, office condominiums, vacant-land or "site" condominiums, and vacation condominiums, including "time-share" properties.[90]

---

85 26 U.S.C.A. §121. The taxpayer must own and use the property as taxpayer's principal residence for 2 of 5 years before sale. Excellent concise guides to federal income tax law are MARVIN CHIRELSTEIN, FEDERAL INCOME TAXATION, 11TH ED. (Foundation 2009), HOWARD E. ABRAMS & RICHARD L. DOERNBERG, FEDERAL CORPORATE TAXATION, 6TH ED. (Foundation 2007); JOSEPH BANKMAN, THOMAS D. GRIFFITH & KATHERINE PRATT, FEDERAL INCOME TAX: EXAMPLES AND EXPLANATIONS, 5TH ED. (Aspen 2008).

86 26 U.S.C.A. §1031 and 26 C.F.R. 1.168(i)-6T. The process by which a taxpayer exchanges or replaces investment or business property is commonly referred to as a "1031 exchange."

87 Federal income tax rates vary from 15% to 39% of income after deductions. *See generally* Chapter XVI, where income taxation is discussed in detail.

88 Association members are often called co-owners.

89 *See Nahrstedt v. Lakeside Village Condominium Ass'n*, 878 P.2d 1275 (Cal. 1994) (discussing restrictions in general and citing cases) and *Laguna Royale Owners' Ass'n v. Darger*, 174 Cal. Rptr. 136 (Cal. App. 1981) (striking down association disapproval of transaction; association "must act reasonably, exercising its power in a fair and nondiscriminatory manner and withholding approval only for a reason or reasons rationally related to the protection, preservation and proper operation of the property").

90 Time-shares were discussed *supra* p. 475.

2. Cooperatives

A "cooperative" is a form of ownership in real estate in which the owner does not own the specific space the owner occupies, but rather owns an interest in the whole building or complex. This lack of an ownership interest in the specific space occupied is the principal difference between a cooperative and a condominium. An organization (usually a corporation) actually holds title to the property. The individual owns an interest in the organization, usually in the form of shares, and he or she comes to possess a unit through a long term lease. This type of lease — usually known as a proprietary lease — typically gives tenants possessory rights that are so extensive that they are effectively the same as condominium ownership. However, the sale of the shares, as well as the owners' rights to sublet their units, are extremely restricted by the organization and often involve the organization's approval of purchasers. "Financing" to purchase shares, similar to mortgage financing, is available to the individual unit owner. "Rent" amounts are usually based on the expenses of the corporation.

Despite their legal differences, condominiums and cooperatives may seem to be quite similar in practical effect. However, there is a significant difference. Condominium units are usually purchased by owners obtaining their own mortgage financing for their own unit, similar to most other real property purchases. Condominium owners are responsible for the payment of the mortgage, taxes and association fee for *their unit alone*, and if those payments are not made, only their unit is subject to foreclosure. Cooperatives are financed by mortgaging the entire project. Thus, owners are each liable for the payment of the mortgage on the *entire* property. If cooperative unit owners fail to make their payments on the cooperative, the other owners are responsible for the share of the non-paying owners. If full payment is not made on the building mortgage, then the *entire building* may be foreclosed.

C. Leasing Property: Landlord-Tenant Law

Landlord-tenant law is important because many individuals and entities rent (lease) their homes or places of business. The basic concepts of leasing are the same for both residential and commercial leasing, but there are several important differences in the legal protections afforded the tenant.[91]

1. Residential Leasing

Since residential tenants are on the whole less sophisticated in business affairs and often in a far weaker bargaining position than landlords, most states and localities have enacted special laws designed to protect residential tenants. For example, nearly all localities enforce laws that require a landlord to have the property inspected and approved by local housing officials before renting to tenants, and every few years thereafter. Many jurisdictions regulate residential leases to ensure that tenants are not subject to unfair agreements.

It was not always the case that residential tenants had such protections. Until the 1960s, leaseholds tended to be viewed as "interests in property" and lease terms tended to be construed under the rules of property law. Notably, a fundamental common law rule of property law, called the doctrine of "independent covenants," undercut tenants' rights. Under this doctrine, landlord promises and tenant promises were independent rather than "mutually dependent." Consequently, even if landlords promised to make necessary repairs but failed to do so, tenants still had to pay rent. Since tenants were not

---

91 *See* DAVID S. HILL, LANDLORD AND TENANT LAW IN A NUTSHELL, 4TH ED (West 2004).

permitted to withhold rent, they were often without any recourse to force the landlord to maintain the premises.

By the 1960s, however, the residential landlord-tenant relationship in the United States had changed significantly. Courts began to analyze leases under contract law rather than property law and ignored the independent covenants doctrine.[92] Today, the landlord's and the tenant's obligations under a lease are mutually dependent. And as part of every residential lease, whether written or oral, is an implied "warranty of habitability." It is a non-waivable warranty.[93] Therefore, clauses in lease agreements that state that tenant takes the residence "as is" or "with all faults" have no effect on warranty violations. The warranty of habitability obligates the landlord to keep the premises in a safe and habitable condition and in compliance with all local building code requirements. Landlord is liable for breach even if tenant had knowledge of breach before renting.[94] Typical breaches include the failure to provide heat in the winter or the failure to provide running water. If the landlord breaches this warranty, the tenant may withhold rent until the landlord makes necessary repairs, or the tenant may repair the problem and deduct reasonable costs from the rent.[95] In addition, a duty under *tort* law may arise. Thus, a landlord who fails to repair premises may be liable in a tort action for injuries suffered by tenants as a result of unrepaired dangerous conditions.[96]

All residential leases also contain an implied covenant of "quiet enjoyment." This means that the tenant has the right to possess and use the property without interference from the landlord.

2. Commercial Leases

The commercial tenant is considered to be more sophisticated and to have greater bargaining power. At the very least, the commercial tenant is probably better able than the residential tenant to inspect the premises and demand that any defects be repaired before signing the lease. As a result, the implied warranty of habitability does not generally apply to a commercial lease, although the implied warranty of quiet enjoyment still applies. Commercial leases are often much longer in duration than residential leases and often give the tenant greater rights to make changes on the property. Often, a condition of a long-term commercial lease will demand that the landlord remodel the property to suit the tenant's planned business use.

D. Succession of Property Interests Upon Death of the Owner

Interests in real and personal property are transferred upon the death of the owner.[97] The transfer, called "succession," can be either "testamentary," meaning

---

92 See *Brown v. Southall Realty*, 237 A.2d 834 (D.C. 1968) (housing regulations were implied part of the lease and landlord's non-compliance relieved the tenant of the obligation to pay rent).

93 *See Randall Co. v. Alan Lobel Photography, Inc.*, 465 N.Y.S.2d 489 (N.Y. Civ. Ct. 1983) (holding that waiver of counterclaim for breach of the implied warranty of habitability may be upheld in commercial leases but not in residential leases).

94 *See Knight v. Hallsthammar*, 623 P.2d 268 (Cal. 1981) (holding that tenant awareness of apartment defects does not preclude tenant cause of action under implied warranty of habitability).

95 *See Javins v. First National Realty Corp.*, 428 F.2d 1071 (D.C. Cir. 1970).

96 *See Sargent v. Ross*, 308 A.2d 528 (N.H. 1973) (landlord held liable for death of child where landlord had exposed tenants to unreasonable risk of harm due to faulty design of stairs and his failure to correct the dangerous condition).

97 For more on wills and testamentary dispositions, *see* WILLIAM M. MCGOVERN, JR. & SHELDON F. KURTZ, HORNBOOK ON WILLS, TRUSTS AND ESTATES, 3D ED. (West 2004), MARK REUTLINGER, WILLS, TRUSTS AND ESTATES: ESSENTIAL TERMS AND CONCEPTS, 2D ED. (Aspen 1998), and ROBERT L. MENNELL & SHERI L. BURR, WILLS AND TRUSTS

transfer with a "will," or "intestate," meaning transfer without a will.[98]

1. Testamentary Succession of Property

Testamentary succession of property is disposition of that property upon death through a will. If a person writes a will, then the property that person owns at the time of his or her death will go to the persons named in the will. If real property passes, beneficiaries are called "devisees." If personal property passes, they are called "legatees."

The "testator," the person writing the will, may generally designate whomever he or she wishes to receive the property. The formalities of proper execution of a will by a testator are governed by state laws. These laws generally require that testators be "competent" (that they understand what they are doing), that the will be in writing, that it be signed by the testator, and that the signing be witnessed by at least two witnesses.[99] A will may be changed or revoked by the testator at any time during his or her life. Changes to a will are often made by drafting an additional document known as a "codicil." A codicil, or any change in a will, must be made with the same formalities as the original will itself.

One constraint on the power of testators to bequeath property is that they may not choose to leave their spouse nothing at all. Typically, state laws give to a surviving spouse one-third of the testator's property, even if the testator has designated a smaller amount in the will. The decision to take a "statutory share" of the property rather than the amount designated in the will is generally known as "electing against the will." Such a share for the surviving spouse is often referred to as a "statutory elective share." The statutory share idea was an effort to protect women, whose economic welfare was often completely dependent on their husband's wishes.[100]

After the testator dies, a special court, usually called a "probate" court, generally supervises the distribution of the testator's property and the payment of testator's debts.[101] This process is called "probate," and sometimes referred to as "probating an estate." When a will is involved, the court will appoint an "executor" to oversee the process. The executor is a person trusted by the testator and named in the will itself. The executor is personally responsible for insuring that the property is distributed to the correct persons and the debts are paid.

2. Intestate Succession

Decedents who die without a will are said to have died "intestate," and their property passes by way of "intestate succession." In such cases, the probate court appoints an "administrator" to oversee the distribution and debt-payment process. The administrator's responsibilities are generally the same as an executor, described above.

The property of people who die intestate goes to their "heirs at law," as determined

---

IN A NUTSHELL, 3D ED. (West 2008). *See also* UNIFORM PROBATE CODE, OFFICIAL TEXT WITH COMMENTS, 11TH ED. (West 1994).

98 A will is a document by which an owner specifies to whom property should go after death. "Testamentary" and "intestate" are derived from the term "testament." "Testament" is an antiquated term referring to a "will." Nonetheless, even today many wills are entitled "Last Will and Testament."

99 In general, these witnesses should have no interest in receiving any property under the will. If a witness is an interested party, the will, in general, will not be invalidated. However, the witness risks losing his or her interest under the will.

100 Marital property rights are discussed in Chapter XIV, pp. 520-521.

101 Such courts may have different names in different states. *See* Chapter V, p. 173.

by state law.[102] These laws vary somewhat, but strongly favor distributing the decedent's estate to the surviving spouse and children, and in their absence, to the parents. State "intestacy" statutes tend to follow a pattern of awarding one-third of the decedent's property to the decedent's spouse and two-thirds to the decedent's children However, the surviving spouse generally makes out much better than this division indicates. This is because most of the important property of the decedent — such as a house, bank accounts, stocks and bonds — are owned jointly with rights of survivorship by husband and wife. Thus, the surviving spouse automatically becomes the sole owner of such property upon the decedent's death and the property is not included in the distribution process of the decedent's estate.

E. Establishment and Operation of Trusts

The concept of a trust was introduced at the beginning of the chapter.[103] As stated there, settlors can convey their property to a trustee, who holds legal title, but also convey a beneficial interest in that property to other persons, called beneficiaries. This allows the beneficiaries to receive the benefits of the property without the burdensome obligations and rights of ownership. Trusts that come into being at the death of a person, usually as part of a plan coordinated with a will, are referred to as "testamentary trusts." Trusts created during the lifetime of a person are called "inter-vivos trusts."

1. Formation of a Trust and Reasons for Its Establishment

An example of a typical family trust might be as follows. A owns considerable stocks and bonds and wishes to have A's children, B, C, and D, receive the income from them. However, managing a securities portfolio takes some skill and time. A is also somewhat concerned that D, the youngest, may not appreciate the value of the securities and may sell them if A gave them as a gift outright. A might wish to set up a trust for the children and transfer the securities to that trust. A can choose anyone to be "trustee." Under the terms of the trust, B, C, and D, the "beneficiaries" of the trust, will receive all of the net income from the securities every year. However, the "legal title" to the securities is actually transferred to the trustee. Since B, C and D have the right to enjoy the benefits of the property in the trust, it is sometimes said that they have "equitable title." This separability of legal and equitable title has been a feature of Anglo-American law for several centuries.

A might name First State Bank & Trust as "trustee." As trustee, the bank owes a "fiduciary duty" to the beneficiaries — the duty to act in the best interest of the beneficiary. The bank must manage the property competently and must distribute the net income from the property in accord with A's wishes, as expressed in the trust document. The distribution designation is entirely up to the settlor. For example, if A wanted B to receive one-half of the net income and C and D the remaining half, then all A would need to do is to specify that division in the trust document. The beneficiaries have no right to interfere with the trustee's management of the trust property. For instance, if D wanted the trustee to sell all the gold mining stock in the portfolio because the mining company involved has been polluting the air, D would have no authority to order the trustee to do so. Only the trustee would have that authority. In general, the trustee must manage the property in the way that a "prudent businessperson" would manage it.

---

102 Technically, in most states, "heirs at law" or "heirs" describes only those who receive real property. Recipients of personal property are referred to as "next of kin."

103 *See supra*, p. 473. For more material on trusts, *see supra*, note 97.

It is not unusual for the trust agreement to provide for certain limited withdrawal rights in beneficiaries. In other words, in addition to paying out the income from the securities, the trustee may be authorized to make lump sum payments up to a certain limit upon request of a beneficiary for certain special needs. Thus, A might provide that B, C, or D may receive up to $10,000 additional money for each year they are enrolled in college, or in the event of an emergency.

2. Avoiding Probate with a Revocable *Inter-Vivos* Trust

Trusts are commonly used, along with wills, as part of "estate planning." Estate planning involves preparing for the distribution of a person's property upon death. *Inter-vivos* trusts are trusts established during the lifetime of the settlor and are commonly used to avoid making the distribution of the decedent's property subject to the probate process, described earlier. A trust avoids probate because the legal title to the property in the trust was already transferred to the trustee during the settlor's lifetime. As a result, there is no distribution of property upon the death of the decedent. Thus, there is nothing for the probate court to supervise.

Trusts designed to avoid probate may be either revocable by the settlor or "irrevocable." In revocable inter-vivos trusts, the settlor has the right to end the trust at any time during the settlor's life and assume direct ownership of the property. Inter-vivos trusts, designed primarily to avoid probate, are usually revocable in order to provide maximum flexibility to the settlor. If the trust is not revoked by the time of the settlor's death, the property therein is not part of the settlor's probate estate, despite the fact that the settlor could have ended the trust and retaken the property while living. However, since a revocable trust effectively allows the settlor the full benefit of the property (if the settlor so wishes) while living, federal income tax must be paid by the settlor on all the *income* from such a trust, just as if the settlor owned the property outright. In addition, federal *estate* taxes will be imposed on the value of the trust at the time of the settlor's death. The federal estate tax laws follow the "substance" rather than the "form" of trust arrangements. Consequently, while this form of trust avoids the probate process, it does not avoid estate taxes upon the settlor's death or income taxes while living.

3. Avoiding Taxes with an Irrevocable *Inter-Vivos* Trust

Avoiding Income Taxes If the settlor wishes to avoid income taxes on income from trust property, the *inter-vivos* trust must be irrevocable so that the settlor cannot regain ownership of the trust property. The *beneficiaries* must pay income taxes on payments they receive, but they are often subject to a lower rate of taxation than the settlor. This is because they have less income and therefore fall into a lower "tax bracket." Often the beneficiaries in a lower tax bracket will be the settlor's children.

Avoiding Estate Taxes Irrevocable inter-vivos trusts are also used to avoid federal estate taxation upon the death of the settlor. However, a transfer to such an irrevocable trust is "complete" at the time of the transfer, so the transfer is subject to the federal *gift tax* at the time of the transfer. Despite the fact that the federal estate and gift taxes are coordinated, the gift tax imposes a lower tax rate than the estate tax. On the other hand, the gift tax must be paid at transfer, whereas the estate tax must be paid at the settlor's death. Estate planning generally requires the help of sophisticated lawyers who specialize in taxation. A proper estate plan must not only minimize federal and state gift, estate and income taxes, but also ensure that there is adequate income for the client.[104]

---

[104] For more on the details of estate and gift tax, *see* JOHN K. MCNULTY, FEDERAL ESTATE AND GIFT TAXATION IN A NUTSHELL, 6TH ED (West 2003).

4. Testamentary Trusts and the Use of a Pour-Over Will with an *Inter Vivos* Trust

Tax and Probate Treatment of Testamentary Trusts   A settlor may wish to set up a "testamentary" trust — a trust that comes into being upon the testator's death. While such a trust provides the benefits of having a trustee control distribution to beneficiaries, testamentary trusts have none of the tax or probate avoidance benefits outlined above. Instead, the entire corpus of the trust is taxed and included in the probated estate.

Pour-Over Wills and Inter Vivos Trusts   To avoid some of the tax and probate disadvantages of a testamentary trust, the settlor may wish instead to place part of the property into an *inter vivos* trust and use a "pour-over" will to dispose of the remainder of the property. A pour-over will is so named because the will directs the transfer of the remaining estate to a trustee. The will recognizes the existence of the trust agreement. Using this device, the settlor-testator gains the benefits of a trust, which provides control over the testator's property distribution, while also making outright unrestricted testamentary bequests.

F. Other Methods of Transferring Interests in Property

1. Transfers Common to Both Real and Personal Property

Gifts   An owner that makes a gift of property is called the "donor," and the recipient of that gift is called the "donee." The donor must possess "donative intent," which is the intent to transfer property as a gift.[105] In addition, for a gift of personal property to be valid, the donor must actually deliver possession and the donee must accept.[106] However, if it is not feasible to deliver the personal property because of its size, a symbolic delivery is sufficient, such as handing over the keys to a car. Real property, like all other property, may be given away. However, unlike gifts of personal property, real property gifts — like all other transactions involving real estate — must be in writing. This generally means that the donor must execute the deed to the donee. A statement of intent to make a gift is not legally enforceable due to lack of "consideration."[107]

Judicial Sale   Judicial sales of property are sales which are ordered and supervised by a court. The most common of these are sales to satisfy civil judgments, which are sometimes called "sheriffs' sales."[108]

2. Transfers Applicable to Personal Property Only

Adverse Possession   Adverse possession of personal property, like adverse possession of real property, can be a means of acquiring ownership, and the same requirements apply in general.[109] The difficulty with personal property, however, is that it is often hard for the adverse possessor to prove that his or her possession was "open and notorious" because of the small size and easily transportable nature of much personal property. Some courts avoid this problem by rejecting adverse possession in

---

105 Of course, a testamentary gift may be made by will. In that case, all of the formalities of a will must be fulfilled. *See supra* p. 493.

106 *See Newman v. Bost*, 29 S.E. 848 (N.C.1898).

107 *See* Chapter X, p. 402.

108 *See* Chapter VII, p. 244, where execution of civil judgments is discussed.

109 *See* discussion *supra*, p. 478.

the case of personal property and basing their inquiry instead upon the diligence of the true owner in trying to recover the property.[110]

Finders Ownership interests in personal property may also be acquired by finding an item. The ownership interest of the finder depends on how the true owner became separated from his or her property. Once lost property is found, the finder receives an ownership interest in the property which is inferior only to the interest of the original owner. If the personal property has been abandoned, the finder gets title superior to that of all others, including the original owner. If the personal property has been mislaid (the property has been put in a specific location purposefully and inadvertently left there), the owner of the real property on which it is found generally has the right to the item, not the finder.

Bailments A bailment exists when one person leaves property in the possession of another for safekeeping or some other temporary purpose. This could include leaving one's car in a parking garage or leaving one's watch at a jeweler's shop for repair. Problems with bailments arise when the "bailee," the person keeping the property, loses it, conveys it, or damages it. There are different standards of care that apply depending on the nature of the bailment. For bailments that are for the benefit of the bailee, as where the bailee charges for the service, the bailee is held to a higher standard of care than where the bailment is gratuitous (where no fee is charged) or the bailment is for the benefit of the property owner.

Accessions and Improvements Under the doctrine of accession, an owner of property gains title to any natural or artificial increases in or additions to that property. For example, the owner of a cow would gain title to any milk produced by that cow. Woodworkers who turn their own wood into a table are entitled to the increased value of the wood. A more complicated scenario arises when a person unites his or her labor or property with the property of another person. In that case, ownership of the finished product is determined on the basis of such factors as the difference in value as a result of the labor, the degree of change in the form of the original property, and the ease with which the personal property of the laborer can be removed from the other's property.[111]

PART III: Intellectual Property

Intellectual property is a form of personal property. However, it differs enough from other forms of personal property and is sufficiently important in its own right to be discussed separately. Intellectual property comprises three distinct bodies of law: copyright law, patent law and trademark law.[112]

---

110 *See, e.g., O'Keeffe v. Snyder,* 416 A.2d 862, 869 (N.J. 1980) (the statute of limitations of an action for return of the property begins to run when the true owner "discovers or should have discovered facts which form the basis of a cause of action").

111 *See, e.g., Austrian Motors, Ltd. v. Travelers Insurance Co.,* 275 S.E.2d 702 (Ga.App. 1980) (tires and other easily removable parts innocently added to another's car remain the property of the trespassing laborer, but materials such as paint that cannot be easily removed as well as the labor employed become the property of the car owner).

112 For more, *see* MICHAEL EPSTEIN, EPSTEIN ON INTELLECTUAL PROPERTY, 5TH ED. (Aspen 2006, 2008); CHARLES R. MCMANIS, INTELLECTUAL PROPERTY AND UNFAIR COMPETITION IN A NUTSHELL, 3D ED. (West 2004); ARTHUR R. MILLER & MICHAEL H. DAVIS, PATENTS, TRADEMARKS AND COPYRIGHT IN A NUTSHELL, 4TH ED. (West 2007); SELECTED INTELLECTUAL PROPERTY AND UNFAIR COMPETITION STATUTES, REGULATIONS AND TREATIES. (West 2010). *See also* JESSICA LITMAN, DIGITAL COPYRIGHT (Prometheus Books 2001).

A. Copyright Law

Copyright law is set out in the federal Copyright Act of 1976.[113] The Act was passed, along with the patent laws to be discussed below, pursuant to Congress's power "[t]o promote the Progress of Science and useful Arts, by securing for limited Times to Authors and Inventors the exclusive Right to their respective Writings and Discoveries."[114] The Supreme Court has emphasized that "[t]he ultimate aim of copyright is not to reward the labor of authors, but '[t]o promote the Progress of Science and useful Arts.'" Thus, the "monopoly privileges" afforded "are limited in nature and must ultimately serve the public good."[115]

1. Works Subject to Copyright Protection

Basic Requirements The federal act protects "original works of authorship fixed in any tangible medium of expression."[116] Works can be literary, dramatic, scientific, musical, artistic or architectural, and can be any form of pictorial or sculptural representations, recorded sounds or computer programs. "Originality" requires that the work involve some creative choices in its production. There is no requirement of complete novelty or artistic merit, but some creative choices must have been involved. Thus, collecting names and numbers in telephone directory is "not remotely creative" even though it may represent a significant amount of work.[117] Producing a "yellow pages" business directory of names and numbers "selected, coordinated, or arranged in such a way that the resulting work as a whole constitutes an original work of authorship" might protected by copyright, but it will have to contend with the limited original choices one can make in organizing such information.[118] Of course, if a person creates a work from preexisting material, as is the case with such a compilation or with a derivative work, such as a translation or abridgement, copyright protection extends only to the creative features added and not to the preexisting material used in the work.[119] A photograph, while it is literally a mere copy of reality, may be protected as an "original work, the product of plaintiff's intellectual invention," because of the author's efforts in composing the subject.[120]

The requirement that the work be "fixed" in some form is met when the work is "sufficiently permanent or stable to permit it to be perceived, reproduced, or otherwise communicated for a period of more than transitory duration."[121] This would exclude

---

113 17 U.S.C.A. §101 *et seq.*

114 Art. I §8 cl. 8.

115 *Fogerty v. Fantasy*, 510 U.S. 517, 526 (1994). *See also Graham v. John Deere Co.*, 383 U.S. 1 (1966) (emphasizing that "[t]he clause is both a grant of power and a limitation."). *But see Eldred v. Ashcroft, infra* note 133 (rejecting claims that additional 20-year extension by Congress was unconstitutional).

116 17 U.S.C.A. §102(a).

117 *Feist Publications v. Rural Telephone Service Co.*, 499 U.S. 340 (1991). *See also Matthew Bender & Co. v. West Publishing Co.*, 158 F.3d 674 (2d Cir. 1998) (selection and ordering of caption and other aspects of non-copyrightable judicial decisions is not copyrightable).

118 17 U.S.C.A. §101 (defining a "compilation"). *See BellSouth Advertising & Publishing Corp. v. Donnelley Information Publishing, Inc.*, 999 F.2d 1436 (11th Cir. 1993) (*en banc*) (rejecting, over a strong dissent, copyright claims regarding such a "yellow pages" business directory).

119 17 U.S.C.A. §§101, 103. However, protection does not extend to any part of the derivative work in which the preexisting material is used unlawfully. *Cf.* 17 U.S.C.A. §106(2) (securing rights in the original owner to "prepare derivative works based upon the copyrighted work").

120 *Burrow-Giles Lithographic Co. v. Sarony*, 111 U.S. 53, 60 (1884).

121 17 U.S.C.A. §101. A work produced on a computer is fixed as soon as it is in random access memory (RAM). It need not be saved to a disk or printed out. *Cf.* 17 U.S.C.A. §117(c) (infringement exception for copying a computer program into RAM, which all computers do when they use a program).

such things as improvisational speeches, choreography or other performances that have not been recorded in some manner. U.S. government works, names, titles, slogans or short phrases cannot be copyrighted.[122]

Notice of copyright is usually provided by a © for visually perceptible works and by a ℗ for sound recordings. And, as discussed below, the work can be registered with the U.S. Copyright Office. However, neither a copyright notice nor registration is necessary to protect the work. And the presence of a notice means neither that the work is protected, nor that it is registered — only that the author claims the work is protected.[123]

Ideas vs. Expression of Ideas Copyright protects the specific *form of expression* the author has chosen, not the underlying concepts, ideas or facts expressed.[124] The treatment of historical research and analysis illustrates this. In one case, the author of a book on the mysterious destruction of the German dirigible, the Hindenberg, published a book that set out his extensive historical research on the subject and posited a theory that the dirigible was sabotaged by a member of its crew to embarrass the Nazi regime. When a film company with access to his book made a movie on the Hindenberg espousing the same theory, a court held that copyright protection extended neither to "documented fact" nor to the "explanatory hypothesis" set out in the book.[125] Quoting or closely paraphrasing the book would constitute infringement.[126]

In rare circumstances, there may be only a few possible ways to express an idea. In such cases, it is said that there is a "merger" of the idea and the expression of it, such that they become one and the same.[127] In such cases the merged expression of the idea is not copyrightable, since "to permit copyrighting would mean that a party or parties, by copyrighting a mere handful of forms, could exhaust all possibilities of future use of the substance."[128]

2. Copyright Owner's Rights

Nature of Rights The law creates rights in authors to control exploitation of their works, including the right to reproduce or copy the work, to prepare or control preparation of derivative works from them (*e.g.*, films based on novels), to control distribution to the public of copies (free or for sale), public performance and display.[129] Protection of "moral rights" of authors — certain rights retained by an author even after a copyright

---

122 Titles, slogans and short phrases may qualify as trademarks, however. *See infra* pp. 511-516.

123 However, the presence of a copyright symbol on a work makes it hard for the infringer to claim "innocent infringement," which reduces the damages recoverable for infringement. 17 U.S.C.A. §§401(d), 402(d). There is no protection for works published before March 1, 1989, without a copyright notice. 17 U.S.C.A. §101 note. As noted *infra* p. 503, registration brings with it important procedural benefits.

124 *See Baker v. Selden*, 101 U.S. 99 (1879) (method of accounting is not copyrightable, although the explanation of it is); *Reyher v. Children's Television Workshop*, 533 F.2d 87 (2d Cir. 1976) (idea for television program not copyrightable). 17 U.S.C.A. §102(b) (no copyright of "any idea, procedure, process, system, method of operation, concept, principle, or discovery"). However, some systems may qualify for patent protection. *See infra* pp. 507-509.

125 *Hoehling v. Universal City Studios, Inc.*, 618 F.2d 972 (2d Cir. 1980).

126 *See infra* p. 505 (different standards for infringement of fiction and non-fiction works).

127 *See Matthew Bender & Co. v. Kluwer Law Book Publishers, Inc.*, 672 F.Supp. 107, 112 (S.D.N.Y. 1987) (categories in the plaintiff-law publisher's chart on verdicts in medical malpractice cases are "the only sensible ones which could have been used to compile the data.").

128 *Morrissey v. Procter & Gamble Co.*, 379 F.2d 675, 678-79 (1st Cir.1967) (despite almost precise similarity between rules of contest setting out how to fill out and send in entry form, no infringement took place because there are "if not only one form of expression, at best only a limited number" involved).

129 17 U.S.C.A. §106.

is assigned — is less strong in the U.S. than in some other countries.[130] An exception is the 1990 Visual Artists Rights Act, which prohibits "any intentional distortion, mutilation, or other modification" of a visual work that "would be prejudicial to [the author's] honor or reputation."[131]

Electronic Protections The Digital Millennium Copyright Act of 1998 seeks to adapt copyright law to the electronic age and, in the process, some believe it has gone too far in its protections. The Act makes it illegal to use, make or distribute programs or other devices that circumvent or "crack" electronic protection of electronic copyrighted material, such as computer programs and audio recordings. Some claim that this allows copyright owners to keep electronic "gates" in place to protect even those portions of works that might be in the public domain or are subject to fair use, and even to make them inaccessible long after the relevant copyrights have expired.[132]

Duration of Copyright Protection Copyright in a work created on or after January 1, 1978, extends from the time of its creation until 70 years following the author's death. The period may not be renewed.[133] Once the statutory period expires, the work is in the "public domain" and has no copyright protection. It may therefore be used by anyone for any purpose, including commercial purposes. Authors may expressly dedicate or abandoned their work to the public domain. However, abandonment cannot be implied from failure to assert the right against infringers.[134] And, contrary to popular belief, placing one's work on the Internet is not abandonment.[135]

3. Ownership and Transfers of Copyrights

Transfers Authors may sell or otherwise assign their rights to someone else, typically to the publisher of their work. Any assignment must be in writing. In addition, title can pass by any means of conveyance, including by will or intestate succession.[136]

Works Made for Hire If the author is an employee and the work is created within the scope of employment, then the work is a "work made for hire," and the employer

---

130 Moral rights include rights of authors to claim authorship, to divulge their work when and how they choose, to have their name appear as author, to oppose distortions, mutilations, or other modifications that would injure their honor or reputation, and to require faithful adherence to the text of their work.

131 17 U.S.C.A. §106A. For a discussion of the Act, *see* 138 A.L.R.Fed. 239 (1997). However, state common-law, particularly defamation, and state art protection statutes may apply to protect non-visual works. For an example of director John Huston's heirs' attempts to enforce his moral rights to prevent colorization of his films in France, *see* Jane C. Ginsburg & Pierre Sirinelli, *Authors and Exploitations in International Private Law: The French Supreme Court and the Huston Film Colorization Controversy*, 15 COLUMBIA-VLA JOURNAL OF LAW & THE ARTS (1991).

132 *See* 17 U.S.C.A. §1201. The Act was held constitutional against 1st Amendment free speech claims as applied in a case enjoining web sites offering software that would disable anti-copying protection of DVDs. *Universal City Studios, Inc. v. Corley*, 273 F.3d 429 (2d Cir. 2001).

133 17 U.S.C.A. §302(a). In 1998, Congress added 20 years to the previous 50-year term. Works produced between 1964 and 1977 enjoy copyright status for 95 years. Works from 1923 through 1963 have 28-year initial and 67-year renewal terms. 17 U.S.C.A. §304(a). The Supreme Court upheld the 1998 extension, rejecting arguments that the additional 20-year period violated the 1st Amendment and the constitutional provision for granted rights in authors for "a limited time." *Eldred v. Ashcroft*, 537 U.S. 186 (2003). Works made for hire (*see infra* p. 501) are protected for 95 years.

134 *National Comics Publications v. Fawcett Publications*, 191 F.2d 594, 598 (2d Cir. 1951) (1939 copyright to comic strips, including "Superman," not abandoned by failure to affix copyright symbol or enforce); *Micro Star v. Formgen, Inc.*, 154 F.3d 1107 (9th Cir. 1997) (copyright owner encouraging players themselves to make other "levels" of computer game "Duke Nukem 3D" and providing editing program to assist in doing so was not abandonment).

135 For a web site guide for librarians setting out a chart showing when works pass into the public domain, *see* http://www.unc.edu/~unclng/public-d.htm.

136 17 U.S.C.A. §204. *See also* 17 U.S.C.A. §201(d)(1) (testamentary and other transfers of copyright).

is considered the author, unless there is a contrary written agreement.[137] A work by an non-employee independent contractor can also be a work for hire, but only if there is a written agreement that it is for hire and it is specially ordered or commissioned as a contribution to a collective work, as a part of an audiovisual work, or as a translation, supplementary work, compilation, instructional text, test, or atlas, or as answer material for a test.[138] Even if the work is not made for hire and the author owns the copyright, the author may have created an implied non-exclusive license in the person for whom the author created the work. This allows the party who ordered the work to use and distribute it to others.[139] A special exception applies to university teachers, whose works are never considered to belong to their university.[140]

Nature of Assignment   The assignment of a copyright gives the assignee all the rights the author had in the work. There have been notable cases of authors who sold their works cheaply early in their careers, only to face relative poverty later in life, while publishers continued to reap profits from their work. In reaction to this, Congress in the 1976 Act created a non-waivable right in authors to "recapture" their copyright by canceling the transfer of the copyright after the expiration of 35 years following the original transfer.[141]

The First Sale Doctrine   The primary limitation on the copyright owner's right to control distribution of a work is the "first sale" doctrine. If the owner sells a copy of the work, the purchaser of that copy may resell it or dispose of it as the purchaser wishes without obtaining the permission of the copyright owner.[142] The most common examples of this doctrine in practice are used bookstores and video rental stores. While the buyer cannot make copies of the copy, even resale of the very copies sold can create problems for the original owner when a product is sold in different markets at different prices. In *Quality King Distributors Inc. v. L'Anza Research International Inc.*[143] a California manufacturer sold its hair care products with copyrighted labels at substantial discount from the U.S. price to a Malta distributor, which subsequently sold them to an importer, which imported the products back into the United States to be sold at lower prices. The manufacturer attempted to stop the "reimportation" and sales. A unanimous Supreme Court held that the first-sale doctrine permitted the practice. Importation might be prohibited through enactment of an international trade law or conclusion of an international agreement with the importer's country, the Court conceded, but copyright laws afforded no protection.[144] Goods like those in *Quality King* are sometimes called "gray-market" goods. The "gray" comes from the fact that they are sold without the

---

137 17 U.S.C.A. §§101, 201(b). *Community for Creative Non-Violence v. Reid*, 490 U.S. 730 (1989) (sculpture not work for hire; sculptor was not employee, despite some supervision or execution or work).

138 *Lulirama Ltd. v. Axcess Broadcast Servs.*, 128 F.3d 872 (5th Cir. 1997) (issue of fact of whether jingles were to be included in audio-visual work so as to be work for hire precluded summary judgment).

139 *See Effects Associates v. Cohen*, 908 F.2d 555 (9th Cir. 1990) (special effects film of "alien yogurt oozing out of a defunct factory" belonged to the company that made it, not the film producer who ordered it, but producer had license to use it and distribute it to others). *See also Lulirama Ltd.*, *supra* note 138.

140 This "teacher exception" is not mentioned in the current Act, but was in the 1909 act. While some have contended that the current Act eliminated it, most agree that is still exists. *See Hays v. Sony Corp. of America*, 847 F.2d 412, 416 (7th Cir. 1988) (while grounds of the "teacher exception" were "scanty," "virtually no one questioned that the academic author was entitled to copyright his writing").

141 17 U.S.C.A. §203. Authors could use this as a limited means of protecting "moral rights" by "recapturing" their work if unhappy with the assignee's treatment of it. *See supra* p. 500 and note 130.

142 17 U.S.C.A. §109(a). Sold copies may be leased as well, except for sound recordings and computer programs. 17 U.S.C.A. §109(b)(1).

143 523 U.S. 135 (1998).

144 The Court noted that executive agreements had been reached with 5 countries on the subject.

approval of the copyright owner, but their sale and resale are completely legal, as *Quality King* shows, at least as a matter of copyright law.[145]

Registration   As noted earlier, no particular procedure need be followed to obtain copyright protection for a work. However, registration of the copyright with the U.S. Copyright Office is available and it is encouraged since it establishes an official public record of the copyright.[146] Registration is also necessary as a precondition for a suit for infringement, though this can be done after the infringement and just prior to filing suit. Registration by a U.S. author within 5 years of publication of the work establishes *prima facie* evidence in court of the validity of the copyright. Registration within 3 months after publication of the work or before infringement entitles the author to statutory damages of between $750 and $30,000 "as the court considers just," plus attorney fees, in any infringement suit.[147]

4. Fair Use of Copyrighted Work

The rights of authors are subject to "fair use" of their works by others. Begun as a common law doctrine, fair use is now set out in the Act, but the intent of Congress was to codify the common law. Unfortunately, the Act does not provide a definition of fair use, only examples and four "factors" to consider. The examples of fair use given are "criticism, comment, news reporting, teaching (including multiple copies for classroom use), scholarship, or research." The factors to consider are: "(1) the purpose and character of the use, including whether such use is of a commercial nature or is for nonprofit educational purposes; (2) the nature of the copyrighted work; (3) the amount and substantiality of the portion used in relation to the copyrighted work as a whole; and (4) the effect of the use upon the potential market for or value of the copyrighted work."[148] Even with this statutory guidance, courts have observed that the doctrine is "so flexible as virtually to defy definition."[149] Its indeterminacy is enhanced by the fact that "[t]he factors enumerated in the section are not meant to be exclusive: '[S]ince the doctrine is an equitable rule of reason, no generally applicable definition is possible, and each case raising the question must be decided on its own facts.'"[150]

Character and Purpose of Copying   The presence of a profit motive has been important in determining that the use was not fair use.[151] While not determinative, the non-commercial nature of consumers recording television programs on their home video recorders was a factor leading to a conclusion of fair use.[152] Educational use, even outside the context of formal education, has been deemed important as well. One court upheld a vacuum cleaner company's reprinting, without permission, an independent

---

145 The Court had reached a similar result with regard to trademarks. *K Mart Corp. v. Cartier, Inc.*, 486 U.S. 281 (1988).

146 The Copyright Office's website is www.copyright.gov.

147 17 U.S.C.A. §§411-412; 504(c)(1). Actual damages are also available. Registration is not necessary if the origin of the work is a foreign country that is a signatory of the Berne Convention.

148 17 U.S.C.A. §107. Since copying exceeding fair use is often an infringement, *see also infra* p. 505.

149 *Time, Inc. v. Bernard Geis Associates*, 293 F.Supp. 130, 144 (S.D.N.Y. 1968) (including copies of parts of Zapruder film of President Kennedy's assassination in a book on the event was fair use).

150 *Harper & Row Publishers v. Nation Enterprises*, 471 U.S. 539, 560 (1985) (quoting House Report on the 1976 Act). For application of the fair use factors, *see A&M Records, Inc. v. Napster, Inc.*, 239 F.3d 1004 (9th Cir. 2001).

151 *Henry Holt & Co. v. Liggett & Myers Tobacco Co.*, 23 F.Supp. 302 (E.D.Pa. 1938) (portions of scientific book used to advertise cigarettes); *Sony Corp. of America v. Universal City Studios, Inc.*,464 U.S. 417, 451 (1984)("every commercial use of copyrighted material is presumptively an unfair [use]").

152 *Sony Corp. of America* case, *supra* note 151 at 448. Analog music recordings may also be copied for personal use. *See* Audio Home Recording Act, 17 U.S.C.A. §1001 *et seq.*

consumer group's favorable review of its product. Among other factors, the court noted that circulating the review served to educate consumers.[153]

Nature of the Work One distinction made by courts under this factor is between fact and fiction. Fiction receives the greater protection on the ground that there are fewer if any uncopyrightable facts involved with fiction.[154] Other courts have used a "published/unpublished" distinction, protecting unpublished works more completely on the grounds that there is a unique value to first publication.[155] A recurring fair use issue is the copying of copyrighted works as materials for courses at educational institutions. While the statute expressly refers to "teaching" and "multiple copies for classroom use," there are limits. If the copies are made, not by the educational institution itself, but by commercial duplicating establishments that sell the materials to students at a profit, fair use has not been found.[156]

Amount of Copying Amount and substantiality of copying is a factor that some have attempted to quantify. A typical editor's guide might list such limits as no more than 300 words from a scholarly text, no more than 150 words from popular books, no more than 2 lines of song lyrics, and no more than 1 sentence from a newspaper. However, as the Copyright Office warns, "[t]here is no specific number of words, lines, or notes that may safely be taken without permission."[157] The issue of the amount of a work that can be copied often comes up in parody cases. The Supreme Court recently made clear that parody copying may be substantial since copying even of the "heart" of the original may be necessary to the work's parodic purpose.[158]

Effect of Use on Value of the Work The "effect of the use upon the potential market for or value of the copyrighted work" has been described as "undoubtedly the single most important element of fair use."[159] Especially where the copier uses the work in precisely the market it was created for, this factor weighs heavily. An example is where material copied for educational use was itself written for educational use.[160] This factor was an important one in determining that consumer home recording of shows offered for free on television was not infringement, but downloading music from the Internet was. The television recording did not pose substantial harm to the potential market for such shows.[161] But digital downloads available for free necessarily harmed the copyright holders' attempts to charge for the same downloads.[162]

---

153 *Consumers Union v. General Signal Corp.*, 724 F.2d 1044 (2d Cir. 1983).

154 Even with non-fiction, the case can be made that the author's particular description of uncopyrightable facts is a large part of the appeal of the work. *See Harper & Row v. Nation Enterprises*, 471 U.S. 539 (1985) (copying former President Ford's memoirs is not fair use).

155 *Salinger v. Random House*, 811 F.2d 90, 97 (2d Cir. 1987) (paraphrase of famous, reclusive author's unpublished letters in biography of that author was not fair use). *But see* 17 U.S.C.A. §107 ("The fact that a work is unpublished shall not itself bar a finding of fair use if such finding is made upon consideration of all the [fair use] factors.")

156 *Princeton University Press v. Michigan Document Services*, 99 F.3d 1381 (6th Cir. 1996) (*en banc*).

157 Copyright Office Document FL102. Law reviews in the United States typically give copying permission without charge. Other academic journals and commercial publications usually insist on a fee.

158 *Campbell v. Acuff-Rose Music, Inc.* 510 U.S. 569, 589 (1994) (copying of the "heart" of Roy Orbison's "Oh, Pretty Woman" by 2 Live Crew rap group in parody may not necessarily be excessive, but remand ordered to determine whether repetition of the bass riff was excessive copying).

159 *Harper & Row*, *supra* note 154, at 566.

160 *See McMillan v. King*, 223 F. 862 (D. Mass. 1914) (teacher copying of substantial portions of an economics text written for the classroom is not fair use).

161 *Sony Corp. of America*, *supra* note 151, at 451-456.

162 *A&M Records, Inc. v. Napster, Inc.*, 239 F.3d 1004, 1017 (9th Cir. 2001). The fact that there was not yet a developed commercial market for downloading music was deemed irrelevant.

5. Infringement

Direct Infringement Authors or copyright owners can recover damages or obtain appropriate injunctive relief for any infringement on their rights.[163] The most common infringement, copying, is proven usually by showing "substantial similarity" between the works and access by the infringer to the original. However, "independent creation" is a complete defense to infringement. Thus, if a person did not have access to the first work, then the infringement suit fails, even though the result is substantially similar to the first work. Infringement need not be intentional to be actionable. A famous case on this point was the successful suit against George Harrison of the Beatles, whose song, "My Sweet Lord," was held to be an unconscious infringement of an earlier song.[164] In music cases, experts are often called to testify on the issue of copying. But the ultimate issue of whether there is substantial similarity is one for the jury, since the issue is whether the infringer took "so much of what is pleasing to the ears of lay listeners, who comprise the audience for whom [the] music is composed," that there was infringement.[165]

As noted above when fair use was discussed, fiction receives greater protection than non-fiction because of its very nature. There is much greater creative choice in fiction, so similarities in the works being compared will be more suspect, such as similar plots, incidents or characters. Copying a fictional character can be infringement if the character is not a stereotypical figure, is well developed and figures prominently in the work.[166] Characters depicted visually provide an added dimension for comparison. By contrast, non-fiction factual works on the same topic are likely to be quite similar in content, so for there to be infringing similarity of expression there will usually have to be verbatim copying or close paraphrasing.

Contributory Infringement The distributor of a device that is capable of being used by third parties to infringe a copyright is not usually liable for the resulting infringements, especially if the device is capable of substantial non-infringing uses. Thus, a manufacturer of VCR recording machines was not liable for inducing infringement even though many purchasers used its machines to copy movies.[167] However, a distributor is liable for the resulting acts of infringement if it promoted the device's infringing use. In *Metro-Goldwyn-Mayer Studios Inc. v. Grokster, Ltd.*, Grokster software could be used by computer users to swap files, including copyrighted material, and was in fact used and promoted for that purpose. While the Supreme Court agreed that a distributor's mere knowledge of the infringing potential or even of actual infringing use of its software would not be enough for liability, purposeful, culpable expression and conduct promoting infringing use was sufficient for contributory liability.[168]

---

163 17 U.S.C.A. §501(a).

164 The infringed song was "He's So Fine" by the Chiffons. *Bright Tunes Music Corp. v. Harrisongs Music, Ltd.*, 420 F.Supp. 177 (S.D. N.Y. 1976).

165 Arnstein v. Porter, 154 F.2d 464, 473 (2d Cir. 1946) (infringement case against Cole Porter).

166 *See, e.g., Sid & Marty Krofft Television Productions, Inc. v. McDonald's Corp.*, 562 F.2d 1157 (9th Cir. 1977) ("McDonaldland" advertisements infringed "H.R. Puff'n'stuff children's show); *Denker v. Uhry*, 820 F.Supp. 722 (S.D.N.Y. 1992), *aff'd* 996 F.2d 301 (2d Cir. 1993) (play "Driving Miss Daisy" depicting relationship between crusty, bigoted, elderly white woman and her black chauffeur did not infringe novel about crusty, bigoted, elderly Jewish man and his black physical therapist).

167 *Sony Corp. of America* case, *supra* note 151.

168 545 U.S. 913 (2005). The Grokster software, as its name suggests, was promoted as a successor to the banned Napster software. *See Napster* case, *supra* notes 150, 162.

Infringements of Computer Programs As mentioned earlier, computer programs are subject to copyright protection.[169] This includes both the programmer-written (source code) and the converted computer-readable (binary code) versions of the program.[170] However, a programmer can avoid copying the very codes used and yet come up with a result that performs the same functions and has the same structure and organization — sometimes called the "look and feel" of the original program. Courts in some cases have held that structure and organization may be copyrighted, not just the literal computer code. This is by analogy to fictional works, from which it is prohibited, not just to copy verbatim, but sometimes also to copy plots, incidents and characters.[171] However, recent cases have tended to treat computer programs — even those with audiovisual animation — more like non-fiction than creative works. As such, virtual identity of the programs will have to be found for there to be infringement. In a case affirmed by an equally divided Supreme Court, the First Circuit Court of Appeals held that Borland's Quattro Pro spread-sheet program did not infringe Lotus's 1-2-3 program even though Borland copied exactly the 1-2-3 menu command terms and hierarchy, and despite the fact that Lotus developers made some expressive choices in arranging the Lotus command terms. The menu, as a "method of operation," could not be copyrighted.[172]

B. Patent Law

A patent is the right granted to inventors to exclude others from making, using, or selling their invention for a limited period of time.[173] Patents are issued by the U.S. Patent and Trademark Office (USPTO).[174] In the patent application, the inventor must describe the invention in specific terms sufficient to enable others to build it. In this way, the inventor's "secrets" are revealed to the public in exchange for patent protection. This *quid pro quo* provides an incentive for inventors to invent, while at the same time promoting the dissemination of knowledge.

1. Inventions Patentable

Basic Requirements Under §101 of the Patent Act, patents can be granted to anyone who "invents or discovers any . . . process, machine, manufacture, or composition" if it is "novel," "useful," and "non-obvious."[175] Novelty raises the question of

---

169 *See also infra* p. 507 where patent aspects of computer programs are discussed.

170 *See Apple Computer v. Franklin Computer Corp.*, 714 F.2d 1240, 1246-1249 (3d Cir. 1983). The 1984 Semiconductor Chip Protection Act protects computer circuitry. *See* 17 U.S.C.A. §§901-914.

171 See, *e.g.*, *Whelan Associates v. Jaslow Dental Laboratory*, 797 F.2d 1222 (3d Cir. 1986) (dental laboratory infringed software copyright of consulting company that developed record keeping program for laboratory; program structure similar despite use of another computer language).

172 *Lotus Development Corp. v. Borland International*, 49 F.3d 807 (1st Cir. 1995), *aff'd by an equally divided Court*, 516 U.S. 233 (1996). *See also Apple Computer, Inc. v. Microsoft Corp.*, 35 F.3d 1435, 1441-1447 (9th Cir. 1994) (in dispute over "Windows" interface, infringement exists only if Microsoft used virtually identical selection and arrangement of windows; no infringement found). Possible *patent* protection for software installed on a computer as a patented "process" is discussed *infra* pp. 507-509.

173 35 U.S.C.A. §101 *et seq.* There are three types of patents: utility, design and plant patents. Design patents cover new and ornamental designs of useful articles, such as furniture and shoes. Plant patents are issued for new plant varieties, such as flowers and fruit trees. Only utility patents — about 90% of all patents — are discussed here.

174 The web site for the office is www.uspto.gov. It contains a variety of useful information.

175 35 U.S.C.A. §§101-103. A "manufacture" refers to the articles that result from the process of manufacturing, the process by which raw or prepared materials are given new forms or qualities either by hand labor or machinery.

whether the invention was invented or discovered before.[176] Usefulness simply means that the invention has some function of benefit to humanity.[177] An invention is obvious if "the differences between [the invention] sought to be patented and the prior art are such that [it] would have been obvious . . . to a person having ordinary skill in the art to which the [invention] pertains."[178] If the invention "could readily be deduced from publicly available material" by the average expert in the field, it is obvious.[179] The novelty and obviousness requirements insure that "concepts within the public grasp, or those so obvious that they readily could be, are the tools of creation available to all."[180]

Exceptions   Patents may be issued for "anything under the sun that is made by man," but not for "laws of nature, physical phenomena, and abstract ideas."[181] Nonetheless, a naturally occurring substance may be patented if the discoverer has made it in purified or altered form. Thus, a new life form of bacteria genetically altered to eat petroleum wastes was held patentable.[182] Human genes can be patented and roughly 4,000 of the total of 24,000 have been.[183]

Business-Method Patents   "Process" patent claims have caused some difficulties. Many computer programs fall into the "process patent" category, as do business methods. As discussed earlier, computer programs are protected under the Copyright Act. But copyright protects only the particular way the software program is written.[184] A patent can protect against copying the *process* and the *result* produced. For years, the USPTO and the courts maintained that software installed on a computer was a mere "method-of-doing-business" involving a "mathematical algorithm" — an "abstract idea."[185] Computer programs also suffer from lack of novelty and from obviousness, since many such programs simply do more quickly what can already be done manually.[186] In recent year, however, the USPTO has issued patents for several business methods that might otherwise be characterized as little more than ideas. An example

---

176 *See, e.g., In re Donahue*, 766 F.2d 531 (Fed.Cir. 1985) (chemical compound not novel; journal described how to make it).

177 Except in the case of new medicines, the utility requirement is usually not hard to meet. *But see Brenner v. Manson*, 383 U.S. 519 (1966) (steroid compound not shown to have usefulness where possible uses were being investigated and related chemical was useful in treating tumors in mice). Usefulness is sometimes important for establishing an invention date. When two inventors simultaneously produce a chemical compound, it is not the first to develop it, but the first to discover a practical use for it who wins.

178 35 U.S.C.A. §103(a).

179 *Bonito Boats, Inc. v. Thunder Craft Boat, Inc.*, 489 U.S. 141, 150 (1989). *See Graham v. John Deere Co.*, 383 U.S. 1 (1966) (improvements on plow obvious).

180 *Bonito Boats*, 489 U.S. at 156. *Bonito Boats* thus these limitation in the Patent Act as protecting free trade in "unpatented design and utilitarian conceptions." Thus, the Court held, a Florida state law protecting an unpatentable process for creating boat hulls was preempted as interfering with this policy.

181 *Diamond v. Chakrabarty*, 447 U.S. 303, 309 (1980).

182 *Diamond v. Chakrabarty, supra. See also Amgen, Inc. v. Chugai Pharmaceutical Co.*, 927 F.2d 1200 (Fed.Cir. 1991) (concentrated amino acid proteins that stimulate red blood cell production).

183 For more on patent law and other legal aspects of genetic research, *see* Michael J. Malinowksi & Radhika Rao, *Legal Limitations on Genetic Research and the Commercialization of Its Results*, 54 Am. J. Comp. Law 45 (2006). One problem with gene patents is that the U.S.'s research exception to its patent laws is narrow, such that basic research using a patented gene is impossible without the permission of the patent holder.

184 *See* discussion *supra* p. 506.

185 *See Gottschalk v. Benson*, 409 U.S. 63 (1972) (algorithm that converted binary-coded decimals into binary numerals could not be patented because it was an abstract idea).

186 *See Diamond v. Diehr*, 450 U.S. 175 (1981) (process for curing synthetic rubber that utilized a computer to process temperature information and recalculate curing time was a potentially patentable "new and useful process"; irrelevant that the process used a well-known mathematical formula that expressed the relationship between temperature, time and cure).

is the online "reverse auction" on the Internet, whereby consumers name the price they wish to pay and the first seller to agree gets the sale, a patent for which was granted to Priceline. Some have criticized business method patents as tantamount to granting a patent for the "process" of ordering pizza by telephone. However, the Supreme Court recently approved business method process patents in principle and set out guidelines for courts in assessing them.

The Circuit Court of Appeals for the Federal Circuit in 1998 upheld a patent for a software program that, when installed on a computer, took stock prices, processed them through a series of mathematical calculations to produce a waveform display on a monitor.[187] The court approved the patent because, as a practical application of an abstract idea, it produced a "useful, concrete and tangible result." The court saw no distinction between chemical and mechanical, as opposed to electronic, "processes." Ten years later, however, the Federal Circuit changed course, perhaps influenced by the explosion of business method patents and their effect in preempting others from using similar methods without obtaining a license.[188] In 2008, the court limited process patents to any business process that is "tied to a particular machine" or "transforms an article."[189] Applying this test, it rejected as nothing more than an "abstract idea" a claim for a patent for a mathematical formula that explains how commodities buyers and sellers in the energy market can hedge against the risk of price changes.

The Supreme Court granted review of the latter decision in *Bilski v. Kappos*.[190] It agreed that business methods are within patentable subject matter under §101. But the applicant in the case sought "to patent both the concept of hedging risk and the application of that concept to energy markets" — an attempt to patent an abstract idea. Unfortunately, the Court did not set out any specific test for determining what is a patentable business method. The Court disagreed with the Federal Circuit that the "machine-or-transformation" test is the exclusive test for determining patentability of a process. It stated that the test provides a "useful and important clue." Yet, the Court did not offer an example of an invention that would *not* be tied to a machine or transform an article, but would still pass the subject matter test.

The Court instead spoke generally about the need to strike a balance between protecting inventors and the danger of granting monopolies over procedures that others could discover by independent, creative application of general principles. It set out a list of factors that courts must consider in determining what is a proper business method patent: (1) the extent to which use of the concept would preempt its use in other fields; (2) the extent to which the claim is so abstract and sweeping as to cover both known and unknown uses of the concept; (3) the extent to which the claim is a statement of the problem versus a description of a particular solution to the problem; (4) whether the concept is disembodied or whether it is implemented in some tangible way; and (5) whether the performance of the process is observable and verifiable rather than subjective or imperceptible.

---

187 *State Street Bank & Trust Co. v. Signature Financial Group*, 149 F.3d 1368 (Fed.Cir. 1998).

188 To mitigate this preempting effect, Congress in 1999 amended the law to provide a defense to any infringement action with respect to claims in a patent directed to a method of doing business, if the prospective infringer, acting in good faith, had reduced the subject matter to practice at least 1 year before the effective filing date of the patent and had used the subject matter commercially before the effective date of the patent. 35 U.S.C.A. §273(b)(1).

189 *In re Bilski*, 545 F.3d 943 (Fed.Cir 2008). Also required was that "the involvement of the machine or transformation in the claimed process [is] not merely . . . insignificant extra-solution activity."

190 ___ U.S. ___, 130 S.Ct. 3218 (2010)

Since *Bilski*, the USPTO has moved to implement the decision by issuing guidelines for patent examiners.[191] However, the guidelines do not have the force of law and, in any event, are not much more concrete than the Court's opinion. Clearly, patent examiners and courts will have to develop workable standards for determining patent eligibility beyond the machine-or-transformation test.[192]

2. Registration of Patents

Procedure A person wishing to obtain a patent must file a patent application, which must set out (1) "a written description of the invention, and of the manner and process of making and using it, in such full, clear, concise, and exact terms as to enable any person skilled in the art to which it pertains . . . to make and use the same," (2) "the best mode contemplated by the inventor of carrying out his invention" and (3) "one or more claims particularly pointing out and distinctly claiming the subject matter which the applicant regards as his invention."[193] Usually, an inventor will seek the services of a "patent attorney" or "patent agent" who is experienced in preparing patent applications.[194] The application is filed with the U.S. Patent and Trademark Office (USPTO) in Washington, D.C., where it is examined by a patent examiner to ensure that it meets the statutory requirements.[195] The examiner will either reject the application or issue a "Notice of Allowance." If the application is rejected, the applicant has the right to respond and seek to persuade the Examiner that the claims are indeed patentable. Alternatively or additionally, the applicant can amend the claims. However, the applicant cannot introduce subject matter that is not already set forth in the application. If an application is twice rejected, the applicant may appeal the Examiner's decision to the Patent Office's Board of Appeals; if such appeal fails, the applicant can then appeal to the Court of Appeals for the Federal Circuit or the federal District Court for the District of Columbia. A patent holder gives notice to all that the invention is patented by placing the word "Patented" or "Pat.," plus the patent number on the item, or "Patent Pending," if one has been applied for, but not yet granted. This is important because the holder can recover damages only for infringements that occur after the infringer is given notice.

When is an Invention Invented? In contrast to most other countries, the United States follows a "first to invent" standard instead of a "first to file" standard. As the Supreme Court has observed, the "meaning of 'invention' in the Patent Act unquestionably refers to the inventor's conception rather than to a physical embodiment of that idea."[196] The most famous example was the patent for the telephone that was issued to Alexander Graham Bell even though he had filed his application before constructing a

---

191 "Interim Guidance for Determining Subject Matter Eligibility for Process Claims in View of Bilski v. Kappos," 75 Fed. Reg. 43922 (July 27, 2010).

192 In one post-*Bilski* case, a district court rejected a patent for a method for allowing Internet users to view copyrighted material free of charge in exchange for watching certain advertisements, in the process rejecting the contention that the Internet or programmed computers were "machines." *Ultramercial LLC v. Hulu LLC*, 2010 WL 3360098 (C.D.Cal. 2010).

193 35 U.S.C.A. §112.

194 Patent agents are nonlawyers who have the right to prepare, file and argue patent applications with the U.S. Patent Office and Board of Appeals. However, agents do not have the right to give legal advice or appear in court. A patent lawyer is a regular lawyer who has passed the patent bar examination — an exception to the generally unified nature of the legal profession. *See* Chapter IV, p. 138.

195 *See* Utility Examination Guidelines, 66 Fed. Register 1092 (Jan. 5, 2001) and "Written Description" Requirement, 66 Fed. Register 1099 (Jan. 5, 2001). Examiner "training materials" are available on the PTO's website.

196 *Pfaff v. Wells Electronics, Inc.*, 525 U.S. 55 (1998) (invention date was when drawings were sufficient to produce it). Congress has plans to change this order to favor the "first to file."

working model of one.[197] Thus, even though one inventor may win the race to the Patent Office or may produce a working model sooner, another inventor can prevail by proving that he or she first conceived of the invention and showed diligence in reducing the invention to practice. This does not mean that the inventor does not have to worry about timeliness in filing. If one year passes after the invention is in public use or on sale in the United States, or it is patented or described in a printed publication or a patent application is filed for it in any country, the inventor loses the right to obtain a patent. Since some of these triggering events can be taken by unknown third parties, inventors need to carefully monitor various sources of information to avoid being foreclosed.[198]

3. Rights Protected

If the patent application is approved, the inventor has the right to exclude others from making, using or selling the invention for the period of the patent, currently 20 years from the date of filing.[199] A patent cannot be renewed, so it enters the "public domain" at the end of the stated period. During the patent period, the patentee can sell it to another or license others to develop it, on either an exclusive or non-exclusive basis, or the patentee may choose not to develop the device at all.[200] However, the patent owner may not infringe on existing, unexpired patents. This is often an issue when a patent is issued for an improvement on a patented invention. For example, assume inventor A invents a new headache pill and receives a patent for it. Inventor B then invents a *buffered* version of the same medicine that makes it is easier on the stomach, and receives a patent for it. A could prevent B from making and marketing his improved product because doing so would infringe A's patent. Such problems are usually resolved by a cross-licensing agreement between the patent holders that permits both patent holders — and the public — to benefit from the improvement.

4. Infringement

Enforcement Procedures A patent owner can sue anyone who infringes any claim of a patent.[201] If successful, the owner is entitled to invoke the same injunctive and damages remedies available in copyright cases.[202] Other ways of raising the issue of the validity of a patent are by way of a suit for a declaratory judgment by the party wishing to use the patent and a request to the Patent Office to re-examine the patent application it has approved.[203] Before 1982, appeals in both categories of cases went to the appropriate regional federal courts of appeal. The result was variation in interpretations of patent law among those circuit courts. In order to remedy this lack of uniformity and to prevent the rampant forum shopping that had developed — and also to foster the development of judicial expertise in patent litigation — Congress in 1982 created the U.S. Court of

---

197 *Telephone Cases*, 126 U.S. 1 (1888).

198 Triggering events are in 35 U.S.C.A. §102. In *Pfaff, supra* note 196, the inventor had completed the invention when he produced drawings and had concluded sales contracts based on the drawings more than year before he sought patent protection, thus disqualifying himself under §102(b).

199 35 U.S.C.A. §154(a)(2). Certain patented inventions that are subject to considerable delay in being approved by the government for distribution, such as new drugs and medical devices, are given an additional 5 years under certain conditions. 35 U.S.C.A. §156.

200 The lack of a requirement that the patentee "work" the patent distinguishes U.S. patent law from that in many other countries.

201 35 U.S.C.A. §281.

202 35 U.S.C.A. §§284-285. However, upon finding an infringement, it is not an automatic rule that a court should grant injunctive relief. *eBay Inc. v. MercExchange, L.L.C.*,547 U.S.338 (2006). *See* Chapter VII, p. 245 (traditional standards for permanent injunction).

203 35 U.S.C.A. §302.

Appeals for the Federal Circuit and gave it exclusive jurisdiction over appeals in patent infringement cases.[204] Beyond the benefits of greater uniformity, some report that the Federal Circuit appeals court has helped to streamline the process for obtaining patents and to strengthen their protection.[205]

Parallel Imports   A problem with patented goods similar to the "gray-market" copyright problem discussed earlier (*supra* p. 502) is the issue of parallel imports — where patented goods are authorized to be sold abroad, but are then imported back into the U.S. and resold at below the U.S. price. As with copyright, the "first sale" doctrine should mean that the patent owner's rights are exhausted by the sale, thus permitting resale anywhere. However, the Federal Circuit has held that exhaustion takes place upon the first sale only if the sale is in the U.S., and a patentee's sales abroad do not exhaust U.S. patent rights.[206] This rule is based on the territorial limits of U.S. patent laws, which can only govern the effect of sales made in the U.S. By parity of reasoning, if the patentee sells the goods abroad (regardless of what protections the patent law of the country where they are sold provide), then it should be able to assert its U.S. patent rights for the first time when the goods arrive in the U.S. So, a patentee can avoid the parallel import problem at least for goods it sells overseas.

C. Trademark Law

Trademark law originated as common law. It has since been adopted and modified by federal statute, the Lanham Act, which provides procedures for protection of trademarks, including a national system for registration of trademarks.[207]

1. What is a Trademark

Trademarks   A trademark is any distinctive word, name, symbol or device, or any combination thereof, that identifies the origin of particular goods sold in the market-place. A trademark is most commonly a word ("Sprite"), phrase ("Kentucky Fried Chicken"), symbol (the scallop shell of Shell Oil Co.), stylized letters ("Coca-Cola" in script) or design (the McDonald's "golden arches"). Also included is "trade dress" — the overall appearance, image or "look" of goods or services as offered for sale in the marketplace. It includes the appearance of labels, wrappers, and containers used in packaging a product as well as displays and other materials used in presenting the product to prospective purchasers. It may also include visible features of the design of the product itself if they are not purely functional.[208]

A primary policy behind trademark protection is protection of the public from mistake, deception and confusion with regard to the origin of a product. At the same time, consumer preference for a good of a particular origin allows the trademark to be used as a marketing and advertising device.

---

204 28 U.S.C.A. §1295.

205 *But see Holmes Group, Inc. v. Vornado Air Circulation Systems, Inc.*, 535 U.S. 826 (2002) (if patent issue arises in a counterclaim, there is no jurisdiction in the Federal Circuit).

206 *Jazz Photo Corp. v. International Trade Com'n*, 264 F.3d 1094 (Fed.Cir. 2001).

207 15 U.S.C.A. §§1051 *et seq.* The Lanham Act was passed pursuant to interstate commerce clause. Consequently, it is supposed to affect only the interstate use of trademarks. However, as with other exercises of the commerce clause power, the statute is read broadly by courts. *See* Chapter I, p. 25. As is the case with many other common-law-based areas of the law, there is a restatement of the law: RESTATEMENT (THIRD) OF UNFAIR COMPETITION §9 (1995) [hereafter "RESTATEMENT"].

208 *See* RESTATEMENT §16. Also protected are "service marks," which are essentially trademarks attached to services instead of goods and "certification marks," such as "UL Tested" or "Good Housekeeping Seal of Approval." 15 U.S.C.A. §§1053-1054.

Distinctiveness To be a protected trademark, a mark must be distinctive. Courts have recognized points on a spectrum of distinctiveness. From most distinctive to least distinctive, marks can be (1) fanciful, (2) arbitrary, (3) suggestive, (4) descriptive and (5) generic.[209] Fanciful marks are made-up words ("Xerox," "Kleenex," "Exxon"). Arbitrary marks are ordinary words with unexpected associations ("Apple" computers, "Camel" cigarettes). Suggestive marks reflect a particular quality of the product (*e.g.*, "Diehard" car batteries, "Ivory" soap, "Downy" fabric softener), but some imagination is required to associate them with the product. These first three types of marks are presumptively distinctive.

Descriptive Marks Descriptive marks simply describe some positive attribute of the product in ordinary, non-fanciful terms. As such, they are presumed not to be distinctive. However, a descriptive mark may become distinctive if, through use, it has acquired a "secondary meaning" that associates it in the mind of the public with a *particular* product of a particular producer. Examples of such marks are "Realemon," as a mark for a *particular* reconstituted lemon juice that supposedly tastes like real lemons, "Animal Crackers," as a mark for *particular* cookies shaped like animals, and "Instant Breakfast," as a mark for a *particular* powdered breakfast substitute that can be prepared instantly.[210] Secondary meaning is usually acquired only after spending a great deal of advertising money promoting the mark. Colors can also acquire such a secondary meaning, such as pink for a particular brand of home insulation, as long as the color is not merely functional.[211]

Generic Marks A generic mark employs the name of an item or the descriptive phrase that is normally used to refer to it. As such, generic words or phrases cannot satisfy the distinctiveness requirement, since they do no more than state what the item is. For example, "apple" could never be a trademark for apples. Aside from creating confusion, merchants would be unable to describe the fruit they have for sale for fear of infringement.[212]

Secondary Meaning and Trade Dress Trade dress may be inherently distinctive and thus constitute a proper trademark without having acquired a secondary meaning. In *Two Pesos, Inc. v. Taco Cabana, Inc.*,[213] the Supreme Court held that a restaurant's "Mexican trade dress" for its dining services that included "a festive eating atmosphere having interior dining and patio areas decorated with artifacts, bright colors, paintings and murals," was sufficiently distinctive "product packaging" to be protected. More difficulty is involved when a *product design* feature is claimed to be the trade dress, both because design is less likely to be identified with a particular producer and because the

---

209 *Abercrombie & Fitch v. Hunting World*, 537 F.2d 4 (2d Cir. 1976) (Friendly, J.). *See also Two Pesos, Inc. v. Taco Cabana*, 505 U.S. 763, 768 (1992) (approving this approach).

210 *Kellogg Co. v. National Biscuit Co.*, 305 U.S. 111, 118 (1938) (secondary meaning is established when "the primary significance of the term in the minds of the consuming public is not the product, but the producer"; holding that long exclusive use of term "shredded wheat" was not sufficient to give it a secondary meaning necessary for trademark status).

211 *Qualitex v. Jacobson Products*, 514 U.S. 159 (1995) (green-gold color of manufacturer's dry clearing press pads can be registered as they have through use acquired a secondary meaning associated with that particular manufacturer).

212 As a mark for *computers*, however, "apple" is distinctive, as noted earlier. Geographical marks, like generic marks, are not proper trademarks unless they are more than merely descriptive (*e.g.*, London Fog). Immoral or offensive terms or phrases may not become trademarks. *See Bromberg v. Carmel Self Service, Inc.*, 198 U.S.P.Q. 176 (Trademark Tr. & App. Bd. 1978) (mark for a chicken restaurant, "Only a breast in the mouth is better than a leg in the hand," disallowed).

213 505 U.S. 763 (1992).

producer can obtain copyright or patent protection. Consequently, the Court has required that claimed product design trade dress features have acquired a secondary meaning that identifies them with a particular producer in the minds of consumers before they will be protected.[214] The fact that a product design feature is functional eliminates its being protectable trade dress, even if it has acquired a secondary meaning. Otherwise, not only is such a functional use already protectable by patent law, but permitting its "exclusive use" as a matter of trademark law "would put competitors at a significant non-reputation-related disadvantage."[215]

Loss of Distinctiveness A trademark may, through use, lose its distinctiveness and become generic. Thus, the term "aspirin" went from a trademark of the Bayer Company to a generic description of the drug.[216] Other examples are "cellophane,"[217] "shredded wheat,"[218] and "escalator."[219] Though it is rare, sometimes a mark that has become generic or descriptive can be "recaptured" by the owner.[220]

Surnames Surname marks usually describe an establishment, product or service as being that of a particular person, such as Smith's Café. Like other descriptive marks, however, if a secondary association has been established through the public associating the surname with a particular product or service, a surname can become a trademark. For example, "McDonald's" evokes in the minds of most people a particular fast-food restaurant chain. As a result, no other persons named McDonald may use their name to market fast-food, though they could use their name for a different kind of business. But even when the same type of business is involved, courts are reluctant to prevent people from using their own names to promote their businesses because of the inherent unfairness of it. An acceptable compromise is to permit use, but to require a disclaimer.[221] But if the later surname-user is trying to deceive the public or exploit the first user's success, then its use will be prohibited.[222]

2. Registration

Ownership and Registration A trademark owner can apply for registration of the mark with the U.S. Trademark Office. The application will be approved if the mark is in actual use, meets the requirements for trademarks discussed earlier and does not so closely resemble a prior registrant's mark that it would create a likelihood of confusion, deceit or mistake. The mark is then published in the Official Gazette of the Trademark

214 *Wal-Mart Stores, Inc. v. Samara Brothers, Inc.*, 529 U.S. 205 (2000) (fabric and design of a line of children's clothes).

215 *Traffix Devices, Inc. v. Marketing Displays, Inc.*, 532 U.S. 23 (2001) (visible double spring feature of collapsible road signs covered by an expired patent was a functional feature and could not be protected even if it had acquired a secondary meaning; functional nature of the design feature is particularly difficult to avoid when a patent based on that feature was obtained, but has expired).

216 *Bayer Co. v. United Drug Co.*, 272 F. 505 (S.D.N.Y. 1921).

217 *DuPont Cellophane Co. v. Waxed Products Co.*, 85 F.2d 75 (2d Cir. 1936).

218 *Kellogg Co. v. National Biscuit Co.*, supra note 210 at 116.

219 *Haughton Elevator Co. v. Seeberger*, 85 U.S.P.Q. 80, 83 (Comm'r of Patents 1950).

220 *See Singer Manufacturing Co. v. June Manufacturing*, 163 U.S. 169 (1896) ("Singer," while originally distinctive, is now a generic term for all sewing machines) and *Singer Manufacturing Co. v. Briley*, 207 F.2d 519 (5th Cir. 1953) (continuous use of the term of "Singer" as a trademark for over 50 years after 1896 ruling has made it once again a distinctive mark).

221 *See Taylor Wine Co. v. Bully Hill Vineyards, Inc.*, 569 F.2d 731 (2d Cir. 1978) (grandson of Taylor Wine's founder may use his name Taylor in selling his own competing wines, but only with a disclaimer).

222 *See Sardi's Restaurants v. Sardie*, 755 F.2d 719 (9th Cir. 1985) (Sardie using his own name in California to denote his restaurant did not infringe rights of famous Sardi's Restaurant in New York City when his use was "honest and straightforward, with no intent to confuse the public").

Office. However, registration is not necessary to obtain rights in a trademark. All that is required is *actual use* of the mark. There must be evidence of actual "use in commerce," defined as "bona fide use in the ordinary course of trade, and not merely to reserve a right in the mark."[223]

While not required, registration is useful for at least two reasons. First, a certificate of registration of a mark on the principal register "shall be prima facie evidence of the validity of the registered mark"[224] and registration plus 5 years continuous use thereafter makes the mark "incontestable" for so long that it is in actual use.[225] Among other things, this means that an infringer cannot raise the defense that a descriptive mark has not acquired its necessary "secondary meaning."[226] Second, registration provides constructive notice to the entire country, thus avoiding the normal common law limits on a trademark that confine rights in it to the geographical areas where it is being used.[227] Thus, a manufacturer that uses the trademark only in the eastern U.S. can gain protection against infringement in California by registering the mark.[228]

Prior Use Registration is often approved despite prior use by another, because the earlier user has not registered the mark. If so, the rights of the prior user must be recognized and protected. For example, if A uses a mark extensively in 3 western states, but does not register it, and then B starts using the same mark nationally and registers it, A will be permitted to continue as before in the 3 western states, while B owns the mark in the other 47 states.[229]

Review of Trademark Office Decisions Disputes over registration between the applicant and the federal Trademark Office are resolved through an examiner's decision and an administrative appeal to the Trademark Trial and Appeal Board. Thereafter, judicial review is possible in the Court of Appeals for the Federal Circuit and under some circumstances in the federal district court. Any person who "believes he would be damaged by the registration" is permitted to file an opposition proceeding within 30 days, which is then handled by the Trademark Trial and Appeal Board, subject to judicial review.[230]

Contingent Registration As just noted, rights in trademarks are established only by actual use. However, the Act set up in 1988 a system of "contingent" registration based

---

223 15 U.S.C.A. §1127. *See also La Societe Anonyme des Parfums Le Galion v. Jean Patou*, 495 F.2d 1265 (2d Cir. 1974) (registration of mark as part of a "trademark maintenance program" without any "serious effort to merchandise" and with only minimal sales was ineffective to show ownership).

224 15 U.S.C.A. §1057(b).

225 15 U.S.C.A. §1065.

226 *See Park 'N Fly v. Dollar Park and Fly, Inc.*, 469 U.S. 189 (1985) (over dissent arguing that "mark 'Park and Fly' is at best merely descriptive in the context of airport parking," upholding the mark as incontestible because Trademark Office had issued a registration). However, even an incontestable mark may be merely descriptive, thus affecting its strength as a mark and whether it is infringed. *See Petro Stopping Centers v. James River Petroleum, Inc.*, 130 F.3d 88, 92 (4th Cir. 1997) (incontestable mark "Petro" is largely descriptive as applied to gas stations and therefore is not a strong mark for purposes of determining likelihood of confusion). Secondary meaning was discussed *supra* p. 512.

227 15 U.S.C.A. §1072.

228 Registration also entitles the trademark owner to more extensive damages, including treble damages, plus attorney fees. 15 U.S.C.A. §1117. Registration lasts 10 years and is renewable for a like period. A "use affidavit" must be filed every 6 years or the mark will be canceled. 15 U.S.C.A. §1058(a).

229 *SweeTarts v. Sunline, Inc.*, 380 F.2d 923, 928 (8th Cir. 1967) (small candy maker's prior use of "SweeTarts" trademark within three western states entitles it to exclusive use of mark there). *But see SweeTarts v. Sunline, Inc.*, 436 F.2d 705 (8th Cir. 1971) (no likelihood of confusion existed in eight additional states where plaintiff showed only slight market penetration).

230 Trademark cases may be brought in federal court. 15 U.S.C.A. §1121.

on intent to use a trademark. Such registration establishes "constructive use" and provides priority over all but earlier users and contingent filers. Contingent registration can ripen into full registration if the applicant files a statement of actual use within 6 months (extendable for additional 6-month periods to 24 months) after notice that the contingent registration has been allowed.[231] Contingent registration later ratified by actual use may well become the standard method for establishing rights in trademarks in the future.

3. Infringement Suits

Likelihood of Confusion   The owner of an infringed mark may sue for injunctive relief and for damages for wilful infringements in federal court.[232] A mark is infringed when a competing mark is such as to create a "likelihood of confusion" among an appreciable number of "ordinarily prudent purchasers."[233] Actual confusion, while not required, is highly probative of likelihood, so consumer surveys are often performed and used as evidence. The degree of similarity of marks and similarity of the products involved is also important. For example, a motion sickness drug called "Bonamine" is likely to be confused with "Dramamine," a preexisting motion sickness drug,[234] but there is little likelihood of confusion with "Bonamine" computers. How goods are marketed also matters. For example, goods with competing trademarks that are stacked together in a supermarket and subject to "impulse buying" will be treated differently than an expensive item, such as a car, which is purchased only after considered deliberation.[235]

Fair Use   Fair use is a defense to infringement. A common example of fair use is where a manufacturer includes a component in another product and advertises the product as containing that part using its trademark. For example, the label on a computer may proclaim "Intel Inside" in referring to its CPU. Reconditioned goods can be advertised with the trademark of the original manufacturer so long as they are not sold as new items. In addition, as with copyright, parody can be fair use.[236]

D. International Intellectual Property Protection

1. Treaties

Copyright Protection   The United States has joined the Berne Convention for the Protection of Literary and Artistic Works (Berne Convention), but the most meaningful copyright protection is provided by TRIPs, discussed below. In addition, several bilateral treaties may apply to countries that are not signatories to these treaties. However, there are still several countries with which the United States has no copyright treaty in common.

---

231 15 U.S.C.A. §1051(b)-(d).

232 15 U.S.C.A. §1117.

233 *See Mushroom Makers, Inc. v. R.G. Barry Corp.*, 580 F.2d 44, 46 (2d Cir. 1978) (Friendly, J.).

234 *G.D. Searle & So. v. Chas. Pfizer & Co.*, 265 F.2d 385 (7th Cir. 1959).

235 There is now protection against "cybersquatting" — the practice of registering domain names on the Internet, including personal names, in order to then sell them to persons and concerns that are identified with them. *See* 15 U.S.C.A. §1125(d)(1). A recent case under the Act is *Newport Electronics, Inc. v. Newport Corp.*, 157 F.Supp.2d 202 (D.Conn. 2001). For an infringement suit involving domain names, *see Strick Corp. v. Strickland*, 162 F.Supp.2d 372 (E.D.Pa. 2001) (Internet searches could locate the trademark holder with reasonable ease, using standard Internet searching techniques, so no dilution).

236 *Jordache Enterprises v. Hogg Wyld, Ltd.*, 828 F.2d 1482, 1486 (10th Cir. 1987) (no confusion likely between "Jordache" jeans and alleged-infringing "Lardache" jeans). *See also Reddy Communications v. Environment Action Foundation*, 477 F.Supp. 936 (D.D.C. 1979) (use of "Reddy Kilowatt," an electric utility industry trademark, in pamphlets critical of electric utilities held not an infringement; critical point of view made confusion unlikely).

Patent Protection Since 1883, the United States has been a signatory of the Paris Convention on patents, trademarks and "industrial property," which covers patents, trademarks and industrial design. The regime set up by the Convention, like the copyright treaties, guarantees non-discriminatory national treatment of foreign inventors. The Patent Cooperation Treaty came into force with the United States as signatory in 1978. However, its protections are largely procedural, facilitating the filing of parallel patents in signatory countries. There is no patent treaty or other mechanism — outside the European Union — by which an inventor can obtain a patent that is recognized as valid internationally. A major step toward harmonization of procedural requirements for obtaining and maintaining patents was taken in 2000, when 40 member of the World Intellectual Property Organization (WIPO) signed the Patent Law Treaty. The treaty standardizes many of the filing formalities, offers electronic filing, eliminates complicated procedures for filing translations, provide procedures to reinstate rights lost as a result of missing deadlines, and other procedural advantages.[237]

Trademark Protection   As with copyrights, the trademark owner usually must comply with the laws of each foreign country to gain protection in that country. Most foreign countries allow for registration of trademarks without evidence of prior use, so rights can be established without a major financial commitment to marketing efforts. The Madrid Protocol of 1989, to the United States is a signatory effective November 2, 2003, provides for an international registration system administered by the International Bureau of WIPO in Geneva, Switzerland.[238] The trademark owner can simply file one application directly with his or her own national trademark office. Once registered, an international mark is equivalent to an application or a registration of the same mark undertaken directly in each of the countries designated by the applicant. If the trademark office of a designated country does not refuse protection within a specified period, the protection of the mark is the same as if it had been registered by that Office.

2. Trade Agreements

Holding more promise in moving toward true international standards for intellectual property are the agreements and rules administered by the World Trade Organization (WTO), of which the United States is a member. The WTO promulgates rules for the conduct of international trade under General Agreement on Tariffs and Trade (GATT) and other international agreements. These agreements concentrate on lowering tariff and other trade barriers, but also establish some international standards for protections of intellectual property rights.

TRIPs The most important trade agreement for intellectual property is the Agreement on Trade-Related Aspects of Intellectual Property Rights, Including Trade in Counterfeit Goods (TRIPs). TRIPs, like the conventions discussed above, takes a national regime approach and emphasizes the obligation of all signatory parties to provide non-discriminatory access to national protection. But it also establishes detailed substantive minimum standards for patent, copyright and trademark law (as well as for trade secrets and unfair trade practices). Perhaps the most important aspect of TRIPs is that is enforceable. It is enforced by the WTO's general dispute process and non-compliance with a decision can result in the imposition of trade sanctions against the offender.

---

237 This and other WIPO treaties are available from the WIPO's web site: www.wipo.org/treaties/en.
238 *See generally* 15 U.S.C.A. §1126 for international aspects of trademarks.

Substantive standards for copyright include required protection for computer programs on the same basis as literary works, protection of compilations of databases or other material to the extent selection or arrangement of their contents constitute "intellectual creations," a minimum term of protection of at least 50 years, provisions for authors to limit rental rights for computer programs and films, and various protections for performers, including the ability to limit recording and broadcasting of performances.

TRIPs patent law standards include minimum exclusive rights, including the right to assign, transfer outright, or license the patent, prescription of the manner in which applicants for patents are required to disclose their inventions, and a required minium 20-year term of patent protection, calculated from the date of filing of the application. Nations are permitted to prohibit or limit inventions concerning human, animal or plant life, patents that seriously affect the environment, or patents on biological processes. While trademark standards permit members to condition registrability on actual use, actual use cannot be a condition for filing an application for registration. They also provide a minimum initial 7-year term and renewal for an indefinite period, and establish "likelihood of confusion" as the test for infringement. Misidentification of geographical origin and disallowance of trademarks with such misdescriptions are prohibited. It also sets forth requirements that must be met for the use of geographic marks in connection with wines or liquor.[239]

---

[239] A course book on international intellectual property is DORIS E. LONG & ANTHONY D'AMATO, INTERNATIONAL INTELLECTUAL PROPERTY (West 2000). Treaties and trade agreements referred to here are set out in the collection of intellectual property laws cited *supra* note 112.

CHAPTER XIII

FAMILY LAW

Family law has traditionally been considered the special province of the states. However, as discussed in the chapter on constitutional law, federal constitutional law has increasingly played a role, especially in the development of the fundamental right to privacy in family matters.[1] Moreover, Congress has intervened with the power and resources of the federal government in some family law areas, notably in providing assistance to needy families and in enforcing child support obligations.[2] The Uniform Law Commissioners have been active in the family law area, but have had mixed success in attracting states to adopt uniform laws, undoubtedly because of the strong feeling that family law policy issues generate in state legislatures.[3] As a result, the law can vary considerably from state to state.[4]

Most state law governing family matter is statutory. Yet, court decisions are of paramount importance because statutory provisions tend to be general. At most, statutes will list factors courts are to consider in making decisions, thus leaving much to the discretion of the court and making much depend on the facts of each case.

A. Marriage

1. Ceremonial Marriages

Legal capacity to marry is fulfilled when an individual is of legal age, mentally competent, and not already married. Age requirements vary among states, ranging generally from 16 to 18 years old. Mental competence, which requires that a person understand the nature and consequences of marriage at the time of the act, is presumed unless it is proven that a person either was mentally ill or was involuntarily intoxicated. In the case of someone who is mentally ill, a legal guardian must give consent to the marriage.[5] Both parties must freely consent to the marriage. If one party is coerced under duress to marry the other, the marriage is invalid. Free and voluntary consent may also be vitiated by fraud, jest or some other ulterior motive. The procedure for marrying begins with the couple obtaining a marriage license issued by the county clerk. This requirement is typically perfunctory unless the applicants have a close blood

---

1 *See* Chapter IX, pp. 364-367.

2 *See infra* this chapter, pp. 535-537.

3 *See, e.g.,* UNIFORM MARRIAGE AND DIVORCE ACT (1979) (UMDA); UNIFORM PARENTAGE ACT (2000, 2002)(UPA); UNIFORM RECIPROCAL ENFORCEMENT OF SUPPORT ACT (1979); UNIFORM STATUS OF CHILDREN OF ASSISTED CONCEPTION ACT (1988); UNIFORM CHILD CUSTODY JUDGMENT ACT (1968); UNIFORM PREMARITAL AGREEMENT ACT (1983); UNIFORM ADOPTION ACT (1994); UNIFORM MARITAL PROPERTY ACT (1987), and others available at www.nccusl.org/Update/. An multi-volume annotated source is UNIFORM LAWS ANNOTATED (West 2010). *See* Chapter I, p. 34, note 155 (Uniform Law Commissioners).

4 For a hornbook treatment of family law *see* HOMER H. CLARK, JR., THE LAW OF DOMESTIC RELATIONS IN THE UNITED STATES, 2D ED. (West 1998). See also JOHN D. GREGORY, PETER N. SWISHER & SHERYL L. WOLF, UNDERSTANDING FAMILY LAW, 3D ED. (Lexis 2005).

5 A legal guardian is a person appointed by a court to supervise the affairs of persons who are mentally or physically incompetent to manage their own affairs. *See infra* p. 547.

relationship[6] or are of the same sex,[7] or one or both lack legal capacity, such as where one of the parties is already married. After an application for a marriage license is submitted, most states impose a brief waiting period, usually 3 days to a week, before a license is issued. Many states require a blood test to check for sexually transmitted diseases, such as syphilis or gonorrhea, though the right to marry is not denied based on the results. Some states have imposed testing requirements for acquired immune deficiency syndrome (AIDS).

Finally, the parties must solemnize their marriage through someone authorized by law to do so. A religious representative will do, such as a priest, rabbi, or minister. Some civil officials have that power, such as a judge or the mayor of a city. Most commonly solemnization involves a ceremony during which the couple announces their intent and desire to be married. The secular purposes for this requirement are to give public notice and to impress upon the parties the serious nature of the commitment they are making.

2. Common Law Marriages

Approximately one-fourth of the states recognize "common law" marriages. These marriages technically meet none of the formal requirements described above. Thirty-seven states have either passed statutes or decided by case law to abolish common law marriages.[8] These informal marriages are entered into by the parties pursuant to an agreement to be married, but without the formalities of a license and solemnization. The agreements are almost never written and are rarely agreed to in explicit detail by the parties. In fact, most often they are implied after the fact by courts, which draw inferences about the existence of an agreement from the conduct of the parties. If a valid common law marriage can be proven, then it will entitle the spouses or children to the same benefits and legal rights outlined above for a ceremonial marriage. The most common situation where common law marriage is sought to be proven is where one partner dies and the other seeks to claim a share of the estate or some form of other benefits tied to marriage, such as workers' compensation payments or Social Security benefits.

Courts determining whether a common law marriage existed will consider whether the couple held themselves out to the public as husband and wife, whether they cohabited, filed joint tax returns, maintained a joint bank account or undertook any other actions which indicated their intent to be married. The couple must also have manifested a present intent to be husband and wife and must have the capacity to marry. An intent to ceremonially marry in the *future* may preclude a finding of a present intent to be husband and wife.[9]

A common law marriage will be recognized by all states if it was valid where and when it was entered into. This follows from the conflicts of law rule that the law of the place of the marriage controls, regardless of where the couple travels thereafter.

---

6 Many states prohibit an uncle and niece and aunt and nephew from marrying. Only a few states forbid first cousin marriages. CLARK, *supra* note 4, at §2.9. The issue of whether relatives are "marriageable" also determines whether sexual relations between them will be considered incest. *See Tapscott v. State*, 684 A.2d 439 (Md. 1996) (defendant's sexual liaison with his half-blood niece violated prohibition against incest; case cites many sources and traces history of incest laws).

7 *But see infra*, p. 537.

8 Some of these states qualify this restriction. For example, in Indiana, a common law marriage may be recognized for worker's compensation purposes if it both occurred before 1958 and was open and notorious for five years before the party's death. West's Ann. Ind. Code §22-3-3-19 (2010). For a complete listing of state statutes, see CLARK, *supra* note 4, at §2.4.

9 *In re Estate of Shepherd*, 646 N.E.2d 561 (Ohio App. 1994) (co-habitant not a "surviving spouse").

Consequently, a common law marriage legally formed in one state will be recognized as valid even by the states that do not permit common law marriages.[10]

3. Marriage and Property Rights

Common Law Under traditional common-law principles, a single women had legal capacities similar to men's. But upon marriage, that all changed. As Blackstone described it, "[b]y marriage, the husband and wife are one person in law; that is, the very being or legal existence of the woman is suspended during the marriage, or at least is incorporated and consolidated into that of the husband . . . ."[11] A married woman could neither enter into contracts, nor could she sue or be sued. Any real or personal property belonging to the wife was controlled by the husband upon marriage. The wife's personal property actually became the property of her husband, and on his death passed to his personal representative. Even such items as clothing and jewelry were owned by the husband, although these did come back to the wife if the husband died. While the wife retained the right to direct to whom real property owned by her *prior* to the marriage would go upon her death, the husband had control over that property, including any rents or profits generated by land, for the duration of the marriage.[12]

Married Women's Property Acts In England, as early as the 1600s and 1700s, equity courts began to develop exceptions to common law rules limiting women's legal capacities. This resulted in creation of the *feme sole* estate. This device permitted married women to control their separate property much like a single woman could, and shielded it from the husband's creditors. The more pervasive solution, however, were the many "Married Women's Property Acts" (MWPAs). By 1900, all states had enacted one. However, the laws fell far short of granting married women full legal capacity. Also, courts had a tendency to interpret the statutes as narrowly as possible. Eventually, the MWPAs provided full rights and responsibilities to the married woman, permitting her to own, convey or sell property, to contract, engage in business, seek employment and keep her own earnings. A married woman could sue or be sued, make a will and testify in court. Finally, she became fully responsible for her own criminal and tortious conduct.

The MWPAs, however, did not undermine the husband's position as head of the household or the wife's duty to provide him with household services. Moreover, by providing that the property of each spouse, whether acquired before or during the marriage, remained that spouse's property, MWPAs hurt most women. Most women had no property of their own. For them, the only effect of a MWPA was the negative one of assuring that wives had no property interest in their husbands' earnings.

---

10 There is an exception where the marriage "violates the strong public policy of another state which had the most significant relationship to the spouses and the marriage at the time of the marriage." RESTATEMENT (SECOND) OF CONFLICTS §283. Section 284 provides that a state usually gives the same incidents to a valid foreign marriage that it gives to a marriage contracted within its territory. RESTATEMENT §284. *See also* Chapter VII, p. 264. The Constitution's "full faith and credit" clause may also require it. *See* Chapter VII, p. 261. *Cf. infra* p. 539.

11 1 WILLIAM BLACKSTONE, COMMENTARIES ON THE LAWS OF ENGLAND 445 (1765-1769) (William S. Hein & Co. 1992).

12 Upon death of the husband, the fact that his property went to his heirs often left the widow destitute. The common law developed the concepts of dower and curtesy to protect surviving spouses. These doctrines permitted the wife to claim a certain portion of the husband's estate (dower) or the husband to claim a certain portion of the wife's estate (curtesy) regardless of the deceased spouse's will. Later these became the "statutory elective share" a spouse can choose instead of what is provided for in the deceased spouse's will. *See* Chapter XII, p. 494.

The Common Law Separate Property Approach Upon Divorce   The vast majority of the states follow the common law separate property approach, as adjusted by MWPAs. But this approach is modified by divorce laws that require, upon divorce, that there be an "equitable distribution" of the property acquired during marriage to achieve a fair settlement between the spouses. This is based on the idea that marriage is a shared enterprise and the assets of this enterprise should accrue to both partners in light of the contributions of each, including homemaking services.

Community Property Approach   A minority of the states have adopted what is called a "community property" approach, borrowed from the civil law systems in Europe. Under this concept, all property acquired during the marriage is community property and both spouses share an ownership interest in it from the time that it is acquired. Property acquired prior to marriage, gifts or inheritances either spouse acquires during marriage and any profits earned on separate property remain separate property, unless commingled. Upon divorce, spouses retain their separate property and the community property is divided equally. While the community property concept seems simple, much litigation has arisen on its application to the many different forms of property acquired during marriage, such as veterans' benefits, damages for personal injuries, and property acquired before marriage but paid for in part with community funds. Rebuttable presumptions have developed that property acquired during the marriage, regardless of who acquired it, is community property.[13]

Premarital Agreements   In most states, the parties may predetermine contractually what marital property or support rights will accrue upon marriage. This is done by means of a premarital agreement, sometimes called a "prenuptial" or "antenuptial" agreement. Traditionally such agreements could affect property rights only upon death of a spouse. Common situations were a marriage of people with grossly disproportionate financial assets or marriage of two older people who wanted to protect the inheritance rights of children from previous marriages. In recent years, however, premarital agreements have had the broader purpose of affecting property distribution upon divorce. Not all courts will recognize agreements in contemplation of divorce, usually on the ground that they encourage divorce.[14] But some courts maintain that there is no real evidence that premarital agreements encourage divorce and that, given that divorce is "such a commonplace fact of life," it makes sense to permit the parties to agree on what property and alimony rights should accrue to the parties "in the event their marriage, despite their best efforts, should fail."[15]

Even in states that honor premarital agreements, however, courts tend to require that there be complete disclosure of both parties' assets and liabilities and that the agreement be "fair." Courts will refuse to enforce an agreement that is grossly unfair or one-sided, especially when it is evident that one party took advantage of the other party's ignorance or lack of knowledge in business affairs. They will also take into account the fact that it may be difficult for the parties to predict what their circumstances will be at

---

13 *See, e.g., Brebaugh v. Deane*, 118 P.3d 43 (Ariz.App. 2005) (when husband had stock options that had not vested before divorce complaint was served, whether they were community property to be divided depended on whether they were compensation for past performance, incentives for future performance or some combination of both).

14 *See Mulford v. Mulford*, 320 N.W.2d 470 (Neb. 1982) (ignoring premarital agreement that waived any right to alimony, attorney fees, costs, property or support in the event of divorce).

15 *Newman v. Newman*, 653 P.2d 728, 732 (Colo. 1982) citing *Posner v. Posner*, 233 So.2d 381, 384 (Fla. 1970). *See generally* J. Thomas Oldham, *Premarital Agreements Are Now Enforceable Unless . . .* , 21 HOUSTON L. REV. 757 (1984).

the time of divorce, and equity will step in if necessary to adjust for such changes.[16] The courts are more willing to enforce a prenuptial agreement when the weaker partner (traditionally the wife) had independent counsel.[17] In 1983, the Uniform Premarital Agreement Act was drafted and has since been adopted in 27 states. It makes such agreements enforceable, but codifies the case law exceptions just described.[18]

B. Dissolution of Marriages

1. Divorce

Grounds A divorce action is a civil lawsuit in equity.[19] Traditionally, to obtain a divorce in the United States, one party was required to show that the other party was at fault. While state statutes have varied somewhat, the traditional grounds have been similar: habitual drunkenness, adultery, physical cruelty, mental cruelty, abandonment, and insanity. However, a revolution in divorce law was spurred by California's enactment in 1969 of a "no-fault" divorce statute.[20] California provides "irreconcilable differences" or "incurable insanity" as grounds for divorce. The Uniform Law Commissioners approved §302 of the Uniform Marriage and Divorce Act in 1970, providing as the sole ground for divorce "that the marriage is irretrievably broken."[21] This means, in general, that a divorce can be granted if one person wants it. The policy behind no-fault divorces is that they avoid invading the family's privacy, reduce the acrimony between the couple and, where both parties want the divorce, eliminate the need to "create" grounds that meet the requirements of the law. Most important, fault can be taken into account in determining child custody, property settlements and spousal support. Fault issues can be especially hard fought when proof of marital fault disqualifies the offending party from receiving any spousal support.[22]

Many statutes impose a waiting period before a divorce judgment can be entered. Typical periods are 60 days for couples with no children and 6 months for couples with children.[23] However, in some states the waiting period may be longer, in some cases up to two years. Also, some states have read the requirement that the marital relationship be *truly* irretrievably broken to require that there be some evidence of unsuccessful attempts to work out problems or to reconcile. Counseling is usually made available for couples who might be able to reconcile.[24]

For many years, New York was the only state that still required that fault to be shown to get a divorce. This situation changed in 2010, when the governor signed a new no-fault divorce law into law. Because of this change, an extensive discussion of how fault regimes work is not necessary here. However, two recent cases illustrate New York's fault system and demonstrate a large part of the reason why it was abolished. In

---

16 *Reilling v. Reilling*, 474 P.2d 327 (Or. 1970) (distinguishing premarital agreements from separation agreements, since the latter affect present, known financial circumstances).

17 *Del Vecchio v. Del Vecchio*, 143 So.2d 17 (Fla. 1962) (where wife had no counsel and full disclosure of the extent of the husband's assets was not made, agreement will not be honored on his death and a court must order adequate provision for wife).

18 UNIFORM PREMARITAL AGREEMENT ACT, *supra* note 3.

19 Equity is discussed in Chapter VII, p. 243. Divorces were first handled in ecclesiastical courts.

20 *See* Cal.Fam. Code § 2310. *See* CLARK, *supra* note 4, §12.1 for a brief history of divorce law.

21 UMDA §302.

22 Fault grounds and defenses for divorce will not be discussed here. The role of fault in other aspects of divorce is discussed *infra* p. 525.

23 Mich. Comp. L. Ann. §552.9f. *See also* Cal. Fam. Code §2339 (6 months for all couples).

24 *See Riley v. Riley*, 271 So.2d 181 (Fla. App. 1972) (statute imposing a three-month period for possible reconciliation and counseling).

one the appellate court denied a divorce on grounds of cruel and inhuman treatment of the wife by means of constant verbal abuse and refusal to spend time with her, since no effect on her health was shown.[25] In another, the same court held the "vastly conflicting testimony offered by plaintiff and defendant" in the case was sufficient to prove that the wife had had an affair.[26] Needless to say, New York's system often causes a "fraud or flight" reaction, as some have called it — people either faking grounds or going to other states for a divorce — not the original intended purpose of trying to preserve marriages. Matrimonial lawyers seemed to like it, however.

Procedural Requirements for Divorce Most states require in general that at least one spouse be "domiciled" in the state where the complaint for divorce is filed, meaning that the state must be the permanent home of that spouse.[27] States impose "durational residency" requirements, mandating that the plaintiff live in the state continuously for a given length of time. This period varies with the state and ranges from 6 weeks to 2 years. The most common length is 6 months.[28] The main reason for the requirement is to provide objective evidence of a party's domicile in a state as proof that that state's court has proper jurisdiction over the divorce action.[29]

Settlement and Alternative Dispute Resolution Many feel that it is a mistake to give the judicial system the primary task of handling marital breakups. Among the reasons are that the judicial setting encourages an adversarial relationship between the two spouses, even when the parties approach it amicably, and that it gives the advantage to the party with the greater resources, a serious concern in marital breakups where one party (usually the wife) is in a much worse financial circumstance than the other. In addition, it is a waste of precious judicial resources, given that over half the civil cases filed in state courts of general jurisdiction are divorces.

No state has taken courts completely out of divorce cases, but courts routinely "lean on" the parties to settle as many issues as possible out of court and efforts have been made to use non-judicial resources whenever possible. Out of court settlement efforts often do little to reduce acrimony, as settlement negotiations can often be as contentious as contested court proceedings.[30] However, mediation has been touted as one option for settling marital settlement disputes in a less hostile environment. Arbitration, like mediation, is an informal procedure that offers the advantage of saving time and money. However, in the family law area, enforceability of arbitration decisions is less sure than in other areas of the law. Courts have been careful to assure that the best interests of

---

25 *Omahen v. Omahen*, 735 N.Y.S.2d 236 (App.Div. 2001) (epithets included "Japanese Polack").

26 *Gentner v. Gentner*, 736 N.Y.S.2d 431 (App.Div. 2001).

27 The Supreme Court has likewise assumed that domicile is necessary for jurisdiction in a divorce case. *See Williams v. North Carolina*, 325 U.S. 226, 229 (1945). For a discussion of jurisdiction and procedural issues in divorce actions see CLARK, *supra* note 4, §§12.2-12.5 and Chapter 14.

28 Residency requirements of up to one year have been held constitutional. *Sosna v. Iowa*, 419 U.S. 393 (1975). *Compare Shapiro v. Thompson*, 394 U.S. 618 (1969) (durational residence requirement for need-based welfare eligibility violates fundamental right to travel).

29 A county residency requirement is also imposed usually. It is shorter in duration than the state residency requirement, usually between seven and ten days. It is imposed to deter parties from flocking to a particular court in the state perceived as more favorable to certain interests and to spread the divorce docket rationally among the courts of the state.

30 See CLARK, *supra* note 4, §14.8 for a complete discussion of alternative methods of dispute resolution.

all concerned, particularly any children involved, are protected in divorce cases. Thus, courts are not likely to approve arbitration decisions without first reviewing them.[31]

2. Annulment and Legal Separation

Annulments When a couple has obtained a license and solemnized the marriage, but has failed to meet the other requirements for a valid marriage, such as consent or capacity, the couple may be eligible for an annulment. An annulment is a legal recognition that the marriage was invalid. Despite annulments declaring that no valid marriage took place, courts usually treat them just as they would a divorce — apportioning property, assets and debts, and determining the custody and support of children. Alimony, however, is generally not awarded. Courts deem such action necessary to restore the parties to the same position they were in prior to the invalid marriage and to protect any children involved. Nearly all states' laws provide that any children of the union will not be made "illegitimate" as a result of the annulment. However, some states require good faith intent to enter into a valid marriage.[32] Because divorce has become more prevalent, more socially acceptable, and easier to get, fewer legal annulments are sought or granted by the courts.[33]

Legal Separations Couples may choose legal separation as a way to gain a perspective on their marriage while deciding whether to divorce. Others, for various reasons, may wish to live apart on a permanent basis, but to remain married. A permanent legal separation of this type is known as a "divorce from bed and board" or divorce *a mensa et thoro*, and is recognized in about half the states. In such cases, a court order is entered specifying the terms of the separation, including resolution of property and child-related issues, much like a divorce. The main difference is that the parties may not remarry. If the parties later decide to divorce, another legal proceeding is necessary. For this reason, many lawyers advise their clients to forego legal separations and either file for divorce or separate without a court order.[34]

3. Alimony and Property Settlement

a. Distinction Between Alimony and Property Settlements

"Alimony," sometimes called "spousal support," is money paid by one spouse to the other for financial support pursuant to court order. Payment can be made either in a lump sum or periodically. Periodic payments can be for a definite or indefinite period of time. Generally, the death of the payer or payee will terminate the obligation to pay alimony. The remarriage of the payee or other major changes in the financial circumstances of either party may be grounds for modifying alimony, unless the alimony order expressly states otherwise.[35]

---

31 Mediation and arbitration in civil cases were discussed in Chapter VII, p. 251. At least one commentator has protested use of mediation in divorces as disadvantageous to women. Trina Grillo, *The Mediation Alternative: Process Dangers for Women*, 100 YALE L.J. 1545 (1991).

32 In the absence of statute, the common law considered all such children to be illegitimate. Because of recent cases holding much discrimination against illegitimate children unconstitutional, the consequences of illegitimacy are not as serious as they used to be. *See* Chapter IX, p 362.

33 Religious annulments are different. Most commonly a religious annulment is sought by a Roman Catholic who wishes to remarry in a Catholic church. Religious annulments and not recognized by law, so the parties to them have usually already obtained a civil divorce.

34 Couples are also considered legally separated pursuant to a formal agreement or a temporary order of the court while the divorce case is pending.

35 Historically, the husband's legal duty to provide for his wife was the basis for the right to alimony, so many state alimony statutes provided that only wives could receive alimony. However, the Supreme Court has held such statutes to be unconstitutional sex discrimination in violation of the equal protection

In contrast to alimony, property settlements try to achieve an equitable division of the *assets* of the marriage and typically divide those assets by way of lump-sum payments or specific awards of particular items of property to one or the other party. Assets are determined and evaluated based on several factors, typically the parties' contributions, including homemaking and child rearing services, and other equities, such as what property the parties brought to the marriage and the duration of the marriage.

Both property settlements and alimony may consist of periodic payments or a lump sum and the payments could well be classified as one or the other. But how they are characterized can have important ramifications. First, a property settlement is not taxable income to the *recipient* under federal income tax laws. Similarly, the transfer of property does not create a tax deduction for the *payer*. Alimony, however, *is* taxable income to the *recipient* and can be *deducted* from the *payer's* gross income in calculating income tax due. Second, although a property settlement may have more favorable tax consequences for the recipient, there are some disadvantages. The obligation to comply with a property award is dischargeable in bankruptcy, while the obligation to pay alimony is not. Finally, while property settlements generally cannot be modified, alimony awards may be modified where warranted by a change in circumstances, as discussed above. Modifiability is a risk factor that may positively or negatively affect a dependent spouse's standard of living in the future. The paying spouse may argue for the entire settlement to be treated as a property settlement so that the receiving spouse cannot modify it in the future. In contrast, the receiving spouse may wish to include some alimony in the settlement to preserve the right to future modification.

b. Determining the Amount of Alimony Awards and Property Settlements

As noted earlier, some states, while retaining no-fault grounds for *divorce*, effectively provide for "fault" grounds to be considered in resolution of issues of alimony, property division and child custody. But these are often the only issues the parties fight about, so reintroducing fault undercuts the purposes of no-fault legislation. Consequently, some states prohibit consideration of fault at any point in the divorce. For example, the UMDA provides that the amount and duration of spousal support is to be determined "without regard to marital misconduct."[36]

Alimony States statutes typically grant the courts broad discretion in determining the amount of an alimony award and provide only factors to be considered. The UMDA[37] is typical in listing in §308 the following factors: (1) the financial resources of the party seeking alimony including marital property received in a settlement, any child support payments which include a sum for the party as custodian, and the party's earning potential; (2) the time necessary for the spouse seeking alimony to acquire sufficient education or training to enable that spouse to re-enter the job market; (3) the standard of living established during the marriage; (4) the duration of the marriage; (5) the age and physical and emotional condition of the spouse seeking alimony; and (6) the financial status of the spouse from whom alimony is sought.

---

clause of the 14th Amendment. *See Orr v. Orr*, 440 U.S. 268 (1979) and Chapter IX, p. 360.

36 UMDA §308. The factors to be considered are discussed below.

37 *See supra* note 3.

Courts today award alimony less often than in the past and for shorter periods of time. One state, Texas, does not allow alimony under any circumstances.[38] Other state statutes strictly limit the situations in which alimony can be awarded. The property settlement is replacing alimony as the principal means of adjusting the parties' financial relationship in most states.

Property Settlements In all states — whether common law separate property" or community property states — courts seek to divide property equitably and have wide discretion in determining which spouse gets what property. The UMDA, for example, requires the court to consider all the assets of the parties, whenever acquired, and (1) the duration of the marriage; (2) prior marriages of either party; (3) any prenuptial agreements; (4) the age, health, occupation, earning power, and employability of the parties; (5) the liabilities and needs of each party; and (6) any alimony received.

c. Agreements on Alimony and Property Settlement

In most cases, the parties will agree to particular financial and other arrangements and present the agreement to the court for approval. One ground for avoiding the effect of a settlement agreement is that it is "unconscionable."[39] Courts have tended to insist that such agreements not only be free of fraud and coercion, but also that they be "fair and sufficient in light of the station in life and circumstances of the parties."[40] Invalidation of a settlement agreement is most likely to be invoked successfully at the behest of the traditionally weaker party, the wife. Husbands have more difficulty arguing that they were forced into one-sided agreements.[41]

If approved by the court, settlement agreements are often incorporated into the divorce decree. This may be done either by referring to a separate agreement or by simply copying the agreement's terms into the divorce judgment. Either procedure allows the agreement to be enforced in the same manner as any other judgment.

d. Property Subject to Division

Virtually any thing that can be evaluated and the value divided between the parties is potentially property that may be divided upon divorce. Divisible property includes not only houses, cars, business property, cash, stocks, bonds, and accounts, but also pension rights, disability payments and medical insurance.[42] Even more intangible things, such as the "good will" generated by a business or professional practice, are considered in most states to be marital property. Such property may be evaluated and part of its value ordered paid to a party.[43]

Recently, there has been a trend to expand the concept of divisible property to include "career assets" or "human capital." These terms refer to a college or profes-

---

38 *See, e.g., Tinsley v. Tinsley*, 512 S.W.2d 74 (Tex.Civ.App. 1974).

39 UMDA §306.

40 *Crawford v. Crawford*, 350 N.E.2d 103 (Ill.App. 1976).

41 *Compare Jameson v. Jameson*, 239 N.W.2d 5 (S.D. 1976) (though the agreement was "harsh" from the husband's standpoint, it would not be invalidated on grounds of unconscionability) *with In re Marriage of Hitchcock*, 265 N.W.2d 599 (Iowa 1978) (agreement invalidated at wife's request even though she was represented by counsel and advised by her brother).

42 *See Schober v. Schober*, 692 P.2d 267 (Alaska 1984) (state policeman's unused personal leave time from work was deemed to be a divisible marital asset by analogy to a pension). *But see Boyd v. Boyd*, 323 N.W.2d 553 (Mich.App. 1982) (refusing to evaluate and divide husband's seniority at work).

43 *See Wisner v. Wisner*, 631 P.2d 115 (Ariz.App 1981) (community property state) and *Moffitt v. Moffitt*, 749 P.2d 343 (Alaska 1988) (common law state). But see *Nail v. Nail*, 486 S.W.2d 761 (Tex. 1972) (good will of medical practice is an attribute of a particular person that cannot be transferred, so it is not community property).

sional degree which one spouse earned during the marriage while the other spouse worked and supported the family. The essence of this development is to allow the court to reach future earnings, which many believe is the only way to achieve economic fairness when one spouse has sacrificed to put the other through school. Traditionally, alimony was awarded to remedy inequities of this sort. However, the growing antipathy toward alimony has caused courts to categorize some professional degrees acquired during marriage as a marital asset that can be divided as part of the property settlement. In *O'Brien v. O'Brien*,[44] a New York court found that the wife had contributed 76% of the household's income during the period the husband pursued his medical degree, determined that the present value of the degree was $188,000 and that the wife was entitled to 40% of that amount.[45] Other courts have refused to categorize professional and college degrees as marital property because degrees are not property that can be transferred, inherited or acquired by merely paying money[46] or because alimony provides the better method of dealing with the issue.[47] But even in these states the contributions of a spouse toward the other spouse's acquisition of an advanced degree is taken into account in determining property settlements or alimony.

4. Custody of Children

The issue of the custody of children most often comes up when there is a divorce, but it may arise in other contexts as well. In general, courts treat custody disputes in an identical fashion whether the parents are married to each other or not. This change over the last 40 years has been brought about in part by constitutional decisions by the Supreme Court[48] and in part by the leadership of the Uniform Law Commissioners, who have amended the Uniform Parentage Act over the years to virtually eliminate the distinction between "legitimate" and "illegitimate" children.[49]

Legal custody of a child includes the right to make all decisions pertaining to the child's upbringing, including education, health care, religion, growth and development. It usually includes physical custody of the child as well. Thus, the child will live with the custodial parent and is under that parent's physical supervision. Custody generally lasts as long as the child remains a minor; it may extend beyond the age of majority for a mentally disabled child.

---

44   489 N.E.2d 712 (N.Y. 1985).

45   *See also Woodworth v. Woodworth*, 337 N.W.2d 332 (Mich.App. 1983) (plaintiff-wife worked to support the family while the husband was in law school; law degree was the product of a concerted family effort and the result of mutual sacrifices and efforts by both the husband and wife).

46   *See In re Marriage of Graham*, 574 P.2d 75 (Colo. 1978) and *In re Marriage of Weinstein*, 470 N.E.2d 551 (Ill.App. 1984).

47   *McLain v.McLain*, 310 N.W.2d 316 (Mich.App. 1981). *See also Graham*, *supra* note 46 and *In re Marriage of Sullivan*, 691 P.2d 1020 (1984) (community property jurisdictions).

48   *See Stanley v. Illinois*, 405 U.S. 645 (1972) (law presuming unwed father to be unfit parent and depriving him of custody after mother's death was unconstitutional). *Compare Quilloin v. Walcott*, 434 U.S. 246 (1978) (state may deny putative father veto right over adoption of child by future stepfather, when birth father had no relationship with child) and *Lehr v. Robertson*, 463 U.S. 248 (1983) (not unconstitutional for adoption to take place without notice to putative father who had established no custodial, personal, or financial relationship with the child) *with Caban v. Mohammed*, 441 U.S. 380 (1979) (mother-only consent to adoption unconstitutional where biological father had lived with mother and child and established a relationship with the child). *See also infra* note 89.

49   Uniform Parentage Act, *supra* note 3. While the most recent versions of the Act have not been adopted in many states, the Act has had a major influence on the laws in most states. For an excellent article on the changing law of parenthood, *see* David D. Meyer, *Parenthood in a Time of Transition: Tensions Between Legal, Biological, and Social Conceptions of Parenthood*, 54 AM.J.COMP.L. 125 (2006).

a. Presumptions and Factors in Awarding Custody

Presumption in Favor of Birth Parents   Contests between a natural parent and a non-parent do not often arise in divorce child custody disputes, but when they do and in other contexts, there is a clear presumption in favor of the natural parent. This presumption can be overcome, but given its probable constitutional underpinnings, it requires "extraordinary circumstances."[50] One such circumstance has been a determination that a stranger-caregiver of the child has become the psychological parent of the child.[51]

Presumptions As Between Parents   Under traditional common law in the 19th century, custody of children was granted to the father. In the first half of the 20th century, this changed to the "tender years" doctrine, under which it was presumed that the mother was best qualified to care for children in their pre-teenage years. The father could overcome this presumption only by proving that the mother was unfit or far less capable than he of caring for the children. Today, the explicit preference for mothers has disappeared because of the dramatic increase in the number of mothers working outside the home, a greater willingness of fathers to be custodial parents, and concerns about its constitutionality.[52] Instead, courts consider the "best interests of the child" without regard to the sex of the competing parents. Nonetheless, this often amounts to a *de facto* custody presumption in favor of the mother, since courts often presume that the best interests of children facing the disruption of divorce are served by maintaining continuity in their care. This presumption in favor of the "primary caregiver" during the marriage in most cases points to the mother.[53] The component factors in determining the "best interests" of the child are (1) the demonstrated ability of each parent to care for the child personally; (2) the nature of the relationship between the child and the competing parents as revealed by the past conduct of parent and child; (3) the desires of the parents for custody; (4) maintenance of the stability of the child's current environment, especially with respect to home, school and friends; and (5) the desires of the child.[54]

Religion and Race   It has been traditional for courts to take into consideration the religious beliefs, or lack thereof, of the parents. However, increased sensitivity to 1st Amendment issues has led courts typically to consider a parent's religious views only if they threaten the health or well-being of a child. The issue of religion arises in its extreme form when a parent refuses to consent to medical treatments for a child on religious grounds. Even then, however, the 1st Amendment allows religion to be considered as a factor only when there is "an immediate and substantial threat to the

---

50   *Bennett v. Jeffries*, 356 N.E.2d 277, 281 (N.Y. 1976) (contest between natural mother and friend of child's grandmother to whom grandmother had entrusted custody).

51   This was the determination of the trial court on remand in *Bennett, id. See also Painter v. Bannister*, 140 N.W.2d 152 (Iowa 1966) (custody awarded to maternal grandparents on this basis).

52   Some courts have held the "tender years" doctrine invalid as violative of the equal protection clause of the 14th Amendment. *Ex Parte Devine*, 398 So.2d 686 (Ala. 1981); *Pusey v. Pusey*, 728 P.2d 117 (Utah 1986). *But see J.B. v. A.B.*, 242 S.E.2d 248 (W.Va. 1978). State constitutional equal rights amendments are a common basis for this conclusion. *See* Annotation, 90 A.L.R.2d 158, 186 (1979).

53   *See Garska v. McCoy*, 278 S.E.2d 357 (W.Va. 1981) (in addition observing that the primary caretaker preference is necessary to prevent non-custodial parents from using their possible custody claim as bargaining leverage in divorce negotiations). *But see Wolf v. Wolf*, 474 N.W.2d 257 (N.D. 1991) (concluding that the primary caretaker factor is not a presumption; only one of many factors to consider).

54   *See* CLARK, *supra* note 4, §19.4.

child's well-being" because of the religious practices.[55] Similarly, race has been routinely considered as a factor in child custody disputes. However, the Court has made clear that the Constitution prohibits using race as the sole basis for a custody award even when based on anticipated difficulties of the child living with a parent of a different race and public attitudes toward interracial families.[56]

Lifestyles of Parents The most difficult questions that arise in many custody cases involve the character and "lifestyles" of the parents and their possible effect on the child. Traditionally, the courts closely scrutinized the moral fitness and character of each parent, particularly as it related to sexual behavior. In the past, an adulterous parent had very little chance of gaining custody. The current trend is to place less emphasis on the parent's morality, except where the parent's behavior or activities could have a detrimental effect upon the child.[57] This is also the view adopted by the UMDA.[58] However, there are many cases with the traditional view. Some courts have refused to grant custody to a parent who is cohabiting with a lover, and they have prohibited overnight visitation. In *Jarrett v. Jarrett*,[59] the Illinois Supreme Court granted the father custody after he proved that the mother was living with her boyfriend. The court stated that the moral values the mother was representing to her children "contravened statutorily declared standards of conduct and endanger the children's moral development." However, that case "does not establish a conclusive presumption" that a child is harmed by a custodial parent's cohabitation with a member of the opposite sex.[60]

Homosexual parents face even more difficulty gaining or retaining custody. While society appears increasingly willing to extend rights to homosexuals and lesbians in certain areas, public opinion is mixed when it comes to child custody and care issues. Thus, in *Roe v. Roe*,[61] the court found that the father's exposure of his 9-year-old daughter to his "immoral and illicit homosexual relationship renders him an unfit and improper custodian as a matter of law." But court decisions have sometimes been based on more than simple moral judgments. Courts have denied custody to a homosexual parent and limited visitation rights because of fears that the child would become homosexual,[62] and that the "children upon reaching puberty would be subject to either overt or covert homosexual seduction . . . ."[63] However, other courts have deemed the homosexual relationship of a parent irrelevant to either custody or visitation rights in the absence of some indication of actual harm to the child.[64]

---

55 *Osier v. Osier*, 410 A.2d 1027 (Me. 1980) (trial court acted improperly in granting custody to the father by giving too much weight to the fact that the mother, a Jehovah's Witness, refused to consent to a blood transfusion for her child).

56 *Palmore v. Sidoti*, 466 U.S. 429 (1984) (award of custody of white child to white father after white mother married a black man was unconstitutional racial discrimination).

57 *See Feldman v. Feldman*, 358 N.Y.S.2d 507 (N.Y.App. 1974) (reversing trial court for "punishing this sexually-liberated divorced woman for her 'life-style' and personal beliefs" and noting that sexually active unmarried men are not so harshly judged).

58 UMDA §401.

59 400 N.E.2d 421, 425 (Ill. 1979).

60 *In re Marriage of Thompson*, 449 N.E.2d 88, 92 (Ill. 1983).

61 324 S.E.2d 691 (Va. 1985). The court also prohibited any visitation in the father's home or in the presence of his lover.

62 *Dailey v. Dailey*, 635 S.W.2d 391 (Tenn.App. 1981); *In re J.S. & C.*, 324 A.2d 90 (N.J.Super. 1974).

63 *In re J.S. & C., id.* at 96. *See also, J.L.P.(H.) v. D.J.P.*, 643 S.W.2d 865, 867 (Mo.App. 1982).

64 *S.N.E. v. R.L.B.*, 699 P.2d 875 (Alaska 1985) (change of custody denied when based on mother having a live-in lesbian lover); *Conkel v. Conkel*, 509 N.E.2d 983 (Ohio App. 1987) (visitation).

Preference of the Child   The child's preference is usually elicited by the judge in chambers rather than in the open court. Although some state statutes set a minimum age for children to state a preference, others leave it to the discretion of the judge. How much weight to give to a child's preference is left to the discretion of the trial court. The greatest weight is given when all the other factors are equal.[65]

b. Visitation Rights

Visitation by the Non-Custodial Parent   The court will generally grant the non-custodial parent visitation rights in order to maintain as much stability in the child's life as possible following the marital breakup, and to enable the non-custodial parent to continue his or her involvement with the child.[66] Only in the event that visitation is found to be of serious harm to the child will it be denied altogether.[67] In such an event, the courts may require that the non-custodial parent see the children in the presence of a social worker or the child's grandparents or that the child not visit overnight.

In most cases courts will leave visitation open-ended, dictating only that the visitation rights be "reasonable." In amicable divorce situations this may be the best approach because it gives the parents flexibility and decreases the court's involvement. However, the court may dictate a visitation schedule with specific times and arrangements. This may be the best approach where the parties are hostile and are unwilling to work together to facilitate visitation. Also, this type of definite and routine arrangement may be better for young children because it gives them a sense of stability.

Interfering with a non-custodial parent's visitation rights is a violation of a court order that renders the violator potentially subject to contempt of court sanction, such as a jail sentence or fine.[68] However, the difficulties and expense of going to court often make minor interferences with visitation not worth pursuing.

A difficult issue of visitation rights and custody is presented when the custodial parent wishes to leave the state, since this will radically alter the ability to visit the children and may even, as a practical matter, terminate visitation. Courts may deny custody to the moving parent if the move is for the purpose of frustrating visitation and has few countervailing benefits for the moving parent or the child. More difficult decisions are where the custodial parent's move is a good faith attempt to improve the custodial parent's life. Nonetheless, many courts have flatly made custody dependent on the custodial parent continuing to live in a particular place[69] or have increased visitation with parties sharing in transportation costs.[70]

Visitation by Others   Concern for the relationship of children to their extended family has caused courts and legislature to give attention to the possibility of visitation rights for grandparents or other relatives. In the last 10 years, nearly all states have passed statutes recognizing the potential for granting independent visitation rights to

---

65   *See Goldstein v. Goldstein*, 341 A.2d 51 (R.I. 1975) (preference for father of 9 ½ girl, very intelligent of her age, given substantial weight where other evidence was "so nearly in a state of equipoise").

66   *See generally* Steven Novinson, *Post-Divorce Visitation: Untying the Triangular Knot*, 1983 U.ILL.L.REV. 119.

67   *See French v. French*, 452 So.2d 647 (Fla.App. 1984) (fact husband failed to recognize the effect of his extramarital affair on the children was not enough to ban all visitation; sexual intercourse in front of the children might be). *See also* UMDA §407.

68   For a brief discussion of the contempt power, *see* Chapter VII, p. 247.

69   *See Carlson v. Carlson*, 661 P.2d 833 (Kan.App. 1983) (custody dependent on living in the county).

70   *Friedrich v. Bevis*, 9 S.W.3d 556 (Ark. App. 2000) (appellant could not restrain his ex-wife from moving out-of-state with their two minor children).

grandparents or other non-parent relatives. The overall test in most of these statutes is the "best interests of the child." Courts will typically consider pre-divorce involvement of the grandparents in the child's life and the psychological bond that may have resulted, plus the child's preferences.

A difficulty with non-parent visitation arises when the custodial parent disagrees with such visitation or its frequency or extent.[71] Often this problem occurs after a divorce when the parents of the non-custodial parent seek visitation with their grandchildren over the objections of the custodial parent.[72] There have been concerns with orders compelling such visitation since they could well violate the due process family privacy right of the custodial parents to raise their children as they see fit.[73] The Supreme Court recently held that a grandparent visitation order violated such due process rights. However, the statute involved in the case was quite broad, permitting a court to order visitation by anyone and the state trial court failed to accord any weight to the custodial parent's decision as to the grandparents' visitation. Also, the case did not involve a complete cut off of the grandparents' visitation. The custodial parent simply wished it to be limited to short visits once a month and on holidays. The Court declined to determine the broader issue of whether due process requires that there be a showing of harm or potential harm to the child as a condition precedent to granting visitation instead of the more general "best interests of the child" standard.[74]

c. Joint Custody Arrangements

"Joint custody" entails the child living alternatively with one parent and then the other on a rotating basis, such that the parents share both decision-making and actual custodial care responsibilities. For example, the child many live at the father's home certain days of the week and at the mother's home on other days. The facts that divorce is more commonplace, that it is granted without regard to fault, and that the traditional roles of fathers and mothers have begun to break down, have generally meant greater cooperation between the separating marital partners regarding care of their children. Proponents of joint custody argue that it helps to assure children that they are loved by both parents and to avoid the sense of loss the non-custodial parent feels, as well as to provide a beneficial effect that both parents share in the pleasure and burdens of raising their children. Opponents argue that joint custody undermines the stability that children of divorce need and that the difficult logistical demands of joint custody make strife between the parents more likely, resulting in unnecessary damage to the children. The desirability of joint custody is still a hotly debated topic and there are indications recently of lessened enthusiasm for it.[75]

Whatever the ultimate benefits or detriments of joint custody, a majority of states have legislation that permits it. In some states, joint custody is the preferred custody arrangement and is presumed to be in the best interests of the child. Courts in a few states have held that joint custody is not in the child's best interest except in extraordi-

---

71 *Compare In re Robert D.*, 198 Cal.Rptr. 801 (Cal.App. 1984) (granting visitation over parent's objections) *with Commonwealth ex rel. Zaffarano v. Genaro*, 455 A.2d 1180 (Pa. 1983) (denying visitation based on friction between parent and grandparent).

72 *See, e.g., Roberts v. Ward*, 493 A.2d 478 (N.H. 1985) (ordering visitation for grandparents when the custodial parent had remarried, despite the objections of the custodial parent and stepparent).

73 *See generally* Chapter IX, pp. 364-367 (right to family privacy).

74 *Troxel v. Granville*, 530 U.S. 57 (2000).

75 *See* Susan Steinman, *Joint Custody: What We Know, What We Have Yet to Learn, and the Judicial and Legislative Implications*, 16 U.C. DAVIS L. REV. 739 (1983).

nary circumstances.[76] The key consideration in determining whether joint custody is in the best interest of the child is the parents' ability and willingness to cooperate in daily decisions affecting the child's welfare. In many cases, the need for cooperation presents an insurmountable barrier to joint custody.

Distinctions between joint *legal* custody and joint *physical* custody can create difficulties. An order for joint legal custody gives an equal say to both parents on all major decisions affecting the child, while an order for joint physical custody allocates the actual times that the child is in the custody of each parent. It is possible for there to be joint *legal* custody, but physical custody in only one parent. In such cases, the physical custodian often resents having to consult with the non-custodial parent, who is not sufficiently involved in the child's life to properly participate in daily decision-making for the child.

d. Interstate Enforcement of Custody Decrees

Custody orders of state courts do not have a direct effect beyond the borders of a state. Problems regularly arose in the past where a parent simply took a child into another state to avoid a custody ruling. However, in 1980 Congress passed the Parental Kidnaping Prevention Act (PKPA),[77] which makes clear the applicability of the full faith and credit clause to child custody decrees and requires states to enforce the custody decrees of other states.[78] In addition, almost all states have adopted the Uniform Child Custody Judgment Act (UCCJA), which requires enforcement.[79]

Though strict enforcement of custody decrees discourages the reprehensible "forum-shopping" that often occurred, some have argued that there should be more flexibility for a court in the second state in appropriate cases to reconsider the issue of custody. However, in a recent case under the federal act involving an attempted adoption that attracted national attention, the Michigan Supreme Court took a strict view of the matter. It held that an Iowa court's award of custody to the natural father prevailed regardless of the best interests of the child and even if it meant removing the child from the would-be adoptive parents with whom the child had lived virtually since birth.[80]

5. Child Support

a. Nature and Duration of the Support Obligation

Traditionally, it was the father's obligation to provide adequate support for his children. The mother became liable for support upon the father's failure or refusal to furnish support. Today both parents have a duty to provide for their children to the extent that they are financially able.[81] This obligation continues even in the event of divorce. It is generally enforced in a divorce case by way of a child support order requiring that the non-custodial parent make periodic payments in a certain amount to the custodial parent.

---

76 *See, e.g., Trimble v. Trimble*, 352 N.W.2d 599 (Neb. 1984); *Lumbra v. Lumbra*, 394 A.2d 1139 (Vt. 1978).

77 28 U.S.C.A. §1738A.

78 Art. IV §1. *See* Chapter VII, pp. 261-262. Doubts about the enforceability of child custody decrees arose because equitable decrees are always modifiable and then only by the court that rendered them.

79 *See supra* note 3.

80 *In re Clausen*, 502 N.W.2d 649 (Mich. 1993).

81 In some states, a stepparent has a duty to support stepchildren. *See Washington Statewide Organization of Stepparents v. Smith*, 536 P.2d 1202 (Utah 1975) (rejecting constitutional objections).

The parents' support obligation normally runs until the child reaches the age of "majority," usually 18 years of age.[82] The statutes in some states limit support awards to support of "minor children," while others refer simply to "children." Some courts have held that support can be ordered beyond the age of 18 for children with physical or mental disabilities.[83] More controversial have been orders for the expenses of a child's college education. The traditional view is not to impose such an obligation because college is not a "necessity." Today most states by statute or judicial decision allow orders for college education when the parents can afford it and the child is making academic progress.[84] In other states, such an order will be made if there are "special circumstances," though the circumstances in the cases often seem to be rather ordinary.[85] The change in approach reflects the belief that a college education is very important and that children from divorced families should have the same advantages as those from non-divorced families.[86]

Minor children who become "emancipated" are no longer owed a duty of support. Emancipation occurs when the child marries or enlists in the army before the age of majority or whenever the child is capable of self-support. In some states there is a procedure for emancipation.[87] The support duty also terminates when parental rights are terminated by a court proceeding. Unlike the duty to pay alimony, however, the duty to pay child support does not always expire upon the death of the parent and is not dischargeable in bankruptcy.[88]

b. Determining Parentage for Support Purposes

Presumptions and Acknowledgments   Children born during a marriage are presumed by the law to be the children of the couple.[89] Consequently, in most divorce situations, the identity of the parents who owe the obligation of support is not in question. Outside of marriage, paternity is usually determined by voluntary "legitima-

---

82 It is unconstitutional for a state to have different ages of majority for males and females that results in differential support obligations. In *Stanton v. Stanton*, 421 U.S. 7 (1975), the Court rejected arguments that girls tend to mature earlier and marry young while boys need extended time to get a good education or training to prepare them for a job. For a discussion of sex discrimination, *see* Chapter IX, pp. 358-362.

83 *See Grapin v. Grapin*, 450 So.2d 853 (Fla. 1984) (based on common law).

84 *Greiman v. Friedman*, 414 N.E.2d 77 (Ill.App. 1980) (order to pay college expenses upheld even though child's academic record was not outstanding); *Childers v. Childers*, 575 P.2d 201 (Wash. 1978) (state statute makes support obligation turn on "dependency," not minority).

85 *In re Marriage of Plummer*, 735 P.2d 165 (Colo. 1987) (order based on finding that both parents have college degrees and "there was an atmosphere in which it was anticipated and expected that the children would go to college and would be supported while they did so.").

86 Even graduate school has been included. *See Ross v. Ross*, 400 A.2d 1233 (N.J.Super. 1979). *But see Brown v. Brown*, 474 A.2d 1168 (Pa.Super. 1984) (no obligation to fund law school). Law school in the United States is graduate study that follows four years of college study. Chapter IV, p. 129.

87 *See* Cal.Civ.Code §7000-7002. Such procedures have been used in some notable cases where a child actor or athlete wishes to gain control of his or her own money. The press has touted such actions as the child "divorcing" the parents and the accompanying acrimony is similar.

88 *See Bailey v. Bailey*, 471 P.2d 220 (Nev. 1970) (order must specifically provide that it is enforceable against the estate); 11 U.S.C.A. §523(a) (bankruptcy). Courts in some states may also require a parent to maintain a life insurance policy payable to the children.

89 *See* Uniform Parentage Act, §4(a), *supra* note 3, which provides a rebuttable presumption of paternity if the child is born during the marriage or within 300 days after its termination. *See also Mock v. Mock*, 411 So.2d 1063 (La. 1982) (rebuttable by preponderance of the evidence); *P.B.C. v. D.H.*, 483 N.E.2d 1094 (Mass. 1985) (rebuttable only by proof beyond a reasonable doubt). The Supreme Court has held (with no majority opinion) that it did not violate due process for a state to prohibit anyone but the married couple who are the presumed parents to contest the presumption, thus disallowing a challenge by the putative father. *Michael H. v. Gerald D.*, 491 U.S. 110 (1989) (father had fathered a child during an affair with a married woman and husband objected; state law barred establishing parentage).

tion" by the father. The father simply signs and files a form with a state agency, usually the county clerk. In other states, less formal methods may be acceptable as well, such as written and even oral contracts[90] or the putative father taking the child into his home.

Paternity Suits When the parents are not married and paternity is disputed, a paternity suit must be filed. This is a civil suit filed by the mother seeking a judgment declaring the defendant to be the father (an order of "filiation") and a child support order.[91] In the past, crude means of proof were used, such as having the jury look at the baby and the putative father to see how much they look alike, but today blood tests can play a key role and the state must pay for blood tests for indigent putative fathers.[92] Depending on the type of test, blood tests can be effective both for excluding and including a particular putative father.[93] The focus of paternity proceedings is the welfare of the child, so the actions of the parents are irrelevant. Consequently, it is no defense that the father was tricked into intercourse by the mother's false statement that she was using contraceptive pills.[94] Recognizing that the original nature of the action was criminal and that claims of paternity are difficult to defend against, some states require proof beyond a reasonable doubt or clear and convincing evidence, but others impose only the normal civil standard of a preponderance of the evidence.[95]

c. The Amount of Support Orders

Guidelines and Discretion The amount of child support orders, whether temporary — during the pendency of the divorce case — or permanent, lies within the discretion of the trial court. Since both parents are responsible for the support of their children, the court will consider the finances of both in making its determination, along with any division of property or awards of alimony provided for in the divorce decree. Federal law requires states to develop and follow guidelines for support amounts, but guidelines vary considerably from state to state.[96] The overall test of a child support amount is that it be "reasonable" considering the limits of the parents' financial abilities.[97] Reasonable needs of the child include clothing, food, education, medical care, and entertainment. The court may also consider the standard of living to which the child had become accustomed prior to the divorce.[98]

Modifications in Amount Most child support orders provide for periodic payments to be made to the custodial parent. The amount of such payments can be modified if

---

90 *See T. v. T.*, 224 S.E.2d 148 (Va. 1976) (oral contract valid where there had been part performance and detrimental reliance); *Peterson v. Eritsland*, 419 P.2d 332 (Wash. 1966) (written contract).

91 Some states and the Uniform Parentage Act §6 permit the child to bring the action (by the child's guardian or "next friend") and some states permit the state agency providing welfare assistance to the child to sue as well.

92 *Little v. Streater*, 452 U.S. 1 (1981).

93 For a summary of the types of tests *see* GREGORY, SWISHER & SCHEIBLE, *supra* note 4, §5.02[F].

94 *See Pamela L. v. Frank S.*, 449 N.E.2d 713 (N.Y. 1983).

95 Though rare, fathers sometimes sue to establish their paternity and the trend is toward allowing such suits. Constitutional aspects were discussed in note 48, *supra*. *See also* note 89 *supra*.

96 42 U.S.C.A. §667. The guidelines are part of the federal government's intervention to ensure child support enforcement. *See infra* p. 537.

97 Common formulas for computing support payments are discussed in GREGORY, SWISHER & SCHEIBLE, *supra* note 4, §8.06[C].

98 *See White v. Marciano*, 235 Cal.Rptr. 779 (Cal.App. 1987) (when the child's parent is wealthy, "the child is entitled to, and therefore 'needs,' something more than the bare necessities of life"). *But see State v. Hall*, 418 N.W.2d 187 (Minn.App. 1988) (despite father's monthly income of $16,000, child's actual expenses did not exceed $1000 per month, so ordering the standard amount was sufficient; any excess would only go to increase the mother's standard of living).

circumstances warrant. Such circumstances might include changes in either party's financial condition, the needs of the child or the cost of living. Decrease is possible where the parent has changed careers or otherwise can no longer pay the amount ordered.[99] A strong case can be made that a change in a parent's career that results in a lower standard of living is possible in an intact family, so it should have a similar effect on the child support order. However, courts will closely scrutinize such cases with some skepticism to determine whether the career change was made for the purpose of lowering the child support amount.[100] While support orders are supposed to reflect the obligor's ability to pay, many cases in this area seem to consider what the obligor *should have* been able to pay.[101] Increases are possible when there is an increase in the child's needs, such as an increase in education or medical expenses. However, an increase may also be ordered based solely on an increase in the non-custodial parent's ability to pay.[102] To discourage parties from constantly seeking modifications, many statutes require that the change in financial circumstances be a major one. For example, the Uniform Marriage and Divorce Act requires that to warrant modification the change in circumstances must be "so substantial and continuing as to make the terms [of the order] unconscionable."[103]

The problem of the adequacy of support orders is often less one of sudden changes than one of gradual erosion of the value of the amount ordered resulting of inflation. Some states have addressed this problem by permitting an "escalation clause" that ties the amount of the order to the Consumer Price Index (CPI) calculated periodically by the United States Department of Labor.[104]

d. Welfare Programs for Needy Families

When child support and the resources of the custodial parent are not sufficient to support the child, a "safety net" of welfare programs is available. From 1935 until 1996, the federal government funded and supervised a cooperative state-federal program that provided cash and in-kind payments to needy families with children deprived of support as a result of the absence, disability or, in some cases, the unemployment of a parent, called Aid to Families with Dependent Children (AFDC). The purpose of the program was to provide a stable source of income at a subsistence level to allow the needy children involved to be cared for at home by their parent or parents. But in 1996 Congress replaced the program with Temporary Aid to Needy Families (TANF) program, based on its judgment that single parents with children at home should work and that financial assistance should be temporary until they can become self-sufficient. The

---

99 *See Guyton v. Guyton*, 602 A.2d 1143 (D.C. 1992) (reduction required when father lost his job).

100 *Compare Curtis v. Curtis*, 442 N.W.2d 173 (Minn.App. 1992) (father who quit job of 10 years to attend school to be electronic repairman one month after support order entered acted in bad faith and was not entitled to a reduction) *with Diagre v. Diagre*, 527 So.2d 9 (La.App. 1988) (father's quitting real estate job to go to law school was not an attempt to evade support obligations, so decrease in order was proper). Courts are generally less sympathetic to lessened ability to pay that results from remarriage and a new family. *See Berg v. Berg*, 359 A.2d 354 (R.I. 1976) (father stopped paying support after he adopted three children of his new wife; contempt sentence affirmed; remand to determine issue of bad faith).

101 *Compare Pierce v. Peirce*, 412 N.W.2d 291 (Mich.App. 1987) (amount should abate while father in jail where he has no resources) *with In re Phillips*, 493 N.W.2d 824 (Iowa 1992) (inability to pay resulting from imprisonment for father's voluntary conduct does not warrant modification).

102 *See Graham v. Graham*, 598 A.2d 355 (D.C. 1991) (allowing downward adjustment when financial ability declined, but denying upward adjustment when it increases, would be unfair to children, who have a right to a higher standard of living when the parent's finances improve).

103 Uniform Marriage and Divorce Act, §316(a), *supra* note 3.

104 *See In re Marriage of Nesset*, 345 N.W.2d 107 (Iowa 1984) (indexing support to CPI approved).

program imposes work requirements and strengthens child support cooperation and collection requirements. A total five-year limit (or less at state option) is set on financial assistance.[105] TANF has had mixed success in moving people from welfare into self-supporting jobs of any duration.[106]

In addition to cash assistance, "food stamps" — coupons redeemable for food — are available to low-income households,[107] as is medical assistance (called "Medicaid").[108] Also, totally disabled people, including children, are entitled to support under the Supplemental Security Income program.[109]

e. Enforcement of Child Support Orders

Non-payment of child support is a major problem in the United States that is only now getting better. Statistics vary from state to state, but one set of data shows that at one point less than half of all custodial parents awarded child support received payment in full.[110] The main problem has been that the custodial parent must hire a lawyer to pursue collection.

One method of collection is to seek to have the defaulting parent held in civil contempt of court. This could lead to the jailing of the non-supporting parent until the order is paid.[111] A second remedy is "garnishment" of the obligor's wages or an order that property be seized and sold. Indeed, federal law requires that wage withholding be included in support orders.[112] Finally, where the party has willfully defaulted on a support obligation, he or she may be charged with criminal contempt or criminal non-support, often a felony. However, these remedies, if they result in a long prison term, generally do not result in the immediate collection of more money.

A major problem with collection remedies is that individuals bent on avoiding their court-ordered support obligations often leave the state where it was ordered. To meet this problem, all states have adopted the Uniform Reciprocal Enforcement of Support Act (URESA) and the Revised Uniform Reciprocal Enforcement of Support Act (RURESA)[113] which require each state to enforce the support obligations of other states. These acts, then, supplement the Constitution's requirement that states give "full faith and credit" to judgments from other states.[114] However, the acts have not been as successful as hoped, largely because of the lack of public resources.

---

105 *See* Title IV-A of the Social Security Act, 42 U.S.C.A. §§601 *et seq.*

106 Rodger Doyle, Welfare Woes: Mixed Success in Getting People on Their Own Feet, SCIENTIFIC AMERICAN (April-May 2006).

107 *See* 7 U.S.C.A. §§2011 *et seq.*

108 42 U.S.C.A. §§601 *et seq.* Also of assistance to families with children are federal programs providing for free or reduced-price hot lunches (and sometimes breakfasts) in public schools.

109 *See* 42 U.S.C.A. §§1382 *et seq.*

110 CLARK, *supra* note 4, at 734, citing LOUISE WEITZMAN, THE DIVORCE REVOLUTION: THE UNEXPECTED SOCIAL AND ECONOMIC CONSEQUENCES FOR WOMEN AND CHILDREN IN AMERICA 283 (1985).

111 Civil contempt was discussed in Chapter VII, p. 247. The indigent non-supporter's right to counsel was initially held not to be constitutionally required, but in recent years this trend has been reversed. *See Mead v. Batchlor*, 460 N.W.2d 493 (Mich. 1990), *overruling Sword v. Sword*, 249 N.W.2d 88 (Mich. 1976).

112 42 U.S.C.A. §666(a)(8), (b)(2), (b)(3).

113 *See supra* note 3.

114 *See* Chapter VII, p. 261, where the full faith and credit clause is discussed.

In response to this, Congress in 1975 decided to devote federal resources to the problem of non-support.[115] The federal law originally sought only to recoup federally funded welfare benefits paid to custodial parents, but many of its provisions now apply to all support orders. The federal law now provides for a Parent Locator Service to assist in finding absent parents and an Office of Child Support Enforcement to assure that state support enforcement programs live up to federal standards. Those federal standards require states to implement numerous administrative reforms in their child support enforcement systems to keep better track of non-supporting parents and to provide for more efficient processing of support orders. In addition, the law authorizes intercepting federal or state income tax refunds.

C. Non-Traditional Relationships and Family Law

1. Unmarried Heterosexual Couples

The increase in the number of couples living together outside of wedlock can be attributed to the rise in the divorce rate and an accompanying skepticism about the institution of marriage, plus a general tendency for couples to wait longer before getting married.[116] But one legal advantage of marriage that has not been available to unmarried couples in most jurisdictions is judicial protection of the financial interests of the partners. This situation has been changing, however. Some courts have applied equitable principles to the breakup of unmarried couples and have held that they may order property divisions and support for unmarried couples who break up in a manner similar to that used in divorces. Awards of property or maintenance payments in these circumstances are sometimes referred to erroneously as "palimony" — "alimony" payments by one's former "pal."[117]

Marvin v. Marvin[118] established the right of an unmarried partner to seek such relief. Marvin and his female companion, Michele Triola, lived together for six years. The court held that Triola could seek to recover support or property from Marvin by showing either an explicit oral agreement or an implied agreement based on a tacit understanding so long as the consideration for the contract was not solely sexual. On remand to the trial court, Triola was unable to prove either theory of recovery, but the legal basis for such recovery was established for other cases. The trial court nonetheless awarded her $104,000 for "rehabilitation," *i.e.*, to learn new employable skills, but this was reversed on appeal.[119] Many states are skeptical about the *Marvin* doctrine and have rejected it altogether even in the face of rather compelling facts.[120]

2. Homosexual Couples

Legality of Same-Sex Marriages Increasing recognition that committed same-sex relationships are no different than committed heterosexual relationships has resulted in quite a few legal developments in recent years. One of these was the Massachusetts

---

115 *See generally* Title IV-D of the Social Security Act, 42 U.S.C.A. §§651 *et seq.* These provisions and other interstate support collection issues are discussed in GREGORY, SWISHER & SCHEIBLE, *supra* note 4, §8.06[F][3]-[4].

116 CLARK, *supra* note 4, at §2.1, n. 36.

117 The option of arguing that a common law marriage existed is often unavailable. It been abolished in many states and there is usually more than ample evidence that the couple had the specific intention not to be married. *See* discussion of common law marriage, *supra* p. 519.

118 557 P.2d 106 (Cal. 1976).

119 *Marvin v. Marvin*, 176 Cal.Rptr. 555 (Cal.App. 1981).

120 *See, e.g., Hewitt v. Hewitt*, 394 N.E.2d 1204 (Ill. 1979) (court concluded woman had no rights to alimony or property even though she lived with her partner, a dentist, for fifteen years and had borne and raised their three children).

Supreme Judicial Court's decision in *Goodridge v. Dep't of Pub. Health* in 2003, in which it declared the Massachusetts marriage statute unconstitutional under the Massachusetts state constitution, finding that the statute violated personal autonomy rights protected by its due process clause and discriminated on the basis of sex in violation of its equal protection clause.[121] The court noted that the ban effectively denied same-sex couples not only the intangible benefits of marriage, but also access to rights and benefits incident to marriage, such as tax breaks, public assistance benefits, community property rights, inheritance rights, child custody rights and spousal support rights.[122]

A 2010 federal case held unconstitutional California's voter-enacted amendment to the state constitution, which restricted marriage to opposite-sex couples.[123] In a suit brought by same-sex couples, the district court found that the amendment, called Proposition 8, violated equal protection by treating opposite-sex and same-sex couples differently without a rational basis related to a legitimate state interest, and violated due process by infringing on the plaintiffs' fundamental right to marry without any compelling state interest.[124] The court found that same-sex couples came within the fundamental right to marry despite a long history of the law excluding them from the official status of being married, and that California's option of a "domestic partnership," discussed below, did not fulfill the state's obligation to the plaintiffs. The court rejected arguments that the ban preserves "the prerogative and responsibility of parents to provide for the ethical and moral development and education of their own children," that it accommodates "the First Amendment rights of individuals and institutions that oppose same-sex marriage on religious or moral grounds," and several other interests, which it characterized as "nothing more than a fear or unarticulated dislike of same-sex couples."[125]

Civil Unions The Vermont Supreme Court in 1999, took a different approach to reach a similar result, holding that denial of the benefits incident to marriage to same-sex domestic partners violated the "common benefits" provision of the Vermont Constitution. However, it held that the defect could be remedied by enactment of a law providing for civil unions or domestic partnerships. The Vermont legislature promptly

---

121 798 N.E.2d 941 (Mass. 2003). *See also Opinions of the Justices to the Senate*, 802 N.E.2d 565 (Mass. 2004). *See* Hillel Y. Levin, *Resolving Interstate Conflicts Over Same-Sex Non-Marriage*, 63 FLA. L.REV. 47 (2011).

122 In both Massachusetts and Hawaii, the state argued that the statute did not discriminate based on sex, because its ban on same-sex couples applied equally to males and females. The court rejected the argument by analogy to cases holding that statutes prohibiting racially mixed marriages, which apply both to whites and blacks, constituted race discrimination. *See Loving v. Virginia*, 388 U.S. 1 (1967). Ten years earlier, in *Baehr v. Lewin*, 852 P.2d 44 (Haw. 1993), the Hawaii Supreme Court issued a similar decision. There, the electorate reacted by approving constitutional amendments prohibiting same-sex marriage. *See, e.g.*, Hawaii Const. art. I §23. The Alaska Supreme Court also rejected the argument that a statutory ban on same-sex marriage would be impermissible discrimination. *Brause v. Alaska*, 21 P.3d 357 (Alaska 2001).

123 *Perry v. Schwarzenegger*, 704 F. Supp.2d 921 (N.D. Cal. 2010).

124 Equal protection and substantive due process are discussed in Chapter IX, pp. 352-356, 362-368.

125 As of this writing, same-sex marriages are not taking place in California, because the case was appealed to the federal court of appeals for the Ninth Circuit.

passed such a law giving parties to such a union rights equal to those of married couples.[126] California has a similar domestic partnership law, as do a few other states.[127]

Federal Defense of Marriage Act By whatever means same-sex unions gain legal status under state law, such status is confined to that particular state unless other states choose voluntarily to recognize their effect. Conflict-of-law and "full faith and credit" requirements normally require states to recognize the legal effect of the marriage laws of the state where a couple as married.[128] However, Congress in 1996 passed the Defense of Marriage Act, providing states with the option of refusing to give effect to any laws of another state "respecting a relationship between persons of the same sex that is treated as a marriage under the laws of such other State."[129] In 2010, a federal district court in Massachusetts ruled that parts of the Defense of Marriage Act were unconstitutional as violating 5th Amendment due process clause's requirement of equal treatment.[130] The court rejected several proffered governmental interests behind the Act, including purported administrative burdens presented by the changing patchwork of state approaches to same-sex marriage in distributing federal marriage-based benefits. In early 2011, the Obama administration stated that it would no longer defend the constitutionality of the Defense of Marriage Act, as it normally would be required to do, opining that the Act discriminates against same-sex couples without any rational basis.[131]

Benefits Without Legal Status Some courts and legislatures have bypassed the issue of the legal status of same-sex marriages, and instead have focused directly on marriage-like benefits for same-sex couples. The New York Court of Appeals prevented the eviction of a gay man from his deceased partner's rent-controlled apartment in Manhattan, finding him to be a "member of the deceased tenant's family" within the meaning of a New York city ordinance governing rent-controlled apartments.[132] Many employers, public and private, extend employment fringe benefits, such as health insurance and pension benefits, to same-sex domestic partnerships. The Alaska Supreme Court held in 2005 that the state's failure to provide such employment fringe benefits to its employees who are in same-sex relationships violates the state constitution's equal protection clause.[133] Alaska was even one of those states where the

---

126 *Baker v. State*, 744 A.2d 864 (Vt. 1999). The "common benefit" clause is essentially a form of equal protection clause. *See* Vt. Stat. Ann. tit. 15 §§1201-07. The law also provides property, and income tax treatment on par with married couples. New York intermediate appeals courts have rejected constitutional challenges to that state's marriage laws. *See Samuels v. New York State Dept. of Health*, 811 N.Y.S.2d 136 (App.Div. 2006).

127 West's Ann.Cal.Fam.Code §297 and *Koebke v. Bernardo Heights Country Club*, 115 P.3d 1212 (Cal. 2005) (registered lesbian partners denied spousal benefits at country club could sue for discrimination based on marital status under state's civil rights laws).

128 *See* Chapter VII, p. 264 (conflicts rule for marriages).

129 28 U.S.C.A. §1738C. Litigation in Massachusetts after the *Goodridge* case has upheld a ban on *nonresident* same-sex couples obtaining marriage licenses in the state unless they can show that their home state has chosen to recognize the marriage. *See Cote-Whitacre v. Department of Public Health*, 844 N.E.2d 623 (Mass. 2006). The federal act also defines marriage for all federal statutes to mean "only a legal union between one man and one woman as husband and wife," thus assuring that benefits based on marriage secured by federal statutes would not be available to same-sex partners. 1 U.S.C.A. §7.

130 *Gill v. Office of Personnel Management*, 699 F.Supp.2d 374 (D. Mass. 2010); *Commonwealth v. Department of Health and Human Services*, 698 F.Supp.2d 234 (D. Mass. 2010). The equal protection component of the 5th Amendment's due process clause is discussed in Chapter IX, p. 351.

131 The Supreme Court's decision in *Lawrence v. Texas* in 2003 at least renders unconstitutional prosecution of same-sex couples for their sexual conduct. *See* Chapter IX, p. 329.

132 *Braschi v. Stahl Associates Co.*, 543 N.E.2d 49 (N.Y. 1989). *But see Samuels v. New York State Dept. of Health, supra* note 126. *Compare* Chapter II, text at note 61 (German Constitutional Court decision).

133 *Alaska Civil Liberties Union v. State*, 122 P.3d 781 (Alaska 2005)

constitution had been amended to provide that a marriage can only be between one man and one woman, but the court held that this related solely to the determination of the marital status and was irrelevant to the issue of whether benefits had to be distributed to same-sex couples on a non-discriminatory basis.

Parentage and Same-Sex Couples Same-sex couples in domestic partnerships, official or unofficial, create additional challenges for the law when children are involved. Most of these issues have been resolved without dealing directly with the relationship between the parenting couple. About half the states permit a same-sex partner to adopt the natural child of the other.[134] The California Supreme Court has gone further, holding that a former lesbian partner was obliged to pay child support to the mother for children who were conceived intentionally during their former relationship. It reasoned that the provision of the law which holds that a man is presumed to be the natural father of a child if he receives the child into his home and openly represents the child as his own, applies equally to women.[135] The Washington Supreme Court upheld the petition of the former partner in a lesbian relationship to have her parental rights recognized, based on common-law principles of "*de facto* parentage." Such status exists, it held, whenever: (1) the natural or legal parent consented to and fostered the parent-like relationship, (2) the petitioner and the child lived together in the same household, (3) the petitioner assumed obligations of parenthood without expectation of financial compensation, and (4) the petitioner has been in a parental role long enough to have established with the child a bonded, dependent relationship, parental in nature. In addition, it noted, *de facto* parent status is "limited to those adults who have fully and completely undertaken a permanent, unequivocal, committed, and responsible parental role in the child's life"[136]

Marvin-Type Grounds for Protection The *Marvin* rationale has been held to apply to same-sex couples, in California at least. It is, of course, subject to all the requirements of that case, including the requirement that sex not be the sole basis for the agreement.[137] It is not known precisely how passage of civil union or domestic partnership laws affect *Marvin* claims.

D. Child Custody Issues Outside Divorce

1. Adoption

In adoptions, a child in essence gets a new parent or set of parents in place of their birth parent or parents. The parental rights of both natural parents must be terminated before a child can be adopted. This can be accomplished voluntarily, by having the parent(s) sign a document agreeing to termination, or involuntarily, through court proceedings in which neglect or abuse has been shown. Where reliance is placed on

---

134 *See, e.g., In re Jacob*, 660 N.E.2d 397 (N.Y. 1995) (interpreting N.Y. statute).

135 *Elisa B. v. Superior Court*, 117 P.3d 660 (Cal. 2005). See also *K.M. v. E.G.*, 117 P.3d 673 (Cal. 2005) (lesbian partner who donated eggs so partner could have children *via in vitro* fertilization is a parent). *Compare infra* p. 542 (artificial insemination done by doctor does not confer parentage on sperm donor).

136 *In re Parentage of L.B.*, 122 P.3d 161 (Wash. 2005). *See also T.B. v. L.R.M.*, 786 A.2d 913 (Pa. 2001) (lesbian partner "assumed a parental status and discharged parental duties with the consent of [the biological mother]" and thus had standing as person *in loco parentis* to bring action for partial custody and visitation). *But see T.F. v. B.L.*, 813 N.E.2d 1244 (Mass. 2004) (while the evidence supported a conclusion that an implied contract existed between a child's mother and her domestic partner to assume the responsibilities of a parent in consideration of the mother's conceiving and bearing the child, this implied contract was unenforceable). *See generally* Child Support Obligations of Former Same-Sex Partners, 5 A.L.R.6th 303 (2005).

137 *Whorton v. Dillingham*, 248 Cal.Rptr. 405 (Cal.App. 1988) (even where sex was an explicit part of the agreement, if there was other adequate consideration for agreement and non-sexual part of agreement was severable, it is valid).

voluntary release of the child for adoption, most states have waiting periods before an adoption can become final, and some require counseling of the birth parent(s) before parental rights are voluntarily relinquished. If the birth mother is acting alone or if the birth father is not known, certain due process rights of notice are required before his rights can be terminated.[138] Like other family law matters, other aspects of adoption laws vary widely among the states, but in general two types of adoptions are possible: "agency" and "private" adoptions.

Agency Adoptions Every state has a system of agency adoptions, either as the sole means of adopting or in addition to private adoptions. Agency adoptions are administered through a public agency or private agencies licensed by the state. In the typical agency adoption, the birth parents' parental rights have already been terminated and the adopting parents have no contact with them. Records are sealed for the privacy of the family and the child. In general, the idea behind agency adoptions is to assure that adoptive parents are carefully screened by professionals before adoption can take place. This is more difficult to assure in private adoptions. In some states, screening is thought so important that all forms of private adoption are banned. A disadvantage of agency adoptions is that they typically take much longer than private adoptions and impatient adoptive parents who live in an "agency state" often consider going to a state or country with private adoptions to get a child.[139] Similarly, some birth parents prefer private adoptions because they have more control over who the adoptive parents will be.[140]

Private Adoptions In private adoptions, no state agency is involved. Many private adoptions involve birth and adoptive parents who know each other or are related to each other, or the birth and adoptive parents might be "matched" by an intermediary, usually a lawyer, a physician or a private company specializing in such matches. The amount of regulation of private adoptions varies in terms of whether a home study must be conducted, the degree to which counseling is required for any of the parties involved and other issues. Most states prohibit profiteering by intermediaries, regulating fees they can charge and permitting lawyers only to charge for the legal services involved. However, such regulations are hard to enforce especially given the eagerness of the adoptive couples to get a baby. As a result, the boundary between permitted adoption and prohibited baby selling is not a bright line, and there is considerable room for the shady intermediary to cross it.

Requirements for Adoptive Parents Usually the statutes require only that the adopting person be an adult, that an adopting couple be married and jointly adopt the child, and in some states age restrictions are imposed to assure a "normal" spread in age between the adoptive parents and the child. But in "agency" adoption states at least, there are various "rules" in the form of standards set by the agency and long-standing practices that are sometime very specific. Traditionally, agencies have looked for "ideal" married couples of similar backgrounds to the birth parents, for placing adoptive children. This has been criticized by some who argue that agencies' criteria are too narrow and result in some children not being adopted who should be or in turning down non-traditional adoptive parents who would be excellent parents.

---

138 *But see Lehr v. Robertson*, 463 U.S. 248 (1983), summarized *supra* note 47.
139 Interstate adoptions are subject to the Interstate Compact on Placement of Children.
140 *See generally* Mitchell A. Charney, *The Rebirth of Private Adoptions*, 71 A.B.A.J. 52 (1985).

2. Reproductive Technology and Child Custody

Artificial Insemination The simplest and most common case involving reproductive technology is artificial insemination of the mother with sperm from a donor. If the mother is married when insemination occurs and the husband agrees, the husband is considered the father rather than the donor of the sperm.[141] The logical result of this rule is that, if the husband did not consent, then the child is considered illegitimate, though this result has been criticized.[142] Where an unmarried woman has a child through artificial insemination, the donor, if identified, is considered to be the father of the child. However, some states provide that if the insemination is done by a doctor, the donor is not considered the father; if no doctor is used, then the donor is the father.[143] This rule applies to "natural insemination" situations as well — where an unmarried woman agrees with a man to get her pregnant and she agrees to waive any right to child support from him. The Indiana Supreme Court refused to allow such an agreement to affect the father's support obligation, holding it invalid on general public policy grounds.[144]

In Vitro Fertilization Medical science is also able to conceive a child in the laboratory and then implant the fertilized egg in the mother's body. In such a case, the legal implications are no different from where there is natural or artificial insemination within the mother's body. However, not all such fertilized eggs may be used and they may be frozen and placed in storage for future use. The Tennessee Supreme Court was faced with the question of the "custody" of such frozen embryos upon the couple's divorce. Because of the husband's constitutional right to decide whether to procreate was involved, the court held that there must be *joint* "custody." This overrode the wife's desire to keep the embryos or donate them to a childless couple.[145] In a similar case, the California Court of Appeals held that the unmarried woman partner of a man who died was entitled to possession of his frozen sperm over the claims of his estate.[146]

Surrogate Mothers More difficult legally than artificial insemination is the situation presented by so-called "surrogate mother" agreements.[147] In a typical situation, a childless couple will hire a woman to bear a child for them. The husband, as provider of the sperm, is the biological father and the surrogate mother consents to adoption by the wife. Difficulties arise when there is a dispute, typically when the surrogate mother refuses to give up the child as agreed to in the contract. When this happens, traditional legal principles dictate the unsatisfactory result of the legal parents of the child being the surrogate mother and the husband.

A famous New Jersey case, *Matter of Baby M*,[148] illustrates the difficulties. The trial court in that case upheld the validity of the contract, awarding custody to the husband and authorizing adoption by the wife, thus terminating the parental rights of the biological surrogate mother. On appeal, the New Jersey Supreme Court held that

---

141 *People v. Sorensen*, 437 P.2d 495 (Cal. 1968) (husband can be prosecuted for non-support); Uniform Parentage Act §5. Consent can be implied. *In re Baby Doe*, 353 S.E.2d 877 (S.C. 1987).

142 *See* CLARK, *supra* note 4, p. 154.

143 *See, e.g.*, Cal. Family Code §7613.

144 *Straub v. B.M.T. by Todd*, 645 N.E.2d 597 (Ind. 1994).

145 *Davis v. Davis*, 842 S.W.2d 588 (Tenn. 1992). *See also Kass v. Kass*, 693 N.E.2d 194 (N.Y. 1998) (enforcing contract requiring consent of both by husband and wife and, if no agreement, donation to medical research).

146 *Hecht v. Superior Court*, 20 Cal.Rptr.2d 275 (Cal.App. 1993).

147 *See generally* CLARK, *supra* note 4, §20.8. The term "surrogate mother" is not technically correct, since the woman is the child's biological mother, but the terminology has stuck and is used here.

148 537 A.2d 1227 (N.J. 1988). *See also* 542 A.2d 52 (Super.Ct. 1988) (decision on remand).

surrogacy contracts were unenforceable because they violated public policy by determining custody without regard to the child's best interests and for their lack of true voluntariness, given the potential for exploiting the poor. It ruled that the case should be treated like any other custody dispute. Consequently, it affirmed the award of custody to the father alone, but granted visitation rights to the surrogate mother. Other states have reached different results. The Kentucky Supreme Court, for example, has held that the state's prohibition on sale of children for adoption did not apply to void a surrogate contract and declined to revoke the charter to do business of a surrogacy agency.[149]

Even more complex are cases where the surrogate mother is essentially a "gestation surrogate" because she is implanted with an embryo produced by the husband and wife. The surrogate is truly the "birth mother" of the child, but the child has none of her genetic material. The Supreme Court of California held that in a true "egg donation" situation, where a woman gestates and gives birth to a child formed from the egg of another woman with the intent to raise the child as her own, the birth mother is the natural mother under California law.[150] A New York court decided that the gestational mother, the wife, is the natural mother of the children.[151] In an even more complicated case, a husband and wife used anonymous sperm and egg donors and had a surrogate mother implanted with the embryo. The California court in this case declared that the husband and wife were the parents of the child.[152]

Since the *Baby M* case, there has been a flurry of legislative activity to deal with surrogacy, with states taking divergent paths. Most have completely prohibited paid surrogacy arrangements[153] while others have chosen to permit, but closely regulate them.[154] Regardless of the legality of surrogacy contracts, however, courts nonetheless will undoubtedly scrutinize very closely the custody arrangements contemplated by the contract to assure that they are in the best interests of the child involved.

E. Problems in the Intact Family

1. Spouse Abuse

Domestic violence against women is a serious problem in the United States. Crime statistics show that 32% of all female homicide victims older age 20-24 are killed by their husbands or other intimate male partners.[155] Over 4 million acts of domestic violence are perpetrated each year and as many as 40% of all police calls concern matters of domestic violence.[156] Despite the prevalence of abuse, it is only recently that measures have begun to be taken to deal with it.

Historical Roots of Spousal Abuse   The delayed reaction of society to domestic violence finds its roots in the common law. At common law, a man had the right to

---

149 *Surrogate Parenting Associates, Inc. v. Kentucky ex rel. Armstrong*, 704 S.W.2d 209 (Ky. 1986).

150 *Johnson v. Calvert*, 5 Cal.4th 84, 93 (Cal. 1993).

151 *Andres A. v. Judith N.*, 591 N.Y.S.2d 946 (N.Y. Fam. Ct. 1992) (N.Y. artificial insemination law precluded declaring wife, whose embryo was implanted, the mother of the child).

152 *Buzzanca v. Buzzanca*, 72 Cal.Rptr.2d 280 (Cal.App. 1998).

153 *See* N.Y. Dom. Rel. §122; Mich.Comp.Laws §722.855. The Michigan statute was held constitutional in *Doe v. Attorney General*, 487 N.W.2d 484 (Mich.App. 1992).

154 *See* Va. Code. Ann. §20-156 *et seq. See* GREGORY, SWISHER & SCHEIBLE, *supra* note 4, §5.07[B].

155 Source: United States Department of Justice data, 1993-1999.

156 *Developments in the Law — Legal Responses to Domestic Violence*, 106 HARV.L.REV. 1528, 1529 (1993). In 1992, the Massachusetts courts issued an estimated 60,000 civil restraining orders to protect women from their abusive partners.

"discipline" his wife (or child) through application of moderate physical violence. And the common law definition of rape excluded even forcible sexual assault by a husband of his wife.[157] In the late 1800s, states legislated specific punishments for batterers, but these laws were seldom enforced. It was only in the 1960s that the advent of the women's movement brought the issue of domestic violence into the national spotlight. Still, courts are reluctant to interfere in family situations; unless the abuse is blatant and serious, and police find domestic violence situations to be among the most dangerous, distasteful and frustrating parts of their job.

Law Enforcement Policy on Domestic Violence   A large part of the solution to the problem has been major revisions in law enforcement policy. In 1984, the Minneapolis police department issued an order requiring police officers "to aggressively utilize arrest powers" in domestic violence situations.[158] This order resulted from the outcome of a National Institute of Justice study analyzing over 300 cases of domestic violence. The study evaluated the three methods police most often use to prevent further domestic violence — arrests, mediation, and ordering the assailant out of the house to "cool off." The most effective method was found to be arrest. Statutes have also been enacted requiring the police to inform victims of available resources to help them extricate themselves from a violent relationship.[159] Other statutes require police to offer transportation to a shelter or other safe place.[160] Where police policy fails to treat domestic abuse complaints on par with other complaints of crime, battered women have sued, arguing that it constitutes impermissible sex discrimination in violation of the 14th Amendment.[161]

Personal Protection Orders   Often more useful than the criminal process are "personal protection orders" for the wife. If a divorce case is pending, a temporary restraining order can be issued by the court forbidding the husband from having contact with the wife. In recent years, a similar remedy has been authorized in virtually all states for unmarried partners. In addition, the enforcement process has been streamlined. Though any battery on the partner is clearly a violation of the court order, traditionally restraining orders could be enforced only by filing a complaint with the court and seeking a contempt of court remedy. Now many states allow the police to arrest violators of restraining orders immediately based upon a reasonable belief that the order has been violated.

2. Child Abuse and Neglect

Civil Abuse and Neglect Proceedings   Child abuse and neglect is often a crime, but more commonly remedial civil proceedings are pursued against the parents instead. Such proceedings are usually brought in the juvenile or family court, most often a division of the state probate court. Once the court takes jurisdiction of the case upon proof of neglect or abuse, it has broad discretion to take whatever action it deems necessary to protect the children and plan for their future. The court cooperates closely with the state department of child welfare services. A social worker is assigned to the case to make recommendations and supervise any court disposition. The court may return the child to the custody of the parents under supervision and conditions, place the

---

157 *See also* Chapter XIV, p. 560.

158 *Arrests of Wife-Beaters Rise In New Policy in Minneapolis,* N.Y.TIMES, July 24, 1984.

159 *See, e.g.,* Mont.Code Ann. §46-6-602.

160 Tenn. Code Ann. §40-7-103(7).

161 *Watson v. City of Kansas City,* 857 F.2d 690 (10th Cir. 1988) (reversing summary judgment dismissing complaint).

child in a foster home until the conditions improve in the home, require counseling or parenting classes for the parents, require therapy or other treatment for the child, or any combination of these measures.[162]

Terminating Parental Rights   When it appears unlikely that any of these measures will improve the child's home sufficiently to permit the child's return, the state may terminate parental rights and make the children "wards of the court." Thereafter, if the child is very young, adoption is a good possibility. However, older children who are permanent wards of the court are difficult to place for adoption. Often the child drifts from one foster home to another, never establishing any real familial ties. Because of these risks and the drastic nature of termination, agencies usually make every effort to return the child home if this is at all possible.[163]   The question in such cases is not whether the child would be better off in foster care than in their parents' home, but whether the parents are unfit. As one state supreme court puts it, "even though it might be in a child's best interests to live with a family of comfortable means rather than a poorer family, this standard may not justify the state's intervention absent a finding of parental unfitness."[164]

Due Process Rights   Abuse or neglect proceedings, while they are civil, have very serious potential consequences for the parents. Consequently, the Supreme Court has held that due process requires that, despite the fact that termination proceedings are civil, the proof standard must be "clear and convincing evidence" rather than the normal civil standard of "preponderance of the evidence."[165]   On the other hand, the Court has held that such proceedings are not so much like criminal cases or other cases involving deprivations of liberty that due process requires appointment of counsel for indigent parents at state expense in every case.[166]   State law often secures this right, however, as well as other procedural protections beyond those afforded in an ordinary civil case.[167] It is also common for the juvenile court to appoint a *guardian ad litem* for the child to directly assert the child's interests in court to the extent that they can be ascertained.

A controversial question involving neglect and abuse statutes has been whether drug-addicted or alcoholic women who give birth to an addicted fetus have committed child neglect or abuse. In *Matter of Smith*[168] a New York court answered this question in the affirmative, holding that an unborn fetus is a child. On the other hand, in *Reyes v. Superior Court in and for San Bernardino County*,[169] the California Court of Appeals refused to view the birth of a drug-addicted baby as evidence of neglect by the mother, because at the time the mother ingested the drugs, she was carrying a fetus, not a developed child. The court felt that neglect or abuse of a child could take place only

---

162 *See generally* GREGORY, SWISHER & SCHEIBLE, *supra* note 4, §5.08.

163 Termination can also result from parental abandonment, mental illness, chronic non-support or from an absent parent unreasonably withholding consent to adoption. *See* Uniform Adoption Act, §19(c), *supra* note 3.

164 *In re Kristina L.*, 520 A.2d 574, 581 (R.I. 1987). *See also In The Matter of The Adoption of Children*, 736 A.2d 1277 (N.J. 1999) ("The termination of parental rights involves consideration of the nature of the right, the permanency of the threatened loss, and an evaluation of parental unfitness. Merely showing that a child would be better off with an adoptive parent rather than the biological parent is not enough.").

165 *Santosky v. Kramer*, 455 U.S. 745 (1982). Standards of proof are explained in Chapter III, p.105.

166 *Lassiter v. North Carolina Dept. of Social Services*, 452 U.S. 18 (1981) (due process may require appointment of counsel in certain cases where the parents are unable to assert their interests, but not all).

167 *See V.F. v. State*, 666 P.2d 42 (Alaska 1983) (state constitution requires appointment of counsel).

168 492 N.Y.S.2d 331 (N.Y.Fam.Ct. 1985). *But see Matter of Fletcher*, 533 N.Y.S.2d 241 (N.Y.Fam.Ct. 1988) (questioning decision in *Smith*).

169 141 Cal. Rptr. 912 (Cal.App. 1977).

after birth because the child abuse statutes do not include fetuses within their definition of "child." If the legislature meant to include a fetus in the definition, it could have specifically stated so, as in the murder statute which specifically defines murder as the unlawful killing of a "human being or fetus."

3. Medical Care

Parents have a duty to provide necessary medical care to their children and a pattern of not doing so may constitute child neglect. However, there are also situations where parents are not providing needed care for a sick child for religious reasons. If the medical procedures indicated involve little risk to the child, courts have not hesitated to step in.[170] If the authorities do not act in time and a child dies, the parents can be convicted of homicide.[171] But if the medical procedure is risky or the risks associated with non-treatment are speculative, courts are less likely to intervene to overturn a parent's decision. Each case is decided on its own facts.

Another issue that has arisen is the medical treatment of newborn children with severe birth defects. Parents in two cases in New York and Indiana withheld consent for lifesaving medical treatment for their severely disabled newborn on the non-religious ground that it was better for them to die. Because of the resulting public clamor, Congress enacted a federal law requiring equal necessary medical treatment for such newborns.[172] Nonetheless, where the parents do not object to withholding treatment, there is an unofficial policy of benign neglect in many hospitals.

4. Juvenile Delinquency

A "juvenile delinquent" is a child who has committed an act that would be a crime were the child an adult, or other anti-social acts, such as repeatedly missing school or disobeying parents. For years the interests of the delinquent and the juvenile court were thought to be identical, so no due process rights were needed like those for adults facing criminal prosecutions. Delinquency was treated like child neglect or abuse cases, in which the court was seen, not really a court, but as a social services agency helping to give guidance to a troubled or confused child. In 1969, the Supreme Court rejected this model and held that juveniles who are subject to confinement for committing an act that would be a crime if committed by an adult, are entitled to the same due process rights as any adult prosecuted for a crime.[173] Since most juvenile delinquency proceedings involve criminal charges, the law of criminal procedure rather than family law is the applicable body of law.[174]

One difference between ordinary criminal proceedings and juvenile delinquency proceedings is the result of the proceeding. If the state proves beyond a reasonable doubt that the minor committed a crime,[175] the court does not apply the penalties set out in the statute. Instead, a "disposition" is ordered that is designed to rehabilitate the

---

170 *Jehovah's Witnesses v. King County Hospital*, 278 F.Supp. 488 (W.D. Wash), *aff'd* 390 U.S. 598 (1968) (blood transfusion necessary to save children ordered despite religious opposition of parents).

171 *See Walker v. Superior Court*, 763 P.2d 852 (Cal. 1988) (parents convicted of manslaughter by denying child medical treatment; religious reasons are no defense). However, some states have made religion-based actions exceptions to child endangerment. *See, e.g.*, Ohio Rev.Code § 2919.22.

172 29 U.S.C.A. § 794 (prohibiting discrimination against the handicapped); 45 C.F.R. § 84.55 (requiring public notice that "nourishment and medically beneficial treatment . . . should not be withheld from handicapped infants solely on the basis of their present or anticipated mental or physical impairments).

173 *In re Gault*, 387 U.S. 1 (1967).

174 *See* Chapter VIII, pp. 283-323.

175 Proof beyond a reasonable doubt is required in juvenile proceedings. *In re Winship*, 397 U.S. 358 (1970).

delinquent minor or otherwise seek to overcome whatever it was that led the minor to commit the offense in the first place. Sometimes this means that in a serious felony case such as murder, a minor could often receive a "sentence" that is much less severe than would be the case with an adult. However, the juvenile court has the option of "waiving jurisdiction" to the normal criminal courts for older minors who do not appear to be amenable to the rehabilitative measures that the court has at its disposal for juveniles. Juveniles in recent years have been committing progressively more serious crimes and presenting a hardened attitude toward changing their conduct. This has resulted in an increased number of instances of juvenile courts waiving jurisdiction to the ordinary criminal courts.

5. Mentally or Physically Disabled People

a. Guardianships of the Estate and the Person

Guardianships of the Estate Adults who are mentally or physically incapable of taking care of their financial affairs can be the subject of a guardianship or wardship "of the estate," under which another person is appointed "guardian" and makes whatever financial arrangements are necessary to provide for them. Such cases are most often filed in the probate or surrogate's court of the state. The guardian, often a close relative of the "ward," the person in need of assistance, has a fiduciary duty to that ward, which requires the highest degree of loyalty and care. To insure that the ward is protected from improper actions or neglect of the ward's affairs, guardians are usually required to file reports with the court and to purchase a bond to cover any losses they cause. In some states, a guardianship can be established, not just when there is full mental incapacity, but where the ward is a "spendthrift."

Guardianship of the Person This form of guardianship is also used when the ward is mentally or physically disabled, but its purpose is not to deal with the ward's finances. A guardian of the person can in general make decisions for the ward with respect to non-financial matters, such as decisions as to medical treatment. Often guardianships of both the estate and the person are established.[176]

b. Civil Commitment of Mentally Ill Persons

All states have some procedure for involuntary commitment of mentally ill persons to a psychiatric facility. Usually the petitioner seeking commitment is a relative of the respondent or a public agency or social worker. However, more than just mental illness must be proven. Constitutional principles permit involuntary commitment only of persons who are a danger to themselves or others, or who cannot take care of their basic needs. In addition, though the proceeding is a civil one, the grounds for commitment must be proven by "clear and convincing evidence" rather than the normal civil "preponderance of the evidence" standard.[177]

c. Issues Involving the Mentally Retarded

Civil Commitment to an Institution The adult mentally retarded are in most states subject to the same procedures for involuntary commitment to an institution as are the mentally ill, although the nature of their institutional surrounding and care is different.

---

176 For more on guardianships, *see* DONALD H.J. HERMANN, MENTAL HEALTH AND DISABILITY LAW IN A NUTSHELL 214-233 (West 1997).

177 *O'Connor v. Donaldson*, 422 U.S. 563, 576 (1975) ("A state cannot constitutionally confine . . . a non-dangerous individual who is capable of surviving safely in freedom by himself or with the help of willing and responsible family members or friends"); *id.* at 432 (proof standard). *See also supra* note 165. For more on mental commitments, *see* HERMANN, *supra* note 176, at 142-183.

Most often, however, the mentally retarded are diagnosed as such early in life and are committed voluntarily by their parents as infants. However, a major effort at "de-institutionalizing" the less severely mentally retarded has come about since the 1970s and more and more of them are taken care of in small group homes or are in independent living situations.

Sterilization of the Mentally Retarded At the turn of the century, the eugenics movement was strong in the U.S. Its followers believed that "science" could improve the human species by eliminating "defective" genes from the human gene pool. One method of doing this was to sterilize those who suffered from mental retardation, mentally illness, epilepsy and other "defective" conditions. Many states passed laws permitting involuntary sterilization. The U.S. Supreme Court in 1927 upheld the constitutionality of these laws. By to analogy to compulsory vaccinations against smallpox, Justice Holmes's majority opinion reflected eugenics theory: "It is better for all the world, if instead of waiting to execute degenerate offspring for crime or to let them starve for their imbecility, society can prevent those who are manifestly unfit from continuing their kind."[178] In 1942, the Supreme Court decided *Skinner v. Oklahoma*, declaring that an Oklahoma statute that provided for mandatory sterilization of "habitual criminals" was unconstitutional because it interfered with the "fundamental right" to procreate.[179] However, *Skinner* did not invalidate involuntary sterilization in all cases. It only required that there be "strict scrutiny" of such laws, thus requiring that they be justified by a "compelling state interest."[180]

Today, involuntary sterilization is possible in many states, either by statute or as an exercise of courts' inherent equity powers. In general, mentally disabled persons who are sexually active, are unwilling or unable to employ other contraceptive methods and are unable to care for a child, will probably be ordered sterilized and that result is probably constitutional.[181]

---

178 *Buck v. Bell*, 274 U.S. 200, 207 (1927). One sentence later he uttered his now-famous dictum "Three generations of imbeciles are enough."

179 316 U.S. 535 (1942). *Skinner* is also discussed in Chapter IX, p. 356.

180 Strict scrutiny and compelling state interest are discussed in Chapter IX, pp. 351-356, 363.

181 *See North Carolina Ass'n of Retarded Citizens v. North Carolina*, 420 F.Supp. 451 (M.D.N.C. 1976). *See also In re Moe*, 432 N.E.2d 712 (Mass. 1982) (sterilization is proper exercise of equity powers; concept of "substituted judgment" to be used, whereby court determines what the retarded person would want were he or she mentally competent).

CHAPTER XIV

CRIMINAL LAW

Crimes usually have private victims, but criminal actions are considered to be offenses against the state and society. As a result, the state has an interest in prosecuting offenders beyond the rights or wishes of any private person.[1]

A. General Considerations

1. Sources and Variety of Criminal Law

State and Federal Law Criminal law in the United States has traditionally been the domain of the state law. Most "ordinary" criminal offenses, such as murder, assault, rape, larceny and robbery are governed exclusively by state law, while federal crimes have historically been limited to conduct having a direct relationship to federal property or legislative programs or interstate aspects of crime.[2] However, just as non-criminal federal legislative activity has grown in recent decades, there has been an increased "federalization" of criminal law. Again like non-criminal federal law, federal crimes do not preempt state law on the same subject, so the result is a mix of state and federal criminal laws that might apply to the same conduct of a person or enterprise.[3] But beyond the creation of new federal crimes pursuant to Congress's broad commerce power, there has been an increased willingness to prosecute "old" federal crimes based on the perception that some crimes present a national problem that states cannot handle alone. The prime example of this is the federal government's "War on Drugs," declared by President Reagan and continued in successive administrations.

Statutory and Common Law Crimes Crimes in England were originally defined by the common law. Given the lack of sufficient notice of potential criminal sanctions involved when criminal offenses are set out exclusively in caselaw, most states have chosen to adopt a statutory approach. A few states retain common law crimes to the extent that they do not conflict with statutes.[4] Federal crimes are completely statutory.[5] However, statutes have tended to codify the common law. This means that there is considerable similarity in crimes among the states. It also means that common law definitions of elements of offenses and defense are still important. Indeed, many state statutes use general common law terms without defining them, such as "murder,"

---

1 Standard criminal law texts are WAYNE R. LAFAVE, HORNBOOK ON CRIMINAL LAW (West 2000) and JOSHUA DRESSLER, UNDERSTANDING CRIMINAL LAW, 4TH ED. (Lexis 2006). An outline with more than average detail is PETER W. LOW, CRIMINAL LAW, 2D ED. (West 2002).

2 *See, e.g.,* 18 U.S.C.A. §2312 (transportation of stolen vehicles across state lines) and 18 U.S.C.A. §1073 (interstate flight to avoid prosecution or giving testimony).

3 The general federalization of the law and mix of federal and state laws was discussed in Chapter I, pp. 21-28, 30-33.

4 *See, e.g., Gervin v. State,* 371 S.W.2d 449, 454 (Tenn. 1963) (common law misdemeanor offense of solicitation to commit a crime was not merged into attempt statute and is still prosecutable as an offense separate from attempt); *State v. Palendrano,* 293 A.2d 747 (N.J. 1972) (common law offense of "common scold," a chronically difficult and argumentative woman, was preempted by statutory offense with common elements). Common law offenses come into the law by way of state statutes or constitutional provisions formally "receiving" English common law. *See* Chapter II, p. 43.

5 *United States v. Hudson and Goodwin,* 11 U.S. (7 Cranch.) 32 (1812) (Article III's vesting judicial power in federal courts did not include the authority to create common law crimes). The reasons for limiting federal court common law powers are discussed in Chapter I, pp. 35-36. One federal crime is defined in the Constitution. Art. III §3 defines treason as "levying War against [the United States] . . . or in adhering to their Enemies, giving them Aid and Comfort."

because it is expected that courts will give those terms their settled common law meaning.[6]

Civil penalties can also be set out in state and federal administrative regulations or orders pursuant to legislative delegation of authority.[7] However, agencies adjudicating violations are limited solely to imposing a fine and may not order imprisonment as a sanction.[8]

The Importance of the Model Penal Code A major step toward greater uniformity and rationality of state criminal codes was taken in 1962 when the American Law Institute adopted the Model Penal Code (MPC).[9] Spurred by the MPC, nearly 40 states have enacted new criminal codes during the past 30 years. Some states have used the MPC almost in its entirety except for certain provisions they believe need modification. Other states have utilized only certain provisions from the MPC which they feel appropriately fit within their pre-existing statutory scheme.

Unlike the Uniform Commercial Code (UCC), which stresses the necessity for uniformity in commercial practices, the MPC is intended to be a "model" for state legislatures to help identify the major issues, and the alternatives to these issues, in criminal law. In fact, it is considered appropriate by many scholars that states should have significant variations in their penal laws, based upon differences in local conditions or points of view.[10]

Because criminal law in the United States is a mixture of the MPC and common law concepts, it has become necessary for students of the criminal law to learn both. Consequently, both common law and MPC approaches will be discussed in this chapter where their differences are major.

Categories of Criminal Offenses A crime can be either a "felony" or a "misdemeanor." Generally, crimes punishable by imprisonment for more than one year or by death are felonies. Those punishable by incarceration for less than a year or solely by a fine are misdemeanors. Some states, however, have a classification of "high misdemeanor," which are crimes punishable by more than one year, but not more than two years of imprisonment.[11] Some states have "civil infractions" that have only monetary penalties and are not considered to be criminal offenses. These include parking and other minor traffic offenses.

2. Constitutional Considerations

Both the federal and state governments have broad powers to criminalize a wide range of behavior, but these powers must give way if they violate constitutional liberties. Many of the cases discussed in the chapter on constitutional law grew out of criminal

---

6 *See, e.g.*, Mich.Comp.L.Ann. §750.317 (punishing "murder" without defining it).

7 *See also Atlas Roofing Co. v. Occupational Safety and Health Review Comm.*, 430 U.S. 442 (1977) (no right to jury trial in civil penalty administrative proceeding for violation of worker safety rules).

8 *See Wing Wong v. United States*, 163 U.S. 228 (1896) (judicial trial necessary before sentence of 1 year at hard labor could be imposed). For federal agencies at least, part of the reason that agencies cannot punish criminal offenses is that crimes are said to involve "private rights" that must be adjudicated by an Article III judge. *See* Chapter VI, pp. 220-222. On the question of administrative powers regarding these issues, *see generally* BERNARD SCHWARTZ, ADMINISTRATIVE LAW, 3D ED., §§2.24, 2.28, 2.29, 9.17 (Aspen 1991).

9 MODEL PENAL CODE, PROPOSED OFFICIAL DRAFT (American Law Institute 1962).

10 *See* LAFAVE, *supra* note 1, at 4.

11 MPC §1.04.

prosecutions.[12] However, there are other constitutional limitations specifically applicable to criminal statutes that should be mentioned here.

The Constitution prohibits bills of attainder and *ex post facto* laws.[13] A bill of attainder is a law passed by a legislature that specifically identifies a person or an easily identifiable person within a group and punishes that person without a trial.[14] An *ex post facto* law operates to make conduct criminal that was not criminal when it occurred. Also included in the definition are laws that increase the punishment for crimes that have already been committed or that change the rules of evidence for such crimes.[15] The prohibition against *ex post facto* laws applies only to legislatively enacted law, not judicially created law.[16] The clauses also do not apply to what courts consider "non-punitive" legislation, such as laws requiring convicted sex offenders to register on a public registry, because the goal of the registry is to protect the public, not punish the offender.[17]

B. Elements of a Crime

Generally, for a criminal offense to exist, there must be (1) a wrongful act or omission, (2) a guilty state of mind, and (3) sometimes, causation of injury. The burden is on the prosecution to prove each element "beyond a reasonable doubt."[18]

1. The Wrongful Act

Nature of Requirement of a Wrongful Act Bad thoughts alone are an insufficient basis of criminal liability. Instead, there must be some wrongful or criminal act (*actus reus*), whether it is an actual physical action taken by the defendant or an omission. In order for an omission to constitute an "act," there must be some duty to act on the part of the defendant. Generally there is no duty to aid another person in peril, even when such aid can be given without inconvenience. One need not reach out to save a drowning child in a pool, nor give warning to a person who is about to fall into an open manhole.[19] A duty to act generally exists only when there is some special relationship created by contract or statute. Thus, parents have affirmative duties to care for and protect their children. Additionally, the law implies a duty to act where one person voluntarily assumes the care of another, where a person creates some peril by an unlawful act that endangers another, or when a landowner hosts business invitees on his or her property.[20]

Voluntariness Requirement The defendant's act must have been voluntary to qualify as criminal.[21] The requirement of voluntariness is based on the principle that

---

12 *See* Chapter IX.

13 Art. I §§9, 10.

14 *See, e.g., United States v. Brown*, 381 U.S. 437 (1965) (federal act that made it a criminal offense for a member of the Communist party to be a labor organization officer held unconstitutional).

15 See *Calder v. Bull*, 3 U.S. (3 Dall.) 386 (1798) (listing types of laws covered by the constitutional prohibition against *ex post facto* laws and determining that a Connecticut law granting a new trial regarding a will was not such a law).

16 See *Ross v. Oregon*, 227 U.S. 150 (1913) (*ex post facto* prohibition does not apply to judicial construction of a state statute).

17 *Smith v. Doe,* 538 U.S. 84 (2003).

18 *See* Chapter VIII, p. 269.

19 *See, e.g., State v. Ulvinen*, 313 N.W.2d 425 (Minn. 1981) (defendant not criminally liable for daughter-in-law's death when he knew of son's plan to kill her and did not warn her).

20 *See, e.g., State v. Benton*, 187 A. 609 (Del. 1936) (railway gateman guilty of criminal homicide for failing to lower gate to prevent an automobile from colliding with a train).

21 MPC §2.01(1).

criminal liability only attaches to conduct that the defendant can control.[22] But what is meant by "voluntary" is not entirely clear. The MPC does not define the term, but it does list acts which are not voluntary: reflex or convulsions, bodily movement during sleep, conduct during hypnosis, and bodily movement that otherwise is not a product of the effort or determination of the actor, either conscious or habitual.[23]

Punishment of Status In *Robinson v. California*,[24] the Supreme Court held it was unconstitutional to punish a defendant for *being* a drug addict. It reasoned that addiction is an illness can be acquired involuntarily and that punishing involuntary status would amount to "cruel and unusual punishment," contrary to the 8th Amendment. However, in *Powell v. Texas*[25] the Court upheld the conviction of a chronic alcoholic for public drunkenness. A synthesis of these two cases suggests that a defendant can be punished for the possession or use of substances to which the defendant is addicted, but cannot be punished for the status of being addicted.[26]

2. Fault or Guilty Mind (*Mens Rea*)

Generally, there can be a crime only if a criminal act (*actus reus*) is combined with some guilty state of mind (*mens rea*). Nonetheless, at least in certain circumstances, liability is possible without regard to fault.

a. The Levels of Fault

Under the modern view, there are three levels of guilty mind requirements: intent, recklessness and negligence. The greatest fault is assigned when defendants act intentionally. A person is said to act with intent to bring about certain harm if that person either (1) acts with the purpose (*i.e.*, desire or design) of causing the harm or (2) voluntarily acts with the knowledge that the harm will almost certainly occur as a result of that act.[27] An example of acting with the intent to kill would be where a person aims and shoots another with a gun.[28] "Recklessness" can be defined as acting with the awareness that one's conduct is creating a significant unjustified risk of harm. For example, a person who fires a gun in the direction of a group of people assembled on the street acts recklessly. Criminal recklessness requires that the defendant actually be aware of the risk of harm. "Criminal negligence" embraces somewhat lesser culpability than recklessness. It is reserved for defendants whose behavior would otherwise be reckless, but who are not subjectively aware of the significant unjustified risk of harm that they are creating. Negligence exists if a "reasonable and prudent" person *would*

---

22 *See, e.g., Fain v. Commonwealth*, 78 Ky. 183 (1879) (person who kills while in a state of sleep or between waking and sleep not guilty of murder).

23 MPC §2.01.

24 370 U.S. 660 (1962).

25 392 U.S. 514 (1968).

26 *See also United States v. Moore*, 486 F.2d 1139 (D.C. Cir. 1973) (declining to recognize addiction as a defense because there is no consensus that addiction overrides free will).

27 The MPC does not use the term "intent." Instead, it distinguishes between (1) and (2) in the text above explicitly as (1) "purposely" and (2) "knowingly." MPC §2.02.

28 Knowledge includes a suspicion that a fact exists with the deliberate avoidance of learning that the suspicion is correct, sometimes called "wilful blindness." *See, e.g., United States v. Jewell*, 532 F.2d 697 (9th Cir. 1976) (defendant knew of a secret compartment in a car which he acquired under suspicious circumstances; this was sufficient to establish the knowledge requirement for importing marijuana even if he did not actually know that it was in the compartment). *But see United States v. Heredia*, 429 F.3d 820, 824 (9th Cir. 2005) ("willful blindness"jury instructions are "rarely appropriate" and should not be used to "close gaps" in the prosecution's case, even the defendant-driver suspects passengers may have hidden drugs in the car).

have been aware of the risk. An example of criminal negligence would be firing a gun out a window without looking to see whether there was anyone there.[29]

b. General and Specific Intent

The requirement of fault demands that at least "general intent" be shown to make out a crime. General intent is satisfied by showing a voluntary act done with an awareness of the probable consequences of that act — essentially the standard of recklessness.[30] "Specific intent" may also be required for some crimes.[31] This extra mental element is essentially a requirement that the defendant have a purpose to accomplish a particular harmful result. Specific intent is usually imposed when the law wishes to single out particular types of behavior for more serious treatment. Usually the basic conduct involved is already punishable, but higher punishment is specified if the conduct is carried out with a particular purpose in mind. For example, a state might punish simple possession of narcotics, but punish more severely the very same act of possession if it is coupled with the intention to sell those narcotics. Similarly, the law may wish to punish more severely assault with intent to do serious bodily harm than a simple assault, even when the same injury is inflicted in both cases. For a conviction on the more serious version of the crime, the prosecution must prove both general intent and the specific intent.[32]

Situations occur where the defendant acts with the intent to cause one result and another result takes place instead. For example, if the defendant shoots at one person intending to kill that person and hits and kills another person instead, the defendant has the requisite *mens rea* for the murder of the person actually killed because the defendant intended to kill *some* person, and therefore satisfied the fault requirement for murder.[33] Because the harm that resulted (killing a person) was the same *type* of harm the defendant intended, then the requisite *mens rea* exists. In such cases, it is said that the intent is "transferred" from the intended victim to the actual accidental one. However, if the defendant shoots at a teacup sitting on a table intending only to destroy it and instead accidentally hits a person, the same type of harm was not intended, so intent cannot be "transferred" from the cup to a person.[34]

c. Liability Without Fault

The common law traditionally requires some level of fault to make out a criminal offense. However, legislatures have dispensed with the *mens rea* requirement in four situations. One is where there is a "public welfare offense" for which strict liability is imposed. A second is where the fault of one person is vicariously attributed to a different person. A third type of liability without fault is the criminal liability of a corporation, which has no mind and thus can have no guilty mind. A fourth is statutory rape, where absence of consent is conclusively presumed.

---

29 These definitions correspond generally with that in tort law. *See* Chapter XI, p. 436.

30 When a crime does not specify intent, the MPC requires at least recklessness. MPC §2.02(3).

31 The MPC does not make this distinction.

32 Specific intent is shown by circumstantial evidence. *See, e.g., United States v. Wilson*, 432 F.Supp. 223 (S.D.Tex.1976) (possession of 493 pounds of marijuana is sufficient to presume intent to distribute. *See also Defries v. State*, 342 N.E.2d 622 (Ind. 1976) (discussing different types of aggravated assault laws).

33 *See, e.g., Mayweather v. State*, 242 P. 864 (Ariz. 1926) (defendant found guilty of murder for shooting one person while intending to kill another).

34 If the teacup was close to the person shot, the defendant might be deemed to have acted intentionally toward the victim, *i.e.* with knowledge that the resulting injury was almost certain to occur. Depending on the distance, the defendant might also be deemed to have acted recklessly, *i.e.* creating an unjustifiable risk of harm.

Public Welfare Offenses Most "public welfare offenses" are minor offenses for which it is difficult to prove intent or other fault. Traffic offenses are the most prevalent.[35] Others involve liquor sales.[36] These offenses are often not thought of as "real" crimes since they usually do not involve morally blameworthy conduct and are usually punished only by fines. Some states have even decriminalized some of them, calling them "civil infractions."[37] This movement for change is not universal, however, and in any event not all such offenses have been decriminalized. In many countries such matters are handled administratively, so it is sometimes a shock when visitors to the U.S. find out first hand that they are crimes.

Other public welfare offenses are more serious but still remove the need to prove fault at least as to some elements. The theory behind this is that the threat to health and safety posed by the activity in question is so obvious that this is sufficient notice to the defendant that it is regulated, thus excusing the need to prove fault. The nature of the object or activity punished, then, may affect the degree of fault required. For example, the Supreme Court held it proper to convict a defendant of illegal possession of an unregistered hand grenade based solely on the defendant's knowledge that what he possessed was a hand grenade. However, conviction for possession of an unregistered machine gun required that it be proven that the defendant knew that the weapon he possessed was capable of firing multiple rounds with one trigger pull, the salient characteristic of a machine gun.[38] In both cases, the person was held strictly liable for knowing that the item needed to be registered, but the characteristics of the item that required its registration differed in terms of their obviousness. For some public welfare offenses, then, it must be proven that the defendant's conduct as to *operative facts* of the offense was undertaken knowingly, though it need not be proven that the defendant knew the consequences of that conduct or its unlawfulness.[39]

Vicarious Liability Vicarious liability is liability imposed on a person without regard to personal fault or even personal conduct. It is automatic liability that results from the conduct of another. The largest number of vicarious liability situations involve the employer-employee relationship, as where a clerk in a store sells liquor to a minor and the employer is held responsible.[40] When a corporation commits a crime, corporate officers can also be vicariously liable if they had a "responsible relation" to the relevant corporate action and the power to prevent them.[41] Laws imposing vicarious liability on parents for the acts of their children are rare, however.[42] And even employer-employee vicarious liability has its limits. The Supreme Court held it was unconstitutional to

35 *See People v. Caddy*, 540 P.2d 1089 (Colo. 1975) (speeding is a strict liability crime, so a defective speedometer is no defense).

36 *City of Dickinson v. Mueller*, 261 N.W.2d 787 (N.D. 1977) (strict liability for sale of liquor to minor).

37 *See* MPC §2.05, which calls such strict liability offenses "violations." rather than crimes. Often the decriminalization is not so much out of concern for the stigma attached as it is about avoiding giving defendants jury trials. Many state constitutions provide for the right to a jury in "all criminal prosecutions."

38 *United States v. Freed*, 401 U.S. 601, 609 (1971) (hand grenade); *United States v Staples*, 511 U.S. 600, 612 (1971) (machine gun).

39 Environmental laws present similar problems and a similar approach has been taken by the lower federal courts. *See United States v. Wilson*, 133 F.3d 251, 264-265 (4th Cir. 1997) (Clean Water Act case with a thoughtful discussion of the issues). *See also* Chapter XV, p. 638 (environmental offenses).

40 *But see Commonwealth v. Koczwara*, 155 A.2d 825 (Pa. 1959) (in liquor sale case, due process does not permit imprisonment of employer for acts of employee, only a fine).

41 *United States v. Park*, 421 U.S. 658 (1975) (not unconstitutional to hold president of national food store chain liable for corporation's shipments of adulterated food).

42 *State v. Akers*, 400 A.2d 38 (N.H. 1979) (law making parents vicariously liable for offenses committed by their children in the operation of snowmobiles is unconstitutional).

convict a store owner of "knowingly and willfully" contributing to the delinquency of a minor just because his employee sold a button with an indecent slogan to a minor.[43]

3. Causation

Some criminal offenses require proof that the defendant's conduct caused harm to a victim. For example, to be convicted of any form of homicide, the prosecutor must prove that the defendant's actions were the legal or "proximate" cause of the victim's death.[44]

Cause-in-Fact and Proximate Cause There are two steps in determining causation. The first is to determine if the defendant's action was a "cause-in-fact" of the harmful result. Cause-in-fact is a cause that is sufficient for the result to occur, a *sine qua non* test. It is most often stated as "but-for" causation: "but for" the defendant's conduct (*i.e.*, without the defendant's conduct), the result or harm would *not* have taken place. If cause-in-fact cannot be shown, then the inquiry is over and causation is not satisfied. If cause-in-fact is shown, then the second step is to determine whether that cause-in-fact was the "proximate cause" of the harm. There can be many "but-for" causes of harm, but the law can punish a defendant's behavior only if it was a *proximate* cause of the harm. In general, "proximate cause" means that there is an uninterrupted causal chain between the defendant's act and the harm. In most cases this is easily determined. For example, if the defendant shoots the victim and the victim dies immediately, there is obviously nothing breaking the causal chain. However, the causal link is sometimes less clear.[45]

Intervening Cause An intervening act can "break the chain" of causation. Whether it will depends in most situations on whether it was a *coincidence* unrelated to the defendant's actions or a *response* to the actions of the defendant. As one might expect, the law permits a longer chain of causation for response than coincidence.

A coincidence will break the chain of causation only if its intervention and result were not foreseeable. For example, assume that the defendant inflicts a non-fatal wound on the victim and leaves the victim lying unconscious in the middle of a road at night. If a passing motorist runs over the victim causing death, then the defendant can be said to have caused the death because such a consequence was a foreseeable result of leaving the victim on the road.[46] On the other hand, if the defendant left the victim on a *sidewalk* and a drunk driver lost control and drove onto the sidewalk and ran over the victim, this would not be foreseeable.

In the case of an intervening *response* to conditions created by the defendant, causation will be found in some cases even if the response was not foreseeable. Only if the response is completely abnormal will the defendant be said not to have caused the ultimate result. An example is a case involving negligent treatment of a crime victims' wounds by health care professionals. Generally, "ordinary" negligent medical treatment

43 *Vachon v. New Hampshire*, 414 U.S. 478 (1974) (button proclaiming "copulation, not masturbation" sold to 14-year-old girl).

44 *See, e.g., People v. Dlugash*, 363 N.E.2d 1155 (N.Y. 1977) (murder conviction reduced to attempted murder where defendant shot victim five times in the face after victim had been shot in the chest by another; prosecution did not show that victim was alive at the time the defendant shot him).

45 *See, e.g., Commonwealth v. Berggren*, 496 N.E.2d 660 (Mass. 1986) (proximate cause existed based on foreseeable chain of events in motor vehicle homicide case when defendant on his motorcycle led police car on a high-speed chase and police office died in accident when his car hit a tree).

46 *People v. Fowler*, 174 P. 892 (Cal. 1918).

is considered "normal" and does not break the causation chain,[47] while grossly negligent or intentional malpractice is considered an intervening cause.[48]

Response actions by the *victim* may also be part of a proper causation chain. For example, when the victim, whom the defendant has beaten, dragged to a river and threatened with more beatings, "voluntarily" jumps into the river and drowns, the defendant is still liable for the victim's death.[49] Responsibility for the result of a victim's suicide is sometimes imposed. Where the defendant has seriously wounded the victim and the victim commits suicide for reasons unrelated to his wounds, the defendant will not be held responsible for the victim's death. But it is not considered abnormal that a victim could commit suicide out of extreme pain from the wounds the defendant inflicted or from mental incompetence caused by those wounds. In such a case, the defendant has been held responsible.[50]

The Common Law "Year and a Day" Rule The common law rule that is still followed by many jurisdictions is that a defendant cannot be found guilty of murder if the victim lives for more than a year and a day after the defendant's act. This rule is based on the premise that it is too difficult to prove that the act of the defendant was the cause of the death after too much time has passed. Due to advances in the medical field, this is clearly no longer the case and many jurisdictions have abandoned the rule.[51]

Other Causation Situations Intervening acts aside, the lack of foreseeability of the *particular* resulting harm does not always break the causal chain. For instance, an illness of the victim that causes the victim to suffer greater harm than was foreseeable to the defendant at the time of the crime does not bar the act from being considered the proximate cause of the harm.[52] As the Indiana Supreme Court once noted, "if one throws a piece of chalk at [a] victim with an eggshell skull, and the chalk strikes the victim and fractures his skull, the perpetrator would be guilty" of aggravated assault, even though he did not intend to do this amount of bodily harm.[53]

C. Specific Offenses

1. Criminal Homicide

Murder Murder is a common law crime, traditionally defined as an unlawful killing of a human being with "malice aforethought."[54] Malice is "the intent to kill, the intent to cause great bodily harm, or the intent to do an act in wanton and wilful disregard of the likelihood that the natural tendency of such behavior is to cause death or great bodily

---

47 *People v. Fite*, 627 P.2d 761 (Colo. 1981) (doctor's discontinuance of antibiotics was not gross negligence, so chain of causation not broken and defendant was guilty of homicide).

48 *People v. Stewart*, 358 N.E.2d 487 (N.Y 1976) (failure of anesthesiologist to provide oxygen to patient in operation to repair hernia following surgery for knife wound defendant inflicted held to break chain of causation and defendant was not guilty of homicide).

49 *State v. Myers*, 81 A.2d 710 (N.J. 1951).

50 *See also United States v. Hamilton*, 182 F.Supp. 548 (D.D.C. 1960) (defendant responsible for death where non-fatal wound he inflicted sent victim to hospital, where victim ripped out life-supporting tubes causing death).

51 *See, e.g., Commonwealth v. Lewis*, 409 N.E.2d 771 (Mass. 1980) (rule is an anachronism in light of advances in showing cause of death and in prolonging life). *See also Rogers v. Tennessee*, 532 U.S. 451 (2001) (Tennessee Supreme Court's abolition of the rule on appeal of defendant's case did not violate due process given that its abolition was "not unexpected and indefensible").

52 *See, e.g., Hopkins v. Commonwealth*, 80 S.W. 156 (Ky. 1904) (it was murder when defendant killed victim weakened by prior illness who perhaps would not have died if completely healthy).

53 *Defries v. State*, 342 N.E.2d 622, 629-630 (Ind. 1976).

54 *See* LaFave, *supra* note 1, §7.1.

harm."[55] These coincide with the intent and recklessness levels of *mens rea* discussed earlier.[56] In defining malice for juries, some courts have used such terms as "wilful and wanton disregard for the value of human life" or "abandoned and malignant heart," while others have stated more simply that intent to kill from any "unlawful and unjustified motives" is sufficient, leaving the matter for the jury to determine.[57]

It is common for criminal codes to divide murder into degrees. This was originally done to single out first degree murder for capital punishment. For example, a statute might classify murder perpetrated by means of poison, lying in wait, or other wilful, deliberate, and premeditated killing, or murder committed in the perpetration of any felony, as murder in the first degree, and provide that all other murder is in the second degree. The MPC provides that a criminal homicide constitutes murder when committed purposely, knowingly, or recklessly under circumstances that manifest an extreme indifference to the value of human life.[58] The MPC does not divide murder into degrees.

Felony Murder One of the more controversial forms of murder is "felony murder," which exists in most states: if any death occurs during the commission of a felony, the defendant committing the felony can be convicted of murder without the requisite mental state for murder and even without directly causing the death of the victim.[59] In theory, the requisite mental state can be imputed to the defendant from the defendant's intent to commit the felonious act.[60] Felony murder is said to deter criminals from committing felonies, or at least to encourage them to commit them safely. However, the felony murder rule has been criticized by scholars, and many courts have limited its application. Courts have (1) required that the felony be inherently dangerous, (2) required the prosecutor to prove malice in addition to proof of a killing and a felony, (3) required that the felony be independent from the act that caused the victim's death, and (4) tightened the causal chain by requiring that the death be at least foreseeable and take place at or near the time of the felony.[61] In addition, some statutes limit felony murder to deaths that take place only during specific felonies enumerated in the statute. The MPC largely rejects felony murder and instead substitutes an evidentiary presumption of malice from commission of certain enumerated felonies.[62] Despite the MPC's stand, most states retain some form of felony murder.

Manslaughter Manslaughter is a homicide under conditions that make it a lesser crime than murder. There are two major types of manslaughter: voluntary manslaughter, which involves intentional killings, and involuntary manslaughter, which involves unintentional killings. Usually a more severe punishment attaches to voluntary man-

---

55 *People v. Goecke*, 579 N.W.2d 868, 878 (Mich. 1998). MPC §210.2(1)(b) requires simply the intent to kill or recklessness manifesting an extreme indifference to human life. Intent to cause merely serious bodily harm alone will not support a conviction.

56 *See supra* p. 552. Negligence is insufficient for murder.

57 *See also People v. Woods*, 331 N.W.2d 707 (Mich. 1982) (substituting intent to kill or do great bodily injury for the term "malice," which court considered to be meaningless and confusing to juries).

58 MPC §210.2(1)(b).

59 *See, e.g., People v. Stamp*, 82 Cal.Rptr. 598 (Cal.App. 1969) (defendant properly found guilty of murder when, during a robbery, a person died of fright). *Compare Commonwealth v. Redline*, 137 A.2d 472 (Pa. 1958) (defendant not guilty of murder where co-felon was shot and killed by a policeman) *with Commonwealth v. Moyer*, 53 A.2d 736 (Pa. 1947) (defendant properly guilty of murder where one victim accidentally shot another victim after being wounded by defendant).

60 *But cf. People v. Dillon*, 668 P.2d 697 (Cal. 1983) (malice is not an element of felony murder, so there is no unconstitutional presumption).

61 *See generally* LaFave, *supra* note 1, §7.5.

62 MPC §210.

slaughter. The MPC and some states do not make a distinction in punishment between voluntary and involuntary manslaughter. However, many jurisdictions maintain the distinction. Other states disregard the distinction between voluntary and involuntary, and, instead, divide manslaughter into degrees.

In the common law understanding, voluntary manslaughter is an intentional killing which is reduced from murder when the defendant is provoked so as to be "acting in the heat of passion." In determining what constitutes an adequate provocation, courts ask whether "reasonable" persons would have had their passions aroused. Moreover, the killing must follow shortly after the provocation. A homicide committed with adequate provocation, but after a sufficient "cooling-off" period, would be considered murder, not manslaughter.[63]

Involuntary manslaughter may be divided into two types. The first type is negligent involuntary manslaughter. The majority of jurisdictions have *mens rea* requirements for involuntary manslaughter that are similar to either the criminal negligence or the recklessness standards discussed earlier.[64] However, a few jurisdictions use a civil negligence standard.[65] The second type of involuntary manslaughter, "misdemeanor-manslaughter," parallels the felony-murder rule. Under this concept, an unintended homicide that occurs in the commission of a misdemeanor constitutes involuntary manslaughter.[66] However, like felony murder, misdemeanor manslaughter has been limited by courts because they deem it too harsh. The MPC abandons the misdemeanor manslaughter rule and some states have done so as well.

2. Burglary

Burglary was defined at common law as breaking and entering the dwelling of another in the nighttime with the intent to commit a felony therein.[67] At common law, "breaking" meant that the burglar had to create an opening to enter the dwelling. Going through an open window or door was insufficient. The rationale was to ensure that homeowners secured theirs windows and doors. However, modern criminal codes rarely require "breaking." Instead, such terms like "unlawfully" are used to describe the type of entry necessary for burglary.[68] Modern statutes do not require much "entering" either. It has been held that as small an entry as a foot entering through a kicked-in window satisfies the requirement.[69] Moreover, if one enters premises when open and remains there surreptitiously until after the premises are closed, that is also an "entry."[70]

---

63 *See, e.g., Sheppard v. State*, 10 So.2d 822 (Ala. 1942) (defendant killed wife several days after discovering her adulterous behavior; conviction of first degree murder, not manslaughter, was proper).

64 *See supra* p. 552. *Compare Commonwealth v. Welansky*, 55 N.E.2d 902 (Mass. 1944) (awareness of high risk of harm not necessary for conviction of manslaughter when 490 people died in fire due to inadequate precautions) *with Bussard v. State*, 288 N.W. 187 (Wis. 1939) (defendant found not to have realized the high risk of harm created by driving negligently and therefore was not guilty of involuntary manslaughter for resulting death).

65 *See, e.g., State v. Williams*, 484 P.2d 1167 (Wash.App. 1971) (civil negligence standard was sufficient for involuntary manslaughter conviction of parents who caused the death of their infant child by failing to get medical care).

66 *See, e.g., People v. Nelson*, 128 N.E.2d 391 (N.Y. 1955) (defendant-landlord's misdemeanor of failing to provide adequate fire precautions in his apartment building which resulted in two deaths held to support manslaughter conviction).

67 *See* LaFave, *supra* note 1, §8.13.

68 The Model Penal Code deals with the problem by simply excluding all entries onto premises when they are open to the public or by a person who is licensed or privileged to enter. MPC §221.1.

69 *People v. Roldan*, 241 N.E.2d 591 (Ill.App. 1968) (defendant's act of kicking in store window, which enabled others to loot store, was sufficient for burglary conviction).

70 MPC §221.1.

Part of the theoretical basis of burglary was the need for special protection of homes. Any building used for habitation is considered a dwelling, even if only part of the building is so used. The requirement that the burglary take place at nighttime is based on the notion that such intrusions will terrorize residents more than daytime entries. Most modern burglary statutes punish both day and nighttime entries as burglary, but some states punish nighttime entries more severely.

Common law burglary also required that the burglar intend to commit a felony within the dwelling. If the intruder merely intended to trespass, then there was no burglary. However, modern criminal codes no longer make it necessary to intend a felony. Instead, all that is required is an intent to commit some offense. Where intent to commit an offense is a required element, proof of specific intent is required.[71]

3. Theft Offenses

Traditionally, larceny, false pretenses and embezzlement make up the three major forms of theft.[72] "Larceny" has been defined as the "trespassory taking and carrying away of the personal property of another with the intent to deprive the other of the property permanently."[73] Larceny includes improperly retaining the lost, mislaid or mistakenly delivered property of another, as well as actually taking property.[74] False pretenses can be defined as knowingly obtaining the property of another, with the purpose to defraud the other, through factual misrepresentation.[75] Embezzlement involves the wrongful conversion to one's own use of the property of another that is already in one's possession. An example is an employee who handles money or property of his or her employer and takes some of it.[76]

Intent to permanently deprive the owner of the property is an essential element of theft and an intent to return property to the lawful owner will absolve the defendant.[77] However, abandoning property with merely a *hope* that the owner will find it does not negate intent to permanently deprive the owner of the property.[78] Problems with young people taking cars temporarily to go "joyriding" have caused many states to pass statutes that remove the need to show intent to permanently deprive the owner in the case of motor vehicles and punish simple taking without permission of the owner.[79]

---

71 Specific intent was discussed *supra* p. 553.

72 The MPC abandons the distinction between the three traditional forms of theft. MPC §223.1.

73 *United States v. Waronek*, 582 F.2d 1158, 1161 (7th Cir. 1978) (dictum). *See also People v. Khoury*, 166 Cal.Rptr. 705 (Cal.App 1980) (defendant guilty of sufficiently carrying away tools when he concealed them in a chandelier box and wheeled them back into the store when the cashier insisted on inspecting the box before accepting payment for the chandelier).

74 *See, e.g., State v. Hector*, 402 A.2d 595 (R.I. 1979) (defendant who retained money after bank teller misread check and overpaid him was guilty of larceny).

75 LAFAVE, *supra* note 1, §8.7. *See, e.g., Rex v. Barnard*, 173 Eng. Rep. 342 (1837) (defendant who purposefully created the erroneous understanding that he was an Oxford student by wearing a cap and gown found guilty of false pretenses for obtaining goods on credit).

76 *United States v. Faulkner*, 638 F.2d 129 (9th Cir. 1981) (embezzlement occurred when truck driver displayed and tried to sell refrigerators he was transporting even though he never took the goods off the truck or sold any of them; possession and control with the intent to convert goods is sufficient).

77 *Impson v. State*, 58 P.2d 523 (Ariz. 1936) (larceny conviction not proper where facts showed defendant took car with intent to use it and return it). *But see Chapman v. State*, 212 P.2d 485 (Okla. App. 1949) (larceny conviction proper where defendant fraudulently rented the car and did nothing to disclose its whereabouts until he saw escape was impossible).

78 *See* MPC §223.0(1) (including, as part of "deprive," disposing of property "so as to make it unlikely that the owner will recover it."); *State v. Davis*, 38 N.J.L. 176 (1875) (defendant-students who took professor's horse and buggy and left it abandoned had requisite intent).

79 *See* LAFAVE, *supra* note 1, §8.5(b).

Modern theft offenses include blackmail, bribery and money laundering. Blackmail involves the threat to expose private information or accuse another of a crime with intent to extort money or certain acts from that person.[80] Bribery of public officials is payment of money or other valuable consideration to seek to influence the official in the discharge of his or her duties. International bribery connected with business deals has recently become a great concern for governments and businesses.[81]

Of recent vintage is money laundering. Money laundering is undertaken in order to be able to openly spend the proceeds of an illegal business operation, such as drug dealing. The money is "dirty" both because it is from drug sales and because it has never been declared as income and no taxes have been paid on it. Spending the money openly would likely alert the tax authorities, who are always on the alert for people who seem to be spending beyond their officially declared means. Typically, to launder money, a person will affiliate with a legitimate business, preferably one that operates on a cash basis, such as a restaurant. The "dirty" money is added little by little to legitimate profits of the business. Profits are declared and taxes paid on what seems to be a successful legitimate business. It is difficult to tell what is legitimate income taken in by the business and what is "dirty" money.[82] Often offenses such as money laundering, bribery, embezzlement and tax evasion are referred to as "white collar" crimes, since they are often perpetrated by persons in business suits and white shirts.[83]

4. Rape (Criminal Sexual Conduct)

Common Law Rape and Modern Definitions The common law defined rape as sexual penetration by a man of a woman who is not his wife, which is accomplished through force or otherwise without her consent. This definition has been abandoned in virtually all states.[84] Each state rape statute differs slightly, but most address forcible penetration of another person without that person's consent.[85] Some states have expanded and revised sexual offenses. For example, Michigan has created four degrees of "criminal sexual conduct" and punishes a variety of forms of "sexual contact" that include more than just actions by males against females. The statute also specifies that resistance on the part of the victim is not necessary.[86]

"Rape Shield" Laws A major change in the law that affects prosecutions for rape has been a modification in the law of evidence. Traditionally, the sexual history of the

---

80 *See State v. Harrington*, 260 A.2d 692 (Vt. 1969) (blackmail conviction proper where defendant intended to extort money by threatening to expose private information). *See generally*, Wendy J. Gordon, *Truth and Consequences: The Force of Blackmail's Central Case*, 141 U.PA.L.REV. 1741 (1993).

81 *See generally* Shada Islam, *Investment: Kickback Setback: OECD Bolsters Fight Against International Corruption*, Dec. 11, 1997 Far E. Econ. Rev. 69.

82 *See* 18 U.S.C.A. §1956; *United States v. Jensen*, 69 F.3d 906 (8th Cir. 1995) (conviction of accepting money from a drug deal to purchase a car held constitutional). *See United States v. Cleveland*, 951 F.Supp. 1249 (E.D.La. 1997) (federal money laundering statute properly passed under Congress' taxing power).

83 *See generally* ELLEN S. PODGOR & JEROLD H. ISRAEL, WHITE COLLAR CRIME IN A NUTSHELL (West 1997). *See also infra* pp. 571-573, where "enterprise criminality" is discussed.

84 *See* DRESSLER, *supra* note 1, §33.02. There has been much recent attention to the issue of rape in non-legal as well as legal circles. Some of the literature is collected in DRESSLER, *supra*, §33.03-33.04.

85 *See State v. Baker*, 441 S.E.2d 551,553 (N.C. 1994) (defendant convicted of first-degree rape for forcing the victim on the bed and penetrating her vagina with his fingers and genitals). *See Wisdom v. State*, 708 S.W.2d 840, 842-43 (Tex.Cr.App. 1986) (Court held that the legislature recognized that forceful and violent sexual penetration is non-consensual and is therefore a crime of violence *per se*). *See generally*, 65 Am. Jur. Rape §1 (1972, 1998)

86 Mich. Comp. L. Ann. §§750.520a-.520n. Sexual contact includes "intentional touching of the victim's . . . intimate parts . . . for the purpose of sexual arousal or gratification," or to inflict revenge, humiliation, or out of anger. *Id.* §750.520a(q). This law is discussed in DRESSLER, *supra* note 1, §33.09(A).

rape victim was admissible to show that the victim consented to the sexual intercourse and to undermine the reliability of her testimony. Presently, the rules of evidence of all states and the federal court system limit such evidence.[87] Behind such "rape shield" laws is a desire to encourage victims to report rapes and a judgment that the sexual history of the victim is generally irrelevant.

The Husband Exemption   A few states still follow the common law rule that non-consensual sexual intercourse between a husband and wife is not rape. Even the MPC states that the victim must not be the wife of the defendant.[88] The "husband exemption" has its origin in the common law treatment of women as not much better than their husbands' property, coupled with the idea that, when a woman marries a man, she has given blanket consent to sexual intercourse with him. Modern justifications for the exemption include the difficulty of proving rape within a marital context, the potential for false claims of rape in divorce, the societal interest in maintaining marital privacy, and the idea that spousal rape is a less serious crime than other forms of rape.[89] Most states have abandoned the husband exemption and some courts have even held it unconstitutional.[90]

Statutory Rape   Most states also have what is called "statutory rape," which prohibits even consensual sexual relations with a female under a certain age, often 16 or 18. This is a strict liability offense in that it does not require that the defendant know that his sexual partner is underage at least when the victim is in her early teens.

D. Defenses to Criminal Liability

It is useful to divide defenses into two categories: "failure-of-proof" (FOP) defenses and affirmative defenses. FOP defenses are defenses which tend to negate some element of the offense, typically the mental element of *mens rea*. Affirmative defenses essentially concede all the elements of the crime and rely on some additional reason as an excuse or justification for the offense.

1. Failure-of-Proof Defenses

Foremost among FOP defenses are "mistake of fact" and "mistake of law." A mistake of fact or law defense is invoked by defendants to show that they lacked the requisite intent to commit the crime because they were mistaken as to the circumstances of the crime.[91] A mistake as to whether something is punishable under the criminal law is not a defense even when that mistake is based on advice from one's attorney. The maxim *ignorantia legis neminem excusat* (ignorance of the law excuses no one) is deeply imbedded in Anglo-American jurisprudence.

Other FOP defenses are "diminished capacity" and "intoxication." Diminished capacity, where recognized as a defense, may be used to show that, due to a mental

---

87   *See, e.g.*, Federal Rules of Evidence 412 (limiting evidence regarding the sexual past of the victim, unless "good cause" is shown, such as to show that the defendant was not the source of semen found in the victim). *Cf.* Federal Rules of Evidence 413-415 (permitting evidence of the defendant's commission of another sexual assault or child molestation in either a civil or criminal case).

88   MPC §213.1(1).

89   For more on spousal rape, *see* DRESSLER, *supra* note 1, §33.07.

90   *See People v. Liberta*, 474 N.E.2d 567 (N.Y. 1984) (husband exemption rule denies equal protection of the law to unmarried men and is therefore unconstitutional).

91   *See, e.g., Green v. State*, 221 S.W.2d 612 (Tex.Cr.App. 1949) (in larceny prosecution, defendant did not have the intent to permanently deprive another of several hogs because he mistakenly thought that they belonged to him). *Cf. Lambert v. California*, 355 U.S. 225 (1957) (due process violated by punishing defendant for violating law requiring convicted felons to register with police when she did not know of law).

defect short of insanity, the defendant was deluded, mistaken or otherwise may not have formed the requisite *mens rea*.[92] Diminished capacity is not available in some jurisdictions. Voluntary intoxication is sometimes used to negate the presence of the requisite specific intent due to the intoxication.[93] But regardless of how drunk the defendant was, that defendant can be convicted of general intent crimes, such as rape.[94]

Limiting FOP defenses to specific intent elements has been criticized as illogical.[95] The limitation to specific intent elements can best be explained, not logically, but as a policy decision that persons with these types of defenses deserve some leniency, but should not be completely exonerated. Thus, the MPC, which does not adopt the distinction between general and specific intent, allows use of any FOP defenses to negate *any* element of culpability of a crime. However, it makes one exception: voluntary drug or alcohol intoxication may not negate recklessness — the MPC's threshold "general intent" requirement for basic criminal liability.[96] Clearly, the exception for intoxication is a policy choice designed to limit defendants' ability to negate culpability based on use of drugs or alcohol.

In recent years, courts have become increasingly reluctant to allow excuses based on impaired capacity for self-control through addiction to drugs or alcohol. The general theory behind this movement is that, while people may not act voluntarily when they are addicts, they did make a voluntary choice when they first decided to use drugs or alcohol, and this is sufficient to impose criminal liability. In *Montana v. Egelhoff*, the Supreme Court affirmed the constitutional validity of eliminating voluntary intoxication as a defense completely when it upheld a Montana law that prohibited the defendant from introducing and the jury from considering *any* evidence of voluntary intoxication.[97]

2. Affirmative Defenses

The successful assertion of an affirmative defense exonerates the defendant even though the prosecution has proven all of the elements of the offense. These defenses are "affirmative" in the sense that new additional facts beyond those placed in issue by denial of the elements must be affirmatively proven for the defense to succeed. In addition, the law often places the burden of proof on affirmative defenses on the defendant. As with other aspects of criminal law, the common law and the MPC versions of these defenses differ somewhat and these differences will be noted.[98]

---

92 The MPC and about a dozen states recognize diminished capacity for all crimes. MPC §4.02(1). A few jurisdictions do not recognize it at all. *Bethea v. United States*, 365 A.2d 64 (D.C.App. 1976). Others reserve it solely for murder prosecutions. *State v. Cooper*, 213 S.E.2d 305, 319 (N.C. 1975), *overruled on other grounds, State v. Leonard*, 266 S.E.2d 631, 636 (N.C. 1980). Yet others limit it to specific intent elements of offenses. *United States v. Brawner*, 471 F.2d 969 (D.C. Cir. 1972), *superceded by statute*, Insanity Defense Reform Act of 1984, Pub L. No. 98-473, 98 Stat. 2057, *as recognized in Shannon v. United States*, 512 U.S. 573 (1994); *United States v. Gonyea*, 140 F.3d 649 (6th Cir. 1998). *See* DRESSLER, *supra* note 1, §§26.01-26.03.

93 *See, e.g., Heideman v. United States*, 259 F.2d 943 (D.C.Cir. 1958) (defendant did not have intent to steal due to intoxication and therefore not guilty of robbery). *See supra* p. 553, where general and specific intent are discussed.

94 *See, e.g., People v. Langworthy*, 331 N.W.2d 171 (Mich. 1982).

95 See DRESSLER, *supra* note 1, at 279-280.

96 MPC §2.08.

97 518 U.S. 37 (1996). *Egelhoff* is also discussed in Chapter VIII, p. 314.

98 It has been customary to categorize affirmative defenses as either "justifications" or "excuses." Justifications are defenses that focus on the conduct of the defendant and exonerate the defendant because that *conduct* is not a crime (*e.g.*, self-defense). Excuses focus on the defendant and exonerate based on a judgment that the defendant is not blameworthy (*e.g.*, insanity). However, these distinctions have no real practical meaning, so they are ignored here. *But see* Joshua Dressler, *Justifications and*

a. Defensive Violence

Self-Defense   One can use deadly force to defend against attack if one actually *and* reasonably believes that there is an imminent threat of death or serious bodily harm such that force is necessary to prevent that harm. This defense most often applies to homicide and assault cases. The majority of courts hold that where the threat is this serious, there is no duty to retreat, even when a retreat can be safely accomplished. The rationale for this belief is the notion that people should be able to stand their ground and not be forced to back down. If the defendant subjectively believes that force is necessary, but the belief is not reasonable, it may be sufficient to negate specific intent, thereby reducing murder to manslaughter. However, objective reasonableness is required to constitute a complete defense to homicide.[99]

Defense of Others and Property   Force may also be used to defend another person, to defend property, to stop crimes, and to apprehend criminals. In a minority of states, defense of others is permitted only if the person the defendant is protecting would have been justified in using the same force in self-defense.[100] The majority, however, hold that defense of others is proper so long as the defendant *reasonably believed* that the other person would have been justified in using the same force in self-defense.[101] Property may be defended with the use of reasonable, non-deadly force if the defendant reasonably believed that it is necessary to do so to avoid imminent theft or trespass to the property. Generally, because human life is more important that property, one can never use *deadly* force in the defense of property.[102] If a person entering property in order to accomplish "forcible" felonies (*e.g.*, rape, murder) or serious bodily harm, then deadly force may be used.[103] Finally, non-deadly force may be used by both police officers and private citizens to prevent the commission of a crime and to apprehend criminals.[104]

Battered Women Cases   In order to have a valid claim of self defense, one must have a reasonable belief of an *imminent* threat of serious harm. This limit has been tested by recent cases in which an abused woman has killed her abusive husband or boyfriend when he was not actively attacking her, often while he slept. Some scholars advocate that courts, instead of applying the traditional self-defense standard, should consider whether the woman's actions were reasonable given a history of repeated abuse or whether she suffered from "battered woman syndrome," which made it

---

Excuses: A Brief Review of the Concepts and the Literature, 33 WAYNE L. REV. 1155 (1987) (arguing the utility of the distinction).

99   *See People v. Humphrey*, 921 P.2d 1, 6 (Cal. 1996) ("If the belief subjectively exists but is objectively unreasonable, there is 'imperfect self-defense,' *i.e.*, 'the defendant is deemed to have acted without malice and cannot be convicted of murder,' but can be convicted of manslaughter.").

100   *See, e.g., People v. Young*, 183 N.E.2d 319 (N.Y. 1962) (defendant's use of force to defend a person who was being arrested by a plainclothes policeman not justified because the arrest was lawful).

101   *See, e.g., State v. Menilla*, 158 N.W. 645 (Iowa 1916) (defendant's reasonable belief that her husband would imminently kill her son justified her use of deadly force against her husband even though her son would not have been so justified because he did not know he was in danger).

102   *Falco v. State*, 407 So.2d 203 (Fla. 1981).

103   *Morrison v. State*, 371 S.W.2d 441 (Tenn. 1963) (defendant was justified in using deadly force when intoxicated victim attempted to enter defendant's house). *Cf. State v. Terrell*, 186 P. 108 (Utah 1919) (burglary of rabbit pen described by court as forcible felony, justifying use of deadly force by defendant).

104   The Supreme Court has held that it is unconstitutional for police officers to use deadly force to apprehend a felony suspect unless it is necessary to prevent the escape and the suspect poses a threat of death or serious physical injury to the officer or others. *See Tennessee v. Garner*, 471 U.S. 85 (1985).

impossible for her to resolve the abuse problem in any other way.[105] Others oppose this trend, arguing that if courts consider each defendant's circumstances, this will leave judge and jury without any guide as to what is reasonable and will permit them to acquit on the improper ground that the defendant "deserved" to be killed.[106]

b. Insanity and Other Mental Illness

The Right or Wrong Test The traditional common law test for legal insanity was the *M'Naghten* test, or "right and wrong" test.[107] Under this test, defendants are considered insane if, as a result of some form of mental disease, they did not know what they were doing (referred to as cognitive incapacity) or failed to realize that what they were doing was wrong (referred to as moral incapacity). The *M'Naghten* test has been criticized because it focuses on cognitive impairment and ignores cases where defendants knew what they were doing, but were unable to control themselves. In response to this criticism, courts have adopted other tests. One is the "irresistible impulse" test, under which defendants were unable, due to a mental disease, to refrain from engaging in the prohibited conduct, though they realized that their conduct was wrong.[108] Another has been the "product" or *Durham* test, which relieves the defendant of responsibility whenever a causal connection can be shown between a mental disease and the criminal conduct. The *Durham* test has been criticized for its heavy reliance on expert evidence. It is not presently followed in any jurisdiction.[109]

The MPC's "Substantial Capacity" Test Under this test, defendants are not responsible for their crimes if they lacked the substantial capacity either to appreciate the wrongfulness of that conduct *or* to conform their conduct to the requirements of the law. The substantial capacity test was used in the federal system until John Hinckley used it successfully to defend himself after his failed assassination attempt on President Reagan. As a result, Congress limited insanity as a defense to cases in which the defendant, "as a result of a severe mental disease or defect, was unable to appreciate the nature and quality or the wrongfulness of his acts." Moreover, "the defendant has the burden of proving the defense of insanity by clear and convincing evidence," as opposed to the lesser "preponderance of the evidence" standard.[110]

Guilty But Mentally Ill In recent years, an increasing number of states have by statute adopted a new verdict option of "guilty but mentally ill" (GBMI).[111] Traditionally, if a defendant raised an insanity defense the jury had only three possible verdicts: guilty, not guilty, or not guilty by reason of insanity. With a guilty-but-mentally-ill verdict, the

---

105 *See, e.g., State v. Hodges*, 716 P.2d 563 (Kan. 1986) (jury could consider "the history of violence" and circumstances leading up to the use of force in battered women syndrome cases); *State v. Kelly*, 478 A.2d 364 (N.J. 1984) (describing the nature of the battered woman syndrome); California Evidence Code 1107 (permitting expert testimony on "the nature and effect of physical, emotional, or mental abuse on the beliefs, perceptions, or behavior of victims of domestic violence").

106 James R. Aker & Hans Toch, *Battered Women, Straw Men and Expert Testimony: A Comment on State v. Kelly*, 21 CRIM. L. BULL. 125 (1985).

107 *Daniel M'Naghten's Case*, 8 Eng.Rep. 718, 10 Cl. & Fin. 200 (1843).

108 *Parsons v. State*, 2 So. 854 (Ala. 1887).

109 *See Durham v. United States*, 214 F.2d 862 (D.C. Cir. 1954) *overruled by United States v. Brawner*, 471 F.2d 969 (D.C. Cir. 1972). States have considerable latitude in defining the scope of its insanity defenses. *See Clark v. Arizona*, 548 U.S.735 (2006) (*M'Naghten* rule is not a constitutional due process minimum for insanity defenses). The case discusses the variety of state approaches.

110 18 U.S.C.A. §17(a). The constitutionality of shifting the burden of proof to the defendant and requiring "clear and convincing" proof has not been evaluated by the Supreme Court, though the lower courts have upheld it. *See, e.g., United States v. Freeman*, 804 F.2d 1574 (11th Cir 1986).

111 *See* 71 A.L.R.4th 702 (1989) (reviewing GBMI statutes).

jury may find beyond a reasonable doubt that the defendant did the criminal acts charged and was mentally ill, but not *legally* insane. The result of a GBMI verdict is that the defendant is sent to prison, but is supposed to get psychiatric treatment there. However, critics point out that psychiatric treatment is generally not available in prisons and that, in any event, overcrowded prisons are hardly an atmosphere conducive to recovering from mental illness. Moreover, critics say jurors will not seriously consider an insanity defense, because they will think that the defendant will get treatment under either option and at least will be sent to prison if the verdict is GBMI.[112]

It should be emphasized that defendants acquitted by reason of insanity do not go free. Instead, they are committed to a psychiatric hospital and may not be released until and unless cured and no longer a danger to themselves or others.[113] An example is would-be presidential assassin John Hinckley, who to date remains in a mental hospital. Even defendants who have been convicted and have completed their prison sentences may be confined in a psychiatric facility. In the recent case of *Kansas v. Hendricks*,[114] Hendricks was a repeat child sex offender who was scheduled for release from prison following completion of his latest sentence, but whose pedophilia had not been cured and who continued to harbor sexual desires for children that he admitted he could not control when he was "stressed out." The Supreme Court rejected constitutional objections to his confinement in a psychiatric facility under Kansas's Sexually Violent Predator Act, which permitted civil commitment of any person who suffered a "mental abnormality" or a "personality disorder" that made them likely to engage in "predatory acts of sexual violence." It did so based on its assessment that the Act was not punitive, but essentially civil in nature.[115] The usual justification for civil commitment is that treatment is provided. In the case of sex offenders, there is evidence that many are not treatable. In those cases, the Court held, the state was justified in confining them for the protection of the public.[116]

Mental Incompetence to Stand Trial   A defendant may not be able to stand trial because of mental incompetence. The standard generally applied is whether the defendant "lacks capacity to understand the proceedings against him or to assist in his own defense."[117] A state may presume competence and require the defendant to prove incompetence by a preponderance of the evidence.[118] If incompetence is found, the criminal proceedings are suspended and the defendant is committed to a mental health facility until competence is restored. Then the criminal case can resume, unless the

---

112 *See* Linda C. Fentiman, *"Guilty But Mentally Ill": The Real Verdict Is Guilty*, 26 B.C.L.Rev. 601 (1985) and Project, *Evaluating Michigan's Guilty But Mentally Ill Verdict: An Empirical Study*, 16 U. Mich. J. L. Ref. 77 (1982).

113 MPC §4.08(1).

114 521 U.S. 346 (1997).

115 *But see Kansas v. Crane*, 534 U.S. 407 (2002) (civil confinement cannot be used for general deterrence and requires some showing that the defendant lacks control).

116 *See also Seling v. Young*, 531 U.S. 250 (2001) (upholding Washington state statute). *See also United States v. Comstock*, ___ U.S. ___, 130 S.Ct. 1949 (2010) (upholding federal statute as within Congress's power under Necessary and Proper clause of Art. I §8).

117 MPC §4.04.

118 *Cooper v. Oklahoma*, 517 U.S. 348 (1996). For a discussion of the various standards of proof, *see* Chapter III, p. 105.

court determines that "so much time has elapsed since the commitment of the defendant that it would be unjust to resume the criminal proceeding."[119]

c. Duress, Necessity and Other Pressures on Free Will

Duress Duress applies when a defendant commits a crime under a threat of death or serious bodily injury. The threat may be to the defendant, a family member or other person, but it must be a real threat with imminent consequences. The defendant's ability to escape (if being physically held) or to report threats to the authorities are relevant.[120] Duress is unavailable if the person helped create the coercive situation.[121]

Most states limit duress to situations where the harm threatened is greater than the harm the defendant is coerced into inflicting. For instance, if the defendant participates in a robbery on threat of being killed, the defense applies.[122] This limit and the inapplicability of duress to murder — effective in about half the states — make duress inapplicable where a defendant kills because threatened with death.[123] However, the MPC provides that a defendant has a duress defense when coerced into performing any crime if a person of "reasonable firmness" in the defendant's situation would not have been able to resist.[124] Under the MPC, then, duress might apply when X threatens to kill D if D does not hold Y while X stabs Y to death.[125]

Necessity While duress deals with psychological pressure applied by another *person*, the defense of necessity involves the effects of *physical* circumstances on a defendant's will. For necessity to apply, (1) defendants must face some force that threatens imminent harm to themselves or others, (2) committing a criminal act must be the only way to prevent that harm, (3) they must not have placed themselves in the position of danger, and (4) the criminal conduct must involve less harm than the harm threatened. For example, if a person is lost in a snowstorm facing death from exposure and starvation, it is not a crime to break into a cabin to seek shelter and food. The law places a higher value on human life than on property.

Economic necessity does not justify a crime, such as where a person steals food out of hunger.[126] Necessity has also been routinely rejected in cases of "civil disobedience" — where protesters violate the law for the purpose of preventing certain conduct from occurring. For example, protesters against abortion cannot assert that blocking entrances to an abortion clinic was necessary to prevent the killing of unborn children,

---

119 MPC §4.06(2). Another issue regarding insanity arises when a defendant sentenced to death become insane after conviction and sentence. States have uniformly prohibited execution of an insane prisoner and the Supreme Court has held the principle to be a constitutional one. *See* Chapter XIV, p. 320.

120 *United States v. Lee*, 694 F.2d 649 (11th Cir. 1983) (defendant who claimed to have been forced to join drug conspiracy because of threats to friend had numerous reasonable chances to inform police). *But see United States v. Riffe*, 28 F.3d 565 (6th Cir. 1994) (opportunity to report drug ring to authorities was not real for prisoner coerced into participating by threats of death, because protective segregation had failed to protect informants in the past).

121 *See* MPC §2.09(2) and *Williams v. State*, 646 A.2d 1101 (Md.App. 1994) (defendant who was allegedly coerced by gang into robbery could not claim duress because he had borrowed money from gang leader and participated in crimes to pay it back).

122 *People v. Merhige*, 180 N.W. 418 (Mich. 1920) (defendant forced to drive getaway car not guilty of robbery or felony murder when robber he assisted shot a bank patron during the robbery).

123 *State v. Nargashian*, 58 A. 953 (R.I. 1904) (A threatened B with death unless B helped hold C so A could kill C; duress instruction refused).

124 MPC §2.09.

125 *See* LAFAVE, *supra* note 1, §5.3(b). *Compare State v. Nargashian, supra* note 123.

126 *State v. Moe*, 24 P.2d 638, 640 (Wash. 1933) (mob of unemployed looted grocery store owned by head of relief committee who had refused to increase their flour allotment; no necessity defense).

nor can opponents of nuclear power who trespass at a power plant claim necessity based on the dangers of nuclear power. In these cases, the law has already anticipated the choice involved and determined the balance between the competing values. Consequently, defendants and courts are precluded from reassessing those values to determine whether certain conduct is justified.[127]

"Medical necessity" did not fare well in the Supreme Court in the recent case of *United States* v. *Oakland Cannabis Buyers Cooperative*.[128] The United States sued for an injunction to halt the Cooperative from continuing to produce and distribute marijuana (cannabis) for medical purposes.[129] The Court of Appeals agreed with the Cooperative that the injunction should be modified to exclude any production or distribution made out of "medical necessity." The Supreme Court, however, refused to graft a "medical necessity" exception onto the federal Controlled Substances Act, which only provided an exception for government-approved research. Similar to the state civil disobedience cases, the Court held that a necessity defense cannot succeed when the legislature itself has made a determination of values in the opposite direction.

Another important limitation on the necessity defense is that it does not excuse intentional homicide. In a famous English case, shipwrecked seamen on a lifeboat with no food or water intentionally killed a young sailor so they could survive on his flesh while awaiting rescue. Despite the seamen's argument that everyone, including the young sailor would have died otherwise, the court found the seamen guilty of murder.[130] American law follows the same rule.[131]

MPC "Choice of Evils" Defense The MPC's version of the necessity defense is the "choice of evils" defense. It is interesting for its effort to generalize the fundamental social issue involved in duress and necessity. The defense is established if it is shown that, in committing a crime, (1) the defendant believed his conduct was necessary "to avoid harm or evil to himself or to another" and (2) "the harm or evil sought to be avoided by such conduct [was] greater than that sought to be prevented by the law." However, it does not apply where the defendant is at fault for creating the difficult choice presented.[132] Notable differences from common law necessity and duress are the lack of a requirement of "imminent" necessity and its applicability to choices imposed both by the forces of nature and by another person.

Like common law necessity and duress, "choice of evils" does not apply to excuse intentional homicide even if the defendant is threatened with death. The rationale is that the choice is between two innocent lives involved — the victim's life and the defendant's life — which have equal value.[133] It has been argued, however, that if the choice of evils

---

127 *Cleveland v. Municipality of Anchorage*, 631 P.2d 1073 (Alaska 1981) (trespass at abortion clinic); *State v. Warshow*, 410 A.2d 1000 (Vt. 1979) (nuclear power plant). *See also State v. Tate*, 505 A.2d 941 (N.J. 1986) (necessity did not excuse paraplegic's use of marijuana to relieve pain).

128 532 U.S. 483 (2001).

129 Injunctive relief is discussed in Chapter VII, p. 245.

130 *Regina v. Dudley & Stephens*, 14 Q.B.D. 273 (1884).

131 *United States v. Holmes*, 26 F.Cas. 360 (C.C.E.D. Pa. 1842) (crew members of sunken ship, who threw 14 male passengers overboard to keep lifeboat afloat, guilty of manslaughter).

132 MPC §3.02. The MPC also requires that it be clear that the legislature did not intend to exclude the choice made by the defendant, such as in the civil disobedience cases just discussed.

133 This is in contrast to self-defense, where the judgment of the law is that the aggressor's life is worth less than an innocent person's.

is between taking one life and saving *several* other lives, then the defense should apply.[134]

Situational Coercion Some argue in favor of a defense even broader than duress and the MPC's "catch-all" choice of evils defense. A defendant, it is asserted, should be able to choose the *greater* of two evils if there was some understandable reason for doing so. Such a "situational coercion" defense would be available if a person of reasonable firmness would bend under the pressure and choose the greater evil. Mercy killing is an example. If a person takes the life of his or her spouse, who is suffering tremendous pain from terminal cancer, after being repeatedly requested to do so, many would not consider such a person morally blameworthy. Such conduct does not qualify for the choice of evils defense because intentional killing is the greater evil. Yet, critics argue, most would understand how a loving spouse of reasonable firmness could well act the same way under the circumstances.

d. Entrapment

It is common for the police to use various undercover methods of operation to catch criminals. These range from simple police purchases of narcotics to more elaborate "sting" operations, such as creating bogus criminal enterprises. For example, police might set up a fake "chop shop," an underground business which purchases stolen automobiles and dismantles them to sell the parts. Such a scheme allows the police to catch offenders in the entire distribution chain of stolen car parts. Even "reverse stings," as where the police sell illegal drugs, are common. Yet, the police should not become so involved in arranging crimes that they pressure or induce innocent people into committing crimes they would not otherwise commit. The doctrine of entrapment deals with this issue.

Subjective Test There are two approaches to entrapment: subjective and objective. The majority of states and the federal courts use the "subjective" approach. Both tests require that it be proven that the idea for the crime originated with the police, *i.e.*, that the police offered the narcotics for sale, delivered the bribe or offered to buy the stolen car. Beyond this, the subjective test focuses on whether the defendant was "predisposed" to commit the type of offense charged — whether the defendant was "ready and willing to commit the crimes such as are charged in the indictment, whenever the opportunity was afforded."[135] One difficulty with the subjective approach is that it opens the door to introducing evidence of the defendant's character, reputation and criminal history. Such evidence is generally not admissible at trial against the defendant except under limited circumstances, because of the risk that the jury will convict the defendant, not for committing this particular crime, but for being a generally bad person.[136] Another problem with the subjective approach is that, if it is followed strictly, there is no limit to how much police deceit or badgering there is in a given case — it is tolerated so long as the defendant was predisposed to commit the offense. Indeed, the police can single out

---

134 *See* Comment to MPC §3.02, Tentative Draft No. 8, at 15.

135 LAFAVE, *supra* note 1, §5.2(b) at 450, quoting jury instructions; *Sherman v. United States*, 356 U.S. 369 (1958) (entrapment established as a matter of law where government informer met the defendant while both were undergoing treatment for narcotics addiction, repeatedly badgered the defendant into assisting him in obtaining narcotics, paid for the drugs and the taxi to go get them).

136 The general inadmissibility of bad character evidence against criminal defendants was discussed in Chapter III, p. 111. The difficulties are compounded by the fact that the subjective test requires that the *jury* rather than the judge determine the defendant's predisposition. *See Sherman v. United States, supra* note 135.

"predisposed" suspects for outrageous treatment, confident that "anything goes" with them.

Objective Test In reaction to these criticisms, an alternative "objective" approach, used by a minority of jurisdictions, has developed. It does not focus on the particular defendant and his or her criminal propensities. Instead, it looks at the effect that the police conduct in question would have had on the *average innocent person*. The particular defendant's character and predisposition are irrelevant. The objective test, then, seeks to determine how bad the police practices were, rather than how bad a person the defendant is.[137]

A recent Supreme Court case imposes an additional limit on the subjective test. In *Jacobson v. United States*,[138] a child pornography case, the government spent some two-and-a-half years trying to persuade the defendant to order sexually explicit materials, using five different fictitious organizations and a bogus "pen pal." After finally receiving a missive from one of the "organizations" decrying international censorship, he ordered a magazine — doing so, he testified later, because he was curious about "all the trouble and the hysteria over pornography and I wanted to see what the material was." The Court reversed his conviction. It held that the predisposition of the defendant must be "independent and not the product of the attention" the government had directed at him over the two-and-a-half years.

Some have argued that entrapment, like many other limits on police investigation techniques, should be constitutionally based — that entrapment is an unfair tactic that violates due process of law. In general, the Court has rejected this idea. The Court has suggested in dictum that truly outrageous police entrapment behavior might violate due process, though no such case has yet reached the Court.[139]

E. Peripheral Actors, Anticipatory Crimes and Enterprise Criminality

1. Accessories and Accomplices

The common law divided participants in a felony into (1) principals of the first degree, (2) principals of the second degree, (3) accessories before the fact and (4) accessories after the fact, punishing each type differently. However, under the law of all jurisdictions in the United States, accomplices and accessories have the same criminal liability as a principal. The terms are nonetheless used to describe the particular participant's role. An "accessory before the fact" is someone who helps the principal out beforehand but is not present when the crime is committed. An "accomplice" is someone who assists in the commission of the crime. By punishing accomplices and principals identically, in effect the acts of the principal participants are imputed to the accessories.[140] To be an accomplice, a person must (1) give assistance or encouragement and (2) intend thereby to promote or facilitate commission of the crime. Thus, the

---

137 The objective test also differs from the subjective test in that it is typically the judge rather than the jury that determines what the effect of the police practices would be on the average person.

138 503 U.S. 540 (1993).

139 *See* Chapter VIII, p. 568, note 134. Because *Jacobson* is not constitutionally based, it is only binding on the federal courts. The extent to which "sexual entrapment" is proper has divided the lower federal courts. *Compare United States v. Simpson*, 813 F.2d 1462 (9th Cir. 1987) ("deceptive creation and/or exploitation of an intimate relationship does not exceed the boundaries of permissible law enforcement tactics) *with United States v. Cuervelo*, 949 F.2d 559 (2d Cir. 1991) (hearing required to examine allegations that federal drug agent had sexual relations with the defendant on 15 occasions, had given her gifts of money, clothes and jewelry, had written her "a number of love letters," and had induced her to come to the U.S. to participate in drug smuggling by procuring a visa for her and paying her way).

140 *See* MPC §2.06(3).

driver of the "getaway" car that brought the robbers to a bank may be subject to the same criminal liability as the robbers who actually went in and robbed the bank and shot the bank manager, unless the driver did not intend the crime (under the MPC) or if the crime was not foreseeable or was not committed in order to further the conspiracy (under the common law). Clearly, providing a weapon, transportation or standing as a lookout qualify, but it is also sufficient if the accessory or accomplice does not supply any assistance but is standing by to render assistance if necessary. The relevant *mens rea* requirement is equal to that of the principal actor for the relevant crime, plus having the purpose to promote or facilitate the principal's commission of the crime.[141] The accomplice is deemed liable for any criminal acts of those he or she assists if they are a natural and probable consequence of the enterprise.

An "accessory after the fact" is someone who helps the principal actor after the crime. Accessories after the fact are usually not held equally accountable with the principal. Generally they are punished separately for crimes such as "obstruction of justice" or "aiding and abetting" an escape.

2. Solicitation, Attempts and Conspiracies

Because of the harmful consequences of criminal activity, society need not wait for a complete crime to take place before acting. "Solicitation" of a crime — encouraging or engaging another to commit a crime — can be punished.[142] Similarly, an "attempt" to commit a crime is punishable, typically by one-half the penalty for the completed crime. An attempt takes place when the defendant has the specific intent to commit a completed crime and takes a substantial step toward doing so, such as the robber who points a gun at the victim, but then runs away without taking anything.[143] Solicitation merges into attempt once some step toward undertaking the crime takes place. Attempt merges into the offense once the offense is completed. This means that the defendant cannot be prosecuted for both the attempt and the completed offense.

A "conspiracy" exists when two or more people agree to commit a criminal act and take some overt step toward committing it. Conspiracy laws have been justified on the theory that groups of criminals are more dangerous, in part because once formed to commit one crime, the group is likely to plan and commit other crimes as well.[144] Conspiracy remains a separate crime regardless of whether the planned crime is carried out. However, if offenses are committed, then every coconspirator is liable for all crimes committed by every other coconspirator that are "within the scope of the conspiracy, are in furtherance of it, and are reasonably foreseeable as a necessary or natural consequence of the conspiracy."[145] Unlike attempt and solicitation, the crime of conspiracy

---

141 *See* MPC §2.06(3) (defining when a defendant is "legally accountable" for conduct of another). Accomplices and accessories before the fact may also be conspirators. The difference between conspiracy and accomplice or accessory liability is that conspirators are responsible for their act of conspiracy — a crime by itself — even if the planned crime does not take place or is not attempted.

142 MPC §5.02.

143 MPC §5.01(1)(c). *State v. Smith*, 621 A.2d 493 (N.J.App. 1993) (defendant, who had tested positive for HIV, could be found guilty of attempted murder upon proof that he intended to kill corrections officer by biting him; it was sufficient that defendant himself believed he could cause death by biting his victim).

144 *United States v. Rabinowich*, 238 U.S. 78, 88 (1915); *Pinkerton v. United States*, 328 U.S. 640, 644 (1946) (reaffirms the conspiracy rule defined in *Rabinowich*).

145 *State v. Walton*, 630 A.2d 990, 997 (Conn. 1993), *citing Pinkerton, supra* note 144; *State v. Bridges*, 628 A.2d 270 (N.J. 1993) (conspiracy was to return to party with loaded guns to intimidate party-goers from beating a friend; although killing was not within the scope of the conspiracy, it was foreseeable that things would escalate and someone would fire into the crowd). *But see Commonwealth v. Wilson*, 296 A.2d 719, 721 (Pa. 1972) (reversing conviction for voluntary manslaughter when Wilson's friends stabbed and killed

does not merge into the substantive offense.[146] For example, a defendant could be guilty of both robbery and conspiracy to commit robbery.

3. Enterprise Liability

a. Criminal Liability of Corporations

Vicarious strict criminal liability of business entities based on the actions of employees was discussed earlier. As stated there, liability is generally limited to social welfare offenses of a minor type, which generally do not require any *mens rea* on the part of the employee.[147] However, there are more serious offenses for which a corporation or other entity can be punished.

The common law's requirement that a criminal actor have the requisite *mens rea* to commit a crime traditionally excluded corporations from criminal liability, since they have no human mind. Today, corporations can be convicted of criminal offenses. The MPC provides, for example, that the corporation is liable when any one of the following applies: (1) the criminal conduct is performed by the corporation's agents within the scope of their employment and the statute's purpose is to impose criminal liability on the corporation, (2) the crime is a failure to act when the law requires the corporation to act or (3) the criminal inaction was authorized or "recklessly tolerated" by "high managerial agents" of the corporation.[148] Though some states limit liability of corporations, crimes for which corporations have been convicted range from theft to homicide. Many of the corporate criminal cases have been for violations of workplace safety requirements that injured employees.[149]

b. Criminal Liability for Racketeering Activities: RICO

RICO Elements The Racketeer-Influenced and Corrupt Organizations Act (RICO), passed by Congress in 1970, imposes criminal and civil liability for various actions related to enterprises.[150] RICO outlaws four activities: (1) investing income that was derived from a "pattern of racketeering activity" in any "enterprise," (2) the acquisition or maintenance of any interest in such an enterprise "through a pattern of racketeering activity," (3) participating in the conduct of an enterprise "through a pattern of racketeering activity" and (4) conspiring to do any of the preceding.[151] "Racketeering activity" is defined broadly as the commission of or threat to commit any of a list of generic types of state crimes set out in the Act or any "indictable" acts proscribed by numerous federal criminal provisions, including mail and wire fraud, bankruptcy offenses, securities fraud or drug-related offenses. A "pattern" of racketeering is defined as commission of 2 such acts in the last 10 years that are related and continuous. "Related" means that the offenses were linked by having a common goal or by some other logical connection. "Continuity" means that the acts must continue or constitute a threat of continuation.[152]

---

someone with whom Wilson had been engaged in a barroom brawl where Wilson did not encourage or acquiesce in nor was he even aware of his friend's use of a knife).

146 *Iannelli v. United States*, 420 U.S. 770 (1975).

147 *See supra* p. 554.

148 MPC §2.07(1).

149 *People v. Pymm*, 563 N.E.2d 1 (N.Y. 1990) (sustaining convictions of corporation and officers for assault and conspiracy based on mercury poisoning of employees; prosecution not preempted by federal law). *See generally The Corporation's Criminal Liability for Homicide*, 45 ALR4th 1021 (1987).

150 18 U.S.C.A. §§1961-1968.

151 18 U.S.C.A. §1962. The enterprise must affect interstate commerce.

152 *See* 18 U.S.C.A. §1961; *H.J., Inc. v. Northwestern Bell Telephone Co.*, 492 U.S. 229 (1983) ("only few weeks or months with no possibility of continuation beyond that" is not sufficient); *Religious Tech. Center*

An "enterprise" can be a formal organization, such as any normal business organization, or it can simply be "any group of persons associated together for a common purpose of engaging in a course of conduct."[153]   RICO applies to a corporate employee who conducts the affairs of the corporation of which he is the sole owner, regardless of whether he conducts those affairs within or beyond the scope of his corporate authority.[154]

Up to 20 years imprisonment (or life if the underlying offense provides) and substantial fines are possible under RICO. Serious forfeiture sanctions are also possible. The statute provides that convicted RICO defendants forfeit any interest they may have in the relevant "enterprise" and "any property constituting, or derived from, any proceeds which the person obtained, directly or indirectly, from racketeering activity."[155]

Criminal Uses of RICO The primary focus of RICO was organized crime's infiltration and use of legitimate business enterprises as a "front" for their criminal activities or for money laundering. Examples are where a "loan-sharking" extortion operation is run out of a bar owned by organized crime figures or where a drug dealing group takes over a bank for money laundering purposes. RICO responded to the concern that the traditional approach of arresting and imprisoning individual members of organized crime groups is not fully effective. RICO was designed to get at the entire organization, its assets and the top leaders who run it. It has been used effectively against the mafia and other organized crime groups.[156] It has also been used to fight political corruption, white collar crime and violent groups.[157]

The broad reach of RICO, however, goes beyond organized crime groups. This is especially apparent in the civil RICO suits filed by private plaintiffs, as discussed below. Use of interstate wire communications or the mails to perpetuate fraud is a federal crime that qualifies as "racketeering," so multiple acts of fraud that involve interstate use of the telephone, fax or postal service can qualify as "racketeering" under RICO if the requisite relatedness and continuity can be shown. In *Sedima S.P.R.L. v. Imrex Co., Inc.,*[158] a Belgian company filed a RICO claim against its joint venture partner for the latter's continued over-billing of expenses for locating aircraft parts. The RICO connection was the fact that the bills were mailed and thus constituted mail fraud. The Supreme Court held that a RICO claim was properly alleged. In so holding, the Court expressly rejected the concerns of the lower court, which was distressed that RICO, "instead of being used against mobsters and organized criminals, . . . has become a tool for everyday fraud cases brought against 'respected and legitimate 'enterprises'" that are then branded "racketeers."

A conspiracy to violate RICO also casts a wide net. In *Salinas v. United States,*[159] a Texas sheriff arranged for a federal prisoner held in his jail to have unsupervised visits

---

v. Wollersheim, 971 F.2d 364, 367 (9th Cir. 1992) (12-month rule of thumb). *But see Allwaste Inc. v. Hecht,* 65 F.3d 1523, 1528 (9th Cir. 1995) (12-months not a per se rule).

153 *United States v. Turkette,* 452 U.S. 576, 583 (1981).

154 *Cedric Kushner Promotions Ltd. v. King,* 533 U.S. 158 (2001).

155 18 U.S.C.A. §1963(a).

156 *See United States v. Brooklier,* 685 F.2d 1208 (9th Cir. 1982) (La Cosa Nostra extortion operation).

157 *United States v. Bustamonte,* 45 F.3d 933, 935 (5th Cir. 1995) (congressman convicted of running bribery scheme); *United States v. Yarbrough,* 852 F.2d 1522, 1526-28, 1540, 1546 (9th Cir. 1988) (members of radical right-wing, white-supremacist group, the "Order," convicted); *United States v. Marubeni America Corp.,* 611 F.2d 763 (9th Cir. 1980) (contractors convicted in bid-rigging bribery scheme).

158 473 U.S. 479, 499 (1985).

159 522 U.S. 52 (1997).

with his wife and girlfriend for $6,000 per month and $1,000 per visit. There was no question of the sheriff's RICO liability, but a question arose regarding the sheriff's deputy. The deputy had been acquitted of RICO charges, but was convicted of conspiracy to violate RICO. The issue was whether the deputy's continuing to permit the visits while in charge of the jail during the sheriff's absence was sufficient for the conspiracy conviction or whether the deputy had to have personally committed the 2 criminal acts required for a "pattern of racketeering activity." According to the Court, all that was necessary was proof that the deputy was involved in the scheme as a co-conspirator and that the *sheriff* had accepted the bribes. The Court observed broadly that, if conspirators have a plan which calls for some conspirators to perpetrate the crime and others to provide support, the supporters are as guilty as the perpetrators and are liable for the acts of their co-conspirators.

Cases like *Salinas* raise the question of the potential RICO liability of "outsiders" — lawyers, accountants, bankers and other professionals — who may be hired to perform services for a business that is violating RICO. Outsiders present an attractive "deep pocket" both for the government and civil RICO plaintiffs, especially when the principal offenders involved have no assets. The Supreme Court has made clear that outsiders are guilty of a RICO violation only if they are involved in the "operation or management" of the RICO enterprise. Consequently, lawyers and other professionals avoid liability by sticking solely to providing services.[160] However, *Salinas* teaches that a *conspiracy* to violate RICO may be exist so long as the outsider had knowledge of what the principal was doing and, through providing professional services, rendered assistance in what was later determined to be a RICO violation.[161]

Civil Uses of RICO As already alluded to, civil suits under RICO are also possible. Private persons or organizations "injured in [their] business or property by reason of a violation" of the Act may obtain treble damages and attorney fees — substantial incentives for civil plaintiffs.[162] A civil suit is proper even though no prior criminal action has been brought.[163] Furthermore, as in *Sedima*, discussed above, the facts that ordinary business fraud is the cause and a legitimate business is the target are irrelevant. Attempts to expand Civil RICO beyond economic racketeering to target nonprofit political "racketeering" have not been successful. Thus, the Court has rejected attempts by abortion supporters to sue individuals and groups for threatening or committing physical violence aimed at closing abortion clinics. It held that such actions could not form the basis for RICO liability because they were not related to robbery or extortion that obstructs, delays, or affects commerce — the requirements of the underlying federal criminal law.[164] To establish that an injury came about "by reason of" a RICO violation,

---

160 *Reves v. Ernst & Young*, 507 U.S. 170 (1993) (accounting firm not liable for understating value of assets where its role was limited to preparing financial reports).

161 W.B. Markowitz, *Expanding RICO Civil Liability for Lawyers and Other "Outsiders": Perspectives of a Plaintiff's Lawyer*, 45 Fed. Lawyer 35 (1998).

162 18 U.S.C.A. §1964(c). The federal court is empowered in §1964(a) to grant appropriate injunctive relief ordering divestiture or limits on future activities of enterprises or persons or dissolution of enterprises. However, the use of injunctive relief in private RICO suits is not well-developed.

163 *Sedima*, 473 U.S. at 486-493. The Court strongly hinted that the normal civil "preponderance of the evidence" standard of proof would apply, but did not decide the question. *Id.* at 491.

164 *Scheidler v. National Organization for Women*, 547 U.S. 9 (2006).

a plaintiff must show that a predicate offense "not only was a 'but for' cause of his injury, but was the proximate cause as well.[165]

F. Criminal Sanctions

The most common criminal sentences are fines and imprisonment. In addition, the death penalty is possible in some states for first degree murder.[166]

1. Imprisonment

Range of Sentences for Particular Offenses The range of sentences varies considerably from state to state. To give a general idea of the ranges for certain offenses, the following prevail in California: 1st degree murder, 25 years to life in prison or death; 2nd degree murder, 15 years to life; kidnaping, 3 to 8 years; armed robbery, 3 to 9 years; rape, 3 to 8 years; arson of an inhabited structure, 5 to 9 years; and burglary, 2 to 6 years in prison.

Indeterminate Sentences Most states still utilize "indeterminate" sentences. Under this method, the statute determines a minimum and maximum term of imprisonment for each crime. Judges, in their discretion, impose a minimum and maximum sentence term which falls within the statutory sentence range. An administrative body called a "parole board" then sets the actual date of release "on parole" somewhere in the sentence range. In deciding on a release date, the parole board considers the offender's behavior while in prison and other factors influencing the likelihood that the prisoner would reoffend, such as the prisoner's job prospects, education obtained in prison, remorse for his crimes, and others. In some jurisdictions the parole board may release an offender before he or she serves the *minimum* sentence based on similar factors. Some states have implemented "truth-in-sentencing" laws, which requires the defendant serve at least the entire minimum, regardless of the parole board's determination.[167] In 2002, 45% of state parolees successfully completed their term of supervision, while 41% were returned to jail or prison, and 9% absconded.[168]

Determinate Sentences Traditionally, judges had wide discretion in sentencing, so long as the sentence fell within the statutory minimum to maximum range. This created great disparity in sentencing, with different defendants guilty of the same crime receiving very different sentences. In response, about half the states and the federal government have adopted sentencing systems that limit or eliminate the discretion of judges in determining the sentence and the discretion of parole boards in determining release dates. Determinate sentencing has benefitted defendants because it allows them to know at sentencing exactly how much time they will spend in prison. It has also reduced inequality in sentencing among offenders who commit the same offense. However, determinate sentencing has deprived society of the benefit of tailoring sentences to individual defendants in each particular case. Furthermore, restricting the parole board's ability to release prisoners weakens the incentive for them to behave well and complete rehabilitative programs in prison. It is not surprising that state inmates

---

165 *Hemi Group LLC v. City of New York*, ___ U.S. ___, 130 S.Ct. 983 (2010) (in RICO suit over sales of untaxed cigarettes, city could not show that failure of defendant, in violation of federal law, to register its customers with the state directly caused it to lose tax revenue).

166 For discussion of the procedure for determining sentences, *see* Chapter VIII, pp. 277-279.

167 *Assessing Consistency and Fairness in Sentencing: A Comparative Study in Three States*, PEW EXECUTIVE SUMMARY (Nat'l. Ctr. for State Courts, Washington, D.C.) May 22, 2008, *available at* http://www.ncsconline.org/images/PEWExecutiveSummaryv10.pdf. The study did find some disparity among within states, with rural courts sentencing more harshly than urban courts.

168 Source: Bureau of Justice Statistics, U.S. Dep't of Justice, www.ojp.usdoj.gov/bjs/pandp.htm.

released from prison as a result of a parole board decision dropped from 50% of all adults entering parole in 1995 to 39% in 2002, while releases by statutory requirement increased from 45% to 52%. By the end of 2000, 16 States had abolished parole board authority for releasing all offenders, and another 4 States had abolished parole board authority for releasing certain violent offenders.[169]

Determinate sentencing systems contain different components including sentencing guidelines, mandatory minimums and enhancements based on specific factors (such as use of a gun), and specific determinant sanctions for repeat offenders.

Sentencing Guidelines Since 1984, the federal system has used sentencing guidelines which assign mathematical values to relevant factors in sentencing, such as the defendant's prior offenses and the nature of the present offense.[170] The judge then calculates a sentencing range based on these values. Despite being called "guidelines," they have been mandatory in the federal courts. States have adopted similar systems.

The guidelines produce a range of sentences, stated in numbers of months, that is a function of two factors: the adjusted offense level and the defendant's criminal history category. The judge focuses first on the "base offense level" for the particular crime and adjusts that level upward or downward for specific aggravating and mitigating factors that are specified in the guidelines. This results in an "adjusted offense level." For example, larceny has a base level of 4. However, if the defendant stole more than $10,000 (but less than $20,000), the judge would increase the level to 9. If the theft involved more than minimal planning, the judge would increase the level to 11. If the crime involved the exploitation of a vulnerable victim, the judge would increase the level to 13. This would be the "final adjusted offense level." Next, the judge looks at the criminal history category into which the defendant falls. Assuming the defendant has one previous conviction, even for an unrelated crime, for which a sentence of more than a year in prison was imposed, the defendant would be classified in "criminal history category II." Based on an adjusted offense level of 13 and being in criminal history category II, the defendant would be subject to a sentencing range of 15-21 months. This means the judge would be prohibited from sentencing this defendant to less than 15 months or more than 21 months in the absence of certain extraordinary circumstances specified in the guidelines, such as rendering substantial assistance to the authorities in uncovering other crimes or capturing other offenders.

Sentencing guidelines have been criticized as "computer justice" and as unduly harsh. Furthermore, trial judges do not like how guidelines circumscribe their ability to tailor a sentence to the individual before them. Nonetheless, one study found that sentencing guidelines in three states enhanced predictability and reduced disparity in sentencing for the same offense. This was so regardless of whether the guidelines were mandatory.[171]

As for the federal guidelines, the Supreme Court upheld their constitutionality in 1989, but in 2005 it held that the guidelines could not be mandatory.[172] Whether judges

---

169 See *Assessing Consistency supra* n. 167

170 Federal Guidelines Sentencing Reform Act, 18 U.S.C.A. §3551. The guidelines are explained with appropriate examples in HARRY L. SUBIN, BARRY BERKE & ERIC TISCHWELL, THE PRACTICE OF FEDERAL CRIMINAL LAW: PROSECUTION AND DEFENSE §17.6 (West 2006).

171 See *Assessing Consistency supra* n. 167

172 *Mistretta v. United States*, 488 U.S. 361 (1989); *United States v. Booker*, 543 U.S. 220 (2005). The Court held that the *mandatory* federal guidelines violated the right to a trial by jury because the judge, rather than the jury, determined the existence of aggravating factors that increased the statutory maximum penalty.

will continue to follow them and whether states will continue to use guidelines systems remains to be seen.

Mandatory Minimums and Sentence Enhancement   Enhancement factors are typically imposed in drug trafficking cases and felony cases in which a gun is used.[173] For example, at the federal level, Congress has imposed mandatory minimum sentences for the manufacture or distribution of narcotics.[174] These sentences are currently set at 5 and 10 years, depending on the quantity of the drug involved.

Dealing with Recidivists   While a prior criminal record is a major determinant of any sentence, special "three-strikes" laws exist in some form in half the states. The name comes from baseball, where the batter has three chances to hit the ball and "strikes out" upon the third attempt. California's law requires a minimum sentence of 25 years to life for a third conviction for a serious felony, and doubles the usual sentence imposed for a crime when it is a second offense. Thus, the commission of a relatively minor offense can lead to a life sentence. In 2003, the Supreme Court upheld the constitutionality of California's law against the argument that it imposed grossly dispro-portionate punishment for the offense that triggered it, in violation of the 8th Amend-ment's ban on "cruel and unusual punishment."[175] The defendant in that case had been sentenced to 25 years to life after his third felony — also chargeable as a misdemeanor — of stealing three golf clubs.

Rates of Incarceration   The most commonly articulated policies behind sanctions in criminal law are deterrence of crime, incapacitation of offenders and rehabilitation of offenders. As discussed above, recent years have seen a decline in the rehabilitative function and a greater emphasis on punishment, incapacitation and deterrence through long prison sentences. The violent crime rate in the United States decreased from 1995 to 2004 by 32.0% and in 2004 was the lowest ever recorded. The property crime rate decreased from 1995 to 2004 by 23.4%.[176] Yet, incarceration rates have continued to increase. In 2005, the United States had 737 per 100,000 of its population behind bars. These rates are quite phenomenal when compared to those of other developed democratic countries: 148 prisoners per 100,000 in England and Wales, 107 in Canada, 85 in France and 62 in Germany. As of 2005, the American incarceration rate rose each year since 1973.[177]

A defendant is entitled to a jury determination of such factual issues. Mandatory increases in a statutory *minimum* penalty based on aggravating factors need not be determined by a jury. *See* Chapter VIII, p. 278.

173 *See, e.g.*, Mich. Comp. L. Ann. §750.227b (Michigan's mandatory 2-year sentence, to be added to any felony involving a firearm); 18 U.S.C.A. §924(c) (mandatory sentences of varying lengths for using different kinds of guns in the commission of a drug offense).

174 *See, e.g.*, 21 U.S.C.A. §841.

175 *Ewing v. California*, 538 U.S. 11 (2003). *See also* Chapter XVIII, pp. 319-321 (8th Amendment).

176 *Incarceration and Crime: A Complex Relationship,* INCARCERATION PUBLICATIONS (The Sentencing Project, Washington, D.C.) January, 2005, *available at* http://www.sentencingproject.org/doc/publications /inc_iandc_complex.pdf.

177 *New Incarceration Figures: Thirty-Three Years of Consecutive Growth,* INCARCERATION PUBLICATIONS (The Sentencing Project, Washington, D.C.) December, 2006, *available at* http://www.sentencing project. org/doc/publications/inc_newfigures.pdf. The second highest rate was 611 per 100,000 residents in Russia. Some have argued that the decrease in the crime rate is the direct result of a higher incarceration rate. However, while it is undoubtedly one factor, comparisons of different states show that between 1991 and 1998, those states that increased incarceration at rates that were less than the national average experienced a larger decline in crime rates than those states that increased incarceration at rates higher than the national average. Moreover, other important and complex variables have simultaneously been in play. *See Incarceration and Crime, supra* note 176.

2. Probation

Where permitted by law, a court can sentence an offender to "probation." Probation is used usually when the circumstances of the crime and the defendant's background make a prison sentence too harsh. Offenders on probation are returned to the community under the supervision of a "probation officer." They will avoid prison if they comply with certain conditions, such as behaving well and not committing more crimes, reporting regularly to their probation officer, and perhaps other more specific conditions, such as payment of restitution, performance of some community service or drug or alcohol abuse therapy. If offenders on probation do not fulfill the conditions, probation can be revoked, and they will begin serving their prison sentence. Probation is a common alternative to incarceration. In 1996 over 3 million adults, or 57.6% of all offenders under correctional control, were on probation.[178] They are divided almost equally between those convicted of a misdemeanor and those convicted of a felony. Those under active supervision comprised 74%, 9% were inactive cases and 9% had absconded. Supervision on probation has been greatly facilitated by the invention of the "electronic tether," a device is attached to a defendant's leg that "reports" on where the defendant is located and whether the tether has been removed.[179]

3. The Death Penalty

The death penalty has been widely available as a punishment in the United States since colonial times. However, in 1972 the Supreme Court held the death penalty unconstitutional as applied by the states, because there were virtually no standards to guide the jury or judge in their decision to impose it.[180] But by 1976 some states had passed laws that met the requirements of the Court's 1972 ruling. The Court's view since 1976 has been that the death penalty is not unconstitutional, so long as there are sufficient standards by which a judge or jury can decide whether to impose.[181]

Today, 34 states and the federal government have capital punishment.[182] Potential methods of execution include lethal injection (34 states and U.S. government), electrocution (10 states), the gas chamber (5 states), hanging (2 states), and firing squads (2 states). However, all jurisdictions permit lethal injection as an alternative.[183]

As of July 2009, there were 3279 inmates awaiting execution, down from a peak in 2000 of 3,593. Of those on death row, 44% are white, 42% black, 12% Hispanic, and 2% other minorities. California has the largest death row, with 690 inmates awaiting

---

178 Christopher J. Mumola and Thomas P Bonczar, *Substance Abuse and Treatment of Adults on Probation 1995*, 2 (1998).

179 Statistics here and in the preceding paragraphs are from Bureau of Justice Statistics, U.S. Dept. of Justice, www.ojp.usdoj.gov/bjs/cvict.htm.

180 *Furman v. Georgia*, 408 U.S. 238 (1972).

181 Constitutional aspects of the death penalty are discussed in Chapter VIII, pp. 311-320. While the MPC originally took no position on the death penalty and in MPC §210.6 simply provided procedures for its imposition, in 2009, the MPC's author institution, the American Law Institute, voted to withdraw MPC §210.6. *See* ALI press release at http://www.ali.org/ _news/ 10232009. htm. This repealed section's factors and bifurcated jury procedure have widely influenced state procedure. *See* Chapter VIII, p. 320, where this procedure is described.

182 In 2004, New York's statute was declared unconstitutional under the New York state constitution, *People v. LaValle*, 817 N.E.2d 341 (N.Y. 2004). A statute repairing the defect and reinstating the death penalty was rejected by the New York legislature in 2005 after intense study by a legislative committee. New Mexico abolished its death penalty in 2009, although the law was not retroactive and two inmates remain on death row in that state. *See* N. Mex. Stat. Ann. § 31-18-14. Illinois abolished its death penalty in 2011.

183 *Facts About the Death Penalty*, DPIC Tools (Death Penalty Information Center, Washington, D.C.) March 31, 2010, *available at* http://www.deathpenaltyinfo.org/documents/FactSheet.pdf. See also http://www.deathpenaltyinfo.org/methods-execution.

execution. Other leaders include Florida (403), Texas (342) and Pennsylvania (225). Since 1976, 1200 prisoners have been executed. The states with the greatest share of these executions are all in or near the southern United States. Texas leads with 452 executions since 1976, followed by Virginia (106), Oklahoma (92), Florida (69), and Missouri (67).[184] Recent studies indicate that race may play a role in death sentencing. While 98% of district attorneys in death penalty states are white, only 1% are black.[185] Studies in North Carolina and California found that defendants who kill white victims are 3 to 3.5 times more likely to be sentenced to death than defendants who kill blacks or Latinos.

There are signs that support for the death penalty may be in decline. A 2006 poll on the death penalty found that, when given a choice between life without parole and the death penalty, 47% of respondents chose capital punishment, the lowest percentage in 20 years. The poll also revealed that overall support for the death penalty in 2006 is 65%, which is significantly lower than in 1994, when 80% supported capital punishment.[186] Additionally, a poll showed that 88% of criminologists did not believe that the death penalty deterred crime.[187] Police chiefs in a 2009 poll ranked the death penalty last among ways to reduce violent crime.[188] One reason for declining support may be several recent high-profile exonerations of death row inmates, some 14 of which were due to DNA testing.[189] In 2004, Congress passed the Innocence Protection Act.[190] One part of it establishes the Kirk Bloodsworth[191] Post-Conviction DNA Testing Grant Program and authorizes $25 million over 5 years to help states pay the cost of post-conviction DNA testing. It provides grants for DNA testing of all who claim actual innocence, both death row inmates and others. Another provision increases the maximum amount of money that the United States may be required to pay in federal cases of unjust imprisonment from a flat $5,000 to $50,000 per year of imprisonment in a noncapital case, and $100,000 per year of incarceration in capital cases. The Act also sets forth the "Sense of Congress Regarding Compensation in State Death Penalty Cases," which encourages states to provide reasonable compensation to any person found to have been unjustly convicted and sentenced to death. However, the Act does not require states to compensate

184 See *Facts About the Death Penalty, supra* note 183

185 Jeffrey J. Pokorak, *Probing the Capital Prosecutor's Perspective; Race of the Discretionary Actors,* 83 CORNELL L. REV. 181 (1998).

186 USA Today - Gallup Poll (May 5-7, 2006), www.pollingreport.com/crime.htm.

187 Michael L. Radelet and Traci L. Lacock, *Do Executions Lower Homicide Rates? The Views of Leading Criminoloists* 99 J. CRIM. L. & CRIMINOLOGY 489 (2009).

188 See *Facts About the Death Penalty, supra* note 183

189 *See* discussion in Chapter VIII, p. 284 (DNA and other exonerations). In the 25 years from 1973 to 1998, there were an average of 2.96 exonerations per year. In the 5 years since 1998, through 2003, the average rose to 7.60 exonerations. There were 6 exonerations in 2004. Exoneration is defined having a conviction overturned on appeal, followed by acquittal or dismissal of all charges on re-trial or being given an absolute pardon by a governor based on new evidence of innocence. Anyone freed by an acquittal on retrial could well not have been actually innocent, since all that is necessary for an acquittal is reasonable doubt. *See* Chapter III, p. 105 and Chapter VIII, p. 313.

190 18 U.S.C.A. §3600 *et seq.*

191 Bloodsworth was the first death row inmate exonerated by DNA evidence.

exonerated defendants.[192] Since 1973, 130 people have been exonerated and released from death row.[193]

192 Recovery for wrongful conviction may be difficult in states because of their sovereign immunity from suit and individual immunity of individual judges, prosecutors and witnesses. Indeed, suit against the federal government would also be impossible had it not waived its sovereign immunity. *See* Chapter VI, pp. 223-228.

193 STAFF OF H. COMM. ON THE JUDICIARY, 103RD CONG., REPORT ON CIVIL AND CONSTITUTIONAL RIGHTS, (Comm. Print 1993)

CHAPTER XV

BUSINESS LAW

This chapter will outline some of the more important legal aspects of doing business in the United States: the law of business organizations, securities law, antitrust law, bankruptcy, labor and employment law and environmental law. Sources for further study are cited in each section.

A. Types of Business Organizations

Most business enterprises are organized in one of four ways: (1) sole proprietorship, (2) partnership (general or limited), (3) corporation or (4) limited liability company. Each business organization shares some common aspects with others, but differs in method of ownership, the degree of personal liability of the investors for the enterprise's debts and in the complexity of the structure. Business organizations are governed primarily by state law, with a few areas governed by federal law.[1]

1. Sole Proprietorships

A sole proprietorship is a business enterprise owned solely by one individual. It is the most elementary organizational form of business. Small new businesses often begin as sole proprietorships because they are the simplest and least expensive to form and operate. Local accountants or attorneys in business for themselves or small retail shops are likely to be sole proprietorships.

The formation, operation, and management of sole proprietorships are generally simple. It is not necessary to file any documents with any governmental office other than local requirements (by a city or county) that the owner register the name of the business to prevent fraud. This registration would notify the public, for example, that John Smith is "doing business as Smith's Hardware Store."

The owner has total control, making all decisions concerning the business. Employees may be hired, and some management authority may be delegated to them, but the sole proprietor maintains ultimate control. Businesses that are sole proprietorships are not considered separate legal entities apart from the owner. Thus, the owner of the business is personally liable for all of the business' debts out of the owner's personal assets. However, the owner also reaps all the fruits of the business and need not pay partners or shareholders anything.

The identity of owner and business entails a tax advantage as well. Unlike corporations, sole proprietorships are not considered to be separate taxable entities by the Internal Revenue Service (IRS), the federal income taxing agency. Therefore, unlike the corporation, the sole proprietorship business itself does not have to pay federal income taxes. Instead, the income and deductible expenses of the business are reported on the owner's personal tax return.

---

[1] For more detail on the legal context of business and business organizations, *see* ROBERT W. HAMILTON & RICHARD BOOTH, BUSINESS BASICS FOR LAW STUDENTS, 4TH ED. (Aspen 2006); WILLIAM A. KLEIN & JOHN C. COFFEE, JR., BUSINESS ORGANIZATION AND FINANCE: LEGAL AND ECONOMIC PRINCIPLES, 7TH ED. (Foundation 2010); ROBERT W. HAMILTON, THE LAW OF CORPORATIONS IN A NUTSHELL, 6TH ED. (West 2009); ALAN R. PALMINTER, CORPORATIONS: EXAMPLES AND EXPLANATIONS, 6TH ED. (Aspen 2009). For fuller treatise coverage, *see* HARRY G. HENN AND JOHN R. ALEXANDER, LAW OF CORPORATIONS, 3D ED. (West 1983, 1986); ROBERT C. CLARK, CORPORATE LAW (Aspen 1986); WILLIAM A. GREGORY, LAW OF AGENCY & PARTNERSHIPS, 3D ED (West 2001).

2. General Partnerships

Nature of Partnerships and Reasons for Choice of Form   A partnership is an association of two or more persons to carry on a business for profit as co-owners. This "association" is in most cases set out in a written partnership agreement, but agreement can be oral and may even be implied from conduct.[2]

Like sole proprietors, partners in a general partnership are exposed to unlimited liability. However, an advantage of a partnership over a corporation is that the partnership does not have to pay income taxes separate from its owners. Instead, the income or loss of the business is reported on the partners' personal individual tax returns. In addition, partnerships avoid the complexities involved in forming and running a corporation.

Formation   The laws of most states are based on the Revised Uniform Partnership Act (RUPA), which governs the formation, operation, and structure of partnerships.[3] Partners may agree to almost any arrangement between them that is not illegal or contrary to public policy, so much of the RUPA provides simply a "default provision" — applicable only in the absence of express agreements in the partnership agreement. However, some RUPA provisions cannot be changed by agreement of the partners, notably provisions declaring that each partner owes a "fiduciary duty" to the partnership and the other partners or any limitation affecting third parties, such as creditors.[4] This fiduciary duty means that each partner must abide by the highest standards of loyalty, good faith, and integrity in matters pertaining to the partnership.[5] Any partner who fails to act in the best interest of the partnership or who acts in personal self interest is liable to the partnership. Thus a partner who uses partnership assets for personal gain is liable to the partnership for all the resulting profits.[6]

Each partner is required to make an initial contribution to the business in the form of cash, property, services, or some combination of these. The amount of each partner's contribution need not be the same. For example, in forming the ABC partnership, partner A might contribute $10,000 in cash, partner B might contribute $5,000 in cash and a $15,000 building, and partner C might agree to perform $20,000 worth of management services as an initial capital contribution. If a written partnership agreement exists, it will usually detail each partner's contribution.

Operation and Management   Partners can agree in the partnership agreement that decision-making authority will be granted to only one or a given group of the partners.

---

2   *Cutler v. Bowen*, 543 P.2d 1349 (Utah 1975) (owner of furnishings, equipment and lease of bar must share compensation for harm to business with bartender-manager because they were partners pursuant to oral agreement to share profits); *Chaiken v. Employment Security Commission*, 274 A.2d 707 (Super. Ct Del. 1971) (true nature of agreement showed that barbers working in shop were employees for whom unemployment tax was due, not partners). *But see Stephanz v. Laird*, 846 S.W.2d 895 (Tex. App. 1993) (referring to someone clearly an employee as a "partner" in correspondence is not sufficient to establish a partnership as a matter of law).

3   Revised Uniform Partnership Act, §202(a) (1997), promulgated by the Uniform Law Commissioners, found at http://www.nccusl.org/Update/. Most states have adopted the RUPA, but there were several made to it between 1992 through 1997, so not all states have it in the same version. There is also a Revised Uniform Limited Partnership Act (RULPA), *infra* text at note 20. These and other laws can also be found in JEFFREY D. BAUMAN, CORPORATIONS AND OTHER BUSINESS ASSOCIATIONS: STATUTES, RULES AND FORMS (West 2005). On the Uniform Law Commissioners, *see* Chapter I, p. 34, note 155.

4   UPS §103.

5   *See Meinhard v. Salmon*, 164 N.E.2d 544 (N.Y. 1928) (Cardozo, J.) (defining fiduciary duty).

6   *Clement v. Clement*, 260 A.2d 728 (Pa. 1970) (fraud not necessary for recovery by one partner against another; only proof that partner freely converted partnership assets to his own personal use).

Or the partners may agree to afford management powers in proportion to the capital contributions of each partner. For example, in the ABC partnership formed above, the partnership agreement might specify that A gets one vote, while B and C get two votes each. But in the absence of such a partnership agreement, each partner has equal rights in the management of the business, so decisions are made based on a majority vote and each partner has one vote.[7]

Partners act as agents for the partnership, so their actions bind the partnership, and partners are jointly and severally liable for all partnership obligations.[8] However, the RUPA imposes an "exhaustion of assets" rule, whereby creditors are required to seek payment from partnership assets first, before seeking to reach personal assets of the individual partners.[9]

Sharing Profits and Losses Partners can elect to allocate profits and losses in any manner they wish, but in the absence of an agreement to the contrary, all partners share in the profits and losses of the partnership equally, regardless of the amount of cash, property, or services contributed by each partner to the partnership.[10] A common arrangement is to make distribution of profits proportional to the amount of capital contribution of each partner. For example, the ABC partnership, in its written partnership agreement, might provide that A is entitled to 20% of the partnership's profits, while B and C are each entitled to 40% of its profits. A partner's shares of partnership profits can be assigned to a third party, but that does not give the third party any management rights in the partnership and could leave the assignee in a difficult situation if the partners elect not to make distributions.[11]

Compensation The partnership agreement can provide that some partners will be compensated for services rendered to the partnership. However, if the partnership agreement does not specifically say so, no partner is entitled to any compensation, regardless of any services provided. Absent express agreement to the contrary, the partners' shares of the profits are considered to be their full compensation.[12]

Withdrawal of Partners and Dissolution Each partner has the inherent power to withdraw from the partnership, but this does not cause a dissolution.[13] Instead, the partnership continues, but the remaining partners agreement is required to buy back the departing partner's interest and specifies the terms for doing so (the terms for which may be varied by agreement).[14] However, any remaining partner my require the winding up of the business — recognition that the withdrawal may have seriously compromised the

---

7   RUPA §401(f), (j).

8   RUPA §§301, 306(a). The act must be apparently for the purpose of carrying on partnership business. However, the act does not bind the partnership if the partner had no authority to act for the partnership in a particular matter, and the person with whom the partner was dealing knew or had received a notification that the partner lacked authority.

9   RUPA §307.

10   RUPA §401(b). Losses may be allocated unequally to provide one partner with tax benefits. *See* Chapter XVI, p. 650 (losses and other deductions from income).

11   *See Bauer v. Blomfield Co.*, 849 P.2d 1365 (Alaska, 1993)

12   RUPA §406(h).

13   This is different from the old UPA §37, which provided that withdrawal resulted in dissolution and winding up of the partnership. However, even under the UPA, partnerships usually did not dissolve, but continued to function as a new partnership after paying the withdrawing partner for his or her interest.

14   RUPA §701. Withdrawing partners are entitled to a buy-out from the partnership, while partners in a judicially-dissolved partnership must be paid from the proceeds of the partnership's liquidated assets. *See McCormick v. Brevig*, 96 P.3d 697 (Mont. 2004).

partnership's business.[15]   However, a partnership agreement may limit intentional withdrawal from the partnership for a period of time. Thus, if money has been borrowed, partners may not be permitted to withdraw until the loan is paid off. Such a provision cannot prevent a partner from exercising the right to withdraw, but the partner will be liable for damages for early withdrawal.

Expulsion of a partner is possible, if the partnership agreement provides for it. Expulsions provided for in the agreement can be for good cause, for business reasons or for no reason, but they are subject to the good faith requirements imposed by the fiduciary duty of partners to each other.[16]

The RUPA also provides a procedure for terminating the existence of a partnership. The first step, dissolution, can come about through voluntary agreement of the partners, judicial order, or the death of a partner.[17] A dissolved partnership must then wind-up its affairs. This entails using the assets of the partnership, including contributions by partners, to satisfy the partnership's liabilities to its creditors, and, if any assets remain, making distributions to the partners in accordance with the distribution provisions of the partnership agreement.[18] Termination of the partnership occurs when a partner files a certificate of dissolution, which cancels a filed partnership agreement, provides notice to potential creditors of the dissolution, and serves as a limitation on the authority of partners to further bind the partnership vis-a-vis third parties.[19]

3. Limited Partnerships

Nature and Business Reasons for Choice of Form   A limited partnership has both general and limited partners. It differs from a general partnership in the fact that the limited partners are not subject to unlimited liability for the debts of the business and risk only the loss of their initial capital contribution to the partnership. Correspondingly, limited partners have little control over the running of the business, which is run by the general partner or partners. Thus, a limited partnership is often the choice of a business-person who wishes to raise capital, but does not wish to give up control over the business as would happen with a general partnership.

Today, general partnerships are often small- to medium-sized businesses operating within the local community and generally have relatively few partners. Limited partnerships, on the other hand, are usually much larger businesses, because, among other reasons, limited partnerships are popular with investors as a tax shelter device, as discussed below.   Limited partnerships will often have one general partner and hundreds or thousands of limited partners. Private equity funds, for example, are often formed as limited partnerships, with many hundreds of limited partners contributing up to several billion dollars in capital contributions to the largest funds.

Formation Limited partnerships can be formed only through compliance with state statutory requirements. Most states have adopted the Revised Uniform Limited Partner-

---

15 RUPA §801. However, a 90 day delay is imposed in such an event to permit the remaining partners to assess the situation. §801 also provides for winding up under other limited circumstances.

16 *See Bohatch v. Butler & Binion*, 977 S.W.2d 543 (Tex. 1998) (no breach of fiduciary duty where partnership expelled a partner for reporting suspected over billing; procedures in partnership agreement followed, which did not specify or limit the grounds for expulsion). A practical article on how to mediate breakups of partnerships is James C. Freund, *Anatomy of a Split-Up: Mediating the Business Divorce*, 53 BUSINESS LAWYER 479 (1997).

17 RUPA §802.

18 RUPA §807(a).

19 RUPA §805.

ship Act (RULPA) to govern the formation and operation of limited partnerships.[20] To form a limited partnership, a "certificate of limited partnership" is filed with a designated state official, usually the state's Secretary of State. This certificate must include specified information concerning the partnership, such as the names and addresses of the general and limited partners, and the like.[21] Limited partnerships are also required to have a written partnership agreement, at least if they wish to modify the default rules of the RULPA. Often, the certificate of limited partnership and the written partnership agreement are the same thing.

Operation and Management   Every limited partnership must have at least one general partner and one limited partner. The general partners have the same rights and duties as partners in a general partnership and manage.[22] Limited partners, on the other hand, are treated as investors. They have no rights to participate in the management of the business, to use partnership property, or to conduct business on behalf of the partnership. However, they are entitled to share in the profits of the business as specified in the partnership agreement.[23]

The exact extent to which limited partners can participate in the business without losing their limited liability status is often undefined. The ULPA states that a limited partner becomes liable as a general partner if the partner (1) "takes part in the control of the business" and (2) the person alleging liability must have reasonably believed, based on the limited partner's conduct, that the limited partner is a general partner.[24] The RULPA has a list of "safe harbor" activities in which a limited partner may engage without losing limited liability, including working as a contractor for the partnership, consulting or advising the general partner with respect to the business, and voting on removing or admitting general or limited partners.[25]

Special Tax Aspects of Limited Partnerships   As stated earlier, the partnership form has great flexibility in allocating income and losses among partners. This characteristic has been capitalized upon to provide a "tax shelter" for money. Typically two groups come together for mutual benefit: entrepreneurs with skill, but no money, and taxpayers with high incomes seeking business losses to claim on their tax returns to offset income.[26] For example, assume that a developer believes that there is a need for an office building in a big city, but it has no money. Often the developer will seek out people with high incomes taxed at a high rate to invest their money as limited partners in a partnership formed to build and then rent out and manage the building. The

---

20 *See supra* note 3.

21 RULPA §201.

22 RULPA §403(a).

23 RULPA §303(a).

24 RULPA §303(a). By contrast, the earlier ULPA required only (1). *See Alzado v. Blinder, Robinson & Co., Inc.,* 752 P.2d 544 (Colo. 1988) (activities of limited partner in promoting boxing match were not sufficient to render him liable). And the trend seems to be toward greater limited partner participation. The *revised* RULPA promulgated in 2001, called "Re-RULPA," provides for limited liability of a limited partner "even if the limited partner participates in the management and control of the limited partnership." Re-RULPA §303. Re-RULPA also permits a limited partnership to elect the status of "limited liability limited partnership" that accords the general partner limited liability as well. Re-RULPA §404(c). This would put the limited partners on equal footing with corporate shareholders and limited liability company members.

25 RULPA §303(b)(6). A general partner's work is judged under the same "business judgment rule" applicable to corporate managers, discussed *infra* p. 595. *See Wyler v. Feuer,* 149 Cal.Rptr. 626 (Cal.App.1978) (no basis for suit by limited partners when partnership's movie did not make money).

26 The federal income tax system is moderately "progressive," meaning that as income goes up, the rate of taxation does as well. In general, the tax rate is between 15% and 40%. *See generally* Chapter XVI.

developer uses the investment to build the building, takes the rents from the building as income and allocates the losses (primarily in the form of depreciation of the building) to the limited partner investors. These losses, taken each year for several years, serve to reduce the amount of income from other sources on which the investors must pay taxes. The developer gets the money needed to build the building, and the investors are protected by limited liability from losing more than their investment, and get a substantial tax savings.[27]

4. Corporations

a. General Nature

Corporations are recognized as legal entities distinct from their owners — "shareholders," so-called because they "hold" a "share" of the overall ownership of the corporation. Corporations can sue and be sued, enter into contractual relations, and own property. Corporations even have constitutional rights separate from their owners or management: since 1868 corporations have been able to sue for violations of their 14th Amendment due process and other rights.[28] In 2010, the Supreme Court held that corporations have First Amendment rights to fund independent political broadcasts in elections.[29] One of the principal values of the corporate form of doing business is its limited liability. Absent exceptional circumstances, the shareholders in the corporation cannot be held personally liable for debts incurred or liability imposed on the corporation. However, this is only one feature of the corporation that must be weighed in deciding whether to incorporate, as discussed below.

Corporation law is principally state law. It is largely statutory, but the common law is often relied upon, especially when defining the fiduciary duties of management. Federal law governs trading in publicly-offered corporate securities[30] and federal income taxation law drives some corporate decision-making.[31] There is a Model Business Corporation Act (MBCA) and Revised Model Business Corporation Act (RMBCA) promulgated by a committee of the American Bar Association.[32] However, the MBCA and RMBCA have not gained as wide acceptance by state legislatures as the uniform partnership laws have.

---

27 The losses taken on the investors tax returns do not relieve the limited partners of tax liability for the benefits of the value of the building. They will pay for the gain their investment has produced when the building is sold years later. But such a "tax deferral," generally for a number of years, provides the limited partners with real benefit. First, they have the *use* of the money that would have otherwise been paid in taxes over several years. Second, their overall tax liability is less when the building is sold years later, because the investors will often be retired and therefore have less income. Taxpayers with lower incomes pay a smaller percentage of their income in taxes. For more detail, *see* sources cited in note 47, *infra*, and *see generally* Chapter XVI, where income and other federal taxes are discussed.

28 *See Paul v. Virginia*, 75 U.S. (8 Wall.) 168 (1868) (corporation is a "person" as that term is used in the 14th Amendment). Corporations have been responsible for raising most of the issues of 1st Amendment commercial speech. *See* Chapter IX, pp. 387-389. Strangely enough, while it is a "person," a corporation is not a "citizen" protected by the privileges and immunities clause of the 14th Amendment or Article IV. *See* Chapter IX, p. 348. This is so despite the fact that a corporation can be a citizen of a state for purposes of diversity of citizenship. *See* Chapter V, p. 190.

29 *See Citizens United v. Federal Election Comm'n*, ___ U.S. ___, 130 S. Ct. 876, 882-85 (2010).

30 *See infra* p. 600.

31 *See infra* p. 589.

32 *See* MODEL BUSINESS CORPORATION ACT ANN., 3D ED. (Prentice Hall Law & Bus. 1985-present). The RMBCA and the corporation acts of several states (including Delaware) are set out in SELECTED CORPORATION AND OTHER BUSINESS ASSOCIATIONS: STATUTES, RULES AND FORMS, *supra* note 3. Professor Hamilton, author of the Nutshell on corporations, *supra* note 1, was the reporter for the RMBCA.

The corporate law of the state of Delaware is very important.[33] Generally, the laws of the state where the company was incorporated control issues of governance of a corporation even when all the corporation's offices and facilities are in other states.[34] Delaware has tried its best to be an attractive state for incorporation by providing perhaps the greatest flexibility for corporate governance. Thus, Delaware has won what some have called "the race to the bottom" that began in the early 20th century — a competition among states to pass corporate laws that least restrict corporate management prerogatives.[35] As a result, over one-third of the corporations listed on the New York Stock Exchange are incorporated in Delaware. The great number of Delaware corporations has in turn produced a great number of cases decided under Delaware law. As a result, Delaware corporate law is by far the most well-developed and therefore the most predictable.[36]

b. Types of Corporations

It is helpful to distinguish between two types of corporations: publicly held corporations and closely held corporations. Both are created under state statutes and are subject to the same basic rules. Both can conduct the same types of business. But they inhabit different worlds in terms of ownership and operation. Among the differences is the fact that publicly held corporations are subject to federal regulation to a much greater extent.

Publicly Held Corporations Publicly held corporations are those whose shares are traded by the general public in organized markets, such as the New York Stock Exchange, other national exchanges or in the "over-the-counter" markets. These include some of the largest corporations in the world, such as Exxon-Mobil, Toyota and General Electric. Their stockholders are numerous, widely dispersed and constantly changing. Most shareholders purchase shares as an investment and have no desire to become actively involved in management decisions or even to attend stockholders' meetings or vote. However, some holders of major blocks of stock serve as directors or managers, are active at shareholder meetings or otherwise seek to affect management decisions.

Closely Held Corporations Closely held corporations, called close corporations, are corporations with shares that are not publicly traded. Usually, close corporations have relatively few shareholders who are close business associates or family members and all participate actively in running the business. In this respect, close corporations sometimes resemble sole proprietorships or partnerships. In fact, closely held corporations are often businesses that were once sole proprietorships or partnerships, but have since incorporated to obtain benefits offered by the corporate form, such as limited liability or advantageous treatment of corporate retirement pension plans. Shareholders often agree to restrict transfers of their stock to any outside investors to ensure that the corporation continues to run as the original shareholders want. Most close corporations are small businesses, but there are some large ones that rival the size of some of the publicly traded corporations.

---

33 For the most comprehensive analysis of Delaware corporate law, *see* EDWARD P. WELCH, ROBERT J. TUREZYN, AND ROBERT S. SAUNDERS, FOLK ON THE DELAWARE GENERAL CORPORATION LAW, 5TH ED (Aspen 2010).

34 *See VantagePoint Venture Partners 1996 v. Examen, Inc.*, 871 A.2d 1108 ((Del. 2005).

35 *See* William L. Cary, *Federalism and Corporate Law: Reflections Upon Delaware*, 83 YALE L.J. 663 (1974). *But see* Daniel R. Fischel, *The "Race to the Bottom" Revisited: Reflections on Recent Developments in Delaware Corporation Law*, 76 NW. L.REV 913 (1982).

36 Delaware's incentive to provide a hospitable environment for corporations is at least in part financial. Currently, 20% of Delaware's state budget comes from fees charged to corporations incorporated there, thereby allowing the state to abolish its sales tax and to lower its residents' income tax.

Whatever their size, close corporations must comply with the same state statutory requirements as publicly held corporations. Thus, while shareholders and officers may be the same people, the corporation must elect directors, appoint officers, conduct board and stockholders' meetings, and comply with other such requirements.[37] However, many states have passed special close corporation statutes that attempt to deal with some of the unique features of the close corporation. For example, the shareholders may be able to manage the corporation without having a board of directors. The goal of these statutes is to allow for internal flexibility within the close corporation, much like that in a partnership.[38]

In a publicly held corporation, shareholders who disagree with how the corporation is being run can simply sell their shares. Dissenting shareholders in close corporations cannot redeem their investment so easily, since the corporation's articles or bylaws usually prohibit shareholders from selling their shares to anyone without the approval of the board of directors or other shareholders. When matters become antagonistic, dissenting shareholders may find themselves "frozen out" of any meaningful role in the business, including having their employment with the corporation or their dividends terminated. Dissenting shareholders who are frozen out may file an action in court seeking an appraisal of their shares and a buyout by the corporation. But unless there is some special statute or agreement providing for a buyout, the dissenting shareholder has to show some breach of fiduciary duty, and this is sometimes difficult to show.[39] The reason for this is that, short of such a breach, corporations are *supposed* to work on a majority-rules basis. Nonetheless, some dissenters do succeed if they can show that actions taken against them by the majority shareholders make little business sense or are clearly in bad faith.[40] The remedy for such actions is one which protects the plaintiff's "reasonable expectation of benefit" from the corporation and provides compensation for past wrongs. This could be back-pay or a forced dividend, but it does not necessarily have to be a forced sale of the plaintiff's shares, which could amount to an economic windfall, given the general lack of a market for shares in closely held corporations.[41]

c. Formation of the Corporation

Despite variations in law from state to state, the basic rules for formation are substantially the same everywhere. The first step is to file "articles of incorporation" with the appropriate state official and to pay a fee. Exactly what these papers must contain varies among the states, but at a minimum they must include the name of the corporation, the number of shares the corporation is authorized to issue, the address of the corporation's registered office in the state, and the incorporators' names and signatures.

---

37 *See* discussion of powers and duties of board of directors *infra* pp. 593-595.

38 See Delaware General Corporation Law, Subchapter XIV: Close Corporations; Special Provisions, 8 Del. C. 1953, §341 et seq.

39 See *Donahue v. Rodd Electrotype Company of New England, Inc.*, 328 N.E.2d 505 (Mass. 1975) (holding that stockholders in close corporation owe each other substantially the same fiduciary duties as partners in a partnership).

40 *See Wilkes v. Springside Nursing Home, Inc.*, 353 N.E.2d 657 (Mass. 1976) (terminating paid employment and failing to reelect dissenting shareholder to paid position as director was breach of fiduciary duty; damages awarded).

41 *See Brodie v. Jordan*, 857 N.E.2d 1076 (Mass. 2006).

When these papers are in the proper form, a state official will issue a certificate of incorporation, and the corporation comes into legal existence.[42]

After obtaining a certificate of incorporation, the incorporators must adopt the corporation's bylaws. The bylaws are a set of rules that govern the internal affairs of the corporation. However, rules set out in the articles of incorporation control over contrary bylaws. The articles of incorporation are a matter of public record, whereas the bylaws are not accessible to the general public for inspection.

d. Business Reasons for Choosing to Incorporate

For many large businesses, the corporate form is the most efficient way to carry on the business. Many small partnerships and sole proprietorships, however, will consider incorporation when they wish to expand their businesses. For these businesses, it is often said that the best advice on whether to incorporate is "when in doubt, don't." It is useful to review some of the advantages and disadvantages of incorporation now before getting into some of the details of corporate operation.

Limited Liability The first advantage of incorporation is the limited liability the corporate form provides for all of its shareholders. If a corporation has 1,000 shares of stock and a shareholder owns 250 shares, that shareholder has a 25% ownership interest in the corporation. Shareholders stand to lose no more than the amount represented by the value of their shares, regardless of the corporation's outstanding debts. Such limited liability allows corporations to raise capital easily since purchasers of shares can own part of a business without incurring its liabilities.[43] While limited partners in an LP also enjoy limited liability, LPs are required to have at least one general partner who remains personally liable for all the partnership debts.

But limited liability is not always as important as it might seem. Liability insurance can often be purchased to cover all but the most unusual losses. Or liability exposure may not be a major worry in a given business. Moreover, banks and other creditors lending money to new and often undercapitalized corporations often insist that shareholders give *personal* guarantees for loans to the corporation. Obtaining loans is often a more efficient method of raising capital than selling shares, since it is often difficult to attract investors in the rather limited market for shares in most small corporations.

Perpetual Existence A second reason for choosing to incorporate is the advantage of the perpetual existence of the corporation. A partnership can dissolve at the insistence of any partner and, absent contrary agreement, the withdrawing partner can insist on payment to each partner of the appropriate share of the enterprise.[44] A shareholder in a corporation generally cannot unilaterally dissolve the entity and withdraw his investment. Yet, a partnership may be almost as durable as many corporations. While the partnership's *legal* continuity is disrupted by various occurrences, its *economic* continuity generally is not. In most cases, as noted earlier, the business continues unchanged while the partnership is reformed.

Ease of Transfer of Shares A third advantage of incorporation is the fact that the ownership interests represented by shares of stock in a corporation can be easily

---

[42] States enacted general incorporation statutes starting in the early 1800s in response to the growth in business activity at that time. Before then, corporations generally could only be created by action of the legislature and then only for limited public or semi-public purposes (such as to build a toll road or canal). *See* HENN & ALEXANDER, *supra* note 1, §12.

[43] *See* discussion of corporate financing and structure *infra* pp. 590-591.

[44] UPA §§31(1)(b), 38(1).

transferred with no effect on the corporation. If a shareholder dies, the shares pass to the estate and then to heirs. If a shareholder wishes to sell to a new investor, this transaction will not affect the corporation. But, while easy transfer is true of publicly-traded companies, small businesses often restrict transfers of shares to maintain control and commonly have the right to buy back shares of deceased or withdrawing shareholders.

Centralized Structure   Another reason often given for incorporating is that the corporation is more centrally governed since management power is vested in directors and officers. In a partnership, all general partners usually participate in management decisions. But this is only a default position. Partnership agreements can provide for centralized control in managing partners.

Tax Treatment   A major consideration in choice of the corporate form is tax treatment of corporate earnings.[45] Consistent with their separate legal existence, corporations must pay their own federal income taxes. Corporate earnings then are effectively subject to a double tax: earnings are taxed once through *corporate* income taxation and then taxed again through *individual* income taxation when the corporation distributes part of those earnings to its shareholders by way of dividends.

But the double taxation problem is not as serious as it might seem for many corporations. In most cases, a closely held corporation can avoid double taxation. If it is an independent domestic and domestically-owned corporation with no more than 75 shareholders and only one class of stock, it may qualify for special tax treatment as an "S corporation" under the Internal Revenue Code (IRC).[46] Such corporations may opt to have corporate income taxed directly to the shareholders. This "pass-through" or "conduit" form of taxation operates much like taxation of partners in a partnership.[47]

Corporations not covered by the exception just explained are called "C corporations."[48] In many relatively small C corporations, shareholders are also employees or creditors of the corporation. Such C corporations may be able to obtain "pass-through" tax advantages similar to an S corporation. The C corporation could make distributions of corporate income by way of payments of reasonable salaries or interest on loans to shareholder-employees or shareholder-creditors. Such "non-dividend" distributions are deductible from corporate earnings. If the C corporation is able to thus "zero-out" its earnings, corporate income ends up being taxed only once — when it is received by the shareholder-employees and shareholder-creditors — just as in the case of partnership or subchapter S distributions.[49] One study found that, because of the large number of deductions and credits available to C corporations in the IRC, the effective tax rate for

---

45 *See* Chapter XVI for more details on this and other points of tax law.

46 26 U.S.C.A. §§1361 *et seq.* "S Corporation" comes from subchapter S of Chapter 1 of subtitle A of title 26 of the United States Code where these requirements are found. Changes in 1996 raised the number of stockholders from 35 to 75, allowed S corporations to own subsidiary corporations under certain circumstances and have them treated as S corporations, and permitted non-profit S corporations.

47 In recent years, the double taxation disadvantage has been lessened by adjustments in tax rates. *See* Chapter XVI, pp. 661-664.

48 26 U.S.C.A. §§301 *et seq.* Subchapter C of the IRC governs corporate taxation in general.

49 Yet, this device may be difficult to use where some C corporation shareholders are not employees and the amount that needs to be distributed in this way is so large that payment in salary or bonuses may violate IRC limits on the reasonableness of compensation for employees that can be deducted.

most corporations is quite low, and nearly half of all C corporations reported no taxable income in 2001.[50]

Whatever the benefits of incorporation, they come at the price of increased complexity. There is much more paperwork and formal requirements must be observed. Annual reports must be filed and shareholder meetings held and a host of other additional work done (including preparation of separate tax returns) that is not involved when the business is a partnership. And one must add to this the lawyers' and accountants' fees in dealing with these complexities. An additional aspect of the various corporate filing formalities is that the filings become public record, thus making the corporate form a less private way of doing business. Not surprisingly, small businesses that have recently incorporated have a natural tendency to continue the business in the same informal way they did when it was a sole proprietorship or partnership. But the consequences of failure to follow essential corporate formalities can be serious because such failures might allow a creditor to disregard the corporate form and reach shareholders' or officers' personal assets.[51]

e. Corporate Finance and Ownership

Corporations raise capital primarily by issuing "securities." Securities are evidence of the obligation to pay money or of the right to participate in earnings. Most corporations issue two types of securities to investors: (1) equity securities or shares of stock (already encountered) and (2) debt securities or bonds.[52]

Stocks As mentioned earlier, shares of stock represent ownership interests in the corporation. In public corporations, shares are generally freely transferable, meaning that shares can be bought and sold by investors without the consent of the corporation and without affecting corporate operations. Similarly, the death of a shareholder matters little to the corporation, as the shareholder's heirs become the new owners.[53] The purchasers of stock do not actually "own" the assets of the corporation. All of the business' assets are owned by the corporation itself. Instead, shareholders are granted certain rights, depending upon the type of stock owned, as outlined below.

Corporate shares are usually divided into two categories, "common stock" and "preferred stock." Common stock is the most basic type of stock and must be issued by every corporation. It confers upon its holders two fundamental rights: (1) the right to vote for the directors of the corporation and on other matters requiring stockholder approval, such as a merger, and (2) the right to the net assets of the corporation upon dissolution of the corporation. Dividends are discretionary payments made by the corporation to the stockholders out of the earnings of the business. Dividends are declared by the board of directors and are usually paid on a quarterly basis. The receipt of dividends is one way for stockholders to earn a profit on their investment in the corporation. However, the board of directors is not required to declare a dividend, and shareholders have no inherent right to the payment of dividends. The other way they profit is by the increase in the market value of their shares. But there is no guarantee

---

50 STEPHEN A. LIND, STEPHEN SCHWARTZ, DANIEL J. LATHROPE, AND JOSHUA D. ROSENBERG, FUNDAMENTALS OF BUSINESS ENTERPRISE TAXATION, 3D ED 25 (Foundation 2005).

51 *See* discussion *infra* p. 595.

52 *See generally* HENN & ALEXANDER, *supra* note 1, §§154-161.

53 As noted earlier in the discussion of closely held corporations, the articles of incorporation may restrict the transferability of shares to assure that control of the business is not lost.

that the stock will increase in value. Its value will depend on the profitability of the business.

Shares of preferred stock also represent an ownership interest in the corporation. However, the owners of preferred stock are entitled to certain rights and privileges that are superior to those of common stock owners. The most common feature of preferred shares is a dividend preference over common stock. This preference does not guarantee the payment of a dividend, but it does guarantee that any dividends declared by the board will be paid first to the preferred stock owners. Preferred stockholders also are given priority over common stockholders in the event of a liquidation of the corporation, though neither class of shareholders can be paid before the corporation's creditors, including bondholders, discussed below. Unlike common stock, preferred shares often come without voting rights for the holder. In addition, some preferred shares are convertible, meaning that they can convert into common shares in certain circumstances. Often the trigger for conversion is a specified event, such as an initial public offering or the sale of the corporation, but it may also be simply at the election of the corporation or the stockholder.

Bonds In addition to equity securities, most corporations also issue debt securities, or bonds, which represent the borrowing of money. In other words, instead of purchasing an ownership interest in the corporation, the bondholder is making a loan to the corporation. The bond represents an unconditional guarantee by the corporation to pay the bond holder a specific amount on a certain date. In addition, the bondholder is generally entitled to periodic interest payments. For example, the ABC Corporation might issue a $1,000 ten-year bond, paying 6% interest. To obtain this bond, the purchaser will pay the corporation $1,000. In return, the corporation agrees to repay the purchaser the $1,000 in ten years. During the ten-year period, the corporation agrees to pay the bondholder annually 6% of the face value of the note, or $60 a year. Unlike shareholders, bondholders are not entitled to voting rights, nor do they receive dividends. Instead, a debtor-creditor relationship is established between the corporation and the bondholder. Corporations can deduct the interest they pay on outstanding bonds for federal income tax purposes.[54]

f. Organizational Structure and Powers

Ownership and management of a corporation involve three tiers: (1) shareholders, (2) directors, and (3) officers. Directors and officers, and occasionally controlling shareholders, comprise the management. Each group has defined powers within the enterprise.

Shareholders' Rights and Duties Shareholders' rights are established in the articles, bylaws and the state's general incorporation law. Shareholders have either the absolute or qualified right to inspect the corporate books and records for proper purposes, such as to become informed of corporate affairs.[55] [In management-friendly Delaware, for example, shareholders must have a "credible basis" from which a court could infer mismanagement, waste, or wrongdoing on the part of the corporation's leadership.][56] Shareholders do not actually run the business, nor do they have the power to act individually on behalf of the corporation. Instead, their powers must be exercised

---

54 I.R.C. §163(a).

55 An improper purpose would be to learn business secrets, to aid a competitor of the corporation, or to secure prospects for personal business.

56 *See Seinfeld v. Verizon Communications, Inc.*, 909 A.2d 117 (Del. 2006).

collectively along with the other shareholders by way of voting, usually at the stockholders' meeting. Most states require a yearly stockholders' meeting with advance written notice.

Each shareholder is entitled to one vote per share of common stock owned. Shareholders do not have to be present at the stockholders' meeting to vote. Through the use of a document called a "proxy," shareholders can appoint someone else to cast their vote on a specific subject. Because of the large number of shareholders in most publicly held corporations and the impracticability of attending shareholders' meetings, voting by proxy is common.

Through their voting powers, shareholders have control over the corporation in three primary ways: (1) they can elect or remove the directors;[57] (2) they can amend the articles of incorporation or bylaws;[58] and (3) they have the right to approve or disapprove extraordinary changes to the corporation, such as a merger with another corporation.[59]

The obligations of shareholders are few. Because of the principle of limited liability, shareholders are not responsible for any of the corporation's debts or other actions, with the extraordinary exception of "piercing the corporate veil" discussed below.[60] If the corporation fails, its shareholders lose only their investments.[61]

Shareholder Rights in Publicly Traded Corporations   In large publicly traded corporations, the governance power of shareholders is virtually nonexistent. Shareholder proxies are delivered to the corporate managers, who elect directors that often reappoint the incumbent managers. Most shareholders do not choose to exert any control over corporate managers. First, they usually view themselves as passive investors, not owners. Second, they often doubt whether they can improve corporate performance by intervening or controlling the choice of managers. Third, even if they did want to be more active, a great deal of time, money and energy is needed for them to inform themselves about corporate matters and to persuade and solicit proxies from other shareholders.[62] Consequently, when shareholder meeting announcements are sent out, along with management proxy forms requesting shareholders to vote their shares as it has recommended, most shareholders simply vote with by proxy in favor of the management or throw the entire announcement away.

If shareholders wish to be come active in exerting control over corporate actions, however, federal law is of some assistance. Section 14 of the Securities Exchange Act and regulations thereunder regulate the procedures by which proxies are obtained from shareholders of publicly traded corporations.[63] In addition to prohibiting fraud and misrepresentation in management communications to shareholders, the Act and regulations require that an annual report be sent that conforms to particular specifica-

---

57 Directors usually serve their full term. If the shareholders are unhappy with a director's performance, the director is simply not reelected. However, the shareholders have the power to remove a director from office *for cause* and some laws expressly provide that shareholders can vote by majority to remove a director at any time *without cause*. *See* RMBCA, *supra* note 32, §8.08(a).

58 *See CA, Inc. v. AFSCME Employees Pension Plan*, 953 A. 2d 227 (Del. 2008) (management was correct to decline to include in annual proxy mailing a shareholder proposal which could interfere with corporate board's exercise of fiduciary duties).

59 *See infra* p. 597.

60 *See infra* pp. 595-597.

61 *See generally* HENN & ALEXANDER, *supra* note 1, §§199-203.

62 A proxy is a document executed by shareholders appointing someone else to vote their shares for them.

63 15 U.S.C.A. §78n.

tions. The content of proxy statements is regulated. Management is required to include in any proxy statement certain shareholder proposals and supporting statements, and to afford shareholders the opportunity to vote for or against management or shareholder proposals in the management proxy. Corporate management rarely loses votes on important proposals. Section 14 has been viewed as embodying a policy of "corporate democracy" and a desire to prevent management from treating corporations as their own personal property.[64]

Directors   Directors are responsible for the management of the corporation and for creating corporate policy. The initial directors are usually named in the articles of incorporation or elected by the incorporators, and serve until the first annual shareholder meeting or until their successors are elected and qualified. Thereafter, directors are elected by majority vote of the shareholders and usually serve a term of one year.[65] The number of directors of a corporation varies; some states require at least three, while others require only one.

Directors meet regularly at board meetings to conduct the corporation's business. Directors do not have the power to act individually for the corporation; they can act only as an entire board. Thus, unlike employees, whose acts in the name of the corporation bind it, directors can bind the corporation only by actions approved by an affirmative vote of the board. They have the responsibility for all major policy-making decisions necessary for the management of all corporate affairs: declaring and paying corporate dividends to shareholders, authorizing major corporate policy and appointing, supervising, and removing officers and employees; and making financial decisions.

Directors, as persons in control of the property of others, are "fiduciaries" who have duties to both shareholders and the corporation. The directors' fiduciary duties include the duty of care and the duty of loyalty.[66] The duty of care entails being honest and using prudent business judgment when conducting corporate affairs. Directors must exercise the degree of care that a reasonably prudent person would use when conducting personal business affairs, including the duty to become informed about corporate affairs.[67] The duty of loyalty prevents directors from, among other things, using corporate funds or confidential corporate information for their personal advantage, competing with the corporation, usurping a corporate opportunity, engaging in insider trading, or selling control over the corporation.[68] A director who breaches either the duty of care or the duty of loyalty is answerable to the corporation and shareholders. A Delaware corpora-

---

64   *Medical Committee for Human Rights v. Securities & Exchange Comm.*, 432 F.2d 659 (D.C. Cir. 1970), *vacated as moot*, 404 U.S. 403 (1972).

65   Directors usually serve from annual meeting to annual meeting, but longer or staggered terms are permissible under most state statutes.

66   Delaware also considers a duty to act in good faith alongside the duties of care and loyalty. *See In re Walt Disney Company Derivative Litigation*, 906 A.2d 27 (Del. 2006). *See also* Melvin A. Eisenberg, *The Duty of Good Faith in Corporate Law*, 31 DEL. J. CORP. L. 1 (2005); John L. Reed and Matt Neiderman, *Good Faith and the Ability of Directors to Assert §102(b)(7) of the Delaware Corporation Law as a Defense to Claims Alleging Abdication, Lack of Oversight, and Similar Breaches of Fiduciary Duty*, 29 DEL. J. CORP. L. 111 (2004); Hillary A. Sale, *Delaware's Good Faith*, 89 CORNELL L. REV. 456 (2004).

67   *Smith v. Van Gorkom*, 488 A.2d 858 (Del. 1985) (rescission of merger allowed in shareholder suit where merger was approved quickly based on a 20-minute presentation by the chairman and without review of merger documents).

68   *See* HENN & ALEXANDER, *supra* note 1, §234; *see also* RMBCA, *supra* note 32, §8.30. *See, e.g., Globe Woolen Co. v. Utica Gas & Electric*, 121 N.E. 378 (N.Y. 1918) (Cardozo, J.) (contract to supply power that grossly favored textile company voided where same person was director and chairman of the executive committee of electric company and chief stockholder and director of textile company).

tion's certificate of incorporation can remove a director's personal liability for breach of the duty of care, but not for the duty of loyalty.[69]

Officers The corporate officers are responsible for the day-to-day operation of the corporation. They are most often selected and removed by the board of directors. Traditional titles include "chief executive officer," "president," "vice-president," "treasurer," and "secretary." The officers carry out the board's decisions and conduct the day-to-day operations of the business. The tenure of the officers is generally pursuant to a contract, though it may also be at the board's discretion.

Officers are viewed as having the same fiduciary duty of care and loyalty to the corporation and its shareholders as directors do when conducting business affairs, as well as the same obligations concerning corporate opportunities and conflicts of interest.[70] Like directors, officers purporting to contract on behalf of the corporation without the authority to do so may be personally liable on the contract or to the corporation. Even authorized officers may be liable on contracts if they do not advise that they are contracting as an agent of the corporation.

Shareholder Lawsuits Many of the above duties of the management of the corporation can form the basis for a shareholder suit for breach of duty. Shareholders may file either a "direct" or a "derivative" shareholder suit. A common example of a direct shareholder suit is a suit to compel the management to declare and pay a dividend.[71] It is "direct" because it enforces a duty owed directly to shareholders.

A shareholder "derivative" suit is one to enforce a duty owed to the *corporation*. Shareholders in such a suit are suing *on behalf of* the injured corporation. In cases where the wrongdoing of officers or directors has injured the corporation itself, the *corporation* has a right to sue its own officers or directors.[72] However, since those very officers or directors control the corporation, they will probably decide that it is not in the best interests of the corporation for it to sue them. A derivative shareholder's suit remedies this problem by allowing the shareholders to "step into the shoes" of the corporation and sue on its behalf. Thus, a shareholder is able to sue on behalf of the corporation, demanding that the corporation be repaid millions of dollars, even though the individual shareholder's loss may be nominal or nonexistent. When the derivative suit is successful and benefits the corporation, the plaintiff-shareholder is entitled to be reimbursed by the corporation for reasonable expenses, including attorney fees.[73]

Because shareholders may not have much personally at stake in a derivative suit, legislatures and courts have imposed limitations on such suits to prevent abuse. For instance, the plaintiff in a derivative action must be a shareholder both when suing and at the time of the alleged misconduct. This means that a person cannot buy shares after the alleged misconduct simply for the purpose of bringing a law suit. Also, shareholders wishing to sue must give management the opportunity to take action to remedy the

---

69 *See* 8 Del.C. §102(b)(7) and *Sutherland v. Sutherland*, 2009 WL857468 (Del. Ch.) (holding that §102(b)(7) of Delaware's corporation law does not allow for limitation of duty of loyalty).

70 RMBCA, *supra* note 32, §8.42; HENN & ALEXANDER, *supra* note 1, §§219-243; *Gantler v. Stephens*, 965 A.2d 695 (Del. 2009).

71 *See* HENN & ALEXANDER, *supra* note 1, §360. *See, e.g., Godley v. Crandell & Godley Co.*, 105 N.E. 818 (N.Y. 1914) (suit over payment of dividends).

72 *See Tzolis v. Wolff*, 844 N.E.2d 1005 (N.Y. 2008) (concept of the derivative suit extends to LLC members as well, even though New York's LLC statute makes no mention of derivative suits)

73 *See, e.g., Tooley v. Donaldson, Lufkin & Jenrette, Inc.*, 845 A.2d 1031, 1036-1039 (Del. 2004) (discussing the difference between direct and derivative actions by shareholders).

problem by serving them with a formal demand. Finally, if *disinterested* directors have determined that the suit is not in the best interests of the corporation, the court may dismiss the action.[74]

Business Judgment Rule If shareholders sue the directors or officers of a corporation, those directors and officers are entitled to the benefit of the "business judgment rule."[75] The business judgment rule is a "presumption that in making a business decision the directors of a corporation acted on an informed basis, in good faith and in the honest belief that the action taken was in the best interests of the company."[76] A hallmark of the business judgment rule is that a court will not substitute its judgment for that of the board if the board's decision can be "attributed to any rational business purpose."[77] This rule allows for honest mistakes and reasonably poor business decisions. However, if the directors permit the corporation to violate the law, the business judgment rule does not apply.[78] On the other hand, directors in a large corporation who are effectively relegated to making broad policy decisions are not required to monitor employees closely to discover illegality, absent some cause for suspicion.[79]

g. "Piercing the Corporate Veil"

The separate legal existence of the corporation and the limited liability it affords shareholders serve important social and economic purposes. However, there are instances where courts may ignore the corporate structure and its protections for compelling reasons of public policy. This is called "piercing the corporate veil." The conditions under which the law permits it to be done vary considerably from state to state.[80] Whatever test is used, it is easy to exaggerate the importance of veil-piercing. Only when stockholders of officers are using the corporate structure to perpetuate a fraud, to evade the law or to escape obligations will "piercing" generally be successful. And when piercing is used, the corporation involved is almost always a closely held one.

Formalistic Approach Under one approach, identified with New York, courts will disregard the corporate structure only when there has been noncompliance with the corporate formalities, such as failing to complete the incorporation process or to hold directors' meetings, or where shareholders treat corporate property as their own.[81] This is a rather permissive test. But even so, the conservative "formalistic" approach can trap

---

74 *See* HENN & ALEXANDER, *supra* note 1, §362. *See also* Federal Rule of Civil Procedure 23.1 (requiring a verified complaint and specific pleading).

75 *See generally*, CLARK, *supra* note 1, §3.4.

76 *Aronson v. Lewis*, 473 A.2d 805, 812 (Del. 1984).

77 *Sinclair Oil Corp. v. Levien*, 280 A.2d 717, 720 (Del. 1971). *See Schlensky v. Wrigley*, 237 N.E.2d 776 (Ill.App. 1968) (rejecting challenge to management decision not to install lights at baseball field to permit games to be played at night); *Herald Co. v. Seawell*, 472 F.2d 1081 (10th Cir. 1972) (rejecting challenge to purchase by corporation of its own shares for use in employee trust plan).

78 *Miller v. American Telephone & Telegraph Co.*, 507 F.2d 759 (3d Cir. 1974) (shareholder suit allowed to contest corporation's failure to collect $1.5 million debt owed by political party, a violation of federal election laws).

79 *Graham v. Allis-Chalmers Manufacturing Co.*, 188 A.2d 125 (Del. 1963) (directors not liable for damage to corporation caused by criminal price-fixing activities of middle-level executive employees). *But see American Int'l Group, Inc. Consolidated Derivative Litigation*, 965 A.2d 763 (Del. Ch. 2009) (holding that defendants' knowing toleration of inadequate internal controls and failure to monitor subordinates' compliance with legal duties amounted to breach of duty of loyalty.)

80 *See* HENN & ALEXANDER, *supra* note 1, §146.

81 *See Walkovsky v. Carlton*, 223 N.E.2d 6 (N.Y. 1966) (refusing to disregard corporate form where separate corporations were set up for one or two taxis in a fleet, thus protecting shareholders-owners of fleet from tort liability).

shareholders and officers of close corporations run by friends or family members, who run the business on an informal basis, ignoring corporate formalities and routinely mixing corporate and personal assets.

Undercapitalization Approach   Other states have given less weight to legal formalities and emphasize "undercapitalization"—where the assets of the company are "trifling compared with the business to be done and the risks of loss."[82] But even under this test, Courts are often unwilling to disregard the protections of the corporate shell when the creditor is a *business creditor* (such as a bank). The reason is that the business creditor voluntarily enters into the relationship with the company, can investigate the company's ability to pay beforehand and require additional security as needed.[83] Most situations where the veil is pierced are where the involuntary creditors are injured tort victims.[84]

"Dummy" Corporations   Often the shareholder of a company whose corporate form is sought to be disregarded is another corporation and the creditor seeks to reach the assets of the "parent" or owner corporation. If the subsidiary is treated as a "dummy" and controlled in every way by the parent corporation, the subsidiary's corporate form can be disregarded to reach the assets of the parent. This will be particularly so if the subsidiary is used to carry on particularly risky functions of a business.[85]

In theory, the piercing doctrine applies to publicly held as well as closely held corporations. However, research reveals no case in which the *shareholders* of a corporation whose stock was publicly traded or widely held were found personally liable for the obligations of the corporation. Instead, when courts pierce the corporate veil of a publicly traded corporation, liability is usually imposed on the individuals who *managed* the enterprise, on a parent corporation that gave orders, or on a group of corporations that were operating as an economic unit.[86]

Many courts have also embraced the logic of "reverse veil-piercing," in which a third-party plaintiff seeks to reach the assets of a corporation or other business entity due to the acts of the corporation's shareholder. At least one state allows reverse veil-piercing in the case of a partnership or even a limited partnership.[87]

Choice of Law in Veil-Piercing   "Internal affairs" of the corporation are usually governed by the law of the state of *incorporation*. However, some courts resolve issues of veil-piercing according to the law of the state where the corporation *operates*.[88] This is especially so if the state of incorporation is one of convenience. Also, there is a

82 *See Minton v. Cavaney*, 364 P.2d 473, 15 Cal.Rptr. 641 (Cal. 1961) (dictum). In this case, there was also evidence that many of the basic corporate formalities had not been followed, including the serious omission of failing to complete the formation of the corporation.

83 *See Kinney Shoe Corp. v. Polan.*, 939 F.2d 209 (4th Cir. 1991) (*applying Laya v. Erin Homes, Inc.*, 352 S.E.2d 93 (W.Va. 1986).

84 *See Consumer's Coop v. Olsen*, 419 N.W.2d 211 (Wis. 1988) (declining to disregard limited liability for business creditor). *But see Victoria Elevator Co. v. Meriden Grain Co.*, 283 N.W.2d 509 (Minn. 1979) (holding major shareholder liable where wide variety of wrongful acts occurred).

85 *But see Craig v. Lake Asbestos of Quebec*, 843 F.2d 145 (3d Cir. 1988) (applying New Jersey law, declining to hold parent liable in tort case where asbestos production had been transferred to wholly-owned overseas corporation for lack of complete "alter ego" control). *Craig* contains a good discussion of controlling authorities.

86 David Barber, *Piercing the Corporate Veil*, 17 WILLAMETTE L. REV. 371, 372 (1981).

87 Kurtis A. Kemper, *Acceptance and Application of Reverse Veil-Piercing–Third Party Claimants*, 2 A.L.R. 6th 195 (2010); *C.F. Trust, Inc. v. First Flight L.P.*, 580 S.E.2d 806 (Va. 2003).

88 This is consistent with the general notion that the state of operation has the greater contacts and interest in the issue. *See* Chapter VII, pp. 265-268.

growing *federal* common law of veil-piercing. For example, federal environmental laws impose environmental cleanup obligations on "owners" and "operators." The Supreme Court has rejected the view that this automatically includes shareholders or any parent corporation heavily involved in the operations of the company that caused the contamination. However, it instructed lower courts to determine "whether, in degree and detail, actions directed to the facility by an agent of the parent alone are eccentric under accepted norms of parental oversight of a subsidiary's facility."[89]

h. Extraordinary Corporate Transactions

Events that transcend ordinary business matters generally require shareholder approval. These extraordinary matters include: (1) mergers, (2) purchases of assets other than in the regular course of business, and (3) terminations.[90]

Mergers A merger is the legal combination of two (or more) corporations, whereby one corporation transfers all of its assets and liabilities to the other, called the "surviving" corporation. After merger, the surviving corporation automatically acquires all of the merged corporation's rights, privileges, and assets, as well as its debts and obligations. The former shareholders of the merged corporation may receive cash, bonds or shares in the surviving corporation, depending on what the merger agreement provides.[91] Both director and shareholder approval of all the merging corporations is generally required. However, shareholders who disapprove of a merger that has been approved by the majority usually have a statutory right of "dissent" and "appraisal," whereby shareholders can require that the corporation buy their stock at the value it had immediately prior to the approval of the merger. However, exceptions to this are often made when the new stock is publicly traded.[92]

Sale of Assets When a corporation acquires all or substantially all of the assets of another corporation, it does not alter the legal status of the acquiring corporation. Thus, shareholder approval of the acquiring corporation may not be required for such a transaction. However, the corporation that is selling substantially all its assets is substantially changing its structure, so that corporation's board of directors and shareholders must approve the transaction. Generally, acquiring all the assets of a corporation does not transfer legal responsibility for its liabilities. Exceptions to this rule exist when the purchasing corporation impliedly or expressly assumes the acquired entity's liabilities, when the sale is truly a merger, when the purchaser continues the seller's business and retains the same management staff, and when the sale is fraudulently executed to escape liability.

Termination The termination of corporate life begins with "dissolution," the legal death of the corporate entity. Following that is "liquidation," the process of selling corporate assets and distributing the cash between creditors and shareholders. Typically, shareholder approval is required for dissolution, and no right of dissent and appraisal is ordinarily provided. Dissolution can be brought about voluntarily, usually by the approval of the shareholders and the board of directors or by unanimous shareholder action, or involuntarily, by court decree. Involuntary judicial dissolution may occur, for example, when a board of directors is deadlocked or in the event of serious mismanage-

---

89 *United States v. Bestfoods*, 524 U.S. 51 (1998). *See also Anderson v. Abbott*, 321 U.S. 349 (1944) (bank holding company).

90 Though filing bankruptcy is also an extraordinary event, shareholder approval is not required.

91 *See* RMBCA §§11.01-11.07.

92 HENN & ALEXANDER, *supra* note 1, §349.

ment. However, courts are hesitant to order dissolution. Whenever dissolution does take place, the directors are responsible for handling liquidation for the benefit of creditors and shareholders. This includes selling the assets, paying the expenses involved, satisfying creditors' claims, and distributing the net proceeds. Corporate creditors are paid first, followed by preferred shareholders (if any) and then common stockholders. Court supervision is generally not required during liquidation.

i. Tender Offers

"Friendly" and "Hostile" Corporate Takeovers One method of acquiring a corporation without dealing with its management is to seek to purchase a sufficient number of the voting shares of the corporation's stock to take control of it. This can be done through market purchases or through a "tender offer" made directly to shareholders. A tender offer is the means by which a would-be acquirer invites shareholders of the "target" corporation to tender their stock for purchase. The purchase price offered is generally higher than the market price of the target stock. If the takeover is against the wishes of the managers of the corporation, it is a "hostile" takeover; if management is in favor of the takeover, it is considered a "friendly" takeover.

Federal Regulation of Tender Offers Because publicly-traded securities are involved, several aspects of tender offers are controlled by federal law, notably the Williams Act.[93] The Act requires any market purchaser of more than 5% of the stock of a publicly traded company to disclose that fact to the federal Securities Exchange and Commission (SEC). In addition, any tender offeror who proposes to purchase at least 5% of a company must disclose that fact and state the purpose of its tender offer and its plans for the target corporation should the offer be successful. Other parts of the Williams Act govern closely the terms, duration, and circumstances of tender offers.[94]

Tactics to Counter Hostile Takeovers A successful hostile takeover generally means that the managers of the target corporation will lose their jobs. With their careers at stake, managers often vigorously oppose takeover bids with various tactics. They may try to persuade shareholders that the takeover is not in the best interest of the corporation. They may file a lawsuit alleging violations of applicable federal securities and antitrust laws, although this is often done primarily to gain time to employ some other device to prevent the takeover. Some common takeover defenses have colorful or evocative names. Target companies can seek out a "white knight" — a rival tender offeror who has promised to treat the managers and shareholders well after the takeover. Another tactic is the "poison pill" plan. This tactic involves giving shareholders extraordinary rights against the target corporation that are triggered by a takeover. This serves to make the target corporation less valuable to the tender offeror. Yet another defense is a "turnabout," under which the target corporation responds with a tender offer of its own for the tender offeror's shares. An expensive method of ending a hostile takeover is for the target company to pay "greenmail" by buying the shares purchased by the tender offeror at a premium, with the understanding that the offeror will stop the takeover.[95]

---

93 15 U.S.C.A. §§78m(d)-(e), 78n(d)-(f). *See also infra*, pp. 600-604.

94 There is little state law regulating tender offer because most of it is either preempted by the Williams Act or violates the dormant commerce clause by imposing an undue burden on interstate commerce. *See Edgar v. MITE Corp.*, 457 U.S. 624 (1982) (holding Illinois anti-takeover law violative of dormant commerce clause). *See generally* Chapter IX, pp. 345-348.

95 These and other tactics are discussed in CLARK, *supra* note 1, §13.6.

Duties of Management in Hostile Takeovers   There is a potential for conflicts of interest to arise between management and the shareholders of the target corporation during a takeover attempt. This raises the question of how far management may go to resist takeover efforts.[96] The answer that has emerged is the *"Revlon* duty," based on the Delaware Supreme Court's opinion in *Revlon, Inc. v. MacAndrews & Forbes Holdings, Inc.*[97] The "business judgment rule" applies generally to management actions in a takeover. However, in a takeover situation a court will scrutinize defensive action of management for signs that it was taken out of self interest rather than in the pursuance of the corporation's or shareholders' best interests.[98] And if defensive tactics fail and sale of the company becomes inevitable, the duty of the management changes from one of preserving the corporate entity to one of maximizing the company's value and assuring that its shareholders get the best deal possible for their shares.[99]

5. Limited Liability Companies

The limited liability company (LLC), first developed in 1977 in Wyoming, is now provided for in all 50 states and the District of Columbia.[100] The LLC is a hybrid entity that is neither a corporation nor a partnership, but combines features of both.

The LLC has several advantages over other enterprise organizations. Comparing it to the limited partnership, it has the same taxation and limited liability advantages for limited partners, but LLC members, unlike limited partners, have the right to participate in control of the business. Further, there is no need for a general partner subject to unlimited liability.[101] The LLC has advantages over the close corporation. First, LLCs are simpler to create and operate. All that is needed is a document called an "operating agreement," similar to a partnership agreement, to set up the capital and management structures.[102] State LLC statutes typically abandon the corporation statutes' mandatory structure and hierarchy of shareholders, directors, and officers, and the attendant rules relating to meetings and voting rights. Second, there is much greater flexibility with LLCs. Members can choose to manage the LLC directly themselves or indirectly through managers. Single-member LLCs can even be used in place of a sole proprietorship.[103]

Perhaps the most important advantage over a corporation is that LLCs can be taxed on a "pass-through" basis like partnerships, thus avoiding the double taxation imposed on corporations.[104] Favorable tax treatment is facilitated by a "check-the-box" procedure implemented by the IRS.[105] This approach allows LLCs to elect how they wish to be

---

96 *Id.* §13.6.3.

97 506 A.2d 173 (Del. 1985).

98 *Revlon, id.; Unocal Corp. v. Mesa Petroleum, Inc.*, 493 A.2d 946 (Del. 1985).

99 *Revlon, supra; Paramount Communications Inc. v. QVC, Inc.*, 637 A.2d 34 (Del. 1994); *eBay Domestic Holdings, Inc. v. Newmark*, 2010 WL 3516473 (2010).

100 *See generally* J. WILLIAM CALLISON & MAUREEN A. SULLIVAN, LIMITED LIABILITY COMPANIES: A STATE-BY-STATE GUIDE TO LAW AND PRACTICE (West 2005). The Delaware Act is set out in CORPORATIONS AND OTHER BUSINESS ASSOCIATIONS: STATUTES, RULES AND FORMS, *supra* note 3.

101 A limited liability partnership (LLP) similarly has no general partner requirement. However, states often allow LLPs only for certain professionals, provide protection only from certain liabilities and require a certain level of liability insurance coverage or a designated fund for payment of claims.

102 See *Kuroda v. SPJS Holdings, LLC*, 971 A.2d 872 (Del. Ch. 2009), holding that the terms of an operating agreement govern the relations among LLC members and are not superceded by the implied covenant of good faith and fair dealing found in all contracts.

103 The operating agreement need not be in writing. ULLCA §103(a).

104 *See supra*, p. 589.

105 *See* 26 C.F.R. §§301.7701-1 - 301.7701-3.

treated for tax purposes: as a corporation or as a partnership or association. This election can be changed, though not more than once in any 5-year period unless there is more than a 50% change in ownership and the IRS gives permission. Even if no election is made, the rules provide the default position that the LLC with two or more members will be treated as a partnership and the LLC with only one member will be disregarded for tax purposes, *i.e.*, it will be treated as a sole proprietorship.[106]

Despite all of their flexibility, LLCs are not completely informal. The statutes all require an official filing for an LLC to be formed. Some of the statutes require the filings to make fairly substantial disclosures with respect to the entity's financing. In addition, LLCs are treated like corporations for purposes of "veil-piercing," and fiduciary duties of management.[107] LLCs have become increasingly popular and may soon render partnerships and subchapter S corporations obsolete.[108]

One might wonder why public corporations do not convert to LLCs. There are at least two reasons. First, pass-through partnership taxation is not available for any publicly traded partnership, negating the principle financial incentive to elect to be treated as a partnership.[109] Second, securities offered by an LLC would be a "non-standard" securities product that could be hard to sell. The very rigidity of the corporate form means that investors who buy shares in a corporation know what they are getting — something that the very flexibility of LLCs makes much less certain.

B. Regulation of Corporate Securities

1. Federal Securities Regulation

Much of the federal law that relates to public corporations involves regulation of issuance and trading in securities.[110] The primary goal of regulation is to protect the investors who purchase them. This is done in two ways. First, issuing corporations are required to disclose accurate and current information about themselves. Unlike most goods, securities have no intrinsic value and can be issued virtually without cost and in unlimited amounts. The value of a security is dependent on the profitability or the future prospects of the entity that issues it. Consequently, accurate information about the company is essential to make a decision on purchase. Second, the federal laws seek to insure that information about the corporation is *equally* available to all shareholders. Thus, those laws penalize those who use special "inside" information about the issuing corporation to make advantageous trades of that company's stock.

---

106 However, some states treat LLCs like corporations for *state* taxation purposes.

107 *See Fielbon Development Co., LLC v. Colony Bank*, 660 S.E.2d 801 (Ga.App. 2008) (LLC held liable on note signed by member) *and* Ann K. Wooster, *Construction and Application of Limited Liability Company Acts–Issues Relating to Personal Liability of Members and Managers of Limited Liability Company with Respect to Third Parties*, 46 A.L.R. 6th 1 (2010).

108 The future of the LLC is discussed in Larry E. Ribstein *The Emergence of The Limited Liability Company*, 51 BUSINESS LAWYER 1 (1995) and *Symposium, Check-the-Box and Beyond: The Future of Limited Liability Entities*, 52 BUSINESS LAWYER 605 (1997). *See also* UNIFORM LIMITED LIABILITY COMPANY ACT (ULLCA) (1995), www.nccusl.org/Update/, which seeks to remedy various deficiencies in state statutes.

109 16 U.S.C.A. §7704. Subchapter S corporations are similarly limited. *See supra* p. 589.

110 Other federal laws relating to public corporation are those governing proxy solicitations (*supra* p. 592) and tender offers (*supra* p. 598). Securities were defined *supra* p. 590. The federal securities acts and rules discussed here and earlier in this chapter are compiled in JOHN J. COFFEE, JOEL SELIGMAN & HILLARY SALE, ED., SECURITIES REGULATION: SELECTED STATUTES, RULES AND FORMS (West 2006). For summaries of the law of federal securities regulation, *see* LARRY D. SODERQUIST & THERESA A GABALDON, SECURITIES LAW, 3D ED. (Foundation 2004); THOMAS L. HAZEN, THE LAW OF SECURITIES REGULATION, 6TH ED. (West 2009); ALAN PALMITER, SECURITIES REGULATION: EXAMPLES AND EXPLANATIONS, 4TH ED. (Aspen 2008).

Principal Federal Statutes Federal regulation of securities began soon after the stock market crash of 1929, which was viewed as a failure of the securities market. The two main federal statutes are the Securities Act of 1933 (SA) and the Securities Exchange Act of 1934 (SEA). Although these two acts are closely related, they affect different stages of the securities market. The SA mainly regulates the issuance of new securities. This act requires that all material facts related to that issuance be publicly filed in a "registration statement" and presented to potential buyers in a "prospectus"[111]. Sometimes an exemption from the registration requirements will be available, and an issuer can then utilize a less-burdensome (albeit smaller) "private placement" rather than a "public offering." The SEA mainly regulates the buying and selling of securities already in the public markets.[112] The SEA requires disclosure of all important information that shareholders and prospective purchasers should know. It imposes a duty of continuous disclosure for all corporations with securities traded on the securities exchanges and for those companies with assets of more than $5 million and 500 or more shareholders. The 1934 Act also established the federal Securities and Exchange Commission (SEC), which is responsible for administering all federal securities law. The 1934 Act authorizes the SEC to prohibit by rule any "manipulative or deceptive devices or contrivances" in connection with the purchase and sale of securities.[113]

Enforcement of Securities Regulations Violations of securities laws and rules are subject to public enforcement by way of criminal prosecutions or civil actions brought by the SEC. However, the primary means of enforcement is private litigation, encouraged by incentives provided in the federal and some state statutes.

Rule 10b-5 Rule 10b-5, promulgated by the SEC pursuant to the 1934 Act, forms the basis for much litigation about unlawful corporate disclosures or non-disclosures.[114] The basic idea is that a person who speaks in a manner reasonably calculated to influence investors has a duty to speak truthfully. Thus, the rule makes unlawful any "untrue statement of a material fact" or misleading omission and "any act, practice, or course of business which operates or would operate as a fraud or deceit upon any person, in connection with the purchase or sale of any security." Any shareholder or other person who is injured can sue for damages. The Act applies to options to purchase stock and to oral misrepresentations.[115] Liability does not extend to the customers or suppliers of an issuer, even if they aid the issuer in its fraudulent conduct.[116]

---

111 15 U.S.C.A. §§77a-77aa. The law is codified here, but virtually everyone uses the section numbers of the original act. That convention will be honored here.

112 15 U.S.C.A. §§78a-78hh-1.

113 15 U.S.C.A. §78j(b). The 1934 Act also provides for SEC registration and regulation of securities brokers and dealers. Other important federal securities laws are the Investment Company Act of 1940, 15 U.S.C.A. §80a (regulating publicly-owned companies engaged in investing and trading securities), the Investment Advisors Act of 1940, 15 U.S.C.A. §80b (regulating and requiring registration of investment advisors); and the Securities Investors Protection Act of 1970, 15 U.S.C.A. §78aaa *et seq.* (providing measures to protect against financial failures of securities firms).

114 *See* 17 C.F.R. §240.10b-5 and §243.100-.103 (2006). *See also* 65 Fed. Reg. 51716-01 (August 24, 2000) (explaining the background for and content of §243.100 *et seq.*) The impact of Regulation FD (for "fair disclosure") that this Federal Register entry introduces is also analyzed in D. Casey Kobi, Wall Street v. Main Street: the SEC's New Regulation FD and its Impact On Market Participants, 77 INDIANA L.J. 551 (2002).

115 *The Wharf (Holdings) Ltd. v. United International Holdings, Inc.*, 532 U.S. 588 (2001) (orally promising an option to purchase stock in return for services while secretly intending not to honor the option is a violation).

116 *See Stoneridge Investment Partners, LLC v. Scientific-Atlanta, Inc.*, 552 U.S. 148 (2008).

The liability of a corporation can be substantial when the class action device is used to recover for all shareholders who lost money as a result of a violation of 10b-5.[117] After several years of growth in the number of suits, the Supreme Court made liability harder to prove by imposing a requirement that plaintiff shareholders prove that every untrue statement or omission was made or done with the *intent* to deceive or manipulate.[118] Still, the issues of fraud and intent can be decided by the judge or jury only after a full trial. Defendant companies often feel pressured to settle even groundless suits. There are the costs of litigation to consider, as well as possible bad publicity for the company and the possibility, however slim, of ruinous class action damages.

Complaints about such "strike" suits prompted Congress in 1995 to provide additional protections in the Private Securities Litigation Reform Act (PSLRA).[119] There is now a "safe haven" for predictive statements accompanied by "meaningful cautionary statements." To be a basis for liability, predictive statements must be "made with actual knowledge" that they are "false or misleading." Causation of loss must be strictly alleged and proven.[120] There are also severe limits on plaintiffs' discovery while a motion to dismiss or for summary judgment is pending, thus protecting defendants from the expense of responding to discovery requests before the court has determined that the suit has merit.[121] In addition, there are mandatory sanctions on plaintiffs for groundless suits, limits on damages recoverable, limits on attorney fees to a certain percentage of the class recovery and qualifications for who can be the member of the plaintiff class, presuming that it will be the plaintiff owning the most shares in the defendant company rather than the plaintiff who filed first.[122] The Supreme Court recently tightened the PSLRA's already stringent rules on allegations of intent (scienter), holding that the allegations in a complaint must give rise to a strong (as opposed to merely plausible) inference of scienter, and that lower courts must consider all plausible, non-culpable explanations for the defendants' conduct as well.[123] Despite these new, more stringent rules, the PSLRA has had a modest effect on the volume of securities litigation. In fact, recent research indicates that the PSLRA has had the paradoxical effect of reducing the filing of meritorious suits without impacting the filing of nuisance suits.[124]

Insider Trading   Less obvious than the use of Rule 10b-5 to police misleading predictive statements by companies is its use to police "insider trading." Insider trading is the buying and selling of securities by persons who have received important "inside" confidential information about the company's condition or business that could have a bearing on the value of its securities. In a series of administrative decisions and

---

117 *See* Chapter VII, p. 234, where class actions are discussed.

118 *See Ernst & Ernst v. Hochfelder*, 425 U.S. 185 (1976). The scienter requirement applies to suits for injunctive relief as well as to damage suits. *Aaron v. Securities & Exchange Comm'n.*, 446 U.S. 680 (1980). On the other hand, the Court has given a very broad reading to the phrase "in connection with the purchase or sale" aspect of 10b-5, holding that it applied to deception in connection with the purchase or sale of any security by anyone, not just the deception of an identifiable buyer and seller. *Merrill, Lynch, Pierce, Fenner & Smith, Inc. v. Dabit*, 547 U.S. 71 (2006).

119 15 U.S.C.A. §77z-2(c).

120 *Dura Pharmaceuticals, Inc. v. Broudo*, 544 U.S. 336 (2005) (allegation that misrepresentation of product caused "inflated price" for stock is insufficient to show causation of any "loss").

121 Discovery and pre-trial motions in civil cases were covered in Chapter VII, pp. 235-240.

122 A symposium on the Act discusses these and other aspects of the changes it makes. *Symposium on the Private Securities Litigation Reform Act of 1995*, 51 BUSINESS LAWYER 975 (1996).

123 See *Tellabs, Inc. v. Makors Issues & Rights, Ltd.*, 551 U.S. 308 (2007).

124 Stephen J. Choi, Karen K. Nelson, and A. C. Pritchard, *The Screening Effect of the Private Securities Litigation Reform Act*, 6 JOURNAL OF EMPIRICAL LEGAL STUDIES 1 (2009).

injunctive actions starting in the 1960s and culminating in *Securities & Exchange Comm'n v. Texas Gulf Sulphur Corp.*,[125] the SEC convinced the courts that the disclosure requirements of Rule 10b-5 impose a duty on persons with inside information either to disclose the information or to abstain from trading until the information is disclosed publicly. In *Texas Gulf Sulphur*, corporate officers made substantial purchases of stock after learning — but before announcing publicly — promising news about exploratory drilling on some of the company's oil and gas properties.

Liability attaches under Rule 10b-5 only to persons who have such a duty to "disclose or abstain." This duty is most clear in classic insider trading cases, where corporate officers or employees owe a fiduciary duty to their shareholders not to take advantage of inside information. However, "outsiders" — persons not employed by the issuer of stock — may also be liable if they "misappropriate" confidential information for securities trading purposes in breach of a duty owed to the source of the information. For example, in *United States v. O'Hagan*,[126] a lawyer bought shares of the target of a tender offer based on confidential information he learned in the process of his law firm representing the tendering company on the tender offer. The advantage of knowing about a tender offer in advance is that the offer for the stock will usually be higher than its market price. The Supreme Court held that this constituted a breach of the duty he owed to his law firm and its client not to misappropriate information acquired in the course of the attorney-client relationship.[127]

Other Liability of Insiders Vigorous enforcement action against insiders has also revolved around §16 of the 1934 Act.[128] Rule 16(b) is designed to discourage insider trading by penalizing "short-swing" profits — profits from securities transactions that take place within a 6-month period — received by officers, directors and 10% shareholders of a public corporation. Suit can be filed by the corporation or by any shareholder. Proof that the defendant actually used insider information is not a prerequisite for recovery. Unlike Rule 10b-5 violations, no intent is required and many if not most 16(b) violations are inadvertent. All that is required is proof of a purchase and a sale (the order is irrelevant) within a 6-month period and a profit as determined by a rather liberal method of accounting. Persons subject to potential 16(b) liability must report their trades to the SEC and the reports are published, thus making violations easy to spot and prove. Indeed, there are lawyers who support themselves quite well reading the SEC reports, notifying the corporation whenever there has been an improper trade, and, if necessary, filing suit on behalf of the corporation. Improper profits recovered against insider violators are payable to the corporation, but attorney fees may be awarded to the plaintiff's lawyer out of profits recovered in successful litigation.[129]

"Tippees" — persons outside the corporation who are "tipped" about inside information and use it to their advantage — may also be liable. However, for tippees to

---

125 401 F.2d 833 (2d Cir. 1968). *See generally* CLARK, *supra* note 1, §§8.9-8.10.

126 521 U.S. 642 (2001). *See also Securities & Exchange Comm'n v. Talbot*, 530 F.3d 1085 (9th Cir. 2008) (holding that a corporate director who bought shares in another company based on confidential information he learned about that company in a board meeting was liable under misappropriation theory).

127 *See also* 17 C.F.R. §240.10b5-2 (SEC rules clarifying misappropriation theory, §240.10b5-1 (defining when trading is "on the basis of" confidential information). These are part of Regulation FD discussed in 65 Fed. Reg. 51716-01 (August 24, 2000). *See supra* note 114.

128 15 U.S.C.A. §78p.

129 *See Magida v. Continental Can Co.*, 176 F.Supp. 781 (S.D.N.Y. 1956) (fact that the lawyer has the principal financial interest in suing in insider suits does not violate lawyer ethical standards; Congress authorized such suits as an incentive to gain enforcement of the securities laws).

be liable, the tipper must have profited in some way from the tipping, whether through pecuniary or indirect "reputational" benefit.[130]

At the urging of the SEC, Congress in the 1980s made insider trading information more serious by authorizing the SEC to recover up to three times the trading profit from the participants, increasing criminal penalties, and providing a further incentive in the form of a 10% "bounty" for private plaintiffs of any amounts recovered.[131]

2. State "Blue Sky" Laws

In addition to the federal laws governing securities, every state has its own set of securities laws regulating offers and sales of securities that take place within their borders, referred to as "blue sky" laws.[132] Similar to their federal counterparts, blue sky laws require disclosure by issuers and sellers of securities and contain anti-fraud provisions. Typically, these laws step in where federal laws do not apply, requiring registration and qualification of securities that are not covered by federal laws. Blue sky laws vary widely from state to state, though most are similar to the Uniform Securities Act, which has been passed in 30 states.[133]

3. Federal Regulation of Corporate Governance

Federal law, as just described, has traditionally imposed disclosure requirements on companies, not substantive corporate governance standards. These were left to state corporate law. However, in 2002, Congress departed from this tradition and enacted the biggest change in federal corporate law since the securities and exchange acts of the 1930s — the Sarbanes-Oxley Act (known as SOX), applicable to all companies that are subject to the federal securities acts.[134] The impetus for SOX was the exposure of fraudulent accounting practices and executives' self-dealing transactions that caused the failures of two highly regarded corporations, Enron and Worldcom, and the Arthur Anderson accounting firm.[135]

Auditor independence was seen as a major failing in these scandals, so much of SOX is devoted to that. It sets up a new government-appointed Public Company Accounting Oversight Board with the power to regulate and discipline accounting firms and practitioners and to set auditing standards.[136] The company's auditor must be hired and report directly to the firm's audit committee, which must be composed of independ-

---

130 *See Dirks v. Securities & Exchange Comm'n*, 463 U.S. 646 (1983) (no liability where tippers were motivated by a desire to expose fraud and received no monetary or personal benefit from revealing information and tippee did not profit either, but communicated information to some stockholders, who then sold their stock). In one case, the tipper's "profit" was that the inside information impressed his girlfriend. *But see Securities & Exchange Comm'n v. Maxwell*, 341 F. Supp. 2d 941 (S.D. Ohio 2004) (holding that tipper was not likely to receive future benefit to his reputation from tip given to his barber).

131 *See* Insider Trading Sanctions Act of 1984, 15 U.S.C.A. §78u-1.

132 "Blue Sky" comes from the purpose of the laws, which is prevent "speculative schemes which have no more basis than so many feet of 'blue sky'." *Hall v. Geiger-Jones Co.*, 242 U.S. 539, 550 (1917).

133 7B Unif.L.Ann. 69-132 (Supp. 1992).

134 15 U.S.C.A. §§7201 et seq.; 17 C.F.R. Parts 210, 240, 249 and 274. For a critical view of the Act, see Roberta Romano, *The Sarbanes-Oxley Act and the Making of Quack Corporate Governance*, 114 Yale L.J. 1521 (2005). For a more charitable view, *see* Lawrence A. Cunningham, *The Sarbanes-Oxley Yawn: Heavy Rhetoric, Light Reform (and It Just Might Work)*, 35 CONNECTICUT L. REV. 915 (2003)

135 Two excellent books on the Enron scandal are KURT EICHENWALD, CONSPIRACY OF FOOLS (Random House 2005) and BETHANY MCLEAN, THE SMARTEST GUYS IN THE ROOM (Penguin Books 2003). The second was made into a documentary movie.

136 *See Free Enterprise Fund v. Public Company Accounting Oversight Bd.*, ___ U.S. ___, 130 S. Ct. 3138 (2010) (upholding the constitutionality of the Sarbanes-Oxley act and the PCAOB while striking down certain provisions relating to the appointment and dismissal of PCAOB members).

ent directors. The audit committee must set up a system of internal accounting controls, including anonymous employee submissions. The lead audit partner must rotate every five years. Auditors are prohibited from providing the company with many non-audit services.

Addressing self-dealing, SOX, with a few exceptions, prohibits personal loans by companies to their officers and directors. Management and principal shareholder stock trades must be reported within two days. Pension blackout periods must be announced 30 days ahead so participants can move their stock if they wish, and insider trades during pension blackout periods are prohibited. Any profit on any insider trades can be recovered by the company.

Companies must disclose all material changes in financial condition and report all arrangements that might have a material effect on the financial health of the firm, particularly "off balance sheet" transactions.[137] Moreover, §302 requires that the chief executive officer (CEO) and chief financial officer (CFO), in separate sworn statements, personally certify every report of financial data, affirming that they have reviewed the report, that it is true to the best of their knowledge, that it "fairly presents, in all material respects, the financial condition" of the company, and that they have established internal controls designed to ensure that material information is made known to them. False statements are punishable by fines of up to $1 million and 10 years in prison or, in the case of false certification accomplished willfully, up to $5 million and 20 years in prison.[138] In addition, if misconduct results in the need to restate financial data, the CEO or CFO must reimburse the company for profits they made for from sales of securities as a result of the inaccurate data.

Obstruction of justice provisions punish destruction of documents by any person with reason to know of a pending federal investigation or bankruptcy. SOX also directs the SEC to promulgate rules of practice requiring the company's attorneys to report any evidence of misfeasance "up the ladder" to the company's CEO, CFO, audit committee or board of directors. A proposal to require that the attorney for the company report such information to the SEC, if appropriate action is not taken, was originally proposed, but dropped by the SEC. Instead, the regulation restates general ethical requirements when it states that the attorney "may reveal to the Commission, without the issuer's consent, confidential information related to the representation" if necessary "[t]o prevent the issuer from committing a material violation that is likely to cause substantial injury to the financial interest or property of the issuer or investors."[139]

The reaction of business leaders in the U.S. to SOX has not been overwhelmingly positive. It has moved from grudging reluctance to a general acceptance and even

---

137 These featured prominently in the Enron scandal, which created hundreds of "special purpose entities" (SPEs) to which it transferred highly indebted assets or to which it made sales, thus permitting it to overstate its income and understate its debt on its balance sheet — all with the purpose of inflating the value of its stock.

138 17 C.F.R. §240.13a-14; 18 U.S.C.A. §1350.

139 17 C.F.R. §205.3(b), 15 U.S.C.A. §7245, Implementation of Standards of Professional Conduct for Attorneys, 68 Fed.Reg. 6296 (Feb. 6, 2003). The SEC rule is identical to ABA Model Rule 1.6(b)(2), as amended in 2003, but not all states have adopted the 2003 change, notably California and New York. *See* Chapter IV, p. 163. For lawyers in states that have not adopted the 2003 amendments, compliance with the SEC rule would apparently constitute a violation of state ethical rules. A proposed SEC "noisy withdrawal" rule, under which attorneys would be required under certain circumstances to withdraw from representing a company and disclose that fact to the SEC, would be a major departure from normal ethical rules in all states, and is still under consideration. *See* Peter J. Henning, *Sarbanes-Oxley Act §307 and Corporate Counsel: Who Better to Prevent Corporate Crime?*, 8 BUFFALO CRIM. L.REV. 101 (2004).

approval. This is no doubt influenced by the fact that any effort to push Congress to radically modify or repeal the Act is not likely to succeed, given the current climate of mistrust, and the bad publicity that would ensue for the companies involved in such an effort. There have been complaints about its costs, however. For example, under §404 of the Act, all companies must submit an assessment of the effectiveness of the internal control structure and procedures for financial reporting. A survey of 217 publicly traded companies in 2005 disclosed that they spent $4.36 million, on average, to comply with §404.[140] But in 2007, the SEC issued new interpretive guidance designed to simplify compliance with §404, with a particular emphasis on assisting smaller companies.[141] A 2007 survey of 185 companies found that §404 compliance costs had declined to an average of $1.7 million.[142]

SOX applies to foreign companies that offer securities for sale in the U.S. market. Some of these companies and their governments resent what they see as an attempt to impose U.S. corporate law and structures on them as a condition of participating in the U.S. capital market. The §302 requirement of CEO and CFO personal certification and its criminal penalties were the main reason that the German company Porsche decided not to list on the New York Stock Exchange, noting that SOX sets up a new criminal liability of the chair of the board and the director of finance that is "irreconcilable with German" law, which instead places liability on a collective of some 20 different people in the company.[143] There is some evidence to suggest that foreign exchanges, particularly the London Stock Exchange, have benefitted from a reluctance of foreign issuers to spend time and money complying with SOX after listing on a US exchange.[144]

C. Bankruptcy

Debtors who file for bankruptcy are usually debtors whose obligations far exceed their ability to pay and who are in massive default. Bankruptcy can result either in a reorganization of the finances of the debtor so that the debtor can continue in business or in liquidating the debtor's assets and applying the proceeds to pay outstanding debts. Bankruptcy law is federal, passed pursuant to Congress' specific authority in Article I §8 of the Constitution to prescribe "uniform bankruptcy laws" for the country. The principal law is the federal Bankruptcy Code. However, it is the law of contracts, property and torts that often defines obligations and property rights in bankruptcy and this law is overwhelmingly state law. Consequently, federal bankruptcy law adopts or necessarily contemplates the application of state law.[145] Federal courts have exclusive jurisdiction over bankruptcy proceedings.[146]

---

140 Jonathan D. Glater, "Here It Comes: The Sarbanes-Oxley Backlash" (N.Y. Times, April 17, 2005).

141 17 C.F.R. §241.

142 Financial Executives International, *FEI Survey: Average 2007 SOX Compliance Cost $1.7 million*, http://fei.mediaroom.com/index.php?s=43&item=204.

143 HAROLD S. BLOOMENTHAL AND SAMUEL WOLFF, 3F SECURITIES AND FEDERAL CORPORATE LAW § 27:317, 2d ed (West 2006).

144 Joseph D. Piotroski and Suraj Srinivasan, *The Sarbanes-Oxley Act and the Flow of International Listings*, November 22, 2006,8 http://www.hbs.edu/units/am/pdf/Piotroski%20Srinivasan%20SOX%20International%20Listings.pdf.

145 For more complete treatment of bankruptcy, *see* DAVID G. EPSTEIN, BANKRUPTCY LAW IN A NUTSHELL, 7TH ED. (West 2005); BRIAN BLUM, BANKRUPTCY AND DEBTOR-CREDITOR:EXAMPLES AND EXPLANATIONS, 5TH ED. (Aspen 2010). *See also* BANKRUPTCY CODE, RULES AND OFFICIAL FORMS, LAW SCHOOL EDITION (West 2006). *See also* ROBERT K. RASMUSSEN, BANKRUPTCY LAW STORIES (Foundation 2006) (stories behind bankruptcy cases).

146 *See* 11 U.S.C.A. §§101-1330. The federal bankruptcy court is attached to the federal District Court in each district and has a separate Bankruptcy Judge who is appointed for 14-year terms. *See* Chapter V, p. 186. Bankruptcy judges are Article I, not Article III judges, and are limited in the powers they can

Both businesses and individuals can file for bankruptcy.[147] A person operating as a sole proprietorship files as an individual and corporations, partnerships and LLCs file as entities. Whether business or personal, the policy behind bankruptcy is debtor rehabilitation — to give the debtor a "fresh start" — and to provide a fair means of distributing a debtor's assets among all its creditors.[148] Bankruptcy can be either voluntary (commenced by the debtor) or involuntary (commenced by creditors).

There are two principal types of bankruptcies that relate to businesses. They are commonly referred to by the chapters of the Bankruptcy Code that regulate them. A Chapter 7 bankruptcy results in liquidation of the debtor's assets and distribution of the corporation's assets to creditors. Chapter 11 provides a procedure for reorganization of an entity which could continue to function if adjustments were made in its debts and structure agreeable with its creditors.[149] All forms of bankruptcy provide the debtor with the immediate relief of immunity from suit by creditors for the duration of the bankruptcy proceedings.

Chapter 7 In a Chapter 7 proceeding, a trustee in bankruptcy is appointed to administer and liquidate the debtor. A trustee is a private person, often a lawyer, who is appointed by the court and is paid by the court. The trustee's job is to gather the assets of the debtor, to notify creditors to file their claims, to adjudicate any matters of dispute involving assets or obligations of the debtor's estate, and finally to pay out the bankrupt's estate to creditors on an equal basis. Individual debtors are permitted to retain certain personal and real property.[150] Individual debtors receive a discharge of their debts — complete relief from the obligation to pay those debts — unless they have engaged in certain fraudulent or wrongful acts, such as concealing assets, making a false statement under oath or violating a bankruptcy court order.[151] Other exceptions to discharge are listed in the federal statute.[152] A partnership or corporation does not receive a discharge, but simply goes out of business and may dissolve itself under state law. Most Chapter 7 bankruptcies proceed without difficulties and are over in a matter of months.

Chapter 11 The purpose of Chapter 11 proceedings is to reorganize the debtor's debt structure in such a way as to enable the business to continue, if that is possible.

---

exercise. *See* Chapter VI, pp. 220-222 and note 146.

147 Individuals can file a for bankruptcy because of consumer debt, which involves much the same procedure as outlined here. Since our topic here is business law, consumer bankruptcies are not discussed. However, it should be mentioned that major changes in the provisions of the bankruptcy law were enacted in 2005 impose major additional obstacles and costs. *See* Henry J. Sommer, *Trying to Make Sense Out of Nonsense: Representing Consumers Under the "Bankruptcy Abuse Prevention and Consumer Protection Act of 2005*, 79 AM.BANKR.L.J. 191 (2005) (pointing out draconian and misdirected provisions).

148 *See Local Loan Co. v. Hunt*, 292 U.S. 234 (1934) and *In re Chicago, Milwaukee, St. Paul and Pac. R.R.*, 974 F.2d 775 (7th Cir. 1992) (discussing bankruptcy policies).

149 There is a Chapter 13 "reorganization" option as well for individual debtors who have regular income. However, it is used almost exclusively by consumers rather than businesses, who use Chapter 11. In 1991, 69% of cases filed were under Chapter 7, 38% were under Chapter 13, and 3% were under Chapter 11. The total number of all cases filed under the Bankruptcy Code that year was 943,987.

150 *See* 11 U.S.C.A. §522(b). Exemptions specified in either federal or state law or both will apply, depending on state option. Typical state exemptions for individual debtors are for tools of the trade, household goods, clothes and jewelry, and certain farm animals, as well as a "homestead exemption" in a limited amount for the house in which the debtor lives. There is considerable variation in exemption laws from state to state and some states, Florida in particular, have extremely liberal exemption laws.

151 11 U.S.C.A. §727(a).

152 Completely non-dischargeable are certain taxes, debts contracted under false pretenses, alimony and child support, and most educational loans for students. *See* 11 U.S.C.A. §523(a).

Reorganization is encouraged since it will allow the business to continue to employ people, pay taxes and otherwise contribute to the economy. This makes the course of Chapter 11 proceedings less predictable and more complex than Chapter 7 proceedings.

Upon filing the Chapter 11 case, the debtor's current management remains in control as the "debtor-in-possession" and continues to run the business.[153] But in this capacity, the managers of the debtor take on the "fiduciary responsibilities of a trustee" to preserve the estate for the benefit of the creditors.[154] A "creditor's committee" is appointed, which consists of the largest creditors of the debtor willing to serve. The creditors' committee's job is to protect the interests of the "general creditors" — creditors who do not hold security or collateral for their debts. However, general creditors' claims to the bankrupt's assets are subject to security interests in those assets (real estate mortgages and liens on personal property). There is also a priority for employees' unpaid wages and any taxes owed.

To successfully conclude a Chapter 11 reorganization, the court must "confirm" a "plan of reorganization." The plan of reorganization will substitute new obligations for the debtor's old obligations. The debtor usually submits a proposed plan of reorganization. To be confirmed, the plan must meet a number of requirements not discussed here.[155] But an important one is that the plan must give each creditor at least what that creditor would receive under a Chapter 7 distribution unless the affected creditor consents to a different arrangement. Further, the court may confirm a plan only if it is either (1) approved by a vote of all classes of creditors[156] or (2) determined by the bankruptcy court to be a "fair and equitable" plan that pays creditors in accordance with the "absolute priority rule."[157] Under the absolute priority rule, all classes of claims must be paid in full first before the shareholders receive anything. Unless the creditors are paid in full or agree otherwise, the result of this rule is that the creditors become the owners of the company.

In practice, most Chapter 11 plans that are confirmed are plans negotiated between creditors and the shareholders and approved by them. Under such a compromise, creditors are paid something less than what they are due and stockholders get to keep some of their stock. In only 17% of cases are reorganization plans finally confirmed. In the remainder of the cases, the case is converted to a Chapter 7 proceeding and the debtor's assets are liquidated.[158] The size of the bankruptcy filer and its debt load are critical variables for predicting the successful confirmation of a reorganization plan. A study of Chapter 11 cases filed in 2002 found that larger debtors were more than twice as likely to confirm plans.[159]

---

153 11 U.S.C.A. §§1101(1), 1107.

154 *Commodity Futures Trading Comm'n v. Weintraub*, 471 U.S. 343 (1985). *See, e.g., In re Tudor Associates, Ltd.*, 20 F.3d 115 (4th Cir. 1994) (manager of limited partnership violated fiduciary duty when he arranged to buy partnership assets through separate company he owned).

155 *See* 11 U.S.C.A. §1129(a).

156 11 U.S.C.A. §1129(a)(8). Approval does not mean a unanimous vote. Two-thirds in debt amount and over one-half in number of each class of creditors voting must approve. 11 U.S.C.A. §1126(d).

157 11 U.S.C.A. §1129(b). The legal slang term for this court-imposed plan is a "cram-down plan" — since it is effectively "crammed down the throats" of the creditors.

158 Edward M. Flynn, "Statistical Analysis of Chapter 11", Administrative Office of U.S. Courts, Statistical Analysis and Reports Division 10 (October 1989) (unpublished).

159 Elizabeth Warren and Jay Lawrence Westbrook, *The Success of Chapter 11: A Challenge to the Critics*, 107 MICHIGAN LAW REVIEW 603, 635 (2009).

D. Antitrust Law

The core of federal antitrust law is set out in the Sherman Act, the Clayton Act, and the Federal Trade Commission Act.[160] Most states have their own antitrust statutes, which are not preempted by the federal statutes.[161] But by far it is federal law that is more important, so in this short summary we will deal only with it.[162]

1. Applicable Law

The Sherman Act   The Sherman Act dates from 1890.[163] Its language is uncommonly broad and vague. Section 1 prohibits "every contract, combination . . . or conspiracy in restraint of trade."[164] Section 2 prohibits actions, attempts or conspiracies to "monopolize."[165] None of these terms is defined in the act. All business contracts limit the freedom of the parties by imposing obligations on them and thus "restrain" free trade. Consequently, the Court has held that Congress intended that the Sherman Act prohibit only *unreasonable* restraints of trade. Since it is up to the courts to define what business practices come within this "rule of reason," judicial decisions define much of federal antitrust law.[166]

The Clayton Act   The general language of the Sherman Act as originally interpreted by the Supreme Court led to some dissatisfaction with its lack of effect on monopolies. This resulted in passage of the Clayton Act.[167] That Act prohibits specific activities and mergers that tend to monopolize or that demonstrate a reasonable likelihood of substantially lessening competition.[168] As will be pointed out later, most practices specifically prohibited by the Clayton Act's provisions are banned under the Sherman Act as well.

The Federal Trade Commission Act   The Federal Trade Commission Act of 1914[169] established the Federal Trade Commission (FTC). Under §5 of the FTC Act, the FTC can initiate administrative proceedings against those who engage in any "[u]nfair methods

---

160 *See generally* HERBERT HOVENKAMP, FEDERAL ANTITRUST POLICY: THE LAW OF COMPETITION AND ITS PRACTICE (West 2005); ERNEST GELLHORN, WILLIAM E. KOVACIC & STEPHEN CALKINS, ANTITRUST LAW AND ECONOMICS IN A NUTSHELL, 4TH ED. (West 2004).

161 For a summary of the law that covers unfair trade practices generally, including state law, *see* CHARLES R. MCMANIS, INTELLECTUAL PROPERTY AND UNFAIR TRADE PRACTICES, 4TH ED. (West 2004). *See also* HOVENKAMP, *supra* §20.8 for a discussion of state antitrust law and its relationship to federal antitrust law.

162 Federal law may be applied only to transactions that affect interstate commerce, but, as has been discussed elsewhere, this includes almost any economic activity. *See* Chapter I, p. 25, and *Summit Health, Ltd. v. Pinhas*, 500 U.S. 322 (1991) (Sherman Act held to apply to alleged conspiracy by local hospital to exclude eye surgeon because conduct would have effect on interstate commerce).

163 The word "antitrust" comes from the cartels and groups of firms that were then called "trusts." Antitrust law is typically referred to as "competition law" in other countries.

164 *See Bell Atlantic Corp. v. Twombly*, 550 U.S. 544 (2007) (in order to state a claim under §1, a complaint must specify "enough factual matter" to demonstrate "plausible grounds to infer an agreement"; merely alleging parallel conduct and asserting the existence of a conspiracy does not suffice to state a claim). *Compare* Chapter VII, pp. 229-230, where general rules of pleading are discussed.

165 15 U.S.C.A. §§1-7.

166 *Standard Oil Co. of New Jersey v. United States*, 221 U.S. 1 (1911) (holding rule of reason did not encompass oil company's pattern of acquisition of rivals, illegal rebates from railroads, industrial espionage and predatory pricing that led to controlling almost 90% of country's oil refining capacity). *See also National Society of Professional Engineers v. United States*, 435 U.S. 679, 688 (1978) (Congress intended phrase in statute prohibiting all agreements "in restraint of trade or commerce" would be "shape[d]" by "drawing on common law tradition").

167 15 U.S.C.A. §§12-27. *See* HOVENKAMP, *supra* note 160, at 56-57.

168 15 U.S.C.A. §13.

169 15 U.S.C.A. §§41-58. The FTC is also authorized to issue regulations on and investigate unfair and deceptive trade practices that affect the consumer. *See* Chapter X, pp. 429, 430, and note 176.

of competition in or affecting commerce."[170] Business conduct that tends to restrain trade or create a monopoly under the Sherman Act often amounts to an unfair method of competition. Consequently, the FTC can proceed against violators of the Sherman Act. In addition, it has joint civil enforcement authority with the Department of Justice to proceed against violators of the Clayton Act. Moreover, it may intervene and conduct administrative proceedings even when there has technically been no violation of antitrust laws if a particular business activity appears to violate the "spirit" of the antitrust laws.[171]

2. Prohibited Practices

These three Acts, when taken together, prohibit principally four kinds of anti-competitive activity: restraints on trade, monopolization, mergers and acquisitions, and price discrimination. When the "rule of reason" is used, anticompetitive effects from the challenged practice must be shown. However, some activities "have such predictable and pernicious anticompetitive effect, and such limited potential for procompetitive benefit, that they are deemed unlawful *per se*."[172] Somewhere in between a full rule-of-reason market effects examination and a *per se* violation is the "quick look" application of the rule of reason. This is employed when "an observer with even a rudimentary understanding of economics could conclude that the arrangements in question would have an anticompetitive effect on customers and markets."[173]

Restraints on Trade   Restraints on trade may be horizontal or vertical. Horizontal restraints are attempts to restrain competition between companies on the same level of production or distribution, such as agreements by companies not to compete on each other's territories or to fix prices. Thus, in *Palmer v. BRG of Georgia, Inc.*,[174] the agreement of competing companies to divide up territory where each would offer bar review courses to bar examinees was held to be a *per se* violation of the Sherman Act.[175] Vertical restraints involve attempts by companies at one level to control what happens at a lower level, such as where a manufacturer seeks to control the price at which the distributor or retailer resells its product. In an early case, the Court held that a drug manufacturer could not use a resale price maintenance agreement specifying minimum price for which resellers could sell its product. In 2007, the Supreme Court sent shock-waves through the antitrust community when it overturned that 96-year-old decision, holding that resale price maintenance agreements could, under some circumstances, have pro-competitive benefits and therefore should be analyzed under the rule of

---

170 15 U.S.C.A. §45.

171 *See Fed. Trade Comm'n v. Brown Shoe Co.*, 384 U.S. 316 (1966).

172 *State Oil Co. v. Khan*, 522 U.S. 3 (1997). *See United States v. Socony-Vacuum Oil Co.*, 310 U.S. 150 (1940) (scheme of oil companies to buy up surplus gas from independent suppliers to prevent them from "dumping" it on depressed market at reduced prices). There is some dispute, however, as to what a *per se* rule is. *See* discussion in Hovenkamp *supra* note 160, at 226-240.

173 *California Dental Association v. Fed. Trade Comm'n*, 526 U.S. 756 (1999) (rejecting "quick look" condemnation of dentists' advertising of discount prices and quality since it involved professional services where the danger of misleading or irrelevant advertising).

174 498 U.S. 46 (1990).

175 *Catalano, Inc. v. Target Sales, Inc.*, 446 U.S. 643 (1980) (beer wholesalers' agreement to abolish short-term credit terms when selling beer to retailers *per se* violation). *But see Texaco Inc. v. Dagher*, 547 U.S. 1 (2006) (joint venture between Shell and Texaco oil companies to sell gasoline in Western states at an agreed-on price did not constitute illegal price fixing where they did not formerly compete in that market).

reason.[176] In these cases, a distinction must be made between setting minimum and maximum prices. The Court had held that maximum price restraints were *per se* violations, but changed course and found that the anticompetitive effects of maximum price restraints are not as serious and that such restraints often result in lower prices for consumers.[177]

Another vertical restraint is the "tying arrangement." If a seller has good market position for one product or service (called the "tying product"), it may try to promote a second product or service (the "tied product") by "tying" its purchase to the purchase of the first, *i.e.*, by selling the first only on the condition that the buyer purchase the second. Not all tying arrangements are unlawful and the courts have increasingly limited liability in this area. The Court's increasingly permissive attitude toward tying arrangements is the result of the fact that they can be pro-competitive, providing "uniquely advantageous deals to purchasers."[178]

As stated in *Eastman Kodak Co. v. Image Technical Services, Inc.*,[179] liability attaches only if (1) the tying and tied goods are two separate products; (2) the defendant has market power in the tying product market; (3) the defendant affords consumers no choice but to purchase the tied product from it; and (4) the tying arrangement forecloses a substantial volume of commerce.[180] In *Kodak*, illegal tying was found when Kodak, a copy machine manufacturer with a 23% market share sold repair parts only to buyers who purchased its repair services. But in another case, no illegal tying arrangement was found where a hospital required patients to use its own staff anesthesiologists, since there was no effect shown on the market for hospital care or anesthesiology services.[181] The need for quality control or other business justifications can be a defense. However, the Court in *Kodak* rejected as "pretextual" Kodak's quality control defense, since many copier owners preferred non-Kodak repair services. Moreover, it was not likely that copier owners would erroneously blame Kodak for bad repairs, as opposed to bad parts, given that buyers of its produce were sophisticated.

In the *Microsoft* antitrust litigation discussed earlier, the tying arrangement alleged to be illegal was Microsoft's tying its Internet Explorer browser program to its Windows operating system. While the trial court found an illegal tying arrangement, the Court of Appeals disagreed and remanded the case for a balancing of the anti-competitive harms and the pro-competitive benefits under the "rule of reason," pointing out that the government had failed to clearly define browsers and the browser market, but precluding it from clarifying these issues on remand. It also observed that "integration of new

---

176 *Dr. Miles Medical Co. v. John D. Park & Sons Co.*, 220 U.S. 373 (1911), *overruled by Leegin Creative Leather Products, Inc. v. PSKS, Inc*, 551 U.S. 877 (2007).

177 *See State Oil Co. v. Khan, supra* note 172, *overruling Albrecht v. Herald Co.*, 390 U.S. 145 (1968) In commenting on *Albrecht*, the Court noted that the defendant newspaper's refusal to sell to the plaintiff distributor because it resold papers to customers at above suggested retail price could well protect consumers from price gouging by monopolist distributors.

178 *See United States Steel Corp. v. Fortner Enterprises, Inc.*, 429 U.S. 610, 622 (1977) (tying sales of homes to financing "nothing more than a willingness to provide cheap financing in order to sell expensive houses").

179 504 U.S. 451 (1992).

180 The mere fact that a tying product is patented does not support a presumption of market power in a patented product. *Illinois Tool Works Inc. v. Independent Ink, Inc.*, 547 U.S. 28 (2006) (requiring printer manufacturers who use patented printer technology to also use unpatented ink was not necessarily an illegal tying arrangement).

181 *Jefferson Parish Hosp. Dist. No. 2 v. Hyde*, 466 U.S. 2 (1984). There was insufficient evidence to determine whether this amounted to exclusive dealing, dealt with next.

functionality into platform software is a common practice and ... wooden application of *per se* rules in this litigation may cast a cloud over platform innovation in the market for PCs, network computers and information appliances."[182]

Yet another vertical restraint is the "exclusive dealing" contract. An exclusive dealing contract is a contract in which the buyer agrees not to purchase goods or services from the seller's competitors. Such agreements, like tying arrangements, are often an effort to use economic power as to one product to promote sales of another. But liability results only if the agreement causes some substantial foreclosure of the market. The classic case on exclusive dealing is *Standard Oil Co. of California v. United States*,[183] where an agreement that retail gas stations only purchase Standard Oil's products was held illegal since it foreclosed competition in 7% of retail gas sales, deemed a "substantial share" of a market that was concentrated and had significant entry barriers for competitors. On the other hand, the Court held in *Tampa Electric Co. v. Nashville Coal Co.*[184] that no substantial share of the coal supply market was foreclosed by a 20-year agreement that the coal company fill the total needs of an electric power utility company. The *Tampa* rule of reason requires a court to examine (1) length of the contracts, (2) likelihood of collusion in the relevant industry; (3) the height of entry barriers for competitors seeking to enter the market (4) alternative distribution avenues that exist, and (5) other obvious effects on competition.[185]

Monopolization Under §2 of the Sherman Act, "every person who shall monopolize, or attempt to monopolize, or combine or conspire ... to monopolize any part of the trade or commerce among the several States, or with foreign nations, shall be deemed guilty of a felony." This involves two elements: "(1) the possession of monopoly power in the relevant market and (2) the willful acquisition or maintenance of that power as distinguished from growth or development as a consequence of a superior product, business acumen, or historic accident."[186] A successful claim of attempted monopolization requires proof that "(1) that the defendant has engaged in predatory or anticompetitive conduct with (2) a specific intent to monopolize and (3) a dangerous probability of achieving monopoly power."[187]

A description of three practices from recent cases will provide a flavor of the kind of conduct that is the focus of §2. The first practice is "predatory pricing" — selling at below cost to squeeze out competitors. But the pricing is not predatory unless the economics of it work out. Thus, when a cigarette manufacturer's sold its name-brand product at below-cost prices that undercut plaintiff's generic cigarette sales, there was

---

182 *United States v. Microsoft, Inc.*, 87 F.Supp.2d 30 (D.D.C. 2000), *aff'd in part, rev'd in part* 253 F.3d. 34, 95-98 (D.C.Cir. 2001). For a good analysis of the tying claim, *see* Andrew Chin, *Decoding Microsoft: A First Principles Approach*, 40 WAKE FOREST L.REV. 1 (2005). For a short overview of the case, the settlement and its aftermath, and Microsoft's antitrust problems in Europe, *see* Amanda Cohen, *Antitrust: Note: Surveying the Microsoft Antitrust Universe*, 19 BERKELEY TECH. LAW JOURNAL 333 (2004).

183 337 U.S. 293 (1949).

184 365 U.S. 320 (1961).

185 Concerted refusals to deal in an effort to affect price are *per se* violations. *Fed. Trade Comm'n v. Superior Court Trial Lawyers Assoc.*, 493 U.S. 411 (1990) (lawyers' boycott, refusing to accept criminal appointment from court because compensation rates were too low, was *per se* violation of §5 of FTC Act). In the *Microsoft* case, exclusive dealing was the only claim Microsoft prevailed on in the trial court. *But see* Shannon A. Keyes, *Legal Update: Microsoft: Exclusive Dealing under Section 1 of the Sherman Act: A New Standard*, 7 BOSTON U. J. SCI. & TECH. LAW 173 (2001) (discussing how *Microsoft* court departed from traditional exclusive dealing analysis).

186 *United States v. Grinnell Corp.*, 384 U.S. 563, 570-71 (1966).

187 *Spectrum Sports, Inc. v. McQuillan*, 506 U.S. 447, 456 (1993).

no violation since there was no proof that the manufacturer would "recoup its investment in low prices."[188] A second practice is a monopolist's development of a new product that is incompatible with the products of rivals whose business depends on their ability to adapt to industry standards. Yet, courts have been forgiving in this area if the monopolist's new products are improvements, even though rivals are hurt, on the ground that to do otherwise would stifle innovation.[189] A third practice is refusing to deal with weaker competitors. While it is a traditional antitrust principle that there is no duty to aid competitors, refusal to sell a product on terms otherwise available to the public can be illegal if undertaken for an anti-competitive end. This includes refusal to share facilities that are essential and hard to duplicate.[190]

The government has won many monopolization cases, but it is significant that it has rarely succeeded in breaking large companies with monopoly power into competing smaller ones. A significant failure was the suit against International Business Machines (IBM) — abandoned in 1982 after 13 years of litigation and 700 days of trial.[191] But a notable success was the breakup of American Telephone & Telegraph, which many have credited with lowering prices and improving service in the telecommunications industry.[192]

Another case that many consider a mixed success at best is the Microsoft litigation. The trial court found Microsoft unlawfully maintained its monopoly in PC operating systems and attempted to monopolize the market in Internet browsers. These were sufficiently serious, in its view, to break Microsoft up into two companies, one providing operating system software and the other providing browser software. However, the Court of Appeals, while agreeing that Microsoft had unlawfully maintained a monopoly in operating systems, found insufficient evidence of attempts to monopolize the browser market to satisfy §2 of the Sherman Act. Given this reduced liability of Microsoft, the Court of Appeals determined that the remedy of breaking up the company was not warranted. On remand, the case was settled by way of a consent decree imposing penalties that were much less severe than those ordered by the trial court.[193]

Mergers and Acquisitions Section 7 of the Clayton Act prohibits mergers and acquisitions that tend to lessen competition substantially or tend to create a monopoly

---

188 *Brook Group Ltd. v. Brown & Williamson Corp.* 509 U.S. 209 (1993). The Supreme Court extended the *Brooke* rule to predatory bidding (intentionally over-bidding to secure a monopoly supply) in *Weyerhauser Co. v. Ross-Simmons Hardwood Lumber Co.*, Inc., 549 U.S. 312 (2007). *See also Pacific Bell Tel. Co. v. Linkline Communications, Inc.*, ___ U.S. ___, 129 S. Ct. 1109 (2009) (plaintiffs cannot state a price squeeze claim when the defendant has no obligation under the antitrust laws to deal with the plaintiffs at the wholesale level.)

189 *Berkey Photo, Inc. v. Eastman Kodak Co.*, 603 F.2d 263 (2d Cir. 1979) (monopolist Kodak need not disclose new camera designed for exclusive use with its new film because disclosure would retard innovation); *California Computer Products v. IBM Corp.*, 613 F.2d 727 (9th Cir. 1979) (new computer design not §2 violation even though it was incompatible with rival manufacturer's peripheral products).

190 *Aspen Skiing Co. v. Aspen Highlands Skiing Corp.*, 472 U.S. 585 (1985) (no valid business reason for refusal to continue joint ski ticket program with one of three competing ski slopes held unlawful); *Otter Tail Power Co. v. United States*, 410 U.S. 366 (1973) (refusal of electric power company to share lines or sell power in effort to delay or prevent development of municipal power systems illegal). *But see Verizon Communications Inc. v. Trinko*, 540 U.S. 398 (2004) (refusing to share telephone network with competitors not antitrust violation; network sharing exclusively covered by Telecommunications Act).

191 *See United States v. IBM Corp.*, 687 F.2d 591 (2d Cir. 1982).

192 *United States v. American Tel. & Tel. Co.*, 552 F. Supp. 131 (D.D.C. 1982), *aff'd sub nom Maryland v. United States*, 460 U.S. 1001 (1983).

193 *United States v. Microsoft Corp.*, 231 F. Supp. 2d 144 (D.D.C. 2002). *See* Cohen, *supra* note 182, for a succinct explanation of the final settlement agreement.

in any line of commerce.[194] The Act mandates government approval for certain kinds of mergers and requires merging entities to notify the Federal Trade Commission and the Justice Department before specified transactions can be completed.[195] Complex guidelines, issued by those agencies, set out criteria by which they will determine what mergers to challenge.[196]

There are three main categories of mergers which the antitrust laws address. The first is the horizontal merger, defined as a company acquiring a competitor company that is in the same geographic area and market.[197] Regulators will examine the resulting market concentration and what barriers exist to new competitors entering the market.[198] The second kind of merger is the vertical merger, defined as a company starting to perform itself some function it would otherwise employ others to do. An example is a manufacturer acquiring a supplier of components for its product.[199] Vertical mergers in recent years have not been condemned except in the most extreme circumstances, because courts have come to view most of them as efficient and not seriously anti-competitive.[200] The third category is the conglomerate merger. This includes all other types of acquisitions not covered in the other two categories. It often deals with potential anti-competitive effects of joint ventures between large companies[201] or mergers of companies whose businesses are not in direct competition.[202]

Price Discrimination Section 2 of the Clayton Act and the Robinson-Patman Act prohibit sellers from engaging in price discrimination, preventing sellers from charging different buyers different prices and preventing buyers from inducing or receiving discriminatory prices.[203] Prohibition of price discrimination was designed largely to help small retailers who were being priced out of their markets by large "chain stores."

---

194 15 U.S.C.A. §7.

195 15 U.S.C.A. §18A requires a pre-merger notification process when a party to the proposed merger has annual net sales or total assets in excess of $100 million and the other merging party has annual net sales or total assets in excess of $10 million and the acquisition price or value of the acquired entity is greater than $15 million. These amounts are updated periodically to reflect changes in the size of the nation's economy.

196 *See* 1992 Horizontal Merger Guidelines, 57 Fed. Reg. 41552 (Sep. 10, 1992). While the guidelines are not binding, courts give deference to them, *See, e.g., Fed. Trade Comm'n v. Cardinal Health, Inc.*, 12 F.Supp.2d 34 (D.D.C. 1998).

197 *See, e.g., Boyertown Burial Casket Co. v. Amedco, Inc.*, 407 F.Supp. 811 (E.D.Pa. 1976) (preliminary injunction entered against tender offer by one casket company to purchase another where there was concentration in the market).

198 *See* 1992 Horizontal Merger Guidelines, *supra* note 196. *See and compare United States v. Philadelphia National Bank*, 374 U.S. 321, 363 (1963) (emphasizing concentration where merging banks would have one-third of Philadelphia market) and *United States v. Phillipsburg National Bank & Trust Co.*, 399 U.S. 350, 368-369 (1970) (relying on high entry barriers to condemn bank merger).

199 *See, e.g., Ford Motor Co. v. United States*, 405 U.S. 562 (1972) (automobile manufacturer acquisition of spark plug manufacturer illegal vertical merger).

200 *Hovenkamp, supra* note 160, §9.4.

201 *United States v. Penn-Olin Chemical Co.*, 378 U.S. 158 (1964) and 389 U.S. 308 (1967) (chemical companies' joint venture to build plant not shown to be violation of Clayton Act).

202 *See, e.g., Federal Trade Comm. v. Procter & Gamble Co.*, 386 U.S. 568 (1967) (violation of §7 when household product manufacturer that did not make bleach acquired bleach manufacturer because buyer was a potential competitor). *See generally* HOVENKAMP, *supra* note 160, §§9.1-9.5 (vertical mergers); 12.1-12.10 (horizontal mergers); and §§13.1-13.5 (conglomerate mergers).

203 15 U.S.C.A. §§13(a), (f), 14. *See, e.g., Best Brands Beverage, Inc. v. Falstaff Brewing Corp.*, 653 F. Supp. 47 (S.D.N.Y. 1985) (preliminary injunction entered rolling back price hike imposed by brewery on only one beer distributor on grounds of price discrimination). *But see Volvo Trucks North America, Inc. v. Reeder-Simco GMC, Inc.*, 546 U.S. 164 (2006) (price discrimination involving bids for the same customer is not a violation).

However, it has been widely criticized as overly complex and ineffective at curbing price discrimination. Some also condemn it as hurting rather than helping smaller businesses when they band together to negotiate a lower price from a supplier.[204] In addition, a seller can escape liability by showing that it charged a lower price in a good faith effort to "meet competition."[205] The fundamental problem with the Act is that it penalizes low prices, thus making price competition more difficult. It also sometimes works at cross purposes with the prohibition against price-fixing. For example, any conversation with a competitor about price could be a *Sherman Act* violation. To avoid this conflict, the Court held that there was no need to verify competitors' prices in order to assert a "meeting competition" defense to price discrimination.[206] Government suits aimed at price discrimination have been significantly reduced since 1977, though private enforcement does continue.[207]

3. Federal Antitrust Remedies and Enforcement Powers

Public Enforcement The federal antitrust laws are unique in that they provide for dual civil enforcement powers in two federal agencies — the Department of Justice and the FTC. In civil actions, equitable relief is usually sought, such as an injunction or a "cease and desist" order. Only the Department of Justice has authority to bring criminal actions for violations of the federal antitrust laws, and it brings many of them. Nearly all of them are for §1 horizontal restraints, such as price-fixing and market division agreements. Under the Sherman Act and the Antitrust Criminal Penalty Enforcement and Reform Act of 2004, the maximum criminal sanction is a $100 million fine for a corporate defendant, and any antitrust felony can result in fines up to double the corporate defendant's monetary gain or double the victim's monetary loss, whichever is greater. Individual violators of the Sherman or Clayton Acts may be fined up to $1 million, and imprisoned for up to 10 years.[208]

Private Enforcement Private persons and companies by far file the greatest number of antitrust actions. Congress has sought to encourage private enforcement by providing substantial incentives. Section 4 of the Clayton Act provides that private plaintiffs may sue for "treble damages" — three times their actual damages. In addition, states can bring actions for treble damages on behalf of their citizens as consumers. Prevailing private plaintiffs can recover reasonable attorneys' fees, while prevailing defendants ordinarily may not.[209]

---

204 *See* William F. Baxter, *A Parable*, 23 STAN. L. REV. 973 (1971) and HOVENKAMP, *supra* note 160, §14.6. *See, e.g., Mid-South Distributors v. Fed. Trade Comm'n.*, 287 F.2d 512 (5th Cir. 1961) (it was illegal price discrimination for cooperative buying group of small manufacturer-suppliers to buy auto parts at reduced cost through volume rebates in order to compete with larger competitors).

205 *Falls City Industries, Inc. v. Vanco Beverage, Inc.*, 460 U.S. 428 (1983) (Congress "intended to allow reasonable pricing responses on an area-specific basis where competitive circumstances warrant them"). *United States v. United States Gypsum Co.*, 438 U.S. 422 (1978) ("good faith" in charging lower price is all that is required, but discussing problem of the "untruthful buyer"); *Rose Confections, Inc. v. Ambrosia Chocolates Co.*, 816 F.2d 381 (8th Cir. 1987) ("meeting competition" defense rejected where seller relied on "assumption and speculation" that competitors were charging lower prices).

206 *See United States v. United States Gypsum Co., supra,* and HOVENKAMP, *supra* note 160, at 523 ("while [the Act] is hostile toward economic competition, it is nevertheless disguised as an antitrust law.").

207 *See* U.S. Dept. of Justice, Report on the Robinson-Patman Act (1977).

208 15 U.S.C.A. §§1-3; 18 U.S.C.A. §3623. The 2004 Act brings antitrust penalties more into line with other white collar criminal penalties, such as violation of the Sarbanes-Oxley Act.

209 15 U.S.C.A. §15.

4. Exemptions and Reach of Federal Antitrust Laws

Exemptions   Exemptions from federal antitrust regulation are provided for labor unions and regulated industries. Thus, each deregulation of an industry expands the reach of antitrust laws. This was true for the airline industry, which was deregulated in 1976.

State Action Doctrine   Another exemption is a "state action" doctrine, which exempts most state or local government regulation from federal antitrust laws. The exemption applies even if the regulation at issue shields private conduct that is clearly anti-competitive, so long as that private conduct that is both: (1) in accordance with a clearly articulated and affirmatively expressed state policy to supplant competition; and (2) actively supervised by the state itself.[210] Thus, monopoly private electric power utility companies regulated by states that supply most of the power in the country are exempt, even though their prices are controlled and entry into the market is restricted. However, there must be active supervision by the state. Thus, where prices or rates are initially set by private parties, subject to veto only if the State chooses, the party claiming the immunity must show that state officials have undertaken the necessary steps to determine the specifics of the price-fixing or rate-setting scheme beforehand. The mere potential for state supervision is not an adequate substitute for the State's decision.[211]

Noerr-Pennington Doctrine   The 1st Amendment protects the right to petition government for redress of grievances, so attempts by businesses to influence government action are exempt despite their anti-competitive effects. This includes not just attempts to influence legislation or rules, but also the filing of lawsuits or counterclaims in lawsuits so long as they are legitimate and not merely a sham.[212] The "sham" distinction is difficult to define. In some recent cases, fine distinctions were made based on intent, while more recently the Court seems to have opted for a more objective test.[213]

Extraterritorial Effect of Antitrust Laws   Antitrust laws have been at the forefront of laws claiming extraterritorial application. Conduct that takes place outside the United States has been held to be subject to liability under U.S. antitrust laws if it has a direct effect on commerce in the United States. More coverage of this issue and the general question of extraterritorial application of U.S. law is set out in Chapter XVII.[214]

E. Labor and Employment Law

Four topics will be covered here: (1) the legal nature of the individual employment relationship, (2) laws protecting workers on the job, (3) laws prohibiting employment discrimination, and (4) employees' rights to unionize and engage in collective bargaining.

---

210 *Parker v. Brown*, 317 U.S. 341 (1943).

211 *Fed. Trade Comm'n. v. Ticor Title Ins. Co.*, 504 U.S. 621 (1992) (setting of rates for title insurance allowed to take effect without state review).

212 *Eastern Railroad Conference v. Noerr Motor Freight, Inc.*, 365 U.S. 127 (1961) and *United Mine Workers v. Pennington*, 381 U.S. 657 (1965) (applying 1st Amendment immunity to activity aimed at influencing a government agency's purchasing decision).

213 *Compare City of Columbia v. Omni Outdoor Advertising, Inc.*, 499 U.S. 365 (1991) (subjective test applied to efforts to influence zoning, because they were aimed at the ultimate product, *i.e.* zoning ordinances, rather than as a means of imposing cost and delay on its rival) *with Professional Real Estate Investors, Inc. v. Columbia Pictures Industries, Inc.*, 508 U.S. 49 (1993) (objectively reasonable legal claim filed in court is immune regardless of subjective intent).

214 *See* pp. 705-714.

1. Nature of the Individual Employment Relationship

The "At-Will" Doctrine   The default legal arrangement for most workers in the United States, defined by the common law, is employment "at will." This means that, unless there is an employment contract providing otherwise, an employer can "discharge or retain employees at will for good cause or for no cause, or even for bad cause without thereby being guilty of an unlawful act *per se*."[215] The at-will doctrine also means that the employer has the right to change any term of employment in its discretion. The employee's only choice is to accept the change or quit.

There several exceptions to the at-will rule, some by statute and some as a matter of common law. One major exception is a dismissal based on racial or other discriminatory reasons, covered below.[216] Another is a dismissal in violation of public policy. Most cases of this type involve firings for performing a civic obligation (such as jury service or testifying in court proceedings), for refusing to commit an illegal act (such as covering up an employer's illegal activity), or for exercising a statutory right (such as filing a claim for workers compensation).[217] Included in the category is firing an employee for "whistle-blowing" — reporting illegal action by the employer.[218] Finally, workers covered by a specific employment contract or a collective bargaining agreement will also be guaranteed employment unless a layoff is needed for economic reasons or there is "just cause" for termination.

"Just Cause" Requirements of Implied Contracts   Starting in the 1970s, courts began to undercut the at-will doctrine, imposing a "just-cause" requirement for termination even in the absence of an express employment contract.[219] Most decisions rely on an implied contract that the company will only dismiss workers for unsatisfactory performance, based on tacit understandings, course of dealing, long and faithful service to the employer, or the employer's personnel manuals or handbooks.[220] In the words of one court, if an employer "creates an atmosphere of job security and fair treatment with promises of specific treatment in specific situations and an employee is induced thereby to remain on the job," those promises will be enforced.[221]

---

215 *Payne v. Western & Atlantic R.R.*, 81 Tenn. 507 (1884) (holding it proper for employer-railroad to discharge anyone who shopped at plaintiff's store). The at-will doctrine at one time was thought to be constitutionally required, *Adair v. United States*, 208 U.S. 161 (1908) (federal statute punishing employer for firing employee for union membership violated employer's rights under the due process clause).

216 *See infra*, pp. 620-625.

217 *Petermann v. International Brotherhood of Teamsters*, 344 P.2d 25 (Cal.App. 1959) (employee fired for refusing to testify falsely as instructed by his employer); *Haddle v. Garrison*, 525 U.S. 121 (1998) (fired for obeying a grand jury subpoena and testifying at a criminal trial); *Nees v. Hocks*, 536 P.2d 512 (Ore. 1975) (fired for going on jury duty).

218 *Garibaldi v. Lucky Food Stores, Inc.*, 726 F.2d 1367 (9th Cir. 1984) (fired for reporting adulterated milk after being ordered to deliver it) (applying California law); *Sheets v. Teddy's Frosted Foods*, 427 A.2d 385 (Conn. 1980) (fired for efforts to insure employer followed state product quality standards). Government employee whistle-blowers can rely on their 1st Amendment free speech rights for protection. *But see Garcetti v. Ceballos*, 547 U.S. 410 (2006) (prosecutor who complained in memo to superiors that application for search warrant was falsified was not protected from discipline; speech was part of his official duties, not a publicly stated dissatisfaction with his employing agency as a citizen).

219 *See generally* MARK A. ROTHSTEIN, CHARLES CRAVER, ELINOR P. SCHROEDER & ELAINE SHOBEN, EMPLOYMENT LAW §§9.3-9.20 (West 2009).

220 *See, e.g.*, *Toussaint v. Blue Cross & Blue Shield of Michigan*, 292 N.W.2d 880 (Mich. 1980); *Duldulao v. Saint Mary of Nazareth Hosp.*, 505 N.E.2d 314, 317 (Ill. 1987); *Foley v. Interactive Data*, 254 Cal.Rptr. 211, 665 P.2d 373 (Cal. 1988).

221 *Thompson v. St. Regis Paper Co.*, 685 P.2d 1081, 1087-1088 (Wash. 1984).

A few cases have based just-cause employment on the theory that such implied employment contracts, like all other contracts, contain an implied "covenant of good faith and fair dealing," requiring both sides to abide by the contract in good faith. If the employer fires an employee for an arbitrary reason, this covenant of good faith is breached.[222] The advantage of this theory of recovery is that, although the duty of good faith is one implied from the existence of a contract, breach of that duty is considered a *tort* rather than a breach of contract, opening up the possibility of punitive damage awards for breaches of good faith that are intentional.[223]

Judicial activity in the "just-cause" area has prompted the Uniform Commissioners on State Laws to act by proposing a Model Employment Termination Act.[224] However, the development of just-cause doctrines has not really had much impact on at-will relationships. The vast majority of U.S. workers are at-will employees and successful wrongful discharge suits are not that common.[225] The first reason for this is that employers have reacted to these judicial doctrines with disclaimers in employee handbooks that say the relationship is only at-will. Second, even in the absence of such disclaimers, proving an implied contract is quite difficult to do. Third, the financial incentive for lawyers to bring wrongful discharge suits is not there. Unlike employment discrimination, where some statutes provide for recovery of attorneys' fees from the defendant, common-law claims for wrongful discharge are governed by the normal "American rule" on attorneys' fees.[226]

Employee Obligations The common law also imposes obligations on employees. These duties are often supplemented by statutes or agreements with the employer. Employees have a duty of loyalty to the employer. This prohibits the employee from competing with the employer during their employment, either working for a competing business or soliciting fellow employees or customers. An employee may work for more than one employer (called "moonlighting") as long as there is no conflict between the two types of employment. An employee may make preparations to start a new business while still employed, and may solicit the former employer's employees and customers after leaving. An employee is also prohibited from taking a business opportunity offered to the employer. Contracts not to compete after leaving employment are allowed in most states, but courts have placed limits on these contracts if they are so broad as to make it impossible for the employee to quit and find new work.

An employee may not reveal the employer's trade secrets or take them for the employee's own use, and the employer may have rights in employee inventions. These duties are usually reinforced by non-disclosure agreements and patent assignment agreements. If another employer assists the employee in violating any of these implied covenants, the new employer may be liable for interference with business or corporate or contractual advantage.

---

222 *See Farris v. Hutchinson*, 838 P.2d 374, 277 (Mont. 1992).

223 *See* Chapter XI, pp. 463-465 (punitive damages for intentional torts).

224 *See* Theodore J. St.Antoine, *A Seed Germinates: Unjust Discharge Reform Heads Toward Full Flower*, 67 NEBRASKA L.REV. 56 (1988).

225 The biggest exception is employees represented by labor unions, almost all of whom have just-cause employment as part of their collective bargaining contract. *See infra* pp. 625-632.

226 *See* Chapter VII, p. 247 (awards of attorney fees). Working on a contingent fee basis is possible, but usually the amount of potential recovery, except perhaps in the case of a highly paid executive, is not high enough to justify a fee on a contingent basis. *See* Chapter IV, p. 145 (contingent fees).

2. Laws Protecting Workers

While most workers in the United States do not have the job security a just-cause regime would afford, there are several important laws that protect them on the job. A worker dismissed without just cause may be eligible for unemployment compensation benefits. These are provided by a state unemployment insurance fund that employers pay into pursuant to a federal-state cooperative program that exists in all the states.[227] While unemployment compensation is not high and is limited in time, it can provide an important source of support when workers are between jobs. Under the federal Worker Adjustment and Retraining Notification Act (WARN), statute, an employer who lays off a large number of workers or closes all or a part of its business may be obligated by to give employees 60 notice or 60 days pay.[228] Wages and hours worked are regulated by the federal Fair Labor Standards Act.[229] The maximum work week set by federal law is 40 hours and "overtime" pay of one-and-a-half times base wages must be paid for any hours worked beyond that. The federal minimum wage is $5.15 per hour. State wage laws can require a higher minimum wage or permit fewer hours a week of work than federal law. State statutes also regulate when wages must be paid and the form of payment. The federal Equal Pay Act prohibits payment to an employee of an amount less than that paid to members of the opposite sex for the performance of equal work.[230]

The federal Employee Polygraph Protection Act (EPPA) prohibits employers from administering lie detector tests to employees in most situations and establishes rights and procedures for instances when they are permitted to be given.[231] Employer psychological, drug, or other testing is permitted, and dismissal for refusal to take a drug test is legal in most states.[232] The rationale is that constitutional limits on invasions of privacy or 4th Amendment rights against unreasonable searches do not apply if it is a private employer who is requiring the test. However, tests must be administered with care to avoid tort liability or running afoul of privacy and other tort rights, as well as violating anti-discrimination laws.[233] Despite the constitutional constraints of the 4th Amendment, federal statutes making drug testing mandatory for transportation workers have been upheld.[234]

The federal Occupational Safety and Health Administration (OSHA) and parallel state agencies inspect workplaces and can fine employers for unsafe working conditions and require that they take remedial action.[235] Workers' compensation benefits for work-

---

227 *See* Federal Unemployment Tax Act (FUTA), 26 U.S.C.A. §3301 *et seq.*

228 29 U.S.C.A. §2102(a).

229 29 U.S.C.A. §201 *et seq.*

230 29 U.S.C.A. § 206(d). *See infra* 625

231 *See* 29 U.S.C.A. §§2002, 2006-2007. Exceptions mainly concern security and law-enforcement.

232 In a recent year, 98% of all Fortune 200 companies and 77.7% of employers in a random survey tested employees for drugs. David W. Lockard, *Protecting Medical Laboratories from Tort Liability for Drug Testing*, 17 J.LEGAL MED. 427 (1996). The Drug-Free Workplace Act of 1988, codified as amended at 41 U.S.C.A. §§701-702, requires drug testing for employees of federal contractors.

233 *See Santiago v. Greyhound Lines, Inc.*, 956 F.Supp. 144 (N.D.N.Y. 1997) (recognizing a common-law claim for negligent drug testing against doctor hired by employer). *Compare Mission Petroleum Carriers, Inc. v. Solomon*, 106 S.W.3d 705 (Tex. 2003) (no duty of reasonable care owed to employee tested).

234 *See* 49 U.S.C.A. § 31306(c) (requiring drug tests for all transportation workers) and *Skinner v. Railway Labor Executives' Ass'n*, 489 U.S. 602 (1989) (imposing tests on railway workers pursuant to federal statute does not constitute an unreasonable search). *Compare Chandler v. Miller*, 520 U.S. 305 (1997) (state statute imposing tests on candidates for political office unconstitutional). The determining factor is how necessary it is that the category of employees be drug free.

235 29 U.S.C.A. §651 *et seq.*

related injuries are provided for in all states.[236] Workers' compensation also promotes increased safety by penalizing with higher insurance rates employers who have high claiming rates or who do not score high on workers' compensation insurance carrier workplace inspections. The federal Family and Medical Leave Act (FMLA) requires employers to give qualifying employees 12 weeks unpaid leave to take care of family members who are ill or to tend to their own medical needs.[237] Federal retirement and long-term disability benefits are provided by the Social Security Administration.[238] If an employer provides retirement or other benefit programs beyond these (they need not do so), the Employee Retirement Income Security Act (ERISA) regulates how those benefits are to be provided.[239]

Notable for its absence among benefits legally required for workers — or anyone else — is medical care.[240] The tradition in the U.S. is that private health insurance plans are provided for employees by their employers as part of their fringe benefits. However, in recent years, the skyrocketing costs of such programs offered by private companies has caused some employers to cut back or eliminate medical coverage. Attempts by President Clinton in his first term as President to persuade Congress to pass a national governmental health program were resoundingly rebuffed by Congress, following a vigorous publicity campaign mounted by vendors of private health insurance. Whether paid for by the individual or an employer, private medical insurance policies are quite expensive. For example, the cost of an individual policy for a family of four with average coverage from Blue Cross and Blue Shield, a major medical insurance company, is approximately $10,900 per year, plus various "co-pay" requirements, including 50% of the cost of all doctor visits. It is estimated that more than 50 million U.S. citizens have no health insurance coverage, and that the most common reason given for not having it is cost.

3. Employment Discrimination

Title VII of the Civil Rights Act of 1964 prohibits discrimination in employment or employment opportunities on account of race, color, sex, national origin, or religion.[241] The Equal Employment Opportunity Commission (EEOC) is the federal administrative agency that has power both to handle administrative complaints of violations and to sue to redress violations in cases it deems sufficiently important to pursue. Title VII applies

---

236 *See* JACK B. HOOD, BENJAMIN A HARDY, JR., & HAROLD S. LEWIS, JR., WORKER'S COMPENSATION AND EMPLOYEE PROTECTION LAWS IN A NUTSHELL, 4TH ED. (West 2004). *See also* Chapter XI, p. 469.

237 29 U.S.C.A. 2601-2654; KURT H. DECKER, FAMILY AND MEDICAL LEAVE ACT IN A NUTSHELL (West 2000).

238 *See* U.S. SOCIAL SECURITY ADMINISTRATION, SOCIAL SECURITY HANDBOOK (Gov't Printing Office, Washington 2010), www.ssa.gov/OP_Home/handbook/ssa-hbk.htm.

239 *See* JAY CONISON, EMPLOYEE BENEFIT PLANS IN NUTSHELL, 3D ED. (West 2003) discussing the federal Employment and Retirement Security Act (ERISA), 29 U.S.C.A. §1001 *et seq. See also* SOCIAL SECURITY HANDBOOK, *supra* note 238.

240 The poor and the aged, blind and disabled are generally covered by federally funded Medical Assistance program. *See* 42 U.S.C.A §1396a *et seq.*

241 42 U.S.C.A. §2000e *et seq.* For more detail, *see* ROTHSTEIN ET AL., *supra* note 219 and GEORGE RUTHERGLEN, MAJOR ISSUES IN THE FEDERAL LAW OF EMPLOYMENT DISCRIMINATION (Fed. Jud. Center 2004). *See also* JOEL W. FRIEDMAN, EMPLOYMENT DISCRIMINATION STORIES (Foundation 2006) (stories of famous cases). The 1964 Civil Rights Act also bans racial discrimination in public accommodations (Title II), in federally-funded programs (Title VI), and in sales or rentals of housing (Title VIII). Only Title VII will be discussed here. It is the most developed of all the titles and much of its doctrine is applied to other titles.

to all employers in all industries that affect interstate commerce and, since 1972, includes state and local governments.[242]

Discrimination Proscribed Title VII prohibits two kinds of employment practices. The first is discriminatory treatment. Discriminatory treatment is proven by showing that a prohibited factor such as race "was a motivating factor for an employment action, even though other factors also motivated the practice."[243] Since discriminatory motive is hard to establish, a three-part proof process is followed.[244] Using a job application example, (1) applicants must prove that they are members of a protected class, that they are qualified for the job for which they applied, and that the employer did not hire them and continued to seek applicants with their qualifications; (2) once this is shown, the burden shifts to the employer to produce evidence of a non-discriminatory reason for the action;[245] and (3) if the employer offers a non-discriminatory reason, applicants must then demonstrate that that reason is merely a "pretext" for discrimination.[246] In individual cases, proof is usually by way of showing instances of discriminatory treatment of the plaintiff in relation to another who is not a member of the protected class, or in some cases, more direct evidence of bias.[247] In class action cases, and in some individual cases, statistical proof of negative treatment of an entire class of employees or applicants, including gross under-representation of minorities in given positions may be offered, with the employer usually responding with evidence that its overall record shows racial balance.[248]

The second form of discriminatory practice prohibited by Title VII is an employment practice that may have no discriminatory motive, but which "causes a disparate impact on the basis of race" or other protected criteria. A similar burden-shifting occurs: (1) the plaintiff must show disparate impact on the protected class; (2) if this is shown, then the burden shifts to the employer to show that the qualification "is job-related for the position in question and consistent with business necessity"; and (3) if the defendant makes this showing, the burden then shifts to the plaintiff to prove that "an alternative employment practice" exists with a smaller disparate impact.[249] Thus, in one case, it was held to be a violation of Title VII to require a high school education or passing of a general intelligence test for a job, where neither standard was significantly related to

---

242 Constitutional challenges to basing anti-discrimination laws on the interstate commerce power have been rejected. *See Heart of Atlanta Motel v. United States*, 379 U.S. 241 (1964). Power to include state and local governments is granted under §5 of the 14th Amendment. *Fitzpatrick v. Bitzer*, 427 U.S. 445 (1976). State and local laws also prohibit discrimination, which federal laws do not preempt. Since 1991, Title VII has applied to U.S. citizens working abroad.

243 42 U.S.C.A. §2000e-2(m).

244 *See McDonnell Douglas Corp. v. Green*, 411 U.S. 792 (1973) and 42 U.S.C.A. §2000-e-(k)(1)(A).

245 The non-discriminatory motive may be malicious, immoral or even illegal, but if it was the real reason for the action, there is no discrimination. *See Furnco Construction Corp. v. Waters*, 438 U.S. 567 (1978) (preference for known over unknown applicants not discriminatory); *Hazen Paper Co. v. Biggins*, 507 U.S.604 (1993) (firing plaintiff so his pension would not vest was not evidence of age discrimination).

246 On the "pretext" issue, *compare St. Mary's Honor Center v. Hicks*, 509 U.S. 502 (1993) (just because trial court disbelieves the employer's stated non-discriminatory reason does not mean that it must find discrimination) *with Reeves v. Sanderson Plumbing Products, Inc.*, 530 U.S. 133 (2000) (*prima facie* case of discrimination, plus sufficient evidence for a reasonable jury to reject the employer's nondiscriminatory explanation for its decision, is adequate to sustain a finding of liability for intentional discrimination). *See also Ash v. Tyson Foods, Inc.*, 546 U.S. 454 (2006) (pretext rules used by lower court incorrect).

247 *See Grant v. Hazelitt Strip-Casting Corp.*, 880 F.2d 1564 (2d. Cir 1989) (in age discrimination case, employer stated that it sought a "young man . . . between 30 and 40 years old").

248 *Hazelwood School District v. United States*, 433 U.S. 299 (1977) (disparities between actual and expected representation of minorities among teachers).

249 42 U.S.C.A. §2000-e-2(k)(1)(A)(i)-(ii).

successful job performance and both operated to disqualify black applicants at a substantially higher rate than white applicants.[250] Similarly, a ban on hiring all who have arrest records is a violation of Title VII since it disqualifies black applicants at a substantially higher rate than white applicants.[251]

Basing discrimination claims on discriminatory impact under Title VII has improved the chances of state and local government employees recovering for discrimination. Absent Title VII, public employees must rely solely on the equal protection clause, which requires proof of intentional discrimination.[252]

Defenses to Discrimination   Other than seeking to show the non-discriminatory basis for its action, employers may rely on the defense of "bona fide occupational qualification" or BFOQ. BFOQ is narrowly construed. First, a protected group may be excluded from consideration for a job only if the relevant characteristic is closely related to the essence of the employer's business.[253] Thus, in an often-cited case, a court rejected as not a BFOQ an airline's requirement that all airline attendants be women. The airline justified its requirement on the ground that women attendants allayed psychological fears of passengers, but the "essence" of the airline's business was providing safe transportation and this requirement had no relationship to that purpose.[254] Second, a BFOQ is proper only if the employer has a factual basis for concluding that all or substantially all applicants in the protected class lack the qualifications for that position or that it is impracticable to determine which can and which cannot perform the job.[255] This narrow definition of BFOQ has resulted in women obtaining jobs that traditionally have gone only to men because physical requirements effectively excluded women, such as police officer, firefighter and construction worker. The Court invalidated a claim of BFOQ as justifying a ban on fertile women working with lead in a battery plant, finding that they were no less capable of doing the job than anyone else. The Court found insufficient the employer's concern about damage to any fetus present in the woman's body, observing that decisions about the welfare of future children must be left to the parents conceive, bear, support, and raise them rather than to the employers who hire those parents or the courts.[256] On the other hand, the Court upheld as a proper BFOQ a ban on women guards in a men's maximum security prison where

250 *Griggs v. Duke Power Co.*, 401 U.S. 424 (1971). *Compare New York City Transit Authority v. Beazer*, 440 U.S. 568 (1979) (ban on employment of methadone users upheld despite statistics showing greater number of blacks and Hispanics are on the drug; lack of other legitimate requirements, such as education, could account for disparity). *Cf. Los Angeles Department of Water & Power v. Manhart*, 435 U.S. 702 (1978) (even though women live longer than men and therefore their pension costs are greater is no basis for requiring women employees to make larger contributions to its pension fund than men employees).

251 *Gregory v. Litton Systems, Inc.*, 316 F.Supp. 401 (C.D.Cal.1970), *modified*, 472 F.2d 631 (1972).

252 *See* Chapter IX, pp. 351-362. Public employees may nonetheless have to resort to the equal protection clause if Title VII is not available, such as when the claimant has missed the 180 or 300-day limitation period for filing Title VII claims with the EEOC. The remedies are cumulative.

253 Race can never be a BFOQ. Yet, there may be jobs that require persons of a particular race, such as an acting job where racial authenticity is desired. While such a job qualification has been considered to be a "business necessity," recent changes possibly place this in doubt. 42 U.S.C.A. §2000e-2(k)(1)(C)(2) (business necessity cannot be a defense to intentional discrimination).

254 *Diaz v. Pan American Airways, Inc.*, 442 F.2d 385, 388 (5th Cir. 1971) ("While a pleasant environment, enhanced by the obvious cosmetic effect that female stewardesses provide," coupled with their women's apparently greater ability to quiet psychological fears of passengers "may all be important, they are tangential to the essence of the business involved").

255 *See Western Airlines v. Criswell*, 472 U.S. 400 (1984) (in age discrimination case, mandatory retirement of flight engineers at age 60 is not BFOQ). *See also Diaz, supra* note 254.

256 *International Union, United Auto Workers v. Johnson Controls, Inc.*, 499 U.S. 187 (1991).

sexual predators were mixed in with the general population and attacks on women guards would also present a threat to the general order in the prison.[257]

Affirmative Action   The circumstances under which affirmative action plans are constitutional have been discussed.[258] In *United Steelworkers v. Weber*,[259] the Court held that Title VII permits employers to give preferential treatment based on race pursuant to a formal affirmative action plan adopted to remedy a "conspicuous racial imbalance in traditionally segregated job categories." In addition, the plan must be "reasonable" in that it must be a temporary attempt to address imbalance and must not "unduly" interfere with opportunities of white males. This last requirement means at least that no white workers may be fired to remedy an imbalance. Thus, in *Weber* the Supreme Court approved a plan the union and an employer had agreed to, whereby 50% of the persons admitted into an apprenticeship program for skilled trades would be black until the proportion of black skilled trade workers approximated the black population in the area. Similarly, when courts order "affirmative action as may be appropriate" as authorized by Title VII, they must follow the same guidelines.[260]

Sexual Harassment   In *Meritor Savings Bank v. Vinson*, the Supreme Court confirmed that Title VII could be used to redress sexual harassment, since sexual harassment can alter the "terms, conditions or privileges" of employment based on sex.[261] There are two legal theories used: "quid pro quo" and "hostile environment." The *Vinson* case was an example of the former, where giving in to the sexual demands of a supervisor was understood to be a *quid pro quo* for continued employment. In a "hostile environment" situation, usually the victim suffers no economic consequences, but unwelcome sexual advances and other acts of gender animosity or sexually charged work behavior are so "severe or pervasive" that they can be said to have altered the victim's employment conditions. In judging whether there has been such a change, the EEOC and many courts have held that an objective standard of the "reasonable victim," usually a woman, is to be applied. This is primarily because a sex-blind reasonable *person* standard "tends to be male-biased and tends to systematically ignore the experience of women."[262]

The facts of hostile environment cases are various. In one case, the court held insufficient five mild sexual advances by a supervisor.[263] In another, the court deemed insufficient "undoubtedly inappropriate" incidents of a supervisor rubbing the plaintiff's leg, kissing her and, after rejection, refusing to speak with her, teasing her about her relationship with a co-worker and being condescending toward her.[264] A situation deemed sufficient was where a supervisor called plaintiff "honey" and "dear," touched

---

257 *Dothard v. Rawlinson*, 433 U.S. 321 (1977).

258 Chapter IX, pp. 354-355.

259 443 U.S. 193 (1979). *See* Chapter II, p. 56, where the statutory interpretation aspects of the case are discussed.

260 42 U.S.C.A. §2000e(5)(g)(1). *Local 28 of Sheet Metal Workers' Int. Ass'n v. Equal Employment Opp. Comm'n*, 478 U.S. 421 (1986). The same standards discussed here apply to affirmative action based on sex. *Johnson v. Transportation Agency, Santa Clara County*, 480 U.S. 616 (1987).

261 477 U.S. 57 (1986). *See also Harris v. Forklift Systems, Inc.*, 510 U.S. 17 (1993) (no need to show psychological injury). Sexual harassment has been held by some lower courts to constitute a violation of the equal protection clause of the 14th Amendment as well. *See Bohen v. City of East Chicago*, 799 F.2d 1180 (7th Cir. 1986).

262 *Ellison v. Brady*, 924 F.2d 872, 878-79 (9th Cir. 1991).

263 *Chamberlin v. 101 Realty*, 915 F.2d 777, 782-83 (1st Cir. 1990).

264 *Saxton v. AT&T*, 10 F.3d 526, 528, 534 (7th Cir. 1993).

her shoulders, asked her what kind of underwear she wore and what kind of birth control she used, and said that it was his turn to have his way with her.[265] Another case deemed sufficient involved six abusive incidents during three weeks of employment including off-color jokes, comments on complainant's appearance, leaning on or rubbing her back, placing a hand on her shoulder, and calling her at home.[266] Sexual harassment by members of the same sex is also actionable, as the Supreme Court made clear *Oncale v. Sundowner Offshore Services, Inc.*[267] In *Oncale*, the Supreme Court held that a same-sex harassment plaintiff "must always prove that the conduct at issue was not merely tinged with offensive sexual connotations, but actually constituted 'discrimina[tion] . . . because of . . . sex.'"

Complications sometimes arise in attributing sexual harassment by a supervisor or fellow employee to the employer, since such actions could be argued to be actions that are not within the scope of the harassing party's employment. If the employer knows about the harassing action and does nothing, there is no problem with liability. In other cases, a court should consider what steps the employer has taken to prevent and correct promptly any sexually harassing behavior with regard to other employers and whether the plaintiff employee unreasonably failed to take advantage of any such preventive or corrective opportunities provided by the employer.[268]

Procedure A person with a discrimination claim may not file suit immediately, but must first file an administrative complaint with the EEOC and give it or any similar state or local agency the opportunity to investigate.[269] The agency will provide a "right-to-sue" letter if it finds no grounds for the claim or if it finds grounds, but is unable to obtain a settlement of the claim. In addition, permission to sue is granted if 180 days have expired and the claimant wishes to sue. Incredible delays in processing administrative claims have made both the EEOC and most state agencies largely ineffective in gaining administrative compliance, thus leaving enforcement by private suits as the most common avenue of relief. A plaintiff can sue for injunctive relief or for damages.[270] An important provision of the law that serves to make private enforcement a reality is the provision for a successful plaintiff's recovery of attorney fees from the defendant.[271]

Remedies Before 1991, Title VII has provided only for equitable relief, primarily in the form of reinstatement and restitution of back pay lost. However, the 1991 amendments to Title VII provide for the award of compensatory damages against an employer if the plaintiff proves intentional discrimination and for punitive damages if the intentional discriminatory practice was carried out with "with malice or with reckless

---

265 *Beardsley v. Webb*, 30 F.3d 524, 528-29 (4th Cir. 1994).

266 *Canada v. Boyd Group, Inc.*, 809 F.Supp. 771, 776 (D.Nev. 1992).

267 523 U.S. 75 (1998) (plaintiff forcibly subjected to sex-related, humiliating actions against him by co-workers and supervisor in the presence of the rest of the crew and to physical assault in a sexual manner and threat of rape).

268 *Faragher v. City of Boca Raton*, 524 U.S. 775 (1998); *Burlington Industries v. Ellerth*, 524 U.S. 742 (1998). But see *Gebser v. Lago Vista Independent School District*, 524 U.S. 274 (1998) (no liability under different statute for teacher-student sexual relationship unless the school knew of the conduct and responded to it with "deliberate indifference").

269 The time limit for filing is 180 days, unless a charge has been filed with an appropriate state or local agency, in which case it is 300 days.

270 42 U.S.C.A. §2000e-5. An EEOC determination of "no reasonable cause" is not binding on the court in a later suit, but it may be admissible in evidence at trial. *Cf.* FRE 803(8).

271 42 U.S.C.A. §2000e-5(k). Though the statute provides that the "prevailing party" is to be awarded fees, this is read as imposing a double standard, with prevailing *plaintiffs* receiving fees as a matter of course, but prevailing *defendants* receiving fees only if the plaintiff's suit was completely groundless.

indifference to the federally protected rights of an aggrieved individual."[272] This has been interpreted as requiring proof that the employer discriminated "in the face of a perceived risk that its actions will violate federal law." It does not require "egregious conduct."[273] However, the employer will not be liable for the discriminatory employment decisions of its managers where their decisions are contrary to the employer's "good-faith efforts to comply with Title VII."

Pregnancy Discrimination   While Title VII protects against sex discrimination, the Supreme Court held in 1976 that differing treatment based on pregnancy did not constitute sex discrimination. Congress responded by passing the Pregnancy Discrimination Act in 1978, making clear that it considered discrimination on the basis of pregnancy to be sex discrimination.[274] The Supreme Court held in 1983 that differing treatment based on pregnancy compared to other medical conditions is discriminatory.[275]

Equal Pay   The Equal Pay Act requires pay for women to be equal to that earned by men who perform "equal work on jobs the performance of which requires equal skill, effort, and responsibility, and which are performed under similar working conditions" in the same place of employment.[276] Thus, in one case, female guards at a women's prison made out an Equal Pay Act violation when they showed that their retirement benefits were lower than those of male guards at a men's prison.[277]

Age and Disability Discrimination   Age discrimination by private and public employers is prohibited by the 1967 federal Age Discrimination in Employment Act (ADEA) and applies to employees over 40.[278] Compulsory retirement at age 65 is prohibited except for certain executive and "high-level policy making" positions.[279] Discrimination against individuals with physical or mental disabilities is redressed by the Americans with Disabilities Act (ADA), which provides remedies similar to Title VII.[280] Discrimination laws apply outside the U.S. citizens under some circumstances.[281]

4. Rights to Unionize and to Act and Bargain Collectively

Workers' collective action to improve working conditions has progressed from

---

272 Civil Rights Act of 1991, 42 U.S.C.A. §1981(a)(1)-(b)(1).

273 *Kolstad v. American Dental Ass'n.*, 527 U.S. 526 (2001).

274 42 U.S.C.A. §2000e(k).

275 *Newport News Shipbuilding & Dry Dock Co. V. EEOC*, 462 U.S. 669 (1983) (based on Pregnancy Discrimination Act, 42 U.S.C.A §2000e(k)).

276 29 U.S.C.A. §206(d).

277 *Marcoux v. State of Maine*, 797 F.2d 1100 (1st Cir. 1986). The Equal Pay Act clearly overlaps with Title VII, but a plaintiff may wish to use the Equal Pay Act since it does not require administrative exhaustion of remedies and has a 2 or 3-year limitations period rather than 180 days. *See Washington County v. Gunther*, 452 U.S. 161 (1981) (discussing intersection of Title VII and the Equal Pay Act).

278 29 U.S.C.A. §623 *et seq.* Discrimination between those between people aged 40 and 49 in favor of those over 50 is not prohibited by the ADEA, only between those over and under 40. *General Dynamics Land Systems, Inc. v. Cline*, 540 U.S. 581 (2004). Other ADEA cases are cited in notes 247, 245 and 255.

279 29 U.S.C.A. §631(c). Disparate impact claims may be brought under the ADEA. *Smith v. City of Jackson*, 544 U.S. 228 (2005). *See also Meacham v. Knolls Atomic Power Laboratory*, 554 U.S. 84, 128 S.Ct. 2395 (2008) (employer bears burden of proving employment action based on "reasonable factors other than age"). State age discrimination laws may provide for discriminatory impact claims. *See* Cal. Gov. Code §12941 ("the use of salary as the basis for differentiating between employees when terminating employment may be found to constitute age discrimination if use of that criterion adversely impacts older workers as a group.").

280 42 U.S.C.A. §12111 *et seq. See Bragdon v. Abbott*, 524 U.S. 624 (1998) (dentist who refused to treat patient with HIV cannot refuse in absence of medical evidence of harm).

281 29 U.S.C.A. §623(h) (age); 42 U.S.C.A. §2000e-1(c) (Title VII). *See* Chapter XVII, p. 705.

criminal conspiracy to a federal statutory right.[282] In 1935, Congress passed the National Labor Relations Act (NLRA), which guaranteed the right of employees — at least employees of private companies — "to form, join or assist labor unions, to bargain collectively" and "to engage in other concerted activities for the purpose of collective bargaining or other mutual aid and protection."[283] The NLRA also created the National Labor Relations Board (NLRB), a five-member federal agency that supervises and enforces the NLRA. The NLRB is one of the "independent" administrative agencies discussed in Chapter VI. Its five members are appointed by the President and confirmed by the Senate for overlapping 5-year terms. The NLRB tends to be more "political" than most independent agencies, with Republican members tending to side with employer's and Democratic members inclined to side with unions. The result has been several reversals and modifications of policy, especially in the area of unfair labor practices. Clarity and stability of the law are further hindered by the fact that the NLRB generally makes policy through case-by-case adjudication rather than by regulation.[284]

Workers Covered Private employers whose activities affect interstate commerce are the principal group regulated by the NLRA. The NLRA applies to employees, other than supervisors and managers, and not to independent contractors.[285] Employees of railroads and airlines are governed by the somewhat different provisions of the Railway Labor Act.[286] Public sector workers (employees of federal, state and local governments and agencies) are not covered by the NLRA, except for federal postal workers. Agricultural workers are outside the protection of the NLRA. Often employees not covered by federal labor laws are covered by similar state laws. California, for example, has an elaborate system governing farm workers.[287]

General Policy Unlike some countries where the *content* of collective bargaining agreements is specified by law or administrative action, U.S. labor laws generally take a "procedural" approach in that they do not dictate the substance of agreements. Instead, they provide the appropriate arena for the union and the employer to "fight it out" with each other using their respective economic weapons, and to come to an agreement if they can.[288]

---

282 *See* DOUGLAS L. LESLIE, LABOR LAW IN A NUTSHELL, 4TH ED. 1-4 (West 2000), citing *Commonwealth v. Pullis* (Philadelphia Mayor's Court 1806) (workers refusing to work except for specified wage and seeking to prevent others from doing so guilty of criminal conspiracy). *See* WILLIAM B. GOULD, A PRIMER ON AMERICAN LABOR LAW, 4TH ED. (M.I.T. Press, Cambridge, Mass. 2004) and ROBERT A. GORMAN & MATTHEW W. FINKIN, HORNBOOK ON LABOR LAW, 2D ED. (West 2004). *See also* LAURA J. COOPER & CATHERINE L. FISK, LABOR LAW STORIES (Foundation 2005) (an in-depth look at the stories behind famous labor law cases).

283 29 U.S.C.A. §§151-168, quoting §157. Federal government employees are covered by the Federal Service Labor-Management Relations Statute (FSLMRS), which provides similar protections. *See* 5 U.S.C.A. §7101 *et seq. See, e.g., Fort Stewart Schools v. Federal Labor Relations Authority*, 495 U.S. 641, (1990) (Army must bargain with school teachers' union formed at school on military facility). State and municipal employees must resort to state labor relations acts and tribunals.

284 *See* Chapter VI, p. 204. Some stability results through the presidential tradition, since Franklin D. Roosevelt, of the President to naming no more than 3 members from his own party to the Board.

285 A case invalidating the NLRB's definition of "supervisor" as used with nurses is *Nat'l Labor Relations Bd. v. Kentucky River Community Care, Inc.*, 532 U.S. 706 (2001).

286 This Act is enforced by a different agency. The reason for having a separate law and bureaucracy for railroad and airline employees is largely one of historical accident.

287 *See* Cal. Labor Code §§1140-1167. Some believe it is superior to the federal NLRA.

288 There is an exception to this rule under which courts may invalidate a provision of a collective bargaining agreement that violates "public policy." However, the exception is narrow indeed. *See, e.g., Eastern Associated Coal Corp. v. United Mine Workers*, 531 U.S. 57 (2000) (there is no public policy against reinstatement of workers who use drugs that would prevent arbitrator from ordering conditional reinstatement of truck driver who was repeat drug user).

a. Union Organizing

When employees want to form a union, they typically must first seek support from a majority of workers in a "bargaining unit" — a group of employees defined by either particular job categories or a particular industry. Employees signal their desire for a union usually by getting other workers to sign authorization cards indicating that they wish to be represented by the union. When 30% of the employees in a bargaining unit have signed such cards, a union election will be set by the NLRB. In such elections, the union organizers will campaign for unionization and the employer often will campaign against the union, but the employer cannot coercively interfere with the union's organizing efforts or the election process.[289] The NLRB oversees elections to ensure that they are fair.[290] If the union obtains cards from a majority of employees, the employer may (but need not) voluntarily recognize the union without the need for an election. But most employers request an election.[291]

Once the union wins recognition from the employer, it becomes the exclusive representative of all workers in its bargaining unit, whether members of the union or not.[292] It will seek to conclude a collective bargaining agreement governing wages and working conditions for its bargaining unit. "Closed shop" agreements, requiring union membership to get a job are illegal.[293] However, the union may and often does negotiate a "union security clause" in the collective bargaining agreement, under which all non-members are required to pay union dues or an amount that represents the portion of union activity related to collective action benefitting all employees in the bargaining unit.[294] If the employer has a "good faith reasonable doubt" that the union continues to enjoy the support of a majority of workers, it may poll employees to find out for sure or it may withdraw recognition or seek a Board-supervised election.[295]

b. Unfair Labor Practices

The NLRB protects fairness during elections and at other times by prohibiting certain unfair labor practices by both employers and unions. For example, an employer is prohibited from interfering with, restraining, or coercing employees in any way in connection with their right to engage in concerted activities, to protect working conditions, and to join labor organizations for the purpose of collective bargaining.[296] Included in this prohibition are threats to close plants, cut pay or withdraw benefits if the union is elected, use of spies or other surveillance of union activities, interrogating employees about their union activities, and threats and promises designed to stop union activity. Similarly, the union may not restrain or coerce workers in the exercise of their right to

---

289 29 U.S.C.A. §158(a)(1).

290 29 U.S.C.A. §§159, 160.

291 *Linden Lumber Division v. Nat'l Labor Relations Bd.*, 419 U.S. 301 (1974).

292 29 U.S.C.A. §159(a).

293 29 U.S.C.A. §§158(a)(3), 158(b)(2).

294 *Nat'l Labor Relations Bd. v. General Motors*, 373 U.S. 734 (1963). Disputes arise over how much is attributable to these activities. *See Airline Pilots Ass'n. v. Miller*, 523 U.S. 866 (1998).

295 *See generally Allentown Mack Sales & Service, Inc. v. Nat'l Labor Relations Bd.*, 522 U.S. 359 (1998) (discussing the standards and sufficiency of evidence of "reasonable doubt").

296 29 U.S.C.A. §158(a). In cases of alleged discrimination against workers for union activities, the Supreme Court has held that, once it has been shown that union membership was a substantial factor in the employer action, the burden of proof shifts to the employer to prove non-discriminatory motivation. Where there are mixed motives, the employer must show that the same result would have occurred in absence of anti-union animus. *Nat'l Labor Relations Bd. v. Transportation Management Corp.*, 462 U.S. 393 (1983). This is similar to the standard used in employment discrimination cases. *See infra* p. 621.

oppose the union or other rights protected by the statute.[297]

The procedure for handling alleged unfair labor practices usually begins with the union, employee or employer filing a charge with the NLRB. If the NLRB issues a complaint, there is a hearing before an administrative law judge (ALJ) that is prosecuted by lawyers from the NLRB General Counsel's office.[298] If a party disagrees with the ALJ's decision, there will be a hearing before the NLRB. However, that hearing will be on the record made before the ALJ. Although the NLRB hearing sounds similar to appellate court review of a trial court, there is rarely any oral argument and the NLRB is not bound by ALJ fact-finding. After the NLRB decision is rendered, the Board can apply to the U.S. Court of Appeals for enforcement of its decision or the losing party can obtain judicial review in the same court.[299] The complaint process is long and involved and unions often complain that this has made the NLRB largely ineffective in protecting the rights of unions and their members.[300]

c. Protected Action for Other Mutual Aid and Protection

The NLRA protects some rights not connected with union organizing and elections — activities engaged in "for *other* mutual aid and protection." Thus, an individual employee's conduct may be protected if it constitutes "concerted" activity, *i.e.*, activity undertaken by two or more employees or by one employee on behalf of others. In *Nat'l Labor Relations Bd. v. Washington Aluminum Co.*,[301] for example, the Court held that the NLRA protected activity of seven non-union employees who left work to protest cold temperatures in their shop. In another case, discussions by employees of non-payment of the full amount of a "safety bonus" were protected.[302] If the concerted activity is protected, then the employer's action constitutes an unfair labor practice that can be redressed before the NLRB. Employee action is also considered "concerted" if it is an effort to enforce an existing collective bargaining agreement.[303] However, employees can forfeit protections for concerted activity that if their conduct goes too far.[304]

d. Collective Bargaining

Both the employer and union are obliged to "bargain in good faith." While good faith *bargaining* is mandatory, agreement is not, and it is a difficult question whether a party who insists that particular terms be in the contract is bargaining in good faith.[305] The good faith bargaining requirement applies to mandatory subjects of bargaining — wages and conditions of work, including issues of layoffs, vacation and sick leave, and

---

297 29 U.S.C.A. §158(b)(1).

298 Federal ALJs and administrative hearings were discussed in Chapter VI, pp. 202-204.

299 29 U.S.C.A. §160(e), (f).

300 Many blame the Board for undermining union and employee rights in recent years, but others see the problem to be hostile court interpretations of the NLRA. *See* ELLEN DANNIN, TAKING BACK THE WORKERS' LAW (ILR Press 2008) (proposing a plan to obtain reversal of such decisions).

301 370 U.S. 9 (1962).

302 *Bowling Transp., Inc. v. Nat'l Labor Relations Bd.*, 352 F.3d 274 (6th Cir. 2003).

303 *Nat'l Labor Relations Bd. v. City Disposal Systems*, 465 U.S. 822 (1984) (refusal to drive a truck with defective brakes concerted activity because collective bargaining agreement stated employer could not require employees to operate any unsafe vehicle).

304 *See St. Luke's Hospital v. Nat'l Labor Relations Bd.*, 268 F.3d 575 (8th Cir. 2001) (nurse's statement on television show that employer had jeopardized the health of mothers and babies in switching shifts and duties of nurses not protected).

305 *Compare Nat'l Labor Relations Bd. v. American National Insurance Co.*, 343 U.S. 395 (1952) (insistence on broad "management functions" clause is still good faith) *with Nat'l Labor Relations Bd. v. Reed & Prince Mfg. Co.*, 205 F.2d 131 (1st Cir. 1953) (refusal of management to find any common ground with union proposals and insistence on management discretion on every issue held not good faith).

fringe benefits. Other non-mandatory subjects that have only an indirect effect on worker life may be the subject of bargaining. However, some decisions of management are not mandatory bargaining issues even though there is clearly a direct impact on workers. For example, it is completely up to management whether the plant will start making a new product. Plant closings that result in layoffs have also been held to be management decisions on the basic scope and direction of the entire enterprise not subject to mandatory bargaining.[306] On the other hand, if an employer decides to subcontract out work previously done by union employees and the subcontractor will perform that work under similar employment conditions, such a management decision has been held to be subject to mandatory bargaining.[307] It is widely assumed that loss of jobs through automation is a managerial decision not subject to bargaining.

e. Strikes, Boycotts and Other Tactics

The good faith bargaining requirement does not suspend the use of actions designed to bring economic pressure to bear on the other side.[308] The union's right to strike is protected by the NLRA and employees may not be discharged or disciplined for engaging in such conduct.[309] However, despite the NLRA's protection of the right to strike, courts have held that employers have the right to replace the striking workers and go on with business if possible.[310] Thus, the Court has drawn the line between discharge, which is not permitted, and replacement, which is. The right to replace exists only for economic strikes (wages, working conditions, etc.), not if the strike is to protest an unfair labor practice.[311] Sit-down strikes (when employees refuse to work, but stay at their work stations) are not protected and may violate state criminal trespass laws, thus making participating workers subject to discharge by the employer or arrest by the local police.[312]

"Secondary boycotts," where workers' activities go beyond the "primary employer" to reach companies that do business with the primary employer, are prohibited. However, action against the second business is permissible if it is working as an "ally" of the first by, for example, allowing a manufacturing step to be performed on its premises.[313] Similarly, the primary employer is not immune from union appeals to secondary workers who come to the work site of the struck employer if they do work that is "related" to that done by the strikers.[314] "Hot cargo" agreements, in which

---

306 *First National Maintenance Co. v. Nat'l Labor Relations Bd.*, 452 U.S. 666 (1981) (company closed division). The union may be entitled to 60-days notice under another law, 29 U.S.C.A. §2101. Moreover, the *effects* of a plant closing on workers is a mandatory bargaining subject, such as issues of the order of layoffs, rights to transfer to other divisions or plants, and the like.

307 *Fibreboard Paper Products v. Nat'l Labor Relations Bd.*, 379 U.S. 203 (1964).

308 *Nat'l Labor Relations Bd. v. Insurance Agents' Int'l Union*, 361 U.S. 477 (1960) (employee slow-down designed as a general "irritant" rather than a promoter of dialogue was not unfair labor practice).

309 29 U.S.C.A. §158(a)(3).

310 *Nat'l Labor Relations Bd. v. Mackay Radio and Telegraph Co.*, 304 U.S. 333 (1938). Overruling the *Mackay* doctrine has been a major legislative agenda item for organized labor for some time.

311 *See Mastro Plastics v. Nat'l Labor Relations Bd.*, 350 U.S. 270 (1956). The distinction between being fired and being replaced is one that is lost on many workers. The difference is that replaced strikers retain the right to be called back to work if positions become available.

312 *Nat'l Labor Relations Bd. v. Fansteel Metallurgical Corp.*, 306 U.S. 240 (1939).

313 *See Nat'l Labor Relations Bd. v. Office Appliances Conference Bd. (Royal Typewriter)*, 228 F.2d 553 (2d Cir. 1955) (picketing of typewriter repair facility performing repairs for struck employer permitted).

314 *Local 761, International Union of Electrical Workers v. Nat'l Labor Relations Bd. (General Electric)*, 366 U.S. 667 (1961) (striking picketers could appeal to maintenance and other workers not to work when they arrived at primary employer's plant).

employers agree with unions not to deal with non-union companies, are illegal secondary boycotts.[315] It is proper for unions to appeal to consumers not to purchase a secondary employer's products as a show of support. However, false statements and public disparagement of the employer's product or services unrelated to the labor dispute are routinely considered unprotected by the courts.[316]

On the employer side, the passage of time without a paycheck during a strike is probably the most potent economic weapon against employees. In addition, the employer can hasten this by imposing a lockout (refusing to permit employees to enter the premises to work), either as a means of exerting economic pressure on workers or as a preemptive device in anticipation of a union strike or other tactic. So long as the use of the lockout is not so hostile to the union's interest in organizing and bargaining as to "destroy or frustrate the process of collective bargaining," the lockout is legal.[317]

From all this it is clear that the effectiveness of a strike or threat of a strike will vary depending on many factors, including the state of the economy and willingness of other workers to support the union's position. In recent bad economic times, workers' need for a job has made strikes less attractive as a weapon. When strikes do occur, replacement has been a successful technique for counteracting them. Replacement was used successfully in the 1990 New York Daily News strike and the 1992 Caterpillar Tractor Company strike, though in the Caterpillar case the replacement workers were not hired permanently. Thus, in recent years, employers have been in a better position than the union to wait out an impasse in bargaining. On the other hand, lower unemployment rates and a generally better economy made the 1997 strike against United Parcel Service a notable success for the union involved.

Regardless of who wins when there is a strike or a lockout, such disputes are costly in both economic and human terms. For this reason, some commentators have argued for mandatory arbitration when voluntary agreement is not possible, but that would require a major change in the law which Congress has been unwilling to make. The percentage of U.S. workers in private industry covered by collective bargaining agreements has declined substantially in recent years. It has gone from 33.2% in 1955 to 12.5% in 2006.[318] This decrease may be due in part to more conservative attitudes among workers in recent years and a perceived lesser need for the protection a union affords. But most of the change is the result of the fact that substantial portions of three of the most heavily unionized industries in the U.S. — steel, automobile and basic manufacturing — have essentially left the U.S. and moved overseas.

f. Disputes Under the Collective Bargaining Agreement

Collective bargaining agreements are governed by federal common law, the Court having concluded that Congress delegated to courts the power to develop a federal

---

315 29 U.S.C.A. §158(e). In a rarely used provision of the law, the President is given special powers to end a strike in a national emergency, including the right to seek an injunction. However, presidential intervention in strikes has almost always been informal efforts to talk or "jaw-bone" the parties into ironing out their differences.

316 *Nat'l Labor Relations Bd. v. Local Union No. 1229, IBEW*, 346 U.S. 464 (1958) ("vitriolic attack on the quality of the company's television broadcasts" not protected). *See also Nat'l Labor Relations Bd. v. Thor Power Tool Co.*, 351 F.2d 584 (7th Cir. 1965) (leeway for "impulsive behavior" must be "balanced against the employer's right to maintain order and respect").

317 *American Shipbuilding Co. v. Nat'l Labor Relations Bd.*, 380 U.S. 300 (1965).

318 Bureau of Labor Statistics News (Jan. 20, 2006). Public employees have a higher rate of unionization (36.5%) — teachers, firefighters and police are the most heavily unionized — but the number of public employees in the U.S. is small.

common law of labor contracts.[319] However, most disputes about the interpretation of collective bargaining agreements do not get to the courts since the parties usually agree to some form of arbitration for all disputes arising under the agreement. These disputes, called "grievances," are then decided by the private arbitrator, whose decision is final. Courts may disturb a grievance arbitration decision only in limited circumstances.[320] Workers, the union and the employer can file grievances, though employer grievances are rare. The union may dispute such things as the meaning of a "no-strike" clause or whether the employer can contract out work. The union may seek relief for an individual worker and "grieve" such things as the proper calculation of seniority rights or severance or vacation pay for a particular worker.[321]

Courts will intervene to order arbitration if the employer or union has ignored the required grievance procedure. This issue arises often with "no-strike" clauses, where the union goes out on strike even though it has given up its right to strike and has agreed to arbitrate disagreements. A seeming obstacle to injunctions against strikes is the Norris-LaGuardia Act of 1932, which prohibits federal courts from enjoining any strike.[322] However, the Supreme Court held that the anti-injunction provision had to be accommodated to the federal labor policy of encouraging arbitration of disputes, so it read the applicable statutes as allowing injunctions against strikes that violate no-strike clauses.[323] Thus, the employer can properly seek to enjoin strikes in breach of the agreement and seek appropriate damages from the union. Consistent with this reasoning, if the strike is over an issue that is not arbitrable (such as a sympathy strike), the Norris-LaGuardia Act applies and injunctive relief is *not* available.[324] A recent illustration of a strike still within the Norris-LaGuardia prohibition on injunctions was the refusal of longshoremen working on a dock to handle cargo from the Soviet Union in protest of its military intervention in Afghanistan. This kind of work stoppage was not arbitrable under the collective bargaining agreement, so it could not be enjoined.[325]

g. The Union's Duty of Fair Representation

The union has a "duty of fair representation" requiring it to represent the interests of all the bargaining unit's employees (both members and non-members), both in collective bargaining and in pursuing grievances under any collective bargaining agreement it concludes. For breach of this duty the union may be sued for damages. Generally, the union has considerable discretion in fulfilling its bargaining duties, and can pick and choose among issues it will assert. However, racially motivated union bargaining for less favorable treatment for minority members constitutes a breach of the

---

319 *Textile Workers Union v. Lincoln Mills*, 353 U.S. 448 (1957); *Local 174, Teamsters v. Lucas Flour Co.*, 369 U.S. 95 (1962). For a discussion of the ordinarily limited nature of federal common law, *see* Chapter I, pp. 35-36. State courts have concurrent jurisdiction and must apply federal common law, *Charles Dowd Box Co. v. Courtney*, 368 U.S. 502 (1962), and the defendant may remove such a case to federal court because it involves an issue of federal law. *Avco Corp. v. Aero Lodge*, 390 U.S. 557 (1968).

320 *See United Paperworkers International Union v. Misco, Inc.*, 484 U.S. 29 (1987) (absent fraud by the parties or the arbitrator's dishonesty, courts cannot reconsider the merits of the award; reinstatement of employee who used drugs affirmed). Arbitration was discussed in Chapter VII, p. 252.

321 Employment discrimination claims are not subject to an arbitration requirement unless there is a clear and unmistakable waiver of the covered employees' rights to a judicial forum" in the collective bargaining agreement. *Wright v. Universal Maritime Service Corp.*, 525 U.S. 70 (1998).

322 28 U.S.C.A. §104.

323 *Boys Markets, Inc. v. Retail Clerks Local 770*, 398 U.S. 235 (1970).

324 *Buffalo Forge Co. v. United Steelworkers*, 428 U.S. 397 (1976).

325 *Jacksonville Bulk Terminals v. International Longshoremen's Union*, 457 U.S. 702 (1982).

duty of fair representation.[326] As for its duty with regard to presenting grievances of its members, the Court has held that the union has some discretion and may refuse to pursue some grievances. However, it may not do so arbitrarily or based on personal animus or other bad faith reason.[327] The union must pursue competently those grievances it does choose to take.

F. Environmental Law

Scope of Environmental Law Prior to the 1960s, industry operated without much regard for the detrimental effects on the environment. This changed in the 1970s.[328] Congress responded to the newfound public concern with new and ambitious legislation on air pollution, water pollution, toxic chemicals, contaminated drinking water, pesticides, hazardous waste, the environmental impact of actions of federal government agencies and protection of endangered species. Most of the efforts to control pollution are aimed at industry and, even where environmental laws focus on the actions of federal agencies, that action commonly concerns the agency's issuance of a permit for private business development or activities. Additionally, laws on endangered species have direct application to private business development on private lands when those lands are part of the critical habitat of a listed threatened or endangered species. Consequently, it is appropriate to address the topic of environmental law in this chapter on business law.

The Environmental Protection Agency Administration and enforcement of environmental laws are the responsibility of the Environmental Protection Agency. The EPA is an independent agency within the executive branch.[329] It was created by Executive Order in 1970 and assigned responsibility for administering environmental laws, previously allocated among the Departments of Agriculture, the Interior and Health Education and Welfare. With a budget of more than $5 billion and 15,000 employees, the EPA is among the largest of federal administrative agencies. The EPA promulgates rules and the enforces the law like other agencies, but it also engages in research. Various bills, popular among environmentalists, have been introduced to elevate the agency to cabinet rank, but to date they have not been successful.

Sources of Environmental Law As suggested by the above, the federal government and federal law have been in the forefront of environmental protection. However, state law is becoming an increasingly important source of environmental law.[330] But on both the federal and state levels, the fundamental debate in environmental law has focused on the trade off between economic growth and environmental protection. Recent conservative trends in the Congress, presidential administrations and the country in general have led to concerns that environmental regulation is retarding business growth and limiting the ability of U.S. industries to 0compete in the international marketplace. The result has been a trend both with the EPA and the states to work with industry rather

---

326 *Steele v. Louisville & Nashville Ry.*, 323 U.S. 192 (1944).

327 *Vaca v. Sipes*, 386 U.S. 171 (1967) (union could decline to press grievance of employee denied the right to return to work for medical reasons where employee's medical evidence was not strong).

328 For more detail, *see* WILLIAM H. RODGERS, JR., ENVIRONMENTAL LAW, 2D ED. (West 1994, 1998); JAMES SALZMAN & BARTON H. THOMPSON, JR., ENVIRONMENTAL LAW AND POLICY (Foundation 2003); JOHN S. APPLEGATE & JAN G. LAITOS, RCRA, CERCLA, AND THE MANAGEMENT OF HAZARDOUS WASTE (Foundation 2006); SELECTED ENVIRONMENTAL LAW STATUTES (Foundation 2005). *See also* OLIVER A. HOUCK & RICHARD J. LAZARUS, ENVIRONMENTAL LAW STORIES (Foundation 2006) (stories behind famous environmental law cases).

329 The distinction between executive and independent agencies is discussed in Chapter I, p. 16.

330 *See infra* p. 638.

than to enforce against it. This has led to a greater number of citizen suits.

1. Pesticides and Other Toxic Substances

The federal environmental market access statute dealing with pesticides is the Federal Insecticide, Fungicide, and Rodenticide Act (FIFRA).[331] The federal statute dealing with other toxics is the Toxic Substance Control Act (ToSCA).[332] FIFRA requires any person distributing, selling, offering, or receiving any pesticide to register the poison with the EPA. Assuming proper labeling and effectiveness of a poison, the EPA will permit its use once it determines that the pesticide will perform its functions without "unreasonable risks to humans and the environment, taking into account the economic, social, and environmental costs and benefits of the pesticides' intended use." FIFRA then imposes official "tolerance levels" — the maximum permissible exposure. Once granted, registrations serve as licenses to market the product. Registrations can be canceled or suspended. A requirement in the statute that the government compensate the manufacturer for all existing supplies of materials that could no longer be marketed was recently repealed. FIFRA does not preempt remedies available under state law for recovery of damages for harm caused by application of a federally registered pesticide.[333]

ToSCA is directed at the chemical manufacturing industry. It is designed to insure testing by manufacturers to identify hazards to human health and the environment associated with chemical substances before they are permitted to be manufactured and sold. The EPA may require testing and disclosure of test results to the government. If the test results are adverse, the EPA may forbid or limit the uses made of a chemical substance. ToSCA also regulates PCB and asbestos hazards and establishes national goals for indoor radon abatement, while offering states technical and other assistance.

2. Air Pollution

The Clean Air Act (CAA), with certain important exceptions, relies heavily on a "command and control" approach in which regulators make technological judgments and determine standards and then enforce them.[334] The EPA is to determine National Ambient Air Quality Standards (NAAQSs) "requisite to protect the public health" with "an adequate margin of safety."[335] This approach allows some pollution to occur. The political and scientific challenge lies in determining the amount of emissions that can be safely assimilated. However, "economic considerations [may] play no part in the promulgation of ambient air quality standards."[336]

Under the CAA, the EPA has authority to develop and administer an air pollution control plan for each state that has failed to adopt an adequate plan of its own.[337] Adequacy of the plans, termed State Implementation Plans (SIPs), depends upon

---

331 7 U.S.C.A. §§136-136y.

332 15 U.S.C.A. §§2601-2671.

333 *Bates v. Dow Agrosciences* LLC, 544 U.S. 431 (2005) (peanut farmers could sue for damage to crops when pesticides stunted growth in soil with high pH levels). *See also* Chapter I, 31 (preemption doctrine).

334 42 U.S.C.A. §§7401-7671q.

335 42 U.S.C.A. §7409(b)(1).

336 *Whitman v. American Trucking Assn., Inc.*, 531 U.S. 457 (2001), quoting *Lead Industries Ass'n., Inc. v. Environmental Protection Agency*, 647 F.2d 1130, 1148 (DC Cir. 1980). *American Trucking* also rejected arguments that Congress had improperly delegated legislative power to the EPA because the quoted language for the NAAQS standard was too vague. *See* Chapter VI, p. 219 (law of delegation).

337 Prior to the extensive 1970 amendments, the CAA had relied almost exclusively on voluntary state efforts to control air pollution, which had not been effective. Part of the problem with state control of air quality was competition among the states to attract industry.

meeting the federally set NAAQSs. These standards set limits on the concentration of certain pollutants allowed in the air for 247 "air quality control regions" and are updated every 5 years. The NAAQSs were intended to reduce pollution to acceptable levels, *i.e.*, levels that do not endanger human health.[338] Clearly, the decision about what to consider a pollutant is an important one and the courts have not hesitated to order the EPA to add an element that has been shown to have a negative impact on health.[339] However, less searching review has been accorded the question of how to determine compliance with NAAQSs. Averaging exposure to pollutants and determining the period over which it should be done are issues that have been left to agency discretion.[340]

In addition to the SIP provisions, the CAA establishes a program to prevent significant deterioration of air quality where the air is clean, such as in wilderness and other pristine areas, including state and national parks.[341] The CAA also sets strict auto exhaust pipe emission standards for cars and trucks. By most accounts, the CAA has improved air quality in the United States considerably over the last 30 years. This resulted primarily from a 90% reduction in lead by phasing out leaded gasoline, but also from significant reductions in sulfur dioxide and carbon monoxide. Ozone is the most pervasive continuing problem, an important component of the "smog" that hovers over large cities and which has become a particularly serious problem in Los Angeles.[342]

There was some doubt whether the EPA has the authority to regulate so-called greenhouse gases from new motor vehicles as "air pollutants" under the Act, since it is the Department of Transportation that has authority over motor vehicle emissions. However, that question was resolved in favor of its power to do so. Indeed, the Supreme Court observed that "[u]nder the clear terms of the Clean Air Act, EPA can avoid taking further action only if it determines that greenhouse gases do not contribute to climate change or if it provides some reasonable explanation as to why it cannot or will not exercise its discretion to determine whether they do."[343] EPA regulation is pending and it has caused somewhat of a political firestorm. As of yet, there has been no congressional action to amend the Clean Air Act, though funding cuts have been threatened.

3. Water Pollution

Regulation of the discharge of pollutants into water is handled under the Federal Water Pollution Control Act, commonly referred to as the Clean Water Act (CWA), enacted in 1972. The CWA set as its goal achieving "fishable and swimable" waters by 1983. This deadline has been extended several times, but the struggle, in the words of the Act, "to restore and maintain the chemical, physical, and biological integrity of the nation's waters," continues.[344] Less success has been achieved than with air quality.

NPDES Under the CWA, the EPA sets technology-based effluent limitations by

---

338 42 U.S.C.A. §§7408-7409.

339 *Natural Resources Defense Council v. Train*, 545 F.2d 320 (2d Cir 1976) (lead must be included).

340 *American Petroleum Institute v. Costle*, 665 F.2d 1176 (D.C.Cir. 1981) (ozone exposure).

341 42 U.S.C.A. §§7470-7491. *See, e.g., Alaska Dept. of Environmental Conservation v. E.P.A.*, 540 U.S. 461 (2004) (upholding EPA authority to enforce this provision by ordering a halt to construction when state agency certification of best available control technology was unreasonable).

342 While the Clean Air Act has been at the forefront dealing with pollution, it preempts conflicting state standards, even if they are stricter than federal standards. *Engine Mfrs. Ass'n v. South Coast Air Quality Management Dist.*, 541 U.S. 246 (2004) (Los Angeles district rules banning sales of fleet vehicles that do not meet state standards held preempted; fact "sales" are regulated does not avoid preemption).

343 *Massachusetts v. Environmental Protection Agency*, 549 U.S. 497, 532 (2007).

344 33 U.S.C.A. §§1251 *et seq.*

category of industry, determined by the type of products manufactured, and by subcategories based on processes or raw materials utilized in producing the products. This forms the basis for a permit system, the National Pollutant Discharge Elimination System (NPDES), implemented by the states with EPA approved NPDES programs or by the EPA itself. Such permits limit effluents and set out other standards, terms and conditions, as well as numerical discharge limitations. The EPA is to incorporate into the permits increasingly strict effluent limitations. Dischargers must use the "best practicable control technology currently available" (BPCT) within an industry. EPA limitations must, for toxic pollutants, be the "best available technology economically achievable" (BAT) and, for discharge of conventional pollutants, represent the "best conventional pollution control technology" (BCT).[345]

New pollution sources in an industry must meet a separate set of standards, called "new-source performance standards."[346] These standards limit the discharge of pollutants from new sources based on the "best available demonstrated control technology" (BDT). Finally, the EPA is authorized to establish "best management practices" (BMPs) to control plant site runoff, spillage or leaks, sludge or waste disposal, and drainage from raw material storage, in order to diminish the amount of toxic pollutants flowing into receiving waters.

Permit applicants are required to test any discharge into water for toxics and other substances and to report its composition and the amount of pollutants present. The permit application will be considered in light of two primary factors. First, the state or the EPA will consider the pollution control technology used by the applicant. The applicant may be required to use either BAT, BCT or BDT depending on the nature of the pollutants discharged. Second, the pollution control authority is concerned with the quality of the water receiving the effluent. States must establish water quality standards for all bodies of water. Generally, an applicant must demonstrate, not only the effectiveness of the pollution control devices, but also that discharge will not cause the receiving body of water to fall below the established water quality standards.[347] "Discharge" is read broadly. In *S.D. Warren Co. v. Maine Bd. of Environmental Protection*,[348] it was argued that water that was merely impounded by a dam did not qualify as a "discharge" for which a permit was necessary. The Court disagreed, holding that Congress intended to "restore and maintain the chemical, physical, and biological integrity of the Nation's waters," including protecting minimum stream flow as established by a state's regulatory authority.

The issuance of an NPDES permit is preceded by public notice and an opportunity for the public to comment on whether the permit should be issued. The EPA retains considerable control over the state NPDES programs and can veto state permit approvals.[349]

Enforcement The enforcement provisions under the CWA are civil, administrative, and criminal. Civil penalties range up to $10,000 per day per violation. In 1987, the CWA

---

345 33 U.S.C.A. §1311.

346 33 U.S.C.A. §1316.

347 33 U.S.C.A. §1313.

348 547 U.S. 370 (2006).

349 In what may be a sign of things to come, the Court recently struck down a regulation broadly defining the scope of the CWA in part because it approached the limits of the Court's new view of Congress's power under the interstate commerce clause. *See Solid Waste Agency of Northern Cook County v. United States Army Corps of Engineers*, 531 U.S. 159 (2001).

was amended to add criminal penalties for any person who "knowingly" violates the Act and "who knows at the time that he thereby places another person in imminent danger of death or serious bodily injury." Criminal penalties range from $2500 to $25,000 per day per violation for first offenders, plus imprisonment up to one year. Habitual criminal offenders may be subject to fines of $50,000 per day of violation and/or imprisonment for not more than two years.[350] In addition, a water polluter faces requirements that it purchase and implement pollution control technology needed to bring it within the regulatory standards. In a recent case against a steelmaker, the EPA levied the largest penalty ever under the CWA.[351] The steel company was convicted of discharging pollutants, including cyanide and ammonia, into the Ohio River in violation of its NPDES permit. The company entered into a consent decree with the EPA in which it agreed to pay $6 million in penalties and also to spend $24 million on pollution control projects.

Intent requirements under the CWA have been relaxed to permit liability even where it could not be proven that the polluter knew precisely the nature of the duties imposed by the CWA or the dangers posed by the particular dumping.[352] However, other limitations have created difficulties. In one 1990 case, a federal court convicted a corporation and its president of intentionally discharging nickel plating waste and nitric acid into a public sewer system. The president, who personally participated in the dumping, faced a maximum 15-year sentence and a $500,000 fine, and the corporation could have been fined up to $2 million. However, the Court of Appeals reversed because the only people endangered by the dumping were the 12 plant employees who were ordered to dump the chemicals, noting that a CWA conviction cannot be premised upon danger that occurs before pollutant reaches publicly owned sewer or treatment works.[353]

4. Cleanups of Sites Contaminated with Toxic Substances

The Comprehensive Environmental Response, Compensation and Liability Act (CERCLA) of 1980[354] is a statutory system for managing and funding environmental cleanups of sites contaminated with hazardous substances. CERCLA was enacted in large part in response to the chemical waste disaster at Love Canal, New York. Hooker Chemical, a major corporation, had buried thousands of drums of industrial solvents under land surrounding its manufacturing facility and later sold parcels of the land for residential purposes. Reports of children becoming seriously ill from playing in their own backyards helped emphasize the urgent need for government-regulated hazardous waste disposal and cleanup programs.

The "Superfund" At the center of the statutory scheme established by CERCLA is the "Superfund," the source of money for cleanups. The Superfund currently obtains its money from a surtax assessed against large companies with incomes of over $2 million per year and from taxes on petroleum and chemical feedstocks. These sums are supplemented by a relatively small amount of general revenue money and money

---

350 33 U.S.C.A. §1319(c), §1321(b)(5).

351 *United States v. Wheeling-Pittsburgh*, 1991 WL 157355 (S.D. Ohio, May 15, 1990).

352 *United States v. Wilson*, 133 F.3d 251, 264-265 (4th Cir. 1997) (discussing CWA scienter requirements). Several lower courts have concluded that the CWA violations are public welfare offenses, which do not require proof of intent at least where the pollutants involved were inherently deleterious. See, *e.g.*, *United States v. Sinskey*, 119 F.3d 712, 716 (8th Cir. 1997) (meat packing plant waste water containing large amounts of ammonia nitrate). *See* Chapter XIV, p. 554, where the public welfare exception to *mens rea* is discussed.

353 *United States v. Borowski*, 977 F.2d 27 (1st Cir. 1992).

354 42 U.S.C.A. §§9601 *et seq.*

recovered from potentially responsible parties (called PRPs). PRPs may be individuals, including corporate officers and directors, or corporations involved in the disposing, arranging for disposing or transporting hazardous waste.[355] Liability of PRPs under CERCLA was intended by Congress to be retroactive and such application has been upheld in the face of constitutional attack.[356]

CERCLA provides a procedure for identifying and ranking the hazards posed by sites of hazardous materials contamination. On the basis of that hazard ranking system, the statute establishes a national priorities list (NPL) that then functions to ensure that the most dangerous sites are remediated first. When CERCLA was first enacted, many thought there would be only a few sites that merited attention. But by 1989, over 30,000 sites had been identified and there are now 1,305 sites on the NPL. About 11 million people in the U.S., including 3-4 million children, live within 1 mile of a federal Superfund site and confront potential public health risks. The average cost of the cleanup of an NPL site is around $25 million.[357]

CERCLA also requires that owners or operators of contaminated facilities notify the EPA of any release of any hazardous substances.[358] When there is contamination or a threat of contamination, the EPA can act to prevent further damage and to perform the cleanup, in which case it can obtain reimbursement for such costs from PRPs, or PRPs can perform the cleanup under EPA supervision.[359] PRPs and others who pay for or themselves clean up contaminated sites have the right to seek contribution from other responsible persons.[360] Liability under CERCLA is strict and the only defenses are Act of God, acts of war, and certain actions or omissions by third parties.[361] If there is "an imminent and substantial endangerment to the public health or welfare or the environment," the EPA can order PRPs to undertake cleanup action and enforce such an order in court.[362]

CERCLA Policy The purpose of CERCLA is to place the responsibility for environmental cleanup on PRPs. Such a policy has the appeal of fairness and it is also thought to encourage voluntary cleanup action and to assist in recovering tax dollars spent on cleanups. The problems with carrying out this policy have been the surprising magnitude of the hazardous waste contamination problem in the country and the difficulties of finding financially solvent PRPs to pay into the Superfund.[363] For example, of the Superfund money spent so far on cleanups, only 9% of it has come from PRPs. However, PRPs performing cleanups under EPA supervision account for a substantial percentage of sites currently being remediated — annually approximately 50 out of 90.

---

355 42 U.S.C.A. §9607(a).

356 *In re Penn Central*, 944 F.2d 164, 165 (3d Cir. 1991).

357 For more information, *see* www.scorecard.org/env-releases/def/land_npl.html.

358 42 U.S.C.A. §9603(a), (c).

359 42 U.S.C.A. §9604(a)(1).

360 42 U.S.C.A. § 9613(f)(1). *But see Cooper Industries, Inc. v. Aviall Services, Inc.*, 543 U.S. 157 (2004) (buyer of an aircraft repair business who voluntarily cleaned up sites purchased cannot sue seller for contribution unless the cleanup was the result of a suit against buyer, thus providing lessening incentives for voluntary cleanups by PRPs).

361 42 U.S.C.A. §9607(b). *See* Elizabeth Glass, *Superfund and SARA: Are There Any Defenses Left?*, 12 HARV. ENVTL. L.REV. 385 (1988). "Act of God" means natural disasters, sometimes called *force majeure*.

362 42 U.S.C.A. §9604(a).

363 A Management Review of the Superfund Program (EPA). Solvency of PRPs is a question in so many cases that issues of PRPs' obligations are often determined in bankruptcy court. *See* HEIDT, ENVIRONMENTAL OBLIGATIONS IN BANKRUPTCY (West 2004, 2006).

A hotly disputed issue in the Superfund program is selection of the means of remediation. Many PRP groups argue that cost must be a major factor in deciding on an appropriate remedy and note that CERCLA requires "cost-effective" remedies.[364] However, the EPA's position is that cost may only distinguish among sufficiently protective alternatives that have already been chosen without regard to cost.[365]

5. Hazardous Waste Management

While CERCLA is aimed at cleanups of hazardous wastes already in the environment, the Resource Conservation and Recovery Act (RCRA)[366] is aimed at preventing release of such materials in the first place. The Hazardous Waste Management subchapter of the RCRA takes what has been called a "cradle-to-grave" approach to waste, regulating everything in its life cycle, from generation to treatment, storage or disposal. The Act regulates generators of the waste, transporters of waste and owners and operators of waste storage, treatment and disposal facilities. It provides a tracking system and sets standards for activities and equipment used by each category of persons to prevent hazardous waste from being introduced into the environment. The RCRA also employs a waste reduction strategy under the assumption that there will be fewer releases if there is less hazardous waste to control.

RCRA standards are enforced largely through operating permits issued by the EPA or parallel state agencies. In addition, the EPA can issue administrative orders and assess civil penalties (essentially a fine) of up to $25,000 per day for each violation of RCRA standards.[367] It may also seek injunctive relief against violators and may pursue criminal penalties of up to $50,000 per day for each day of violation and up to 5 years in prison for violation of permit requirements, and up to $250,000 per day and up to 15 years in prison for violations that endanger people.[368]

6. State Environmental Laws

The EPA and federal law have been the primary guardians on the environment. Most state law and regulatory activity have been the product of the federal-state partnerships created by the various federal laws already discussed. However, state law has significance of its own in at least three areas.

"Command and Control" Regulation Some states have statutes analogous to the federal statutes just discussed, but which impose different or stricter standards. New Jersey, for example has environmental standards that exceed those of the federal government and California, Florida and Michigan have fairly comprehensive environmental statutes. The laws of most serious consequence to industry are CERCLA-like

---

364 42 U.S.C.A. §121(a)-(b).

365 Nonetheless, a recent memorandum from the EPA allows as a consideration in determining remedial action "reasonable anticipated future land use or uses," thus implying that less stringent standards for remediation should be applied to sites that are likely to be used in the future only for industrial, as opposed to residential purposes. For an article discussing problems with this approach, *see* George Wyeth, *Land Use and Cleanup: Beyond the Rhetoric*, 25 ENVTL. L.REP. 10358 (1996).

366 42 U.S.C.A. §§6901 *et seq.*

367 42 U.S.C.A. §§6925, 6928(a)(1).

368 42 U.S.C.A. §6928(d), (e). A recent issue in hazardous wastes is racially discriminatory issuance of permits resulting in concentration of waste facilities in areas where minorities live. *See, e.g., Chester Residents Concerned For Quality Living v. Seif*, 132 F.3d 925 (3d Cir. 1997) (recognizing right to sue where minority town had disproportionate share of hazardous waste facilities in the county).

laws imposing liability for contamination of industrial sites.[369] Perhaps most noticeable to the general public are the higher emission standards imposed on automobiles by the State of California. The problem of "brownfields" is another area that has been addressed by state regulation. "Brownfields" are tracts of previously developed land that could be cleaned up sufficiently for new development so that more undeveloped "greenfields" would not have to be used. At least 38 states now have voluntary cleanup programs that offer certain benefits for voluntarily remediating brownfield properties, including clear cleanup standards, streamlined environmental review and liability caps for owners who are innocent of wrongdoing. The purpose of such programs is to try to prevent additional "urban sprawl" — inexorable expansion of development into previously undeveloped land — by making the choice of redeveloping previously developed land more attractive than purchasing farm, forest or other pristine land.[370]

Local Building, Health and Sanitation Laws   State and local governments have always been the primary regulators of local building, health and sanitation. For example, sewer and septic tanks systems are regulated and controlled through the issuance of building permits and inspections. Also regulated primarily by states are landfills — sites where garbage is buried. And, as already alluded to, the same state and local governments have a role in assisting the implementation of federal requirements with regard to air and water quality.

Toxic Torts   In "toxic tort" litigation, the state law of relevance is the common law, primarily the doctrines of negligence, nuisance, trespass and strict liability for ultra-hazardous activities.[371] Toxic torts have taken various forms, from asbestos exposure to residential communities built on old toxic waste dumping sites. The latter sort of case was the subject of a popular book that detailed the struggle of one private lawyer to gain redress for a neighborhood inflicted with the lingering effects of the environmentally unsound practices of a large corporation.[372] While the book illustrates a rather dramatic case where tort remedies were used to redress massive damage caused by pollution, there are thousands of smaller toxic tort actions that have been filed throughout the country.

7. Environmental Impact of Actions of the Federal Government

The National Environmental Policy Act   Congress enacted the National Environmental Policy Act of 1969 (NEPA) in order to set a general policy of environmental protection for the country.[373] Among other things, it requires the President to report to the nation on the state of the environment. Aside from its bold statements of general policy, the most important requirement of NEPA is that any "recommendation or report on proposals for legislation and other major Federal actions significantly affecting the quality of the human environment" be accompanied by an environmental impact statement (EIS) on "the environmental impact of the proposed action."[374] This statement is to be produced in cooperation with the EPA. The EIS must "accompany the proposal [for

---

369 *See* Lynda Butler, *State Environmental Programs: A Study in Political Influence and Regulatory Failure*, 31 WM.& MARY L.REV. 823 (1990) and Wendy E. Wagner, *Liability for Hazardous Waste Cleanup: An Examination of New Jersey's Approach*, 13 HARV.ENVTL. L.REV. 245 (1989).

370 Work has been done on a federal brownfields law, but no statute has yet been passed.

371 For a case discussing all three theories of recovery, *see National RR. Passenger Corp. v. New York City Housing Authority*, 819 F.Supp. 1271 (S.D.N.Y. 1993). The law of torts was discussed in Chapter XI.

372 JONATHAN HARR, A CIVIL ACTION (Vintage Books, NY 1995).

373 42 U.S.C.A. §4331 *et seq.*

374 42 U.S.C.A. §4332(2)(C). Smaller actions that are not "major actions" are not covered by NEPA.

federal action] through the existing agency review process" and must be circulated to interested federal, state and local agencies. This requirement of NEPA might seem irrelevant to business law. However, businesses must often seek and obtain federal agency permits or other authorization to proceed, so a wide range of proposed private business development and other activities have been scrutinized for their environmental effects under NEPA. For example, permits by the U.S. Army Corps of Engineers are needed for dredging and filling waterways and a license from the Nuclear Regulatory Commission is essential for construction and operation of a nuclear power plant. Decisions of the Civil Aeronautics Board to license private activities resulting in greater air traffic and a decision of the Food and Drug Administration to authorize use of nonreturnable plastic beverage containers require EISs.[375]

By requiring preparation and circulation of an EIS, NEPA is purely "procedural." It affects the *way* agency decisions are made by forcing the agency to consider environmental factors. It does not specify the *content* of those decisions. An agency may issue a finding of no significant environment impact (called a FONSI), but the validity of FONSIs, like the sufficiency of any EIS prepared, is reviewable both administratively and by way of a citizen suit, discussed below.

Role of the Council on Environmental Quality The Council on Environmental Quality (CEQ) is set up by NEPA to conduct research and advise the President on the state of the environment, and to mediate between the EPA and other agencies in disputes over environmental effects. These latter functions involve it in determining the need for or sufficiency of an EIS. The CEQ has issued highly specific rules to guide agencies in their compliance with NEPA requirements, and these rules have been accepted as authoritative by the courts.[376] Ultimately, if no resolution can be reached, the matter can be referred to the President for resolution. However, the CEQ does not have the power to stop the agency action and, barring presidential intervention, the only real threat of legal intervention is a citizen suit.

Citizen Suits By far the most common litigation under NEPA has been citizen suits contesting failure to prepare an EIS or inadequacy of an EIS. While there is no explicit statutory right to sue, courts have implied a right of action. Since NEPA is a procedural rather than a substantive law, a court reviewing proposed agency action may enjoin it only if the agency has filed a FONSI instead of an EIS or where the EIS it has filed is inadequate. If there is an adequate EIS, the court generally has no power to enjoin the action, no matter how serious the environmental effects might be. Theoretically, the court could enjoin the proposed action if its benefits are so far outweighed by environmentally disastrous effects that it would be "arbitrary and capricious."[377] However, research discloses no case where this has happened. Quite likely, this is because of the success of NEPA's procedural "stop, think and inform" approach. Agencies whose proposed actions entail very serious environmental effects have uniformly abandoned their initial decisions or have modified them substantially to minimize the environmental consequences. This can result from internal agency concerns or intervention or pressure from Congress, the President, cabinet-level policymakers or the public. Most environmental lawyers believe that in this respect, NEPA's procedural approach has

---

375 *See* RODGERS, *supra* note 328, §9.1.

376 *See* 40 C.F.R. Pt. 1500. *See Andrus v. Sierra Club*, 442 U.S. 347, 358 (1979). Also given weight are CEQ's "Forty Most Asked Questions Concerning CEQ's National Environmental Policy Act Regulations," 46 Fed. Reg. 18026 (March 23, 1981).

377 *See* Chapter VI, p. 204.

worked well. Perhaps because of this success, a similar approach has been adopted by the European Union.

A recent innovation of agencies has been to issue a FONSI with a statement of how the agency intends to mitigate the planned action to ensure that it entails only a "non-significant impact." This approach has been approved by the courts. However, one difficulty is assuring that the promised mitigating actions are actually carried out effectively. It has been held that they may not be enforced by way of a citizen suit. The same is true when mitigation action is promised as part of an EIS, discussed earlier.[378] However, if the deviation from the planned mitigation is sufficiently substantial to be considered a new "major federal action," suit could be filed to compel the preparation of a supplemental EIS (SEIS).[379]

8. Endangered Species

The Endangered Species Act of 1973 (ESA) prohibits any federal governmental or private action that "takes" threatened or endangered species anywhere in the United States or its territorial seas, and requires federal agencies to insure that any actions funded by them do not entail such consequences anywhere in the United States or the high seas.[380] Section 7 applies to governmental action while §9 applies to private action. Section 7 of the ESA was read strictly in *Tennessee Valley Authority v. Hill*, to prohibit completion of a $100 million dam because of the danger such development presented to the tiny endangered snail darter fish. Arguments that a "hardship exception" should be read into the ESA were rejected by the Court. It noted that "[t]he plain intent of Congress in enacting this statute was to halt and reverse the trend toward species extinction, whatever the cost."[381] The ESA is administered by the Departments of Interior and Commerce. Among its interesting features is that the Secretary of the Interior has the option, in cooperation with the states, of purchasing the property to prevent or mitigate a "taking."[382] In addition to its other protections, the ESA provides serious civil and criminal penalties to those who knowingly violate the Act. However, courts, while taking a firm position that ignorance of the law or the list of species is no excuse, have imposed rather light punishment in cases of conviction.[383]

Listing of Endangered and Threatened Species   The list of endangered and threatened species is determined by the Secretary of the Interior, who is required to make list determinations "solely on the basis of the best scientific and commercial data available," taking into account existing efforts to preserve the species. The list may include any plant or animal species in the world and, as of 1991, included 651 species, with an additional 600 being considered as serious candidates and an additional 3,000

---

378 *Robertson v. Methow Valley Citizens' Council*, 490 U.S. 332 (1989) (NEPA does not impose a substantive duty on agencies to mitigate adverse environmental effects, only to file a sufficient EIS).

379 *Environmental Defense Fund v. Marsh*, 651 F.2d 983 (5th Cir. 1981) (Army Secretary modified water project in a major way during implementation requiring an SEIS).

380 16 U.S.C.A. §1531 *et seq.* A good summary of the ESA and cases under it is provided in RODGERS, *supra* note 328, at 993-1023. Originally, regulations of the Secretaries of Commerce and Interior extended the scope of the ESA to federally funded projects in foreign countries, but subsequently limited the scope to the United States and the high seas. A suit challenging this limitation foundered for lack of standing. *See Lujan v. Defenders of Wildlife*, 504 U.S. 555(1992).

381 437 U.S. 153, 193 (1978). The statutory interpretation issue was discussed in Chapter II, p. 59. Unfortunately for the snail darter, Congress amended the ESA to permit completion of the dam.

382 16 U.S.C.A. §1534.

383 *See, e.g., United States v. Clark*, 986 F.2d 65 (4th Cir. 1993) (sale of Siberian tiger and Bengal tiger skin rugs; sentence of 1 year supervised probation, 6 months home detention and 500 hours of community service; but rejecting as a defense reliance on advice that sales of wildlife killed before the ESA were legal).

identified as potentially eligible. Species may be deleted or added depending on the degree of danger of their extinction. The degree of extinction danger is obviously difficult to determine, even with the best scientific help. But the ESA's listing has served to focus public attention on the extinction threat to many species, from the 3-inch snail darter of the *Tennessee Valley Authority v. Hill* case, to sea turtles, to the lowly furbish lousewort flower of Northern Maine, to the elderberry longhorn beetle.[384]

The Scope of a "Take" Under §9, which prohibits private actions that "take" listed species, the statutory definition of "take" includes within it "harm" to the species. The Secretary of the Interior has defined "harm" as including "significant habitat modification or degradation where it actually kills or injures wildlife by significantly impairing essential behavioral patterns, including breeding, feeding, or sheltering."[385] In areas of the United States which remain in undeveloped states, this can be a significant limitation on business development, particularly in the residential building and wood products industries. The Secretary's broad definition of taking was recently approved as within his power under the ESA by the Supreme Court in *Babbit v. Sweet Home Chapter of Communities for a Great Oregon*.[386] In *Sweet Home*, landowners and logging companies challenged the Secretary's prohibiting "habitat modification" of the endangered red-cockaded woodpecker and the threatened northern spotted owl.[387] Despite the resulting broad scope of the ESA, a 1982 amendment was added to accommodate private development. It allows private parties to "take" a listed species provided the taking is "incidental" to otherwise lawful activity and it is accompanied by a "habitat conservation plan" approved by the Department of the Interior. The plan must specify the impact on the species, the means that will be used to "minimize and mitigate" it, and the reasons why any "alternatives" to the taking are not being used.[388]

---

384 *See* 50 C.F.R. §§17.11-17.12. Endangered species throughout the world are listed because of the prohibitions on possession, importation, delivery or sale of such species.. 16 U.S.C.A. §1538(a)(1).

385 50 C.F.R. §17.3.

386 515 U.S. 687 (1995).

387 Justice Scalia dissented, noting that the Court's holding "imposes unfairness to the point of financial ruin, not just upon the rich, but upon the simplest farmer who finds his land conscripted to national zoological use."

388 16 U.S.C.A. §1539(a)(1)(B). Interestingly, some courts have permitted the species itself to be a named plaintiff. *See, e.g., Marbled Murrelet v. Pacific Lumber Co.*, 83 F.3d 1060 (9th Cir.1996) (marbled murrelet is a rare seabird which nests primarily in old-growth coastal coniferous forests; evidence supported finding that there was imminent harm to them from company's intended logging operation).

CHAPTER XVI

TAX LAW

This chapter will discuss the taxes in effect in the United States. On the federal level there are taxes on income (individual and corporate income tax), taxes to support the social security system (payroll taxes), taxes on certain products (excise taxes), taxes on gratuitous transfers (estate and gift taxes), and various minor taxes. There is no federal sales tax, property tax or value-added tax.[1]

In 2009, the federal government, collected over $2.3 trillion in taxes. The federal income tax on individuals and corporations raised approximately 60% of these revenues. Of this amount, about $1.2 trillion came from the federal income tax on individuals, and about $225 billion came from the federal income tax on corporations. About $858 billion came from payroll taxes to support the social security system, about $47 billion came from federal excise taxes, and about $25 billion came from federal estate and gift taxes.[2]

State and local governments also raise revenues through taxes. In the year ending in December 2008, state and local governments collectively raised approximately $1.3 trillion dollars, or about one-half of federal tax revenues. Most of the revenues (about 55%) were raised through sales and property taxes, while another large portion (about 23%) were raised through individual taxes. The next two largest revenue contributors were corporate income (about 4%) and motor fuel sales (about 3%).[3]

The principal focus of this chapter is on the federal income tax because it raises by far the most revenue, and it typically imposes the most significant tax on the taxpayer. To a limited extent, the chapter also discusses some of the other forms of federal taxation.

A. Sources of Law and Basic Concepts in Federal Tax Law

1. Sources of Law

The Constitution The 16th Amendment of the Constitution grants Congress the power to levy an income tax. It was ratified in 1913.[4]

The Internal Revenue Code As may be expected, many additions and changes have shaped tax laws over the years. The first income tax was enacted in 1916. It underwent annual revenue act changes, including the addition of a tax on estates and gifts, resulting in the Internal Revenue Code ("IRC") of 1939. The IRC of 1939, too,

---

1 The most important federal tax statutes and regulations (except for those related to international tax) are set out in Selected Federal Taxation Statutes and Regulations (West 2008). Useful sources on tax law include the following: Marvin A. Chirelstein, Federal Income Taxation, 11th ed (West 2009); John K. McNulty & Daniel J. Lathrope, Federal Income Taxation of Individuals in a Nutshell, 7th ed. (West 2004); Karen C. Burke, Federal Income Taxation of Partners and Partnerships in a Nutshell, 3d ed. (West 2005); Karen C. Burke, Federal Income Taxation of Corporations and Stockholders in a Nutshell, 6th ed. (West 2008); Douglas A. Kahn & Jeffrey S. Lehman, Corporate Income Taxation, 6th ed. (West 2009); John K. McNulty, Federal Estate and Gift Taxation in a Nutshell, 6th ed. (West 2003); Camilla E. Watson, Tax Procedure and Tax Fraud in a Nutshell, 3d ed. (West 2005); Richard L. Doernberg, International Taxation in a Nutshell, 8th ed. (West 2009). For more detailed information, *see* CCH Standard Federal Tax Reporter, Research Institute of America (RIA) Federal Tax Coordinator 2d, BNA Tax Management Portfolios.

2 Source: Internal Revenue Service Data Book 2009, Table 1.

3 Source: U.S. Bureau of the Census, "Quarterly Summary of State and Local Tax Revenue" (2005).

4 As pointed out in Chapter I, p. 27, the use of conditional spending, backed by the increased economic power of the federal government derived from its receipt of income taxes, has been a real factor in increasing the power of the federal government *vis-a-vis* the states in the 20th century.

endured multiple additions and amendments until its recodification as the Internal Revenue Code of 1954. Next and last in this evolutionary line came the Internal Revenue Code of 1986, the current Code. This behemoth encompasses almost all of the taxes levied at the federal level. The current Code, which continues to be revised and amended annually, is now about two thousand pages long. The IRC is codified in Title 26 of the United States Code.[5]

The IRC's Subtitle A, which is about a thousand pages long, is the primary source of law for the federal income tax. All other sources of law focus on interpreting the language of the Code.

The Treasury Regulations The second major source of law with respect to the income tax (and all federal taxes, for that matter) are the Regulations issued by the Department of the Treasury (the "Treasury Regulations," or just the "Regulations"). The purpose of the Regulations is to interpret the language of the Code. The Regulations are issued by the Treasury pursuant to specific legislative grant of authority found in §7805 of the IRC. The Regulations are about four times longer than the Code, or about eight thousand pages. The Regulations are codified as Title 26 of the Code of Federal Regulations.[6]

The courts give great deference to the interpretations of the Code found in the Treasury Regulations and rarely overturn a Regulation. Indeed, the standard of judicial review seems to require that a Regulation have no plausible basis as an interpretation before a court considers overturning it.[7]

There is a second class of Regulation that is given even greater weight and is generally considered to have the force of law itself. This kind of Regulation must be promulgated by the Treasury Department pursuant to a specific grant of authority found in a specific section of the Code. These Regulations are sometimes referred to as "legislative regulations" in that they are, in effect, a delegation of the legislative authority of Congress to the Treasury Department.[8]

Revenue Rulings As discussed below, the administration of tax laws is assigned to the Internal Revenue Service (the "IRS"), which is a division of the Treasury Department. The IRS is a very large government bureaucracy which oversees the assessment and collection of federal taxes. In addition, the IRS also issues rulings on various aspects of tax law. The most common form of ruling is called a Revenue Ruling, of which the IRS issues about 300 each year.[9] Each Revenue Ruling interprets a particular aspect of the Code or Regulations. These rulings are issued in a general form and often address

---

5 The formal citation to a section of the Internal Revenue Code would refer to Title 26. In other words, §61 of the Internal Revenue Code is formally cited as "26 U.S.C.A. §61." In most circumstances, however, it is both acceptable and common to cite this section as "IRC §61." This form of citation will be used here.

6 The numbering scheme of the Treasury Regulations tracks that of the relevant IRC section. For example, the income tax regulations concerning §61 of the IRC are to be found in Part 1 of Title 26 of the Code of Federal Regulations. In general, Part 1 of the Regulations deals with the income tax. As such, the third regulation under §61 would bear the formal citation "26 C.F.R. §1.61-3." In practice, however, this regulation usually would be cited as "Treas. Reg. §1.61-3" or even more simply as "Reg. §1.61-3." The "1" before the ".61" refers to Part 1 and informs the reader that the regulation concerns the income tax.

7 *See also* Chapter II, p. 60 (deference to administrative interpretations of statutes).

8 *See, e.g.*, IRC §385 for an example of such a grant of authority.

9 Revenue Rulings are numbered by year and the order in which they were published. For example, the 125th Revenue Ruling of the year 1997 would bear the citation, "Rev. Rul. 97-125." Revenue Rulings are published weekly in the Internal Revenue Bulletin ("I.R.B.") and are collected annually in the Cumulative Bulletin ("C.B."). If the above ruling were to be found starting at page 347 of the 1997 Cumulative Bulletin it would also carry the parallel citation, "1997 C.B. 347."

important or recurring tax matters, as viewed by the IRS. Thus, they are deeply informative of the IRS's current thinking, not only on the specific examples offered in the ruling, but also on other transactions that share substantial similarity to the examples. These rulings, however, do not carry the legal weight of Regulations, and thus the rulings are more easily challenged in the courts.

Private Letter Rulings   In addition to Revenue Rulings, the IRS also issues Private Letter Rulings (sometimes referred to as just "Letter Rulings") in response to a specific taxpayer's question concerning a specific transaction. Prior to executing a transaction, taxpayers sometimes seek an advance assessment by the IRS of the transaction's tax consequences. The IRS may respond to such a request by issuing a Letter Ruling that is based on the hypothetical facts of the transaction. The Letter Ruling is applicable only to the taxpayer who sought the ruling, and it has no precedential value. The IRS issues about 300 such rulings annually.[10] The Letter Rulings are published, but all identifying information about the taxpayer or the transaction is deleted. Similar to Revenue Rulings, Letter Rulings also provide useful information to other taxpayers confronting similar situations. Generally, however, Letter Rulings carry less legal weight than Revenue Rulings.

Legislative History   Since the IRC, with its various amendments and revisions, is a product of Congress, the legislative history is sometimes useful in helping the courts interpret arguably ambiguous language in the Code.[11] Of particular import are three committee reports: the report of the Ways and Means Committee of the House, which originates all revenue legislation;[12] the report of the Senate Finance Committee, which handles all tax measures for the Senate; and the report of any Conference Committees set up to reconcile differences between House and Senate versions of the bill.

There is also a standing committee of Congress called the Joint Committee on Taxation. The Joint Committee tends to be fairly active in studying various proposals for tax reform. It issues frequent studies and reports describing the current law as well as the reform proposals. Reports of the Joint Committee on Taxation are often very thorough and useful in getting an overview of a particular tax area as well as an overview of current reform proposals.

Case Law   The various federal courts, including the U.S. Supreme Court, have had, and continue to have, a substantial number of taxpayer cases that advocate interpretations of the Code or Regulations different from that enforced by the IRS or its agents. The body of case law in the tax area is large in comparison to many other areas of law, but the significance of judicial interpretation, in contrast to other sources of law, is relatively small. The overwhelming majority of cases deal with fact-specific issues and have little applicable significance to other matters.

2. Basic Concepts in Tax Law

It is perhaps not surprising in a common law country that judicially created doctrines would be important despite the overwhelmingly statutory and regulatory nature of tax law. Certain judicial doctrines pervade tax law, and tax planners must be aware of these.

The Business Purpose Doctrine   Roughly, the business purpose doctrine looks

---

10   Private Letter Rulings are numbered sequentially for the year and month they are issued. For example, the 23rd ruling in the month of February 1997 would bear the citation, "L.R. 9702023.

11   Legislative history is discussed in Chapter II, pp. 56-57.

12   All revenue bills must originate in the House. *See* Chapter I, p. 6, and Art. II §7 cl. 2.

askance at transactions motivated solely by tax reasons. The doctrine requires a non-tax purpose such as an independent business purpose, for a given transaction to be given its tax effect. Transactions that have only tax motivations are to be disregarded. There is some disconnect here between theory and practice. Businesses routinely make decisions to cut costs, so businesses naturally look to cut down their tax burdens as just another form of cost-cutting. For example, moving to a new state may be a *worse* business decision overall, but due to tax incentives provided by the new state (i.e., cost-cutting for the business), many businesses would make the move solely for the benefit of paying less taxes. Still, the business purpose "requirement" is a well-established cornerstone of tax law.[13] Although not explicitly required by the Code, this doctrine has been judicially mandated and is now "codified" in various sections of the Regulations.[14]

The Step Transaction Doctrine In a like manner, the step transaction doctrine holds that a court may look at the end result of a series of transactions and "collapse" the intervening steps if the steps were merely steps without any independent economic significance and they were predetermined to reach the end result.[15] In other words, if a taxpayer wants to go from situation "A" to situation "B" but doing so would incur the unfavorable tax result "X," that taxpayer may find a way to get first from "A" to "C" without any unfavorable result and then get from "C" to "B" also without any unfavorable result. The net result would be that the taxpayer got from "A" to "B" without incurring the unfavorable result "X." If the intervening steps from "A" to "C" and from "C" to "B" do not have independent economic significance and the transaction was planned to end up at "B" then the courts may invoke the step transaction doctrine to disregard the intervening steps and cause the taxpayer to suffer the unfavorable result "X" anyway.[16]

The Substance-Over-Form Doctrine Although tax laws place great weight on following the allowable form of a transaction in order to attain the desired tax result, there are circumstances in which the courts will look beyond the form of the transaction to its substance. In a sense, both the business purpose doctrine and the step transaction doctrine are applications of the substance over form doctrine in that they both nullify for tax purposes transactions with proper form.[17] In particular, a court might look to apply the substance over form doctrine where the taxpayer's motivation was solely for tax evasion.

B. Federal Income Tax

It is helpful to look at the federal income tax from several perspectives: who pays the tax (the taxable unit), what is taxed (the tax base), and how much is the tax (the tax rate structure).

1. Taxpayers, the Tax Base and Taxable Income

Taxpayers The federal income tax has a broad sweep. All U.S. citizens are subject to the tax. All U.S. residents, even if they are not citizens, are subject to the tax. All U.S.

---

13 *See* Robert S. Summers, *A Critique of the Business-Purpose Doctrine*, 41 OREGON L. REV. 38 (1961), for a comprehensive criticism of the business purpose doctrine.

14 The level of strictness of the business purpose requirement varies depending on the transaction; for instance, it is much harsher under §355 than under §368.

15 *See, e.g., Minnesota Tea Co. v. Helvering*, 302 U.S. 609, 613 (1938). ("A given result at the end of a straight path is not made a different result because [it is] reached by following a devious path.").

16 *See, e.g., McDonald's Restaurants of Ill., Inc. v. Comm'r*, 688 F.2d 520, 524-25 (7th Cir. 1982). The step transaction doctrine consists of three parts: the binding commitment test, the end result test, and the mutual interdependence test.

17 *See Long Term Capital Holdings v. United States*, 330 F. Supp. 2d 122, 136-37 (D. Conn. 2004).

corporations are subject to the tax. In addition, all individuals and business entities doing business in the U.S. or having U.S. source income are subject to the tax.

Tax Base The tax base comprises what is being taxed. Here, too, the sweep of the income tax is broad. When looking at tax base, it is helpful to divide potential taxpayers into two categories. In the first are U.S. citizens, U.S. residents and U.S. corporations. All these taxpayers are liable for income tax on all of their income from anywhere in the world. A U.S. citizen who is living in Denmark and who has income only from Danish sources is subject to the income tax in the U.S. on that Danish income. Likewise, a U.S. corporation that does business only in Japan is subject to U.S. income tax on its Japanese income.

This broad rule could clearly result in double taxation for this category of taxpayers. These are dealt with in the U.S. law and tax treaties. The principal mechanism for this is the granting of a "foreign tax credit" to the U.S. citizen, resident, or corporation for taxes paid to a foreign government.[18] This credit will offset any U.S. income tax liability by the amount of any *income tax* paid to a foreign government. But the initial position of the U.S. income tax is that all income from any source located anywhere is taxable if the taxpayer is a U.S. citizen, resident or corporation.

In the second category are individuals who are neither U.S. citizens nor residents and non-U.S. corporations. These taxpayers are generally taxed only on income that comes from U.S. sources. For example, a Brazilian corporation that does business in Brazil, Argentina and the U.S. will be subject to U.S. income tax only on its income from U.S. activities.

Taxable Income The income tax is levied on the "taxable income" of the individual or entity. As we will see in more detail later, taxable income is defined as "gross income" (essentially all income) minus certain specified deductions. Thus, a corporation may earn $1,000,000 in gross income but if it has spent $900,000 in allowable business expenses (such as employee salaries, office rent, etc.), it has a taxable income of $100,000. It is only on this $100,000 that the income tax is levied.

2. Tax Rates

The U.S. income tax has a graduated, "progressive" rate structure. As a taxpayer earns more income, the taxpayer pays not only more tax but also an increasing percentage of taxable income, i.e., pays a higher tax rate.

Corporate Rates The taxation rate for corporations begins at 15%.[19] This applies to the first $50,000 of taxable income. Thus a corporation with $20,000 of taxable income owes $3,000 in income tax (15% times $20,000 = $3,000). Taxable income above $50,000 and up to $75,000 is taxed at the rate of 25%. Thus, a corporation with $70,000 of taxable income owes $12,500 in income tax. This is calculated as follows: the corporation owes a tax of 15% of its first $50,000, or $7,500 (15% times $50,000 = $7,500). In addition, since the corporation earned $70,000, it owes a tax of 25% on the $20,000, the excess of its $70,000 in taxable income over the first $50,000. This second tier of tax is thus $5,000 (25% times $20,000 = $5,000). Its total tax bill is $12,500 ($7,500 plus $5,000 = $12,500). It would be common to speak of this particular corporation as being in the "25% marginal bracket." This is because the last dollars that the corporation earned were taxed at the "marginal rate" of 25%.

---

18 26 U.S.C.A. §§901 et seq.

19 The corporate income tax rate schedule is found in §11 of the Internal Revenue Code, 26 U.S.C.A. §11.

This concept of "marginal rate" or "marginal tax bracket" is a useful shorthand. If, for example, we are told that a taxpayer is in the middle of the 25% tax bracket then we know that the federal government will take 25 cents out of the next dollar it earns. When a taxpayer is considering expanding its business, it may be helpful to realize that it will get to keep only 75 cents (or less) out of every dollar that it earns.

After the 15% and 25% brackets come the 34% and 35% brackets, which are the broadest brackets. Every dollar above $75,000 and up to $10,000,000 is taxed at a rate of 34%. Then, every dollar between $10,000,000 and $15,000,000 is taxed at a rate of 35%, for $15,000,000 and $18,333,333 the rate is 38%, and then it goes back to 35% for anything over $18,333,333. As shown, when a corporation earns more it not only pays more in taxes, but it also pays "progressively" more with the higher tax rates applied to greater income.[20]

Individual Rates　In a like manner, individuals are also subject to a progressive rate structure.[21] The income tax rate varies depending on the taxpayer's filing status.[22] The taxable income of a single individual earning up to $8,350 a year is taxed at a 10% rate. Between $8,350 and $33,950, the tax is $835 plus 15% of the amount over $8,350; between $33,950 and $82,250, the tax is $4,675 plus 25% of any amount over $33,950; between $82,250 and $171,550, the tax is $16,750 plus 28% of any amount over $171,550; between $171,550 and $372,950, the tax is $41,754 plus 33% of any amount over $372,950; and for anything over $372,950, the tax is $108,216 plus 35% of any amount over $372,950.

There are also special rates on certain types of income, such as capital gains and corporate dividends. A capital gain is gain on the sale or exchange of a "capital asset." In addition, capital gains must be "netted" against capital losses, meaning that the losses are deducted from the gains. In general, net capital gains are taxed at a flat 15% rate. Until recently, corporate dividends were taxed at ordinary income rates. In 2003, new legislation changed the tax rate for most dividends to the capital gains rate, and this change continues at least through 2010.

3. Taxable Income

The federal income tax is a tax on net income only, i.e., on gross income minus specified allowable deductions. In the language of the Internal Revenue Code (the "Code"), the income tax is imposed on the "taxable income" of the taxpayer. The two principal sections imposing the tax are §1 (on individuals) and §11 (on corporations). "Taxable income" is a term of art that is defined in §63 of the Code as "gross income minus the deductions allowed by this chapter . . ."

a. Gross Income

"Gross income," also a term of art, is the starting point for determining taxable

---

20　When a corporation earns more than $100,000, it starts to pay another small amount in income tax which is calculated to eliminate the benefit it received of the lower tax rates on the first dollars it earned. In effect, the taxes "saved" by virtue of the lower rates on the first dollars are "recaptured" once the corporation starts to earn more than $100,000. It is still appropriate for most purposes to think of the maximum marginal corporate tax rate as being 35%. Indeed, as a corporation earns somewhat over $100,000 one can also view its tax burden as resulting from a "flat (non-progressive) tax" of 34 or 35%.

21　The individual income tax rate schedule is found in §1 of the Internal Revenue Code, 26 U.S.C.A. §1. The rates presented above are for the 2009 tax year.

22　Currently, there are five possible filing statuses for individuals: unmarried (single), married filing jointly, married filing separately, head of household, and qualifying widow(er) with dependent children. 26 U.S.C.A. §1.

income. It is defined as "all income from whatever source derived . . ."[23] The word "income" itself is not defined in the Code, but has been consistently interpreted by the courts (including the U.S. Supreme Court) very broadly.[24] This tax concept of income is roughly equivalent to the definition used by many economists as "anything that results in an increase in net worth." For example, if Marcia, a lawyer, received a fee of $1,000 in cash, Marcia would have $1,000 of gross income. There are a few statutory exclusions from this general rule. For example, if Marcia received a birthday gift of $1,000 she would have income in the economic sense, but the Code specifically excludes gifts from gross income.[25] The statutory exclusions[26] are generally motivated by social policy concerns.

Of course, if the tax system were purely based on such an economic concept of income it would be unwieldy to administer. Market values fluctuate over time. For example, assume Bill purchases a building in April for $100,000 and the building, because of market forces, is valued at $110,000 in June, but declines in value to $105,000 in July. How should he be taxed? There are several aspects of the tax system designed to deal with matters such as this one. In Bill's case, he will not be taxed until he sells the building and "realizes" the gain. This "realization requirement" has been read into the Code by the courts and will be discussed below.

b. Arriving at Taxable Income

"Horizontal Equity" Allowing of deductions is necessary for the fair application of the system. "Horizontal equity" demands that taxpayers in like situations be treated (or taxed) in a like manner, and that taxpayers in unlike situations be treated differently. For example, if Lora receives $100,000 from her business without having to spend any of her own capital and Jesse receives $100,000 from his business but only after spending $90,000 of his own money to get it, both Lora and Jesse would have $100,000 of *gross* income. But in an economic sense Jesse is only $10,000 better off while Lora is $100,000 better off. A fair system would impose a tax only on the *net* increases in their economic positions. In the example of Lora and Jesse, the Code would allow Jesse a deduction for all "ordinary and necessary" business expenses incurred by him.[27] Assuming that the $90,000 he spent was both ordinary and necessary in his business, Jesse would be allowed a deduction of that amount in computing his taxable income. In recognizing that Jesse has $10,000 of *taxable* income and Lora $100,000 of *taxable* income, the Code accomplishes a rough approximation of horizontal equity by taxing the two differently situated taxpayers in different manners. Similarly, if Charles received $500,000 of business income as a result of spending $400,000, he would be treated the same as Lora, i.e., as having $100,000 of *taxable* income.

Deductions and "Legislative Grace" While "gross income" is interpreted broadly,

23 26 U.S.C.A. §61. The U.S. Supreme Court has held that in determining whether a transfer of property is a "gift" under §102 the law looks to the donor's subjective motivation. If that motivation is from "detached and disinterested generosity" or "out of affection...or like impulses" and *not* because of some duty and *not* with anticipation of some benefit, then a transfer should be considered a "gift" for purposes of §102. *Comm'r of Internal Revenue v. Duberstein*, 363 U.S. 278 (1960). The test for a gift under this Code section is not the same as the test for a gift under the federal gift tax (26 U.S.C.A. §§2501 *et seq.*) or the test for the making of a gift under common law. In other words, "gift" is a technical term whose "meaning" depends very much on the context in which it is used.

24 *See, e.g., Comm'r of Internal Revenue v. Glenshaw Glass*, 348 U.S. 426 (1955).

25 26 U.S.C.A. §102.

26 26 U.S.C.A. §§101-137.

27 26 U.S.C.A. §162.

"deductions" are generally interpreted narrowly. Deductions are generally considered to be a matter of "legislative grace." In other words, if the item one wishes to deduct is not allowed *explicitly* by some section of the Code, it is not deductible. In dealing with deductions it is important to be able to point to a section of the Code that explicitly allows the deduction.

c. Deductible Expenses

Allowable deductions are specifically set out in the Code.[28] Among the more common deductions available to all taxpayers are business expenses (§162), interest paid on borrowed money (§163), certain taxes (§164), certain losses (§165), and depreciation (§167). In addition, there are provisions applicable only to individuals.[29] For example, individuals are allowed to deduct ordinary and necessary expenses incurred in the production of income that is not part of a "business" (§212), and certain medical and dental expenses (§213).

It is also important to note that the sections allowing deductions are also subject to other specific Code provisions which may specifically *disallow* a deduction.[30] An example is the disallowance deductions for "capital expenditures." A capital expenditure consists of "improvements . . . made to increase the value of property."[31] For example, assume Donald spends $20,000 to put a new roof on the warehouse where he runs his business. Although the expenditure seems to fall under the category of an "ordinary and necessary" business expense, it would likely be considered to be a "permanent improvement" and thus not currently deductible. On the other hand, if Donald spent $7,000 merely *to repair* the old roof, it is *possible* (but not certain) that the $7,000 would be allowed as an ordinary and necessary business expense.

The difference between an "expense" (which is currently deductible) and a "capital expenditure" (which is not deductible) is often hazy. A very rough "rule of thumb" is to ask whether the item is likely to last more than one year. If it will last more than one year, its cost is likely not to be currently deductible. Thus, the cost of routine semi-annual maintenance on the heating system of a building is likely to be viewed as a currently deductible expense, whereas the cost of replacing the furnace (which is likely to last many years) is likely not to be currently deductible.

However, just because the amount paid is a capital expenditure does not mean that no deduction can ever be claimed. The Code allows for recovery *over time* of the cost of most capital expenditures by allowing deductions for depreciation, depletion, and amortization, as discussed next.

d. Capital Cost Recovery: Depreciation, Depletion Allowances, and Amortization

Depreciation Depreciation is an annual deduction allowed for the "exhaustion, [and] wear and tear" on property that is used in trade or business or held for the production of income.[32] The most basic type of depreciation allowance is calculated using the "straight line method." For example, assume Regina buys a truck for use in her business for $20,000 and expects to use the truck for four years, after which she expects

---

28 26 U.S.C.A. §§161-249.

29 26 U.S.C.A. §§211-249.

30 Section 161 makes it clear that all of the sections following it that allow deductions are subject to the explicit *disallowance* provisions of §§261 *et seq.*

31 26 U.S.C.A. §263.

32 26 U.S.C.A. §167.

to sell the truck for $12,000. Regina will be allowed a deduction for $2,000 for each of the four years she owns the truck. The straight line deduction is calculated by figuring the amount of the expenditure that is expected to be "used up" and then dividing that amount by the expected "useful life" of the asset. In Regina's case, she spent $20,000 but expects to recover $12,000 when she sells the truck 4 years later.[33] In essence, Regina expects to use up $8,000 of the asset over a 4-year period. The straight line method simply allows the taxpayer to prorate this $8,000 amount over the 4-year useful life, and allows Regina her $2,000 per year deduction. The straight line method of depreciation is the touchstone for all other methods of depreciation.

The taxpayer may have the possibility of claiming greater depreciation in the earlier years of using the asset. Increased early deductions are usually more valuable to a taxpayer because they will usually result in a lower *current* tax bill and the taxpayer may invest these current tax savings. There are "accelerated" methods of depreciation available that, in special cases, can accomplish this. For instance, a taxpayer may qualify to use a "declining balance" method of depreciation. Such a method allows a taxpayer increased deductions in the early years of an asset's life and may more closely model the actual economic depreciation of the asset. The Code also establishes an "Accelerated Cost Recovery System" (often referred to as "ACRS") for depreciation related to tangible property.[34]

Because different kinds of capital expenditures may qualify for differing depreciation methods, it is generally wise for a business to seek the advice of a tax lawyer or tax accountant when planning any large asset acquisition. In addition to different methods of depreciation, intangible assets, such as "goodwill" or customer lists, may not be deductible if they are found to last indefinitely and thus deemed to have no calculable useful life. It is important to know the potential tax consequences of allocating values to such intangible assets when purchasing an entire business in order to estimate the amount of depreciation deductions that will be available to deduct from future income. Such allocations should be done carefully to be able to accurately assess the potential after-tax income of the business.

Depletion The Code allows for capital cost recovery in other areas (such as oil, gas, and minerals), through allowances for depletion of the asset. There are various methods of calculating such allowances. The potential tax benefits in these areas can be significant in analyzing the overall economic value of an investment. Here, too, a taxpayer would be prudent to seek the advice of a tax professional.

Amortization A deduction for amortization is similar to a deduction for depreciation of an asset. Amortization allows the taxpayer who had to "capitalize" the cost of the asset under §263 the ability to recover that cost over time by annual deductions. Sometimes the word "amortization" is used relatively loosely to mean recovery of the cost of any (usually intangible) asset. For instance, if Ed pays an up-front premium of $5,000 for the right to lease a certain office space for 10 years he will (1) be required to capitalize that expenditure (i.e., not be allowed to deduct it currently)[35] and (2) be allowed to amortize that cost over the life of the lease (i.e., be allowed annual deductions of $500 for the 10 years.)[36]

---

33 This $12,000 figure is referred to as the "salvage value" of the asset.
34 26 U.S.C.A. §168.
35 26 U.S.C.A. §263(a).
36 26 U.S.C.A. §178.

4. Adjusted Gross Income

"Adjusted gross income" is defined[37] as gross income minus certain specified deductions (19 in all). The concept "adjusted gross income," commonly referred to as "AGI," serves as a touchstone for calculations in other sections of the Code that are applicable only to individuals. For instance, §170 allows a deduction for charitable contributions. However, there is a limit on the amount of charitable contributions an individual may deduct in a given year. That limit (or "ceiling") is stated as a percentage of AGI. For the most preferred class of charities, that annual limit is 50% of the taxpayer's AGI (with one modification).

In a conceptual sense, AGI can be seen as the economic income of the taxpayer. The specified deductions can be very loosely viewed as an indication of the economic cost of earning the gross income. AGI is also used outside the field of tax law in economic policy studies where it is sometimes used as a measure of income for comparison of individuals.

5. The Sale or Disposition of Property

Realization and Recognition The Code requires that gross income include "gains derived from dealings in property."[38] Whether gain is included in gross income is a two-step process of determining (1) if the taxpayer had "realized" any gain and (2) if so, whether any of the realized gains are to be "recognized."[39] Most "dispositions" of property are an "event of realization." However, any gain from such a disposition will be taxable only if it is "recognized."[40]

a. Non-Realization and Non-Recognition of Gain

Non-Realization Some kinds of dispositions, gifts, for example, are not an event of realization. For example, if Valerie mortgages a piece of real estate in exchange for a loan, this "disposition" is not an "event of realization" that will trigger gain or loss.[41]

Non-Recognition There are numerous Code sections that provide for the "non-recognition" of gain. These sections are generally motivated by policy and fairness concerns. For instance, if Nancy exchanges an office building for another office building in an even exchange (i.e., she receives no additional cash), that exchange *is* an "event of realization." Normally, the Code would require recognition of that gain and its inclusion in gross income. However, forcing Nancy to recognize gain (and to thus include it in gross income) seems unduly harsh for at least two reasons. First, Nancy's position has changed little. Before the transaction she owned one building and now, after the transaction, she owns a similar building. Pursuant to the principle of horizontal equity, it could be argued that she should be treated, for tax purposes, as if no exchange occurred. Second, since Nancy received no cash, she would be forced to use other assets to pay any tax due or forced to mortgage the property to get cash to pay the tax. This would violate a fundamental theoretical tenet of fair tax systems — that taxes should, if possible, be "market-neutral." In other words, taxes should not unintentionally force a taxpayer to engage in a market transaction to satisfy a tax burden (or to obtain

---

37 26 U.S.C.A. §62.

38 26 U.S.C.A. §61(a)(3).

39 26 U.S.C.A. §1001 *et seq.*

40 26 U.S.C.A. §1001(c).

41 There are other "dispositions" of property that are also not events of realization. For example, the making of a gift can be viewed as not being an event of realization in that no gain or loss is generally triggered by that act.

a tax benefit).

These two concerns, among others, led to the enactment of §1031 of the Code, which specifically provides for non-recognition of gain when that gain was realized by an exchange of one property for a "like-kind" property, so long as both properties are used in the taxpayer's trade or business or as investment property.[42] Nancy would thus qualify for non-recognition treatment. Of course, §1031 also provides that any gain that Nancy had that was not recognized on the exchange will be "preserved" in the new property. When Nancy actually sells the new building for cash she will have to recognize (and be taxed on) any gain that was carried over from the original building. Thus, non-recognition provisions generally only *defer* the payment of taxes; they do not forgive or decrease the payment. The mechanisms for accomplishing this deferral are discussed below.

b. Gain or Loss Realized from Disposition

Gains More common than gifts or exchanges are sales of property. If Chris buys a building for $60,000 and then sells it two years later for $80,000 cash, common sense (sometimes a rare commodity in tax law) tells us that he should be taxed only on the $20,000 gain he had in the transaction. This is exactly what the Code does,[43] although not before going through several intermediate steps.[44]

Gain Defined: Amount Realized Minus Adjusted Basis Gain from a sale or other disposition is "the excess of the amount realized therefrom over the adjusted basis provided in §1011 for determining gain."[45] The terms "amount realized" and "adjusted basis" are both terms of art and are defined in the Code.

"Amount Realized" Defined The "amount realized" is defined as "the sum of any money received plus the fair market value of the property (other than money) received."[46] So, if Miles sells a building he owns for $200,000 cash plus $30,000 worth of stock in ABC Corp., Miles's amount realized on the sale is $230,000.[47]

"Adjusted Basis" Defined The "adjusted basis" is a little more complicated. It is the "original basis" "adjusted" by other provisions of the Code. Generally, the original basis is the cost of the property.[48] If Miles purchased the building four years ago for $120,000 cash, then the original basis was the building's cost of $120,000. As for adjustments to

---

42 There are many non-recognition provisions in the Code. We will see some others later in the sections on corporate tax.

43 26 U.S.C.A. §1001(a).

44 Section 1001(a) tells how to calculate the gain or loss resulting from "the sale or other disposition of property." In a sense, this is a codification (albeit a somewhat vague one) of the realization requirement discussed above. In other words, if the taxpayer has neither sold nor otherwise "disposed" of property, there will be no gain or loss to calculate. Although the term "sale" is fairly clear, the term "other disposition" is not. For instance, is the mortgaging of a property in exchange for a loan a "disposition"? Although the answer to this question is generally "No", it is less than clear why this is so. After all, the taxpayer who mortgages property does give away an interest in the property and will have cash from the loan that could be used to pay taxes. It has generally been left to the courts and the Regulations to clarify on a case-by-case basis what is and what is not a "disposition."

45 26 U.S.C.A. §1001(a).

46 26 U.S.C.A. §1004(a).

47 As discussed later, a taxpayer may also have additional amount realized if on the sale of property he is "relieved" of any liability associated with that property (such as a mortgage liability). As we will see, this is so even if the taxpayer was not personally responsible for the debt.

48 26 U.S.C.A. §1012. In addition, as discussed later, a taxpayer may also count as part of the original basis of property purchased the amount of any liability (such as a mortgage liability) assumed by him or if the property is taken subject to such a liability even if he assumes no personal responsibility for the debt.

the basis, two of the most common ones are "(1) for expenditures ... properly charge-able to the capital account ...[and] (2) for exhaustion, wear and tear, obsolescence, amortization and depletion."[49]

Adjustments for Capital Expenditures and for Depreciation The cost of the capital expenditure is *added* to the *basis* of the building. If Miles, in the example just given, had spent $20,000 to place a new roof on the building just after he bought the building, that $20,000 would be *added* to the original basis in the building. Miles's *adjusted basis* in the building would then be $140,000. Further, assume Miles properly depreciated his $140,000 cost of the building and roof and properly took, say, $3,000 as a depreciation deduction on his taxes for each of the 4 years he owned the building. If so, Miles's basis must be *decreased* by the amount of the deduction.[50] So, every time Miles took a $3,000 depreciation deduction (in each of the four years) the basis in the building would have *decreased* by $3,000 in that year. Miles's basis would thus have decreased by a total of $12,000 (to $128,000) as of the time of the sale.

These adjustments have the proper effect. If Miles's building had *actually* de-creased in value by $12,000 by the time Miles sold it, and he sold it for $128,000 cash, Miles would have realized *neither gain nor loss on the sale*. His amount realized would be the $128,000 cash he received and his adjusted basis would be the $120,000 original cost plus the $20,000 cost of the roof, minus the $12,000 adjustment for depreciation deductions allowed while he owned the building (thus, also equal to $128,000) which would yield no gain or loss. This is the correct result since Miles's claimed depreciation mirrored perfectly the economic depreciation of the building and roof.

However, experience tells us that most buildings usually *increase* in value over time. Consequently, one might wonder if Miles is getting away with something by being allowed to depreciate the building. But the Code controls for this when Miles sells the building. Assume that Miles is able to sell the building (and roof) for exactly what he paid four years earlier, $140,000 total. Since his adjusted basis at the time of the sale is $128,000, he will realize (and recognize) gain of $12,000. In essence, the Code causes Miles to *recapture* the $12,000 of depreciation deductions he took earlier in the form of gain later.[51]

Other Basis Provisions There are basis provisions in the Code other than those discussed above. In general, these provisions are of two types: *transferred* and *substi-tuted* basis.

Transferred Basis For example, assume Susan gives a gift of one share of stock of XYZ Corporation, worth $100, to her daughter Whitney as a birthday present. If Susan bought the share of stock for $80, she would have had a cost basis of $80 in the stock. Assuming no adjustments to basis, Susan's adjusted basis in the stock would be $80. In essence, Susan transferred appreciated property to Whitney, i.e., stock which had an "inherent" gain of $20. In other words, if Susan had chosen instead to sell the stock for $100 cash, she would have realized a gain of $20 and all that gain would have been

---

49 26 U.S.C.A. §1016(a)(1) and (a)(2).

50 26 U.S.C.A. §1016(a)(2).

51 In this manner, "excessive" depreciation deductions only give a temporary benefit to the taxpayer. They will be "recaptured" later when the taxpayer sells the property. Depreciation deductions can thus be seen as providing a potential for tax *deferral*. Of course, if all other things are equal, a taxpayer will prefer to pay tax later rather than earlier since the current tax savings can be invested. Even when the taxpayer ultimately has to pay the tax, he still gets to keep the investment returns on the tax savings. In a sense, tax deferral is like getting an interest-free loan from the government. Tax benefits, such as tax deferral, commonly influence the economic viability of an otherwise marginal business deal.

recognized. However, a *gift* of property, despite its seeming to be a "disposition," has never been considered an event of realization. So, Susan would realize no gain on making the gift to Whitney.

As we saw earlier, Whitney, one receiving the gift would have no gross income under §61 because of the exclusion of gifts from gross income under §102. But, a question remains: What is *Whitney's* basis in the stock? We need to know this to determine any gain or loss to Whitney when she sells the stock. The Code provides generally that Susan's basis is "transferred" to Whitney along with the gift itself.[52] This mechanism preserves the gain inherent in the stock and insures that it will be taxed eventually. Thus, if Whitney sells the stock later that same day for $100 cash (because she would rather have the cash to buy new jeans), then Whitney will realize and recognize gain of $20.

Substituted Basis A similar result occurs when there is an exchange of property, except that it is called a "substituted basis." Returning to the case of Nancy, who exchanged one office building for another, the basis of Nancy's old building is *substituted* into the new property.[53]

Apply this to Nancy's exchange of her office building by assuming that the fair market value of Nancy's office building was $250,000 and that it had an adjusted basis in her hands of $210,000 (original price paid). If Nancy had chosen to sell the building for $250,000 cash, she would have a realized and recognized $40,000 gain. If Nancy instead exchanges her building for another office building also worth $250,000, she would *realize* a gain of $40,000 but would *not recognize* that gain. The basis of Nancy's old building is substituted for the basis of the new building. Later, when Nancy sells the new building, Nancy's gain of $40,000 is taxed if the sale price is still $250,000.

Thus, whenever there is an "event" which either does not cause current realization of gain (as with a gift) or does not cause current recognition of gain (as with the like-kind exchange of property), there must be always an applicable provision that accounts for any economic gain by preserving the original basis.

Discharge of Debt as Gross Income If Miles borrows $100 from his employer, Tess, Miles will not have any income since his net worth will not have changed. Although he has $100 more in cash, he also has $100 more in liabilities. His net worth did not change. If Tess later relieves Miles of his obligation to pay the debt back to her, Miles then receives an economic benefit because his net worth now has increased. At the moment of debt discharge, Miles's liabilities decreased by $100, and his net worth increased by the same amount. The Code treats this discharge of indebtedness as gross income.[54] A similar but even more extensive set of rules applies to debts related to property transactions.

---

52 26 U.S.C.A. §1015 (basis for the donee "shall be the same as it would be in the hands of the donor").

53 26 U.S.C.A. §1031(d) ("the basis [of the new property] shall be the same as that of the property exchanged [i.e., the old property]").

54 26 U.S.C.A. §61(a)(12). Of course, if the reason for Tess's discharge of Miles's debt was that of "detached and disinterested generosity" and without any anticipation of a future benefit to her, then the discharging of the debt could be viewed as a "gift" within the purview of §102 and the *Duberstein* case discussed earlier and thus excludable from gross income. However, if the only relationship between Tess and Miles is that of employer-employee, it will be very hard to sustain this claim for "gift" treatment. Thus, one should always look at the *reason* behind an act in order to determine its significance for tax purposes. In the case of discharge of indebtedness, there is also potential direct statutory relief in §108 of the Code, where discharge of indebtedness is excluded from gross income if the taxpayer is insolvent or in formal bankruptcy proceedings (or in one of a few other narrowly defined situations).

Relief of Liabilities as Part of the Amount Realized The amount of any liability of which a taxpayer is relieved in conjunction with the sale of property constitutes an economic "benefit" to him just as in the case of any other discharge of debt. In this context it is functionally the same as if the seller were given cash by the purchaser with which to pay off the debt. Assume Joe owns a building worth $200,000 and the building was subject to a mortgage liability of $160,000. A potential purchaser might be willing to assume the $160,000 mortgage debt, but would then only be willing to give Joe an additional $40,000 cash since the building is only worth $200,000. If the sale is concluded this way, Joe would get a total economic "benefit" of $200,000 in the form of the $40,000 cash and the relief from the $160,000 liability.

The case law and Treasury Regulations make clear that "the amount realized from a sale . . . of property includes the amount of liabilities from which the transferor *is discharged*."[55] This makes obvious sense if the seller is being relieved of a personal obligation. However, it is not uncommon in large commercial purchases of real estate for the potential owner to arrange mortgage financing so that *no one* is personally liable on the debt and the lender's interest is secured by the property. This type of financing is called "non-recourse" financing because the lender has no "recourse" against the borrower directly if the debt is not paid. All the lender can do in such a situation is to foreclose on its security interest in the property. The Regulations take the position (correctly as we shall see) that even if the liability that Joe was "relieved" of (in the above example) was a non-recourse mortgage liability (i.e., one for which Joe was not personally liable), then Joe must count the amount of that liability as part of his amount realized on the sale. The Regulations state that for purposes of calculating the amount realized, "the sale . . . of property that secures a nonrecourse liability *discharges* the transferor from the liability."[56] Such a deemed "discharge" is thus included in the amount realized.

Liabilities Assumed as Part of the "Cost" It is well-established, originally by the U.S. Supreme Court and later by the Treasury Regulations, that if a taxpayer purchases property and part of the purchase price is the assumption of a liability on the property, then the amount of that liability is included in the "cost" of the property for figuring the basis of the property. For example, if Peggy purchases an apartment building for $10,000 cash plus the assumption of a $120,000 mortgage liability, then her basis in the property is $130,000. Thus, in essence, the basis includes any loans that are part of the financing. This is true *even if the liability is a non-recourse liability* (one for which she is not personally liable). Since Peggy is required to include the amount of non-recourse debt in her basis when she buys the property, she will be able to use that basis of $130,000 for purposes of figuring how much depreciation she may take on the property.[57] In essence, Peggy will be treated *just as if she had borrowed the money and was personally liable*. This principle was needed in order to treat the property of non-recourse borrowers the same as that of full-recourse borrowers. Peggy will also get to use that same basis (adjusted, of course, for depreciation and such) as her basis when she sells the property. We can now see the symmetry and logic of requiring Peggy, or any seller, to include *in her amount realized* the amount of any non-recourse liability outstanding at the time when she sells the property. She was treated for tax purposes as if she were personally liable on the loan (even though she was not) at the purchase of the property, and she

---

55 Treas. Reg. 1.1001-2(a)(1) (emphasis added).

56 Treas. Reg. 1.1001-2(a)(4)(I) (emphasis added).

57 26 U.S.C.A. §167(c)(1).

will be treated the same at the sale of the property.

Losses The first step in calculating a loss is to subtract the amount realized from the adjusted basis. A loss occurs when the adjusted basis is higher than the amount realized. For example, if Martin buys vacant land for use in his business for $100,000 cash and later sells the land for $70,000, he would realize and recognize a loss of $30,000 since his adjusted basis would be $100,000 and his amount realized only $70,000. Martin will be able to deduct the loss against his other income (if any).[58]

On the other hand, if Martin had bought the land *for his personal use only* (e.g., camping for his family) for the same $100,000 and sold it for the same $70,000, then he would have a problem. The Code provides that "[e]xcept as otherwise expressly provided in this chapter, no deduction shall be allowed for personal, living, or family expenses."[59] The loss, although realized and recognized, would not be allowed to offset other income because the property was being used for personal purposes rather than business purposes. This "personal" loss exception makes the treatment of gains and losses asymmetrical. If Martin had purchased the vacant land for personal use and resold it at a *gain*, he would be taxed despite the fact that he had no business use in mind.

It is worth noting that a taxpayer can change her mind and *convert* personal use property into business use or "for profit" property and thus potentially qualify for a deductible loss on sale.[60] However, the courts have generally held that this conversion must be an *actual* conversion of *actual* use, and not just a change of intent. Even so, the Regulations hold that the basis for determining ultimate loss on sale is the *lower* of the taxpayer's actual basis or the fair market value at the time of conversion.[61] For example, assume Taylor bought for $100,000 a large tract of vacant land for personal use which she did use for several years that way. If she then actually converted the property to

---

58 Losses are permitted to be deducted by §165(a) ("There shall be allowed as a deduction any loss sustained....").

59 26 U.S.C.A. §262(a). Even though §165(a) (quoted in the last footnote) would apparently allow the deduction, there are two other issues to deal with. First, §165(c) limits the losses deduction allowed to individuals to (1) "losses incurred in a trade or business"; (2) losses incurred in any transaction entered into for profit"; and (3) other losses but only if they "arise from fire, storm, shipwreck, or other casualty, or from theft." Martin could attempt to argue that he bought the land with a profit motive and thus should qualify for a deduction under §165(c)(2). However, taxpayers are usually not successful in this line of argument which often arises in the context of personal residence that is sold at a loss. Courts usually hold that if the primary purpose was for personal use there is no deduction allowed. Indeed, §161 makes it clear that the deduction allowed in the sections following §161 (Part VI of Subchapter B of Chapter 1 of Subtitle A of Title 26 of the U.S. Code) are "subject to the exceptions provided in part IX (sec. 261 and following...)." Since §165, which Martin hoped would allow the deduction of the loss, is in part VI, it is subject to disallowance by §262, which is in part IX. Although §262 does allow for the possibility of another section which would expressly override it somewhere in Chapter 1 (which is the whole income tax chapter), there is none. As this demonstrates, the Tax Code is inordinately complex even when it comes to trying to find the answer to simple questions. As noted before with respect to acquiring property, it is always advisable to consult with a tax lawyer before engaging in the selling of property as well.

60 26 U.S.C.A. §165(a) allows the loss, and §165(c)(1) and (c)(2), respectively, would then exempt the loss from the limitations §165(c) otherwise imposes on individuals if the property is "incurred in a trade or business" or was part of a "transaction entered into for profit." If the taxpayer actually converts the property to business use, (c)(1) would clearly govern. If the taxpayer actually converts the property to "profit" use (such as by actually renting out the former personal use property), then (c)(2) would govern, although it would seem that the "transaction entered into for profit could not likely be the ultimate sale since the taxpayer would know she was going to sustain a loss. And, we already know that the original purchase was not entered into for profit but for personal use. The only other possible "transaction" is the "transaction" (using this word rather loosely) of the conversion itself. The reader can be left to decide the somewhat metaphysical question of how an individual goes about entering into a transaction with herself.

61 Treas. Reg. 1.165-9(b)(2).

business use (say, by starting a sheep ranch) or to "profit" use (say, by leasing it to sheep ranchers) at a time when the property was worth $80,000, then Taylor's basis *for loss calculation purposes* would be $80,000. If she ultimately sold the ranch land for $70,000 she would be allowed a $10,000 loss. This seems reasonable because the property lost that amount of value since the time of its conversion. It is interesting to note that Taylor's basis for gain still remains her $100,000 cost basis. If she sold the property for $120,000, she would recognize $20,000 of gain. Of course, this leaves an interesting middle ground where Taylor would have neither gain nor loss. If she sold the property for $90,000, she would have no gain (because her basis for gain purposes was $100,000). Also, she would have no loss (because her basis for loss purposes was $80,000).

"Characterization" of Gains and Losses: Capital Gains and Losses There is a class of gains and losses that has a long history of being given special treatment under the Code. In general, capital gains are taxed at a lower rate than other income for individuals.[62] This preferential rate for individuals is imposed only on the "net capital gain," namely the amount of capital gain left over after subtracting the capital losses for the year, and then making some minor adjustments. Over the last few decades the rate at which capital gains have been taxed has varied widely. Many restrictions apply to the deduction of capital losses. As of 2010, the maximum rate of tax on a taxpayer's "net capital gain" is generally 15%.

The terms "capital gain" and "capital loss" are technical ones and should not be used loosely. A "capital gain" is a gain that results from the sale or exchange of a "capital asset."[63] A capital asset is defined as all property except certain listed types of property. However, the listed items tend to be interpreted broadly, and thus the term "capital asset" tends to be interpreted narrowly. A typical *non-capital asset* is inventory. The sale of inventory in the regular course of business will not generate capital gain.[64] A typical *capital asset* is stock in a corporation if the stock is owned by a taxpayer who is *not* in the business of buying and selling corporate stock. If the taxpayer were in that business, then the stock would be considered inventory and thus excluded from the definition of capital asset. Thus, the corporate stock portfolio of an individual usually contains only capital assets.

There is also a serious potential disadvantage to an asset being classified as a capital asset. Allowance of deductions for capital losses is very limited. As we have discussed, the Code generally allows a deduction for losses.[65] However, for corporate taxpayers, deductions for capital losses are allowed only to the extent of capital gains.[66] For individual taxpayers, deductions for capital losses are allowed only to the extent of capital gains plus $3,000 per year.[67] Furthermore, any losses not allowed in a given year may be carried to other years under a rather complicated set of rules.[68]

The debate about the propriety of a preferential rate on capital gains and limitations

---

62 26 U.S.C.A. §1(h). The maximum rate of tax on "net capital gain" for individuals, as of 1999, is 20%. This should be contrasted with the maximum rate of tax on ordinary income of nearly 40%. Corporations are taxed on their "net capital gain" at the same rate as they are taxed on other income. However, both corporations and individuals are subject to the limitation on deductions of capital losses discussed below.

63 26 U.S.C.A. §1221.

64 26 U.S.C.A. §1221(1).

65 26 U.S.C.A. §165(f).

66 26 U.S.C.A. §1211(a).

67 26 U.S.C.A. §1211(b).

68 *See* 26 U.S.C.A. §1212 for the rules.

on the deductibility of capital losses has been going on for several decades. Congress modifies the treatment of capital gains and losses every few years, sometimes radically so. It does not look like this pattern of change is going to stop any time soon.

6. The Taxable Year and Accounting Methods

The "Taxable Year" The Code requires that taxable income "be computed on the basis of the taxpayer's taxable year." "Taxable year" is defined as "the taxpayer's annual accounting period."[69] In general, the annual accounting period is either the calendar year or a "fiscal year." A fiscal year is defined as "a period of 12 months ending on the last day of any month other than December."

The timing of when a taxpayer has income or loss is significant. Assume that Elizabeth, a calendar-year taxpayer, owns a manufacturing corporation that is also a calendar year taxpayer and that Elizabeth is the chief executive officer of the corporation. If the corporation receives $60,000 of cash from a customer on December 31, 2006, it will have $60,000 more gross income for 2006. However, if it pays Elizabeth a compensation bonus of $60,000 on December 31, 2006, it will have a deduction for that amount and thus have no net effect because the receipt of the $60,000 from its customer will be offset by the compensation paid. Elizabeth, on the other hand, will have gross income for 2006 and will have to pay tax (around $24,000 at current maximum rates) on that income by April 15, 2007, which is the day her 2006 tax return and payment are due.

Assume, on the other hand, Elizabeth's corporation had elected to be a January 31 fiscal year taxpayer when it was formed. When it receives its $60,000 payment from its customer on December 31, 2006, it would have gross income for its fiscal year ending one month later. If, instead of paying Elizabeth her $60,000 bonus on December 31, 2006, it waits until January 1, 2007, *it* will receive a deduction for the compensation paid in the same *fiscal* year as it had income. However, when *Elizabeth* receives the income on January 1, 2007, she would have additional gross income for her calendar year *2007*, and would have to pay tax on that income by April 15, *2008*, which is the day her 2007 tax return would be due. In other words, by virtue of having received the income *just one day* later, she gets to defer the payment of the $24,000 for *one full year*. If she could invest that money at 8% interest, this *deferral* of one year would be worth nearly $2,000 to her.

This example is intended to point out that there are sometimes deferral advantages to having a corporation and its shareholders on different taxable years. There are some limitations on the ability to defer income. For instance, Elizabeth's corporation could not have been a "personal service corporation," that is, a corporation whose "principal activity is the performance of personal services . . . by its employee-owners." In addition, Elizabeth *may* have to make an estimated tax payment on the expected tax due on the $60,000 early on in the year 2007 (which would seriously limit the time of deferral), but that question depends on other facts about her.

It is important to remember that a taxpayer (an individual or a corporation or other entity) makes the election of its annual accounting period at the time of the filing of the first tax return. Any change in annual accounting period must be approved by the IRS.[70] Thus, it is important to choose the annual accounting period carefully at the time of the first return.

---

69   26 U.S.C.A. §441(a) and (b).

70   26 U.S.C.A. §442.

Tax Accounting Tax accounting and regular financial accounting are related, but by no means identical systems. For instance, a corporation cannot simply file its annual financial accounting income statement as its tax return for a given year. Thus, there is a cost to maintaining a set of tax records as well as a set of regular financial records.

According to the Code, taxable income "shall be computed under the method of accounting on the basis of which the taxpayer regularly computes his income in keeping his books."[71] There are numerous permissible methods of accounting authorized by the Code. However, the two most common permissible methods of tax accounting are "the cash receipts and disbursements method" and the "accrual method."[72]

The "Cash Method" Under the cash receipts and disbursements method (often simply called the "cash method"), the taxpayer must report any income or loss only in the year in which she actually receives "payment." If a business deal "closes" on December 27 of a given year, but the cash-method taxpayer receives the proceeds on January 3 of the following year, the taxpayer is treated as having gain or loss only in the second year. Of course, if the taxpayer was actually offered payment in the first year, but refused to accept it until the second year, she is considered to have "constructively" received the payment in the first year and is taxed as if she had received it in the first year. Regarding expenses, the cash-method taxpayer is entitled to an expense deduction only in the year in which she actually pays for the expense. For example, if the cash-method taxpayer receives an invoice on December 14 for an amount due, but pays the invoice on January 12 of the next year, a deduction will be allowed only in the second year.[73] Almost all individuals use the cash method of accounting in their personal returns.

The Accrual Method Under the accrual method, a taxpayer is deemed to receive income in the taxable year "when all the events have occurred that fix the right to receive the income and the amount of the income can be determined with reasonable accuracy."[74] A like rule applies with respect to the taxable year for a deduction of a liability incurred.[75] It is irrelevant when the taxpayer actually receives money or pays the bill. All "C corporations"[76] and any businesses that use inventories are required to adhere to the accrual method of accounting.[77]

Installment Sale Method of Accounting A taxpayer may use "any other method permitted by [the Code]."[78] One of those methods is the "installment sale" method of accounting. For instance, if a cash-method taxpayer sells property at a gain but receives installment payments that extend beyond the end of the taxable year, then the taxpayer

---

71 26 U.S.C.A. §446.

72 26 U.S.C.A. §446(c)(1) and (2).

73 Treas. Reg. 1.446-1(c)(1)(i).

74 Treas. Reg. 1.446-1(c)(1)(ii).

75 *Id.*

76 A "C corporation" is defined in §1361(a)(2) as any "corporation which is not an S corporation." An "S corporation" is defined in §1361(a)(1) as any "small business corporation" which makes an election to be taxed under subchapter S of the Code rather than Subchapter C of the Code. As discussed later, electing the "pass-through" treatment of subchapter S is very restricted. C corporations constitute the vast majority of corporations. They are taxed under the regular corporate tax rules of subchapter C of the Code (§§301 *et seq.*).

77 26 U.S.C.A. §448(a)(1)(C) governs the limitation on C corporations. Treas. Reg. 1.446-1(c)(2)(I) addresses the limitation on businesses with inventories.

78 26 U.S.C.A. §446(c)(3).

may report a portion of the gain in each year.[79] In general, the percentage of gain to be reported in each year will be proportional to the percentage of the total price received in that year.[80] This type of installment reporting is automatic unless the taxpayer elects not to have the transaction treated in this manner. See also §453A for special rules relating to non-dealers, and §453B for special rules relating to gain or loss on the disposition of installment obligations.

Other Permissible Methods of Accounting There are other specific methods of accounting permitted in the Code.[81] It is advisable to check with a tax lawyer when planning a transaction in order to see whether the method of accounting used by the taxpayer in its financial reporting is a permissible method under the Code. Whatever method is used by a taxpayer, the Code requires that the method "clearly reflect income."[82] If it does not clearly reflect income, the IRS is authorized to recompute the taxable income of the taxpayer using a method that does clearly reflect income.

7. Tax Credits

As noted earlier, the income tax is imposed on the taxable income of the taxpayer. However, a taxpayer may receive a dollar-for-dollar *credit* against the tax liability in certain circumstances. For example, if a taxpayer has prepaid part of the tax liability through employer withholdings (or through quarterly payments of estimated tax liability), then the taxpayer is entitled to offset its tax liability by the amount prepaid.[83] In a like manner, income taxes paid to a foreign government are creditable against a U.S. income tax liability.[84] There are also various other types of credits available to some taxpayers as mechanisms of promoting social policies.

8. Income Tax on Corporations

All the basic concepts already discussed apply also to corporations. However, there are some aspects of the tax system that present unique issues with regard to corporations.

a. Double Taxation of Corporate Income

As pointed out in the last chapter's discussion on the choice of business form, the federal Internal Revenue Code imposes a tax on the taxable income of corporations.[85] In addition, the individual income tax includes dividend income received from corporations.[86] However, the Code does *not* allow corporations to deduct from *its* gross income dividends paid to shareholders. The result of this structure is that corporate income is in effect taxed twice – once at the corporate level and then again when the income is distributed to shareholders.

This result deserves some explanation by way of a brief detour into the philosophy of taxation. It is generally agreed that a tax system (and, in fact, government in general) should adhere at a fundamental level to at least four basic principles: horizontal equity, vertical equity, market neutrality, and economic efficiency. The U.S. corporate tax

---

79 26 U.S.C.A. §453(a) and (b)(1).

80 26 U.S.C.A. §453(c).

81 See 26 U.S.C.A. §446(c)(3). If a combination of accounting methods is used by a taxpayer the taxpayer must comply with the requirements of Treas. Reg. 1.446-1(b)(2)(iv).

82 26 U.S.C.A. §446(b); Treas. Reg. 1.446-1(c)(1)(ii)(C).

83 26 U.S.C.A. §31.

84 26 U.S.C.A. §901.

85 26 U.S.C.A. §11.

86 26 U.S.C.A. §61(a)(7).

system has been criticized for running afoul of each of these principles. There have been numerous proposals to reform the system of double taxation, but none has ever gained much momentum. As a result, in the last decade new forms of business structures have emerged which have allowed taxpayers to have the benefits of doing business in corporate form (such as limited liability for investors) without the burden of double taxation. These newer forms are discussed later.

Horizontal Equity This principle requires that "persons in similar situations should be treated in a similar manner." The corporate tax, however, can be viewed as treating similarly situated persons differently. For instance, if Victoria owns a toy store as a sole proprietor she will be taxed on the net income (taxable income) of the business. If the store generates $100,000 of taxable income, her tax liability is maximally $35,000, using the highest marginal rate for individuals (35%). If Helen uses the corporate form to run a similar toy store as the sole shareholder, the *corporation* is taxed first on its net income (taxable income). If the corporation distributes its net earnings (after paying the corporate income tax) to Helen as a "dividend," then Helen is taxed personally on the dividend. Thus, if Helen's store generates the same $100,000 of taxable income that Victoria's did, Helen's corporation has to pay a tax of $35,000 (using the highest marginal rate for corporations, which is 35%), leaving it with $65,000. If Helen then takes the $65,000 out of the corporation as a dividend, she is taxed again. The $65,000 is gross income to Helen. Normally, an additional $65,000 of income would generate a tax of $22,750 (again using the highest marginal rate for individuals of 35%). However, because of recent changes in the Code, this $65,000 of corporate dividends is taxed at a maximum rate of 15%, thus yielding a maximum tax on Helen of $9,750. The result is that Helen is left with $55,250 after all taxes are paid while Victoria ends up with $65,000 after her taxes are paid. The effective tax rate on Helen's profit, generated through a corporation, is thus about 45%, while Victoria's is only 35%.[87]

Vertical Equity The principle of vertical equity in simple form requires that the burdens of a system be distributed among the members of society in a fair manner. In a sense, this principle requires us to look at *differently* situated persons and decide how to allocate the burdens of society in a fair manner. This can be seen as part of the tax concept of progressivity discussed earlier, under which rates of taxation increase as income increases. Turning to the corporate tax, one could argue that the double taxation effect unfairly burdens those doing business in corporate form. As the example of Victoria and Helen demonstrates, there would not seem to be much basis for saying that everyone who uses the corporate form is better able to bear a higher tax burden. And even if one does view corporations as meriting an additional tax, we must still ask how much additional burden should be placed on them. As the example of Victoria and Helen demonstrates, the difference is large indeed.

A second way in which vertical equity is offended has to do with the question of who *actually* pays the corporate tax. Although a tax may be imposed on a particular person or transaction, the burden of that tax may be *shifted* to another. The corporate tax falls immediately on the corporate entity. However, the corporation will often have the ability to *shift* the *burden* of the corporate tax from itself to other sectors of the

---

87 This disparity is even more striking when we realize that Victoria could choose to use one of the newer entities, such as a "limited liability company," and get all of the benefits of using true corporate form (such as limited liability, centralized management, etc.) and still be taxed only once at the individual rate. The only benefit she could not easily get is the free transferability of shares, thus limiting her ability to raise capital by selling shares to the public.

economy. It can pass on the burden to its workers in the form of lower wages, to its suppliers in the form of lower prices paid for raw materials, to its shareholders in the form of lower returns on investment, or most likely, to its consumers in the form of higher prices. To the extent that the actual burden of the corporate tax is borne by the consumer, it is arguably "regressive" because it impacts low-income consumers and taxpayers disproportionately heavily. The analysis of who actually pays the corporate income tax is a complex one and the answer will vary from industry to industry. What is clear is that the ultimate burden of the corporate income tax may be far from what is intended.

Market "Neutrality" Ideally, taxes should not affect the market decisions of the taxpayer. If two "products" are similar but one carries with it the additional burden of a tax, the consumer of the products would be inclined to avoid the taxed product and purchase the non-taxed product. A tax that forced such a decision would violate the desirable goal of market neutrality. Seen in this light, the corporate income tax is not neutral since the burden imposed by the corporate tax leads a rational person to avoid the corporate form (all other things being equal). In addition, doing business in corporate form affects decision-making (and is thus non-neutral) in several areas. One key area in which the corporate tax affects market choices is the preference for debt-based financing over equity financing in the capitalization of the corporation since interest paid on debt is deductible while dividends paid on stock are not. Discussed in the next paragraph, this distortion may also lead to market inefficiencies.

Economic Efficiency Interest payments on debts are deductible by the corporation under the Code.[88] Dividend payments to shareholders are not deductible. Thus, dividends incur a higher rate of tax than interest payments since profits that are distributed as dividends are effectively taxed twice. This arguably encourages economic inefficiency by encouraging corporations to raise funds by borrowing rather than by seeking more investment capital. Such encouragement also violates the policy of market neutrality.

For example, assume Kate forms a corporation that needs $100,000 of capital to operate and expects to generate $10,000 of gross income. First, assume Kate contributes the $100,000 to the corporation as paid-in capital. If the corporation earns the expected $10,000, the corporate level tax is about $3,500 (assuming the highest marginal rate for the purpose of this example). Kate's corporation will then have $6,500 to distribute to Kate as a dividend. That $6,500 is gross income to Kate. Since that $6,500 qualifies as a corporate "dividend," it would be taxed at a maximum rate of 15%. Thus, Kate personally has to pay a tax of $975, making the after-tax return $5525.

Now, instead, assume that Kate only puts in $1 as paid-capital, and *loans* the corporation the other $99,999 at an interest rate of 10%. When the corporation earns its expected $10,000 it will have $10,000 of *gross* income. When the corporation pays Kate $9,999.90 of interest, the corporation enjoys a *deduction* under §163 for that amount. Thus, the corporation's *taxable* income is *zero*. Kate, of course, treats the interest as gross income under §61(a)(4) and pays a tax of $3,500 on that amount. Kate now has an after-tax return of $6,500.

This example shows how the corporate tax can distort market decisions by encouraging debt-based financing over equity-based financing. It is a well-established fact that most new business ventures fail early in their lives. One of the principal causes

---

88 26 U.S.C.A. §163.

of business failure is the inability of young businesses to meet their fixed obligations (such as payment of interest on their debts). Viewed in this way, the corporate tax not only causes market distortions (by preferring debt over equity), but also arguably causes dead-weight losses in the economy at large and is thus economically inefficient. Another inefficiency and market distortion that occurs is that the corporate tax encourages companies to retain their earnings at the corporate level rather than distributing them to shareholders where the earnings would be taxed again. Corporations do so because raising financing for new projects is cheaper with retained earnings than with new capital.[89]

b. Income Tax Issues in Formation of the Corporation

Exchanges of Stock Forming a corporation often involves transferring assets into the corporation in exchange for shares of stock. This is an "exchange" of property for stock. This exchange is an "other disposition" of property and is thus considered to be an event of realization.[90] If the assets are appreciated (i.e., their fair market value exceeds their adjusted basis) there will be a gain *realized* on the transfer. In a like manner, the exchange of depreciated assets will cause a loss to be realized. However, if the corporation is controlled by the transferor of the property, there is little of substance that has changed. The transferor once owned an asset and now owns a corporation which owns the asset. Imposing an income tax at this point on the realized gain seems inappropriate if we view this as more of a change in form rather than in substance. In addition, there is a practical problem. The transferor would have to get the cash to pay any tax imposed, thus potentially forcing her to sell some of her stock or to borrow money.[91]

The Code states that "no gain or loss shall be *recognized* if property is transferred to a corporation . . . solely in exchange for stock in such corporation" but only if "immediately after the exchange" the transferor (or group of transferors) is "in control of the corporation."[92] Three important points should be made about this provision.

First, it allows the taxpayer to receive *stock* in the corporation in order to get non-recognition treatment. If the taxpayer receives cash, bonds, or other property, then that *gain* is recognized up to the amount of the fair market value of property received, but no loss shall be recognized. This provision makes some sense. If one of the reasons for allowing non-recognition in the first place was to avoid imposing a tax on a taxpayer who did not have the means to pay the tax, then it seems proper to impose a tax when the taxpayer receives cash or other property. Since gain is recognized only up to the amount of cash or other property received, the tax imposed will always be less than that amount and thus affordable. The denial of loss recognition seems somewhat less justified since the taxpayer could have sold the loss property in a separate transaction.

Second, stock issued to a transferor in exchange for *services* is not considered as

---

89 There have been many proposals over the years to eliminate the corporate tax but none has gained widespread acceptance. However, some of the difficulties have been eliminated by the advent of the relatively new limited liability company and the efficiency of "check-the-box" options for tax treatment of an entity either like a corporation or like a partnership. *See* Chapter XV, p. 599.

90 26 U.S.C.A. §1001(a).

91 This interference with market decisions would violate the tenet of "market-neutrality."

92 26 U.S.C.A. §351(a). Being "in control" means "ownership of stock possessing at least 80% of the total combined voting power of all classes of stock entitled to vote and at least 80% of the total number of shares of all other classes of the corporation's stock." §386(c).

having been given in exchange for property.[93] Thus, a person receiving stock for services *cannot* be counted as part of the group of property transferors for purposes of the 80% control tests. It is fairly common for smaller corporations to have one person contribute services and one person contribute property. The formation of such a corporation requires careful tax planning if the property transferor is to get non-recognition treatment. Of course, if the non-services transferor is going to contribute only money, the issue of non-recognition does not arise (since the basis of cash is its fair market value).[94]

Third, non-recognition, as discussed earlier, is almost always just a deferral mechanism. Any gain (or loss) will be recognized on the later disposition of the asset. As in the like-kind exchange example earlier, this inherent gain or loss is preserved by means of substituted and transferred basis provisions.

Here is an example of how this works. Assume Marjorie owns 100% of the stock of ABC Corporation and also owns an airplane with fair market value of $50,000 and an adjusted basis of $30,000. If Marjorie transfers the airplane into the corporation in exchange for $50,000 worth of stock (a fair exchange), Marjorie has a realized gain of $20,000 since this is an event of realization and her amount realized of $50,000 exceeds her adjusted basis of $30,000 by $20,000. However, since Marjorie is in control of the corporation immediately after the transfer, none of this realized gain is recognized. Marjorie's basis in the new shares of stock will be $30,000 and she will *substitute* her basis in the airplane as her basis in the stock.[95] Marjorie's transfer of the airplane to her wholly-owned corporation will not incur any *immediate* taxes.[96] However, Marjorie had $20,000 of potential gain *inherent* in the airplane before she transferred it. If she had sold the *airplane* for its value of $50,000, she would have realized (and recognized) a gain of $20,000, because her amount realized would have been $50,000 and her adjusted basis was $30,000. This is only a deferral, however. Marjorie will realize and recognize that same $20,000 of gain when she sells the new *stock* in the corporation that now owns the airplane, since Marjorie's $30,000 basis in the airplane has been substituted as the basis for the new stock.

Effect of Stock Exchanges on the Corporation The effect of stock exchanges on the corporation are similar to those discussed for the recipient of the stock. ABC Corp. recognized no gain or loss on the issuance of its shares to Marjorie in exchange for the airplane. The corporation takes a *transferred* basis of $30,000 in the airplane from Marjorie. Of course, if the corporation sells the airplane for its $50,000 fair market value it will realize and recognize a gain of $20,000, just as Marjorie would have had she sold the airplane herself.

One should note how the Code in this manner preserves the policy of double taxation of corporations. It has not only preserved Marjorie's $20,000 inherent gain for later taxation, but it has also insured double taxation — once when Marjorie sells her

---

[93] 26 U.S.C.A. §351(d).

[94] We should note that §351 will apply to the transfer of property not just to new corporations, but to any controlled corporation so long as "immediately after" the transfer the transferor (or group of transferors) is in control of the corporation. We should also note that the corporation itself, under §1032 of the Code, does not recognize any gain or loss on the issuance of its own stock in exchange for money or property. Finally, while taxpayers generally prefer to not recognize gain, they generally *do* like to recognize losses. Thus, some creative tax planning may be necessary if the transferor wishes to recognize her losses on depreciated property that would otherwise be transferred to the corporation.

[95] 26 U.S.C.A. §358. This section is part of a larger set of sections in Subchapter C of the Code, which deals exclusively with corporations.

[96] Nor will it for the corporation. *See infra* note 96.

stock and once when ABC Corp. sells the airplane.

When Both Stock and Cash are Involved: "Boot" If instead of $50,000 worth of stock Marjorie instead receives $45,000 of stock and $5,000 cash from the corporation, the Code requires that Marjorie recognize her realized gain up to the amount of money and other property received.[97] Thus, Marjorie would have to recognize $5,000 of her $20,000 of realized gain. This additional money (or property) received in a non-recognition transaction is most commonly referred to as "boot."[98] Since she will now have recognized $5,000 of her $20,000 in realized gain, the basis of her stock and the corporation's basis in the airplane should reflect this recognition. Consequently, Marjorie should increase her basis in the stock by the amount of gain recognized.[99] Thus, Marjorie's basis in the stock would be $35,000: her substituted basis of $30,000 increased by the $5,000 of recognized gain caused by her receipt of $5,000 of boot. This outcome is logical since if Marjorie were to sell her stock for its $50,000 value, she would recognize the remaining $15,000 of gain. In a like manner, the corporation's basis in the airplane would be $35,000: Marjorie's transferred basis of $30,000 increased by the $5,000 amount of gain recognized by Marjorie.[100]

This same pattern of dealing with non-recognition of gain or loss appears throughout the Code. In almost all cases the pattern is this: (1) If one engages in an exchange of something *solely* for something else, and (2) if one meets certain criteria, then (3) neither gain nor loss is recognized. However, (4) if one gets boot in addition to the permitted exchange of property, then (5) realized gain is recognized but only up to the amount of boot received. Moreover, (6) the basis in the new property received is the basis in the exchanged old property, increased by the amount of gain recognized because of the boot received.[101]

c. Income Tax Issues in Operating the Corporation

As discussed earlier, a corporation, like an individual, is a taxable entity. As with an individual, gross income is reduced to taxable income by subtracting allowed deductions.[102] The most likely deductions for a corporation are operating expenses (e.g., all ordinary and necessary business expenses),[103] depreciation,[104] and any interest paid on debt.[105] However, there are special issues for corporations in two areas: distributions made to shareholders and compensation of employees.

(1) Distributions to Shareholders

This area of taxation is fairly technical, but the concepts are relatively easy to understand. First, we should briefly explore the possible sources of a distribution to a shareholder.[106]

Distributions in the Absence of Profit Assume that David forms a wholly-owned

---

97 26 U.S.C.A. §351(b).

98 The etymology of this term goes back to Anglo-Saxon times in England (before the 11th century) when "*bot*" was an amount paid by one person to another person in certain custom-based transactions.

99 26 U.S.C.A. §358(a)(1)(B)(ii).

100 26 U.S.C.A. §362(a).

101 Although we did not look at the issue of boot when we explored the non-recognition of like-kind exchanges under §1031, that section calls for the same treatment.

102 26 U.S.C.A. §§61, 63.

103 26 U.S.C.A. §162.

104 26 U.S.C.A. §167.

105 26 U.S.C.A. §163.

106 26 U.S.C.A. §301.

corporation to manufacture toys by contributing $100,000 as paid-in capital. He would then have a basis of $100,000 in the stock.[107] If the corporation, before earning any money distributes $10,000 back to David, then that distribution should be seen as a mere return of capital and not as income to David. Also, as we would expect, David's basis in his stock would be reduced by $10,000 to $90,000.[108]

Distributions When There is Profit If the corporation earns profits and then makes a distribution to David, the distribution is considered to have come first from those profits. Since the corporate tax is premised on the double taxation of profits, that distribution is also taxable as a dividend to David. To use a concrete example, if the corporation (before any distribution to David) earns $10,000 of taxable income, it must pay a corporate tax of about $3,500 (assuming the maximum marginal rate of 35%). This would leave the corporation with $6,500 of after-tax profits. If the corporation then distributes $5,000 to David, the entire $5,000 amount would be included in David's gross income as a "dividend" and thus subject to the individual income tax. If, on the other hand, the corporation distributed $8,000 to David, only $6,500 would be considered to come from its "profits," because the corporation's *economic* profit (i.e., its "after-tax profit") is only $6,500. The remaining $1,500 would be treated as a return of capital, and David's basis in the stock would be reduced, just as in the first part of this example.[109]

The Definitions of "Dividend" and "Earnings and Profits" "Dividend" is a term of art in the Code and should not be confused with Wall Street's definition of a dividend. The Code provides that if a distribution is made to a shareholder, then that distribution is a "dividend"[110] if it is made out of "current earnings and profits" or out of "accumulated earnings and profits."[111]

"Earnings and profits" (commonly referred to by tax lawyers as "e&p") is also a technical tax term. It has virtually no relationship to the financial concepts of "retained earnings" or "current earnings."[112] In essence, the e&p of a corporation is *very roughly* equivalent to its after-tax economic profits. However, the exact calculation of earning and profits is very complex. The following is a brief explanation.[113]

The Code essentially splits the earnings and profits of a corporation into two "accounts." The first account consists of "current earnings and profits."[114] The second account consists of "accumulated earnings and profits."[115] The current earnings and profits account holds, simply, the earnings and profits for the current taxable year. The accumulated earnings and profits account holds, as it implies, any earnings and profits that have accumulated over the years. The reason for this split is mainly historical, but the key point is that a distribution to a shareholder is a "dividend" (and thus included in the shareholder's gross income) to the extent that there are earnings and profits in *either*

---

107 26 U.S.C.A. §358.

108 As we will see below, this is exactly how §301 of the Code treats such a distribution in the absence of profits.

109 26 U.S.C.A. §301(c)(1)-(3).

110 A dividend is included in gross income under 26 U.S.C.A. §61(a)(7).

111 26 U.S.C.A. §316(a)(2) and (1), respectively.

112 26 U.S.C.A. §312. Actually, the term "earnings and profits" is not defined in the Code. Section 312 of the Code, however, does provide some guidance by giving us several pages describing the "effect on earnings and profits" of various transactions and occurrences.

113 26 U.S.C.A. §316.

114 26 U.S.C.A. §316(a)(2).

115 26 U.S.C.A. §316(a)(1).

account.[116] Thus, even e&p from 50 years ago has the potential to cause a current distribution to be taxable as a dividend to a shareholder.

Referring back to David's corporation, we can see that it had earned a taxable income of $10,000 in its first year. It also paid a corporate-level tax of $3,500. That payment reduces the corporation's earnings and profits to $6,500. Assuming no other adjustments to the earnings and profits account, a distribution of $5,000 would be seen as coming from the current earnings and profits first and, thus, would be included in David's gross income as a dividend. Since the distribution also reduces the corporation's economic capacity, the $5,000 will further reduce the corporation's current earnings and profits to $1,500.[117]

If the first tax year ends without any further distributions, that $1,500 of current earnings and profits would be shifted over to the *accumulated* earnings and profits account. If in the next taxable year the corporation *loses* money and has a net loss and no taxable income it may very well have a *negative current earnings and profits account* for that second year. If the corporation then makes a distribution to David of $4,000 in the second year, David would nonetheless have a dividend of $1,500, because of the $1,500 in the *accumulated earnings and profits account*, even though the *current* earnings and profits account would be negative. The remaining $2,500 of the distribution would be treated as a return of capital and would reduce his basis in the stock by that amount.[118]

Distributions in Excess of Both E&P and Basis If a corporation has large amounts of capital (perhaps because it borrowed money) and no current or accumulated earnings and profits, and it makes a distribution to a shareholder, the distribution reduces the basis of the shareholder's stock. If the distribution exceeds that basis, then the Code treats the excess as "gain from the sale or exchange of property."[119] This has two effects. First, the shareholder must recognize the gain as gross income. Second, since that gain is treated as if it were from the "sale or exchange" of property, that gain may be *characterized* as "capital gain" *if* the stock was a "capital asset" in the hands of the shareholder. If so, as discussed earlier, it may be taxed at a preferential rate afforded to "capital gains."[120]

The Deduction for Corporate Dividends Received To avoid triple and quadruple taxation of corporate profits, the Code provides a deduction for a percentage of the dividends received from another corporation.[121] The percentage amount of deduction depends on the percentage amount of stock ownership. If the receiving corporation is a member of the same "affiliated group" as the distributing corporation, then there is a 100% deduction.[122] The term "affiliated group" is a technical one. In essence, it refers to a chain of corporations owned by a common parent where at least every link in any ownership chain consists of 80% of the total voting power and 80% of the total value of any subsidiary corporation.[123] If the receiving corporation is not part of an affiliated group with the distributing corporation, but owns at least 20% of its stock "by vote and value,"

---

116 26 U.S.C.A. §§301(c)(1) and 61(a)(7).

117 26 U.S.C.A. §312(a)(1).

118 26 U.S.C.A. §301(c)(2).

119 26 U.S.C.A. §301(c)(3).

120 26 U.S.C.A. §1201 *et seq.*

121 26 U.S.C.A. §243.

122 26 U.S.C.A. §243(a)(3).

123 26 U.S.C.A. §243(b)(2) referring to §1504(a).

then the Code grants a deduction of 80% of the dividend received.[124] Finally, if the receiving corporation owns less than 20% of the stock, then a deduction of 70% of the dividend received is provided.[125]

Distributions of Stock A distribution of additional stock of a corporation, commonly referred to as a "stock dividend," is generally not a dividend at all in the tax sense. The Code provides that "gross income does not include the amount of any distribution *of the stock* of a corporation made by such corporation with respect to its stock."[126] Of course, in the inimitable style of the Internal Revenue Code, there are then two pages of exceptions to this general rule. In general, however, an ordinary pro-rata distribution of common stock on common stock will not be included in gross income.

Redemptions of Stock A corporation may redeem ("buy back") some of its stock from a shareholder for various reasons. Since a redemption resembles a sale or exchange, it is treated like one.[127] This gives several potential tax advantages to the shareholder. First, the amount received for the stock surrendered is treated as the amount realized and only the excess of the amount realized over the adjusted basis in the stock is recognized as gain.[128] Indeed, if the adjusted basis exceeds the amount realized, the taxpayer would have a recognized loss that may be deductible. Second, since the Code grants "exchange" status, if the stock is a capital asset in the hands of the taxpayer, then the gain would be capital gain and potentially taxable at a preferential rate.[129]

The rationale for treating the redemption as an exchange can be understood better by examining the qualifications for sale or exchange treatment and the consequences of alternative tax treatment. If the redemption of stock is pro-rata among all the shareholders, it is seen as a mere subterfuge for a distribution of earnings and profits. In a pro-rata redemption, all shareholders would own exactly the same percentage of stock as before, and the only difference is that shareholders have now received money from the corporation. The distribution is treated as a dividend to the extent of earnings and profits. Thus, the consequences of failing to qualify a stock redemption as an exchange can be disastrous.

Since a pro-rata redemption is archetypally what is *not* accorded exchange treatment, it is reasonable to expect that a *non-pro-rata* redemption *would* qualify for exchange treatment. In fact, this is the case. For instance, if the redemption terminates the shareholder's interest in the corporation, i.e., if it is a complete redemption of all of the shareholder's stock in the corporation, then it qualifies for exchange treatment.[130] This makes sense since such a redemption could not be a subterfuge for a distribution from e&p. Such a shareholder should be treated the same as if he "sold" his entire interest to a third party. Likewise, a "substantially disproportionate" redemption of stock also qualifies for exchange treatment.[131] This disproportionality is determined by looking

---

124 26 U.S.C.A. §243(c).

125 26 U.S.C.A. §243(a)(1).

126 26 U.S.C.A. §305(a) (emphasis added).

127 26 U.S.C.A. §302(a) and (b).

128 26 U.S.C.A. §1001(a).

129 26 U.S.C.A. §302. Capital asset is defined by §1221. Of course, if there is a recognized loss on the redemption and the stock is a capital asset in the hands of the taxpayer, then the deductibility of the loss is limited by §1211 and §1212.

130 26 U.S.C.A. §302(b)(3).

131 26 U.S.C.A. §302(b)(2).

at the shareholder's percentage interest in the corporation's stock, both voting and common stock, before and after the redemption. If the shareholder's percentage interest after the redemption is less than 80% of his interest before, then the shareholder qualifies for exchange treatment. If the shareholder cannot meet either the termination test or the substantially disproportionate test, the shareholder may yet qualify under a more nebulous test if the redemption was "not essentially equivalent to a dividend."[132] There is substantial case law analyzing particular fact patterns that either meet or fail this test.[133] The key issue is whether there was a "meaningful reduction" in the shareholder's interest in the corporation.[134]

Partial Liquidations There is one other type of redemption that qualifies for exchange treatment — when the redemption of stock from an individual constitutes a "partial liquidation."[135] This term is defined as a distribution that "is not essentially equivalent to a dividend."[136] Although "not essentially equivalent to a dividend" is the same language found in the nebulous exception just discussed, the contrast is that this subsection looks at the corporate level for dividend equivalence not the shareholder level. This section and its precursor have a long history. In general, the courts look to see if there has been a significant *contraction* in the size of the corporate business before finding that a distribution is not essentially equivalent to a dividend. This provision also now provides the taxpayer with a technically drafted safe harbor if a corporation is ceasing one of its long-established businesses.[137]

(2) Compensation of Corporation Employees

The compensation paid to a corporate employee is deductible to a corporation if it is an "ordinary and necessary" expense and if it is "reasonable."[138] In most small corporations, the principal shareholders are often also highly positioned employees of the corporation. Since compensation to those employees is potentially deductible, there is pressure (caused by the double taxation system) to take money out of the corporation as compensation (salary and/or bonus) rather than as a dividend. As discussed earlier, one of the most highly contested areas in tax audits is that of the "reasonableness" of compensation paid to employees who are also shareholders. Before paying high compensation to an employee-shareholder one should do some homework on comparable compensation paid to similarly situated employees whose compensation is a matter of public record. In addition, one should be ready to demonstrate the true economic value of that employee by looking at the business profits generated by her.

Loans to Shareholders: A Word to the Wise Because of the double-tax effect of the corporate tax, there is a strong tendency, especially in smaller corporations, to find ways to take money out of the corporation without paying the double tax. One way to do that is through large loans to shareholders. Knowing this, the IRS tends to scrutinize such

---

132 26 U.S.C.A. §302(b)(1).

133 *See, e.g., Comm'r v. Sullivan*, 210 F.2d 607 (5th Cir. 1954); *Northup v. United States*, 240 F.2d 304 (2d Cir. 1957).

134 Section 302(c) requires that, in applying the substantially proportionate test of §302(b)(2) and the termination test of (b)(3), it is not just the stock actually owned by the taxpayer that is examined, but also the stock *constructively* owned by him or her before and after the redemption, as defined by §318. Section 318 is complex. Suffice it to say that stock ownership is attributed to a taxpayer from certain family members, as well as from various partnerships, estates, trusts and corporations.

135 26 U.S.C.A. §302(b)(4).

136 26 U.S.C.A. §302(e).

137 26 U.S.C.A. §302(e)(2).

138 26 U.S.C.A. §162(a)(1).

loans.[139] Any loans to shareholders should be well documented with formal notes. Although the topic of interest-free loans is a complex one, in general a loan to a shareholder should bear market interest. Further, the shareholder-borrower should make all payments when due. Dire consequences await those who are careless with these steps. The entire loan may be recharacterized by the IRS as a distribution to the shareholder with respect to stock and thus be taxable as a dividend to the extent of earnings and profits.

d. Income Tax Issues in Corporate Mergers and Liquidations

Corporate Mergers and Reorganizations   Mergers and reorganizations were discussed in Chapter XV.[140] When a corporation acquires the stock or assets of another corporation in exchange for its own stock, changes its place of incorporation, or undergoes a recapitalization, each of these transactions is likely to be an event of realization that triggers realized gain or loss for at least one of the participants. But most of these transactions result in owners of stock in one corporation ending up with stock in another corporation or with different stock in the same corporation, while all the corporate assets remain in place. Consequently, it seems *inappropriate* to impose an income tax on them at that time. Consistent with this, the Code lists seven basic transactions in which the participants are granted "reorganization" status.[141] This status ensures that every "party to a reorganization" will not recognize any realized gain or loss.[142] Like the other non-recognition exchanges discussed earlier, any realized gain or loss is preserved in the form of a substituted or transferred basis.[143] Also, similar to other non-recognition exchanges, any cash or other property received as "boot" triggers recognition of realized gain up to the amount of boot received.[144]

Liquidations   Just as the Code grants "exchange" status to amounts received in a qualifying redemption or partial liquidation, it grants that same status to shareholders who receive a "distribution in complete liquidation of a corporation."[145] The shareholders are treated as if they had "sold" their stock, and they get to setoff their basis in the stock against the amount realized. As with a qualified partial liquidation or redemption of stock, the shareholders may also receive capital gain or capital loss treatment. At the corporate level, the corporation is treated as if the property distributed "were sold to the distributee at its fair market value."[146] If the corporate assets have fair market values in excess of their adjusted bases, a gain is recognized and taxed.[147] In a final twist of fate, losses, although recognized and allowed, may not be used at all unless there is sufficient other current income to set them off against or they can be carried back to prior taxable

---

139 26 C.F.R. 1.162-1. Also, the Sarbanes-Oxley Act, enacted in response to the most recent wave of corporate misconduct, provides additional limitations prohibiting most loans to executives in registered corporations. *See* Chapter XV, pp. 604-606, where the Act is discussed.

140 *See* p. 597.

141 §368(a)(1).

142 §368(b). Shareholders are covered under §354 or §356 and corporations under §361.

143 *See* §358 for shareholders and §362 for corporations.

144 26 U.S.C.A. §368(a)(2). Reorganizations are very complex. Briefly, this Code section covers the following types of reorganizations, listed according to their subparagraph in the statute: (A) statutory mergers; (B) stock-for-stock transactions; (C) stock-for-assets transactions; (D) divisive and non-divisive reorganizations; (E) recapitalizations; (F) mere changes in form; (G) bankruptcy-related reorganizations. It also has complex rules for triangular reorganizations involving subsidiaries and the use of parent (or related company) stock.

145 26 U.S.C.A. §331.

146 26 U.S.C.A. §336(a).

147 26 U.S.C.A. §336.

years under other Code sections.[148]

9. Taxation of "Pass-Through" Entities or "Fiscally Transparent" Entities

The Code has always treated certain entities as conduits for income and loss rather than as entities to be taxed. The most common of these "pass-through" entities is the partnership. In general, under the partnership tax rules of subchapter K of chapter 1 of the Code, all items of income and loss are passed through to the partners in the proportion of their partnership interests. From a business viewpoint, partnerships have long been a favorite form of doing business because of the flexibility afforded the partners in arranging the details of the partnership. Limited partnerships even afford the limited partners limited exposure to liability. In contrast to the corporate form, virtually every detail of a partnership can be a matter of agreement of the partners. From a tax viewpoint, partnerships, especially limited partnerships, are very popular entities for at least two reasons. First, they are business entities that avoid the double taxation of corporations. Second, the fiscal "transparency" allows the pass-through of *tax losses* to the individual partners even if the partnership is operating at an economic profit.[149]

The most common use of this loss pass-through feature is in real estate ventures where accelerated depreciation of buildings can generate losses that pass through to the partner's tax return (to offset other income of the partner) even though at the same time the venture itself generates a positive cash flow. Of course, since the accelerated depreciation lowers the basis in the partnership property, the end of the partnership usually requires a recapture of these losses by the realization of a significant gain and its concomitant tax liability. However, the deferral of that tax liability and the use of the losses in the earlier years against income provides substantial benefits to investors.

Because of the widespread and "creative" use of partnerships in areas such as real estate in the last three decades, a substantial body of Treasury Regulations, case law, and scholarly commentary has developed around the partnership rules of subchapter K. These rules have been extended to cover the newer forms of pass-through entities, such as limited liability companies, which are treated for tax purposes as if they were partnerships.

Choice of Entity: "Check-the-box" Regulations For several decades the IRS battled with taxpayers over whether a particular entity was more like a corporation, and thus subject to double taxation, or more like a partnership, and thus allowed a pass-through of income and losses. In the mid-1990s, the IRS finally decided to allow unincorporated business organizations, such as limited liability companies, the *choice* of being taxed as an "association" (the technical classification of a corporation) or as a partnership. The so-called "check-the-box" regulations that allow this choice were issued in late 1996.[150]

S Corporations Until the advent of the limited liability companies in the last decade, there were only two ways to both get the limited liability protection afforded to corporations *and* the pass-through tax treatment of income and losses. One way was to use a limited partnership. However, such a partnership always carried some risk of being classified by the IRS as a corporation. The other way was to use an "S corpora-

---

148 26 U.S.C.A. §1501 grants an "affiliated group" of corporations the privilege of filing a consolidated tax return for all members of the group instead of individual tax returns. The definition of an "affiliated group" was discussed when the deduction for dividends received was explained. The area of consolidated returns is quite complex and entails very detailed regulations.

149 Partnerships are discussed in Chapter XV, pp. 581-585.

150 Treas. Reg. 301.7701-1 et seq. *See* Chapter XV, p. 599.

tion." The S corporation takes its name from subchapter S of chapter 1 of the Code.[151] The S corporation allows pass-through of items of income or loss to its shareholders in much the same fashion as does a partnership. However, the S corporation has a rather limiting set of requirements in order to qualify. For instance, an S corporation can have no more than 75 shareholders. All its shareholders have to be individuals (with very limited exceptions). It can only have one class of stock.[152] Despite these limitations, the S corporation played a significant role for small businesses. The limited liability company, even before the issuance of "check-the-box" regulations, had already significantly displaced the S corporation. It remains to be seen whether it will end up replacing it entirely.

Trusts and Estates Trusts (which are commonly used in personal "estate planning") and estates (which are used to wind down the affairs of a deceased person) are technically taxable entities.[153] However, they are granted a deduction for income distributed to beneficiaries. Thus, if all their income is distributed currently, they are effectively a "pass-through" entity. However, failure to distribute income may cause a tax at the level of the trust. Despite the seeming simplicity of this scheme, the income taxation of trusts and estates is a fairly complex one.[154]

C. International Tax Issues

1. Tax on Foreign Income of U.S. Taxpayers

General Policy In general, the United States asserts jurisdiction to tax U.S. citizens, U.S. residents, and U.S. corporations on their worldwide income. However, the United States taxes non-resident aliens and foreign corporations only on income that has a certain connection with the United States.

In a like manner, the United States generally does not impose a tax on the income earned by a foreign corporation even if that corporation is owned by U.S. shareholders until that income is actually repatriated to the United States in the form of a dividend. However, to prevent perceived abuses of this deferral, the United States currently taxes the income of certain foreign corporations that have U.S. shareholders.

In conformity with norms of international taxation, the United States cedes to foreign governments the primary right to tax income arising in their countries. To prevent double taxation, the United States grants a tax credit against U.S. income taxes for taxes paid to a foreign government on income earned in that country.

Bilateral income tax treaties, which are essentially contracts between two governments, may modify these basic rules. For instance, a treaty may waive the right of a country that is the source of income to tax that income when the recipient of the income is a citizen of the other contracting party.

The U.S. Corporation Doing Business Overseas A U.S. taxpayer may have foreign source income in two different ways. First, it may be doing business directly in a foreign country in the form of a branch operation. Second, it may be doing business in a foreign country indirectly through a subsidiary that is incorporated in a foreign country.

Doing Foreign Business Directly The U.S. corporation that does business abroad

---

151 26 U.S.C.A. §§1361 et seq. *See* Chapter XV, p. 589.

152 See 26 U.S.C.A. §1361(b)(1).

153 *See* Chapter XII, pp. 493-497.

154 In general, subchapter J of chapter 1 of the Code provides the rules for the taxation of trusts and estates.

directly is taxed currently on its domestic and foreign income in the same manner as any other domestic corporation. There are rather detailed rules regarding the matter of currency translation of the foreign operations and very complex rules regarding the application of the foreign tax credit.[155]

The foreign tax credit is an elective provision. The taxpayer may, in certain circumstances, choose to *deduct* the foreign income taxes paid.[156] In general, a credit would be preferable because it would offset U.S. taxes on a dollar-for-dollar basis. However, if the U.S. taxpayer has foreign income in one country that is taxed in that country and an equal foreign loss in another country in the same year, the Code requires that the loss be offset against the gain to determine the *net* amount of foreign income available for the credit. In this circumstance the credit for the tax paid to the first country would not be usable and a deduction would be preferred. The election to take or not take the credit is made each year.

The foreign tax credit is subject to a complex set of limitations in order to prevent the use of the credit against U.S. income taxation of U.S. source income. The Code requires the taxpayer to look at several defined categories of foreign income and losses before applying the limitation rules.[157]

The foreign tax credit is available only to offset *income* taxes imposed by foreign governments. Although the Code does not define "income tax," the Treasury Regulations attempt to do so. In essence, in order to be considered an income tax the foreign tax must be "likely to reach net gain."[158] Given the wide variety of taxes in the world, the tests laid out in the regulations often fail to give clear answers to income tax categorizations. The issue of foreign tax credits is an important subject of bilateral treaty negotiations.

Doing Foreign Business Indirectly Through a Subsidiary When the foreign source income of a foreign subsidiary of a U.S. corporation is repatriated to the U.S. in the form of a dividend, the parent corporation is entitled to a credit under the Code, for the foreign income taxes paid by that subsidiary. This credit is usually referred to as the "indirect" or "deemed-paid" foreign tax credit.[159]

In order to be eligible for the indirect credit the U.S. parent must be at least a 10% shareholder (by vote) of the foreign subsidiary paying the dividend. This same rule applies to second and third tier subsidiaries so long as the *product* of the ownership percentage of each corporation down the chain equals at least 5%.[160] The three-tier limit imposed difficult restrictions on multinational corporations with highly hierarchical structures of subsidiaries. Many such corporations needed to use additional levels of entities for business purposes as well as for compliance with local foreign rules. These corporations were thus forced to use pass-through entities, such as partnerships and limited liability companies, at levels below the third if they wished to avail themselves of the indirect credit since those entities were by their nature deemed to pass through to their owners the foreign taxes paid. Since 1997, *corporate* subsidiaries down to the sixth level are now permitted to pass indirectly back to their parent the taxes paid to a

---

155 26 U.S.C.A. §901.

156 26 U.S.C.A. §164(a)(3).

157 26 U.S.C.A. §904.

158 Treas. Reg. 1.901-2.

159 26 U.S.C.A. §902(a).

160 26 U.S.C.A. §902(b).

foreign government. However, in addition to also having to meet the 10% tests, there are further restrictions on the corporations in levels four through six. Among other things, any such lower-tier foreign subsidiary corporation must also be a "controlled foreign corporation."[161] Such "CFC's" are discussed below.

"Grossing Up" the Dividend In order to create a parallel structure to the treatment of dividends from domestic corporations, the parent corporation is required to add to the actual dividend paid the amount of the foreign tax actually paid and include *both* in gross income. This "grossed-up" amount is thus equivalent to the pre-tax foreign income (*i.e.*, the foreign income before any foreign tax is paid).[162] The U.S. tax on the U.S. parent would thus be imposed on this grossed-up amount of income, and it is against this U.S.-taxed income that the indirect credit would be applied.

"Controlled Foreign Corporations" and the Anti-Deferral Provisions A "controlled foreign corporation," commonly referred to as a "CFC," is any foreign corporation in which U.S. persons own more than 50% of the corporation's stock by vote or value. However, in applying the 50% test, one must take into account only those U.S. persons who own at least 10% of the stock by vote only.[163] The stock ownership that counts here is not just direct ownership, but also constructive ownership determined by applying attribution rules for related parties and entities.[164]

The consequences of a foreign corporation being classed as a CFC are that certain classes of income, commonly called "subpart F income," are taxed *currently* to the U.S. shareholders, even if not repatriated. The CFC is thus not permitted the deferral generally accorded to other foreign subsidiaries. When a CFC earns subpart F income, that income is currently taxed to the 10% U.S. shareholders in accord with their pro-rata holdings. In addition, the U.S. will generally tax the U.S. shareholders on their share of the CFC's earnings that are invested in the United States and in certain other assets. The foreign tax credit may be available to offset some or all of the tax on these items. Subpart F income is generally income that is fairly movable from one country to another, and it is subject to relatively low rates of tax.[165]

Transfer Pricing Since a U.S. parent corporation may own a foreign subsidiary completely, there is potential for abuse in the way the two corporations set the prices for intercompany transactions and allocate items of expense and income between them. The Code gives the IRS express authority to allocate and apportion any items of income, deductions, credits or allowances between the two companies in order to ensure that the tax returns of the companies "clearly reflect the income" of the individual companies.[166] The area of intercompany pricing is a highly contested area and results in many disputes with the IRS. Intercompany pricing analyses are typically very complex and require the services of expert economists. It is often possible and advisable to get advance rulings from the IRS in this area.

2. Tax on U.S. Source Income of Foreign Taxpayers

There are four basic schemes for the taxing of foreign taxpayers with U.S. source income.

---

161 26 U.S.C.A. §957(a).

162 26 U.S.C.A. §78.

163 26 U.S.C.A. §957.

164 26 U.S.C.A. §958.

165 *See* 26 U.S.C.A. §§952-954 for the details of what is included in subpart F income.

166 26 U.S.C.A. §482.

"FDAP" Income and 30% Gross Taxation　Foreign persons (including corporations) are subject to a flat 30% tax[167] without regard to any deductions on gross income derived "from sources within the United States."[168]　The income subject to this tax is generally recurring income from investments.　Indeed, the Code refers to this income as "fixed or determinable annual or periodical gains, profits, and income" (commonly referred to as "FDAP" income).　The most common forms of FDAP income are interest, dividends, rents, and royalties.　Income from personal services rendered in the U.S. is also considered FDAP income.　The 30% tax on gross income is, subject to exceptions, required to be withheld at the source by the U.S. payor.[169]

"ECI" and Net Taxation　The U.S. also taxes the income of foreign persons that is "effectively connected" with the conduct of a trade or business in the U.S., whether or not it is sourced in the U.S.　This tax is imposed on a net basis, in the same way and subject to the same rates to which U.S. persons are subject.[170]　The term "effectively connected" income, sometimes referred to as "ECI," is defined as including income from sales, services, and manufacturing in the U.S.[171]　Some *foreign* source income of a foreign person may be effectively connected with the conduct of a U.S. trade or business and thus may also be subject to tax in the U.S.[172]　Of course, such effectively connected foreign source income may also qualify for the foreign tax credit for any foreign taxes paid on it.[173]

"Occasional" Gains and No Taxation　If a foreign person has an occasional gain that is not FDAP income (because it is not recurrent) and no "effectively connected" income, then, subject to several major exceptions, the foreign person is not subject to any tax in the U.S.　The most significant exception is for the gain from the sale of U.S. real property (or the stock in a holding company owning U.S. real property).　The sale of such U.S. real property (or of the stock in such a holding company) is treated as effectively connected income (ECI), discussed above.　It is therefore subject to the same net taxation scheme applicable to all ECI.

Modification by Treaty　Bilateral tax treaties may reduce or eliminate some of the above taxes.　For instance, it is not uncommon for a treaty to reduce or eliminate the 30% withholding tax on FDAP income.　Also, U.S. tax treaties tend to *modify* the taxation scheme for effectively connected income by looking to see if the foreign person has a "permanent establishment" in the U.S.　Only if one exists will the "business profits" or "commercial and industrial profits" (depending on the particular treaty) be taxable in the U.S.　Even then, the treaties often state that U.S. tax will be imposed only on the business profits attributable to the permanent establishment.

Maintaining Parity with the "Branch Profits Tax"　If a foreign corporation does business in the U.S. through a U.S. subsidiary, then that subsidiary would be taxed on its income just like any other U.S. corporation.　When the subsidiary pays a dividend to its foreign parent that dividend would be FDAP income subject to the flat 30% withholding tax.　If, on the other hand, the foreign corporation chose to do business directly in the U.S. through a "branch" operation rather than through a U.S. subsidiary, its U.S. source

---

167　26 U.S.C.A. §§871(a), 881.

168　26 U.S.C.A. §§861-865.

169　26 U.S.C.A. §§1441, 1442.

170　26 U.S.C.A. §§871(b), 882.

171　26 U.S.C.A. §864(c).

172　26 U.S.C.A. §864(c)(4)(A) and (B).

173　26 U.S.C.A. §§864(c)(4), 906.

income would effectively be connected income and would be taxed in a manner similar to other U.S. corporations. However, when the U.S. branch office sends its profits back to the foreign home office, there would be no additional tax on this intra-company transfer. When the foreign corporation then pays a *dividend* to *its* shareholders, that dividend would technically be FDAP income from a U.S. source. However, it is virtually impossible for the U.S. to collect a tax from a foreign corporation on its dividend distribution. As a result, the U.S. enacted a "branch profits" tax, which imposes a 30% flat tax on the earnings repatriated (or deemed so) by the U.S. branch office to the foreign home office.[174] This tax, like the 30% tax withheld by a U.S. subsidiary on the dividends it pays, is in addition to the regular net tax paid by the branch office on the effective connected income (ECI).

D. Other Federal Taxes

1. The Payroll Tax

The federal social security system is funded by payments from taxpayers deducted from their payroll and paid at the source by the employer. Employers are liable for about one-half of the tax and employees the other half. Self-employed individuals also must contribute to the system. The general level of tax is 15.3% of one's wages or equivalent self-employment earnings. The maximum amount of wages or earnings subject to the tax was $106,800 in 2010.[175]

2. Excise Taxes

There are numerous federal excise taxes on particular items. Perhaps the most common of these are the taxes on sales of alcohol and tobacco.

3. The Estate and Gift Taxes

The federal estate and gift taxes of chapters 11 and 12 of the Code[176] and the tax on generation-skipping transfers of chapter 13[177] are a relatively well-coordinated set of taxes on gratuitous transfers. Although the generation-skipping tax is a relatively recent addition to the Code, the estate and gift taxes have been around almost as long as the income tax. All three taxes are imposed on gratuitous transfers. The gift tax is imposed on transfers made during life. The estate tax imposes a final tax on the transfers made after the taxpayer's death. One of the premises of these taxes is that the intra-family transfer of wealth should be taxed once each generation. The generation-skipping tax, put simply, is imposed on transfers that avoid these taxes by transferring wealth in a manner that "skips" over an intervening generation.

The estate and gift taxes have a unified rate structure[178] that, as of 2006, effectively taxed only those gratuitous transfers or estates of individuals that exceeded $2,000,000 *in the aggregate*. The tax-free amount for estates jumped to $3,500,000 in 2009 and to $5,000,000 in 2011. All amounts above the tax-free amount are taxed at the flat rate of 45%.[179] These amounts and rates are likely to fluctuate since the very existence of an estate tax is a hot political issue and proposals for its elimination are an annual event in Congress.

---

174 26 U.S.C.A. §884.

175 Source: Social Security Administration. *See* www.ssa.gov/pressoffice/factsheets/colafacts2010.htm.

176 26 U.S.C.A. §§2001 *et seq.* and 2501 *et seq.* respectively.

177 26 U.S.C.A. §2601 *et seq.*

178 26 U.S.C.A. §2001.

179 As noted earlier, the recipient of the gratuitous transfer does not have gross income because the Code excludes transfers "by gift, bequest, devise, or inheritance." 26 U.S.C.A. §102(a).

E. State and Local Taxes

1. The Sales Tax

Sales taxes, imposed at the point of sale to the ultimate consumer, are a major source of revenue for most states. Some cities also impose sales taxes. It is fairly common to see sales tax rates of about 5%.[180] Sales taxes have been heavily criticized as being regressive in their effect since the greatest proportional burden of the tax falls on lower-income consumers. Attempts to correct this inequity are usually in the form of exempting staples such as food from the tax base.

2. The Property Tax

Property taxes are another major source of revenue for states. These were discussed in Chapter XII.[181]

3. Franchise Taxes

Many states impose franchise taxes on the privilege of doing business in the state. These taxes are sometimes viewed as a substitute for more comprehensive income taxes.

4. State and Local Income Taxes

Many states tax the income of residents and those non-residents doing business in the state. Some cities also impose income taxes in a like manner.[182] Many of the state income taxes are based on federal income tax or on the federal adjusted gross income with further adjustments. State income tax rates vary widely, but are usually less than 10%. Some states have no income tax.[183]

F. Administration of Tax Laws

The U.S. tax system is based on self-assessment of taxes made by the taxpayer on a "tax return" form. In other words, the taxpayer calculates the amount of taxes due and submits the amount due along with the tax return to the IRS. The taxpayer generally submits these forms without submitting any of the underlying documents (such as receipts for claimed expenses). But while the honesty of individual taxpayers is important and is relied upon heavily to produce accurate taxation, the system is not a complete "honor" system. For example, many taxes are collected "at the source" by withholding potential taxes from payments. Similarly, the federal income tax is collected from all employees by requiring that all employers withhold appropriate amounts of tax from every payment to the employees.

If necessary, audits and even criminal investigations may be undertaken to follow up on the taxpayer's self-assessment. Investigations of potential criminal matters are conducted by "special agents" of the IRS Criminal Investigation Division (the "CID"). An investigation by the CID is essentially the same as an investigation by any other law enforcement agency of the government (such as the FBI) and should be treated accordingly. The general rule in normal audits is for the taxpayer to cooperate with the

---

180 Currently, California has the highest rate of 8.25 % while 5 states do not impose sales tax at all (Alaska, Delaware, Montana, New Hampshire, and Oregon), *at* www.taxadmin.org/fta/rate/sales.html.

181 *See* p. 481.

182 "Tax-free Day," usually in the month of May, is the day when most taxpayers in the U.S., who have been working since January 1st, stop "working for the government" and start working for themselves.

183 Alaska, Florida, Nevada, South Dakota, Texas, Washington, and Wyoming impose zero state income tax. New Hampshire and Tennessee also have zero income tax with the exception of dividends and interest income which are taxed. *At* http://www.taxadmin.org/fta/rate/ind_inc.html.

government's requests. If the audit turns into a criminal investigation, the taxpayer should not have any further contact with the government agents before she contacts a lawyer who specializes in criminal defense.

1. Initial Screening of Returns

Tax returns are initially reviewed only for mathematical errors. They are then reviewed by sophisticated computer programs designed to highlight potential problems. If the computer finds an area of the return in which the amounts claimed for an item are outside the average range of amounts, then that area of the return is marked for further review by an IRS agent (a "revenue agent"). If the review shows potential problems, the return is marked for an "audit." An audit is an official review of the tax return by an agent of the IRS.

2. Tax Audits

In General If the tax return is marked for audit the taxpayer will be notified by the IRS of the time and place for the review of the tax return. The notification to the taxpayer includes a list of the issues that are to be examined and a request by the IRS to see the documents supporting the taxpayer's position on the return. The notice also tells whether the audit will occur at the local IRS office (an "office audit") or at the taxpayer's place of business (a "field audit"). Audits of individuals are usually office audits and will take place at the local IRS offices and are conducted by tax auditors. Audits of businesses are usually field audits and will take place at the place of business of the taxpayer and are conducted by revenue agents. The reason for the difference in the place of the audit is that access to records is usually easier on site at a business, while the individual taxpayer can usually bring in the requisite records without difficulty.

Audits are conducted informally. Most audits start with a revenue agent, who is usually not a lawyer or accountant, looking at supporting documents, such as receipts for expenses, to support the taxpayer's position on the tax return. The great majority of audits end when the revenue agent is satisfied that the taxpayer has sufficient documentation to support the item on the return. However, some audits continue beyond this factual inquiry and concern legal issues or mixed issues of law and fact.

An audit comprises both a factual part and a legal part. Among the most common issues in audits is the propriety of "deductions" from income. The allowance or disallowance of a deduction affects the important issue of how much taxable income the taxpayer had. For example, among the more common deductions that get raised in audits are those permitted for business expenses, interest paid on loans, depreciation of business property, and gifts to charities.

The "Factual" Part of the Audit In this part of the audit, the basic facts of the claimed deduction are established. If a business deduction is questioned, the taxpayer is asked to substantiate the claim that the business-related item was in fact purchased by production of a receipt and evidence of payment. If a charitable deduction is questioned, the taxpayer is asked to produce a receipt and canceled check for the donation.

The "Legal" Part of the Audit The legal part of the audit will involve whether the expense for which a deduction has been claimed is a legitimate one from the standpoint of the law. If the taxpayer claimed a deduction for business expenses for using his car to take his children to school and to soccer practice, this would not be allowed as a business expense as a matter of law. On the other hand, if the taxpayer is a salesperson who travels by car in her business, the deduction of transportation expenses would probably be proper.

It does not matter in which "order" the audit is conducted. In practice the two "parts" are often intermixed. The legal part may be conducted first if it disposes of the issue. Thus, if it is clear that the taxpayer's deduction is for taking the children to school and soccer practice, it will not matter whether the taxpayer can substantiate the expense or method of calculating it.

3. Administrative Protests and Appeals

When the revenue agent is satisfied that there is enough information the agent will issue a report (commonly called a "revenue agent's report" or "RAR").

The "Thirty Day Letter" The RAR is attached to a letter (commonly called a "thirty day letter") to the taxpayer that gives the taxpayer thirty days to appeal the conclusions in the report to the Appellate Division of the IRS. If the taxpayer wishes to dispute the conclusions she will generally be required to file a "protest" (or "protest letter") with the IRS within thirty days.

The Appellate Division of the IRS Upon receipt of the protest the IRS will transfer the case internally to the Appellate Division where it will be assigned to an "appeals officer." The appeals officer will review the file anew and will schedule a hearing with the taxpayer and the taxpayer's representative (typically her lawyer or accountant). The original revenue agent will generally not be present. Appeals officers are generally better trained and more sophisticated than revenue agents. They also have the authority (which auditors do not have) to "settle" a dispute with a taxpayer based on the possible risk to the IRS of losing the case if it were to go to litigation. The appellate hearing will also be an informal proceeding. The taxpayer will again be allowed to present her view of the issues. Then, the appeals officer will issue a final report, typically in the form of a letter stating the conclusions of the appeals officer.

The "Ninety Day Letter" If the taxpayer chooses not to protest the original revenue agent's conclusions, or at the end of the IRS appeals process, the IRS will send the taxpayer another letter (typically called a "ninety day letter") which tells the taxpayer that she has ninety days to either pay the tax or to file a lawsuit in the U.S. Tax Court. As discussed below, the taxpayer may take the matter to the Tax Court and contest the findings of the IRS without first paying the claimed tax. The taxpayer may also choose to pay the tax and then sue for a refund in the U.S. District Court (where there are juries) or in the U.S. Claims Court. These courts are discussed below.

4. Judicial Review

As mentioned earlier, if a taxpayer disagrees with the IRS as to the treatment of an issue and wishes for judicial review of the IRS decision, the taxpayer can bring the matter to one of several courts. The taxpayer has the choice of three quite different tribunals: the Tax Court, the U.S. District Court, and the Claims Court.[184]

The Tax Court If the taxpayer wishes to challenge the IRS's decision without first paying the newly assessed tax, the Tax Court is the only possibility. All cases in the Tax Court are tried to a single judge. There are no jury trials. The judges of the Tax Court are specialists in tax matters, and they hear no other kinds of cases. Tax Court dockets tend to move quickly. Although the same types of pre-trial discovery are available in the Tax

---

184 The Tax Court and the Claims Courts are Article I courts, while the U.S. District Court is an Article III court. This means that only the U.S. District Court has a judge with lifetime tenure. *See* Chapter VI, pp. 220-222.

Court as in other courts, the judges tend to place great pressure on the parties to narrow the issues in the case. Indeed, Tax Court judges tend to make far more extensive use of stipulations than judges in other courts. In general, Tax Court judges will require that the parties stipulate to all facts about which there is no dispute. In this manner, trials in the Tax Court tend to be fairly streamlined. Although the Tax Court has its administrative offices in Washington, D.C., its judges hold court throughout the country. It is not uncommon for the Tax Court to hold court for several days each month in major U.S. cities. Appeals from Tax Court rulings are taken in the U.S. Court of Appeals for the Circuit in which the taxpayer resides. It is not uncommon for the tax law on particular points to vary from Circuit to Circuit.[185]

The taxpayer also has the option of paying the newly assessed tax and then suing the government for a refund. An important advantage of paying the tax early in the dispute process is that the payment halts the accrual of interest on the alleged deficiency balance.[186] A refund suit may be brought in either the District Court or the Claims Court.

District Court A suit for a refund in the District Court where the taxpayer resides is conducted in the same manner as any other civil matter. This is the only forum that provides juries to a contesting taxpayer. However, as in all civil jury cases, the jury will resolve only the factual issues in dispute. The District Judge will resolve any legal matters. District Judges are rarely specialists in tax matters. Depending on the nature of the case, it may or may not be to the taxpayer's advantage to have the case heard by a jury or by a non-specialist judge. Appeals from District Court decisions go the Court of Appeals for the circuit of which the district is a part and the District Court is bound to follow the precedents of its circuit.

Claims Court The U.S. Claims Court has jurisdiction to hear claims, including claims for tax refunds, against the United States. Cases in the Claims Court are heard only by a judge. There are no juries. Some tax lawyers believe that the judges of the Claims Court are fairly sophisticated in handling large and business-related claims and are not as deferential to IRS interpretations of the Code as the Tax Court judges are sometimes perceived to be. Although the Claims Court is based in Washington, D.C., its judges will travel wherever necessary to hear evidence in a case. Unlike other courts, a trial in the Claims Court may occur in several sittings rather than all at once. These matters may make litigation in the Claims Court a more attractive option. Appeals from decisions of the Claims Court go to the Court of Appeals for the Federal Circuit.

Thus, the taxpayer must make some strategy choices based on the type of issue presented and the type of tribunal involved. Among the factors to consider are the presence or absence of a jury, the state of the law in the Federal Circuit, as opposed to the taxpayer's home Circuit, and the facts that Tax Court judges are sophisticated in tax law and Claims Court judges are expert in complicated business matters, while federal district judges tend to be generalists.

5. Tax Lawyers and Advisors

As noted in Chapter IV, despite the general nature of the license to practice law, U.S. lawyers tend to specialize in particular areas of practice. A few states have set minimum

---

185 Although the Tax Court once tried to establish nation-wide standards for its decisions by claiming that it did not need to follow the decisions of the Court of Appeals of the circuit where the taxpayer resides, this attempt to establish an independent Tax Court jurisprudence was rejected by the Tax Court itself in *Golsen v. Comm'r of Internal Revenue*, 54 T.C. 742 (1970). Appeals of Tax Court decisions are heard in the taxpayers's circuit Court of Appeals and the Tax Court is bound to follow its precedents.

186 26 U.S.C.A. §6601.

standards of competence in various specialties. Most "tax lawyers" are highly specialized and tend to do only tax-related work. It is fairly common, but by no means universal, for tax lawyers to have had additional formal post-graduate education beyond their basic JD law degrees. A typical graduate tax program consists of one year of full-time course work, or three years of part-time course work, after the J.D. degree. It typically results in a Master of Laws degree, i.e., an LL.M. in Taxation. Most of the large American cities have at least one law school that offers at least a part-time graduate tax program.[187]

Most large businesses and large law firms have a separate department that deals only with tax matters. It would not be uncommon for a 200-lawyer firm to have a tax department with 20 tax lawyers. The large accounting firms also have large tax departments staffed with tax accountants and tax lawyers.

Tax lawyers are usually intimately involved in tax and business planning for their clients. The need for tax advice stems from the fact that there are usually several different ways to achieve the business result desired by a client. The different ways may have very different tax consequences. The tax lawyer helps the client assess, with respect to taxation, the potential impact and risks of the myriad transactional possibilities while keeping in mind the client's ultimate goals.[188]

---

[187] LLM programs in law schools were discussed in Chapter IV.

[188] Businesses are not the only taxpayers in need of tax planning. As discussed in Chapter XII, estate planning is essential to minimize estate, gift or income taxes upon one's death. Most lawyers who practice in the estate planning area are tax specialists.

CHAPTER XVII

INTERNATIONAL ASPECTS OF
UNITED STATES LAW

Globalization of the economy and communications in recent years has made the subject of this chapter one of increasing importance, as international law and litigation have become a part of the practice of the many lawyers in the United States. In this chapter we will examine two international aspects of U.S. law. The first, discussed in Part I, deals with how international law norms and institutions intersect with the law and legal system of the United States, including the important issue of the status of international law in the U.S. system and how it is applied by U.S. courts. The second aspect, discussed in Part II, covers issues of U.S. law that arise in the context of litigation in the U.S. that has international dimensions.[1]

A few issues of terminology, concepts and categories should be mentioned. First, "domestic" or "municipal" law is the technical name given by international lawyers to the national or internal law of a particular nation. In most instances here, "domestic" law will mean applicable federal or state law of the United States. Second, international lawyers discuss issues dealing with nations, and refer to them as "states," thus creating the possibility of confusion with a state of the United States. In what follows, the context of the term's use should differentiate its meaning. However, to avoid confusion, when an international nation-state is intended, the word "state" will be capitalized ("State") and when a state of the United States is meant, it will be written in lowercase ("state").

PART I: International Law and Its Application in the United States
A. Sources, Forms and Hierarchy of International Law Rules
1. Sources and Forms

International law comes from three sources: (1) treaties or other agreements, (2) customary international law and (3) general principles of law.[2]

a. Treaties

Nature of Treaties All written agreements between States are considered to be "treaties" regardless of what name is attached to them.[3] Thus, it does not matter whether a given international agreement is called a treaty, agreement, convention,

---

1 For more detail on these subjects, *see* Restatement (Third) of Foreign Relations Law of the United States. RESTATEMENT (THIRD) OF FOREIGN RELATIONS LAW OF THE UNITED STATES (American Law Institute 1987), hereafter simply "RESTATEMENT." *See also* PHILLIP R. TRIMBLE, INTERNATIONAL LAW: UNITED STATES FOREIGN RELATIONS LAW (Foundation 2002); DAVID J. BEDERMAN, INTERNATIONAL LAW FRAMEWORKS (Foundation 2001); JOHN M. ROGERS, INTERNATIONAL LAW AND UNITED STATES LAW (Dartmouth-Ashgate 1999); JORDAN J. PAUST, INTERNATIONAL LAW AS LAW OF THE UNITED STATES, 2D ED (Carolina Academic Press 2006); GARY B. BORN, INTERNATIONAL CIVIL LITIGATION IN UNITED STATES COURTS (4TH ED. 2007); SEAN D. MURPHY, PRINCIPLES OF INTERNATIONAL LAW CONCISE HORNBOOK (West 2006). *See also* RALPH FOLSOM, MICHAEL GORDON & JOHN A. SPANOGLE, HORNBOOK ON INTERNATIONAL BUSINESS TRANSACTIONS, 2D ED. (West 2001).

2 RESTATEMENT §102. See Chapter II, p. 76, for an explanation of restatements of the law.

3 Art. 1-2, Vienna Treaty on the Law of Treaties, 23 May 1969, Art. 2(1)(d) (eff. 27 January 1980), 8 Int.Leg.Mat. 679 (1969). The treaty became effective after 35 countries had ratified it. Although the President in 1971 transmitted it to the Senate for its consent, the Senate has not acted and the treaty remains unratified. Nonetheless, the Department of State treats it as authoritative and several federal courts have applied its provisions. RESTATEMENT, Introductory Note, pp. 144-145.

covenant or compact.[4] Any form of agreement entered into by States is a treaty.[5] A bilateral treaty is one that is agreed to by only two States, while a multilateral treaty is one agreed to by more than two States.

Treaties and Customary Rules   As the international law system strives for greater consistency and clarity, customary international law has increasingly been "codified" in multilateral treaties. Thus, while treaties are the principal method of creating international law today, much of the law thus "created" already existed in the form of customary law. A prominent example of this is the Vienna Convention on the Law of Treaties — a "treaty on treaties" that codifies customary rules for interpretation of treaties. Another is the rule on the limits of territorial waters. In turn, as discussed below in subsection b., treaties are also the principal method of creating new customary international law binding on States that are not parties to it.

Reservations   A State may file a "reservation" to a treaty. A reservation is a unilateral statement made by a State when it signs a treaty that purports to exclude or to modify the effect of certain provisions of the treaty with regard to that State. However, reservations may not be made if prohibited by the treaty or if they are "incompatible with the object and purpose of the treaty."[6]

Terminations   A party to a treaty can terminate a treaty in accord with its provisions for termination or with the consent of the parties to it. However, even where the treaty does not so provide, an implied right of termination may exist.[7]

b. Customary Rules of International Law

(1) Criteria for Customary Rules

Development Through Practice   Customary rules result from (1) "a general and consistent practice" of States (2) that is observed "from a sense of obligation."[8] The first inquiry is a historical one of determining what States have done on the subject over the years. There is no set formula for determining how many states must follow a practice or for how long it must be followed before it becomes a rule of customary law. Some rules take centuries to develop. For example, the rule that coastal fishing vessels of an enemy State are immune from seizure during war was thought by the English High Court of Admiralty in 1798 not to be sufficiently established as a rule at that time, but was determined by the U.S. Supreme Court to have crystalized into one by 1900.[9] Other practices have become "instant custom" over a just few years. For example, the rule that States can claim offshore oil and gas deposits within its own continental shelf proved so instantly popular among States that it developed over a mere 15 years.[10] Proof of consistent practice can be a difficult task. The burden is on the party relying on the

---

4   Other less commonly heard names are charter, statute, act, declaration, *concordat*, exchange of notes, agreed minute, memorandum of agreement or understanding and *modus vivendi*.

5   U.S. law distinguishes between treaties and other international agreements for domestic purposes, primarily to determine which agreements must be ratified and which need not be. *See infra* pp. 688-693.

6   Art. 19, Vienna Convention; RESTATEMENT §313.

7   *See generally* Art. 54-56, Vienna Convention; RESTATEMENT §332. Conclusion of a later treaty that is seriously incompatible can also effect an termination. Treaties can be suspended and modified by the parties under certain circumstances. *See* RESTATEMENT §§333-334.

8   RESTATEMENT, §102(2).

9   *Compare The Young Jacob*, 165 Eng. Rep. 81 (Adm. 1798) *with The Paquete Habana*, 175 U.S. 677 (1900).

10   *See North Sea Continental Shelf Cases*, 1969 Int'l Ct. of Justice Reports 3, 43-44. *See* RESTATEMENT, Reporter's Notes to §102.

existence of the rule.[11]

Opinio Juris A consistent practice becomes a customary rule *only if* states observe it from a sense of *obligation* (called *opinio juris sive necessitatis*). It is this sense of legal obligation that distinguishes customary rules from practices observed out of mere "comity." Comity is the natural courtesy and respect that States owe each other and may act on when appropriate in the international arena. A "rule" of conduct observed out of comity — no matter how consistently or how long it is observed — fails this second requirement for the establishment of a customary rule of international law.[12]

(2) How Customary Rules Develop

Historical Practice The process of developing a customary rule of international law has been said to be a "process of continuous interaction, of continuous demand and response" among States.[13] The evidence of a customary rule includes not just judgments of national and international tribunals, but also the works of scholars and "pronouncements by states that undertake to state a rule of international law, when such pronouncements are not seriously challenged by other states."[14]

Influencing History Knowing the significance of their actions and pronouncements in creating the practice requisite for development of an international rule, States actively seek to act, issue official statements and file diplomatic protests in such a way as to promote the establishment of some customary rules and to defeat development of others. Thus, a State must be alert to developing practices and trends in the international arena to make sure that the appropriate actions are taken or statements of agreement or protests made. Silence could cause a State to be "accidentally" bound by a customary rule it disagrees with. This accounts for many international protests that might seem to the layperson to be pointless. It follows that, if a customary rule is established despite a State's decidedly minority, but consistent protests and action opposed to it, a State will not be subject to the rule. However, the instances of this exception being successfully invoked are few.[15]

(3) Nature of Customary Rules

The idea of customary norms based on the practice of States may sound somewhat vague and indeterminate when compared to rules established by multilateral treaties. Drawing a line between "hard" and "soft" international law is useful, but as Professor Handl has noted, there are examples of "treaties, whose ineffectiveness relegates them to the ranks of nonlegal . . . or . . . soft norms," while there are some customary norms

---

11 *See The S.S. Lotus (France v. Turkey)*, 1927 Perm. Ct. of Int'l Justice (Ser. A) No. 10 (in dispute with Turkey, France was unable to prove that exercise of criminal jurisdiction over its national for negligent homicide of Turkish nationals on the high seas violated any customary rule).

12 *See Hilton v. Guyot*, 159 U.S. 113, 163-164 (1895). Comity figures prominently in the question of the extraterritorial reach of laws. *See infra* pp. 705-714. The requirement that the practice be engaged in out of a sense of obligation has raised theoretical difficulties, particularly the question of how a practice can be engaged in out of a sense of obligation before the law that arises out of the legal obligation has fully developed. For this and other theoretical mysteries of customary international law, *see* PARRY, THE SOURCES AND EVIDENCES OF INTERNATIONAL LAW (1965).

13 Myers McDougal, *The Hydrogen Bomb Tests and International Law of the Sea*, 49 AM. J. INT'L LAW 356, 357-358 (1955).

14 RESTATEMENT §103(2).

15 An example of a State carving out an exception for itself in this way is the *Fisheries Case* (United Kingdom v. Norway), 1951 Int'l Ct. of Justice Rep. 116 (despite otherwise unanimous agreement on 3-mile territorial waters, Norway would be not be subject to the rule because it had sufficiently protested application of the rule to itself).

"which have proven to be highly effective . . . ."[16] Customary rules of international law can be as specific as any treaty. For example, the rule applied in *The Paquete Habana*,[17] that small coastal boats are immune from capture during a war unless they can be shown to be participating in the war effort, is a specific and clear rule of customary international law.[18]

(4) Documentary Sources of Customary International Law

Treaties As mentioned earlier, multilateral treaties "may lead to the creation of customary international law when such agreements are intended for adherence generally and are in fact widely accepted."[19] There are several such "objective regime" treaties, such as the Charter of the United Nations, which is adhered to by all states, even the few remaining nonmember states. Another is the operation of the norms of the Vienna Convention on Treaties in those States, such as the U.S., that have not yet ratified it.

Acts of International Bodies or Conferences States also act through international organizations in passing resolutions and other agreed statements. If their content and the circumstances of their adoption reflect an expectation that the international community will abide by them, they can be a source of customary law. In this category are the various resolutions, declarations and statements of principles adopted by the General Assembly of the United Nations. In a similar though less formal manner, multilateral conferences may voice a consensus on particular principles, thus making them potential sources of customary rules.[20] The strength of the particular act may depend on the majority it commanded and who the dissenting nations were.[21] An example of instant customary law being created by the U.N. was the Outer Space Declaration of the U.N. General Assembly for which all the "space powers" voted and which both the United States and the U.S.S.R. promptly announced they would follow.[22] On the other hand, an arbitrator of a dispute between Libya and a U.S. oil company whose property it had expropriated rejected Libya's attempt to rely on three General Assembly resolutions. The arbitrator felt that the resolutions had not been supported by a sufficient cross-section of States, all the economically developed and capital-exporting cases having either abstained or voted "no."[23]

---

16 *A Hard Look at Soft Law*, 82 PROC., AMERICAN SOCIETY OF INTERNATIONAL LAW 132 (1988), quoted in relevant part in PAUST, FITZPATRICK & VAN DYKE, *supra* note 1, at 34.

17 175 U.S. 677 (1900).

18 Another was the traditional rule of 3-mile territorial waters established in the 18th century, which has since been replaced by a 200-mile rule. *See* WESTON, FALK & CHARLESWORTH, *supra* note 1, at 1007.

19 RESTATEMENT §102(3).

20 An example of the International Court of Justice relying on a resolution of a multilateral conference on law of the sea is the *Fisheries Jurisdiction Case (United Kingdom vs. Iceland)*, 1974 Int'l Ct. of Justice Rep. 4, 31.

21 As a memorandum of the Office of Legal Affairs of the U.N. Secretariat explained that a declaration by the General Assembly "may be considered to impart, on behalf of the organ adopting it, a strong expectation that Members of the international community will abide by it. Consequently, insofar as the expectation is gradually justified by State practice, a declaration may by custom become recognized as laying down rules binding upon States." E/CM.4/L. 610, quoted in RESTATEMENT Reporter's Notes to §102 at 31.

22 Gen. Assembly Res. 1962, 18 U.N. GOAR, Supp. No. 15, at 15.

23 *Texaco Overseas Petroleum Co. (TOPCO) v. Libyan Arab Republic*, 17 Int'l Legal Materials 1 (Arb. 1978).

c. General Principles of Law

General principles are a supplementary source of international law because they are most often used to fill gaps in international agreements or customary international law rules. However, some general principles are as clear and forceful as the provisions of any treaty. The general principles are not general principles of *international* law. They are general principles of *domestic* law of States. In the words of Article 38 of the Statute of the International Court of Justice (the "World Court"), the source is "the general principles of law recognized by civilized nations."[24] This includes not just nations of the common-law and civil-law traditions, but also major religious legal cultures (*e.g.*, Jewish and Islamic) and the "socialist" legal tradition, as practiced in China and Cuba.

The difficulty with general principles is that the greater the consensus among nations and legal systems as to their existence, the more generalized and diluted their content becomes. Thus, all agree that the principle of good faith in the fulfillment of legal obligations (called *pacta sunt servanda*) exists in some form in all legal cultures. There is far less agreement about its meaning as applied to specific disputes.[25] More specific substantive examples are prohibitions on slavery and *ex post facto* punishment.

2. The Hierarchy of the Forms and Sources of International Law

Treaties and Customary Law Treaties and customary law are considered to be of equal force. Among other things, this means that the rule that is adopted later in time will govern. Thus, a treaty could overrule a prior rule of customary law and a later-developed custom could potentially override the provisions of a treaty. In practice, it is most often the case that international agreements change earlier rules of customary law. However, it must be clear that the treaty in fact did replace the customary rule. For example, in World War I, before the United States entered the war, it successfully objected to the British stopping its ships and arresting German nationals found on board. The United States relied on the customary rule granting immunity to vessels of neutral powers. Britain relied on a network of treaties, but none of them treated the precise issue. Thus, the customary rule remained unaffected.[26]

Cases of customary rules "trumping" international agreements are less often encountered. However, if a practice has great political appeal, it can become an "instant custom" without any action being taken to replace a previous treaty. Examples are the practice of States establishing 200-mile exclusive resource zones in the sea, thus effectively superceding contrary law in the 1958 Law of the Sea Conventions.[27]

Jus Cogens There are certain customary rules of international law that are said to be higher than the others. These are called "peremptory norms" or, in Latin, *jus cogens* — principles so fundamental that no State, whether by treaty, protest or practice, can exempt itself from them. Most experts agree that such "super-norms" exist and they are

---

24 Art. 38(1)(c), Statute of the International Court of Justice, quoted in RESTATEMENT, §102, Reporters' Note 1.

25 Even more general concepts of equity have been applied as well: "abuse of right," where an actor having the right to engage in certain conduct may not do so in an abusive manner; "unjust enrichment," where benefits accrue to a party to the disadvantage of another; and the "clean hands" doctrine, whereby a party may be denied relief if it has engaged in the same kind of activity of which it complains or has otherwise conducted itself in a morally improper way.

26 *The S.S. China Incident,* 1916 Foreign Relations of the U.S. Supp. 667.

27 *See* RESTATEMENT §514 and Reporter's Notes to §102 at 33. A new and extraordinarily detailed U.N. Convention on Law of the Sea (UNCLOS) was finally adopted in 1982 as a U.N. Convention after "the longest-running international law negotiation ever." BEDERMAN, *supra* note 1, at 119. UNCLOS codified the basic customary rule on economic zones, although there is still debate over some of the details.

acknowledged in the Vienna Convention on Treaties.[28] It is harder to say exactly what they are. Most experts would agree that prohibitions on genocide, slave trade and slavery, apartheid, torture and other such gross violations of human rights, and attacks on diplomats are among them. Some would also include the prohibition on the use of force as set out in the U.N. Charter, and the International Court of Justice has so held.[29] However, one might question whether, in light of recent history, the actual practice of nations is unanimous on the point.

B. International Law in the U.S. Legal System

1. U.S. Law of Treaties and Other International Agreements

a. Treaty Power Under the Constitution

(1) Procedures for Making and Ratifying Treaties

Ratification In popular speech and probably the speech of most lawyers, the President negotiates a treaty and the Senate "ratifies" it.[30] In fact, the President "makes" the treaty and the Senate gives its "advice and consent" and "concurs" by a two-thirds vote.[31] The President then continues the ratification process and at the appropriate point "proclaims" the treaty "ratified." Or the President may choose not to ratify it if, for example, the Senate has attached unacceptable conditions to its approval.[32] "Ratification" is a generic term used to denote the entire domestic legal process needed to finally approve a treaty following the initial signature by the relevant representatives of a State.[33] Since the ratification process is ultimately under the President's control and is successfully concluded only when so proclaimed by the President, it is most accurate to say that the President is the one who ratifies the treaty after obtaining Senate consent.[34]

Reservations and Conditions Outright refusals by the Senate to approve treaties are relatively rare. There have been only 21 refusals to consent since 1789. The last was the 1999 rejection of the Comprehensive Nuclear Test Ban Treaty. Perhaps the most serious was the Treaty of Versailles, which included the Covenant of the League of Nations championed by U.S. President Woodrow Wilson. The Senate has often given its consent conditioned on a particular understanding of the treaty's meaning or on the United States filing reservations to the treaty to a particular effect.[35] There have been notable delays

---

28 *See* Art. 53 and 64.

29 RESTATEMENT, Reporter's Notes to §102, at 34; *Nicaragua v. United States of America*, 1986 Int'l Ct. of Justice 14, 103-123.

30 *See, e.g., El Al Israel Airlines, Ltd. v. Tsui Yuan Tseng*, 525 U.S. 155, 160 (1999) (referring to the Warsaw Convention protocol (Montreal Protocol No. 4) as "recently ratified by the Senate").

31 *See* Constitution, Art. II §2 (the President "shall have Power, by and with the Advice and Consent of the Senate, to make Treaties, provided two thirds of the Senators present concur."). "*Advice* and consent" is a term of art. It really only requires consent and is not read to require that the President seek the advice of Congress during the entire treaty-making process

32 RESTATEMENT §303, Reporter's note 3, §312, comment d, §314, comment b. An example of a President refusing to ratify because of unacceptable reservations was President Taft's refusal to proceed with a 1911 arbitration treaty with France and Great Britain. *See* 4 CHRISTIAN L. WIKTOR, ED., UNPERFECTED TREATIES OF THE UNITED STATES, 1776-1976, 217-218, 225-226 (1979).

33 When a treaty is signed, but subject to later ratification, it is referred to as being signed *ad referendum*.

34 *See* RESTATEMENT §303, Reporter's note 1 ("Properly speaking . . ., the Senate gives its consent to ratification. The President makes, ratifies, or accedes to a treaty on the behalf of the United States.") The President is also the one responsible for depositing the instruments of ratification with the depository designated by the treaty.

35 *See* RESTATEMENT §314, Reporter's note 1, discussing Senate declarations attached to the 1976 Treaty of Friendship and Cooperation with Spain and SALT II.

between initial signature and ratification. For example, the 1958 U.N. Convention on the Recognition and Enforcement of Foreign Arbitral Awards of 1958 was submitted swiftly to the Senate, but did not receive Senate consent until 10 years later and the United States did not accede to it until two years after that.

Termination of Treaties   The issue of how a treaty is terminated as a matter of international law has been mentioned. The question here is how a treaty can be terminated as a matter of U.S. domestic law. Unfortunately, the answer to it is unclear and not likely to become clearer anytime in the near future because of the "political question" doctrine applicable to the federal courts in the United States. In the case of *Goldwater v. Carter*,[36] Senators sued seeking to have President Carter's unilateral termination of a Mutual Defense Treaty with Taiwan declared invalid for the President's failure to seek Senate approval for such action. The Court declined to decide the case on the ground that it presented a "political question" to be resolved by the President and Congress, not by the courts. While *Goldwater v. Carter* involved the narrow issue of treaty abrogation, one can easily see how the political question doctrine could prevent courts from deciding other foreign affairs issues when there is a dispute between Congress and the President.[37]

(2) Scope of the Treaty Power Under the Constitution

As discussed in Chapter I, the federal government of the United States is one of limited powers. All its actions must be authorized by some grant of power set out in the Constitution.[38] Since Senate approval of a treaty is legislative, the question arises whether a treaty, to be constitutional, must come within one of the "enumerated" powers set out in Article I §8.

At least one Supreme Court case stands for the proposition that treaties need not fall under one of Congress's enumerated powers to be valid. In the 1920 case of *Missouri v. Holland*,[39] Congress passed a law to protect migratory birds. The law was challenged as unconstitutional for its lack of authorization under Article I §8, in view of the fact that wildlife management had traditionally been governed by state law. Two lower courts had held the act unconstitutional on this basis. Undeterred, the federal government in 1916 entered into the Migratory Bird Treaty with Great Britain and Canada and passed a federal law implementing it that was similar to the original law. The Court upheld the validity of the law in *Holland*. The Court assumed that the first statute was not within Congress's Article I powers to, but held that the second one enacted pursuant to the treaty was constitutional. It observed that there are matters "that an act of Congress could not deal with, but that a treaty followed by such an act could."[40]

Holland is regularly cited for the proposition that Article I §8 limits on congressional power do not apply to treaties.[41] However, there are at least two problems with this reading. First, the *Holland* opinion made reference to the statute and treaty dealing with

---

36   444 U.S. 996 (1979).

37   For a discussion of the political question doctrine, *see* Chapter IX, pp. 333-335.

38   *See* Chapter I, p. 4.

39   252 U.S. 416 (1920).

40   *Id.* at 433.

41   *See, e.g.,* ROGERS, *supra* note 1, at 92-95. In fact, in 1953-55, Senator Bricker led a movement in the Congress to amend the Constitution to deny the power to Congress to enact a law pursuant to a treaty that it could not enact in the absence of a treaty. The "Bricker Amendment" failed, however. *See* RESTATEMENT §111, Reporters' Note 10.

"matters of the sharpest exigency for the national well being,"[42] thus suggesting that *Holland* is limited only to such cases. On the other hand, the statement does not seem significant as a practical matter. If dealing with migratory birds in the pre-conservation era of *Holland* was considered a matter of "sharpest exigency for the national well-being," then most matters important enough to be governed by a treaty today would seem to qualify.[43] Second — and perhaps more important — the Supreme Court has held that treaties are subject to the limitations set out in the Bill of Rights.[44] Indeed, *Holland* itself acknowledged that a treaty cannot violate the "prohibitory words" of the Constitution. While one can argue that the "prohibitory" limits of the Bill of Rights are different from mere absence of constitutional power,[45] the Court has applied no such distinction in any other areas of constitutional law. Indeed, it has tended to equate Article I's implied limitations with the "prohibitory words" of the 10th Amendment.[46]

For years it did not matter whether *Holland* meant that treaties were confined to the limits of Congress's Article I enumerated powers. Until recently, the Court took a very broad view of Congress's powers, particularly the power to regulate interstate commerce. So, to say that the treaty power was limited to the enumerated subjects set out in Article I was to say that it was not limited very much. However, since 1995 the Court has taken a more restricted approach to Article I powers. The argument that any activity that has some form of economic impact comes within Congress's interstate commerce power is no longer sufficient, if it ever was, since almost all human conduct can be shown to have some economic impact. While any subject appropriate for treaty treatment will in most cases concern more than one state, recent caselaw suggests that its subject matter will have to be commercial relationships or non-commercial activities closely connected with them.[47]

(3) Enforcing U.S. Treaties: Self-Executing and Non-Self-Executing Treaties

Even if a treaty is properly made, approved by the Senate and ratified, it may still not qualify as "supreme" federal law enforceable in the courts if it is not "self-executing." Treaty provisions are not self-executing if they contemplate that domestic legislation will be enacted to effectuate its provisions or if such steps are required by the Constitution or a condition of the Senate's consent to the treaty.[48]

The concept of a non-self-executing, unenforceable treaty comes from a 1829 Supreme Court case, *Foster v. Neilson*.[49] The most often-cited case on the subject, which relied heavily on *Foster*, is *Sei Fujii v. State*,[50] a 1952 California Supreme Court

---

42 252 U.S. at 433.

43 *See, e.g.,* BEDERMAN, *supra* note 1, at 159-161. Any effort to limit the treaty power to "matters of international concern," as has been suggested by some, flies in the face of the facts of *Holland* (migratory birds) and cases like *De Geofroy v. Riggs*, 133 U.S. 258 (1890) (right to inherit land), and is fraught with conceptual difficulties. *See* RESTATEMENT §302, Reporter's note 2. Moreover, protection of human rights of a State's own nationals within its own territory is a constant subject of modern treaties.

44 *See* discussion *infra* p. 696.

45 This appears to be the position of the Restatement. *See* RESTATEMENT §302, Reporter's note 1.

46 *See* Chapter I, pp. 25-27, and Chapter IX, pp. 337-339.

47 *See id.* Not coincidentally, the current Court takes a narrow view of Congress's power under §5 of the 14th Amendment as well. *See* Chapter IX, pp. 343-344.

48 RESTATEMENT §111(4).

49 27 U.S. 253 (1829) (Marshall, C.J.).

50 242 P.2d 617 (Cal. 1952).

case.[51] In *Sei Fujii*, the Japanese plaintiff challenged the state's "alien land law," which provided that aliens who were not eligible for U.S. citizenship could not own land and further that any land purchased by such aliens was escheated (forfeited) to the state.[52] The court held the statute unconstitutional on grounds of its violation of equal protection of the laws under the 14th Amendment.[53] However, the plaintiff also argued that the law was invalid under the then recently ratified United Nations Charter. The court admitted that treaties were the "supreme law of the land" under the supremacy clause. However, a treaty "does not automatically supersede local laws which are inconsistent with it unless the treaty provisions are self-executing."

The California court found that the relevant provisions of the preamble and of Article 1 of the UN Charter are not self-executing since they state only the "general purposes and objectives of the United Nations Organization and do not purport to impose legal obligations on the individual member nations or to create rights in private persons." Indeed, it observed, member nations "pledge themselves to take joint and separate action in cooperation with the Organization for the achievement of the purposes" of equal rights. Since "it was contemplated that future legislative action by the several nations would be required to accomplish the declared objectives, . . . there is nothing to indicate that these provisions were intended to become rules of law for the courts of this country upon the ratification of the charter."[54]

The court contrasted the Charter with treaties that have been held to be self-executing. In *Clark v. Allen*,[55] the treaty dealt with rights of a national of one country to inherit real property located in another country. It specifically provided that "such national shall be allowed a term of three years in which to sell the [property] . . . and withdraw the proceeds" free from any discriminatory taxation.[56] And in *Nielsen v. Johnson*,[57] the signatory parties agreed that "no higher or other duties, charges, or taxes of any kind, shall be levied" by one country on removal of property therefrom by citizens of the other country "than are or shall be payable in each state, upon the same, when removed by a citizen or subject of such state respectively."[58]

In the process of considering treaties, the Senate has made reference to whether a given treaty is self-executing or not. While courts are likely to give deference to what the Senate thought it was giving assent to, such observations are not controlling.[59]

---

51 The concept that only self-executing treaties are enforceable in courts has spread from the U.S. to other countries. The concept remains controversial. For a debate on the issue, *see* PAUST, *supra* note 1, at 51-64 (doctrine requires belief in "one of the most transparent of judicial delusions" and a defense of the doctrine in ROGERS, *supra* note 1, at 76-87).

52 242 P.2d at 620.

53 *See* Chapter IX, pp. 351-362, for a discussion of equal protection. It is clear today that such a law would also be infirm as an improper interference with federal foreign policy power. *See infra* p. 695.

54 242 P.2d at 620-621.

55 331 U.S. 503 (1947).

56 *Id.* at 507.

57 279 U.S. 47, 50 (1929).

58 *See also Asakura v. City of Seattle*, 265 U.S. 332, 340 (1924), discussed *infra* p. 695. The court in *Sei Fujii* observed that the U.N. Charter did contain some self-executing provisions, such as those permitting the United Nations to own land for its permanent site in New York City. A New York state court had held these provisions were sufficiently clear and direct as to be self-executing without the need for any implementing legislation. *See Curran v. City of New York*, 191 Misc. 229, 77 N.Y.S.2d 206, 212 (Sup. Ct Queen's Co. 1947).

59 See Rogers, *supra* note 1, at 86-87.

b. Executive Agreements

An executive agreement is an agreement between the President and a foreign State. The difference between a treaty and an executive agreement is irrelevant for the purposes of international law, which considers both to be binding treaties. But as a matter of U.S. law the distinction is crucial since treaties must be approved by the Senate, while executive agreements need not be.

Though there is no explicit authorization for executive agreements in the Constitution, they have been used for many years in foreign affairs. Indeed, some of the most important international obligations of the country have been made by way of executive agreement implemented by executive orders.[60] And Presidents have not generally used executive agreements as a means of avoiding Senate opposition to a treaty. Indeed, most executive agreements have been authorized by ratified treaties or have been otherwise explicitly authorized by Congress.[61]

There are two types of executive agreements: (1) congressional-executive agreements entered into pursuant to some congressional authorization and (2) freestanding executive agreements made exclusively by the President pursuant to an exclusive presidential power.

(1) Congressional-Executive Agreements

For congressional-executive agreements, the task of a court reviewing the propriety of the agreement is to find some form of congressional approval. Usually, this is not hard as the approval required need not be very explicit.

In *Dames & Moore v. Regan*,[62] President Carter negotiated an end to the Iranian hostage case at the American Embassy in Teheran. Embassy employees were released pursuant to a complex agreement that provided, among other things, that the U.S. would "nullify all attachments and judgments" against Iranian assets in the United States and "prohibit . . . litigation based on such claims, and . . . bring about the termination of such claims through binding arbitration" before an international claims tribunal. The Court held that the executive order transferring the encumbered assets was valid on the ground that Congress had given the President emergency economic powers in an earlier statute, and that the purpose of that statute was to permit the President to use the foreign assets as a "bargaining chip" when negotiating with a hostile nation. Although there was no such statutory support for nullifying claims in U.S. courts, the Court relied on the "long continued . . . practice" of the President settling international claims of citizens "acquiesced in by Congress."[63] It determined that this "raises a presumption that the action has been taken in pursuance of [Congress's] consent."[64] Quoting from an opinion in an earlier case on presidential power, the Court observed that "a systematic, unbroken,

---

[60] For example, U.S. participation in the all-important General Agreement on Tariffs and Trade (GATT) was accomplished by way of an executive agreement. *See generally* JOHN E. NOWAK & RONALD D. ROTUNDA, HORNBOOK ON CONSTITUTIONAL LAW, 7TH ED. §6.9 (West 2007).

[61] Moreover, the executive agreement route is sometimes the politically wise move if additional funding will be needed for activities provided for in the agreement, since the Constitution requires that all revenue bills be initiated and approved by the House. *See* Art. I §7 cl. 1 ("All Bills for raising Revenue shall originate in the House of Representatives . . .")

[62] 453 U.S. 654 (1981).

[63] *Id.* at 685.

[64] Despite this reference to "consent," the second part of the President's executive agreement nullifying claims in U.S. courts is considered as having involved solely implied presidential power. *See* RESTATEMENT §115, Reporters' Note 6, p. 69. Thus, Congress's *acquiescence* or *acceptance* in the longstanding history supporting this presidential act is not the same as Congress's explicit *required approval*.

executive practice, long pursued to the knowledge of the Congress and never before questioned . . . may be treated as a gloss on 'Executive Power' vested in the President by §1 of Article II."[65]

In the absence of circumstances such as existed in the *Dames & Moore* case, however, courts have not hesitated to invalidate executive agreements. For example, in *United States v. Guy W. Capps, Inc.*,[66] the Court of Appeals struck down an executive agreement on imports when such action was inconsistent with an earlier congressional enactment. The court held that the power to regulate foreign commerce was one held by Congress. A claim of general executive power to enter into such agreements was rejected.[67]

(2) Free-Standing Executive Agreements

The Constitution also sets out certain "freestanding" presidential foreign affairs powers that authorize the President to take action alone, without the consent or authorization of Congress. When acting pursuant to one of these powers, the President can conclude executive agreements with foreign governments that do not require congressional or Senate approval.

Most of the law of freestanding presidential powers involves the President's right to recognize foreign governments and to appoint ambassadors to them.[68] In *United States v. Pink*,[69] the Court approved the Litvinov Agreement made by President Franklin Roosevelt. Among other things, the agreement recognized the Soviet government as the legitimate government of Russia and assigned all assets to which the Soviet government had any claim in the United States to the U.S. government.[70] When the U.S. government sought to collect those assets by seizing the New York accounts of a Russian insurance company nationalized by the Soviets, the action was challenged on the ground that the assignment in the Litvinov Agreement was unconstitutional. The Court held that the agreement was a valid exercise of the President's foreign policy powers to recognize foreign governments. It reasoned that the President has the sole power to recognize foreign governments and that such recognition may sometimes be conditional rather than absolute. Thus, the President had the power to enter into an agreement that dealt with those conditions.

---

65 435 U.S. at 674, quoting *Youngstown Sheet & Tube Co. v. Sawyer*, 343 U.S. 579, 637 (1952) (Jackson, J., concurring). *Youngstown Sheet & Tube,* or the *Steel Seizure Case*, was discussed in Chapter I, p. 14. In that case the Court invalidated the President's wartime seizure of privately owned steel mills because Congress had at one point rejected legislation that would have given the President such power.

66 204 F.2d 655, 659 (4th Cir. 1953), *aff'd on other grounds*, 348 U.S. 296 (1955).

67 The 4th Circuit relied in large part on the *Steel Seizure Case, supra* note 65. At one point, the Supreme Court posited a "dual track" for presidential power. In domestic affairs, the President's power was said to be limited to the enumerated powers granted by the Constitution. But in foreign affairs, the role of the President as "representative of the nation" brought with it broad inherent powers that were not so limited. *United States v. Curtiss-Wright Corp.*, 299 U.S. 304 (1939). While *Curtiss-Wright Export* continues to be cited as support for broad presidential power in foreign affairs, both the breadth of the statements made in it and the historical support offered to support them have been discredited. However, cases like *Dames & Moore* may signal a return to its broader concept of presidential power.

68 *See* Art. II §2 cl. 2.

69 315 U.S. 203 (1942).

70 These assets would then be used by the U.S. government to satisfy claims of U.S. citizens against the Soviet government.

2. The Place of International Law in the U.S. Domestic Legal Order

a. The United States as a "Dualist" State

Monist and Dualist Regimes International law scholars posit two models of States based on how their domestic legal regimes treat international law — monist states and dualist states. A monist state is one that considers that international law is (1) part of its domestic system of laws and (2) superior to all domestic sources. Thus, in a monist system, when international law is added to the normal domestic hierarchy of laws, there is one single and continuous hierarchy of laws that extends from international law at the top, down to the lowliest city ordinance or regulation. Thus, international norms apply automatically without any need to "convert" them into domestic law.

A dualist state is one which considers that domestic law and international law operate in separate spheres and that the only law that controls within the domestic legal system is domestic law. If international law is to be enforceable in domestic courts, it will have to be "converted" into some form of domestic law. And there is no guarantee that, as converted, international law will occupy the highest level in the domestic legal hierarchy. Thus, it is entirely possible that it will be overridden by various forms of domestic law. Because of this "disconnect" between international law and domestic law, a dualist State can be in complete compliance with its domestic law, but in violation of its treaty or other international law obligations.

There are few monists States in the world. In fact, conservative observers would point to only one — the Netherlands, whose constitution appears to permit treaties to "trump" all domestic law. Other countries have tendencies toward monism, with Germany, Italy and Austria providing in their constitutions that "general rules of public international law" take precedence over domestic laws.[71] But even so, the Dutch would appear to be only "treaty monists" and the Germans, Italians and Austrians only "customary law monists."[72]

The U.S. Approach Judging solely by the supremacy clause of the U.S. Constitution, one might think the United States to be a monist State. The supremacy clause provides that, like the Constitution and federal statutes, "all Treaties made, or which shall be made, under the Authority of the United States, shall be the supreme Law of the Land." The supremacy clause is silent as to customary international law. However, the Supreme Court has held that it is also part of U.S. domestic law. In *The Paquete Habana*,[73] it observed:

> International law is part of our law, and must be ascertained and administered by the courts of justice of appropriate jurisdiction, as often as questions of right depending upon it are duly presented for their determination.[74]

---

71 The articles are in the Netherlands, Articles 93-94, Germany, Article 25, Italy, Article 10(1) and Austria, Article 9. However, the debate continues in Germany about the domestic effect of European Court of Human Rights decisions. *See* 100 AM.J.INT'L L. 196 (2006) (comment on *Von Hannover v. Germany*).

72 Russia may be a treaty monist as well. Art. 15 of the 1993 Russian Constitution provides that "[i]f an international treaty of the Russian Federation establishes rules other than those established by law, the rules of the international treaty shall apply." However, while the Russian Constitutional Court has held that several domestic statutes violate international law (principally European human rights law), no court has yet clearly held that international law prevails over contrary Russian *constitutional* law. *See generally* WILLIAM BURNHAM, PETER B. MAGGS & GENNADY DANILENKO, LAW AND LEGAL SYSTEM OF THE RUSSIAN FEDERATION (4th ed. 2009).

73 175 U.S. 677, 700 (1900).

74 In the *Paquete Habana*, the Court applied the customary rule that coastal fishing boats are immune from seizure in wartime, ordering the release of Cuban fishing boats seized by the U.S. Navy.

Despite the first impression of monism, however, the United States is decidedly dualist in the way that it treats international law in its domestic jurisprudence. As the discussion in the next section makes clear, the fact that international law may be "the supreme Law of the Land," along with the Constitution and statutes, does not make it superior to either the Constitution or statutes.[75]

b. International Law in the U.S. Domestic Hierarchy of Laws

Enforceable treaties and customary international law are federal law.[76] What level of federal law they occupy is a more complicated subject. The two issues are addressed below.[77]

(1) "Federal" International Law's Relationship to State Law

As "supreme" federal law, treaties prevail over contrary state law. For example, in *Asakura v. Seattle*,[78] a treaty between the U.S. and Japan permitted nationals of the two States "to carry on trade" and "to own or lease and occupy houses . . . and shops" in the other State.[79] Based on this treaty, the Supreme Court struck down a Washington state statute that required that all pawnbrokers in the state be U.S. citizens. Non-treaty executive agreements have the same status.[80] As for customary international law, there is no Supreme Court authority directly on point, but it is generally agreed that customary norms are part of federal law and therefore prevail over conflicting state law.[81]

It is also noteworthy that state law may be preempted by the mere existence of exclusive federal foreign policy power — even in the absence of any treaty or customary rule adopted using that power. For example, in *Zschernig v. Miller*,[82] the Court invalidated an Oregon law that prohibited foreign heirs or legatees from receiving inheritances from Oregon residents if the property would be confiscated by their government or if U.S. heirs and legatees could not reciprocally receive property from abroad. The Supreme Court held that this "kind of state involvement in foreign affairs and international relations matters — which the Constitution entrusts solely to the Federal Government" — threatens foreign relations. Most recently, in *Crosby v. National Foreign Trade Council*,[83] Massachusetts passed a law barring state agencies from buying goods or services from companies doing business with Burma out of its opposition to the military

---

75 Once a treaty or customary rule of international law is determined to be relevant, the issue of the its content and meaning is one of law for the judge (and not the jury) to decide. *See* Chapter III, p. 87. Official evidence of treaties is set out since 1950 in a compilation called "United States Treaties and Other International Agreements." 1 U.S.C.A. §112a. Treaties before 1950 are set out in the U.S. Statutes at Large and collections of treaties published commercially. Despite the fact that the content of international law is a legal question, judges sometime take testimony from international law experts as to its content. *Cf.* Federal Rule of Civil Procedure 44.1 (permitting this practice as to foreign law). Or if they think the issue is clear enough from the briefs of the parties and the judge's own research, the court will take judicial notice of the rule.

76 The fact that international law is federal law means that it can be enforced in federal courts under the "federal question" prong of federal court jurisdiction. If international law issues are adjudicated in state court, the U.S. Supreme Court has the power to review that determination. *See* Chapter V, pp. 176, 188.

77 For a discussion of the hierarchy of laws in the U.S. legal system, *see* Chapter II, pp. 38-42.

78 265 U.S. 332 (1924)

79 *Id.* at 340.

80 *See United States v. Belmont*, 301 U.S. 324, 331 (1937) (assignment of Russian government's rights to the U.S. as part of the Litvinov agreement recognizing the Soviet government and settling conflicting claims between U.S. investors and Russian companies could not be affected by New York law or public policy).

81 PAUST, *supra* note 1, at 6-7 and note 47.

82 389 U.S. 429 (1968).

83 530 U.S. 363 (2000). *See also* Chapter I, p. 31 (preemption aspects).

regime in that country. While Congress had imposed mandatory and conditional sanctions on Burma, there was no conflict with any federal statute. Nonetheless, the Court struck the state law down because its law interfered with the President's flexibility in foreign affairs.[84]

(2) International Law Among Other Forms of Federal Law

All Forms of International Law Subject to the Constitution In a long line of cases, the Court has made clear that all forms of international law are subject to superior constitutional commands.[85] To cite but one example, in *Reid v. Covert*,[86] the wife of an Air Force sergeant killed her husband on a U.S. base in England. She was tried and sentenced for his murder by a military court, which asserted jurisdiction based on an international agreement between the United States and Great Britain, which permitted U.S. military courts to exercise exclusive jurisdiction over offenses committed in Great Britain by American servicemen or their dependents. The Court held that the due process and jury trial rights set out in the Constitution prevailed over that international agreement.[87]

Treaties Ratified, self-executing treaties are on the same hierarchical level as federal statutes. This means that a "later in time" rule applies.[88] Thus, following ratification of a treaty, Congress could pass and the President could sign legislation that rendered that treaty ineffectual — or Congress could do it alone by mustering a two-thirds majority sufficient to override a presidential veto. In the *Head Money Cases*,[89] the Court applied this principle to uphold a tax on foreign passengers pursuant to a statute, even though the statute conflicted with an earlier treaty. And in *Whitney v. Robertson*,[90] the Court held that acts of Congress imposing duties on imported sugar enacted subsequent to a contrary treaty were valid.

Executive Agreements The place of executive agreements in the hierarchy of federal law depends on what kind of executive agreement it is. As discussed earlier, there are two types: congressionally authorized executive agreements (called "congressional-executive agreements") and executive agreements based on a freestanding executive power, such as the power to appoint ambassadors.[91]

As creatures of federal legislation or a federal treaty, congressionally authorized executive agreements are subject to the superior authority of Congress. This principle is illustrated by *United States v. Guy W. Capps, Inc.*[92] In that case, the President and Canada agreed on conditions under which Canadian potatoes could be imported into the United States. Congress by statute had specified that such regulation problems be handled through the Tariff Commission. The Court held that the statutory command prevailed over the contrary executive agreement.

Freestanding executive agreements are made by the President without any need for

---

84 *See also infra* p. 707. Another federal power set out in the Constitution that similarly operates in its "dormant" state to preempt state laws is the interstate commerce clause. *See* Chapter IX, pp. 345-348.

85 *See* RESTATEMENT §115(3).

86 354 U.S. 1, 19 n. 38 (1957).

87 The agreement was an executive agreement, which is on the same level as a ratified treaty. Such Status of Forces Agreements (SOFA) involving U.S. military bases abroad are discussed *infra* p. 713.

88 RESTATEMENT §115(1)(a) and (2).

89 112 U.S. 580, 598-599 (1884).

90 124 U.S. 190, 192-195 (1888).

91 *See supra* pp. 692-693.

92 204 F.2d 655 (4th Cir. 1953), *aff'd on other grds*, 348 U.S. 269 (1955).

congressional authorization and are valid actions of the President in and of themselves. Although the point is not entirely free from doubt, such agreements, being the product of a constitutional power not subject to congressional approval, should not be subject to congressional undoing. Thus, presidential action recognizing a particular foreign government as legitimate could not be reversed by a congressional enactment declaring the government illegitimate and recalling the ambassador. The "Litvinov Agreement" recognizing the Soviet government that went on to deal with other issues between the two countries is an example of this.[93]

The issue of congressional power to overrule executive agreements came up recently in the controversy over Congress's consideration of a bill to recognize Jerusalem as the capital of Israel and to mandate the establishment of an embassy there. The Department of Justice issued a memorandum opposing the bill as unconstitutional for its infringement on presidential foreign affairs powers.[94] Support for ranking freestanding executive agreements above statutes can be gleaned from the way the Court has dealt with another freestanding power of the President — the power to issue pardons.[95]

Customary International Law As Federal Common Law The "law of Nations" is the term used by the Framers to denote customary international law. The Constitution empowers Congress to "define and punish . . . Offences against the Law of Nations,"[96] so Congress could incorporate customary norms into a statute. Congress has done this in only a few narrow areas.[97] However, as noted elsewhere in this book, federal common law exists in areas where there are strong uniquely federal interests in need of protection, but there is no federal statute.[98] Thus, like maritime and admiralty law, disputes between the states of the United States and regulation of federal government property and financial paper, foreign relations is an area in which there are strong, uniquely federal interests. Even in the absence of statutory incorporation, customary international law — as federal law existing independently of statutes or treaties — is a species of federal common law.[99]

---

93 *See United States v. Belmont, supra* note 80 and accompanying text.

94 *See* Malvena Halberstam, *The Jerusalem Embassy Act*, 19 FORDHAM INT'L LAW JOURNAL 1379, 1381 (1996), citing Memorandum of Walter Dellinger, Assistant Attorney General, to Abner J. Mikva, Counsel to the President (May 16, 1995). The bill was later enacted, but in its final form provided for the President to postpone opening the embassy in Jerusalem six months at a time.

95 *See* Art. II §2 and *United States v. Klein*, 80 U.S. 128 (1867) (federal statute unconstitutional in part on the ground that it sought to reverse the effects of a pardon) (*dictum*). The issue of abuse of the pardon power comes up periodically at the end of presidential terms, when Presidents sometimes grant pardons too controversial to be granted mid-term. For example, when President Clinton left office in 2000, many were dissatisfied with some of his pardons. While there were rumblings in Congress about reversing them, experts were in agreement that there was nothing it could do. *See also* ROGERS, *supra* note 1 at 104-105 and RESTATEMENT, Reporter's Note No. 5 to §115.

96 Art. I §8 cl. 10.

97 *See* 10 U.S.C.A. §818 (authorizing courts-martial to try "any person who by the law of war is subject to trial by a military tribunal") and *Ex parte Quirin*, 317 U.S. 1, 29-30 (1942) (finding that spying is an offense against the laws of war triable in courts-martial rather than civilian courts).

98 *See* Chapter I, pp. 35-36, and Chapter II, p. 40.

99 *In re Estate of Ferdinand E. Marcos Human Rights Litigation*, 978 F.2d 493, 502 (9th Cir. 1992) ("It is . . . well settled that the law of nations is part of federal common law.") RESTATEMENT §111, comment d ("International law is considered to be like common law in the United states, but it is federal law.") and §112(2), comment a. *But see* Louis Henkin, *International Law and Law of the United States*, 82 MICHIGAN LAW REV. 1559, 1561-67 (1983) (principal author of the Restatement distinguishing between "authentic" federal common law and international customary law as federal common law) and Curtis A. Bradley and Jack L. Goldsmith, *Customary International Law as Federal Common Law: A Critique of the Modern Position*, 110 HARVARD LAW REV. 815, 821 (1997) (position that customary international law is federal common law is based on "mistaken interpretations of history, doctrinal bootstrapping . . ., and academic

The standard hierarchy of laws ranks common law below all the forms of enacted law.[100] Thus, customary international law is subject to being trumped by contrary federal constitutional provisions, statutes, treaties, and even agency regulations. *The Paquete Habana*, which established that customary international law is part of federal law, confirmed the lowly place of customary law in the hierarchy of laws. The Court observed that "resort must be had to" customary international law "where there is *no treaty, and no controlling executive or legislative act or judicial decision.*"[101]

Rationale for the "Later in Time" Rule   The fact that a simple statute can abrogate a duly signed and ratified treaty with a foreign State or a congressionally approved executive agreement might not appear to be the best arrangement for the orderly conduct of international relations.[102] But the arrangement has its own internal constitutional logic. Even if the President and two-thirds of the Senate at one point agreed to assume particular international obligations — as would be the case if the Constitution's treaty process were followed — it would make sense that the President and the majority of the whole Congress or two-thirds of the whole Congress overriding a presidential veto should be able to determine otherwise. Thus, it is consistent with democratic values to permit the consensus of the political branches to decide whether the country should breach its treaty obligations. This is the rationale of the principal case cited to support the proposition that treaties are no higher than ordinary statutes.[103] However, it should be remembered that the President does not have a "line item" veto and may be forced to sign a bill containing a treaty abrogation if it is inserted in a bill the President otherwise wants.[104]

c. Compensation for the Low Hierarchical Position of International Law in the Domestic U.S. Legal Order

(1) Vested Private Rights Under Treaties

It is settled law that "Congress has no constitutional power to settle or interfere with rights under treaties, except in cases purely political."[105] However, this exception applies only to property rights and other tangible rights that are "capable of sale and transfer." Thus, the Court rejected arguments by Chinese aliens who departed the U.S. with certificates under a treaty granting them the right to return, but who were excluded because of an intervening exclusionary federal statute. These were merely rights that were "personal and untransferable in their character."[106]

The origin of the Court's general rule for vested property rights is probably found in

---

fiat.").

100 *See* Chapter II, p. 41.

101 This statement appears as the next sentence in the text quoted at note 74 (emphasis added). Professor Henkin has argued that the statement is *dictum* and that customary rules should be considered on the same level as treaties and federal statutes. *See* Louis Henkin, *The Constitution and United States Sovereignty: A Century of Chinese Exclusion and Its Progeny*, 100 HARVARD LAW REV. 853, 873-878 (1987).

102 *See* Louis Henkin, *Treaties in a Constitutional Democracy*, 10 MICH. J. INT'L LAW 406, 426 (1989).

103 *See Head Money Cases* and *Whitney v. Robinson*, discussed *supra*. *See also* ROGERS, *supra* note 1, at 88-92.

104 *See Clinton v. New York*, 524 U.S. 417 (1998)(holding line item veto unconstitutional). *See* Chapter VI, p. 219 note 138.

105 *Holden v. Joy*, 84 U.S. 211, 247 (1872) (Cherokee Indian lands granted by prior treaty could not be taken back by Act of Congress). *See also Jones v. Meehan*, 175 U.S. 1, 32 (1899) (grants to Indian chiefs).

106 *Chae Chan Ping v. United States*, 130 U.S. 581 (1889).

general understandings about the inalienability of vested rights.[107] However, the 5th Amendment states that "private property" shall not "be taken for a public use, without just compensation." This may provide an explicit textual basis for compensation for property rights lost as a result of treaties.[108] A stumbling block to such claims, however, is the "treaty exception" to the jurisdiction of the U.S. Court of Claims, the court with jurisdiction over claims against the U.S. government. It excludes jurisdiction over "any claim against the United States growing out of or dependent upon any treaty entered into with foreign nations."[109] However, in *Dames & Moore v. Regan*, the Iranian hostage case discussed earlier, the Court suggested that the executive order in that case could have effected a compensable "taking" of property for public purposes in its nullification of claims against the Iranian government. The Court did not think the issue ripe for review yet, but it did go out of its way to hold that if a taking were shown, any such claim would not be barred by the "treaty exception." Moreover, it rejected the "treaty exception" as inapplicable.[110]

(2) Narrow Interpretations of Statutes to Avoid Conflict

Holding more promise as a means of mitigating the harshest effects of the "later-in-time" rule is the *Charming Betsy* rule — named for the 1804 case that established it.[111] This doctrine of statutory interpretation maintains that "an Act of Congress ought never to be construed to violate the law of nations if any other possible construction" is possible.[112] The presumption behind the rule is that Congress would not wish to violate international law. The rule's effect is to require that Congress be crystal clear in its intention to abrogate a prior treaty or international agreement.

The case of *United States v. Palestine Liberation Organization*,[113] demonstrates the usefulness of the rule in avoiding diplomatic embarrassment. Congress passed an "Anti-Terrorism Act" that declared it "unlawful . . ., notwithstanding any provision of law to the contrary, to establish or maintain an office, headquarters, premises, or other facilities or establishments within the jurisdiction of the United States at the behest or direction of, or with funds provided by the PLO." The executive branch supported the PLO having such a mission. The U.N. Headquarters Agreement required the United States, as the host country, to permit all missions to the United Nations to come to U.N. sessions. The court held that this included the right to establish an office. It observed that there was no clear evidence of an intent to alter the Headquarters Agreement. In support, it pointed out that the statute failed to mention the Agreement specifically and there was

---

107 *See, e.g.*, 1 JAMES KENT, COMMENTARIES ON AMERICAN LAW 424-29 (1826) ("A retrospective statute, affecting and changing vested rights is . . . unconstitutional and void."). *See also* Art. 70 of the Vienna Convention on Treaties.

108 For a discussion of compensable "takings," *see* Chapter XVII, pp. 482-487. *Cf.* Art. I §9 ("No State shall . . . pass any . . . Law impairing the Obligation of Contracts . . .").

109 28 U.S.C.A. §1502.

110 453 U.S. 654, 689-690 (1981)("to the extent petitioner believes it has suffered an unconstitutional taking by the suspension of the claims, we see no jurisdictional bar to an appropriate action in the United States Court of Claims"). *See also id.* at 690-691 (Powell, J., concurring and dissenting)("The Government must pay just compensation when it furthers the Nation's foreign policy goals by using as 'bargaining chips' claims lawfully held by a relatively few persons.") For a criticism of this interpretation, *see* Phillip Trimble, *Foreign Policy Frustrated* — Dames & Moore, *Claims Court Jurisdiction and a New Raid on the Treasury* 84 COLUMBIA LAW REV. 317 (1984). *Dames & Moore* was discussed *supra* p. 692.

111 *Murray v. Schooner Charming Betsy*, 6 U.S. 64 (1804) (Marshall, C.J.). *See* RESTATEMENT §114 and §115(1)(a).

112 6 U.S. at 81.

113 695 F.Supp. 1456 (S.D.N.Y. 1988).

no consistent legislative history expressing an intent to override that agreement.[114]

The *Charming Betsy* rule does not resolve all conflicts in favor of the international rule, however. An example of its failure to do so is *South African Airways v. Dole*.[115] In that case, a 1947 treaty with South Africa permitted air service between the countries. In 1986, however, in reaction to the apartheid regime in South Africa, Congress passed and President signed a statute that directed the Secretary of Transportation to revoke the air service rights of any airline-designee of the South African government. The Court of Appeals, after first trying unsuccessfully to reconcile the two documents under the *Charming Betsy* rule, held that the statute prevailed over the earlier treaty.[116]

C. War Powers and Military Intervention Under U.S. Law

1. Shared Powers of the President and Congress

The Constitution gives both Congress and the President specific powers in the area of war and military intervention. Under Article I §8, Congress has the power to "declare War, grant letters of Marque and Reprisal, and make Rules concerning Captures on Land and Water," to "raise and support Armies," to "provide and maintain a Navy," to "make Rules for the Government and Regulation of the land and naval Forces," and to regulate the state militias and to call them into federal service. The President under Article II §2 is the "Commander in Chief of the Army and Navy of the United States, and of the militia of the several States when called into the actual Service of the United States."

2. Presidential Action Independent of Congress

Role as Commander-in-Chief The mix of powers just set out has raised the issue many times in history of the ability of the President, as Commander in Chief of the armed forces, to engage in military action abroad without a formal declaration of war from Congress. Certainly a concurrent resolution (a resolution passed by a majority of both houses) granting authority to the President to take military action is sufficient, and such resolutions were passed before commencement of the Gulf War in 1991 and in several other interventions before it. But the President has used American troops numerous times in history without going to Congress for a declaration of war or other congressional authorization, leaving Congress simply to react after the fact. Once troops are committed, it is difficult for Congress to mount opposition to the President's course of action. It was largely the result of the President leading and Congress following that the United States became involved in the disastrous Vietnam War.[117]

Power of the Purse As a Check It is not likely that the Supreme Court will clarify the extent of the President's power in this area, as it would likely be considered a non-justiciable political question.[118] However, Presidents have tended not to act contrary to

---

114 *Id.* at 1468-1471. The reason the President did not veto the bill, despite his disagreement with it was that it was a "rider" attached to an appropriations bill for the entire State Department. One reason there was no little evidence of the requisite clear intent was that the rider was added to the bill without any discussion.

115 817 F.2d 119 (D.C. Cir. 1987).

116 In actuality the 1947 document was an executive agreement rather than a treaty as defined under U.S. law.

117 Vietnam and later incursions were only the latest in a long line of presidential military actions taken without a declaration of war. Between 1789 and 1970, one author counted 130 transfers of troops or war matériel abroad without Congressional involvement. *See* NOWAK & ROTUNDA, *supra* note 60, §6.10.

118 *See* Chapter IX, pp. 333-335, where the political question doctrine is discussed. The constitutionality of the Vietnam War was raised in the lower federal courts, but most held the issue non-justiciable under the political question doctrine. The Supreme Court avoided deciding either the political question issue or the constitutionality of the war by exercising its discretionary power to deny review. *See Mora v.*

a restriction specifically imposed on the use of funds by Congress pursuant to its "power of the purse."[119] Thus, this would seem to be a permissible way for Congress to protect its interests.[120] However, legislation containing such a restriction must be signed by the President or passed over his veto.[121] While this might seem to be a difficult hurdle for Congress when only a simple majority opposes presidential action, the President may feel compelled to sign the bill despite the funding restriction in it because of other positive provisions it contains.[122]

Short-Term Military Action   The Commander-in-Chief power probably allows the President to order some military action without Congressional authorization on a short-term emergency basis, such as an armed attack on the United States or a threat to American citizens or property in a foreign country. This basis for military intervention was relied on by President Reagan when he sent American troops into Grenada in 1983, claiming that the safety of Americans attending a medical school in Grenada was in danger. Such power to launch short-term interventions could also be argued to support the bombing of Libya by President Reagan in 1986 in reprisal for a terrorist attack in Germany that killed American military personnel. The same could be said of the invasion of Panama by President Bush in 1990 to capture General Noriega and bring him to trial in the United States for alleged violations of American drug laws.[123]

D. Remedies for Violations of International Law

What States are supposed to do when they violate international law is relatively clear. They should "terminate the violation and . . . make reparation, including . . . restitution or compensation for loss or injury."[124] However, as noted earlier, the system of international law is at its weakest when it comes to providing coercive remedies in the event States fail in their obligations. As a result, most disputes involving claims of violations between states are settled by negotiation. If a solution is not reached by negotiation, the parties may resort to arbitration by a third party, either *ad hoc* or pursuant to an applicable treaty. The International Court of Justice (World Court) is available as a permanent tribunal to resolve international disputes, but it is available only if the parties (1) agree to submit the particular dispute to it or (2) have agreed to submit to the Court's jurisdiction in general categories of disputes which include the current one.[125] If none of these approaches is availing, the aggrieved state can resort to proportionate, unilateral counter-measures that do not violate applicable treaties or customary international law. However, the use or threat of the use of force is subject to the

---

McNamara, 389 U.S. 934 (1967) (denying certiorari over two dissents). *But see Orlando v. Laird*, 443 F.2d 1039 (2d Cir. 1971) (finding the issue justiciable and finding sufficient congressional authorization). Certiorari was also denied in *Orlando*.

119 *See also Train v. City of New York*, 420 U.S. 35 (1975) (President may not impound money Congress has directed to be spent).

120 A recent example of this was Congress's specific prohibition any use of appropriated funds to provide assistance to the "contras" in Nicaragua. Congress's action forced certain officials in the Reagan administration to seek to fund the "contras" by means other than appropriated funds. One method was by selling arms to Iran, which led to the "Iran-Contra" scandal.

121 For this reason, the section of the War Powers Resolution of 1973 that allowed Congress to halt military action ordered by the President by way of a joint resolution of Congress that is not subject to the presidential signature requirement, is unconstitutional. *See* Chapter VI, p. 218, where *Immigration and Naturalization Service v. Chadha*, 462 U.S. 919 (1983), the "legislative veto" case, is discussed.

122 The President does not have the right to a "line item" veto. *See supra* note 104.

123 Whether such action is constitutional is separate from the question of whether such military intervention comports with international law.

124 RESTATEMENT §901.

125 RESTATEMENT §903.

prohibitions on its use in the U.N. Charter, which are also considered to be *jus cogens*. Article 2(4) of the Charter forbids the "threat or use of force against the territorial integrity or political independence of any state, or in any other manner inconsistent with the Purposes of the United Nations." However, Article 51 preserves "the inherent right of individual or collective self-defence if an armed attack occurs."

1. U.S. Law on Remedies in General

From the standpoint of U.S. law, it is up to the President to determine what measures will be resorted to and the severity of the response. It may be that to take some measures, the President will have to seek approval of Congress. The power to suspend or limit diplomatic relations is clear. The power to terminate international agreements is also generally acknowledged. However, if the interests of individuals are affected, authorization by Congress of the action is usually thought to be necessary. There are several statutes which grant power to the President to freeze assets, impose trade sanctions or alter tax laws in response to violations of international law.[126]

From the discussions of the limited role of courts in adjudicating the legality of actions of the executive branch in foreign relations, one could perhaps surmise that U.S. courts have no real role in adjudicating the appropriateness of any of the measures just discussed. The decision is considered to be political rather than legal.

2. U.S. Amenability to Jurisdiction of International Tribunals

Discussion of the International Court of Justice (World Court) and the U.S. relationship to it is beyond the scope of this chapter on international aspects of U.S. law. But because of the nature of that relationship and what it demonstrates about U.S. attitudes toward that court, a few words should be said about it.

The U.S. accepted compulsory jurisdiction in 1946 when President Truman submitted the appropriate declaration, as approved by two-thirds of the Senate, accepting that obligation for "all legal disputes" that concern interpretation of a treaty and any question of international law, and appropriate fact-finding that would be needed to apply such norms. However, it exempted, as had several other States, "disputes with regard to matters which are essentially within the domestic jurisdiction" of the U.S., as determined by the U.S.. Upset in the U.S. over the court's decision in the 1984 case brought by Nicaragua over U.S. funding of the "contra" guerillas in that country then led President Reagan and the government to formally terminate its acceptance on October 7, 1985, effective 6 months thereafter.[127] The reason given was that the U.S. had never been able to successfully bring another State before the court on its compulsory jurisdiction, because of the principle of reciprocity. Since the U.S. has reserved to itself the right to except itself from the court's jurisdiction for matters that it has determined are issues of its own domestic law, other States use the U.S.'s reservation against it. It also noted that a majority of the judges in 1985 were from States that had not accepted compulsory jurisdiction under any circumstances and that there were only 47 States in that category.

---

126 *See*, *e.g.*, 19 U.S.C.A. §2102; 50 U.S.C.A. §5(b); 50 U.S.C.A. §1701 *et seq.*; 26 U.S.C.A. §891. There may be some free-standing presidential power to affect individuals as well. *See Dames & Moore v. Regan*, 453 U.S. 654 (1981), discussed *supra*, p. 692.

127 *See supra* note 29.

3. Enforcement of International Law in U.S. Courts

a. Enforcement of Private Rights Under Treaties

Most treaties and customary rules of international law govern the relationship between international States and do not create judicially enforceable private rights. As discussed in the earlier outline of the doctrine of self-executing treaties, any private rights must be secured either in self-executing treaties or by appropriate domestic legislation implementing the treaty.[128] When these conditions are met, treaty rights are judicially enforceable in the same way any other right secured by federal law.[129]

b. Private Rights Under Customary International Law: The Alien Tort Statute

Since 1789, U.S. courts have had "original jurisdiction of any civil action by an alien for a tort only, committed in violation of the law of nations or a treaty of the United States" under the Alien Tort Statute (ATS).[130] The origin and purpose of the ATS have been lost to history, though scholars have suggested that it was intended at the time of its passage to be applied in cases of violations of diplomatic immunity, to piracy or to the international slave trade. The existence of the ATS is perhaps surprising, given the dualist nature of the U.S. approach to international law. But the ATS only establishes subject-matter jurisdiction in the federal courts. It does not create a right to sue. For that, there must be rights secured either by a self-executing treaty or customary international law from which the federal court can imply a cause of action. This involves the exercise of a federal court's limited federal common-law powers.

The ATS sat dormant for almost two centuries before beginning a new life as a means for redressing violations of human rights in the case of *Filartiga v. Pena- Irala.*[131] In *Filartiga*, a Paraguayan citizen sued a Paraguayan government official found living in the United States for torture. The court rejected several objections to the use of the statute for this purpose. Then, on remand, the district court awarded a judgment that included punitive damages.[132] The use of the ATS to redress violations of human rights was affirmed by the Supreme Court in 2004, in *Sosa v. Alvarez-Machain,*[133] a case involving a claim that Alvarez-Machain was abducted from Mexico by U.S drug enforcement agents to stand trial in the U.S. The Court concluded that the ATS was only a jurisdictional statute, but that any substantive international law rights and any implied right to sue to redress their violation would have to be found in federal common law. However, the Court emphasized, federal common-law powers of federal courts are

---

128 *See supra,* pp. 690-691.

129 If Congress incorporates treaty standards into legislation, then those standards are judicially enforceable in a suit by an individual. Thus, in *Hamdan v. Rumsfeld,* 548 U.S. 557, 642 (2006), the Court applied a 1949 Geneva Convention requirement that trials of prisoners of war take place before "a regularly constituted court affording all the judicial guarantees which are recognized as indispensable by civilized peoples," because a federal statute required that all military tribunals comply with the "law of war," of which the Geneva Conventions are a part. The Court so held even though the sole remedy for violations provided for in the Convention was diplomatic intervention by political and military authorities. *See* Third Geneva Convention, Art. 3, ¶1 and ¶1(d), Relative to the Treatment of Prisoners of War, 6 U.S.T. 3316, 3318, T.I.A.S. No. 3364 (1949) and 10 U.S.C.A. §821. *See also* Chapter I, p. 14.

130 28 U.S.C.A. §1350, Judiciary Act of 1789, Act of September 24, 1789, § 9, 1 Stat. 73, 77.

131 630 F.2d 876 (2d Cir. 1980).

132 *Filartiga v. Pena-Irala,* 577 F.Supp. 860, 865 (E.D.N.Y 1984). The district court applied Paraguayan law to determine liability and compensatory damages. It awarded punitive damages even though Paraguayan law did not permit them because "it is essential and proper to grant the remedy of punitive damages in order to give effect to the manifest objectives of the international prohibition against torture."

133 542 U.S. 692 (2004).

rather limited.[134] Thus, federal courts may enforce only those standards of customary international law that have a specificity and concreteness comparable to those of the norms that existed in the 18th century (such as piracy, slave-trading and torture) and must take into account the practicalities of a decision to recognize a claim in U.S. courts, particularly its disruptive effects on the foreign state involved. Applying these guidelines on the merits of the claim in the *Sosa* case, the Court rejected Alvarez-Machain's claim. Ignoring the cross-border nature of his abduction and taking his claim to be only that the abduction was "arbitrary" because it was not authorized by law, the Court found that "a single illegal detention of less than a day, followed by the transfer of custody to lawful authorities and a prompt arraignment, violates no norm of customary international law so well defined as to support the creation of a federal remedy."[135]

The precise meaning of *Sosa v. Alvarez-Machain* is not clear. However, it would seem to be, in general, consistent with the lower federal court cases that had been developing since *Filartiga*, some of which the Court explicitly cited with approval. Among the earlier cases have been cases using the ATS to redress summary executions and "disappearances,"[136] detention for the purposes of extortion,[137] torture and false imprisonment,[138] assassination of opponents,[139] and violations of diplomatic immunity.[140] Two cases it cited were suits against Radovan Karadzic for genocide in Bosnia-Hercegovina and against the estate of Ferdinand Marcos of the Phillippines for torture, arbitrary arrests and detention.[141]

Claims that have been rejected include claims against a private party who benefitted from expropriation of property based on the owner's religion,[142] unseaworthiness of a vessel,[143] environmental spoliation,[144] claims for corporate fraud, conversion and waste[145] and detention pursuant to legal process, even if wrongful under state law.[146]

At least one set of rights enforceable under the ATS has been specifically authorized by Congress when it passed the Torture Victims Compensation Act of 1991 as an amendment to the ATS.[147] It provides for a 10-year statute of limitations for torture and extra-judicial killing cases and for exhaustion of remedies (unless its exhaustion would be futile or dangerous). U.S. ratification of the United Nations Convention Against

---

134 The nature of this restraint and the reasons for it are covered in Chapter I, p. 35-36.

135 542 U.S. at 738. The Court had earlier held that Alvarez-Machain's abduction did not violate an extradition treaty between the U.S. and Mexico or otherwise prevent his prosecution. *See United States v. Alvarez-Machain*, 504 U.S. 655 (1992), discussed *infra* p. 719. He was acquitted after a trial.

136 *Xuncax v. Gramajo*, 886 F.Supp. 162, 172 (D.Mass. 1995) (actions of police in Guatemala).

137 *Eastman Kodak Co. v. Kavlin*, 978 F.Supp. 1078 (D.Fla. 1997)(detention of Kodak's representative in Bolivia in order to secure favorable economic settlement).

138 *Paul v. Avril*, 812 F.Supp. 207 (S.D.Fla. 1993) and 901 F.Supp. 330 (S.D.Fla. 1994)(against former military ruler of Haiti).

139 *Letelier v. Republic of Chile*, 488 F.Supp. 665 (D.D.C. 1980).

140 *Von Dardel v. Union of Soviet Socialist Republics*, 623 F.Supp. 246 (D.D.C. 1985) (Raoul Wallenberg seized in violation of diplomatic immunity), *vacated on other grounds* 736 F.Supp. 1 (D.D.C. 1990) (USSR had sovereign immunity).

141 *See Kadic v. Karadzic*, 70 F.3d 232 (2d Cir. 1995) and *In re Estate of Ferdinand Marcos*, 25 F.3d 1467 (9th Cir. 1994).

142 *Bigio v. Coca-Cola Co.*, 239 F.3d 440 (2d Cir. 2000).

143 *Damaskinos v. Societa Navigacion Interamericana*, 255 F.Supp. 919 (S.D.N.Y. 1966).

144 *Beanal v. Freeport-McMoran, Inc.*, 197 F.3d 161 (5th Cir. 1999).

145 *IIT v. Vencap, Ltd.*, 519 F.2d 1001 (2d Cir. 1975) (Friendly, J.).

146 *Martinez v. City of Los Angeles*, 141 F.3d 1373 (9th Cir. 1998).

147 *See* 28 U.S.C.A. §1350 note.

Torture in 1990 strengthens the reach of the Act in its application. None of this, however, removes what are the principal roadblocks to successful use of the Act — lack of personal jurisdiction over defendants and inability to enforce judgments against them.

PART II: International Litigation in U.S. Courts

A. Extraterritorial Reach of U.S. Law and Judicial Process

The issue of the extraterritorial reach of the law of an international State has to do with that State's assertions of "jurisdiction" over people, transactions, occurrences or things that have a connection with another State. There are three types of jurisdiction: (1) a State's "jurisdiction to prescribe" normative rules for extraterritorial conduct, also called "legislative jurisdiction" (2) a State's jurisdiction to adjudicate disputes involving foreign parties, called "judicial jurisdiction"; and (3) a State's jurisdiction to enforce its law on the territory of other states.

1. Legislative Jurisdiction

a. The Territoriality Principle

It was routinely maintained in the 18th and 19th centuries that legislative jurisdiction completely ceased at the physical borders of a State. In the 20th century, however, this concept of strict territoriality began to break down. The United States and other countries in recent years have increasingly passed laws that purport to regulate conduct that takes place outside their borders.

In keeping with the bedrock principle of territorial limits, U.S. courts generally presume in the face of such silence that Congress did not intend extraterritorial application.[148] For example, in *Equal Employment Opportunity Comm'n v. Aramco*,[149] the Supreme Court applied the presumption to hold that a U.S. citizen working overseas for a U.S. company was not protected by Title VII of the Civil Rights Act of 1964 against allegedly discriminatory discharge based on his race, religion and national origin.[150] The *Aramco* Court repeated the policy behind the presumption — "to protect against unintended clashes between our laws and those of other nations which could result in international discord."[151] On the other hand, the Court has held that foreign-flagged cruise ships operating in United States waters were places of "public accommodation" and "specified public transportation" within meaning of Title III of the Americans with Disabilities Act. However, it held that barrier removal for the disabled was not "readily achievable" if it would result in the vessel being out of compliance with the International Convention for the Safety of Life at Sea (SOLAS) or any other international legal obliga-

---

148 The sources of the territorial principle in U.S. law are the writings of Justice Joseph Story, which are fashioned after the ideas of the 17th century Dutch academic, Ulrich Huber. JOSEPH STORY, COMMENTARIES OF THE CONFLICT OF LAWS, 2D ED. (1834), relying on Huber's *De Conflictu Legum* (1689). The 1824 case of *The Appollon*, 22 U.S. 362, 369 (1824), also gave Story the opportunity to expound on his view of the "law of nations" as it related in that case to extraterritorial reach of U.S. customs laws to vessels on the high seas. He concluded that such an application would be improper for its violation of the territoriality principle.

149 499 U.S. 244 (1991).

150 *See also Morrison v. National Australia Bank, Ltd.*, ___ U.S. ___, 130 S.Ct. 2869 (2010) (anti-fraud provision of the Securities Exchange Act did not apply extraterritorially to provide cause of action to foreign plaintiffs suing foreign and American defendants for misconduct in connection with securities traded on foreign exchanges).

151 Id. at 282. Congress apparently decided that the Court's reading of its intent was wrong. It quickly reversed the result in *Aramco* by amending Title VII to cover U.S. citizens working in foreign countries. Civil Rights Act of 1991, 42 U.S.C.A. §2000e(f). However, there is an exception if compliance with Title VII "would cause [the] employer . . . to violate the law of the foreign country in which such workplace is located."

tion.[152]

b. Exceptions to Territoriality

There are four more or less standard exceptions to the territorial principle on which extraterritorial legislative jurisdiction has been based: (1) the nationality principle; (2) the protective principle, (3) the passive personality principle, and (4) the universal offense principle.[153]

(1) The Nationality Principle

The nationality principle permits nations to apply their laws to the conduct of their own nationals wherever they may be located in the world.[154] One well-known example is U.S. income tax, which applies to all citizens of the United States regardless of where they live.[155] Another is the Foreign Corrupt Practices Act, which is aimed at the conduct of U.S. "domestic concerns" paying bribes to officials of foreign governments in connection with securing or retaining contracts.[156] Trade sanctions commonly rely on the principle. The Comprehensive Anti-Apartheid Act of 1986 provided that "[n]o national of the United States may, directly or through another person, make any new investment in South Africa."[157] As Chief Justice Hughes has written, "the United States is not debarred by any rule of international law from governing the conduct of its own citizens upon the high seas or even in foreign countries when the rights of other nations or their nationals are not infringed."[158]

Regulating U.S. Subsidiaries Abroad The nationality of a corporation is determined by its place of incorporation.[159] The nationality of the owners, directors or managers or principal place of business are irrelevant. Nonetheless, the United States has tried to apply its laws to foreign subsidiaries of U.S. corporations as "United States persons" on the theory that those who control them are located in the United States. One vehicle for this has been the Trading with the Enemy Act,[160] which asserts jurisdiction over "persons subject to the jurisdiction of the United States" who are abroad, including corporations or other legal entities, wherever organized or doing business, owned or controlled by U.S. citizens or other persons in the U.S. This has sometimes resulted in conflicts with States, primarily over trade sanctions. Usually, U.S.-owned multinational companies are located in the State subject to the sanctions or in a State that has a friendlier trade policy toward the sanctioned State than the United States would prefer. For example, in the 1950s and 1960s the United States prohibited Canadian companies owned by U.S. corporations from trading with China. This conflicted with Canada's policy of seeking

---

152 *Spector v. Norwegian Cruise Line Ltd.*, 545 U.S. 119 (2005).

153 *See United States v. Rivard*, 375 F.2d 882, 885 (5th Cir. 1967) ("The law of nations permits the exercise of [extraterritorial] criminal jurisdiction by a nation under five general principles. They are the territorial, national, protective, universality and passive personality principles.").

154 RESTATEMENT §402(2).

155 *See Cook v. Tait*, 265 U.S. 47 (1924)(rejecting arguments based on the constitution and international law against taxing income received in other countries by U.S. citizens).

156 15 U.S.C.A. §78dd-1-2. A "domestic concern" is defined as "(A) any individual who is a citizen, national, or resident of the United States; or (B) any corporation, partnership, association . . . or sole proprietorship which has its principal place of business in the United States or which is organized under the laws of a State of the United States . . . ."

157 Pub.L. 99-440, *repealed by* Pub.L. 103-149, § 4(a)(1) (Nov. 23, 1993).

158 *Skieriotes v. Florida*, 313 U.S. 69, 73 (1941); *Blackmer v. United States*, 284 U.S. 421 (1932) (subpoena to attend criminal case served on U.S. citizen living in France was valid). *See also* 28 U.S.C.A. §1783 (providing for issuance of subpoenas to a U.S. "national or resident . . . who is in a foreign country").

159 RESTATEMENT §213.

160 50 U.S.C.A. Appx. §5(b).

increased trade with China.[161] In 1979-1980, similar sanctions were imposed against Iran over the hostage crisis and against the Soviet Union over the invasion of Afghanistan. And in 1985, anti-apartheid sanctions were directed against South Africa.

The concept of a "United States person" is defined even more broadly in the anti-boycott provisions of the Export Administration Act[162] — a law that attempted to prevent U.S. overseas subsidiaries from assisting in the Arab boycott of Israel. Congress included "any foreign subsidiary or affiliate" of a U.S. company that is "controlled in fact by" the U.S. company "as determined by regulations of the President."[163] In 1997, federal statutes and executive action subjected Myanmar (Burma) to trade sanctions. Statutes required that "United States persons" refrain from "new investment" in that country if the President determines that the Burmese Government harmed, rearrested, or exiled the opposition leader or committed "large-scale repression of or violence against the Democratic opposition."[164] In the Foreign Corrupt Practices Act, Congress chose not to include all U.S.-owned or controlled subsidiaries in its prohibition on bribing foreign officials, but made it clear that any domestic U.S. corporation that engaged in such bribery through its subsidiary would be liable under the statute.[165]

(2) The Protective Principle

Under the protective principle, a State may apply its laws to conduct that takes place abroad if that conduct threatens its national security. Laws against espionage, sabotage, and counterfeiting, as applied to extraterritorial conduct, are laws justified by this principle.[166] The protective principle has also been used to justify application of U.S. laws to drug smuggling on the high seas.[167]

(3) The Passive Personality Principle

The "passive personality" principle would base legislative jurisdiction on the nationality of the *victim* of a crime. At its broadest, it would permit a State to apply its law to actions undertaken against its citizens wherever they might be. As a basis for applying general criminal or tort law, the principle is not generally accepted. However, it "has been increasingly accepted when applied to terrorist and other organized attacks on a state's nationals by reason of their nationality, or to assassinations of a state's ambassadors, or government officials."[168] For example, article 5(1)(c) of the Convention Against Torture and Other Cruel, Inhumane and Degrading Treatment or Punishment, authorizes States to proscribe conduct involving a "victim [who] is a national of that State if the State considers it appropriate."

---

161 A similar conflict arose with France. *See* William L. Craig, *Application of the Trading with the Enemy Act to Foreign Corporations Owned by Americans: Reflections on* Fruehauf v. Massardy, 83 HARVARD L. REV. 579 (1970).

162 50 U.S.C.A. Appx. §2407. The act was an attempt to prevent U.S. enterprises from assisting in a boycott of Israel organized by Arab countries.

163 50 U.S.C.A. Appx. §2415(2).

164 *See* Burma Executive Order, Exec. Order No. 13047, 3 CFR 202 (1997) and summary of the Act's provisions in *Crosby v. National Foreign Trade Council*, 530 U.S. 363 (2000).

165 *See* 15 U.S.C.A. §§78dd-1-2. Another area where clashes over who can regulate the conduct of subsidiaries of U.S. corporations is international banking — now governed by the Basle Concordat of 1983, 22 Int'l Legal Materials 901 (1983). Other issues of international banking not covered are those arising from discovery orders against assets in possible foreign subsidiary banks, discussed *infra* pp. 724-726.

166 RESTATEMENT §402(3).

167 *See United States v. Cardales*, 168 F.3d 548 (1st Cir. 1999) (protective principle justified U.S. legislative jurisdiction over Venezuelan-flag ship stopped 150 miles south of Puerto Rico that was carrying illegal drugs bound for the U.S.).

168 RESTATEMENT §402, Comment g.

The United States has accepted the "passive personality" principle in its passage of the Omnibus Diplomatic Security and Antiterrorism Act of 1986, specifically the section making it a crime to kill or injure a citizen of the United States. Indicative of the fact that this principle is not yet generally accepted under international law is a provision of the Act that requires certification by the Attorney General that the act was in fact directed against the U.S. government or civilian population as a whole.[169] No such certification is needed for a prosecution under the Hostage Taking Act, which proscribes taking U.S. hostages "in order to compel a third person or a governmental organization to do or abstain from any act."[170] Another example of this principle is a case where a Colombian was charged with conspiracy to murder a U.S. federal narcotics agent in Colombia, the court noting that "the nationality of the victims, who are United States Government agents, clearly supports jurisdiction."[171] In another case, a Palestinian airline hijacker was held to be properly subject to U.S. criminal laws for killing U.S. citizens in Egypt.[172]

(4) The Principle of Universal Jurisdiction

Certain crimes are considered to be offenses against all of humankind, so any State that catches the perpetrators may prosecute them under its own law, regardless of where the crimes were committed. Among the crimes subject to universal jurisdiction are piracy, slave trade, attacks on or hijacking of aircraft, genocide, war crimes and possibly some acts of terrorism.[173] The United States is also a party to numerous conventions punishing those who endanger civil aviation or diplomats, or who hold hostages. Other examples of offenses covered by universal jurisdiction are piracy and ship or airline hijacking on the high seas or outside United States air space.[174]

The concept of universal jurisdiction was applied in the proceedings for extradition of John Demjanjuk. Israel sought to try him for offenses he was alleged to have committed as a guard in Nazi concentration camps in Eastern Europe. In approving extradition, the court noted that Israel had jurisdiction to try the case. Referring to universal jurisdiction, it noted that "[i]nternational law provides that certain offenses may be punished by any state because the offenders are 'common enemies of all mankind and all nations have an equal interest in their apprehension and punishment.'"[175]

c. Effects as a Basis for Extraterritorial Jurisdiction

If a person stands in one State and shoots a gun across the border into another State and kills someone there, most would agree that the second State should be permitted to apply its laws to punish that conduct. Indeed, one might assert that the crime is one that is committed in both States, since an essential element of it — killing the victim — took place on the territory of second State. Increasingly, States have sought to apply this "effects principle" to less tangible economic effects.

International Limits on the Effects Principle International law has generally been permissive where effects are concerned. The premier case on the subject is the 1927

---

169 18 U.S.C.A. §2231 *et seq. See* RESTATEMENT §402, Note 3.

170 18 U.S.C.A. §1203. Other bases for extraterritorial application are where the offender is a U.S. national, the offender is found in the U.S. or the government sought to be compelled is that of the U.S.

171 *United States v. Benitez*, 741 F.2d 1312, 1316 (11th Cir. 1984).

172 *United States v. Rezaq*, 134 F.3d 1121 (D.C. Cir. 1998).

173 RESTATEMENT §404. The Restatement notes that the concept is not limited to criminal law and may apply to tort or restitution liability for victims of such criminal offenses, such as under the Alien Tort Claims Act, discussed *supra* pp. 703-705.

174 *See* 18 U.S.C.A. §7 (maritime offenses); 18 U.S.C.A. §1651 (piracy).

175 *In the Matter of Demjanjuk*, 776 F.2d 571 (6th Cir. 1985).

decision of the Permanent Court of International Justice (PCIJ) in *The S.S. Lotus (France v. Turkey)*.[176] In that case, a French officer in charge of a French ship on the high seas allegedly caused a negligent collision of his vessel with a Turkish ship, causing injuries to or killing several Turkish sailors. Turkey brought criminal charges in its courts and France protested. The court rejected the territoriality principle as argued by France, observing that international law did not require States to confine the reach of their laws to their own territory. More broadly, the Court asserted that international law "leaves [States] . . . a wide measure of discretion" and that "every state remains free to adopt the principles which it regards as best and most suitable." The court noted that many countries have considered offenses as having taken place on their territory "if one of the constituent elements of the offense, and more especially its effects, have taken place there."[177] Not only that, the court proclaimed, State assertions of extraterritoriality are presumptively valid and the burden of proving that there is an exception is on the State opposing its assertion.[178]

The Effects Test in U.S. Law The application of the effects test in U.S. law has been one of the more contentious issues in the area of legislative jurisdiction. And battles of it have principally been fought in the arena of antitrust regulation.[179] In a 1945 decision, the Court of Appeals for 2d Circuit in *United States v. Aluminum Co. of America (Alcoa)*[180] created what has been called the "*Alcoa* effects" doctrine. *Alcoa* involved an alleged conspiracy between U.S. and foreign insurance companies to refuse to agree to reinsurance contracts without certain limited liability provisions. Under the *Alcoa* effects test, U.S. antitrust laws apply to foreign conduct if it is (1) intended to affect U.S. commerce and (2) has an actual effect on U.S. commerce. Moreover, once the government proves intent, actual effect is presumed unless the defendant can show there was in fact no effect or *de minimis* effect.[181]

Criticism of U.S. Applications of the Effects Doctrine The *Alcoa* effects extension of antitrust jurisdiction of U.S. courts has met with considerable objections from other countries, particularly in Europe. The theoretical objection is that it is improper to apply an effects test outside the context of concrete immediate physical effects — such as the example of the person shooting someone across an international border. When extended to less tangible consequences, such as the cross-border effects of economic activity, the doctrine can provide a basis for almost limitless extraterritorial jurisdiction.[182] U.S. authorities have responded that the price of choosing to enter the lucrative U.S. market is to be subject to the rules that apply to all others who participate in it.

---

176 PCIJ, Ser. A, No. 10 (1927).

177 *Id.* at 23.

178 Another classic case on effects is the *Trail Smelter Case*, an international arbitration case in which the U.S. successfully claimed against Canada for cross-border pollution by a Canadian smelter. *See* 3 Reports of Int'l Arb. Awards 1905 (1949).

179 15 U.S.C.A. §§1-7. For more on antitrust law generally, *see* Chapter XV, pp. 609-616.

180 148 F.2d 416, 444 (2d Cir. 1945) (L. Hand, J.).

181 The Supreme Court approved and applied the doctrine, most recently in *Hartford Fire Insurance Co. v. California*, 509 U.S. 764 (1993) (also involving reinsurance agreements). But the outer limits of the effects test have been superceded by the Foreign Trade Antitrust Improvements Act of 1982 (FTAIA), 15 U.S.C.A. §6a, which requires a "direct, substantial, and reasonably foreseeable effect" on U.S. commerce. Where alleged price-fixing of vitamins by a Germany company that significantly and adversely affected both customers outside and within the United States, the Supreme Court approved dismissal of foreign purchasers from the lawsuit. *F. Hoffmann-La Roche Ltd. v. Empagran S.A.*, 542 U.S. 155 (2004).

182 Jennings, BRITISH YEARBOOK OF INT'L LAW 146, 159 (1957). Other situations involving less tangible effects are the effects of seditious acts and defamation.

Some nations objecting to U.S. extensions of jurisdiction have gone beyond diplomatic protests and have enacted "blocking statutes." An example was the United Kingdom's Protection of Trading Interests Act.[183] It prohibits enforcement of any "multiple damage" awards — a clear reaction to antitrust "treble" damage awards.[184] It also authorizes British executive officials to prohibit compliance with discovery orders. And, in what has been called a "clawback" provision, it permits a non-U.S. party to recover back in a U.K. action two-thirds of any award it has paid. As the head of U.S. antitrust enforcement remarked recently, "[u]ntil the 1990s, the not infrequent reaction of foreign governments to 'U.S. antitrust investigations' was to leap to the defense of 'their' firms, accuse the U.S. of 'extraterritorial' tendencies, threaten to invoke blocking statutes, and express astonishment that any country should even want to have pro-competitive laws, much less enforce them."[185]

Some of the friction over application of U.S. antitrust laws has lessened in recent years for two reasons. The first is the convergence of antitrust standards and vigorous enforcement policies, as requirements in the rest of the world have become more similar to U.S. requirements and the dangers of cartels have become more apparent. Particularly in the European Community, standards have stiffened to protect its markets from unfair competition and the European Court of Justice has been active in enforcing them based on the effects principle.[186] Second, there have been attempts to harmonize enforcement efforts and avoid friction, both under U.N. auspices and through bilateral arrangements, particularly between the United States and Canada, Germany and Australia.[187]

Criminal Cases and the Effects Test   The Restatement notes that assertions of criminal jurisdiction should be approached more cautiously than assertions of civil jurisdiction because they "may be perceived as particularly intrusive." But it also notes that foreign States are less likely to object to regulation of "serious and universally condemned offenses, such as . . . traffic in narcotics" — the most frequently encountered applications of U.S. extraterritorial legislative jurisdiction.[188] Thus, extraterritorial application of U.S. civil antitrust laws has been greeted with greater concern than

---

183 U.K. Statute 1980 c. 11. *See* Edward T. Swaine, *The Local Law of Global Antitrust*, 43 Wm. & Mary Law Rev. 627 (2001).

184 Treble damages awards were discussed in Chapter 15, p. 208.

185 Joel I. Klein, The Antitrust Division's International Anticartel Enforcement Program (Washington, D.C., April 6, 2000).

186 National law has also been applied. *See Organic Pigments Case*, 74 BGHZ (May 29, 1979) (regulation of acquisition of a U.S. firm by subsidiary of a German firm in the U.S. based on potential for and intent to compete in Germany). *See also* the United Kingdom's recent White Paper, "Productivity and Enterprise: A World Class Competition Regime" (July 31, 2001), which condemns international cartels in the strongest terms and promotes criminal penalties for those involved.

187 *See* RESTATEMENT §415, Reporters' Note 9. Some foreign objections to U.S. assertions of antitrust jurisdiction are sometimes based less on antipathy to antitrust regulation or extraterritorial jurisdiction, as to the uneven and biased interpretations of U.S. law by U.S. courts, by the treble damages penalty, by extensive pre-trial discovery methods, and the fact that most such actions are brought by private parties. *See* Chapter XV, pp. 609-616 (antitrust law) and Chapter VII, pp. 235-240 (discovery). Discovery in international cases is discussed *infra* this chapter, p. 724. Many countries do not allow penalties to be imposed in civil litigation; most do not permit lawyers to engage in discovery of such broad scope as authorized in U.S. courts; and many insist that enforcement of government regulations be undertaken by public agencies accountable to the government, not by private persons.

188 RESTATEMENT §403, Reporter's Note 8.

application of U.S. criminal drug laws.[189]

If effects of conduct can provide the basis for legislative jurisdiction over conduct outside a State, then it is only a small step further to punish conspiracies to cause an effect. Punishing extraterritorial conspiracies to import drugs even when they are not successful has been approved under the theory that the whole purpose of many drug laws is "to halt smugglers *before* they introduce their dangerous wares into and distribute them in this country."[190]

d. The Overall Reasonableness Test

Restatement Position According to §403 of the Restatement, even if a particular assertion of legislative jurisdiction meets one of the exceptions to the territoriality principle just outlined, it must still be tested for its overall "reasonableness."[191] The determination of reasonableness is to be guided by several factors, the most important of which are (1) the link of the conduct to the State's territory, including whether it has a "substantial, direct, and foreseeable effect" within the territory; (2) the link between the principal parties or the victims involved and the State; (3) the relative importance of regulation to the regulating State and other States involved and the degree to which such regulation is generally accepted or might conflict with those of other States; and (4) justifiable expectations. Other factors include less specific criteria, such as "the importance of the regulation to the international political, legal, or economic system" and the "extent to which the regulation is consistent with the traditions of the international system." Section 403 concludes with an additional caveat that, even if "it would not be unreasonable to exercise jurisdiction . . . , but the prescriptions of the two states are in conflict, . . . a state should defer to the other state if that state's interest is clearly greater."

There is some dispute as to whether the reasonableness rule exists at all. Commentators point out that it is not really followed. Courts tend simply to look to see if the facts of the case support jurisdiction under territorial, nationality, protective, universal jurisdiction and effects, and that is the end of the inquiry.[192] Critics argue that "the judiciary possesses neither the special training nor the resources necessary to analyze the economic, political and social interests that underlie a state's policies." Moreover, "it is not part of the judicial function to decide whether a law or policy is justified by what the court conceives to be in the national interest. That is a political function."[193]

The Reasonableness Test in U.S. Law As a result of overseas objections, the Supreme Court and U.S. authorities have become more sensitive to potential conflicts with foreign law and sovereignty. It has been said that U.S. extraterritorial assertions of

---

189 There have been objections over application of U.S. narcotics laws, but those objections have been less about legislative jurisdiction than about irregular *enforcement* action taken in other countries, particularly abductions of criminal suspects from the territories of other States. *See infra* pp. 719-720.

190 *United States v. Wright-Baker*, 784 F.2d 161, 168 (3d Cir. 1986)(affirming drug conspiracy charges against marijuana smuggler arrested on the high seas); *United States v. Noriega*, 746 F.Supp. 1506, 1513 (S.D.Fla. 1990) (upholding drug conspiracy charges against former Panamanian dictator Manuel Noriega).

191 RESTATEMENT §403(2).

192 Phillip R. Trimble, *The Supreme Court and International Law: The Demise of Restatement Section 403*, 89 JOURNAL INT'L LAW 53, 55-57 (1995) ("there is no general practice and hence no customary international law like that advanced in section 403").

193 Address to the American Bar Association by Senator Paul Durack, Attorney General of Australia, made in 1981, quoted in PAUST, FITZPATRICK & VAN DYKE, *supra* note 1, at 441-444. *See also Laker Airways Ltd. v. Sabena*, 731 F.2d 909, 948-51 (D.C.Cir. 1984) (criticizing use of §403 by the 9th Circuit in *Timberlane, infra* note 197).

jurisdiction are subject to overall "international comity" concerns that are similar to the "reasonableness" factors of Restatement §403, and the Supreme Court has suggested as much in its caselaw.[194] However, in evaluating particular instances of extraterritorial legislative jurisdiction, the Supreme Court has done little analysis and balancing of interests.[195] In an antitrust case, *Hartford Insurance Co. v. California*,[196] the Court assumed without deciding that "international comity" applied to assertions of antitrust jurisdiction. In the end, however, it required that there be some actual conflict between U.S. and foreign law before the extraterritorial application of antitrust laws would be questioned. In denying the comity claim of British reinsurance companies, supported by their government as *amicus curiae*, the Court observed that they argued nothing more than that British Parliament regulated the area and the challenged conduct was perfectly consistent with British law and policy. Unless compliance with the laws of both countries is impossible, the Court saw no conflict with British law and therefore no reason to limit the reach of U.S. law.[197]

Securities Regulation and Other Areas Laws barring fraud in the advertisement and sale of securities have been applied extraterritorially on much the same basis as antitrust laws. However, often securities or commodities fraud is actually consummated on a U.S. exchange, thus making the link more concrete than just effects.[198] In addition, the conflict with foreign interests is less likely as few foreign states encourage misrepresentation or insider trading. The Lanham Trade-Mark Act, which protects U.S.-registered trademarks has also been applied extraterritorially.[199]

Constitutional Limits on Extraterritorial Effect U.S. due process constitutional limits on U.S. states' power of extraterritorial legislative jurisdiction with regard to other states were discussed in Chapter VII.[200] Those limits apply equally to state assertions of jurisdiction over conduct in foreign international States. However, due process limits are quite permissive and rarely present a problem.[201] Some of the recent cases suggest

---

194 *See Societe Nationale Industrielle Aerospatiale v. United States District Court*, 482 U.S. 522, 546 (1987) (reasonableness must be determined by the trial court "based on its knowledge of the case and of the claims and interests of the parties and the governments whose statutes and policies they invoke.").

195 Congress has also ignored any comity factors test in the international criminal statutes it passes. *See, e.g.*, the Torture Victim Protection Act, 28 U.S.C.A. §1350 note; the Antiterrorism Act, 18 U.S.C.A. §2331-2337; the Hostage Taking Act, 18 U.S.C.A. §1203; the Protection of Internationally Protected Persons Act, 18 U.S.C.A. §112(a), (b), (e); and the Destruction of Aircraft Act, 18 U.S.C.A. §32.

196 509 U.S. 764 (1993).

197 In so concluding, the Court cited and quoted comments e and j of RESTATEMENT §403. *See also United States v. Nippon Paper Industries Co.*, 109 F.3d 1, 798-99 (1st Cir. 1997) (law after *Hartford* is that voluntary forbearance is a matter of grace and applicable "only in those few cases in which the law of the foreign sovereign required a defendant to act in a manner incompatible with the Sherman Act or in which full compliance with both statutory schemes was impossible."). *But see Timberlane Lumber Co. v. Bank of America*, 549 F.2d 597 (9th Cir. 1976) (pre-*Hartford* case requiring lower court to use all the §403 factors to evaluate use of antitrust laws to conspiracy that had its situs primarily in Honduras).

198 *See Psimenos v. E.F. Hutton*, 722 F.2d 1041 (2d Cir. 1983)(upholding jurisdiction over claim regarding transaction on U.S. commodity exchange). *See also* RESTATEMENT §416. Securities regulation is covered and the relevant statutes and rules are cited in the discussion in Chapter XV, pp. 600-604.

199 15 U.S.C.A. §§1091-1096. *See Wells Fargo & Co. v. Wells Fargo Express Co.*, 556 F.2d 406 (9th Cir. 1977). Trademark law is discussed in greater detail in Chapter XII, pp. 511-516. At least one court has held that the U.S. Copyright Act does not apply extraterritorially. *See DeBardossy v. Pustri*, 763 F.Supp. 1239 (S.D.N.Y. 1991).

200 *See* Chapter VII, p. 263.

201 The one international case discussed in Chapter VII in which due process made a difference was *Home Insurance Co. v. Dick*, 281 U.S. 397, 408 (1930), where the Supreme Court rejected Texas's efforts to apply its law to an insurance contract concluded in Mexico, but assigned to a Texas resident because "nothing in any way relating to the policy sued on, or to the contracts of reinsurance, was ever done or

that due process limits are essentially identical to international law limits, noting that "[p]rinciples of international law are 'useful as a rough guide'" to deciding the due process issue.[202]

e. Legislative Jurisdiction by Consent

U.S. Overseas Military Bases Prime examples of consent extraterritorial legislative jurisdiction are found in "Status of Forces Agreements" (SOFA) agreements under which U.S. military bases have been established in foreign countries.[203] Such treaties and the administrative agreements under them commonly provide that the United States will exercise "primary" jurisdiction over service-connected offenses ("offenses arising out of any act or omission done in the performance of official duty") and offenses involving U.S. property or personnel, while the host country will have primary jurisdiction over all other offenses.[204] However, other SOFAs are more restrictive. U.S. offenses are most often handled under the Uniform Code of Military Justice.[205]

Friction has arisen when military personnel commit serious offenses against the host countries nationals in the course of their official duties. For example, in 1998 U.S. Marine fighter pilots from the airbase at Aviano, Italy flew too low and cut the cable supporting an Italian cable car near Cavalese, Italy, killing its 20 occupants. Since the tragedy was service-connected, an Italian court ruled that the U.S. military had jurisdiction over the case against the pilots. The pilots were later acquitted of manslaughter charges in a court-martial trial, much to the consternation of the relatives of the dead. However, in a 2001 case in Japan, a U.S. Air Force sergeant who was accused on the rape of an Okinawan woman was turned over to Japanese authorities since the crime was not service connected. In addition, the U.S. may voluntarily waive its right to exercise jurisdiction and turn the person over to host country authorities.[206]

The Status of Diplomatic Premises Diplomatic or consular premises in a foreign country — because they are owned and controlled by another country with the consent of the host country — might be thought to be analogous to military bases. However, as the Restatement notes, the fact "[t]hat premises are inviolable" by the host government and protected by both treaties and customary international law "does not mean that they are extraterritorial. Acts committed on those premises are within the territorial jurisdiction of the receiving state . . . ."[207] Diplomatic "premises and related property are subject to the host state's jurisdiction to prescribe, adjudicate, and enforce law except by means

---

required to be done in Texas." States may act based on the normal exceptions to territoriality, such as the effects test. *See, e.g., State v. Tickle*, 77 S.E.2d 632 (N.C. 1953) (non-payment of child support having effect in the state). This could well include effects within the state of conduct engaged in outside the United States. Certainly, a state could not base its legislative jurisdiction only on U.S. citizenship. A state can base legislative jurisdiction on the fact that the person is a domiciliary of the given state. *See Skieriotes v. Florida*, 313 U.S. 69, 73 (1941).

202 *Caicedo, infra* note 256, at 372, quoting *Davis, infra* note 257.

203 *See, e.g.,* North Atlantic Treaty Status of Forces Agreement, 4 U.S. Treaties 1792, TIAS No. 2846 (1951).

204 *See* the Administrative agreement with Japan, quoted in *Wilson v. Girard, infra* note 206.

205 10 U.S.C.A. §§801 *et seq.* The U.S. federal military courts on these bases in the past handled cases against both civilian and military personnel. However, the Supreme Court held that this practice violated the constitutional rights of civilians. *Reid v. Covert*, 354 U.S. 1 (1957). But if the offender is a member of the military, there is court-martial jurisdiction even if the crime is not "service-connected." Solorio v. United States, 483 U.S. 435 (1987).

206 *See also Wilson v. Girard*, 354 U.S. 524 (1957) (upholding waiver over jurisdiction to Japanese authorities in case where soldier killed a Japanese civilian).

207 RESTATEMENT §466, Comment a.

or in circumstances where an exercise of jurisdiction would violate the premises or interfere with their use for [their] designated purposes."[208]

2. Extraterritorial Judicial Jurisdiction

Jurisdiction to adjudicate and jurisdiction to prescribe are closely related, though conceptually distinct. While jurisdiction to prescribe concerns a State's power to create a rule of conduct applicable to extraterritorial conduct, jurisdiction to adjudicate has to do with the State's power to compel an offender against that rule to answer a claim in its own courts and to bind that offender to its courts' judgments.

Like extraterritorial legislative jurisdiction, extraterritorial judicial jurisdiction is a familiar concept in U.S. law because of its federal system. Indeed, in most respects, the law of extraterritorial judicial jurisdiction in the international context is the same as it is in the domestic interstate context. Interstate jurisdiction over defendants, called the law of "personal jurisdiction," is governed by a "minimum contacts" test of the defendant's conduct to determine if asserting jurisdiction would be fair. The details of the test employed were discussed in Chapter VII.[209]

a. International Application of the Minimum Contacts Test

(1) Minimum Contacts with U.S. States in the International Setting

The factor in the "minimum contacts" due process analysis that is most commonly at issue in international cases is usually not whether some contacts exist. Rather it is the character of those contacts — whether they were "purposely directed" toward the forum state. For product liability, this means that the foreign manufacturer must have "purposefully availed" itself of the benefits of markets in the forum state either directly or by injecting products into the "stream of commerce" that runs through the forum state. In determining this question, courts focus on whether the defendant has "targeted the market" in the forum state. Some examples of factors courts have found relevant to show such targeting are where the foreign manufacturer has designed the product for U.S. export,[210] has sent advertising literature or personnel to the forum state,[211] or has granted distribution licenses for sale in the forum state.[212] Some cases have found targeting based on presence of a substantial number of sales made in the U.S. state,[213] just as the absence of a substantial number has been deemed probative of an absence of targeting.[214] Again, these are the same factors that are applied in domestic out-of-state

---

208 *Id.*, Comment c. *See United States v. Erdos*, 474 F.2d 157 (4th Cir. 1973) (holding a federal statute applicable to a senior diplomat who killed another embassy employee) and Jordan J. Paust, *Non-Extraterritoriality of "Special Territorial Jurisdiction" of the United States: Forgotten History and the Errors of Erdos*, 24 Yale Journal Int'l Law 305 (1999).

209 *See* pp. 253-259.

210 *In re Perrier Bottled Water Litigation*, 754 F.Supp. 264, 268 (D.Conn. 1990) (among other things, bottles had ounce rather metric labels).

211 *Weight v. Kawasaki Motors Corp.*, 604 F.Supp. 968 (E.D.Va. 1985) (literature); *Heins v. Welhelm Hlh Wetzlar Machinery GmbH*, 522 N.E.2d 989 (Mass.App. 1988) (employees sent to current and prospective clients).

212 *Lister v. Marangoni Meccania SpA*, 728 F.Supp. 1524, 1527 (D.D.C. 1985) (Italian manufacturer of tire retreading machine had concluded agreement with U.S. distributer of its machines).

213 *Oswalt v. Scripto, Inc.*, 616 F.2d 191 (5th Cir. 1980) (3-4 million units in annual sales sufficient); *Allen v. Canadian General Electric Co.*, 410 N.Y.S.2d 707 (N.Y.App. 1978) (1% of sales constituting $9 million sufficient).

214 *Hapner v. Rolf Brauchli, Inc.*, 273 N.W.2d 822 (Mich.1978) (no personal jurisdiction over Swiss manufacturer of hair dryer that injured the plaintiff where only a few were exported and there was no evidence of manufacturer targeting the Michigan market).

assertions of personal jurisdiction.

(2) Minimum Contacts with the Entire U.S. for Federal Claims in Federal Court

As explained in Chapter VII, when federal courts handle state-law claims, their powers of personal jurisdiction are limited to those of a state court of the state in which the federal court sits. However, when the claim is a federal one, federal courts are not so confined and may exercise jurisdiction in any manner "consistent with the Constitution and laws of the United States."[215] The Supreme Court has formally reserved judgment on the precise constitutional limits of jurisdiction as it relates to federal courts.[216] However, the lower courts have approved personal jurisdiction by analogy to the *International Shoe* test. Since federal courts are national courts, when handling federal claims they have personal jurisdiction over foreign defendants who have the appropriate contacts with the entire territory of the United States.[217] Thus, if a foreign national sells an investment package to one customer in each of 40 states, this may not constitute sufficient contacts for any of these customers to sue that foreign national on a state-law claim in any one of the 40 states. But if the sales violated federal securities laws, all 40 contacts count and this may be sufficient volume for there to be personal jurisdiction in a federal court.[218]

(3) Special Treatment of International Defendants

Legislative jurisdiction is said by some to be subject to an overall reasonableness requirement under Restatement §403, although there is some doubt whether the overall reasonableness test of §403 is really a rule of international law or is actually applied by U.S. courts.[219] However, in the case of *judicial* jurisdiction, U.S. law of personal jurisdiction does have an overall reasonableness test. As discussed in Chapter VII, in the 1987 *Asahi Metals* case, the factors to be considered are (1) the actual burden on the defendant of defending in the forum, (2) the interests of the forum state in the case, (3) the plaintiff's interest in getting relief and (4) "efficient resolution of controversies" and "fundamental substantive social policies."[220] On the facts of *Asahi*, 8 justices of the Supreme Court agreed that the reasonableness test would defeat personal jurisdiction over the foreign defendant in that case because "[t]he unique burdens placed upon one who must defend oneself in a foreign legal system should have significant weight in assessing the reasonableness of stretching the long arm of personal jurisdiction over national borders."[221] The Court also quoted an earlier opinion asserting the need to exercise "great care and reserve" when extending personal jurisdiction into the international field. Based on these concerns, the Court concluded that the California

---

215 FRCP 4(k)(2). *See* Chapter VII, p. 258.

216 *See Omni Capital* case, *infra* note 218, 484 U.S. at 103 n. 5.

217 *ISI International, Inc. v. Borden Ladner Gervais LLP*, 256 F.3d 548 (7th Cir. 2001) (Canadian defendant's contacts with the U.S. included sending letters to California falsely claiming patent infringement, hired Michigan lawyers for the patent and signed production contract with Texas company); *United States v. Swiss American Bank, Ltd.*, 191 F.3d 30 (1st Cir. 1999) (federal government seeking to collect money laundered by U.S. defendant from foreign bank).

218 These were essentially the facts of the case that enactment of FRCP 4(k)(2) was meant to remedy. *See Omni Capital International v. Rudolf Wolff & Co., Ltd.*, 484 U.S. 97 (1987).

219 *See supra* pp. 711-712. It is interesting to note that, in contrast to §403, the Restatement does not have such an overall reasonableness test for judicial jurisdiction. *See* RESTATEMENT §421.

220 480 U.S. at 113. The case was discussed in Chapter VII, pp. 255-257.

221 480 U.S. at 114.

court could not exercise personal jurisdiction over the Japanese defendant.[222]

Some have suggested that *Asahi Metals* recognizes a special rule for foreign defendants. However, the facts of the case were that the injured California plaintiff had settled with one of two foreign defendants and had been dismissed from the case. This left a lawsuit between two foreign nationals in the California courts over who was responsible for what was paid to the plaintiff. In dismissing the case, the Court relied on this fact, indicating that since the remaining Taiwanese manufacturer "plaintiff is not a California resident, California's legitimate interests in the dispute have considerably diminished."[223] Thus, where an injured U.S. resident plaintiff is still in the case, it is not at all clear that any special solicitude is due the foreign defendant.[224]

b. *Forum Non Conveniens* as a Basis for Declining Judicial Jurisdiction in International Cases

Just because a U.S. court has judicial jurisdiction to go forward with a lawsuit, does not mean that it must hear the case. As discussed in Chapter VII, the doctrine of *forum non conveniens* may be a basis for rejecting the case.[225] This doctrine authorizes dismissal of a case whenever it appears that the place it has been brought is not a convenient forum for it. In U.S. law, this doctrine has most often been applied in the U.S. domestic interstate context to dismiss a case in the courts of one state so that it could be brought in another state. However, it has also been used in the international context to dismiss a case in U.S. state or federal court on the ground that the case would best be brought in a foreign court system.

The factors to be considered in deciding whether to dismiss are those set out in the Supreme Court case of *Gulf Oil Corp. v. Gilbert*.[226] They were summarized in Chapter VII and will not be repeated here.[227] However, three points should be mentioned as specifically bearing on the doctrine as applied in international cases.

The first point is important because it goes to the heart of why a foreign plaintiff might wish to bring a case in the United States — the desire for more favorable law. These are principally procedural advantages of discovery and jury trials, but sometimes substantive liability law as well.[228] In *Piper Aircraft Corp. v. Reyno*,[229] Scottish plaintiffs sued U.S. aircraft and propeller manufacturers in the United State arising out of a plane crash that took place in Scotland. Defendants moved to dismiss on *forum non conveniens* grounds, arguing that the case should be brought in the Scottish courts. Plaintiffs opposed dismissal on the ground that Scottish law did not follow strict liability for defective products and that it disallowed recovery of some elements of damages

---

222 *Asahi*, 480 U.S. at 115.

223 *Id*. at 113.

224 *See* BORN, *supra* note 1, pp. 137-138 for a discussion of the issue. For a case rejecting a higher standard in international cases, *see Roth v. Garcia Marquez*, 942 F.2d 617, 623 (9th Cir. 1991) (defendant being a foreign national cannot be "dispositive, because . . . it would always prevent suit against a foreign national. . ."). A foreign manufacturer cannot avoid personal jurisdiction by passing title of products to a foreign distributor. *See Vermeulen v. Renault, U.S.A., Inc.*, 965 F.2d 1014, 1025 (11th Cir. 1992) (fact that Renault's title to cars passed to its distributor in France is irrelevant for personal jurisdiction over Renault).

225 *See* pp. 259-261.

226 330 U.S. 501 (1947).

227 *See* p. 259 note 168. The *Gulf Oil* factors have been widely copied by state courts, but they are not binding on states. States may adopt any considerations it wishes or may reject the doctrine entirely.

228 In addition, there is evidence that, for whatever reason, "foreign plaintiffs and defendants win substantially more often than domestic litigants." Kevin Clermont & Theodore Eisenberg, Xenophilia in American Courts, 109 HARVARD LAW REV. 1120 (1996).

229 454 U.S. 235, 247 (1981).

available in the United States. The Court rejected the plaintiffs' arguments, holding that "[t]he possibility of a change in substantive law should ordinarily not be given conclusive or even substantial weight in the forum non conveniens inquiry" unless "the remedy provided by the alternative forum is so clearly inadequate or unsatisfactory that it is no remedy at all." Applying the *Gulf Oil* factors, the Court dismissed the suit so that it could be brought in Scotland.

The second point about *forum non conveniens* is of even more specific relevance to foreign plaintiffs. As a general rule, a plaintiff's choice of forum is given deference since it is often convenient at least for the plaintiff, who chose it. Thus, it is only when the *Gulf Oil* factors clearly point to a different forum that the presumption is overcome. However, for a foreign plaintiff, the United States is most often *not* a convenient forum. Thus, a foreign plaintiff's choice of forum "deserves less deference."[230]

The third point about international *forum non conveniens* is that it runs counter to the almost invariable rule in civil law countries that it is always permissible to sue a defendant in that defendant's home State. While the fact that the forum is the defendant's home or place of doing business is a relevant factor under *Gulf Oil*, it is far from conclusive in determining convenience.[231] A well-known case involving international application of *forum non conveniens* was the disaster at the Union Carbide company's Bhophal, India, plant. The Indian plaintiffs sued Union Carbide in federal court in New York, where it was located. The Court of Appeals dismissed the case, relying on the facts that virtually all the witnesses were in India, all the plant records were in Hindi and Indian law would undoubtedly govern liability in the case.[232]

3. Jurisdiction to Enforce

A State's extraterritorial jurisdiction to enforce its laws is closely related to its legislative and judicial jurisdiction. Jurisdiction to enforce is especially close to judicial jurisdiction, since judicial proceedings are often used to enforce the law. However, this may not always be the case.

There are two types of enforcement action: administrative and judicially allied. Administrative enforcement comprises executive, police or administrative sanctions employed against a respondent outside the immediate context of and without any contemplation of a future judicial proceeding. For administrative enforcement, a State need not have judicial jurisdiction, but it must have legislative jurisdiction. Judicially-allied enforcement action can be either criminal or civil. In criminal cases, enforcement actions may involve investigation by police agencies and physical arrest of a suspect preparatory to initiating criminal judicial proceedings. In civil cases, the actions are initiated by the parties, but resort may be had to process from the court to effectuate service of process. To take such judicially allied enforcement actions, a State must have both judicial and legislative jurisdiction.

---

230 *Piper Aircraft*, 454 U.S. at 266. *See also Bergquist v. Medtronic, Inc.*, 379 N.E.2d 508, 512 (Minn. 1986) ("Why should the United States taxpayers, or taxpayers of Minnesota in the present case, be presumed to pay for the costs of trial for a plaintiff who is a citizen of a foreign nation; who has a remedy in his own country; and whose defendant consents to being sued in the foreign country?").

231 *See Silver v. Great American Ins. Co.*, 278 N.E.2d 619 (N.Y. 1972) (residence of defendant only one factor to consider); *Russell v. Chrysler Corp.*, 505 N.W.2d 263 (Mich. 1993) (same). *See also Gulf Oil Corp. v. Gilbert, supra* (New York is inconvenient even though defendant is licensed to do business there).

232 *In re Union Carbide Corp. Gas Plant Disaster*, 809 F.2d 195 (2d Cir. 1987).

a. Administrative Enforcement Action

To extract a fine or other sanction from a person, a court order — or the threat of one — is usually necessary. However, if a State is already in possession of money belonging to that person or controls the grant of some license or other privilege sought by the person, all it need do to sanction that person is to withhold the sum of money or privilege. To accomplish this, administrative action is sufficient. Often administrative enforcement actions are not necessarily designed to punish, but more to persuade the respondent to change its behavior or to remove the opportunity for the respondent to violate the law.[233]

Regulated Markets and Tax Withholding An example of administrative enforcement action is the denial of an export license to a business that may sell strategic technology to unfriendly powers.[234] Another is disqualification from bidding on government contracts. Administrative penalties are widely used in regulated markets, such as commodity exchanges, maritime commerce, and civil aviation. Perhaps the most widespread use of administrative enforcement is income tax withholding. Though it is applied to U.S. citizens, income tax withholding applied extraterritorially as well. When foreign nationals receive income from sources in the United States, whether as landlords, lenders, licensors or even as recipients of alimony from U.S. ex-spouses, the federal Internal Revenue Code requires that the *U.S. payers* of the money withhold and pay to the Internal Revenue Service (IRS) a portion of the payment sufficient to cover the taxes due. If there is any balance due a foreign payee, that payee, as a taxpayer, can file a nonresident tax return to obtain that balance.

Requirements The party subject to enforcement action must be given reasonable notice of the claims or charges and an opportunity to be heard in opposition to them before the action becomes effective as a final matter. In addition, whatever sanction is imposed must be a proportionate response to the violation.[235] If the party does not respond to the notice of violation, the State is justified in withholding the benefit or privilege, but this action does not determine that there was a violation in fact. In addition, if the State administrative machinery is facing an urgent situation, it can take action immediately without waiting for the party to be heard and even without notice if circumstances demand it.[236]

b. Judicially-Allied Enforcement Actions: Criminal Cases

(1) Extraterritorial Investigation and Arrest

Investigatory Activities The general rule of international law is that a State's law enforcement officers may carry out their activities on the territory of another State only with the consent of the second state.[237] The law enforcement action need not be particularly coercive or intrusive for it to be taken seriously by the State on whose

---

233 Sometimes judicial action is necessary for enforcement to be effective. If so, the State's courts must have judicial jurisdiction. However, if the party voluntarily resorts to the State's courts to challenge an administrative decision on its merits, that party is deemed to have consented to judicial jurisdiction.

234 *See* Berne C. Kluber, *Global Distributions: The Effect of Export Controls,* 23 HOUSTON J. INT'L LAW 429 (2001) (outlining the law and its enforcement, including recent statistical information).

235 RESTATEMENT §431(2) and (3).

236 *Id.*, Comment e. These requirements resemble closely what the procedural due process doctrine requires as a constitutional minimum for deprivations of property. *See* Chapter VI, pp. 205-209.

237 RESTATEMENT §432(2). The consent may be a one-time consent for a particular investigation or blanket consent granted by an international agreement, such as Status of Forces Agreements. *See supra* p. 713.

territory the enforcement action takes place. In one case, two French customs officials traveled to Switzerland to interrogate a former official of a Swiss bank about French citizens believed to be hiding funds from French tax authorities. The two officials were arrested for acting as agents of a foreign state and violation of Swiss banking and economic intelligence laws. They were convicted and given substantial sentences.[238]

Abductions of Suspects From Other Countries International arrests and abductions of criminal suspects are a more extreme violation of foreign sovereignty. A notable such case was that of Adolph Eichmann, the Nazi war criminal who was abducted from Argentina by Israeli agents. If an abduction takes place, the foreign State involved has the right to protest and, if it does, it may receive reparations from the offending State or may obtain the return of the person abducted.[239] However, under the rule of *mala captus, bene detentus*, which almost all states follow, the fact that the abduction violated international law is generally no bar to prosecution of the offender, if the State where the abduction took place does not demand return. Thus, in the Eichmann case, after Israel and Argentina reached a settlement that did not require Eichmann's return, Eichmann's defense of forcible abduction was denied by the Israeli court.[240] The most common justification for the *mala captus* rule has been that cross-border abductions are an issue of State sovereignty, so the State is the only party that has standing to protest the incursion. Some have argued that this ignores international human rights conventions, such as the Universal Declaration of Human Rights and the International Covenant of Civil and Political Rights, which protect against arbitrary deprivations of freedom and allied rights. In one case from 1981, the U.N. Human Rights Committee so declared in a case involving abduction of a Uruguayan refuge from Argentina by Uruguayan security forces.[241]

Cross-Border Abductions Under U.S. Law The United States follows the so-called *Ker-Frisbie* rule, under which the process by which the defendant got before the court is irrelevant and does not bar prosecution.[242] The rule was reaffirmed in 1992 in *United States v. Alvarez-Machain*,[243] a case that attracted considerable attention from the international community. In *Alvarez-Machain*, federal narcotics agents forcibly abducted a Mexican national from Mexico whom they believed to have been involved in the torture and murder of a U.S. narcotics agent in Mexico. Vigorous protests demanding the defendant's return were made by the Mexican government. However, the Court held, unless abductions are *expressly* prohibited by treaty, "the rule of *Ker* applies, and the court need not inquire as to how [defendant] came before it."[244] Moreover, any decision on release and return of the person was one for the executive branch, not for the courts.

238 *See* Schellenberg, *Proceedings Against Two French Customs Officials in Switzerland*, 9 INT'L BUSINESS LAWYER 139 (1981).

239 RESTATEMENT §432, Reporter's note 3.

240 *See* RESTATEMENT §432, Reporter's note 3 at 332. For an example of where a protest gained the return of a captive, *see Kear v. Hilton*, 699 F.2d 181 (4th Cir. 1983) (on protest, Florida bail jumper was returned to Canada; also bail bondsmen who abducted him were extradited to Canada and convicted there of kidnaping).

241 *See* RESTATEMENT §432, Reporter's note 1 and PAUST, FITZPATRICK & VAN DYKE, *supra* note 1, at 478-479, and citations therein.

242 In *Ker v. Illinois*, 119 U.S. 436 (1886), a private person had abducted a U.S. citizen-fugitive from a foreign country and in *Frisbie v. Collins*, 342 U.S. 519 (1952), state officials abducted the defendant from another U.S. state.

243 504 U.S. 655 (1992).

244 *Alvarez-Machain*. 504 U.S. at 662. Three justices dissented, protesting "[t]he Court's admittedly 'shocking' disdain for customary and conventional international law principles." In the dissent's view, *Ker* was distinguishable because the *Ker* Court assumed that a private person carried out the abduction there.

The decision has met with almost unanimous international condemnation.[245]

The Constitution and Law Enforcement Abroad In 1990, the Court held in *United States v. Verdugo-Urquidez*[246] that a warrantless search carried out by U.S. and Mexican law enforcement officials completely in Mexico was not governed by the 4th Amendment at all because the Constitution does not have extraterritorial force. In *Verdugo-Urquidez*, The Court worried that having the Constitution "travel" with U.S. officials wherever they act in the world would interfere with deployment of U.S. armed forces abroad. And, in any event, it concluded: "If there are to be restrictions on searches and seizures which occur incident to such American action, they must be imposed by the political branches through diplomatic understanding, treaty, or legislation."[247]

It was suggested in *United States v. Toscanino*[248] that there is an exception to the *Ker-Frisbie* rule if shockingly brutal treatment is employed by U.S. agents in the process of apprehension and abduction. In *Toscanino*, the defendant, an Italian citizen convicted of U.S. narcotics offenses who was kidnaped from Uruguay, claimed he was tortured and beaten for 17 days before being brought to the United States for trial. The Court of Appeals ordered that he be provided with a hearing on the allegations he made. However, research discloses no defendant who has gained release on this ground, including Toscanino himself.[249] Moreover, the Supreme Court in *Alvarez-Machain* implied that issues of "shocking" behavior are matters for the executive branch to consider in deciding whether the person should be released, not for the courts.[250]

(2) Extradition from a Foreign State

Extradition is the preferred way to obtain custody of a criminal suspect or escapee in another country. Extradition is beyond the scope of this brief chapter. However, three points should be made that relate directly to U.S. law.[251] First, the doctrine of "specialty" requires that the extraditing nation specify what crimes a prisoner is being extradited to face and this specification is enforceable in U.S. courts.[252]

Second, the principle behind the specialty rule — that a U.S. criminal prosecution cannot proceed in violation of an extradition treaty — means that abductions could be

---

245 *See* testimony of Alan J. Kreczko, Deputy Legal Advisor of the U.S. Department of State, before the House Judiciary Subcommittee, 3 U.S.Dep't of State Dispatch 614 (1992), reprinted in PAUST, FITZPATRICK & VAN DYKE, *supra* note 1, at 493-496. Alvarez-Machain was subsequently acquitted and sued under the Alien Tort Statute, but lost his civil claim. *See Sosa v. Alvarez-Machain*, 542 U.S. 692 (2004), *supra* p. 703.

246 494 U.S. 259 (1990).

247 It perhaps goes without saying that the U.S. Constitution does not apply to foreign police agents — even when the arrestee is a U.S. citizen. *Rosado v. Civiletti*, 621 F.2d 1179, 1189 (2d Cir. 1980)(no challenge to Mexican conviction permitted based on U.S. due process of law). For a discussion of the deterrence rationale for the exclusionary rule, *see* Chapter VIII, pp. 303-306.

248 500 F.2d 267 (2d Cir. 1974).

249 The district court on remand rejected the defense, finding after a hearing that there were several serious abuses by Uruguayan and Brazilian police, but that U.S. agents were not involved. *United States v. Toscanino*, 398 F.Supp. 916 (E.D.N.Y. 1975). *See also United States v. Noriega*, 746 F.Supp. 1506 (S.D.Fla. 1990) (capture of defendant on drug charges by means of invasion of Panama no defense).

250 *Compare* RESTATEMENT §433(1) (permitting U.S. extraterritorial law enforcement action only with consent *and* "in compliance with the laws both of the United States and the other state").

251 The U.S. extradition law is found at 18 U.S.C.A. §3181 *et seq.*

252 *United States v. Rauscher*, 119 U.S. 407, 411-12 (1886) (defendant could only be tried for murder, not for cruel and unusual punishment of seaman under his command, since he was extradited only for murder; also latter charge was not a listed offense in the extradition treaty). There is a split of opinion among the courts on the question of whether a protest from the asylum State is a prerequisite to the accused raising speciality as a defense. *Compare United States v. Puentes*, 50 F.3d 1567 (11th Cir. 1995) (accused has standing) *with United States v. Miro*, 29 F.3d 194, 200 (5th Cir. 1994) (no standing).

prohibited by extradition treaties.[253] Indeed, the principal issue in the *Alvarez-Machain* case was whether a 1978 extradition treaty with Mexico contained an implied term that abductions were prohibited. The Court held that it was neither intended by the parties as shown from the history of the treaty nor was it as an unspoken assumption based on well-established international law.

Third, it is not uncommon for U.S. extradition treaties to provide — at the insistence of the other State — that it can deny extradition for any offense punishable in the U.S. by death unless the U.S. provides assurances that the death penalty will not be imposed or, if imposed, that it will not be carried out.[254] Moreover, the European Court of Human Rights unanimously held in 1989 that the U.S. "death row phenomenon" of the condemned prisoner living in close confinement for years as execution dates are continually set and postponed — not so much the death penalty itself — constitutes "inhuman and degrading treatment and punishment" in violation of Article 3 of the European Convention on Human Rights and Fundamental Freedoms.[255] Consequently, it held, a member of the Council of Europe has a duty not to extradite prisoners to the United States unless the death penalty can be avoided upon their return.

(3) High Seas, Customs Waters and International Airspace

High Seas When conduct takes place on ships on the high seas that are registered in a State, the ship is treated like the territory of that state. This is in contrast to a stateless vessel, which can be stopped and boarded by the authorities of any State.[256] The flag State involved usually has no interest in refusing permission if criminal activity is suspected, so permission to board is given much more readily than consent to law enforcement action on the State's actual physical territory. The U.S. is active in interdicting vessels on the high seas that are suspected of drug smuggling and then seeking permission of the flag country to board and search them.[257] The U.S. Coast Guard also benefits from the "right of approach" doctrine in drug interdiction on the high seas. The right of approach permits a nation's warship to hail and board an unidentified vessel to ascertain its nationality. If suspicious about the vessel's nationality, the inquiring nation may board the vessel and search for registration papers or other identification in order to verify the vessel's nationality.[258]

"Customs Waters" Drug law enforcement actions against flagged vessels are facilitated by the Marijuana on the High Seas Act, a federal statute that permits enforcing U.S. law on board "any vessel within the customs waters" of the United States. "Customs waters" includes the waters along the U.S. coast up to 12 miles out. However, it also includes any place on the high seas that the United States and the flag registry State of

---

253 *See United States v. Rauscher,* 119 U.S. 407 (1886) (defendant could be tried only for the offense for which he was extradited).

254 *See, e.g.,* Canada-U.S. Extradition Treaty, 1976 T.S. No. 3; Italy-U.S. Extradition Treaty, 1983 T.I.A.A. 10837.

255 *Soering Case,* 161 Euro.Ct.Hum.Rts. (Ser. A) (1989) (U.K. acceding to Virginia's request for extradition would violate Art. 3). *See also Ng v. Canada* (1993), Comm. No. 469/1991, 98 I.L.R. 479 (UN Human Rights Committee) (execution by gas asphixiation does not comply with the Int'l Covenant on Civil and Political Rights).

256 *United States v. Caicedo,* 47 F.3d 370 (9th Cir. 1995) (35-foot power boat 200 miles off the coast of Nicaragua and 2000 miles from San Diego was properly boarded by U.S. authorities even though there was no evidence that it was headed for the U.S.).

257 *See, e.g., United States v. Davis,* 905 F.2d 245 (9th Cir. 1990) (British flag ship coming from Hong Kong and heading toward the California coast turns away from the coast when intercepted by Coast Guard helicopter; British authorities are contacted and consent to search).

258 *See* art. 22 of the Convention on the High Seas, 13 U.S.T. 2312, T.I.A.S. No. 5200 (1958).

the vessel in question agree, by "treaty or other arrangement," constitute U.S. customs waters. The term "other arrangement" includes *ad hoc* permission granted through diplomatic channels.[259] Using this device, borrowed from anti-smuggling laws from the 1930s, the U.S. has either entered into blanket agreements with several States for boarding suspicious vessels flying those States' flags or regularly seeks *ad hoc* agreement that U.S. "customs waters" include a moving zone of water around the vessel.[260]

International Airspace The United States has established "special aircraft jurisdiction" which asserts legislative jurisdiction over conduct on board any aircraft, even a foreign one, that has the United States as "its next scheduled destination" if the aircraft "next actually lands in the United States."[261] The original laws establishing special aircraft jurisdiction were passed to effectuate the Tokyo Convention on Offences and other Acts Committed on Board Aircraft, ratified in 1969, and other treaties. However, the U.S. laws are broader in that they reach offenses that are not specified in the treaties. Nonetheless, their validity has been upheld.[262]

c. Extraterritorial Reach of U.S. Civil Process and Court Orders

In U.S. civil litigation, the issues of extraterritorial enforcement action revolve around issues of service of process on foreign defendants and how evidence is obtained from abroad.

(1) Service of Process on Foreign Defendants

A Clash of Legal Cultures Under U.S. law, for personal jurisdiction to exist, due process requires (1) the appropriate "minimum contacts" for judicial jurisdiction plus (2) adequate notice of the suit.[263] When the defendant is outside the territory of the court of the forum, notice is sent by mailing a copy of the summons and complaint to the defendant — a practice followed in the U.S. with respect to both interstate U.S. defendants and foreign defendants that raises no sovereignty issues in the minds of U.S. lawyers. However, mailing the copy of the summons and complaint is the enforcement action that implements judicial jurisdiction over the person. As a result, many foreign States consider that such action is "a sovereign act that may be performed in their territory only by [that] state's own officials and in accordance with its own law."[264] As such, it must be handled through diplomatic channels. More than one diplomatic protest has been lodged by Switzerland, France, Germany and other countries protesting mailing court documents directly to defendants located on their territory.[265]

The Hague Service Convention Difficulties arising out of service of process by U.S.

---

259 18 U.S.C.A. §955a(c). *See, e.g., United States v. Bent-Santana*, 774 F.2d 1545 (11th Cir. 1985) (permission to board, search and seize Panamanian flag vessel 100 miles off U.S. coast communicated by Panamanian government to U.S. authorities after reports that bales of marijuana were being off-loaded to small boats).

260 *See United States v. Romero-Galue*, 757 F.2d 1147, 1154 (11th Cir. 1985) ("nothing in international law prohibits two nations from entering into a treaty . . . to extend . . . the reach of the domestic law of one of the nations into the high seas.").

261 18 U.S.C.A.App. §1472(k)(1).

262 *See United States v. Georgescu*, 723 F.Supp. 912 (E.D.N.Y. 1989) (applying the act to a criminal sexual act by a Romanian against a Norwegian minor that took place on a Scandinavian Airlines flight to New York) (Weinstein, J.).

263 *See* Chapter VII, pp. 253-259.

264 RESTATEMENT §471, comment b.

265 *See generally* BORN, *supra* note 1, at 774-779 (reproducing diplomatic protest notes). Switzerland and others even impose criminal penalties for mailing such actions — and it takes foreign enforcement actions in *civil* cases on its soil almost as seriously as it does *criminal* enforcement actions. *See id.* p. .

courts have been substantially reduced by two events: ratification of the Hague Convention on Service of Process in 1969[266] and changes in Federal Rule of Civil Procedure 4 in 1993.[267] The Hague Service Convention provides an approved means of serving process in both federal and state courts.[268]

The Hague Service Convention provides several methods for service of process, but the key one is the creation of a "Central Authority" in each signatory State "to receive requests for service coming from other contracting States" and to serve or arrange for service of documents that comply with Convention requirements.[269] This is done by sending a "letter rogatory" or "letter of request" along with the process that is sought to be served. Three methods of service can be used: (1) a method provided by domestic law; (2) a manner specified by the applicant unless it is "incompatible" with domestic law; and (3) "serv[ice] by delivery to an addressee who accepts it voluntarily," subject to the same incompatibility proviso.[270]

Serving U.S. Subsidiaries An easier route to service of process on foreign companies may be to serve their subsidiaries in the United States. This was approved by the Supreme Court in *Volkswagen AG v. Schlunk*.[271] The Court found it unnecessary for a plaintiff to resort to the Hague Service Convention service if the plaintiff serves foreign defendant's subsidiary, which acts as its principal's agent for service of process on the territory of the United States.

Service on a U.S. Citizen Abroad In *Blackmer v. United States*,[272] a prominent case on use of the nationality principle to establish judicial jurisdiction over U.S. citizens abroad, the Supreme Court addressed the question of what enforcement action should be taken to establish judicial jurisdiction. In *Blackmer*, a subpoena from a U.S. federal administrative agency was served in France by a U.S. consul on a U.S. citizen. The Supreme Court rejected the suggestion that this might violate French sovereignty. It characterized the action as "mere giving of . . . notice to the citizen in the foreign country of the requirement of his government that he shall return" and as such "is in no sense an invasion of any right of any foreign government."[273] Even the Swiss make an exception for foreign consuls serving process on their own nationals. The Hague Convention similarly permits a foreign State to object to service by consuls from another State,

---

266 *See* Hague Convention on Service Abroad of Judicial and Extrajudicial Documents in Civil and Commercial Matters, 20 U.S.T 361-73, T.I.A.A. No. 6638, 658 U.N.T.S. 163.

267 For a discussion of the Federal Rules of Civil Procedure, *see* Chapter VII, p. 229.

268 *Volkswagen AG v. Schlunk*, 486 U.S. 694, 699 (1988) (dictum; court found service on subsidiary under U.S. law sufficient). If service abroad is required in a country that is not a signatory, Rule 4(f) provides for alternative procedures to be followed.

269 Art. 2, 5, Hague Service Convention. The U.S. Central Authority is the Office of International Judicial Assistance of the Civil Division of the Department of Justice.

270 Art. 5(a), (b), Hague Service Convention. Other means of service are set out or preserved in the Convention: (1) service through diplomatic or consular agents; (2) service by "judicial officers or other competent persons" (such as a marshal or court officer); (3) service in accord with internal law, as where parties need not go through any central authority; and (4) sending documents by mail. Art. 8, 19, and 10. Signatory States have the option of objecting to any of these alternative methods and many states have objected to some or all of them. So the lawyer will have to determine for the State where service is to be made whether a Central Authority must be used or some easier method is an option. Service options for the various signatory parties are set out in annotations to 28 U.S.C.A. FRCP 4.

271 486 U.S. 694 (1988).

272 284 U.S. 421 (1932).

273 *See also Securities & Exchange Comm'n v. Briggs*, 234 F.Supp. 618 (N.D. Ohio 1964) (service of SEC subpoena on a U.S. citizen in Canada, a violation of Canadian law, does not violate Canada's sovereignty).

except when they are serving their own nationals.[274]

The Hague Service Convention is most commonly invoked for service of a summons and complaint when a case is started. However, it may also be used for service of other court process, such as discovery orders issued during the case. The procedural aspects of serving such orders are covered by the Convention, but it does not regulate their substance, such as where they require conduct that is incompatible with the foreign law to which the party subject to the order is subject, an issue that is discussed next.

(2) Discovery of Evidence Abroad

(a) Another Legal Culture Clash

As set out in Chapter VII, the parties to a civil case in U.S. courts have a wide variety of discovery tools that they can invoke to obtain information, documents and other items of evidence from their opponent in a civil case, and from anyone else as well.[275] If the person does not voluntarily comply with discovery, a court order compelling discovery can be obtained and sanctions ordered for its violation, including contempt of court. When the person subject to a discovery order is a foreign national located in a foreign country, difficulties arise. This issue has sovereignty overtones like those involved with service of process.

In other countries, particularly those of the civil law tradition, taking evidence is a judicial undertaking that is conducted and controlled by the trial judge, not the parties. Thus, the automatic reaction of many is that international discovery for a case in a U.S. court is proper only if performed by a judicial official in the country where the evidence is located. Second, in no other country is the scope of discovery as broad as it is in the U.S. This opens U.S.-style discovery to the charge that it permits wide-open "fishing expeditions." As one commentator put it, "[t]he rest of the world . . . thinks U.S. lawyers, agencies and prosecutors start lawsuits or investigations on minimal bases, and rely on their adversaries or targets to build their cases for them."[276]

On the U.S. side, discovery has deep roots in our understanding of the adversary system, in which the judge plays no proactive role in seeking out the facts and the parties are expected to find and develop the evidence. Indeed, it would be considered improper if the judge were to take the initiative in or to control or direct evidence-taking except in a very general way.[277] U.S. lawyers also feel that other systems' broad bank and business secrecy rules and weak discovery systems are a "conspiracy of silence" that both hides the truth and serves as a form of economic protectionism. Thus, they argue, large corporations can get away with all manner of illegal behavior without any legal consequences so long as they are careful not to leave any public trail of clues.[278]

Hague Convention as an Alternative The Hague Service Convention discussed earlier is available for the purpose of obtaining evidence abroad. However, the Supreme

---

274 Art. 8, Hague Service Convention. A cynic might suggest that the lack of objection demonstrates that foreign objections have less to do with performing an "act of sovereignty" on the territory of the foreign state — which serving a subpoena on a U.S. citizen would be — than it has to do with foreign states protecting their own nationals from suits brought against them.

275 *See* pp. 235-240.

276 Andreas Lowenfeld, *Some Reflections on Transnational Discovery*, 8 J. COMP.BUS.&MKT.L. 419, 419-20 (1986). Diplomatic protests and blocking statutes associated with overseas discovery, including a German one dating from 1874, are reproduced and discussed in BORN, *supra* note 1, at 849, 852-855.

277 *See* Chapter III, pp. 80-85 (adversary system theory).

278 As an illustration of this point, they might refer to the recent attempt of Swiss banks to avoid being forced to account for Holocaust victims' assets.

Court held in *Societe Nationale Industrielle Aerospatiale v. United States District Court*[279] that Convention procedures are optional with courts and litigants — unlike its completely preemptive effect of the Convention on service of process accomplished by Rule 4(f) of the Federal Rules of Civil Procedure. Thus, litigants in U.S. courts may use the Hague Convention if they like, but are free to continue unilateral discovery efforts as before. The remainder of the discussion here will deal with U.S. unilateral discovery methods abroad.

(b) Types of Discovery Disputes

In general, the international discovery issues in U.S. transnational litigation are of three types: discovery from parties where there is no conflict with foreign law, discovery from non-parties located in a foreign country, and discovery where compliance with the order may conflict with foreign law.

Discovery From Parties Where There is No Conflict This category of cases is the least problematic. However, even when there is no conflict with foreign law or public policy, there is still room for foreign parties and States to think that the unilateral assumption of a power to order evidence located in another country to be produced is both presumptuous and a violation of sovereignty.[280]

Discovery from Non-Parties Discovery from persons not named as parties to the suit is more problematic. Normally, this is done pursuant to a subpoena issued under Rule 45 of the Federal Rules of Civil Procedure.[281] It is permitted only when the subpoena can be served within the territorial limits of a federal district court (usually through service on an agent or branch office of a foreign corporation in the U.S.), where the court has personal jurisdiction over the non-party and prudential considerations do not militate against it.[282] In litigation against corporations, U.S. courts consider the officers, directors and managing agents of the corporation to be parties, and thus more easily subjected to discovery. However, lower level employees are often treated as non-parties. Depositions can sometimes be held in the foreign country if it is not one of the many that prohibit such actions on their territory. Or, if the witness agrees and is given the needed funding, the deposition can be in the U.S. If neither is possible, judicial assistance pursuant to the Hague Convention will have to be sought.

Discovery in Conflict with Foreign Law The most difficult problems occur when discovery orders conflict with foreign law. While U.S. courts at one point generally declined to order discovery abroad in violation of laws of the place where the evidence was located, they now simply order the discovery without regard to foreign law. Then, if compliance is not forthcoming, they consider the issue of any conflict with foreign law in deciding whether *sanctions* should be imposed for non-compliance. This aggressive approach derives from *Societe Internationale v. Rogers*,[283] a 1958 case involving a claim

---

279 482 U.S. 522, 536 (1987). *Compare Volkswagen AG v. Schlunk*, discussed *supra*, p. 723 (service of process under the Hague Service Convention is mandatory where the Convention applies).

280 An example of this kind of case is *In re Uranium Antitrust Litigation*, 480 F.Supp. 1138, 1144 (N.D. Ill. 1979) (U.S. court has the power to order a party over which it has personal jurisdiction to produce documents under its control; "the location of the documents is irrelevant").

281 *See* Chapter VII, pp. 236-237. Continuing the theme of legal cultural clashes, the fact that Rule 45 permits the *lawyers* to issue a subpoena to appear comes as a surprise and a shock to foreign lawyers.

282 An example of a case approving discovery of this type is *Laker Airways Ltd. v. Pan American World Airways*, 607 F.Supp. 324, 327 (S.D.N.Y. 1985) (vacating subpoena *duces tecum* in an antitrust case in part of the ground extraterritorial jurisdiction in such cases "has long been a sore point with many foreign governments...").

283 357 U.S. 197 (1958).

by a Swiss firm for return of its property seized from a German national as enemy property during World War II. Banking records located in Switzerland were sought as necessary to clarify the Swiss company's relationship to the German owner of the property. While not disputing the relevance of the documents, the Swiss company argued that compliance would violate Swiss criminal laws. The Court held that, given the importance of the documents to the case, the discovery order was justified despite its possible conflict with Swiss law. The Swiss company could certainly "plead with its own sovereign for a relaxation of [its] penal laws."[284] However, the sanction of dismissal of the Swiss national's claim was not considered proper, given that it "had not been in collusion with the Swiss authorities to block [discovery]. . . and had in good faith made diligent efforts to execute the production order."[285]

The Third Restatement sets out the current standards that are applied when disclosure is prohibited by foreign law. It requires that a court consider a variety of factors in determining the importance of the material sought to be discovered. Then if disclosure is prohibited by foreign law, a good faith effort to secure permission from foreign authorities must be made and the court may not impose serious sanctions unless there is deliberate concealment or other bad faith action. However, the court may in appropriate cases "make findings of fact adverse to the party that has failed to comply with the order for production."[286]

B. International Enforcement of Judgments

1. Enforcement of U.S. Judgments by Foreign Courts

Enforcement of U.S. judgments abroad is closely linked to issues of legislative and judicial enforcement jurisdiction just discussed, since absence of jurisdiction is the most common reason for denying enforcement of judgments. However, a few additional considerations apply. First, when it comes to enforcement of judgments we need to add to the list of "legal cultural clashes" already mentioned with regard to legislative and judicial jurisdiction. We must add the facts that U.S. jury awards are often perceived abroad to be excessive in amount and that U.S. civil judgments sometimes include punitive damages, a remedy civil law systems consider appropriate only in criminal law. Second, lawyers in civil law countries often do not understand why the U.S. plaintiff did not come to the defendant's home country to litigate, since that is the usual practice if not the requirement in most civil law systems.[287] Third, civil law countries approach issues of international enforcement of judgments in a different manner. While common-law countries, as discussed below, tend to enforce foreign judgments liberally as a matter of course, the civil law has tended to require reciprocity as a condition of recognition and to take a broader view of the "public policy" exception to enforceability. Moreover, civil law countries tend to view judgment enforcement as an issue properly dealt with by a treaty with the country involved, an approach which the U.S. has tended not to pursue until only recently.

After some initial negative reactions, most civil countries have been relatively

---

284 *Id.* at 205.

285 *Id.* at 208. A modern example of a court struggling with this form of discovery is *Reinsurance Company of America, Inc. v. Administratia Asigurarilor de Stat*, 902 F.2d 1275, 1279 (7th Cir. 1990) (no need to require good faith effort to secure permission from authorities given clear evidence that Rumanian "service secrets" law was strictly applied).

286 RESTATEMENT §442(1)-(2). This section of the Restatement remains controversial.

287 Indeed, in some cases, under the U.S. doctrine of *forum non conveniens*, the defendant's home court might not be considered an appropriate venue at all. *See supra* p. 716.

hospitable to U.S. judgments, despite these potential sources of friction and misunderstanding. Germany, for example, has readily conceded reciprocity. While it refuses to enforce U.S. punitive damage awards, it has enforced compensatory "pain and suffering" awards, in one case doing so despite the fact that this component made the judgment some 11 times higher than a comparable award under German law.[288]

2. Enforcement of Foreign Judgments by U.S. Courts

The Uniform Act The full faith and credit clause of the Constitution does not require states of the United States to recognize judgments of the courts of foreign countries. Nonetheless, most states recognize and enforce foreign money judgments as a matter of course so long as the procedures followed are compatible with due process.[289] A total of 28 states and the District of Columbia do so because they have passed the Uniform Foreign Money-Judgments Recognition Act. The Act provides in §3 that any foreign-country judgment "is conclusive between the parties to the extent that it grants or denies recovery of a sum of money" and that it is "enforceable in the same manner as the judgment of a sister state which is entitled to full faith and credit."[290] In §4 exceptions are provided where the procedures in the foreign forum "are not compatible with the requirements of due process," where there is no personal or subject-matter jurisdiction or where there has been fraud. An exception for judgments that violate the "public policy" of the state is set out, but it tends to be narrowly construed.[291]

Reciprocity The Uniform Act requires no proof of reciprocal recognition by the foreign country as a precondition for validity, nor do states without the Act that enforce foreign judgments tend to require reciprocity. This is so despite old Supreme Court caselaw requiring reciprocity.[292] However, reciprocity could be a problem in one of the 7 states of the U.S. that retain a clear statutory reciprocity requirement.[293]

---

288 *Judgment of June 4, 1992*, 1992 NJW 3073 (Supreme Court of Germany). And at least some kinds of U.S. judgments have been met with a cool reception in some fellow common-law countries, such as England and Australia, despite similarities in approach to the issues. *See, e.g.*, the reaction of the U.K. to U.S. anti-trust judgments, discussed *supra* p. 710.

289 For more on enforcement of foreign judgments in the U.S., *see* EUGENE F. SCOLES, PETER HAY, PATRICK J. BORCHERS & SYMEON C. SYMEONIDES, CONFLICT OF LAWS, 4TH ED. §§24.33-24.45 (West 2004). Many of the principles parallel recognition of interstate judgments, discussed in Chapter VII, pp. 261-262.

290 13 UNIFORM LAWS ANNOTATED 261 (1986, 1998) (originally promulgated in 1962). The ALI's RESTATEMENT OF CONFLICT OF LAWS, 2D (1971) has provisions similar to the Uniform Act, but is slightly more cautious than the Uniform Act's automatic rule.

291 *See, e.g., Nepoorany v. Kir*, 173 N.Y.S.2d 146 (App.Div. 1958) (Canadian judgment for seduction and criminal conversion recognized even though such actions had been abolished in New York). *See generally* SCOLES ET AL., *supra* note 289, §24.44. *But see Stein v. Siegel*, 377 N.Y.S.2d 580 (App.Div. 1975) (Austrian decree containing a claim waiver is no a bar to bringing the claim in New York since New York law would not prevent re-litigation).

292 *Hilton v. Guyot*, 159 U.S. 113 (1895). *Hilton* is based on federal common law, so it has not been considered binding on the state courts or on federal courts in diversity. This is because conflict of laws issues in federal diversity cases are determined according to state law. *See* Chapter V, p. 192, Chapter VII, p. 263, *Klaxon Co. v. Stentor Electric Mfg. Co.*, 313 U.S. 487 (1941), and SCOLES ET AL., *supra* note 289, §24.35 at 1311 (*Hilton's* "authority seems negligible"). *Cf. Semtek International, Inc. v. Lockheed Martin Corp.*, 531 U.S. 497 (2001) (effect of a judgment based on a state-law claim brought in a federal court is governed by *federal law*, though it incorporates state law of the state where federal court is located).

293 *See* SCOLES ET AL., *supra* note 289, §24.35-.35. State laws requiring reciprocity may be preempted under the Constitution as an interference with foreign policy, because of *Zschernig v. Miller*, discussed *supra* p. 695. However, *Zschernig* may only apply to bar states from making a *political* evaluation of certain foreign legal systems across the board, not from applying long-standing conflicts rules in individual cases. *See* SCOLES ET AL., *supra* note 289, at 1311 n. 5. *But see* RESTATEMENT §98, Comment c.

3. A Potential Treaty on Judgment Enforcement

In an effort to reform the remaining conservative states and to seek better enforcement of U.S. judgments abroad, the U.S. proposed that the Hague Conference on Private International Law draft a convention on international recognition and enforcement of judgments. Since the question of the enforceability of foreign judgments often turns on issues of whether the foreign court had jurisdiction, the Convention deals with that topic as well.[294] A Preliminary Draft Convention on Jurisdiction and Foreign Judgments in Civil and Commercial Matters was produced in 1999. In broad outline, the draft convention parallels European practice as set out in the EEC Brussels Convention. However, work has been suspended, because the United States and other important potential signatory nations have expressed dissatisfaction with various provisions. Under the *status quo*, then, courts in the U.S. enforce foreign judgments as a routine matter by force of U.S. domestic law, while many foreign countries reserve the right to decline to enforce U.S. judgments.[295] The reintroduction of reciprocity into U.S. judgment recognition law would change this one-way dynamic, but, as noted above, the trend at the present time is in the opposite direction.

4. Enforcement of International Arbitration Awards

It is perhaps surprising given the difficult negotiations over enforcement of judgments at the Hague that there is a quite successful and long-standing convention on reciprocal recognition of arbitration awards — the 1958 U.N. Convention ("New York Convention").[296] The New York Convention provides for enforcement both of agreements to arbitrate and of any arbitration awards rendered in contracting States. There is no need to have the award confirmed by a court in the arbitral state and signatory States may not impose any conditions more onerous than those that apply to domestic arbitration awards.[297] The Convention states that a court "shall confirm" the award unless one of the exceptions is met. There is a "public policy" exception, but courts have limited it to cases of procedural unfairness.[298]

C. Suits Involving Foreign States and Their Official Acts

If a suit is brought against a foreign State in the courts of another State or an issue arises regarding the validity of the sovereign acts of another State, sovereign immunity or the "act of state" doctrine may issue. These are discussed in the next two sections.

1. Sovereign Immunity

Like most international States, the U.S. recognizes and protects the sovereign immunity of foreign States in its courts. The scope of that immunity and the procedures for invoking it are governed by the Foreign Sovereign Immunities Act of 1976 (FSIA).[299]

---

294 *See generally* SCOLES ET AL., *supra* note 289, §24.39 and Linda Silberman, Comparative Jurisdiction in the International Context: Will the Proposed Hague Judgments Convention be Stalled?, 52 DEPAUL L.REV. 319 (2002). Members of the European Economic Community have for some time participated in the Brussels Convention and non-EEC members in Europe have joined with EEC members in the parallel Lugano Convention of 1988. It was the Hague Conference that produced the convention on service of process discussed earlier.

295 *See* Kevin M. Clermont, *Jurisdictional Salvation and the Hague Treaty*, 85 CORNELL LAW REV. 89 (1999).

296 *See also Scherk v. Alberto-Culver Co.*, 417 U.S. 506 (1974) (applying the convention).

297 *See* Chapter VII, p. 252 (U.S. law on arbitration).

298 *See generally* SCOLES ET AL., *supra* note 289, §§24.46-24.48 and sources cited therein; GARY BORN, INTERNATIONAL COMMERCIAL ARBITRATION: INTERNATIONAL AND U.S. ASPECTS (2009). A related question is the enforceability of decisions of foreign administrative agencies. *See id.* §24.46 at 1213 and *Johnson v. Berger*, 273 N.Y.S.2d 484 (Family Ct. 1966) (recognizing Danish administrative paternity decree).

299 28 U.S.C.A. §§1330, 1602-1611 *et seq.*

Before the FSIA, these issues were governed by federal common law, incorporating customary international law.[300] A major role was also played by "letters" of "advice" from the State Department, which considered sovereign immunity issues as they arose in court cases brought to its attention. Because of the cumbersome nature of this procedure and the uneven, often politically motivated results it produced, the task of applying the doctrine was transferred by the FSIA to courts.[301] In addition to defining the scope of the immunity and exceptions to it, the FSIA governs the procedural issues of service of process and enforcement of judgments. The FSIA is the sole basis on which foreign States can be sued in U.S. courts.[302]

a. Scope of the Foreign Sovereign Immunity Act

The FSIA provides immunity for all "foreign states" for their "sovereign" acts, but makes exceptions for their "commercial" or "private" acts.[303] The exceptions are in recognition of the wide variety of activities of States on the world scene and the unfairness of States engaging in ordinary commerce in a commercial capacity and then hiding behind their immunity in their sovereign capacity. The FSIA affects only immunity and does not specify any other rule of decision. Claims are governed by the relevant contract or tort law — usually U.S. state law, foreign law or international law.

Jurisdiction The FSIA provides for both subject-matter and personal jurisdiction in federal courts for plaintiffs who wish to have their case decided in federal court.[304] Jurisdiction is not exclusive, however, so suit may be brought in state court. If it is, the state court must apply the immunity provisions of the federal statute. The grant of jurisdiction to federal courts is for "non-jury civil" actions. Actions handled in state court can be tried to a jury, but the defendant may remove the action to federal court, thus avoiding a jury.[305]

What is a Foreign State In general, to qualify as a "foreign state," a State must be officially recognized by the U.S. government. Acrimonious relations will not disqualify a State from claiming immunity.[306] A "foreign state" entitled to immunity "includes a political subdivision of a foreign state or an agency or instrumentality of a foreign state as defined in" the FSIA.[307] Political subdivisions include lands, cantons, regions, states,

---

300 For a discussion of customary international law as federal common law, *see supra* p. 697.

301 *See* BORN, *supra* note 1, at 199-285; RESTATEMENT §§451-460.

302 *Argentine Republic v. Amerada Hess Shipping Corp.*, 488 U.S. 428 (1989).

303 The FSIA does not bar suits against foreign officials for damages for actions taken in their official capacities. *Samantar v. Yousuf*, ___ U.S. ___, 130 S.Ct. 2278 (2010) (suit for damages against former high-ranking Somali government officials for alleged acts of torture and human rights violations).

304 With respect to the federal courts, the FSIA is stated in jurisdictional terms, that is, if a State has immunity, the federal court has no jurisdiction over the claim, while if the State does not have immunity, there is jurisdiction over the claim. Because the standards of the FSIA are to be applied in determining the immunity question, jurisdiction was held to be authorized by the "federal question" head of jurisdiction in Article III even though non-federal law was the law that governed the claim. *Verlinden B.V. v. Central Bank of Nigeria*, 461 U.S. 480 (1983). *Compare* Chapter VII, p. 189 ("well-pleaded complaint" rule requires that to qualify for federal question jurisdiction under 28 U.S.C.A. §1331, federal issue be part of the claim, not defenses).

305 *See* Chapter V, p. 190 (removal). Lower federal courts have held that these provisions do not violate the 7th Amendment right to a civil jury trial in federal court because there was no right to sue a foreign sovereign at common law when the 7th Amendment was ratified. *See, e.g., Baily v. Grand Trunk Lines*, 805 F.2d 1097 (2d Cir. 1986). *See generally* Chapter VII, pp. 243-244 (historical test for jury trial right).

306 In addition, one court held that a quasi-national entity, the Pacific Ocean Trust Territory, is a foreign State because it exercises many of the powers of a State. *Morgan Guaranty Trust Co. v. Republic of Palau*, 639 F.Supp. 706 (S.D.N.Y. 1986).

307 28 U.S.C.A. §1603(a).

provinces, cities and the like.

Entities Separate from the State In defining an "agency or instrumentality of a foreign state," there are two issues and two consequences of determining these issues. First, if the agency or instrumentality belongs to a foreign State, it *is* the "foreign State" that potentially qualifies for immunity. States have a wide variety of entities and arrangements to carry out their affairs and this determination is often a matter of sifting through the facts of individual cases. However, the FSIA makes clear that a separate entity that is an organ of a State or "a majority of whose shares or other ownership interest is owned by a foreign state" is a State instrumentality that may enjoy the protections of the FSIA to the same extent that the State itself does.[308]

The second issue concerns what property can be executed upon in the event of a judgment against the foreign State. This is important because execution on the property of the foreign State itself located in the United States, in contrast to the question of the State's suability on a claim, is not subject to the "commercial activity" exception. Thus, the armed forces of a state may well be "an integral part of the state itself," and not a mere "agency or instrumentality" of the State.[309]

The general rule is that liability of a corporate entity will not be attributed to its owner unless there are special reasons to "pierce the corporate veil."[310] However, exceptions have been made under the FSIA as they have been in corporate law. In *First National City Bank v. Banco Para El Comercio Exterior de Cuba*,[311] a Cuban state bank sued a U.S. bank to collect on a letter of credit in support of a contract for delivery of sugar to a U.S. buyer. The U.S. bank counterclaimed to recover assets that it asserted the Cuban government had wrongfully seized. The Cuban bank asserted that it was a separate legal entity and could not be sued for actions of the Cuban government. The Court noted the extensive control of the bank by Cuban government officials. Relying on established exceptions to the separate status of corporations, it held that it would not "adhere blindly to the corporate form where doing so would cause an injustice."

b. When Sovereign Immunity Does Not Apply

Waivers of Sovereign Immunity The FSIA permits suit when the State "has waived its immunity either explicitly or by implication."[312] Explicit waiver by treaty is possible, but it must be clear.[313] As for implicit waiver, the legislative history makes reference to several forms, such as a choice-of-law agreement pointing to U.S. law, agreement to arbitrate, or by failure to mention it immunity in its answer to the complaint. However,

---

308 28 U.S.C.A. §1603(b). It does not matter that the stock is owned by a State agency rather than the State itself. *O'Connell Machine Co. v. M.V. Americana*, 734 F.2d 115, 116 (2d Cir. 1984) (Italian line that was owned by maritime financing company which was owned by the state financial management entity of the Republic of Italy was a State agency or instrumentality). It is also important in terms of whether the "contacts" of one entity with the U.S. "count" for purposes of determining personal jurisdiction over another entity or the State itself, discussed next. The contacts test of personal jurisdiction was discussed in Chapter VII, pp. 253-259.

309 *Ministry of Defense of Islamic Republic of Iran v. Elahi*, 546 U.S. 450 (2006) (case remanded to Court of Appeals to determine this question).

310 *See* Chapter XV, pp. 595-597.

311 462 U.S. 611 (1983).

312 28. U.S.C.A. §1605(a)(1).

313 *Amerada Hess, supra* note 302, at 442-443 ("signing an international agreement that contains no mention of a waiver of immunity to suit in United States courts or even the availability of a cause of action in the United States" is not a proper waiver).

some courts have tended to read implicit waiver narrowly.[314]

Commercial Activities The FSIA denies immunity for certain commercial activities of States, but only if they have the requisite connection with the U.S. Thus, there is no immunity for any claim "based upon" (1) "a commercial activity carried on in the United States by the foreign state," (2) "an act performed in the United States in connection with a commercial activity of the foreign state elsewhere," or (3) "an act outside the territory of the United States in connection with a commercial activity of the foreign state elsewhere and that act causes a direct effect in the United States."[315]

The FSIA does not define "commercial activity" and the task has been largely left to the courts.[316] "Commercial" activity is to be distinguished from "sovereign" activity, which is the core State function that immunity is designed to protect. But in one sense, all activities of a State — even a State enterprise purchasing goods abroad for resale at a profit — serve to promote sovereign purposes. One thing that is clear from the FSIA's definition of "commercial" is that it relates to the *nature* of the activity, *not* its purpose. Thus, purchasing boots for a public purpose, such as to equip a State's army, is just as "commercial" in terms of the activity engaged in as purchasing boots for resale at a profit. The Supreme Court in *Republic of Argentina v. Weltover, Inc.*[317] applied this concept when it decided that Argentina's default on certain bonds as part of a plan to stabilize its currency was "commercial activity" outside the U.S. that had a "direct effect in" the U.S. The fact that the purpose of the default was to stabilize Argentina's national currency — a sovereign purpose — was irrelevant. Since the bonds were "in almost all respects garden-variety debt instruments" that could be held and traded on the international market, any action with regard to them constituted commercial activity.[318]

"Based on" Commercial Activity The Court has also interpreted the requirement a claim be "based upon" commercial activity. In *Saudi Arabia v. Nelson*,[319] Nelson was an employee of a hospital owned by Saudi Arabia and got into a dispute with his employer over repair and reporting of safety hazards at the hospital. He alleged that because of the dispute, he was arrested, held for 39 days, beaten and tortured. The Court held that the arrest and detention were not themselves commercial acts and that the fact that he could prove that they were in retaliation for action arising out of his employment contract did not mean that his suit was "based upon a commercial activity."[320]

Nexus with the U.S. The FSIA requires that an act with respect to the commercial

---

314 *See, e.g., and compare Frolova v. U.S.S.R.*, 761 F.2d 370, 377 (7th Cir. 1985) (courts have "narrowly construed" waiver); *Castro v. Saudi Arabia*, 510 F.Supp. 309, 312 (W.D. Tex. 1980) ("intentional . . . relinquishment of the legal right") *with Proyecfin de Venezuala, S.A. v. Banco Industriale de Venezuela, S.A.*, 760 F.2d 390, 392 (2d Cir. 1985) (waiver in loan agreement; "broad reading of implicit waivers"). In one case, over a strong dissent, the Court of Appeals held that Nazi Germany did not implicitly waive its sovereign immunity from claims by Holocaust survivors through its violation of fundamental norms of the law of nations (*jus cogens*). *Princz v. Federal Republic of Germany*, 26 F.3d 1166 (D.C. Cir. 1994).

315 28 U.S.C.A. §1605(a)(2).

316 *See* Chapter II, p. 40 and p. 41 note 15, where other examples of legislatively delegated power to make common law are discussed.

317 504 U.S. 607 (1992).

318 *Compare MOL, Inc. v. People's Republic of Bangladesh*, 736 F.2d 1326 (9th Cir. 1984) (revocation of license to export monkeys was a sovereign act, not a commercial activity); *In re Sedco*, 543 F.Supp. 561 (S.D. Tex. 1982)(oil exploration by Mexican state oil company was not commercial activity). *Cf. IAM v. OPEC*, 649 F.2d 1354 (9th Cir. 1981)(participation in oil cartel was not commercial), discussed *infra* p. 735.

319 507 U.S. 349 (1993).

320 Because it resolved the suit on this basis, the Court did not have to reach the issue of whether the activity involved had the required nexus to the United States.

activity on which suit is based either take place in the U.S. or have a "direct effect" in the U.S. for suit to be proper. The *Argentina* bond default case discussed above also dealt with this issue. The Court rejected the argument that the effect in the U.S. must be substantial or foreseeable, only that it has to be "direct," which the Court defined as an effect that follows as an immediate consequence of the activity.[321] It found direct effect in the U.S. on the facts of that case, since Argentina had designated its accounts in New York as the place of payment and had made some interest payments to those accounts before default.[322]

Noncommercial Torts in the U.S. The FSIA denies sovereign immunity for non-commercial torts committed in the U.S. — tort actions for "money damages . . . for personal injury or death, or damage to or loss of property occurring in the United States."[323] To qualify under this provision, at least part of the tortious conduct — not just the resulting harm — must take place in the U.S.[324] Although this provision of the FSIA was prompted by concerns about automobile accidents involving diplomats, the wording of the section is clearly broader than that and could well include sovereign as well as private actions.

Discretionary Functions A major limitation on the non-commercial tort provision is that it disqualifies claims regarding conduct that is based on "discretionary functions regardless of whether the discretion be abused."[325] This exception is based on similar protections afforded the U.S. government in suits against it.[326] The Supreme Court has determined that discretionary conduct is conduct as to which "there is room for policy judgment and decision."[327] The exception is designed to "prevent judicial 'second-guessing' of legislative and administrative decisions grounded in social, economic, and political policy through the medium of an action in tort."[328] In *In re Sedco*,[329] a suit against the Mexican state oil company for damages caused by a disaster on one of its off-shore oil drilling rigs, the district court held that any wrongful acts complained of were discretionary, since they were "done in furtherance of Pemex's legal mandate to explore Mexico for hydrocarbon deposits." In another case, the court held that confiscation of travel documents and forcible confinement of servants of the Saudi royal family while they were in the U.S. were discretionary.[330] But in *Letelier v. Republic of Chile*,[331] the court held that the decision to assassinate a critic of the regime in power, while it would have to have involved a policy judgment and decision, did not come under the discre-

---

[321] *Republic of Argentina, supra* note 317 at 617 (internal quotations omitted).

[322] The nexus requirement is deemed to establish personal jurisdiction, but it must, of course, also satisfy due process. *See* Chapter VII, pp. 253-259. The Court in the *Argentina* case held that due process was satisfied as well, since the presence of the accounts in New York constituted "minimum contacts."

[323] 28 U.S.C.A. §1605(a)(5).

[324] *Compare In re Sedco, Inc.*, 543 F.Supp. 561 (S.D. Tex. 1982) (all of the tortious conduct must be in U.S.) *with Olsen ex rel. Sheldon v. Government of Mexico*, 729 F.2d 641 (9th Cir. 1984) (sufficient if part of the conduct takes place in the U.S.).

[325] 28 U.S.C.A. §1605(a)(5)(A), (B). Also excluded are claims for malicious prosecution, libel, misrepresentation, interference with contract relations and similar torts.

[326] *See* Chapter VI, p. 224 and note 164.

[327] *Dahelite v. United States*, 346 U.S. 15, 36 (1953) (decision to make and store fertilizer and failure to take precautions against it exploding were discretionary and nonactionable).

[328] *United States v. Varig Airlines*, 467 U.S. 797, 814 (1984) (decision of aviation agency to use only a "spot-check" compliance method, resulting in it approving airplane with an unsafe lavatory trash receptacle, involved discretionary duty).

[329] 543 F.Supp. 561 (S.D. Tex. 1982).

[330] *Alicog v. Kingdom of Saudi Arabia*, 860 F.Supp. 379 (S.D. Tex. 1994).

[331] 488 F.Supp. 665 (D.D.C. 1980).

tionary function exception because a foreign State "has no 'discretion' to [cause an] assassination . . ., action . . . contrary to the precepts of humanity as recognized by both national and international law."[332]

2. The Act of State Doctrine

a. Scope of and Rationale for the Act of State Doctrine

The classic American statement of the act of state doctrine is that "the courts of one country will not sit in judgment on the acts of the government of another, done on its own territory."[333] While the sovereign immunity is an issue only when a foreign State or one of its instrumentalities or agencies is sued, the act of state doctrine applies even if all the parties to the case are private parties. Expropriation of property is a common example. If a state nationalizes property in a way that violates international law and then sells that property someone else, the seizure is considered to be legal and the purchaser has good title. Thus, the original owner will lose any suit to recover it.[334]

A Changing Rationale and Scope The act of state doctrine has been justified as part of comity — the respect owed by one State to another that is essential to maintaining good international relations. It has also been stated in choice of law terms. Under this latter view, the doctrine is simply directing a court to apply the only law that it can apply to actions by a government on its own territory — the law of the foreign State as demonstrated by its own "rule of decision" in taking the very action at issue. The U.S. version of the doctrine, as stated in the case of *Banco Nacional de Cuba v. Sabbatino*,[335] is said to be required by separation of powers considerations. Specifically, U.S. courts "passing on the validity of foreign acts of state may hinder rather than further this country's pursuit of goals both for itself and for the community of nations." In more recent years, the Court in its unanimous decision in *W.S. Kirkpatrick & Co. v. Environmental Tectonics Corp.*,[336] returned to the choice of law approach, observing that "the act of state doctrine is not some vague doctrine of abstention but a *'principle of decision'* binding of federal and state courts."

Narrowing of the Doctrine The Court in *Environmental Tectonics* not only changed the rationale for the doctrine, it also suggested a narrower scope for it. In that case, the unsuccessful bidder on a Nigerian defense contract sued the successful bidder for damages, claiming violations of antitrust laws and the Racketeer-Influenced and Corrupt Organizations (RICO) Act. The plaintiff claimed that Nigerian officials accepted a competing bid because the bidder paid certain "commissions" to those officials.[337] The Supreme Court disapproved several lower court decisions setting forth expansive versions of the act of state doctrine and held that "[a]ct of state issues only arise when a court *must decide* — that is, when the outcome of the case turns upon — the effect of

---

332 *Id.* at 673. *See also Liu v. Republic of China*, 892 F.2d 1419 (9th Cir. 1989) (same). The *Liu* court also determined that the assassination was nonetheless "within the scope of employment" of the Vice-Admiral who ordered it — despite his undertaking it without his superiors' knowledge and despite it being a violation of ROC law and regulations. *Id.* at 1425. The Court applied California law on the point.

333 *Underhill v. Hernandez*, 168 U.S. 250, 252 (1897) (dismissing claim of U.S. citizen imprisoned by Venezuelan revolutionary commander). *See also* RESTATEMENT §443.

334 *See, e.g., Oetjen v. Central Leather Co.*, 246 U.S. 297 (1918) and *Recaud v. American Metal Co.*, 246 U.S. 304 (1918) (property seized by Mexican revolutionary forces). In declining to afford relief, parties were not necessarily completely remediless. Claims of private parties in those situations are often pursued by U.S. diplomatic personnel and are often successful.

335 376 U.S. 398, 423 (1964).

336 493 U.S. 400, 406 (1990).

337 *See* Chapter XV, pp. 609-616 (antitrust law) and Chapter XIV, pp. 571-573 (RICO).

official action by a foreign sovereign." It found that "nothing in the present suit requires a court to declare invalid, and thus ineffective as 'a rule of decision for the courts of this country,' . . . the official act of a foreign sovereign."[338] At most, the federal court decision would determine that the Nigerian officials awarded the contract based on bribery. This determination might impugn their *motivation* for acting and it might be embarrassing to the Nigerian government, but it would not constitute a determination that the contract award was *invalid* under Nigerian law. The act of state doctrine, the Court held, "does not establish an exception for cases and controversies that may embarrass foreign governments, but merely requires that . . . the acts of foreign sovereigns taken within their own jurisdictions shall be deemed valid."[339]

What is an Act of State   In *Alfred Dunhill of London, Inc. v. Republic of Cuba,*[340] the Court rejected application of the act of state doctrine to Cuban officials' refusal to pay back royalties, because there was "[n]o statute, decree, order, or resolution of the Cuban Government itself" produced in court. It observed that there must be some "public" or "sovereign" act by someone with "authority to exercise sovereign powers." The statements of counsel for the Cuban government during the litigation that their clients denied liability and refused to make repayment were not enough. This is a narrow ruling, however. The fact that the immediate refusal might be carried out by a low-level official does not make them any less an act of state so long as it was the State that had made the decision. For example, in a case involving wrongful deportation, a federal court explained that the issue for act of state purposes was whether the action of Swiss police in forcibly putting her on a Swiss Air plane was an action "ordered in the exercise of the sovereign authority of Switzerland, or whether it was simply an ad hoc decision of local police officers."[341] But even if a high-level State official is the actor, the fact that the acts are so improper and pursued for personal rather than State purposes may mean that they constitute "private" acts of the individual rather than "public" acts of the state.[342]

b. Exceptions to the Act of State Doctrine

"Bernstein" Exception   The act of state doctrine as applied in the U.S. is in part based on the separation of powers problem concern of avoiding court interference with the executive branch's conduct of foreign relations. It makes sense then to modify application of the doctrine if the executive branch certifies that a particular suit does not present any such problems. This is referred to as the *Bernstein* exception from the name of the case from the Court of Appeals for the Second Circuit that recognized it.[343] In that case, Jewish businessmen sued to recover property seized from them by the Nazi regime in Germany. The court at first dismissed the case on act of state grounds, but then reversed itself after the State Department sent a letter suggesting the court should exercise jurisdiction.[344]

---

338 493 U.S. at 405 (emphasis in original).

339 *Id.* at 409.

340 425 U.S. 682, 694 (1976). *Cf.* Born, *supra* note 1, at 710-711 (suggesting that a law "can authorize an act of state, but is generally not itself an act of state until it is implemented").

341 *See Galu v. Swiss Air Transport Co.*, 873 F.2d 650, 654 (2d Cir. 1989).

342 *Filartiga v. Pena-Irala*, 630 F.2d 876, 889 (2d Cir. 1980 (torture cannot be an act of state since state did not authorize the conduct); *Jimenez v. Aristeguieta*, 311 F.2d 547, 558 (5th Cir. 1962) (financial crimes in violation of official position are "as far from being an act of state as rape . . . .").

343 *Bernstein v. N.V. Nederlandsche-Amerikaansche,* 173 F.2d 71 (2d Cir. 1949) and 210 F.2d 375 (2d Cir. 1954).

344 A head count of Supreme Court justices in *First National City Bank, supra* note 311, reveals that five and perhaps 6 of them disapprove of the *Bernstein* exception in *dictum*. Nonetheless, many lower courts continue to apply it, others reject it and the greatest number consider *Bernstein* letters as significant, but

"Commercial" Exception A "commercial" exception to the act of state doctrine has been developing along the lines of the similar exception in foreign State sovereign immunity. At least similar cases in both areas have been decided similarly on the issue of whether natural-resources exploration is a "sovereign" or merely a "commercial" activity. In *IAM v. OPEC*,[345] an antitrust suit against OPEC for price-fixing of petroleum was dismissed on act of state grounds. Parallel to the result in the *Sedco* case involving Mexico's State petroleum company,[346] the court considered but rejected the application of the commercial exception, characterizing the activities of each member of OPEC as each "foreign sovereign['s] . . . chosen means of allocating and profiting from its own valuable natural resources."

Treaties A treaty with the U.S. has sometimes been held to make the act of state doctrine irrelevant. For example, treaties securing property of the citizens of the contracting States from being taken by the government without payment of just compensation have been held to permit claims to be made against the governments of Iran and Ethiopia.[347]

Federal Statutes Congress has on one occasion passed legislation directing that the act of state doctrine not be applied in a class of cases. In the wake of the Supreme Court's unpopular use of the doctrine in the *Sabbatino* case to dismiss suits against Castro's Cuba for expropriation of the property of U.S. nationals, Congress passed the so-called Second Hickenlooper Amendment. It forbade any court in the U.S. from invoking "the federal act of state doctrine" on grounds of any violation of international law. However, the Amendment only applies to suits to recover property *located in the U.S.* In addition, it provides an exception when the President had certified that the suit would interfere with U.S. foreign policy. The Amendment has been read narrowly by the courts and has had limited effect in practice.[348]

---

not conclusive evidence that they should proceed with the case.

345 649 F.2d 1354, 1361 (9th Cir. 1981).

346 *See supra* note 318 and text. In the *Alfred Dunhill* case, only four justices agreed that a "commercial" exception existed. But lower federal courts continue to apply it, as the OPEC case shows.

347 *Kalamazoo Spice Extraction Co. v. Provisional Military Government of Socialist Ethiopia*, 729 F.2d 422 (6th Cir. 1984); *American International Group v. Islamic Republic of Iran*, 493 F.Supp. 522 (D.D.C. 1980).

348 BORN, *supra* note 1, at 744. The Amendment is found at 22 U.S.C.A. §2370(e)(2).

APPENDIX A

Contents

Philip Francis HOFFMAN, Jr., and

Pav-A-Way Corporation, a Florida corporation,

Petitioners,

v.

Hazel J. JONES, as Administratrix of the Estate

of William Harrison Jones, Jr.,Deceased,

Respondent.

No. 43443.

Supreme Court of Florida.

280 So.2d 431 (1973)[1]

78 A.L.R.3d 321[2]

Widow brought wrongful death suits both in her individual capacity and as administratrix of deceased husband's estate. The Circuit Court, Brevard County, William G. Akridge, J., denied plaintiff's requested instruction predicated on comparative negligence, and rendered judgment for defendants, and plaintiff appealed. The District Court of Appeal, 272 So.2d 529, reversed and certified decision on question of whether contributory negligence rule should be replaced with principles of comparative negligence. On writ of certiorari, the Supreme Court, Adkins, J., adopted comparative negligence rule and delineated time when such rule is to be applied at trial and appellate levels.[3]

Remanded.

Roberts, J., dissented and filed opinion.[4]

---

1 All footnotes in this appendix are by the author of this book and are inserted to point out features of the opinion.

2 A.L.R.2d, the American Law Reports, second series, publishes selected cases that have an important impact on the development of the law. Such cases are followed by an annotation commenting on the significance of the decision and analyzing that area of law in depth with citations from other jurisdictions.

3 This paragraph summary of the case was written by the editors of the case reports employed by West Group, the private publisher of the regional reporter in which this opinion appears. Florida is one of several states that do not themselves publish a reporter, but rely on the West regional reporters.

4 What follows at this point in the opinion are "headnotes" — summaries of all the major points and holdings of the opinion. These are written by case editors, not by the court. Because of space considerations, only the first 6 headnotes are reproduced here, starting on the next page. There are 16 headnotes in the original. Headnotes are collected in a "digest," which the lawyer can scan to decide what judicial decisions might be useful without reading the entire opinions of all relevant cases. Note that some

[1] Courts k91(1)

District Court of Appeal is without power to overrule Supreme Court precedent.

[2] Courts k216

Mere certification to Supreme Court by a District Court of Appeal that the latter's decision involves a question of great public interest does not vest Supreme Court with jurisdiction; if neither party involved petitions for writ of certiorari, Supreme Court does not have jurisdiction to answer questions certified or review district court's action.

[3] Courts k91(1)

[3] Courts k216

District Courts of Appeal are free to certify question of great public interest to Supreme Court for consideration and to state their reasons for advocating change; however, they are bound to follow case law set forth by Supreme Court.

[4] Common Law k8

[4] Constitutional Law k55

Supreme Court has power to replace rule of contributory negligence with that of comparative negligence; in view of fact that prior to 1809 English case implicitly pronouncing that rule the theory of contributory negligence was a matter of judicial thought rather than judicial pronouncement, it could not be said that the common law was clear and free from doubt so as to make it part of the statute law of Florida by virtue of statute adopting the English common law. F.S.A.Const. art. 5, §3(b)(3).

[5] Common Law k11

Supreme Court may change a common-law rule where great social upheaval dictates.

[6] Negligence k547

[6] Negligence k549(2)

[6] Negligence k549(10)

A plaintiff in an action based on negligence is no longer to be denied any recovery because of his contributory negligence; if it appears from the evidence that both plaintiff and defendant were guilty of negligence which was, in some degree, a legal cause of injury to plaintiff, plaintiff's recovery is not to be entirely defeated; negligence of plaintiff and that of defendant is to be apportioned with plaintiff receiving only such an amount proportionate with his negligence and negligence of defendant.

. . .

Edna L. Caruso of Howell, Kirby, Montgomery, D'Aiuto, Dean & Hallowes, West Palm Beach, for petitioners.

Sammy Cacciatore of Nance & Cacciatore, Melbourne, for respondent.

E. Harper Field and Frank C. Amatea of Keen, O'Kelley & Spitz, Tallahassee, for amicus

---

headnotes are listed in more than one category in the digest, such as headnote 4, which is appears in both "Common Law" and "Constitutional Law." Before the title of the headnote (in bold) is a bracketed number that corresponds to a bracketed number at the beginning of some paragraphs in the opinion. The numbers to the right and below the title of the head note are "key numbers" that allow the lawyer to find the headnote and others on the same topic in the digest of key numbers. The use of digests in legal research is discussed in Chapter II, p. 79.

curiae, Fla. Defense Lawyers Ass'n.[5]

C. Graham Carothers and C. DuBose Ausley of Ausley, Ausley, McMullen, McGehee & Carothers, Tallahassee, for amicus curiae, Fla. Railroad Ass'n.

Kenneth L. Ryskamp, of Bolles, Goodwin, Ryskamp & Welcher, Miami, for amicus curiae, Fla. East Coast Railway Co.

William B. Killian, of McCarthy, Steel, Hector & Davis, Miami, for amicus curiae, Fla. Power & Light Co.

Sam H. Mann, Jr. and John T. Allen, Jr., of Harrison, Greene, Mann, Davenport, Rowe & Stanton, St. Petersburg, for amicus curiae, Fla. Power Corp.

Raymond Ehrlich and James E. Cobb, Jacksonville, for amicus curiae, American Mutual Ins. Alliance, American Ins. Asso., and National Asso. of Independent Insurers.

Thomas W. McAliley of Beckham & McAliley, Miami, for amicus curiae, United Transportation Union, Fla. Legislative Boards of Railroad Brotherhoods and the Fla. AFL-CIO.

ADKINS, Justice.

This cause is here on petition for writ of certiorari supported by certificate of the District Court of Appeal, Fourth District, that its decision (Jones v. Hoffman, 272 So.2d 529) is one which involves a question of great public interest. See Fla.Const., art. V, §3(b)(3), F.S.A.[6]

The question certified by the District Court of Appeal is:

Whether or not the Court should replace the contributory negligence rule with the principles of comparative negligence?[7]

The District Court of Appeal answered the certified question in the affirmative and reversed the trial court in the case *sub judice* for following the precedent set down by this Court in Louisville and Nashville Railroad Co. v. Yniestra, 21 Fla. 700 (1886). This early case specifically held the contributory negligence rule to be the law of Florida, and it has uniformly been followed by the courts of the State ever since. The District Court of Appeal attempted, therefore, to overrule all precedent of this Court in the area of contributory negligence and to establish comparative negligence as the proper test. In so doing, the District Court has exceeded its authority.

In a dissenting opinion, Judge Owen stated well the position of the District Courts of Appeal when in disagreement with controlling precedent set down by this Court:

[I]f and when such a change is to be wrought by the judiciary, it should be at the hands of the Supreme Court rather than the District Court of Appeal. . . . The majority decision would appear to flatly overrule a multitude of prior decisions

---

5 Several *amicus curiae* or "friend of the court" briefs were filed by lawyers for the organizations listed. When an appellate court is faced with deciding an important issue, appearances of *amici* are one way it can get additional points of view beyond those of the plaintiff and defendant. *See* Chapter II, p. 43 note 26.

6 A "writ of certiorari" is a discretionary order issued by a higher court to a lower court requiring it to "bring up the record" of a case the higher court wishes to review. Florida thus follows the normal pattern of state appellate courts taking cases on the Supreme Court level only at its discretion. *See* Chapter V, p. 169. *Certiorari* practice in the U.S. Supreme Court is discussed in Chapter V, p. 176.

7 The subject of recovery for negligent actions is discussed in Chapter XI, pp. 440-443. Reading the cited pages would assist in understanding the discussion in the opinion.

of our Supreme Court, a prerogative which we do not enjoy.

Jones v. Hoffman, 272 So.2d 529, p. 534.

The other District Courts of Appeal have recognized the relationship between their authority and that of this Court. Griffin v. State, 202 So.2d 602 (Fla. App.1st, 1967); Roberts v. State, 199 So.2d 340 (Fla. App.2d, 1967); and United States v. State, 179 So.2d 890 (Fla. App.3d, 1965). To allow a District Court of Appeal to overrule controlling precedent of this Court would be to create chaos and uncertainty in the judicial forum, particularly at the trial level. Ever since the District Court rendered its opinion there has been great confusion and much delay in the trial courts of the District Court of Appeal, Fourth District, while the attorneys and judges alike have been awaiting our decision in this case.

[2] We point out that the mere certification to this Court by a District Court of Appeal that its decision involves a question of great public interest does not vest this Court with jurisdiction. If neither party involved petitioned here for a writ of certiorari, we would not have jurisdiction to answer the question certified or to review the District Court's action.

[3] This is not to say that the District Courts of Appeal are powerless to seek change; they are free to certify questions of great public interest to this Court for consideration, and even to state their reasons for advocating change. They are, however, bound to follow the case law set forth by this Court.[8]

[4] Prior to answering the question certified, we must also consider our own power and authority to replace the rule of contributory negligence with that of comparative negligence. It has been suggested that such a change in the common law of Florida is properly within the province only of the Legislature, and not of the courts. We cannot agree.

The rule that contributory negligence is an absolute bar to recovery was — as most tort law — a judicial creation, and it was specifically judicially adopted in Florida in Louisville and Nashville Railroad Co. v. Yniestra, *supra*. Most scholars attribute the origin of this rule to the English case of Butterfield v. Forrester, 11 East 60, 103 Eng.Rep. 926 (K.B.1809), although as much as thirty years later — in Raisin v. Mitchell, 9 Car. & P. 613, 173 Eng.Rep. 979 (C.P.1839) — contributory negligence was held not to be a complete bar to recovery. Maloney, From Contributory to Comparative Negligence: A Needed Law Reform, 11 U.Fla.L.Rev. 135, 141-142 (1958). Although "contributory negligence" itself had been mentioned in some earlier cases, our research reveals that prior to 1809 (as well as for a time after that date) there was no clear-cut, common law rule that contributory negligence was a complete defense to an action based on negligence. Most probably, the common law was the same in this regard as English maritime law and the civil law — *i.e.*, damages were apportioned when both plaintiff and defendant were at fault. See Maloney, *supra*, page 152. Many authorities declare that early references to "contributory negligence" did not concern contributory negligence as we are familiar with it — *i.e.*, lack of due care by the plaintiff which contributes to his injuries — but that it originally meant a plaintiff's own negligent act which was the effective, *direct* cause of the accident in which he was injured. *e.g.*, Turk, Comparative Negligence on the March, 28 Chi-Kent L.Rev. 189, p. 196 (1950).

---

8   The Florida Supreme Court was obviously somewhat upset by the Court of Appeals' going ahead and deciding to use comparative negligence — despite the fact that Supreme Court ultimately agreed with that position on the merits. It thus demonstrates the traditional relationship that exists between superior and inferior courts. However, one frustration for lower appellate courts is the possibility that issues will remain unsettled for years because the supreme court in a system chooses not to decide them. What the Florida Court of Appeals did is one way to force the issue to be decided.

Hoffman v. Jones

Prior to Butterfield v. Forrester, *supra*, there was no clear-cut pronouncement of the contributory negligence rule, so it must be said that "judicial thinking" culminated in the implicit pronouncement of the contributory negligence rule in the 1809 decision of Butterfield v. Forrester, *supra*. In view of the fact that prior to Butterfield contributory negligence was a matter of judicial thought rather than judicial pronouncement, it cannot be said that the common law was "clear and free from doubt," so as to make it a part of the statute law of this State by virtue of Fla.Stat., §2.01, F.S.A.[9]

As we stated in Duval v. Thomas, 114 So.2d 791, 795 (Fla.1959), it is "only when the common law is plain that we must observe it." We also said in this case,

> [W]hen grave doubt exists of a true common law doctrine . . . we may, as was written in Ripley v. Ewell, *supra*, (61 So.2d 420), exercise a "broad discretion" taking "into account the changes in our social and economic customs and present day conceptions of right and justice."

[5] Even if it be said that the present bar of contributory negligence is a part of our common law by virtue of prior judicial decision, it is also true from *Duval* that this Court may change the rule where great social upheaval dictates. It has been modified in many instances by judicial decision, such as those establishing the doctrines of "last clear chance," "appreciable degree" and others. See Negligence: Application of the Last Clear Chance Doctrine by Kenneth M. Myers, 8 Fla.Law.Rev. 336 (1955). In a large measure the rule has been transfigured from any "statutory creation" by virtue of our adoption of the common law (if such it were) into decisional law by virtue of various court refinements. We have in the past, with hesitation, modified the common law in justified instances, and this is as it should be. Randolph v. Randolph, 146 Fla. 491, 1 So.2d 480 (1941), modified the common law doctrine that gave a father the superior right to the custody of a child; Banfield v. Addington, 104 Fla. 661, 140 So. 893 (1932), removed the common law exemption of a married woman from causes of action based on contract or mixed contracts in tort.

In Waller v. First Savings & Trust Co., 103 Fla. 1025, 138 So. 780 (1931), this Court refused to follow the common law principle that an action for personal injuries was abated upon the death of the tort-feasor, the Court saying:

> This court has expressly recognized the principle that in specific instances certain rules which were admittedly a part of the old English common law did not become a part of the Florida common law, because contrary to our customs, institutions, or intendments of our statutes on other subjects. (p. 784)

This Court receded from the common law and held, in Hargrove v. Town of Cocoa Beach, 96 So.2d 130 (Fla.1957), that a municipal corporation may be held liable for the torts of police officers under the doctrine of *respondeat superior*, saying:

> Tracing the rule to its ultimate progeniotr we are led to the English case of Russel v. Men of Devon, 2 T.R. 667, 100 Eng.Rep.R. 359 (1788).
>
> Assuming that the immunity rule had its inception in the Men of Devon case,

---

9 The cited statute is a "reception" statute, officially receiving the English common law as the law of the State of Florida as of July 4, 1776. *See* Chapter II, p. 42. This explains why the majority has spent the last few paragraphs determining exactly when contributory negligence came into English common law. The Florida reception statute is quoted in the dissenting opinion *infra* p. A12. The dissent asserts that contributory negligence came into English law much earlier and thus the decision to change it is one for the legislature, not the courts. *See infra* p. A12.

A5

and most legal historians agree that it did, it should be noted that this case was decided in 1788, some twelve years after our Declaration of Independence. Be that as it may, our own feeling is that *the courts should be alive to the demands of justice. We can see no necessity for insisting on legislative action in a matter which the courts themselves originated.* (Emphasis supplied) (p. 132)

Gates v. Foley, 247 So.2d 40 (Fla.1971), established the right of a wife to recover for the loss of consortium as a result of her husband's injuries. This decision receded from Ripley v. Ewell, 61 So.2d 420 (Fla.1952) and abrogated a common law principle, saying:

> It may be argued that any change in this rule should come from the Legislature. No recitation of authority is needed to indicate that this Court has not been backward in overturning unsound precedent in the area of tort law. *Legislative action could, of course, be taken, but we abdicate our own function, in a field peculiarly nonstatutory, when we refuse to reconsider an old and unsatisfactory court-made rule.* (Emphasis supplied) 247 So.2d 40, p. 43.

All rules of the common law are designed for application to new conditions and circumstances as they may be developed by enlightened commercial and business intercourse and are intended to be vitalized by practical application in advanced society. One of the most pressing social problems facing us today is the automobile accident problem, for the bulk of tort litigation involves the dangerous instrumentality known as the automobile. Our society must be concerned with accident prevention and compensation of victims of accidents. The Legislature of Florida has made great progress in legislation geared for accident prevention. The prevention of accidents, of course, is much more satisfying than the compensation of victims, but we must recognize the problem of determining a method of securing just and adequate compensation of accident victims who have a good cause of action.

The contemporary conditions must be met with contemporary standards which are realistic and better calculated to obtain justice among all of the parties involved, based upon the circumstances applying between them at the time in question. The rule of contributory negligence as a complete bar to recovery was imported into the law by judges. Whatever may have been the historical justification for it, today it is almost universally regarded as unjust and inequitable to vest an entire accidental loss on one of the parties whose negligent conduct combined with the negligence of the other party to produce the loss. If fault is to remain the test of liability, then the doctrine of comparative negligence which involves apportionment of the loss among those whose fault contributed to the occurrence is more consistent with liability based on a fault premise.

We are, therefore, of the opinion that we do have the power and authority to reexamine the position we have taken in regard to contributory negligence and to alter the rule we have adopted previously in light of current "social and economic customs" and modern "conceptions of right and justice."

Use of the terms "contributory negligence" and "comparative negligence" is slightly confusing. The two theories now commonly known by these terms both recognize that negligence of a plaintiff may play a part in causing his injuries and that the damages he is allowed to recover should, therefore, be diminished to some extent. The "contributory negligence" theory, of course, *completely* bars recovery, while the "comparative negligence" theory is that a plaintiff is prevented from recovering only that proportion of his damages for which he is responsible.

The demise of the absolute-bar theory of contributory negligence has been urged by many American scholars in the law of torts. It has been abolished in almost every common law nation in the world, including England — its country of origin — and every one of the Canadian Provinces. Some form of comparative negligence now exists in Austria, France, Germany, Portugal, Switzerland, Italy, China, Japan, Persia, Poland, Russia, Siam and Turkey. Maloney, *supra*, page 154.

Also, our research reveals that sixteen states have so far adopted some form of the comparative negligence doctrine.

One reason for the abandonment of the contributory negligence theory is that the initial justification for establishing the complete defense is no longer valid. It is generally accepted that, historically, contributory negligence was adopted "to protect the essential growth of industries, particularly transportation." Institute of Judicial Administration, Comparative Negligence-1954 Supplement, at page 2. Modern economic and social customs, however, favor the individual, not industry.

We find that none of the justifications for denying any recovery to a plaintiff, who has contributed to his own injuries to any extent, has any validity in this age.

Perhaps the best argument in favor of the movement from contributory to comparative negligence is that the latter is simply a more equitable system of determining liability and a more socially desirable method of loss distribution. The injustice which occurs when a plaintiff suffers severe injuries as the result of an accident for which he is only slightly responsible, and is thereby denied any damages, is readily apparent. The rule of contributory negligence is a harsh one which either places the burden of a loss for which two are responsible upon only one party or relegates to Lady Luck the determination of the damages for which each of two negligent parties will be liable. When the negligence of more than one person contributes to the occurrence of an accident, each should pay the proportion of the total damages he has caused the other party.

In an effort to ameliorate the harshness of contributory negligence, other doctrines have evolved in tort law such as "gross, willful, and wanton" negligence, "last clear chance" and the application of absolute liability in certain instances. Those who defend the doctrine of contributory negligence argue that the rule is also not as harsh in its practical effect as it is in theory. This is so, they say, because juries tend to disregard the instructions given by the trial judge in an effort to afford some measure of rough justice to the injured party. We agree with Dean Maloney that,

[T]here is something basically wrong with a rule of law that is so contrary to the settled convictions of the lay community that laymen will almost always refuse to enforce it, even when solemnly told to do so by a judge whose instructions they have sworn to follow. . . .

[T]he disrespect for law engendered by putting our citizens in a position in which they feel it is necessary to deliberately violate the law is not something to be lightly brushed aside; and it comes ill from the mouths of lawyers, who as officers of the courts have sworn to uphold the law, to defend the present system by arguing that it works because jurors can be trusted to disregard that very law. 11 U.Fla.L.Rev. 135, pp. 151-152 (1958).[10]

---

10 This demonstrates how the jury, which is only supposed to decide fact questions and follow the *judge's* instructions on the law, can ultimately have a cumulative effect on the shape of the law. The division of labor between the judge and the jury and the question of jury power to judge the law is discussed in Chapter III, p. 87. This is one area where consistent jury action "bending" the law contributed

In Connolly v. Steakley, 197 So.2d 524, 537 (Fla.1967), Mr. Justice O'Connell referred to contributory negligence as a "primitive device for achieving justice as between parties who are both at fault." Even Mr. Chief Justice McWhorter, in authoring the decision which specifically held the contributory negligence doctrine to be the law of this State, referred to it as "unjust and inequitable." Louisville and Nashville Railroad Co. v. Yniestra, *supra*, 21 Fla. p. 738.

Eighty-seven years after that decision, we find ourselves still laboring under a rule of law that has long been recognized as inequitable. The Legislature did enact a statute in 1887 which applied the principle of comparative negligence to railroad accidents. We held the statute unconstitutional under the due process and equal protection clauses of the Federal and State constitutions because it was of limited scope and not of *general application*. Georgia Southern & Florida Railway Co. v. Seven-Up Bottling Co., 175 So.2d 39 (Fla.1965). Our Legislature again addressed the problem in 1943, when a comparative negligence statute of general application was passed by both houses. This bill was vetoed by the Governor and the Legislature would not override the veto. Senate Journal, Regular Session, 1943, pp. 716-717. One man thus prevented this State from now operating under a much more equitable system of recovery for negligent personal injuries and property damage. Since that "defeat," the Legislature has done little to discard the harsh and inequitable contributory negligence rule, perhaps because it considers the problem to be a judicial one.

Since we definitely consider the problem to be a judicial one, we feel the time has come for this Court to join what seems to be a trend toward almost universal adoption of comparative negligence. A primary function of a court is to see that legal conflicts are equitably resolved. In the field of tort law, the most equitable result that can ever be reached by a court is the equation of liability with fault. Comparative negligence does this more completely than contributory negligence, and we would be shirking our duty if we did not adopt the better doctrine.

[6] Therefore, we now hold that a plaintiff in an action based on negligence will no longer be denied any recovery because of his contributory negligence.

If it appears from the evidence that both plaintiff and defendant were guilty of negligence which was, in some degree, a legal cause of the injury to the plaintiff, this does not defeat the plaintiff's recovery entirely. The jury in assessing damages would in that event award to the plaintiff such damages as in the jury's judgment the negligence of the defendant caused to the plaintiff. In other words, the jury should apportion the negligence of the plaintiff and the negligence of the defendant; then, in reaching the amount due the plaintiff, the jury should give the plaintiff only such an amount proportioned with his negligence and the negligence of the defendant. See Florida Cent. & P.R. Co. v. Foxworth, 41 Fla. 1, 25 So. 338, 79 Am.St.Rep. 149 (1899).

[7][8] This rule should not be construed so as to entitle a person to recover for damage in a case where the proof shows that the defendant could not by the exercise of due care have prevented the injury, or where the defendant's negligence was not a legal cause of the damage. Stated differently, there can be no apportionment of negligence where the negligence of the defendant is not directly a legal cause of the result complained of by the plaintiff. A plaintiff is barred from recovering damages for loss or injury caused

---

to changing the law. It is also noteworthy that here and earlier in the opinion, the majority relies heavily on scholarly commentary in support of its decision.

by the negligence of another only when the plaintiff's negligence is the sole legal cause of the damage, or the negligence of the plaintiff and some person or persons other than the defendant or defendants was the sole legal cause of the damage.

[9] If plaintiff and defendant are both at fault, the former may recover, but the amount of his recovery may be only such proportion of the entire damages plaintiff sustained as the defendant's negligence bears to the combined negligence of both the plaintiff and the defendant. For example, where it is found that the plaintiff's negligence is at least equal to that of the defendant, the amount awarded to the plaintiff should be reduced by one-half from what it otherwise would have been.

[10] The doctrine of last clear chance would, of course, no longer have any application in these cases. See Martin v. Sussman, 82 So.2d 597 (Fla.1955).

We decline herein to dissect and discuss all the possible variations of comparative negligence which have been adopted in other jurisdictions. Countless law review commentaries and treatises can be found which have covered almost every conceivable mutation of the basic doctrine. Suffice it to say that we consider the "pure form" of comparative negligence — as we have phrased it above — to be the most equitable method of allocating damages in negligence actions.

[11] In the usual situation where the negligence of the plaintiff is at issue, as well as that of the defendant, there will undoubtedly be a counterclaim filed. The cross-plaintiff (just as plaintiff in the main suit) guilty of some degree of negligence would be entitled to a verdict awarding him such damages as in the jury's judgment were proportionate with his negligence and the negligence of cross-defendant. This could result in two verdicts — one for plaintiff and one for cross-plaintiff. In such event the Court should enter one judgment in favor of the party receiving the larger verdict, the amount of which should be the difference between the two verdicts. This is in keeping with the long recognized principles of "set off" in contract litigation. The Court's primary responsibility is to enter a judgment which reflects the true intent of the jury, as expressed in its verdict or verdicts.

In rare cases the net result of two such claims will be that the party more responsible for an accident will recover more than the party less responsible. On the surface, this might seem inequitable. However, using an extreme example, let us assume that a plaintiff is 80 per cent responsible for an automobile accident and suffers $20,000 in damages, and that the defendant — 20 per cent responsible — fortunately suffers no damages. The liability of the defendant in such a case should not depend upon what damages he *suffered*, but upon what damages he *caused*. If a jury found that this defendant had been negligent and that his negligence, in relation to that of the plaintiff, was 20 per cent responsible for causing the accident then he should pay 20 per cent of the total damages, regardless of the fact that he has been fortunate enough to not be damaged personally.

Petitioners in this cause, and various amicus curiae who have filed briefs, have raised many points which they claim we must consider in adopting comparative negligence, such as the effects of such a change on the concept of "assumption of risk," and no "contribution" between joint tortfeasors. We decline to consider all those issues, however, for two reasons. One reason is that we already have a body of case law in this State dealing with comparative negligence, under our earlier railroad statute. Much of this case law will be applicable under the comparative negligence rule we are now adopting generally.

[12] The other reason is that it is not the proper function of this Court to decide unripe issues, without the benefit of adequate briefing, not involving an actual controversy, and

unrelated to a specific factual situation.[11]

We are fully confident that the trial court judges of this State can adequately handle any problems created by our change to a comparative negligence rule as these problems arise. The answers to many of the problems will be obvious in light of the purposes for which we adopt the rule stated above:

(1) To allow a jury to apportion fault as it sees fit between negligent parties whose negligence was part of the legal and proximate cause of any loss or injury; and

(2) To apportion the total damages resulting from the loss or injury according to the proportionate fault of each party.

In accomplishing these purposes, the trial court is authorized to require special verdicts to be returned by the jury and to enter such judgment or judgments as may truly reflect the intent of the jury as expressed in any verdict or verdicts which may be returned.[12]

[14] We recognize the thousands of pending negligence cases affected by this decision. In fact, the prospect of a general upheaval in pending tort litigation has always been a deterring influence in considering the adoption of a comparative negligence rule. See Annotation, The Doctrine of Comparative Negligence, 32 ALR 3d 463, p. 487. We feel the trial judges of this State are capable of applying this comparative negligence rule without our setting guidelines in anticipation of expected problems. The problems are more appropriately resolved at the trial level in a practical manner instead of a theoretical solution at the appellate level. The trial judges are granted broad discretion in adopting such procedure as may accomplish the objectives and purposes expressed in this opinion.

Determining the time when the comparative negligence rule shall be applied at the trial level presents another problem. The confusion created by the premature adoption of the comparative negligence rule by the District Court of Appeal is further exemplified by the fact that some trial judges, relying on the decision, have applied the rule in the trial of many cases. Other trial judges have conducted their trials in accordance with the law of contributory negligence.

[15] We hold that a District Court of Appeal does not have the authority to overrule a decision of the Supreme Court of Florida. In the event of a conflict between the decision of a District Court of Appeal and this Court, the decision of this Court shall prevail until overruled by a subsequent decision of this Court.

[16] Under the circumstances, we hold that this opinion shall be applied as follows:

1. As to those cases in which the comparative negligence rule has been applied, this opinion shall be applicable.

2. As to those cases already commenced, but in which trial has not yet begun, this opinion shall be applicable.

3. As to those cases in which trial has already begun or in which verdict or

---

11 The Court adopts the traditional judicial stance of declining to declare any law beyond what is essential to resolution of this case and gives the traditional adversary system reasons for doing so — the lack of sufficient incentive for the parties to "fight it out" over an issue that does not directly affect them. *See* Chapter III, pp. 83-88, where the value of a partisan clash of views is discussed, and Chapter IX, pp. 323-324, where the adversarial basis for limitations on judicial power are discussed.

12 A "special verdict" is one that requires the jury to provide a justification for its decision by way of specific findings of fact, rather than rendering a "general verdict" stating nothing more than who wins and in what amount. *See* Chapter III, p. 107.

judgment has already been rendered, this opinion shall not be applicable, unless the applicability of the comparative negligence rule was appropriately and properly raised during some stage of the litigation.

4. As to those cases on appeal in which the applicability of the comparative negligence rule has been properly and appropriately made a question of appellate review, this opinion shall be applicable.

5. This opinion shall be applicable to all cases commenced after the decision becomes final.[13]

The certified question having now been answered in full, this cause is remanded to the District Court of Appeal, Fourth District, to be further remanded to the Circuit Court for a new trial.

In order to finalize the determination of the question in this case as expeditiously as possible, this decision is made effective immediately and a petition for rehearing will not be allowed.

It is so ordered.

CARLTON, C.J., and ERVIN, BOYD, McCAIN and DEKLE, JJ., concur.

ROBERTS, J., dissents with opinion.

ROBERTS, Justice (dissenting).

I must respectfully dissent from the majority opinion in this cause. My primary concern is whether this Court is empowered to reject and replace the established doctrine of contributory negligence by judicial decree.

The sovereign powers of this State are divided into three coordinate branches of government — legislative, judicial and executive — by the Constitution of Florida, Article II, Section 3. Our Constitution specifically prohibits a person belonging to one of such branches from exercising any powers "appertaining to either of the other branches unless expressly provided herein." This Court has been diligent in preserving and maintaining the doctrine of separation of powers, which doctrine was imbedded in both the state and federal constitutions at the threshhold of constitutional democracy in this country, and under which doctrine the judiciary has no power to make statutory law. State ex rel. Hanbury v. Tunnicliffe, 98 Fla. 731, 124 So. 279 (1929), Carlton v. Matthews, 103 Fla. 301, 137 So. 815 (1931), State v. Herndon, 158 Fla. 115, 27 So.2d 833 (1946), Hancock v. Board of Public Instruction of Charlotte County, 158 So.2d 519 (Fla.1963), Holley v. Adams, 238 So.2d 401 (Fla.1970), State v. Barquet, 262 So.2d 431 (Fla.1972).

In the case of Ponder v. Graham, 4 Fla. 23, 25 (1851), this Court emphatically stated, "The fundamental principle of every free and good government is, that these several co-ordinate departments forever remain separate and distinct. No maxim in political science is more fully recognized than this. Its necessity was recognized by the framers of our government, as one too invaluable to be surrendered, and too sacred to be tampered with. Every other political principle is subordinate to it — for it is this which gives to our system energy, vitality and stability. Montesquieu says there can be no liberty, where the judicial are not separated from the legislative powers. 1 Spirit of Laws, page 181. Mr. Madison says these departments should remain forever separate and distinct, and that there is no political truth of greater intrinsic value, and which is stamped with the authority

---

13 In view of the great change in the law that this decision represents, the court decides to give its decision only partial retroactive effect. *See* Chapter II, p. 48.

or more enlightened patrons of liberty. Federalist, 270." Applying this well established doctrine, we held that the matter of changing statutory law is not one to be indulged by the Court, but is a legislative function. Kennedy v. City of Daytona Beach, 132 Fla. 675, 182 So. 228 (1938). Therein, this Court also reaffirmed the principle that the common law, if not abrogated by statute or constitutional provision, is in full force and effect in this state. See also Bryan v. Landis, 106 Fla. 19, 142 So. 650 (1932), Wilson v. Renfroe, 91 So.2d 857 (Fla.1957), Brooks v. City of West Miami, 246 So.2d 115 (Fla. App. 1971).[14]

It is the statutory law of this state that, "The common and statute laws of England which are of a general and not a local nature, with the exception hereinafter mentioned, down to the fourth day of July, 1776, are declared to be of force in this state; provided, the said statutes and common law be not inconsistent with the constitution and laws of the United States and the acts of the legislature of this state." Florida Statutes, Section 2.01, F.S.A.

The doctrine of contributory negligence was a part of the common law of England prior to July 4, 1776, and therefore, is part of the common law of this state pursuant to Florida Statutes, Section 2.01, F.S.A., and is secure from the desires of this Court to supplant it by the doctrine of comparative negligence, provided that it is not inconsistent with the Constitution and laws of the United States and the Constitution and acts of the Legislature of this state. Ripley v. Ewell, 61 So.2d 420 (Fla.1952), Duval v. Thomas, 114 So.2d 791 (Fla.1959). Furthermore, we have held that courts are bound by the rule of *stare decisis* to follow common law as it has been judicially declared in previously adjudicated cases. Layne v. Tribune Co., 108 Fla. 177, 146 So. 234 (1933).

The question presently before this Court is whether this Court should replace the doctrine of contributory negligence with the concept of comparative negligence. *Sub judice*, by applying the doctrine of contributory negligence, the trial court correctly followed the precedent set down by this Court in Louisville and Nashville Railroad Co. v. Yniestra, 21 Fla. 700 (1886), and its progeny. This Court in *Yniestra* recognized and described contributory negligence as "the law as it unquestionably stands," 21 Fla. 700, p. 737. We said, "If Mr. Yniestra was himself negligent, and that negligence was the proximate cause of his death, the *law* calls that contributory negligence, and the plaintiff could not recover."

Although the case of Butterfield v. Forrester, 11 East 60, 103 Eng.Rep. 926 (K.B.1809), is recognized as a leading case in the area of contributory negligence, such case was not the first pronouncement of the common law doctrine of contributory negligence. Lord Ellenborough wrote in Butterfield v. Forrester, *supra*, "One person being in fault will not dispense with another's using ordinary care for himself. Two things must concur to support this action, an obstruction in the road by the fault of the defendant, and no want of ordinary care to avoid it on the part of the plaintiff." 11 East 60, 61.

The brief opinions of Bayley, J. and Lord Ellenborough in *Forrester* were merely a restatement of the concept of common law contributory negligence. If this case was the origin of common law contributory negligence, then clearly it would not have been adopted as part of the statutory law of this state through Florida Statutes, Section 2.01, F.S.A., because that decision was rendered subsequent to July 4, 1776.

I note with much interest the comment by Wex S. Malone in, "The Formative Era of

14 The dissenting justice is setting out a limited view of Florida courts' power to make common law based on the state constitutional separation of powers principles which are similar to limits on the federal courts's common-law powers, but are unlike that of most state courts. *See* Chapter I, p. 30 and Chapter IX, pp. 321-325 (limitations on federal court power based on separation of powers).

Contributory Negligence," 41 Illinois Law Review, 151, to the following effect: "The concise opinions of Bayley and Lord Ellenborough in Butterfield v. Forrester (1809) afford no indication that either of those judges felt at the time that he was charting new paths for law."[15]

Contributory negligence was adopted much earlier as a part of the common law. In Bayly v. Merrell, Cro.Jac. 386, 79 Eng.Rep. 331 (1606), the Court explicated, "(I)f he doubted of the weight thereof, he might have weighed it; and was not bound to give credence to another's speech; *and being his own negligence*, he is without remedy." (Emphasis supplied) Cro.Jac. 386, p. 387, 79 Eng.Rep. 331.

Charles Beach in 1882 traced the doctrine of contributory negligence back to its origin in his treatise on contributory negligence, wherein he set out, "Our Anglo-American law of Negligence, including, as of course, that of Contributory Negligence, has come down to us, in ordinary generation, from the civil law of imperial Rome. It is a part of that great debt which the common law owes to the classical and the scholastic jurisprudence." Beach on Contributory Negligence, §1, p. 1 (1882). See also: Beach on Contributory Negligence, 2d Ed., §1, p. 1 (1892), and Beach on Contributory Negligence, 3d Ed., Crawford, §1, p. 1 (1899).

Although he expressed a personal view of dislike for the operation of the principle of contributory negligence, Chief Justice McWhorter recognized in Louisville and Nashville Railroad Co. v. Yniestra, *supra*, the inability of this Court to change the common law rule of contributory negligence when he applied the existing law required to the facts of the case before him. He observed, "The law, in cases at least where human life is concerned, certainly needs *legislative* revision." (Emphasis supplied) 21 Fla. 700, p. 738.

By virtue of Florida Statutes, Section 2.01, contributory negligence is in force and said doctrine can be modified or replaced only by legislation to the contrary. Interposition of judicial power to make a legislative change in a statute which the Legislature on numerous occasions has refused to do is a clear invasion of the legislative.

Co-Operative Sanitary Baking Co. v. Shields, 71 Fla. 110, 70 So. 934 (1916), involved a personal injury suit wherein plaintiff sought to recover damages for injuries sustained through the alleged negligence of defendant. Therein, this Court stated, inter alia, that at common law a plaintiff could not recover for injuries to himself caused by the negligence of another if he in any appreciable way contributed to the proximate cause of injury, upon the theory that there is no apportionment of the results of mutual negligence. See also German-American Lumber Co. v. Hannah, 60 Fla. 76, 53 So. 516, 30 L.R.A.(N.S.) 882. In the *Shields* case, this Court explicitly recited, "The only modification of this common-law principle which the Legislature of this state has seen fit to make is in regard to injuries occasioned by railroad companies. See sections 3148, 3149, and 3150 of the General Statutes. *If this common-law principle is to be still further modified, it must be done by the Legislature, as it is beyond the power and province of the courts.* We would also refer to Coronet Phosphate Co. v. Jackson, 65 Fla. 170, 61 So. 318, and Wauchula Manufacturing & Timber Co. v. Jackson, 70 Fla. 596, 70 So. 599, decided here at the last term, wherein we followed the principles enunciated in German-American Lumber Co. v. Hannah, *supra*. If the evidence adduced in the instant case established the fact that the plaintiff's own negligence contributed to the proximate cause of the injuries which he received, then he

---

15 The dissenting judge relies on scholarly commentary in his favor to support his position. *See supra* note 10.

cannot recover, even though it is also established by the evidence that the defendant was likewise guilty of negligence, whether by acts of commission or omission, which contributed to or formed a part of the proximate cause of the injury. In order to determine this point a careful examination of the evidence is requisite." (Emphasis supplied) *supra*, 70 So. at p. 936.

In fine, the primary question is not whether or not the law of contributory negligence should be changed, but rather, who should do the changing. Contributory negligence was recognized in the common law as far back as A.D. 1606 and made a part of the statute law of this State in A.D. 1829, and thus far not changed by statute. If such a fundamental change is to be made in the law, then such modification should be made by the legislature where proposed change will be considered by legislative committees in public hearing where the general public may have an opportunity to be heard and should not be made by judicial fiat.[16] Such an excursion into the field of legislative jurisdiction weakens the concept of separation of powers and our tripartite system of government.

For the foregoing reasons, I respectfully dissent.

---

16 Here, the dissent is making an argument about the relative institutional competence of judges and the legislature to fully consider and decide on changes in the law. *See* Chapter II, p. 45.

CONSTITUTION OF THE UNITED STATES

[drafted 1787, ratified 1789][1]

PREAMBLE

WE THE PEOPLE of the United States, in Order to form a more perfect Union, establish Justice, insure domestic Tranquility, provide for the common defence, promote the general Welfare, and secure the Blessings of Liberty to ourselves and our Posterity, do ordain and establish this Constitution for the United States of America.

ARTICLE I [Legislative Power]

Section 1. [Legislative Power Vested in Congress] All legislative Powers herein granted shall be vested in a Congress of the United States, which shall consist of a Senate and House of Representatives.

Section 2. [House of Representatives] [1. Election and Term of Members] The House of Representatives shall be composed of Members chosen every second Year by the People of the several States, and the Electors in each State shall have the Qualifications requisite for Electors of the most numerous Branch of the State Legislature.

[2. Qualifications of Members] No Person shall be a Representative who shall not have attained to the Age of twenty five Years, and been seven Years a Citizen of the United States, and who shall not, when elected, be an Inhabitant of that State in which he shall be chosen.

[3. Apportionment of Representation] {Representatives and direct Taxes shall be apportioned among the several States which may be included within this Union, according to their respective Numbers, which shall be determined by adding to the whole Number of free Persons, including those bound to Service for a Term of Years, and excluding Indians not taxed, three fifths of all other Persons.}[2] The actual Enumeration shall be made within three Years after the first Meeting of the Congress of the United States, and within every subsequent Term of ten Years, in such Manner as they shall by Law direct. The Number of Representatives shall not exceed one for every thirty Thousand, but each State shall have at Least one Representative; and until such enumeration shall be made, the State of New Hampshire shall be entitled to choose three, Massachusetts eight, Rhode Island and Providence Plantations one, Connecticut five, New York six, New Jersey four, Pennsylvania eight, Delaware one, Maryland six, Virginia ten, North Carolina five, South Carolina five, and Georgia three.

[4. Vacancies] When vacancies happen in the Representation from any State, the Executive Authority thereof shall issue Writs of Election to fill such Vacancies.

[5. Speaker of the House; Impeachment Power] The House of Representatives shall chuse[3] their Speaker and other Officers; and shall have the sole Power of Impeachment.

Section 3. [Senate] [1. Composition, Election, and Term of Office] {The Senate of the United States shall be composed of two Senators from each State, chosen by the Legislature thereof, for six Years; and each Senator shall have one Vote.}[4]

---

1 Footnotes and material in square brackets [ ] are explanatory and added by the author. Material in braces { } is superseded or changed by amendment, as explained in the accompanying footnote.

2 The mode of apportionment of representatives among the several states was amended by the 14th Amendment §2. Taxes on incomes without apportionment was authorized by the 16th Amendment. The reference to "other Persons" is to slaves. *See* Chapter I, p. 5.

3 This is the 18th century spelling of "choose."

4 The paragraph in braces was superseded by the 17th Amendment.

[2. Staggered Terms and Vacancies] Immediately after they shall be assembled in Consequence of the first Election, they shall be divided as equally as may be into three Classes. The Seats of the Senators of the first Class shall be vacated at the Expiration of the second Year, of the second Class at the Expiration of the fourth Year, and of the third Class at the Expiration of the sixth Year, so that one third may be chosen every second Year; {and if Vacancies happen by Resignation, or otherwise, during the Recess of the Legislature of any State, the Executive thereof may make temporary Appointments until the next Meeting of the Legislature, which shall then fill such Vacancies.}[5]

[3. Qualifications of Senators] No Person shall be a Senator who shall not have attained to the Age of thirty Years, and been nine Years a Citizen of the United States, and who shall not, when elected, be an Inhabitant of that State for which he shall be chosen.

[4. Vice President as President of Senate] The Vice President of the United States shall be President of the Senate, but shall have no Vote, unless they be equally divided.

[5. Officers] The Senate shall chuse their other Officers, and also a President pro tempore, in the Absence of the Vice President, or when he shall exercise the Office of President of the United States.

[6. Senate's Power to Try Impeachments] The Senate shall have the sole Power to try all Impeachments. When sitting for that Purpose, they shall be on Oath or Affirmation. When the President of the United States is tried, the Chief Justice shall preside: And no Person shall be convicted without the Concurrence of two thirds of the Members present.

[7. Effect of Conviction in Impeachment] Judgment in Cases of Impeachment shall not extend further than to removal from Office, and disqualification to hold and enjoy any Office of honor, Trust or Profit under the United States: but the Party convicted shall nevertheless be liable and subject to Indictment, Trial, Judgment and Punishment, according to Law.

Section 4. [Congressional Elections and Meetings of Congress] [1. Congressional Elections] The Times, Places and Manner of holding Elections for Senators and Representatives, shall be prescribed in each State by the Legislature thereof; but the Congress may at any time by Law make or alter such Regulations, except as to the Places of chusing Senators.

[2. Meetings of the Congress] The Congress shall assemble at least once in every year, and such meeting shall begin at noon on the {first Monday in December, unless they shall by Law appoint a different Day.}[6]

Section 5. [Power of Each House Over Internal Operations] [1. Each House as Judge of Qualifications and Election of Members; Quorum] Each House shall be the Judge of the Elections, Returns and Qualifications of its own Members, and a Majority of each shall constitute a Quorum to do Business; but a smaller Number may adjourn from day to day, and may be authorized to compel the Attendance of absent Members, in such Manner, and under such Penalties as each House may provide.

[2. Rules of Proceedings; Punishment and Expulsion of Members] Each House may determine the Rules of its Proceedings, punish its Members for disorderly Behaviour, and, with the Concurrence of two thirds, expel a Member.

[3. Journal and Voting] Each House shall keep a Journal of its Proceedings, and from

---

5 The phrase in braces was superseded by 17th Amendment.
6 The material in braces was superseded by 20th Amendment.

time to time publish the same, excepting such Parts as may in their Judgment require Secrecy; and the Yeas and Nays of the Members of either House on any question shall, at the Desire of one fifth of those Present, be entered on the Journal.

[4. Consent of Each House to Adjournment] Neither House, during the Session of Congress, shall, without the Consent of the other, adjourn for more than three days, nor to any other Place than that in which the two Houses shall be sitting.

Section 6. [Compensation and Immunities; Incompatible Offices] [1. Compensation and Immunities] The Senators and Representatives shall receive a Compensation for their Services, to be ascertained by Law, and paid out of the Treasury of the United States. They shall in all Cases, except Treason, Felony and Breach of the Peace, be privileged from Arrest during their Attendance at the Session of their respective Houses, and in going to and returning from the same; and for any Speech or Debate in either House, they shall not be questioned in any other Place.[7]

[2. Incompatible Offices] No Senator or Representative shall, during the Time for which he was elected, be appointed to any civil Office under the Authority of the United States, which shall have been created, or the Emoluments whereof shall have been increased during such time; and no Person holding any Office under the United States, shall be a Member of either House during his Continuance in Office.

Section 7. [Legislative Process] [1. Revenue Bills to Originate in House] All Bills for raising Revenue shall originate in the House of Representatives; but the Senate may propose or concur with Amendments as on other Bills.

[2. Passage of Bills by Both Houses and Presentment to President] Every Bill which shall have passed the House of Representatives and the Senate, shall, before it become a Law, be presented to the President of the United States; If he approve he shall sign it, but if not he shall return it, with his Objections to that House in which it shall have originated, who shall enter the Objections at large on their Journal, and proceed to reconsider it. If after such Reconsideration two thirds of that House shall agree to pass the Bill, it shall be sent together with the Objections, to the other House, by which it shall likewise be reconsidered, and if approved by two thirds of that House, it shall become a Law. But in all such Cases the Votes of both Houses shall be determined by yeas and Nays, and the Names of the Persons voting for and against the Bill shall be entered on the Journal of each House respectively. If any Bill shall not be returned by the President within ten Days (Sundays excepted) after it shall have been presented to him, the Same shall be a Law, in like Manner as if he had signed it, unless the Congress by their Adjournment prevent its Return, in which Case it shall not be a Law.

[3. Presentment of Orders and Resolutions] Every Order, Resolution, or Vote to which the Concurrence of the Senate and House of Representatives may be necessary (except on a question of Adjournment) shall be presented to the President of the United States; and before the Same shall take Effect, shall be approved by him, or being disapproved by him, shall be repassed by two thirds of the Senate and House of Representatives, according to the Rules and Limitations prescribed in the Case of a Bill.

Section 8. [Powers of Congress] [1] The Congress shall have Power To lay and collect Taxes, Duties, Imposts and Excises, to pay the Debts and provide for the common Defence and general Welfare of the United States; but all Duties, Imposts and Excises shall be

---

7 The 27th Amendment amended this section by adding a sentence on compensation of members of Congress.

uniform throughout the United States;

[2] To borrow Money on the credit of the United States;

[3] To regulate Commerce with foreign Nations, and among the several States, and with the Indian Tribes;

[4] To establish an uniform Rule of Naturalization, and uniform Laws on the subject of Bankruptcies throughout the United States;

[5] To coin Money, regulate the Value thereof, and of foreign Coin, and fix the Standard of Weights and Measures;

[6] To provide for the Punishment of counterfeiting the Securities and current Coin of the United States;

[7] To establish Post Offices and Post Roads;

[8] To promote the Progress of Science and useful Arts, by securing for limited Times to Authors and Inventors the exclusive Right to their respective Writings and Discoveries;

[9] To constitute Tribunals inferior to the supreme Court;

[10] To define and punish Piracies and Felonies committed on the high Seas, and Offences against the Law of Nations;

[11] To declare War, grant Letters of Marque and Reprisal, and make Rules concerning Captures on Land and Water;

[12] To raise and support Armies, but no Appropriation of Money to that Use shall be for a longer Term than two Years;

[13] To provide and maintain a Navy;

[14] To make Rules for the Government and Regulation of the land and naval Forces;

[15] To provide for calling forth the Militia to execute the Laws of the Union, suppress Insurrections and repel Invasions;

[16] To provide for organizing, arming, and disciplining, the Militia, and for governing such Part of them as may be employed in the Service of the United States, reserving to the States respectively, the Appointment of the Officers, and the Authority of training the Militia according to the discipline prescribed by Congress;

[17] To exercise exclusive Legislation in all Cases whatsoever, over such District (not exceeding ten Miles square) as may, by Cession of particular States, and the Acceptance of Congress, become the Seat of the Government of the United States, and to exercise like Authority over all Places purchased by the Consent of the Legislature of the State in which the Same shall be, for the Erection of Forts, Magazines, Arsenals, dock-Yards, and other needful Buildings;—And

[18] To make all Laws which shall be necessary and proper for carrying into Execution the foregoing Powers, and all other Powers vested by this Constitution in the Government of the United States, or in any Department or Officer thereof.

Section 9. [Powers Prohibited to the United States]

[1. Importing Slaves] {The Migration or Importation of such Persons as any of the States now existing shall think proper to admit, shall not be prohibited by the Congress prior to the Year one thousand eight hundred and eight, but a Tax or duty may be imposed on such

Importation, not exceeding ten dollars for each Person.}[8]

[2. Suspension of Writ of Habeas Corpus] The Privilege of the Writ of Habeas Corpus shall not be suspended, unless when in Cases of Rebellion or Invasion the public Safety may require it.

[3. Bills of Attainder and Ex Post Facto Laws] No Bill of Attainder or ex post facto Law shall be passed.

[4. No Direct Tax] No Capitation, or other direct, Tax shall be laid, unless in Proportion to the Census or Enumeration herein before directed to be taken.[9]

[5. No Taxes or Duties on State Exports] No Tax or Duty shall be laid on Articles exported from any State.

[6. No Preferences to Ports Nor Duties on Vessels] No Preference shall be given by any Regulation of Commerce or Revenue to the Ports of one State over those of another: nor shall Vessels bound to, or from, one State, be obliged to enter, clear, or pay Duties in another.

[7. Appropriations; Statements and Accounts] No Money shall be drawn from the Treasury, but in Consequence of Appropriations made by Law; and a regular Statement and Account of the Receipts and Expenditures of all public Money shall be published from time to time.

[8. No Titles of Nobility or Emoluments From Foreign States to Officers of United States] No Title of Nobility shall be granted by the United States: And no Person holding any Office of Profit or Trust under them, shall, without the Consent of the Congress, accept of any present, Emolument, Office, or Title, of any kind whatever, from any King, Prince, or foreign State.

Section 10. [Restrictions on the States] [1. Powers Restrictions and Rights Restrictions] No State shall enter into any Treaty, Alliance, or Confederation; grant Letters of Marque and Reprisal; coin Money; emit Bills of Credit; make any Thing but gold and silver Coin a Tender in Payment of Debts; pass any Bill of Attainder, ex post facto Law, or Law impairing the Obligation of Contracts, or grant any Title of Nobility.

[2. Import-Export Clause] No State shall, without the Consent of the Congress, lay any Imposts or Duties on Imports or Exports, except what may be absolutely necessary for executing its inspection Laws: and the net Produce of all Duties and Imposts, laid by any State on Imports or Exports, shall be for the Use of the Treasury of the United States; and all such Laws shall be subject to the Revision and Controul of the Congress.

[3. Powers Restrictions] No State shall, without the Consent of Congress, lay any Duty of Tonnage, keep Troops, or Ships of War in time of Peace, enter into any Agreement or Compact with another State, or with a foreign Power, or engage in War, unless actually invaded, or in such imminent Danger as will not admit of delay.

ARTICLE II [The Executive Power]

Section 1. [Executive Power Vested in President; Term and Election of President and Vice-President; Qualifications of President; Removal and Succession; Compensation; Oath of Office] [1. Executive Power Vested in President; Term of Office] The executive Power

---

8 Congress duly passed a prohibition of further importation. To the extent that this clause condones slavery, it is superseded by the 13th Amendment.

9 This clause, together with Art. I §2 cl. 3, was repealed by the 16th Amendment.

shall be vested in a President of the United States of America. He shall hold his Office during the Term of four Years, and, together with the Vice President, chosen for the same Term, be elected, as follows:[10]

[2. Election of President and Vice-President] Each State shall appoint, in such Manner as the Legislature thereof may direct, a Number of Electors, equal to the whole Number of Senators and Representatives to which the State may be entitled in the Congress: but no Senator or Representative, or Person holding an Office of Trust or Profit under the United States, shall be appointed an Elector.[11]

[3. Method of Selection] {The Electors shall meet in their respective States, and vote by Ballot for two Persons, of whom one at least shall not be an Inhabitant of the same State with themselves. And they shall make a List of all the Persons voted for, and of the Number of Votes for each; which List they shall sign and certify, and transmit sealed to the Seat of the Government of the United States, directed to the President of the Senate. The President of the Senate shall, in the Presence of the Senate and House of Representatives, open all the Certificates, and the Votes shall then be counted. The Person having the greatest Number of Votes shall be the President, if such Number be a Majority of the whole Number of Electors appointed; and if there be more than one who have such Majority, and have an equal Number of Votes, then the House of Representatives shall immediately chuse by Ballot one of them for President; and if no Person have a Majority, then from the five highest on the List the said House shall in like Manner chuse the President, the Votes shall be taken by States the Representation from each State having one Vote; A quorum for this Purpose shall consist of a Member or Members from two thirds of the States, and a Majority of all the States shall be necessary to a Choice. In every Case, after the Choice of the President, the Person having the greater Number of Votes of the Electors shall be the Vice President. But if there should remain two or more who have equal Votes, the Senate shall choose from them by Ballot the Vice President.}[12]

[4. When Electors Vote] The Congress may determine the Time of chusing the Electors, and the Day on which they shall give their Votes; which Day shall be the same throughout the United States.

[5. Qualifications] No Person except a natural born Citizen, or a Citizen of the United States, at the time of the Adoption of this Constitution, shall be eligible to the Office of President; neither shall any Person be eligible to that Office who shall not have attained to the Age of thirty five Years, and been fourteen Years a Resident within the United States.

[6. Succession] {In Case of the Removal of the President from Office, or of his Death, Resignation, or Inability to discharge the Powers and Duties of the said Office, the Same shall devolve on the Vice President, and the Congress may by Law provide for the Case of Removal, Death, Resignation or Inability, both of the President and Vice President, declaring what Officer shall then act as President, and such Officer shall act accordingly until the Disability be removed, or a President shall be elected.}[13]

---

10 To the extent that this implies that the President may be elected to more than two terms, it is amended by the 22nd Amendment.

11 This clause was altered by the provisions of the 23rd Amendment, which authorizes Presidential Electors for the District of Columbia, thus for the first time giving District residents the right to vote in presidential elections.

12 This clause was superseded by the 12th Amendment. Parts of the 12th Amendment were in turn superseded by §3 of the 20th Amendment.

13 This clause was superseded by the 25th Amendment.

[7. Compensation] The President shall, at stated Times, receive for his Services, a Compensation, which shall neither be encreased nor diminished during the Period for which he shall have been elected, and he shall not receive within that Period any other Emolument from the United States, or any of them.

[8. Oath of Office] Before he enter on the Execution of his Office, he shall take the following Oath or Affirmation: — "I do solemnly swear (or affirm) that I will faithfully execute the Office of President of the United States, and will to the best of my Ability, preserve, protect and defend the Constitution of the United States."

Section 2. [Powers of the President] [1. Commander in Chief; Executive Opinions; the Pardon Power] The President shall be Commander in Chief of the Army and Navy of the United States, and of the Militia of the several States, when called into the actual Service of the United States; he may require the Opinion, in writing, of the principal Officer in each of the Executive Departments, upon any Subject relating to the Duties of their respective Offices and he shall have Power to grant Reprieves and Pardons for Offenses against the United States, except in Cases of Impeachment.

[2. Treaty Power and Appointments Power] He shall have Power, by and with the Advice and Consent of the Senate, to make Treaties, provided two thirds of the Senators present concur; and he shall nominate, and by and with the Advice and Consent of the Senate, shall appoint Ambassadors, other public Ministers and Consuls, Judges of the supreme Court, and all other Officers of the United States, whose Appointments are not herein otherwise provided for, and which shall be established by Law: but the Congress may by Law vest the Appointment of such inferior Officers, as they think proper, in the President alone, in the Courts of Law, or in the Heads of Departments.

[3. Recess Appointments] The President shall have Power to fill up all Vacancies that may happen during the Recess of the Senate, by granting Commissions which shall expire at the End of their next Session.

Section 3. [Powers with respect to Congress; Ambassadors; Enforcement of the Laws; Commissioning of Officers] He shall from time to time give to the Congress Information of the State of the Union, and recommend to their Consideration such Measures as he shall judge necessary and expedient; he may, on extraordinary Occasions, convene both Houses, or either of them, and in Case of Disagreement between them, with Respect to the Time of Adjournment, he may adjourn them to such Time as he shall think proper; he shall receive Ambassadors and other public Ministers; he shall take Care that the Laws be faithfully executed, and shall Commission all the Officers of the United States.

Section 4. [Impeachment of the President and Other Federal Officers] The President, Vice President and all civil Officers of the United States, shall be removed from Office on Impeachment for, and Conviction of, Treason, Bribery, or other high Crimes and Misdemeanors.

ARTICLE III [The Judicial Power]

Section 1. [Federal Judicial System and Federal Judges] The judicial Power of the United States, shall be vested in one supreme Court, and in such inferior Courts as the Congress may from time to time ordain and establish. The Judges, both of the supreme and inferior Courts, shall hold their Offices during good Behaviour, and shall, at stated Times, receive for their Services, a Compensation, which shall not be diminished during their Continuance in Office.

Section 2. [Jurisdiction of the Federal Courts] [1. The Bases of Federal Jurisdiction]

The judicial Power shall extend to all Cases, in Law and Equity, arising under this Constitution, the Laws of the United States, and Treaties made, or which shall be made, under their Authority; —to all Cases affecting Ambassadors, other public Ministers and Consuls; —to all Cases of admiralty and maritime Jurisdiction; —to Controversies to which the United States shall be a Party; —to Controversies between two or more States {; —between a State and Citizens of another State}; —between Citizens of different States; —between Citizens of the same State claiming Lands under Grants of different States {, and between a State, or the Citizens thereof, and foreign States, Citizens or Subjects.}[14]

[2. Supreme Court Original and Appellate Jurisdiction] In all Cases affecting Ambassadors, other public Ministers and Consuls, and those in which a State shall be a Party, the supreme Court shall have original Jurisdiction. In all the other Cases before mentioned, the supreme Court shall have appellate Jurisdiction, both as to Law and Fact, with such Exceptions, and under such Regulations as the Congress shall make.

[3. Jury Trial in Criminal Cases] The Trial of all Crimes, except in Cases of Impeachment, shall be by Jury; and such Trial shall be held in the State where the said Crimes shall have been committed; but when not committed within any State, the Trial shall be at such Place or Places as the Congress may by Law have directed.

Section 3. [Treason] [1. Definition and Proof] Treason against the United States, shall consist only in levying War against them, or, in adhering to their Enemies, giving them Aid and Comfort. No Person shall be convicted of Treason unless on the Testimony of two Witnesses to the same overt Act, or on Confession in open Court.

[2. Punishment] The Congress shall have Power to declare the Punishment of Treason, but no Attainder of Treason shall work Corruption of Blood, or Forfeiture except during the Life of the Person attainted.

ARTICLE IV [States; Federal Property]

Section 1. [Full Faith and Credit] Full Faith and Credit shall be given in each State to the public Acts, Records, and judicial Proceedings of every other State. And the Congress may by general Laws prescribe the Manner in which such Acts, Records and Proceedings shall be proved, and the Effect thereof.

Section 2. [1. Privileges and Immunities] The Citizens of each State shall be entitled to all Privileges and Immunities of Citizens in the several States.

[2. Extradition] A person charged in any State with Treason, Felony, or other Crime, who shall flee from Justice, and be found in another State, shall on Demand of the executive Authority of the State from which he fled, be delivered up, to be removed to the State having Jurisdiction of the Crime.

[3. Fugitive Slaves] {No Person held to Service or Labour in one State, under the Laws thereof, escaping into another, shall, in Consequence of any Law or Regulation therein, be discharged from such Service or Labour, but shall be delivered up on Claim of the Party to whom such Service or Labour may be due.}[15]

Section 3. [1. Admission of New States] New States may be admitted by the Congress into this Union; but no new State shall be formed or erected within the Jurisdiction of any other State; nor any State be formed by the Junction of two or more States, or Parts of

---

14 The two phrases in braces in this clause were superseded by the 11th Amendment. *See* Chapter I, p. 37, and Chapter VI, pp. 225-226.

15 This clause was repealed by the 13th Amendment's prohibition of slavery and involuntary servitude.

States, without the Consent of the Legislatures of the States concerned as well as of the Congress.

[2. Power Over Federal Property] The Congress shall have Power to dispose of and make all needful Rules and Regulations respecting the Territory or other Property belonging to the United States; and nothing in this Constitution shall be so construed as to Prejudice any Claims of the United States, or of any particular State.

Section 4. [Guaranty of Republican Form of Government] The United States shall guarantee to every State in this Union a Republican Form of Government, and shall protect each of them against Invasion; and on Application of the Legislature, or of the Executive (when the Legislature cannot be convened) against domestic Violence.

ARTICLE V [Amendment of the Constitution]

The Congress, whenever two thirds of both Houses shall deem it necessary, shall propose Amendments to this Constitution, or on the Application of the Legislatures of two thirds of the several States, shall call a Convention for proposing Amendments, which, in either Case, shall be valid to all Intents and Purposes, as Part of this Constitution, when ratified by the Legislatures of three fourths of the several States, or by Conventions in three fourths thereof, as the one or the other Mode of Ratification may be proposed by the Congress; Provided that no Amendment which may be made prior to the Year One thousand eight hundred and eight shall in any Manner affect the first and fourth Clauses in the Ninth Section of the first Article; and that no State, without its Consent, shall be deprived of its equal Suffrage in the Senate.

ARTICLE VI [Debts, Supremacy and Oaths]

Section 1. [Debts] All Debts contracted and Engagements entered into, before the Adoption of this Constitution, shall be as valid against the United States under this Constitution, as under the Confederation.

Section 2. [Supremacy of Federal Law] This Constitution, and the Laws of the United States which shall be made in Pursuance thereof; and all Treaties made, or which shall be made, under the Authority of the United States, shall be the supreme Law of the Land; and the Judges in every State shall be bound thereby, any Thing in the Constitution or Laws of any State to the Contrary notwithstanding.

Section 3. [Oath of Office] The Senators and Representatives before mentioned, and the Members of the several State Legislatures, and all executive and judicial Officers, both of the United States and of the several States, shall be bound by Oath or Affirmation, to support this Constitution; but no religious Test shall ever be required as a Qualification to any Office or public Trust under the United States.

ARTICLE VII [Ratification of Original Articles]

The Ratification of the Conventions of nine States, shall be sufficient for the Establishment of this Constitution between the States so ratifying the Same.

DONE in Convention by the Unanimous Consent of the States present the Seventeenth Day of September in the Year of Our Lord one thousand seven hundred and Eighty seven and of the Independence of the United States of America the Twelfth. IN WITNESS whereof We have hereunto subscribed our Names,

[signatures of delegates omitted]

AMENDMENTS TO THE CONSTITUTION[16]

AMENDMENT I [Freedom of Religion, Speech, Press, Assembly and Petition]

Congress shall make no law respecting an establishment of religion, or prohibiting the free exercise thereof; or abridging the freedom of speech, or of the press; or the right of the people peaceably to assemble, and to petition the Government for a redress of grievances.

AMENDMENT II [Militia; Right to Bear Arms]

A well regulated Militia, being necessary to the security of a free State, the right of the people to keep and bear Arms, shall not be infringed.

AMENDMENT III [Quartering of Soldiers]

No Soldier shall, in time of peace be quartered in any house, without the consent of the Owner, nor in time of war, but in a manner to be prescribed by law.

AMENDMENT IV [Searches and Seizures]

The right of the people to be secure in their persons, houses, papers, and effects, against unreasonable searches and seizures, shall not be violated, and no Warrants shall issue, but upon probable cause, supported by Oath or affirmation, and particularly describing the place to be searched, and the persons or things to be seized.

AMENDMENT V [Grand Jury Indictment; Double Jeopardy; Self-Incrimination; Due Process of Law; Taking of Property]

No person shall be held to answer for a capital, or otherwise infamous crime, unless on a presentment or indictment of a Grand Jury, except in cases arising in the land or naval forces, or in the Militia, when in actual service in time of War or public danger; nor shall any person be subject for the same offence to be twice put in jeopardy of life or limb; nor shall be compelled in any criminal case to be a witness against himself, nor be deprived of life, liberty, or property, without due process of law; nor shall private property be taken for public use, without just compensation.

AMENDMENT VI [Speedy and Public Trial; Trial by Jury; Notice of Charges; Confrontation; Assistance of Counsel]

In all criminal prosecutions, the accused shall enjoy the right to a speedy and public trial, by an impartial jury of the State and district wherein the crime shall have been committed, which district shall have been previously ascertained by law, and to be informed of the nature and cause of the accusation; to be confronted with the witnesses against him; to have compulsory process for obtaining witnesses in his favor, and to have the Assistance of Counsel for his defence.

AMENDMENT VII [Jury Trial in Civil Cases]

In Suits at common law, where the value in controversy shall exceed twenty dollars, the right of trial by jury shall be preserved, and no fact tried by a jury, shall be otherwise reexamined in any Court of the United States, than according to the rules of the common law.

---

16 The year each Amendment was ratified is indicated in parentheses, except for the Bill of Rights (first 10 amendments), which were all ratified together in 1791. *See* Chapter I, p. 3.

AMENDMENT VIII [Bail; Cruel and Unusual Punishment]

Excessive bail shall not be required, nor excessive fines imposed, nor cruel and unusual punishments inflicted.

AMENDMENT IX [Rights Retained by the People]

The enumeration in the Constitution, of certain rights, shall not be construed to deny or disparage others retained by the people.

AMENDMENT X [Powers Reserved to the States]

The powers not delegated to the United States by the Constitution, nor prohibited by it to the States, are reserved to the States respectively, or to the people.

AMENDMENT XI [Immunity of States from Suit in Federal Court] (1798)[17]

The Judicial power of the United States shall not be construed to extend to any suit in law or equity, commenced or prosecuted against one of the United States by Citizens of another State, or by Citizens or Subjects of any Foreign State.

AMENDMENT XII [Separate Electoral Vote for President and Vice-President] (1804)[18]

The Electors shall meet in their respective states and vote by ballot for President and Vice-President, one of whom, at least, shall not be an inhabitant of the same state with themselves; they shall name in their ballots the person voted for as President, and in distinct ballots the person voted for as Vice-President, and they shall make distinct lists of all persons voted for as President, and of all persons voted for as Vice-President, and of the number of votes for each, which lists they shall sign and certify, and transmit sealed to the seat of the government of the United States, directed to the President of the Senate; — The President of the Senate shall, in the presence of the Senate and House of Representatives, open all the certificates and the votes shall then be counted; — The person having the greatest number of votes for President, shall be the President, if such number be a majority of the whole number of Electors appointed; and if no person have such majority, then from the persons having the highest numbers not exceeding three on the list of those voted for as President, the House of Representatives shall choose immediately, by ballot, the President. But in choosing the President, the votes shall be taken by states, the representation from each state having one vote; a quorum for this purpose shall consist of a member or members from two-thirds of the states, and a majority of all the states shall be necessary to a choice. And if the House of Representatives shall not choose a President whenever the right of choice shall devolve upon them before the fourth day of March next following, then the Vice-President shall act as President, as in the case of the death or other constitutional disability of the President. — The person having the greatest number of votes as Vice-President, shall be the Vice-President, if such number be a majority of the whole number of Electors appointed, and if no person have a majority, then from the two highest numbers of the list, the Senate shall choose the Vice-President; a quorum for the purpose shall consist of two-thirds of the whole number of Senators, and a majority of the whole number shall be necessary to a choice. But no person constitutionally ineligible to the office of President shall be eligible to that of Vice-President of the United States.

---

17 *See supra* note 14.

18 *See supra* note 12.

AMENDMENT XIII [Abolition of Slavery] (1865)

Section 1. Neither slavery nor involuntary servitude, except as a punishment for crime whereof the party shall have been duly convicted, shall exist within the United States, or any place subject to their jurisdiction.

Section 2. Congress shall have power to enforce this article by appropriate legislation.

AMENDMENT XIV [Citizenship; Privileges and Immunities; Due Process of Law; Equal Protection of the Laws] (1868)

Section 1. All persons born or naturalized in the United States, and subject to the jurisdiction thereof, are citizens of the United States and of the State wherein they reside. No State shall make or enforce any law which shall abridge the privileges or immunities of citizens of the United States; nor shall any State deprive any person of life, liberty, or property, without due process of law; nor deny to any person within its jurisdiction the equal protection of the laws.

Section 2. Representatives shall be apportioned among the several States according to their respective numbers, counting the whole number of persons in each State, excluding Indians not taxed. But when the right to vote at any election for the choice of electors for President and Vice President of the United States, Representatives in Congress, the Executive and Judicial officers of a State, or the members of the Legislature thereof, is being denied to any of the male inhabitants of such State, being twenty-one years of age, and citizens of the United States, or in any way abridged, except for participation in rebellion, or other crime, the basis of representation therein shall be reduced in the proportion which the number of such male citizens shall bear to the whole number of male citizens twenty-one years of age in such State.[19]

{Section 3. No person shall be a Senator or Representative in Congress, or elector of President and Vice President, or hold any office, civil or military, under the United States, or under any State, who having previously taken an oath, as a member of Congress, or as an officer of the United States, or as a member of any State legislature, or as an executive or judicial officer of any State, to support the Constitution of the United States, shall have engaged in insurrection or rebellion against the same, or given aid or comfort to the enemies thereof. But Congress may by a vote of two-thirds of each House, remove such disability.}

{Section 4. The validity of the public debt of the United States, authorized by law, including debts incurred for payment of pensions and bounties for services in suppressing insurrection or rebellion, shall not be questioned. But neither the United States nor any State shall assume or pay any debt or obligation incurred in aid of insurrection or rebellion against the United States, or any claim for the loss or emancipation of any slave; but all such debts, obligations and claims shall be held illegal and void.}[20]

Section 5. The Congress shall have power to enforce, by appropriate legislation, the provisions of this article.

---

19 The first sentence of §2 amended the provisions of Art. I §2 cl. 3 governing apportionment of representation in the House of Representatives by requiring states to count former slaves as whole persons and providing a penalty in the event that state interfered with the voting rights of newly freed slaves.

20 Sections 3 and 4 are obsolete. They concerned matters regarding the aftermath of the Civil War.

AMENDMENT XV [Prohibition Against Racial Discrimination in Voting] (1870)

Section 1. The right of citizens of the United States to vote shall not be denied or abridged by the United States or by any State on account of race, color, or previous condition of servitude.

Section 2. The Congress shall have power to enforce this article by appropriate legislation.

AMENDMENT XVI [Income Tax] (1913)

The Congress shall have power to lay and collect taxes on incomes, from whatever source derived, without apportionment among the several States, and without regard to any census or enumeration.[21]

AMENDMENT XVII [Direct Election of Senators] (1913)[22]

[1] The Senate of the United States shall be composed of two Senators from each State, elected by the people thereof, for six years; and each Senator shall have one vote. The electors in each State shall have the qualifications requisite for electors of the most numerous branch of the State legislatures.

[2] When vacancies happen in the representation of any State in the Senate, the executive authority of such State shall issue writs of election to fill such vacancies: Provided, that the legislature of any State may empower the executive thereof to make temporary appointments until the people fill the vacancies by election as the legislature may direct.

[3] This amendment shall not be so construed as to affect the election or term of any Senator chosen before it becomes valid as part of the Constitution.

AMENDMENT XVIII [Prohibition on Alcoholic Liquor][23]

Section 1. After one year from the ratification of this article the manufacture, sale, or transportation of intoxicating liquors within, the importation thereof into, or the exportation thereof from the United States and all territory subject to the jurisdiction thereof for beverage purposes is hereby prohibited.

Section 2. The Congress and the several States shall have concurrent power to enforce this article by appropriate legislation.

AMENDMENT XIX [Women's Right to Vote] (1920)

[1] The right of citizens of the United States to vote shall not be denied or abridged by the United States or by any State on account of sex.

[2] Congress shall have power to enforce this article by appropriate legislation.

AMENDMENT XX [Presidential and Congressional Terms] (1933)

Section 1. The terms of the President and Vice President shall end at noon on the 20th day of January, and the terms of Senators and Representatives at noon on the 3d day of

---

21 The 16th Amendment gave Congress the power to levy an income tax. *See* Chapter I, p. 27.

22 The 17th Amendment amended Art. I §2 cl. 1-2, which had provided for election of Senators by the state legislatures.

23 The 18th Amendment, which established "Prohibition," was repealed by §1 of the 21st Amendment. *See* Chapter IX, p. 361 note 363.

January, of the years in which such terms would have ended if this article had not been ratified; and the terms of their successors shall then begin.

Section 2. The Congress shall assemble at least once in every year, and such meeting shall begin at noon on the 3d day of January, unless they shall by law appoint a different day.[24]

Section 3. If, at the time fixed for the beginning of the term of the President, the President elect shall have died, the Vice President elect shall become President. If a President shall not have been chosen before the time fixed for the beginning of his term, or if the President elect shall have failed to qualify, then the Vice President elect shall act as President until a President shall have qualified; and the Congress may by law provide for the case wherein neither a President elect nor a Vice President elect shall have qualified, declaring who shall then act as President, or the manner in which one who is to act shall be selected, and such person shall act accordingly until a President or Vice President shall have qualified.

Section 4. The Congress may by law provide for the case of the death of any of the persons from whom the House of Representatives may choose a President whenever the right of choice shall have devolved upon them, and for the case of the death of any of the persons from whom the Senate may choose a Vice President whenever the right of choice shall have devolved upon them.

Section 5. Sections 1 and 2 shall take effect on the 15th day of October following the ratification of this article.

AMENDMENT XXI [State Control Over Intoxicating Liquors] (1933)

Section 1. The eighteenth article of amendment to the Constitution of the United States is hereby repealed.

Section 2. The transportation or importation into any State, Territory, or possession of the United States for delivery or use therein of intoxicating liquors, in violation of the laws thereof, is hereby prohibited.

AMENDMENT XXII [Limitation on Presidential Terms] (1951)

Section 1. No person shall be elected to the office of the President more than twice, and no person who has held the office of President, or acted as President, for more than two years of a term to which some other person was elected President shall be elected to the office of the President more than once. But this Article shall not apply to any person holding the office of President when this Article was proposed by the Congress, and shall not prevent any person who may be holding the office of President, or acting as President, during the term within which this Article becomes operative from holding the office of President or acting as President during the remainder of such term.

Section 2. This article shall be inoperative unless it shall have been ratified as an amendment to the Constitution by the legislatures of three-fourths of the several States within seven years from the date of its submission to the States by the Congress.

---

24 See supra note 6.

Constitution of the United States

AMENDMENT XXIII [Presidential Electors for the District of Columbia] (1961)

Section 1. The District constituting the seat of Government of the United States shall appoint in such manner as the Congress may direct:

A number of electors of President and Vice President equal to the whole number of Senators and Representatives in Congress to which the District would be entitled if it were a State, but in no event more than the least populous State; they shall be in addition to those appointed by the States, but they shall be considered, for the purposes of the election of President and Vice President, to be electors appointed by a State; and they shall meet in the District and perform such duties as provided by the twelfth article of amendment.

Section 2. The Congress shall have power to enforce this article by appropriate legislation.

AMENDMENT XXIV [Prohibition on Poll Tax in Federal Elections] (1964)

Section 1. The right of citizens of the United States to vote in any primary or other election for President or Vice President, for electors for President or Vice President, or for Senator or Representative in Congress, shall not be denied or abridged by the United States or any State by reason of failure to pay any poll tax or other tax.

Section 2. The Congress shall have power to enforce this article by appropriate legislation.

AMENDMENT XXV [Succession to Presidency and Vice-Presidency; Presidential Disability] (1967)

Section 1. In case of the removal of the President from office or of his death or resignation, the Vice President shall become President.

Section 2. Whenever there is a vacancy in the office of the Vice President, the President shall nominate a Vice President who shall take office upon confirmation by a majority vote of both Houses of Congress.

Section 3. Whenever the President transmits to the President pro tempore of the Senate and the Speaker of the House of Representatives his written declaration that he is unable to discharge the powers and duties of his office, and until he transmits to them a written declaration to the contrary, such powers and duties shall be discharged by the Vice President as Acting President.

Section 4. Whenever the Vice President and a majority of either the principal officers of the executive departments or of such other body as Congress may by law provide, transmit to the President pro tempore of the Senate and the Speaker of the House of Representatives, their written declaration that the President is unable to discharge the powers and duties of his office, the Vice President shall immediately assume the powers and duties of the office as Acting President.

Thereafter, when the President transmits to the President pro tempore of the Senate and the Speaker of the House of Representatives his written declaration that no inability exists, he shall resume the powers and duties of his office unless the Vice President and a majority of either the principal officers of the executive department or of such other body as Congress may by law provide, transmit within four days to the President pro tempore of the Senate and the Speaker of the House of Representatives their written declaration that the President is unable to discharge the powers and duties of his office. Thereupon

Congress shall decide the issue, assembling within forty-eight hours for that purpose if not in session. If the Congress, within twenty-one days after receipt of the latter written declaration, or, if Congress is not in session, within twenty-one days after Congress is required to assemble, determines by two-thirds vote of both Houses that the President is unable to discharge the powers and duties of his office, the Vice President shall continue to discharge the same as Acting President; otherwise, the President shall resume the powers and duties of his office.

AMENDMENT XXVI [Prohibition Against Discrimination in Voting on Basis of Age] (1971)

Section 1. The right of citizens of the United States, who are eighteen years of age or older, to vote shall not be denied or abridged by the United States or by any State on account of age.

Section 2. The Congress shall have power to enforce this article by appropriate legislation.

AMENDMENT XXVII [Compensation of Senators and Representatives] (1992)[25]

No law, varying the compensation for the services of the Senators and Representatives, shall take effect, until an election of Representatives shall have intervened.

---

25 This recent amendment amended Art.I §6 cl. 1. It is notable for having the longest period between proposal and ratification — over 200 years. *See* Chapter IX, p. 325 note 56.

DIAGRAMS

Structure of the Federal Government

Legislative Branch

CONGRESS

SENATE   HOUSE

Architect of the Capitol
U.S. Botanic Garden
General Accounting Office
Government Printing Office
Library of Congress
Congressional Budget Office

Executive Branch

PRESIDENT
EXECUTIVE OFFICE OF THE PRESIDENT
VICE PRESIDENT

White House Office
Office of Management and Budget
Council of Economic Advisers
National Security Council
Domestic Policy Council
Office of National Drug Control Policy
Foreign Intelligence Advisory Board
Office of the U.S. Trade Representative
Council on Environmental Quality
Office of Science and Technology Policy
Office of Administration
National Space Council

Judicial Branch

SUPREME COURT
U.S. Courts of Appeals
U.S. District Courts
Specialized Courts
Administrative Office of U.S. Courts

Agricultural Department

Commerce Department

Defense Department

Education Department

Energy Department

Health and Human
Services Department

Homeland Security Department

Housing and Urban
Development Department

Interior Department

Justice Department

State Department

Transportation Department

Treasury Department

Veterans Affairs
Department

Independent Establishments, Government Corporations and Quasi-official Agencies

African Development Foundation
Appalachian Regional Commission
Board for International Broadcasting
Central Intelligence Agency
Commission on Civil Rights
Commodity Futures Trading Commission
Consumer Product Safety Commission
Corporation for Public Broadcasting
Corporation for National and Community Service
Election Assistance Commission
Environmental Protection Agency
Equal Employment Opportunity Commission
Export-Import Bank of the United States
Farm Credit Administration
Federal Communications Commission
Federal Deposit Insurance Corporation
Federal Election Commission
Federal Housing Finance Board
Federal Labor Relations Authority
Federal Maritime Commission
Federal Mediation and Conciliation Service
Federal Mine Safety and Health Review Commission
Federal Reserve System, Board of Governors
Federal Retirement Thrift Investment Board
Federal Trade Commission
General Services Administration
Institute of Museum and Library Sciences
Inter-American Foundation
International Broadcasting Bureau
Legal Services Corporation
Merit Systems Protection Board
National Aeronautics and Space Administration
National Archives and Records Administration
National Capital Planning Commission
National Credit Union Administration
National Endowment for the Arts
National Labor Relations Board
National Mediation Board
National Railroad Passenger Corporation (AMTRAK)
National Science Foundation
National Transportation Safety Board
Nuclear Regulatory Commission
Occupational Safety and Health Review Commission
Office of Government Ethics
Office of Personnel Management
Office of Special Counsel
Panama Canal Commission
Peace Corps
Pension Benefit Guaranty Corporation
Postal Rate Commission
Railroad Retirement Board
Securities and Exchange Commission
Selective Service System
Small Business Administration
Social Security Administration
Tennessee Valley Authority
Trade and Development Office
U.S. Agency for International Development
U.S. Information Agency
U.S. International Trade Commission
U.S. Postal Service

Diagram of State and Federal Court Systems and Hierarchy

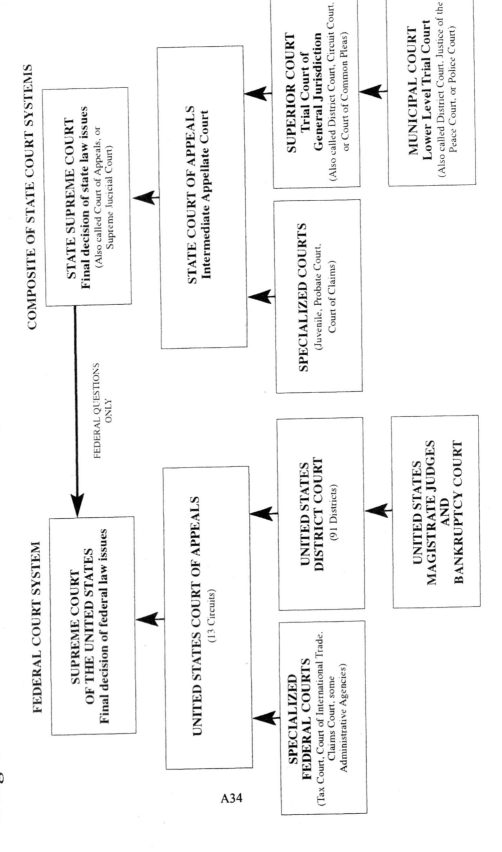

COMPOSITE OF STATE COURT SYSTEMS

STATE SUPREME COURT
Final decision of state law issues
(Also called Court of Appeals, or Supreme Judicial Court)

STATE COURT OF APPEALS
Intermediate Appellate Court

SPECIALIZED COURTS
(Juvenile, Probate Court, Court of Claims)

SUPERIOR COURT
Trial Court of
General Jurisdiction
(Also called District Court, Circuit Court, or Court of Common Pleas)

MUNICIPAL COURT
Lower Level Trial Court
(Also called District Court, Justice of the Peace Court, or Police Court)

FEDERAL COURT SYSTEM

FEDERAL QUESTIONS ONLY

SUPREME COURT
OF THE UNITED STATES
Final decision of federal law issues

UNITED STATES COURT OF APPEALS
(13 Circuits)

UNITED STATES
DISTRICT COURT
(91 Districts)

UNITED STATES
MAGISTRATE JUDGES
AND
BANKRUPTCY COURT

SPECIALIZED
FEDERAL COURTS
(Tax Court, Court of International Trade, Claims Court, some Administrative Agencies)

A34

Typical Trial Courtroom

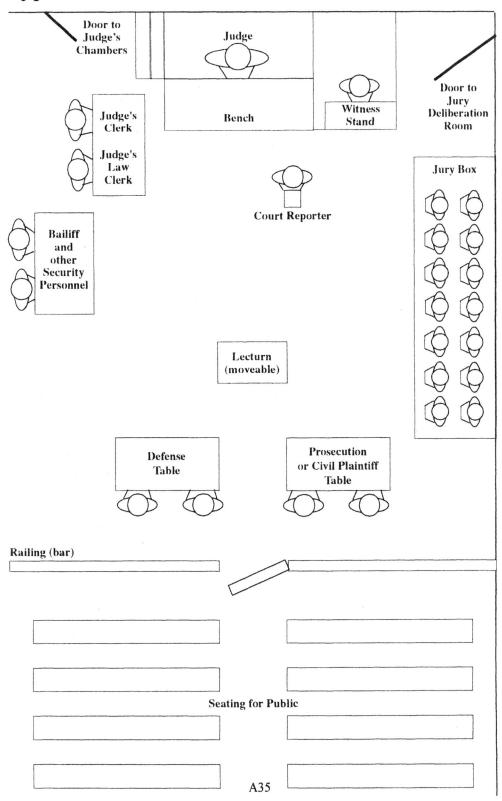

A35

APPENDIX B

ADDRESSES OF MAJOR PUBLISHERS OF U.S. LEGAL EDUCATIONAL MATERIALS AND SOURCES OF U.S. LAW ON THE INTERNET

These companies specialize in legal materials for law students and law teachers, though some have extensive materials for practitioners as well. Most readers of this book will be interested only in the law school materials and will want contact the law school division of the publishers or go to the law school section of the website. An explanation of the kinds of books and materials available is set out in the *Reader's Guide and Bibliographic Introduction* at the beginning of this book (pp. x-xii).

West Academic Publishing
610 Opperman Drive
Eagan, Minnesota 55123

Telephone: 1-800-313-9378
www.westacademic.com/

Foundation Press (owned by West)
610 Opperman Drive
Eagan, Minnesota 55123

Telephone: 1-877-888-1330
www.westacademic.com/

Wolters-Kluwer Aspen Publishers
7201 McKinney Circle
Frederick, Maryland 21704-8356

Telephone: 1-800-234-1660
lawschool.aspenpublishers.com/

LexisNexis Matthew Bender
1275 Broadway
Albany, NY 12204

Telephone: 1-800-424-4200; 1-518-487-3000
www.lexisnexis.com/academic/

SELECTED INTERNET SITES FOR LEGAL INFORMATION

The amount of legal information and materials available on the Internet is expanding and the sites listed below are subject to change. Further comments on Internet sources are set out in the Reader's Guide and Bibliographic Introduction following the preface.

Legal Research Sites

http://www.findlaw.com/

Legal Search Engines

http://www.law.cornell.edu/

Links to Other Legal Sites

https://gsulaw.gsu.edu/metaindex/

Legal News

http://www.law.com/jsp/law/index.jsp

U.S. Congress

http://thomas.loc.gov/

Library of Congress

http://www.loc.gov/topics/government.php

Federal Judiciary

http://www.uscourts.gov/Home.aspx

National Center for State Courts

http://www.ncsc.org/

Department of Justice Bureau of Judicial Statistics	http://www.ojp.usdoj.gov/
American Judicature Society	http://www.ajs.org/
American Bar Association	http://www.americanbar.org/aba.html
Attorney Finders	http://www.martindale.com/
U.S. Government Printing Office	http://www.gpoaccess.gov/

APPENDIX C: TABLE OF CASES

Table of Cases

Table of Cases

Table of Cases

Table of Cases

Table of Cases

Table of Cases

C35

C38

Index